The Book of

POTTERY AND PORCELAIN

VOLUME I

The Book of
Pottery and Porcelain

BY

WARREN E. COX

*3000 illustrations. Pictures selected by the
author. Lay-outs by A. M. Lounsbery*

REVISED EDITION

VOLUME I

CROWN PUBLISHERS, INC.
NEW YORK

Library of Congress Catalogue Card Number: 75-127511
ISBN: 0-517-539314

Published simultaneously in Canada by General Publishing Company Limited

PRINTED IN THE UNITED STATES OF AMERICA

10 9 8 7 6 5 4 3 2

This book is dedicated

to

ELIZABETH AND ETHELYN

who kept things going while I had the fun of doing it

INTRODUCTION

This book is both a history and a description of the processes of making pottery, stoneware, soft paste, faïence, "delft," porcelain and other wares together with criticisms of their various appeals and defects, both practically and artistically speaking, and suggestions as to methods for searching out such criticisms. It is intended for all craftsmen who would make things of fired clay, for collectors in any branch of ceramics who would like to widen their general outlook and knowledge, for students of art who are searching in the field of aesthetics for that which man calls beautiful, and finally for the layman who, I hope, will be caught by a little of that interest which already burns so brightly in many men.

Like all ancient arts of world-wide appeal, the art of ceramics or fired clay has grown about it much mossy bunk that demands a gentle scraping before one can get down to the real beauties that have made it appeal to all sorts of men through all sorts of ages. The very names which we must use for different kinds of fired clay vessels or figures, for the different processes with which they are made and for the colors applied to them are taken from half a dozen different languages because certain things were discovered or were famous in one place while others were famous in a far distant place and habit has associated these places with these things. We call the ox-blood color of certain K'ang Hsi period vases *"sang de boeuf"* because it was greatly appreciated in France during the 18th century and also because it was the fashion in England and America during the 18th century to think a French name added considerable class and distinction to anything. We also call it *"lang yao,"* *lang* being a Chinese name, perhaps of a viceroy of the times or perhaps of a family of potters. We are not certain which. And *yao* meaning simply ware. Thus we shall find words and names from France, Italy, China and many other places in such common use that we have to continue to use them to make ourselves understood.

Another thing is obvious at once and that is that few so-called authorities agree even on their definitions of such basic terms as *"soft paste"* or *"porcelain"*; the latter being derived from an Italian term used for a shell, that of the "purple-fish" or "Venus-shell" called also *"porcellana"* because "the curved shape of the upper surface resembles the curve of a pig's back,"—to quote from the Century Dictionary, because the Chinese ware brought to Venice earlier than the 15th century was thought to resemble this shell in texture. The term *"soft paste"* is properly applied to an imitation of porcelain which really was not at all like the original Chinese article either in composition or characteristics. Thus the often heard term *"soft paste porcelain"* is anomalous and contradictory to begin with. We need not now go into the

vii

various discussions concerning whether porcelain is necessarily translucent, whether it is porous, whether it must necessarily be white, etc., etc., for we are doing that towards the end of this book so that the reader, knowing how these terms came about, and how they were generally used, can make up his own mind in the end as to how they should be used. Meanwhile we shall leave the hair splitting of definitions to those who are interested in them. We shall try also to be consistent, though this we do not promise as it is almost an inhuman achievement save perhaps to lawyers, schoolmasters and successful businessmen. Most porcelain is translucent but we are certainly not going to throw out of this category some Ming wares which are so dense and thick as not to be. Those gentlemen who argue for translucence as a needed attribute answer that, if such porcelains were split to thin enough flakes, they would be translucent. We can only answer sadly that good authorities say that anything under God's heavens can, under these conditions, be called translucent. Gold, as an example, is quite a dense substance, yet gold leaf is quite translucent and of greenish hue.—But let us waste no more time with such nonsensical arguments. My warning is simply and solely that the reader must be tolerant with me because the words at my disposal are bound to fall far short of making everything perfectly clear. How can they help but do so, when they start out by being confused and far from clear themselves?—The man who has never held a piece of porcelain in his hand and looked at it could never understand what it is from a word description. The man who has never made a piece of porcelain can never really understand it either. All we really attempt, therefore, is to round up a few ideas which may be intriguing.

A lady came into my shop a while ago and asked me if I would show her my "best vase." There were three or four I thought of at once but finally brought out one and you should have seen her face fall. It wasn't a big vase and, aside from firing, I don't believe it could have taken the potter more than a few hours to have made it. It was not perfect. It wouldn't even make a very good vase for holding flowers. She asked me why I liked it and, knowing that she was an intelligent and understanding person, I undertook to tell her to the extent of about three hours of conversation, or perhaps we had better say oration. As the reader may imagine, my success was not of the best, accomplishing in her mind, very likely, a lowering of opinion of me rather than a raising of opinion of the vase. She was courteous but I notice she has not been back to ask about the second-best vase.

In the book, I shall probably not be one bit more successful in telling why I like this vase and dislike that one; such things are entirely personal and cannot very well be defined. Why does a man love one girl and pass another without a look? Is it associations? Is it his own endocrinal condition? Or is it, as the ancients contended, all in the stars? Certainly no one could tell by looking at him. And just as certainly he, himself, would be the very last to give a reasonable accounting. However, with half a chance he could tell you veritably a thousand reasons—none of which would be worth much to you. Therefore, as I consider the matter in cold blood, I don't believe one man or woman will ever turn collector or maker of potteries because of reading this book. I doubt if all these little words will make one reader love one vase the more or the less and I shall probably accomplish nothing more than a reduced opinion of myself. However, my kind publisher has given me the chance and, like the lover, I cannot resist putting down my thousand reasons for that which is largely reasonless.

There are some terribly dry parts of this book, not at all worth reading, and I don't have to tell you to skip them for you will anyhow, but let me tell you that I have saved you, the reader, an awful lot that is dryer yet, by making charts of much of this sort of material and by glossing over much scholarly proof of this or that point. I may add that my publisher has saved you more. Naturally I don't thank him now but probably will ten years from now.

As you probably know, all *"Introductions"* are written *after* a book is finished. It is only when the hull is launched that the leaks are discovered. And I am not the first to discover that one can get in apologies for shortcomings in the front of a book and get them read while after the reader has ploughed through some quarter to half a million words he gets into a state of semi-consciousness in which all the apologies in the world will do no good. However, they are not of much use anyhow so let us proceed.

Acknowledgments

Thanks should be extended to Charles Henry, through whom I met Jack Blitzer, who took me to lunch with Joseph Aronson, who brought Nat Wartels to my place, who in turn made this book possible. Many others have contributed, though in some cases without knowing it, such as those early instructors H. Kevorkian, the late Demottes both father and son, Matachia Miya, Oto Fukushima, the late Isaac Voron, the late Lee Van Ching and his son, L. Y. Lee as well as Quill Jones, the late Dr. Riefstahl and Dr. Berthold Laufer, and my instructors in painting Emil Carlsen and Harry Watrous both of whom have also passed away before their valued criticisms could be obtained. A very real debt is also owed to those great authorities who wrote articles for me in the 14th Edition of the Encyclopaedia Britannica and who, each in his own field, discussed various phases of aesthetics and also pots with a very young and not very well grounded "editor," who knew only just enough to trot to the best men available. These are too numerous to list but outstanding among them besides Dr. Laufer were R. L. Hobson, Percy Gardner, Bernard Rackham, Herbert Read, Ananda K. Coomaraswamy and H. R. H. Hall.

To the Metropolitan Museum of Art as a whole and to the staff individually a great debt is owed. To Evelyn B. Grier and her staff together with all those who aided in the selection of photographs to be used in illustration and for providing notes on color, period and sizes of the hundreds upon hundreds of objects too much thanks cannot be extended. Mr. Theodore Y. Hobby gave constant and unflagging help and advice in his kindness and enthusiasm for Far Eastern ceramics, a field in which he is leading authority. Mr. Alan Priest, Miss Josephine Hadley, Mr. James J. Rorimer, Miss Gisela M. A. Richter, Miss Christine Alexander, Mr. S. H. Han and Lt. Commander William Christopher Hayes were all very helpful in their kind assistance at various times over the past five years as was also the Vice-Director, Mr. Horace H. F. Jayne.

But the Metropolitan Museum was no more helpful than were many of the museums all over this country and such authorities as Mr. Howard Hollis of the Cleveland Museum of Art, Mr. James Marshall Plumer of Ann Arbor, Michigan, Mr. Charles Fabens Kelley of the Art Institute of Chicago, Miss Alice Wilson Frothingham of the Hispanic Society N. Y., Mr. Kojiro Tomita of the Boston Museum, the late Mr. John Lodge and also Mr. Carl W. Bishop of the Freer Gallery of Art, Washington, Mr. Langdon Warner of the Fogg Museum, Cambridge and Mr. Richard E. Fuller of the Seattle Museum should be especially thanked for their aid in both text matter and illustration.

Again the greatest of thanks must be given to many who are, although in the trade, among our really studious and serious scholars in their various fields, and who devoted much valuable time to consultation, help and advice, and to these I must express my gratitude. Such friends as Mr. C. Edward Wells, Mr. Walter Hochstadter, Mr. C. F. Yau, Mr. C. T. Loo, the late Mr. Zado Noorian, Mr. Benjamin Ginsburg, Mr. Quill Jones, Mr. Frank Stoner, Mr. Frederick Lunning, Mr. Howard Back, Baron van Haersolte, The Bluett Brothers, Mr. Morris S. Cuthbertson, Mr. Nasli Heeramaneck, Mr. Ralph M. Chait, Mr. Ellis Munroe, the late Mr. John Gibbons, Mr. H. Kevorkian and Mr. Lem Sec Tsang have been invaluable.

Finally among collectors again there are those who, not content with mere ownership, are serious students and who have helped me immeasurably and to whom I owe the fullest of appreciation for their assistance. These run into a great many but outstanding among them are the late Mrs. Christian R. Holmes, Mrs. Ogden K. Shannon, Jr., Mr. Delos Chappell, Mr. Benjamin d'Ancona, Mr. Fritz Low-Beer, the late Mr. Samuel T. Peters, the late Mr. Ernest Dane, the late Mr. Shepard K. DeForest, Mr. Nai-Chi Chang, Mr. Edgar Worch, Mrs. Charles Porter Wilson, Mr. Diedrich Abbes, Mr. K. M. Semon, Mrs. Louise Higgins, Miss Ethelyn C. Stewart, Mr. George Eumorfopoulos, Sir Percival David and Mrs. Warren E. Cox, from whose private collections I have in several cases illustrated a number of objects.

For technical advice throughout I have raised all questions to Mr. Walter Howat who has given me exact and practical advice. No one could be better equipped than he to assist in this field. However, Mr. Paul Freigang also lent aid in several matters of both technical and aesthetic consideration. To both of these friends I owe a debt of gratitude.

In conclusion undoubtedly the man who had most to do with this book, with the education of the author, with his opportunities with the Encyclopaedia Britannica and with the actual making of a large part of the Warren E. Cox Collection, is my good father, William J. Cox.

CONTENTS OF VOLUME ONE

DEFINITIONS

ALUMINA is CHINA CLAY or KAOLIN. It fires white and opaque and can withstand high temperatures. Bernard Leach says that some 10% to 40% is present in most bodies. It is this content which actually determines whether or not a ware is porcelain.

BALL CLAY is a plastic clay which stands high temperatures without wilting.

BASALT WARE is the name given to a certain ware of hard black quality by Wedgwood.

BELLEEK was made in Ireland and a similar ware made chiefly in Trenton, N. J., and called *Lenox* is made of pre-fused feldspar, flint and alkalis in a glassy mass, and is glazed with a very brilliant borosilicate of the alkalis lime, lead and zinc. The firing temperature is considerably below that of other types of so-called "porcelain," though the use of the term is incorrect.

Characteristics

1. It is highly translucent, even more than European soft paste as a rule.
2. It has a natural ivory color.
3. It is easily scratched.
4. It is decorated with gold or low-fired enamels, but recently slip in contrasting color to the body has come into use.

BISCUIT is unglazed porcelain. Unglazed pottery is usually referred to as TERRA-COTTA.

BISQUE, *see* PORCELAIN.

BONE CHINA, *see* ENGLISH SOFT PASTE.

CHINA, *see* PORCELAIN.

CHINA CLAY is thought to be decomposed granite and is made up of silica and alumina and appears as a white amorphous powder. It is usually hydraulically mined. It is this clay that gives plasticity to the mixture before firing, but it is the non-fusible part of the mixture which the Chinese call *Kaolin*.

CHINA STONE, or *Petuntse,* as the Chinese call it, is mined and quarried like stone. It is sold in four grades:

1. "Hard purple" (white with purplish tinge and hard).
2. "Mild purple" (the same but softer).
3. "Dry white" or soft (a soft white rock).
4. "Buff" (similar but with slight yellow tinge).

Silica is about 80% in the colored varieties and 74% in the white. Alumina is about 18% in the white and 7% to 10% in the others. The china stone gives the body its translucency. Its function is that of flux. The Chinese say that Kaolin is the "bone" and Petuntse the "flesh" of porcelain. (Of course, this does not mean that it has any actual bone in its makeup in the Far East.) It is not always clear in the minds of students that china clay turns hard and china stone turns soft in the firing, exchanging characteristics as it were.

CHINESE SOFT PASTE is a porcelain to which has been added steatite (soap stone) or some similar substance which produces a softer ware fired at a lower temperature. Soft paste slip may also be added to a hard porcelain.

Characteristics

1. It is lighter in weight.
2. Its body can be scratched with a steel point.
3. It often has a slightly undulating surface.
4. It usually has a lower fired glaze, sometimes inclined to craze.

CLAY is a plastic substance composed largely of aluminum and silica and is simply decomposed rocks usually also containing some iron and also vegetable remains in its natural state.

CREAM WARE, *see* QUEEN'S WARE.

DELFT, *see* POTTERY.

EARTHENWARE is correctly used to name pottery whether glazed or unglazed in its more definite sense excluding all porcelains and stonewares. It is incorrectly used in the trade to designate a semivitreous or white ware sold to hotels and restaurants for heavy usage. Its composition is about 13% English ball clay, 13% feldspar, 25% English china clay, 10% North Carolina kaolin, 6% Florida kaolin and 33% flint and the firing is done at about 2,200° F. or pyrometric cone 8, the glost firing at 2,150° (cone 5) and the decorating at 1,350° (cone .017). The glaze is a boro-silicate of the alkalis, lime, lead and zinc in various compounds. The ware is similar to that made in Staffordshire, England, except that it is higher fired. Much of it is made in the U. S. at East Liverpool. Practically no underglaze decoration is used. This ware might more appropriately be called *white stoneware.*

ENAMELS are low fired colored glazes usually applied over harder glazes. When they are used over a biscuit the distinction between them and glazes becomes indefinite though generally speaking they are supposed to be less hard.

ENGLISH SOFT PASTE or BONE CHINA is a hybrid composition in which china clay is partly replaced by ashes of calcined bones. It should, of course, not really ever be called "china" for the Chinese never made any such ware, nor, in a sense, should it be called "soft paste" but habit has formed the two designations and they will probably continue to be used.

Characteristics

1. It is easily scratched but is not so soft as European soft paste.
2. It is more opaque than European soft paste yet it has some translucence.
3. It can be made nearly white.

ENGOBES are slips.

EUROPEAN SOFT PASTE was originally made in attempts to imitate real Chinese porcelain in such examples as "Medici porcelain," St. Cloud, Rouen, Chantilly, etc. Kaolin had not been discovered in the western hemisphere and the body was simply mixed with a frit or ground up glass in various proportions in an attempt to obtain translucency. The firing was done at very low temperatures, about those in which glass will melt.

Characteristics

1. It is easily scratched with a steel blade.
2. It is likely to warp in the kiln.
3. It is highly translucent.

4. It can be made nearly white but usually greenish or greyish by transmitted light.

The French term for it, and they were really chief makers of it, is *pâte tendre.*

FAÏENCE, *see* POTTERY.

FELDSPAR or FELSPAR is any one of several minerals, silicates of aluminum with potassium, sodium or calcium. It is usually white or pinkish and it melts at about 1200° to 1300° C. It loses its alkaline content through decomposition and then becomes china clay.

FLINT is the hard stone which we have all seen at times in the form of pebbles on a beach, but there are different flints and not all are useful to the potter. Some of the best come from France though there are many sources. They are calcined (heated), which turns them opaque and white and softens them so that they can be more readily crushed into powder which can be mixed with the clay. The ground flint when mixed with water appears a thin liquid paste of whitish or greyish color. It can withstand very high temperatures.

FLUX is a substance used to promote the melting of metals or minerals. It also causes overglaze colors to vitrify. Such materials as lead, borax or lime are so used.

FRIT is simply ground glass of various kinds and is composed of silica and alkaline salts.

GLOST FIRING is firing of the glaze often at a lower temperature than the body was fired, though many wares are fired only once.

GRÈS is the French term for stoneware.

HARD PASTE means PORCELAIN or CHINA as opposed to SOFT PASTE.

KAOLIN, *see* ALUMINA.

LEAD as galena or lead ore containing sulphide, red lead, white lead, litharge and massicot or lead monoxide of reddish or yellowish color, are all used as fluxing agents for low and medium temperatures. The metal fluxes at 326° C. It is, of course, highly poisonous and must be used with care.

LUSTRE is a thin metallic sheen applied usually over a tin glaze. It consists actually of finely divided metals of various sorts, and is fired at low, reducing atmospheres.

MAJOLICA or MAIOLICA, *see* POTTERY.

PARIAN WARE is a vitreous porcelain left

unglazed and composed of one part china-clay and two parts feldspar. It does not in the least resemble Parian marble from which the name is derived.

PÂTE-SUR-PÂTE is a French term for the process of building low relief decorations by repeated touches of a brush charged with thin slip. It is perhaps best known in some Minton wares.

PETUNTSE, *see* CHINA STONE.

PORCELAIN or CHINA are synonymous as true porcelain was found and developed in China and, though this country made other wares, it was porcelain to which Europeans referred when they used the term china. It is made of fusible silicates of alumina (called petuntse) and nonfusible silicates of alumina (called kaolin), called by the English "china stone" and "china clay."

Characteristics

1. It is not porous even when unglazed.
2. The body cannot be scratched with a steel knife.
3. It is naturally of a whitish color caused by the kaolin but the body may be stained many colors by mineral oxides.
4. It is generally more translucent than *pottery* or *stoneware* and less so than "*soft paste porcelain,*" though translucency is not an absolute test for some of the denser porcelains are not visibly translucent even in fairly thin flakes.
5. It is fired in saggers at first for about 24 hours at low temperature and then raised to about 1300° C. or in some cases to about 1450° C. for another 20 to 30 hours. Present day spark plug insulators, etc., are fired to 2650 to 3000° F. (cone 17 to 30).

Porcelain may be left unglazed and is then called *biscuit, bisque* or, in some cases by some English and American collectors particularly if it is of fine texture, *parian* ware.

Porcelain may also be originally fired with a glaze on it or may have a softer glaze added in a second firing and may also be decorated with enamels in a third firing as low as 700° to 800°.

POTTERY. 1. The term may be used inclusively to cover all types of baked wares, earthen, stone and porcelain. 2. It can also be applied to a factory in which any or all wares are made and fired. 3. More definitely it is used to name all classes of baked clay wares which are not stoneware or porcelain.

It is a slightly calcareous clay which when baked even at low temperatures hardens somewhat and has the following characteristics:

1. It is always porous.
2. It can be scratched with a knife or sometimes even with a hard wood stick.
3. It is opaque save in very thin flakes such as those ground for microscopy.
4. The color is usually reddish brown, yellow, brown or grey depending upon the content of the clay with which it was made and the temperature under which it was fired.
5. It may be sun baked.

Pottery is synonymous with *earthenware, red-ware, black-ware, primitive ware* and *terra cotta.*

When coated with glaze, which is usually of the lead type as pottery is frequently not fired at a high enough temperature to volatilize salt, it is called the same. When covered with a slip or when it has decorations on it in slip, it may be called *slip-ware.* When tin is mixed in the lead glaze so as to make it opaque to hide the body of the ware, it may be called *faïence, majolica* (or *maiolica*), or *delft* as the case may be depending chiefly upon the geographical location.

QUEEN'S WARE is plastic clay, freed as much as possible from iron so that it can be near white, but with some quartz and feldspar, and sometimes a little kaolin is added. It is fired in saggers but at fairly low temperatures. Is also called "*cream ware.*" Was first made by Wedgwood.

SAGGERS are boxes of fire-clay into which objects to be fired are put for protection against direct contact with the flames. The word is spelled in various ways.

SALT GLAZED WARE is, as its name implies, a ware which is glazed by throwing salt into the kiln, which volatilizes at about 800° to 900° C. and deposits itself upon the surface of the ware as a glaze. These temperatures are higher than those at which many earthenwares are fired and, therefore, we usually find salt glaze on a stoneware or some type of porcelaneous ware.

Characteristics

1. The glaze can never deposit itself perfectly evenly and the surface is always slightly roughened.

2. The glaze is very thin and transparent so that all oddities of the biscuit show through it.

SHERDS or SHARDS are pieces of broken pottery and they are often ground and introduced into the body instead of grog or silica as a means of reducing shrinkage.

SLIP is simply a thin mixture of clay that is the consistency of thick cream. It is frequently identically the same composition as the body but thinned down with water.

SOFT PASTE, see EUROPEAN SOFT PASTE, CHINESE SOFT PASTE, ENGLISH SOFT PASTE.

STEATITE or TALC is a soft friable rock with slight plasticity and is used in glazes and bodies. It was thought the Far Eastern "Soft paste" was made with it but this is incorrect. It is a magnesium silicate, also known as SOAPSTONE, and is #1 on the Moh's scale. In glazes it makes viscous silicates with a long range of vitrification.

STONEWARE or GRÈS is a high fired and porcelaneous type of ware which differs from porcelain only in that its materials have been less well purified. It is fired usually without saggers at around 1190°.

Characteristics

1. Its natural color is ash-like or with higher temperatures red-brown.
2. It cannot be scratched readily with a steel point on the body.
3. It is nonporous even when unglazed.
4. A superior type called by the French "grès kaoliné" is really porcelain and the color of ivory.
5. It rings higher than soft paste.

TERRA COTTA, *see* POTTERY.

VITREOUS WARE in the present day designates a non-porous harder ware for hotels and restaurants. It is made of about 15% feldspar, 38% flint, 6% ball clay, 40% of china clay or kaolin and 1% of whiting and fired at 2,300° F. making a "stony" type of vitrification rather than a "glassy" type.

Thanks for assistance must be given Mr. Bernard Leach as much of the above material comes from his very excellent book, *A Potter's Book,* which is a fine and scientific handbook for practicing potters. Also to my friend Mr. Walter Howat who has been of constant help upon all technical questions in this book.

CHAPTER I

FUNDAMENTAL AESTHETIC APPEALS

CERAMICS, the art of making things in clay and baking them, is among the most ancient arts of man. Before man learned to chip stone (the paleolithic periods) he had learned to make clay cups. Young children instinctively love to make mud pies and from the mud pie to the mud cup is a short step. These first potteries have gone but the most ancient, as proven by the layers of earth from which they were dug, are so sophisticated in design that we can only conclude that thousands of years of practice must have preceded their making. Some are so good, in fact, that they have set styles of design which have lasted through many thousands of years.

Ceramics is not only one of the most ancient of arts but one of the most important. Here we meet with a strange misconception on the part of many; that the only works of fine art are those done in oil colors on canvas. The reason for this is that after the Renaissance, during which great craftsmen and great painters were honored equally, and great painters were proud to declare themselves craftsmen, the Gothic architecture with its slender columns and lack of wall space left no room for paintings. The Dark Ages provided few wealthy patrons for the painters. And even later when pictures became popular in the Low Countries, the rooms were small and wall space confined. Thus painting was no longer an applied art or a necessary art and it became a necessity for the painter to do "easel pictures," and to practice art for art's sake. Soon a defensive snobbery appeared and the term "fine art" began to imply that all other art was less fine because it served not art but utility. This is false reasoning but purposeless art became "fine" while all other art was classed as "minor." Even sculptors were excluded and one heard the reference, "Artists and sculptors," as though the latter were not also artists.

I believe that this condition is directly responsible for much misunderstanding and lack of appreciation of the arts. In the great periods no such distinction was made and, as I have written before, the Greeks did as fine things for a pediment as for a pedestal. The Egyptians, Romans, people of India and of China value a knife, a cup, a perfume vial or a carpet as much as a painting. Let us approach the study of this art, which is the very embodiment of form and color, without prejudice and see what ages of man have done with it.

To try to define beauty is like trying to stuff life itself into a box. We may like a thing one day and dislike it intensely the next, and the causes of our

1

likes and dislikes are subconscious and cannot be defined. Croce and others who have tried to define art, beauty, taste, etc., are attempting the impossible, for these are not single things around which we can draw a line and say that which lies within belongs and that which lies without does not. There is no one thing which is beauty; there are thousands of beauties and more are added every day. But I prefer a broader term and would' suggest that we consider some of the unlimited number of *appeals* that men have enjoyed through ceramics.

Man derives his happiness in life through the normal functioning of his body and is likely to associate the pleasant experiences of existence and of procreation with what he calls beautiful or appealing. Certain bowls make our mouths water for a fine soup, a stoneware tankard makes us think of cool beer, or a smooth surface and soft curves may consciously or unconsciously recall a beautiful woman's body. I am reminded of a circumspect lady who handed me a globular vase covered with a glaze called by the Chinese "ostrich egg" or "chicken skin" and saying, "Isn't it perfectly thrilling? Just hold it in your hands and feel it!" I sincerely hope she did not guess what went through my mind and the vase was no less beautiful for it.

The wise Chinese have a saying that the proper size for a tea-cup is that of a young girl's breast and they have a vase which is called "woman's form." Is there not an obvious amount of such appeal in a Rubens nude or a Franz Hals drinking scene? And perhaps in the ceramic arts it is less obvious, less conscious and, therefore, longer lasting and more intriguing.

Just as death is part of life, so the ancient potters made their wares also to serve in death or to help carry life over into the tomb and to some of these we owe our knowledge of past ages, of the aspirations of these men, of their hopes, their pleasures and their pursuits in peace and war. But it is interesting to note that the ceramic arts were never any aid to man in war. Weapons were made of wood, stone, brass, iron and many other substances, but pottery stands alone in being nondestructive.

First Developments

It is safe to say that the older appeals are the stronger. Man instinctively mistrusts that which is new and very little do any of us change from the habits of thought of our parents though we may strut and declare that we are original beings. Let us consider, therefore, the most primitive pots we know.

Certainly the first cups made were hand patted and took the place of leaves and shells. The first were sun baked and later it was found, probably when it was attempted to cook food in them, that they hardened with the fire.

Weaving is probably a less old art but still very ancient and where baskets were made an attempt may have been made to make them watertight by applying clay to the inside. Possibly again the basket was burned away and it was found that the clay had hardened. In any event many primitive potters have used mats to help them form clay vessels. Most of the earliest of such wares are more or less globular or pointed-bottom beakers, and man, having become used to the mat surface, imitated it consciously in many of the earliest known wares.

In Africa in one tribe the women make round pots by patting the clay over an original pot, allowing it to dry partly and then slipping the model out and pressing in the lip to form a narrower mouth. Perhaps a head or round stone was used for the first model.

Another primitive method is that of coiling a sort of rope of clay around and around on itself and finally scraping the inside and outside surface to flatten it. This is related to basket weaving again, of course, and it naturally led to cylindrical forms. In certain instances in America we will find that beautiful patterns were also developed. The scraper was a natural parent of the templet which later was not so beneficial, as it often took away all the impressions of the potter's hands.

The wheel may have come into being through making coiled vessels when it was found easy to place them on a stone so that they could be turned round and round. Later a stone wheel was made in truer form and a helper kept it turning, and then came the foot operated wheel of wood, the use of water power and of more modern means. However, the wheel itself is just about the same instrument as that used thousands of years ago. The power of electricity may have made the work easier, but the relationship of the speed and the action of the artist's hands in "throwing" a vessel is so delicately felt that some modern potters prefer the old foot wheel to power driven ones.

There are few more sensitive instruments than the potter's wheel and the clay can respond as sensitively to the potter's slightest touch as does the string of a violin or the brush of a Chinese painter. Every nervous tremor, every ghost of a touch is translated through the fingers into the imperishable clay which, if treated properly, will freeze it forever for the eyes of those who understand.

The mold is a much later method of making figures and also vase forms. It should never be used to make a round vase which can better be thrown on the wheel. Unfortunately for the art a mold is a cheap short cut and always is called into use when commercialism demands a quantity of pieces in one shape. When a sculptor does make use of a mold he should, of course, go over his work in detail removing suture marks, sharpening details and putting the hand of man freshly upon the work again. But at best this is repetition and his work will lack the first spontaneity. Moreover, casts should not be made from metal or wood or any other substance than clay or it will be obvious that they are not of clay structure or technique.

With these simple processes the potter makes his wares. There was a reason for everything he did and "modern art" creators would do well to consider some of the whys and wherefores before discarding them. As an instance, it was found at an early date in all places that a pot without a foot-rim would be easily broken when it was set down and therefore foot-rims came into general use. It was also found that if the throwing of a pot was not exactly true, the foot-rim could be slightly ground to make it stand straight. Different potters made these foot-rims in different ways and the collector can tell by the rim alone if a piece is likely to be of Near Eastern, of a certain period of Chinese potting, of Korean or Japanese workmanship.

Methods for handling a pottery vessel are interesting. A globular jar can be readily lifted only by using both hands or by grasping the lip-rim and therefore handles were found necessary or at least convenient. The simplest handle is the slightly curved projection to be held between thumb and hand on the Han period Chinese food bowls. Loop handles attached to the shoulder of a vessel and brought up to the neck or lip-rim are more structural, but all handles are easily brok n. The bottle neck is easily grasped and when designed properly has strength through good structure. But it is dif-

FIG. 1. Rice bowls placed in the tomb for the use of the deceased. These are of heavy, red body and with green iridescent glaze of silver tone. Warren E. Cox Collection.

ficult to pour liquids into a neck small enough to be readily grasped and therefore flaring lip-rims were made to act as funnels. This flaring rim became a hazard in itself and was treated in various ways to avoid breakage. Another form is the alberello developed first in Mesopotamia or Persia and this is simply a cylindrical jar with concave waist small enough to get a hold on. These jars could be stood on a shelf side by side and almost touching yet could be easily removed, as there is room to get one's fingers between them. Therefore, the form came to be used as an apothecary jar in Spain, Italy and elsewhere. A modification of the bottle

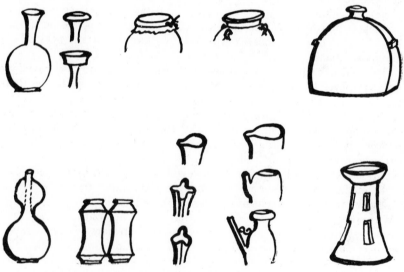

FIGS. 2–8. Elements of Form.

is the Chinese gourd shape with a bulging neck which holds more contents and yet permits an easy hold about the waist. Still another form that is well nigh universal is the pilgrim bottle, a circular flattened vessel with small mouth and often having loops for suspension. This form is undoubtedly derived from metal containers which were slung to a saddle or pack.

Pouring devices also dictate restrictions of form. At times the flaring lip of a bottle is pinched up in one place to make pouring from it easier. Some bottles, such as the small marbled clay T'ang one which I sold the Metropolitan Museum have the lips so pinched as to form quatrefoil or trefoil shapes. The pinching up of the lip was also used on cylindrical and globular pots and this became deeper until it was covered over and became a spout. But it should be remembered that all spouts are easily broken, if they are not made particularly sturdy and well supported.

Methods for covering also have developed many types of pottery covers, prominent rims over which a cloth or leather could be drawn and bound tightly, and various loops about the shoulder to help bind down covers. These should always be distinguished from "handles," as they are often called although they may be so small that one could not get the little finger through one. Covers also had to be so designed for pouring vessels that they would not fall off when the vessel was tipped.

Supporting collars, stands and legs were worked out so that vessels could be stood over fire. Thus we see large spool-like forms all over the world used to hold the pointed and round-bottomed vessels, tall reticulated hollow columns in Anau and Japan, and the well known three-legged "Ting" form of China.

THE USEFUL BEAUTIFUL

Early potters considered the practical reasons for forms and spent very little time on whimsy or endeavors to be different. It would seem, in fact, that the less the potter paid attention to artistic considerations the more pure, moving and enduring was his art. No vase form has ever lasted through the ages if it was not the result of such practical reasoning. What beauty then can lie in such things? How can appeals occur where there was not even the intention to create an appeal?

Michelangelo said that a piece of sculpture should be such that it could be rolled down hill without breaking. He did not follow out his theory but good potters did. We all dislike seeing things which look unstructural. The old broken-handled pitcher sits on the shelf so long that we get sick of it and throw it out. When we buy a new one, we look at it to see if the handle is more strongly made. It is not so much the losing of the pitcher but the pity that it was perfectly good except for that broken handle. Thus a piece of pottery should be so made that it at least appears to have good, sound structure.

You may say, "But surely everyone knows that!" Yet we will find that among the worst offenders in this respect are the so-called "classic" Greek vases which we have been taught to look upon as the greatest of ceramics.

I say that a work of art should be beautiful, satisfying and useful so long as it is recognizable and should meet the onslaught of time and usage with dignity, collapsing utterly rather than fall into the hideous wreckage of crippled distortion. It may be argued that if a thing is beautiful, what does anyone care how it will break? The answer is that one instinctively knows the weak points and subconsciously realizes what it will look like when broken. We cannot deny the appeal of structure.

The appeal of fragility is a corollary to the above. Certain works of art are like a "Prince Rupert's drop" or "glass tear" and will endure forever unless the careless hand destroys them and then they fly to pieces in utter destruction. Eggshell porcelain and Venetian glass are of this sort and it is astonishing how they have come down through the ages when handled by hands more roughly suited to the sword or knife than to their delicacy. An ear, a nose or a foot missing disgusts to the point of discard while the threat of utter demolishment seems to command respect and therein lies the appeal of fragility. Delicacy and fragility in some women may also influence our general judgment of these qualities in a work of art.

There is a human appeal in objects which show the hand of man in their manufacture or use. The arm of an old chair, the handle of a knife, a silver snuff box or an old walking stick recall love, respect and honor. They have served well and something of the character of those who have owned them has entered into them through the years. Of course our ceramic arts do not show such wear but they do bring out the character of the men who made them. In Japan tea-cups are made in what at first appear to be crazy shapes but when held properly they are found to fit the hand perfectly. To obliterate the form and even accidents which the potter put into a work is to sacrifice the human element for the purpose of gaining a cold perfection less appealing to the open mind of a true connoisseur.

There is also *tactile appeal* which is as important to some as visual appeal. As a young man I disliked oil paintings because they looked sticky like "molasses on sand paper" as I used to say. Later when I saw a Chinese gentleman lightly run his fingers over the old silk of a fine Sung painting, I found that there are others who understand this. So it is that some wares feel right in weight and form and some glazes are far more pleasant to the touch than others. Those potteries which can be handled gain great appeal and the real lover of such wares cannot be contented with looking at them. He must pick them up, turn them around, run his hand over the glaze, look at the foot, stand them on the table and frequently even then he keeps his hand on them turning them this way and that as he looks at them. One can easily tell how much a person likes a certain ware and how much he understands it by watching him handle it. And then there are those who can add to the value of a vase simply by the way they handle it. Such was Oto Fukishima, my first master.

Patination also has its appeal for we distrust the new. A soldier will work for days with saddle soap on his leather to make it look old. All boys will scuff their new shoes to take off the newness. Most men hate a new hat. The sculptor will patinate his bronze to make it fit better into the landscape, not for any purpose of faking age. The Chinese Taoists and Zen Buddhists have perhaps thought this out more clearly. They have a belief that one should live in the flow of the universe; should live naturally and to be rather than to seem. They say, I have heard, that a vase should be such that it might be put down in the woods and passed as a mushroom or some other natural growth.

Natural patination is the benediction of nature bestowed as a mark of honor which a fine work of art wears to prove its worthy age. Few of the weak survive to show it, as will, I fear, be proven by many of our modern creations. Upon no other work of man does nature place such brilliant and varicolored fire as upon the common pot of clay glazed with a bit of sand. It would seem that the original ordeal of flame which made it is recalled in the blaze of light.

But, it may be claimed, the potter had no knowledge of this, and that is true. However, a fundamentally poor pot, with glaze chipping off and ill made, would not wear its decorations any better than a war profiteer.

I delighted in reading in Lin Yutang's "The Importance of Living" about an old Chinese rule for the painting of rocks beneath pine trees. It seems that such rocks should be painted so that they will look very old and "stupid," old and solid and dull. Such rocks must wear their moss well and all the moss in the world would not help the brittleness of our sharp city stones. The artist then, although he has no part in making the patination itself, can, nevertheless, make an object which will wear it well, and perhaps a really fine vase can be built which is sturdy enough to last, so natural as to belong to nature itself and as stupid as an old rock under a pine tree.

"Modernists" say that ornamentation is out of place and unnecessary on a work of art and I am the first to agree that many vases are beautiful and most appealing in form, color and texture alone, but who could resist the ornamentation of clay? The vase is turned and smoothed. It has dried to a leather-like consistency and then perhaps been turned and polished. The least scratch can be made even with the fingernail. A clay of a different color and thinner consistency (slip) can be painted on or the vase may be dipped into the slip and have parts scratched away allowing the body to show through. Little patted or pinched up lumps of clay ("barbotine process") can be added to the surface. A glaze or glazes can be applied and decoration over or under these can be made in different colors. It is as hard for a potter to leave the surface of his vase alone as for a boy to resist marking a newly-made cement sidewalk.

An unornamented surface is as unknown as a perfect vacuum in nature. The smoothest pure white stone soon develops stains and cracks which slowly but surely bring it back to harmony with its surroundings in nature. The artificiality of plainness has been a recent cult in decoration and for a short time white rooms were attempted. But a white room is no more restful than a dead calm at sea which is so terrible an ordeal to man's momentum. It is the plainness of prison which punishes to the limits of endurance. What a world this would be if there were no shadows! And, if there are shadows, could they not be indelible and would they not then constitute design? Nature is forever making design before our eyes and we are simply resisting nature and becoming unnatural, if we think we can get along without it. An excellent example of such resistance to nature is the house designed by Frank Lloyd Wright for Edgar Kaufmann. It is built across a brook in a dense grove of trees and the architect made it in the character of great horizontal white slabs of concrete unrelieved save by plain areas of glass. It looks new.

It contradicts all that is about it. It is hard and tiring. It is a challenging place that the aborigines would look upon with fear and mistrust. It is the antithesis of Lin Yutang's "stupid rocks." But never mind, for nature will take care of all that in time although the process will not be a pleasant one.

Of course ornamentation and decoration can be carried too far and can become oppressive or disturbing. We may agree that much Italian majolica with its pictures of nude ladies writhing around among foliage and decorated with scrolls and grotesquerie have their faults. Many feel that perspective which makes a hole in a vase or plate is out of place. *In truth it is dangerous to go much beyond shadows in the decoration of a vase.* Shadows conform to the surface and fit well. Shadows are likely to have colors which contain something of the color of the vase. *Above all they help to define the form rather than distort it.*

Compare the decoration of a "Hawthorn" Chinese blue and white vase with that of a majolica plate. Then look at the beautiful brushwork on the Sung period Tz'u Chou wares. Finally turn to some of the Sultanabad bowls, and you will see what is meant by suitable design and how it is like shadows.

Size itself can be appealing or the opposite and size should be carefully considered in judging a vase or figure. Think of a pearl two feet in diameter. Who would want it? Thus a perfect "clair de lune" vase in its most delicate palest blue perfection would be unpleasant if it were a yard high. We expect a "sang de boeuf" or ox blood vase to be a good size, but who would want a peach bloom vase of the same size? Here we are considering an appeal most difficult to analyze but perhaps, if we use what Henri Bergson might call dream logic, we can make up our minds just about how big an object should be. I have heard people say that they were shocked and surprised when they first saw the Mona Lisa because it was so much smaller than they had expected. Can it be that the picture would have been more appealing had it been painted somewhat larger? Some vases gain power by being larger while others gain preciousness by being small. Of course purpose must be considered, but experiment with projecting things on the stereopticon screen leads to interesting results and size is a factor of appeal.

These are but a few considerations of appeal. Again I quote Lin Yutang, "There are so many kinds of beauty, beauty of quaintness, beauty of tenderness, of gracefulness—of majesty, of austerity, of ruggedness, of sheer strength and of a suggestion of the antique." He was referring to a pine tree, but all these beauties can be found in pottery and there are many more such as the beauty of stillness and there are vases as still as the moon, the beauty with which a vase can stand on tiptoe and slowly turn, the beauty of a jar which can hunch itself up as cosily as a cat, the beauty which suggests the comfort of a well-filled stomach and the beauty of a tall and graceful woman.

CHAPTER II

THE EARLIEST POTTERIES

Neolithic and Early Bronze Age Potteries

After the days of Napoleon it was natural that Europeans should believe that the most ancient culture in the world was in Egypt and, of course, we do find one of the earliest cultures along the Nile, but it soon became apparent that the Danube, the Tigris and Euphrates, and the Yellow River valleys had their own very ancient cultures, while other areas challenged the antiquity of these.

In pre-dynastic Egypt as early as 4321 B.C., red and black pottery was made and decorated with some angular ornament and freely drawn human and animal motives. Sir Flinders Petrie found at Qua an even earlier ware of fine clay, thinly hand potted in true symmetry and containing iron ore which gave it a black polish resembling glaze. In neolithic times, it is claimed by A. J. Butler on good evidence, there were made, about 5500 B.C., votive tiles having a ribbed surface and blue-green glaze with inlaid hieroglyphics in color, and also examples of two colors of glazes blended. Also, still in the pre-dynastic times can be located two green glazed tiles, one with a figure of a Negro and some characters and one with a ram in relief, which were found at Abydos. It is established fairly certainly that it is to Egypt that we owe the first development of glaze and that naturalistic ornament is to be found there at an early date. (I dislike using the word *invented* because glaze, like many of the developments in ceramics, probably occurred more or less accidentally and may have been consciously used, lost and refound at different places in different times.)

Also at a very early date the Egyptians carved out bowls from rock and it was natural enough that later some pottery was made with mixed clays or painted to give an effect of the striations of rock. This technique we will find spread throughout the world and it led to "marbled" wares of many kinds.

At about 4000 B.C., it is thought, a conquering people from the North, possibly from Syria, brought the bronze age to Egypt and around 3500 to 3000 B.C. started the First Dynasty.

In Europe we know that in paleolithic times (that is generally speaking when man was able to make chipped stone implements but had not found out how to polish them smooth) very beautiful and sophisticated naturalistic animal drawing had been accomplished as is proven by the paintings of the Altamira caves and others. Yet no pottery has been identified with this culture though undoubtedly some must have been made. After the arctic

9

FIG. 9. Smooth buff ware tall pottery vase made in predynastic Egypt. Height 11½". Metropolitan Museum of Art.

FIG. 10. Predynastic Egyptian double vase of red polished ware and white line decoration. Metropolitan Museum of Art.

FIG. 11. Vase of predynastic Egypt of the well made red polished ware with primitive decoration in white lines. Metropolitan Museum of Art.

FIG. 13. Predynastic Egyptian tall vase of smooth buff ware. Height about 14". Metropolitan Museum of Art.
Note: This general form of tall jar with pointed bottom seems to have been made by most primitive potters the world over. It, the globular pot and the shallow bowl are the most fundamental forms in all potting.

FIG. 12. Predynastic Egyptian vase, suggesting a stone model but decorated with wavy lines suggestive of water design in weaving. Metropolitan Museum of Art.

FIG. 14. Black ware incised decorated bowl of predynastic Egypt having a good form and well related design. Dia. 5¾". Metropolitan Museum of Art.

10

conditions of this early stone age had modified, some men with the rest of the old quaternary fauna drifted north and various more or less isolated cultures developed. One of these, the "Kitchen Midden," located on the south shores of the Baltic Sea and in Southern Scandinavia, produced a primitive pottery with pointed bottom and rough decoration just below the rim. This form was developed in a number of places probably because it could be leaned against a rock or tree in country so uneven as to make a flat-bottomed or round-bottomed vessel difficult to place. It has been suggested that primitive man spent much of his time in making stones and sticks pointed and thus became what might be called point minded, but this seems to me doubtful.

Toward the end of mezzolithic times Europe began to feel influences from the South and East and among the most important advances were those in pottery. Mr. Miles Burkitt has pointed out, as I did, that it is impossible for man to leave alone the beautiful and so easily impressionable surface of unbaked clay. Thus, now we find red and also black wares (depending upon conditions of firing) which are incised, painted and sometimes first incised and then the incisions filled in with a white or colored clay inlay in contrast to the body. The designs of these wares are a series of deep zigzags running up and down about the body, and those in Central and Eastern Europe are better made and more vigorous and deeply incised than those in the western sections which are coarse and rough. Small ladles and cups were also made.

Probably between the Rhine and Elbe rivers there originated a culture identified by a type of beaker which the people buried with their dead. These beakers are also found in Holland, Denmark, Bohemia and even Britain. The graves contain little metal and that is supposed to have been imported. The theory has been advanced that these people came from the steppes of South Russia and it is admitted that the manner of burial is similar to that of the Russian kurgans (mounds). In Northern Germany cord-ornamented vessels are made with globular bodies and long cylindrical necks while possibly in Spain originated a similar vessel with wider body and widely expanding mouth decorated with bands of geometrical ornament. This latter is found also in Portugal, Sardinia, Sicily, Northern Italy and parts of France. In Bohemia are found both types, but the so-called "bell beakers" of Spanish type are not so good and there is a larger number of the Northern type. Either the former ware came from the Ukraine and was later developed in Spain, or the Bohemian ware shows a degeneration. We are not sure which.

In Greece during the early copper age the Thessalian peasants had been pushed from the East by South Russians and brought with them the painted pottery known as "Dhimini" ware, but before the bronze age this had deteriorated and its place was taken by a plain gray-black or red pottery decorated with light red and white. Finally all decoration ceased at about 2000 B.C. and "Minyan" ware, which was wheel-made of gray clay (sometimes burnt red), was either brought from Asia Minor or developed from the Thessalian plain pottery of earlier times. This plain ware lasted from about 2000 B.C. to 1625 B.C. when the Minoan influences of Crete became strong. (See Chapter III.)

EARLY POTTERY FROM THE BLACK EARTH REGION

1. Erösd; 2 and 4. Cucuteni; 3. Oltszem; 5–10. Government of Kiev.
Scale (Nos. 1–4) 1:6; (Nos. 5–10) 1:10

Note the S designs which have also been pressed into angular forms on the pot stand to upper right in the same way that they appear on Shang (1766–1154 B.C.) bronzes of China.

Note also the prominent "nose and two eye" design on # 6 and # 10 which also became a feature of Shang design.

Both may possibly have originated here in the "Black Earth Region."

Plate 1

Thus, to sum up the first Western European known potteries, they were either red or black, were 1.—decorated with incised or string-impressed designs, 2.—decorated with painted designs or 3.—left plain. The designs are all simple zigzags or bands with various hatched and line patterns; that is the sort that any child or primitive decorator would arrive at in a certain stage of development without any outside influence being necessary. Representations of animals or men were not used, either in freely drawn but naturalistic style, as in Egypt, or in compacted or conventionalized style.

Now coming to the "Black Earth Region" of Transylvania, Bukowina, Galicia, Bessarabia and the Ukraine as far east as Kiev we find the earliest wares of 3000 B.C. or older to be well-made bowls, pot-stands with slightly curved sides and flaring bases and jars having bottoms not pointed but so sharply rounded as to suggest it, stem-cups and, in

FIG. 15. Development of design of Pl. I, No. 1 by Dr. H. Frankfort in his "Studies in Early Potteries of the Near East."

Galicia, diamond-shaped jars having the upper half decorated as though they were made to set into a stand of some sort. They are decorated with black on red, or on a buff ware and parallel with them are plain wares which appear to be contemporary. The most obvious characteristic is the varied use of a horizontal S spiral or what is called a "pot hook" design. These at times are hooked end to end and at times are applied to the pot without regard to its structure. To quote Dr. H. Frankfort ("Studies in Early Potteries of the Near East II") "We see then that, underlying the peculiar designs in which pot-hook spirals, concentric circles, and animal representations are used, there appears persistently a framework of rectilinear bands. On some vessels these latter form the sole decoration." These would impress us at once as being remnants of earlier habitual designs. To continue, "Its correlative seems to be the use of black-painted designs on a polished surface, i.e., that technique which we have found to be characteristic of Cappadocia and the regions further east; and as at Anau I we find designs which may conceivably be a primitive stage of the 'Rautenstil,' there is the probability that the 'Rautenstil' is an aboriginal style of Eastern Asia Minor."

We will come to the Anau examples shortly, but here we find something quite different from anything in Western Europe or in Egypt. It is true that the reverse spiral is typical of the Halstadt Bronze Culture of Austria, but it was not found on potteries and this use of spirals is not so early. It is to be noted too that here we come for the first time to buff colored potteries, all the others being red or black, and also, for the first time in European wares, animals are mentioned.

This "Black Earth Area" northwest of the Black Sea is closely related to our next section of Syria, Mesopotamia and Persia where careful excavations tell us a clearer story.

Ur, near the mouth of the Euphrates, has attracted public attention due to the gold and precious stone objects found there, but the pottery is no less remarkable. Here many civilizations had built upon the crumbled ruins of foregoing civilizations and to give an idea of how these excavations are carried out let us see what Mr. C. Leonard Woolley, director of the joint expedition of the Pennsylvania University Museum and the British Museum,

FIG. 16. Animal Jug on Wheels which is of the Flood period found with jars with lumps of clay stamped with seals on top and dated by inscriptions to the first dynasty of *Ur* (3100 B.C.). Pennsylvania University Museum.

FIG. 17. Pottery of the Flood Period in Mesopotamia which is not wheel made and was found over 30 feet below the level which represented 3200 B.C. It is of whitish or greenish clay with designs in black, or of reddish clay with designs in chocolate brown. Note also the comb decoration in the bottom of one bowl. Pennsylvania University Museum.

FIG. 18. Figures of the period of the Flood —found in the graves with painted pots at *Ur*, these figurines are of white clay with Bitumen headdresses. Another was of green clay with black markings. They represent not human women but some goddess or demon and are about the only objects which were found to show religious significance. The square shoulders, prominence of breasts and general pose suggest some "goddess or demon" of our present age. Pennsylvania University Museum.

says about it. Starting at a level established as being of the date of about 3200 B.C. where were found clay seals for the tops of jars, tablets and the remarkable animal on wheels illustrated, they dug down *two levels* and found potteries painted in sealing-wax red and also in red, black and buff some of which had lead tumblers covering the tops. At the *fourth level* there were potteries quite unlike any of the others found. They were covered with a light slip and wiped off to make a crude sort of pattern. At the *fifth level* were pots of light clay decorated with bands of red paint. At the *sixth level* more three-colored sherds (broken pieces of pottery) were found of the

"Jemdet Nasr" type and then came a level of an entirely different type. At this *eighth level* the remarkable discovery of an intact pottery kiln was found with the last batch of pots stacked in it. Nearby was a clay potter's wheel with burnishers and other potter's tools. Here the pottery was of black on white and chocolate on pink of the "el Obied" type, after the later ones of plain red sometimes burnished and of plum-colored mat. Here was the end of the wheel-made wares and all below are hand patted. Then there was waterlaid sand about eleven feet thick and thirty feet down, but under that a layer of household rubbish and more pottery. In one place were lumps of clay burnt red and black and grooved. To quote, "In other words they were the remains of a reed hut plastered with clay which had stood and been burnt down before the Flood overwhelmed this part of the country."——— This, I must intercede, is another way in which pottery could have been discovered.———But to go on, it was found that these people lived in brick houses also. And finally below this level came indications of sea plants, hard clay and other signs that this was the bottom of Mesopotamia below sea level. Mr. Woolley says that the civilization after the flood was the same as that before but feebler and degenerate and it died soon. The potteries are whitish and greenish decorated with designs in black, and also of reddish clay decorated with chocolate brown. Note the illustration which shows a pot with spout of this culture which seems to show a considerable sophistication and could only be the result of a number of generations of development.

In some of the graves female figurines were found, one of green clay with black markings and others of white clay with bitumen headdresses on their strange misshapen heads. They are nude and either have their hands on their hips or are holding a child. It is thought that these represent some goddess, for anyone who formed the bodies could have made the heads more lifelike, if he had so wished.

Other expeditions of the Pennsylvania University Museum have made discoveries at sites called Tepe Gawra and Tell Billa in the headwaters of the Tigris river. At the former place there are twenty strata and we know nothing of the origin of the "Painted Pottery People" who settled there before 5000 B.C. I show a boat-shaped bowl which is unique and decorated with alternating wave and fern patterns. (Upper right hand corner of plate.) A round bowl has an alternating panel design on the outside and is well potted. The globular jar with cross-hatched triangles about the shoulder is a more usual round bottomed early type, but the flattened pot with spout handle and alternating design about the upper surface is unique.

Billa VII & VI—From about 3000 B.C. to 1500 B.C. the two mounds have a parallel development, although the occupation of Billa did not begin until Gawra had already been covered up by fourteen meters of occupational débris. Here are, beginning with about 3200 B.C., goblet forms with painted bands having cross-hatched panels and rows of highly conventionalized birds and animals as well as plain pots wheel-turned and finished with a wash. They were first fired at about 1600° F and later up to 2000° F. They are similar to the Jemdet Nasr or first predynastic period of the south wares. The colors are purplish brown, black and red on buff, brown and gray. Later

TEPE GAWRA AND TELL BILLA SITES
At Head Waters of Tigris
Potteries found by the Joint Expedition to Persia of the University Mus.
and the Pennsylvania Mus. of Art of 1931

Potteries from Tepe Gawra in northern Iraq of the
al Obied period 4000 B.C.

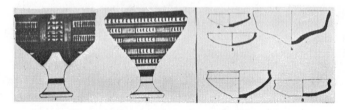

Rows of birds in silhouette, cross hatching, etc. Notice alternating areas in bands.

Painted designs become rare.

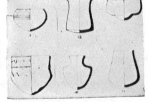

Tell Billa Potteries VII and VI 3200–2900 B.C.
Chalices in brown, black, and red on buff or grey.
Flat and pointed bases on bowls. Plain pieces finished
with a wash, early ones fixed at 1600° F., later ones
fixed at 2000° F.

Incising and relief become popular.

PLATE 2

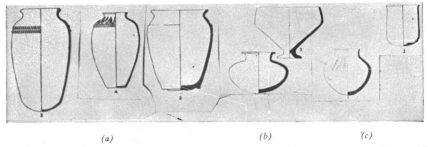

(a)   (b)   (c)

(a) Tell Billa Potteries V 2900–2700 B.C. Copper age begins and potteries become scarcer. Slips, red bands about shoulders, occasionally black paint spots. Note first foot rim on large pot in center. *(b)* Chalice has a lower foot. *(c)* Straight cup with round or flat bottom is characteristic.

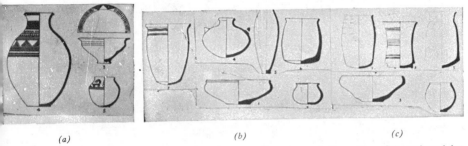

(a)   (b)   (c)

(a) Tell Billa Potteries IV Rustolian Period c. 1900 B.C. New shapes, better potting, flat or rimmed bottoms, well-defined lip-rims. Ribbing, knot handles perpendicularly pierced for suspension. Painting and incising. *(b)* Note alternating principle on rim of bowl and shoulder of pots. *(c)* Cream slips are frequent.

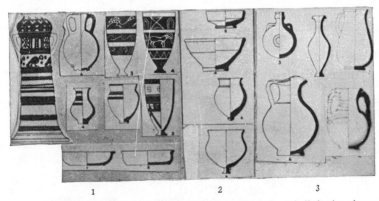

1   2   3

1. Tell Billa Potteries Stratum 3 Hurrian Period 1600–1400 B.C. New and distinctive shapes, small cups with button bases, bowls made into dishes or cups. Buff, grey or reddish. Cream slips and light red, dull black and white used in painting. Naturalistic designs confined to birds, goats, and fish. No humans or trees except as figurines with decoration. Bowls return. Button bases replaced by nipple type. Decoration almost disappears. 2. Tell Billa Potteries Stratum 2 Middle Assyrian 1300–800 B.C. Red predominant. Bowls return. Button bases replaced by nipple type. Decoration almost disappears. 3. Tell Billa 1 Late Assyrian 800–700 B.C. Jugs, pitchers and amphoras appear. Post Assyrian. Glazes frequent, of a silvery sheen, bluish and greenish by accident. The pilgrim flask and slender bottle are new. Relief and incised ornamentation return.

PLATE 3

toward 2900 B.C. they become more elaborate in shape, greenish gray or buff, and painting gives way to incising and molding.

Billa V—Between 2900 and 2700 B.C. comes the copper age and the wares are mostly incised about the shoulder with touches of bitumen and red bands. There are no new shapes.

Billa IV—It is probable that the foregoing period had seen more interest in copper as a novelty than in the potteries. Ring bases are introduced and painting resumed with more angular shoulders and well made lip-rims. This is the Anatolian Period, and extends from around 1900 B.C.

FIG. 19. Iranian ewer from Siyalk of about 1000 B.C. with spout possibly also used as handle. Height about 10". N. M. Heeramaneck Col.

FIG. 20. Iranian unglazed pottery pitcher of buff clay with dark red decoration dating about 1100 to 1000 B.C. Height about 6". Metropolitan Museum of Art.

Billa III—The Hurrian Period of 1600 to 1400 B.C. brings more new shapes and designs, a return to the lower 1600° F firing and much more painting along with Egyptian influences.

Billa II and I—Then we find the design entirely disappearing around 1300 B.C. in our middle and late Assyrian wares until in post-Assyrian times we come to the glazed Syro-Roman wares, etc.

A similar course is found at Damghan just south and east of the Caspian Sea, starting with angular stem cups and pointed-shaped bowls all painted in Hissar I around 3000 B.C., and then in Hissar II (2500 B.C.? to 2000 B.C.) going to nearly all plain wares which in Hissar III (1500 B.C. to 1200 B.C.) become more involved including vessels with hollow or deeply-grooved handle-spouts. These are not unlike the one we illustrate except that the loop handle was evidently a later addition and does not occur on those before 1200 B.C.

In the fertile valley between Askhabad and Merv just east of the southern tip of the Caspian Sea lies Anau where two sites have been found and the northern and earliest one is dated about 3900 B.C. to 3300 B.C. There the potteries are not wheel-made, have no handles and no incising and are painted with diamond cross hatched or solidly filled in bands and some with simple fern designs in bands. From the beginning at Anau there are light wares as well as red wares.

Again at Susa are most beautifully developed designs of animals and birds set in oddly shaped sections which, it has been suggested by Professor Meyers,

TEPE HISSAR "CASTLE HILL" EXCAVATIONS AT DAMGHAN

Potteries found by the Joint Expedition to Persia of the University Mus. and the Pennsylvania Mus. of Art of 1931.

HISSAR I (3000 B.C.)
Buff pottery painted with red, brown, or grey slips.

Note conventionalized leopard on first bowl. The ibex, gazelle, sheep and long horned cattle were known. Other designs are lines and chevrons. Jar second from end is very close to Han Chinese shape.

HISSAR II (2500–2000 B.C.)
Many shapes are identical with Hissar I. Grey wares, with some shapes further developed.

Base stands are eliminated, perpendicular rim disappears, base becomes less flat. Conical bowls are more rounded, all angular lines are eliminated. Spouts occur hollow topped and closed.

HISSAR III (1500–1200 B.C.)
Painted potteries survive as rituaiistic objects. New forms had small loops for covers, no handles yet, spouts further developed.

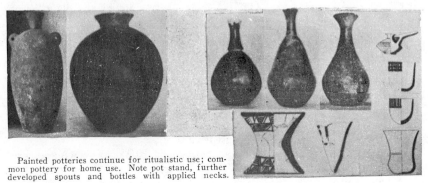

Painted potteries continue for ritualistic use; common pottery for home use. Note pot stand, further developed spouts and bottles with applied necks.

PLATE 4

may have followed the shapes which cut out of leather could have been sewn together to make round forms. The masterful conventionalizing of the animals and birds shows northern nomadic influence, that is from a people who would have naturally worked in leather. In any event these are highly sophisticated and beautifully painted wares of somewhat later period.

Fig. 21. Persian dish said to date about 3000 b.c. with an interesting spotted cat on the rim, perhaps a cheetah judging by its long legs. Part of a similar figure remains on the opposite wall. Length 8½". Brown on light buff. Boston Museum of Fine Art.

Fig. 22. Persian jar said to date about 3000 b.c. which shows interesting associations with those from Ur in Iraq and from Assyrian examples. Note the alternating design. Height about 7". Boston Museum of Fine Arts.

There are many other sites waiting for the spade of the excavator, but these will help to give a general idea of what took place. Now moving on to India we find at Mohenjo Daro a common unpainted ware and around 2000 b.c. a painted ware at the Chanhu-daro site which shows definite Assyrian influence in its alternating bands of foliate, chevron, hatched and similar designs. These again have purplish black and red designs on a white or pinkish white slip, or on a definite red slip. At this site are also earlier potteries of the Harappa times, perhaps going back to about 5000 b.c., with very little difference except that the earlier wares have a little more detail and are more firmly painted, the plant forms being more naturalistic.

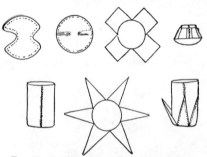

Fig. 23. An ingenious and probably true way in which the pointed designs and slotted circular ones on Susa pottery may have come about. It is suggested by Professor Meyers that these first occurred in sewn leather vessels.

In Eastern Baluchistan in the Zhob valley is the Tell Kaudeni site of early bronze age which is productive of similar wares, and so there are also sites in Turkestan, Sistan and Afghanistan, and we are led to believe that the Iranian Plateau, which is now desert, must once have been the center of a great culture.

In China, J. G. Andersson found at An-yang in Honan province and also in Kansu province further up the Yellow River, a largely wheel-made pottery having well-made loops and handles and of a hard baked red or brown color decorated with black, brown, purple, white and red designs. One of the first things that strikes the eye of the observer is that here again we have the well-defined horizontal S and concentric circular designs very similar indeed to those from the Black Earth Region. Perhaps at times a little more involved, perhaps applied with a better understanding of adaptation to the

Ancient Indian Pottery from Chanhu-daro with Influence of Assyrian Art In its Designs.

FIG. 24. Indian painted potteries of the Jhukar culture (c2000 B.C.) and one, center right, of the earlier Harappa culture (c5000 B.C.).

FROM THE
ILLUSTRATED LONDON NEWS,
Nov. 21, 1936

FIG. 26. Harappa figurine showing appliques of breasts, necklace, eyes and headdress. (c. 5000 B.C.) found at Chanhudaro at Jhukar, near Larkana, in central Sind.

form of the pot, but having so many details in common that it is difficult to believe that there is not some definite connection between the two. These wares are supposed to date about 3200 B.C. to 2900 B.C. although Mr. Liang Ssŭ-Yung, in an excellent paper brought before the American Anthropological Association some years ago, says they are more likely between 2500 and 2000 B.C.

Alongside of this painted pottery there was a coarse, gray earthenware seemingly contemporary, but made without the wheel and often impressed with lines suggesting that they had been wrapped in mats or that strings had purposely been pressed into the moist clay to give this texture. Some of these are globular jars of the fundamental shape, but others are in the form the Chinese call a Li (or hollow-legged Ting), and this is a complicated form to make and most interesting. It is my theory that the earliest potters in China as elsewhere made pointed-bottomed beakers, and that, finding that three of these could be leaned together over a fire, some bright potter thousands of years ago, made up his mind that he would put the three together

POTTERY FROM SUSA I, IN THE LOUVRE
SCALE ABOUT 1:3

Note the beauty of the conventionalized antelope and running dogs on # 1, the long necked birds on the neck of # 4 and # 5 as well as the slotted circular treatments of the bowls and pointed treatments of the cups.
The points particularly occur on Shang bronzes of China.

PLATE 5

FIG. 27. An excellent example of the An-yang painted ware with black and red rope design. It is very thinly potted for its size. Note that cord from the two loops would pull sideways against the body and not upward so as to pull loops off when tying on a cover. Height 18½″. Nasli Heeramaneck Collection.

FIG. 28. Neolithic jar from Kansu province in north western China, found by Andersson and said to date between 2000 and 3000 B.C. Note the reverse spiral which is a favorite design on these wares and is very similar to that on the pots from The Black Earth region. Height 15¼″. Brooklyn Museum.

22

and give them a common mouth, thus making a Li. This theory is fully backed by Andersson and seems most logical.

The Chinese bronze Ting is of generally deep bowl form with three solid and untapered legs and usually having handles added above the rim. Thus Albert J. Koop is incorrect when he says in his "Early Chinese Bronzes" that, "It is generally accepted that the most ancient type is the Ting," for obviously our pottery Li form is closer to the three pointed pots leaned to-

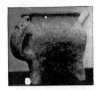

FIG. 29. Chou period unglazed gray pottery jar with incised decoration of horizontal lines and impressed perpendicular lines. Height 9¼". Ex D. Abbes Collection.

FIG. 30. Unglazed pottery Li of the neolithic period, north China, Manchuria or Mongolia string impressed and showing prototype of many bronze vessels. The author thinks that this form was derived from the custom of leaning three pointed type vessels together over a fire. From the Palmer Collection, Art Institute, Chicago.

FIG. 31. Li, or hollow legged tripod, of gray ware from An Yang and certainly reflective of earlier wares. Length about 5¼". Ralph M. Chait Col.

FIG. 32. Two An Yang vessels of Li form and, though of Shang period and contemporary with the great bronzes, probably reflective of much earlier pottery forms. Gray ware. Heights about 4" and 5". Ralph M. Chait.

gether and, therefore, it came first. It is also interesting to note that the general conception, due to Mr. R. L. Hobson's writings, that most of the early pottery shapes copied bronze forms is not quite true, for here is a simple pottery form taken over by the bronzes.

From Hsi-yin come also wares painted much like those of An-yang or Yang Shao. There was little incising and the painted designs give the impression that they are made up of bands containing celts pierced for a cord.

I do not go so far as to suggest that this is the actual source of the design, though certainly the celt is a basic design the world over. In Mongolian and Manchurian sites the wares are more crude and the designs are made up of dots, short lines, diamonds, curves, loops, etc., but are different from the Chinese ones. There are also string-impressed wares there. Mr. Liang Ssŭ-Yung concludes that these wares are later.

In Japan in the Todoroki shell mound, the one of many which lies nearest Korea, are wares similar to the Manchurian, as we would expect, but no string-pressed wares. Ornamentation on many is done by pinching up and pressing with the fingernail. Incising and reticulation are both characteristic. The wares from Cambodia are astonishingly like those in Japan.

Mr. Liang Ssŭ-Yung comes to the conclusion that during the times of the Hsi-yin and Yang Shao cultures a painted pottery flourished on the base of a string pottery from Kansu to Fêngtein in the Northeast. The string-impressed pottery, he thinks, came east and plain pottery from the south northward and met in Korea and Japan. At the end of neolithic times, the incised type with high stand and hollow foot appeared from around the northern borders of the Gobi Desert into Kingan and Yinshin and moved southward. He points out that it reached Anau (Culture III) near the Caspian about the same time. He does not venture to say that the relationship between China and Anau is solved.

However, Dr. Andersson has published a table with motives common to Honan and Anau I. Mr. Percival Yetts and Prof. L. Franz have endorsed and elaborated his views. Among these motives are the slanting oval. It may also be noted that Dr. Andersson found at Sha Ching on the Mongolian-Kansu border two sherds having rows of conventional birds much like those of Susa I and painted in red on a reddish ware. "Thus," to quote Dr. H. Frankfort again, "it seems that occasionally there appear in China, Armenia and Southwest Persia pot fabrics which present similarities in style of decoration as well as in technique."

FIG. 33

Anyone acquainted with Chinese bronzes would agree that the design on the pot-stand #3 (Oltszem) shown on the plate of potteries from the Black Earth Region has much in common with the design of the background of some Shang period (1766–1123 B.C.) Chinese bronzes, and this is nothing but the "pot hook" or "horizontal S" or reverse spiral. Perhaps there is no direct connection, but *this motive does not come into use anywhere else in the world at any such early time.*

Also near An-yang are found pieces of hard white pottery in sites associated also with black pottery usually accompanied by pieces of bone and ivory and which Mr. Yetts has dated about 1800 B.C. These are carved with the same designs seen on pre-Han bronzes. They are technically far ahead of any of the earlier wares we have discussed and on them occurs the horizontal S squeezed as it were into a rectangular form and made up of angles instead of curves. Other very refined potteries of black, hard ware, wheel-turned and thin have been found at Ch'êng Tzŭ Yai east of Tsinan, hence the name

Two important examples of Shang white pottery. A *lei* dating 13th to 12th century B.C. from The Freer Gallery of Art, Washington. Ht. 14″ and the only perfect piece of sculpture in the round and only piece known with turquoise inlays; the head of a cane, Warren E. Cox collection, New York, Ht. 3⅛″. The latter dates 14th century B.C. It is a staff handle.

PLATE 6

Firmly potted dark grey ware of fine form and with rope handle design, Shang period from An Yang. Height 4". Ralph M. Chait Collection.

Grey pottery jar covered with a fine evenly impressed pattern suggestive of a basket weave. Note the reverse spiral appliques on shoulder which had become a basic motive. Late Chou. Height 13½". C. T. Loo & Co.

Black pottery jar of grey body with thin black slip incised, impressed and combed with basic designs. The form is that of Han potteries but without tall base or attached pot-stand. Early Western Chou. Height. 13½". C. T. Loo & Co.

Black pottery Hu with incised decoration and two relief Tao-tieh handles. This is of grey body covered with thin black slip. Said to be "Early Eastern Chou" though very much like the one called Han in the Eumorfopoulos Col. Height 13½". C. T. Loo & Co.

BLACK AND GREY POTTERIES OF SHANG AND CHOU DYNASTIES OF CHINA

PLATE 7

"Lung Shan" ware, and with them refined white wares showing technical proficiency.

In an interesting article in *Asia* (Jan. 1941), Mr. Sterling S. Beath writes of the black pottery as follows: "Some was found in a district near Lung Shan in Shantung and was called 'Lung Shan ware,' also this place is called Cheng-tzu-yai. Other sites are at Liang Cheng, Feng Huang Thai, Shang Ts'un and Wang She Jen Chuang, all in Shantung, also at Hou Kang, Honan province near An Yang and on the Kiangsu-Shantung border. The ware is found only in Eastern China. In the same sites there was gray impressed pottery which is probably later. In Chekiang near Hang Chou at Liang Chu and near the Chin Shan Lake there is more found, but with larger quantities of gray pottery."

He continues that the typical "black pottery" is shiny and glazed and that the body is at times less than a millimeter in thickness. Some of it is black outside and gray inside and this is later. It is wheel-made as a rule and wheel-burnished. (I do not think he means the ware is glazed, for it certainly is not; the term is synonomous with burnished.) He says the painted pottery is only found in the West from Honan to Kansu provinces. Then he says, "It seems possible that the Black Pottery People laid the foundation for Shang civilization," and points out a similarity between their pottery beakers and the bronze form "ku." He also speaks of "li" forms with hollow legs having been found, but no "ting" forms. Perhaps it was this culture, developed as a separate entity in Northeastern China and Manchuria, that provided the technique necessary for the making of the great Shang bronzes and very probably it was not until the design from the West met their skill that the An-yang white wares were made possible.

Max Loehr has shown that certain simple vessels having no decoration other than three low relief ridges set about ⅜ inches apart running around the bodies are pre-Anyang of early Shang period and relate to pre-Shang black pottery. (See "Relics of Ancient China" from the collection of Dr. Paul Singer, Pl. 6, and "Ritual Vessels of Bronze Age China" p. 38, Pl. 11.) He has developed a series showing how the designs became more ornate as techniques improved. Of course, it is quite logical to state that man must have been able to make the beginnings of the bronze forms and the beginnings of bronze design in clay first, and a long time before he gained mastery of the more difficult medium. Thus it is likely that among potteries we find the pre-Shang roots of the great bronze art.

Moreover, it is my contention that the models, as well as the molds for the bronzes, were of ceramic materials. This is based upon the fact that the background is of even surface with the cutting away of equal depth at all points. I think this could only have been done by applying a slip to a partly fired piece and carving down to the harder surface. I shall go into more detail on this theory in my book titled *Drinking Vessels and Drinking Customs*.

The *t'ao-t'ieh* seen on most Shang bronzes, miscalled an "ogre mask," is actually perhaps an owl, a buffalo head, a tiger and can, when divided perpendicularly, become the side view of dragons, cloud patterns and other things.

This *t'ao-t'ieh* appears crudely indicated on a large painted pottery bowl from the Andersson finds, now in the Buffalo Museum. Mr. Priest says of the *t'ao-t'ieh*, "At first glance it is simply an elaborately conventionalized

Fig. 34. Large buff–colored pottery bowl painted with black, two large eyes and a prominent nose on either side with conventional meaningless design between. Dia. about 15″. Philip Rosenbach Col., Buffalo Museum.
Note: Compare with jar # 10 on plate of Black Earth potteries.
Painted Pottery Bowl from Kansu in Northwestern China with T'ao T'ieh Face.

animal head. Look closer and you find it is an intricate composite of animal and bird forms." He shows that it is often a more or less conventionalized owl, a bird, one would immediately conclude, natural to associate with moon worship. We shall later trace the spread of the *t'ao-t'ieh* around the whole Pacific Ocean and on down to Peru where moon worship was the fundamental religion. The *t'ao-t'ieh* is not found on the early potteries of Western Asia or Eastern Europe, or, if it is, it is so highly conventionalized as to be hardly recognizable as in #6 and #10 of our plate showing the potteries of the Black Earth Region. Each has alternating prominent circles, possibly eyes, and perpendicular long areas, possibly a nose; but even, if the head itself is not recognizable, its component parts, the "pot hooks" and reverse spirals are certainly often seen.

One noticeable difference between the Western and Eastern Asian styles is that in the Western sections and particularly in Mesopotamia *bands of alternating design* form a prominent part of the designs. We shall take up this

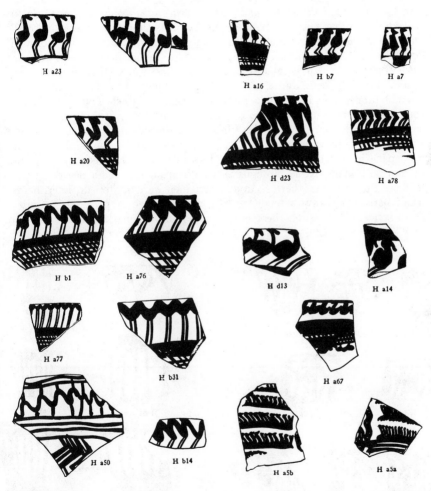

HISSAR I SHERDS—BIRD DESIGN AT VARIOUS STAGES OF CONVENTIONALIZATION. SCALE 1:3

FIG. 35. This plate is reproduced from The Museum Journal (Vol. XXIII, # 4, 1933) of the Hissar excavations of the Joint Expedition of the University Museum and the Pennsylvania Museum of Art. They are beautiful examples of what may be ter ied *degenerating conventionalization* brought about through repetition which grows more and more careless until unrecognizable.

This sort of conventionalization is quite different from that brought about in nomadic civilizations through having to compress a picture into a small given space. See # 1 on Hissar plate, and also # 1 on Susa plate.

method of design in the section on the potteries of Ashur, but it should be noted here that alternation plays an unimportant part in the earliest arts of China most of which are based rather upon a strictly symmetrical division of left and right with either a two front, or front and back section, *i.e.*, four quarters as are found in biological arrangements. Whether this was because study of life was closer to the Chinese and habits of weaving were closer to the Mesopotamians, we can only guess, but the difference is marked.

Finally it is obvious in the study of these early wares that *conventionalization was born and developed in the Northern and nomadic sections.* So far as I know this has not been pointed out, but it is simple to understand. The hunter-nomads lived exciting lives in which records of achievement, and magic demands for the bolstering of courage, were found desirable. They had little space on which to make such records and signs; they had to carry everything with them, and a piece of leather, the handle of a knife or later a small bronze buckle afforded the only areas available. Thus they had to compact their records into a sort of shorthand and this was the first source of conventional design. In the paleolithic cave paintings in Spain and Southern France, in Egyptian art and in that of India we find naturalism, for there was space in which to draw animals, birds and humans freely moving and as they are. The Greeks brought this naturalism to a high degree of perfection. But in the northern sections where men were hunters or, later, herdsmen, there was always a tendency to conventionalize or pack design into a given space. To be sure, there is no exact line of demarcation and we find each style penetrating the other but the separate influences are obvious.

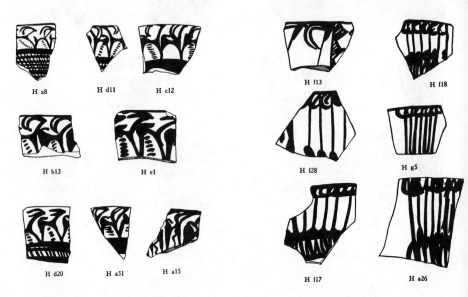

H a8   H d11   H c12   H f13   H f18

H b13   H e1   H f28   H g5

H d20   H a51   H a15   H f17   H a26

HISSAR I SHERDS—GAZELLE DESIGN AT VARIOUS STAGES OF CONVENTIONALIZATION. SCALE 1:3

FIG. 36. Another plate from The Museum Journal of the Pennsylvania University Museum similar to the preceding.

This type of conventionalism is quite different from that decadent, more and more careless, writing of a design until at times the whole meaning of it is lost. Here all vital qualities disappear and the subject matter is simply used because nothing else comes to mind. Even in early wares there are signs of such decadence as we can see in our first plate of the Tell Billa wares where the cup is decorated not only with cross-hatching, saw-tooth patterns, etc., but also with a row of birds that are not only hardly recognizable but also have lost all action and vitality, as again in the Hissar plate.

Thus we have two distinctly different types of conventionalization: (1) that brought about by lack of space, and (2) that of carelessness due to too often repeated a design. The first is to be seen in perfection in the so-called "Scythian bronzes" or those found across the top of Asia in such sites as those about Minusinsk, and the latter as shown here in the Hissar I sherds.

Other types of conventionalization are brought about by the methods of construction such as the modification of the objects represented by weaving of materials, as in rug designs, or the making of baskets, or, as Professor Meyers has shown, in the sewing of leather. (See Fig. 23, p. 20.)

Finally, and quite different from these early forms, there have grown up in "modern art" self-imposed restrictions of forms in "cubism" and "vorticism," among others. These latter have no real reason for being and lack integrity. Often they are carried to such a degree that all meaning is lost, as in the "abstract art" of today.

CHAPTER III

CRETE, EGYPT AND THE AEGEAN

ABOUT 3500 B.C. TO 1100 B.C.

HEINRICH SCHLIEMANN, a poor German boy, read Homer and became con-vinced that Troy really existed. After many years of hard struggle he set out amid jeers to find it and discovered not only the site of Troy but also that of Mycenae and Tiryns. These discoveries with others all pointed to Crete as a great center and later Sir Arthur Evans and Dr. Federigo Halbherr made their discoveries at Knossos, the home of King Minos of labyrinthian fame and of the Minotaur which Theseus and Ariadne slew. Crete lies mid-way between Egypt, Greece and Syria at the mouth of the Aegean Sea and became a crossroads of the ancient world.

Sir Arthur Evans divided the Minoan Culture into nine parts roughly paral-leling the 1st Egyptian dynasty of 3500 or 3400 B.C. to the 20th dynasty of 1100 B.C. and also the first half of the Northern European bronze age and of the Hallstadt Culture as well as the Italian developments up to the Etruscan age.

The early development of Crete was due to Egyptian influences and Mesopotamian and Syrian influences through Egypt. In pre-dynastic Egypt we have noted that glaze was developed but also a crude, unglazed pottery was made and it deteriorated as the art of making stone vessels improved.

FIG. 37. Predynastic Egyptian bowl of the white line decorated ware showing a typical primitive border design on the shoulder and the reminiscent feeling of a basket origin. Dia. about 7". Metropolitan Museum of Art.

FIG. 38. Early Pre-dynastic Egyptian pot-tery figure of reddish clay dating about 4000 to 3600 B.C. Metropoli-tan Museum of Art.

FIG. 39. Painted terracotta figure dating about 4000 to 3600 B.C. and found in Egypt. Metropolitan Museum of Art.

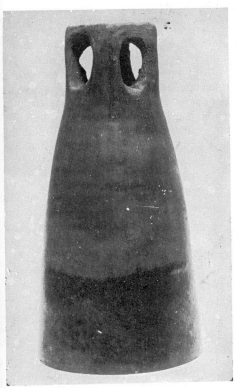

"Black topped" vase which, I am informed by Dr. William C. Hayes of the Metropolitan Museum of Art, was fired with the black part down in the ashes of the open fire, the upper part receiving more heat and less carbon deposit as it was inverted. This makes an interesting comment upon the black or gray wares and the red wares of China and other countries and shows how closely allied they were. Height 9″. Metropolitan Museum of Art.

Predynastic Egyptian vase province unknown but certainly strongly reminiscent of the geometrical wares of Mesopotamia. Metropolitan Museum of Art.

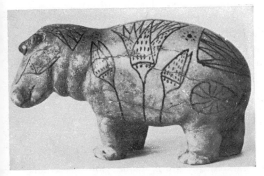

Egyptian 12th dynasty of turquoise faïence with black decoration of lotus blossoms and buds conceived as though they were perhaps thought of as shadows cast upon the hippopotamus. Length 8″. Metropolitan Museum of Art.

Flower vase of a form which we see used later in Persia, Mesopotamia and in the wares of Yüeh in China with spouts from the shoulder, though it undergoes many variations. This one is of the 12th dynasty Egypt and is of blue faïence with decoration in black. Height 3½″. Metropolitan Museum of Art.

EGYPTIAN POTTERIES, PREDYNASTIC AND 12TH DYNASTY

PLATE 8

Vases have been found, like the one illustrated, with a row of ibex and flamingos which are strongly comparable with certain ones of upper Mesopotamia and their place of origin is unknown. Crude female figures with great avoirdupois about the hips are not unlike those of neolithic times in Europe and even of modern times among certain African natives. Some heavy oblate jars are direct copies of the stone ones. And finally a peculiar type of "black-topped vase" demonstrates to us at once the close relationship between black and red wares, for the part of these vases that rested in the fire is black and that above the fire is burnt to a deep red. Alternation is not marked but does occur. Simple chevron, diagonally hatched, fern, wavy line, and point designs are general.

Early Minoan I (3500–3100 b.c.)

(Note:—I am using the dates given by Miss Gisela M. A. Richter, Litt.D. of the Metropolitan Museum, which are a little earlier than those given by E. J. Forsdyke, M.A., F.S.A. of the British Museum, but all of these are only approximate.)

In the early Minoan I period we find Crete also making stone vessels with more artistry than is shown in those of Egypt. The pottery is a rough reddish ware decorated with black slip in herring-bone, squares and various groups of parallel lines and dots. The same ware is also incised. The shapes are sturdy reflecting those of the stone vessels. Immediately we see reflected Mesopotamian influences in round-bodied stem cups and the trough spout used on ewers.

Early Minoan II (3100–2600 b.c.)

This was the great time of Imhotep and Zoser in Egypt, of the Great Pyramids, and during it there was a well-potted, bright red and highly polished ware. In Crete rectangular paintings were done in brown or black and red on a buff ground and many varied and even fantastic shapes were imported from Syria, Mesopotamia and Egypt such as the trough-spouted ewers with handles added and tall inverted conical cups with loop handles, all undoubtedly influenced by the tenuous forms of metal now becoming popular.

Early Minoan III (2600–2200 b.c.)

Pottery in Egypt developed along the line of perfection of the red ware, but after the 7th Dynasty invasion and civil war eliminated her influence and the Aegean Culture became predominant. "Vasiliki Ware" of red, covered unevenly with a black glaze and painted in white, came into use. The mottling of red and black was an attempt to reproduce the effect of stone. "Kamares Ware" (found in the Kamares Cave) with black ground decorated in bands of strongly stylized naturalistic motives in white, yellow and red, started and was carried through the next three periods until about 1600 b.c., becoming more and more naturalistic and decadent.

Fig. 40. Pre-historic Cretan vases dating from about 3000 to 1100 B.C. Of light buff unglazed clay. Heights from 5¾" to 11¼". Metropolitan Museum of Art.

Fig. 41. A group of Cretan stone vases dating before 2200 B.C. all said to be of steatite and measuring from about 3" to 6". Metropolitan Museum of Art.

Fig. 42. Early Minoan II cup with grooved spout dating between 2800 and about 2500 B.C. showing a sturdy and well made rim and an indented line about the foot-rim to set it off. Height 3¾". Metropolitan Museum of Art.

Fig. 43. Early Minoan III cup made between 2500 and 2200 B.C. with white on black design well suited to the intelligent and well potted form. Length 4½". Metropolitan Museum of Art.

Fig. 44. Cretan jug of about 2200–2000 B.C. of very light buff pottery unglazed. Height 3¼". Metropolitan Museum of Art.

Fig. 46. Limestone figure of Cynocephalus glazed, of the 12th dynasty Egyptian found at Sakkara.

Fig. 47. Middle Minoan II terracotta figure of athletic appearance with what appears to be a knife in his belt. Ht. 6½".

Fig. 48. Jar from Knossos of the Middle Minoan II–III period (2000–1600 B.C.) with conventional polychrome decoration. The handles would suspend it in balance. Height about 5¼". Metropolitan Museum of Art.

Fig. 45. Pottery model of a house. Egyptian 12th dynasty. Length 12".

MIDDLE MINOAN I (2200–2000 B.C.)

The Middle Minoan period broadly corresponds with the Middle Kingdom or 9th to 12th Dynasties of Egypt during which the arts reached a crest of achievement. The potteries include scarabs in blue faience, small seated figures of males, many animals of glazed stone and pottery including the well-known hippopotamus in turquoise with black plant forms, like shadows, of lotus painted on it, which has been so admired at the Metropolitan Museum of Art. The stone vessels continued to be well made and the red ware became less frequent.

Crete was developing a large foreign trade and the wares became less thick and more like metal having also polychrome decoration. Relief sculpture was a natural result of the influence of metal work.

MIDDLE MINOAN II (2000–1800 B.C.)

In Egypt a general decline takes place between the 12th and 18th Dynasties and Crete is now dominant. The potter's wheel was developed and tended to simplify some of the over-playful shapes. For the first time there appear natural renderings of flowers and undersea plants, the octopus and similar forms. It is as though the Cretan artists had suddenly looked about and found that many things in their lives could supply pleasing design. I doubt that this was due to any outside influence for the designs are too local in subject and natural in treatment.

The wheel had the effect of developing a tendency toward the use of horizontal bands. The ware from the Kamares Cave seemed to reach its height and, in fact, Miss Richter is of the opinion that *all* of the vessels decorated in white, red and orange are of this period while the white-decorated wares were either Middle Minoan I or III such as those from Pachyammos.

Now, either through conquest or trade, or both, the culture at Mycenae, west of Athens near the tip of Greece, began to follow that of Crete in all arts but particularly in pottery. About this time the northern part of Greece was invaded by a people carrying bronze weapons and they brought with them "Minyan Ware" of red or light gray body and also another ware of mat, painted texture. These wares are common to the islands and to Mycenae but not to Crete and, therefore, are likely to have come from Western Asia. A small goblet from Lianokladi which has a horizontally ribbed column shows East Indian influence.

MIDDLE MINOAN III (1800–1600 B.C.)

During this period the Cretan influence was continuously growing. It seemed that by 1625 B.C. the overlords of this island held sway over all of the Aegean land areas.

Natural design developed on pottery in polychrome style and then gave way to a buff pottery decorated in a lustrous black. This brought the end of the Minyan Ware. Other wares show a sprinkling of white dots to imitate stone and a return, or feeble continuation, of the old designs of spirals and scrolls.

The most interesting development is shown by the "Snake Goddess" found at Knossos together with attendants and other objects. She stands about a foot high and is dressed in a six-flounced skirt with narrow waist and an open bodice showing very prominent breasts, entirely unveiled. The ware is light and treated with a polychrome glaze. Two remarkable reliefs are of a cow and a goat with nursing kid. These are of the highest quality of ceramic art, simple as an air from Beethoven and as sure in their beauty.

LATE MINOAN I (1600–1500 B.C.)

The Late Minoan period roughly parallels the New Kingdom of Egypt or the 18th to 20th dynasties. The potteries there were becoming over-ornate and in bad taste. Green scarabs replaced blue ones. Polychrome glazes fol-

FIG. 49. Middle Minoan III (1800–1600 B.C.) jug of very primitive form, probably for everyday use. Height 5½". Metropolitan Museum of Art.

FIG. 50. A Knossian faience figure of a snake-holding goddess with a pard on her headdress. (c. 1575 B.C.). Sir Arthur Evans.

FIG. 51. Cretan vase said to be from Knossos, Late Minoan I painted in brown on a buff body. Here, instead of the naturalism often spoken of in this period, we have pure, strong conventionalized design on a structural and beautiful form. (The neck and lip are repaired none too well.) Height about 12¼". Metropolitan Museum of Art.

lowing the development of glass were many shades of blue, violet, yellow, brown and green, but they slowly became less bright and generally decadent while the blue-glazed wares slowly became less good and returned to the turquoise color. This pale turquoise was used by the Greeks, but was soon given up.

Crete retained her position of supremacy, and naturalism continued less vigorously. The dark on light technique was used with red and white touches added, but soon the former and then the latter disappeared. This was also a period of renaissance at Mycenae and Thebes.

LATE MINOAN II (1500–1400 B.C.)

This was the approximate time of Tutenkhamun at Luxor. Greece is gaining dominance and the best that can be said about Cretan wares is that some were very large, of the so-called "Palace style."

A reconstruction of the famous "Harvester Vase" showing a procession of men singing and marching to the music of an Egyptian sistrum. Many are carrying "winnowing forks." The whole is in relief and shows some 26 figures. It was carved from steatite and shows the fine handling of relief by these very early artists. Late Minoan I or about 1600 to 1100 B.C. Height 7". Metropolitan Museum of Art.

Late Minoan I pottery ewer found in Lower Egypt. Height 8⅝". Brooklyn Museum.

Late Minoan I–II period vase but not from Crete; it was found in Mycenae, Greece, and has such strong Cretan feeling that it may show important trade relations at this time. Note the beautiful shape with naturalistic but wonderfully conventionalized design, due to northern influence either in Crete or Mycenae. Height about 24½". Metropolitan Museum of Art.

This vase is called the "Boxer Vase" and is modeled in low relief with figures, some wearing visors and cheek-pieces, in fighting attitudes. The band second from the top shows not a "bull hunt" as it has been called but probably the bull-baitings indulged by the Cretans and possibly the source of the old Minotaur legend. Red terracotta. Height about 19½". Late Minoan I (1600–1500 B.C.) Metropolitan Museum of Art.

LATE MINOAN I POTTERIES FROM CRETE

PLATE 9

FIG. 52. Terracotta figure of the late bronze age, Cypriote, dating about 1500–1200 B.C. with marbled effect obtained with slip painting. Height 3⅜". Cesnola Collection. Metropolitan Museum of Art.

FIG. 53. Four exceedingly primitive, though rather amusing figures from Mycenae of the Late Helladic Period III (1400–1100 B.C.) to be compared with Late Minoan III, which have similarities with figures from Ur. Heights about 2" to 4¼". Metropolitan Museum of Art.

FIG. 54. A none too well developed shape and unevenly potted basin dating c. 1400–1150 B.C. from Greece not at all up to Minoan standards. Dia. 15". Metropolitan Museum of Art.

FIG. 55. A rather ingenious ladle of Prehistoric Greek ware c. 1400 to 1150 B.C. or the Late Minoan III age of Crete. Length 9¼". Metropolitan Museum of Art.

FIGS. 56–57. Two cups with tall stems (Kylix). The one said to date about 1400–1150 B.C. and the other with an octopus design said to be from Mycenae and to date about 1350–1100 B.C. Heights about 7". Metropolitan Museum of Art.

FIG. 58. An early "Lekythos" or small ewer from the city of Sardis in Lydia, on the mainland of Asia Minor where the Greeks cut off access to the sea. The alternating wavy band decoration and form shows both Egyptian and Eastern influences. Height 8". Metropolitan Museum of Art.

FIG. 59. Egyptian 18th dynasty jar painted to imitate stone and with an inscription "One honored with Osiris—the official of Amun, Mery." Found at Gournah. Height about 8". Metropolitan Museum of Art.

Late Minoan III (1400–1100 b.c.)

An invasion at the end of this period destroyed the palace at Knossos and overran the island. The old Cretan stock which had settled in Greece now invaded Western Asia and Greece was also invaded from the north. The islands were troubled among themselves as the Egyptians have written and the end of the glory of Crete had come.

CHAPTER IV

GREECE

THE IRON AGE (1000 B.C. TO A.D. 100)

WHEN CRETE lost power it was assumed by Mycenae, a city on the eastern part of the Peloponnesus, that tip of Greece which is almost an island, but soon the whole situation was to be changed by the use of iron as a weapon. Since 4000 B.C. Egypt had made beads of iron and a tool found at Khufu at Gizeh, inside the great pyramid, dates about 3100 B.C. Iron weapons had been found together with bronze ones dating about 1350 B.C. at the site of Hallstadt near Vienna, but these are thought to have been brought there perhaps by the Celts and possibly from the Caucasus Mountains. Jacques de Morgan is quite right when he says, "The Celts and the Dorians must have been the principal propagators of the iron industry," and it was the Danube Valley by which it entered Europe.

THE DARK AGES OF GREECE (1100 TO 700 B.C.)

The so-called "Achaeans" are thought to have invaded Greece from the north and this was very likely a Germanic tribe. It did not happen all at once but more as a slow infiltration, for the invaders are described as speaking Greek but also as being tall and blond. The Ionians, who had come from the Eastern Mediterranean shores, were short and dark. Some old authorities have said that three invasions took place from the north, the Ionian, Achaean and Dorian, but this is not correct for in Homer's time (*Odyssey* XIX.177) the Dorians were known only in Crete. This explains why most Dorian influences are in the southern part of Greece.

THE GEOMETRIC PERIOD (c. 1100–700 B.C.)

We have said that about 1625 B.C. the Minoan influences were strong in Greece and these brought Egyptian styles, somewhat translated, and then the more naturalistic styles of Crete itself.

FIG. 60. "The Warrior Vase" vessel of Late Minoan III period found at Mycenae and showing neither Cretan nor Greek types but bearded warriors with long noses which are probably representative of those from the Western Asian mainland. Height about 15". Metropolitan Museum of Art.

41

A very well known example, the famous "Warrior Vase," found by Schliemann himself, gives us a good idea of the style around 1350–1100 B.C. The long-nosed and bearded warriors speak for themselves and the form is certainly derived from those of the Babylonian-Mesopotamian areas. Miss Richter says that the artist of this piece was afraid to break away from the fixed conventions, for he knew little of anatomy and nothing of perspective, and this may be partly true but I cannot help but feel he was trying for something else again and I find such touches as the curl which forms the back of the neck and ear in one stroke both amusing and clever.

FIG. 61. "Geometric period" (c. 1100–700 B.C.) "Dipylon" vessel, bowl derived from primitive cooking vessels. 9th to 8th century B.C. Height 9½". Metropolitan Museum of Art.

FIG. 62. A "Kantharos" or "Cantharus," a two handled drinking cup of the "Geometric style" dating between 750 and 700 B.C. from Athens showing that not all of these pieces were crowded with design. Height about 5". Metropolitan Museum of Art.

FIG. 63. A "Dipylon" bowl or "Skyphos" of the geometric period from Athens of the 10th–9th century B.C. Height 3¼". Metropolitan Museum of Art.

Now, as for the "Dipylon" vases found in the cemetery of that name near Athens, and others of the "Geometric Period" of 1100 to 700 B.C., we must declare at once that we like them for their design quality and rhythmical arrangements far more than do those who measure the excellence of all Greek art by its approach to perfect rendering of the natural, while, on the other hand, we dislike them for their slender, projecting and unstructural handles which have never been condemned by these same old-school Greek art worshippers. One might as well accuse Beethoven and Brahms of not

FIGS. 64–68. Elements of Design.

reproducing natural sounds as accuse the makers of these vases of not reproducing natural forms. Of course, they had no such intention whatsoever. We see at once, in the forms of the potteries, the old Western Asian influences and in the design, the alternating rhythms, the animal and bird forms strongly conventionalized, and other characteristics of this influence. Added to these are human and horse figures in the same feeling. Note the figures with long

Two "Dipylon" vases (so called because many were found in the Dipylon cemetery of Athens) of buff ware painted in brown glaze with typical "Geometrical period" decorations of horses and chariots, men and animals with three bustled dancing women on the neck of one. Heights about 25" and 28". Metropolitan Museum of Art.

An immense "Dipylon," of the typical geometric style from Greece and dating about 8th century. Height 39". Metropolitan Museum of Art.

DIPYLON VASES OF THE GEOMETRIC PERIOD: GREECE

PLATE 10

legs, triangular torsos and rectangles formed of the arms, with circles in the center for the heads, on the colossal "Dipylon" vase on stand. Note also the soldiers with shields, below them. These later were used without the heads and two legs as on the "Phaleron" jug found at Athens, now in the Metropolitan Museum. In other words the northern constructive conventionaliza-

Fig. 69. Cypriote animal on wheels with two vases of the early iron age which here was about 1200–1000 B.C. Height 8⅞".
Note: comparison should be made with the animal on wheels from Ur.

Fig. 70. A ship with helmsman of the Early Iron Age (or "Dark Ages") of Greece showing influence of the Northern invaders, about 1200 to 500 B.C. and probably made as a votive offering. Length 7½". Metropolitan Museum of Art.

Fig. 71. Early Iron Age terracotta group c. 1000–600 B.C. of a cart with two wheels on which is a woman and a boy playing a double flute. The prominent chins and noses are like those of the bronze centaur and man of the "Morgan group" and those on the "Dipylon vases." Height 4¼". Metropolitan Museum of Art.

Fig. 72. Early iron age pottery figure of a bearded man with a vase in either arm riding a horse. The same sort of pointed chin is often seen in figures of the "Geometric period." This piece dates about 1000 to 600 B.C. Height 5". Metropolitan Museum of Art.

Fig. 73. Terracotta head broken from a statue dating about 8th to 7th century B.C. and of the "Geometric" or "sub-Geometric" period. It shows definite early traces of Western Asian influences particularly in the treatment of the eyes. Height about 7¼". Metropolitan Museum of Art.

Fig. 74. Painted terracotta head found at the shrine of Athena Chalcioecus and said to be of the 8th century B.C. British Museum.

Fig. 75. M. E. L. Mallowan of the British Museum published this head-cup found at the Habur Region, north Syria. Yellowish clay painted in black, wheel-made with the modeling of the features done while the clay was still damp. Contemporary with Atchana-Billa-Hurrian ware about 1500 B.C. Height 5". British Museum.

tion is strong in these wares but, as was usual in each place we study, it soon descended to mere written conventionalization. However, while it lasted, these artists could catch the tense prancing of the chariot horses or the movement of dancers, as seen in the three bustled ladies on the neck of the larger of the "Dipylon" amphoras, as cleverly as any modern cartoonist.

On these potteries we find "Greek Key Fret" borders frequently used and always drawn with double lines diagonally hatched. It also appears at the same time in Northern Italy in Villanova bronzes and potteries and as there is no record of any connection between the two countries, it is likely that it was introduced from the North and descended from the Hallstadt and La Tène cultures, the double spirals having been pushed into a rectangular form so that it would fit into a band of parallel lines or into a square just as it was in China on the Shang bronzes of 1766–1122 B.C. Let us, therefore, call this a *rectangular maeander,* a *swastika* or a *squared spiral,* as the case may be, for the general forms belong to no country. (See "Design" *Encyclopaedia Britannica,* 14th edition, Vol. 7, p. 259.)

A group of crudely-modeled figurines roughly coincide with this period. A small ship seems to have many things in common with northern types and the prominent noses and chins (or beards) show Western Asian types. The wheels on the small cart and also on the animal from Cyprus recall those on the animal found at Ur. The painted terra-cotta head of the girl found at the shrine of Athena Chalcioecus of the 8th century, with sharp nose and staring large eyes, is similar to the Syrian one of about 1500 B.C. which shows a wonderful sense of humor on the part of the artist. In fact this innocent wench could well be the girl friend of the charming Syrian, found at Brak, although he is some 700 years older.

These heads and the vases of the period are all of buff or yellowish buff clay and are decorated in a warm black.

The "Oriental" Period
c. 700 to 550 b.c.

In the 9th century the Greek colonies on the shores of Asia Minor had brought closer the not exactly happy contact with Persia. By the 7th century the influence became predominant. Corinth became the great trade center and the Phoenicians brought much metal work and potteries there. The shapes were exotic and not well adapted to pottery in many instances. Red and white on black drawing was popular. Lions, antelopes and winged griffins or human-headed animals of Babylonian type along with the palmette, lotus and other designs from Egypt by way of Mesopotamia and Persia were similar to Hittite types. We see occasionally the variegated ware imitating stone and in general the design shows the well-known "horror vacui" or horror of vacant spaces which has been much discussed, but this is not always the case and some very beautiful results were obtained as in the Caeretan Hydria, or water jar, in the Louvre and the Cameran style jug, (Pl. 11—3) from the Metropolitan Museum.

Gradually the Oriental style became more free. The structural bands of the Geometrical style widened until they disappeared and the vase became

FIG. 76. An "ary-
ballos" (oil flask) of
"Proto-Corinthian"
or late geometric
style c. 750–700 B.C.
Height about 2".
Metropolitan Mu-
seum of Art.

FIG. 77. Three ewers or "Oinochoe" of 8th century and 7th century Proto-Corinthian period and one of Corinthian period about
625–600 B.C. The first two were found at Attica. All show the tenuous
form better suited to metal than pottery. Metropolitan Museum of Art.

FIG. 78. Early Corinthian "Pyxis" or toilet box typically painted in dark brown with red added
and incised lines for details, c. 600 B.C. and showing animals as well as mythical monsters. Height
about 5". Metropolitan Museum of Art.

FIG. 79. A "Pyxis" or toilet box of Middle Corinthian style c. 575 B.C. Height 5". Metropolitan
Museum of Art.

FIG. 80. Corinthian "Krater" c. 575 B.C. showing a Trojan scene of horsemen with shields
and spears as well as the expected animals. Height 16". Metropolitan Museum of Art.

FIG. 81. "Black figured pottery" plate or "Pinax" of middle Corinthian style showing a poet
on his death-bed with a symbolic lyre, c. 575 B.C. Dia. 9". Metropolitan Museum of Art.

FIG. 82. An "Alabastron" or small ewer, Corinthian c. 625–600 B.C. with opposing lions looking
almost heraldic, and a parrot. Height 5". Metropolitan Museum of Art.

FIG. 83. "Aryballos" with winged lion in red and black on tan ground of the Late Corinthian
style I c. 575–550 B.C. Height 2¼". Metropolitan Museum of Art.

FIG. 84. An Eastern Greek hollow pottery duck, perhaps a vase as the hole is at the top of the
head, dating c. 530 B.C. The feathers of the breast are rendered much like the "scales" on some small
vases. The body is black with red decorations. Length 6⅝". Metropolitan Museum of Art.

FIG. 85. A Proto-Corinthian "Lekythos," Greek of the 7th century B.C. with typical scale design
and petals of alternating colors about the shoulder. Height 4¼". Metropolitan Museum of Art.

FIG. 86. Ewer from Sardis, Lydia, Asia Minor of about 600 B.C. of variegated black and tan to
represent stone. Height 6½". Metropolitan Museum of Art.

46

Early Athenian or "Proto-Attic" vase showing "Oriental" influence derived from Minoan and the "Geometric" vases. The Corinthian ware is, of course, more "Oriental." On one side is represented a combat between Herakles and the centaur Nessas and on the other a chariot with a woman in it. Note the animals about the neck. Height 42¾". 7th century B.C. Metropolitan Museum of Art.

An "Oinochoë" (wine jug) in the style transitional from proto-Corinthian to Corinthian with quite recognizable cats and rams about the body. c. 640 to 525 B.C. Height about 7". Metropolitan Museum of Art.

Jug of the Cameran style, "East Greek" of about 700–650 B.C. The decoration is in black, brown and red on a dull white ground. Height 14⅛". Metropolitan Museum of Art.

Jug showing transition between Proto-Corinthian and the typical Corinthian wares. There are winged animals with human heads of Assyrian origin, geese, lions and antelope probably of Egyptian origin, etc. Height 15¾". Metropolitan Museum of Art.

Probably due to an early Phoenician settlement in Corinth, the "Oriental style" consisting of monsters and very assyrian-like designs is found there on such examples as this "Pyxis" c. 625–600 B.C. Height about 7". Metropolitan Museum of Art.

A rather squat little "Hydria" from Corinth of about 575 to 550 B.C. with a black figure design of Herakles and a centaur. Height 7⅞". Metropolitan Museum of Art.

PROTO-CORINTHIAN AND CORINTHIAN VASES OF "ORIENTAL" STYLE

PLATE 11

FIG. 87. Terracotta two toned vase in the form of a right foot with sandal, c. 600–550 B.C. Greek. Height 2 5/16″, length 4⅛″. Metropolitan Museum of Art.
FIG. 88. Greek vase of the 6th century B.C. in the form of the head of the river god "Acheloos." Height 3¾″. Metropolitan Museum of Art.
FIG. 89. Lydian "Aryballos" in the form of a siren said to have been found at Sardis. It is of brownish clay. Length 4⅞″. Metropolitan Museum of Art.
FIG. 90. Terracotta funerary mask from Kameiros, Rhodes, of Greek workmanship late 6th century B.C. Note conventionalized hair design, almond shaped eyes, etc. Metropolitan Museum of Art.

FIG. 91. Fragment of a head from South Italy c. 560 B.C.? Note fleeting expression of resolute smile which is very alive. Larger than life size, the piece measures about 7½″. Terracotta. Metropolitan Museum of Art.
FIG. 92. A typical seated female figure of late 6th century B.C. probably from Western Sicily and likely a goddess. The stiff pose of this terracotta and its dwarfed proportions of the lower body do not spoil its life-like expression and quiet dignity. Height about 9″. Metropolitan Museum of Art.
FIG. 93. Terracotta figure of a seated goddess of the last quarter of the 6th century B.C. and said to have come from Tanagra. It is typical of the Archaic Period. Metropolitan Museum of Art.
FIG. 94. Late 6th century between 550 and 500 B.C. terracotta statuette of a woman with traces of the stiff early style with one arm straight down the side. Height 7¼″. Metropolitan Museum of Art.
FIG. 95. Terracotta figure of a maiden of the early 5th century and probably from Western Sicily. It still shows the archaic stiffness, though the features of the face are less conventional. Height nearly 10″. Metropolitan Museum of Art.
FIG. 96. Greek antifix, Gorgonion, said to have been found in Tarentum, of terracotta with traces of color originally applied, it is of the late 6th or early 5th century B. c. Width 10¼″. Metropolitan Museum of Art.

FIG. 98. A stand with black figured design on top, a mask of Medusa from Athens of about 560 B.C. and signed *Kleitias* and *Ergotimas*. Note similarity of treatment to that of antefix in relief (above). Dia. 3½″. Metropolitan Museum of Art.

FIG. 97. Three terracotta figurines of the 6th century from Greece. The center is said to be a seated goddess and the animals are typical of the Western Asian influence. It will be remembered how prominent the goat figures in Assyrian art. Height 3½″ to about 10″. Metropolitan Museum of Art.

an open field on which anything could be painted. The painting became more naturalistic and separated into various local types.

CORINTHIAN AND OTHER WARES

From the 7th to 6th centuries a wider divergence took place. In the pottery center, Corinth, the wares were at first distinguished by simplicity and by distinctive miniature sizes. The clay was a smooth, pale yellow-buff and the design of black touched with red and white. Another ware has incised scales painted red and white. Still another ware, probably copied from Egypt, was of small figure vases, shells, animals, squatting men, birds, heads, etc., many having holes for suspension and were probably used for oils or unguents.

"IONIAN WARES"

The "Ionian wares" of Rhodes include vases in the forms of heads, especially with helmets, and are made of the buff pottery and also a black ware similar to "bucchero ware" of Italy. There are also large stoneware jars worked with plastic friezes from engraved cylinders. But the general type is covered with white "pipe clay" (we would suppose a refined slip) and this set off the designs well. Egyptian influence is great and the animals are generally better drawn than in the other oriental wares. A later continuation of these Ionian types will be found in the Etruscan wares of Italy.

In Boeotia and Cyrene the wares were similar although the latter had a reddish white slip, a bolder decoration and predominant black and white check and step patterns as well as the lotus, pomegranates, etc. This ware developed into some of those vases found around Sparta decorated in black silhouette with mythological or genre scenes. Other localities were similar with slight differences: we have Aeolic, Clazomenian, Milesian, Samian (which had drunken dancing figures, etc.) Rhodian, Delian, Melian, Corinthian, Chalcidian, Boeotian, Laconian and other sites both in Greece and Italy and finally Attic wares, the latter finally becoming the great "black figure" style wares which were traded to Etruria, Italy and all other parts. It takes much experience to compare and allocate all these wares, and the job is hardly worth the effort. The actual center of the manufacture is not known. Three of the pieces in the Metropolitan Museum are said to have come from Tarentum and two from Cyprus.

ATHENS AND THE BLACK-FIGURE WARES
c. 600 B.C.

To quote the Rev. Edward M. Walker, "In the Great Age the Greeks had learned to despise the Persian and the Persian to fear the Greek. In the 6th century it was the Persian who despised, and the Greek who feared." Thus the oriental styles were not particularly popular, while at the same time the Panhellenic festivals made athletic prowess and physical beauty much sought after. The beauty of well muscled men usually in the nude and of slender women usually lightly draped became the artist's ideal.

FIG. 99. This *"Skyphos"* (drinking cup with handles below the rim) is from Boeotia, Greece and shows a parody of the myth of Herakles hunting the Erymanthian boar. Metropolitan Museum of Art.

FIG. 100. 18th Dynasty Egyptian alabaster amphoras reflecting a type undoubtedly copied in pottery. Ex H. Kevorkian Collection.

FIG. 101. Amphora of red clay with a black slip. Shows in the form of the handles and lip rim as well as the general shape of the body a close resemblance to the alabaster vases of 18th dynasty Egypt. The addition of the base is a bad feature as it is frequently found broken. Height 16½″. Athenian 5th century. Warren E. Cox Collection.

FIG. 102. Black figured "Amphora" from Capua decorated with a horseman on each side and having a good sturdy shape, well proportioned and usable. Greek c. 550–575 B.C. Height 14″. Metropolitan Museum of Art.

FIG. 103. *"Amphora"* with less than usual distinction between neck and body but tapered foot. Athenian c. 525 B.C., "black figure style." The departure of a warrior on side not shown, and Dionysos and a satyr, Athena and Hermes shown. Height 23½″. Metropolitan Museum of Art.

FIGS. 104–105. Panathenaic amphorae, given filled with olive oil as prizes in the games held at Athens. Scenes are of horse racing, foot racing, a chariot race and the *"pankration,"* a mixture of boxing and wrestling, etc.

This shows Athena, as always shown fully armed, standing between two columns on which are cocks, symbols of strife. The writing says, "From the games at Athens."

The shape has been over weakened by stylization; the handles too small, the base over tapered, etc. Height 24″. Metropolitan Museum of Art.

Attributed to the "Euphiletos Painter" and said to have been found in Etruria. It would date about the end of the 6th century or Archaic Period. Height 22″. Metropolitan Museum of Art.

FIG. 106. "Krater (Stamnos)" from Athens, Greece, of the early 5th century with thin black glaze. Height 15½″. Metropolitan Museum of Art.

FIG. 107. Toy *"Oinochoë"* "showing children imitating the spring festival of the ceremonial marriage of Dionysos, Athenian about 420 B.C. Many such small pieces have been found in children's graves. Height 2¾″. Metropolitan Museum of Art.

FIG. 108. Late free style Athenian *"Bell Krater"* red-figure vase showing on one side three youths and on the other satyrs dancing. Attributed to Polion, c. 420 B.C. Height 10¼″. Metropolitan Museum of Art.

FIG. 109. A red-figured *"Column Krater"* of the ripe archaic style showing a youth on one side and *Dionysos* on the other with effective restraint of other decoration. Athenian c. 500 B.C. Height 13½″. Metropolitan Museum of Art.

50

To be sure the Egyptians had already started the fashion and though their attitudes were sometimes stiff and the anatomy not always correct, they could draw a man's arm to look hard as iron and a woman's torso and breast full of life and sexual beauty. There is at times a stupid hardness that goes with much training of the muscles and the athlete is not the sum total of human beauty. We, therefore, find at times a certain coldness in the art of the Greeks. It is as though they preferred a straight line to a curve.

Figures could not be fitted very well to the shoulders and neck of a vase form, therefore, some design was found necessary to fill such spaces and the Greeks did not invent ornament so much as refine such motives as ivy, lotus, palmette, laurel, the maeander and various ray and tongue patterns. Shapes were of less and less interest and so by the middle of the 6th century a comparatively few were formalized and used over and over again. Many of the old writers treat the Black-figure period as that cumulative time which lead to *"the greatest art of the ceramist ever known on this earth."* In this I distinctly disagree for some of the following reasons:

The *Amphora,* which had its beginnings in the round-bottomed Egyptian form, has two handles curving from the neck down to the shoulder. In sticking out of the neck they were never as graceful as were the T'ang, Chinese vases derived from them, on which the handles meet the lip-rim. The handles do not as a rule widen out where they touch the shoulder, thus they are not strong at this point and are often broken there. The excessive tapering, almost to a point, of the bottom necessitated a flat attached base which spoils the rhythm of the curves and is often broken because of bad structure.

The *Panathenaic Amphora,* a taller and more slender type, simply exaggerates these faults.

The *Hydria,* or water jar, is similar except that it has two usually useless small close horizontal handles on the lower shoulder and a long, slender and easily-broken perpendicular handle at the back.

The *Stamnos* is simply a more squatty hydria with the third handle left off, while the *Pelike* is like an amphora with a sagging, fat-bellied sack of a body.

The *Oenochoe* with its wide spout does not pour very well, although otherwise it is a fair ewer form.

The *Kelebe* or wine-mixing vessel is like a large, wide-mouthed amphora but has two lugs from the lip-rim from which drop double, straight handles to the shoulder. It has some dynamic strength of design but the same weak foot. It is sometimes called a *Column Krater.*

This may be said also of the *Bell Krater;* and the *Calyx Krater.*

The *Kalpis* is nothing but a Hydria on which the third handle joins the neck instead of the lip-rim and it is often stood on a high stand serving no particular purpose but inherited from those reticulated early ones which were used over fire.

The *Skyphos* or *Kotylē* is a clumsy, deep cup with two horizontal handles indicating a two-handled grip for drinking.

The *Kylix* in its very wide shallow form with foot stem and horizontal handles would seem to be a good example of our fragility challenge in ap-

FIG. 110. Greek (Attic) black figure *"Skyphos"* c. 550 B.C. but still showing the "Oriental influence" with its lion which does not occur in Greece and a crane. Height 3½". Metropolitan Museum of Art.

FIG. 111. Important signed piece of this period, a *"Kylix"* inscribed, *"Nikosthenes made me."* There are about 80 signed pieces known by this artist. Dia. 17½". Metropolitan Museum of Art.

peal. The other forms might lose an ear or other part while this actually looks as though it would break completely if broken at all.

Other cups are the *Kaythos,* like a teacup with loop handle twice its height and the *Kantharos* having two such unstructural loops sometimes further supported, as though the potter knew his mistake, by horizontal supports, and having a long stem to boot.

FIG. 112. An exceedingly interesting and really beautiful *"Aryballos"* has a clever device of crescents in four colors about the body and opposing crescents about the shoulder, while the lip shows a spirited battle between the pygmies and cranes with explanatory inscriptions. Height 2⅞". 6th century. Metropolitan Museum of Art.

FIG. 113. Athenian *"Aryballos"* in the form of a group of cockleshells with a black glazed mouth. Late 6th century. Height about 2". Metropolitan Museum of Art.

FIG. 114. Greek (Attic) *"Lekythos"* of black figured type with lion and deer c. 550 B.C. and showing remains of "Oriental influence." Height 7". Metropolitan Museum of Art.

The *Pyxis,* a small cylindrical box and cover, seems a satisfactory form.

The *Aryballos* originally meant bag or purse and is a small globular ewer for oil but was larger and used for carrying water to the bath. It is a good and well devised form.

The *Lekythos* is a tall and pleasant form of bottle with an extraneous handle, for the neck could as readily be grasped, and the same flat base as we have criticized on the Amphora.

The *Alabastron* came direct from Egypt and has usually a round bottom and two handles or loops, perhaps for tying on a cover.

Black figured Oinochoe with painting of Europa riding the Bull. Greek 6th century B.C. Height 8". Cleveland Museum of Art.

"Lekythos" of black figured Athenian ware c. 550 B.C. Height 6⅛". Metropolitan Museum of Art.

Athenian black figure vase c. 550 B.C. showing perhaps the height of this form in Greece, but with weak base flange and sharp edge at lip to chip and break. Height 17". W. R. Hearst Col. International Studio, Inc.

"BLACK FIGURE" VASES, GREECE

PLATE 12

The *Olpe* is a pitcher with a round mouth and no spout. At times it has a body like the unpleasant Pelike, but others are good in form as the one shown.

There are also the *Rhyton, Lebes, Askos, Hemikotylin* and others, which the reader may judge for himself, but perhaps one of the worst is the tall and involved *Loutrophoros*.

Fig. 115. Once in a while the Athenians of the 5th century made a fine pottery vessel without the usual over-decoration. Such an example is this *"Olpe"* of very perfect lines and proportions. Height 8″. Metropolitan Museum of Art.

Fig. 116. A *"Pelike"* of the 6th century B.C., said to be from Ban. Distinguished from the amphora by having a less definite neck and body distinction and more rounded bottom with wider foot. Height 10½″. Metropolitan Museum of Art.

Fig. 117. A *"Psykter"* (wine cooler) of the early red figure style marked by formalized drapes, stiff action and eyes painted in profile faces as though seen in front view. Attributed to *Oltos*, Athenian c. 520–510 B.C. Height 13″. Metropolitan Museum of Art.

Fig. 118. A black figure *"Loutrophoros"* used by Athenian maidens to bring water for the bridal bath. They were also placed in the tombs of unmarried youths or maidens and libations were poured into them. In such cases they had no bottoms as with the specimen shown. The significance was that the marriage had taken place with Hades c. 500 B.C. Height 29½″. Metropolitan Museum of Art.

Most of these forms had suffered very much from the influence of attenuated metal shapes and I believe that the Greeks were not truly pottery conscious; they merely used their ceramic vessels as objects on which to paint. This is further proven by the fact that they utterly ignored the beautiful glazes which they knew full well and had seen when brought from the Near East and Egypt. Thus those who study these vessels often think more of the painting than of the pot and the study really lies out of the scope of this book.

Only a few of the makers of the vases signed them but many of the painters did and we find that among the first of the black-figure artists were *Cleitias* and *Ergotimus*. Others are *Execias, Amasis* and *Nicosthenes;* the first had a style reminiscent of the Near Eastern designs and the second

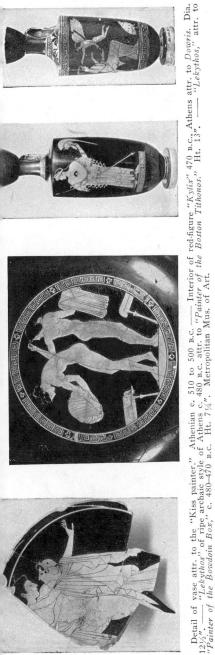

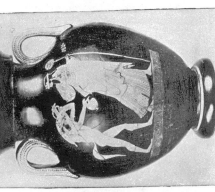

Detail of vase attr. to the "Kiss painter." Athenian c. 510 to 500 B.C. —— Interior of red-figure "Kylix," 470 B.C., Athens attr. to *Douris*. Dia. 12½". "*Lekythos*" of ripe archaic style of Athens c. 480 B.C. attr. to "*Painter of the Boston Tithonos*." Ht. 13". —— "*Lekythos*," attr. to "*Painter of the Bowdoin Box*," c. 480–470 B.C. Ht. 7¼". Metropolitan Mus. of Art.

PLATE 13

RED FIGURE POTTERIES OF GREECE

"Bell-Krater," c. 460–450 B.C. from Athens. Attr. to "*Villa Guilia Painter*." Ht. 14½". —— Early free style "*Amphora*," attr. to "*Painter of the Syracuse Pelike*." Athenian c. 470–460 B.C. Ht. 18". —— Early free style "*Stamnos*" c. 460–450 B.C. attr. to "*Villa Guilia Painter*." Ht. 13½". Metropolitan Mus. of Art.

drew in a formal and dignified manner. His name would suggest that he might have been Egyptian, or was at least of Egyptian heritage.

RED-FIGURE WARES

About 520 B.C. the style changed and instead of painting the figures in black on a buff yellow, light red or dark red ground, depending upon the locality, or a white slip ground, as was sometimes done, the artists began to reverse the process and paint the backgrounds in black leaving the figure the color of the ground, and then touch in the details with more black. Some artists used both styles. *Andocides* and *Pamphaios* were among these and belonged to the circle of *Epictetus* which quickly took up the style. Sometimes a yellow or brown color was added. These colors were made of an alkaline flux mixed with iron earth and are half way between a glaze and a slip.

Personal styles developed and we hear of the "Strong Red-figure Style" (*c.* 500–460 B.C.), the "Fine Red-figure Style" (*c.* 460–430 B.C.), the "Poly-

Fig. 119. Early red-figure style *"Kylix"* showing on the inside a youth running and on the outside revelers c. 510 B.C. Attributed to the *"Epeleios painter."* Dia. about 14½". Metropolitan Museum of Art.

Fig. 120. Miniature "Lekythos" from Greece of the 5th century. Height is about 2½". Metropolitan Museum of Art.

Fig. 121. Miniature "Lekythos" of Greek 5th century. The decoration is a rather startled looking owl. Height about 2½". Mrs. Warren E. Cox Collection.

Fig. 122. Athenian free style "Calyx Krater" c. 450–440 B.C. with two friezes, the above showing Nekyra, Heroes and Divinities, the lower the punishment of Tityas; contest of Zeus and Hermes against a giant. Height 15⅜". Metropolitan Museum of Art.

Fig. 123. A "Column Krater" early free style, 5th century attributed to "The Pig Painter." It shows a Satyr pursuing a Maenad on one side and a Satyr on the other. Height 17". Metropolitan Museum of Art.

An Athenian "Oinochoë," early free style red figured pottery c. 450 B.C. The painting is attributed to "The Manheim Painter" and shows three Amazons starting for battle. Height 13⅛". Metropolitan Museum of Art.

Red figure free style "Amphora" of about 440 B.C. with a warrior bidding farewell to his family on one side and a libation scene on the other. Attributed to the "Lykon Painter." Height 24⅛'. Metropolitan Museum of Art.

A "Lekythos" and "Amphora" of the red figure style and attributed to the *"Painter of the Boston Phiale,"* the first showing the departure of a warrior and the second Herakles in the garden of the Hesperides. Heights 18" and 9½". Metropolitan Museum of Art. c. 460–420 B.C.

Athenian "Volute Krater" dat.ng about 450 B.C. of the early free style attributed to the "Painter of the Shaggy Silenus." Height 25". Metropolitan Museum of Art.

Probably a *"Lebes gamikos"* (marriage-vase) the use for which is not known, this piece shows the bride during the *"Epaulia"* or day after the wedding when it was customary to bring her gifts. The whole is too crowded and confused. Height 22". c. 430–420 B.C. Metropolitan Museum of Art.

A Pelike of Greek Asia Minor of the 4th century B.C. showing "the florid style," in its form, and crowded design. Height 16¼". Metropolitan Museum of Art.

RED FIGURE PAINTERS OF GREECE

PLATE 14

gnotus Style" named after one artist (*c.* 460–445 B.C.), the "Pheidias Style" (445–430 B.C.), and the "Florid Style" (*c.* 430–400 B.C.). Among the best known artists were *Euthymides* who painted bacchanalian scenes without subdivisions of the pot surface, *Euphronius*, the famous kylix painter whose touch was exceedingly sensitive, *Sosias*, a pupil of his who developed a style strong and angular, restless but well composed, *Duris* whose style was something like that of *Euphronius*, and *Brygus*, the dramatic painter. *Hieron* was another but his anatomy was bad and his compositions less interesting. It was about this time that the artists learned to paint the face in three quarters. The effect of the sculpture of *Pheidias* was also felt, particularly by *Aristophanes* and *Erginus*.

WHITE-GROUND WARES

The white ground was usually used on lekythi, the inside of bowls and occasionally on pyxis and kraters. *Euphronius* and *Duris* signed typical bowls finished with white slip inside while the outside was treated with red-figure technique. The earlier lekythi are harder and slightly yellowish with figures in the black-figure style but later the white was less well fixed and whiter, with figures freely drawn in red, black or other colors. This technique necessitated a quick and sure fluency and might have developed something greater had it not been against the taste of the period. The best that can be

FIG. 124. "Aryballos," Greek c. 500 B.C. with all-over design of black palmettes on white ground. Height 5″. Metropolitan Museum of Art.

FIG. 125. White "Lekythos" of the early type which show both red-figure and black-figure styles. This one shows Persus escaping with the head of Medusa while from the neck of Medusa springs the winged steed Pegasos. Greek c. 485–460 B.C. Height 10″. Metropolitan Museum of Art.

FIG. 126. Plate of red figured Campanian ware with touches of white, of about 400 to 300 B.C. Dia. 8¾″. Metropolitan Museum of Art.

Athenian *"Lekythos"* of black figured type showing women working wool about 550 B.C. Height 6½". Metropolitan Museum of Art.

Painting on white ground was heightened by solid washes in various colors. *"Pyxis"* showing Hermes leading the three goddesses for the judgment of Paris, in black, brown, purple and white. Height 6¼". Metropolitan Museum of Art.

"Lekythos" side view of representation of Hermes conducting a man to Charon's boat. The artist was too lazy to continue the key-fret border around under the handle. Greek latter half of the 5th century. Height 11½". Metropolitan Museum of Art.

Lekythos with white ground showing mourning figures, Greek 6th century B.C. Height 19½". The John Huntington Col. Cleveland Museum of Art.

GREEK WHITE GROUND WARES

PLATE 15

said is that the figures were well placed and well drawn, though the weak outline can hardly be seen at a short distance and could hardly be said to form a proper vase decoration. The brush technique never reached the heights of that of Sung China as seen in the Tz'u Chou wares.

The placing of figures on all Greek vases was difficult. If they are too high the heads give a flattened effect due to the curve of the shoulder, and if they are lowered, they seem to sag about the bottom.

IV CENTURY GREEK POTTERY

By the 4th century B.C. Greece had come to the end of all true artistic achievement in ceramics. In the now prevalent "Florid Style" richly draped women toy with winged love-gods and other involved and saccharine subjects predominate. Poor craftsmanship and overcrowding of design are everywhere present. Blue, green, red and gold were added to the palette. These vases are called "Kertch Ware" and many were found in North Africa, and also in South Russia in the town after which they are named.

FIG. 127. Four terracotta figures from an Athenian grave showing actors of comic and tragic roles of the 4th century B.C. Hts. 4⅛" and 4¼". Metropolitan Museum of Art.

At the same time charming little figures were made and painted in pastel colors. The first of these found were in Tanagra and, therefore, the whole group has been given that name though they were made elsewhere in Boeotia, and in Greece, Asia Minor, the Crimea, in Rhodes, North Africa, Sicily and Italy. The Tanagra figures are distinguished by their simple grace and quiet charm. The Asiatic ones are more lively and the Italian less tasteful. In size they vary from 2 inches to 20 but about 7 or 8 inches in height is usual. They may have been temple offerings and some were buried with the dead but I think they were simply toys for grownups and served various purposes from that of a bachelor's etchings to decorations for the what-not, if the Greeks had such things. The subjects are varied and comprise youths, women and children of ordinary dress of the times, quite sexy girls of coy mien, some pensive ladies, actors, slaves and beggars. One amusing one at the Metropolitan Museum of Art is of Herakles with his finger in his mouth. Those of the Hellenistic period (c. 325 to 200 B.C.) are of divinities such as Aphrodite and Dionysus with Erotes, satyrs, Sileni and Maenads with some hetaerae, warriors, etc.

FIG. 128. Modeled vase with figure of Silenus of the 4tb to 3d century B.C. Greece. Height 4¼″. Metropolitan Museum of Art.

FIG. 129. Terracotta statuette representing Niké flying, of the III century or later. Height 9⅜″. Metropolitan Museum of Art.

FIG. 130. This tragic mask of the Hellenistic period is from Thebes, Greece. It is of terracotta. Height 6⅞″. Metropolitan Museum of Art.

Two out of every three that one sees are fakes, for the supply was quickly outrun by the demand. We can only suggest that fakes are likely to have a bit too much color left on them, to be a little busy and too detailed and also to lack true feeling. The sexy ones have always sold well so many fakes are of this nature. Most of the larger museums have collections of real ones and, much to their disgust, a fair number of fakes.

After the Tanagra ones, those from Myrina are valued highest. Here the subjects are from mythology as a rule, more nudes were tried with varying success and the figures are likely to have small heads and slender limbs.

Many of these figures were made in molds, usually of two pieces, and are naturally hollow. Holes were left in the backs so that a finger could press together the sutures from the inside and also so that the gasses could escape. The good ones were then worked over by the artist before firing, but less and less interest finally led to even leaving the suture marks on them.

Man seems always to come to a point when he likes to make little figures of himself, his wife, children and dog. They are inspired at first and get technically better as time goes on until the process of duplicating them with the mold is found, and then they die of their own cheapness. Verily, the preacher against idolaters should present them with the techniques and materials for making molds and all worship of the figures would soon cease!

OTHER MODELED AND RELIEF WARES

Metal had always been the inspiration and also the curse of Greek ceramics. Since the "Harvester Vase" of Crete the reproduction of repoussé had been

Left—Figure of 4th to 3d cent. B.C., Tanagra type. Height 9¼". *Right*—Tanagra type figure of 4th to 3d cent. B.C. Height 12". Metropolitan Museum of Art.

TANAGRA TYPE FIGURES

Left—Tanagra figure, 4th cent. B.C. Height 6½". *Right*—Greek figure in terracotta of Tanagra type of 4th cent. B.C. Height 8¾". Metropolitan Museum of Art.

PLATE 16

FIG. 131. Terracotta mask, which seems to have been a votive copy of an actual mask used in ritual dances in honor of the goddess Artemis Orthia, at whose shrine they were found in Sparta. c. 500 B.C. Photographs by the British School of Archaeology, Athens.

FIG. 132. Etruscan antefix probably of a Maenad from the roof of a temple. Though this is said to come from Italy it has strong Greek feeling and may have been brought from there. About 500 B.C. Height 16". Metropolitan Museum of Art.

FIG. 133. An almost portrait quality is seen in this Hellenistic "Aryballos" or oil jug. Height 2¾". Metropolitan Museum of Art.

FIG. 134. A *"Kantharos"* having a woman's face on either side and a red figure design attributed to Brygus, Athenian, about 490 to 480 B.C. Height 7". Metropolitan Museum of Art.

FIG. 135. *"Rhyton"* c. 475 to 450 B.C. from Athens of the "red figure" type. These vessels were used as drinking cups and some are pierced with a small hole for the liquid to spurt into the mouth of the drinker. Length 4¼". Metropolitan Museum of Art.

FIG. 136. A red-figure *"Kantharos"* (drinking-cup) of the free style having on one side a modeled head of a satyr and on the other that of a woman. Height 7¾". Metropolitan Museum of Art.

FIG. 137. Athenian red-figure *"Askos"* in the form of a lobster claw decorated with a mule. c. 460 B.C. Length 6½". Metropolitan Museum of Art.

FIG. 138. An "Askos" in the form of a rat made in South Italy 4th to 3d century B.C. It is of orangy buff color with black glazed decoration. Length 6⅞". Metropolitan Museum of Art.

sought. Now there was the added desire for ornate detail. *The art of the Greek had at best been a technical development rather than a spiritual one* and now the painted technique was as perfect as they could conceive it had any possibilities of ever being. Therefore, the artists could only turn to the more difficult technicalities of sculpture. Long since, all taste as to the *appropriateness* of the decoration for a vessel had been lost so there was nothing to hold them back from perpetrating the monstrous vases of "Kertch ware," the head vases and cups, odd rhytons in various forms and even the askos in the form of a lobster's claw.

CHAPTER V

ITALY

IF GREECE started the trend toward the worst of bad taste, Italy carried it on to its ultimate conclusion. The Greek influence on Italian ceramics came when Grecian art had already deteriorated. But let us begin at the beginning in Italy.

If one were going to pick stepping stones, one might say that the stone age art was in Egypt and Crete, the bronze age in Greece and the iron age

FIG. 139. Cauldron stand of "Red ware" from Etruria c. 7th century B.C. Remarkably like those of prehistoric Japan showing how men's minds work alike in the solution of simple problems. Height 32″. Metropolitan Museum of Art.

FIG. 140. Bowl and stand of the first half of the 7th century B.C. found at Capena in Latium. Buff terracotta with black finish. Note the sgraffito decoration of animals much in the style of Western Asian metal work. Height 29″. Metropolitan Museum of Art.

FIG. 141. "*Oinochoë*" or pitcher of Italian "*bucchero*" ware with incised decoration showing Western Asian influence. Most of this ware is found in chamber tombs dating from the 7th to early 5th centuries B.C. 625–600 B.C. The red ware is earlier. Height 11″. Metropolitan Museum of Art.

FIG. 142. "*Bucchero*" "*Oinochoë*" with a frieze of animals and monsters incised and touched with purple and yellow, a sort of Italic imitation of Corinthian ware. Etruscan 625–600 B.C. Height 12¾″. Metropolitan Museum of Art.

in Italy. This country seemed destined to be the center of the metal industries. As early as the 12th or 11th century B.C. the "Villanovans," so called because the first finds of their wares were made at a little village of that name about 8 kilometers from Bologna, came from the north and probably from the Danube basin. They seemed to have had some connection with the Hallstadt Culture but were a different people because their burial customs were quite different. With them they brought an advanced bronze culture and also iron used as weapons. They also brought the conventionalized spiral, angular elements of design and the expected animal motifs.

Following this settlement came the Etruscans in about the 9th to 7th centuries and they grew ever stronger, at least in aesthetic influence, until about 500 B.C. Finally in 474 B.C. the Battle of Cumae started the series of disasters from which they never recovered. The Etruscans seem to have come by sea from some place in the Near East between Syria and the Hellespont. After their downfall we reach the Greek influence.

FIG. 143. Etruscan brazier with roller stamped friezes of grazing deer and boars of about 600 to 550 B.C. of red bucchero ware. Dia. 18¾". Metropolitan Museum of Art.

FIG. 144. Etruscan 6th century B.C. Canopic jar with cover in the form of a head of black Bucchero ware. Height 17". Metropolitan Museum of Art.

FIG. 145. Etruscan 6th century Canopic jar with cover in the form of a male head of red bucchero ware. Height 21¾". Metropolitan Museum of Art.

The Villanova pottery was based on a crude ware sometimes incised but never painted. When the Etruscans arrived there were, in the southern tip of the boot, wares painted in rectilinear patterns similar to those of Crete but showing no slightest connection; the people had simply reached the same stage of development. The Villanova pottery is crude and decorated with knobs, ribs and sometimes grotesque handles ending in crescents and horns. Other vases and probably earlier ones have globular bodies tapering somewhat toward the foot and tall truncated conical necks taking half the height. The mouth is left fairly wide and prominent lip-rims are usual. They are found with bowls or helmets turned over the mouths. In the south, burial urns were also made in the form of little huts, probably representative of the deceased one's home.

As early as 900 B.C. decoration came into use with geometric designs very like those which came into Greece, and probably from the same source, but this was a crude red, brown or black pottery and the designs were incised rather than painted. The same maeanders, swastikas and simple borders were more crudely used. The wheel had not been discovered and the designs

Fig. 147. Etruscan bucchero ware black cup on high foot dating about 610 to 560 B.C. Height 8½". Metropolitan Museum of Art.

Fig. 148. Etruscan amphora c. 520 B.C. with cover which seems to have been made for it and a decoration of winged horses possibly of Assyrian inspiration originally. Height 15¼". Metropolitan Museum of Art.

Fig. 146. Head of a satyr, Etruscan, 5th century B.C. Metropolitan Museum of Art.

were in spots about the body with a few bands above and below as the tendency of the wheel to induce many band designs was lacking.

By the 8th century the Etruscan influence was dominant and we must not think of these people as simply an offshoot of Greek art for they brought ideas from the whole Mediterranean and even from Assyria. Their first homes were at Targuinii and Vetulonia, north of Rome on the western shore. They used winged monsters, tree designs and flower designs much like those of Mesopotamia. They were strong and warlike but could never organize sufficiently to stand against Rome. Some of the early sculpture does have an "archaic smile" resembling that found in early Greek art. Others are more closely allied to central European developments. But whether these were actual influences, or just natural stages of development is difficult to tell. There is evidence surprisingly frequently come upon that men's minds do develop along similar lines where no possible relationship could exist.

I must add a note that the monumental head and full figure of a warrior illustrated in my former edition were discovered to be fakes by Iris Cornelia Love and the Metropolitan Museum of Art.

No trace of Greek influence can be found in the tombs of the 8th and 7th centuries. Trade was with the Phoenicians and the feeling was Egypto-Syrian. Toward the end of the 7th century came traces from Corinth and then by the beginning of the 6th century began the flood of Athenian painted wares. So many were found there that old collectors thought they were Etruscan vases and some even speak of them so today.

"Bucchero" ware or the black type called "bucchero nero" was made after

ETRUSCAN TERRACOTTA
HEADS

PLATE 17

Head of a youth (broken from a statue), 6th century B.C. showing elf-ish expression.

Head of a girl wearing earrings and showing archaic smile, 6th to 5th century B.C. Metropolitan Mus. of Art.

the Villanovan ideas. It is rarely wheel-made and usually molded or impressed. Small toothed wheels, cylindrical seals like the Egyptian and Babylonian ones, and various punches and stamps made possible an effect much like repoussé metal. Thus more and more mechanical means were employed, until finally the mold was brought into use. Some of this ware was red and both the black and red types were also treated with white and polychrome decoration which was poorly fired and is usually worn off. As the Greek influence gained it is easy to see how these wares grew into Hellenistic shapes such as those found at Cumae, Apulia, where finds were made at Gnathia, and in Campania at Cales, as well as in Etruria. Those from Etruria were not glazed and may have been gilded all over.

Fig. 149. Etruscan bucchero ware vase of black color dating from about 560 to 500 B.C. Height about 12″. Metropolitan Museum of Art.

Fig. 150. Etruscan amphora of black bucchero c. 6th century or before. Note the animals similar to those in Corinthian wares. Height 20″. Metropolitan Museum of Art.

Fig. 151. Etruscan "bucchero ware" pitcher or "Oinochoë" with Assyrian looking sphinxes in relief. c. 560–500 B.C. Height 12″. Metropolitan Museum of Art.

The Etruscans did not cremate as did the Villanovans and sarcophagi were made of terra-cotta shaped like a couch on which reclined the figure of a man and his wife in an easy and lifelike pose as though conversing. Some of the figures are quite heavy but others are slender and have an elfish smile which, with their almond-shaped and slightly upturned eyes, are typical

Fig. 152. Etruscan "bucchero ware" drinking cup or "Kantharos" with stippled decoration. c. 635–600 B.C. Height 12″. Metropolitan Museum of Art.

Fig. 153. Etruscan bucchero tray with pots and spoons c. 6th century B.C. The color is black or gray-black. Length about 22″. Metropolitan Museum of Art.

Fig. 154. Black bucchero ware "Krater," Etruscan of about 560 to 500 B.C. Height 16⅛″. Metropolitan Museum of Art.

It seems strange that at the same time that some Apulian wares were showing every sign of decadence others like this fine bell-shaped "Krater" could be made. 4th cent. B.C. Ht. 36½". Metropolitan Mus. of Art.

Apulian Hydria with thin black glaze or slip decorated with white and a dull, dirty yellow. The third handle is not visible. Ht. 16½". Warren E. Cox Coll.

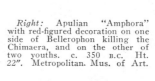

Left: An involved "Krater," Apulian 4th cent. B.C. with a scene of offerings at a tomb, handles having masks and four small goose-head loops on the shoulder. Ht. 36". Metropolitan Mus. of Art.

Right: Apulian "Amphora" with red-figured decoration on one side of Bellerophon killing the Chimaera, and on the other of two youths. c. 350 B.C. Ht. 22". Metropolitan. Mus. of Art.

APULIAN POTTERIES FROM ITALY

Plate 18

Etruscan faces and give them a sprightly expression. The modeling is simple
and good and these are real achievements for the 6th to 5th centuries.

In South Italy, from the earlier geometric wares "Peucetian" and later,
came those flower motives called "Messapian." These wares, known as
Apulian, Lucanian, Campanian and Paestumian, all have brown clays and
are usually of bad and involved design. The last two are heavily ornate on
one hand and mundane and stupid on the other. Here, of course, is another
sign of decadence. How different the attitude of an artist who only does the
side that shows (and overdoes that) from the true artist like the Chinese
ones who make wonderful "secret designs" that do not show at all to the
casual eye! The subject matter is just as uninteresting as the technique.
It consists of unfelt mythological subjects, girls lounging in ornate grandeur
among flowers, ribbons, pet animals and other sloppy ideas of design. In
this, so-called, red-figure style we find also yellow, white and other colors
dabbed on to enhance the effect.

The Hellenistic Period of the 3rd to the 1st century brought from Athens
new ideas of perfume bottles of not heads, but whole busts, of women surrounded by scarves and swirls. Hannover has written, "These objects, with
a jug in the form of Aphrodite and Adonis grouped together, are considered
to be among the greatest treasures of the museums that possess them." (The
Louvre, the Hermitage, the British Museum and the Berlin Museum)—But
he does add, "—although they are in every way more curious than beautiful."
But these fantasies are simple and compact as compared with the masterpieces from Canosa with gorgon masks, front halves of horses or centaurs
plunging out of the sides and large statues or half statues of winged goddesses,
cupids, ladies in distress and such, jumping out of them in the most surpris-

FIG. 155. "Oinochoë" from Apulia of the 4th century B.C. with a design of the chariot of
Aurora. Height 16". Metropolitan Museum of Art.
FIG. 156. "Rhyton" with stag's head. At the lip is a painting of Eros with a bowl of fruit. 4th
century B.C., Apulian. Length about 8". Metropolitan Museum of Art.
FIG. 157. "Amphora" of the 4th century, Apulian, said to be from Tarentum and having a scene
of mourners at a tomb and of the dispute of Persephone and Aphrodite over Adonis. Height 42".
Metropolitan Museum of Art.
FIG. 158. A very much degraded Olpe shaped pitcher of Roman make; buff pottery with green
glaze. Decoration applied. Thought to date c. 1st century B.C. Height 7½". Metropolitan Museum
of Art.

ing, fantastical and god-awful taste that man ever perpetrated. Here at last I am able to point out the *worst* that has ever been done in the art of potting.

The period was one of confusion. Realism had become the fanatical aim of artists (see the figure of Diadoumenos) and caricature and the grotesque became substitutes for sincere style. Invention replaced inspiration. Masks

FIG. 159. Roman vase with movable ring around the neck made of unglazed gray pottery and supposed to date between the 1st and 4th century A.D. Height 14¾". Metropolitan Museum of Art.

FIG. 160. Roman lamp of the sort given as New Year's presents. This one is of red clay and shows Victory in relief holding a shield inscribed with a New Year's wish. 1st century A.D. Length 4½". Height 1". Metropolitan Museum of Art.

FIG. 161. Roman vase of the 1st century B.C. of unglazed gray pottery with scratched and applied design. Height 9¼". Metropolitan Museum of Art.

FIG. 162. Mask of a satyr's head late Greek, made of terracotta. Height 9". Metropolitan Museum of Art.

FIG. 163. Hellenistic period (3d to 1st century B.C.) jug in the form of a sleeping youth. Height 7½". Metropolitan Museum of Art.

FIG. 164. Terracotta Roman "rattle" or hollow pig with glass inlays. Length 3½". Metropolitan Museum of Art.

FIG. 165. Graeco-Egyptian of the Roman period figure of a camel with four large jars attached to the saddle, found at Ephesos. Height 4¼". Metropolitan Museum of Art.

FIG. 166. Terracotta figure of Eros riding a lion found at Tarentum and said to be of the 3d century B.C. or the beginning of the Hellenistic period. Height 6¾". Metropolitan Museum of Art.

and antefixes reflected the trend. In some parts simple and even crude work was done but it was not good. It was the old story of the combination of too many undigestible influences. On top of that and beyond all the usual bad results was the terrible result of the everlasting urge of realism that the Greeks were responsible for.

CHAPTER VI

HAN CHINA

206 B.C–A.D. 220

GENERALLY speaking, the known history of China begins with the Han dynasty. What went before that is divided into four periods, Hsia, Shang, Chou, Ch'in.

The *Hsia* period (2205–1766 B.C.) is purely legendary but when one reads H. G. Creel's book "The Birth of China" he is likely to be amazed at the amount we know about the *Shang* period (1766–1122 B.C.) and also at the state of culture that did exist even in those ancient times.

The *Chou* period (1122–249 B.C.) is the longest in Chinese history and we know that the rulers came from the North West and settled in Honan on the Yellow River. This was on the same caravan route that Anau and Samarkand touched in the West. The period was one of high attainments. During it Confucius, Mencius and Lao Tzŭ devised their great philosophies. But the state finally was divided and overcome by the rulers of *Ch'in* (249–207 B.C.) a land lying west along the Wei River. This was a short period but during it China enthroned its first emperor who set up a central govern-

FIG. 167. Rubbing from a tile found at Loyang in the tombs. It shows a street scene with an old man followed by a Confucian scholar with his bamboo book and two women. Length 6 feet. Royal Ontario Mus., Toronto.

ment, the Great Wall was built, standard weights and measures were instituted, and the territory was extended to Fukien and Kwangtung provinces south and east on the coast. It was this same first emperor, nevertheless, who despite his enlightenment had all the existing books burnt.

The *Han* period is counted as from 206 B.C. to 220 A.D. after a period of civil war and Liu Pang carried his territory well into what is now Sin-Kiang

73

province, halfway to the Caspian Sea, making contact with the Hellenistic world. A Chinese embassy reached the Persian Gulf and the Romans traded iron and silk with them. Meanwhile, from India came Buddhism, bringing a new system of thought, more Hellenistic designs carried there by Alexander the Great, etc.

We do have a very few potteries which can be called pre-Shang or Shang and of these the most notable is the crude gray ware described in Chap. II.

Fig. 168. Front and back rubbings from a Loyang 3d cent. tile with stamped designs. Royal Ontario Mus., Toronto.

Fig. 169. Loyang tomb-tile of hard grey pottery with impressed border and incised design of geese, dogs and stags. Late Han or first part of 3d cent. Royal Ontario Mus., Toronto.

During the Chou and Ch'in period this gray ware seemed to continue with its string-impressed design (though the pointed wares we know seem to have stopped). Such gray wares have been found in Chinese Turkestan and Szechwan province. So far as we know, the hard white pottery with fret patterns carved in it or stamped, which was found on the site of the Yin emperors' tombs (1401–1122 B.C.) at Hsiao-tun in Honan, also ceased.

HAN WARES, 206 B.C.–A.D. 220

If one looks at the chart of Hissar I potteries, the #5 form is identical to many of the early Han wine jar forms. It was derived from the old original primitive pointed pot which had to be set into a ring stand which was made separately for a time and then sometimes made attached to the pot. This had become a bronze form in China, called a *"Hu"* but it did not appear until late Chou times, or about 500 B.C., some 2000–2500 years after the Hissar I potteries and it was not until Han times that it was frequently used. Thus Hobson is right when he says that this, among other Han pottery forms, was copied from bronzes, but he neglected to go far enough back to find that they in turn had been copied from potteries.

FIG. 170. A primitive form of Han pottery vase very much like one form of the Hissar I jars and probably arrived at in the same way though very likely the one was not influenced at all by the other. Ht. 17″. Warren E. Cox Coll.

FIG. 171. A further advanced pottery form in which the foot has widened to become more a part of the body and the lip-rim takes on a cup shape. Ht. 16″. Warren E. Cox Coll.

FIG. 172

A large part of Hu wares are unglazed gray, reddish or dark brown painted with designs in unfired or lightly fired pigments and molded or stamped appliqués. Only occasionally was a fine black dressing applied and polished, not unlike the finish of some American Indian potteries. Many of the painted designs are of dragons or animals, some show the floral motives or key fret bands of Hellenistic wares, but a large number have the sharp points that we described in the Susa potteries and the "pot hook" reverse spirals found on those of the "Black Earth Region." On these the bands are wide and the spirals are no longer angular as on the early bronzes but curved again almost exactly like the originals, flowing in a free and interlacing movement.

With these indications of a Western Asian heritage we are not surprised to find that at this time a simple alkaline glaze, transparent and varying from yellowish to brown, and in many shades of green due to the addition of copper, was introduced probably through association with the so-called Syro-Roman two-handled jars which have a closely allied glaze allowing for local differences in materials. These latter we know to have been found at widely different places (see last figure on Tepe Gawra Chart) and some are likely to have found their way to China through trade. They are contemporary and earlier than the Han period.

This was the first glaze used in China. It appears on a rather soft reddish

Hollow tile of grey pottery with stamped decoration made by applying several blocks over and over. Han dynasty. Length 41½" The Cleveland Mus. of Art.

Grey pottery tiles said to have come from a tomb near Hsianfu and to be of the Han dynasty. Lengths 10¾" to 12¼". The Cleveland Mus. of Art.

HAN DYNASTY TILES (206 B.C.–A.D. 220)

PLATE 19

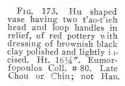

FIG. 173. Hu shaped vase having two t'ao-t'ieh head and loop handles in relief, of red pottery with dressing of brownish black clay polished and lightly incised. Ht. 16¼″. Eumorfopoulos Coll. # 80. Late Chou or Chin; not Han.

FIG. 174. Han pottery Hu showing very prominent use of the pot-hook and also the points (about the neck) which we have spoken of as probably originating in the Black Earth Region and at Susa. Ht. 21″. Mus. of Fine Arts, Boston.

FIG. 175. Han pottery wine jar of usual reddish color covered with a white slip and showing traces of painting. The precision of potting and the fact that the loop handle is made free rather than in relief would possibly indicate that this piece was of early origin. Russell Tyson Coll. (Art Institute of Chicago).

and fairly heavy body and was often streaked and mottled purposely. Like its Near Eastern prototype, it takes a beautiful iridescence from burial, which is more often silver but at times golden and full of fire. The Chinese potters were quick to see the advantages of relief decoration in catching and holding this glaze for a rich effect and we have a type known as "Western Han"

FIG. 176. Han dynasty painted pottery vase of dark buff gray ware with traces of white, red, and green. This type originally had a shallow pyramidal cover, but seldom the loops for ring handles. Perhaps metal ones were affixed to these. Ht. 23″. Fuller Coll. Seattle Art Mus.

FIG. 177. "Syro-Roman" vase said by the museum to date between 100 B.C. and 100 A.D. but possibly a little later. The glaze is a deep green and has considerable iridescence from burial. Ht. about 11″. Metropolitan Mus. of Art.

FIG. 178. Two miniature Han vases, one a reproduction of a typical wine jar even to the three spurs on the bottom, and the other a flattened bottle. Both pieces stand about four inches high, while the average wine jar is 14 inches to 18 inches in height and the granary urns the same.

These miniature pieces are rarer than the full sized ones and their particular use has not been discovered. Warren E. Cox Coll.

which always has a band, about the shoulder, of imaginary and actual animals, dragons, tigers, men riding great galloping lizards or dinosaurs while shooting bows and arrows or hurling spears and such. Some of these were also made in a mold but during the period, strangely, did not seem to lose their vitality thereby.

FIG. 180. Pair of strong wine jars with nine sided bases and curved bronze-form bodies of reddish buff clay with traces of light green glaze and some iridescence. A comb incised wave band is used about the body and lip rim. The rings are omitted from the loops of the usual Tao Tieh design. Note: These two jars are much like # 11 Plate 3 the Eumorfopoulos Coll. which Hobson calls "Late Han" but I think they may be looked upon as perhaps even later. Ht. 16¼". Warren E. Cox Coll.

FIG. 179. A remarkable wine jar with cover made to fit it. This is unusual for most of these are found simply with material tied over the top or a bowl inverted over it. The ware is the usual red pottery with iridescent green glaze. Ht. 18½". The Cleveland Mus. of Art.

FIG. 181. Shensi province or "Western Han" wine jar with relief band of the "Flying gallop." Dark red-brown, covered with a thick and very rich green glaze part of which is smeared over the bottom. Ex Thomas B. Clark Coll. Warren E. Cox Coll.

FIG. 182. Most Han wine jars are fired upside down so that the drips of glaze are at the lip rim, but this very strong example with its high relief handles and three wedge-shaped spurs was fired right side up. Ht. 18". Warren E. Cox Coll.

FIG. 183. Two Han wine jars showing contrast in sizes. The smaller is 3 inches high and the larger 15 inches. The shapes are much alike as are also the bodies of red clay and the glazes. Mrs. Ogden K. Shannon. Warren E. Cox Coll.

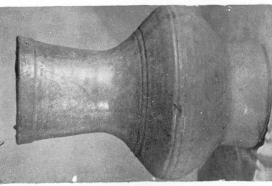

Han vase of beautifully slender form with rhythmical lines and also having its three spurs. It is of red clay with silvery pale green iridescent sheen. Ht. 16½". Warren E. Cox Coll.

Han vase such as usually contain wine in the tombs. Rarely examples are found with faceted bases, always octagonal. Possibly these represent stone plinths supporting bronze vessels which had round bottoms. This piece is of red clay with a bright apple green glaze showing large areas of silver iridescence. Ht. 16½". Warren E. Cox Coll.

The most powerful and dynamically designed Han dynasty vase or wine jar the writer has ever seen with fine high relief loop handles. The clay is of dark red and the glaze of a very dark green with blotches of iridescence. Best known example with the octagonal faceted base. Ht. 17¾". Warren E. Cox Coll. Note t'ao-t'ieh heads holding loops.

Red pottery vase covered with green glaze corroded to a silver iridescence through burial. The form is the primitive Hu with well defined foot which in some earlier forms in the Near East were pot-stands. Ht. 14½". Warren E. Cox Coll.

HAN DYNASTY WINE JARS

PLATE 20

The simple vase form described was used as a wine jar and may or may not have had the plinth base attached but all have wide and strong lip-rims about which were tied thongs, probably, to keep the covers on. Rarely a specimen is found with cover intact so we know that covers were used but no provision was made for seating them and in fact a peculiarity of most of these vases is that they were fired upside down so that the lip-rim often has irregular drops of glaze projecting from it.

It was the custom in Han times to bury a personage surrounded by pottery images of everyone and everything which he treasured in life. It had been the custom to bury the whole household alive in earlier days but Confucius had put a stop to this. He was even opposed to the inclusion of pottery images for fear of a relapse to the older custom, but because of it we know more about life in China 2000 years ago than we do about many intervening periods. How they dressed, how the women did their hair, what were their amusements, what food they ate and how it was prepared, their musical instruments, tools and weapons, the architecture of the times, the dance steps, the legends and even the humor is all becoming more and more clear as excavations proceed. Not many years ago, in our present generation, this was all found. For it was when the first railroads were cut through that grave mounds were opened against the religious laws of the country.

Fig. 184. Detail of Western Han jar c. 100–200 from Shensi showing men on horse-back shooting bows and arrows at tigers. Olive brown with golden iridescence. Ht. 13″. Warren E. Cox Coll.

Fig. 185. Flat foot of Han wine jar which was cut off the wheel with a cord, forming what the Japanese call an "ito-kiri" mark not usual in Han jars. Warren E. Cox Coll.

There are many forms of the "wine jars" but all have oblate bodies and strong concave tapering necks on which are the strong rims. They vary in size from 3 inches to 2 feet or more. It seems the finer ones have a hollowed plinth from the bottom up while most are made with the hollow of the vase extending down into the plinth. The glaze is sometimes thinly applied and almost mat while at other times it did not associate well with the body and had a tendency to chip off, a trouble carried well into T'ang times. The forms are from slender and graceful to the most dynamic and powerful to be found in all the art of potting. Some are fired right side up and are then stood on three or more "spurs" or small triangular pieces which adhered, due to the glaze, to the bottom. The t'ao-t'ieh head is used on the shoulder, usually one applied on either side, with a loop from the beak or mouth which holds a ring handle. In the earlier specimens the rings were made separately and stuck on with the glaze but later the whole handle was cast in the form of the vase in shallower and shallower relief and weaker design. Many are wheel-turned vessels and well defined grooves were usually left about the widest part of the body and at points above and below—such as where the neck joins the body, perhaps reminiscent of the bronzes which were joined at these points. The later "Western Han" vases and also the late Han porcelaneous vases have poorly formed bases or none at all and this may be taken into consideration in dating them for the tendency was toward a rounded softness in the following period, perhaps brought about by southern influences.

FIGS. 186–188. Two Han period granary urns, one of a slender shape and light green iridescence and the other more sturdy and showing an indication of a tile roof at the top. The feet of both represent bears for some reason as yet unknown. It is thought that these silos were set upon feet and floored so as to keep the rats out, but little credence need be given the idea, for the same feet appear on the "hill jars." Warren E. Cox Coll.

Granary urns in the form of a farmer's silo are less numerous than the wine jars and, as these do not occur in bronze, they must have been taken directly from architectural structures. They are usually nearly cylindrical or a little wider toward the top. They stand on three feet of the form of seated bears, perhaps some magical defense against marauders or vermin, and the tops are often made to simulate tile roofs. I have never seen a cover on one of these vessels and the lip-rim is not well defined enough to tie onto so we must assume that they were left open in the tomb. They are found filled with rice and other grains. The same variation is found in them from graceful to strong forms and from well potted early ones to more casual later ones.

"Hill Jars" are shorter cylindrical vessels also set upon three bear feet, usually having a band of relief decoration consisting of waves and strange animals about the body and always surmounted by a cover modeled in the form of a mountain with dashing waves about it. These jars are called *"po shan lu"* by the Chinese or "braziers of the vast mountain," representing the "Isles of the Blest." The great Wu Ti (140–86 B.C.) of the house of Han was a Taoist as were also his successors. The Emperor Shih Huang Ti of the 3rd century B.C. is said to have sent an expedition to find these islands. It was in command of a magician who appropriately took with him a group of young men and beautiful maidens, but in spite of all these precautions, contrary winds drove them back.

FIG. 189. Han dynasty or later gray pottery covered "Ting" copied from a bronze form. Courtesy of the Palmer Coll., The Art Institute of Chicago.

"Hill Censers" have similar covers set upon cups having slender stems and wide shallow saucers attached. Some are pierced as though for incense and some are not. This form also occurs in bronze.

FIG. 190. Watch tower of usual red Han pottery with green glaze and a well of buff pottery with green glaze. Hts. 29" and 19½". Eumorfopoulos Coll. # 48 and # 49.

FIG. 191. A glazed pottery "house," as the Art Institute calls it, which is probably a watch tower with indications of machicolations, a tile roof, etc., and interestingly set upon bear feet such as are also used on the hill jars and the granary urns. Buckingham Coll., Courtesy of the Art Institute, Chicago.

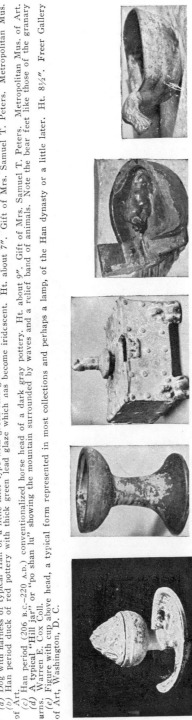

(a)

(b)

(c)

(d)

(e)

(f)

(g)

(h)

(i)

(j)

(a) Dog with harness of typical Han or a little later type with green lead glaze and iridescence. Length 8¼". Freer Gallery of Art, Washington, D. C.

(b) Han period duck of red pottery with thick green lead glaze which has become iridescent. Ht. about 7". Gift of Mrs. Samuel T. Peters. Metropolitan Mus. of Art.

(c) Han period (206 B.C.–220 A.D.) conventionalized horse head of a dark gray pottery. Ht. about 9". Gift of Mrs. Samuel T. Peters. Metropolitan Mus. of Art.

(d) A typical "Hill jar" or "po shan lu" showing the mountain surrounded by waves and a relief band of animals. Note the bear feet like those of the granary urns. Warren E. Cox Coll.

(e) Figure with cup above head, a typical form represented in most collections and perhaps a lamp, of the Han dynasty or a little later. Ht. 8½". Freer Gallery of Art, Washington, D. C.

(f) "Incense burner" (Po-Shan-Lu) of red pottery with a green glaze showing considerable iridescence. The cover is not pierced and is probably therefore, simply a symbol made to be placed in a tomb. Ht. 7½". Warren E. Cox Coll.

(g) Han pottery object called a "lamp" but may be the lower part of a "hill incense burner" or a pot-stand. Usual red body and green iridescent glaze. Ht. 6". Warren E. Cox Coll.

(h) Han "alms box," with a pottery bell so suspended inside that the dropped coin makes it ring and the figure bob. About the rim of the bell are round coins with square holes in relief. Length about 12". Gift of Robert E. Tod to Metropolitan Mus. of Art.

(i) Han pig-sty of buff clay with dark olive glaze showing some iridescence from burial. The incline and corner platform to the left is rather a characteristic suggestive construction. Length 8¼". Warren E. Cox Coll.

(j) Han ladle (or Tou) in the form of a rectangular bowl with flat bottom and dragon-headed handle. Similar to Eumo. Coll, Vol. I, # 53 and of red pottery with green glaze incrusted with iridescence and earth from burial. Length 8". Mrs. Charles Porter Wilson.

HAN DYNASTY POTTERY OBJECTS

PLATE 21

The Ting, it will be remembered, was derived from the Li and became a bronze form. Now we find pottery examples showing every sign of having been in turn copied from bronze ones. Some have lip-rims for covers and others have not.

Among the architectural forms are tall stage towers called "hunting towers" by the Chinese and made by setting one structure upon another, each with its balcony and rail, and the top one having a wide, projecting tile roof. It has been said that the Chinese shot birds from such towers and frequently they have bird finials or birds about the rails for decoration. Another form seems to be a barn set upon bear feet and with small windows set high up. The remarkable group from the Hoyt Collection in the Museum of Fine Arts in Boston shows a whole country house probably much as they were built. Then there is the goat yard, in Boston, with a little figure wearing a pointed

Fig. 192. A glazed Han pottery "pavilion" which is undoubtedly the upper part of a structure similar to the watch tower from the Freer Gallery and showing a similar bird finial and tile roof. The latter is interesting as it shows the decorative modeling at the ends of the tiles. The timber supports for the roof at each corner are also interesting. Buckingham Coll., Courtesy of the Art Institute, Chicago.

Fig. 193. An interesting glazed figure of the Han dynasty showing distinct semitic characteristics with high bridged nose and beard. The purpose for which these were put in the tombs is unknown. A number of later type seem to represent merchants and some have packs on their backs. Ralph M. Chait Coll.

cap and playing on a piccolo under his small private shed at the back, and my own porker in a pen provided with an inclined approach to a platform for feeding him and also for toilet facilities.

There are many animals and birds, chiefly domestic but not invariably, and all spirited and characteristic in modeling.

Furniture was provided, including chairs and tables laden with food and pot-stands incorrectly called "oil lamps," deep cups set upon a plain or human-figure base, but one of the most ingenious pieces of furniture that I have seen is a small chest set on human rather than bear feet and studded all over, but having a slot just above the lock in front and a figure suspended above it. When a coin is inserted there is a clink and the figure bows. This is probably the earliest mechanical bank known. It is in the Metropolitan.

The human figures are usually fairly natural and quite active. There are soldiers, dancing girls, servants, concubines and members of the household. Of course all sorts of people did the modeling and some are very fine while others are childlike.

Added to these things were stoves, well heads and a number of different types of eating bowls, buckets, dishes, etc.

Generally speaking the Han people were great and powerful potters so long as they stuck to their simple vase forms; their representative work is more curious and interesting than imbued with any aesthetic appeal.

SOUTHERN HAN WARES

Definite separation of northern and southern types of Han pottery is difficult due to lack of archaeological data but in general we know the southern wares to be more rounded and soft in form. Globular jars of true pottery forms often lack the horizontal ridges or have them only faintly indicated.

FIG. 194. Southern Han ovoid jar without horizontal grooves or ridges such as were copied on the northern ones from bronze examples. Ht. 9½". Warren E. Cox Coll.

FIG. 195. Late Han employment of the old texture representing mat marks. This vase has also imprints of a seal, perhaps the owner's.

FIG. 196. Ewer of softened Chinese wine jar form with loop handle seen in Neolithic potteries in various places, and an elephant spout closely resembling a North Chinese t'ao-t'ieh head. Found at Thanh-hoa.

In northern Annam Prof. O. Janse made extensive excavations and found potteries reflecting both Chinese and Indonesian wares. I think his contribution from the field of great value, but do not agree with many of his deductions. For instance, in the ewer shown, he sees Indonesian influence in the elephant-head spout and loop handle at the top. We know that the elephant head appears as one modification of the t'ao-t'ieh head on early bronzes from An Yang and that elephant or mastodon forms have been frozen in the ice of Siberia, while the loop handle occurs in the ewer found at Ur and other very early and not necessarily southern sites. He also shows a vessel which looks like a spittoon, jumps to the conclusion that it is a spittoon, and states that it is a vessel "employed above all by people who chew betel-nut" and then goes on to state that the Chinese are not a betel chewing people, which

Mortuary model of a house: "Rectangular enclosure with gate and spirit walls in south, main hall in north, kitchen in east and storehouse in west. Mortar and grist mill; seven figures and saddle horse. Clay: buff, washed with white clay, traces of black trim. Ornamental rockery painted in black on main spirit wall. Ht. 17″, plan about 32″ by 36″. Hoyt Coll. Mus. of Fine Arts, Boston.

Han pottery barn yard with goats and the goatherd in a small shed in the background playing a pipe. Length about 8″. Boston Mus. of Fine Arts.

HAN DYNASTY POTTERY HOUSE AND GOAT YARD

PLATE 22

FIG. 197. Unique South China Han Dynasty pottery jar and cover with red body and green, glossy glaze which was crackled before burial and makes the iridescence appear like confetti. Ht. 8″. Ex Warren E. Cox Coll. Cleveland Mus. of Art.

FIG. 198. A vessel not necessarily a spittoon as Prof. Janse concludes but with a rim for tying down a cover. (See chart of Hissar II potteries.)

FIG. 199. Han jar from Annam of the usual Chinese shape except that it is softer and more rounded in form, lacks the t'ao-t'ieh and ring handles and has loops on the shoulder and slots in the base.

FIG. 200. Southern Han wine jar (hu) of hard red body with a transparent amber finely crack'ed thin glaze over it. Type found at Chang-sha, Nan yang, etc., and probably extends well into the 6th cent. or possibly even T'ang. Ht. 13¾″. Warren E. Cox Coll.

FIG. 201. An Annam incense burner with bird top which does recall certain East Indian brass and bronze treatments.

FIG. 202. The use of the cock-head suggests a connection with Yüeh.

FIG. 203. Pot-stand incorrectly called a "lamp" by Professor Janse. It bears a close relationship to Silla and earlier Korean ones and also those of Japan.

FIG. 204. A *Ting* formed vessel with one horizontal handle added instead of the usual two perpendicular loops. This is undoubtedly a Chinese form derived from the *Li*. (See neolithic section.)

FIG. 205. A typical eating bowl quite similar to Han examples but called a "saucepan" by Prof. Janse. Such forms are used in China to-day.

FIG. 206. Iron cook stove of late Han or 3d cent. type with writing in style of period. Found in the same grave with one of the porcelaneous vases in Shen-si province. Field Mus., Chicago.

is all a little fast as reasoning. Furthermore he calls the pot-stand a lamp. However, the wares are interesting. The reticulated pot-stand and globular vessel show a technique close to that of Korea and Japan. The smooth, rounded shapes are distinctive. But most interesting is the Ting found at Qui-giap, Han-loc in Thanh-hoa province with rooster head spout much like those found on vessels from Chiu yen of the Yüeh ware.

THE FIRST PORCELAIN

FIG. 207. Actual vase of earliest type porcelain. The body is of greyish buff and appears to contain iron while the glaze is yellowish-green, vitrified and covers only the upper part of the jar. The bottom is flat and shows spur marks. Ht. 6⅝″. Field Mus., Chicago.

Through a vessel found on an iron cook stove in Shensi province and dated thereby, it was discovered by the late Dr. Berthold Laufer, assisted by the analysis made by Mr. H. W. Nichols, that the Chinese made a much harder ware than the pottery, and that this ware contained kaolin and was a true porcelain. The body is a gray porous substance coated with a white engobe covered with a transparent greenish-yellow glaze which is inclined to run unevenly over the shoulder and thin out toward the bottom. Frequently it was so badly chemically fitted to the body that it chips off in large areas. An unexplained feature of these wares is that none of them ever have the typical cylindrical bases that are found on the pottery vases and many do not even have base rims of any sort. They look as though they were meant to stand upon pot-stands but so far as I know no stand of this ware has ever been found. The loss of the bases would also indicate a later development around A.D. 200 or a little later.

It has only been some fifty years or a bit more that these early wares have been known. They were first discovered when railroads were permitted to cut straight across country and in grading, opened several grave mounds. It had been against the laws of the country and the religious laws to excavate such mounds before, but when the wares came to light and it was found that they brought high prices, the Chinese began to do some digging of their own and recently a large number of pieces have been exported.

However the 2nd World War put a stop to that and it is very unlikely that any such amount of wares will ever be found and shipped again. Of course, to the porcelain lover or perfectionist these wares may seem crude but to the collector who can look with an open eye they have superb form and are fine pieces of craftsmanship.

FIG. 208. Porcelaneous pottery vase of grey ware covered partly with brown slip and a glaze over that of light green variable color. The weight is great, being nearly six pounds. This piece has both loops with rings in relief and free loop handles, a treatment not found on pottery examples. Ht. 14″. Field Mus., Chicago.

FIG. 209. Han porcelaneous vase of typical type with yellowish-olive thin glaze on upper part. Ht. 13″. Warren E. Cox–Mrs. Gibson L. Douglass Coll.

FIG. 210. Han porcelaneous jar of *lei* shape. Buff gray ware with lower part covered with brown-red slip, upper part and inside of bottom with greenish-yellow glaze. Decoration is combed wave type, handles cast in animal-head design. Ht. 10¼″. Field Mus., Chicago.

I am adding two rare pieces of pottery, not protoporcelain. One is a modified granary urn similar to Figs. 186 to 188 but with rounded shoulder and five sections undoubtedly a prototype of the Yueh ones Pl. 34 top center and lower right. The other is a *lien* (toilet box) like a hill jar (Pl. 21 [d]) but with cover similar in design to that of a bronze mirror. One sees about one of these to a hundred hill jars.

FIG. 210 B. Pottery wine container of modified granary urn form showing five sections representing stacked bowls of grain offerings. Ht. 14¾″. Warren E. Cox Coll.

FIG. 210 C. A very rare *lien* or "toilet box" of Han pottery of "hill jar" form, but with cover having a design similar to that of a bronze mirror. Ht. 7½″. Warren E. Cox Coll.

CHAPTER VII

"SIX DYNASTIES"
(A.D. 220–587)

AND SUI PERIODS
(A.D. 581–617)

OF CHINA

DECADENT WEAKNESS of the ruling family permitted the Han period to break up into three parts sometimes called the "Three Kingdoms," the *Wei* in the north, the *Wu* in the central part and the *Shu* in the west. The last was ruled by descendants of the Hans. The civil wars made opportunity for invasions by people from the north where much of the territory north of the Yangtze was taken. Thus we may list the *Western Chin* (A.D. 265–317), *Eastern Chin* (A.D. 317–420), *Liu Sung* (A.D. 420–479), *Northern Wei* (A.D. 386–636), —— the longest and most dominant period, —— then the *Ch'i* (A.D. 479–502), *Liang* (A.D. 502–557) and the *Ch'en* (A.D. 557–589) which, considering the two Chin dynasties as one, are called *"The Six Dynasties."*

This was a period of chaotic conditions, but during it much transpired that indirectly affected our art of ceramics. Liu Pei (later called Kuan Ti, the god of war) and his two aids Chang Fei and Kuan Yü along with Chu-ko Liang, the strategist and inventor of war machines, made history and are often portrayed. The conquering Tartars, Tibetans and "Hsiung Nu" or barbarians to the North West brought many strange things and new beliefs. Buddhism gained power. It was a formative period.

Horses had been known in Han times but not so generally and we now see attempts to model them, with uneven results. Camels were at times strange in anatomy but often more alive and full of nasty camel character than those which followed in the T'ang period. Dogs are not often seen but the superb bitch and pup shown illustrates how wonderfully the great black and brindle dogs which ran with the horses in the hunt and in war could be caught in character. All the woodenness of the Han dogs had gone out. Some more or less imaginary animals, like the curled and snarling cat-like one shown, were made repeatedly, as though they had some well known significance. The beginning of the development of "Earth Spirits" from animistic forms to the human "Lokapala" was made, as can be seen in the very interesting two illustrated. And human figures show a great divergence

90

FIG. 211. Horse of Northern Wei. Black and olive pottery coated with white slip and painted in red and green. Ht. 8¾". The Cleveland Mus. of Art.

FIG. 212. One of two very crude but spirited camels probably of Wei or even earlier origin. The pottery is buff in color. Ht. 10½". Fuller Coll., Seattle Art Mus.

and variety in technique. There are little silly ones dancing around like dwarfs and gnomes, stupid soldiers on horseback so clothed as to hide the faults of anatomy, strange symmetrical doll-like forms like inverted beakers with heads stuck on, and also some beautifully expressive sculptures. A certain elfish smile is rather significant. The group of small dancers, musicians

FIG. 213. Wei period (221–265 A.D.). One of the "Three Kingdoms" curled catlike animal of gray pottery covered with a white slip. Dia. about 10". Gift of Robert E. Tod. Metropolitan Mus. of Art.

FIG. 214. Two early transitional forms of the "Earth spirits" partly animistic and partly human demon-like forms, of grey clay without sign of polychrome coloring. Hts. 7" and 8". Eric Mansfield.

and attendants (from the Metropolitan Museum of Art) are beautifully conceived and masterful in the portrayal of movement. Other standing figures of women show a great dignity and strength of character in these wives of fighters and farmers and herdsmen, a great dignity and restrained charm.

FIG. 215. Grey, pottery unglazed, box-like object without a bottom, said by Hobson to be a well head (see similar example in the Eumorfopoulos Coll. # 100). He calls that one "3d or 4th cent." but it is quite likely that this piece was made during the Han period (206 B.C.-A.D. 220). Length 9¾", width 6½", ht. 5". Fuller Coll. Seattle Art Mus.

FIGS. 216–220. Nine small figures of the Wei period, (6th cent.), of dancers, servants and a musician in buff pottery showing traces of polychrome decoration. Ht. about 4". Metropolitan Mus. of Art.

These are not the pretty ladies usually portrayed in T'ang times but staunch supporters of the household.

One of the most interesting and often occurring animal forms is the Triceratops-like form illustrated. Mr. Hobson describes it as "remotely resembling a rhinoceros." That it definitely is not a rhinoceros is convincingly proven by Dr. Laufer in his "Anthropological Series" (Vol. XIII, No. 2 Publication 177, page 158) where he states, "There can be no doubt of two points,—first, that the ancient Chinese, from the very beginning of their history, were acquainted with two species of rhinoceros, the single-horned and two-horned ones, distinguished as 'Se' and 'Si'; and, second, that the former is identical with the present *Rhinoceros indicus unicornis* (as proven above all by the linguistic relationship of the word Se with Tibetan Bse and Lepcha Sa), and the latter with the present *Rhinoceros sumatrensis*." In the same treatise we find that the Chinese used rhinoceros hide for armor and at very early dates drew perfectly recognizable likenesses of them.

FIG. 221. Sui or Early T'ang figure of groom. Ochre-colored clay with traces of polychrome. Expression strangely like that of Mussolini. Ralph Chait Coll-

FIG. 222. Typical Six Dynasties conventionalized woman with bell shaped skirt. Grey clay with brown, red and white pigments. Ht. 14". L. R. Mintz.

FIG. 223. Wei merchant traveler in reddish unglazed ware with Eastern Mediterranean type face. Ht. 12½". C. T. Loo & Co.

Now the form we are considering is not at all like a rhinoceros in several features: 1.—It invariably has three large horns. 2.—It always has prominent lumps (usually five in number) on the back ridge. 3.—It has a smooth hide not plaquetted as is the rhinoceros hide. 4.—It always has indications of an armored jowl. Certainly a people who knew the rhinoceros could not have made all these points as errors in construction! and repeated them many times! And finally, 5.—It has a very large and prominent tail which is entirely uncharacteristic of the rhinoceros.

Northern Wei figure of grey ware covered with white and then red slip except for face and hands which show light pink traces. This remarkably modeled bearded figure with the tremendously vigorous hand and tall shield with relief lion's head is unique and appears to be a Tartar or North Russian type, certainly not Mongolian. The shield has a Roman lion mask. Ht. 12½". Warren E. Cox Coll.

Six Dynasty figure of dignified woman. Lifelike face but little anatomical modeling. Upturned toes to shoes usually associated with T'ang costume, yet of very heavy potting. Dark grey, almost black, with traces of white, red and pale green. Ht. 15¾". Warren E. Cox Coll.

Right: Gray pottery woman of 5th or 6th cent. showing typical treatment of skirt but more detailed treatment of face than usual. Ht. about 10". Metropolitan Mus. of Art.

SIX DYNASTY FIGURES

PLATE 23

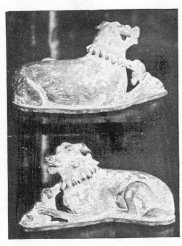

Wei or Six Dynasty bitch and pup of gray clay with traces of white and red encrusted with buff earth. Typical of modeling of period, sometimes lacking in true anatomical detail but imbued with life. Length 9". Warren E. Cox Coll.

Grey terracotta figure of tiger dressed with white pigment. Wei period. Ht. 8½". C. T. Loo & Co.

Left: Camel of gray pottery. Wei (one of "Three Kingdoms") period (A. D. 221–265) or earlier. *Right:* Northern Wei dragon-like animal with a head already beginning to be somewhat ornate.

Pair of painted Six Dynasty horses. Nickerson Coll., Art Institute, Chicago. Length 31".

SIX DYNASTIES POTTERY ANIMALS

PLATE 24

Dr. Laufer goes further and tells of the finding of rhinoceri in Miocene or Pliocene deposits (6 to 12 million years ago) in Europe, India and Northern China, the latter by A. R. Wallace, and of two found between the Yenisei and Lena Rivers frozen and quite recognizable with their hairy coats and two horns, "The skin being smooth and without the characteristic folds of the now living species." But here we have two horns again!

Mr. Roy Chapman Andrews states (*Ency. Brit.* 14th edition, Vol. 15, page 713), "Four days after starting it was found that the main trail between Kalgan, China and Urga, the capital of Mongolia, which had been traversed by several geologists, runs directly through the rich fossil beds—one of Oligocene and one of Eocene, of the age of mammals, and one *Cretaceous* of the age of reptiles." Mr. Andrews found the dinosaur eggs in this section. But here his finds were of the protoceratops, a small dinosaur similar to our animal but without horns.

I then had a talk with the eminent Dr. Barnum Brown and found that the triceratops, or three-horned dinosaurs had only been found in the northern part of North America to date but he stressed the point that field research had not been able to "scratch the surface" on the Asiatic side of the

Fig. 224. The finest of the Chinese reconstructions from Triceratops remains that I have found. Note the power of modeling. Length 12½". Warren E. Cox Coll.

Bering Straits and such negative results are not to be taken too seriously. He pointed out that the buffalo and early elephant types are identical on both sides and also stated that migrations of men had not only been from Asia to America but also in the opposite direction.

Mr. Andrews further states, in reference to the dinosaur eggs, "Three had broken out of a small sandstone ledge and lay exposed," and later he says, "The skeleton of a small dinosaur was found, lying 4 inches above the eggs in loose sediment on top of the rock."

With this evidence I present the, so far as I know, new theory that *these animal forms are actual reconstructions made by the Chinese from dinosaur bones found along the caravan routes of Mongolia.* The alignment of the horns is easily explained by the fact that skulls of triceratops when found are

Triceratops-like form of animal found in Mongolia or Alaska. Grey clay with white slip and red under the encrusted earth. Length 12″. Detroit Institute of Arts.

A Six-dynasty "Ting" having handles showing Hellenistic design. Red ware with green glaze having some iridescence. Dia. 7″. Warren E. Cox Coll.

Jar c. 2nd to 4th cent. One of earliest of this type later developed by Yüeh, Lung ch'üan and southern Kuan kilns. The figures include a dog, dragon, guardians of a portal and front view of flying bird. Ht. 12″. Warren E. Cox Coll.

T'ang or earlier gray stoneware pilgrim bottle with olive brown glaze. This type with grape and phoenix design (and sometimes Bacchanalian figures) shows very strong Roman influence. Ht. 8″. Metropolitan Mus. of Art.

SIX DYNASTIES OBJECTS

PLATE 25

almost always crushed flat. All other points could be observed from the skeletons *en situ*, these bones were often not greatly disturbed and they were right along the caravan route.

This puts a different light on our ideas of the source of the t'ao-t'ieh, "thunder monster," and dragon forms, the original sources of which were much less imaginary than may have been supposed. It is known that the legend of a meteorite will live in the memories of a people for centuries. Add to such legends the finding of actual bones of dinosaurs much larger than those of any living animal and it is easy to see how the well founded belief in a fiery dragon descending from the heavens could take hold of the minds of a people and become part of their religion and a source of many of their art motives.

Vase forms like the Han wine jars, but showing decadence in the use of lower relief and softer forms, continued and I am convinced that many which are now called Han will, when we learn more, be placed at somewhat later dates. As for the "proto-porcelain" which I described under the Han

FIG. 225. Smaller vase of type found in Shensi province. Typically heavily potted with border about shoulder which Reinach has named "the flying gallop" but which occurs on bronzes only of a later epoch.

Larger vase probably Six Dynasties or later T'ang dynasty. More thinly potted, has even and thinner, greener glaze and the body is more brown than the reddish Han type. Though these vases are later copies of Han ones, they are more rare and costly. Warren E. Cox Coll.

FIG. 226. T'ang or Sui dynasty flask with circular body, concave neck and broad tapering lip-rim, set upon flaring base. The clay is of reddish buff and the glaze brownish green. Ht. 9". Buckingham Coll., The Art Institute of Chicago.

period, some of it belongs in that period but most of it was made around A.D. 300 or later. I placed it in the earlier period because it began then. The style seemed to tend toward the use of a gray ware rather than red, perhaps because the clay was not so well fired or so well protected from smoke in firing, but it is entirely wrong for dealers to make up their minds that all gray wares are Wei while all red wares are Han. Glaze seemed not so generally popular as the use of painted slips much like those of the Han period and in some cases hardly distinguishable at all, but it is not reasonable to assume that glaze was entirely discontinued and we actually find improvements in it.

Glaze was used on new types of wares. The flattened bottles or "pilgrim bottles" of red ware covered with a green or brown glaze and decorated with relief designs very similar to those of Han or slightly later bronze mirrors and showing strong Hellenistic influences in grape motives and dancing figures such as existed from about 3rd century B.C. to 4th century A.D. in the Western World, are undoubtedly earlier than T'ang although the form does continue into the later period. We find it represented hanging to the saddles of T'ang camels and rarely even in the T'ang streaked yellow and green glazes on a white ware. (See my example.)

Another red stone-ware, usually globular jars, decorated with various scallops, applied rosettes, etc. and covered with a dark brown glaze seems to have all the characteristics of a pre-T'ang ware and is so called by Hobson

Fig. 227. Pottery jar with cover, grey body coated with thin greyish glaze, foot not glazed. About body are Zodiac figures in high relief. Said to be Wei. Ht. 14". C. T. Loo & Co.

Fig. 228. Pottery jar and cover of red ware with mottled olive brown glaze, called Sung or earlier by museum but actually of pre-T'ang times. Ht. 10½". Hoyt Coll. Mus. of Fine Arts, Boston.

Fig. 229. Vase and cover on stand of the Six Dynasty period (A.D. 386–589) of buff gray pottery decorated in white and red slip. Ht. about 19". Metropolitan Mus. of Art.

in the Eumorfopoulos Collection (see #159) on the authority of an association between that piece and one published by Prof. F. Sarre and attributed to the Sassanian period (3rd to 7th century A.D.). The one illustrated from the Boston Museum is incorrectly called "Sung or earlier." These are not to be confused with the similar looking globular jars of brown ware with brown glaze of Ming and later times which come from Indo-China and South China although their general look and perhaps even their province is the same.

A rarer type is represented by the brown-gray jar shown herewith. It is decorated with the pinched-up or very crudely modeled decoration consisting of a portal with guards with arms akimbo on either side, a dragon, a running figure, a horse (head missing), dog, etc. including an amazing bird flying directly head-on toward the spectator. The glaze is of very thin "tea-dust" type sunk into the body so that it is mat in texture and brown in color. This appears to be a prototype to the tall pale celadon mortuary jars of the T'ang period. Its cover is missing.

That Yüeh ware was made before the T'ang period we now have full evidence. Yüeh is the name of an ancient district now called Shao-hsing in Chekiang province and we shall speak of the three Shang-lin-hu kiln sites in

Yüeh yao writer's water vessel made in an ingenious manner. Body is a vase, neck of which potter cut off and applied near bottom to form animal's mouth, adding legs, nose, eyes, ears and handle-like a tail afterwards. Typical light grey-green glaze. Length 4″. Warren E. Cox Coll.

Rare Chiu-yen Yüeh box with grey-green glaze and evenly spaced iron-brown spots. A prototype of the Lung-ch'üan ware called "tobi seji" by the Japanese. That it was considered an important work even in Yüeh days is proven by beautifully fitting and very thin rim of cover. Bottom is slightly concave and fired on spurs. c. 6th cent. Dia. 3⅞″. K. M. Semon Coll.

Ewer from Chiu-yen kiln, made c. 2nd to 4th cent. Finely modeled rooster-head spout and dragon-head handle, incising on the shoulder and typical two squared loops make this an interesting piece. Ht. 15″. Fuller Coll., Seattle Mus.

Small Yüeh yao jar with stamped design and applied heads with ring handles. The glaze is the usual frosty grey green. Ht. about 4″. Judge Edgar Bromberger Coll. Brooklyn Mus.

Important Yüeh yao jar probably from the Chiu-yen or "nine rocks" site. The glaze is mat olive green of greyish tint. Ht. about 11½″. Nasli Heeramaneck Coll.

SIX DYNASTIES YÜEH WARES
FROM CHIU-YEN (NINE ROCKS) SITE

PLATE 26

the T'ang section for the wares from there are of that period, but the late Mr. A. D. Brankston has published (*The Burlington Magazine*, 1938, December issue) another site called the Chiu-yen (Nine rocks) section near Shao-hsing where a type of Yüeh ware was also made at earlier times. The basin from the Sir Percival David Collection corresponds exactly with bronzes dated A.D. 101, 132 and 194. The small jar from the Judge Edgar Bromberger Collection with its cross-hatched pattern and t'ao-t'ieh heads is like,

FIG. 230. Small Six Dynasty Yüeh jar from the Chiu-yen site. Glassy, crackled glaze is characteristic of the heavier sort of these wares. K. M. Semon Coll.

FIG. 231. This jar shows small figure of Buddha applied to shoulder on either side. K. M. Semon Coll.

FIG. 232. Jar with doubled loop handles, which came into use on T'ang wares. Ht. 7″. Warren E. Cox Coll.

Right: Yüeh, Chiu-yen, basin which A. D. Brankston placed as between 1st and 3d cent. A.D. Dia. 12¾″. Sir Percival David, Bt.

Writer's coupe of frog form similar to one illustrated by Brankston belonging to Mr. P'an Hsi and inscribed Kê-erh meaning "guest child" and, therefore, said to be of 5th cent. A.D. Length 3½″. Miss Grandin Baldwin.

FIG. 234. Ewer c. 7th cent. or before having typical Six Dynasty glaze of mat olive but similar to T'ang examples set on separate stands. Form is from the Near East. Ht. 14¾″. Warren E. Cox Coll. C. T. Loo.

FIG. 235. Six Dynasty jar of grey ware with olive green glaze finely crackled. Note the double loops on the shoulder which originated in Han times. Ht. 9½″. John Platt—Warren E. Cox Coll.

FIG. 233. Chiu-yen Yüeh ewer with cock spout. A small circular or star-shaped tool was used to press down clay around spout, places of attachment of loops and handle. Usual grey ware with olive green glaze. Ht. 8″. K. M. Semon Coll.

in many details, several in the Historical Museum, Peking, which were made in Chê-ho-chên, Honan province and were found in a tomb dated A.D. 99. Finally the ewer corresponds in all details, the cock spout, the tapered handle, the squared loops (probably for suspending it to make pouring easier) and the hard gray ware covered with transparent green glaze, with the one owned by Sir Herbert Ingram and placed by Brankston in the 2nd to 4th century. It will be noted that this piece also has incised points on the shoulder, and, what other known specimens lack, the fine dragon at the top of the handle so often seen in later T'ang amphoras. (See Pl. 26)

Another hard gray stoneware dressed with a very thin brown slip or burnt brown where exposed is covered about two thirds of the way down with a rusty olive green glaze almost identical to the early Yüeh glaze. It will be noted that the stopping of the glaze part way down first puts in appearance on these jars and the one with pinched-modeled figures, and this is quite definitely a Near Eastern technique used much earlier in Western Asia. It is also to be noted that the characteristic double loops, three of which are set on the shoulder, correspond with those of the Han example shown and were used to tie on a cover. (Fig. 235)

Finally the two ewers, one without handle but with trefoil lip and one with handle and spout, the one having a buff body and the other gray again, have the same sort of mat olive green glaze heavier and darker than we expect in T'ang times. The one without handle corresponds to those of the

Fig. 236. Six Dynasty painted pottery house with what appear to be tile roofs beamed walls and sliding doors. Buckingham Coll., The Art Institute of Chicago.

T'ang period which were stood upon tall pot-stands and was probably so equipped.

The architectural potteries include a further development of the detail of forms, such as beam ends, and of structural details. One seemingly new trick was the making of loose sliding doors set in grooves. The polychrome painting in blue, green, red, white and black seemed to be favored for these as for the large jars but here structure governs the designs rather than the traditional and merely decorative pot hooks and scrolls.

It is obvious that our information is fragmentary concerning this period of some 400 years and it offers a fascinating field for future collectors, but a word of warning must be inserted. In a period in which the styles varied so much and in which the potteries offer no great technical obstacles the forger finds a happy playground and it is conservative to estimate that out of all the Wei and T'ang pieces on the market not one third are correct. Some are cast from old pieces and some are made whole by the Japanese and modern Chinese.

CHAPTER VIII

T'ANG PERIOD OF CHINA

A.D. 618–906

WE NOW enter upon one of the great periods of world art. One thinks of T'ang, Sung and Ming in the Far East as one thinks of Egypt, Greece and the Renaissance in the West, though they are not, of course, contemporary, and are quite unlike in styles. The first represents *simple beauty* and perfected craftsmanship, the second the *pinnacle of the classic* and the third the *ornate but not yet too decadent flowering*. Actually the T'ang period was much influenced by Hellenistic art but so strongly burnt the flame that no amount of smoke could serve to dull its light.

The Northern Wei lost power to the southern Liang dynasty with its capital at Nanking (A.D. 502–557) and Buddhism came strongly there by sea through the straits of Malacca. The art which represented this religion

FIG. 237. Globular jar of polished black pottery with incised peonies much in technique of rare Han examples but having design more like that of Sung. In London exhibition of 1935–6 it was given the attribution: "Probably T'ang." Ht. 9½". D. Abbes Coll. Mrs. Margot Holmes Coll.

FIG. 238. T'ang coupe and cover of white pottery with a very thin, light, straw-colored glaze. Ht. 4½". Metropolitan Mus. of Art.

FIG. 239. T'ang white pottery cup with transparent white glaze. Well proportioned and thinly potted. Ht. 2¾". Fuller Coll. Seattle Art Mus.

was not much affected by that of Gandhara but rather that of the Maurya dynasty of the 3rd century B.C. With it came the great winged lions and also the fluted column. In 589 China was again united for a short period until 618. This is loosely known as the Sui period (A.D. 581–617) and may be thought of so far as we are concerned as a continuation of the Six Dynasties.

The territory of the first great T'ang emperors after their conquests extended into Tibet and Turkestan and intercourse with the West was exten-

Superb pilgrim bottle of the T'ang period showing strong classic influence in the carved low relief foliate design. It is of white ware with straw colored thin glaze. Ht. 13". Gift of Mrs. H. O. Havemeyer. Metropolitan Mus. of Art.

Pedestal of red ware covered with a buff and green glaze somewhat iridescent from burial. This piece shows some Hellenistic influence. T'ang. Ht. about 12". Metropolitan Mus. of Art.

Rare small T'ang pilgrim bottle similar to the larger brown glazed Six Dynasty ones. It is of light buff body with mottled green and amber glazes inclined to chip off as is usually the case with T'ang glazes. Ht. 5¼". Warren E. Cox Coll.

T'ang coupe of white pottery with light straw colored glaze showing very strong resemblance to Roman ones which are often found with green lead glaze. Ht. about 4". Gift of Mrs. Samuel T. Peters. Metropolitan Mus. of Art.

T'ANG DYNASTY WARES
SHOWING GREEK AND ROMAN INFLUENCE

PLATE 27

sive. It was during this time that Wu Tao-tzŭ, the greatest of Chinese painters, lived. Wood block printing was extensively developed. Much of the classic literature and poetry was written, and the famous Li Tai Po lived, who, like our Poe, drank heavily and wrote well.

Ever since the conquest of Alexander the Great into India and the formation of Greco-Bactrian states north west of India, communications between China and Western Asia had been continuous. The drapery of all Buddhistic figures is really Greek as are also the features of many and the poses. An examination of many T'ang potteries will disclose Greek origins or at least Western Asian ones. Portraiture in the figures is not at first frequent just as it was not in Greece but during the T'ang period a revolt against this principle occurred just as in Rome, although the portraits were pretty much confined to pottery rather than wood, stone, or bronze. Most early T'ang paintings were of a religious nature and symmetrical in design as well as conventional in treatment. Only during the later part of the period did masterful landscape and animal painting commence. The Chinese were close observers of distance and could render aerial perspective better than many western artists but they were more interested in design, in catching the struggle of a tree branch against the prevailing wind, in the movement of the wind at the moment of painting, that the water (and there is usually water) be flowing or rippling or full of water life and spirit. In other words the transition from the static qualities of Buddhistic art were cast aside during this time and an interest in movement and life was assumed which has not been lost since.

FIG. 240. T'ang candlestick of hard white ware with greenish white glaze. Ht. 11¾". Cleveland Mus. of Art.

The technique of potting had been improved and we find T'ang wares usually whiter in body and varying from soft to porcelaneous, though some are also buff, light gray, and reddish. Thus the mere color of the body is no final criterion of period. It was generally thinner in the smaller pieces especially. The old lightly fired pigments, red, black, white and rarely blue and green were continued, though sparingly. The most usual glaze is transparent and straw colored, thinly applied but finely crackled and likely to chip off because it was not well associated with the biscuit. The Chinese did not learn how to govern crackle until the end of the Sung period and some T'ang glazes are not crackled at all though this is rare and was only luck. This glaze is simply a refined type of the old alkaline lead glaze of Han times and the same greens, browns, amber tones, etc. were used a little more purified and brighter. Quite rarely cobalt was added to make a blue but no manganese was ever consciously employed and it occurs only by accident in some of the browns, some of which have a purple cast. This is strange for the blue was undoubtedly learned from the Near East where the purple also had been used for thousands of years. Many splashed, dripped and running effects were employed, perhaps because the glaze tended to act that way and the Chinese made use of its characteristics rather than tried to curb them. However, that the glazes could be controlled by the use of incised outlines may be seen by the beautiful pillow illustrated. It is interesting to note that glaze had first been employed in the Near East because the wares were porous and were thus aided in being liquid-tight, here it became a style to let the glaze just splash over the edge and come part way down on the body. In China the Han wares were denser and did not need glaze inside but the association with bronze made the potters glaze the outside down to the bottom carefully so as to imitate metal. We see the first Near Eastern stopping of the glaze short of the foot-rim in the Six Dynasties times and now it becomes prevalent.

At Samarra, half way between Baghdad and Ashur, on the Tigris River were found sherds of stoneware and true porcelain with feldspathic glaze of high fire, and corresponding with Chinese wares. This site is definitely dated as of the 9th century. The glazes were yellowish white, closely crackled and a green mottled transparent type. Others were sea green (or "celadon"), pure white, ivory, chocolate brown verging on black and of mat texture, watery green, gray and finally a group of transmutation glazes of brown splashed with frothy gray with bluish and whitish tinges. Of the latter it is not easy to distinguish between the T'ang and Sung wares and reliance must be placed mostly on the style of the foot.

It is typical of the T'ang foot that it was flat bottomed and beveled before firing, but the disadvantages of such a bottom were discovered and some T'ang wares have simple foot-rims. Thus we cannot depend too much on this characteristic.

Continuation of the animals and human forms of Han times and Six Dynasties times was, of course, to be expected and others were added while here again we find them ranging in sculptural qualities and beauty or appeal all the way from childlike attempts to masterpieces. This was natural for some tombs were of great importance while others were for minor officials or family heads. The movement and action of the Six Dynasties is usually preserved and forms come closer to nature with greater details. Horses seem to vary from Arabian types to heavy fellows almost like Percherons, but they were rare and costly animals in China and were all used for saddle purposes while carts were drawn by oxen. In different sections there were different styles but so little is known of the tomb sources of many that no clear plan of these sources has yet been laid out, though Dr. Laufer did take some steps in this direction.

He states generally that horses from Honan are: 1.—more realistic, 2.—more lifelike, 3.—always harnessed, 4.—in various poses with turns of the neck, 5.—have grace of motion, 6.—have narrower chests, 7.—the hair of the mane hangs straight downward, 8.—carry riders of which the women are bet-

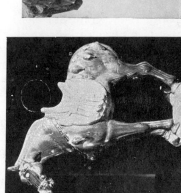

Fig. 241. T'ang lion or dog of white ware with a transparent glaze. Ht. 4¾". Fuller Coll. Seattle Art Mus.
Fig. 242. T'ang dynasty glazed pottery duck. Many animals were made during this time to place in the graves. Buckingham Coll. The Art Institute of Chicago.
Fig. 243. T'ang or earlier pottery camel coated with greyish finely crackled glaze. Note game and pilgrim bottle hung on saddle. C. T. Loo & Co.

Fig. 245. T'ang unglazed pottery horse with faint traces of color on a cream white ware. Ht. 16½". Fuller Coll. Seattle Art Mus.
Fig. 246. T'ang horse with yellowish brown glaze and green glazed trappings. The saddle is left in biscuit. Ht. 21". Warren E. Cox Coll.
Fig. 247. T'ang horse, bactrian type, made of almost white ware covered with a rich brown glaze. This animal, though heavy, is spirited and shows certain points of possible Arabian strain. Ht. 22". Gift of Mrs. Edward S. Harkness. Metropolitan Mus. of Art.
Fig. 248. T'ang pottery horse with light straw colored glaze and green and yellow trappings and saddle. Length about 30" or a little more. Boston Mus. of Fine Arts

T'ang bullock cart. The wheels are unique in that spaces between spokes are carved open. The two figures are of identical red pottery and white slip. Length about 20″. Mrs. Charles Porter Wilson.

T'ang pottery lion chewing his leg. The glazes on these pieces are usually yellow of a brownish tone and clear grass green, though rarely blue was used. Ht. 7½″. Freer Gallery of Art, Washington.

T'ang hound not unlike a present day greyhound but with fuller tail hair. Ears not so long nor hairy as Afghan hound's. The ware is white and the thin glaze is cream and green. Ht. about 9″. Metropolitan Mus. of Art.

T'ang pottery pillow decorated with beautifully drawn design of two ducks in yellow and white against a green ground. Length about 14″. Judge Edgar Bromberger Coll. Brooklyn Mus.

T'ANG POTTERY ANIMALS

PLATE 28

ter seated than the men of Shansi province, 9.—have ears pricked up, 10.—necks elegantly curved, 11.—the manes are either upright or fall to the right side, 12.—when they have riders stirrups are always represented.

Those from Shensi province he says are: 1.—usually a bare horse, 2.—sober and mechanical, 3.—massive dimensions, 4.—not well modeled harness, 5.—strong build, 6.—broader chests, 7.—curly manes combed and parted to the sides, 8.—men riders wore a pompom on the front of their round hats, and 9.—they were poor riders. He shows one with left foot pressed forward and right foot backward and the hands too near the horse's neck and seem-

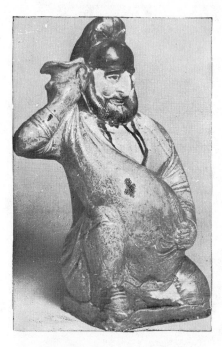

FIG. 249. T'ang figure of lady dancing. K. M. Semon Coll.

FIG. 251. T'ang figure which is not Chinese and looks semitic in type. The large head also suggests that this may have been a dwarf. Ht. 5". Warren E. Cox Coll.

FIG. 252. T'ang merchant portrayed, as was the custom, clutching his money-bag. The glazes are of green, brownish-yellow and almost black on a whitish ware. Ht. 14¾". Fuller Coll. Seattle Art Mus.

FIG. 253. Pair of T'ang pottery ladies in spotted green, yellow and straw colored glazes, the heads as usual left in biscuit. The tall slender proportions give dignity and charm. Ht. 14". Ex Warren E. Cox Coll. Courtesy of Mrs. Alvin Thalheimer.

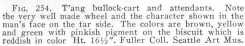

FIG. 254. T'ang bullock-cart and attendants. Note the very well made wheel and the character shown in the man's face on the far side. The colors are brown, yellow and green with pinkish pigment on the biscuit which is reddish in color Ht. 16½". Fuller Coll. Seattle Art Mus.

Fig. 250. Two T'ang unglazed figures of ladies quite similar to the pair in the Eumorfopoulos Co'l. # 181 and # 182 of pinkish white pottery decorated in gold, black, red and green pigment. Ht. 15¼". Fuller Coll. Seattle Art Mus.

ingly moving. He says, "Whoever has observed Chinese riding will have witnessed such performances; and in this case the potter must be granted all credit for his power of observation." Finally there is one type of rider which seems to be seizing the bridles with the left hand while his right is pressing against his chest.

All of these horses are made on thin rectangular bases and are potted hollow inside with an opening in the belly. The tails are usually made sepa-

Famous T'ang period horse of buff ware with glaze of straw color with blue mottlings. The saddle shows traces of original red pigment. I know of only three "blue horses." Length and ht. 11½". Ex Warren E. Cox Coll., Mr. Delos Chappell.

Fine large Honan horse of T'ang period with brown body and green and yellow as well as straw colored glazes. Ht. about 36". Nasli Heermaneck Coll.

T'ang female rider perhaps representing a polo player on large Bactrian running horse of reddish clay with white slip. Length 14". Mrs. Charles Porter Wilson.

Arabian type horse. Light buff clay with straw colored transparent finely crackled glaze. Mane of yellow brown, hooves and saddle-blanket of green glaze, saddle is unglazed and shows traces of iron red. Length 21". Warren E. Cox Coll.

T'ang horse of Arabian type with fine trappings, of light buff colored ware and showing faint traces of red and other colors as well as gold. Ht. 15½". Ex D. Abbes Coll.

T'ang horse of rather heavy body and slender legs. A brocade cover seems to have been thrown over the saddle. The horse is of buff pottery with a transparent glaze and there is some green and yellow. Ht. 22½". Fuller Coll. Seattle Art Mus.

T'ANG POTTERY HORSES

PLATE 29

rately and sometimes glazed on and sometimes just stuck in a hole left for the purpose. Slots occur in the mane ridges and it is possible that real hair may have been used for both tails and manes though none has been recorded. Some are glazed and some left in the biscuit and more or less painted. The glazed ones may have a plain straw-colored glaze or may be treated with splashes of green or amber or very rarely blue. Others have a body color of brown, straw or amber with saddles in biscuit and harness in various other of the colors mentioned.

Although T'ang painting and the sculptures in wood, stone and bronze are largely religious and also symmetrical in the early T'ang times, these pottery figures being intended for tomb use are not, although we do have animistic demons, "Earth Spirits" (which Hobson says are properly so named "T'u Kuai" when they have human faces only), and the tall symmetrical dignified

Fig. 255. Group of T'ang pottery figures of dancers of buff ware decorated with white and dark red pigment. Ht. 8". C. T. Loo & Co.

figures often holding a "kuei" (or symbol of authority representative of a sort of jade scepter) in their two hands clasped before them. These have variously been designated as legendary or mythological personages, or, on the other hand, possibly contemporary dignitaries. I am inclined to the former belief because they are always perfectly symmetrical in pose. However, the large preponderance of figures represent entertainers, musicians, lovely ladies, soldiers, boxers, etc. and a group which it is difficult to understand such as merchants, curly-haired Western Asian types which might have been slaves, and other characters which it is hard to imagine could have been thought necessary for the happiness of the deceased. The treatment of glazes or pigments on figures is much like that described for the horses and other potteries. The faces and hands are often left in biscuit, probably because the glaze tended to cover the delicate modeling, but sometimes a thin straw-colored glaze was used and at times darker colors to show the character of the skin color.

The Lokapala is an interesting form. It represents a guardian of one of the quarters of the Buddhistic Heaven. This figure originated in the Civaitic worship of India and spread to Tibet, Turkestan, China and Japan. Dr. Berthold Laufer (*Chinese Clay Figures*, Part I, Field Museum, Chicago) says

Figure of a harpist in buff white terracotta glazed brown, blue and yellow except for face and hair which are painted. Ht. 12⅝". The Cleveland Mus. of Art.

Early T'ang gray pottery figure decorated with slip colors of white on the skirt, mustard and red on the coat and pink face and hands with touches of green on the shoes. Ht. about 18". Metropolitan Mus. of Art.

Early T'ang or Six Dynasty figure of red terracotta covered with a white slip. Ht. 22¼". Nasli Heermaneck Coll.

A Mongolian gentleman shown with fur hat and a small parrot. It is of buff white body with blended green and amber glazes on coat and boots. Ht. 16¾". Warren E. Cox—Lem Sec Tsang Coll.

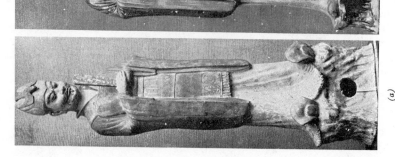

(a)

(b)

(a) Unglazed pottery T'ang period tomb attendant with polychrome decoration. Ht. 48½". Fuller Coll. Seattle Art Mus.
(b) T'ang figure, possibly a tomb guardian, but certainly a man of importance. Glazed in green, yellow and with the face left in bisque. Ht. 41". Fuller Coll. Seattle Art Mus.

T'ANG POTTERY HUMAN FIGURES

PLATE 30
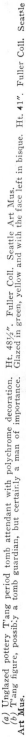

Two figures from Shen-si and Ho-nan
having horns still but human faces of
a bull-like type, the first having a hole
in the right hand probably for holding
a weapon. They also have armor and
a plumed head-dress. One is standing
on a demon. These were developed
from *Yama* as triumphant warriors.
Hts. 18″ and 12″. Field Mus., Chicago.

Left: This figure, according to Berthold Laufer is *"Yama,"* God of Death, standing on a body of a
sow. His head is that of a bull and he has three-clawed hands and feet. The head is surrounded by
flames. From Shen-si province, T'ang period. Traces of red pigment, the eyeballs being black. Ht.
23½″. Field Mus., Chicago.
   Center: Further development from animistic to human forms of guardians. This figure, from Shensi
Province, shows Yama standing on a bull. Ht. 25″. Field Mus., Chicago.

| (a) | (b) | (c) | (d) |

   (a) Glazed T'ang figure from Honan with flame from the head similar to above and a winged animal
body but distinctly human face. Buckingham Coll. The Art Institute of Chicago.
   (b) The human warrior in full armor standing on a demon represents the Triumphant God of Death.
It is all glazed in green, blue and brown save the head. Ht. 21″. Shen-si. Field Mus., Chicago.
   (c) Shen-si figure of the God of Death standing on a reclining bull, unglazed clay. T'ang period. Ht.
26½″. Field Mus., Chicago. Note that the figure has now become passive except for the facial expression.
   (d) Honan tomb guardian lacking all trace of the demon expression. Note dragon repoussé metal
shoulder plates and helmet and skirt of leather with padding in the helmet and a knitted sweater
under the armor. Ht. 23½″. Warren E. Cox Coll.

T'ANG POTTERY FIGURES OF LOKAPALA
ZOOMORPHIC TO ANTHROPOMORPHIC

PLATE 31

Fig. 256. Ovoidal pot on three legs of light buff clay with yellow and buff glazes on blue glazed ground. This blue color, rarely found, was evidently developed during this period. Ht. 4¾″. Ex D. Abbes Coll.

Fig. 257. The rare blue glaze covers this sturdy formed jar which is probably after a bronze form. Ht. about 6″. Freer Gallery of Art, Wash.

the variations may be classed under Dharmapāla (protectors of the dead) or as Yama (the God of Death). He proves his case clearly that they originated as zoomorphic and developed into anthropomorphic types. It is not necessary here to go into the full series and I have, therefore, picked a few representative high spots. A study of the sequence of illustrations will show the development.

Vase forms are largely much simplified. The globular jar seems to have

Fig. 258. Typical T'ang jar of warm white clay and decorated with a design of green, yellow and transparent colorless glaze finely crackled. Ht. 7″. The Buckingham Coll., The Art Institute of Chicago.

Fig. 259. T'ang period jar of pinkish-buff ware with iridescent green glaze. The decoration is of appliqués with slight incising on shoulder. Ht. 4¼″. Warren E. Cox Coll.

One of pair of unique deep green vases on mustard yellow bases. The green glaze has brilliant silver iridescence in large areas. Ht. 10½". Ex Warren E. Cox Coll. Courtesy of Mrs. Alvin Thalheimer.

7th cent. "Kalása" or "vase for holding amrta (ambrosia); symbol of Maitreya, Man-la, Padmapani, Amitayus, Kubera, Usnisavijaya, Vasudhara and Cunda." (The Iconography of Tibetan Lamaism by A. K. Gordon.) Ht. 16". Base is restoration. Warren E. Cox Coll.

Amphora showing Hellenistic influence in general form and in shoulder ornamentation. White pottery with light grayish-green crackled glaze covering the upper two thirds. The handles have been changed to dragon forms by the Chinese. Ht. 18". Warren E. Cox Coll.

T'ang vase of usual white body and cream glaze finely crackled but also showing suggestions of "tear drops" similar to those found on Ting yao. Ht. 6". Ex D. Abbes Coll.

Vase of light buff white pottery with thin finely crackled cream glaze down to near foot. Ht. 10".

T'ang period vase of white ware covered with a rather rough white glaze and having yellow green in the foliated mouth. The crude striping about the foot is done with dark brown. This shape was developed and simplified into better proportions in the Sung period. Ht. about 11". Metropolitan Mus. of Art.

A beautiful T'ang period small bottle of simple and growing form more classic than almost anything the Greeks ever did. The glazes which run down over it are yellow, brown and green. Ht. 7¾". Fuller Coll. Seattle Art Mus

Ewer and stand of light buff pottery and green glaze almost entirely covered with silver iridescence. The tall, tapering neck and the gracefulness of the body make it one of the most beautiful specimens known. Applied relief ornaments show this technique to perfection. Ht. 37½". Freer Gallery, Washington, D. C.

Jar of the same period and ware but having a glaze with a slight greenish tinge. Ht. 5¾". Ex D. Abbes Coll.

T'ANG POTTERY VASE FORMS

Plate 32

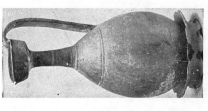

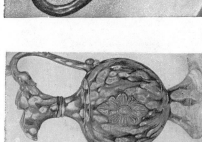

T'ang pieces of "marbled ware" with light and dark clays and glazed with transparent brown. Distinct East Indian influence. Bottle ht. 7". Ex Warren E. Cox Coll.

Incense burner of brown and light buff clays covered with straw colored transparent glaze splashed with green. Supported by lions rampant with hind legs braced against rim of stand. Dia. 6". Warren E. Cox Coll.

T'ang "marbled vase," form from Han bronze. Unglazed. Ht. 8¼" Warren E. Cox Coll.

Late T'ang or Sung grey marbleized porcelaneous stoneware with transparent glaze. Dia. 6½". Fuller Coll. Seattle Art Mus.

Left to Right: Ewer with characteristics of Greek oenochoë and certain Near Eastern metal forms, of pinkish buff clay with amber and green glaze. Ht. 10½". Eumorfopoulos Coll. # 330.—Ewer after Near Eastern form with relief designs of a bowman on one side and a fenghuang (sacred bird) on the other. The glazes are straw, amber, green and blue. Ht. 11½". Warren E. Cox Coll.—Pottery ewer with saucer of yellowish buff body with partly iridescent green glaze. After bronze form characteristics of which originated in Near East.—T'ang vessel used for drinking water as Ananda Coomaraswamy has pointed out. Filled from side and spout squirted water into mouth just as a Frenchman uses a wine-skin. Hts. 7" and 8¼". Cleveland Mus. of Art.—John Platt-Warren E. Cox Coll.—T'ang or perhaps a little later "Marbled" or "Wood Grain" vase made by mixing dark gray and buff clays and glazing over with a transparent brown glaze. Though shape suggests T'ang origin, fragments were found by Sir Aurel Stein in Sung and Yüan sites. Buckingham Coll., Art Institute of Chicago.

T'ANG EWERS AND MARBLED WARE

been most frequently used and collections show a great number or these all with different glaze patterns consisting of spots, streaks, cross hatching and chevrons. They are frequently found with covers to match and probably all had them, though usually no rim was provided, the cover being held in place simply by a rim, usually unglazed, on the bottom of it. At times this form was fitted with three claw feet, making it a "ting." Infrequently the form might have loops on the shoulder and even a spout in short cylindrical form and also a few are found with small round and leaf-shaped low relief appliqués. Some of the thinnest and best potted jars of this shape were treated simply with near-white glaze and these are usually somewhat larger, being nearly a foot in height rather than 8″ or 9″. In fact it is noticeable that many of the finest vase forms and ewer forms were treated with plain light cream glaze depending upon the beauty of form alone. Other simple forms, but perhaps more bronze-like, such as the ewers with tall and sometimes ribbed necks, that stood upon pot-stands, are covered with green glaze and are unornamented except for occasional appliques.

The old marble-cake or imitation stone technique was introduced and evidently used quite extensively. Probably the earlier ones, and possibly these are even of the Six Dynasties period, were unglazed and of sturdy form recalling Han bronze forms, although ewers and bowls were also done in this heavy ware. An interesting gourd bottle also of very heavy and thick ware is treated simply with glazes rather than the clays. But as the period develops these marbled wares became thin and beautifully potted while the Chinese, not contented with making haphazard patterns, devised means of doing circles, rings and such, of the mottled clays, set off by plain areas. A beautiful example of this is shown in the small bottle having strong Indian influence which we illustrate from the Metropolitan Museum of Art.

Ewers after Near Eastern metal forms and occasional vases such as the unique rectangular pair shown (Pl. 32), were often cast complete in molds but they lost no strength thereby and in fact often represent the strongest shapes in T'ang pottery.

Finally we see the beginning of real decorative technique as it appears on plates, small wrist rests for writers, occasional boxes, etc. The artist in most instances resorts to incising the outline and then freely applying his glazes within these bounds, but he also uses what might be called his blending technique as may be seen around the edges of the six-lobed dish shown and in the dappling and rim painting of the beautiful spotted dish from the Eumorfopoulos Collection.

FIG. 260. T'ang plate on three small spiral legs. Front iridescent straw color with green rim, design in green, deep blue and dark amber. Back in mottled, iridescent, amber tones. Dia. 8⅝″. Warren E. Cox Coll.

Although the Chinese poets wrote appreciatively of some wares, there is little real data concerning famous kiln sites and it is generally true that American and European collectors know as much about the wares as the

Chinese themselves. In the *Book of Tea,* which describes the fact that this beverage had become popular, two wares of outstanding merit are mentioned —*Yüeh Chou Yao* and *Hsing Chou Yao.* (The first two words refer to the location and the last means simply ware.) Yüeh Chou was near Hangchow

FIG. 261. T'ang pottery pillow with incised decoration and glazes of green and yellow on straw color. Length 14″. Warren E. Cox Coll.

FIG. 262. Small T'ang pottery object called a pillow by museum but actually a wrist rest for painter or writer. Length 4″. Boston Mus. of Fine Arts.

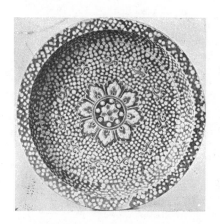

FIG. 263. Dish with rounded sides and flat rim, flat base and three elephant-tusk supports of soft white ware with straw colored glaze and design in brown and green. Dia. 15″. Eumorfopoulos Coll. # 403.

FIG. 264. Shallow T'ang bowl with flat bottom and rounded sides decorated with incised and painted design in green and amber on cream. Finely crackled glaze. Dia. 9¼″. K. M. Semon Coll.

in Chekiang province and Hsing Chou was in the southern part of the same province. It is said that Yüeh Yao was valued because it made the tea look green; and Hsing Yao, because it made the tea look red, being itself white. Yüeh Yao is described as being the blue of distant hills or "Ts'ui," the color of kingfisher wings or that of certain jades. The Hsing Yao was supposed to be white as snow. Both were also used for "musical cups" by Ku Tao-yüan. Other wares were said to have been made in *Ting Chou* in

An exceedingly beautifully proportioned Yüeh yao vase with cover having the usual d nse but sandy gray body burnt reddish brown where exposed and covered with a transparent olive green crackled glaze. This piece shows a distinctly classic tradition. Ht. 14¾". Warren E. Cox Coll.

Yüeh wine jar beautifully made of grey body with the usual transparent, olive-green, crackled glaze. Note below that the potter signed the piece with his thumb-print on the bottom. Such pieces always are glazed underneath while the Lung-ch'üan ones are not. Ht. 16". Warren E. Cox Coll.

Yüeh vase of pale greenish grey color and fine form from Shang-lin-hu site. Cover missing. Ht. 11⅞". K. M. Semon Coll.

Yüeh yao Sung period bowl beautifully carved in a low relief design of dragons among waves. The ware is a dense gray stoneware and the glaze the typical olive gray green of pale tone. Dia. about 9". Metropolitan Mus. of Art.

Wine jar of Yüeh ware with grey body and pale grayish-green glaze. Ht. 16". Ex Warren E. Cox Coll. Now Metropolitan Mus. of Art.

YÜEH WARES FROM THE SHANG-LIN-HU SITES

PLATE 34

FIG. 265. Yüeh yao vase with deep inverted lotus petal cover modeled in relief, and hexagonal knob. The lightly incised large flowers are bifurcated in each case by one of the five ridges from the "spouts" which are not round as is usually the case but seven sided. The glaze is light grayish green. Ht. about 10″. From the K. M. Semon Coll.

FIG. 266. The small jar is rarer than the typical taller funerary jars and the potting is thinner. It is of dense gray clay burnt reddish brown where exposed and the glaze is the same as that on the others. Ht. 8″. Warren E. Cox Coll.

FIG. 267. Yüeh yao vase of fine style with interesting applied ornaments of flying birds on the shoulder. Later these jars were made with spouts and then the style developed into the placing of dragons, animals, etc., about the shoulder, chiefly at Lungch'üan and the Southern Kuan yao site. Nasli Heeramaneck Coll.

Shensie province, *Wu Chou* in Chekiang, *Yo Chou* in Hunan, *Shou Chou* in Anhwei and *Hung Chou* in Kiangsi. The poet Tu Fu also mentions *Ta-yi* in Szechwan which was also white as snow and would ring like jade when

FIG. 268. Yüeh yao tea or wine pot of the incised type, specimens of which were found also at Samarra, Persia and Fostat, Egypt. Others have relief decoration as well as the incised. Ht. 5″. The Metropolitan Mus. of Art.

FIG. 269. Yüeh yao bowl-stand showing interesting incised petal decoration. Nasli Heeramaneck Coll.

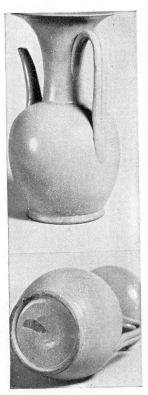

Yüeh dish with incised decoration, light olive green glaze and an incised mark under the glaze under the foot meaning "Bamboo," which might have been the mark of some potter or of some certain kiln. Note typical smooth and well turned foot-rim with marks from the supports. Dia. 6″. Mr. K. M. Semon.

A beautiful ewer from the "nine rocks kiln site" of Yüeh yao with the usual grey body and dull, mat, grey-green glaze. Note the way the handle foll ws the lines of the neck and body and how nicely it would fit the hand for pouring. Ht. about 7½″. T'ang period. Yamanaka & Co.

Yüeh wine-jar of grey stoneware, burnt orange where exposed and covered inside and out with a pale yellow-green glaze. This piece, though it leaned in firing, shows rare curved spouts about the shoulder and a beautifully designed cover the knob of which was actually set in a hole to make it secure. Ht. 14″. Warren E. Cox Coll.

DETAILS OF YÜEH WARES FROM THE SHANG-LIN-HU SITES

PLATE 35

struck. The wares from Yo Chou were "Ch'ing" (green?) (or "natural color") and yellow, and those from Hung Chou brownish "like coarse cloth" or "Ho" or yellowish black making the tea appear black. This latter ware was made not far from Ching-tê Chên, later famed as the greatest pottery center in the world, and it is probable that it was from here that some of the wares found at Samarra were sent. Yo Chou has now been identified.

The allocating of most of these wares is pure speculation and personal opinion to date, but the Chinese descriptions should be taken quite seriously, contrary to the opinion sometimes expressed by the late R. L. Hobson, for when we do find a kiln site, we are often made to feel foolish because the descriptions have fitted so perfectly. Thus much has recently been learned about Yüeh Yao and we find that it has been more or less under our noses for some time, all unrecognized. Probably Mr. Yuzo Matsumura was the first to recognize the mounds of kiln wasters and he published an article in *Oriental Ceramics,* a Japanese periodical in 1936. Hobson and Sir Percival David had identified two fine bowls in the latter's collection through sherds sent them by Dr. Nakao. In 1937 Mr. J. M. Plumer visited three kiln sites at Shang-lin-hu and described them in detail and Mr A. D. Brankston followed him in the same year. They found the natives still using the precious wares as building materials and the clay for making bricks. Previously Dr. Manzo Nakao had visited the neighboring site of Yü Yao Hsien to the east and nearer the seacoast and had found the very similar ware which Sir Percival says, in an article in the January, 1929, issue of *Eastern Art,* was believed by the editor of the *T'ao lu* to be the actual ware described by the ancients as Pi-sê Yao, or "secret color ware." Thus we have now sorted out the Shang-lin-hu kilns, the Chiu-yen kilns and the Yü Yao kilns all of which made Yüeh Yao.

Sir Percival quotes the collated literary allusions brought together by the author of the T'ao Shuo as translated by Dr. Bushell after warning, "Translation at its best can only be like the reverse side of a brocade—the threads are there, but the subtility of color and design is lost." Here, then, is the list:

1.—Lu Kuei-mêng, a T'ang poet, uses these terms:
"The misty scenery of late autumn appears when Yüeh kilns are thrown open;
"The thousand peaks have been despoiled of their color for the decoration of the bowls."

2.—Ku K'uang, also contemporary, says:
"The cups of Yüeh-chou paste like jade."

3.—Mêng Chung refers to them:
"Yüeh-chou cups like molded lotus leaves."

4.—Hsü Yin in a verse composed to accompany some teacups made for presentation to the Emperor says:
"Like bright moons, cunningly carved and dyed with spring water;
"Like curling disks of thinnest ice, filled with green clouds;
"Like ancient moss-eaten bronze mirrors, lying upon the mat;
"Like tender lotus leaves, full of dewdrops, floating on the riverside!"

And it would be difficult to better describe these beautiful wares! Here is what Mr. Plumer says he found: "Specimens of the ware are all but totally lacking in museums or private collections, though unidentified pieces doubtless exist. A hard, light grey porcelaneous stoneware was found at them all" (He refers to the three Shang-lin-hu kiln sites.) "with a thin, transparent glaze, the color effect covering a rather limited range of greens, yet including numerous gradations. The idea came to me that we might almost call it 'subtile color' rather than 'secret color' ware. Greyish-greens and olive greens predominated; a light bluish green was sometimes in evidence, and occasionally a brownish-yellow, lacking any greenish tinge. Discoloration in the form of small accidental Chün-like blue and purple splotches was sometimes found."

He goes on to say that there were bowls, saucers, vases, pots for tea and wine, tiny cosmetic boxes, flower-pot stands, etc. including a type of "mortuary jar" usually having spouts about the shoulder. The technique was that of incising, also low relief modeling and low relief appliques molded and applied, with infrequent use of the comb and also of reticulation. Some were crude and some recalled Mêng Chung's words, "like tender lotus leaves." And one was incised under the foot before firing, with a date corresponding to our A.D. 978.

Brankston says others have been found with the date A.D. 987 but he did not produce them. He also warns against clever imitations so dated.

As we look at these wares could the Chinese descriptions have been better? And yet *after* we learned about them I found I had about a dozen in my collection which had never been thought of except as "Northern Sung Celadon," and I must confess that I have made lamps out of a few just as fine as the one I sold the Metropolitan Museum in 1937. Thus the collector often says to himself, "If I had only known! If I had only had the eyes with which to see!"

In the 11th century these Yüeh kilns met the strong competition from the Lung-ch'üan kilns in the southern part of the province and near the capital Ch'u Chou which also later became a great ceramic center. Many of the Yüeh shapes were made with modifications at Lung-ch'üan but the wares there had a beautiful glaze quality (the finest "celadon" wares, so called) and it was probably this, rather than finer potting which made them more popular. (Actually Lung-ch'üan potting is always more crude.)

It is agreed that the Shang-lin-hu kilns did not operate any earlier than the 7th century although those of Chiu-yen were probably, to quote Brankston, "nearer to Han than T'ang in date."

Another ware which we find usually in the form of very high wine jars with a row of 12 figures about the shoulder and a dragon coiled around the tall slender neck on which are also appliqués of birds, stags, cloud scrolls, etc., sometimes with the "pearl of purity," a disc standing off perpendicular to the surface, is similar to Yüeh yao but cruder and rougher in potting and thicker. This ware gives every indication of being pre-Sung but, so far as I know, the kiln site has not been found. Just as was the case with the Yüeh yao many pieces have come on the market and the value has been proportionately low, but some day we shall find the source of this ware and

FIG. 270. Wine jar from Fu Liang just north of Ching-tê Chên. They occur with celadon, ying-ch'ing and brown glazes. Ht. about 15". Ex Warren E. Cox Coll.

FIG. 272. T'ang wine jar (cover missing) of grey ware with thin grey-green glaze and of the usual form with twelve immortals about the shoulder, a dragon, fêng huang or sacred bird, etc., including a "pearl of purity" standing off the neck. Ht. 30". Warren E. Cox Coll.

FIG. 271. Two T'ang ewers of white ware, the one glazed with mat brown and the other with cream, crackled glaze. Hts. 7" and 7½". The dark one C. T. Loo Coll. The light one Warren E. Cox Coll.

it will then become important to the museums. The range of color and the texture of the glazes are so close to those of Yüeh yao that it is likely that the kilns are somewhere near that great center in northern Chekiang.

Perhaps from Hung Chou may come the first of the brown glazed wares although many of these were made in Honan and elsewhere by Sung times. In any event the transition seems to be from the thin olive-green glazes to thin, and therefore mat, greenish brown and finally, in T'ang times, to an even mat brown or "tea dust" type glaze. The ewer shown, similar to that in the Eumorfopoulos Collection #430, has all the characteristics of T'ang ware; a white body, flat beveled foot, the cylindrical spout, etc. It is interesting to note in passing that the white glazed ewer is very similar in shape and technique and is undoubtedly of the same period. Another brown glazed example with typical T'ang neck and lip-rim, with the double loops inherited from Han times and with the same flat beveled foot has also splashes of the Chün-like blue mentioned in connection with the Yüeh ware by Plumer. These are evenly spaced about the shoulder and, therefore, certainly intentional. The effect is not unlike that produced in the "Kian Temmokus" of the Sung period and this seems to be one of the earliest of the "transmutation glazes." Mr. Walter Hochstadter says these were made in Yu Chou and are the first Chün type.

There is a quantity of white wares which, far from being able to allocate in certain kiln sites, we are not sure as to whether they are late T'ang or early Sung. A good example is the globular ewer mentioned above which we are fairly certain is of the T'ang period because of the flat foot. However, some of the wares found at Samarra did have foot-rims and, therefore, we must assume that during T'ang times they were at least occasionally used in some places. Often the glaze of these wares is not pure white but has a very slight yellowish tinge, and this glaze at times shows only a slight tendency to crackle where it runs thicker.

Ewer of almost white stoneware with olive green glaze of "tea dust" texture. Six dynasties. Ht. 9½". John Platt–Warren E. Cox Coll.

Early Lung-ch'üan vase perhaps even of T'ang period. The base is nearly flat and the ware is grey. Ht. 8". Warren E. Cox Coll.

T'ang jar of white stoneware with "tea-dust" brown glaze with large patches on the shoulder symmetrically arranged of pale blue. The foot is flat and the double loops are a T'ang or earlier characteristic. Ht. 9¼". Warren E. Cox Coll. Note: Many of these wares are found about northern Honan and may have been made at Yu chou, being a sort of prototype of the Chün wares.

CHAPTER IX

THE FIVE DYNASTIES

A.D. 906–960

AFTER THE T'ang period China split into various warring states certain of which gained ascendency for short periods of time. The periods are generally called 1.—Later Liang, 2.—Later T'ang, 3.—Later Tsin, 4.—Later Han and 5.—Later Chou, but these do not particularly interest us as the potteries were simply transitional between T'ang and Sung.

As short a time ago as 1926 Mr. Hobson in writing the Eumorfopoulos Catalogue said that the period was only mentioned in Chinese annals for two kinds of ware both of which were "somewhat mysterious," and yet one of the wares was Yüeh which seems perfectly reasonable to us of today and which I have just described in some detail.

The other ware was "Ch'ai yao" and Ch'ai was the family name of the Emperor Shih Tsung of the posterior Chou, or last period, who ruled at K'ai-fêng Fu between 954 and 959, in northeastern Honan just about where the Yellow River divides into its north and south outlets. It is said that the potters of Chêng chou about 60 miles south of the capital were able to make this ware colored "blue as the sky after rain." Hobson jumps to the conclusion that they made it "only four or five years," which I think is foolish first of all because potters cannot perfect an imperial ware in so short a time and secondly because there is no indication that they stopped. Just as several of the Yüeh kilns made wares for many years and were taken under imperial patronage for a comparatively short time, so could it have been with the kilns of Chêng chou.

The *Ko ku yao lun*, a book I shall speak of in the first part of the next chapter, says Ch'ai yao was rich, refined, unctuous and with crackled lines. It also states that in many cases there was yellow clay on the foot of the ware. The more poetical Master Kao in his book the *Tsun shêng pa chien* and also the author Ku Ying-t'ai of the *Po wu yao lan* state that the ware was as blue as the sky, brilliant as a mirror, thin as paper and resonant as a musical stone.

Hobson suggests, and we quite agree with him, that among the wares which have been given the broad name of *ying ch'ing* there are some that answer all of these characteristics. The bodies of these are white but burn a yellowish buff where exposed. They are thin, translucent, ring when struck and of the pale sky-blue. Some are of a remarkable delicacy of potting particularly when the age in which they were made is taken into consideration. The Chinese have always lauded their finer wares highly and this quite justly. On the other hand modern collectors who now praise the delicacy and charm of a fine Yüeh yao vase could not see anything in it five or ten years ago. I think that the kilns made much more than we suppose and that right before our eyes there are probably Ch'ai wares to be seen.

"Earth worm marks" in a Chün yao glaze at just about normal size.

Typical "crab's claw" crackle as it appears on a Lung-ch'üan "kinuta" of finest quality. Full scale.

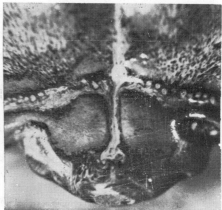

Crackle and flow of glaze on what Hobson calls "Kuan type Chün yao." The crackle is like the "ice crackle" of Southern Kuan but the ware is far heavier.

Foot of a Chün yao bowl showing how glaze runs in mixed blues and purples. About full size.

LUNG-CH'ÜAN AND CHÜN GLAZES

CHAPTER X

THE SUNG DYNASTY

A.D. 960–1280

THE STATEMENT that during the Sung period, "The reins of government were more securely held over a unified, though diminished China," is false for during this time there was internal conflict, intrigue and constant threats from the North which finally ended in conquest and flight. General Chao Kuang-yin (called T'ai-tsu) attacked the Khitan Tartars to the Northeast and they reacted by taking some territory while to the Northwest the kingdom of Hsia fought both sides. In the reign of Hwei-tsung (1101–1126) the terrible mistake was made of persuading the Chin or Nuchih Tartars to help against the Khitan Tartars which they did and then promptly took over all the territory north of the Yangtze River forcing the Sung rulers to move their capital to Nanking and then in 1127 to Hang Chou. Close on the heels of the Chins came the Mongols under the great Jenghiz Khan in 1214 and his son Ogodai was left heir to the whole northern section at his death in 1227. Another alliance was made between the Mongols and the Chinese to fight the Chins and the promise was made that Honan would remain to the Chinese but a quarrel led to the Mongolian conquest south until the last Sung emperor cast himself into the sea in despair and Kublai Khan became emperor of all China and much more in 1280.

Strangely the art of Sung China is not martial but rather poetic and transcendental, not lacking in strength but with the strength of the willow which bends before the storm that breaks the oak; having the strength of the foil rather than that of the broad-sword. It was so close to nature that it did not seem so much to copy nature as to be a very part of it. This art was not so much due to any one group or to patronage as it was lived by almost everyone. I think that critics often try to explain a great flowering of art by some glibly caught phase of history which the artists of the day, perhaps living more apart than might be supposed, had never heard of. A tree shows no interest if one of its branches is broken off; it goes right on growing and eventually the open space fills in. So it is that war simply does not affect some people.

Another very vital fact must be understood before one can understand Sung art and that is that the Far Easterner can be a tough fighter and at the same time a sensitive soul. The good fencer holds his foil cupped in his hand gently as though he were holding a bird, not to let it get away but not to crush it. An old Chinese saying goes, "He who knows the cherry blossom bough can best handle the sword." We men of America suffer more than any others from a masculine-complex; we feel that a real man should enjoy base-ball, whisky and poker rather than fencing, wine and art. A real man is not supposed to take his women too seriously at least in talk with h:s companions. Before World War I it was considered sissy to wear a wrist watch or carry a cane until expedience and necessity dictated the use of both. This manly swagger seems childish to the Chinese for the Chinese man knows his own qualities of courage and in his country life is held cheaply. Thus it was possible for many artists in the troublous Sung times to think philosophically and spend time searching for little beauties of nature without any idea of having to prove themselves worthy or masculine.

One thing the wars did was to shut off to some degree the foreign influences which had poured into China ever since Han times. A chance was provided to search the inner soul and to develop what was undoubtedly the most clear strain of purely *Chinese* art that the country ever knew either before or after. We materialists can perhaps grasp the greatness of the times through the reports of Marco Polo who visited the country in 1280 in which he tells of the city of Hang Chou with its many canals bridged, it is said, by 12,000 stone bridges, its hundreds, literally, of hot water baths, its many markets, the great lake covered with pleasure boats and the fine streets thronged with busy people. He tells of the good lives of the merchants and of the craftsmen, and speaks of the fact that no person carried arms, a wondrous thing to an Italian of that day. Little did the roll of distant thunder disturb them and they made life merry and productive, and among their products was pottery valued quite as highly as jade or bronze. The wares as we know them were no longer always laid away in tombs. Wooden, paper and clay figures long ago fallen to dust in many places were used for this purpose, much that we have is the precious inheritance of ancient families and the wasters cast aside at the kilns. Thus when one looks at a Sung vase one often sees the purest Chinese taste, expressed by an inspired artist of a great age and cherished and held dear for well-nigh a thousand years by generation after generation of sensibly sensitive people. But even the wasters from these great kilns, often as perfect as the day they were potted, carry to us the inspiration of the artists as studio sketches sometimes show a freshness not always preserved in a finished painting.

The Chinese themselves have always loved the wares of Sung and we can turn to their books for much of our information. Of these the best known are:—

1.—The *Cho Keng Lu* (1368) a miscellany on art.
2.—The *Ko Ku Yao Lun* (1387) (2nd edition 1459)
3.—The *Album of Hsiang Yüan-p'ien* (1561)
4.—The *Tsung Shêng Pa Chien* (1591)
5.—The *Ch'ing Pi Ts'ang* (1595)
6.—The *Po Wu Yao Lan* (1621–1627)
7.—The *T'ao Shuo* (1774) which incorporates the information given in the former works and others.
8.—The *Ching-tê Chên T'ao Lu* (1815) which also covers much of the same ground, and which has to do with the famous potteries at Ching-tê

Chêng in the Ch'ang-nan district east of Po Yang Lake in Kiangsi province, given its name by Ching Tê (1004–1007) and which in the 18th century was commanded by the Emperor Yung Chêng to make reproductions of Sung wares for which purpose specimens were sent down from the Imperial Palace Collection.

We read of the wares of Ju (pronounced Ru), Kuan, Ko, Lung-ch'üan, Chün, Chien, Ting and Tz'ŭ Chou but these were only a few of the best known factory products and many others copied the famous wares and also made wares of their own. It should also be stressed that none of these kilns started at the beginning of the Sung period and stopped at the end of the period. Also the beautiful wares of Lung-ch'üan were carried on with slight differences at the capital of Chekiang province, Chü-chou, and these together with the Ting and Tz'ŭ Chou were sent to the ends of the earth and copied by potters in Japan, the Near East and Europe.

In general the bodies are now high-fired and porcelaneous though the change was not an abrupt one. This body clay usually contained iron so that it was white, grey or buff where protected but often burnt reddish-brown where exposed due to iron oxide. It was usually well refined and smooth to the touch though some of the buff bodies are rough and some of the more vitreous ones gritty as in certain Ying Ching wares which are also translucent.

The glazes are frequently of one color or combinations of two colors ranging from palest blue or green to deep blue or to brown and even black. There is no doubt but that the Sung Chinese collectors preferred the restraint and simplicity of single colors rather than dramatic decorations of color as we find in Chün wares for instance and later in Ming wares. T'ang glazes were soft lead types, thinly applied and minutely crackled much like those of the later Ming period but Sung glazes are hard, feldspathic types which are either not crackled at all or are definitely and boldly so, at first by accident but soon by direct intent as in Ko ware. A few of the terms used by Chinese critics are "tzŭ jun" (rich and unctuous), "hsi ni" (fine and glossy), and "jung" (lustrous). So beautiful are these glazes that, though the whole world has tried, and the Chinese of later days tried, they have never been truly copied. Mr. W. Burton has explained this as follows: "The Chinese method of firing naturally produced glazes in which the oxide of iron and copper were present in the lowest state of oxidization; and this is the explanation of the seeming paradox that the green glazes, known to us as celadon, and the copper-red glazes, were amongst the earliest productions of the Chinese porcelain makers, while in Europe they have been among the latest secrets to be acquired." Thus it is perhaps so that this was another natural development rather than abrupt invention but this takes nothing away from the glory of these artists who made so much of what they had in hand. The same general principles of potting were probably used in all the kilns and the same glaze due to differences in local clays and other materials might turn out green, grey, lavender or turquoise blended with red.

One of the difficulties in reading the Chinese descriptions is their seeming lack of a definite meaning for the terms used for the colors. Thus the word "ch'ing" which annoyed Hobson to the point of distraction might refer to a blue, a sea-green of celadon, a pale bluish shade of clair de lune, grey, brown and even black. The Chinese dictionaries define it as the "color of nature," and this seems to me a perfectly understandable qualification. Our own Western terminology is vague and most misleading and few of us designate a color by its three elements. We speak of a leaf green which may include hundreds of different hues and various values of each and various qualifications of each. The Chinese mean by ch'ing a color of nature rather than an artificial appearing color such perhaps as the horrible green seen on cheap Japanese toys. Perhaps they are not so interested in the actual hue as in its quality just as they think of the *consistency* of shark-fins or of bird's nest soup as much as of the taste. We Westerners pay less attention to consistency unless the steak is too tough to chew. But there are certain colors which we see more often in the world about us and which are pleasant therefore, like the colors of vegetable dyes so qualified as to be soft and pleasing. Later chemistry produced colors which, like the sound of the klaxon horn, had never been on this earth before and which are most unpleasantly shrill and hurtful and which have to be qualified to be tolerated. These colors are not ch'ing.

There are great varieties in the weights of Sung wares from paper thin to well-nigh an inch in thickness, but they are all of a heavy feeling for the thickness used and the glazes always adhere perfectly though at times they were not applied evenly over the whole surface and there may be small areas where they round down to the body when melted in the kiln.

Ju Yao & Ying Ch'ing

Our knowledge of Ju yao is scanty. We do know that Hsü Ching visited Korea in 1125 and wrote that Korean pottery was "like the modern Ju and the ancient Yüeh wares." Other contemporary writers wrote that it was of ch'ing color. Furthermore it was written that the potters at Ju Chou south of the Yellow River in central Honan province were ordered to supply their ch'ing ware to the Imperial Court in place of the wares of Ting Chou because flaws occurred in the Ting yao. Whether the potters were actually moved to the court in K'ai-fêng Fu is debatable. The *Cho kêng lu* quotes a 13th century writer, Yeh Chih, as saying that the Ju potters were chosen because they were better than those at T'ang and Teng (in southern Honan) and Yao (in Shensi) where the wares were similar. So much is fairly strong evidence.

As second rate evidence we have the *Ko ku yao lun* stating that the glaze was "tan ch'ing" or pale ch'ing. Kao Lien says in the *Tsung shêng pa chien,* "Ju ware I have actually seen. In color it is egg white 'luan po' the glaze is transparent and thick like massed lard." This "luan po" could refer to ducks' eggs which are usual in China and are pale bluish or greenish. Hsiang Yüan-p'ien illustrates three pieces, two of which are described as of "yü lan" (sky blue) and one as of "fên ch'ing" (pale ch'ing) and the glaze is crackled. Finally the 19th century imitations were made of the "blue like the sky after rain" which was also the description of Ch'ai yao which it was

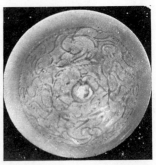

FIG. 273. Ying Ch'ing Sung dish of white porcelain with clear pale blue transparent glaze of considerable brilliancy. Dia. 5¾". Charles Porter Wilson. Warren E. Cox Coll.

FIG. 274. Ying Ch'ing bowl of white porcelain covered with a clear pale blue transparent glaze slightly crackled. The dynamic whirling design has been scratched into the body with a sharp instrument with flattened tip. Sung. Dia. 6½". Ex Warren E. Cox Coll. Now K. M. Semon Coll.

FIG. 275. Incised Ying Ch'ing type bowl showing "happy boys" among flowers, a favorite design for a certain type of fairly heavy ware with glossy glaze. Dia. about 7½". K. M. Semon Coll.

said was made in Chêng Chou in the same district. None of the early writers gives any description of the body.

One of the world's greatest collectors and students, the late Mr. George Eumorfopoulos has advanced the theory on this evidence that Ju yao may be searched for among the wares which we now arbitrarily label Ying Ch'ing. His points are all well taken and particularly it does seem impossible that

FIG. 276. Ying Ch'ing bowl of rather heavy porcelaneous ware and having a somewhat gritty foot burnt light brown. The design of a swimming duck is swiftly incised as is also the outside petal motif. The glaze is clear light blue. Dia. 6½". Surg Period. Warren E. Cox Coll.

FIG. 277. Ying Ch'ing type incense burner with three legs, two handles on shoulders and two added loose ring handles. The ware is white and porcelaneous and the glaze a very bright pale blue. It is perhaps of late Sung period. Ht. 6". Metropolitan Mus. of Art.

FIG. 278. One of pair of Ying Ch'ing type incense burners of white and porcelaneous ware with very brilliant pale blue glassy glaze. The period is late Sung. Ht. 9". Metropolitan Mus. of Art.

any such group of wares showing such beauty and subtility could have gone unnoticed by the ancient Chinese writers. Thus they must have been described under Ch'ai, Ju, Kuan or Ko wares and we are fairly certain that they were neither of the last two. Moreover the testimony concerning Korean wares is to the point for in that country we do find many of the Ying Ch'ing types of ware either imported or perhaps made there by Chinese potters. I am inclined to give greater credence to this theory than to the later one expressed by R. L. Hobson in the Sir Percival David Catalogue (1934).

FIG. 279. Cup-holder of early Korai period Korean ware having a green glaze with crackle on a white body browned where exposed and fired on seven spurs. Dia. 7". John Platt, Warren E. Cox Coll.

FIG. 280. The upper bowl is rather heavy in potting and has an imperfect glaze pitted and having, "numerous pin holes and shallow depressions," as Hobson says. The foot-rim is glazed and it was fired on three spurs. Dia. 5".

The cup-holder is similar and even more heavy in potting. Dia. 6½".

Both of these are termed Ju ware by Hobson, I think arbitrarily for they appear to be rather ordinary Korean wares of heavy potting and not at all of imperial quality. Sir Percival David Coll.

FIG. 281. Oval "brush-washer" of the Sir Percival David Coll., called Ju ware by Hobson. There are two sesamum flowers incised in the bottom. I think it a Korean piece not very well made. Note the poor spacing of the spur marks, fire crack in glaze of bottom and irregular shape. Length 5½".

Hobson thought that Ju yao would have been compared with the "common Korean wares" or the celadon type but I see no reason why a rare ware should not be compared with another rare ware in the mind of a traveller and the Ying Ch'ing wares found in Korea are not so very rare at that. He more or less takes the word of a poet of the Ch'ien Lung (1736–96) period or perhaps that of the emperor poet himself that two rather heavy dishes (#B100 Eumo. Cat.) (Pl. II David Cat.) may be Ju yao though they certainly do not rival Ting yao in potting, and only by a long stretch of imagination could be thought to resemble the clear sky color. The only slightest resemblance these have to Korean wares is that they are glazed over the foot rim and fired on five spurs. They certainly do not represent any general type of ware, being odd and not very fine pieces. Having established in his own mind that these are possibly Ju yao, he includes a cup-holder in the

"Ying Ch'ing" type vase of white porcelain burnt brown where exposed and covered with a clear, pale blue crackled, transparent glaze which is silvery iridescent on one side on which it probably rested in burial. Ht. 9". Sung Dynasty. John Platt—Warren E. Cox Coll.

Ying Ch'ing type jar with cover of buff clay and finely crackled glaze showing pale blue toward bottom shading up to buff probably due to over firing. Ht. 9½". Warren E. Cox Coll.

Ewer reported found near Kinkiang, of the Sung period, and of the so called Ying Ch'ing type though it is paler and more buff than blue. The form is a Near Eastern one and the potting excellent. Ht. about 9". Metropolitan Mus. of Art.

A beautiful small pillow of Sung period ware which we call Ying Ch'ing. It is heavily potted and porcelaneous. The glaze is pale blue. Metropolitan Mus. of Art.

Ying Ch'ing type ewer of rather rough pottery with a pale blue glaze discolored red-brown by earth in which it was buried. The potting is thin and well done. Ht. 7⅛". John Platt–Warren E. Cox Coll.

YING CH'ING WARES OF SUNG DYNASTY

PLATE 36

Sir Percival David Catalogue which is typically Korean and quite like ours in the John Platt Collection Fig. 279 as may be seen by comparison, and neither of these, though they are very fine potting, can actually rival the Ting yao in thinness of potting or perfection. (Fig. 280)

It must be remembered that the *Tsung shêng pa chien* was written in 1591, the latter part of the Ming period and that Ming writers frequently used the phrase that we have had translated "like massed lard." This may have an entirely different connotation than we give it, that is, it may not mean a thick glaze at all but rather a soft, unctuous quality which certain of the Ying Ch'ing wares do have to a marked degree. Moreover, it seems obvious to me that the Ying Ch'ing thinner wares are even thinner and more truly potted than the Ting ware while none of the other Sung potteries even including Yüeh, which is perhaps next in thinness, can rival these two. (Note the three delicate small bowls which are well-nigh paper thin.) Thus I feel we must still grant Mr. Eumorfopoulos the more sound theory.

Ying Ch'ing porcelain has a hard, white vitreous body and the glaze is full of bubbles which give it a soft effect. This glaze is of palest blue show-

Figs. 282–283. Three Ying Ch'ing bowls of exceedingly delicate and true potting with thin foot rims and very thin lip rims certainly finer than any Ting yao specimens. The ware is a white porcelain and the glazes all palest blue. Dias. 3½″ to 6″. John Platt–Warren E. Cox Coll.

ing darker where it runs thicker.

The blue was made by the slightest possible trace of iron in the glaze—about .05 percent. The glaze sometimes crazes though often it does not. The lip-rims are usually glazed and the bottom is often not glazed sometimes showing the marks of a ring on which it was fired. The body turns brown where exposed. Rarely the Ting technique was copied and the bowls were fired with the lip-rims for support and the bottoms glazed. They were then mounted

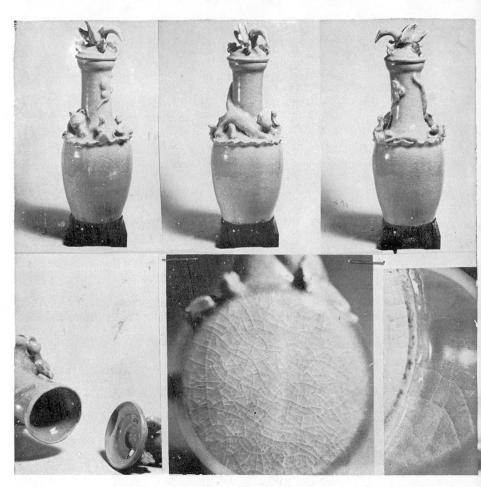

Superb specimen of the rare Southern Kuan yao from "below the Suburban Altar" site. The only large and perfect piece known. It is of grey "wu-ni yao" beautifully potted and more thin than the finest Lung Ch'üan "kinuta" type ware. The glaze is of grey-blue shading to olive-brown and has the "ice crackle" with long curved "crab's claw" crackle. The form is traditional, inherited from T'ang mortuary jars and found with modifications in Yüeh, Lung Ch'üan and other wares but the beautiful proportions with the long neck, stalking tiger and "Feng-Huang" bird show the work of a master potter as technically can also be seen in the fine finish of the inside of the cover. Ht. 13⅜". The Freer Gallery of Art, Washington, from Ralph M. Chait and Warren E. Cox.

SOUTHERN KUAN WINE JAR FROM "BELOW THE SUBURBAN ALTAR" SITE

PLATE 37

with a metal rim. This may have been during the times that rivalry was set up between the two kilns. The decoration consists of incising, modeling, molding, appliqué and even reticulation but all was conservatively used and in good taste until the Ming period. The designs are of ducks, boys among flowers, "happy boys," fishes, etc., and seem to be similar to those of Northern Sung celadons. Beautiful vase forms reflect those of Tz'u Chou and tall ewers called "hu p'ing" are of Near Eastern and probably metal origin. The *Ko ku yao lun* tells us that these were introduced first by the Mongols in the Yüan period (A.D. 1280–1368) but we know this to be untrue for we have proven conclusively that Near Eastern relationship was very strong and continuous in Tang and earlier times.

The quality and thickness of these wares varies more than any other and this is, of course, explained by the various sources. South and east of Ching-tê chên alone there were five sites: Nan shan, Hu-tien, Hsiang-hu, Fu-tien-ts'un, and Wang-ts'un where it was made in pre-Ming times according to Brankston.

KUAN YAO

Kuan yao literally means simply "imperial ware," but the term was used by the early Chinese writers to designate that which was made in the Im-

FIG. 284. Pair of Lung-ch'üan jars of Kuan (Imperial) type thinner in potting even than the "kinuta" type. One is olive-green and almost without crackle. The other is pale grey-green with a prominent "crab's claw" crackle. Note the thin foot-rims. Ht. 9¼". Warren E. Cox Coll.

perial Factory near the capital of Honan, K'ai-fêng or K ai-fêng Fu. This ware was called Ta Kuan by later writers. It was supposed to have been made during the Ta Kuan (1107) and Chêng Ho reigns (1111–1117) and the factory was established by the Emperor Hui Tsung but in 1127 when the court fled the potters were taken along to Hang Chou where two kilns were set up, one under Shao Ch'êng-chang in the Imperial precincts at Hsieu Nei Ssŭ near the Surveyor's Office, and one, "Below the Suburban Altar."

The ware from K'ai-feng Fu has not been identified but that from the Altar site has. It was said to imitate the Ta Kuan ware but the potters had difficulty with the new materials. The first or, "Surveyor's Office site," made "Nei yao" or Palace ware. Meanwhile at Yü-hang Hsieu, near Hang Chou, still another ware was made imitating Kuan yao, and shortly after the Lung-ch'üan kilns also made a "Kuan yao." (Figs. 284 & 285)

Early descriptions say that Ta Kuan yao was "fên ch'ing" (pale blue), "ta lü" (deep green), "yüeh pai" (moon white), and finally, *"Ch'ing t'ai fên hung,"* (ch'ing with a tinge of pale red). It had a large crackle called "crab's

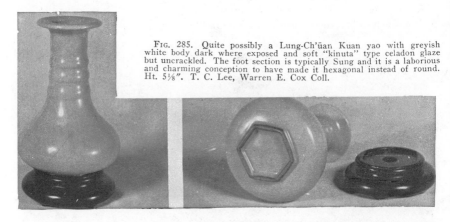

FIG. 285. Quite possibly a Lung-Ch'üan Kuan yao with greyish white body dark where exposed and soft "kinuta" type celadon glaze but uncrackled. The foot section is typically Sung and it is a laborious and charming conception to have made it hexagonal instead of round. Ht. 5⅛". T. C. Lee, Warren E. Cox Coll.

claw" and a finer "fish roe" one. There is no word of the body color of the original ware but the second was said to be "tzŭ" (dark brown or purple) which caused a "brown mouth and iron foot." And finally it was stated by Hobson that, "yellow, black, red and purple (or brown) forms of great beauty," appeared on the surface and took the forms of natural objects such as, "butterflies, birds, fishes, unicorns, leopards and the like." This is translated from the *Tsung Sheng pa chien* (1591) and Ko ware is included in the description. The *Ch'ing pi Ts'ang* (1595) by Chang Ying-wên speaks of, "ice crackle with lines as red as eel's blood," and of, "plum blossom crackle with lines ink colored." This might apply to crackles stained from oxidation of the body or artificially colored by soaking in dye.

Here we get into one of those common difficulties in making translations. Hobson, jumping to the conclusion that, "ch'ing t'ai fên hung," meant, *"splashes* of red on blue color," built a whole theory to the effect that certain

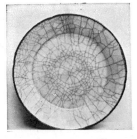

FIG. 286. For imperial potting one would search far before
finding a finer specimen than
this jar of blackish stoneware
with brownish-grey glaze and
black (probably stained) crackle.
It is, I bel'eve incorrectly, called
Ko by Hobson but may well be
Ta Kuan. Ht. 3.9″. Eumor-
fopoulos Coll. # B64.

FIG. 287. "Küan yao plate"
of black ware with gray-blue
glaze having brown crackle. It
is thinly potted and mounted
with a metal rim. Dia. about 7″.
Metropolitan Mus. of Art.

FIG. 288. "Küan yao" beg-
ging bowl of the Sung period
of dark stoneware with black
rim and blue-green or green-
blue glaze and dark brown
crackle. Dia. about 5″. Metropolitan Mus. of Art.

of the more refined and thin (though still fairly heavy) Chün wares, with
their brown or olive green edges, dark bod'es, blue and often crackled glazes
and red splashes, were Southern Kuan ware. On the other hand the translation should really be, "a bluish or greenish color *tinged with* red," which any
person, used to mixing color, would agree would produce browns, lavender,
dull green fawn and vinaceous or cinnamon colors depending on the proportions. The point is important as we shall see.

The *Ko ku yao lun* (1387) said the ware was, "fine and unctuous, the
color ch'ing with a flush of pale red *and varying*," according to Hobson's own
translation. It also says specimens with black body are called "wu-ni yao,"
which I take to be an inference that there may have been other kinds. It
further states that Kuan yao made at Lung-ch'üan has no crackle. We know
that crackle was not under control there until the very end of Sung or even
later times though it did occur slightly at times. This type is quite possibly
represented by our small bottle with hexagonal foot. (Fig. 285)

The *Cho Keng Lu* (1368) states, "Southern Kuan is of fine clay with
translucent color and brilliant right through." This is quoting Yeh-chih. The
meaning may be that the ware is translucent or that the color (or glaze) is
translucent as seems to be the case.

Our present day findings are beginning to make this ware quite certain.
Dr. Menzo Nakao found shreds in the Surveyor's Office site including dark
bodied wares, a greyish white bodied "kinuta" type "celadon" probably
from Lung-ch'üan, a crackled "celadon" and others with a thinner and more
bubbly glaze; at least four types. Mr. Karlbeck, Dr. Burchard and Peter
Boode found others of great variety both in color and glaze which are in the
British Museum. It is upon these that some sort of classification has been
attempted though many of the wares at first called Ko are more likely to
be Kuan and vice versa. Perhaps the most sensible way to approach the
matter is to assume that certainly *the Imperial Ta Kuan and Southern Kuan
wares would have been better potted than the more ordinary Ko ware*, all
of Mr. Hobson's bubble theories to the contrary, and, if we apply this simple

FIG. 289. Southern Kuan vase (neck cut) from the Suburban Altar site. Thin grey ware burnt brown, with lavender-brown transparent glaze crackled typically. Note ogival plan. Ht. 4". Benjamin d'Ancona Coll.

FIG. 290. Sung bowl of black stoneware thinly potted, the foot having a narrow and shallow rim and six black spur marks. The glaze is of greenish oyster gray with black crazing, broader on the outside and denser on the inside. Called Kwan yao. Dia. about 4". Metropolitan Mus. of Art.

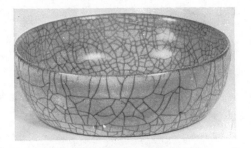

rule certainly the Eumorfopoulos example #B64 (Our Fig. 286) would belong in the Kuan category as it is a superb piece of potting.

Just before World War II a few dozen small and mostly broken pieces of an exceedingly thin and beautifully potted ware came onto the American market and it was stated that they had been found "below the Suburban Altar." The pieces were said to have come from a dealer named Chow of the Rue Bron Gros, French Concession, Shanghai. The body is invariably dark grey or brown and the glaze is bubbly and transparent so that you can, "see right through it," and prominently crackled with what may well be described as an "ice crackle." The colors of no two are alike and vary even on a single piece. The range is through soft blues and greens to buff, lavender and reddish browns perhaps best described as near the colors of moth wings and all consisting of "ch'ing tinged with red." So thinly potted is it that it compares with the thinner Ying-Ching. It makes Pai-Ting Yao feel heavy. Lung-ch'üan even of the "kinuta" type is crude and heavy by comparison. Thus master potters must have made it. The forms are often derived from bronze shapes but made in ogival plan at times with the suture marks so exaggerated as to become actual flanges. Other forms are simple potters' forms but with great charm and beauty of proportion.

Just recently Mr. Ralph M. Chait and I acquired the finest specimen of this ware which has ever been seen (Pl. 37), and which I illustrate in detail. This piece clears up one interesting point. It had worried collectors that although the ware was exactly as described in every detail the reference to

Early Lung-Ch'üan jar and cover having a dragon, chicken and reclining figure about the shoulder and the "Feng-Huang" bird on the cover. Note the similarity of the form to the Southern Kuan ware example but the much finer potting of the latter. Early Sung. Ht. 13″. Warren E. Cox Coll.

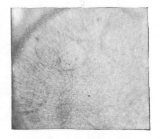

Two interesting examples, the one of Southern Kuan (the darker) and the other of Lung-Ch'üan ware, showing how closely the former took up the designs of the older kilns, and how much better the potting was. Late Sung. Hts. 3″. Warren E. Cox–John Platt Coll. The Kuan example is from C. T. Loo.

EARLY LUNG-CH'ÜAN WINE JAR PROTOTYPE OF A SOUTHERN KUAN FORM

PLATE 38

various animals appearing on the surface as quoted from the *Tsung shêng pa chien* could not be explained. Some had suggested that one with imagination could envision animal forms in the crackle but this stretched the imagination altogether too far. In our jar this final question is settled. The animals appear *not painted,* as Hobson assumed in working out his Chün type theory, but beautifully *sculptured* in the round and covered with the glaze so they appear in color. They include a tiger, a dog and two human figures. The cover is surmounted with a most beautiful bird with half opened wings.

FIG. 291. Brush-washer (hsi) of water-chestnut flower (ling hua) shape called "Ko ware" by Hobson. It must be admitted that the potting is heavy but the glaze of buff, bluish and brown at edges, with its "ice crackle" is much like that of the Southern Kuan ware from below the Suburban Altar site. Dia. 7.35″. Sir Percival David Coll.

FIG. 292. Southern Kuan incense burner from below the Suburban Altar of thin brown-grey ware covered with a transparent deep green-blue glaze. Ht. 3″. N. M. Heeramaneck Coll.

It so happened that I had an early Lung-ch'üan jar (Pl. 38) in my collection which is a likely prototype and represents an ancient, traditional form dating at least from the second century A.D. (See brown jar Pl. 25, Fig. 3), but in this Southern Kuan example the form reaches its greatest beauty. The color of the body of this jar is dark grey and the glaze is gray-blue shading to buff and greenish-buff. The thinness of the lip and cover rims speaks for itself. So far as we know, no comparative example is in existence, and when it is placed near one of the Lung-ch'üan jars of similar form but with squat bodies, short necks, flattened covers and heavy potting, its aristocratic beauty stands out clearly. (See Pl. 40 for late example.)

Ko Yao

Ko yao (or the "Elder Brother's ware") is invariably associated with Kuan yao in the ancient Chinese texts which in most cases make no distinction between them. It was supposed to have been made by the elder brother Chang in the latter part of the Southern Sung period (A.D. 1127–1280) in the Lung-ch'üan district in Ch'u Chou Fu (Chekiang province) at a place called Lin-t'ien. The other brother made a celadon very much like Lung-ch'üan yao and treated under that section.

The story has been doubted but there was some potter who made this ware and he may have had a brother. It is immaterial and the story persists. The dark clay from Phoenix Hill at Hang Chou was imported and this

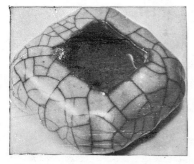

FIG. 293. "Ko yao" writer's coupe with grey body which burns brown about the foot and mouth, and a translucent gray glaze filled with just visible bubbles and crackled in brown and black. Yung Chêng period (960–1280 A.D.). Width 3½". Judge Edgar Bromberger Coll. Brooklyn Mus.

FIG. 294. "Ko yao" Sung period bowl of dark gray stoneware and having a greenish gray glaze with black crackle and dark gray lip rim. Dia. about 6". Metropolitan Mus. of Art. Comparison should be made of the crackles.

made the "brown mouth and iron foot" similar to Hang Chou Kuan yao (see preceding section). Crackle was purposely developed in Ko yao and Hsieh Min of the Yung Chêng period (A.D. 1722–1736) said "Ko glaze on an iron body of two kinds—mi sê (millet-colored) and fên ch'ing both copied from ancient specimens sent from the Palace," in the descriptions of the wares he was ordered to copy. The least good color according to the older critics was hui sê or ash-colored, but the poet Ku Liu describes a Ko yao

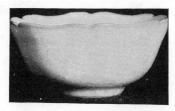

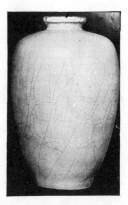

FIG. 296. Termed "Kuan yao" by the museum but doesn't fit requirements, is heavily potted, has light body, etc. Possibly Ko. Sung. Freer Gallery of Art. Washington, D. C.

FIG. 295. Bottle called "Kuan type" by the museum, of black body and bluish-grey glaze which is crackled. The heavy and none too sure potting makes it difficult to suppose this a real imperial ware. Sung. Ht. 8½". Metropolitan Mus. of Art.

FIG. 298. Ovoid vase with black stoneware body and thick opaque glaze of pale bluish-grey with irregular crackle of the "crab's claw" type. "Ko type." Ht. 10.75". Eumorfopoulos Coll. # B60.

FIG. 297. "Ko ware" bowl, said to be Sung. Grey-green with a definite crackle and also a fainter one. The glaze full of quite perceptible bubbles. Dia. 4¾". Gift of Mrs. Thos. D. Stimson. Seattle Art Mus.

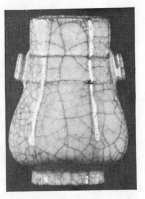

A typical Ko vase of grey stoneware with opaque gray-buff glaze having strong black and lighter brown crackle. Inside the lip is engraved a poem by Ch'ien Lung:
"Despite the hundred-fold crackle lines, its surface is smooth to the touch.
"This, the ware of Ch'u-chou, was the work of the talented Elder Brother.
"When one has once discovered the worth of undecorated wares,
"The elaborate products of Hsüan and Ch'êng will be less esteemed."
Ht. 5.9". Sir Percival David Coll.

"Ko yao," Sung vase after a bronze form, having a dark body and bluish gray glaze filled with small bubbles but not having the "brown mouth" often found in such wares. Ht. about 4". Freer Gallery of Art, Washington.

Small vase called "Kuan yao" by the museum but so proportionately heavy and comparatively crude that should say it was "Ko yao" if of either type Ht. 4". Freer Gallery of Art. Washington, D. C Is also called "Sung but may be later.

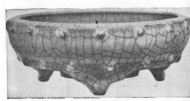

Ko ware bulb-bowl (shui hsien p'ên) c blackish brown ware burnt red-brown when exposed and covered with a slightly greenis buff-grey glaze crackled in black and brow probably stained. Sung. Dia. 7". Sir Percival David Coll.

"Ko ware" fairly heavy incense-vase (hsiang lu) or leys jar (Cha-tou) of dark brown stoneware with brown crackled pale green glaze. The lip-rim is copper. Dia. 4.6". Imperial Coll., Peking. Cf. Eumor-fopoulos Coll. # B64. Sir Percival David Coll.

Wide necked bottle on flaring foot in which there are two rectangular holes. Thinly potted dark ware covered with a pale gray green glaze, similar to that of Lung Ch'üan yao, which is irregularly crackled with what may be called a "crab's claw" crackle. Called Ko yao. Sung period. Gift of Mrs. Samuel T. Peters. Metropolitan Mus. of Art.

Lung Ch'üan Sung period bulb bowl c white porcelain with rich and translucen green glaze. Dia. about 6½". Gift of Mr Samuel T. Peters. Metropolitan Mus. of Ar Note similarity of form to the Ko or above, which tends to bolster the theory of the Brothers Chang.

KO WARE OF THE SUNG DYNASTY
PLATE 39

ink-stone as lü (green) as the waves in spring. This may have been poetic license or perhaps he simply got mixed up. In any event, as has been explained, the glazes of these wares may vary considerably in color and should be judged chiefly by their texture. The *Ch'ing pi ts'ang,* a book not on our list and of doubtful authority, speaks of crackle varying from "the crab's claw of Kuan yao to the fish-roe of Ko yao, which was less beautiful," but this general description of a small crackle is not borne out by other authorities. However, it is true that the small privately owned kiln did perhaps make a ware less good than the Imperially patronized Kuan yao. The old reports also speak of "touches," "splashes," or "tinges" of warm contrasting color (see preceding discussion) and I believe these to be similar to those in Kuan yao. The Hobson theory that Kuan might have been a kind of Chün yao type ware should also receive its fatal blow when the ancient writers associate Kuan and Ko so closely together. Certainly we cannot admit Ko yao into this same category of Chün-like wares.

Perhaps here a word should be said about crackle in general. It is caused by a different rate of expansion and contraction under heat and cold of the body and the glaze. Thus a tension is set up which results in a cracking of the weaker part, the glaze. This is not usually sufficient to crack the glaze off the body. The *T'ao lu* (1815) says that the potters of Yung-ho Chên during the Sung dynasty used a special clay called "hua shih" in the glaze and it may be that they added some ingredient to make a wider divergence between the rates of expansion and contraction. However, this was no invention and again was a simple adaptation of a phenomenon which occurred by accident. Another method said to have been used was to heat the piece in the sun and then plunge it into cold water. This might *aid* to develop a crackle but it could hardly *cause* a crackle if the tension was not already present. It must be explained that the crackle does not take place entirely in the kiln as the piece is cooling off. I have heard a modern piece of porcelain sitting on my desk days after it was made suddenly begin to snap and crack and have watched the crackle developing further on it.

Ko yao was greatly copied from the time of its origin and the collector therefore must be careful. But although it is rare, and beautiful, pieces can be had for a price running from a few hundred dollars up, we need hardly go to the lengths of at least one old Chinese eunuch who, it is reported in the *Pi chuang so yü,* had a man thrown into prison simply because he was jealous of the ownership of a piece of Ko yao "about two inches in height."

CH'ING TZ'U (GREEN PORCELAIN)
LUNG-CH'ÜAN YAO, CH'U-CHOU YAO AND OTHER "CELADONS"

I have already used the word "celadon" a number of times in reference to such wares as Yüeh yao, Kuan yao, Ko yao, etc. It further applies to Lung-ch'üan yao, Ch'ü-chou yao, some Northern Honan wares, some Korean wares and imitations made both in the Far East and Near East as well as Europe. Stretching its meaning to cover cheap green oil lamps, as some department stores have recently, is wrong for they have nothing whatsoever to do with the original Far Eastern ware which has been so popular in nearly every country in the world for over 500 years. We are not sure of the origin of the word. Some say it was derived from the name Saladin but the best known theory is that it came from France where a play featured a shepherd who wore the then new and popular color in the 17th century.

Fig. 299. Early Sung Lung-ch'üan bottle. Grey clay burnt red where exposed and covered with transparent crackled glaze shading from buff to olive green. Ht. 9¾". Warren E. Cox Coll.

Fig. 300. Lung-ch'üan square bottle c. A.D. 1100 with grey body burnt red where exposed and transparent pale green crackled glaze. Ht. 9¾". K. M. Semon Coll.

Fig. 301. Pair of important Sung vases of Lung Ch'üan yao which are very close to the shape of the T'ang period mortuary jars. White and porcelaneous; foot-rims show brown where exposed. Glaze of soft yellowish green color without crazing. c. after A.D. 1127. Ht. 31". Formerly Warren E. Cox Coll.

Chinese "celadon" of various types has been found extensively in the Near East in Persia and Egypt where it is called "martabani" from the port of Martaban on the coast of Pegu from which the wares were shipped, we know at least from the 9th century on. They are in the form of bowls, jardinieres, vases, bases for hubble pipes, etc., and were thought to make harmless any poison that might be poured into them. In China these wares are known as "ch'ing tz'u" (green porcelain) and in Japan as "seiji."

The body of Lung-ch'üan yao the best known site is a hard, high-fired porcelain varying from light grey (not so deep as that of Yüeh yao) to pure white. It is likely that the whiter wares are later and were due to better perfected methods of refining the clay. There is one type in particular made by the younger Chang, it is related, which shows white where the glaze runs thin and is generally more refined than the ordinary Lung-ch'üan wares. (Pl. 46) This was toward the end of the Sung period. The bodies all contain a large amount of iron and therefore burn a yellowish or reddish brown where exposed but they are so light that no "brown lip" occurs.

As the finds at Samarra prove, the Lung-ch'üan factory must have started well before the 9th century in T'ang times. I show an example which has a flat almost rimless foot and a form which might well be T'ang and from

Left: Early Lung-ch'üan wine jar. Grey ware burnt red where exposed and covered with rich, transparent, green, crackled glaze. Ht. 14″. Warren E. Cox Coll.
  Center: Lung-ch'üan jar after Yüeh type but heavier. Glossy olive green glaze, full of bubbles. Ht. 10½″. Early Sung. Warren E. Cox Coll.
  Right: Lung Ch'uan yao jar and cover. Reflects some characteristics of Yüeh yao, but is much heavier and glaze is more glossy, transparent and thicker. Ht. 10½″. Warren E. Cox Coll.

Two wine-jars, smaller from Lung-ch'üan with white body burnt brown where exposed and covered with transparent olive-green glaze except under foot. Note perfunctory potting of cover.
  Taller jar from Imperial Yüeh kilns at Shang-lin-hu. Of grey body burnt brown where exposed, covered with similar transparent olive glaze even under foot. Thin, deep lip on cover shows greater care taken in potting. Hts. 11″ and 13½″. Warren E. Cox Coll.

Right: Lung Ch'üan vase of late Sung to early Ming period, of heavy white porcelain with rich, beautiful green glaze without crackle. Ht. 8″. Metropolitan Mus. of Art.

DEVELOPMENT OF LUNG-CH'ÜAN WINE JARS

PLATE 40

Jar called "Northern Celadon" in Percival David Catalogue but which is Yüeh or Lung-ch'üan (I have not examined it) inscribed as follows:

"On the 15th day of the intercalary 9th month of the 3d year of the Yüan Fêng period (Oct. 30th 1080 A.D.), I have baked this first class urn in the hope that it may hold fragrant wine for thousands and myriads of years; that after a hundred years, it may be handed down to my descendants; that I may have a thousand sons and ten thousand grandsons; that they may have wealth and occupy high positions in the government continually: that they may live long and enjoy good fortune and unlimited happiness; and that the world may be at peace." Ht. 14.8″. Sir Percival David Coll.

Early Lung-ch'üan jar and cover of gray ware with crackled olive green glaze. On cover, protected with glaze, is inscription, "chu shih pa lang ch'ien nien chiu ku tzu," or "Chu the 18th thousand-year-wine store made." The last word may also be rendered "chih." Thus this jar along with Sir Percival David one illustrated prove that these were made to contain wine.

Possibly spouts having holes that do not enter main compartment were to hold flowers.

Yüeh examples are lighter in potting and have glaze on bottom which this has not.

Thanks must be given to Mr. Nai-Chi Chang, chairman of the translations committee of the Chinese Art Society of America, to Mr. C. F. Yau and Mr. Hsuge K. Pao as well as Mr. Shinzo Shirae for working out this translation. Ht. 12¾″. Warren E. Cox Coll.

UNIQUE WINE JARS WITH INSCRIPTIONS PROVING USE

PLATE 41

this kiln. Other early examples such as the one illustrated clearly show the influence of the Yüeh yao jars with covers and we are led to believe that this factory took away the trade from the Yüeh kilns. In this type the glaze is glassy and crackled but thinner and very different from the much later Ch'ü-chou types largely of Ming and Ching periods. It also shows, on close examination, roughened frosty spots like the beginning of iridescence from action of the soil in which it was buried. Still others which are perhaps even

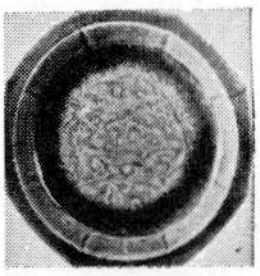

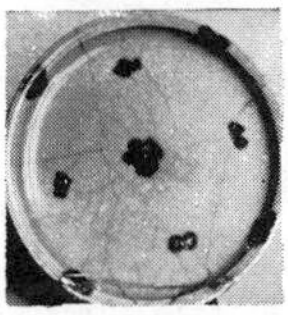

FIG. 302. Chekiang celadon dish (p'an) of greyish porcelain with pale emerald-green transparent glaze crackled. On base is wide unglazed ring burnt reddish brown, enclosing disc of glaze beneath which is incised mark "ta sung nien tsao" (made in great Sung period). Dia. 14.8". Sir Percival David Coll.
FIG. 303. A pao pie (leopard skin) Lung-ch'üan or, as Japs say, "tobi seiji" (buckwheat celadon) of light grey-green with spots of brown caused by iron. Sometimes these have silvery sheen. Ht. 10¾". Sir Percival David Coll. # LV.
FIG. 304. Lung-ch'üan bottle of pale green with silvery-brown iridescent spots evenly spaced. In 1931 a similar piece brought some $45,000 in a Japanese auction. Ht. 10¾". Eumorfopoulos Co'l.
FIG. 305. "Celadon" dish of Lung Ch'uan ware spotted by iron. Dia. 6½". Metropolitan Mus. of Art.

earlier are almost exact imitations of Yüeh jars with the spouts around the shoulder, incised decoration, etc., but the ware is a little heavier and the glaze more glassy. (Pl. 40, 41) These early wares are all definitely green without any bluish and little greyish cast. The crackle on them is never stained and appears to be entirely accidental.

In Sung times it appears that the glaze was constantly improved along with the potting until at the end of the period it reached its apex when it declined under Mongol influence, as did all wares of the time, through the Yüan into Ming times. The T'ao lu tells us that at the beginning of Ming times the Lung-ch'üan kilns were moved to Li-shui Hsien in Ch'u-chou Fu and that the ware was known as Ch'u yao but this must not be taken to mean that Lung-ch'üan kilns did not continue to operate or that the Ch'ü-chou kilns only started at that time. As a matter of fact we have dated Sung Ch'ü-chou wares as well as Lung-ch'üan ones bearing Ming dates. It is exceedingly difficult, therefore, to distinguish between the two wares or between Sung and Ming wares from either. The T'ao lu says simply that the Ming wares were not so good and that they were more grey and had a ring of brown unglazed under the base on which the pieces were fired but this

Fig. 306. Lung-ch'üan late Sung bottle or "hsien wên (string-lined) p'ing," of greyish porcelain with clear green "kinuta" glaze glossy and uncrackled. Ht. 12½". Sir Percival David Coll.

Fig. 307. Lung-ch'üan bulb-bowl of white porcelain with grey-green transparent glaze. Dia. 7". Sir Percival David Coll.

Fig. 308. Lung-ch'üan dish in form of lotus leaf with fire crack possibly intentional as it occurs just where leaf would split and such a piece is easy to fire. Glaze of deep, rich green. Dia. c. 5". Ethelyn C. Stewart Coll.

Fig. 309. Lung-ch'üan dish with relief three clawed dragon in biscuit fired brown with soft grey-green glaze. Under bottom is a raised seal mark: "Kien Chung, Tsing Kwoh of the Hwei Tsung reign" (or A.D. 1101). Dia. c. 4". T. C. Lee Coll. Warren E. Cox Coll. Mrs. L. G. Sheafer.

has all been discredited by Mr. Hobson and others. Generally speaking the Lung-ch'üan wares have a more creamy and unctuous and less glassy glaze while they are also thinner in potting, though this is not always the case as may be seen by the large vase illustrated. As a rule, the Sung examples are less ornate in both factories and less heavy for the ornate taste was that of the Mongols and the greater weight came with the increased export trade, but this again is open to exception.

Fig. 310. Rare small dish with sharp, beautifully molded design of birds and clouds in unglazed relief. Ware is white but burnt red-brown where exposed. Glaze clear pale green. Dia. c. 6". Formerly John Platt–Warren E. Cox Coll., (Boston Mus.)

Fig. 311. Incense burner (ting) of "Chang, Lung-ch'üan ware." Grey-white porcelain with green glaze. Known in Japan as "hakama-goshi koro" (skirt-shaped incense-burner). Dia. 5.3". Sir Percival David Coll.

Fig. 312. Pair of Lung Ch'üan yao vases which leaned together in the kiln during process of firing and glaze stuck them at body and rim. Unique and interesting example of difficulties confronting ancient potters. Ht. 6". John Platt Coll.

Fig. 313. Sung period Lung Ch'üan dish with bluish green glaze and two fishes in relief left unglazed. Clay reddish brown where left exposed. Dia. 5". Mrs. Charles Porter Wilson.

Modern celadon glaze is made by adding a small amount of iron to a clear glaze and sometimes the least bit of cobalt to make the color bluer. In Chinese wares the same coloring agents were used and in the beginning at any rate may have been simply due to the iron content of the materials used for glaze. The color was developed to imitate jade and is described as "ts-'ui pi" jade green. The late Mr. Shepard de Forest, one of our greater collectors of the ware, went so far as to state that he thought the brown clouding, far from being an accident of the kiln, was welcomed by the Chinese potters because it is like that in the "skin of jade"; the outer covering which has become further oxidized and also in clouded areas inside a piece of jade of the "fiet-sui" or jewel type. The word "fiet-sui" not only designates this type of jade but also has the literal meaning of "green brown" which seems also to bear out his theory. In any event although the Chinese writers of earliest days never wrote disparagingly of the brown areas sometimes seen in Lung-ch'üan yao they certainly did point out that the red and purple splotches of Chün yao were not desirable.

Much more definite than the clouding referred to above are actual spots of dark brown with roughened surface which probably occurred accidentally at first, but which, due to their careful placing, force us to believe they were entirely intentional later on. They are never large, being about the size of a five cent piece and of irregular form. These are undoubtedly due to the introduction of iron in the body or glaze and occur very rarely on some of the finest pieces. The Japanese have named this particular kind "tobi seiji" meaning literally "buckwheat celadon" and prize it very highly some pieces having fetched close to $50,000 at auction. These may have been made at Lung-ch'üan or some other kiln site. The Chinese call them "pao-pie" or leopard-skin celadon. (Figs. 303–305)

The bluer wares some of which were thought to have been made by Chang the younger and some of which were probably not are also loved by the Japanese who have called them "kinuta" meaning "mallet" from a celebrated vase of mallet shape preserved in one of the old temples. (Pl. 42) The actual "kinuta" vases may be seen in our illustrations of the one from the Freer Gallery of Art and in the Nai-Chi Chang collection formerly in my own collection, and that of Mrs. Charles Porter Wilson and it will be noted that the better ones have delicately modeled fish or bird's head handles. A heavier type has handles in the form of seals or are perhaps less detailed fish. The kinuta type, however, includes wares with the same glaze and of various shapes.

In decoration the potters made use of incising, appliqués and modeling for the glaze was transparent enough to show up the first and hung richly in deeper thickness over the latter two techniques. A variation was developed in which the design was left in unglazed relief so that it burnt reddish brown and the background was glazed giving a beautiful contrast. Small dishes were generally so treated but the figure illustrated of the seated Kuan Yin in bisque on a rocky grotto and with her feet in waves is so far as I know the only Lung-ch'üan example of a figure so treated during the Sung period. (Pl. 43) Later rocky grottoes were made, which we will touch upon in the

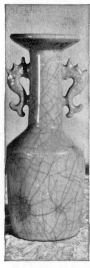

Lung-ch'üan "Kinuta" with delicate fish handles. Irregular crackle probably intentional. Ht. 11½". Warren E. Cox Coll. Nai-Chi Chang Coll.

Late Sung or perhaps later Lung Ch'üan bottle of fine form. These more ornate pieces probably made to suit Mongol taste. Ht. 13½". Warren E. Cox Coll.

Late Sung or early Ming bottle with glaze more glassy than that of usual Lung Ch'üan yao but very beautiful in shape. Ht. c. 10". Warren E. Cox Coll.

Pair of small "Kinuta" vases of white ware showing gray at foot and covered with soft gray-green clear glaze. Handles seem to represent foreparts of flying birds. Sung period. Ht. 6¾". Mrs. Charles Porter Wilson–Warren E. Cox Coll. Nai-chi Chang Coll.

"Kinuta" (Japanese term) or club-shaped vase of Sung dynasty Lung Ch'üan yao. White porcelaneous ware covered with bright grey green glaze without crazing. Ht. 10". Freer Gallery of Art, Washington, D. C.

LUNG-CH'ÜAN "KINUTA" AND BOTTLE-FORMED VASES

PLATE 42

Ming section, although the body and glaze of those too would tend to suggest Lung-ch'üan rather than Ch'ü-chou as their source. The dishes or shallow bowls usually have fish, dragons or birds and clouds for decoration although some are known with floral treatment. (Pl. 44 & Figs. 309–313)

Large jardinieres and "temple vases," some of which at least we know by inscriptions were offered to the temples, began to come into use toward the end of the Sung period. They were heavily made and often decorated with either carved or cast appliqué floral decorations. (Pl. 45) One interesting feature is that the bottoms were often made separately and, in the vases, the bodies of which were made in upper and lower sections, placed in the open foot before the upper half of the body was put on and stuck into position with the glaze alone. In the large example shown, which incidentally has the finest color I know, this bottom disc has slipped and attached itself at a slant. Collectors give the general period of late Sung to these but many of them are of the Ming period I am convinced.

Another classic Chinese vase form which was made in celadon and other wares such as Ting yao and Ko yao, is the "tsu ts'ung" or symbol of the deity Earth. In this case the form is taken from ancient jades which were, when first found, thought to be wheel hubs or axle supports, a theory entirely confuted by Dr. Berthold Laufer (see "Jade" page 125) in his criticism of the *Ku yü t'u p'u*. The form represents that of a cylinder thrust lengthwise through a square vase and projecting above and below (see Pl. 46). A pottery one of the Han period has the inscription "grain vessel." A jade one in the *Fang-shih mo p'u* published by Fang Yü-lu in 1588 has three characters "shih ts'ao p'ing" meaning "vase for plant shih" which is a species of Achillea the stalks of which were used for divination. In any event this is a most sturdy and beautiful form and the eight divisions on each corner, perhaps representing the eight divisions of the earth, take the glaze in a beautiful soft and undulating manner.

OTHER CELADON KILNS

Besides the two mentioned there were other kilns in Chekiang province such as the ones at Chin-ts'un and Li-shui the wares of which have not been segregated to date and, of course, the one at Liu-t'ien run by the younger Chang brother. In the Northern Sung days before A.D. 1127 there were a number of kilns in Honan near the capital Kai-fêng and in other northern provinces. For years the Yüeh yao was included in this group but there are a number of wares quite as thinly potted and with beautiful incised and molded decoration which have a more transparent and bubbly sort of glaze and which are in design closely associated with the Ying ch'ing and Korean wares which may be allotted to these kilns. The ewers often show Near Eastern influences and some of these wares were found at Samarra and along the overland route in Chinese Turkestan, Kharakhoto, etc. At Ch'ên-liu, southeast of Kai-fêng Fu, was one of the most important of these kilns.

It must also be remembered that the kilns at Ching-te Chên operated from early times. Here also a celadon ware was made distinguished by its white body which in more recent times was dressed on the exposed parts with earth

Beautiful and unique Lung-ch'üan figure (unglazed and burnt brown terra cotta color) seated on a glazed rocky throne with waves below. Probably made c. A.D. 1050 to 1127. Ht. 12″. Lem Sec Tsang–Warren E. Cox Coll.

LUNG CH'ÜAN BISQUE FIGURE OF KUAN YIN

PLATE 43

Heavenly shrine with Buddha in the center and Kuan-yin above while adoring disciples stand to either side. At the bottom is a tortoise and snake as though on a seal while toward the top is a lotus flower and above that a lichen-scroll. The figures are in bisque burnt brown. The objects, including also the halo about Buddha's head, and a bird and vase to either side of Kuan-yin are brown but seemingly glazed with a transparent colorless glaze. The rest is in typical Lung-ch'üan green glaze of good quality. Late Sung to Early Ming Period. Ht. 13½". Warren E. Cox Coll.

BUDDHISTIC HEAVENLY SHRINE OF LUNG CH'ÜAN WARE

PLATE 44

Lung-ch'üan amphoras of similar materials and potting. One has straight foot-rim; the other a bevelled one more associated with Ming wares. Late Sung and Early Ming. Hts. 12½" and 17¼". Mrs. Charles Porter Wilson.

Two Sung Lung-ch'üan bowls with straight, narrow foot-rims and frosty line where glaze meets body. Dias. 8½" and 9⅛". John Platt–Warren E. Cox Coll.

Lung-ch'üan amphora (neck cut) with finest glaze to be seen on such wares. This perfection of glaze, appliqué design, heavy, bevelled foot-rim all would indicate Ming rather than Sung origin. No frosty line appears on these pieces where glaze meets body clay. Note bottom saucer dropped in and stuck with glaze. Ht. 18½". Warren E. Cox Coll.

One of pair of small Lung-ch'üan vases rare in that they have a slip-trailed decoration. (Note enlarged detail showing where it smudged on lower left part of body.) Enlargement of foot-rim shows typical frosty white line on glaze where it meets body-clay, due to corrosion in burial. Usually present on Sung period Lung-ch'üan wares and is sure sign of authenticity as I have never seen it on any Ming or later example. Ht. 6". K. M. Semon Coll. Note: This also appears on Southern Kuan wares.

LUNG CH'ÜAN VASES SHOWING FOOT-RIMS
PLATE 45

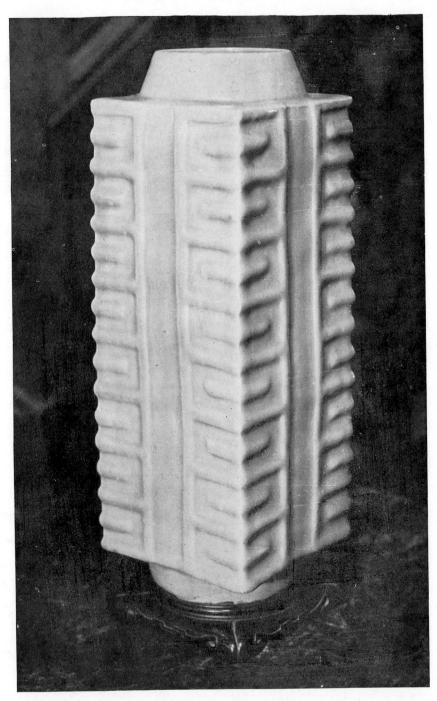

Lung-ch'üan late Sung vase in form of jade "ts'ung" or ritual vessel used in worship of earth and intended to hold divining rods. Of greyish porcelain with rich and glossy green glaze having brown clouds and showing white through it on ridges. (Of type supposedly made by Chang the Younger.) The only comparative one in size and quality is that of the Sir Percival David Coll. Ht. 16¼". Warren E. Cox Coll.

LUNG CH'ÜAN "TS'UNG" OR SYMBOL OF EARTH

PLATE 46

Fig. 314. Lung Ch'uan large jar of thinly potted white porcelain covered with clear green glaze and showing iron red brown foot where exposed. Ht. 10½". Warren E. Cox Coll.

Fig. 315. Chü Chou large jar of white ware with frosty green glaze of rich color and light and dark brown crackle. Foot and lip rims, unglazed, show red brown. Probably late Sung. Ht. 10". Warren E. Cox Coll.

containing iron to simulate the wares made of iron containing clay. Ching-tê Chêng also used a coarse yellowish clay. In Kwangtung not far from Canton a ware was made with reddish brown body.

The factory at Ch'ên-liu mentioned above made the well known "tung yao" or "Eastern ware" which the *Ko ku yao lun* describes as "pale green with fine crackle and in many cases with brown mouth and iron foot." It is, we are told, "similar to Kuan yao but lacks the red tinge and the material is coarse and wanting in fineness and lustre while at the present day it is not often seen." (1387) We find that there was a light and dark Tung yao imitated in Yung Chêng times. A poem by Chang-lei of the 11th century compares the glaze with green jade (pi yü). For some unknown reason Mr. Hobson in the Eumorfopoulos Catalogue jumps to the conclusion that the ware must be, "a superior kind of Northern Celadon," and indicates two bowls, "conspicuous for the beauty of their celadon glaze, but not obviously referable to the Lung-ch'üan type; and these may be regarded as possible specimens of true Tung yao."

Actually Tung yao has a copper containing glaze more related to green Chün yao and is not a celadon at all, the green of which is caused by iron. There are two ewers in the Cleveland and Boston museums and one oblate melon-shaped box ex Warren E. Cox and now Cyrus Churchill collection.

Deep bowls of heavy potting and often having impressed designs inside, of figures standing and on horse-back and characters (jên) benevolence, (shou) longevity and (fu) happiness were dug up at Showchow in Anhwei province and are probably of local manufacture. They are of a white ware which burns brown where exposed and are covered including the lip and also the foot-rim with a thick, frosty, crackled glaze often of an olive green but at times, as in the small plain bowl illustrated, with a bright pea-green color of great beauty. These have also a dab of glaze under the foot and it is a mystery how they were fired for there are no spur marks and no regular ring under the foot. Some of these may be pre-Ming, but their weight would seem to indicate a Ming feeling.

Left: "Northern Sung Celadon" bowl with incised decoration and crackled olive green glaze. Nasli Heeramaneck Coll.

Center: Sung Honan celadon bowl. Dense gray stoneware with impressed and carved design of "Happy boys and chrysanthemums." Dia. 6". Gift of Sadajiro Yamanaka. Metropolitan Mus. of Art.

Right: "Northern Sung Celadon" bowl from Honan. Grey body burnt brown where exposed and covered with a vetiver green or tea green semi-mat glaze. Design carved in relief, not incised or impressed. Dia. 8". Warren E. Cox–John Platt Coll.

"Northern Sung Celadon" bowl. Grey body and watery grey green glaze with many large bubbles. Dia. 4¾". Warren E. Cox Coll.

Bowl of dense gray ware thinly potted with carved design under transparent olive green crackled glaze. Type found in northern provinces. Dia. 5". D. Abbes Coll.

Center: Northern Sung celadon bowl dating about A.D. 1200. Grey burnt to tan and glaze very light olive green full of bubbles and roughly applied. Dia. 6¾". Warren E. Cox Coll.

Left: Sung celadon bowl from Honan province with gray body and olive brown transparent glaze over an incised design. The potting is refined and well done. Dia. 5¾". Warren E. Cox Coll.

Center: "Northern Sung Celadon" bottle probably before 1127. Well potted grey porcelain body burnt brown where exposed around foot-rim and in scraped out symbols, which are seven in number and not all so clear as two shown. Glaze olive green filled with tiny bubbles. Ht. 7¼". Warren E. Cox Coll.

Right: Sung period Honan celadon coupe of light gray stoneware with olive green glaze filled with tiny bubbles and quite transparent where it runs thin. Ht. c. 5". Metropolitan Mus. of Art.

"NORTHERN SUNG CELADON" WARES FROM DIFFERENT KILNS

PLATE 47

Fig. 316. Small ewer from Northern Honan, possibly Yu Chou. Buff grey stoneware body, "tea-dust" greenish brown glaze and splashes of blue produced by copper added to glaze. Loops and handle repaired. T'ang period and perhaps a prototype of Chün wares. Ht. 6½". Warren E. Cox Coll.

Fig. 317. Flower pot from Chün Chou. Gray stoneware body covered with light blue glaze turning to olive green at edges and on ridges where thin. These plain blue Chün wares were valued highly by the Chinese. Sung. Ht. c. 8". Metropolitan Mus. of Art.

Fig. 318. Bulb bowl made in Chün Chou. Gray stone ware covered with pale blue and blue and purple glazes. Sung. Dia. c. 7½". Metropolitan Mus. of Art.

Fig. 319. Chun yao porcelain flower pot dish, having purple glaze flecked with grey and marked # 7 under base. 2½" by 8⅛". Gift of Mrs. Thos. D. Stimson. Seattle Art Mus.

In Sawankhalok, Siam, a heavy ware was made also possibly in Sung times. It is heavily potted of a greyish-white porcelaneous ware reddish brown where exposed and covered with a transparent glassy glaze often tinged with blue. The plates often have rings on the bottom where they were supported in the kiln, much as have the crude blue and white ones from the same section.

In Persia a ware with beautiful celadon glaze was made which can be distinguished simply by the porous and sandy body.

Finally there were many Japanese factories which made celadons and which we shall treat under that section and then some of the modern Japanese and Chinese factories have made exceedingly close copies, so close in fact that the collector must be careful.

CHÜN YAO

There are not so many kinds of Chün wares as there are celadons but at least five or six can be distinguished. The first was made in the early part of the Sung period not at Chün Chou as has often been said, but at Chün-t'ai (Chün terrace) in a place which is now Yü-chow in central Honan province and it continued well into the Ming period, for we learn from the *T'ao kung pu hui k'ao* that in Hsüan Tê and Chia Ching reigns vases and wine jars were supplied the court.

Fig. 320. Plates # 24 and # 25, Vol. II of the Eumorfopoulos Coll. showing four typical shapes of thinner and finer wares which Hobson surmised were of Kuan type although they were made at Chün chou, the place now known as Yu chou. Dish and bowl with ogee-edged flange are pale lavender blue grey. Dia. of foliated dish 10", of plain mottled dish 7½", of bowl 7" and ht. of jar 3½".

"Celadon" vase from Siam. Crudely potted light gray body burnt red-brown where exposed, covered with glassy transparent glaze faintly crackled. Ht. 5". John Platt–Warren E. Cox Coll.
Fig. 321. Plate # 27, Vol. II, of the Eumorfopoulos Coll. showing various shapes of "Kuan Chün." Hts. 2" to 4".

This ware is heavy grey stoneware burnt brown where exposed and sometimes particularly under the base and at the lip-rim showing brown, under the very thin parts of the glaze, or olive, where it is a little thicker. Chinese numerals 1 to 10 are carved on the bottom before glazing on this type and the *Po wu yao lan* tells us it is the best. The glaze slips from the upper edges where it is very thin down to thick pools in the bottom of the bowls and hangs in heavy ridges and even drops about projections or near the bottom. In this particular sort it is not crackled but shows Y and L shaped marks called by the Chinese "earthworm" marks which were caused by a crackle or uneven flowing together of the glaze which has not quite melted together, leaving no surface depression but little denser lines in which there are fewer bubbles than in the surrounding parts. The general color seems to be olive green in which there is an opaque pale blue occurring in the tiny bubbles with which the glaze is filled and which, having burst on the surface, cause pores which are called by the Chinese "ant tracks." Sometimes this whole glaze is infused with plum color or red but still preserves the olive at the thinnest places. At other times the warm colors run in streaks and mottlings in the blue which yet again may become quite definite patches or splotches sometimes taking on the vague forms of animals and birds or even of Chinese characters as may be seen in the pillow illustrated. (Fig. 324)

Fig. 322. A wonderful Chün bottle of grey stoneware burnt brown where exposed, and covered with blue and purple to plum clouds. Glaze under the base. Ht. 11½". Sir Percival David Coll.

This ware is confined almost entirely to bulb bowls, small jardinieres or flower pots with saucers and similar useful objects of heavy potting. The forms, though heavy, are accurate and well designed and well made.

Associated with this ware and probably from the same factory is the rougher type which the *Po wu yao lan* calls "coarse and thick and not beautiful." This is of buff sandy ware roughly finished at bottom with a foot-rim often deeper on the center edge than on the outer edge and a shallow cone unglazed under the foot. This same style is sometimes of grey ware burnt brown and with a glaze inside the foot. In both of these the colors are essentially the same but the glaze itself is more like thick glass and crackled. These never have the numerals and the glaze usually stops short of the base. It has been a silly collector's habit to call these all Yüan in period but they are certainly contemporary with the first described type and show many characteristics which would indicate that they are even earlier. Among these is the lack of scroll feet and other such involved forms, for they are all very simple and beautifully proportioned bowls, nearly globular vases, etc. (Pl. 48)

What even Hobson himself admitted may be an entirely arbitrary division

Sung dynasty Chün yao bowl of greyish white stoneware burnt brown where exposed and covered with a thick, blue, crackled, translucent g'aze which runs thin and shows olive green at the lip. Dia. 5¾". Warren E. Cox Coll.

Small Chün yao vessel with three legs after a bronze form, of porcelaneous ware with a blue glaze and purple clouding. Ht. 2⅜". Ex D. Abbes Coll.

Refined Chün dish of thin and careful potting of the type Hobson termed "possibly Kuan or Imperial ware." It is grey and dense, the foot-rim feeling smooth to the fingernail, and the glaze is pale blue shading to olive at the edge. Dia. 6". Ex John Platt– Warren E. Cox Coll. Mrs. Ogden K. Shannon, Jr.

Wide mouthed jar, Eumorfopoulos Col. # B80. "Grey porcelaneous ware, brown on the raw edges. Warm lavender glaze irregularly crazed and with splashes of purple shading to crimson. A wash of glaze under the foot. Kuan Chün," says Hobson. Ht. 4.9".

Rare Green Chün jar of dense grey stoneware which Hobson called "Chün ware of Kuan type," covered with a transparent, bubbly olive green glaze much like that of some Yüeh and Lung-ch'üan pieces. Ht. 5". John Platt–Warren E. Cox Coll. Note: The Chinese texts mention "crab-shell green" and also "parrot-green" which was a favorite color of Chün, yet few examples exist in western countries.

Left: Chün yao flower pot of grey ware with pale blue and lavender glaze. It has five drainage holes in the bottom and the incised numeral ssŭ (four) under the streaky brown glaze on the bottom. Ht. 8¼". Eumorfopoulos Coll. # C1.

Center: A Cha-tou (leys jar), possibly an incense burner of grey ware with white slip and transparent glaze of yellowish tone where thick. Sung period, said to have come from Yu Chou. Ht. 4". Baron C. T. von Seidlitz Coll.

Right: "Kuan Chün. Emorfopoulos Coll. # B78. Bubbly lavender glaze shading to pale brown at the mouth and splashed with plum-purple patches which break into grey and crimson." Hobson. Dia. 7.6".

"KUAN CHÜN" AND CHÜN WARES

PLATE 48

is probably simply a finer ware of the same kilns which is thinner in potting, has regular and narrow foot-rims and a perfectly controlled glaze that stops just short of the foot and is evenly applied under the foot. These too are not numbered but include many more delicately potted pieces than the first group such as small jars with covers, small "ting" (three legged incense burners), large foliated bowls, etc. The colors are essentially like the others again although one which I illustrate is of an even olive green similar to Yüeh yao celadon. They again are fairly evenly crackled and do not show "earthworm" marks. In the Küan yao section I have explained why I do not think these can possibly be maintained in that category and I believe them to have been made from early to late Sung times and perhaps even into Ming, for the shapes range from simple and beautiful ones to somewhat involved and unstructural forms.

Hole

Fig. 324. Southern Chün type pillow of late Sung or Yüan period (1127–1368 A.D.) of buff stoneware covered with a slightly opaque blue glaze and having a large character drawn on it in purple-red. This confutes the earlier theories to the effect that the color was due "to inequalities of heat in firing." The marks are actually made by the introduction of iron oxide in the body of the ware before glazing. Length about 11". Gift of Mrs. Samuel T. Peters. Metropolitan Mus. of Art.

Fig. 325. Small Southern Chün yao bowl ground down to show the introduction of iron in the body to produce the purple markings in the glaze on both outside and inside. When one surface only is to be marked the iron is pressed into the body under the glaze. Dia. 3½". T. C. Lee–Warren E. Cox Coll.

Fig. 323. Collapsed sagger with Chün bowl in it. Note the small hole at the side wall for transmission of gases. Also note that purple mark is far to the right of this hole. It has been said that the purple was due to inequalities of heat but it is obvious that such variations would be hard to make inside a sagger. Actually they are produced by iron particles in the body of the ware. Dia. 9". T. C. Lee–Warren E. Cox Coll.

These, then, are the three original Chün wares. Hseih Min lists the colors as "mei kuei tzŭ" (rose purple), "hai t'ang hung" (cherry-apple red), "ch'ieh hua tzŭ" (aubergine purple), "mei tzŭ ch'ing" (plum-bloom green), "lü kan ma fei" (donkey's liver and horse's lung), —— probably in derision —— "shên tzŭ" (deep purple), "mi sê" (millet color), "t'ien lan" (sky blue), "yao pien" (furnace tranmutation), etc. (I am using the Bushell-Hobson translation.) One thing was made clear and that is that the *Cho kêng lu* and the *Ko ku yao lun* do not even deign to mention these wares and even in Ming times the *Ch'ing pi ts'ang* says, "The best is uniform in color and has the numerals underneath. The mixed colors are not worth collecting." During the Yung Chêng period four kinds had to be sent for outside the Palace Collection for reproduction. Thus it was not until taste in China had become decadent that the ware was taken note of and it took our Western hemisphere millionaires to boost the demand because the color so appealed to their child-like instincts. The plain colors which the ancient collectors thought worth while were, "cinnabar red, parrot green and dark aubergine purple along with the 'ch'ing' or pale blue." A white ware was also made at Yu-Chou. (Pl. 48) For green Tung yao, similar to green Chün yao, see p. 160.

The numerals mentioned have been proven to indicate simply sizes although much nonsense was talked in the earlier days of our century about their indicating various qualities, etc. Numerals and poems cut in the glaze are of course of fairly recent date and mean nothing.

Mr. Hobson has written (*Chinese Pottery and Porcelain* page 118) (1915), "How far the old Chün effects were due to opalescence it is impossible to say, but we know that all of them can be obtained, whether turquoise, green, crimson, or lavender grey, by that 'Protean medium,' oxide of copper, according as it is exposed in the firing to an oxidizing or reducing atmosphere, conditions which could be regulated by the introduction of air on the one hand, or wood smoke on the other, at the right moment into the kiln." Through this passage the general impression has gained footing that the Chün splotches are accidental or uncontrolled. Perhaps they were at first but, as I have said, the potters soon became sufficiently proficient to be able to write characters on pieces. Now Chün wares were fired in individual saggers of heavy clay either set slightly apart so air could enter and escape or having a small hole to one side. How then in the world could a potter vary the conditions of his kiln so as to produce a given symmetry of splotches or even to write a character?—Obviously the explanation is not correct.

Through the offices of my friend Mr. T. C. Lee a small Chün "bubble bowl" was sent to me from China which had been examined by the Acadamei Sinica. This had been so broken as to expose a cross section at a point where the purple mark occurred and we found upon analysis of a small dark place in the body at this point that it is iron in an oxidized state. The placing of slight iron filings in the body made the purple mark *on both sides*. It is possible that simply pressing them into the clay on one side would affect that surface only. In any event we must come to the conclusion that this slight use of iron so affects the copper glaze as to make the irregular marks in it.

"Soft Chün yao" or, as the Chinese call it, "Ma-chün" was supposed to have been originated by a potter named "Ma" who worked in the late Sung period. It has a buff earthy body and a glaze more waxy and less glossy than Chün yao. It is a pale lavender blue or a deep peacock blue and seems not to run or slip so much as the Chün glaze. There is always a crackle and the splotches are usually of crimson color. These pieces are rare and have a beauty of their own in some ways more appealing than the original wares.

Finally there were imitations made at Yi-hsing and in Kwangtung during late Ming times and even down to the present, while at Chêng-tê Ching really beautiful copies were made in the 18th century but with white porcelain bodies as a rule. This rule was not always followed, however, and the ones with stoneware bodies are even more deceptive. Just recently I have seen pieces

FIG. 326. "Soft Chün yao" gallipot of buff stoneware covered with an opaque and porous blue glaze. These are usually called Yüan but I believe them to have been made from 1127 A.D. to well into the Ming dynasty. Gift of Mrs. H. O. Havemeyer. Ht. 9". Metropolitan Mus. of Art.

FIG. 327. Soft Chün small vase which shows a prominent crackle and opaque quality of the glaze. Ht. 5¾". Ming or later. Warren E. Cox Coll.

FIG. 328. Double gourd of "soft Chün" ware made of reddish buff stoneware covered with a thick glaze of lavender-blue and splashed in front with dull purple. Ming. Ht. 7½". Sir Percival David Coll.

FIG. 329. Green Chün ware jar with the rough, sandy buff foot of the "soft Chün type," Southern Sung. The glaze is thick, crackled and full of large bubbles many of which have burst on the surface. Ht. about 5". K. M. Semon Coll.

of the 20th century made at Yü-chow which are very close to the old wares indeed and these were of the type of shallow dishes having the olive green to brown glaze underneath and all characteristics very close to the old wares. In Japan the wares of Hagi, Akahada and Seto include similar glazes and some streaky Cantonese wares are similar and are called "Fat-shan Chün."

FIG. 330. Honan Tsung Sê tz'ü jar of rough and porous light buff stoneware covered with a lustrous blue-black glaze shading to tan at lip and lighter and more bluish about lower half. Sung. period. Ht. 6½". Warren E. Cox Coll.

TSUNG SÊ TZ'Ü
DARK BROWN COLORED POTTERY

It is recommended that we cease to use the name "Honan Temmoku" for these wares as they were made elsewhere and it is anomalous to use a Japanese word for a Chinese ware. "Chien yao" is also too narrow a term and can only properly be applied to the wares from certain sites in northern Fukien. I, therefore, at the suggestion of Mr. C. F. Yau have adopted the term TSUNG SÊ TZ'Ü meaning "palm leaf brown colored pottery" or "dark brown colored pottery." The word Tsung according to Giles derives from the brown leaves of the palm used in China for the making of brooms. Various other suggestions seem less good. Mr. Hochstadter says that he has used "Hei Sung tz'ŭ" successfully in asking for the wares in China but this literally means "black Sung pottery." A common term is Tzŭ chin tz'ŭ meaning "lustrous brown pottery," but this also has the implication of "purple brown," which is not always the case. Let us then adopt ᴛꜱᴜɴɢ ꜱᴇ̂ ᴛᴢ'ŭ as a more reasonable term generally covering all brown potter¡es wherever made and at whatever time.

The possibility has been pointed out that the thin mat brown glaze developed from the olive mat glazes of the Six Dynasties and we have illustrated an ewer which is likely of this period and another of the T'ang period having the brown glaze. As most of these glazes look like ground up brown or greenish brown tea-dust, I shall use this term to describe them. A sort of intermediate type may be called chocolate and then we finally come to the glossy or treacly glazes which I do not believe developed until toward the latter part of the Sung dynasty. No kiln had an exclusive use of these earlier glazes. They are about as natural and simple to come by as the old alkaline glazes of the Han period. Once our colored maid was dusting my collection and made the remark that they looked just like her old "mammy's salt pot " This is about true for they do not differ much from our Early American kitchen wares save in the fine techniques.

Mr. Hobson gives them the arbitrary name of "Honan Temmokus" and then proceeds to say at once that they also come from Chihli, Shantung, Shansi, Shensi, Anhwei and Kiangsu but he might have added all the other provinces that made pots, with perfect safety, for certainly the use of brown glaze was as universal as that of the green or celadon types, or for that matter the cream or Ting and Tz'u Chou types, these three being easiest to make and most pleasant for general use.

The word "Temmoku" is foreign and also narrow in its true application as is also the Chinese name "Chien yao" and neither should be used for this entire classification. There is an old Japanese tradition that their pirates used to swoop down on the Fukien province coast to loot and kidnap and that tea-bowls were demanded as ransom. In 1888 Hippisley published the information that these bowls came from "the department of Chien-chou, the present district of Chien-yang in the department of Chien-ning, Fukien province." That is in the most northern part. Pelliot is reported to have located the kiln site in the T'ien-mu Shan in Che-kiang. And recently Mr. Plumer has published further kiln sites. Hetherington says, "There was a mountain in the neighborhood of the place of manufacture called T'ien-mu Shan or the 'Eye of Heaven' mountain. In Japanese T'ien-mu Shan becomes Temmoku-zan. The name Temmoku is now applied to all tea-bowls with hare's fur marking whether made in Chien-yang or not." Now the term has unfortunately been broadened to include all brown wares as has also Chien yao with no better reason. I propose that these be called simply "Brown Wares" or, if we must have a Chinese term let us adopt "Tsung Sê tz'ŭ" (dark brown ware), even though this was not used by the ancient Chinese writers. One could so ask for them in China today and be understood.

Plumer went to the little villages of Hou-ching, Ta-lu and T'ieh-tun on the left bank of the Chien Ch'i river just north of Kien-ning in the northern part of the Fukien province, and found three large piles of sherds. At Shui-chi there was an open cut where the natives had mined their bowls for years. In Hou-ching a pig was eating from a sagger. There were only bowls varying from a few inches to a foot or more in diameter; no vases. They all had a grey body almost black and reddish where exposed and the glazes were typical

FIG. 331. Four Tsung Sê tz'ŭ tea-bowls. The top is an "oil spot" with grey body and black glaze silver spotted. The two on either side are of the Kian-fu, Kian-si province, type with greyish bodies and brownish black glazes with yellowish and buff floral and leaf motives. The bottom is said to have been found in Tz'u Chou and has a brownish black glaze with white sl.p and glazed rim. Dias. 5½" to 8". C. T. Loo & Co.

Chien yao type which we will describe. Mr. Plumer believes the kilns to have started in late T'ang times and to have run into Ming.

The *T'ao shuo* quotes a supposedly 10th century work, "In Fukien are made tea-bowls with ornamental markings like the mottling and spots on a partridge (chê ku pan). The tea-testing parties prize them." We need not quote the other books but they all speak of this Chien yao in the early texts. In the Ming period little was said but in Japan, due to the development of the tea ceremony (cha no yu) Chien yao came into great favor. These bowls are properly called Chien yao or, in Japanese, Temmoku.

The real ones have a rough stoneware body of very dark brown best described as reddish-black. It is open grained and earthy in feel. The glaze is of blue-black streaked and mottled with brown which appears to have forced its way up through the glaze making "hare's fur" or "partridge marking" effects. Rare specimens have small silver spots all over called by the Chinese "oil spots."

Mr. Hetherington quotes William Burton in explanation of these markings, "The glistening appearance as well as the fine striation both arise from

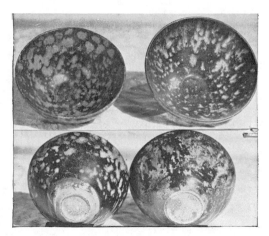

Two bowls of the so called "Kian Temmoku" type made of the typical greyish white ware and having the dull brown glaze and pale blue spots. This type would certainly appear to be earlier than those with ornate but skillfully handled designs in them. Dia. 4½". John Platt Coll. Warren E. Cox Coll. Note later type in lower right corner.

Honan tea-bowl (wan) of white porcelaneous ware dressed with brown-black where it is exposed and having a thick, black glaze showing silver "oil spots" so prized in Japan where it is called "yu teki temmoku." Dia. 3½". Sung. Sir Percival David Coll.

Three Chien yao or "Temmoku" tea-bowls showing "hare's fur" markings, the irregular drips of glaze near the bottom and the heavy dark rough body. Dias. 4½". Warren E. Cox Coll.

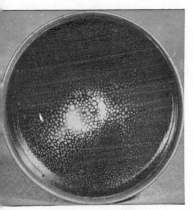

Honan tea-bowl reported to have a dark body, black glaze and showing the silver, "oil-spots." Dia. about 3". N. M. Heeramaneck Coll.

"Kian temmoku" bowl of the ware reported to have come from central Kiangsi. It is a rather crude gray stoneware with transmutation glaze of brown, yellow and bluish gray. Dia. 5½". Gift of Mrs. Thos. D. Stimson. Seattle Art Mus.

CHUNG TZE TEA BOWLS OF CHIEN, KIAN AND NORTHERN HONAN TYPES

PLATE 49

the fact that microscopically thin plates of artificial mica crystals segregate from the cooling glaze, while it is still somewhat fluid, and arrange themselves with their long axes parallel to the lines of flow of the glaze, thus producing the effect." He goes on to say that the "hare's fur" ones are Phlogopite glazes or those containing a considerable amount of iron called Biotite while the silvery spotted ones are either Phlogopite or Muscovite.

Usually the glaze slips so that the lip-rim is actually exposed and at times the Chinese added a silver rim but not, as was the case with Ting yao, because the piece was fired on its rim. A heavy irregular ridge of glaze forms near the bottom and there is a thick pool inside. No vases occur in this ware.

"Kian Ware" or Chi Chou Yao

Through hearsay alone, but which has never been confuted, Hobson gave the name of Kian Temmoku to another class of ware consisting of bowls and

FIG. 332. Vase called "Honan Temmoku" by the museum but actually quite like the so'called "Kian Temmoku" bowls in its rather soft buff body, glossy blue black glaze and small brown and blue spots. Probably Yüan or Ming. Ht. 13″. Gift of Mrs. Samuel T. Peters. Metropolitan Mus. of Art.

occasional vases. It is said that they are found near the old kiln sites at Yung-ho Chên in the department of Kian or Chi-an Fu in south central Kiangsi province. We hear that the bowls are found by dragging the river at this place and Hobson points out that it is likely that this would then be the "Chi Chou Yao" spoken of in the *Ko ku yao lun* and described as being brown (tzǔ), like that of Ting Chou but thick and coarse and "not worth much money." There is also a white ware, and a crackled ware like Ko yao was also made here, and during the Sung period there were five kilns of which that run by the Shu family was the best. This is the place where it was reported that when the Sung minister passed all the wares in the kilns turned to jade and the potters fearing that this portent might reach the ears of the Emperor fled to Chêng-tê Ching.

Actually there is a considerable divergence in technique and taste shown in the wares so lumped together, some being perhaps over refined and too ornate while others are exceedingly crude, but this may be due to the long time the kilns were working.

Probably fairly early are the bowls two of which are shown with rudimentary footrims and of thick and none too sure potting, covered with a mat brown glaze having splotches of pale blue both outside and in. The body is buff and gritty but more so on one than on the other. Perhaps a little later is the vase with the same glaze and technique of potting but on a slightly more refined body long called "Honan Temmoku" by the museum but certainly of this classification. And then toward the end of the Sung period and later we came to the bowls which have leaves, birds, etc., actually roughly drawn in them in dark brown against the blue and brown flecked ground. Perhaps the earlier ones of this type had the designs so roughly indicated that they seemed like natural accidents and one can imagine what a stir they must have caused in Japan. Some again show light decorations against dark brown glaze.

"KOREAN RED TEMMOKU" OR "RED TING?"

Almost certainly from Chihli province comes a fine white ware often as thinly and beautifully potted as Ting yao. It is covered either in part or all over (except for the foot rim on some, or the whole base on others) with a soft, mat, brownish red glaze which is amazingly absorptive and which often

FIG. 333. Light buff ware bowl with dull reddish brown glaze very similar to a sherd found in Samarra. This piece was found in Korea and is given a Korean attribution by the museum. Dia. 6″. Metropolitan Mus. of Art.

FIG. 334. Brown glazed bowl with well made light buff body. The glaze is washed in so as to leave an exposed area in the bottom. The foot rim is a strong argument that these wares are Chinese. Dia. 5¼″. Warren E. Cox Coll.

FIG. 335. Bowl given "Korai Korean" attribution at the museum as are all of their similar wares, but more likely Chinese in origin. Dia. 7¼″. Metropolitan Mus. of Art.

runs very thin (though it is all thinly applied) at the lip, and there has olive green tinges. Sometimes where it is a little thick it takes on the blue-black and glossy look of other glazes of the sort and even shows the "partridge breast" effect. In two bowls illustrated the thin glaze is used outside and the thick inside with drips running down the outside. When moisture is applied to these bowls they take it up almost as fast as blotting paper. Another beautiful treatment is like tortoise shell as can be seen on the outside of the finest specimen (Pl. 50) and this bowl is remarkable in another way, for just faintly traceable inside can be seen a charming floral design. I am told that this design was originally in gold and that slight traces of the metal itself can be seen on two specimens in the Rioke Museum in Seoul, Korea. This was reported by Sir Percival David who said he had seen no other specimens similar. Whether the gold was fired on or not he did not say.

The Metropolitan Museum and others have for years labeled these pieces "Korean" simply because a number have been found in that country although Bernard Rackham as far back as 1918 in the Catalogue of the Le Blond Collection put them in the doubtful category. They were called "kakigusuri" by the Japanese who attributed them to the T'ang period. Since our more detailed study of Sung ceramics there can be no slightest doubt but that they are of Sung period and made in China. It has been guessed that they might be the famous "red Ting" ware spoken of by ancient writers and, in truth, some of the pieces such as the bowl just described might be, but recently Mr.

Walter Hochstadter has said that he heard on good authority in China that they come from Ching-ho Hsien east of Tz'u Chou in Chihli province. There the matter will have to rest until excavations give us clearer evidence.

FIG. 336. Wine ewer of red glazed light buff ware often found in Korea but probably made in China. Ht. 7". Metropolitan Mus. of Art.

FIG. 337. White bodied vase with terracotta red glaze called by the museum "Tz'u Chou type," but which is often found in Korean tombs. Ht. 7½". Gift of Mrs. Samuel T. Peters. Metropolitan Mus. of Art.

FIG. 338. Vase called by museum "Korai Ting" and having a mottled red-brown glaze running to olive at lip where it is thin. It is more likely the "Red Ting" of tradition. Ht. 7¼". Metropolitan Mus. of Art.

TSUNG SÊ TZ'Ŭ, TZ'U CHOU YAO
BROWN POTTERY INCISED

The Tsung Sê tz'ŭ (Brown Pottery) found in the general district of Tz'u Chou in Chihli province has a similar glaze more brown than red and with a silvery sheen by reflected light. The body is buff and heavy but well potted

FIG. 339. Jar of the Tz'u Chou type although none of these may have actually been made there but just as likely in Chihli or Shansi as in Honan. Ht. 8". Ex Warren E. Cox Coll.

FIG. 340. Tsung Sê tz'ŭ vase possibly from Tz'u Chou, of buff-gray ware with dull, middle Sung type glaze of chocolate brown incised through and into body. Ht. 14". The Cleveland Mus. of Art. Dikran G. Kelekian Coll.

FIG. 341. Bowl possibly made at Tz'u Chou during the Sung period. The body is buff-grey and the glaze olive brown. Dia. 13¼". Mus. of Fine Arts, Boston.

Three finely potted examples with red glaze shaded at the lip-rims with olive green. The one on the right has a beautiful mottling of the back and the tracery of flowers which were in gold inside. Dias. about 4½″ and 3¼″. John Platt–Warren E. Cox Coll. Note: The kiln-site of these pieces are unknown and they vary considerably but the white body and thin potting makes it possible that some were made at Ting Chou and that they may be the "red Ting ware," mentioned in the old texts.

Jar of the "Kian Temmoku" from south western Kiang-si province of the same ware as the early type tea-bowls with rough body and streaked brown glaze. Early Sung. Note numeral five incised before firing. Ht. 10½″. Warren E. Cox Coll.

Two conical bowls such as are used for drinking tea in summertime, with glossy black glaze touched with red-brown inside and having the light red-brown glaze outside. The ware is greyish white. Dia. 5¾″; John Platt–Warren E. Cox Coll.

TSUNG SÊ TZ'U (DARK BROWN WARES)

FROM KIANG FU, CHING-HO HSIEN AND POSSIBLY TING CHOU

PLATE 50

Early Sung vase of the type made in northern Honan, Shansi and Chihli provinces. It has a brown body and olive green-brown "tea-dust" type glaze. The foot-rim is crude and low. (c. 960–1000 A.D.) Ht. 10½". Warren E. Cox Coll.

The mat glaze on this piece would indicate that it was of fairly early Sung period (c. 1100 A.D.) even though the design is florid and somewhat decadent. Ht. 12½". Ex Warren E. Cox Coll. C. T. Loo Coll.

Early Sung (c. 1000–1100 A.D.) Tz'u Chou vase with brown body and incised "tea dust type" brown glaze. Ht. 14½". Metropolitan Mus. of Art.

The more refined grey stoneware body and more glossy, better perfected glaze would indicate that this piece is of middle Sung period (c. 1100 to 1127 A.D.). Surely it shows no Mongol influence in the design. Ht. 11¾". Warren E. Cox Coll.

TSUNG SÊ WARES OF TZ'U CHOU TYPE

PLATE 51

Tsung Sê jar of the Tz'u Chou type with deep buff body and the typical mat brown glaze of Early Sung to possibly T'ang origin. The foot is very slightly concave. The neck is cut. Ht. 16". Warren E. Cox Coll.

One of the earliest Sung types of brown globular jars dating about 1000 to 1100 A.D. It has a brown body and greenish, tea-dust type glaze simply incised. Probably made in Shansi province. Ht. 13½". Warren E. Cox Coll.

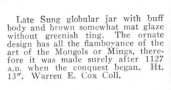

Late Sung globular jar with buff body and brown somewhat mat glaze without greenish ting. The ornate design has all the flamboyance of the art of the Mongols or Mings, therefore it was made surely after 1127 A.D. when the conquest began. Ht. 13". Warren E. Cox Coll.

Vase of Tz'u Chou type with buff body and mat brown glaze. The broad, low foot-rim places this as probably Sung and the glaze as of the early part of this dynasty. Ht. about 14". Diedrich Abbes Coll.

Tz'u Chou wine jar of light buff body covered with a mat brown glaze of typical late Sung type and incised with a very beautiful design of lotus blossoms and leaves. Ht. 9¾". Ex Samuel T. Peters Coll. Warren E. Cox Coll.

TSUNG SÊ INCISED JARS T'ANG TO LATE SUNG PERIOD

PLATE 52

and very much like that of the light glazed wares from Tz'u Chou and Chü-lü Hsien. The glaze is evidently applied all over and reaching down nearly to the foot, and then the design is scratched out with a sharp point which often cuts even into the body, and finally the background is scraped away on some pieces.

Although we give these the general name of T'zu Chou wares and though the body clay is quite similar to proven Tz'u Chou examples we must admit at once that the slightly bulging cylindrical forms, angular shoulders and rather flat everted lip-rims do not occur in the light glazed wares. Perhaps this was due to the personal taste of some one potter or perhaps they come from some nearby kiln.

Nearer to the usual Tz'u Chou form of tapered melon shape with everted lip-rim are several which I illustrate. The first has a nearly white body and chocolate brown glaze while the second is of a buff grey very hard stoneware with glossy brown glaze having a very slight greenish tinge where it is thickest. Certainly these must come from different kilns as undoubtedly yet again does the shorter one of buff ware with a distinctly olive glaze and the large globular one with a sort of oatmeal body and olive brown glaze. All of these are of Sung shapes but widely different materials. Let us tentatively place them in Chihli and Shansi provinces and it is fair to associate them with the Tz'u Chou type in general. Of these incised glaze wares the only ones which I should assign to Honan are the heavy globular large jars similar to the one shown but with more treacly glossy almost black glazes which we shall touch upon in the Yüan and Ming sections.

Smaller examples with the same rough body heavily potted and covered with a blue-black glaze running to brown streaks or sometimes brown with thick blue black areas running over them are also likely from Honan and of late Sung or later periods. These are set apart also by their uneven and poor potting, wobbly lip-rims, etc. They are not quite so rough as the Kian wares but exhibit more careless craftsmanship. Perhaps a few are of the Sung period but even this is doubtful. None of these have painted or incised designs. (See Ming Section.)

Returning to the more northerly provinces, there is one type of wide mouthed globular jar with perpendicular arrangements of ridges and two small loops from lip to shoulder which Mr. Hochstadter says have been found at Ch'ing-ho Hsien. The shape is certainly one of that region but these show none of the usual staining from submersion that the light wares do. Perhaps that is due to the denser glaze. Again there is the grey stoneware olive green tea-dust glazed pear shaped bottle with flying phoenix decoration in near black which he claims was found near Ho-chou in Shansi province and which is truly and beautifully potted. This is just a little heavier than the beautiful buff ware bottles with glossy brown glaze having a silvery sheen and silver birds or brown ones painted on them which I think may very well be actual Tz'u Chou pieces. Their shapes are among the most graceful and well proportioned of all ceramic wares, and the counterparts in the same body but with cream slip and brown decoration are of the same size and shape. Others with buff and buff-grey bodies are covered with glazes ranging from the

Vase with wheel marks about the body. Buff stoneware covered with a dull "tea-dust" type of glaze which I believe was used on the earlier type. Probably early Sung. Shansi province. Ht. 14½". Ex Warren E. Cox Coll. Walter Hochstadter Coll.

"Honan temmoku" jar of hard, smooth grey stoneware covered with a blue black glaze having streaks of light brown. Late Sung to Early Ming (c. 1127 to 1400 A.D.). Ht. 8". Warren E. Cox Coll.

Late Sung or early Ming jar carefully designed with rounded shoulder so that they would roll and not break when knocked over, and a small neck with wide mouth and heavy lip which is easy to grasp. Dark brown stoneware with dull brownish black glaze. Ht. 11". Warren E. Cox Coll.

Buff stoneware vase covered with a dull chocolate colored glaze, unlike earlier examples which have a slightly greenish tinge. The everted lip has degenerated into a simple cylindrical mouth with a bulge. Late Sung or even later. Ht. 14". Warren E. Cox Coll.

"Honan temmoku" jar. Buff grey body over which is a thin dressing of brown slip, and a thick black iridescent glaze showing light brown at lip-rim and on handle loops. Sung period. Ht. 8". Warren E. Cox Coll.

Jar of typical Sung shape attributed to Ch'ing-ho Hsien. Grey stoneware, glossy blue-black glaze streaked with brown. Ht. 9". Ex Warren E. Cox Coll. Walter Hochstadter Coll.

Jar possibly from Honan but having a grey stoneware body heavily made and a black glaze of plum tone showing iridescence. Sung period. Ht. 6¾". Ex Warren E. Cox Coll. Mrs. Ogden K. Shannon, Jr.

Flower pot with five holes in the bottom. Brown stoneware covered with black glaze running in brown and bluish streaks. Ming period. "Honan Temmoku." Ht. 8½". Warren E. Cox Coll.

TSUNG SÊ UNDECORATED WARES EARLY SUNG TO MING

PLATE 53

tea-dust to the glossy type and are of typical Tz'u Chou shape (an elongated tapering melon form) but have somewhat modified lip treatments and for decoration only more or less prominent helical grooves executed in turning. These again are beautiful examples of potting in which is caught the very touch and movement of the potter's hand. They must certainly be from southern Chihli or eastern Shansi if not from Tz'u Chou itself.

FIG. 342. Tz'u Chou bottle of beautiful form, of light buff stoneware with glossy varicolored brown glaze and painted with flying birds in iron lustre. Late Sung (1100–1127 A.D.). Ht. 11½". Warren E. Cox Coll.
FIG. 343. Ching-ho Hsien jar of almost white ware with mat black glaze having iron-rust spots evenly distributed. Ht. 5". Warren E. Cox Coll.
FIG. 344. Grey stoneware jar treated with white slip, brown decoration and yellowish transparent glaze. Dr. Oscar Rücker-Embden called it Tz'u Chou which it probably is. Ht. 9¾".
FIG. 345. The close similarity in shape and design treatment of the Tsung Sê tz'ǔ globular jars to the Tz'u Chou one shown would seem to indicate that they too were made in Tz'u Chou. Buff-grey stoneware, greenish "tea-dust" type glaze which I associate with early Sung wares. Ht. 14". Warren E. Cox Coll.

Another closely associated group and very likely from the same source consists of globular jars with small mouths having modified everted lip-rims and made from light buff to dark brown clay. These too have tea-dust to glossy glazes and painted bird or floral designs.

Finally there are many odd wares which have body clays ranging from white to dark red-brown or hard grey stoneware and glazes of plain, rich, lustrous, iridescent black, of rich brown, of mottled and even of the "tobi seiji" technique which we have seen in the celadons, which we cannot place at all but which have characteristic shapes of the Sung period and techniques of Sung potting. These indicate many kilns some of which we hope will be found in the future.

The appeal of these wares is not at once apparent but for flower containers against a light background there is a beauty in them which grows upon one. They have always commanded fairly high prices and have not missed the attentions of imitators in Japan and elsewhere. Others of the Tsung Sê tz'ǔ yao group will be described under the Yuan and Ming sections.

TING YAO

Hirth (*Ancient Chinese Porcelain,* op. cit., p. 4) discovered a passage in the *T'ang pên ts'ao* (pharmacopoeia of T'ang dynasty) compiled about A.D. 650 which mentions "pai tz'ǔ" or "white ware" made at Ting Chou and it is likely that some of the pieces found at Samarra came from this site in central

Amphora made in Ching-ho Hsien north east of Tz'u Chou dating before 1108. Greyish white, black glaze with splashes of iron rust some of which are on the foot and the unglazed body inside the mouth showing they were applied by hand and were not glazed accidentals. Ht. 11″. Warren E. Cox–Mrs. C. P. Wilson Coll.

"Tz'u Chou" bottle of hard grey stoneware with brown glossy glaze and a design of flying bird quite typical in silvery lustre. Late Sung period (1100–1127 A.D.). Ht. 12″. Ex Warren F Cox Coll.

Two "Tz'u Chou" jars of the usual well potted buff-grey or brown stoneware. The one on the left has a greenish "tea-dust" glaze with black design and is earlier than the other which has a glossy blue-black glaze and design in iron-lustre-brown. Hts. 8½″ and 7″. Warren E. Cox Coll. Note: The close similarity in the body materials, the development of the glazes and the flying bird designs, almost always seen, make it fairly certain that these globular jars and the pear shaped vases were both made in the same place and that is very likely Tz'u Chou.

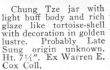

Chung Tze jar with light buff body and rich glaze like tortoise-shell with decoration in golden lustre. Probably Late Sung origin unknown. Ht. 7¼″. Ex Warren E. Cox Coll.

Bottle of buff stoneware with "tea dust" type of glaze and birds painted on it in black said to have come from Shan-si province. Sung period. Ht. 10½″. Ex Walter Hochstadter Coll. Warren E. Cox Coll.

Two jars of almost white body, heavily potted and with broad foot-rims. Blue-black glaze with iron-brown spots at even intervals. Probably late Sung to Early Ming, province unknown, possibly Honan. Hts. 12″. Warren E. Cox Coll.

CHUNG TZE DECORATED WARES

PLATE 54

western Chihli province just southwest of Peking. The place is now called Chên-ting Fu. In the *Ko ku yao lun* we find that the best wares were made during the years A.D. 1111 to 1125, therefore the ware must have improved after the royal patronage was taken from it because of flaws in the glaze and given to the Ju Chou potters. In 1127 when the court fled the potters went along and settled near Chêng-tê Ching where they made "nan ting" or Southern Ting supposedly almost undistinguishable from the former product. Actually identified pieces have not been established by western collectors. That some of the potters remained is proven by the Administrative Annals

FIG. 347. Ting yao bowl of the Sung period with a graceful design of lotus incised on the outside which is less often seen than decoration on the inside. Dia. 6½". Ex D. Abbes Coll.

FIG. 346. One of a pair of pai-ting dishes with molded design of mandarin ducks, symbols of marital fidelity. Note that the lip-rim has been left unglazed though the flat rim would not permit its having been fired upside down. Dia. 4". N. M. Heeramaneck Coll.

FIG. 348. Rare black Ting yao bowl with typical cream white glaze inside showing spur marks, an unglazed rim and the outside coated with a brown-black teadust type glaze of considerable richness. Dia. 8½". Ex John Platt–Warren E. Cox Coll. Judge Edgar Bromberger Coll., Brooklyn Mus

of the Ming Dynasty which states that wine jars were supplied the court in the Hsüan Tê period (1426–1435) and again in 1553 and 1563. There is also a mold in the B.M. which bears the "nien hao" or honorific title of the Emperor Ta Ting (the actual date corresponds with A.D. 1189) of the Chin Tartar dynasty.

The *Ko ku yao lun* gives the earliest description mentioning the "lei hên" or tear-stains which are slightly straw colored places usually on the outside of the bowls where the glaze runs thicker and were regarded as a sign of genuineness. It also mentions "hua hua," engraved decoration, "yin hua" impressed decoration and "hsiu hua" which can only mean painted designs although we have never seen any of these. The wares in order of their importance are "fên ting" or flour ting, "pai ting" or white ting and "t'u ting" or earthy ting which had a yellower glaze. The Chinese writers also speak of "tzǔ ting" which would be brown or purple, "huang ting" or red ting "like carved red jade," purple ting and black ting. The *T'ao shuo* mentions Ting

FIG. 349. Group of Ting ware of Sung period including a rare and beautiful small dipper and a heavy pure white bowl in the center of upper shelf. John Platt–Warren E. Cox Coll. C. T. Loo & Co.

yao "mottled like hare's fur." Of these wares we are certain of the first three classifications and the black Ting yao which is surely the type of bowl with black outside and creamy glaze inside or on rare occasions black all over. These are of the same ware and identical style of potting and some of them have a slight indication of the "hare's fur" markings. But of the purple which

FIG. 350. One of pair of stem cups stated on good authority to be Sung although the shape would certainly be more expected in the Ming period, of creamy white porcelaneous ware with cream glaze. Ht. 4". Ex D. Abbes Coll.

FIG. 351. Ting yao "cup stand" or cup attached to stand of what appears to have been a pure white ware but now somewhat stained brownish. Ht. about 3½". Gift of Mrs. Samuel T. Peters. Metropolitan Mus. of Art.

FIG. 352. Ting yao bowl rather heavily potted but of clear white color and with a freely and beautifully incised design of lotus flowers. Foot is glazed, lip rim left unglazed and mounted with a silver rim. Dia. 8". Gift of Mrs. Samuel T. Peters. Metropolitan Mus. of Art.

appears in Hsiang Yüan-p'ien's *Album* none has appeared and we are inclined to believe that he relied on a misconception of the ancient texts. And of red Ting yao there is nothing except the very fine white bodied Tsung Sê tz'ŭ yao often called "Korean" and mentioned previously. This probably is not the

Pai-ting bowl with center medallion only decorated with incised design of two fish among waves. Has original silver rim. John Platt–Warren E. Cox Coll. Dia. 8¼".

Typical bowl from Ting Chou with incised floral design and sharply raised radial lines to give it a floral form. Dia. 7½". N. M. Heeramaneck Coll.

Fine dish with low relief design made over a mold. Sung dynasty. Dia. 8⅜". Metropolitan Mus. of Art.

Fine Pai Ting shallow bowl with small foot. This is the type made by patting the clay over a mound on which was the engraved design so that in reverse it appears on the bowl in low relief. Note the fine drawing in the flying goose. Dia. 6½". Has original metal rim. John Platt–Warren E. Cox Coll. This is perhaps the finest known to Western collectors.

T'ING WARES INCISED AND MOLDED

Plate 55

ware (though it is fully as delicate) because the method of potting is different, the foot ring being left unglazed and the bowls being fired right side up.

Ting yao is of white or slightly greyish, dense porcelaneous ware usually high fired enough to ring but not always. It is slightly translucent and is covered with a more or less transparent glaze of pure white or light ivory tone usually not crackled in the fên and pai classes but with crackle in the t'u ting. It has always been written that the bowls were fired upside down on the lip-rims to keep them from wilting and distorting their shapes during firing. Here we come to an interesting modern finding. Mrs. Ogden K. Shannon Jr. of Fort Worth, Texas, brought in the observation that the running of the tear-stains was usually *toward the bottom* and not away from it as we should expect, if the above statement is correct. Upon examination of many bowls her observation was found to be true, though amazingly enough hundreds upon hundreds of collectors had never raised the question. There seemed no reason to the thing. The bowls simply could not have been fired right-side up for there was so sign of spur marks or other support and the foot-rims were covered with glaze which surely would have stuck had they

FIG. 353. Sung period Ting yao vase of bronze form. The ware is nearly white and the glaze an impure white. Ht. about 8″. Gift of Mrs. Samuel T. Peters. Metropolitan Mus. of Art.

FIG. 354. Sung period Tu Ting pilgrim bottle. Form similar to those which showed Roman influence in the T'ang period but with simplified design. Light buff, glaze brownish, purplish and gray due to staining during firing. Ht. about 8″. Gift of Mrs. Samuel T. Peters. Metropolitan Mus. of Art.

rested upon the foot-rim. In a general discussion I brought the problem to the attention of Mr. Walter Hochstadter and, after considerable deliberation, he suddenly hit upon the only reasonable solution:—The bowls were fired standing upright on edge, probably in a rack of some sort into which the unglazed edge could be slipped. Upon more careful examination it was found that the glaze does not *all* run toward the foot-rim, though it appears to, for the heaviest accumulation is at that point of stoppage; it does run

Tu Ting (earth Ting) cove
with cream colored glossy glaze l
ing brown crackle. Foot and bott
both glazed, rim being ungla
and bound with metal rim. 1
6½". John Platt–Warren E. (
Coll.

Left to Right: Unique Ting yao jar with typical white glaze showing "tear stains" and forming a large globule
greenish brown where it runs thick inside of bottom. The body is white and porous and left exposed at bottom.
4½". Warren E. Cox Coll.—Greyish white vase probably made at Ting chou, heavily potted, covered with w
slip over incised design. Transparent glaze inclined to darken into "tear stains" where thick and even into a gre
brown drop as shown just below the shoulder. Ht. 12⅜". Warren E. Cox Coll.—Sung period Ting yao bottle of p
white or pai ting ware. Note that the potter has purposely left the marks of his templet with which he shaped
Ht. 11". Ex Warren E. Cox Coll. C. T. Loo Coll.

Left: Tu Ting vase of the Sung period. Thinly potted buff gray porcelaneous ware covered with a crea
glaze. The design of four clawed dragons on front and back is in relief from the mold while the sides are de
rated with incised clouds. It is of the bronze form called Hu and hexagonal in plan. Ht. 12¾". Ex Samuel
Peters Coll. Ex Warren E. Cox Coll.—Baron C. T. von Seidlitz.
Center: Sung period Tu Ting gourd shaped bottle of buff ware with glossy, finely crackled glaze over an incised
sign. Note the typical horizontal ridges where the sections are joined together. Ht. 12". Metropolitan Mus. of A
Right: Two Tu ting vases with incised design under a soft creamy and glossy glaze which is mottled with I
ender about the shoulder of the larger piece. Hts. 8¾" and 9¾". Warren E. Cox Coll.

PAI TING AND TU TING WARES SUNG DYNASTY

PLATE 56

away on one side opposed to that side where the tear stains show most markedly. Our thanks to two enthusiastic and most observant collectors!

It was the custom to cover the unglazed lip-rim with a copper or silver rim but these are often missing or have been replaced by modern ones usually of heavier construction. When replaced the collector should beware of hidden chips in the rim.

The impressed ornamentation was done by means of a mold in the form of a mound carved with the low relief design. The clay for the bowl was pressed down over this and when partially dry shaved off with a knife to the proper thinness. A detail of this beautiful work is illustrated. (Pl. 55) The incising was swiftly done with a sharp instrument and was in outline only. Collectors have a mistaken idea that the incised pieces are more to be desired than the impressed, for only one of a kind was made. However there are no duplicates of the impressed ware known, there was nothing careless in their execution and they appear in the very finest quality of pieces. This is once when the use of the mold shows not the slightest decadence.

Besides the bowls vases were made in ancient bronze forms and occasionally in the most beautiful slender pear shaped forms such as the one illustrated. Some of these are of the true fên and pai quality. Most of the t'u ting ware consists of vases, some also of sensitive and beautiful form, and all well potted though just slightly heavier and lower fired than the others. The body may appear slightly greyish or ivory where exposed. In the Eumorfopoulos Collection is a bowl #188 with the mark under the bottom "ta sung hsi ning ni en tsao" or "made in the Hsi period of the great Sung dynasty" (A.D. 1068–1077). (See Burton & Hobson *Marks on Pottery and Porcelain.*) Therefore these are definitely of the Sung period although some of the more ornate and involved forms may be later or at least after A.D. 1127 when the Tartar taste would have had effect. Due to impurities which may or may not have been accidental in the body clay, many of these wares of a basic ivory tone have cloudings of subtle rosy and lavender tints that enhance their beauty. Some were molded in low relief while others have "secret design" decoration delicately incised so as often to be hardly visible under the quite transparent glaze. (Pl. 56)

So far as I know there were no wares made at Ting Chou with a slip while those at T'zu Chou being of darker clay were always dressed with a slip, therefore it seems confusing to me to include, as Hobson does in his descriptions, slip treated wares under the heading of Ting yao. Let us make this arbitrary division and call the light bodied wares Ting type and the dark bodied, slip dressed ones Tz'u Chou type.

Besides the Southern Sung Ting yao made at Chêng-tê Ching a great many other places copied this ware more or less accurately but never approaching the original in conception or technique. Hsiang yao is described by the old writers as being rich and lustrous with "crab's claw" crackle and valued when fine but not when it was coarse and yellow. This was probably made at Hsiang-shan in Chekiang near Ning-po south of Hang-chow Bay. Fêng-yang had a substitute at Su Chou in Anhwei but it was inferior. In Ssŭ-chou in the same province there was a "bargain lover's" Ting yao and at Hsüan Chou another. Brinkley speaks of a ware "Nyo-fu" which has an earthy looking body and is very light in weight. We have seen an example of this with poorly impressed design and a pitted glaze having slight hardly perceptible Ying-ching bluish cast. At the "White Earth Village" Pai-t'u Chên near Hsiao Hsien in northwestern Kiangsu or southern Shangtung a ware was noted "very thin, white and lustrous, beautiful in form and craft," and here were some thirty kilns employing hundreds of potters. Actually sherds found there are greyish, slip covered and with a warm creamy crackled glaze, probably not of the type described at all. We illustrate an interesting vase reported to have been found at Hsiang-hu Shih southeast of Chêng-tê Ching in Kiangsi province which is well potted from a white clay that is slightly pinkish where exposed perhaps due to the earth in which it was buried. The glaze is glossy white with irregular places of crackle. The foot is roughly potted not unlike the Kian Tzŭ Chin wares, but it grows thinner higher up and the lip-rim is thin and well potted.

Hobson states that the *T'ao shuo* speaks of four factories in Shansi under the heading of Hsi yao. They are P'ing-yang Fu in the southern part, Ho Chou also in that part, Yu-tzŭ Hsien in the T'ai-yüan prefecture in the north and P'ing-ting Chou in the west. These probably all date from T'ang times and the Ho Chou was supposed to be the best ware of "fine, rich material, the body unctuous and thin, the colour usually white." The poorest was from Yu-tzŭ Hsien, "a coarse pottery."

Many other kilns are recorded and many wares have been found which do not seem to fit any of the descriptions. It is a field upon which many books will be written in future years as the evidence piles up.

Tz'u Chou Yao

Always loved and cherished by the Chinese people and crystallizing into one medium perhaps the best of the taste of this purest and most Chinese of all periods was the T'zu Chou type pottery embodying at once the greatest mastery of form with the uttermost perfection of restrained decoration. In the *Ko ku yao lun*, later quoted by the *T'ao lu* almost verbatim, it is said that "The good kinds are like the Ting ware, but without tear stains. Some specimens have engraved ornament (hua hua), while others are painted (hsiu hua). For even the plain ones the price is higher than that of Ting ware." When Mr. Hobson gives this passage he notes that, "None of them, however, can be said seriously to challenge the Ting ware." And here I beg to differ for reasons we shall state as we go along. The one is a very perfect and beautiful ware within a narrow scope; the other shows more breadth of conception, greater mastery of technique, a human quality closer to the hand of the potter, a natural quality full of the Taoist or Zen Buddhist spirit, moods of power, of delicate beauty, of humor and of many other human emotions.

The most important center of manufacture was Tz'u Chou now in southern Chihli but formerly included in northern Honan. The place was called Fu-yang but the name was changed in the Sui dynasty (A.D. 589–617) because of the "tz'u" stone found there and according to Chinese authorities it was a pottery center even at that time. This may be true for there were

Three Tz'u Chou type vases with blue glaze. Larger of brown stoneware with white and brown slip under deep sapphire blue, crackled glaze. Flat foot, swift drawing and shape indicate that it is Sung.—The smaller one beside it has typical S form of early Ming, deep foot-rim and glaze, though deep, is not so fine as first. It is also not crackled.—The other example is typical later Ming with paler blue glaze, crowded design and double foot-rim. Hts. 17½″, 9½″, and 10″.—Largest vase Warren E. Cox Coll. Others Ex Warren E. Cox Coll. Note: Blue glazed Ts'u Chou wares are rare and all are inclined to have the glaze chip away from the body.

BLUE GLAZED T'ZU CHOU TYPE JARS OF SUNG AND MING

PLATE 57

pieces of the ware in the 9th century site of Samarra and old Chinese writing records finding it in T'ang tombs. The K'ang Hsi encyclopaedia notes that wine jars were furnished the Court in Hsüan tê and Chia Ching Ming times, and the *T'ao lu* mentions the continued existence of the factories there in the 18th century. Thus there must have been a tremendous and varied output.

In general the body of this ware is described as putty colored or buff-grey

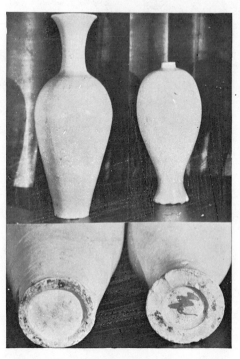

FIG. 355. Two early Sung Tz'u Chou type vases both having buff stoneware body, white slip somewhat imperfectly applied and transparent glaze. The larger is slightly yellowish. Note completely different methods of potting of bases which indicate different kilns. Hts. 21¼" and 15¼". Warren E. Cox Coll. and Warren E. Cox–John Platt Coll.

FIG. 356. A simple and fine form of a Tz'u Chou vase called by the Chinese "Woman form." A number of the undecorated wares have dark brown tea dust type glaze at lip-rim and in mouth. Metropolitan Mus. of Art.

and the Sung period ones are dense and smooth to the touch. The later Ming period ones are inclined to be either sandy buff or harder porcelain. Some of the wares from other kilns are also buff but less gritty during the Sung period. Over this ware and usually down to near the foot or right to the foot a slip was applied probably by dipping. This slip is nothing but a refined white or cream colored clay brought to the consistency of cream. It was used to fill the small imperfections in the body and to make a light ground. The decoration then consists either of cutting lines or removing areas of this slip so that the grey body color shows through, or of painting the design on it

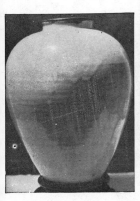

Fig. 357. Superbly classic form and rich cream-white glaze make this an outstanding example of Tz'u Chou art. Buff stoneware, lip and inside treated with a mat brown glaze. Note "wheel-marks" use of the drips of slip to give interest to an otherwise plain surface. Ht. 13". Ex Warren E. Cox Coll. Delos Chappell Coll.

Fig. 358. Tz'u chou type vase. Gray stoneware covered with creamy slip and transparent glaze making it eggshell color. The design is incised in the slip and rubbed in with brown pigment under the glaze to give an inlayed effect not unlike what the Japanese call "mishima" in Korean celadon wares. Note the way the stems enclose the flowers and also the vigorous spiral drawing of the lotus petals at the bottom. Ht. 16¾". Ex Samuel T. Peters Coll. Warren E. Cox Coll.

Fig. 359. Tz'u Chou type vase found at Chü-lu Hsien and dating before 1108 A.D. Buff gray covered with a slip and incised with a beautiful all over design of flowers toned to old ivory through action of the soil. Ht. about 11". Metropolitan Mus. of Art.

Fig. 360. Tz'u Chou buff body covered with white slip painted in dark brown over the finely crackled glaze. Russell Tyson Coll. Courtesy of The Art Institute of Chicago.

Fig. 361. Three typical Chu-lu Hsien vases. Early Sung type buff stoneware. White slip and cream glaze showing crackle and stains due to inundation in A.D. 1108. Hts. 10" to 11". Warren E. Cox Coll.

Fig. 362. Chü-lu Hsien ewer showing Near Eastern influence in shape. Grey stoneware covered to near bottom with white slip, having colorless transparent glaze finely crackled and slightly stained from burial. Ht. 11½". Ex D. Abbes Coll.

Left: Rare dated Tz'u Chou type vase. Characters about neck read, right to left or clockwise: "Great Sung Kia T'ai three made," and as Kia T'ai took throne in 1201, this would indicate the year 1203. Body buff, glaze straw colored and not crackled and design in black. From southern kiln site perhaps near Hang Chou. Ht. 7". Ex Warren E. Cox Coll. Metropolitan Mus. of Art.

Right: Wine jar designed to be rolled on side for pouring. Body yellowish buff, decoration brown and glaze yellow tinted and transparent without crackle. Characters are a *chiang ch'en tsze* or "flute lyric." Finest of the type ever to come to western hemisphere. See text for translation of poem made by Mr. Nai-Chi Chang and Mr. C. F. Yau. Ht. 14¾". Ex Tonying & Co. Warren E. Cox Coll.

RARE T'SU CHOU VASES WITH INSCRIPTIONS

PLATE 58

in dark brown or black over which the transparent glaze is applied. Many variations were developed which we can note as we proceed, and many of the vases were made simply with the slip and glaze without decoration. The glaze is usually slightly straw color and sometimes finely crackled and sometimes not. By adding copper or cobalt a rich green or light blue could be obtained and toward the end of the period a deep sapphire blue was made which continued into Ming times in the well known gallipots on which are painted figures under a blue glaze. The finest of these prototypes is illustrated herewith along with an early Ming example and a typical later Ming example. It may be Late Sung to Early Ming.

Fig. 363. Vase from Chü-lu Hsien, similar to one at Metropolitan Mus. but with more dynamic, stylized design. Ht. 8¾". Freer Gallery of Art, Washington.

Fig. 364. Vase reported found at Chü-lu Hsien. Grey stoneware with usual black and white slip decoration and incised lines. Form similar to those in Tz'u Chou, but somewhat wider. Ht. c. 11". Metropolitan Mus. of Art.

Fig. 365. Vase probably from Ch'ing-ho Hsien. Yellow-brown glaze typical of that place painted into incised design over white slip and transparent glaze. Ht. 13". Metropolitan Mus. of Art.

Other sections which produced this beautiful Tz'u Chou yao have been traced. Just northeast in Chihli province is Chü-lü Hsien only about 70 miles from Tz'u Chou where we know that an inundation occurred in 1108. Here are found wares of a soft, creamy feeling which have been stained a reddish brown in some places and this stain has accented the crackle of the glaze pleasantly. The body clay is buff here but also dense and smooth. The foot-rim is usually a little heavier than that of the Tz'u Chou wares. Gallipots usually have flaring horizontal lip-rims rather than everted ones. Large ovoidal bowls are typical as are also small amphora shaped vases on conical bases and with widely flaring lip-rims. Many of what appear to be the earlier wares have T'ang characteristics and are plain. Incising of the body was practiced and later incised designs were filled in with a black glaze with details scratched in it while the background was filled in with white. The style of the design was vigorous and smart as may be seen by the illustrations.

Just a bit further along the river is the site of Ch'ing-ho Hsien where a

Rare type vase. Buff-grey ware with white slip, black decoration and over-all green glaze. Ht. 12″. Benjamin d'Ancona Coll.

Incised vase. Soft ivory brown stained color with beautiful design. Ht. 13″. Ex Warren E. Cox Coll.

Fish-bowl of buff stoneware with white slip and cream glaze showing brown irregular crackle. Five spur marks inside. Dia. 9½″. Warren E. Cox Coll.

Bowl said to have been found at Chü-lu Hsien. Gray ware with incised black and white design of slips. Ht. c. 6″. Metropolitan Mus. of Art.

Buff pottery vase with black decoration and filled-in white slip. Ht. 19½″. Ex C. T. Loo & Co. Mr. Hsieh's Coll.

SUNG T'SU CHOU TYPE WARES FROM CHÜ-LU HSIEN

PLATE 59

similar ware was made but instead of the black glaze a greenish brown glaze was employed in a similar manner and also painted on over the glaze quite thickly. Sir Percival David has said that on the whole the Ch'ing-ho Hsien wares are potted better and are more choice than the Chü-lü Hsien ones. The body clay here is a bit more grey and seemingly denser.

Still other sections produced similar wares in abundance for they were very popular, and slowly we are gaining ground in the identification of certain types. Thus in Shansi province to the west at Ping yang Fu just south of Ho Chou a type was made which is crude in technique, quite possibly intentionally to produce a natural or close to earth feeling, but which are often beautiful in form as may be seen in the example shown herewith.

At Wei Hsien in Shantung province were found some Tz'u Chou type painted wares in a Sung tomb and some of these had the light blue glaze.

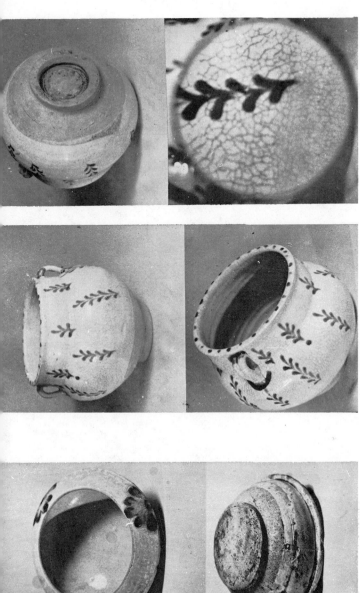

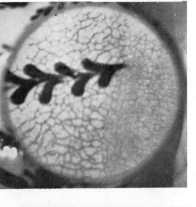

(b)

(a)

(a) Ching-ho Hsien or Chü-lu Hsien bowl of T'ang period. Buff stoneware with straw colored slip and glaze, decorated with peculiar green-brown transparent glaze. Chinese had written that these kilns were in operation in T'ang times but this is the only example which has come to light. Note flat bottom and heavy potting. Dia. 6⅞". Warren E. Cox Coll.

(b) Ching-ho Hsien jar of buff-grey stoneware with white slip and creamy, crackled glaze decorated in greenish brown transparent enamel with delicate sloping design of leaf-stems. Ht. c. 7". Given Metropolitan Mus. by Mrs. Wilfred H. Wolfs, Mr. John Platt's daughter, in his memory.

T'ANG AND SUNG WARES FROM CHING-HO HSIEN

PLATE 60

Hobson seems to decide out of hand that these were made at Po Shan Hsien where he says kilns have been in operation "time out of mind," but this is doubtful for the only wares we have which can definitely be attributed to Po Shan are quite different. Laufer described some of the Wei Hsien pieces as having a light reddish or reddish buff body which was often completely dipped in white slip as though to hide it. The glaze is also a little more glassy than that of the Tz'u Chou Yao and where painted decorations occur

FIG. 368. Pilgrim bottle which was made at Po-shan according to its inscription. Buff-grey with white slip, painted in black under a transparent glaze. Note the slanting keyfret border and the rather close decoration of cloud scrolls about it. Ht. 16½". Eumorfopoulos Coll. # C299.

FIG. 366. Vase made in Shansi province probably at Ping Yang Fu or Ho chou, of gray stone ware, incised and then covered all over with white slip and a transparent glaze showing crackle in some areas. The background of the design is then covered with a brownish black glaze. Ht. 15¾". Ex Samuel T. Peters Coll. Warren E. Cox Coll.

FIG. 367. Two vases possibly from Po-shan. The vase on the left with script decoration is of gritty buff clay with black specks though the glaze is of a creamy sort over white slip more usually associated with Tz'u Chou. Base is more crudely potted, without glaze under it.

The vase on the right is of gritty buff clay, lighter in weight, glaze is transparent and of light straw color over white slip. Both have the typical "tea dust" type brown glaze around the lower parts. Sung period. Ht. 13". Warren E. Cox and John Platt Colls.

they are nearly black but being underglaze are not as strong a black as the Chü-lü Hsien color. Another type found at Wei Hsien is buff to brown rough ware heavily potted in melon shaped vases with small mouths and slightly flaring heavy lip-rims. There are usually three or four small loops on the shoulder as though for tying on a covering. The lower third and under the foot, but leaving the rim exposed, is covered with a tea-dust mat type of brown glaze. The upper third is covered with a white slip on which are very summarily painted flying birds and plant or flower forms and rarely four characters in the same brown under a yellowish transparent uncracked glaze. Hobson again assigns these to Po Shan but the attribution is now somewhat doubtful. Judging by our findings of the dull mat glaze of brown on T'ang wares and its displacement by the glossy blue-black brown flecked glaze during Sung times, I think it fair to assume that these Wei Hsien pieces are of the first part of the Sung period.

It is interesting to note that aside from the beautiful deep sapphire glaze the technique and the form of the large blue vase shown are not unlike these vases. To be sure the potting is thinner and the ware darker brown. Also the piece has a flat bottom rather than the low board foot-rim but these changes might have been due to an endeavor to make a superfine pot. Of course the painting is much finer also but it is in the same dark brown glaze with a wide band of brown at the bottom and I assign this piece to northern Shantung, tentatively at least.

At Po Shan Hsien there was a cream ware with black decoration as is proven by the well known pilgrim bottle in the Eumorfopoulos Collection #C299 on the shoulder of which is an inscription "yang kao chiu," "lamb wine," and also "po shan ho chia tsao" "made by the Ho family at Po Shan." This is a pilgrim bottle with buff-grey stoneware body dense and hard, covered with a white slip and cream colored transparent glaze not at all like the above described ware, the breezy willow landscape on it being far more skillful than the broad painting on any of the part-brown part-cream pots. This is also called "Yüan?" by Hobson probably because the design fills the space rather fully but the ware is certainly Sung in craftsmanship and I am certain that in these northern sections the decadence due to the Mongolian conquest was felt first or that is immediately after 1127 in any event. We show a small jar (with mouth cut) which seems to be of a similar if not identical ware in the paragraph on humor because of the painting of the rabbit on it, and this again is typically Sung in all respects. A disconcerting pot #295 in the Eumorfopoulos Collection has a very similar key fret border (though more cautiously rendered) to the one on the Po Shan pilgrim bottle and a rather curlicue style of decorative painting quite similar. It too is described as of grey porcelaneous stoneware with white slip and cream glaze with black painting and remains of brown glaze inside and it is dated "chêng t'ung shih i nein wu yüeh ch'u i jih" or "the first day of the fifth month of the eleventh year of Chêng T'ung" (A.D. 1446). Does it make the pilgrim bottle Ming in period or did the style persist?

To add evidence, the flower on this jar is almost identical to that on a pear shaped vase I recently acquired which again has all of what we have known as Sung characteristics. We know these designs were copied but were they done so well four or five hundred years afterwards? I am still of the opinion that the pilgrim flask and the bottle are Sung, but this gives an idea of the difficulties in dating these wares.

A similar problem is posed by the "ku hsiang" (or Old Hsiang) pillows. A number of these are known containing the above words in inscriptions and some of them the potter's mark containing his name, "Chang." Hsiang, Mr.

FIG. 369. Tz'u Chou bottle which in its sort of curlicue linear technique suggests it may be "Ku Hsiang" or "Old Hsiang." Ht. 9¾". Warren E. Cox Coll.

FIG. 370. "Old Hsiang" type pillow of typical character and having an inscription in the border reading, "Made by the idler of the bank of the Chang." On the bottom is a bell shaped stamped mark reading, "Mr. Wang Shou-ming." Sung, and probably made at Tz'u Chou. Length 16¾". Eumorfopoulos Col. # C310.

Hobson found, is the name of the old prefecture now Chan-tê Fu in which Tz'ŭ Chou is located. Judging by the style of the potter's mark and also by the fact that there came a number of these on the market at once, Mr. Hobson came to the conclusion that they were of the 17th century. However, subsequent comparisons have led us to place them back into the Sung period and certainly from the Tz'ŭ Chou kilns. They have the typical buff-grey stoneware body and cream slip with transparent glaze. The painting in underglaze black consists of landscapes with animals and figures in economical and direct Sung style. These are set off in ogival medallions set upon rather closely decorated grounds of clouds, rock and wave and such all-over patterns.

FIG. 371. "Ku Hsiang" type jar of grey stoneware made without foot-rim, as are most of these large jars, and covered with white slip and transparent glaze under which is a vigorous drawing of a dragon on one side and a Fêng-huang bird on the other. Ht. 17". Warren E. Cox Coll.

FIG. 372. Tz'u Chou type jar with the usual cream glaze over a white slip and brown decoration of a dragon and bird. Several very similar ones in shape and decoration are glazed with the turquoise color. Ht. 10⅞". The Cleveland Mus. of Art. The Dikran G. Kelekian Coll.

A remarkable jar illustrated herewith has similar characteristics and one of the finest drawings of a dragon I have ever seen on one side with a Fêng-huang on the other. Both are tearing their way through tattered clouds in an ogival medallion while a band about the shoulder has a fine rock and wave pattern. The ware is typically Sung Tz'u Chou with a pinkish stain on one side. The dragon style is reminiscent of the paintings by Ch'ên Jung in the Boston Museum and these are dated A.D. 1244 and our potter may have seen such pictures.

Probably also from the main center come the slip incised wares with almost white transparent glaze sometimes crackled but pure and clear. We show a bowl stand and a vase having bands of foliage, coins, ducks and

FIG. 373. Large painted Tz'u Chou wine jar with flying cranes and a poem reading, "Keep the cover on and you keep the fragrance inside. Remove the cover and the fragrance greets your nostrils. Keep the cover off and a beautiful golden glow comes over your countenance." Ht. 24½". Sung Dynasty. Warren E. Cox Coll.

FIG. 374. Tz'u Chou type jar of Sung period made of buff stoneware with carved white slip and transparent glaze. Ht. 4". Note: This is almost identical to # C404 Emorfopoulos Coll. Warren E. Cox Coll.

FIG. 375. Tz'u Chou vase of gray stoneware covered with white slip which is then incised with the design and glazed over with a transparent glaze. This piece, though noble in size and proportions, is roughly handled and of a gray tone due to the impure glaze running unevenly. Sung period. Ht. 20". Gift of Mrs. Samuel T. Peters. Metropolitan Mus. of Art.

lotus petals of this type. Of the same ware is the larger Samuel T. Peters incised vase from the Metropolitan Museum of Art, and again the partly painted and partly incised vase which I think is the greatest one known.

This example shows a simple mastery of brush work beyond any other known. The petals of the lotus are nearly an inch in width and the pigment has been applied so that it hangs thickly at the bottom of each petal. Yet so wonderfully did the painter handle his brush that the pigment had just about been used up at the end of each stroke, giving a shaded effect. On close examination it will be seen that the petals actually seem to grow out of the stem.

Above: An amazing similarity in style and treatment leads us to believe this vase was made by the same master. The same characters are incised in the same style. The form is similar. But most of all the brilliant and feeling brush work is so alike that only some great master could have done both.

The bodies of both are of gray stoneware and the slip and glaze give a brown or old ivory color. Ht. 14½″. Warren E. Cox Coll.

Left: The finest Tz'u Chou vase I have seen, interesting because it combines the incised-through-slip technique with masterful brush work and fine form. The vigorous characters mean "snow," "moon," "wind," and "flower" and constitute a sort of short poem perhaps painting a landscape of snowflowers being blown by the wind in the light of the moon. Ht. 14″. Warren E. Cox Coll.

T'ZU CHOU MASTERPIECE

PLATE 61

In the incising too, partly done with a stylus and partly with a comb, the fluid and yet dynamic writing of the characters makes the incising of most other vases seem mere child's play. The characters used mean "snow," "moon," "wind," and "flower"; a sort of poem or impression of a landscape but also expressive of the seasons, and of such duality of the universe as "wind" movement and "moon" quiet, of "flower" life and of "snow" death.

Tz'u Chou type pillow with carved slip decoration under a transparent glaze. The color is buff to cream white. Ht. 4¾″. Fuller Coll. Seattle Art Mus.

Tz'u Chou type pillow of grey stoneware with white slip beautifully incised and covered with a greenish straw colored crackled glaze. It is said to have come from Shansi province and is of the Sung period. Length 9¾″. Warren E. Cox Coll.

Left: One of a near pair of Sung period tz'u Chou type vases with carved slip under a transparent glaze. This was purchased from Lee van Ching the famous Chinese collector in 1927. An almost identical one was bought in 1941. Ht. 14″. Warren E. Cox Coll.

Right: Cup stand with incised band about the wide lip. It will be noted that a comb was used in doing the background of the cloud scrolls. Sung period. Ht. 6″. Warren E. Cox Coll.

T'ZU CHOU TYPE INCISED SLIP WARES

FROM T'ZU CHOU, CHÜ-LU HSIEN AND SHANSI PROVINCE

PLATE 62

This vase was surely made by one of the greatest potters that ever lived, and amazingly I recently found another lesser work by the same hand as can be judged without a doubt by the brush work and also by the script.

In Shansi, mainly at Ho Chou a grey ware was made with the usually white slip incised with a free and charming manner and covered with a yellowish-greenish closely crackled distinctive glaze. Two excellent examples of this are the vase #C390 in the Eumorfopoulos Collection and the pillow from my own. The ware is rare and beautiful equaling that of Tz'u Chou. This attribution is given through the research of Walter Hochstadter and several pieces have been traced to the neighborhood. Of course it may be that they were actually made in one of the other three large kilns of the province, but unless otherwise proven let us assume that they came of Ho Chou, the largest and most central.

In Kiangsu a grey ware was made and also a red ware which Mr. Hochstadter says was made in Tan-yang Yu in northwestern Honan just southwest of Chang-tê. I show an excellent example of this ware with red body dipped, foot-rim, base and all in white slip which has been incised in a sort of checkerboard pattern and with a band of the same key fret we saw on the Po Shan pilgrim bottle, and with the body exposed by incising carefully covered by a painted-in grey slip to hide the red color that might have been very effective. Cne other small jar has plain white slip and glaze outside and grey on the inside. Where the slip goes over the bottom of these and is not covered with glaze it is inclined to crack and curl up and comes off easily when picked.

Note should be made that most of the sherds found by Sir Aurel Stein in Turkestan and at Kharakhoto are of yellowish buff body. This is all the information we have to date on the kiln sites and it is just as difficult to date these wares. Style is the best criterion and style is difficult to define. Some of these wares are aristocrats of slender and tall form, thinly potted, true and beautiful in conception. They are likely always to be Sung. Other Sung pieces are peasant wares squat and of the soil, heavily potted and without pretense. They may at first be confused with the fatter bellies of the Ming period which are also heavily potted but the feeling is quite different between the two.

I have criticized perhaps severely the Greek forms. Their parallels and derivations can be found in these Sung wares and a glance at the accompanying illustration will make my point clear. I show an Apulian vase which in simple proportions has perhaps reached the height of the Mediterranean art. See how useless the little handles at the sides are, note that the neck has grown so thick that it cannot be used to grip in one hand, note that by trying to taper the bottom overmuch a rounded almost pot belly is obtained and an added pan-cake base made necessary and see how the sharp edged lip-rim is nicked. Now compare the Chü-lü Hsien and Tz'u Chou vases which are like trim athletes and turn back to the other forms. The "wheat sheaf" and slender pear shaped bottles, the melon shaped jars and globular ones all have simplicity and firmness such as no Near Easterner or European can achieve. There was a self-discipline in the Chinese heart that tells its story here.

FIG. 376. Reddish brown jar treated all over with a white slip which is carved and filled with a grey slip under a transparent glaze. Walter Hochstadter claims this ware is made in Tan-yang yu in north western Honan near the Shansi border. Ht. 6″. Warren E. Cox Coll.

FIG 377. Chü-lu Hsien vase of gray stoneware decorated with a white slip and finely crackled glaze turned cloudy brownish from the inundation in 1108 before which it was made. Ht. 7½″. Warren E. Cox Coll.

FIG. 378. Vase of beautiful form and having spirited bamboo design. The body is buff stoneware, the slip and glaze are cream in color and the decoration is in a warm grey almost black. Tz'u chou Sung. Ht. 15¾″. Warren E. Cox Coll.

FIG. 380. Fine simple forms with beautiful tints to the glazes. Note the delicately formed full throat of the bottle, the sturdy quality of the "wheat sheaf" vase. Hts. 8″ and 9″. Warren E. Cox Coll.

Apulian amphora (see text, p. 202).

FIG. 379. Late Sung ware made at Yu chou in central Honan. Body is of thickly potted gray stoneware not unlike that of some Chün types, covered with white slip and creamy glaze inclined to show faint greenish yllow, and crackle where it runs thick. Ht. 8¾″. Ex Samuel T. Peters Coll. Warren E. Cox Coll. Baron C. G. von Seidlitz Coll.

Finally the superb example of both useful and decorative form is again developed from the amphora in the example shown which I recently acquired from the Peters collection. This piece was made at Yu Chou, where the Chün wares were made. It has a similar hard, grey stoneware body but is covered with a white slip and thick, glossy, creamy glaze which turns yellowish and crackles where it runs thick. This ware is very rare and always beautiful in form.

The painting on these vases is truly like shadows cast across them and adds to the meaning of the forms, becoming an integral part of them. The old saying was that a leaf touched with the brush twice dies, and the Chinese brush has, therefore, to be large enough to carry all the pigment necessary for one stroke however long it may be. The brushes are not trimmed but made rather of tapered hair of mink, sable, mouse whiskers and such. Mr. L. Y. Lee

Fig. 381. A beautiful example of Sung Tz'u Chou yao with white flower on one side and dark on the other. The wide band about the shoulder is vigorous and interesting. It is all painted in brown under a glossy glaze. Ht. 13¾". Warren E. Cox Coll.

has told me that children are made to practice painting and writing with the water cup balanced on the quarter inch end of the bamboo handle, the brush perfectly perpendicular. Thus a spiral can begin thin and end up wide, or it can begin wide and taper. Thus a leaf can be made in any given direction and a swift writing of the design becomes possible. An ancient master is said to have condemned his student's work many times without seeming reason because in painting the long tapering lily leaf bent down toward the earth he had not put into it the upward pull of "sky longing" which all green things have. Old men are palsied and beginners need wrist rests but the artists held their brushes far up the handle and moved them freely. What a vehicle! Compared with this the violin bow resting upon the strings is a heavy and crude instrument. No effort was made here toward the careful and painstaking drawing in truest possible anatomy of cavorting or posed human figures with heads and shoulders bent over a vase form. Here instead is caught the fleeting mood, the instant beauty of the still, full blown lotus flower lifting proudly to the heavens, of the fragile willow and bamboo bent before the wind, of the instantaneous flash of the wings of a flying bird, of a child playing with a kite, of an old man observing the flight of a bat the symbol of happiness, of the twitch of a rabbit's nose or of the forgetful pause of a rambling professor. Here we have dragons and waves that thunder, and peace, and the observance of a single leaf. The artist is exuberant and in love with the world about him.

FIG. 382. Sung period Tz'u Chou vase of typical buff grey stoneware covered with white slip down to within about an inch from base, painted with black which is freely handled and scratched out for the veins in the leaves at shoulder, and then covered with a straw colored transparent glaze. Ht. 11¼″. Formerly Mrs. Charles Porter Wilson Coll. now the Warren E. Cox Coll.

FIG. 383. Tz'u Chou small jar with neck cut but showing a humorous and life-like painting of a rabbit, a crane and a "happy boy" in three medallions about the body and a beautiful floral band about the top. Ht. ″. Sung period. Warren E. Cox Coll.

FIG. 384. Sung Tz'u Chou bowl of buff grey ware covered with white slip and transparent glaze allowed to run down unevenly on the outside. Beautifully painted picture of a philosopher observing the flight of a bat, the emblem of happiness, and holding a book in his hand. Dia. 6″. Mrs. Charles Porter Wilson.

FIG. 385. Tz'u Chou type jar with buff stoneware body, white slip and transparent glaze, of rare molded type, having four heads about the shoulder. The eyes and cheeks are touched with brown accents. Ht. 6″. Sung period. L. G. Sheafer Coll. Formerly Warren E. Cox.

FIG. 386. Tz'u Chou jar showing two medallions with sages and one with a black flower. Note the half forgetful pose of the sage and conventionalization of verdure, clouds and rocks. Ht. 12″. Warren E. Cox Coll.

FIG. 387. Tz'u Chou Sung Dynasty water vessel for a writer's table. Buff ware with white slip and transparent, glossy, crackled glaze decorated on slip with black and tan painting of great charm. Ht. 3¾″. Warren E. Cox Coll.

FIG. 388. Amusing pillow said to have come from Chü-lü Hsien with design of a baby and duckling. Length about 10″. Nasli Heeramaneck Coll.

FIG. 389. Tz'u Chou pillow of the Sung period humorously showing a boy riding a bamboo hobby horse. The painting is black on cream. Length about 10″. Nasli Heeramaneck Coll.

205

Fig. 390. Small figure of a child showing an almost Disney-like humor. Length 2¼″. Warren E. Cox Coll
Fig. 391. Small dog probably made in northern Honan. Buff ware with light greenish brown glaze. Lengt
1⅜″. Warren E. Cox Coll.
Fig. 392. Tz'u Chou pillow with writing meaning, "Wise men agree that when you have nothing to d
go early to bed." The color is soft cream and the writing in brown. Length 9¾″. Warren E. Cox Coll

Humor is not lacking. I illustrate a few examples, the philosopher and the rabbit, a jar with jolly masks that peer out between flowers arranged in it, a Walt Disney child on hands and knees, a most sensitive and bashful soul with his umbrella over his shoulder, a yellow pup of "coon-dog" indeterminate breed with ribs showing and a playful and expectant flap of the ears and finally a small horse that is everything that a T'ang horse is not, being large of head and small of rump, narrow of chest, fat of belly and short of leg. Certainly no artist could better poke fun at the great T'ang animals! The superb bowl showing a philosopher's studies interrupted by a bat (fu) symbol of happiness, and the babies on the pillows and vase, playing horse, posing with a fat duck and flying a kite are other unmistakable examples of light humor.

THREE COLOR TZ'U CHOU WARES

Toward the end of the Sung period and into the early Ming these figures were made of a grey clay covered with the usual white slip and transparent somewhat glossy glaze. Black outlines of the details were painted underglaze and often also overglaze on the faces particularly. Bowls and dishes usually have no outlines or if they do, they are in the iron red. The bowls are usually of buff rather than grey ware. This pigment red which is nothing but ground up iron oxide or more properly hydro ferrous oxide 2 Fe_2O_3 3 H_2O (rust) was applied to the glaze and after firing became ferric oxide Fe_2O_3 the brown of the one being changed to the red of the other, by driving out the water in the heat of the kiln. It had been used a little in T'ang times or earlier but here it appears for the first time on a glaze. The potters did not succeed in fixing it perfectly at first and we frequently find it partly rubbed off but shortly they learned to handle it better. Added to the old green and yellow or amber of the T'ang glazes now used as enamels on the cream glaze it became a new medium of overglaze decoration very rarely applied to vases and usually seen on small bowls and figures.

Of the figures the *Liang ch'i man chih* of the early 13th century says, "In Kung Hsien (in the Honan Fu) there are porcelain (tz'ŭ) images called by

ate Sung incense burner of buff eware covered with creamy slip transparent glaze and de orated in ow, g.een, brown (outlines) and iron-red. Largest and finest speci- of this ware I know. Ht. 7¼". Warren E. Cox Coll. Mr. Delos ppell.

A boy with portrait-like quality, of rare "Three color" S ng Tz'u Chou ware with yel'ow, green and iron red decoration. Ht. 5¾". Warren E. Cox Coll.

Two Tz'u Chou figures possibly made at different kilns but both of Sung period and showing masterful character- ization of both dog and gentleman. Ht. 8". Warren E. Cox Coll. Yamanaka & Co.

vo figures with yellow and green en- and iron red decorations. The little has much the same expression as has Metropolitan Mus. one and the man a polite and unctuous look. Hts. 7" and Ralph M. Chait Coll.

Figure of grey clay covered with white slip and painted with iron red, green en- amel and black. Ht. c. 6". Metropolitan Mus. of Art.

Small horse, the opposite in all features of the great Bactrian or Near Eastern breeds so celebrated by T'ang p tters. Ani- mals in this ware are rare and humor of this makes it a valuable example. Ht. 4". Mrs. Warren E. Cox.

T'ZU CHOU "THREE COLORED" FIGURES OF LATE SUNG PERIOD

PLATE 63

the name of Lu Hung-chien. If you buy ten tea vessels you can take one image. Hung-chien was a trader who dealt in tea—unprofitably, for he could not refrain from brewing his stock. Hung-chien formerly was very fond of tea, and it brought him to ruin." This is Hobson's translation and he adds, "Possibly the images of Hung-chien, which were given away with tea vessels, were made at Tz'u Chou or Hsü Chou." I do not place entire confidence in this, our only report of the times and it occurs to me that again the meaning might have been that, if you were collecting you might find ten vessels to one figure. The proportion is even greater today.

Left: Three bowls of late Sung period Tz'u Chou. Buff body covered on the inside and down to near bottom with white slip and transparent finely crackled glaze. Decorated with low fired iron red and green and yellow enamels. Note that red is considerably worn as usual. Dias. 6¼" and 6". John Platt—Warren E. Cox Coll.

Right: Sung period Tz'u Chou bowl of "three color" type but having deeper and stronger red and more sophisticated design. Dia. 7". Warren E. Cox Coll.

Tz'u Chou type bowl with grey-buff stoneware body, white slip and creamy transparent glaze decorated with iron red, green and yellow enamel. Red is of a deep color which would indicate this bowl is of Ming, rather than Sung period. Dia. 3½". Seattle Art Mus.

T'ZU CHOU "THREE COLOR" BOWLS OF LATE SUNG AND MING DYNASTIES

PLATE 64

Another late Sung technique for vases was the application of actual leaves to the body after which the piece was dipped in slip, the leaves plucked off so that the body was exposed where they had been and then as usual glazed and fired. Hobson calls one of these in the Eumorfopoulos Collection Ming with a question mark and it is a rather heavy and clumsy one. However, the typical grey stoneware body and all other characteristics of the one illus-

FIG. 393. Figures of Tz'u Chou type with muddy yellow and green enamels and iron red decoration on cream glaze. These figures rare and almost never unbroken. Made in molds and show some decadent features but are amusing and portrait-like character studies. 6″ to 10″. Late Sung. Miss Ethelyn McKinney the smaller and center figures and Mrs. L. G. Sheafer the standing dignitary. Ex Warren E. Cox Coll.

FIG. 394. Tz'u Chou figure of rare "three color" type. Buff and slightly gritty ware, covered with white slip and transparent glaze minutely crackled and decorated with iron red and yellow, green and black enamels. Sung. Ht. c. 10″. Gift of Mrs. Samuel T. Peters. Metropolitan Mus. of Art.

trated have convinced me that it is Sung. The tall and very beautiful vase is made in the same manner but cut-out patterns, perhaps of paper, have been used instead of the leaves. When the leaf or pattern is plucked up it causes the edge of the slip to come up slightly to a sharp edge quite different from that of an incised pattern. It should be noted how beautifully the potter of the tall vase has used his various bands of biscuit, biscuit with glaze, drips of slip, a plain band of slip and glaze and then the two with pattern.

Besides the lustrous brown wares or Tsung Sê tz'ŭ, as we have decided to call them, are certain ones which combine this glaze with the Tz'u Chou technique. Fairly frequently we see tea-bowls with a dull mat brown set off by a white slip and glazed edge. The beautiful bowl from Mrs. Charles Porter Wilson's collection has the outside in dull brown glaze as has also the brush holder shown. Both of these are of buff ware the holder being lighter,

Fig. 395. Vase of smooth grey stoneware covered with white slip which has been dipped over leaves stuck on the surface and then plucked off. Vase then glazed with transparent glaze showing yellowish and lavender tinted stains and fine crackle where thick. Sung. Ht. 8″. Warren E. Cox Coll.

Fig. 396. Brush holder of Tz'u Chou type ware. Brown glaze at foot. Slip and brown painted treatment on upper part. Body of rough, buff stoneware. Sung. Ht. 10″. Warren E. Cox Coll.

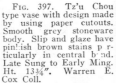

Fig. 397. Tz'u Chou type vase with design made by using paper cutouts. Smooth grey stoneware body. Slip and glaze have pinkish brown stains particularly in central band. Late Sung to Early Ming. Ht. 13¾″. Warren E. Cox Coll.

and possibly of Ming date though the bowl has painting in perfect Sung taste.

Finally on Plate 58 I am able to show two unique and wonderful examples of Tz'u Chou type ware. One is a small jar with free, beautiful, feathery foliage design and about the shoulder an inscription reading in a clockwise direction, "Great Sung Kia T'ai three made," and as Kia T'ai ascended the throne in 1201, probably indicates the year 1203. According to Sir Percival David's theory this should indicate a Chinese workman as the Mongol or Tartars begin their writing in the upper left hand corner and write downwards in columns moving toward the right while the Chinese begin in the upper right, moving downwards and toward the left. Therefore, it is likely that this piece was not made in the north, which at the time was in the hands of the Nuchih Tartars, but perhaps near Hang Chou and for imperial use. Certainly this is one of the earliest *nien hao* marks known, and I am delighted that the piece has passed from my hands to the Metropolitan Museum of Art.

The other example is a globular wine jar of nearly 15 inches in height and able to contain some three and a half gallons. At first glance it may appear a clumsy shape necessitating two hands to lift it but it is a well known Chinese shape often seen in Tsung Sê and Tz'u Chou wares in various sizes. The everted lip-rim is, of course, designed so that a leather or cloth cover can readily be tied on, but why the shape? I am proud to say that it occurred to me and I have seen no reason given for it elsewhere: —Such a jar can be rolled over easily, though very heavy even when partly filled, and one can pour into a small cup from it while it would be almost impossible to *lift* a pot containing three gallons and pour steadily from it. Hence we find once again the practical good sense behind the Chinese pottery forms.

The jar is of yellow-buff stoneware, covered with a white·slip on which the design is painted in brown and over which there is a thin, yellowish glaze showing no tendency to crackle. I think it likely to have been made in some southern Sung kiln not yet located as I guess the other small jar (see above) to have been, though Walter Hochstadter is of the opinion that this type of globular jar comes from Shansi. The potter used his thumb to finish the inside of the foot-rim and the whole has a sturdy handmade look about it. Around the shoulder is a beautifully designed lotus border about four inches in width and the whole remainder of the body is covered with the characters of a poem which, through the kind labors of Mr. Nai-Chi Chang and finally of Mr. C. F. Yau together with Mr. Hsuge K. Pao, was translated into English form. It is entitled a

FIG. 398. Sung period bowl of Tz'u Chou type. Rounded form with cylindrical foot and wide, perpendicular slightly concave rim treated with white slip and transparent glaze inside and brown "tea dust" type glaze outside unevenly applied below rim. Body is buff and sandy. Brushed design inside of brown-b'ack and swiftly executed with a whirling feeling. Dia. 7". Mrs. Charles Porter Wilson.

"Chiang Ch'eng Tzu," or "Flute Lyric" which Mr. Chang explains was a form composed to be sung or chanted to the accompaniment of a flute as certain Greek poems were composed for lyre music, but Mr. Yau also says it may have been the poetic name of the composer. Thus let us think of the following words as though associated with the cool, wavering notes of the Chinese flute:

CHIANG CH'ENG TZU
(A Flute Lyric)

Despite the cold, she eagerly seeks the prunus blossom amid the snow.
Still she ponders—
From whence comes the subtile fragrance?
But soon the waiting perfume guides her to the blooming branch beyond the
    Bamboo Grove
And here she meditates in the chilly twilight, until the moon arises
Casting its varied shadows
Around the Tower of the Winds (Feng T'ai).
With slender fingers she breaks the jade-like blossom and brings it home
Where its enchanting fragrance permeates the draperies and screens
Reminding her that Spring is now returning.
She sways with the rhythm of the flute coming from the tower top
And all is tranquil.
Ever we cherish this sweet isolation that induces our poetry to song.
Shall we linger a moment longer?
Then let us partake of the golden cup.

The beauty of the Tz'u Chou type pottery is, therefore, not only compounded of the beauty of fine forms, of rich and lovely textures and subtilely thrilling colors; of the superbly masterful painting but also of words. Is it any wonder that the Chinese for ages have loved it and can I be blamed for ranking it among the highest arts of the life of mankind? Greatest of the ceramic arts it stands alone.

SUNG BLUE AND WHITE WARES

Generally speaking it is agreed that blue and white wares did not originate until the end of the Sung or beginning of the Yüan period and even this is doubtful so far as records go being based on a vague reference in the *T'ao lu*, and yet some pieces are so nearly Sung in taste that we are inclined to believe that it will eventually be proven the underglaze blue painting was attempted by some of the Sung factories. I submit two bowls, one of a buff ware with creamy crackled glaze stained café au lait and under which there is a soft lavender grey blue design of conventionalized flower and foliage scrolls. The one side of this bowl has been fired brown and the blue has disappeared. The other small bowl is of a white porcelaneous ware covered with a sort of bismuth-paste white glaze also slightly café inside and decorated with an underglaze blackish lavender blue with very smart bird and flower design. There is a floral medallion inside and a character (undistinguishable) under the bottom. These two last point to Ming characteristics but the handling of the blue seems to be experimental and not entirely satisfactory from a technical viewpoint. Both of these look life early experiments in underglaze blue decoration

FIG. 399. Possibly late Sung bowl with decoration in impure blue. Dia. 4". Mr. B. d'Ancona.

FIG. 400. Bowl with buff body and white slip decorated in greyish-lavender-blue under greenish-white crackled glaze burnt brown on one side. Probably late Sung. Dia. 5¾". John Platt–Warren E. Cox Coll.

and may possibly be Sung. Finally a dated ewer is again not clear to the naked eye but may give us evidence under ultra-violet examination. (See the illustration.)

KWANGTUNG SUNG WARE

At the ancient kilns in Kwangtung province, south China, there were made wares far thinner than the usual Yüan and Ming or later types and with even more beautiful, softly blended glazes. These are undoubtedly Sung. Mr. Hochstadter says that all of these have light bodies and that later wares have dark bodies or are more coarse in potting. Of course some Chün and "Celadon" copies are early but most are of 18th century or later.

FIG. 401. Pilgrim bottle of Kwangtung ware, hard brown and thin, covered with café-au-lait glaze streaked with brown and blue in beautiful tones. Sung. Ht. 8". Mr. B. d'Ancona.

CHAPTER XI

KOREAN POTTERIES AND PORCELAINS

THE influences of Sung China naturally spread also to Korea. The love of nature expressed by the Zen Buddhists and Taoists, the well digested Hellenistic forms from India and the wonderful craftsmanship of the Sung artists were bound to have their effect.

We know little more about Korean history than that it was a chaotic land beset by Tartar hordes to the north and island invaders from the east. About the middle of Han times there were the "Three Kingdoms":—1.—The Shiragi

FIG. 402. Silla cooking bowl with hollow foot and pierced outer frame holding it at rim. Ware is gray with thin brownish primitive glaze. Ht. 4″. Warren E. Cox Coll.

FIG. 403. Silla dynasty (A.D. 632–936) Korean jar and cover tu.ned on wheel and decorated with stamped design. Handle stuck on. Mr. Hobson gives this type dating of 9th cent., while the type following early Japanese potteries he calls 5th cent. Slate gray. Ht. 7½″. Freer Gallery of Art, Washington.

(Japanese) or Silla (Chinese) in the south founded about 57 B.C., 2.—The Kokuri or Koriö (Jap.) or Kao-li (Chin.) in the center c. 37 B.C. and 3—The Kudara (Jap.) or Po-chi (Chin.) in the north c. 18 B.C. They continued until about A.D. 632 or the beginning of T'ang China in A.D. 618 when the southern dynasty, the Silla gained dominance.

The monk Shuntao (Jap.) or Tat'ung (Chin.) is supposed to have come in 372 from China to the Kokuri court and it was the old story of missionary followed by soldier, followed by tax collector and in time by the artist, and great artists must have come for the great bronzes and frescoes are of very high art, the latter being as fine as those of Ellora and Ajunta caves in India. Much of the sculpture is also great. Then in T'ang times the calendar, many laws, clothes and customs were of T'ang taste. This Silla dynasty lasted from A.D. 632 to 936 although the Korai had already taken hold in the north in A.D. 918.

The Silla pottery does not compare with T'ang wares probably because potters are craftsmen at heart and it takes time to have them settle and to translate the beauties about them. The single sculptor or painter may do

214

several works of art and the critics call it a great era of art. Pottery more closely expresses what *all* the people know and feel. In any event the ware was unglazed or had a colorless glaze that appeared to emanate from the body itself. It was of reddish or grey tones. The wheel had been introduced and pieces found at Taiku and Fusan in the extreme south are like those in tombs in Japan. The subtility of line was not entirely missing and for decoration there was reticulation, incising, stamped designs and very occasional pinched-up technique. Tiles and architectural grotesques were made and some have a green Han type glaze.

FIG. 404. Silla dynasty pottery bowl and cover called "sacrificial vessel" by museum. Gray clay partly incised, partly stamped with pattern of various bands arranged horizontally. Ht. 8¾". Freer Gallery of Art, Washington.

The Korai period started between (A.D. 918 and 946 as one counts the conquest and lasted until A.D. 1392 or into the beginning of Ming times, roughly paralleling the Sung period. The capital was at Song-do and the country took its present name of Korea. We hear that late in the 11th century the courts interchanged ambassadors after the Sungs had saved the Koreans from Khitan Tartar invasion in 1016 and there was peace for about 200 years until at the end of the 12th century the Mongols invaded and the king fled to an island called Kokwato in 1232.

Most Korean wares are found in tombs rather than at kiln sites and were not "Imperial wares" in any sense so they were not very much affected but by 1280 the Chinese government fell and then Korea simply became a vassal state to Khublai Khan and finally was invaded and sacked by the Japanese who had never been invaded by the Mongols. Thus we visualize a very unhappy time for artists.

The Yi or Ri dynasty was started by Yi Taijo or Litan in 1392 and paid homage to the Ming emperors again for a few hundred years of comparative peace but in 1592 Hideyoshi started his "conquest of the world," by sending 300,000 troops to Korea. China aided the Koreans with 60,000 men and there were six years of strife. The capital which had been moved to Seoul was raided and art and artists were carried off to Japan. In 1598 Hideyoshi died but Korea never recovered from the hate of the islanders. This country has ever been between the devil (the Tartars) and the deep blue sea (the Japs). Undoubtedly its present capital "Chōsen" meaning "Morning Calm" is now filled with boiling hate and takes joy in the war between her ancient enemies. Yet strange are the ways of this world, for it was through Korea that Japan was brought Buddhism, that religion which has meant so much in peace and beauty.

The Korean wares are found (what the Japs have left) in Kaijo, on the island of Kowato, Keisho, Zenra, Chūsei and rarely in the district of Kōkai, in Kōgen, Kanyakō and Heian. Many other objects were placed in the tombs such as jewels, seals, ewers of metal, bronze mirrors, knives, boxes, glass beads, hawk bells and other valuable or useful things. The *Ko ku yao lun* says of Korean ware, "It is of pale green color and resembles Lung Ch'üan ware. Some are covered with white sprays of flowers, but this kind is not worth much money." This is, of course, either ignorance or a bit of local bias, for the wares are most economically decorated and not "covered" with flowers and the quality was high. Other authorities compared it more favorably with Yüeh yao, Pai ting yao, and even Ju yao and Pi-se yao. But here we do not have to rely so much on the Chinese writings.

My good friend and fellow collector, the late John Platt, many of whose things I was able to sell after they spent some fifteen years on loan at the Metropolitan Museum, wrote in the Burlington Magazine in 1912, "We may infer that the perfectly formed specimens, with thin body and uniform glaze, of the color of Ju-Chou porcelain, were in all probability made about 1100 A.D.; the heavier undecorated pieces with fine, soft, wax-like glaze and thick tomb oxidation being of earlier date."

He continues, "Our study of a great number of specimens leads to the assumption that the earliest Korean porcelain was undecorated, and that it had a hard grey proto-porcelain body, which invariably showed the iron color where exposed to the heat of the kiln and not covered with the glaze. The glaze was of a very soft uncracked texture, the best color being either green or blue, both of them generally merging into a soft grey.

"There is also evidence that the pieces of a single color, with engraved scroll work and modelling in low relief, were of an early date, having been made before A.D. 1125.

"But by far the greatest number of pieces taken from the tombs has 'mishima' decorations and is of varying thickness and quality. Most of these wares were undoubtedly made between the years A.D. 1100 and 1392; the heavier ones with harder and more glass-like glaze being made probably between the years 1250 and 1392, as during this period the art was said to be on the decline."

The word "Mishima" is a Japanese term said to have derived from the semblance of the designs to the columns of characters in an almanac compiled in Mishima a town in Japan, or from the small islands called Mi shima (Three islands) now Koybunto which had a harbor at which ships may have stopped between Japan and Korea. Mr. Platt was speaking only of the celadon wares and not the white and other types found, of course.

Dr. Nakao has drawn up a similar outline of the wares and it may be well to compare them:

1.—Heavy undecorated wax-like glazed wares showing oxidation. Platt says before 1100. Dr. Nakao does not distinguish them.

2.—Thin well made wares with carved decoration only and "Ju-Chou glaze" no crackle and apt to lose shape in firing. Platt says about 1100 and modeled ones before 1125. Dr. Nakao says from 1050 to 1170 and the BEST PERIOD.

Left: Excellent example of earliest type of Korai pottery. Well potted, decorated with vigorous carved lotus petal design on outside. Glaze blue gray green and has only few lines of wandering crazing. Dia. 6¾". John Platt–Warren E. Cox Coll.

Center: Bowl of olive green color with well designed but ornate "mishima" decoration and crudely made foot showing four sand supports. Dia. 6½". John Platt–Warren E. Cox Coll.

Right: Large fish bowl probably of 2nd period or c. 1200 of Korai era. Fired evidently with circular support like some Ming period celadons of Chinese, rather than usual three spurs. Dia. 10¼". John Platt–Warren E. Cox Coll.

Left: Fine simple bowl of first and best period according to Dr. Nakao dating between about A.D. 1050 and 1170. Gray-white clay which turns brown where exposed and glaze is thin bluish gray green uncrackled. Slight radial lines on outside and indentations at lip with delicate line incised around about ¾" below lip inside. Dia. 8¼". John Platt–Warren E. Cox Coll.

Center: Bowl with tasteful "mishima" design and partly green, partly olive glaze, fairly thin and well potted, dating c. 1280. Dia. 7½". John Platt–Warren E. Cox Coll.

Right: Bowl probably dating c. 1300 or in the 3rd period of Dr. Nakao (A.D. 1274–1350) or our period of 1250–1392. No spur marks and rough foot-rim. Dia. 7½". John Platt–Warren E. Cox Coll.

KORAI BOWLS OF THE FIVE PERIODS

PLATE 65

Rare stem-cup of 3rd Korai period or later with fair potting and well designed all-over inlayed pattern. At least as early as Sung Dynasty Ting ware. Ht. 3½". John Platt–Warren E. Cox Coll.

Korai cup and saucer of c. 1250 or earlier with inlayed flowers in white and black under transparent crackled glaze. The repair at the lip is of gold lacquer done in Japan. Potting not so fine as cup with incised decoration only. Dia. of saucer 6¼". John Platt–Warren E. Cox Coll.

(c)

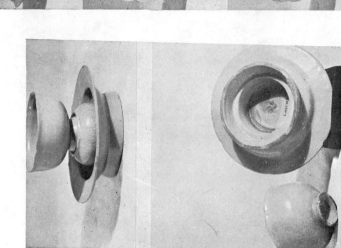

(b)

(a)

(a) Finest wine cup I have seen of Korean ware of early Korai period. Delicately potted and has wax-like gray green glaze. Delicately incised flowers in six sections of outside of cup and on rim of saucer with inverted lotus petals also on saucer base. Dia. 6". John Platt–Warren E. Cox Coll.

(b) Cup with stand attached dating between c. 1050 and 1170 according to Dr. Nakao. Grayish white ware with glossy blue gray green glaze. Foot with covered rim and four spur marks would almost certainly designate this piece as Korean. Beautifully incised. Edges cut to form six-petal flower pattern. Dia. 5¾". John Platt–Warren E. Cox Coll.

(c) Cup and saucer of crude, thick potting. Inlayed and incised decoration. c. 1300 or Dr. Nakao's 3rd period. (A.D. 1274–1350). Ht. 5". John Platt–Warren E. Cox Coll.

KORAI CUPS AND CUP STANDS

PLATE 66

Left: Wine pot of sturdy form with fine pouring spout and handle which fits hand. Covered with smooth gray green glaze having little crazing which was unintentional. Agrees in quality with those of Dr. Nakao's first period of about 1050 to 1170. Ht. 9½". Warren E. Cox Coll.

Right: Excellent specimen of gourd shaped ewer with twisted handle and slight incised design. c. 1200 or earlier. Ht. 14". Freer Gallery of Art, Washington.

Wine ewer of interesting form indicating turtle on lotus blossom, with dragon head. Twisted rope-like handle. Between 1250 and 1392, that is Yuan to Early Ming. Mus. of Fine Arts, Boston.

Wine ewer with ornately modeled cover finial and some inlay. Glassy glaze and heavy, insecure potting place. c. 1250 to 1392. Ht. 9". Metropolitan Mus. of Art.

KORAI EWERS

Plate 67

Korai period, made c. 1280 to 1300, inlayed or "Mishima" set of boxes for the toilet or for condiments. This is the only complete one I know. Dia. 7⅝″. The Cleveland Mus. of Art.

KORAI SET OF BOXES

PLATE 68

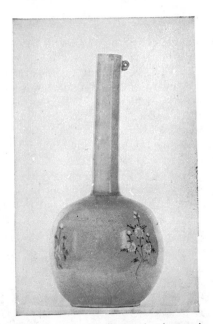

Left: Bottle with usual hexagonal tall neck and loop near top, heavily potted and covered with rich crackled blue gray green glaze. Early Korai. Ht. 13½". Warren E. Cox Coll.
Right: Heavily potted bottle with incised and also inlayed design called by Japanese "mishima" and usual loop near top perhaps for securing a stopper which is missing. c. between 1200 and 1250. Ht. about 13¼". Freer Gallery of Art. Washington.

Korai period bottle dating between 1280 and 1300 with "mishima" inlayed decoration. Ht. about 13". Mus. of Fine Arts, Boston.

Unique bottle with "mishima" design and reticulated body having rich crackled glaze somewhat thicker than usual. According to Dr. Nakao, not later than c. 1300. Only pieces in China with such carved bodies are of Ming period, 1368–1644. Perhaps special technique originated in Korea. Ht. 10½". Warren E. Cox Coll.

KORAI BOTTLES

PLATE 69

3.—Thinnest and best quality "Mishima" type wares without crowded decoration. Platt says 1100 to 1392. Dr. Nakao says "First inlays," stamping molding, etc. and tribute to Emperor between 1170 and 1274.

4.—Heavier wares with more crowded inlays and glaze "like glass." Mr. Platt says 1250 to 1392. Dr. Nakao says that the Tz'u Chou types, with painted design in underglaze black and often coarse, were between 1274 and 1350.

5.—Finally Dr. Nakao says that inferior, dull and cement-like brown wares were between 1350 and 1392.

It will be seen that essentially the two are in entire agreement Mr. Platt, probably correctly, allowing for a bit more overlapping of types. With this material in hand it is not difficult to date our specimens fairly accurately but

Early (1st period) Korai vase dating according to Dr. Nakao between A.D. 1050 and 1100. Thin gray-white ware with bluish gray green glaze uncrackled because thinly applied. Ht. c. 12½". Metropolitan Mus. of Art.

Graceful typical-shaped gallipot of light gray green with "mishima" decoration and dating c. 1280 or earlier. Ht. 11½". John Platt–Warren E. Cox Coll.

Large "mishima" decorated jar dating c. 1300 and showing both combed incising (around shoulder) and free hand incising filled with white slip and covered with transparent green glaze over brown body. Ht. 15". Warren E. Cox Coll.

Right: Two gallipots labeled 15th to 16th cent. in museum but probably better allocated in latter part of 13th cent., one without inlay or "mishima" decoration perhaps being a little earlier. Hts. about 12'. Metropolitan Mus. of Art.

Two bottles, one of early Korai period c. 1100 (with cup mouth) and other of last part of period, according to Dr. Nakao, 1350 to 1392. Hts. 8¼" and 9½". Warren E. Cox Coll. and John Platt–Warren E. Cox Coll.

KORAI VASES

PLATE 70

when it comes to making clear distinctions between the places of manufacture we are met with an unsolved problem and, in fact, several wares are likely to have been made almost alike in China and Korea.

Mr. Bernard Rackham in his catalogue of the Le Blond Collection in the Victoria and Albert Museum (1918) makes three divisions:—1.—Wares undoubtedly made in Korea, 2.—Wares probably Chinese imports, 3.—Wares which we are sure are Chinese.*

In the first category Mr. Rackham places:

1.—Pure white porcelain with translucent body of granular fracture; soft translucent, readily scratched bluish or aquamarine tinged glaze full of tiny bubbles; crackled exceptionally and occasionally showing slight brownish tone where body is exposed. In the form of small boxes, flat dishes, cups and other small objects, these pieces have incised foliage, combing, pressing and modeled slip or relief from mold. One small box in the collection has the name Ch'ên Shih-i, in relief on the bottom. As it was in the mold we may infer that it is the maker's name. It is the only possibly signed piece we know.

Another group of small objects are of the same glaze but coarser in body and with sandy bottoms. These are said to be toys but I am wary of the toy theory unless it includes toys for grownups. There are so many other reasons for making miniatures other than the fitting of the hand of a child, such as the making of small testers and the universal novelty appeal of "cute little things." This is another of our appeals which artists should take account of in passing.

Fig. 405. 1st period (according to Dr. Nakao) dish of gray white ware with bluish gray green glaze with slight tendency to crackle in one place, having the thin covered foot rim and three spur marks. Dia. 7". Ex Warren E. Cox Coll. N. M. Heeramaneck.

Another class similar to these two is probably later and with greyish glaze and even coarser body.

All of these are more vitreous than Ting yao and more closely associated with the "Ying ching" or "Ju types."

2.—Porcelaneous celadons with hard, dense body having a slightly violet tinge and burnt reddish brown where exposed; covered with a thick semi-transparent greyish-greenish-bluish glaze varying in translucency and resembling jade in texture. This ware varies to grey and greenish-brown and has a soft satiny feeling. The bases are covered with glaze, even the foot rims, and show three clean spur marks rather than three piles of sand as do the coarser

*The Study of Korai Potteries and Porcelains by Ken Nomori, pub. Sei Kan Sha, Kyoto, is a valuable contribution to this study.

FIG. 406. Cup with handles of crude T'ng yao imitation, heavily potted and having imperfect and glassy glaze. Ricio or Yi period (1392–1910) probably made in the late 17th cent. Dia. 4½″. Metropolitan Mus. of Art.

FIG. 407. Korai vase of white porcelain with glassy glaze quite different from its T'ang prototype. Ht. 5⅛″. Metropolitan Mus. of Art.

wares. Mr. Rackham does not mention crackle but the examples he shows all have a transparent crackle of "ice type" while only a few in the Platt-Cox collection are without it. Note should be made that the heavier type has usually a more translucent glaze while the slightly later very thin type rivaling Ting yao in weight has a more satiny glaze, applied thinner and usually without crackle. The two finest examples I know of this ware are shown, the bowl of Ting-like form, the cup and saucer. (Pl. 66a & Pl. 65, lower left.) Mrs. Langdon Warner states, "Korean pottery glaze is watery, transparent, vitreous, seldom greasy, and though brilliant in color is neither opaque nor jade-like." Perhaps she had not seen this type for they are undisputably Korean, not watery, not vitreous nor transparent in glaze and not brilliant in color though they are distinctly soft and jade-like.

Mrs. Warner moreover states, "The collector who enters the field today must content himself with mediocre examples or else pay exorbitantly for the occasional good piece that is offered for sale." I have heard from the Warners that they bought a number of pieces "for a song in Korea," but in general these best pieces bring no more than comparative Ting examples and about as many hundreds as Chün wares bring in thousands. Therefore the collector should not be discouraged.

Our illustrations will speak for the subtile and lovely shapes of the refined wares. A characteristic which the bowls share with Ting ones is the very slight indentation of the edge dividing it into six sections which are further set off by very slightly indented lines from the outside making a floral form. Melon shaped gallipots have a cup shaped lip-rim of modified T'ang form. Pear shaped bottles are slender and graceful and a distinctive type has a globular body and tall slender neck of hexagonal tubular form. Ewers express Near Eastern forms in metal but are well modified to suit pottery technique. Bottles with spouts at top and small open mouthed spouts at the side for filling are after bronze forms said to have been ritualistic but originated for quite practical drinking without touching the vessel to one's lips.

Small ewers of melon form are typical and of them Mr. Rackham says, "By a strange singularity, tea-drinking, though practiced from early times in China and Japan, was unknown in ancient Corea; the vessels which might

FIG. 408. Gallipot with inc' ed d. ign a d gray green crackled glaze quite similar to the one in the Eumorfopoulos Coll. which Mr. Hobson dates about 1200 or in Dr. Na^kao's 2nd period. Metropolitan Mus of Art.

FIG. 409. G aceful bottle, notable for the adaptation by the Koreans of the delicate floral design alternating with grooves and lines setting them off. 3rd Dr. Nakao period and may be dated about 1280 to 1300. Ht. 13". Warren E. Cox Coll.

FIG. 410. Ewer of gourd shape with rather irregularly potted spout and handle. The cover and handle have small loops for attachment by a cord. The glaze is of light gray green and uncrazed. This is probably of the first period, dating about 1150, of the Korai times.

be mistaken for tea-pots were used for pouring out wine, and the small bowls and cups for drinking it." Emil Hannover, R. L. Hobson and S. C. Bosch Reitz seem to agree while Mrs. Warner says, "But the Koreans of the Korai period are known to have been great tea-drinkers, and it is safe to assume that many of these (referring to the ewers) are tea-pots. Bronze and stone tea-pots of the same period have been found." I have no doubt but that all

FIG. 411. Wine pot in the form of an eggplant which is a favorite one in Korea. This piece, which has been on loan at the Metropolitan Mus. of Art for many years, is full of simple charm. Ht. 6". John Platt—Warren E. Cox Coll.

FIG. 412. Group of small flattened bottles probably used for oil or other precious lquids and dating around 1280 or in Dr. Nakao's tentative 3rd period. John Platt—Warren E. Cox Coll

of these authorities have ample reason for such definite statements. We can only wish that they had given reasons and more definite evidence where such contradiction occurs. The tall ewers are, of course, descendants of bronze forms of the Near East, but as to whether or not the melon shaped ones are is a question and I have never seen the stone ones mentioned. I see no reason why the melon and gourd shaped ones are not designed after the fruits and vegetables for the potters even went to the trouble to place a stem on the cover in many instances.

We have said that the Koreans were masters of carving and modeling but it is strangely true that when they attempted brush decorations they

Fig. 413. Mishima type ewer showing Western Asian influence. The design has been impressed with small tools and then inlayed a good deal as was done with the Henry II or "Orieon" ware of France. This piece was made about 1280 to 1300. Ht. 11". (Spout repaired). Warren E. Cox Coll.

Fig. 414. A rather well painted Korai vase after the Tz'u Chou style and dating between 1300 and 1350. The glaze is greenish brown. Ht. 10½". Warren E. Cox Coll.

Fig. 415. Late Korai period vase with decoration inspired by the Tz'u Chou Chinese type but losing all the spirit and beauty of the original brush work. The glaze is brownish green. Ht. 9¾". Warren E. Cox Coll.

were clumsy. Perhaps this is because the painted wares were done in the decadent period toward the end of the Korai period, but it is often the case that good carvers and etchers are poor at handling the far more facile medium of the brush. This may be because they cannot lean on the brush and a better control of the nerves is necessary. Perhaps it is because of a different speed of thinking; the carvers being slower and more methodical. In any event the Koreans were great carvers and even when they wanted a painted effect they devised the means of getting it through carving known to the Japanese as "mishima." The technique is very simple and quite ancient for we find it practiced in neolithic times elsewhere but the Koreans brought it to a fine degree of perfection. It is simplicity itself for it consists of nothing more than incising the design with a sharp instrument and then, after the clay is dry and fairly hard, of rubbing into the incisions, white or black clay, over which the glaze is then applied. It is a sort of simple inlay and let me say here that it is not "inlayed jade" as some super salesmen have declared.

The designs consist chiefly of small well spaced floral sprays, flying birds among cloud scrolls and sometimes trees or grasses. A Near Eastern influence, due to the fact that the Northern Caravan Route terminated not far from where Korea joins the mainland, is sometimes prominent as in the beautiful tile from the Boston Museum laid out much as a Persian rug would be.

Ting yao was found in large quantities in Korea and although it has been stated that all of this ware was imported we are inclined to doubt it for there are also several Ting types not readily traceable to known Chinese sources and we do know that Chinese potters worked in Korea. The habits of a potter are hard to change. Mr. Rackham quotes Mr. Bosch Reitz, "The record of Hsü Ching, already cited, refers not only to green ware or celadon as being made in Korea, but also to bowls, cups, platters and other vessels, all closely copying the style and make of Ting ware." "This statement," says Mr. Rackham, "taken with the large quantities of white ware found, is good evidence in favor of a Korean manufacture, although it is not easy to differentiate the indigenous from the imported specimens." Many collectors are inclined to believe that any ware with a regular foot unglazed and well potted, instead of the usual foot on many of the celadon wares; shallow, glazed over and with three spur marks, cannot be Korean yet an exami-

Fig. 416. Inlayed plaque variously described as a "rug design to be shipped to the Near East to copy," a "writing board," etc., but showing certainly a strong Near Eastern influence. Length 12½". Ex John Platt—Warren E. Cox Coll. Boston Mus.

nation of the fine little cup and saucer and of some of the bowls which have typical Korai celadon glaze of the best sort will show them to be comparable with many of the better Chinese wares.

Moreover Ting technique has many things in common with Korai such as: 1.—the indentation of edges, 2.—the use of carved petals on the outside, 3.—incised and low relief molded design, 4.—the glazing of the foot-rim and 5.—the making of a very thin ware.

Much of the "Northern Sung celadon" in the form of bowls large and small with molded all-over floral design is also found in Korean tombs and it presents much the same problem. However, these are slowly being located in definite places in China and we can now definitely recognize the Yüeh, early Lung Ch'üan, and some of the Honan wares so that these are eliminated. It is also true that they do not so closely approximate the other Korean techniques of potting as do the Ting wares.

The marbled pottery wares with transparent glazes are recognized as T'ang Chinese and there are comparatively so few found in Korea that there is no doubt but that they are imported.

Some of the type of Tz'u Chou wares such as were found at Wei Hsien and attributed to Po Shan Hsien are undoubtedly of Shantung make and logically enough would be carried the short distance to Korea. The Japanese have called this ware "Yegōrai" meaning "painted Korean" but this was simply

FIG. 417. Bottle of the latter part of the Korai period made probably between 1350 and 1392 or in Dr. Nakao's last period. Ht. 11½". Metropolitan Mus. of Art.

FIG. 418. Gourd shaped ewer of ornate and badly involved design with celadon glaze and red outlines to the petals. The conception of the frog for the loop on the handle is an amusing feature. Ht. 12". Freer Gallery of Art, Washington.

FIG. 419. Very crudely potted and with a poor glaze, this vase dates in the Richo period, about the middle of the 18th cent. Ht. 11¾". Metropolitan Mus. of Art.

because they had not traced them back to their place of manufacture much as we speak of "Coromandel screens" and as the Italians speak of "maiolica" or "Majorca pottery" simply because these things were shipped from those sources.

Nothing of importance was made after the first Japanese conquest. Some wares copied "Imari" such as was made at Arita in Hizen province, Japan

FIG. 420. Korean bowl of the 17th cent. and seemingly somewhat influenced by some Japanese wares though not to be compared exactly with any of them. Dia. 6¾". Metropolitan Mus. of Art.

FIG. 421. Drinking vessel similar to the earlier examples in general form but far more crudely potted and having a brown green glaze. Ht. 12". John Platt–Warren E. Cox Coll.

FIG. 422. Jar with blue and red underglaze decoration made probably about 1700 to 1800. The ground color is pale greenish buff, the glaze glassy and crackled. Ht. 15". Metropolitan Mus. of Art.

During the 17th and 18th centuries a coarse white porcelain of heavy appearance was made and sometimes painted in more or less spirited decorations of a dull underglaze blue of muddy and greenish tone. Some of this ware was influenced by late Ming characteristics. A dark underglaze brown developed into a rusty red and a fiery crimson. Overglaze colors particularly green enamel with underglaze blue and also rather poor copies of "five color" wares were made, and some reticulation but in bad taste was practiced.

Modern pottery in imitation of the old "mishima" ware was imported to America up to about fifteen years ago by The Japanese Fan Co. It began as crude but fairly tasteful and fairly close copies of the old but was soon "improved" by the addition of red blotches and then was discontinued.

CHAPTER XII

JAPANESE POTTERIES AND PORCELAINS

EVEN before the war there was a wide divergence of opinion in the West concerning Japan, her people and her art: some were enthusiastic while others find everything Japanese anathema. I recently talked with a lady of significant culture and she told me that she had always longed to live in Japan, but after she had seen the country and gone on to China she decided that she preferred the latter. "In spite of all the smells and dirt, there is something *real* about China," she said. That others have felt differently was proven by Fenellosa, Freer, Binyon and Havemeyer to mention only a few. Let us try to clear our minds of all prejudices concerning California, the Philippines and the war and remember that the artists are not like the business men, the soldiers or the politicians. Let us see what they have had to offer.

The earliest people on the islands were the Ainus who were not unlike European prehistoric people so far as we can determine by the shell mounds. These people were driven north by invasions of people from Korea, who may have originated in central Asia, and by the Polynesians. Even later invasions from Korea left records in the dolmens dating from about 300 B.C. to A.D. 700 where are found potteries not unlike that of the Silla period, not yet glazed but well modeled figures of men in armor, horses, boats, etc. all showing influences of China and Siberia. It was these invaders who brought the use of iron. These northern as well as the southern influences both came from the south simply because it is there that the Korean peninsula most closely approaches the islands. As could be expected this caused a confusion of influences and that confusion of traits which persists in all Japanese and can be seen clearly in their art.

Perhaps the dominant characteristic of Japanese art is the love of nature. No other people have been able to build their houses to blend so well with the landscape. No other people have written poetry which so expresses the moods of nature of the sea and land. Only the Chinese of Sung times ever surpassed them in painting landscapes, but where the Chinese go to the mountains and look at them the Japanese bring their mountains into their gardens and live with them.

NARA OR TEMPYO, HEIAN AND KAMAKURA PERIODS
(A.D. 710–794) (A.D. 794–897) (A.D. 1185–1336)

Pottery did not develop except from outside sources and even in the Suiko and Hakuho periods (A.D. 552–710) there was a yearning for Chinese ways and many Chinese settled in Japan. Buddhism did not become at once popular but increased as time went on and received a stimulus from Shotoku Taishi and the Chinese writings. By 710 the T'ang influence was strong, the language was worked out with Chinese script and dress, architecture, the calendar and customs all were as nearly Chinese as possible. The Shoso-in, a wonderful storehouse has actually been kept from that time to this and contains much of general interest but little pottery and that of the mottled T'ang type. Mr. Langdon Warner says, "preserving every jot of their teacher's skill, they lent to continental shapes and styles something that we shall, as soon as the eighth century reaches its second decade, recognize as peculiarly Japanese."

Mr. Warner points out that the volcanic structure of the rock of Japan made it impossible for them to carve colossal rock sculptures so they made the DAIBUTSU-DEN the largest bronze figure ever seen and housed it in a temple. Here we find another point of interest, for the Japanese are masters of *scale* and from this great Buddha down to the smallest netsuki in ivory (button for holding the cord of an inro in the belt) or the little animals in Dōhachi yaki (yaki means ware as yao does in Chinese) things are scaled so that they may appeal to our child-like instincts or so that they cause awe and wonder. This conscious struggle for significant scale does not please some Westerners. A friend of mine once said that in Japan everything was too big or too little. Towels are either little shreds good for nothing or so big you cannot handle them and cups are either thimbles or soup bowls. It is strange but in the Sung Chinese art we never think of scale and this shows that it is far better.

Nothing of interest so far as pottery goes occurred in the Jogan or Early Heian period (A.D. 794–897) or in the Fujiwara or Late Heian (A.D. 897–1185) and we may pass over this time except to note that taste became ornate with a fondness for gilding, Buddhism became involved and to quote Warner, "The very names of the gods became legion and each was different from the others in attitude and attributes." 1000-armed Kwannons were made and other feats of amazing patience. It was a time of *vulgar appeal of number*. If one god is good, a hundred are better. If two arms are good, why not a thousand? But the Japanese corrected this attitude in their tea ceremony as we shall see.

The Kamakura period (A.D. 1185–1336) began to feel the Sung culture of China. In 1223 the priest Dōyen is said to have taken Kato Shirazaemon to China to study the work of Sung potters and after a while he opened a kiln in Seto, Owari province and made a thin ware of purplish-black body glazed in brown with a brilliant black overglaze applied unevenly over it. Other glazes were "ko-Seto" (old Seto) wh'ch is yellowish or reddish in tone over a gray body and also a little later black, yellow brown and chocolate. But these are exceedingly rare.

Zen Buddhism, the sect for the individualist and self-reliant, has no scriptures and teaches that one should not heed the words of others but learn to know one's self and try to find out where one fits into both the spiritual and physical worlds. It encouraged portrait painting of its priests and also the type of pottery which is a part of nature. A jar should look as though it were growing rather than simply to have a picture of a growing plant on it. But still there was little in ceramics to interest us.

The Mongolian invasion stopped at the coast because of a typhoon which sunk the Mongolian boats.

Ashikaga Period (a.d. 1392–1568)

Now, a hundred years after the Sung period was through and done with, its influence became dominant in Japan and Sung paintings and ceramics were easy to obtain for they were not exciting enough for the Ming Chinese people. The Ashikaga period is looked upon as a sort of Sung Renaissance.

In order to understand the aesthetics of this time it is necessary to grasp the significance of the Tea Ceremony in Japan. This again was started in China by "Tea testing competitions" which were of ancient practice. A game was played and still is played in which the Chien yao tea-bowls were bet against each other in the following manner:—All were filled then drained and the bowl to hold the remaining moisture the longest time or the shortest time as decided upon won the others. This may sound silly until we find out that some of these bowls brought the equivalent of as much as $40,000 each and perhaps it is no more silly than watching a little ball skip around a roulette wheel. This, however, had another element involved, namely, the judgment of the bowls, for who would bet a very fine one against a mediocre one? And thus it was that much aesthetic and critical ability was developed and what started out to be a mere gambling game became one of the most powerful influences in the art of Japan.

By the time of the Ashikaga period the old Chinese game had changed to the Tea Ceremony. In this ceremony the tea is powdered and is highly selected and cured. Sometimes it is the brilliant green of "apple green porcelain" or of jade. It is kept in a small jar with ivory cover and small ivory spoon of just such a size. (I give the names of most of these implements below the illustration of the ceremony equipment.) This tea is very expensive. There are never more than a few guests, perhaps four at most, and they are served individually by the host who then washes the tea-bowl carefully and prepares another. Only a tiny amount of tea is used and hot water is placed in the bowl and the mixture frothed up with a small piece of bamboo split at the end so that it looks like a shaving brush. The guest often compliments the host on the tea-bowl and then drinks his tea in three and a half sips, making the proper noise of enjoyment and showing the proper expression of delight. The water is kept to just the temperature so that it makes a noise like wind through the pine trees as it simmers over a charcoal fire. A pottery jar of about eight or nine inches in height and provided with a lacquer cover receives the water with which the bowl is washed out.

The room is just two and a half mats square or about nine feet and ostentation and rank are cast aside in it. One enters not through the house but from the garden after carefully washing at a special pool arranged for that purpose. The door is so low that one has to enter on hands and knees. Everything must be simple and the idea is to show the best of taste with cheap materials. This is not entirely adhered to for I have heard of a single piece of

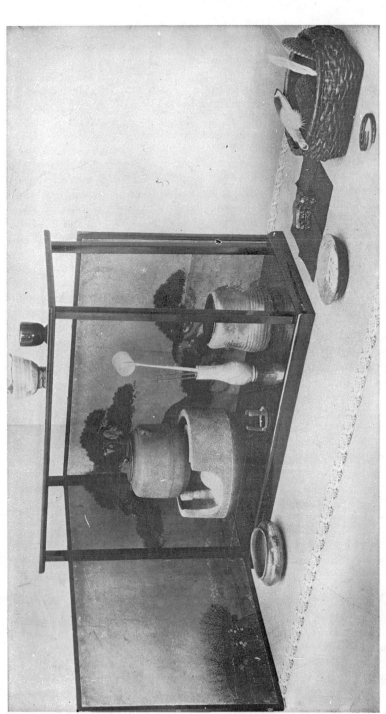

Japanese tea ceremony equipment including a "tea screen," the charcoal stove and iron kettle, a vase with iron chop sticks to handle the charcoal and the bamboo dipper for the hot water, the large jar into which the bowl is washed, etc. Metropolitan Mus. of Art.

JAPANESE TEA CEREMONY EQUIPMENT

PLATE 71

driftwood bringing hundreds of dollars, if it was just what was wanted. The only ornamentation is a simple arrangement of a painting and a few flowers or some object of art on the little platform which is raised about six inches from the floor and called the "takanoma." This is made for the one occasion only and great care is taken. Girls spend half their lives learning flower arranging in Japan and are not considered expert until they have spent years at it.

The Tea Ceremony was started after a time of internal strife and the originator, or that is he who made a cult of it, did so for the purpose of getting men's minds off of worldly advancement, ambition and ostentation. Its very essence, therefore, is economy and this great appeal in art the Japanese came to understand as no other people. The story is told of the man who first brought the morning glory to Japan. The mysterious and wonderful vine was talked of far and wide. Its beautiful flowers which appeared only in the early dawn, which were clear blue on bright days and purple toned when the humidity was high seemed impossible and a great prince of state traveled a long distance to come to see them. When he arrived the gardener's grounds were bare; all the flower beds were empty and strewn with white sand. It was an insult, a personal affront, unforgiveable! Perhaps the gardener did not know that the prince was friendly with the local governor and could have his head chopped off! But, as a samurai should be, the prince was punctilious and when he was received for the Tea Ceremony decided that he would go through with it first.

He washed his face in the cold springwater, sat a few moments which were supposed to be devoted to the enjoyment of the garden and were not, and removing his shoes, entered the softly lighted tea room. No picture hung in the "takanoma" (the little alcove with raised floor) but there stood a slender vase with one beautiful morning glory blossom, a few leaves and a curling tendril. After such an understanding of the appeal of economy in art the Japanese of culture did not go on with that cloying appeal of mere numbers like the 1,000 arms on a Buddha, until in the 18th century commerce made it popular again.

In the Momoyama period (A.D. 1568–1615) the great conqueror Hideyoshi took Korea and brought from there potters who were, shall we be kind enough to say, "under Imperial patronage" in Japan. The great hunger for good taste was about to be satisfied. The longing for culture could be fulfilled but, alas, the Mings of China were setting another standard and the inclination was to force more and more labor into a work of art. Craftsmen were but slaves to a ruling class which demanded more and ever more and thus all taste was lost. Only here and there among the Zen Buddhists do we find traces of appreciation of the Ashikaga art and the art of Sung China. And finally came the blight of western influence which we shall describe in the late 17th, 18th and early 19th centuries in China, of factory work, mass production and commerce.

JAPANESE POTTERY

The study of Japanese pottery is full of confusion for different wares may be called by the same name or one ware may be called by the name of the city in which it was made, the province, the place where it was extensively sold, the name of some "tea-master" who recommended it, or any one of the often many names of the potter who made it. In Hizen, Nagato and Tosa provinces the wares were not signed. Many ådherents of the Tea Ceremony were amateurs who made their own pieces. Great artists in other fields occa-sionally made a pot while on the other hand great paintings were copied by the potter on his ware and given the original artist's signature as tribute. When commercialism started many intended forgeries resulted. It would take a volume many times this size to sort out much of this but I shall simply

Fig. 423. Raku water jar of 3rd generation. Coarse red clay covered with yellowish glaze, dating about 1600. Said to be by Do-niu or Nonko. Ht. 6¾". Metropolitan Mus. of Art.
Fig. 424. Shino flower vase named from the tea-master or *chajin* Shino Sōshin who dictated the style, it is said, near the end of the 15th cent. This piece dates 18th cent. Ht. 9¾". Colman Coll. Metropolitan Mus. of Art.
Fig. 425. "Oribe ware" tea-bowl from Narumi near Seto in Owari province. Dating about 1780. Dia. 4¾". Havemeyer Coll. Metropolitan Mus. of Art.

touch upon the most famous wares and cover some of the others in the follow-ing charts giving full warning that the collector can only depend upon his understanding and taste plus a large amount of technical knowledge in order to collect these wares. Marks mean little or nothing.

The earliest Seto ware of the Kamakura period, about the 13th century, was symmetrical and wheel made. It was a close copy of the Tsung Sê tz'ŭ (or according to Hobson the "Honan Temmoku") wares, and consist of small bottles, jars and cups. In the Ashikaga period (A.D. 1392–1568) the potters were no longer content with the simple irregularities of glaze and began to scorn the wheel, making wares entirely by hand and not even trying to make them straight. This was a new thought about pottery; the endeavor to return to the primitive without improvement; the natural making of a piece of pottery in the easiest and simplest way. Of course it is an artificial attitude and we see altogether too much of it in our present day "modern art," the decadent sophisticate who tries to be the simple primitive. However, many wares resulted such as Shino-yaki, Oribe, Karatsu, Bizen, Hagi-yaki, Raku-yaki, Dohatchi-yaki, Chōsa-yaki, and early Satsuma and all were undecorated or only slightly and crudely decorated with dabs of the brush or finger, depending chiefly upon the irregular running of the glazes, splashes and splotches. It has been suggested that the appeal of asymmetry might have started from some Korai pieces which were not perfectly fired or had wilted in the kiln but, in any event, the appeal of the impression of the human hand fitted into the Zen Buddhistic philosophy of personal expression. Some potters used the wheel just a little. Some dispensed with a foot-rim or even a flat bottom. Many indented or pressed their wares between the palms when in the "leather state," partly dry before firing.

Asymmetry once discovered was found also to be true in many instances in nature and the flower arrangements, the arrangement of furniture and of the tray for eating all followed asymmetrical patterns quite the opposite of the Chinese symmetrical arrangements. We find precedent for this in Sung bird and flower painting but all Buddhistic art is symmetrical in China. It was a step forward and a great contribution which, if started in China, nevertheless should be largely credited to Japan. The little American newlywed will invariably try her best to make her room "balance," will put pairs of vases on the mantlepiece and buy pairs of lamps. Hundreds of American living rooms have a pair of lamps either side of a sofa and directly opposite another pair on either side of the fireplace. Symmetry is stiff, formal and uninteresting while asymmetry gives motion and life to an arrangement and it can regain a certain balance so as not to be disturbing. The dance has been described as a successive loss of one's balance and the regaining of it. Asymmetrical arrangements may be, like the dance, pleasant or unpleasant.

KENZAN

Some things which look like just nothing on first sight slowly impress themselves on us in time as the very soul and essence of an expressive art stripped of every last unnecessary and hampering detail. Such is the art of Kenzan, one of the greatest potters of Japan and one of the greatest artists

FIG. 426. Small jar of Japanese Musashi pottery by Kenzan.

FIG. 427. Kyoto ware writer's box, from Yamashiro province (1690–1741 A.D.) attributed to Kenzan. Length about 10″. Bequest of H. O. Havemeyer. Metropolitan Mus. of Art.

FIG. 428. Incense burner of Japanese Musashi pottery by Kenzan from Tōkyō. Freer Gallery of Art, Washington, D. C.

FIG. 429. Fire-pot of Japanese Musashi pottery by Kenzan, Tokyo. Flowers of this sort were also designed by his brother, Korin, who used them on wood block prints. Freer Gallery of Art, Washington, D. C.

the world has known. He was typically also called Ogata Shinshō, Sanshō, Shinzaburō, Shcko, Suiseidō, Shisui, Reikai, Tōin and other names. He was the younger brother of Korin, one of the greatest lacquer artists and painters that ever lived. Kenzan lived between A.D. 1661 and 1742 and was not only a potter but a poet, painter and master of the Tea Ceremony. As he enjoyed a fair sized surface on which to work, he made chiefly the "hiire" (brazier), the "kōgō" (incense box), the "sara" (tray), the "chawan" (tea-bowl), desk screens, writer's boxes and such things. Flowers, landscapes, occasional figures, birds and trees were his subjects and they were rendered with the fewest possible brush strokes in a few simple colors. He was never a static

Fig. 430. Dish of Japanese Musashi pottery by Kenzan, Tōkyō. Freer Gallery of Art, Washington, D. C.

Fig. 431. *Ogata Shinsho* or *Kenzan* pottery tray of the province of *Musashi* Japan 18th cent. This is c. 1720. Ht. 1½", length 9¾". Metropolitan Mus. of Art.

Fig. 432. Incense-box of Japanese Musashi pottery by Kenzan, Tokyo. Freer Gallery of Art, Washington, D. C.

artist and his styles varied. Many followed his various styles in all sincerity and unfortunately many in later years made outright fakes. The Japanese love his work and there are many enthusiastic collectors of it the world around, but many of the things even "in the style of" Kenzan are in our largest museums and are beautiful works of art.

Fig. 433. Fire-pot of Musashi pottery by Kenzan, showing his simple and direct brush work. Freer Gallery of Art, Washington, D. C.

Fig. 434. Screen for writer's desk from *Musashi* province, 18th cent. attributed to Kenzan. Ht. 10¼". Length 15¾". Metropolitan Mus. of Art.

Fig. 435. Bowl signed by Kenzan and dating about 1840. Decorated only with the face of Uzume modeled in low relief. Dia. 14½". Metropolitan Mus. of Art.

"MISHIMA" AND OTHER KOREAN WARES

As early as A.D. 1200 glazed pottery was made at the town of Karatsu in Hizen province and to the Japanese "karatsumono" (things from Karatsu) is an old term meaning pottery. Here imitations of "Korean" potteries and stonewares were made, many of which were black bodied like Chien yao and probably were not Korean at all. Some of these were intentionally of irregular shape and had splotches and daubs of different glazes. These are called "Chosen Karatsu."

There was also "e-Karatsu" (painted ware touched with swift strokes), "kenjō Karatsu" (presentation ware) and "mishima Karatsu" (inlayed ware) said to have been made as early as 1530 and in production by 1592 after the return of Hideyoshi. At Yatsushiro more naturalistic designs were also made in "mishima" ware with flying birds, etc. The earlier wares are more geometric.

Kenzan jar, Kyoto ware province of Yamashir[o] with crackled buff glaze decorated in dark brow[n] and gray. Ht. 4". Metropolitan Mus. of Art.

Interesting pottery tray with a painting signed by *Korin* and a poem signed by *Kenzan*. Length 8½". Morse Coll. # 4035. Boston Mus. of Fine Arts.

Two trays, the iris painted in green and brown, the bracken in vivid green, brown and blue and bot[h] bearing the signature of Kenzan. Dimensions 9¾" by 9½". Fuller Coll. Seattle Art Mus.

JAPANESE POTTERIES IN KENZAN STYLE

PLATE 72

FIG. 437. 17th cent. Bizen tea-jar. Ht. 1⅞". Metropolitan Mus. of Art.

FIG. 436. Bizen figure of a "Shishi" dating about 1800. Ht. 8". Macy Coll. Metropolitan Mus. of Art.

FIG. 438. Bronze-like bottle made in Imbe, Bizen province during the 18th cent. Ht. 6". Colman Coll. Metropolitan Mus. of Art.

BIZEN WARES

At Bizen a ware was made much like the Yi-hsing yao (described in the Ming Dynasty) or what is loosely called "Chinese bucchero" from a clay that burned smooth and hard at times looking like bronze, or again "aka" (red)

FIG. 440. 18th cent. figure of Shoki seated on waves about a rock, of hard pottery with metallic sheen of brown. Ht. 12¾". Freer Gallery of Art, Washington.

FIG. 439. Bizen 18th cent. glazed or partly glazed pottery incense burner showing excellence of modeling which was often associated with this place. Ht. 8½". Fuller Coll. Seattle Art Mus.

FIG. 441. Bizen 18th cent. incense burner of Kinko sitting on a carp. Ht. 9¾". Metropolitan Mus. of Art.

or "ao" steely blue. This unglazed ware was modeled into vases, animals, incense burners of fantastic shapes and plates. More recently bricks and drain pipes were made there. The amount of detail possible to achieve led to ornate and tasteless naturalism. Here again we find a too easy medium leading to mere virtuosity.

At best we can give in a book of this scope a general idea of the types of potteries made and, as we have tried to do, a method of approach to further study. The following chart will serve as a rough outline on which to build:

Left to Right: A symmetrical wine bottle of Seto ware from Owari province of 18th cent. Ht. 8". Colman Coll. Metropolitan Mus. of Art.—Owari province Seto ware "oil-bottle." According to museum of "Shino ware," named after chajin Shino. 17th–18th cent. Ht. 9½". Freer Gallery of Art, Washington.—19th cent. Shino square bottle, Owari province. Ht. 8½". Colman Coll. Metropolitan Mus. of Art.—Owari ware saki bottle signed "Shun-Tai" dating from 19th cent. Ht. 9". Metropolitan Mus. of Art.

Left to Right: "Ki-Seto" (yellow Seto) vase from Owari province, showing influence of Ming "three color" ware. Ht. 13⅜".—Owari province Seto ware called "Shino-yaki" after *chajin* Shino who is supposed to have set the style. Ht. 13½".—Owari province flower vase called "Akatsu" by museum. Ht. 9½". Freer Gallery of Art, Washington.—rown crackle glazed bottle with exaggerated neck. 17th cent. Seto ware from Owari province. Ht. 11½". Colman Coll. Metropolitan Mus. of Art.

Left: Water jar from Narumi near Seto in Owari province, of the Oribe type following the traditions of Furuta Shigeyoshi. Ht. 5". Warren E. Cox Coll. *Center:* 18th cent. Shino type, Owari tea-jar. Ht. 3¾". Warren E. Cox Coll. *Right: Chawan* or tea bowl of *"Ki-seto"* from Owari province of brownish greenish ware with incised decoration in some ways resembling the heavy "celadons" found at *Showchow in Anwei* province, China. 18th cent. Ht. 3". Metropolitan Mus. of Art.

OWARI PROVINCE POTTERIES

"Ko-seto" or old Seto bowl of the type # 3. Dia. 5½". Metropolitan Mus. of Art.

Seto late 18th cent. glazed pottery dish painted in black and blue. Dia. 9½". Fuller Coll. Seattle Art. Mus.

"Chōsen Karatsu" bowl from Hizen province of the 18th cent. This is of the "hakeme" type and the inlayed design makes it possible also to call it "mishima." Dia. 9¾". Colman Coll. Metrópolitan Mus. of Art.

| (a) | (b) | (c) | (d) |

(a) "Shigaraki" (Omi province) oil dish c. 1770. Such dishes were placed under hanging oil lamps to catch the drip. Dia. 8½". Metropolitan Mus. of Art.

(b) "Ye-Karatsu" or "E-Karatsu" water jar painted in brownish black after the Tz'u Chou style. Ht. 6¼". Freer Gallery of Art, Washington.

(c) Asymmetrical bottle of Imbe ware, Bizen province, with a metallic sheen over it. Late 17th or early 18th cent. Ht. 7½". Freer Gallery of Art, Washington.

(d) 19th cent. (c. 1820) Takatori group comprising Kanyan and Jittoku. Ht. 8". Macy Coll. Metropolitan Mus. of Art.

Left: Takatori, (Chikuzen province) water jar for the tea-ceremony. Dark reddish-brown clay and a splashed glaze. 18th cent. Ht. 7¼". Colman Coll. Metropolitan Mus. of Art.

Center: Kôda ware bottle (Yatsushiro) of gray clay with white decoration. Ht. 9". Freer Gallery of Art, Washington.

Right: A Kôda (Yatsushiro) water jar from Higo province. Ht. 6½". Freer Gallery of Art, Washington.

JAPANESE POTTERIES

PLATE 74

Rikei type bowl from Hagi in Nagato province showing the strong brush work called *"hakeme"* Korean style. Dia. 5¾". Freer Gallery of Art, Washington.

Left: Late 19th cent. Yatsushiro vase. Ht. 8½". Macy Coll. Metropolitan Mus. of Art. *Right:* 19th-cent. Kutani vase, crude in manufacture but with spirited writing. Ht. 16½". Freer Gallery of Art, Washington.

Shidoro type water jar of 19th cent. Ht. 5½". Colman Coll. Metropolitan Mus. of Art.

Tea-jar with ivory cover. Japanese Awaji ware attributed to Mimpei, first generation, c. 1830. Freer Gallery of Art, Washington.

Center: From Rakuzan, this bottle, given date c. 1835. Izumo province. Ht. 9¾". Freer Gallery of Art, Washington.

Jar into which water is poured after washing tea cup. Kyoto ware, Yamashiro province, attr. to Koyetsu. Glaze red and green. c. 1620. H. O. Havemeyer Bequest. Metropolitan Mus. of Art.

Raku-yaki tea-bowl marked "Banjen" 1790, of 9th generation. Dia. 3½". Mus. of Fine Arts, Boston.

Center: "Onohara" saki bottle. Probably a Tachikui piece, date, 1750. Ht. 9½". Freer Gallery of Art, Washington.

JAPANESE POTTERIES

PLATE 75

Left: A tobacco box said to be of Raku ware dating 1840. Macy Coll. Metropolitan Mus. of Art.
Center: Awata (Yamashiro province) tea-jar by Ninsei (Nonomura Seibei) c. 1660. Dark body with thick metallic brown-black and dull white glaze. Ht. 3″. Metropolitan Mus. of Art.
Right: Vase from Awata (18th cent.) probably by Takahashi Dōhachi, who was a bamboo carver too. Perhaps it reflects a slender bamboo feeling. Ht. 11½″. Colman Coll. Metropolitan Mus. of Art.

Left: Awata saki bottle of the 18th cent. Ht. 8¾″. Metropolitan Mus. of Art.
Center: Awata, kettle and stove perhaps made by the Hōzan family. Late 18th cent. Macy Coll. Metropolitan Mus. of Art.
Right: "Daikoku, god of luck" figure of so called "Kyōto ware" but actually from Kiyomizu, Yamashiro province. Ht. 8″. Metropolitan Mus. of Art.

Awata, bowl made about 1800. Dia. 11¾″. Metropolitan Mus. of Art.

Left: Kyoto (Yamashiro province) tea-jar supposed to have been decorated by "Zengoro Hozen" but certainly very strongly like the design of a late Sung or Early Ming Lung-ch'üan "celadon." Ht. 5½″. Metropolitan Mus. of Art.
Right: Awata, incense burner of the old Taoist symbol of a child on a water-buffalo. c. 1720. Metropolitan Mus. of Art.

JAPANESE POTTERIES

PLATE 76

Musashi province statue of Manzai dancer probably by Kōren, Tōkyō c. 1825. Ht. 18½". Freer Gallery of Art, Washington.

Bowl from Kishū province, copy of Chinese *san ts'ai* or three color type with cloisonnes. 19th cent. Dia. 4¼". Macy Coll. Metropolitan Mus. of Art.

Satsuma tea-jar of the late 19th cent. far better than most of the time and place. Ht. 2½". Freer Gallery of Art, Washington.

Saki bottle from Kiyomizu, (Yamashiro province). Buff body, faun colored finely crackled glaze, decorated with underglaze blue of grayish tone. c. 1750. Havemeyer Coll. Metropolitan Mus. of Art.

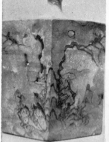

Soma ewer c. 1840 from Iwaki province with greenish gray buff ground and colored glazes on the relief decoration. Ht. 9¾". Macy Coll. Metropolitan Mus. of Art.

Kiyomizu (Yamashiro province) saki bottle. Faun color with irregular stains and underglaze decoration in gray-blue. c. 1750. Ht. 7". Havemeyer Coll. Metropolitan Mus. of Art.

A *cha wan* or tea bowl of black Satsuma pottery from the island of Kyūshū c. 1680. Dia. 4⅛". Metropolitan Mus. of Art.

Satsuma vase said to be of Korean form and covered with a dark brown glaze. Ht. 12½". Freer Gallery of Art, Washington.

Satsuma flower vase of the type called *"mishima"* by the Japanese. Inlayed in imitation of the Korean wares. Some of this ware was made by actually Korean potters who settled there. Ht. 9½". Freer Gallery of Art, Washington.

Yamashiro charcoal fire bowl by Dōhachi. Possibly by Dōhachi II the most famous member of the family, the one who practiced first this entirely Japanese style. Dia. about 12". Freer Gallery of Art, Washington.

Dish by Miura Kenya which has much the feeling of the art of Kenzan. Length 6½". Freer Gallery of Art, Washington.

Finely crackled cream ware of the Boku Heii type. This Satsuma water jar is good in form and well decorated after the Tz'u Chou style of the Ming period. Ht. 6". Freer Gallery of Art, Washington.

JAPANESE POTTERIES

PLATE 77

IDENTIFICATION CHART OF JAPANESE POTTERIES

OWARI PROVINCE

Town	Chajin or "Tea-man"	Artist	Description of wares
Town not known for certain—for first ware.	The priest *Dōyen* set out for China in 1223 and took "Tōshirō I," with him, to learn Chinese potting.	*Katō Shirozaemon* was a potter called "*Tōshirō I.*" Did not sign his work.	*First type.*—Clay brought from China was purplish brown and finely washed, potting done with very thin walls and foot smooth and flat or "*hon-itohiri*" that is with lines swinging clockwise around to the right from the thread with which the piece is separated from the wheel. A first glaze of brown was applied evenly and a black glossy second glaze was poured over showing streaks and spots.
The town of *Seto* was center for later types.			"*Old Seto*" or "*ko-Seto*" grey body of yellowish or reddish tone, coarsely and more heavily potted. This clay was first from Seto and with Japanese glaze. It has a reddish-brown underglaze and black brilliant overglaze.
			Variations:—Two more variations are: a.—with light spots strewn over the brown primary glaze and b.—with the reverse.
			Unglazed type:—Brinckmann has called attention to a piece in the Hamburg Museum, a "chaire" or small tea-ceremony jar of age-darkened pale grey body with a chestnut brown glaze inside only (see Hannover—Pottery & Porcelain of the Far East Fig. 350). This piece has relief decoration, and Hannover suggests that it may be one of those made from "clay from strange parts" such as Tōshirō is said to have tried such as from Asahi in Mino.
Also *Seto*		*Toshiro II*, no signature on pieces.	Brinkley says have a similar body to "ko-Seto" and a brilliant, thick and not very transparent glaze. From them Hannover says descended the thin and transparent, pale yellow glazes, crackled and sometimes shaded with blue of the 16th century called "yellow Seto" or "ki-Seto." (See Ki-Seto from Freer Gallery c. 1630 vase.) The piece illustrated certainly shows Ming Chinese influence strongly though the earlier bowls do not.
Seto		*Toshiro III.* Did not sign his work.	Tōshirō III is said to have made a new glaze of golden color called "*kin-kwa-zan.*" Hannover states that no examples from these masters are known in the Western hemisphere, though later pieces of similar style are well known.
Seto	"chajin" *Shino Sōshin.*	This style set by the tea-master was followed by many artists.	*Shino-yaki* was ordered to be made in Seto near the last of the 15th century by the tea-master Shino Sōshin and lasted to the end of the 19th century. It is thick, and coarse, of irregular shapes and high-fired with bubbly and large crackled only slightly fluid glaze decorated in blue, brown or iron oxide with very brief painting of a few strokes only.

245

Town	Chajin or "Tea-man"	Artist	Description of wares
Narumi near Seto	*Furuta Shigeyoshi* commonly called "*Oribe*" founded a school in 1585.	Many artists.	*Oribe-yaki* as a style was set by Oribe when he ordered 66 tea-jars of strange shapes a few of which were very roughly painted with cranes, plum blossom, etc. in dark brown, moss-green and other colored glazes.
Nagoya		*Chin Gempin* was a Chinese potter who did sign his wares.	*Gempin-yaki* is grey stoneware with a soft crackled glaze with brief decorations of figures, cranes and bushes, flowers etc. in blue and black. These were made in the 16th century.
(See Marks, Japanese)			
Tokoname		Various artists.	A coarse, red and unglazed earthenware decorated with cord marks and also incised designs of trees, birds, etc. Near end of 15th century was making a glazed ware which more recently was decorated with dragons, clouds, scrolls, etc. stamped on.
Nagoya		*Oki Toyosuke* 19th century potter.	One sort of earthenware with white glaze opaque and crackled and decorated with "Raku-like green spots" according to Hannover. Another with black or dark green lacquer and designs in gold, silver and colors.
Inaki near Nagoya			"*Inuyama-yaki*" has a grey, stoneware body with thick, opaque glaze of Shino type but more even and is decorated with trees and leaves in brown, vivid green and red. The name comes from a castle nearby. Imitations bear a spurious Kenzan signature. (See Hannover, Fig. 347.)
	HIZEN PROVINCE		
Karatsu		Corean potters brought to Japan by Hideyoshi's officers.	"*Oku-Kōrai*" or "old Corean" ware was probably of typical Corean type including the "mishima" or inlayed type and others. In fact the collector can differentiate these only by surmise from the clay; an odd piece of Corean ware is likely to have been made in Japan. "*Chōsen Karatsu*" is a later ware for the name Chōsen was given to Corea during the revolution of Yi Taijo.—Some are of blue-black clay with glaze which looks like cast iron, and others are smeared with streaks of white or olive green over a brown, green or black glaze. This is called "*hakeme*" or brush streaked. "*Mishima Karatsu*," previously mentioned and above under oku-Kōrai. "*E-Karatsu*" means painted Karatsu ware which is usually swiftly touched with black or brown in a rude manner. "*Kenjō-Karatsu*" is similar to the above but finer having been made for the prince of Hizen for a "presentation ware." This is of a fine yellowish or brownish clay with transparent crackle glaze and generally has *mishima* work on it.

246

Hizen	*Goroshichi* may be a purely legendary potter but according to Ninagawa he is supposed to have worked somewhere in Hizen c. 1530.	"*Goroshichi*" is used to designate all large tea bowls, but also a special type are supposed to be like the ones he did (if he existed) and they are large, of brownish clay with white crackled glaze and decorated in a not very good blue.

BIZEN PROVINCE

Imbe	Many Kyōto artists over a long period of time not definitely established as yet. In 1400 a large kiln 120 feet by 15 feet is reported built. Firing lasted 60 days and cooling the same length of time. A short while ago *Mimura Mosaburo* tried to revive the industry but failed.	Bizen ware or *Bizen-yaki* fires dark grey on the inside and brown or bronze colored on the outside. It is not glazed but has a glossy look and sometimes it appears to have a brown glaze or black glaze over it. Nearly all bear a stamped mark—circle, rectangle or rhomb with numerals in it. Figures, vases, tea-ceremony vessels (after the 16th century), were made but the best are of the 18th century, technically speaking, at any rate. "*Aka-Bizen-yaki*" is the common red Bizen ware and "*Ao-Bizen-yaki*" is steel blue. Bizen plates were made in the Meiji period (1868–1912) for European use in competition with Chinese *Yi-hsing yao* or so called "*buccaro*." (See Chinese and Roman sections.)

SETTSU PROVINCE

Sanda		*Sanda-Seiji* is a celadon porcelain and is further mentioned in the porcelain chart.
Kosobe	*Igarashi Shimpei* c. 1800 studied in Kyōto and made imitations of Ninsei and Raku. *Shinzō* his successor took his ideas from Takatori, Karatsu and also Corea. In the third generation the shop followed Rokubei. *Komatsuya Tasuke* was an amateur potter who worked at times for the 4th generation.	*Kosobe-yaki* is a stoneware with a hard and sandy body ranging from dark grey to buff or reddish white. The glaze is pearly grey, reddish grey-yellow, or white. The sketchy decoration is in black or brown. It is hardly recognizable from other wares except for being stamped KOSOBE and sometimes TAINEN the art name of *Komatsuya Tasuke*.

ŌMI PROVINCE

Shigaraki in the *Na-gano* district.	There was a very ancient pottery made here. Beginning the 16th century. chajin *Fōō*. *Rikyū* lived at the close of the 16th century. *Sotan* c. 1630. *Enshū* c. 1650 prince of *Tōtōmi* and a famous chajin.	"*Fōō Shigaraki*" ware is grey clay turned reddish in firing and has a reddish-brown or brown primary glaze with an olive or grey green glaze running down irregularly and sometimes with small pieces of unfused quartz in it. "*Rikyū Shigaraki*" is a grey crackled stoneware. "*Sotan Shigaraki*," a variety like the others and various. "*Enshū Shigaraki*," also similar. All are perhaps distinguished by a certain feeling of rough and irregular shape and surface.

IDENTIFICATION CHART OF JAPANESE POTTERIES—*Continued*

Town	Chajin or "Tea-man"	Artist	Description of wares
Zeze, a district on the Lake Biwa.		Only from c. 1650 to c. 1700.	Chaki (articles for the tea-ceremony) resemble old Seto and not inferior to Takatori masterpieces. The body is dark grey and fine. The glazes are golden brown, brownish-red and purple.
CHIKUZEN PROVINCE			
Takatori n.e. of Hizen.	*Enshū* c. 1650 also liked this ware.	Originally by two Coreans carried from that country by Hideyoshi's generals: *Shinkurō* and *Hachizō*. Shinkurō dies c. 1825 and (as we find in Hannover) *Hachizō* is thought to have gone to Enshū although this would seem to make him about 175 years old! Brinkley says that there are three kilns only one of which is now copying the old wares but not very well.	Chaki for the tea-ceremony. *Ko Takatori* (old Takatori) is dull brown, yellow or black spotted in glaze. *Enshū Takatori-yaki* was produced by *Hachizō*, his son and also by *Igarashi Jizaemon*, a potter from *Karatsu* experienced in Seto glazing. Wheel thrown shapes and golden Autumn brown glazes. Morse says, "The usual form is cylindrical, slightly tapering below, often with two ears or knobs on the shoulder. The thread-mark (itokiri) is right handed and finely cut. Other forms occur, some short and wide, others globular; the double gourd form is not unusual. The clay is very fine, usually a grey-drab, though sometimes a light or dark brown or fawn. The glaze is rich, dark-brown often subdued in lustre. All shades of brown are seen, such as olive-brown, golden-brown, purplish-brown etc. Sometimes a light fawn glaze appears. A splash of fawn overglaze is usually seen on one side." Hannover continues, "The only tea-jars with which those of *Takatori* can be confused are those of *Buzen* and *Zeze* in certain of their forms. In order to procure fresh material, the pottery works were repeatedly shifted from place to place. According to Brinkley, it should therefore be possible to determine the approximate age of *Takatori* ware from the clay. In the earliest period (1600–1660) it is said to have been light grey, then (1660–1700) nearly white, and in the third period (1700–1800) reddish and at times purple tone. The glazes are usually grey or greyish-yellow with touches of green, brown or blue.
BUZEN AND HIGO PROVINCES			
Agano in Buzen.	*Enshū* influence also.	1602 founded by *Sonkai* who called himself *Agano Kizō* and died in 1646. 1632 when the Prince of Buzen was given charge of *Higo* province *Kizō* established himself at *Yatsushiro*. His son remained in Agano. There are still endeavors in this town to imitate old wares.	*Sonakai's* first work was like the Corean of coarse clay, and with black glazes. Some later wares are of reddish clay with a purplish brown or brownish-yellow glaze with texture like melon skin. In *Yatsushiro*, Kizō resumed his Corean style and made partly *hakeme* and partly *mishima* ware with white or rarely black inlay but always more loosely and less formalized than the Corean, some are "*unkaku-de*" or cranes flying among clouds. In *Agano* c. 1820–30 large bowls were made very light in weight of yellow clay with transparent glaze or harder fired white. Some have poured over them "robin's egg" or other colored glaze sometimes alternating from the center radially with a rich brown glaze.
Yatsushiro in *Higo*			

248

BUZEN AND HIGO PROVINCE

Yatsushiro in *Higo*. and *Kōda* a town nearby.	These towns have also revived the old wares but they lack the "soft and mild sheen."	*Yatsushiro-yaki* or *Kōda-yaki* has a cold grey clay which does not offer the same contrast with the white that the old clay does, which was reddish. Larger pieces are always modern. In the old ware the inlay is restrained to white, only rarely is black or blue used. The glaze is yellowish-grey or olive-brown-grey or greyish coffee-colored. Larger pieces such as vases are always modern.

NAGATO AND IZUMO PROVINCES

Hagi in *Nagato*.	*Rikei* a Corean adopted the name *Kōraizaemon*.	*Hagi-yaki* is developed from the Corean stoneware called *Ido-yaki* has a grey crackled glaze clouded with salmon. *Rikei* also produced Corean *hakeme* with its powerful brush strokes in grey and later in pale green and light lavender-blue or on grey and yellowish-white grounds. *Oni-Hagi* was made by *Gombei* and it means "demon Hagi."
Rakuzan in *Izumo*.	*Gombei* was a pupil of the master *Kōraizaemon* and was summoned to *Rakuzan* in c. 1675.	
Matsumoto and *Fukagawa* also in *Nagato*.		*Matsumoto-yaki* and *Fukagawa-yaki* Morse says cannot be distinguished except occasionally from those of *Hagi*. *Hagi's* late reproductions are not of interest except perhaps a *mishima* similar to *Yatsushiro-yaki*.

KAGA PROVINCE

Ōhi (See *Kutani* porcelain also in *Kaga*.)	A member of the Raku family came in 1683,—Haji Chōzaemon. (See *Yamashiro* province.)	Brown glazed ware like *Raku* sometimes brownish-red in the early 15th century but similar to Raku since 1683, has a reddish-yellow, honey or amber colored glaze and bears the mark Ōhi stamped—

ISE PROVINCE

Banko	Mostly from 1868 and made in great quantities all over *Ise*, especially at *Yokkaichi*.	Usually tea-pots, flower-vases, etc. usually of thin walls and shaped by hand showing finger marks or molded and bearing sprays in relief or flowers in enamel colors on the unglazed grey ground, but sometimes made of "marbled clays," of different colors. Old Banko appears in many forms many of which copy Karatsu, Shino, ki-Seto, Raku, Kōda and some Satsuma wares, so closely that they would be indistinguishable save for the mark.
Kuwana? *Yedo?*	*Old Banko-yaki* perhaps made by "*Gozaemon*," who was a wealthy amateur potter whose real name was *Numanami* but there is some doubt about this. By 1878 there were 21 potters from Ise showing at the Paris International Exposition.	

IDENTIFICATION CHART OF JAPANESE POTTERIES—*Continued*

YAMATO PROVINCE

Town	Chajin or "Tea-man"	Artist	Description of wares
Akahada-yama, a mountain province.	The prince was a *chajin* and painted some articles.	Derived from an older kiln which was reorganized in 1761 by the prince of Kōriyama with potters from Kyōto.	Marked or it would be hard to tell from Takatori, Hagi or Kyōto wares save that it is perhaps a bit more sandy in body. 2nd period ware have brown or reddish yellow brown glazes, not bright, with designs painted over in enamels delicately. Some are in low relief with designs such as Fuji. Others had white crackled glazes, monochromes and flambé. Still another type have dull gold ground on which are painted flowers and ornaments sometimes also laid on in pipe-clay or paste.

AWAJI ISLAND

Town	Chajin or "Tea-man"	Artist	Description of wares
Iga	*Kashū Mimpei* was a rich *chajin* also called *Toyonosuke*.	c. 1830 a Kyōto potter named *Ogata Shūhei*. His nephew *Sampei* kept up with his son and a pupil.	*Awaji-yaki* has a yellow glaze similar to Imperial Chinese and also a deep green similar to Chinese apple green and later a greyish-white and a black. Later still tortoise-shell effects were obtained. Also understood gold and silver. *Ogata Shūhei*'s own ware is of pale grey, has a dense and hard body and the glaze has a yellow crackle (small) and resembles Awata ware (see below). This is rare.
Sumoto		Also a new kiln at Sumoto was established in 1883.	The nephew and the Sumoto wares are of earthenware like Kyōto with a yellow crackled glaze decorated in enamels and gold.

IZUMI PROVINCE

Town	Chajin or "Tea-man"	Artist	Description of wares
Minato		It is amusing to know that it was here that the potter's wheel was said to have been invented *in the 18th century* by *Gyōgi-bosatsu*, a priest. Also *Dōraku* called *Kichibei* and brother of the 3d *Raku* started a kiln in 1655 and adopted *Yakei* a Kyōto potter. 8 generations lasted to 1861.	An early ware has grey, purple or blue glaze, and there are also unglazed pieces, all with a light body similar to Raku. Most of the generations used the name *Kichiemon*, and do even to-day. They made a light Raku-like ware with a colorless and transparent glaze and an opaque, mat, dark yellow glaze over it. The family used also a green glaze, as well as white, yellow and green combined.

IGA PROVINCE

Town	Chajin or "Tea-man"	Artist	Description of wares
Marubashira	*Enshū* was the *chajin*.		Stone-ware like that of the nearby *Ōmi* province in the town of *Shigaraki* though not quite so reddish. Usually of rough and crude shape and undecorated.

TŌTŌMI PROVINCE

Shidoro	Enshū c. 1670–1730. Also later activity in kiln.	*Shidoro-yaki* is quite simple in form and undecorated but has autumn yellows and browns, rich brown-black, alternating with yellow- or red-browns covering a darker glaze as with a net.

IZUMO PROVINCE

Fujina	*Gombei* went to *Rakuzan* c. 1675 for 18 years and about 1750 to *Fujina*.	The wares attributed to him look like *Hagi-yaki* being very primitive and sometimes with a granulated glaze. From *Fujina* come wares with yellow or flambé glazes.

TAMBA PROVINCE

	Originally in *Onohara* but c. 1650 moved to *Tachikui*.	*Tamba-yaki* is said to "combine the beauty of *Takatori-yaki*," with the simplicity of *Seto-yaki* and the solidity of *Shidoro-yaki*," by the Japanese collectors. It is a hard fired ware of reddish body with chocolate, mahogany and bluish-black glaze and at times with splashes of yellow. To *Tachikui* are also attributed saki bottles with colored liquid glazes also unglazed ones in grey with a crane or flower painted in white or brown.

YAMASHIRO PROVINCE

Kyōto or also called *Yamashiro* but also *Awata* *Iwakura* *Mizoro* *Kiyomizu*	2nd half of the 16th century many *Seto* potters came to the city of *Kyōto*. Also the Corean, *Ameya* or *Masakichi* came perhaps c. 1525 or a bit later. His sister continued work. Ameya's son *Chōjirō* who died sometime between 1592 and 1610 was given a golden seal by *Hideyoshi*, with the character *Raku* meaning "contentment." The family is still working and using the same seal. Also Honnami *Kōetsu* and his son *Kūchū* made *Raku-yaki*.	The Corean style was used in the capital before elsewhere, perhaps 50 years before. After *Ameya's* death his widow as a lay sister or *"ama"* carried on making *Ama-yaki*. *Raku-yaki* is of coarse clay and lightly fired, is of grey or light brown and shaped by hand into thick walled bowls with carved or scraped surfaces. First it was black glazed, then red was added, then, still later a green glaze was used and finally a straw-yellow and even white. The glaze may be thin and porous or thick and glossy and often covers the foot. This ware does not transmit heat readily and is valued for tea-drinking. It is usually not decorated but sometimes has a lightly sketched design in a contrasting colored glaze or even gold. The firing only lasts a few hours and the pieces are taken from the kiln with tongs the marks of which are to be often seen. Such pieces are called *"hasami-yaki"* or *"tong-ware."* There were many copyists and also forgeries so the oldest looking piece may be quite new.

Note:—Hannover says truly, "The value of Raku ware can hardly be fully appreciated by Europeans, as it depends to a great extent on refinements connected with the enjoyment of tea, such as only the Japanese *chajin* can thoroughly relish." We can hardly agree with Mr. Hannover's modest statement, however, for we cannot help but enjoy these wares so honestly made to show attributes we have already discussed.

IDENTIFICATION CHART OF JAPANESE POTTERIES—Continued

Town	Chajin or "Tea-man"	Artist	Description of wares
Kyōto		*Ninsei* was a painter and amateur potter from about 1630 to 1640. The Japanese say of him that he could turn out anything but porcelain or celadon.	*Ninsei-yaki* at first was like *Takatori*, Seto, Shigaraki or Chinese and Corean models. Now it is interesting to note that at this early period the search for the secrets of potting was going on and he, *Ninsei*, had to get his ideas surreptitiously from the potters of *Arita*, who were masters of enamels. His stoneware is of red or yellowish clay and is dense, smooth and hard fired. His crackles formed a circular mesh of yellow or fish-belly-grey color, and quite regular. Among his monochromes is a metallic black over a grass green, to give it life. Over such grounds he painted flowers or ornamental patterns in gold, silver, red and other enamels with economy.
	Note:—Many imitations exist, and some bear his mark. But these are among the most costly rarities.		
Kyōto *Iriya* in the *Musashi* province.		*Kenzan* or *Ogata Shinshō* or (see text) 1661–1742. *Kenzan* spent his old age in *Iriya*.	He made all sorts of *chaki* or tea-ceremony potteries except the little jars for holding the powdered tea which are called *chaire*. He painted usually the *hire* or braziers, the *kōgō* or incense-box, the *sara* or tray and less often the *chawan* or tea-bowl. The older he became, the bolder was his brush work, on pieces called *Iriya-Kenzan*. So many were the types of rough and swiftly painted wares that he made and so many many more are the imitations by such men as *Dōhachi, Kenzan, Sandai, Kenya, Makuzu* and many others right up to the present day that competent distinction can hardly be made. Some have considered **Brinckman**, who depends upon Ninagawa, as the best authority but I have heard Japanese collectors laugh at his attempts. Perhaps this is more a problem for the study of the styles of Kenzan's painting than the actual technical aspects of his potting. The illustrations will give the reader some notion at least.
Iwakura and later at *Awata*.		*Kinkōzan* family.	A crackled yellow or grey Awata export ware with bright coloring and shiny enamels in scratchy designs but originally the ware was not unlike a sort of thin Kenzan type of design.
Was first in *Ōmi* but came to *Kyōto* at *Awata*		*Taizan* family:—*Takahashi Tōkurō* was the founder coming to Kyōto c. 1680 and later to *Awata* in 1711. The early generation called themselves *Yohei*.	A blue glazed ware was made for the Imperial Household. Export wares in modern times with red or blue glaze or with colored decoration on a mat yellow glaze.
Awata		*Hōzan* family after the 18th century and even to to-day, though not in *Awata*.	Blue underglaze ware with a finely crackled thick glaze over a yellow or white slip which is sometimes even laid on in relief.

252

Kiyomizu near Kyōto.	*Seibei Yahyō* c. 1700 who was also called *Ebisei*.	*Ebisei-yaki* is not unlike *Ninsei-yaki*.
	Eisen was a pupil of *Ebisei* and he founded the first true porcelain factory in Kyōto.	He imitated Chinese Lung Ch'üan yao and also Ming painting in red, green and gold.
	Robukei was still another pupil (1738–99). He was of the Kotō family which continued through *Rokubei II, Shichibei,* and *Shorin Rokubei*.	His work shows great technique in enamels and a certain artistic, though over sweet taste in application. He followed *Maruyama Ōkyo's* realistic ideas and also *Gekkei* or *Goshun* and even at times had these masters decorate his wares. His monochromes are famous and sometimes he worked in decoration in reserve and often in underglaze blue.
Awata	*Takahashi Dōhachi* was a pupil of *Eisen* (1740–1840) and he carved bamboo as well as making pottery.	He did porcelain, earthenware and stoneware, and different from the Chinese styles; more of the *Shijō* or realistic school and some speed and directness.
Gojōzaka near Kiyomizu.	His son *Dōhachi II* came in 1811 to *Gojōzaka*.	
Momoyama	*Dōhachi III* in 1842 moved to *Momoyama*.	
	Dōhachi IV was recently president of the Kyōto Potters.	
	Aoki Mokubei—(1767–1833) was another pupil of *Eisen*.	Porcelain and stoneware of some considerable variation and no great importance.
	Kitei.	Followed Dōhachi and also made porcelain.

Then the *Yosobei*, the *Zōroku* or *Ōtani*, *Hiaku ju*, etc. families began to make porcelain and the conditions were not unlike those which held sway in Europe.

Kyōto	Moderns. *Seifū Yohei* is the third of a family. The 1st died 1861. The 2nd in 1878. His art name is *Baikei*.	*Baikei* makes porcelain, pottery and stoneware specializing in celadon and blanc de Chine, also underglaze blue porcelain and blue and red. His work suffers from the same fussy over ornate quality which is prevalent in Japan to-day.
In 1870 he moved to Ōta near Yokohama, in Musashi province.	*Miyagawa Kōzan* has the art name of *Makuzu*.	Imitations of Satsuma ware, they are earthenware with high relief, and naturally colored birds, fishes, flowers etc. These are terrible, but later he made copies of many of the Chinese monochromes and enamelled pieces of the K'ang Hsi and Yung Chêng periods. He also made forgeries of Ninsei ware.

Thus we see that in the 18th and 19th centuries the Japanese were not behind in the merry game of copying and stealing designs and technical "dope" from every hand, but it is not necessary to go further into the iniquitous practices.

253

Town	Chajin or "Tea-man"	Artist	Description of wares
Asahi (Uji) in *Yamashiro* province.	*Zōroku* 17th century.		Yellowish-white or greyish-yellow glazes.
		MUSASHI PROVINCE	
Tōkyō also *Irya* and *Imado*.		*Kenzan* settled at *Irya* in his old age and died in 1743, at 81.	See Kyōto.
		The *Hanshichi* family worked for several generations in *Imado*.	*Imado-yaki* in the first generation is unglazed *chaki* (tea-ceremony wares), in the 2nd a sort of *Raku* ware.
		Haritsu or *Ritsuō* was a pupil of *Kōrin* and *Kenzan*.	He made flowers, insects etc. of low fired *Raku-yaki* to inlay in his lacquer of gold etc.
Asakusa north of *Tōkyō*		*Miura Kenya* came from *Kyōto* (c. 1830–1840).	He too fired at low temperatures a sort of *Raku* ware in flowers and insects to use in inlaying similar to that of *Haritsu*. (See just above.)
Tōkyō		*Hattori Tsuna* is a woman called *Kōren*, worked in the last part of the 19th century.	Plastic figures modeled in an unglazed ware resembling wood in appearance.
		IWAKI PROVINCE	
Iwaki		The artist *Kanō Naonobu* once visited *Iwaki* province and did the design or model of the horse. He died in 1650.	"*Sōma-yaki*" named from the house of *Sōma* have, as a rule only one design, that of a *tethered horse*. The ware is of coarse, grey stone-ware with a thin, transparent glaze of brown-speckled, or pin-holed type or at times with various colors of a sort of transmutation type,—or it may be without glaze. The decoration is painted with a few strokes in black or blue, brown or white or infrequently in gold. It is also rarely incised or in relief having been moulded and applied. A type with granulated glaze but same designs is of the late 18th century.

254

Satsuma also *Nawashirogawa* near *Kagoshima.*

Korean potters settled here in the 15th century and made dark Korean wares. In the last of the 16th century a prince of *Satsuma* brought from Korea 17 potters who soon scattered.

Boku Heii, one of them, found a fine clay from which he made a finely crackled cream ware and with *Kanyu* from c. 1640 made "white Satsuma" which is fine and good.

Late ware not over fifty years old is terrible, ornate and over detailed export ware on a finely crackled, glassy, cream colored ground, in all colored enamels and gold, made only for the Japanese conception of European taste. Much of this ware does not even come from Satsuma.

Chaki were made by the Koreans of fine, brown stoneware with greenish or golden brown fluid glazes. The earlier Koreans made a dark colored stoneware.

Nawashirogawa is where the clay was found. They worked at *Tadeno.*

"White Satsuma" is very finely made and without decoration but covered with an ivory colored very finely crackled glaze. (See also below.)

ŌSUMI PROVINCE

Chōsa or *Chūsa* in *Ōsumi* province still subject to the prince of *Satsuma.*

Hōchu another of the 17 potters (see above) came from *Korea.*

Both here and at *Nawashirogawa* (see above) monochromes with finely crackled glaze such as apple greens, straw yellow, black and gold dusted black were made. Also rough wares with fluid glazes in two or more layers including *jakatsu-gusuri* (dragon-scale glaze) which is speckled with milky white, and highly prized in Japan.

Mishima wares were also made inlayed with white and dark clays like the Korean ones. But the above are both very rare indeed and seldom seen in the West.

Satsuma nishikide (Satsuma Brocade) design was first made in *Chōsa.*

Kōno Senemon by royal command, added gold to the muffle colors at the end of the 18th century.

Kinrande (gold brocade) style is, though bad, not so overladen as the later wares. They used a dry iron red, bluish green enamel, a glossy blue, a soft purple, black, a yellow and the gold was subdued mat relief. Few are ever seen in the West.

"*Old Satsuma*" is even later than this ware and has already become ornate and offensive. It used the dragon and phoenix but never human figures.

Awata, Ōsaka Ōta, Tōkyō and *Kōbe.*

Imitations were made about 1860 and with dragons, the phoenix figures. The peacock followed.

Imitations introduced the human figures, peacock, and even faked antique stains; the red is thinner, and it is less dry, the blue less pure and more muddy,—the purple, black and yellow are seldom seen,—but pink is added from c. 1830 and later a mat black and dull brown. There are many, old and undecorated pieces which have modern painting on them.

255

Japanese Porcelains

Some Japanese pottery was original in conception; most Japanese porcelain is imitative and not particularly attractive even to the Japanese themselves. A man of taste there would far prefer a Sung Tz'u Chou or piece of Korai pottery or stoneware first and secondly an old "chawan" of rough shape. Thirdly he would like a piece of Chinese porcelain and only after that the porcelain of his own country. It is true to state that it was largely export ware, but, as was the style in Europe in the 18th century, some princes gave porcelain royal patronage and some things of real beauty were made.

In the Japanese word "yaki" they include pottery, stoneware and porcelain, making no distinction but their porcelain is a true, hard porcelain much like that of the Chinese. Luckily enough the chief source of materials, Mountain Izumi-yama, provides both kaolin and petuntse already mixed by nature, but the material is difficult to handle for it is inclined to wilt in the kiln and must be given a light firing first and then a higher one.

In earlier days the underglaze blue was imported from China and specimens with the right "gosu" are always of antique make. Later a thinner, more purple and less pure blue was used. At Hizen bowls were made resembling Ming ones and supposedly by a potter named Goroshichi in the late 16th or early 17th century. The blue of these is poor and the painting flabby rather than direct and primitive. These were not porcelain but other potters such as Shonzui made porcelain ones which were widely copied. Arita porcelain also from Hizen province, and "Hirado" made for Prince Hirado's own use were decorated with delicate underglaze blue and the latter was of fine milky white quality. The motives were landscapes, children at play, etc.

The enamel colors were also much like those of China and in the so-called "Imari" ware we have a chance to compare them. There are these obvious differences between the Chinese and Japanese:

1.—The Chinese porcelain is thinner and denser in body and the glaze has a greenish tinge while the Japanese has a coarser and more sandy body with a glaze of greyish tint and of what Emil Hannover calls a "muslin" texture.

2.—The Chinese iron-red is thin and coral colored; the Japanese is opaque, thick and Indian-red.

3.—The Japanese wares were fired on spurs which will never be found on Chinese.

4.—The Japanese yellow is greyish and yet lighter than the Chinese impure Ming yellows.

5.—The Japanese green enamel is bluish as compared with K'ang Hsi greens.

Imari is in Hizen province and about 1650 Sakaida Kakiemon and Toshima Tokuzaemon decided to go to China to study but got only to Nagasaki where they met a Chinese potter who helped them. The result is the ware known as "Kakiemon" which was copied so extensively in Meissen and elsewhere in Europe. It is a refined type of Imari ware painted in iron-red, blue-green, light blue, violet and greyish-yellow and rarely with gold added and rather thin but tasteful designs. Other "Imari" had "nishikide" (brocade) patterns taken from actual brocades and distasteful to the

Left: Typical censer with *nishikide* or brocade pattern made at Arita and shipped from *Imari* during 18th cent. Ht. 7″. Macy Coll. Metropolitan Mus. of Art.

Center: Arita (Imari) porcelain from *Hizen* province, by *Kakiemon.* This style was often copied in Meissen and other European factories and some are difficult to tell from originals. Dia. 9⅝″. Metropolitan Mus. of Art.

Right: Hizen province 17th to 18th cent. dish by Kakiemon painted in blue under transparent glaze, with enamels of various colors. Dia. 12½″. Mus. of Fine Arts, Boston.

Late 17th-cent. Arita blue and white porcelain bottle with nicely graded crackle shading down from shoulder. Ht. 14¼″. Lent by Mrs. Russell Robb. Mus. of Fine Arts, Boston.

Many wares made for *Prince Nabeshima* resembled those of *Kakiemon.* This vase a good example. Ht. 9⅞″. Metropolitan Mus. of Art.

IMARI WARES, PARTICULARLY THOSE OF KAKIEMON

PLATE 78

Japanese themselves. This "Imari" ware was made in Arita, the name coming from the port from which it was shipped. At Arita also was made a finer ware decorated in lilac blue, reddish-brown, purple, black and pale-yellow up to about 1830 but chiefly for home consumption, after which time it lost its quality, and finally ended up in the "Nagasaki vases" with exaggerated

FIG. 442. Japanese "Imari ware" of 18th cent. in imitation of so-called "Lowestoft" ware made around Canton for western trade. Dia. 11¾". Boston Mus. of Fine Arts.

FIG. 443. Ko-Kutani dish from *Kaga* province in northwestern Japan. Technically crude porcelain but considered artistically superior, including underglaze blue, of poor quality, red, yellow, green, gold and silver. Dia. 10". Freer Gallery of Art, Washington.

FIG. 444. Late 18th or early 19th cent. Kutani ware from Kaga province, of Imari style, probably made by Honda Teikichi. Dia. 14½". Smith Coll. Metropolitan Mus. of Art.

flaring mouths and decorated in cold lacquer. Arita is also known for pierced ware, low relief ware, celadon with enamel colors and old and new blue and white ware, there having been about forty factories all told.

Another of the early sites was Kutanimura in Kaga province which from about 1650 had used a local porcelain earth. From here Prince Maeda sent Gotō Saijirō to Hizen to study. The ware is decorated in deep green glaze with purple, yellow and a soft greenish prussian blue called "ao (green) Kutani." The enamels of Arita were also used but the green and red were

FIG. 445. Satsuma vase c. 1800. Finely crackled buff colored glaze. Decorated in low-fired enamels. Ht. about 9½". Macy Coll. Metropolitan Mus. of Art.

FIG. 446. Arita porcelain vase of "Imari" type from province of Hizen. Decorated in underglazed blue and iron red, etc. Ht. 8⅜". Metropolitan Mus. of Art.

FIG. 447. Hizen province white *"Hirado"* porcelain vase decorated in underglaze blue of purplish cast. Typical shape. 1740. Ht. 10½". Metropolitan Mus. of Art.

FIG. 448. Hirado bottle, made between 1830 and 1843 by Furukawa in Tempō period. Less delicately painted than early wares under patronage of Prince Matsura. Ht. 10¼". Lent by Mrs. Russell Robb. Mus. of Fine Arts, Boston.

supplemented by purple, yellow, overglaze blue, gold and silver. It is the most impure porcelain of all Japan, and the enamel colors thick. Some look like attempts to get celadon effects but the green is bright and unpleasant. "Ko-Kutani" (old Kutani) is covered with a close pattern in red with medallions reserved and containing small compositions of ornaments in yellow, green, purple and red. Underglaze blue gave·them difficulties and is rarely, and always badly, used.

Another "five colored" ware was "Eiraku" with its "kinrande" type decoration in gold, which in this case is on a red ground first applied solidly.

Not all of the enamels were employed on porcelains. Ninsei, one of the most famous potters, used various enamels on black or grey or cream grounds with some taste and artistry. Other similar wares came from Iwaki and Yamashiro but those from various places and known as "Satsuma" are perhaps the best known and the worst.of taste. The real Satsuma ware was first of Korean influence and consists of a closely crackled white ware with ivory glaze, a "white Satsuma" of close hard paste almost microscopically crackled and of ivory color, an apple green, a straw yellow, a pure black, a gold dusted black and also a crude looking ware with several glazes including the famous "dragon-scale glaze" or "jakatsugusuri."

These are types reaching up to the 18th and 19th centuries and few of which interest us at all artistically speaking, but we must bear in mind that during this time decadence had set in over the entire world and the Chinese and European potters were showing little better taste.

The following chart, on pages 260–267, will give some slight aid in identifying Japanese Porcelains.

Other towns mentioned by Brinkley are in part as follows:

Higo (from 1791) similar to *Arita,* still producing.

Izumo (from 1873) poor blue and white.

Iwami (from 1860) similar coarse blue and white.

Iyo (from 1796) same.

Nagato (from 1846) ivory colored porcelain and other wares.

Kotō province of *Ōmi* (from 1830 to 1860) blue painting, enamel painting, and red and gold.

Himeji province of *Harima* (from early 17th cent. to 1868) blue and white and celadon.

Meppo-dani province of *Kishū*—celadon with relief decoration under glaze and stamped *"Zuishi,"* the name of a grass of similar green.

Aizu or *Wakamatsu* modern porcelain blue and white.

Ōta province of *Musashi* (from 1879) *Miyagawa Kōzan* who called himself *Makuzu* made copies of Chinese wares.

Koishikawa a suburb of *Tōkyō* (from c. 1900) blue and white, and pale red Chinese imitations.

Tōkyō (from 1863) European exports of wares looking as though they were painted in oil colors, some with gold spotted grounds.

This charming little dish made c. 1750. From Ōkōchi. Length 5½". Macy Coll. Metropolitan Mus. of Art.

Porcelain covered dish made by *chajin, Kashū Mimpei* in *Iga* on Island of *Awaji* c. 1830–1840. Greyish white with transparent glaze. Dia. 7". Mus. of Fine Arts, Boston.

Mokubei bowl, Kyōtō, Yamashiro province dating about 1785, decorated in red, yellow, green, and aubergine enamels with gold. Dia. 9". Metropolitan Mus. of Art.

Late 18th- or early 19th-cent. Kutani jar with cover, from Kaga province. Slightly greenish toned in glaze decorated with landscape in purple, yellow, green and black with borders in red. Ht. 8½". Mus. of Fine Arts, Boston.

Ko Kutani wine bottle from Kaga province, 17th cent. Greyish white painted in red, yellow, green, aubergine and black enamels. Ht. 9½". Gift of Marshall H. Gould. Mus. of Fine Arts, Boston.

Left: "Sanda ware," Japanese vase of porcelain with clear "celadon" glaze. Mark "Kotō" incised under glaze on base. Ht. 11½". Morse Coll. Mus. of Fine Arts, Boston.

JAPANESE PORCELAIN
Plate 79

Geisha girl playing samsen in *Kaga* province ware dating c. 1870. Ht. c. 12″. Macy Coll. Metropolitan Mus. of Art.

Satsuma figures c. 1800 or later showing life-like modeling and soft naturalistic coloring. Ht. of rider about 7″. Belonging to Mrs. Frederick Fish.

Teapot from Kyoto, 1790, potted by Kentei. Decorated by Ogata Shūhei in enamels. Ht. 4¼″. Metropolitan Mus. of Art.

Porcelain water-pot from *Bishu, Owari* province, made by *Hansuki,* c. 1820. Ht. 7¾″. Smith Coll. Metropolitan Mus. of Art.

JAPANESE PORCELAIN

PLATE 80

IDENTIFICATION CHART OF JAPANESE PORCELAINS

HIZEN PROVINCE

Town and Province	Chajin or "Tea-ceremony Master."	Artist	Description of wares
North west corner of the island of *Kiūshū* in *Hizen* province.		*Gorodayū Go Shonzui* went to Ching-té Chén in the start of the 16th century and brought back porcelain art to Japan. Some examples bear his name and some a Ming mark, if attributions are correct.	A fine porcelain decorated in Japanese style with birds, trees, flowers etc. in underglaze blue. There are many imitations the best from China, which in turn imitated the imitator, and from a factory in Japan started for that purpose (1825-40).
Arita in *Hizen* province.		The Korean potter *Risampei* c. 1605 discovered an already mixed porcelain clay containing both *kaolin* and *petuntse* in mountain *Izumiyama* and started a kiln in *Arita*.	The early Arita porcelain was also blue and white (See Hannover p. 210 Guide to the Pottery and Porcelain of the Far East). Hobson says that green and red enamels were used in the earliest Arita porcelain. (See Guide to the Pottery and Porcelain of the Far East, British Museum, 1924, p. 146.) However so few really proven examples exist in the Western Hemisphere that statements concerning them include considerable speculation.
Imari in *Hizen* province.		*Sakaida Kakiemon* and *Toshima Tokuzaemon* c. 1650 started for China but met a Chinese in *Nagasaki* who showed them how to paint in enamels over the glaze.	Kakiemon porcelain called by the French the "*première qualité coloriée de Japan*" was painted in iron-red, blue-green, light blue, violet, greyish-yellow and rarely with gold. It competed with some Chinese wares in export trade. It is not always easy to tell the Chinese wares from these, therefore the following points should be noted:—
Arita and other places also produced similar ware in Japan.			1.—Japanese added flower-baskets or *hanakago* and simpler colored landscapes often only underglaze blue, iron red and gold. 2.—"Old Imari" is the more fully colored type. 3.—Huge quantities came from both Japan and China. 4.—The designs cannot differentiate them for China copied Japan as Japan copied China. 5.—The Chinese ware is thinner and denser and has a greenish tinge. 6.—The Japanese is more sandy, coarser, and has a greyish tint with "muslin" surface. 7.—The Japanese underglaze blue is muddy and darker than the Chinese. 8.—The iron-red of the Chinese is clear and coral color; that of the Japanese is Indian red, thicker and opaque. 9.—There are spur marks on the Japanese dishes which never occur on the Chinese ones. 10.—The Japanese dishes are undulating to the touch while the Chinese are perfectly potted. 11.—On vases the Chinese allowed the wheel marks while the Japanese did not.

All of which is technically interesting in that it shows us another sidelight upon the differing mental processes of the two people, but hardly necessary as Japanese on the whole certainly did not appreciate the wares and they are truly more expressive of European taste, particularly that of August the Strong, than of the Far East, though they were made there.

Arita

A finer ware was made at Arita for Japanese taste from c. 1750 to c. 1830.

It was decorated in lilac-blue, reddish-brown, purple, black and pale yellow.

It also slowly descended to the depths of decadence of the so called "Nagasaki vases" decorated in red and gold and cold lacquer colors and of monstrous shapes.

Recently old *Arita* has been revived but with a poor red and blue.

Other wares made in *Arita* are perforated and relief decorated as well as celadon types decorated in enamels and gold.

"Arita egg-shell" occurs in underglaze blue decoration and a more modern ware with figures of women and warriors in gold, red, blue and sometimes with a fine net work over them called *ajirogumi*.

Mikōchi also in *Hizen* province.

Many of the blue decorated type are marked:—

Zōshun-tei Miho sei meaning "Made by *Miho* in the *Zoshun* pavilion. (See 321—2 Hannover) *Miho* only worked from about 1825 onward.

The *Fukagawa* family worked in Arita from c. 1650, and there were about 40 factories in this province all told.

Some of these are *Koransha* and *Seijisha* which was founded by *Tsuji* and are still working.

Nagasaki

These were blue and white wares cleverly painted but with a less deep blue and of cruder potting than good *Arita* ware.

Kameyama in 1803 made wares near *Nagasaki*.

Sakaida Shibunosuke was founded by *Sakaida Kakiemon* (1615–53).

Ōkōchi eight miles from *Arita*.

The wares made were purely Japanese taste. It is whiter, cleaner and more lustrous than *Arita* porcelain. The enamel decorations resemble *Kakiemon's*. Gold was used moderately, as was also underglaze blue which is sometimes omitted. New enamel is lilac-purple, and the iron-red is more orange and lighter. Another kind is painted in a fine but pale underglaze blue. Red and blue were also combined.

A finely crackled celadon *"seiji"* porcelain was also made. The paste is either white or red stoneware-like material.

A later ware is a coarse crackled brown or celadon glazed stoneware ornamented in red and gold.

In 1660 *Prince Nabeshima* founded a kiln with *Korean* potters. No marks are found, but many have a comb-like pattern *kushide* around the foot, but this is also found on *Kaga* porcelain and modern forgeries. (Hannover Fig. 321–7.) Protection ceased in 1868 and its importance as well.

Town and Province	Artist	Description of wares
Mikōchi in *Hizen* province, (see also above) on the island of *Hirado*.	*Chajin* or "Tea-ceremony Master."	
	In 1650 some Koreans started a factory, but porcelain was not made until 1712 after the ingredients were found on *Amakusa* island. In 1750 *Matsura*, prince of *Hirado* became patron. Between 1750 and 1830 it was the finest porcelain in Japan. The fine work ceased in 1868, but it has been revived. It is rarely marked, though those with the name of the potter belong to the *Tempō* period (1830–43).	"*Hirado porcelain*" is largely plastic and usually of small objects and was only made for the prince himself; its sale being strictly forbidden. It is even cleaner and more brilliant than *Nebeshima*. Decorated usually in underglaze blue, it sometimes had added a pale brownish tone imported from China. The painting is miniature in delicacy and often shows Chinese children playing under a fir tree called *karako*. This is, of course, a well known Ming design. The number of children seems to indicate the class of the ware there being seven boys in the best, five in the second and three in the third. Freely modeled fish, dragons, and figures were also made and colored in blue, red-brown or black. Very delicate perforated wares were also made.
	A smaller factory existed as an independent venture.	This place made egg-shell decorated in a fine brilliant blue underglaze color.
Kyōto	*Chajin Eisen.*	Imitations of Chinese celadon and Ming porcelain in green, red and gold.
	In the 18th century porcelain was produced by *Eisen*. The mark was his name painted in red or stamped.	He imitated blue and white, enamelled porcelain, celadon or a ware called *Kōchi-yaki* imported from China, a semi-porcelain decorated with brilliant enamels of purple, yellow, green and bronze.
	Aoki Mokubei (1767–1833) was a pupil of *Eisen.* He also marked with his name which has often been copied on modern forgeries. *Ogata Kichisaburō* or *Shūhei* signed as another individual.	He did coral red glaze with decoration in gold or enamels painted over it.
	Nishimura Zengorō died in 1855. He was also called *Zengorō Ryōzen* or simply *Ryōzen*, but later he adopted the name *Eiraku* meaning Yung Lo, after the Ming Emperor and then *Kahin Shiryū* which means "scion of *Kahin*," *Kahin* being the name of a mythological ceramic product.	Coral red glaze was one of his best achievements, and it was this that gained for him his last two names from the prince of *Kishū*. His *Eirakukinrande* or "Yung Lo gold brocade pattern" and his *akaji-kingwa* or "gold pattern on red ground" are considered the most precious. He made, too, celadon porcelain, blue and white and copies of *Kōchi-yaki* which he called after his kiln name *Kairaku-en* and also *Onizva-yaki* or "Royal Park ware" as he had been asked to place his kiln in the grounds of the prince's palace near Wakayama. The blue he obtained in the medallions in his red glaze is almost as bright as any known.

264

Kaseyama near *Nara* in *Yamashiro* province.
Omuro
Ōtsu on *Lake Biwa*

He worked a while at *Kaseyama* and then became an instructor at *Settsu* and in the same year 1840 he started a kiln at *Omuro* to copy *Ninsei* pottery. Later in 1850 he moved to *Ōtsu* and changed his name to *Butsu-yu*.

Wazen one of his sons took the style to *Kaga* province in 1857.

Here he made *akaji-kingawa* (see above).

Very similar to the above.

Both also made "three colored" ware in glazes of three or more colors painted within raised outlines after the Chinese ware.

Eiraku's wares have been copied in *Otoko-yama* (1847–66) and *Ota* (1874——) in *Kishū* province.

Kyōto

Rokubei Seisai was a son of the famous *Rokubei* in the early 19th century.

Mashimizu Jūtarō with the art name of *Zōroku* (1849–78).

Seifū III. Yohei (1861–).

Blue and white signed with his father's name in a hexagon.

Celadon and other wares.

Blue and white and red and gold wares.

There are, of course, still many potters in *Kyōto* but they are of little real account so far as we can judge in later exhibitions.

KAGA PROVINCE

Enuma

Prince Maeda sent *Gotō Saijirō* to Hizen to get secrets.
Made from the latter part of the 17th century to about 1750 and called *Old Kutani*.

Old Kutani was seldom if ever marked by the potter but at times bore the inscription:—*Dai Nihon Kutani tsukuru*, "Made at Kutani in Great Japan."

Deep green glaze predominant with purple, yellow and a soft greenish blue made *ao-*(green) *Kutani* ware.
The glazes were used in close patterns or washed over designs in black on the biscuit (manganese).
Arita porcelain was also copied without green and red but with purple, yellow, overglaze blue, gold and silver.
Old *Kutani* porcelain is technically the worst in Japan but among the most valuable and artistic. It has also a typical opaque red-brown or brown-red. The designs are of landscapes, flowers and simple bird and flower ones of the "Kano school." Seldom there are Chinese children at play called "*kara-ko*."
Ko Kutani (a special sort of old Kutani) has a close ground of red pattern with medallions in reserve having designs in yellow, green, purple and red. Underglaze blue is much less used than in *Arita*. That with blue only is rare and poor in quality. The ware is gray or brownish and the glaze too is grayish and often crackled. It is only rarely a true porcelain.

Town and Province	*Chajin* or "Tea-ceremony Master."	Artist	Description of wares
Wakasugi		*Honda Teikichi* came from Hizen with three other potters, and worked until 1822.	The ware was a sort of Imari style.
		In 1832 *Hashimoto Yasubei* reopened the same shop and Yujiro won fame.	*Akae Yujiro-aka-e* means "painted only in red," but he worked in the other enamels.
		From 1830 *Matsumoto Kikusaburō* in work with *Aōda Genemon*, occupied the same place but moved in 1850 to 1867 to *Komatsu*, in the *Nomi* district where 200 workmen were employed.	They reproduced the old Kutani.
			Old Kutani was also reproduced here.
Enuma continued		Meanwhile *Yoshidaya Denemon* (1809–1840) at *Kutani* and later at *Yamashiro-mura* also copied old Kutani. "*Hachiroe ware*," which was continued by *Zengorō Wazen*, the son of the great *Eiraku*, was first made by *Iidaya Hachiroemon* about 1840.	Old Kutani designs.
			This style uses red for outlines and also ground color. Wazen used underglaze blue for the inside of some bowls and red on the outside painted over in gold. It is usually marked *Kutani ni oite Eiraku tsukuru* "made by Eiraku at Kutani."
		The revolution of 1868 stopped all endeavors but in 1885 some 2,700 workers were making true porcelain.	These again were copies of Old Kutani and of Eiraku styles. Various other porcelains from different parts of Japan were sent there to be decorated.
		About 1850 the potters in *Kaga* province began to mark their work with painted marks in red, black, green enamel or gold, the last two more seldom.	The modern Kaga province wares are very inferior export wares of no value.

266

OWARI PROVINCE

Seto

Porcelain began to be made only in the 19th century when *Katō Tamikichi* in 1807 returned from *Hizen* and was backed by Prince of Owari.

The best period was between 1830 and 1860 when such artists as *Kawamoto Jihei*, the modeller, and the potter *Kawamoto Hansuke* were working there.

Seto-mono became the term meaning porcelain in parts of Japan.

Sometsuke was the earliest and was underglaze blue of Japanese cobalt until 1832. Later European blue was used for the export wares.

They made famous large vases, painted plaques, etc. One type had raised designs on white with blue grounds. Enamels were more recent as a rule though *Michihei* did use them as early as c. 1835.

Other techniques were used and even imitation cloisonné was made.

Maruyama-yaki or copies of old Chinese tea ceremony wares were also made, and the *Nabeshima* style was copied.

Seto ware was also sent to Tōkyō to be decorated, though this should not be confused with "*Seto-suke-yaki*" which is a coarse ware made in *Yedo (Tōkyō)* before 1860.

MINO PROVINCE

Tajimi-mura

Kato Gosuke was one distinguished artist

Wares were influenced by both *Seto* and *Kutani*. Most of the pieces are smaller than *Seto* ones. Many eggshell blue and white pieces were made with delicate designs of flowers, landscapes etc. *Gosuke's* wares were of this sort and were protected by fine basket work from *Suruga*.

Modern "*Tajimi* porcelain" is white with floral designs in high relief.

Kaga style porcelain has been made since 1878.

SETTSU PROVINCE

Sanda

Merchant, *Kanda* Sobei erected 12 kilns and obtained men from Kyōto and Hizen.

Blue and white wares and a vivid green celadon "*Sanda seiji*" of unpleasant quality was made and is today.

CHAPTER XIII

POTTERIES OF PERSIA, WESTERN ASIA AND EGYPT

HISTORICAL BACKGROUND

PERSIA is a large country equalling in size Greece, Bulgaria, Albania, Yugo-Slavia, Rumania, Austria, Hungary, Czecho-Slovakia, Germany and half of Poland. It was a center of travel East and West as well as North and South. When we add to Iran the other countries of Iraq, Syria and Turkey we have a country as large as Europe and touching the Aegean culture on the west and that of Asia on the east. This territory is loosely called the Near East.

The people are of Indo-European origin. It was called Ariana (the land of the Arians) hence the Middle-Persian Eran and modern name Iran. South Russian names are largely Iranian and we suppose that migrations took place, before our history begins, from the North into Eastern Iran and down the Indus valley as well as west as far as the borders of the Semitic world.

The first historical records of any country tell of invasions from the North simply because the histories were written by the stay-at-homes in the South. These agriculturalists were easy meat for the hunters of the north who were always called savages but they were not necessarily racially different and were mentally more alert being hunters. Their minds were no less keen and active, in fact quite the contrary. Joseph Strzygowski, in "The Northern Stream of Art from Ireland to China, and the Southern Movement," says "On the European side we have the Celts, Germans and Slavs, together with all those races which burst out of Asia and penetrated to the West of Europe in all the first millennium, namely, the Huns, Avars, Magyars and, later, the Mongols. These peoples, all of them nomads of the North, were bearers of Asiatic ideas of art to Europe in historic times; but they must have been preceded by similar movements long before the Christian era during the Bronze Age and the La Tène period."

Horses, which became the subject of much western art and of the Han through T'ang period of China, were introduced into Babylonia, Egypt and Greece about 1700 B.C. as war instruments by the Medes, Persians, Hyrcanians, Bactrians and Sogdians in various conquests.

And so we may imagine a seething to and fro of the northern nomads with every now and then a sally southward for conquest which nevertheless always brought a new spirit and life to the arts of the southern peoples. Such was the condition when in 715 B.C. the Assyrians led by Sargon penetrated into the mountains to the east and subdued a few Medean tribes. In 612 B.C. the Medeans and Babylonians conquered not only the Assyrians but also the territories of Persia, Armenia and Cappadocia south of the Black Sea.

KING CYRUS AND THE ACHAEMENID EMPIRE (558 TO 330 B.C.)

About 558 B.C. King Cyrus revolted and overthrew Astyages, the Medean king. He called himself "King of the Persians," and by 550 B.C. had founded the Persian Empire but had lost in the process the allegiance of Babylonia, Egypt, Lydia and Sparta which were in 546 B.C. beaten and finally brought into line along with all the Greek littoral towns, Cilicia, the whole Chaldean Empire, Syria and Palestine. Then the great Cyrus turned to the east and fought the Dahae Scyths and Massagetae until he finally died in 528 B.C.

His son took Egypt, Cyprus and the other islands off the coast of Asia Minor. This then was one of those great amalgamations which bring together many different arts.

One of the greatest factors in this conquest was the expert use of the short bow from horse back. In Turkestan even today I understand that riders can gallop full tilt past a post and leave several arrows sticking into it while White Russian cavalry could not do so well with army automatics. Many ancient legends tell of achievements with this bow. Perhaps the best known is that of Bahram Gur, the Sassanian king (A.D. 420–438) and

FIG. 449. Persian tile of lustred pottery probably from Kashan of about 1300 A.D. portraying Bahram Gur and Azadeh on a camel. Length about 13″. Metropolitan Mus. of Art.

Azadeh, often pictured on ceramics. It seems the king saw two gazelles, an old male and a young female and asked "the moon of his delight" which he should kill. Azadeh answered, as the passage of Firdusi's "Shahnameh" is translated by Dr. R. Meyer Riefstahl.

" 'Oh lion,
A man does not fight gazelles.
But transform this female with thine arrow into a male,
And change the male into a female,
Then goad on the dromedary (on which they are usually portrayed)
And when a gazelle runs away from thee,
Hurl the dart of thy crossbow, (short bow)
So that she bends her ears along her shoulder.
The dart shall tickle her ear without hurting her

And she shall raise her foot toward her shoulder,
Then thou shalt pierce her head, foot and shoulder,
And then I will call thee the light of the world.' "

Nothing daunted, Bahram shouted and, when the gazelles ran, he used a double tipped arrow to shoot the horns off the head of the male, thus making it a female. He then planted two arrows in the head of the female appearing like horns and quickly touched the tip of the ear with another so that she raised her foot to scratch it when he sewed together the foot, ear and head. Azadeh, moved to pity and with the contrary whim of a woman, told him he was inhuman and had the nature of an evil spirit at which the kindly gentleman

"——stretched out his hand,
He threw her from the saddle to the ground
And bade his dromedary
Trample the girl with the face like a moon.
He covered her breast, her hand and her lute with blood.
He said:
'Oh, senseless lute-player,
Why didst thou try to trick me?
If I had missed my shot, my family would have been covered with shame!'
Azadeh died under the hoofs of the dromedary
And Bahram never again took a woman with him
When he went out to hunt."

You may draw what lessons from this tale you wish but in any event it is often illustrated.

DARIUS THE GREAT (521–485 B.C.)

Six noble Persians helped the young Darius to kill a usurper in 521 and take the throne. The colonies revolted and Medea, Sagartia and Margiana rose with kings of their own while Babylonia had two revolts and Susiana three. With a small army made up of Persians and Medes he finally brought order and then subdued the nations of the Armenian and Pontic mountains bringing the Persian rule to the Caucasus. Though an ardent Zoroasteran he permitted the Jews to build the Temple of Jerusalem and he himself built temples in Memphis, Edfu and the Great Oasis in Egypt.

GREEK WARS

In 512 he started a series of unfortunate wars with the swift Scythians. Then came the revolt of Egypt, inevitable war with the Greeks, the defeat of Marathon in 490 and the death of Darius in 485 B.C. Soon the Athenian fleet met the Perso-Phoenician armada at Salamis and added further defeat. Persia neither wanted the Greek coastal cities nor could she let them go. A way out seemed possible in the formation of a league against Sparta. Then in 387 Greece had to join the Persians again renouncing all claim to Asiatic possessions and even proclaiming Persian suzerainty over her but this was due to Greek weakness rather than Persian strength and although the Persian Empire reached its greatest geographical extent by 338 B.C. it was rotten at the core.

ALEXANDER THE GREAT AND THE FALL OF THE PERSIAN EMPIRE

Philip of Macedon was trying to liberate the Greek coastal cities of Asia Minor when he was assassinated and his young son Alexander, later known as Alexander the Great, took his place with a keen mind for both war and organization. In five years he had the situation well in hand. In 331 the victory of Gaugamela took place and shortly after Darius III was assassinated being the last of the twelve Achaemenid Dynasty kings. Alexander adopted the dress and ceremonial of the Persian kings and in 330 drafted 30,000 young Persians and trained them in Macedonian war technique. In 324 he held a great marriage feast at which all of his superior officers and about 10,000 more Macedonians were wedded to Persian wives. He then disbanded his veterans and used Persians in his army. Persia then was again a great melting pot where many of already mixed race were mixed again just as they were in North Europe, in the "Celtic basin" and about the Mediterranean, and we see Hellenistic influences brought into India from where they were later spread to China.

THE SELUCIDS (319–190 B.C.)

Alexander died in 323 B.C. leaving no heir. Most of the wives of the mass marriage had been discarded but one general or "Diadochi" kept his and, making Babylon his headquarters, struck at the strategic moment and took the whole of Iran except Northern Medea and the frontiers of the Indus river. He founded Selucia on the Tigris river and a circle of Greek towns about Medea one of which was Rhages, Rai or Rhagae about which we will hear much to do with potteries later. It was now an Hellenic city.

THE PARTHIAN EMPIRE OR ARSACIDS (C. 250 B.C.–A.D. 224)

Meanwhile Justin Arsaces, chief of the Parni tribe of the Dahan Scythians who came from the steppe east of the Caspian Sea, with the help of his brother Tiridates, founded the Parthian kingdom in 248 B.C. It was during the same times that Rome was threatening and the Selucid Empire was finally shattered by Rome to which it paid tribute in 190. The Parthians were much overrated by early historians and actually owed their gains to Roman interference in Asia Minor. During the years between 159 and 139 B.C. the Scythians of further east, called Yue-chi by Chinese, and true nomads living chiefly from the loot of the caravans between Han China and the Romans, took first Sogdiana and then Bactria. The Parthians were always between the slowly encroaching Romans and the lashing attacks of their cousin Scyths. In the period between about 147 B.C. and A.D. 77 there were two and sometimes three kings ruling at once and in 113 to 117 Trajan reduced Armenia, Babylonia and Mesopotamia to imperial provinces. In 162 Marcus Aurelius and Aelius Verus attacked Armenia and Osroene and in 164 Avidius

Cassius finally destroyed Selucia and Hellenism was no more heard of east of the Euphrates. Ardashir I (Artaxerxes) now started his career by killing his neighbors in Medea, then his brothers and so started a conquest in A.D. 212 finally ending up in 224 with the finish of the Parthians and the beginning of the famous Sassanian Empire.

The Sassanian Empire (A.D. 224–633 or 226–251)

When Selucia was destroyed by the Romans and Hellenism in the Near East with it, the culture of the Aramaic section began to take its place. Palestine, Damascus and Mesopotamia, the old section through which Persians had travelled to Egypt was now influenced culturally by the fast growing power of Christianity. At the same time the vitality of Persia continued the Zoroasterian beliefs, and at this time Vologaeses III collected the Avesta. The new Persia was more like the old original Achaemenid period than the intervening Arsacid period. It recovered from its illness and at the same time Rome was having distracting troubles, and finally when the Goths defeated Decius in 251 the whole empire collapsed. Now the Persian empire was not much enlarged and the old title "King of Kings" could hardly apply, but there was a growing strength.

Christianity versus Zoroasterianism

Armenia had become Christian under the Romans and what had started out as a fight between the Romans and Persians now became not only a national duel but a religious duel. To quote Edward Meyer, "The time was come when, in the western and eastern worlds alike, the religious question was for large masses of people the most important question in life, and the diffusion of their own creed and the suppression of all others the highest and holiest of tasks." But the opponents could not clinch, for Rome was harried by the Goths and Persia by the Scyths, yet about 390 Armenia was divided and by A.D. 430 the Persians had removed all trace of the Arsaces' kings who had taken refuge there.

Chosroes II raided Syria, Antioch in 611, Damascus in 613, Jerusalem in 614 and Egypt in 619 but in 623 Heraclius, the Roman, repaid him with interest and finally Chosroes was killed by his son and chaos reigned. Wars had now weakened both Rome and Persia softening them and preparing them for the conquest by Islam, that other great weapon of religion which had been forged in Arabia.

Islamic Persia (A.D. 633–1235)

The Arabs had devised a heaven which promised fountains running with wine and beautiful damosels of willing nature and the key was sure for those who died fighting the unbelievers. The Arabs were toughened by desert and sea. They entered Persia in A.D. 633, the fate of the Sassanians was decided in 637 and by 650 they occupied every province of the country north to the Oxus and Balkh. Zoroasterianism disappeared. For about 150 years Persia was governed by Muhammedan caliphs in Medina and Bagdad who wished only to destroy its nationality and religion and to grow rich on the spoils. Turkish officers were favored to do the work and they held sway until Isma'il b.Ahmad, the Samanid stepped in.

THE SAMANIDS (A.D. 900–1229)

The Samanids were the first important non-Arabic Persian dynasty since the fall of the Sassanian kings. The Arabs had not harmed art for, although they had no art of their own, they had like other nomads a hunger for that of the peoples they conquered. Finally in 999 the last of the Sassanids were cleaned out by the Ilek-Khans of Turkestan.

GHAZNEVIDS AND SELJUKS

Alptagin, a slave of Mansur I, ran away to Afghanistan where he founded a semi-independent group, the first of the Ghaznevids. The Seljuks were another band of nomads from Turkestan who settled in Transoxiana and in the 11th century crossed the Oxus river which flows north west into the Sea of Aral from what is now northern Afghanistan, and plundered eastern Persia making Merv their capital in 1040. Three of their leaders took Balkh, Jorjan, Tabristan, Khwarizm, Hamadan, Rhages, Isfahan and finally Bagdad in 1055 thus introducing once again the northern animistic art and a new blood. The Syrian dynasty of the Seljuks came into contact with the Crusades and ended in three generations. In 1172–1199 Tukush and later in 1199–1220 Ala ed-din Mohammed subdued Khorasan, Rhages, Isfahan, practically all of Persia, Bokhara, Samarkand and Otrar finally reaching Ghazni where he was stopped by Jenghiz Khan.

MONGOLS (A.D. 1220–1335)

It is reported that Jenghiz Khan wished only to trade in the West, but the unfortunate killing of a camel train in Otrar and later of his envoy sent to Mohammed Shah led to war. It was planned carefully and the army was of Chinese and Mongols trained for the march. Juchi, the oldest son moved south into the old trade route while the main body continued westward. Chepé Noyon was already in Turkestan. Across the "Roof of the World" they moved and some starved, some fell and never arose, wagons and horses were left behind and the cold was killing but by Spring they had reached Lake Balkash and approached the frontiers of Islam. Soon the Turks learned a costly lesson from the ragged fur-clad hordes and Mohammed was pushed from pillar to post until he finally took refuge on an island in the Caspian Sea where he died. As the cities fell the useless were put to death, the women taken for the amusement of the troops and able bodied men beaten into slaves, chained like animals, and fed with the dogs. The system was thorough and every living thing and every object was used if possible, or destroyed if it was not of use to the horde.

Chepé Noyon and Subotai drove north into Russia and turned west to the Dnieper meeting a hastily assembled Russian army and annihilating it. They were about to enter Europe when Jenghiz Khan recalled them some 2,000 miles and they returned loaded with treasure having taken two divisions on a march across 90° of longitude in less than two years and having made careful note of the resources of the country and captured many men of learning. Subotai liked the "black earth" region of South Russia and years later he returned from the other side of the world to overrun Moscow and crossed the Dnieper to invade Europe. A generation later Marco Polo was to visit Kubhlai Khan the grandson of Jenghiz in the grandeur of Yüan China (A.D. 1280–1368).

THE ASSASSINS

Persia had been divided after the death of Jenghiz, 1272, by two of Jenghiz Khan's sons Jagatai and Tului. Hulagu was the son of the latter and he set himself to rid the world of the Assassin stronghold called "Alamut" or "Eagle's Nest." Hasan, the "Old Man of the Mountains" had organized a secret society of believers in the Muhammedan heaven who were fed hashish derived from hemp to boost them on this earth. Young men were allowed to live for a time in a sort of artificial heaven where they disported themselves with wine, women and hashish until suddenly they were commanded to fulfill a mission of death. The system should not be hard for us to understand for our own gangsters operate on a similar basis. One of the first victims was Hasan's former friend, one of the Seljuks, whose son also met the same fate. After Hasan died a separate branch was started in Syria and in Persia the last ruler of the Assassins was Rukn ad-Din whom Hulagu captured. The story is that he sent him to the other ruler Mangu who in true gangster style immediately put him to death sending word to Hulagu to do away with his competitive followers. Hulagu, the true Mongol, was nothing loath and promptly liquidated about 12,000 of them.

The Mongol rule now stretched from the dominions of Jagati on the north to Egypt in the south and from the Byzantine Empire on the west to China in the east.

TIMUR OR TAMERLANE (A.D. 1336–1405)

In the Northeast was bred another conqueror, Timur of the "green city" Shahr-i-Sabz or Kesh just 50 miles south of Samarkand. He was scholarly and so poor a military type in the beginning that he had trouble holding Transoxiana. However, later he took Balkh (in what is now Afghanistan). He then turned to the north west to the Caspian and later crossed the Volga. In the south he took all of Persia. After he was 60 in 1398 this energetic gentleman was "informed of commotions and civil wars of India," and went down to stop them, crossing the Indus River and sacking Delhi. It is said by Clavijo that ninety elephants worked one quarry in carrying stones for Timur for a mosque at Samarkand. Later he also took Bagdad, Aleppo and Damascus, beating the Turks at Angora. His final holdings were from the Volga to the Irtish and from the Hellespont to the Ganges.

Timur died in 1405. By 1447 the Timurid dynasty ceased to hold sway over Persia and here we leave what might be called the arena of the Near East. Other things happened there and will happen there but the world turned over and Europe took the stage as the most important center. Of course the conquest of Islam crossed Egypt and spread along North Africa jumping to Spain and nearly half way up into France but that we shall trace later.

THE STORY OF GLAZE

We know that glaze was used on stone and potteries very early in Egypt. We have also very early records in Mesopotamia (now Irak) and Persia (now Iran) but we do not know where the first conscious use of it came into being. Certainly it appears so suddenly and so late in China that it must have been an imported art. Not until the Han period 206 B.C. to A.D. 220 is there any real glaze there.

In the Near East we have found wonderful and brilliant blues that never were made elsewhere. Lustre made to imitate metal and actually made of metallic oxides blazed forth all unforeseen with its iridescence as beautiful as that created by nature on some glazes and seemed to catch the very fire of the kiln and preserve its smoldering lights for ever. These wares appeal not with sensitive forms or colors but with the royal pagan beauty of the wares of kings, and shahs, of caliphs and khans. They have the blazing of hot skies and ominous sunsets as well as the blue black cobalt of nights with stars too many and too large. They are vessels which held precious wines and poisons. They are bizarre, voluptuous, fantastic and as defiant of the laws of nature as were the devils who handled them and broke so many thousands of them in passions of love, lust or cruelty. Some escaped the trembling hands of slaves who lost their lives therefore and others were crushed by the rough shod march of conquest. Anything may be found among them except the firm and disciplined simplicity which only the artist of the Far East has ever mastered. From Arabia to the frozen steppes, from India to Greece, from Egypt to Samarkand, from China to the coast of Spain the pendulum swung and in the center of it all was Persia, Iran, land of kings.

EARLY DEVELOPMENTS

Whether glazed pottery was first made in Egypt or in the land of the Tigris and Euphrates called Mesopotamia we do not know. Its development was probably almost parallel for, as we know, the countries were often under one rule. One reason that the Greeks did not make use of glaze is that they were inclined to draw pictures on their vases and the glazes were not readily controlled. Perhaps for this reason we find many tiles in the earliest wares of the Near East for they could be fired flat and there was less likelihood that the design would be ruined by running glaze. As early as the III Dynasty in Egypt tiles were made and they have been found also in Mesopotamia of even date. Some claim that there are earlier records from Syria.

Butler tells us that at Tell el Yahudia in the palace of Rameses III dating about 1200 B.C. and in Tell el Amarna (about 1370 B.C.) tiles were found showing variety of color, modeling and flat inlay. Walter Andrae tells us that at Ashur on the Tigris were found many tiles and several pot sherds placed about 1300 and showing distinct traces of glaze. Emil Hannover speaks of a fragment of a vase on which the name of King Mena is inlayed in violet glaze, which he, therefore, reasons must belong to a period of about 3300 B.C. but this sort of evidence does not prove any place of origin nor any definite date, and my opinion is that glaze may have been found and lost in a number of places before it came into general use.

EGYPTIAN GLAZED POTTERY

Tiles and bricks with one face glazed seem to show the earliest conscious efforts to make glazes in Egypt as elsewhere, though some accidental salt glazes did occur early in bowls. In the VI Dynasty (about 2550–2350 B.C.) a dark blue was added and in the XIII Dynasty (2000–1788 B.C.) a light blue

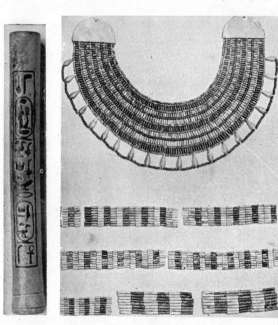

FIG. 452. Fragment of a sistrum of green faïence of Saitic origin showing Isis. Ht. 5¼". Metropolitan Mus. of Art.

FIG. 450. Kohl tube of blue faïence made during the reign of Amenhotep III of the 18th dynasty. Ht. 5½". Metropolitan Mus. of Art.
FIG. 451. Egyptian 12th Dynasty collar, anklets and bracelets of faïence of various colors found in the Cemetery of King Amen-em-het. Metropolitan Mus. of Art.

and soft manganese black were added but it was in the XVIII Dynasty (1540–1350 B.C.) that the greatest development of the art of ceramics took place. Beautifully formed "lotus cups" and other graceful forms were devised. Added to the earliest copper oxide blues and greens obtained by the addition of iron were manganese purples from bluish to violet, chrome yellows and oranges, iron reds, brighter greens and a glaze which through the addition of tin was milk white. Pieces of inlay for architectural purposes, small scarabs, beads, vases, bowls and "ushabti" figures shaped like mummies and supposed to aid or protect the dead were also made. These "ushabti" sometimes hold in their hands, with arms crossed, a basket and a hoe. They

FIG. 455. Heavy cup of faïence inscribed with the name of Ramses the Great made during the 19th dynasty. Ht. 4″. Metropolitan Mus. of Art.

FIG. 453. Dish of blue faïence with black rim and cartouche of Thut-mose II, from Thebes, Egypt. Dia. 3⅛″. Metropolitan Mus. of Art.

FIG. 454. Figure of Horus made during the late dynastic times. Blue faïence. Ht. 3″. Metropolitan Mus. of Art.

have also, on the bottom, an inscription from the VI Chapter of the Book of the Dead. Others represent *Hathor* with the head of a cow (the Egyptian Aphrodite), *Thoth* with the head of an ibis, *Amen* with human head and a crown of plumes, *Pasht* with the head of a lion, *Bast* with the head of a cat, *Isis* with *Horus* and finally *Nephthys*. Until the XXVI Dynasty hundreds of

FIG. 456. Fragment of a vase of pale blue faïence, Ptolemaic Egyptian. Ht. 1⅛″. Metropolitan Mus. of Art.

FIG. 457. Egyptian Early Roman period (about 1st cent. A.D.) faïence ram feeding. Metropolitan Mus. of Art.

FIG. 458. Miniature pylon of blue faïence, Ptolemaic Period, Egypt. Ht. 3½″. Metropolitan Mus. of Art.

figures were placed in tombs with scarabs which are faithful images of the "dung beetle" or "tumblebug" (Scaraebus sacer) which lays its eggs in a ball of dung and then pushes it up a mound with its hind feet and allows it to roll down several times probably to pack it harder. We uncertainly have come to the conclusion that the Egyptians associated it in some way with rebirth and that the small globe was compared to the sun. The beetle was sacred to the sun-god. It was mummified at Heliopolis, many figures of it were placed about the bodies and a large figure with outspread wings was placed over the heart. Many were pierced longitudinally so that they could be worn on cords. A large group of stone ones bear royal names but the pottery ones never do unless made for tourist trade.

18th dynasty blue faïence tile with finely drawn charioteer and plant forms in black. This is quite static in feeling but charming decoration. Length 6¼". Metropolitan Mus. of Art.

Egyptian Late Dynastic period about 500 to 350 B.C. polychrome faïence inlays for a wooden shrine. Not only the drawing but the soft colors of these are very beautiful. Metropolitan Mus. of Art.

EGYPTIAN TILE AND FAÏENCE INLAYS

PLATE 81

21st dynasty pectoral of Entui-ny in blue faïence. Ht. 3¾". Metropolitan Mus. of Art.

19th or 20th dynasty (1350–1090 B.C.) faïence cup of graceful shape with a lotus stem and base and relief figures in two bands about the body. Ht. 5¾". Metropolitan Mus. of Art.

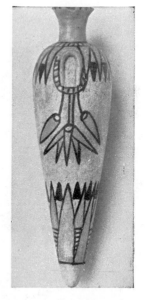

Pectoral of blue faïence. 20th to 26th dynasty. Ht. 4¾". Metropolitan Mus. of Art.

26th dynasty two handled amphora of light colored faïence. Ht. 6". Metropolitan Mus. of Art.

EGYPTIAN 19TH TO 26TH DYNASTY FAÏENCE

PLATE 82

EGYPTIAN USHABTIS AND FIGURES OF DIVINITIES

PLATE 83

Most amazing is the sameness of Egyptian pottery from the beginning of the Middle Kingdom, the IX Dynasty right through to the 17th century A.D. Even in the Roman and Arab epochs little change is seen. As an example the bowl in the British Museum, having portraits of Constantine and Fausta is located in the 4th century yet in its color, blended blue on the back and manganese inside, and technique it is no different from the Islamic wares of centuries later.

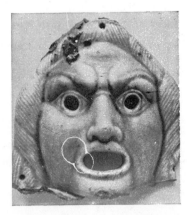

FIG. 461. Egyptian faïence tragic mask in turquoise color of the Early Roman Period about 1st cent. A.D. From the Carnarvon Coll. Metropolitan Mus. of Art.

FIG. 459. Blue faïence figure of the Ptolemaic period, Egypt. Ht. 2¾". Metropolitan Mus. of Art.

FIG. 460. Fragment of a vase of faïence of the Ptolemaic period. Metropolitan Mus. of Art.

NAUCRATITE POTTERY

At the "Potter's Gate" near the extensive kilns in Naucratis was found many pieces. This was not only the most important town of the Greek colony in Egypt from the middle of the 7th to the middle of the 6th centuries B.C. but also a shipping port for wares from Athens, Corinth, Miletus, Samos, Lesbos, Clazomenae and Cyrene. Three pieces only were also said to have been found from Phoenicia or Assyria, but this is not hard to understand when we remember that in 612 B.C. the Medeans and Babylonians were fighting and probably had little time for pottery exports to Egypt. Egypt was on the outskirts of the Near Eastern civilizations and was less disturbed. When conquered, Egypt could draw back into herself up the Nile like a sea-worm and on the other hand there was little incentive for her to reach out beyond her own fertile valley. This accounts for her slow development, her uninspired but basically sound art. She was unwhipped by the constant raids of the nomads and her artists saw little to shock them into new endeavors.

The local Naucratite ware was of soft creamy ground on which was polychrome decoration. The inside was usually black with lotus designs of red and white. The designs were of lions, stags, lotus borders and buds, dancing figures, winged griffins, human headed birds and various other animals and birds, all drawn as well and as life-like as possible but without the compacting of them into given spaces or what we know as conventionalism. It is likely that we find here ancient ideas from the Tigris and Euphrates plus contemporary observation.

ALEXANDRIAN POTTERY

Rhacotis, for centuries a pottery center, had new kilns built in 310 to 230 B.C. for Greek potters, and there is an unbroken succession of dated pieces from 271 to 239 B.C. Most of these potteries are not glazed but enamels were used as were also the application of both silver and gold. In the Alexandrian Museum is a skyphos of blue enamel with horizontal band of olive leaves, a design often seen later. Another fragment with portrait of Arsinoe or Berenice is from an Oenochoe and has traces of gold leaf on it.

At this time there was considerable warlike activity in Asia Minor, Spain, Etruria and Magna Graecia, therefore the Egyptian kilns were probably by far the most active. Prof. Griffith found at Tell el Amarna 150 houses in every one of which were molds for making small ornaments, and from Meroe to Wadi Ghâzai there were many kilns.

COPTIC POTTERY

Most Coptic pottery is crude and badly decorated, made only for common use. One fine example is in the Metropolitan Museum and has been assigned to the 8th or 7th century by Dimand and 6th century by Butler. In the Monastery of Epiphanius at Qurnah were found some typical Egyptian and small Arretine ware bowls interesting because they are glazed on the inside only with the lip-rim covered. Lamps have been found that cover the transition between classical and mediaeval, including Roman forms and those with deeper bodies, more open spouts, higher handles and a definite rim around the oil hole. The later ones have a higher neck and lengthened spout like those found at Fostât.

FIG. 462. Babylonian 6th cent. B.C. panel of enameled bricks from the "Procession Street." The colors are white, tan, blue and green. Length 7 feet 5½ inches. Metropolitan Mus. of Art.

MESOPOTAMIAN GLAZED POTTERIES

From the 9th to the 6th centuries B.C. were placed in the temple of Saragon's citadel, Khorsabad, figures of bulls, lions, eagles and trees wonderfully designed in glazed brick, of various colors. There were also glazed bricks in the archivolt of the town gate, and the walls and floor tiles of the palace of the Assyrian Kings at Calah, now in the city of Nimrud or Kalakh, were also decorated with colored glazes. Unfortunately some of the glazed bricks from Babylon were lost by the excavations forever in the Tigris but the few known give us an idea of the splendor that must have enshrouded this city. From Susa excavated by the French, from the royal citadel of the Akhaemenes dating about 500 B.C. came the parts of the relief of the "Immortals" and the famous "Frieze of Archers" which we hope is still in the Louvre. The colors used are bright yellow, yellow brown, white and soft olive green, now of course tempered by time but with beauty undiminished. With anatomy the artists who made these were fully acquainted but the dignity of feeling and organization of design raises them to a rating with the greatest of fine arts. Only fragments were found of Nebuchadnezzar II's gigantic frieze from the "Procession Street" and the walls of the Ishtar Gate and the Throne Room in Babylon of his time but the Germans have made remarkable restorations of them.

ASHUR

The Deutsche Orient-Gesellschaft's excavations at Ashur have taken us still further back for they reach from the fall of the Assyrian Empire in 606 B.C. back to the 13th century B.C. In the Temple of Ashur were found bricks stamped as made for the Temple of Adad and they must be earlier than the time of Tiglath-Pileser I of the 12th century B.C. for he alone we know restored that temple. Still older are the potteries from Kar-Tukulki-Enurta on the left bank of the Tigris opposite Ashur for they are fully matured and show a well-developed style, already stiff and altered from the original craftsmanship of prehistoric vase painting of Susa from which they are directly descended. Patterns are of the palm, pomegranate and only later about 1500 B.C. does the lotus appear from Egypt for it grows on the Nile and not on the Tigris and Euphrates. But the most startling characteristic of the Ashur pieces is the strong predominance of alternation in design.

ALTERNATION IN DESIGN

Here is another principle of art appeal. In nature the alternation of leaves up a stem or that of two sizes of petals on a flower or that of the effect of calyx and petals at the back of a flower is about all one finds. In the stripes of animals to be sure it occurs in simple form but not often. Alternation implies an abrupt cutting off of one state for another which is in turn severed for a reintroduction of the first or for the introduction of still a third. Nature is largely continuous so this is to a great degree an invention of man. An alternating border may have two or any number of separate blocks unrelated but recurring at stated intervals. There may be a connecting flow but this is unnecessary and simply acts as a softening of the effect. Alternation undoubtedly grew out of the art of weaving and is essential to it. These are the simple facts but the true artist is seldom contented with static alternation of 1-2-1-2 type or even of 1-2-3-1-2-3 type, or the ascending and descending type 1-2-3-2-1-2-3 type, and he may develop constantly varied types such as the enclosing of three dots in a box and four dots in the next but always arranged differently or he may develop growing alternation which introduces a simple pair or more of subjects and makes them ever more complicated always retaining the given forms in some certain rhythm until a crescendo is reached as in a rhapsody. He often imposes rhythm upon rhythm as 1-2-3-5-2-1-2-4-3-2-1-5-2-3-2-4 etc., in which our ascending and descending rhythm has a simple alternation imposed on its every fourth beat.

There is a strange liking for alternation in Mesopotamia and Persia which is lacking in the art of the Far East. It is probably due to the constant invasions of nomadic peoples to whom the weaving of unbreakable baskets and also rugs or other fabrics to protect them against the cold are very important arts. Therefore, we have here another perfectly reasonable explanation of why the Northern and nomadic art was responsible for the development of conventionalization. Those people of the warmer climates made pottery for they did not have to move and carry it with them. In Mesopotamia and Persia we find the two arts meeting to the benefit of ceramic design.

But to return to the potteries of Ashur and to quote Mr. Andrae, "Originally the fruit-bearing turioniferous palm, and probably the rosette, and the he-goats, represented symbolically the cult of the goddess Ishtar; but later palmettos and pairs of facing goats generally on their knees, became simple ornaments with no deeper meaning." This would imply a long development and beginning decadence. Mr. Andrae gives the following list of characteristics peculiar to the Assyrian pottery:

1.—Hardness of curves shown in the palm leaves and tree of life.
2.—Preference for the compact, heavy and almost cumbrous with an apparently willful avoidance of all delicacy and lightness.
3.—The interlacing of patterns and filling of ornaments with other forms such as the leaves with many colored geometrical figures or other plant forms. This, he says is carried for 3,000 years down to the patterns of Islamic carpets and printed cottons.
4.—The pomegranate is probably an Assyrian invention, he thinks, while the palm, which is not indigenous was developed in another form.
5.—The use of the chevron is at its height in the 9th century and was lost by the 7th.

Finally tin glaze is thought to have been consciously discovered and made use of in about 1100 B.C. and through its ability to cover a colored surface and make a clear ground on which to paint decorations, brought about the use of glazed bricks in greater numbers. The colors used were much the same as those used in Egypt though this does not imply that they came from there. The colors were well used and did not run into each other, which implies high technical ability.

ORTHOSTATS AND PROBABLE ORIGIN OF THE CLOUD MOTIF

Large bricks measuring more than 45 inches by a foot and 4 or 5 inches thick were used to protect the lower parts of the walls from blows or damp and are called orthostats. They were usually unglazed but the kings had theirs beautifully decorated. One was found which was dated by its inscription (890–884 B.C.) while a much earlier one shows the god Ashur flying above a charioteer and drawing his bow while about him is a nimbus shown by double yellow rings and to either side is a design of clouds like bags holding dots to

FIG. 464. Tin enamel faced bricks, many having the following inscription stamped on the upper surface:
"Tiglath-Pileser,
The Great King, The Mighty King, the King of All, the King of the Assyrians,
Belonging to the 'Kigal' of the bulls
Of the Gate of Adad's Temple."
(Tiglath-Pileser reigned in 1120–1100 B.C.) Found at Ashur. The colors are turquoise and green ground, white cufic characters and yellow and orange designs with brown outlines. The tiles had been reassembled about 300 years after they were made. Length 5' 9". From *Coloured Ceramics from Ashur* by Walter Andrae.

FIG. 463. Brick orthostat with colored enamel painting of Ashur, the chief national god, receiving an Assyrian noble. He is either thanking or petitioning against a plague of locusts (see one above his head). Above the god's head are symbols of the three other chief gods,—the sun (Shamash), the moon (Sin) and Venus (Ishtar). On his head he has the crown with horns, feather trimming and the eight-rayed disk supported by a lily as in the relief in Malthai, which is well known. Ht. 22", width 10¾". From *Coloured Ceramics from Ashur* by Walter Andrae.

represent drops of rain. It may be that these are the first of that motive which became so prominent in later Chinese design. I know of nothing in China as early.

ASHUR POTTERY VESSELS

Most of the pottery vessels belong to the two last centuries of the Assyrian Empire and almost exclusively to the reign of Sargon ("The legitimate King") who assumed the name of the famous king of Babylon who ruled some 2,000 years before. He lasted from 722 B.C. to 705 B.C. and his conquests included,

FIG. 465. A flat truncated conical "bucket shaped vase" the sherds represented as lying out flat, the biggest and most beautiful one found in Ashur. Note the pair of double handles or loops near the top. The ground is sky-blue. The other colors are mustard yellow and white. Note the alternation of coloring of the flowers and the upper borders. Ht. about 16½". From *Coloured Ceramics from Ashur* by Walter Andrae.

Jar, light buff and sandy clay. Greenish-blue, light grey (which was dark blue), yellow and black outlines. Ht. 14″.

Vase with pointed panels in blue, grey and yellow (grey having been dark blue probably), and rare treatment of kneeling goat and flower in wide band about the body. Ht. 14½″.

Oblate vase with wide mouth and small base of late Assyrian period having interesting check-ered arch design around lotus blossoms and buds arranged in symmetrical panels. Green which was once more blue, white, yellow and brown. Ht. 8⅝″.

Possibly from temple of Anu and Adad. Late or post-Assyrian date. Light blue, yellow, dark blue, black outlines and white. Shape typical. Ht. 11⅝″.

ALL PHOTOGRAPHS FROM *Coloured Ceramics From Ashur*, BY WALTER ANDRAE

ASSYRIAN (ASHUR) POTTERY VESSELS

PLATE 84

Egypt, Damascus, Palestine and the Philistines, as well as eastern Armenia, the Hitites and Moschi 717 B.C. It is said he sent a statue of himself to Cyprus. Probably the empire's fall was a signal for looting of the temple and the vases were broken then or subsequently in handling.

Mr. Andrae makes three classifications:—1.—buckets, 2.—pots, 3.—bottles. The first are all about the same shape though they vary in size, and some have handles. The bottles are close to the prehistoric forms of many countries. The pots are wide-mouthed forms without the appendages which ruined the forms of many Greek vases. They were probably used for daily life, for burial and also for ceremonies. The colors are warm golden yellow, light wine-yellow, ivory, blue (said by Andrae to have faded from the original depth, but very pleasing) and dark violet. The designs are in bands which seem to be suspended on the sides from above rather than supported from below. This is unique.

FIGURES FROM ASHUR

Fragments of figures include a horse head, a torso and the body of some small fat animal which might have been on wheels like the one found at Ur. All show fine craftsmanship and the horse head is as good as most found on

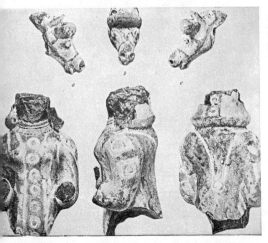

FIG. 466. Polychromed horse's head said to be from the figure of a mounted man. Ht. 2¾". Part of a figure of a woman in the position, with hands raised before her, of prayer. Ht. 4¾". The probable height of the figure was 9½". From *Coloured Ceramics from Ashur* by Walter Andrae.

FIG. 467. A few knob-plates of Neo-Assyrian times restored from fragments. The circular ones 20" in dia. The square 15" on a side. From *Coloured Ceramics from Ashur* by Walter Andrae.

T'ang Chinese specimens 1,200 to 1,400 years later. These are covered with white and decorated with the same colors as were used on the vases. They may have been small household gods though I think to pin this theory of so serious use on every ancient object is not to allow for simple human reactions.

KNOBS AND KNOB PLATES

The walls were ornamented with plaster painting and the orthostats while inner walls were almost covered with pottery and besides that the upper parts had crenelles and friezes of polychrome bricks and having unglazed or polychrome enameled knobs stuck into them, called by the Assyrians "zigat." These knobs were also found in Nineveh and Calah but were thought to be vases. In Babylon they were cones with inscriptions on the shaft or head. Mr. Andrae says they are established as being in use in the third millennium B.C. and thinks they were put in as "key stones" on the completion of the building just as little inscribed barrels, prisms and tablets were put in as "foundation stones."

FIG. 468. Possibly restorations by Dr. Herzfeld of an ena elled knob-plate from Ashur of King Ashur-nazirpal III. Inscription about the base of the knob, PALACE OF ASHUR-NAZIRPAL, KING OF ALL, KING OF ASSYRIA, SON OF TUKULTI-ENURTA, KING OF ALL, KING OF ASSYRIA. Shows that even to the words there is a sort of alternation. Width and ht. 14½". The knob extends 5". From *Coloured Ceramics from Ashur* by Walter Andrae.

FIG. 469. Knobs found in a heap of rubbish in the Old Palace in Ashur. Middle 9th cent. B.C. Such objects were thought to be vases when first found. Greatest length 7½". From *Coloured Ceramics from Ashur* by Walter Andrae.

They are not phallic and derived from pegs. Later ones in Assyria have larger and flatter heads. As bases for these pegs there were found concave square and round plates which Mr. Andrae thinks were alternated. In the 9th century the round ones are larger and this has cast some doubt on his assumption but I see no reason why it should. Some were under the crenellation while others seem to have been placed at about the height of a man. I cannot help but wonder if they did not serve as pegs on which to hang clothing, etc., or if they did not support cords of some sort perhaps for wall hangings.

Such, then, was the general state of the great ceramic art of Assyria during the Sargonid period when she was at the height of her culture. The forms were sound and strong. The designs were alive and full of the rhythm of alternation. The colors were masterfully handled and there is a sureness which seems to grow out of stone carving (at which they were also masters) which disciplines the brush into a secure and definite handling. There are no fancy flourishes here, none of the later Persian sweetness, and yet there is a ferociousness, almost cruelty, in the movement which is entirely lacking from the Egyptian things. These potteries have come a long way up from those we found in the 12th layer at the bottom under the sand of Mesopotamia. They have reached their peak. Now follows the Babylonian and Medean conquest and turmoil with·later King Cyrus of Persia.

ACHAEMENID EMPIRE POTTERY (558–330 B.C.)

This was not a productive time in Persia but it was during the Achaemenid Empire that the "Frieze of Archers" was made and important finds have been made in Susa. The main stream of art came from Assyria and such things as the great winged lions with human heads (Propylaeum at Persepolis) and animals were well drawn but with less power in Persia. The tall slender fluted column with Indian feeling was now developed. The modeling of animals was carried from extreme conventionalism as in Luristan to the purely naturalistic of the South. But perhaps most significant is the discarding of the old Semitic modesty concerning the human body. Finally King Cyrus, as also at a later time King Darius, will be found often portrayed as are George Washington and Abraham Lincoln in the United States.

GLAZED POTTERY NOTES OF THESE TIMES

The glazes used in Egypt and the Near East are composed of silicic acid or simple quartz sand combined with some medium which helps it to fuse at a lower temperature, called a "flux." It is this flux which determines the type of glaze. The palette of colors could not be broadened because the glaze we are discussing was alkaline and would be acted upon by the most diluted acids. It is this which also explains how they easily became iridescent. An interesting point is that the silicates of lime and soda with a little alumina used in the Near East would not stick to ordinary potter's clay but only to a body similar to itself and made of siliceous sand. Such a body is not plastic and had to be mixed with a potter's clay in order to be made so. Therefore it is clear why the beautiful effects accomplished in Persia to Egypt were not obtained elsewhere, for it would be difficult to find all the ingredients; proper sand, clay and the oxides with which to color the glazes all in one place.

Glazes containing lead oxide were used in both sections as far back as Ptolemaic times and, though the Romans with their Greek heritage used little glaze, the pottery that succeeded theirs in Western Europe and Byzantium was generally glazed with a substance rich in lead. These glazes are more or less transparent and showed the texture of the body but the sometimes unpleasant imperfections were hidden by dipping the piece first in a "slip" or what the French call "engobe" and then glazing over that. It will be remembered what a wonderful use the Chinese made of slip treatments in the Sung period. Similar and earlier treatments though less beautiful are found in what is known as "Gabri ware" in the Near East.

Tin glaze is quite as early as lead glaze and probably originated in Assyria. The tiles or glazed bricks found at Nimroud, Khorsabad and Nineveh as well as the famous wall pictures at Susa were stanniferous. This takes such glazes back to at least 500 B.C. In the buildings of Muhammed I at Brusa the tin glaze was decorated with low-fired enamels easily melted in the "muffled kiln." This is all definitely Assyrian for in Egypt even up to and after the Islamic times the older alkaline glazes persisted.

FIG. 470. Roman terracotta or unglazed pottery bowl on foot with four handles painted in slip to imitate marble like those of Egypt and Crete of far earlier date. 1st cent. A.D. Ht. 3¾". Metropolitan Mus. of Art.

PTOLEMAIC EGYPTIAN POTTERIES
(End of 4th century to 1st century and Roman Period)

The Egyptians had always tried to imitate the veining of their marble vessels by mixing potter's clay and we see similar effects done in Crete. By the time the idea reached China not only the body clays but slips and even glazes were so mixed. Then the idea was reflected back from T'ang China (A.D. 618–906) to Samarra. Of course the technique persisted simply because it was pleasing and not with any conscious idea of imitating stone. In the XXVI Dynasty ushabtis were made with a mixture of sand and turquoise glaze all through the body and shortly after bowls were made which look as though they had been carved from dark blue veined onyx.

ASSYRIAN AS WELL AS GREEK INFLUENCES IN EGYPT

The conquest of Egypt by Cambyses in the Achaemenid period during the 6th century had little influence on Assyria but brought designs from there to

FIG. 471. Egypto-Roman vases, first two said to be of 2nd or 3d cent. and having green-blue glaze. Lower two of 1st cent. and glazed in deep manganese blue with turquoise inside and green relief decoration. From Islamic Pottery by A. J. Butler Coll. of Eton Mus.

FIG. 472. Heavy pottery vase with swan handles crudely and unevenly potted and covered with green glaze. Found in Greece and thought to date c. 100 B.C. to A.D. 100. Ht. 5". Metropolitan Mus. of Art.

Egypt and tended to a refinement in potting. The art of making portrait figures started about 500 B.C. and continued until in 200 B.C. the casting process cheapened and destroyed it.

Jars with globular bodies and wide necks had been made for many centuries and the one with cover of about 800 B.C. is little different in general potting from the more graceful example of the 1st or 2nd century B.C. from the Kelekian Collection save that the handles of the latter are joined to the body with a leaf-like spread probably Hellenistic in origin. Another without handles but with horizontal bands of decoration reminiscent of the "Oriental Period" of Greek vases but rendered in beautiful light and dark turquoise is also of the 2nd or 1st century B.C. The one at the Metropolitan Museum has been badly restored but the two published by Butler from the Eton Museum show the real shape with flaring foot of more or less weak classic form and flaring mouth. Of the same period of Egypto-Roman potteries are the jars with more angular shoulders and squared handles. These are usually covered with dark blue glaze on which are modeled plant forms in low relief and picked out in turquoise. A piece with green glaze but showing similar characteristics was found in Greece. It has swan handles and a weaker form.

SYRO-ROMAN POTTERIES

A type of jar thought to have been made in Syria from about the 3d or 2nd centuries to about A.D. 100 shows certain similarities of form including the angular shoulder and double handle although in these the two parts of the handles are sometimes twisted to give a braided appearance. They are about 12 to 14 inches high as a rule, are of sandy body and covered with a green glaze of alkaline type turned, through action of the soil, to beautiful iridescence at times. They inherit the unstructural Greek foot but are otherwise sturdily made and powerful in proportion. At times appliqués in low relief were added but this was a development toward the end of their period and not at all unlike the relief decorations found on typical Roman cups of the day both from the continent and the islands such as Cyprus. It has been suggested that this type of vase is the sort which was sent to China and thus introduced the glaze of the Han period. I do not know of any having been found there although examples have come from all over the Near East, yet similarities in form and the very similar glaze point to this as a reasonable theory. In any event these vases are stronger than those of Rome and the Chinese are stronger than these

IRIDESCENCE

Collectors of Near Eastern wares and those from Han China pay greater prices for pieces showing fine iridescence. This is entirely an accident of nature and the potters never had any slightest idea that their wares were to be so beautified. Iridescence is not color nor any sort of pigment but refraction of light and may be thought of as caused by millions of tiny prisms making "rainbows." These prisms are simply the irregularities caused by the rotting away of the glaze due to chemical action in the soil in which the potteries were buried, and every color from deep violet to brilliant red can be found

Egyptian covered vase with rich, deep
turquoise glaze over usual buff pottery dating c. 800 B.C. Ht. 6½″. Eton Mus.

Beautiful Egypto-Roman vase
with glaze of mottled pale green
and turquoise dating c. 1st or 2nd
cent. Ht. 8¾″. Ex Kelekian Coll.,
Victoria and Albert Mus.

Egyptian vase, light and dark turquoise color.
Middle Ptolemaic period (200–100 B.C.) showing similarity in design to Oriental Period Greek vases, though
latter are not carried out in glaze and relief. Foot
and neck are repairs. Metropolitan Mus. of Art.

Egyptian, Roman-period vase dating c. 1st
cent. A.D. Faience, heavily potted, dark blue
and turquoise. Ht. 7″. Metropolitan Mus. of
Art.

JARS SHOWING GREEK AND ROMAN INFLUENCES IN EGYPT

PLATE 85

"Syro-Roman" vase, excavated at Bagdad. Light buff clay with glaze which varies from blue to green and with brown areas, also iridescence from burial. Ht. 13¼". Warren E. Cox Coll. Ex Demotte Coll.

Roman or "Syro-Roman" vase with unusual appliqués about neck and fine iridescence due to burial. Ht. 14¼". Metropolitan Mus. of Art.

Left: Roman vase dating about 1st cent. B.C. Much like that called Syro-Roman because much of it was found in Syria. Beautiful iridescence from burial. Ht. 9½". Metropolitan Mus. of Art.

Roman cup with pressed design in relief, from Cyprus 100 B.C. to A.D. 100. Ht. c. 2½". Metropolitan Mus. of Art.

Right: Roman buff pottery cup with two ring handles, decorated with moulded relief design under greenish glaze dating c. 100 B.C. to A.D. 100. Ht. 2¾". Metropolitan Mus. of Art.

SYRO-ROMAN POTTERIES

PLATE 86

in all sorts of combinations. Far more beautiful than the color of a peacock's tail or that of a South American butterfly are these subtle sheens of ever-changing light.

I have in my collection from the Kevorkian Collection an ewer of the 12th to 13th century found at Sultanabad which is covered with a silvery lavender colored iridescence. When it is wet the moisture fills all the little interstices between the tiny prisms and makes an even surface. Then it can be seen that the glaze is of deep blue and that it has a design in black painted on it. When the piece dries again this disappears under the sheen of silver and lavender again. Many pieces do not respond so quickly because their

Fig. 473. This ewer shown first dry and then partly wet so that the black of the design shows clearly on the blue ground. When dry the whole is a lavender, silver color. Sultanabad Persian piece of 12th to 13th cent. Ht. 9¾″. Ex Kevorkian Coll. Warren E. Cox Coll.

iridescence is deeper but all will show the original color underneath if soaked in water for some time. I do not advise doing this to repaired pieces for they will fall apart and never under any conditions should a rag be touched to such a surface for it will only rub in dirt and dull the effect. The piece should be wet with clear water and allowed to dry of its own accord.

PARTHIAN AND SASSANIAN WARES (190 B.C.–A.D. 224 AND A.D. 224 TO 633 OR 175–226 AND 226–651 ACCORDING TO DIMAND)

Of the Parthian wares little is known and in truth probably the art of pottery was in an absorptive period rather than productive. We have said

Fig. 474. Sassanian pottery jar, 2nd to 6th cent. More powerful shape than usually seen. Glaze olive green with silver iridescence. Ht. about 22″. Nasli Heeramaneck Coll.

Fig. 475. Dark green glazed earthenware vase, Parthian 1st to 2nd cent. A.D. Ht. 13½″. Metropolitan Mus. of Art.

Fig. 476. Sassanian, Mesopotamian, large jar of unglazed earthenware. Buff colored clay with impressed design, irregular and crude. 3rd to 4th cent. found at Takrit, Iraq. Ht. 16¾″. Metropolitan Mus. of Art.

that the nomadic influences are usually inspirational and this is true but their inventions take some time to digest and they are seldom seen at once. This period was also one of decline both in Rome and in the Near East and during it the great religious wars were starting. If the Parthians won their power chiefly through the weakness of Rome, their pottery also shows a rather weak character. The Sassanians continued a relief technique and some show a "barbotine" or slip treatment in their wares. They also decorated the unglazed water jars with impressions from seals possibly after the Parthian influence. Sassanian metal work was superb and many of the potteries were influenced by this craft. Sassanian and early Islamic pieces have been found at Kufa, Takrit, Samarra, Ganaur and Bagdad.

ISLAMIC POTTERY

From the days of late Rome to Islamic times there is little identified Sassanian pottery and the "Parthian," "Syro-Roman" and a few Egyptian continuations are all we have though excavations in Constantinople may bring to light the Byzantine sequence.

"Gabri" Types

The "Gabri" (or "Guebri") ware was so-called because its enthusiastic discoverers believed it to have been made by the fire-worshiping Pre-Islamic peoples before 633 but it is now agreed that most of these wares are actually of the 8th to 10th century. The body of these wares is usually reddish and they are coated with a white slip over which is a yellowish or green transparent lead glaze sometimes given green, yellow or purplish brown areas. The usual type has the slip cut away to form designs in contrast with the body color, a technique expertly handled in Sung Chinese Tz'u Chou type wares. Here, however, the designs are bold and show northern animal and bird forms, floral scrolls and figures often within geometrical diapers. The wares have been excavated chiefly in Northern Persia at Zendjan, Rhages, Hamadan, Susa, Kermanshah and in Amul just south of the Caspian where yellow and an ocherous red were added, with very rare examples of white

FIG. 477. Hamadan-Zenjan bowl. Reddish brown ware with thick white slip incised and covered with yellowish white glaze having splashes of green. 9th to 10th cent. Dia. about 15". Nasli Heeramaneck Coll.

FIG. 478. Bowl from Samarkand in Western Turkestan. Samanid period, 10th cent. Glazed pottery with cream glaze and design in olive green, red-brown, and black. Dia. 10¾". Metropolitan Mus. of Art.

Bowl of brown pottery with white slip and lead glaze showing green at rim but otherwise colorless and transparent. Located near Amul or Rei (Rhages). c. 8th to 9th cent. Dia. 13″. Dikran G. Kelekian.

Bowl, 9th cent. Green glaze over carved slip decoration on brown ground. Found at Zendjan, Persia and shows Sassanian influence. Note filling in of rump with circular design. Dia. 7¾″. Dikran K. Kelekian Coll.

Left: Reddish pottery bowl of conical form with low concave base having white slip and scratched out design under green transparent glaze. Slip and glaze cover only part of exterior. Note spur marks inside. Zendjan type, so-called because many were found there, though there is no proof of their manufacture there. 10th to 12th cent. Eumorfopoulos Coll. # F356.

Center: "Gabri type" green incised tile for top of stove or for outlet plaque for running water. Nas'i Heeramaneck Coll.

Right: "Gabri" type slip-covered sgraffito pottery. Red-brown ware with lead glaze having streaks of purplish-brown. Found at Hamadan or Zendjan. 10th to 11th cent. Dia. 8¾″. Metropolitan Mus. of Art.

INCISED SLIP WARES OF SO-CALLED "GABRI TYPE"
PLATE 87

painted on a ground of black slip. A red ware of the Samanid period (A.D. 819–1004) painted with colored slips is found as far east as Samarkand, in Western Turkestan.

The Amol potteries are similar with polychrome decoration on white slip of Kufic writing and medallions in orange-red, aubergine, olive-green and white.

T'ANG TYPE SAMARRA WARE

Professors Sarre and Herzfeld made systematic excavations at Samarra on the Tigris (where the Affasid Caliph Matasim lived between 836 and 883 when he left for Bagdad), and found a distinctive close grained buff ware with opaque greyish white tin glaze painted at times with lustre of golden brown, green or blood red tones, or at times with dark cobalt blue with now and then touches of green and dark manganese brown. This lustre was both monochrome and polychrome. Another ware is thin and reddish buff with designs in relief under a green glaze and much like Roman wares. The buff ware is also treated with white, yellow and green monochrome glazes, and

FIG. 480. Samarra bowl. White reserved in red lustre. 9th cent. Mesopotamian. Dia. 6¾". Metropolitan Mus. of Art.

FIG. 479. Samarra dish. Conventionalized character is undoubtedly Arabic, in brown lustre. 9th cent. Dia. 2¼". Metropolitan Mus. of Art.
FIG. 481. Samarra bowl. Incised yellow and green glazes of T'ang type. Dia. about 11½". Nasli Heeramaneck Coll.

also with splashed and mottled treatments very much like those used in T'ang China (A.D. 618 to 906) which they copied without a doubt. There is also an unglazed pottery; water jars with stamped, molded or applied decorations of Kufic writing (angular Arabic letters) arabesques and animals; designs which became more elaborate later in the 11th and 12th centuries.

RAKKA WARES

In Mesopotamia on the Euphrates about 100 miles east of Aleppo is Rakka which was important between the 8th and 15th centuries. It was the home of Caliph Harun Al-Rashid (A.D. 786–809) with his magnificent following, but most of the pottery is of the 12th century. Much of the ware found there is probably not of local manufacture but some types are more plentiful than elsewhere. The body of these is gritty and easily crumbled. It is of a nearly white color. It is often covered with a transparent greenish white or green glaze which becomes opaque when colored blue of deep turquoise hue. Kiln sites yield a white ware of the 11th to 12th century with engraved designs under a clear glaze frequently splashed with blue. Very similar examples come from Rhages with the added colors of yellow, green and purple. Among other decorations are used Naskhi characters (round Arabic letters).

Chatfield Pier's book shows a bowl which is dated 831 and it is painted with a black design under a pale blue glaze, which is characteristic. Other vases and bowls have painting in both black and blue and this is typical of Syrian and Egyptian wares of the 13th to 15th centuries. Thus they are known as Syro-Egyptian. Many are decorated with a brown lustre often with added turquoise and blue touches and in some cases over bold relief and these reach back to the 10th or 11th centuries or earlier. (See following discussion of lustre.) The glaze is transparent and greenish. The various decorations are often confined in compartments. At "Rusapha," Syria, near

Left: Bowl, Samarra type, 9th cent. Dia. 10″. Eumorfopoulos Coll. # F377.
Center: Bowl found at Nishapur. Probably 9th cent. Design incised, with green and brown on cream ground. Nasli Heeramaneck Coll.
Right: Samanid (c. 10th cent.) deep conical bowl found at Nishapur. Salmon, rose and white. Dia. 7¼″. Dikran G. Kelekian.

Left: "Rhages" bowl. 10th cent. Aubergine on cream ground. Boston Mus. of Fine Arts.
Center: 9th–10th cent. bowl found at Amol. Umber, sienna and olive green on cream ground. Nasli Heeramaneck Coll.
Right: Amol bowl. 9th–10th cent. Raw umber, sienna and olive green. Nasli Heeramaneck Coll.

Samarra jug. Black on cream ground. Dia. c. 12″. Nasli Heeramaneck Coll.

Center: 9th cent. Persian jar from Susa. Glaze transparent and crackled. Decoration in green and dark blue. Ht. 8″. Metropolitan Mus. of Art.
Right: Early Rakka vase. Sandy ware with greyish green pale toned design in reserve on black ground. Brilliant silvery iridescence. Ht. 7″. Dikran K. Kelekian Coll.

9TH–10TH CENT. WARES FROM NISHAPUR, AMOL, SAMARRA, SUSA, AND RAKKA

PLATE 88

Vase, typical Western Asian. Writing around shoulder in relief. Turquoise glaze. Ht. about 10". Freer Gallery of Art, Washington.

12th cent. mosque-lamp-shaped vase which may or may not have actually been intended for use as lamp. Pierced neck supports former possibility. Ht. 6¾". Metropolitan Mus. of Art.

Mesopotamian jar of 12th cent. Rare because of inscription about body. Ht. 19⅞". Metropolitan Mus. of Art.

Mesopotamian jar with relief decoration and iridescence from burial. Reconstructed. Ht. 15¾". Metropolitan Mus. of Art.

Rare type ewer with one handle and narrow mouth. Light buff clay with deep turquoise blue glaze and golden iridescence. Ht. 21". Warren E. Cox Coll.

Syrian or Mesopotamian vase. 14th cent. Crowded design in blue and black under grayish glaze. Ht. 12¾". Metropolitan Mus. of Art.

RAKKA POTTERIES (12TH–13TH CENT.)

PLATE 89

Rakka are found similar lustred wares of deeper colors, red, gold, etc., over purplish-blue and colorless glazes.

Some of the most powerful heavy pottery comes also from this site and is likely to be found to reach back earlier than its present dating of 12th to 13th centuries. Certainly it is reminiscent of the Sassanian and Parthian wares. This is usually covered with a turquoise glaze turned brightly iridescent through burial.

Left: Stem sweetmeat dish of Rakka or Rhages ware. Light blue arabic writing in cups under transparent aquamarine tinted glaze largely covered with golden iridescence. 13th cent. or older. Dia. 11½". Warren E. Cox Coll.

Right: Rakka 11th to 12th cent. plate of deep turquoise with spirited black design of bird drawn with great verve. Dia. 14". Ht. 3¾". Dikran G. Kelekian.

Right: Syria or Mesopotamia bowls of 12th–13th cent. with charming and spirited decorations. Black on light ground. deep turquoise glaze. Dias. 3¾" and 4½". Metropolitan Mus. of Art.

Vases of 13th cent. having crude but graceful form and simple design in black under transparent turquoise glaze. Iridescent. Ht. 10¼". Warren E. Cox Coll.

RAKKA POTTERIES (12TH–13TH CENT.)

PLATE 90

RHAGES WARES

The Mongols sacked Rhages in 1220 but it was not abandoned until the 17th century. It was a great trade center in the 12th and early 13th centuries and probably only to a small extent a pottery center for few wasters are found there. Most of the wares are the typical sandy white body finer and thinner after the 12th century and the glaze is usually creamy and opaque frequently decorated with a light golden brown lustre, typical of Persia. Many of the wares are decorated in relief or are actually modelled or molded

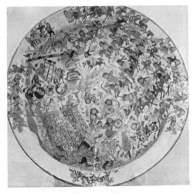

Largest and one of finest Rhages poly-chrome plates known. On front, batt'e scene between Iranians and Turanians. On back (except for center inside foot-rim), con-tinuous hunting scene. 13th cent. Dia. 19". D:kran G. Kelekian.

One of finest Rhages 13th cent. bowls. Deep blue wall inside, with white ground center and beautiful polychrome decoration. Dia. 6¾". Dikran G. Kelekian.

Jug probably after metal design. Relief decoration in gold and blue, green and tan slips. 13th cent. Ht. 7¾". Metropolitan Mus. of Art.

Ewer with reticulated outer wall in turquoise-blue, black and lapis-blue. 13th cent. Ht. 8¾". Dikran G. Kelekian.

Persian 13th cent. vase with enamel decorations of horsemen, seated figures, in polychrome. Ht. 7½". Metropolitan Mus. of Art.

PAINTED WARES FOUND AT RHAGES

PLATE 91

in the round sometimes pierced and covered with a white, turquoise or cobalt blue glaze. Some of these are further enhanced by touches of leaf gold and enamel colors, and finally there is a whole class of the so-called "Minai" technique which is carefully painted from miniature sources with pictures in enamel and gold over white or pale blue grounds. The enamels include cobalt, turquoise, manganese purple, red, green, brown and black and colors mixed with white. They are all mat except the blue and adhere well to the

Bowl with purplish-blue glaze and incised decoration. Persian 12th–13th cent. Dia. 12½". Metropolitan Mus. of Art.

"Lakabi" Persian dish, probably 12th cent. Cream ground and harpy in purplish-blue, aubergine and yellow. Dia. 12¼". Metropolitan Mus. of Art.

Small dish found at Rhages (or Rei), 11th to 12th cent. Cream white ground and three fish in cobalt blue, turquoise and aubergine. Dia. 8⅞". Dikran G. Kelekian.

Persian 12th cent. bowl. Creamy-white with incised decoration glazed deep blue, turquoise green and manganese. Dia. 16". The Cleveland Mus. of Art.

EARLY SELJUK RHAGES INCISED WARES

PLATE 92

ground. Such enamels are also found on unglazed water jugs of porous body often molded in relief and are found all over the Near East. Frequently the lustre ware has lines or touches of blue. Most of these wares were made between the 12th and early 14th century. Great prices have attached to the miniature decorated wares which do not merit them from an artistic viewpoint but which are full of human interest and tell us much of the life of the times.

From various sources comes an early Seljuk ware forming a link between the "Gabri" and 13th century wares. It has incised outlines of the decoration

Rhages bottle with typical fluted cup mouth to aid in pouring into it and fine relief design about shoulder. Commonly covered with cobalt or turquoise blue but some have aubergine glaze. Transparent and crackled. This is turquoise. 12th to 13th cent. Ht. 9". Boston Mus. of Fine Arts.

Ewer in form of seated lion cub found at Sarah (Persia). Ht. 7¼". 13th cent. Dikran G. Kelekian.

Cylindrical jar of white sandy ware with turquoise glaze. Said to be from "Rayy" by mus. Hobson shows one in Eumorfopoulos Coll. and calls it Sultanabad 13th or 14th cent. Ht. about 13¼". Boston Mus. of Fine Arts.

Typical Rhages vase. Light sandy pottery with deep blue glaze. Ht. about 12". 13th cent. Boston Mus. of Fine Arts.

Persian ewer, 13th cent. Cock's head mouth and conventionalized tail for handle. Light buff and blue glaze on whitish sandy ware. Ht. 10½". Metropolitan Mus. of Art.

"Rhages" type light buff ware with turquoise glaze. 13th to 14th cent. Ht. 10¾". Metropolitan Mus. of Art.

POTTERIES FOUND AT RHAGES AND SARAH

PLATE 93

13th–cent. tile with turquoise ground and dark blue writing of "Rhages" type. Length 12¼". Metropolitan Mus. of Art.

"Rhages" 13th–cent. tile. Conventionalized writ covered with bright turquoise glaze touched with lines. Length 14". Metropolitan Mus. of Art.

Glazed tile of 14th to 15th cent. Length 15¼". Metropolitan Mus. of Art.

Iranian or Persian wall tile. Beginning of 1 cent. Relief letters and birds show Chinese influe Sandy light buff, glaze cobalt. 15¾" × 14½". M ropolitan Mus. of Art.

Turquoise blue glazed light buff pottery tile from Persia. 13th to 14th cent. Length 13½". Metropolitan Mus. of Art.

PERSIAN POTTERY TILES

PLATE 94

filled in with turquoise, cobalt and purple under a transparent glaze and often on a white ground. The bold birds and figures suggest the 12th century.

SULTANABAD WARES

From the ruins of Sultanabad in Kazvin come lustre wares without the added blue, relief wares under green, blue or turquoise and also wares painted in blue, green and brown under a clear glaze. Others are painted in black with frequent touches of cobalt with turquoise, cobalt or creamy transparent glazes. This is the most characteristic and often the design of foliage, birds or human figures is in relief against a painted background having spirals or dots in deeper tone. The designs are strongly Chinese in character and pure Chinese motives are seen in the dragons and fêng-huang birds, probably indicating that the wares are to be dated after the Mongolian conquest or late 13th century.

FIG. 482. Rare and beautiful mosque lamp inscribed with statement that maker is Ibn al Ghaibi from Tabriz. Second half of 14th cent. Decoration blue and white on black. Ht. 13″. Metropolitan Mus. of Art.

Many other sites have been found such as those at Khar, where many Rhages wares were found, and Nishapur the source of white ware decorated with highly styled and very beautiful black designs, black and red designs and even one 9th century bowl of buff clay with light slip upon which was drawn a horseman with straight sword in black outline. There are filled-in black areas on the horse and elsewhere on which is painted a bright yellow pigment which is also carried around the ground leaving the design in black and buff. Over this was placed a transparent glaze having splashes of green. The entire background is covered with birds, flowers and the word *"barakeh"* (blessing) in tiny *Kufi* letters and the body of the horse is filled with the yellow scrolls showing the typical horror vacui of much Iranian art. The design was taken from that of a Sassanian silver dish but lacks all the movement and vigor of such pieces. At Nishapur was also found a bowl of the type ascribed to Samarkand of the time of the Samanids having interlacing scrolls with writing about the rim reading "Blessing, prosperity, good will, peace and happiness to you," the whole in dull red and black. But there will undoubtedly be many more sites found and we must wait for the deductions from them before more closely allocating the various wares.

LUSTRE

Lustre ware is pottery that has a brightly shining metallic overglaze that has become iridescent. The art of lustre consists of the special technique of so handling the metallic overglaze that it will become lustrous.

The somewhat biased Dr. A. J. Butler feels a grievance because Dr. Sarre and Dr. Herzfeld believe that "The art of lustre-painting arose in Mesopotamia and thence spread to Syria, Egypt and Spain, and eastward to Persia." This is thought to be of the 9th century. We need not go into

Type found at Rhages but more extensively at Sultanabad. Sandy light buff body with turquoise glaze over which is black left open to show writing and decoration through in turquoise. One of finest examples known. Ht. 11″. Warren E. Cox Coll.

Sultanabad vase having black design painted under transparent glaze. Late 13th cent. Ht. 8½″. Warren E. Cox Coll.

Sultanabad deep dish of glazed pottery with underglaze decoration of black, green and white. 14th cent. Dia. 7⅛″. Metropolitan Mus. of Art.

Jars, called *albarellos* by Spanish who adopted it for lustre apothecary jars and transmitted it to Italy. From Rhages. 13th cent. Hts. 6″ and 11″. Warren E. Cox Coll.

Right: Jar of great importance. Deep blue-green glaze and black underglaze decoration. Ht. 28″. Dikran G. Kelekian.

POTTERIES FOUND AT SULTANABAD

PLATE 95

the well-known and unsound arguments of Dr. Butler save to list them:—

1.—He quotes a letter from Hadrian who was traveling in Alexandria in A.D. 130 and sent a present of *"calices allassontes versicolors"* which he translates as "challices color-changing" but which anyone can well imagine might mean polychrome, and which certainly does not definitely indicate lustre ware.

2.—He claims Egyptian origin for many lustre wares found at Fostat which agree in body and glaze (being white) with Mesopotamian examples but not with any known Egyptian ware which has a red body as a rule.

3.—He claims that a Persian, Nâsir-i-Khusrau while in Egypt in 1035 to 1043 saw "bûqalimûn," a ware which "changes its color according to the time of day,"—that this was lustre, that Nâsir did not recognize it at once,

Large flat plate in light and dark lustre. Many fragments of this sort found in Samarra (complete pieces rare). Said to have come from Rhages and to be of 10th cent. Dia. 15⅛″. Dikran G. Kelekian.

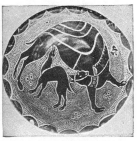

Persian lustre bowl of greyish pottery with reddish yellow design. 9th to 10th cent. Dia. c. 9″. The Louvre.

Bowl described by the museum as "West Asian, 9th to 10th cent., Samarran type." Interesting design in ʈre. Dia. 14¼″. Freer Gallery of Art, Washington.

Fine example of ware found at Fostat, dating 11th to 12th cent. Lustre heavy and brilliant of varying copper color. Dia. 10″. Dikran K. Kelekian Coll.

Lustre bowl found at Fostat (old Cairo) of Fatmid period (11th to 12th cent.). Rare, for fragments only usually found. Dia. 9⅞″. Dikran K. Kelekian Coll.

EARLY LUSTRE FOUND IN PERSIA AND EGYPT

PLATE 96

and, therefore, that there was no lustre in Persia at this time. It is rather obvious I believe that Nâsir may possibly not have known the right people. I have heard of people even of culture having been in London and not going to see Mr. Eumorfopoulos when he was living at 7 Chelsea Embankment.

4.—Nâsir-i-Khusrau went to Rakka and Rhages and did not report on the kilns, thus Dr. Butler declares flatly that there was no lustre there either of local manufacture or imported from elsewhere in Persia or Mesopotamia.

5.—He admits that some of the pieces from Samarra are of the 9th century but contends that they were not made there and particularly one being in a tripod form is certain to have come from Egypt because, to quote a Herr

Gallois, "The tripod is very rare in Eastern ceramics, while it is common in Coptic bronze-work." One would recall the ancient Ting form in ancient Chinese bronzes and wonder.

6.—He argues against the well-founded theory that metallic lustre was applied with the idea of imitating more or less actual metal, though this would seem the most natural thing in the world to do.

7.—He then says, "The truth is clear—that Nâsir was not speaking of lustre ware in general, and the kind of lustre which impressed him as novel was exclusively the brilliant counterchanging lustre." Consequently we are likely to assume that all the foregoing arguments were just kidding and that it was "counterchanging lustre" that was being written about all the time!

Of course this is all so much nonsense and I give it simply because there are still those who take this man Butler seriously even though R. L. Hobson of the B.M., Miss Alice W. Frothingham of the Hispanic Society of America and others have taken care to expose him. The real fact is that in using metallic substances in thin glazes and to paint on glazes would be sure to lead to lustrous effects which might be found pleasing and tried for again. Of two pieces fired in the same kiln and treated exactly alike one may be brightly iridescent while the other shows a plain metallic sheen. Lustre was probably found and lost by dozens of potters and invented in several places as an intended result after it had happened accidentally in perhaps many other places. It is likely that glaze perhaps did originate consciously in Egypt and that much design also came from there but it does not follow that lustre technique was also an Egyptian invention.

DATED PERSIAN LUSTRE

Dr. Ernst Kuhnel has brought together a very interesting study of actual dated examples. The earliest piece is a jar in the B.M. with broad and sure design on a light ground and also reserve design on a lustre ground, and it is marked 573 A.H. which would be A.D. 1179. (Pl. 97, top.)

The next is a bowl we show from the Chicago Art Institute and which shows a more delicate technique. It is dated 587 A.H. or A.D. 1191. (Fig. 485)

Next comes the dish from the Havemeyer Collection and that from the Eumorfopoulos Collection which we show and both of which are dated 607 A.H. or A.D. 1210. Both have a ground filled with delicate spirals and the first is perhaps finer in painting but the latter superior in the lovely treatment of scailoped rise to the rim, and the interesting and typical use of the row of faces to make pattern. (Pl. 97, center left)

The next one dated 608 A.H. or A.D. 1211 is more crude but has an interesting treatment of the birds and leaves of the background in that they are so nearly alike as to make even texture. This bowl is in the Pennsylvania University Museum, Philadelphia and it is possibly from the same atelier as the Boston Museum one which is not dated. I would also place the remarkable figure of an antelope with vase on its back, in the Seattle Museum, at about this same time and place. (Pl. 97, lower right; Pl. 99, upper left.)

The next dated piece known is in the Kelekian Collection and was made in 1227, after the Mongolian Conquest of 1220 it will be noted. It is, as we

Broken jar which is the earliest dated lustred piece known (575 A.H. or 1179 A.D.) and which shows a broad treatment quite unlike the minute drawing at the beginning of the 13th cent. Note also that the decoration is partly reserved. British Mus.

Below Left: Dish found at Rhages of sandy white ware covered with a creamy glaze and decorated in brown lustre having ruby reflections. The design is reserved and plants and scrolls etched out. The inscription reads —"Made by Saygid Shamr al-din al-Husaini in the month Tumada II in the year 607" (or 1210 A.D.). The illustration is of King Khosrau discovering the Princess Shirin bathing. Eumorfopoulos Coll. # F403.

Below Right: Lustre bowl found at Sultanabad and dated 624 A.H. (or 1227 A.D.) with grey ground and blue, green and brown lustre. There are two borders of Arabic inscription, one inside and one outside which bears the date. Dia. 7¾". Dikran K. Kelekian.

Bowl found at Sultanabad and dated in an inscription inside the rim 668 A.H. (1270 A.D.). The decoration is in light olive brown lustre on a cream ground. Dia. 7". Dikran K. Kelekian Coll.

Right: Lustre bowl dated 608 A.H. (1211 A.D.) showing interesting bird and foliage treatment in wide border. Dia. about 18". University Mus. of Philadelphia.

DATED PERSIAN LUSTRE

PLATE 97

would expect, quite different. Dr. Kuhnel says, "The former brown and gold metal tones have given way to a cobalt blue and turquoise and the drawing has become decidedly more scant and summary. Furthermore, it is said to have been found in Sultanabad, which for a long time, but perhaps wrongly, has been considered the home of a large number of Persian faiences, especially those of the Ilkhani." (Pl. 97, center right)

FIG. 483. Late 12th cent. lustre bowl of characteristic style. Dia. 18½". N. M. Heeramaneck Coll.

FIG. 484. Rhages bowl of the late 12th or early 13th cent. with brown lustre on white glaze having a fine crackle. Dia. 19¼". Sears Memorial. Boston Mus. of Fine Arts.

FIG. 485. Rhages lustre bowl dated 1191 A.D. and typical of this period. Dia. 15". Logan–Patten–Ryerson Coll. The Art Institute of Chicago.

FIG. 486. Early 13th cent. lustre plate of brown lustre and with direct but less detailed drawing. Dia. 16". N. M. Heeramaneck Coll.

A jump of 43 years now takes us to the next known piece which is also in the Kelekian Collection and dated 668 A.H. or A.D. 1270 in which the technique is similar but shows decadence.

An entirely different ware was made in the Safvid period under Shah Abbâs I, showing strong Far Eastern influence, but the only dated piece is marked 1084 A.H. or A.D. 1673.

Center: Rhages type bowl of almost white clay covered with tin glaze and having sectors of cobalt blue, turquoise and white outlined in lustre and with lustre spots, a suggested arabesque design, and figur s on the white. The outside is coated with cobalt and has lustred writing. Similar to Eum.rfopoulos Coll. # F406. Dia. 7". Warren E. Cox Coll.

Right: Two lustred 13th cent. pieces both having a brown lustre on a transparent greenish white ground and the larger plate having crossed marks of dark blue and turquoise showing iridescence from burial. Dias. 8½" and 4¼". Warren E. Cox Coll.

Bowl said to have been found at Samarcand, extreme north eastern Persia, and to be of the 11th cent. Freer Gallery of Art, Washington.

Left: "Rhages" lustred pottery bowl of the 13th cent. Dia. 8⅞". Metropolitan Mus. of Art.

PERSIAN LUSTRED BOWLS—11th TO 13th CENTURY

PLATE 98

Center: Vase of the Rakka, Mesopotamian, type with pale aquamarine glaze and dark copper brownish lustre design. 12th cent. Ht. 8½". Metropolitan Mus. of Art.

Right: Persian lustred ewer found at Rhages and belived to be of the 13th cent. The lustre is of a golden brown quality. Ht. 8¾". Metropolitan Mus. of Art.

"Rhages" lustred pottery animal with whitish glaze and brown lustre, of the first half of the 13th cent. This is one of the best specimens I have seen. Ht. 17½". Fuller Coll. Seattle Art Mus.

Center: Rakka greenish glazed pottery jug with underglaze blue and dark lustre decoration. 12th cent. Ht. 6". Metropolitan Mus. of Art.

Right: Pilgrim bottle from Veramin, but perhaps not made there, made during the 13th cent. The lustre is pale and golden and considerably worn. Ht. 14½". Metropolitan Mus. of Art.

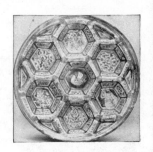

Lustre "Veramin" pottery tazza, Persian about 1300 (Compare style with dated bowls.) having a rather dark toned brown lustre. Dia. about 8¼". Metropolitan Mus. of Art.

Left: "Rhages" ewer of late 12th to early 13th cent. with brown lustre decoration on greenish cream white. Note alternation of panels in rhythm of 1 2 2, 1 2 2 and also the use of conventionalized arabic script. Ht. 10½". Metropolitan Mus. of Art.

Right: "Rhages" 13th cent. lustre sweet meat dish of the general form of a lotus pod made hollow with a hole in the bottom for air escape in firing. Decorated with brown lustre on cream. Alternating cups have portraits and the rims of all show alternating bold and delicate designs. Dia. about 9¾". Metropolitan Mus. of Art.

PERSIAN LUSTRED WARES—12TH TO 13TH CENTURY

PLATE 99

Lustred Tiles

We have tiles through the 14th century and one in the B.M. is dated 810 A.H. or A.D. 1407 while the earliest known is dated 600 A.H. or A.D. 1203 and has a design of four seated figures. (See Herz Bey Catalogue #50, page 240 from Musee Arabe, Cairo.) This is about 25 years later than the first dated vessel but there is no doubt but that the lustred tiles are among the first wares made. They are rectangular or star-and-cross tiles with the dates on the stars. The technique is much like that of the vessels but less well executed. The Mongols did not have much influence on the traditions and the Seljuk designs are much like the earlier ones.

From Veramin come a large number of tiles of both sorts with typical purely floral designs and Dr. Kuhnel points out that they must have worked about two years on the sanctuary Imâmzâdeh Yahya for there are tiles dated 1262, 1263 and 1264 with the mihrab completed during the following year.

A series thought to have come from Damghan in 1267 have not only lustre on white ground but sparing touches of turquoise blue. In these the animals are drawn in their most mature form. A tile now at Breslau shows that there was an increased use of cobalt blue next to white as early as 1240.

The Sultanabad center must have been important about 1271 as is shown by the style of a dated tile in the Berlin Museum which is strongly Mongolian, while another shows a loosening up of the tight arabesques by 1283. There are many showing relief in the similar style and one dated as late as 1407 in Timurid style.

Lustred Mihrabs

A mihrab is made up of one or more tiles with a border of inscription sometimes added and is used instead of a deep niche to indicate the "Qibla" wall

Fig. 487. Persian early 14th cent. Mihrab arch with mosque lamp suspended and the usual writing in gold lustre and blue. Metropolitan Mus. of Art.

Fig. 488. Mihrab of faïence mosaic or tin glazed pottery pieces set in plaster. This piece came from the Midrasah Imami, Isfahan which was built in A.H. 755 or 1354 A.D. Ht. 11' 3", width 7' 6". The colors are cobalt, turquoise, white, golden yellow and dark green. Metropolitan Mus. of Art.

Fig. 489. Mihrab of lustred tiles probably made in Kashan about the beginning of the 14th cent. Ht. 43". Metropolitan Mus. of Art.

Small star tile found at Rhages but quite possibly not made there. Buff clay with cream glaze containing tin and has brown lustre inscription. Dia. 4". 12th to 13th cent. Metropolitan Mus. of Art.

Kashan star tile with lustred decoration of the first half of the 13th cent. Dia. 12⅜". Metropolitan Mus. of Art.

Star tile with tin enamel and lustre decoration found at Veramin and dated 663 A.H. which would be 1265 A.D. Dia. 15". Metropolitan Mus. of Art.

A "Veramin type" tile with copper lustre on a white ground and blue outlines. 13th cent. Dia. 7¾". Metropolitan Mus. of Art.

Kashan wall tile with the writing in blue and the ground design in brown lustre, dated 707 A.H. or 1309 A.D. Length about 14¼". Metropolitan Mus. of Art.

Kashan corner tiles (2) from a prayer niche with lustre decoration of the second half of the 13th cent. The lustre is gold with dark blue and turquoise. Relief parts in cobalt. Ht. 17¼". Metropolitan Mus. of Art.

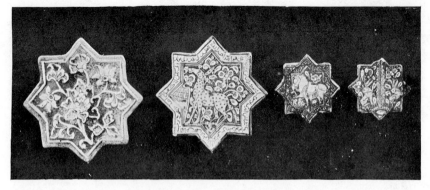

Persian tiles 13th cent. "Veramin" and 14th cent. "Sultanabad." Dias. about 8½" and 3½". Metropolitan Mus. of Art.

PERSIAN LUSTRED TILES

PLATE 100

This beautiful Mihrab is dated 661 A.H. (1264 A.D.) and came from the mosque in Veramin about 10 miles from Teheran. It was brought by Mostofi el Mamalich and sold to H. Kevorkian. On exhibition at the Pennsylvania University Mus., Philadelphia.

PERSIAN LUSTRED MIHRAB

PLATE 101

of a mosque or other holy building. It consists of a variously formed arch with sometimes a suspended mosque lamp. The inside of the arch is also filled with script, which is usually in relief and at times touched with blue to make it legible against the background of arabesques. Large mihrabs often have more than one arch set one within another, and supported with columns.

The earliest mihrab known is in the Berlin Museum and came through H. Kevorkian from the Median mosque in Kashan. It is 2.84 meters high (about 9 feet) and bears the name of the potter, Hasan ibn'Arabshâh and the date 622 A.H. or A.D. 1225. It is generally assumed that while Rhages was making vessels and tiles, Kashan was making mihrabs. The second, still in the possession of H. Kevorkian, is also probably from there and bears the date 661 A.H. or A.D. 1264 though it was found in the mosque in Veramin or about ten miles from Teheran. They look very much alike in style. It is possible that the star and cross tiles found near the Veramin one and the mihrab itself were not made in Kashan. The 14th century ones show little difference in style or writing but are perhaps less imposing.

Thus by comparisons of the dated pieces we reach the conclusion that the earlier pieces except those at Rakka are of light gold as a rule and that later this changes to a more bronze or copper tone. Hannover states that blue was found on the border of the oldest known tiles dated 1217 but we see by Kuhnel that there are at least four earlier and he does not speak of blue being used until 1240 on tiles, although he does mention a bowl having lustre and turquoise as early as 1213. One amusing thing is that the potters thought so little of the writing which they copied over and over that it finally became unreadable design only.

Pottery Mosaic

The tomb-mosque of Khudabanda Khan dating about 1316 shows an early method of covering the cupolas and minarets with slabs of blue glazed pottery, with white ones used now and then, but this system could only be employed on rectilinear or geometrical patterns. Later curved lines were achieved by sawing out pieces of various shapes from slabs of faïence and finally by the 15th century even the backgrounds were so covered. A large color range also had been achieved including transparent cobalt-blue, black, green, yellow and brown with opaque white and turquoise, and all had brilliance and depth. The masterpiece of this technique is in the Blue Mosque at Tabriz (1437 to 1468) but it was also used in the Green Mosque at Brusa, at Konieh and in Constantinople in the Chinili Kiosk (Faïence Pavilion) while to the east it spread to Samarkand and finally by the 17th century to India and later to North Africa and Spain.

Later Persian Tiles

Tiles of the Shah Abbas period 1590 are of similar technique to the Brusa tiles with tin glaze and muffle-painting in designs very much like those of carpets. The tiles no longer made a complete design in themselves but were part of a larger scheme. At the same time tiles used on civil buildings showed contemporary life (though those in the mosques never have figures,

That a considerable amount of good taste and excellent craftsmanship remained even in the late 18th cent. in Persia is shown by this wonderful set of tiles measuring 14″ × 7″ and consisting of 198 matched tiles in many colors. Ex Quill Jones Coll.

SET OF 18TH CENTURY PERSIAN TILES

PLATE 102

of course). Either miniatures or fabrics may have inspired these. They are often strong in yellow while red hardly occurs before the 18th century and strangely even later it was the custom to leave out one of the primary colors. Perhaps the intention was to establish a mood of color harmony. Still later came the use of cobalt blue and white only.

FIG. 490. Wall panel of assembled tiles showing merchants in the royal grounds. 17th cent. The colors are blue, black, and yellow. Length 78″. Ht. 40″. Metropolitan Mus. of Art.

In the late Safawidian times tiles were made with transparent or semi-transparent glaze of hunting scenes, amatory groups, etc., and these were copied in more glassy glazes with even worse taste. By the end of the 18th century the poor copies of famille rose Chinese designs are not worth consideration.

LATER "SOFT PORCELAIN" WARES

Few examples exist between the 14th and 17th centuries when the ware became "soft porcelain" of white body or buff covered with slip used with a creamy transparent glaze. Some wares were treated with blue outside and white inside. The lustre varies from greenish to ruby red and is brilliant. The shapes are somewhat simpler than the early ones. The kiln sites have not been established save that Ispahan the capital of Shah Abbas I (1587–1628) was important. Concerning the style it can be noted that reserve was not used, the use of animals or birds with trees or plant forms is usual and the technique is naturalistic rather than conventional. Chinese influence was strong and Chinese marks sometimes were copied. Such wares are of the Shah Abbas period but died out during the 17th century and only poor imitations have been attempted since.

This same soft paste which is somewhat harder than the European type was also decorated with underglaze blue and black, and overglaze colors sparingly used. It was even treated with the *pate sur pate* technique as may be seen in the example from the Metropolitan Museum.

Another very similar ware is that called "Gombroon" or "Gombrun" from the name of the port from which it was shipped in South Persia. The decoration consists of incisions through the body which are filled with glaze like the Chinese ware which the French term "grain de riz" (grain of rice). Sparse painting in blue and black underglaze colors is also used. Like all such wares it is inclined to distort in firing.

Left: Early 17th cent. ewer of soft porcelain ware with dark lustre decoration. Ht. 5". Metropolitan Mus. of Art.

Center: Porcelaneous ware though not high fired, with decoration of black and blue underglaze on a white ground. 17th cent. Ht. 17¼". Metropolitan Mus. of Art.

Right: Pottery base for a nargile or waterpipe with greenish glaze decorated with sage green and black. 1700 to 1750 A.D. Ht. 10¼". Metropolitan Mus. of Art.

Left: "Gombrun" semi-porcelain bottle of early 18th cent. Incised tracery and white glaze of glossy sheen somewhat pitted on the upper neck. Ht. about 13". Metropolitan Mus. of Art.

Center: Lustre ewer with spout to one side and strainer and spout to the front. The lustre is pale gold with red and green reflections. The dragon and flower design is filled in with a purplish underglaze blue. Ht. 11". Quill Jones Coll.

Right: Persian porcelaneous ware of the early 17th cent. with a design of birds and clouds. Ht. about 12½". Metropolitan Mus. of Art.

Left: 18th cent. semi-porcelain tazza of "Gombrun" ware, decorated in blue and black on white and the body incised all the way through in a pattern with the glaze filling the incisions, a technique like that of the "rice grain" bowls of China and probably derived from that source. Dia. 6½". Metropolitan Mus. of Art.

Right: Two bowls of the "Gombrun" ware of the 18th cent., one having black underglaze design and both having the usual incisions through the rim. They are glossy and of light ivory tone. Dias. about 7⅛". Moore Coll. Metropolitan Mus. of Art.

PERSIAN 17TH TO 18TH CENTURY WARES

PLATE 103

OTHER 17TH AND 18TH CENTURY POTTERIES

A large class of heavy potteries called by the trade incorrectly "Kashan" or "Kubatcha" where many were found come from unknown potteries of small towns of the Caucasus mountains, Syria and all the way through Persia. Mr. K. Kelekian has brought to attention 4 pieces actually dated 15th century although most of them are of the late 16th and 17th centuries. The body is of the same gritty quality that we always find in the Near East but it is often

FIG. 491. "Gombrun" bowl with an amusing riot of pagodas all over the center and sort of lambrequin border in underglaze black and blue. Dia. 10¼". 18th cent. Metropolitan Mus. of Art.

FIG. 492. Kubatcha turquoise plate with design in black painted underglaze. Dia. 13". Persia 17th cent. Fuller Coll. Seattle Art Mus.

stained brown by oil used in them and frequently on the vases the stain has penetrated through the body giving a not unpleasing mottled ivory to brown effect. These are largely painted by farmers who were instinctive artists or by other primitive and untutored painters using the same old traditional designs of flowers, fish, animals, etc., with now and then a Chinese motive such as high hills, peculiar pagodas and even stranger human figures. One type has aubergine added and is usually a bit more refined but given to allover patterns rather than pictorial designs. Crackle was not intentional but occurs on some pieces. Others of the same sort are painted in black or blue under a deep turquoise glaze. Still others have decoration in yellow, brown, blue, green, black, and bolus red though these are often later than the Safavid period (1507–1736). The simple directness of conception has made these wares popular and they have been badly copied by weak imitators the designs showing more flowery feeling, having relief treatment or added colors and imitation staining.

This completes the Near Eastern wares except for the tin glazed enamelled wares from Turkey or Damascus. This group will be taken up under the section on European enamelled wares.

The illustrations show a group of typical Near Eastern pottery forms and it will be seen at once that many of these followed metal in their slender

FIG. 493. Plate found at Koubatcha in Daghestan and dated 873 A.H. (or 1480 A.D.) made by a Persian artist. Turquoise decorated in deep blue. This piece gave first direct evidence of the period of the wares found in this place. Dia. 14¼". Dikran K. Kelekian Coll.

FIG. 494. Plate said to have come from Kubatcha. May have been made in Daghestan. Turquoise glaze with reserved design against a black ground partly scratched out. 15th cent. Dia. 14". Metropolitan Mus. of Art.

FIG. 495. "Kubatcha" glazed pottery jar which may or may not have been made there. Brown stained cream glaze slightly greenish in tint and decorated with black and blue underglaze colors. Ht. 8". Metropolitan Mus. of Art.

FIG. 496. "Kashan" bowl showing conception of Chinese landscape in the center and with glaze-filled piercing in the side design. Creamy white with blue and black design and some greenish tinge. Dia. about 10". Ex Warren E. Cox Coll. Mrs. Bernard Jolis.

FIG. 497. Persian Kerman pottery plate with underglaze blue and black decoration, of the 17th to 18th cent. Dia. about 18". Metropolitan Mus. of Art.

FIG. 498. "Kashan" jar of pottery with greenish cream ground stained brown and blue and black underglaze decoration. Ht. 8¼". Metropolitan Mus. of Art.

FIG. 499. "Kashan" or "Kubatcha" peasant potteries showing the Chinese influence in the drawing of pagodas and high hills. 17th to 18th cent. Jar ht. 9". Warren E. Cox Coll.

FIG. 500. Kutahia plate dated 1719 A.D. Decorated in clear yellow, black, deep blue, green, turquoise and red with the Armenian Saint Sergius on horseback carrying off a Greek woman. Signed with potter's name. Dia. 6". Dikran K. Kelekian Coll.

handles, involved and not always structural (in pottery at least) shapes, in the relief which imitates the repoussé and finally, of course, in the use of actual metallic lustre. The fact that there was a great pottery tradition also must never be lost sight of and some beautiful and suitable forms were made ranging all the way from the most solid and sturdy to those of graceful delicacy. Nowhere else was the ewer so varied and at times so charming. The albarello or apothecary jar of concave cylindrical form was certainly invented in the Near East and became tremendously popular in Spain, Italy and spread through the whole world. The bowls of inverted conical form with delicately flaring sides curving only slightly from the straight are of great beauty. If these potters were not so disciplined as the Chinese, they nevertheless showed delicacy and a strength of their own more colored by emotion but not lacking in power.

CHAPTER XIV

EUROPEAN POTTERY

(FROM LATE ROME THROUGH SPANISH AND ITALIAN LUSTRE WARES)

THE OLD wars were simple struggles for territorial rights and were fought over geographical boundaries. We have seen that religion was a growing power, as in the spread of Buddhism in the Far East, and though it had profound indirect results upon art the effects were not like those of conquest. Now at the beginning of the Christian era there came into use the fanatical manipulation of *religion as a weapon* which, like flood or fire often destroyed aggressor and defender alike. There had, of course, been wars brought about by medicine men of the most ancient tribes and by priests of the higher developed civilizations, but never before had such huge masses of men thrown away their lives simply because they were sure that they believed in the true god while the poor benighted enemy believed in none at all or the wrong one. It was found possible to overthrow the strongest ruler by outlining a code of laws of supposed moral value, by promising a heaven and by exorcising the masses to be good. Their goodness often grew in enthusiasm to the zeal of a crusade against all who did not believe as they did.

Rome had become all powerful but just as the Greeks had become involved in wars with Persia, so Rome made the mistake of diverting power to Byzantium, now Constantinople. This city had, since it was founded in 657 B.C. by the Greeks, been a bone of contention and had been destroyed by Darius Hystaspes, recolonized in 479 B.C. by the Spartans, then became Athenian, Spartan and Athenian again. It was besieged by the Macedonians and, it is interesting to note, was saved from a surprise attack by a flash of moonlight wherefore the Byzantines stamped a crescent on their coins, a device adopted by the Turks and kept to this day. Later the Rodians and then Goths attacked it. In about A.D. 288 Constantine the Great was born and after having been sent to Byzantium as a hostage returned with that city well in mind so that when his father died and he was declared head of his army he became a Christian and the head of the Roman Christian Empire and took the city calling it "New Rome." It was the capital of the Roman Empire of the East from about A.D. 330 to 1453 when it was taken by the Ottoman Turks.

Meanwhile Rome itself in the 5th century lost its western territories to Teuton invasion and in 486 its Gaulish territories to the Franks and was threatened by the expansion of the Slavs and Saracens in the 7th century. Suddenly the forces of Islam arose and swept Persia to the Oxus, Syria and

323

Egypt, Alexandria falling in A.D. 643, and Carthage in A.D. 698, and finally extended to Spain which was absorbed by A.D. 714. Thus Rome was girt about on three sides by Islam while on the North her ancient enemies were always ready to strike. Little of the old power was regained while Byzantium became the greatest city in the world up to that fateful date 1204 when the Crusaders delivered it to Venice which sucked it dry until it was taken by the Turks.

The Muhammedans had swept much of the world with their holy wars and Jerusalem was in the hands of the unbelievers. The pestilence had scourged Europe in the 10th and 11th centuries and finally the Church had preached penitentiary pilgrimages. There was also, of course, the promise of rich loot in the Near East. Therefore, not holy knights in shining armor, but adventurers, fugitives, tramps, villains, bankrupts, camp followers, hucksters and the like made up the Crusades. In 1096 the "People's Crusade" started and killed some 10,000 Jews, won the complete dislike of the Greeks in Constantinople and were finished up by the Hungarians, Bulgarians and Seljuks. The "Crusade of the Princes" reached Constantinople in 1097 about 150,000 strong. Alexius Comnenus had appealed to Rome for aid in his fight against the East and one can imagine his chagrin at being beset by this motley mob. We need not go into detail but the Franks had control of the caravan routes from Persia to Egypt and from Damascus to the Red Sea until the "Jihad" or counter crusade was started and Nureddin took Damascus in 1154 and opened the way for the Atabegs who finally were fatal to the Franks.

In order to gain some understanding as to what all this meant to art and the ceramic arts particularly let us see the description given by Mr. Ernest Barker in the 14th edition of the Encyclopaedia Britannica of the life of these Franks, these Crusaders: "They returned from the field of hard fighting to divans with frescoed walls and floor mosaic, Persian rugs and embroidered silk hangings. Their houses, at any rate those in the towns, had thus the characteristics of Moorish villas; and in them they lived the Moorish life. Their sideboards were covered with the copper and silver work of Eastern smiths and the confectioneries of Damascus. They dressed in flowing robes of silk, and their women wore oriental gauzes covered with sequins. Into these divans where figures of this kind moved to music of Saracen instruments, there entered an inevitable voluptuousness and corruption of manners. The hardships of war and excesses of peace shortened the lives of the men. While the men died, the women, living in comparative indolence, lived longer lives. They became regents to their young children; and the experience of all mediaeval minorities reiterates the lesson—'woe to the land where the king is a child and the regent a woman.'" Thus as Crusade upon Crusade took place, as Barker puts it, "Native Franks with commercial intercourse and diplomatic negotiations could not feel the urge to make a dash for the 'infidels' as the newcomers wished." The 2nd Crusade burned itself out by 1150, the 3rd and 4th by 1202–1204 and the 5th and 6th by 1229.

Meanwhile, the weapon had been forged and crusades became nothing more or less than a game of politics just as they have been ever since. The French barons launched a small crusade of their own against the heretics of

Southern France whom they exploited quite successfully. When Frederick II after several trials did get off on the 6th Crusade the papal soldiers of the church invaded his territories. And so it went. But though they wrought a great deal of unhappiness in this world the Crusades did develop the first ideas of colonization in Europe, they developed the first "chartered companies" which began as charitable groups, developed into military organizations and then became commercial companies owning banks, territories and navies for their protection, they brought about a spirit of toleration which, in a sense, made the Renaissance possible, and finally above all they discovered the East to Europe. Lemons, melons, maize, cotton, muslin, damask, lilac and purple, powder, mirrors and even the rosary itself were introduced through these contacts.

Thus we shall see that as Islam brought the *art of lustre* to Spain where it spread to Italy, so the Crusades brought the *art of tin glazed, enamel decorated pottery,* along with Chinese designs and those of Turkey and Damascus, to Italy where it spread throughout Europe. These two brilliant and colorful arts were emplanted upon the modeling and molding arts which had become so decadent in the Hellenistic world and the three: LUSTRE, ENAMEL DECORATION and RELIEF DECORATION were the basis of all the ceramic arts that followed. We shall take them up in the order named tracing each to the beginning of the 18th century.

Background of Earliest Spanish Pottery

The center of production of ceramics seemed to move ever westward and just as it was in Greece and then Italy so it came in time to that third large peninsula, Spain. But let us begin with the earliest days there:—The rock paintings show us that there was a fairly even paleolithic and neolithic culture over the entire peninsula. We have spoken of the bell-shaped crude pottery called "campaniform" and during this aeneolithic or Late New Stone Age period there are indications of North African contacts and affinities between Spain and the Baleric Islands, Sardinia and Sicily from about 3000 to 2500 B.C. After this time a period of retrogression set in and there are no reflections from Crete. It is true that spasmodic trading was done with the Greeks, but this so-called "Almeria Culture" lasted without influence up to the time of Christ when it was absorbed by the Roman culture. The indigenous people were entirely submerged about the 6th century by the Celtic invasion of the iron age (that same wave which swept over Greece and Italy), except for the Basques who retreated into the mountains. By 70 B.C. the southern districts were Roman.

In A.D. 406–407 the barbarians burst the Rhine frontier and flooded Gaul and Spain. The potteries were Roman but did not reach the point of decadence that they did elsewhere perhaps simply because the Spanish people were too primitive to have reached this bypass.

By 712 Musa b.Nosair the Arab had completed the conquest of Spain and by 732 the North African troops had reached Poitiers, France where they were turned back by the Austrasian Franks, but this Muhammedan conquest was made up of Syrians and Berbers as well as Arabs and there was no govern-

Late New Stone Age pottery from *El Acébuchal* of polished uneven brownish black with chalk white incised design. Ht. 4¾". Hispanic Society of America.

Bowl of brick red glazed pottery of the bucchero type, Gallo-Roman of late 1st cent. or early 2nd. Dia. 3¾". Found at Carmona. Hispanic Society of America.

Left: Amphora used for wine by the Romans. Pitch-lined light yellow, sandy clay. Found near Sevilla. The Hispanic Society of America.

Center: A Pre-Roman pottery cinerary urn from *La Cruz del Negro* of unglazed soft tan clay with reddish-orange and brown circles, thought to date about 500 B.C. Ht. about 13¾". Hispanic Society of America.

Right: Cinerary urn found at *Mérida*. Cream unglazed pottery with incised design. It appears to have been done with a comb. Roman period. Ht. about 6½". Hispanic Society of America.

Gandul bowl of taupe-gray glazed Roman pottery. Ht. 2¾". Hispanic Society of America.

Right: Gallo-Roman flask or pilgrim bottle of brick red lead glazed pottery of the 1st cent. A.D. Ht. 7". Hispanic Society of America.

ROMAN AND EARLY SPANISH POTTERIES

PLATE 104

ment or organization. In 750 there was the plague followed by drought and famine. During the 9th and 10th centuries the Norse pirates raided the coast. Christianity was tolerated and gained a new foothold. In 1037 or thereabouts Fernando I established a kingdom in Castile. Another invasion of Berbers took place in 1120 and it was not until 1212 that the king of Castile organized a crusade against the Almohades which overthrew them and from that time onward Muhammedan Spain was under the control of the Christians. Finally the marriage of Ferdinand of Aragon to Isabella of Castile brought comparative order.

Meanwhile much was accomplished:—Vasco da Gama reached India in 1498, Columbus had found the New World, Cortes had conquered Mexico and by 1535 Pizarro had conquered Peru. Toward the end of the 16th century took place the golden age of literature boiled up from this cauldron of racial and religious hatreds. It was in 1502 that the Muhammedans were expelled, and even converted Muhammedans were sent out in 1610, and with them went most of the true culture that had been the heritage of Spain. Ferdinand had entered a war with Italy in 1497 which proved the might of Spain but also wasted much of it.

Charles V (of Hapsburg) had been educated in Flanders and could not even speak the Spanish language. His only interest in the country was what he could get out of it. His son Philip II (1556–1598) was much the same and the vices and elegance of the court were at the expense of the country. The Reformation had taken place and Philip's Absolutist tendencies were feared by the Netherlands. Finally he became involved with the religious wars with England and the defeat of the famous Armada of 1588 resulted in tumbling his attempts to rule all western Europe. Meanwhile Drake in 1587 swept the West Indies and burnt a number of Spanish ships in the harbor of Cadiz.

The decline had long been due and now it was felt. The war with the Netherlands made shipping unsafe. An attempt to send troops through France ended in a war with that country. In 1640 Portugal separated without a blow being struck. The revolt of Naples and of the Catalans followed. Charles II was an imbecile and the government was directed by his mother and her successive favorites (1665–1700). By the 18th century there is nothing left of interest. Like a multi-colored gleam from one of her beautiful Hispano-Moresque plaques Spain flared and was gone but she preserved and developed one of the greatest of ceramic arts.

HISPANO-MORESQUE POTTERY

From the 8th to the beginning of the 12th centuries the Arab culture under the caliphate of the Ommiads at Cordova was high. They were overcome by the Almoravide who brought a different culture with them but all Moorish tribes were confined to Granada in the southeast part on the coast after the crusade of 1212. In 1566 the Moorish writing, dress and style of decoration were prohibited until 1610 when these people were put out for good.

Our potteries are therefore easily divided into two groups:—

1.—Those *before 1566* with *pure oriental style.*

2.—Those between *1566 and 1700* which show *Italian Renaissance style,* and almost continuous decadence.

Tiles similar to those in Persia were made but used only along the lower part of the walls. The earliest are from the Alhambra and were sawed or molded into symmetrical convex polygonal shapes meant to be set in mosaic designs of geometrical nature. These were colored black, white, greyish-blue, green and brown.

FIG. 501. *"De cuerda seca"* architectural finial with yellow peak, stripes in green, yellow and black and horizontal arrow band of green and white with touches of yellow. Late 15th or early 16th cent. probably at Toledo. Ht. 20½". Hispanic Society of America.

"Cuerda seca" technique is a labor-saving device. Instead of having to lay each piece of mosaic carefully, larger square tiles were made in molds having very slight relief designs in outline, which produced slightly depressed outlines in the tile. These were filled with a greasy manganese medium which formed compartments in which lead and tin enamels of blue, green, brown, black and white were filled. At first the manganese had simply been painted on and later a cloisonné effect was produced by the use of wooden molds which left the outlines in slight relief, on which manganese was also applied. These tiles were cheap, and in Spain when they wanted to say a person was poor they would say "non ava casa azulejos" or "His house has no tiles." However some have spirited and pleasant designs reminiscent of Near Eastern ones. These tiles along with finials, etc., were made at Puente del Arzobispo and in Andalucia before the 15th century. Those for the palaces of the Dukes of Alba and Medinaceli were made in Sevilla in the late 15th and early 16th centuries. The Toledan ones are probably a little later. A water pitcher formed like the bust of a woman and an aguamanil of a crouching animal that looks like a sheep are at Sèvres while in Valencia and Sevilla are also a vase, a large bowl and an albarello.

Tiles made like those described above, with the pattern sunk but a little more so and without the manganese outline, were called "de cuenca." Only the very oldest are of Moresque mosaic, the others being of foliage, palmettes and flowers. These were made in Toledo in central Spain and Sevilla and Triana in the south.

Terracotta tiles of the 14th and 15th centuries are found in Aragon and have some decoration in slightly fired black, brown and occasionally red.

From Valencia of the 15th century are a type that is not Moorish but almost exactly taken from the Italians. These are square or lozenge forms so proportioned that the square can be fitted into the center and four of the others about it making an octagon: The earliest have Gothic designs in blue but early in the 16th century when Spain wanted nothing to do with Martin Luther or the Reformation, they changed the designs to Italian

14th cent. dish from Paterna of tin enameled earthenware, white ground, with green and manganese design. Dia. about 11½". Metropolitan Mus. of Art.

Bowl of cream-colored clay with white slip and lead glaze over blue decoration. Dia. 9½". Hispanic Soc. of Am.

Left: "Cuerda seca" or *"Puente del Arzobispo"* plate probably made at Sevilla. Rabbit yellow-brown with blue tail. Rim green and foliage blue, yellow, green and black on white ground. Dia. 8⅞". Hispanic Soc. of Am.

Left: Vase made at Teruel. Red clay with tin enamel decorated in manganese purple and green. Three shields about the body have (1) triple-tower, (2) green basket, and (3) initials AT in Gothic letters. Ht. 15¾". Hispanic Soc. of Am.

Right: Late 15th or early 16th cent. jar. Light buff colored ware with green glaze. Sevilla. Ht. about 14½". Hispanic Soc. of Am.

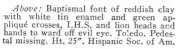

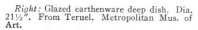

Above: Baptismal font of reddish clay with white tin enamel and green appliqué crosses, I.H.S. and lion heads and hands to ward off evil eye. Toledo. Pedestal missing. Ht. 25". Hispanic Soc. of Am.

Right: Glazed earthenware deep dish. Dia. 21½". From Teruel. Metropolitan Mus. of Art.

SPANISH 15TH CENTURY WARES

PLATE 105

ones. They were said to be floor tiles and in the latter part of the century the output was increased and many were also made in Portugal.

From the latter part of the 16th century Talavera de la Reyna (or Reina) was the center of all earthenware production decorated with tin glaze of soft opaque cream color containing small black specks and with decoration having manganese outlines and a purplish grey-blue both sunk in the glaze

Right: 17th cent. plate of buff ware covered with peachy-white ground, design outlined in aubergine and filled in with deep blue and orange-red hatching. Dia. 10″. Warren E. Cox Coll.

Left: Talavera de la Reina plate designated "Valencia?" by museum but typical in technique and substance. Dia. *c.* 10″. Gift of Miss Theodore Lyman. Mus. of Fine Arts, Boston.
    Center: Plate perhaps earlier than typical 17th cent. type which is usually badly overcrowded in design. Near Eastern influence. Brown body and glaze with decoration in yellow, brown and green. Mus. of Fine Arts, Boston.

Bowl with usual crude but vigorous drawing in lemon and golden yellows, green, blue, and manganese. 17th cent. Dia. 19¾″. Hispanic Soc. of Am.

Jar decorated in violet-blue, green, lemon, golden-yellow and orange. 17th cent. Ht. 21″. Hispanic Soc. of Am.

TALAVERA DE LA REINA POTTERY
PLATE 106

and an orange-red on the surface probably fired at lower temperature. This was not unlike the rare Paterna ware of the 14th century. Paterna was a small town not far from the capital of Valencia. In it was made a ware *par excellence* with tin enamel and design in manganese purplish-black and green which predated the early lustre ware and finally gave way to it. The beautiful plate from the Metropolitan Museum is a fine example. In the 16th century copies of this ware were made at Teruel, and continued down to

Left: This albarello has band about neck of conventionalized Naskhi writing, also wide band of *alafia* characters about middle. Blue and gold on tin glaze. Valencia. 15th cent. Hispanic Soc. of Am.

Center: Jar said to have been made in late 14th or early 15th cent. Ht. 13⅛″. Metropolitan Mus. of Art.

Right: Albarello with device of double crown about middle. Tin glaze with gold and blue decoration. 15th cent. from Valencia. Ht. 12″. Hispanic Soc. of Am.

Left: 15th cent. from Valencia with flowers in blue and lustre having copper and lavender reflections. Ht. 12″. Hispanic Soc. of Am.

Center: From *Talavera de la Reina* bearing coat of arms of Order of Our Lady of Mercy in shades of grayish blue on white tin enamel over buff pottery. 17th cent. Ht. about 12″. Hispanic Soc. of Am.

Right: Possibly 17th cent. Decorated with blue, yellow, orange and manganese purple on white tin enamel, from Sevilla (Triana). Ht. 7½″. Hispanic Soc. of Am.

SPANISH ALBARELLOS

PLATE 107

modern times, but the Talavera de la Reyna ones are of Italian influence with conventional floral scrolls, birds and the like. Very soon, however, by the 17th century the style became more ornate and detailed showing the sloppy pictorial inclinations of the Italian majolica.

HISPANO-MORESQUE LUSTRE WARE

Lustre was not unknown in Europe as early as the 12th century. Examples are found in the walls of buildings in Italy and France of the Romanesque period. An account by El Idrisi, an Arabian geographer, says that in the 12th century lustred faïence was made at Calatayud in Aragon. In the 13th century it was made in Andalusia and shipped from Malaga but we have not one single piece which can be authenticated as before the 14th century. A. J. Butler claims a 10th or 11th century gold lustre was found at Madinah al Zahrah, by Cordova, on the site of the Muslim city but goes on to say that this has not been proven of Spanish manufacture.

In 1492 the Moorish king, Boabdil, was driven by Ferdinand and Isabella from the Alhambra, his palace at Granada, back to Africa and some 200 years later a large vase was found of amphora form with strange wing-like handles so broad as to be useless for lifting it and seemingly over styled. This Alhambra vase and six others were supposed to have come from the grounds of the palace. One is, so far as we know, still there. Another is in the Hermitage. The neck of one is in the Hispanic Society of America, etc. I have examined none of these except the latter piece and it is of terracotta colored clay with blue and white glazes and pale golden lustre. The vase in the National Museum in Stockholm is 4 feet 5 inches high and has a band of arabic inscription above which is an open field with gazelles reserved in cream and golden lustre on a blue ground. The rest of the body and handles are covered with compartments with arabesques and inscriptions in the same colors and the neck is not unlike ours here. The others have arabesques and writing but not the gazelles. The dates of these are not entirely agreed upon but it is supposed that they are late 14th or early 15th century. The technique is similar to that of a much discussed wall tile with an inscription supposed to refer to Yusuf I, II or III depending on which authority you believe.

Since there is considerable confusion concerning these vases I quote an excerpt from a letter to me by Alice Wilson Frothingham which clears up the matter in good shape, "As for the 'Alhambra' vases, that name, of course, leads to much confusion, since all of them were not found at the Alhambra. Actually excavated from the grounds of the Palace in the 17th century were two vases and the fragments of a third. One of these vases is the example, until recently in the *Hall of the Two Sisters* and now installed in the *Museo de Arte Arabe, Palacio de Carlos V*, also in the Alhambra. It was in this new location in 1940, and to the best of my knowledge is still there. The second vase, a few years previous to 1837, had been broken, but not before detailed drawings of it had been made. In 1869, the collar of this vase was in the home of Rafael Contreras y Muñoz, architect in charge of conserving and restoring the Alhambra. Later, the collar and fragments of the body found their way into the art

Right: Neck of late 14th–early 15th cent. vase. Reddish body with blue and white glazes and golden lustre. Ht. 17". Hispanic Soc. of Am.

"Tinaja" with globular body and short neck. On the shoulder are useless handles with which it would be very difficult to lift such a jar. Ware is coarse red clay. Museum says design is incised but I think it is impressed. Probably made in Andalucia toward end of 15th cent. Ht. c. 2'. Mus. of Fine Arts, Boston.

Left: One of several vases of "Alhambra type" but found at Salar. Probably made at Malaga. In Hermitage, St. Petersburg. Lustre of darker and heavier color. Probably early 15th cent. Ht. c. 4'.

Center: Pale golden lustred vase made at Manises. Perfectly functional form for it pours very well when three fingers are inserted into handle. May be derived from a form which predated even the "Alhambra vase" on theory that handles are useless on these huge pieces and were maintained simply through habit. Ht. 15". Warren E. Cox Coll.

Right: Drawing of one of two actual "Alhambra vases" said to have been found filled with gold pieces in 16th cent. in vault under the Comares tower, Granada. Reddish body with blue and white glazes and golden lustre. 14th to early 15th cent. Ht. about 4' 3". Muses Espanol de Antiguedades, Madrid.

"ALHAMBRA TYPE" POTTERIES

Plate 108

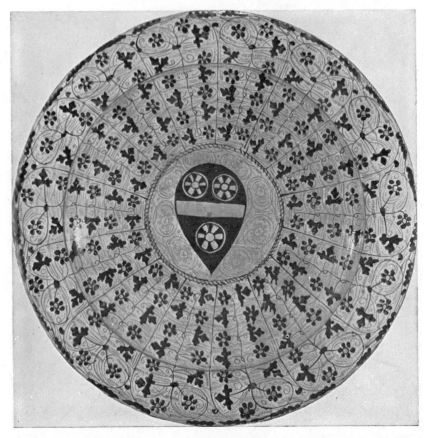

Fig. 502. Hispano-moresque plate of 15th cent. said to have come from Malaga. Decorated with blue and gold lustre. Dia. 18¾". Ex W. R. Hearst Coll. International Studio Coll.

market; the collar was purchased for the Hispanic Society in 1913 from a Persian art dealer.

"All the other vases which are similar to these two in shape and design, but which have come from different sites, should I suppose be distinguished by another term, but they have become known popularly as 'Alhambra' or 'Alhambra type' vases. The Leningrad vase came from Salar, a town near Granada. I do not know from where the Stockholm vase was excavated, but it appears to have been manufactured at Málaga. According to Ferrandis, it belonged to Queen Louise, sister of Frederick the Great; it was transferred from the castle at Drottningholm to the National Museum at Stockholm in 1866."

Hannover who usually displays good taste waxes enthusiastic over the Alhambra vase calling it, "one of the immortal works of ancient craftsmanship." We are, however, privileged to differ and to look upon these vases as monstrous and degenerate forms which imply a more sound and practical prototype. A reproduction of such a prototype I think I have found. This

Deep dish with white enamel glaze and decorations of blue and gold *"alafia"* reflecting red and blue green. Reverse has eagle, fern leaves and scrolls also in gold. Valencia, 15th cent. Dia. 19″. Ht. 2¾″. Hispanic Soc. of Am.

Large bowl of early 15th cent. from Valencia probably at Manises in imitation of Malaga model. Decorated with blue and gold of coppery tint with red and blue *"reflejos."* Four small loops from lower to upper surface of rim. Dia. c. 18″. Ht. 5½″. Hispanic Soc. of Am.

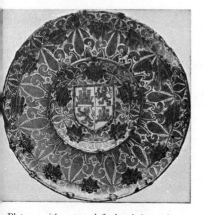

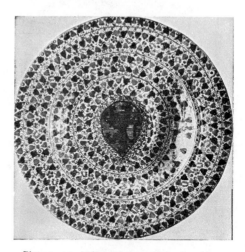

Plateau with outward flaring brim and near center another brim. Pinkish tan clay with white enamel and blue roses surrounded by green-gold lustre leaves having opalescent *reflejos.* Two holes in foot-rim for hanging. Dia. 16¾″. 15th cent. From Valencia. Hispanic Soc. of Am.

Plate c. A.D. 1450–1500 from Valencia with coat of arms probably for Tedali family of Florence. Brim pierced by two holes. Dia. c. 17½″. Hispanic Soc. of Am.

SPANISH LUSTRE PLATES

PLATE 109

15th to 16th cent. Valencia semipherical bowl with four ears. Usual type called *"escudelles ab orelles"* or bowls with ears, have two only. Handles are concave both top and bottom for easy grip. Lustre yellowish gold and faded. Dia. tip to tip 12″. Hispanic Soc. of Am.

15th or 16th cent. plate painted in pale gold lustre. Note use of patterns to break plain area of body of bull and rabbit and leaping wolf. Dia. 16⅛″. Nasli Heeramaneck Coll.

15th or 16th cent. Valencia plate with rampant lion outlined in blue and gold lustre. Details yellowish brown metallic color. Dia. 18½″. Hispanic Soc. of Am.

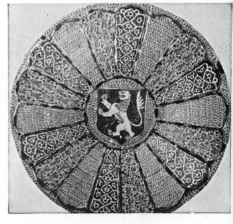

15th to 16th cent. Valencia plate with wide rim of wheel pattern in relief, sectors having triple alternation effectively used. Gold is reddish brown and reflects mother-of-pearl tints. Dia. 17¾″. Hispanic Soc. of Am.

SPANISH LUSTRE PLATES

PLATE 110

vase is of a type of lustre dating from the 17th century and made at Manises so it cannot be an original but it was undoubtedly copied from some now nonexistent one which is perfectly beautiful in proportion and the handles of which we find are, in this size, well fitted to the hand, structural and of great beauty. One need only insert three fingers in the notches to find that it pours as well as the best of ewers. It is my theory that the large vases were a debased and pretentious development of this charming form which must have existed in normal size in early 14th century examples which have all been destroyed.

A beautiful bowl in the Sarre Collection, Berlin is of this ware and has similar decorations. The inside is divided into eight segments showing the effective use of continuously changing alternating designs (see section on

An *"orza."* Clay pinkish tan, glaze known as stanniferous, as it has tin in it. Lustre is gold. Spot of green under one handle. Valencia 15th–16th cent. Ht. 10½". Hispanic Soc. of Am.

Ewer of pinkish tan clay with white tin enamel and gold lustre which reflects purple. 16th cent. from Valencia. Hispanic Soc. of Am.

Vase, early 16th cent. from Valencia. Base and lip of ormolu added later. Pinkish tan clay with white enamel and gold-brown lustre reflecting lavender. Ht. 19½". Hispanic Soc. of Am.

Right: One of a pair of covered vases bearing the arms of Camillo Borghese, who reigned as Pope Paul V 1605–1621. Two shields with between them busts of men wearing morions with chin pieces and plumed crests. Pinkish tan clay with tin enamel and copper colored lustre, from Valencia. Ht. 19½". Hispanic Soc. of Am.

Left: Pharmacy jar or *"botijos"* of early 16th cent. Valencia. Lustre of yellow-gold. Ht. 8⅜". Hispanic Soc. of Am.
Center: Blue glazed vase with delicately painted horizontal bands of bright copper lustre. This type once believed made in Caltagirone, Sicily by Moors and was called "Siculo-Arab ware," but what evidence there is points more truly to Manises as its real source. Ht. 10¼". 17th cent. (?) Hispanic Soc. of Am.

SPANISH LUSTRE VESSELS

PLATE 111

Ashur). On the bottom is a mark construed as meaning "Málaga" thus con-firming the general location of Granada as a source and the possibility that they were all made in Málaga. In 1487 Málaga passed into the hands of the Christians and it would be reasonable to suppose that the pottery either ceased or commenced to change. There is also some possibility that the ware was actually made at Granada in a royal manufactory.

VALENCIA LUSTRE WARES

Several writers have made an error in stating that the family of Manises in the town of the same name made a later lustre ware. This was due to the misconception concerning the evidence of Eximenes at first supposed to date 1499 and found actually to date 1383. The wares were undoubtedly similar to those of Málaga and in fact are referred to in general by the name of "Obra dorada de Málaga." In Manises the ware was evidently made chiefly

FIG. 503. Tazza from Valencia, 16th cent., deco-rated in coppery gold. Sacred monogram IHS placed in square medallion inside. Raised gadroons painted in designs in alternating rhythm 1,2,3,–1,2,–1,2,3, ex-cept where they do not come out right. Dia. 12½". Ht. 8½". Hispanic Soc. of Am.

FIG. 504. "Orza" or globular vase. Fluted neck and four loop handles. Decoration yellow gold color with mother-of-pearl tints. Vertical gold stripes inside neck. 15th or 16th cent. Valencia. Ht. 8¾". Hispanic Soc. of Am.

FIG. 505. Late 18th–early 19th cent. barber's basin or "bacia" made at Manises. Potter's initials are on bot-tom As. Rim pierced so it could be hung on wall. Yel-low, grey-green, lavender, blue and deep cobalt blue. Dia. about 18". Hispanic Soc. of Am.

for the Buyl or Boil family who were overlords levying taxes and occa-sionally making sales.

Other locations are Paterna in Valencia where we have already said an enamelled ware was made in the 14th century and those near the Valencia center:—Mislata, in 1484 Gesarte, in 1507 Calatayud and 1589 Muel which is also in Aragon. Blue and white wares were also made in this section.

DATING OF SPANISH LUSTRE WARE

Our evidence is still too vague to make it possible to assign certain pieces to definite kiln sites and the best we can do is classify them in more or less definite categories so far as dates go. Generally speaking the following facts will help the student:

1.—Those pieces showing pure Moorish style are likely to be earlier. This style is marked by arabesques, the "tree of life," palm motives, animals

Deep dish of *"Brasero"* shape showing interesting use of radial alternating design on inside and of three fish on bottom outside. Probably Valencia, 15th to 16th cent. Dia. 18½", depth 2". Ex W. R. Hearst Coll. International Studio, Inc.

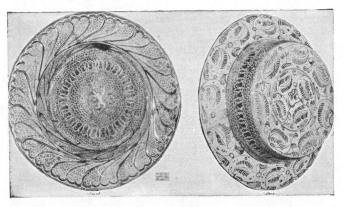

Hispano-moresque plate shaped like *"Brasero"* or Spanish hat. Decorated inside with gold lustre and blue, outside with lustre only in feathery leaf design. 15th–16th cent. Dia. 19¼", depth 4⅝". Ex W. R. Hearst Coll. International Studio, Inc.

SPANISH LUSTRE PLATES, FRONT AND BACK

PLATE 112

showing Western Asian style and Arabic inscriptions such as the word "alafia" (blessing) repeated in formalized characters.

2.—Rare instances of Spanish inscriptions misspelt would be by Moorish craftsmen and therefore early.

3.—Vice versa, Moorish or Arabic inscriptions misspelt are by Spanish Christian craftsmen and would be later, as are also such highly conventionalized inscriptions as to be not legible.

4.—Often the centers of the plates bear the coats of arms of the Buyl family, of the king or queen of Aragon or of other Valencian or Italian families and these aid greatly in dating.

5.—Emil Hannover proves neatly the correctness of the date of one type

Lustre plates, one with soldier of the reign of Philippe II–late 16th to early 17th cent. Dia. 13¾″.
Other with turbaned head has probably portrait of Sultan Suliman II (1520–1566). Dia. 13½″.
Below are backs of these two plates which show verve and spontaneity typical of fine examples.
Dikran G. Kelekian Coll.

PLATE 113

of alberello or apothecary vase decorated with blue and lustred foliage for one was painted in the foreground of a picture by Hugo van der Goes in the famous altar-piece of Portinari which is definitely dated between 1474 and 1477.

The greatest number of pieces are dependent upon style. We no longer believe that the blue color was used only after 1500 and in fact it may have even predated the lustre itself. The Moors or Moriscoes were driven out in 1609–1610 and took with them the secret of the pale gold lustre. After this time the lustre is copper colored and becomes ever more heavy. Earlier in the 15th century there were animals in blue against a lustred ground of spirals. From 1450 the heraldic designs were made for export to Italy and are set among Gothic diapers and foliage. Some alternate the flowers in blue with the leaves in lustre. By the middle of the 15th century alternation has descended from the use of large panels to small details and soon the principle is lost. By the 17th century we see no trace of it. In the earliest wares and up to the 16th century the spirals form a separate background in another plane behind the design but later they become more heavy until they clutter up the main design. Another motive is the "chain mail" so called because it resembles meshes. Hannover says there is no known origin for this but it must surely descend from the "scale" patterns of the Damascus and Turkish wares.

The backs of the plates were more freely and broadly painted with lustre and here we can tell more about the artist for no imitator can get the same swift feeling in his strokes as can a man who has done hundreds in his own way.

A word may be said about shapes:—The wide shallow conical plates with concave, narrow bottom and small raised center, and also the flat plates with straight sides and flat rims are of the 15th and 16th century types while the more ornate raised center ones with a trough around and a wide rim having a shallow second trough around are of the 17th century. The alberello was brought direct from Persia and Mesopotamia. Other of the shapes will be found on comparison to resemble more or less Near Eastern prototypes, but all have a scale and boldness seen only in the early Assyrian wares

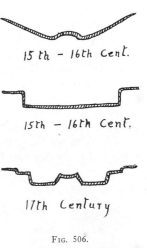

15th – 16th Cent.

15th – 16th Cent.

17th Century

Fig. 506.

before. Both modeled and pictorial designs were well modified to the general forms and aid rather than detract from them with the only exception perhaps the late wares from Talavera de la Reyna which are strongly Italian.

CHAPTER XV

NEAR EASTERN AND EUROPEAN TIN SLIP AND TIN GLAZED WARES

Butler describes the finding of kiln sites at a place on the western border of Algeria called "Tilimsân" or "Tlemcen" which M. Bel believes to date 10th century. The wares are said to be similar to those found at Madînah al Zaharah except that they all consist of the enameled type with manganese and green decoration.

He also describes bricks enameled only on three quarters of the surface with one end left untreated. These were found at the Fortress of the Bani Hammâd, further eastward. At Qalàh were found both partially and wholly glazed bricks which are white, yellow and brown as well as green. M. Marçais is quoted as placing certain tiles, also found there, as before those of Koniah

FIG. 507. Drinking vessel or "cántaros" with filling spout and squirting spout which delivers a thin stream of liquid into mouth when held above head at right angle. Brick red with polished design. Generally left unglazed so evaporation on outside kept them cool. Modern but an old form.

FIG. 508. Jar and cover from North Africa and made at Meknès, 16th to 17th cent. Ht. 19½". Warren E. Cox Coll.

FIG. 509. North African faïence plate from Meknès. Difficult to date but design similar to those of Paterna. Wider range of colors which include manganese brown, blue, turquoise and yellow, indicate perhaps the 16th to 17th cent. Dia. 14½". Warren E. Cox Coll.

or "presumably not later than A.D. 1150." One of these was not believed to have been made on the spot as the drawing of a leopard is much finer than the other animals portrayed. This may or may not be a good reason. Good artists occur in poor kilns just as poor artists occur in good kilns but less frequently.

It is obvious from these and other finds that all the wares were of

342

Egyptian or Western Asian inheritance and that nothing of interest was indigenous. The one plate from my own collection closely resembles Paterna ware but has added colors.

TURKISH ENAMELED WARES

Tin had been used for many centuries to make a white, opaque glaze over an impure, buff or reddish body. We have traced the one great art of *lustre* which was almost entirely developed on this beautiful white surface. Now let us go back to the Near East again and pick up the thread of the other art of ENAMEL DECORATION. Finally we shall see how they unite in Italy, how the use of color supplants that of metallic lustre and how both arts are, though debased, spread throughout the whole of Europe.

The development of tin glaze was certainly directly brought about by the constant attempts to get an effect something like that of the beautiful porcelain which was being made in China. By the 16th century or the Chêng Tê reign

FIG. 510. Pottery globe for suspension as a weight made in Damascus, 16th cent. Silicious tin glaze with enamel decorations. Dia. about 10″. Metropolitan Mus. of Art.

FIG. 511. Well potted and decorated faïence bowl from Turkey 17th cent. Usual blue, green and red colors. Ht. 9″. British Mus.

FIG. 512. Turkish enamel decorated tin glazed earthenware mosque-lamp shaped vase. Ht. 11¾″. Metropolitan Mus. of Art.

of the Ming dynasty in China (1506–1521) the "Muhammedan blue" had long been used, had run short and a new supply was acquired. We learn that "hui hui wen" or "Muhammedan scrolls" were a popular sort of design borrowed from the Near East and adapted to Chinese taste. It is of this period that we find the writer's equipment with Arabic writings and quotations from the Koran, on them. By the following reign, that of Chia Ching (1522–1566) such things had not only become popular for Muhammedans in China but a considerable export business was under way and objects like the bases for hubble pipes and the rose water sprinkler I illustrate in that section are extensively found in the Near East. We must also note that the art of "five color" enamel decoration on white porcelain had by now become highly developed on China which did not need the tin glaze or a slip treatment because the bodies of the wares were naturally so white.

If the Chinese borrowed Near Eastern designs, the compliment was returned and how closely the process went on can readily be seen by comparing

Fig. 514. Turkish dish of blue on white ware dating 16th to 17th cent. and very similar in decoration to the Chia Ching bowl shown. Dia. 11⅜″. James J. Rorimer Coll.

Fig. 515. Turkish blue on white plate of the 16th to 17th cent. with strong Chinese influence shown in the drawing. Dia. 15″. James J. Rorimer Coll.

the first blue and white dish I am illustrating from the wonderful sequence belonging to James J. Rorimer to the liver and white bowl shown among the Chia Ching wares. It is not much of a stretch of imagination to say that one might serve for the saucer of the other, if the colors had been the same, yet the one was made at Ching-tê Chêng while the other was made in Turkey. Another bowl with blue on white decoration and having a pomegranate design could also, technique aside, be of earlier Ming make. Mr. Rorimer conservatively places these as 16th–17th century and 17th century but I think it quite reasonable to call them both 16th century and undoubtedly made from contemporary Chinese originals as models.

At first glance there seems to be a definite break between the enameled wares of Damascus and Turkey and those of the 12th to 13th century of

Fig. 516. Turkish glazed earthenware with blue, green and red design. Note the scale ground copied extensively in European wares of later date. Dia. 13½″. Metropolitan Mus. of Art. Gift of James J. Rorimer.

Fig. 517. Turkish plate of the general appearance of a "Kubatcha" type. Note design of reversible landscape. Glossy, crackled glaze. Dia. 12½″. James J. Rorimer Coll.

Fig. 518. "Damascus type" plate probably made in Turkey, 16th cent. symmetrical design extending to edge shows strong East Indian influence rather than Chinese. Dia. 12⅛″. James J. Rorimer Coll. Metropolitan Mus. of Art.

Persia and Mesopotamia. Yet near Damascus there are kiln sites where large amounts of the so-called "Syro-Egyptian" ware was found. It is painted in blue and black under a clear glaze and was made up to the 14th century. Tiles have also been found nearby with delicate Persian scroll designs in black under a blue glaze and of a style which seems to indicate the 15th century. Butler shows one from Broussa and another from Turkey which is green with gold decoration. All of these are symmetrical. The tin glaze may have been first used at Ashur, for a vase found there and of about 1300 B.C. has tin in the glaze. But it must have been the renewed Chinese contact that was responsible for this art.

The ware itself is of sandy, whitish body and all the better pieces are also dressed with a fine white slip often containing tin. Upon this is painted the design in black outlines which are filled in with brilliant blue, turquoise, green, and, if the ware be Turkish, a thick red, or, if the ware be from Damascus, a soft manganese purple, and over all is a thin glassy glaze. In these wares of Turkey and Damascus the tin was not at first used in the glaze but in the slip, if at all, and the colors are actually, technically *underglaze* colors. This may seem strange when we know that in China to date there had been developed only an underglaze blue and a very uncertain underglaze red, but the answer lies in the difference of temperature. The one ware was a high fired porcelain reaching 2200° F. or more while the other had a feldspathic glaze which melted at so low a temperature that the heat did not harm the colors used underneath it.

Another distinction between the two types is that the Damascus plates have the design reaching to the edge while the Turkish ones have the rim treated with separate motives, very often Chinese "rock and wave," "cloud scroll" or the slanting key frets such as we have seen on Tz'u Chou type Sung wares. But this is not always to be counted on for a large Syrian, Damascus one in the V. Everit Macy Collection of the 17th century has the separate border treatment.

It will be remembered that the "Kubatcha" ware described in the last section and dating from the 15th century is technically very similar. The Chinese influence is probably from the time of Shah Abbas I (1587–1628)

FIG. 519. A very simple and beautiful asymmetrically designed Turkish plate of the 16th to 17th cent. Dia. 12⅛". Coll. of Mrs. James J. Rorimer. Metropolitan Mus. of Art.

FIG. 520. Turkish pottery plate with tin glaze and enamel decoration including red. These are usually about 14" in dia. Boston Mus. of Fine Arts.

FIG. 521. A rare Turkish plate with animal decoration in the center and a petal formed edge. Decorated in blue, turquoise, green and red on white ground. 16th to 17th cent. Dia. 12⅝". James J. Rorimer Coll.

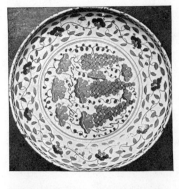

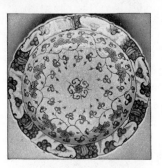

Left to Right: Turkish plate 16th to 17th cent. with symmetrical quatrefoil design. Dia. 12″. James J. Rorimer Coll.—16th to 17th cent. dish decorated in dark and light blue on white ground and showing strong Chinese characteristics. Dia. 11⅞″. James J. Rorimer Coll.—Plate 16th to 17th cent. Decorated with blue on white with a conventional design of Chinese derivation. Dia. 12½″. James J. Rorimer Coll.—Plate reminiscent of the bronze mirror designs of Roman origin with clusters of grapes on them. 17th cent. Dia. 13¾″. James J. Rorimer Coll.

Left to Right: Plate with simple design which is so beautiful in the earlier ones during the transition from the symmetrical to the asymmetrical. Dia. 11¼″. James J. Rorimer Coll.—Plate with symmetrical design in usual colors. Dia. 12⅞″. James J. Rorimer Coll.—Plate with typical asymmetrical design and cloud scroll border in usual colors of blue, green and red on white ground. Dia. 13⅝″. James J. Rorimer Coll.—Plate of 16th to 17th cent. showing the later trend toward over crowding of decoration in red, green, gold, green, blue and black on white ground. Dia. 11″. James J. Rorimer Coll.

TURKISH ENAMELED PLATES: 16TH TO 17TH CENTURIES

PLATE 114

for it is known that he imported Chinese potters and great quantities of Ming wares. But the Turkish wares also were influenced strongly by Persian craftsmen and we see little of the loose Caucasian feeling but rather formal flowers at first symmetrically arranged. It is conceded that the Damascus, Syrian, ones came first and the symmetrical flowers are very likely of East Indian, via Persia, origin. It would seem that during the latter part of the 16th and early part of the 17th centuries the Chinese style also brought about the asymmetrical arrangement of the flowers as on the Turkish plates. Possibly it was the Chinese who also helped with the red color. The fact that the red was very difficult to handle is testified to by many Chinese examples in which it has become liver color or suffered other catastrophes. It is furthermore shown by the fact that when imitations of Turkish wares were made at Candiana near Padua in the 17th century, the Italians were unable to produce the red. This then seemed to need first hand supervision to learn.

The elements of decoration were now: 1.—Natural flowers, 2.—Ornamental imaginative flowers, 3.—Persian scroll stems, 4.—Geometric designs and arabesques, 5.—Animals and birds, 6.—Human figures and 7.—Sailing

Fig. 522. Turkish mug of 16th to 17th cent. with the usual colored enamel decoration. This type is probably earlier than those with colored ground. Ht. 8¾". James J. Rorimer Coll.

Fig. 523. Turkish mug of early 17th cent. with enamel ground of green, blue and white borders at top and bottom. Red, blue and white design of animals. Ht. 7⅝". Metropolitan Mus. of Art.

Fig. 524. Jug of Turkish pottery of early 17th cent. Decorated in white, blue and red on an emerald green ground. The glaze contains tin as well as some of the enamels. Ht. 8⅜". Metropolitan Mus. of Art.

ships. The last two are most rare and perhaps least pleasing. The animals are also not so well drawn as they are on the earlier Persian wares. But the drawing of the flowers is sure and beautiful. The ground was usually left white as possible but sometimes a green ground, as in the mug with animals, or the jug with ships would be used on a scale pattern, as may be seen in one of the plates, given by Mr. Rorimer to the Metropolitan Museum of Art.

The shapes are rather sturdy jugs and mugs, plates, rarely mosque lamps and even more rarely stem-bowls with covers. Marks do not occur as a rule, except for the false Chinese characters that we do see on some Persian wares, but in the Godman Collection there is a small jug which has an Armenian inscription stating that it was made by "Abraham of Kutaia" in the 16th century. The wares from Kutaia, Demitoka, Lindus and Nicaea are hardly distinguishable from one another and they all deteriorated in the 18th and 19th centuries so that they do not interest us.

ITALIAN MAJOLICA

Even by the time of the fall of the Roman Empire nothing had been developed in Italy except the old red or black pottery. A somewhat new technique applied to it was discovered at the Forum in Rome. It is of coarse, red clay with "sgraffito" design and a yellowish, transparent glaze sometimes stained a vivid green with copper oxide. This carried on the technique of the T'ang Chinese, the "Gubri" or "Gabri" wares and some of those of Rhages or Rakka, Persia but the designs are generally more crowded and ornate and less spirited. "Mezza-majolica" or "half majolica" was a step forward being covered with a white slip which was incised and painted with colors and was closer to the prototypes. The earliest of this type is said to date about the 12th century or earlier. The technique continued so long as the fusible colors tended to flow together.

As we have said, tin glaze came from the Near East but, though the technique had been known, tin was as costly as gold and very little was used. It was first employed as a tin ash mixed with the slip to make that creamy

FIG. 525. Stem-cup of mezza-majolica found in Cyprus, dating 9th to 11th cent. This Italian ware is decorated in green and treacle-brown on cream ground showing similarity to T'ang Chinese wares. Ht. 4¾". Metropolitan Mus. of Art.

FIG. 526. Italian (Ferrara) dish with incised decoration and brown and green glazes on tan. 14th to 15th cent. Dia. 9¾". James J. Rorimer Coll.

FIG. 527. Italian tazza of the *sgraffito* majolica ware dating about 1500 and, in a way, carrying on the technique of T'ang and "gabri" Persian wares having similar transparent yellow and green lead glazes. Ht. 2¼". Dia. 9¾". Mortimer L. Schiff Coll. Metropolitan Mus. of Art.

clay white and opaque. About a hundred years before the sgraffito wares were made in Italy tin enamel, that is a lead-silica glaze with tin added, had been introduced but actual use was not made of it until about 1500, although the mezza-majolica sometimes had a sparing touch of it here and there. The introduction had come through Spain, and the early wares were made at La Fratta, Citta di Castello, where the ware called "alla Castellana" was

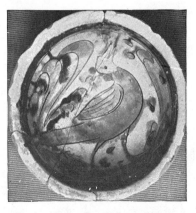

Sgraffito decorated pottery bowl from Italy (Lombardy?) late 15 cent. Dia. 7″. Ht. 3″. Ex Count Bracciforte Piccenza Coll. James J. Rorimer Coll. Metropolitan Mus. of Art.

Bovl with sgraffito design swiftly executed and with dabbed spots of colored glaze on a cream white ground, attributed to Ferrara and of the late 14th or early 15th cent. Dia. 5½″. Ht. 2¼″. James J. Rorimer Coll. Metropolitan Mus. of Art.

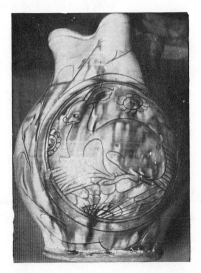

Sgraffito decorated jug with spirited design attributed to Ferrara c. 1400–1450. Apparent is a strong Persian and Chinese influence and the glazes are richer in colors and applications than this place is usually given credit for. Ht. 7½″. James J. Rorimer Coll. Metropolitan Mus. of Art.

"Sgraffito decorated earthenware bowl, Italian (probably Ferrara) 1400 to 1450." The mottled glaze has a T'ang feeling. Dia. 5½″. Ht. 1⅞″. James J. Rorimer Coll. Metropolitan Mus. of Art.

ITALIAN MAJOLICA: 15TH CENTURY

PLATE 115

made, and at Padua and Pavia. In Padua a potter named Nicoleti signed a large round medallion showing the Madonna seated amongst saints. In Pavia the Cuzio family signed a number of pieces in brown or green glaze.

"Orvieto Ware" of the 14th Century

The general name "Orvieto Ware" means little for very similar wares were found at Siena (the best ones), Cortona, Rome, Perugia and Faenza as well

Fig. 528. Majolica 15th cent. bowl very probably from Orvieto with light buff ground inside and yellow outside, the design being in pale green and aubergine. Dia. 12". Metropolitan Mus. of Art.

Fig. 529. Italian 14th to 15th cent. jug probably from Orvieto with a shield with fleur de lis in relief and leaf also in studded relief. Ht. 11". Metropolitan Mus. of Art.

Fig. 530. Todi jug (Boccali) of Italian majolica of about 1400 decorated in black on a white slip ground. The ware is red at the bottom where exposed and the inside shows red glaze effect. Ht. 10⅞". Metropolitan Mus. of Art.

as in Orvieto. The earliest of these wares were dipped in tin enamel to cover only about two thirds to four fifths of their heights and the bottoms were covered with lead glaze. Later the tin covers to the bottom and to the edges of plates but even then the backs are in lead glaze. The ware is crude and reddish, rudely wheel thrown and without sheen. The colors are copper-green, light blue of copper or cobalt, manganese-purple and yellow-ochre, the light blue and yellow being rarer. Some crudely modeled relief heads or fruit were used. The painted designs are degenerated Near Eastern, Gothic and some have Coptic crosses. Animals, fish, birds and monsters are frequent as are also cross hatched backgrounds, which were used to replace flat washes with which the potters seemed to have trouble. Fakes have been cleverly made but the glazes are usually smoother and it is difficult to reproduce primitive drawing simple as it seems. During the 15th century a deeper cobalt blue, a brown and a clearer ochre-yellow were added. The wares also became less pictorial. Many were made for hospitals after the plague of the 14th century in which a quarter of the people of Europe died. Show pieces also occur in the 15th century and the factories and painters began to sign their wares.

"Green Florentine Ware"

"Green Florentine ware" is in the transition between the Middle Ages and the start of the Renaissance. It is finer with thicker glaze, it often has a soft grey tone, the colors are richer, the outlines are of manganese-purple (prob-

Florentine 15th cent. Nativity; five figures forming a persepio of painted terracotta. Ht. of Virgin 34⅞″. Metropolitan Mus. of Art.

FLORENTINE 15TH CENTURY NATIVITY IN POTTERY

PLATE 116

FIG. 531. Majolica jug (Boccali). Outside covered with a creamy glaze and the inside ochre-yellow. c. 1400. Ht. 11". Metropolitan Mus. of Art.

FIG. 532. Florentine albarello of majolica decorated in blue, manganese and yellow on light ground. c. 1450–1475. Ht. 9". Metropolitan Mus. of Art.

FIG. 533. Albarello from Florence of 1425–1450 decorated in blue and manganese on white slip ground with arms of the Hospital of Santa Maria della Scala, at Siena. Ht. 12¾". Metropolitan Mus. of Art.

FIG. 531a. Florentine? plate of brown clay with pinkish tin glaze, incised decoration and glazes of blue and yellow. Note Arabic inscriptions in roots of tree. Probably early 15th cent. Bequest of Mrs. Edward Wheelwright. Mus. of Fine Arts, Boston.

FIG. 533a. Italian 16th cent. carved slipware plate made in very much the same technique as the Gabri and Samarra types. Dia. 15⅛". James J. Rorimer Coll.

ably learned from the cuerda seca of Spain) and the predominant color is a strong bluish green. The decoration is of animals, human figures and heads of portrait character. Two new shapes are the large dishes with broad horizontal rims and squat jars with two flat handles on the shoulder.

"Impasto Blue Florentine Ware"

"Impasto Blue Florentine ware" was undoubtedly inspired first by Chinese importations to the Near East. Also the Egypto-Syrian vases which had underglaze blue and black decoration and are of the 13th century may have built tradition. There are only a few pieces showing the transition from the

FIG. 534. "Green Florentine" 15th cent. jar with the twisted rope handles seen on some Greek wares and a design showing Western Asian influences. It is of brown pottery with tin glaze and green and manganese decoration. Ht. 14⅛". Metropolitan Mus. of Art. Gift of V. Everit Macy.

FIG. 535. Florentine drug-jar c. 1425–1450, decorated with thick enamel-like impasto blue. Note also the Near Eastern tendency to break up the heavy mass of the animal with circular designs. Ht. 8". Mortimer Schiff Coll. Metropolitan Mus. of Art.

FIG. 536. Early 15th cent. Italian majolica jug with lion head and studded leaves in relief and decoration in yellow, green and manganese of dull and impure quality. Ht. 9¼". Metropolitan Mus. of Art.

air of majolica albarelli of the 16th cent. decorated with medal-s in green wreaths of St. John and of a courtesan against grounds canary yellow and a general background of cobalt blue having ige yellow floral ornaments. Ht. 12½". Ex E. H. Gary Coll. and R. Hearst Coll. International Studio, Inc.

Trilobate *Vasque* of Urbino ware of the 16th cent. decorated with grotesque figures and satyrs in low relief on the outside and "The Abduction of Hippodania" on the inside. Dia. 15". From the W. R. Hearst Coll. International Studio, Inc.

ITALIAN 16TH CENTURY MAJOLICA

PLATE 117

green style to the blue, one a dish showing Adam and Eve in the Musée Céramique, Rouen, which is strongly Near Eastern in style, has a slightly pinkish ground and various animals, dogs, etc., about the rim. Fern-like spots in deep blue are about the rise of this plate. Another has an Italian coat of arms and seven small animals with human faces again of Near Eastern type and this has both colors. It is in the Musée Céramique, Sèvres.

The blue technique drove out the green almost at once and was in turn supplanted by the Hispano-Moresque because of the rise of Spanish power. The animals, fish and birds are now similar to those seen on Saracenic silks and all of the space is crowded with design. This was a growing urge as can also be seen in the Kutaian wares of the 16th and 17th centuries. Mixed with these influences the Italian coats of arms and Gothic leaves are entwined. Very large vases were made and signed with factory marks below their handles. Many are from the pharmacy of Santa Maria Nuova and bear the hospital emblem, a crutch, while others from Santa Maria della Scala are marked with a ladder or bier.

The Florentines did not understand the technique of lustre but made similar designs in what is called "Hispano-Moresque-Italian ware" in blue or blue, manganese and yellow, with Gothic trefoils and six-petaled flowers, palmette leaves and twisted stems, tendrils and dots. The blue was no longer in thick lumps but light, transparent and greyish more like that seen on lustre ware.

FIG. 537. Albarello of the Hispano-Moresque style but decorated in heavy blue. It is probably Florentine. Italian 15th cent. Ht. 12″. Mortimer Schiff Coll. Metropolitan Mus. of Art.

Polychrome effects with direct Western Asian, and not Hispano-Moresque, motives came into being by 1470. The "peacock-eye," "pomegranate" from Turkish sources were combined with the "scroll leaf" which now started all

over Italy. Alberelli and large jars with two handles and a wide mouth were usual forms. Also tiles were made with the scrolls as can be seen in those from the Caracciolo chapel in the church of San Giovanni a Carbonara at Naples dating about 1440, those from San Petronio c. 1487 and those of the Bologna chapel at Bentivoglio in San Gaicomo of about 1490.

FIG. 538.

FAENZA AND "FAÏENCE"

While these various things were happening in Florence and spreading out over Italy, Faenza the great center for the Italian Renaissance style in pottery was growing. It was here that the art of Venice, Siena, Caffaggiolo, Ferrara and elsewhere had its origin. So important was this center that the name "faïence" became a universal term meaning tin enameled earthenware. The term was

Castel Durante dish of the 16th cent. painted by Giovanni Harin, 1508 with the arms of Pope Julius II surrounded by swags of fruit, figures of satyrs, dolphins, birds, etc., on a dark blue ground. Dia. 12¾". Ex Col. Duke of Newcastle. W. R. Hearst Coll. International Studio, Inc.

16th cent. Urbino dish showing Venus combing her hair and Vulcan heating a piece of metal over a fire. Dia. 10¾". Ex Baron Adolphe de Rothschild Coll. and W. R. Hearst Coll. International Studio, Inc.

Deruta 16th cent. dish with lustred design in relief. The center shows Judith with the head of Holofernes. Dia. 15½". Ex J. P. Morgan Coll. W. R. Hearst Coll. International Studio, Inc.

ITALIAN 16TH CENTURY MAJOLICA PLATES

PLATE 118

accepted in France in 1574 when a factory was started at Lyons. It is syn-onymous with "majolica" generally speaking and also technically with delft but is misapplied and wrongly used to designate porcelain.

The great contemporary authority on the beginning of majolica or faïence was Cipriano Piccolpaso who was a master potter himself and who detailed for us every step of the progress. I take the following from his notes:

1.—At Urbino and Castle Durante the clay was taken from the bed of the river in summer when the water was low.

2.—It was either dried or buried in deep pits in the ground.

3.—He notes that clay was traded; that for Venice from Ravenna and Rimini, Battaglia (near Padua) and Pesaro.

4.—After throwing on the wheel or modeling, the object was given a slight firing just to harden it enough to handle. This was called "a bistugio."

5.—It was then dipped in the enamel or the latter was poured over it.

6.—The "enamel" was prepared with greatest of care being crushed, pounded, sieved and mixed with water.

7.—After the "enamel" had dried the decoration was painted on with decision and certainty for the surface was porous and very absorbent so that the color took immediately into it and any hesitation meant a blotch.

8.—Sometimes the lees of wine with sand were burned forming an alkali which when blended with the colors formed a sort of extra glaze strengthen-ing the colors and giving them brilliance. (Note:—This may have also been done with the Turkish and Damascus wares but I am not certain.)

9.—Another transparent glaze was then applied over the enamel decoration which gave a certain depth, whereas French and German wares lacked this overglaze as did also the Chinese enameled designs, borrowing their brightness from the enamel undercoat with which they united in firing. (Note:— Each man's own way is the best in his mind. The Chinese enamels had a glaze texture all their own and none of the underglaze came up over them. They were also so high fired a porcelain that the enamels had to be fired at a second and lower temperature.)

10.—The pigments were:

    1.—"Bianchetto" oxide of tin making opaque white.

    2.—"Verde" green from copper oxide with the addition of oxide of anti-mony or lead.

    3.—"Zallo" yellow from lead oxide, antimony and iron rust.

    4.—"Zallolino" light yellow from lead oxide, antimony and a little cooking salt and potash.

    5.—"Zaffara" cobalt blue was imported from the Near East through Venice.

    6.—Brownish purple was the manganese ore from several places in Italy.

He says that the red was not understood in his country. Odd examples he had seen but the color was uncertain and not to be depended upon. (We may say that this was probably copper red.) He says it was mixed from "Armenian bole" with lees of wine and painting the solution on a ground of "zallolino,"—which sounds a bit odd. However, the "Armenian bole" may have been earth containing iron and copper or may have actually been the prepared red the Turks were now using. It must not be confused with ruby lustre which was prepared, according to Piccolpasso, only by Maestro Cencio at "Ugobio" now called Gubbio. Hannover suggests that he refers to one Maestro Vincencio, son of Giorgio Andreoli who was celebrated for his ruby lustre.

11.—Brushes or "panelli" were made from donkey or goat hair while the finest were made from the whiskers of a mouse. (Whether this was simply legend brought from China I do not know but the Chinese do make fine brushes from mouse and other animals' whiskers.)

12.—A clean brush must be used for each color he says and this is an excellent rule for any painter to adhere to.

13.—The designs were traced on the ware by means of a pricked outline on a paper over which a sponge filled with black or red color was passed.

14.—The outlines were drawn in purple or blue.

15.—When painting the vessel was usually held by the artist on his left knee and supported with his left hand. (Amongst the earliest pieces bearing the Caffaggiolo mark there is a plate painted about 1511 showing an artist working just so. It is in the Victoria & Albert Museum.)

16.—With very fine work a table was sometimes used.

17.—The formulas for each part of the painting had been worked out as follows:

   a.—The morning sky and brightly lignted paths were painted in zallolino and bianchetto.

   b.—Woodwork and details of streets were in zallo and bianchetto.

   c.—Sky and sea were in zaffara and bianchetto.

   d.—Plowed land, ordinary roads, ancient ruins, etc., were in zaffara, manganese and bianchetto.

   e.—Green meadows and trees had zallolino with "ramina" (copper ashes).

   f.—Flesh tints were made without red by using zallo, zallolino and high-lights of bianchetto. They all look yellow, therefore.

18.—Each color was mixed light "mista chiara," and dark "mista scura."

19.—After the decoration was completed the vessels received their coat of "marzacotto" and were fired in "cassette" or saggers, which were made with three small cones at the bottom called "pironi." (As the pieces were fired upside down there are always three small scars left in the glaze on authentic examples.)

20.—Firing was not done during the wane of the moon for the pieces would then lack brightness. This again is from the Chinese, and reminds us of the constant mystery which surrounded the making of pottery.

21.—The kiln was heated slowly and cooled even more slowly.

22.—Sometimes a second coat was given of lead oxide which would fuse at the low temperature of the muffle-kiln and add another layer of brilliant glaze. This was called "coperta."

So much for the process. About 1500 *pictorialization* and *show pieces* began. Either of these principles would be fatal sooner or later and both together made ruin certain. The plates were made with holes in the foot-rims for suspension and called "istorati" and "piatti da pompa" (state dishes) or again "bacili amatori" (lover's gifts) and have legends "bella" (beautiful), "diva" (divine), or "paragon di tutte" (the paragon of all) beneath portraits of women and sometimes an added pierced heart, flaming heart or clasped

FIG. 539. Urbino ewer of the 16th cent. with blue dragon spout, blue scrolls around handle and blue and yellow foliage. The inscription reads, "Sy Urbino II" around base. Barber called it Caffagiolo. Mus. of Fine Arts, Boston.

FIG. 540. Large majolica bottle from Faenza late 15th cent. showing a woman with the inscription "Fumisterre." Ht. 16". Ex Lord Tabley Coll. and W. R. Hearst Coll. International Studio, Inc.

FIG. 541. Faenza 16th cent. ewer of tin enameled earthenware. This shows some of the characteristics of German stonewares in design.

hands for good measure. An amusing example in the Louvre is in blue and yellow lustre such as was made in Deruta or Pesaro and has the portrait of a girl and the legend, "Who steers well his ship will enter the harbor." Still others are called "tondino" and have deep centers to be filled with sweets and are ornamented with cupids, portraits and love emblems.

Pharmacies of the times were places of grandeur combining meeting houses, confessionals and gossip centers. As our present day display of sanitation and scientific atmosphere was not known the customers were impressed by grandeur and elegance. Part of the show was made by the many jars upon each of which was a flowery abbreviation indicating the mysterious contents and set·off with scrolls and foliage. Dishes and ewers for rose water showed Venus rising from the sea attended by sea-gods and bathing nymphs. "Vasi gamelii" were made for wedding presents and had scenes from the story of Cupid and Psyche or from the metamorphoses of Jupiter. "Nuzziali" were similar. Princely persons could buy vessels with scenes from the lives of Caesar or Alexander and sacred vessels had subjects from the life of Moses, St. Paul or Aaron.

Of course Raphael had nothing to do with the so-called "Raffaelle ware," nor did other artists of prominence paint these terrible potteries. Actually the potters helped themselves to anything they could get their hands on in the way of a design and made up tales to bolster the sale of their wares. When a drawing was made from a painting the signature was not forgotten. Thus there are pots signed by Raphael, Giulio Romano, Mantegna, Campagnola and the German painters, Durer, Cranach and Schongauer. Scenes from Ovid and Virgil were popular while biblical subjects were taken from the Old Testament as being richer in possibilities for luscious nudes. We are told that landscapes appear alone as decorations from about 1550 but were not general until the "decline" of the next century.

Certain subjects were well known and copied round about such as the:

"Trofei"—from the duchy of Urbino—weapons, armor and musical instruments "pleasantly" arranged in a reserve on colored ground.

"Rabeschi"—from Venice—interlaced lines and foliage in the manner of arabesques of damascened work.

"Cerquate"—principally from Urbino—oak leaves because of the connection with the della Rovere family (Rovere means oak-tree).

"Groteschi"—were ornaments ending in human figures or heads not to be confused with those of Rafaello del Colle, Giovanni da Udine and Battista Franco later at Urbino.

"Foglie"—leaves—at Venice and Genoa sometimes reserved on a colored ground or elsewhere on a white ground.

And so there are listed also "fiori" (flowers), "paesi" (landscapes) which came chiefly from Castel Durante, Genoa and Venice, "alla porcellana" (in the manner of porcelain) something like arabesques but with more lumpy spots of foliage, "tirate" (interlacements), "bianco sopra bianco" (white upon white) which was made chiefly at Urbino and Faenza and which has a cool white color on a warm white glaze, "quartieri" (compartments) and "candalieri" (literally candlesticks) which are said to resemble groteschi but are of greater symmetry of drawing. There are many more but these are the best known in the patter of collectors. Actually tons of majolica were turned out. There were

Fig. 542. Dish showing the "Foglie" type of pattern on a two colored background, made at Faenza about 1535–40. Metropolitan Mus. of Art.

fifty towns making it in the 16th century and twice as many in the 17th and 18th centuries. Thus by mass alone they accomplish as much as some other potters have by excellence.

From about 1540 onwards there are signatures usually in the form of monograms and often dates. In services usually only the largest pieces were marked or the largest piece (the "cappo mazzo"). Painters wandered from shop to shop so their signatures do not tell us much. The following chart may help to locate some of the wares:

Left: Castagiolo plate dated 1522 with the coats of arms of Siena and of the Della Rovere Family. *"Bianco sopra bianco"* border. This plate is one of seven known showing the Seven Virtues in Italian Museums. They were made for the Papal Conclave of 1522. Dia. 10¾". From the W. R. Hearst Coll. International Studio, Inc.
Center: Siena plate of the 17th to 18th cent. Metropolitan Mus. of Art.
Right: Castel Durante dish with portrait and masks, dated 1546. Metropolitan Mus. of Art.

Left: 16th cent. Castel Durante dish with typical grotesques. Dia. 16½". Ex J. P. Morgan Coll. W. R. Hearst Coll. International Studio, Inc.
Center: 16th cent. Gubbio deep dish both painted and lustred. Dia. 10⅝". Ex J. P. Morgan Coll. W. R. Hearst Coll. International Studio Coll.
Right: Gubbio dish signed M. Giorgio in Ugubio and dated 1527. Painting shows St. Margaret and the Dragon. Dia. 9⅞". Ex J. P. Morgan Coll. W. R. Hearst Coll. International Studio, Inc.

Gubbio writing case of the 17th cent. showing the ornate baroque style. Metropolitan Mus. of Art.

Left: Castel Durante albarello of the 16th cent. showing a portrait of a Moor with large turban. Metropolitan Mus. of Art.
Right: Siena albarello with polychrome decoration, made about 1515. Metropolitan Mus. of Art.

ITALIAN WARES 16TH TO 18TH CENTURIES

PLATE 119

CHART OF ITALIAN FAIENCE

Mark	Date	Location	Subject	Technique
Casa Betini 1487	1487	Church of San Petronio at Bologna / At present same	1200 tiles for pavement / Scrolled leaves	In blue outline, and blue, manganese purple, turquoise blue, yellow
One bears mark "Faenza" another date 1500	1500	Faenza / Musée de Cluny	Alberello with grotesques	Yellow ground
1507 Faventine	1507	Now in the Bargello Florence	Dish with David and fallen Goliath	Polychrome
By this piece we attr. to the same hand: 1.—A plate in the Schlossmuseum, Berlin, with reproduction of Dürer's Prodigal Son, 2.—Another with ruins and "putti" cupids after Dürer, 3.—At Brunswick another with the death of Marcus Curtius, 4.—British Museum another with death of Virgin.				
TB. style of Melozzo da Forli	1510 about	1.—Now in the Bargello / 2.—Now in Victoria and Albert Mus.	Panel with Martyrdom of St. Sebastian / Panel with the Resurrection	
F.R. Signed on front	About 1510	1.—Schlossmuseum Berlin / 2.—V. & A. Mus. / 3.—Salting Collection	Plate with legend of the Vestal Tuccia / Panel with Road to Golgotha after Lo Spasimo di Sicilia by Raphael / Dish with Dido and Aeneas	
(Faenza)				
Signed:— / Fata in Fae(nza)— / Josef I(n) Ca(sa) / Pirota 1525	1525	From Faenza earliest dated piece. Now in Gustave de Rothschild Collection	Dish with Joseph finding the cup in the sack of Benjamin	
Fato in Faenza in Caxa Pirota	About 1525 When the Coronation took place	Faenza probably Now in the Museo Archeologico at Bologna	Dish with coronation of Empe or Charles V in church of San Petronio	
Crossed circle with dot or small circle in one quadrant P.F.B.F. around 1525	All about 1525	1.—Schlossmuseum / 2.—British Mus. two panels without date	Plate with Adoration of Magi Madonna and Child Adoration of Magi	Green with all yellow and lavish use of blue, strong highlights

Note: In Faenza it seems that blue was used not only for the outlines but also for the ground. Also the backs have concentric rings of blue and purple. Urbino plain backs.

Casa Pirota the backs are with blue stems "alla porcellana," of the embossed dishes with blue and yellow coils.

Faenza, in the case of enclosed compositions blue "alla porcellana" stems occur also on front decorations.

Faenza at first but later in other sections, "a berettino" or "sopra azzurro" technique where the body is covered with a light blue enamel instead of the white. Sometimes combined with "bianco sopra bianco" on rise of plate.

Faenza as Hannover says, "A long full faced satyr's mask with tufted crest and foliated beard is of such frequent occurrence that it may often play the part of a missing signature in cases where the piece does not present other special characteristics unfavorable to its attribution to Faenza." Faenza and Casa Pirota produced the "scannellati" or pressed spiral dishes in relief with small centers containing one figure against yellow ground as a rule.

Mark	Date	Location	Subject	Technique
		(From Urbino)		
B.M. or Manara 1528 to 1536	About as dated probably 1535	1.—Earliest lost sight of 2.—Unknown 3.—Berlin Museum	Resurrection Adoration of Magi	Drawing in purple painting in more naturalistic colors with too strong orange
		(Faenza)		
MF or ML and Giano Brame dj pallermo 1546 in Faenza	1546	From Faenza now in the Museum at Sigmaringen	Descent from the Cross after Marcantonio	Same style as above but "brilliant" technique
V R in Faencia	? Same time	Faenza Now in the Schlossmuseum Berlin	Death of Marcus Curtius	Same style
Faenza 1562	1562	Faenza Berlin	The head of Hasdrubal being thrown into the camp of Hannibal	Same style Raphaelesque but showing decline of technique
		(Caffagiolo)		
Cafaggiolo or Chafagguolo or SPR or a trident The SPR probably being "Semper" a motto of the Medici. Also si volg meaning "Glovis." Also S.P.Q.F. or	About 1511 to 1570	1.—Caffagiolo Now in the V. & A. Mus. 1511 2.—V. & A. Mus. has a late example with "Semper" mark in lustre	Majolica painter at work Among earliest pieces marked from Caffagiolo	Backgrounds for figures of deep lapis-lazuli blue in rough brush strokes. Use of stick to scratch designs in the ground

S.P.Q.R. meaning: "Senatus populusque Florentinus or Romarus"
And many of the best ones have no mark at all perhaps because they were forbidden side by side with the "Semper" mark of the royal family.

(Siena)

fata ī Siena da m° Benedetto plate in V. & A. Mus. thought to date around 1510 to 1520 or a little later. Also B° or M°B but they are various in quality.

Mark	Date	Location	Subject	Technique
Bartolomeo Terchi Romano 1727 Siena	1727	Now in Berlin Museum	Oval picture panel with Triumph of Galatea	Pale tones after Marcantonio Raimondi and Agostino Caracci
Ferdinando Maria Campani	1733 1733	1.—Berlin Museum 2.—British Museum	Dish with the story of Moses after Raphael Dish with the Creation of the Stars, after Raphael	Same as above

362

Mark / Signature	Date	Location	Description	Notes
1747 The latest known piece from Siena.	1747	V. & A. Mus.	Dish with a pastoral or vintage subject by Campani in the Castelli Manner	
		(Castel Durante)		
1508 a di 12 de Seteb. facta fu i Castel Durat. Zona Maria Vro	1508	Castel Durante Now in Hearst Collection	Basin with the arms of Pope Julius II of the della Rovere Family	Arms on blue ground with yellow palmettes and trophies reserved in white on blue
Pietro dal Castelo fecit on a scroll	1508 or a little later	Castel Durante Now in Bologna	Basin with Arms of Farnese family on blue, with palmettes, trophies, candakieri and putti	Palmettes in yellow, rest white on blue and blue on yellow
Bastiane 1510 meaning Sebastiano	1510	Castel Durante Oppenheim Coll. Now in Cologne	Plate with woman hung by feet for being unfaithful	Trophy border in yellow, ochre-brown and light green on blue
Same as above Bastiane 1519	1519	1.—Castel Durante Now in British Mus. 2.—Also a companion in V. & A. Mus.	Alberello with weapons and grotesques	Yellowish tones on dark blue and green ground
1524-1526 in Castel Durante	Same	1.—Now in Louvre 2.—Louvre	1.—Bowl with the Rape of Ganymede 2.—Bowl with Apollo and Marsyas	Raphaelesque but devoid of character, pale insipid
		These are similar to the following from Urbino		
		(Urbino)		
1521 with a monogram composed of all the letters of his first name	1521	Urbino or Castel Durante Now in the Basilewsky Coll. in Leningrad	Dish with enthroned king	Similar to above
Nicola da U. Same as above artist	?	Urbino British Mus.	Dish with a sacrifice to Diana	Similar
Nicola da Urbino	?	Louvre	Dish with Parnassus after Raphael	Similar

Mark	Date	Location	Subject	Technique
Nicola da Urbino fata in botega de guido da castello durante in Urbino 1528 Monogram made up of all the letters of his name *Orazio Fontana* to which is added: *questo fu fatto nella botega de Mº Guido vasaro da castello durante in Urbino . . . 1542* The Guido is a son of Nicolo whom he seemed to have joined from about 1526 to 1540.	1528	Bargello at Florence	Large dish with thirty-four figures representing the martyrdom of St. Cecilia	Similar
		Berlin Mus.	Contest between the Musea and the daughters of Theseus	
		(Castel Durante)		
P. Mastro Simone in Castel Durante 1562	Same	Was in the Cajani Coll. Rome	Large covered jar with inverted pear shaped body on slender pedestal with a shield and grotesques	Similar
Hippolito Rombaldotti Pinse (pinxit) in Urbania	after 1635 1678 added	1.—Now in Louvre 2.—Milan in private possession	Bowl with Triumph of Flora Large vase with snake handles and a design with allegorical figures	More like a slightly tinted pen-drawing Similar to above
Giovanni Rocco de Castelli 1732	Same date 1732	Now in the Berlin Museum	Panel with the Baptism	
	It was painted at Urbania, formerly Castel Durante, but in pure Castelli style.			
		(Deruta)		
I Deruta 1503	1503	From Deruta was in Castellani Collection. Now?	Votive-tablet with two women seated on a bed in presence of four kneeling figures	
1521	Same	Arezzo Mus.	Bowl with gold lustre with (in relief) Adoration of the Shepherds	
el frate in Deruta (on a few pieces from 1541 to 1554)	1550	Present location not known	Large dish with the Marriage of Alexander and Roxana	Blue outline and painted in blue and lustre like old pieces
1545 in Deruta frate fecit	1545	Louvre	Bowl with a scene from the Orlando Furioso of Ariosto	Drawing and shading in bistre, draperies blue and white with yellow highlights, green sward and dress of female in green

Note: Also lustre usually poor by this maker.

Inscription	Date	Museum	Subject	Style / Notes
(Pesaro)				
1540 fatto in Pesaro	1540	Ashmolean Museum Oxford	Dish with Creation of the Beasts	Commercial and poor quality of Urbino style
Girolamo da le Gabice in Pesaro ?	?	Now in British Museum	Bowl with Cicero expounding the law to Julius Caesar	Markedly superior though by same hand
Note: Many of these wares if not marked *fatto in Pesaro* (with the usual 16th century dates) would be mistaken for Urbino.				
(Rimini)				
in Arimini, in Rimino or in Ariminensis or 153 Iulio da urbino in botega de mastro Alisandro in arimino			Found only on a few fragments at Rimini much like Urbino ware with brown tree trunks instead of black.	
(Ferrara?)				
Thomas Masselli Ferrarien Fec	18th	V. & A. Mus.	Dish with Bacchanalian rout	In manganese purple
Not necessarily from Ferrara and there are no other marked pieces.				
(Verona)				
1547 . . . in Verona	1547	Kunstindustrimuseum at Copenhagen	Bowl with arrival of Aeneas in Italy	Beautiful Urbino style, fine in composition and technique
1563 a di 15 genaro Guiseppe Giovanni Battista da Faenza— in Verona—M. Also the scrolls as stems on the back are not known at Urbino		Bacon Hall Norfolk	Dish with Alexander the Great with the family of Darius	Same style and by same artist
(Venice)				
1540. Adi. 16. del. Mexe. de. Oturbe		Ashmolean Museum Oxford	Dish with mermaid with wide border of arabesques with fruits, flowers and birds	Painted in blue on grey enamel
In Venetia in Co(n)trada dj Sta Polo in botega di M° Lodovico		V. & A. Mus.	Dish entirely covered with arabesques	Style like above

Mark	Date	Location	Subject	Technique
Jacomo da Pesaro a Sᵗᵃ Barnaba in Venetia	1542	Sigmaringen Museum	Large "smaltino" Dish with Venus with Vulcan and Cupid	Painted in blue
1568 Zener Domenigo da Venecia feci in la botega al ponte sito del Andar a San Paolo		Museum at Brunswick		Center picture with rim divided into panels with single figures
		(Gubbio)		
Maestro Giorgio (FIRST SIGNED WORKS) As a rule signed *M.G.* or *M.G. da Ugubio* or on important works *M° Giorgio 1520 a di 2 de O'tobre in Ugubio*	1517–18	V. & A. Museum British and Berlin Museums	Service with housemark of owner (a pointing hand) surrounded by arabesques	Berlin dish is embossed and shows Oriental and Deruta influence. Others more freely curved grotesques like those from 1519 on. Golden Lustre has reddish tone. Also has ruby lustre.
		(Rome)		
Alfonso Patanazzi fecit. Urbini. 1606		V. & A. Mus.	Romulus and the Sabine Women on a large basin	Style like that of second type Urbino
		(Urbino)		
Fabrica di Maiolica fina di monsieur Rolet in Urbino, A 28 aprile 1773		V. & A. Mus.	Tall Roman oil lamp with four nozzles with dec. of clusters of berries	Red, blue and purple on white ground
		(Castelli)		
L.G.P. or *Liborio Grue* as he signed	(1701–1776)	V. & A Mus.	Tureen with naked figures after **Annibale Carracci**	General type
Also Carmine Gentili who signed *C.G.P.* or *Cⁿᵉ Gˡⁱ P.*		(Savona)		
Six pointed star with letter S (Girolamo Salomini)		Sèvres Museum		Coarse and crude scalloped large dishes, etc.

Note: Star and S also appear enclosed in: *L'anno 1721 Agostino Ratti Fece in Sauona.*

366

A few added notes follow:

Faenza about 1560 produced a fine white enamel by Don Pino and Vergiliotto on bowls with perforated rims and dishes with radial embossments decorated in manganese outlines filled with light blue and touches of yellow. The subjects were "putti" (cupids) and such.

Caffaggiolo was a "castello" on the road between Florence and Bologna built by Cosimo de' Medici. Famous pieces from this kiln are the plate with a figure of Fame in Berlin, Diana and Endymion in the style of Botticelli in the Basilewski Collection and the one with St. George in the V. & A. Museum.

Siena is said to have had so many kilns in 1262 that they became a danger and were called to the attention of the authorities. The oldest product of Siena known today is the tile pavement in the oratory of Santa Caterina at Fontebranda which has much rich Renaissance design. Such tiles are distinguished by orange and "terra di Siena" red and it is these two colors that make it possible to associate certain dishes and alberelli with the place. The backs are distinctive and are drawn in blue and orange. Another stunt was the use of a blue shadow behind the profile on a plate. This was also done at Deruta but not in the same way. The oldest ware shows a diapered design made by the repetition of thin blue stems and yellow flowers recalling the Hispano-Moresque style of Florence but different. Some plates have numerous concentric borders, at times only lines and sometimes with scale or leaf ornament. Some are also made with "bianco sopra bianco" decoration combined with "alla porcellana" ornament in blue but most are polychrome, which included red, orange, orange yellow, copper green, deep blue, etc. but with warm colors dominating.

Castel Durante and "Urbino" called "Urbania" after 1635 is the general ground of much contention. It is where our friend Piccolpasso lived. A certain Nicola da Urbino was thought to have been the artist who painted the "Correr service" so called because it is now in the Correr Museum in Venice, but we do not agree for the service is classed very high among the "istorati" and has a delicate yellow in the flesh tints with also a pale pink from manganese; it is drawn by a man who knew anatomy and the general effect is soft. It is now agreed that it dates about 1515 (instead of 1482) and at this time we know that Nicola did some very insecure anatomy with hard outlines on the Gonzaga service and on a plate showing Solomon worshipping an idol. The artist who did the Correr service in 1515 thought in masses while the one who did the Gonzaga service in 1520 thought in outlines only. One real peculiarity of Nicola is that he coils and indents his clouds very much as the Chinese did. These clouds appear typically in the Gonzaga service, a point which may or may not be taken as vital evidence.

If the artists of other places wandered, those from Castel Durante did to a greater degree. Francesco Durante went to Urbino and then to "Monte Bagnolo near Perugia" though we cannot find that place. Guido di Savino went about 1535 to Antwerp. The Gatti family went to Venice as did also Francesco del Vasaro in 1545. But Urbino profited by this drifting.

Castel Durante did various wares but the best known are of the "trofei" type painted en grisaille. They also had the following properties: pale greyish yellow clay, dishes and plates only exceptionally showing black decoration; those with figures are bordered with a yellow line, while those with ornamental designs have a light grey instead of the yellow in most specimens and the designs are in a light greyish olive-green which is peculiar to them. Outlines are in blue or grey. At times a clear reddish-brown is used in the trophies instead of grey.

FIG. 543. Plate still showing strong Spanish feeling. Sa'd to date c. 1500. Phoenix holding shield charged with arms of Raniere Family, Perugia. Lustred brown and blue. Dia. 16". Metropolitan Mus. of Art.	FIG. 544. Deruta majolica plate with lustre decoration similar to one in Louvre attr. to c. 1520–1530. Tan, ivory and blue. Hercules and the lion. Dia. 15¾". From Prince Kudacheff Coll., Florence, the W. R. Hearst Coll. International Studio, Inc.	FIG. 545. Majolica dish from Deruta. 16th cent. painted and also lustred probably about 1550 when painted technique replaced much of lustre. Dia. 16¼". Ex J. P. Morgan Coll. W. R. Hearst Coll. International Studio, Inc.

Now returning to lustre ware which we left off with in Spain we come to the making of it in Italy which was a very different matter as one might guess after having looked over the other wares. At Deruta on the Tiber not far from Perugia and on the road between Todi and Orvieto they first made wares similar to those of Siena but these are difficult to distinguish

FIG. 546. Deruta lustred dish of about 1530 with decoration only. The outlines are blue. Metropolitan Mus. of Art.

and the place is known chiefly for its lustred pottery. Why or how this was the place to receive the seed from Spain is impossible to tell but about 1497 it came into being. One example, a votive tablet with two women sitting on a bed, is dated 1503 and marked "I Deruta." Also a relief of St. Sebastian in the V. & A. Museum bears the date 1501. The tin enamel had been known in this place at least as early as 1475.

The forms are of jars in the shape of pine cones, two-handled vases, goblets, and heavy wide-rimmed dishes often painted with a woman's bust and such adages as the one about steering well one's ship, previously mentioned. The ware is of red or yellow clay and the backs have a simple transparent glaze much as did the Spanish ones. In fact it is said by no lesser authorities than Mr. R. L. Hobson and Mr. William Burton that "The earlier examples are hardly distinguishable from Spanish ware, and to the last the ware remained technically like earlier ware, though with perfectly Italian decorative treatment." The front is covered with tin enamel and fired and the painting is done with a peculiar light blue used as outline and shaded only slightly up from that without any attempt to do any real modeling. Finally this painting was covered and a third and lower firing given to the lustre. This has a thin, transparent glaze which in direct light has a delicate yellowish-olive or perhaps olivish-yellow tone, but when the light reflects obliquely it has a glow like gold or redder than gold, or sky-blue or iridescent like mother of pearl from which it gets its name "madre-perla" as it is called in Italy. Many of these wares have the clever device of low relief designs which make an uneven surface from which the light reflects with more variance.

The designs alone are rather stupid and flabby. Figures are often set on tile floors either flat or in perspective. The wide rims are usually divided "a quartieri" in scrolls or at other times in thirds with a sort of alternating plan but which is crude and non-rhythmical. The best period is between 1520 and 1540.

Unlustred Deruta wares are similar in style to Deruta lustre but are painted in intense shades of yellow and deep blue, ochre, and green. Strangely enough they show many three-quarter faces rather than the profiles used in lustre ware. These also have better borders. Piccolpasso's statement that as a rule out of a hundred pieces of lustre only six come out good may explain this. For we can hardly blame the workmen for slighting painting on wares which were likely to be destroyed anyhow. Here lies the reason for the decline and final obliteration of lustre. The Italians had an unconquerable desire to draw and paint pictures and lustre was just not the medium for them.

At the little city of Gubbio, on the eastern slope of the Apennines, pottery had been made through the middle ages, but in 1498 there came a potter exiled from Pavia and he called himself "Maestro Giorgio" being also a sculptor by profession. The place was owned by the Dukes of Urbino and they did not mind having him. He started to carry out some of his figures in glazed terracotta like that of the della Robbias and now we know of pieces in the church of San Domenico, in the Louvre, the Städelschs Institute at Frankfort and elsewhere. But none of his figures ever bore any lustre.

It is not known whether or not he brought the gold lustre with him but the red "ruby lustre" was certainly not made before his time nor afterwards to such perfection. His lustre colors were known as, "cangiante, madre-perla, reverbero and rubino," and became so famous that they were applied not only to wares made in his factory but others sent for the purpose. He created no new designs but his quality was high.

At first he followed Deruta designs but by 1518 he branched out and included grotesques and trophies after Castel Durante. When this change took place his dishes became light and more graceful. His first signed piece is a service made between 1517 and 1519 and shows the transition from embossed plates showing Oriental influence to large and freely curved grotesques. Most of the larger museums have examples of his work.

Little is known of the small towns of Pesaro and Rimini except that they did make similar wares. We illustrate two plates which are very much like the Deruta wares. Ferrara was under the protection of the Duke of Ferrara, Alfonso I. The ware was famous for its brilliant glaze of white. The potters came from Faenza and a large industry was carried on through

Fig. 547. Two polychromed plates from Pesaro showing similar border treatments to those t, pical of Deruta. Dias. 16¼″ and 16″. Ex Peyta Coll. and W. R. Hearst Coll. International Studio, Inc.

the first half of the 16th century, but there are no dated pieces and it is exceedingly difficult to make attributions. The dish with bacchanalian rout in the V. & A. Museum may have come from there for the artist called himself a "Ferrarian." Verona we only know through two pieces listed in our chart.

Venice passed laws prohibiting the importation of pottery in 1426, 1437 and 1455, yet we have little to go on until 1520 when it came under the influence of Faenza until 1550. Later they resemble the wares of Urbino but the wares from Venice are poor in tin and, therefore, have a comparatively transparent glaze. To try to counteract this the glaze was applied thickly and it is bluish or greyish in tone and seldom white. The name it is called by the Italians is "smaltino." The drawing is done in blue and shaded in blue while the highlights are painted in in white. The backs are decorated with a simplified "alla porcellana" scroll and at times radially fluted or striped with alternate thick and thin lines. The design, generally a shield, is enclosed in a circle considerably smaller than the bottom and the wide rim is filled with design in Persian or Chinese characters and we must remember that there was much communication with the East from this port. One of the earliest works is a service of which several pieces are known in the Knustgewerbe-museum, Berlin, bearing the arms of two Nuremberg families, Imhof and Schlaudersbach, impaled, and it is dated about 1520. For other pieces see chart.

The name Maestro Ludovico appears on pieces from about 1530 to 1550 which are strongly of Eastern influence and painted in blue on an enamel ground stained greyish-blue. Here is a distinct link in the entrance of "blue and white" wares to Europe. Another specialty of Venice was "foglie da duzena" (dozen foliage ware), which is also "smaltino" and painted in large curving leaves with round fruit in blue with touches of white for highlights. They were probably a common ware in their day and Piccolpasso says they could be bought for about forty lire for a hundred pieces but it is interesting to note how a slight touch of Chinese influence called the attention even of the Venetians to the beauty of decoration as such.

Venice also made globular jars and alberelli with strong yellow, green and blue decorations in acanthus scrolls, flowers, rosettes and fruits around medallions of women's busts and warriors, old men, etc. These were painted on a white ground with a blue background also painted in with scratched spirals and scrolls. This mode reflected the Venetian school of oil painting and did produce some decorative effects but soon deteriorated.

Some ware was made with architectural drawings poorly drawn and having blue mountains and yellow clouds in the background. The drawing was done in indigo or manganese.

Guido da Marlingo seems to have come to Venice about 1542 from Urbino and Domenigo da Venezia also copied the Urbino style. The white ground vases are particularly close to the style, but can be distinguished by the spottiness of their colors and usually also have four or five concentric rings on the back.

Black glazed ware painted in gold and lacquer colors similar to those used on Venetian glass date from about 1600. In the 18th century a high fired and resonant ware with decoration of landscapes in blue and brown with sparing touches of gold on a pale blue or greyish white ground became the vogue. The molded technique was also used and passed on to Germany and eventually England.

Venice influenced other towns:—Padua made the sgraffito work and smaltino glaze was applied over relief flowers. Verona, Candiana and Treviso copied the Venetian "Turkish wares."

Urbino was the birthplace of Raphael (1483–1520) and also an ancient pottery center but we hear nothing until in 1477 Nicolo Pellipario who called himself Nicolo da Urbino made the Gonzaga service. His followers were Guido da Castello Durante, Maestro Guido Fontana Vasaro and Guido Durnatino in Urbino. He had three descendants, Orazio, Camillo and Nicolo the last two of whom are not known as potters. But Orazio Fontana, the grandson of Nicolo da Urbino was a great competitor of Xanto Avelli.

This Xanto Avelli was born at Rovigo and became a free lance painter in Urbino. He signed his work and ocasionally put the factory name on it. He never called himself "Maestro." He worked between 1528 and 1542 following the style of Nicolo the master of narrative "istorato" painting. He also took motives from engravings, woodcuts, Ovid's "Metamorphoses" (Venice 1497), Raphael's paintings, the Bible, Virgil, Livy and Ariosto. He was not so good a draughtsman or colorist as Nicolo and aside from the fact that he used a certain bluish green in clothing and drapery his work is not distinctive. Perhaps his best known piece is the dish in the Louvre with the Rape of Helen on it after Raphael.

Orazio Fontana signed his work, as did his grandfather, with a monogram

Fig. 548. Urbino bowl of first half of 16th cent. Metropolitan Mus. of Art.
Fig. 549. Pilgrim bottle in style of Orazio Fantana of 16th cent. showing "Bacchanalian Triumph." Metropolitan Mus. of Art.
Fig. 550. Urbino plate with figure of Justice and grotesques of type supposedly influenced by Raphael and dating c. 1565 or later. Dia. 19". Metropolitan Mus. of Art.

of all the letters of his name. He started about 1542 and became the favorite of all the dukes of Urbino. He made a great service which was presented by Guidobaldo II to Philip II of Spain, and also the equipment of the pharmacy of the ducal castle after designs of Battista Franco and Raffaelle del Colle. The story goes that Louis XV wanted to trade these pieces for statues in gold and Queen Christina of Sweden offered the weight of the service in gold. It consists of about 380 pieces and much of it is in the Sanat Casa at Loreto. Between 1565 and 1571 Orazio found a new style in Raphael after the Loggia in the Vatican. This was a contrast to all that had gone before. It was a frame, and concocted of baldacchinos, genii, chimaeras, masks and various terminal figures lightly drawn but in rich colors around small medallions placed symmetrically and simulating gems with figures in blue camaïeu or grisaille. Large snake-handled vases, great jugs, salt-cellars, etc., typical of the High Renaissance started about this time, and lasted to the 17th century and were widely copied afterwards. This kind of thing was made by the Patanazzi family; but the decline soon set in and the only revival was made by a Frenchman named Rolet who started a kiln in 1770 to fake Roman oil lamps.

Castelli was a town near Naples and there they used only blue, yellow, green and purple. It built up to between 30 and 40 factories about 1743 and used gold instead of lustre. The usual Bible and historical subjects were added to by genre in the style of Berghem and also landscapes with and without ruins. The work was technically fine and plates have rims and centers treated separately. Many were made to hang on the wall. Perhaps the best painters were the Grue family from Francesco Grue whose first signed piece was in 1647 to Saverio Grue who died in 1806. There was Carlo Antonio (1655–1723) who signed C.A.G., and Liborio (1701–1776) who signed L.G.P. Finally Saverio who was later the director of the Capo di Monte factory. Also notable was the Gentili family: Bernardo, Carmine who signed C.G.P., Giacomo and Bernardo the younger.

With the beginning of the 18th century Chinese porcelain had such an

FIG. 551. Urbino plate by Francesco Xanto (1534) showing Alexander presenting crown to Roxana, dated on back and inscribed including signature Xanto :A·. Metropolitan Mus. of Art.

FIG. 552. Small faïence vase from Italy and dated 1777 which shows that this primitive sort of treatment and simple acanthus decoration carried later than might otherwise be supposed. Ht. 5¾". Plummer, Ltd.

influence that places like Delft copied it. At this time the wares of North Italy become more important and we can come to those later.

Meanwhile let us briefly review our findings:

1.—Lustre reached its greatest artistic perfection in Europe in Spain. The Italians brought it to greater technical perfection but almost from the beginning misapplied it trying to paint pictures with it.

2.—As an aid to the variations of color of lustre we find molding and modeling of surfaces in Spain and then much more in Italy.

3.—Color of all things in art seemed to appeal to the Italians most of all and it was heaped on to all ware as much as was possible and more than was good taste.

4.—The pictorial and narrative element which was entirely out of place on pottery became dominant and most destructive to the art. The Italians never seemed to grasp the beauty of an object in itself but always had a yen to wrap it with stories, sentiments and emotions.

Thus these wares were like horrible nightmare fantasies or potteries out of a dream. They had gnomes and giants, rapes, murders and all manner of unholy things, all daubed on them with glowing but often displeasing colors. They offended all but the cruel, the gluttonous and the depraved; they, better than all the tales of the Renaissance of sudden death and treachery, of hate and love unnatural, tell what the Renaissance was really like, and in them, so strange to the soul of man, we find a beauty of horror and fascination; we look at them as a city crowd will look at an accident and stand and shiver at the blood. They constituted an honest outpouring in the main but God preserve us from the sort of people who made them!

CHAPTER XVI

FRENCH, GERMAN AND NETHERLANDS TIN-GLAZED WARES

FAÏENCE OR DELFT

FRENCH FAÏENCE

THE art of lustre died because of the Italian desire to paint pictures for which it was too difficult a medium. The old art of modeling inherited from the Romans, Greeks and from the Near East, had been kept alive by the added beauty that uneven surfaces give to lustre. However, we shall drop it for this chapter and continue with the development of tin slip, tin enamel or tin glaze and the opportunities this metal made possible for decoration.

EARLIEST FRENCH FAÏENCE AND LYONS

The Italian potters taught the French the art of faïence and up to the 17th century it was sporadic. The earliest examples are from Provence, Agen and the church at Brioude where tiles were found decorated with manganese-purple and green and thought to date from the late 14th century. Benedicto Angelo de Laurent, the Italian potter, started work at Lyons in 1512 and continued until 1536. In 1556 Sebastiano Griffo from Genoa and Domenico Tardessir from Faenza made Urbino style wares, and in 1575 Giulio Gambino and Gian Francesco da Pesaro opened another kiln. Generally speaking the characteristics of the wares are these:
1.—Three conical mountains in the background of the landscapes. 2.—Waves arranged in regular rows in seascapes. 3.—Flesh tones which are reddish-yellow or orange. 4.—A distinctive light blue for sky and sea and the inscriptions refer to the compositions on the front of the plates just as they did in Italy. None are dated.

ROUEN

From 1540 to 1560 Masseot Abaquesne made tiles at Rouen with French Renaissance designs and the first dated example comes from there. There are two paving tiles from the Château d'Écouen, one at Chantilly and one still at Rouen all inscribed "à Rouen 1542." In the Musée de Cluny there is an altar step from the chapel of the Château de La Bâtie d'Urfé decorated with canopies, flaming urns, winged female figures and angels playing musical

374

ínstruments in pale blue, yellow, light green and manganese on a white ground. A cartouche in the center dates these 1551.

Nothing more is known until in 1644 Nicolas Poirel started a kiln followed by Edme Poterat and his son and we are told that during the reign of Louis XIV their wares were noted for large sizes and were decorated in blue, or in blue combined with red or yellow-ochre. The designs were of palmettes, scrolls and festoons in radial arrangements on the wide borders and Chinese elements were combined with "classical baroque."

Fig. 553. Panel of faïence tiles from Rouen. 17th cent. Length 19¾". Metropolitan Mus. of Art. Note: These tiles are not correctly assembled.

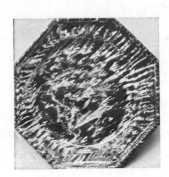

Fig. 554. Rouen 16th cent. panel of tiles, Masseot Abaquesne. Length 38". Metropolitan Mus. of Art.
Fig. 555. 16th cent. Rouen faïence dish. Interesting glaze of mottled type which we have seen from Crete, through Near East and Far East, and finally which was Rockingham and Benton ware of later times. Dia. 18⅛". Metropolitan Mus. of Art.
Fig. 556. Faïence albarello from Laurent Abaquesne, Rouen. 16th cent. showing strong Italiaṇ influence. Metropolitan Mus. of Art.

MOUSTIERS

The Clérissy family made pottery at Moustiers before 1700 and these wares were also large and were decorated with hunting scenes from the engravings of Tempesta. They also made large rectangular trays with light baroque decorations after Bérain, first in blue on white and then polychrome. About 1677 one of the Clérissy family went to Marseilles in St. Jean-du-Désert where he made potteries like the Moustiers ones.

NANTES, NÎMES AND NEVERS

Gian Ferro established himself in Nantes in 1588. In Nîmes the potter Sigalon signed a pilgrim bottle of Italian style in 1581. In Nevers the three brothers named Conrade, kinsmen of Giulio Gambino of Lyons and Faenza, started in 1578 but there is also evidence that Scipio Gambini had been there before that. Lastly by rumor there was supposed to have been a potter named Oratio Borniola at Le Croisic to whom is attributed the ribbed dishes with fine scrolls in blue and orange-yellow dating around 1630, but similar things were also made at Antwerp and other northern cities.

The wares at Nevers followed Urbino and Faenza in both blue and white and polychrome but great baroque jugs with dragon handles were distinctive and had hunting scenes on them. Large oval basins such as the one in Cluny with the Triumph of Amphitrite were made, the outlines being in manganese, nude figures in two shades of yellow or also in manganese and a typical use of the same color, in draperies, tree trunks and other details, which never occurs in Urbino. The rims of these are also treated separately from the centers as is not the case in Urbino ware.

FIG. 557. Polychrome dish of Nevers ware showing Italian influence particularly in grotesqueri of border. Dia. 9¾″. 1644. Metropolitan Mus. of Art.

FIG. 558. Nevers, so-called "Persian style" (A.D. 1640–1700) faïence plate. Dia. 9¾″. Metropolitan Mus. of Art.

The Conrade family copied the della Robbia sculptured ware. The third brother, Augustin, founded a school of potters and Pierre Custode made the "Bleu Persan" ware typical of the second period of Nevers. It has charm but little to do with Persian design. There are three types: 1.—blue glazed ground with white decoration and at times gilding, 2.—yellow glazed ground painted with white and on top of it blue so that the blue does not turn green over the yellow, 3.—white tin enameled ground with polychrome, blue alone or less frequently, green decoration. The first is common, the second rare and the third almost nonexistent. There are Chinese figures in green on white, blue on white and also manganese on white, the latter showing distinct Delft influence. There were also "marbled" wares splashed with white on blue as in the wine cooler from Vestlandske Museum, Bergen. Note how again the old Egyptian technique crops up as we have seen it in Crete, Italy, T'ang China, Persia and elsewhere.

Nevers, being a large pottery center a little later than Rouen and Moustiers, copied both wares. It was a strongly Catholic city and the potters made sacred figures and holy-water stoups to set in niches at street corners. It is here also that "Faïence Patriotiques" were plentiful; jugs, cisterns, barrels and plates painted with childish crudity with such subjects as the Bastille,

FIG. 559. Nevers pilgrim bott'e dating between 1640–1700. Ht. 9¾". Metropolitan Mus. of Art.

FIG. 560. Nevers ewer of faïence (1640–1700). Ht. 12¾". Metropolitan Mus. of Art.

tree of liberty, etc., and inscribed with "La Liberté ou la Mort," or "Ca Ira Vive la Nation," etc. These are of course late and of little value but many have been sold in America since the late craze for French provincial antiques, just as also hundreds of "Empire" vases which are not even made in France have been sold. The Nevers ware is of whitish-buff clay, can easily be scratched, and the blue glaze is warm, soft, very smooth and apparently even but when seen with the magnifying glass is full of tiny sunken holes or specks. The white pigment is chalky and in the same detail may vary from an enamel-like thickness to transparent thinness. The brush strokes are apparent and the handling is pretty rough. Lastly the weight of the ware is surprisingly light for the thickness of the walls.

The course that these wares went through is much like that so often seen in Europe: First Italian feeling, second in the 17th century Chinese influences, third the polychrome gave way to the blue and white with manganese outlines probably because it was easier to make, fourth classical themes again giving way to late Ming and a reversion to polychrome; and at the end of the 18th century the growing effects of Napoleon's conquests and the Revolution.

GERMAN FAÏENCE

The faïence of Spain, Italy and France had little to do with that of Germany. There is as much difference as there is between Latin country music and German music. The north country liked stoneware and the craving for color is replaced by a demand for modeling. The earliest example we know is a plate dated 1526 in Nuremberg. It purports to show Samson and Delilah but it is in the style of Burgkmair and they are all dolled up with puffed sleeves and other details of the costumes of the period. The colors are in the Italian manner, manganese, blue, yellow and light green. Another dated 1530 is in blue only, similar to the Venetian wares of even date and shows the Madonna and Child on a crescent while still another dated 1531 is of similar treatment and shows a half figure of a woman in German costume.

FIG. 561. Lower Rhine earthenware plate decorated in brown, green and yellow with border dated 1783. Dia. 8¾". Metropolitan Mus. of Art.

A fluted bowl in the museum at Sigmaringen recalls the embossed dishes of Faenza and Castel Durante and here also is a ring shaped bottle of 1544. This shape originates with the metal work of the Near East and was also made in pottery there, later coming to Italy and thence throughout Europe; but it became especially dear to the hearts of the Germans. It is an impractical form holding little and unfitted to the hand of man, but it offered the potters a chance to show off their technical skill. At Ulm there is an alberello with a portrait of a woman on it and a dish in the style of Deruta is in the Hamburg Museum. I know of nothing much more of this type.

One note that Hannover makes which is of interest is that some of these plates have been called Swiss but are proven to be of German origin because the Swiss plates have a small loop set on the back perpendicular to the rim and radially, for the purpose of hanging them on the wall. How infallible this is I do not know.

Owl jars or "Eulenkrugen" were not only made in stoneware but also in the imported tin glaze on pottery and there is one believed to have been made by Augustin Hirsvogel of Nuremberg which has underglaze blue and shields on its breast modeled in relief and is seemingly painted with oil colors and

gilded. Between the legs is the date 1540. The heads on these jars are removable from the neck. They were supposed also to be Swiss but are now
allocated to South Germany. Many fakes are made by Fleischmann of
Nuremberg and others. A double eagle is spoken of by Robert Schmidt (*Der
Cicerone,* II, p. 667 f.) also treated with underglaze blue and with shield
painted with oil color. It is now in Coburg. The owl jars remind us of the
Shang period (1766–1122 B.C.) bronze ones of China. These could never
have been seen by the German potters and one wonders what the origin of
their jars could have been. Perhaps the owl is just a good solid form
which is sufficiently jar shaped to suggest itself. There is one theory for the
design which we shall quote under the stoneware section but it does not
seem fundamental.

From about Kreussen came cylindrical jars (one of which is dated 1618)
which are painted in blue on white. Hamburg produced similar ones the
earliest of which is dated 1624 and from Hanau again similar ones reach
from 1661. They might be called alberello forms but with convex rather than
concave sides. They have escaped the blight of Italian pictorial ideas and
are decorated with symmetrical flowers of Indian origin which came in
via Holland. However the constant use of the spiral with them seems indigenous when we remember the Halstadt Culture, but how the motives
of that very ancient culture could have been brought to the 17th century
is a question. Toward the end of the century the quality of these wares
deteriorated, the blue getting darker and heavier, the glaze coarse and
glistening and the brushwork less deft.

Faïence of Hamburg

Another early ware which reached its height about 1640 to 1650 has been
found around Hamburg and the arms of Hamburg and of Hamburgers are
commonly painted on it. The last dated piece is 1656. Some have letter
signatures which have not been identified. There are a few dishes but not
in quite the same direct spirit as the jugs which are more numerous. These
latter are well formed with flaring foot and narrow cylindrical neck from
which springs a strong handle down to the body. The ground color is warm
due to the body toning through the tin enamel. The blue is strong and bright
and touches of yellow are used. Most of them have a front medallion of a
merchant's mark, an emblem, a shield of arms or something of the sort. Only
one is known with flowers and it is probably of a different source.

Other German Faïence

With the opening of the factory at Hanau in 1661 by two Dutch potters
and another in Frankfort-on-the-Main in 1666 Far Eastern influences are
felt as translated by the Dutch, and the latter factory is renowned for its
large blue and white jars and plates in a sort of remote late Ming style.
Erfurt, in Thuringia, Potsdam (where powder blue was tried), Berlin, Dresden, Ansbach, Nuremberg and Bayreuth also made poor copies of Chinese
blue and white and polychrome wares. French painting of naturalistic flowers
was done by the glass painters such as Johann Schaper and Abraham Helm-

hack of Nuremberg who did landscapes and figures in black and called "schwarzlot," or in polychrome. This influence came through Strasbourg and Marseilles and was carried on to rococo forms by Johann Tännich, Ludwig Ehrenreigh and Johann Eberhardt among others who followed in factories at Kiel and Mosbach.

But it is obvious that faïence was a poor thing in Germany and the preference was all for the stoneware which we shall take up shortly.

"Delft" or the Faïence of the Netherlands

In the Low Countries things were different for "Delfsche porselyn" was a great influence in Europe in the 17th and 18th centuries. It was Italy again that was the first source. In 1548 Guido di Savino set up shop in Antwerp where his sons had already been struggling and this started the work. A tile memorial to them and dated 1547, now in the Vleeschhuis Museum, Antwerp, is considered the oldest work of faïence made on Netherlandish soil. It is definitely Italian in all respects.

There are also many small alberelli from the hospital at Middleburg which was destroyed in 1570. Some tiles are found so frequently in certain places that they would seem to have been made in the Netherlands rather than in Italy, though they show very close similarity to pieces from Florence. Bernard Rackham says in the 14th edition Encyclopaedia Britannica, "About 1560–70 maiolica potters from Antwerp carried their art as Protestant refugees to the northern provinces which were to be Holland (by 1579) and England." Rotterdam and Haarlem became centers of production of earthenwares and wall-tiles with animal, flower and fruit motives in strong coloring, and large tile work pictures with figure subjects. Toward 1650 Delft came to the fore and for more than a century continued with its numerous potteries, known by their signs (the Peacock, the Star etc.) as a thriving center of industry exporting its wares all over the civilized world. It is difficult to prove any piece actually of this period but it is agreed that several dishes with overloaded design in blue may possibly be.

Strangely, it was the failure of the beer business that helped Delft ware. Strong competition had made the breweries fail and someone had the idea that the new industry of potting might be housed in them. Men were out of work, thus capital, a roof and willing hands were all ready. The Guild of St. Luke founded in 1611 had only ten members up to 1640. Now between 1651 and 1660 there were 20 and between 1662 and 1663, 12 more were admitted. The "plateelbakkers" became so important that they took family names. Up to that time they had passed the baptismal name in the genitive form to their children. This great success was in spite of the fact that the clay had largely to be imported from Tournai and Mülheim.

As this was a purely commercial influence let us digress for a moment and consider this new

Fig. 562. Dutch cup of red earthenware ornamented with a cock inside and borders outside in green and yellow slip under transparent glaze. Italian in feeling. 15th–16th cent. Dia. 5″. Metropolitan Mus. of Art.

Right: Large deep dish with brown body and tin white glaze decorated in blue underglaze. Text is the Ten Commandments, etc. 17th or 18th cent. Dia. 15¼″. International Studio Art Corp.

Right: Ewer made at "Rose factory," marked *Roos* in blue, having typical famille rose design but shape showing Near Eastern influence. c. 1700. Ht. c. 12″. Metropolitan Mus. of Art.

Left: Plate, 17th cent., probably of Ster factory. Dia. 12″. Metropolitan Mus. of Art.

Left: Dish with grotesques in Urbino, Italian style. c. 1600. Decoration in yellows, browns and blue on white ground. Back also white. Dia. 5½″. Metropolitan Mus. of Art.
Center: Plate with mark of Miss Amerensie van Kessel, proprietress in 1675 of factory "De Dubbele Schenkkan." Kakiemon style with light colors of red, blue, green and gold with turquoise. Dia. 12¼″. International Studio Art Corp.

Polychrome plate with mark of A. Pynacker. The border in three shades of blue and center with "carnival figure" in blue, red, green and yellow. Dia. 15¾″. 17th cent. International Studio Art Corp.

DELFT OF VARIOUS STYLES

PLATE 120

Set of 12 Delft plates from the Porceleijne Bijl (Porcelain Axe) under Huibrecht Brouwer and dating late 17th to early 18th cent., representing the months of the year. Dias. 9 1/16".

DELFT PLATES FROM "PORCELAIN AXE" FACTORY

PLATE 121

Set of "month of year" plates continued.

DELFT PLATES FROM "PORCELAIN AXE" FACTORY

PLATE 122

force: I have spoken about religion as a weapon and its effect in bringing lustre to Spain, nay the East to Europe. We have noted how art was, as it were, turned off and on by the ancient conquests of arms. Here we meet a new and powerful force *which may be devastating to all art for centuries.*

Briefly it seems to follow in about this way: First there were chieftains of brawn and brains who led tribes or nations as naturally as a stag leads his herd. When they conquered they looted, and artists were employed to make glorified statues of them or to please their tastes. Secondly there stood in the market place an unarmed man who spoke about a Heaven to come after death and put ideas of good and evil in the heads of the masses so that they would rise up and overthrow the chieftains. When these men conquered there was not much for artists to do, but soon the various churches again put the artists to work glorifying Heaven and helping to keep the masses impressed. Thirdly came the invention of the real use of money as a weapon and it was found that with wealth the churches could be bought, arms could be hired and one could sit on top of the world. Men said, we shall skip the trouble of fighting for an earthly heaven, we shall skip all ephemeral promises of some heaven to come after death, we can see clearly that we can buy our own heaven with money. Of course artists were needed to decorate this heaven. But certain troubles arose which are not yet solved.

The invention of the new weapon *money* did not stop the efficiency of the old ones and when one man got all the chips at times those who wielded *religion* would talk of the evils of wealth and the masses would rise up and take away the money from the rich man, or some gentleman who believed in the more direct weapon of *force* would simply pull a gun and take what he liked. Each time the power becomes too great in one of these forces the other two upset it. We have recently seen great stacks of wealth in the world and we are seeing them melt away under the rising of the masses on the "religious principles" of the trade unions, revolutions, strikes and such, but these mass movements even in Russia have finally given way to the old original primitive power of a leader and the use of force. I predict that the chieftains will fight it out, then there will be a revival of the talkers with new principles and then again will come the laxity which permits accumulation of personal wealth. Only to go through the cycle again. As we later trace the results of money-getting on the arts of the 18th century it will be seen exactly how the blight works. Now in the 17th century the mass movements of the churches both Christian and Muslim as well as Buddhistic had had their day; we enter upon the day of the merchant and we shall see what his effect is upon the 18th and 19th centuries so far as ceramic art is concerned.

The Dutch continued the Italian habit of taking designs from the painters of the period. Biblical and genre subjects surrounded with baroque ornament prevailed. Lastly great interest had centered in China and Japan because of the rising power of the Dutch East India Company.

This company had been chartered in 1602 for the purpose of regulating trade in the Indian Ocean and to help in prosecuting the long war for independence against Spain and Portugal. It was a long and arduous route necessitated by the war with these countries, around the Cape of Good Hope, but it seemed to pay and many companies were formed in competition pursuing it and fighting among themselves. The formation of one company was accomplished to do away with the contention and it had the rights to maintain sea forces, plant colonies, erect forts, make peace or war, coin money and maintain full administrative, judicial and legislative authority from the Straits of Magellan westward to the Cape of Good Hope. The headquarters were in Batavia, Java. In 1638 to 1658 it expelled the Portuguese from Ceylon and Malacca. It grew throughout the century and in 1669 it had 150 ships for trading, 40 war ships, 10,000 soldiers—and it paid a dividend of 40%. It had eight governments:—Amboyna, Banda, Ternate, Macassar, Malacca, Ceylon, Cape of Good Hope and Java, while trading posts were placed in Bengal on the Coromandel Coast, at Surat, Gambroon (or Bunder Abbas) in the Persian Gulf and in Siam. Thus we see that it had *no direct contact with China* and although many porcelains and other works of art were brought to Holland by trade, they were little understood. *This accounts for the whole spirit of 18th century appreciation of Chinese art, or lack of it.* It was thought exotic and strange and was never taken seriously. Few, if any, could tell Japanese design from Chinese and who cared? Both were frequently mixed with Renaissance design and baroque scrolls surround Chinese figures or what were thought to be Chinese figures. But some craftsmen did make remarkable copies of Chinese vases even if they knew nothing about their reason for being, and this is the second great wave of Chinese influence. The first came across the top of the world on the Northern Caravan Route to Turkey, Damascus and on to the shores of the Mediterranean. This second came the long way around to the coast of Holland. It was borne solely by commercialism and probably no other cargo was so precious even from the long range dollars and cents basis.

DELFT PAINTERS

Frederick van Frijtom was a great landscape painter from 1658. The only fully signed panel by him is in Amsterdam and was done about 1660 in blue on white and has most interesting trees and rock formations, figures, and

FIG. 564. Shaving basin with buff body, tin glaze and underglaze blue with iron red and gilding added. Late 17th cent. Delft ware. Length 12". International Studio Art Corp.

FIG. 563. Late 17th cent. blue and white plate with Chinese design. Dia. 10". Metropolitan Mus. of Art.

a bridge. It has a fine feeling of depth. Also attributed to Van Frijtom are a number of plates with centers painted and wide rims left plain.

Abraham de Cooge was also a well known painter in oils who came from Haarlem but as he only dated and did not sign his pieces they are difficult to identify.

G. 565. Set of twelve plates showing "The Passion of Christ" with a four line inscription on the back and monogram of W. Kleffius the maker who worked in the style of Lambertus van Eenhoorn and sta.ted his factor, 1663. Dias. 10¼". From the W. R. Hearst Coll.

Aelbrecht Cornelis de Keizer did sign his work AK in monogram and in the Louvre there is a beautiful bottle by him which has a fanciful Chinese bird surrounded by feathery flowers and foliage. There is also a well established small square tea caddy with a "happy boy" in medallion on a ground of conventional flowers very like the Chinese. But his style was soon copied even to the monogram. Mr. Hannover says he translated the Japanese and Chinese porcelain pictures with "dauntless fantasy" but I think him a bit too dauntless myself. He was followed by his two sons-in-law; Jacobus and Adriaen Pijnacker. All worked in polychrome as well as blue on white. Adriaen signed his work APK usually in red and many forgers also copied him. He later made blue, red and gold ware after Imari with figures and less formal than the originals.

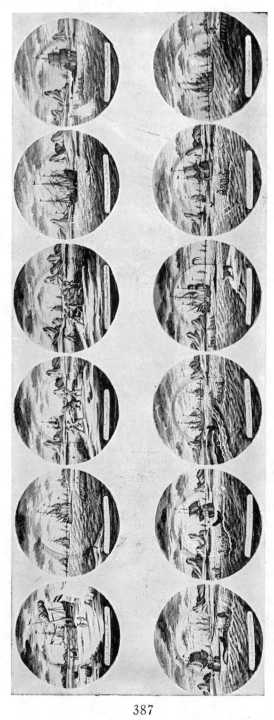

Fig. 566. Set of twelve plates possibly by Justus Brouwer or at least very much in his style and of about 1700. Dia. 10″. From the W. R. Hearst Coll.

387

Among other great painters were the family of Wouters van Eenhoorn, his sons Lambertus and Samuel, and their rival Louwijs Fictoor whose signature LF is hardly distinguishable from their LVE. They all made blue

FIG. 567. Pair of vases decorated in Chinese manner, Delft, late 17th or early 18th cent. Ht. 5½″. Metropolitan Mus. of Art.

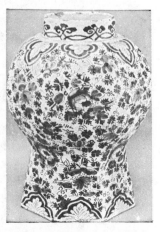

FIG. 568. Blue and white Delft jar of strong Chinese influence, dating late 17th or early 18th cent. Ht. 10″. Metropolitan Mus. of Art.

FIG. 569. Delft 17th cent. candlestick with blue decoration on white, probably copy of Ming Chinese example. Samuel van Eenhoorn, 1674. Mark SE VIII in blue. Gift of Seth K. Sweetsor. Mus. of Fine Arts, Boston.

FIG. 570. Cruet and stand marked AP in red and to Adriaen Pijnacker c. 1680. "Old Imari" style in red, and gold. Ht. 6¾″. Metropolitan Mus. of Art.

and white and liver colored styles making a specialty of the "cachemire" style which was supposed to have originated with Lambertus van Eenhoorn. Others were Ghicbrecht Lambrechts Kruyk who did blue and white on a bluish glaze, Samuel Pererius van Berenvelt, Claas Jansz Messchert, Jores Mesch specializing in blue and white, Jacob Wemmersz and his son Rochus Hoppestyn, Cornelis Cornelisz van der Hoeve, Augustijn Reijgens and many others including Lambartus Kleffius who claimed to have invented a red stoneware, on down to David Kam who purchased the old factory of Claas Messchert and made pieces with colored glaze over slip.

Toward the end of the 17th century the factories came into the hands of merchants who ran them simply for profit and deterioration set in with only a few of the older potters standing out a while for quality in work.

Potting Methods

These potters worked in two ways. In one process the colors, which were green (a mixture of cobalt and antimony), red (made from the finest sifted bole) and less extensively yellow (of antimony) and violet (from oxide of manganese) were painted, having been mixed with water, within an outline made of cobalt and iron oxide or merely an impure blue called "trek" upon the dry and dusty tin-enamel in which the piece had been dipped after a preliminary light firing. The tin enamel had not yet been fired, of course, and was very absorbent and unpleasant to work on. When the painting was finished it was powdered by the so-called "vloerwercker" with a "kwaart" which was a fine dust of colorless lead glaze. Then the piece was fired at a high temperature and at a single opera-tion the tin glaze, the metallic oxide colors and the lead glaze were fused into one. The "kwaart" acted like the Italian "marzacotto" and gave more brilliance to the colors just as varnish does to a painting. The undecorated side did not receive this treatment and is therefore more rough, while the face of the piece has typically tiny specks as though pricked with a needle. With the blue and other colors, of course, there was no possibility of really imitating Chinese wares in anything but the drawing, which we have already criticised.

Fig. 571. "Hoti" or god of wealth and happiness, made and signed by Lambertus van Eenhoorn. Decoration blue on white. Ht. 8½". From W. R. Hearst Coll.

The other method was the same with the addition of another (or third) firing for iron red which was painted on the fused glaze, and a fourth for the gilding. Each of these colors takes successively lower heats to set them and will not stand the higher temperatures. This is the way the Japanese wares were copied. Similarly in attempting to reproduce some of the Chinese wares the blue was painted on the tin enamel surface and fired while the other colors were added later, these usually being an enamel-like green and iron-red. In all these methods requiring a third firing the "kwaart" was omitted. Up to about 1650 they stuck to the blue and white technique and then with great suddenness developed a full palette adding to the above colors black, and by the 18th century a rose similar to the famille rose of the Chinese.

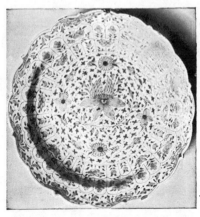

FIG. 572. Blue and white Delft plate with Chinese design. 18th cent. Dia. 12⅛". Metropolitan Mus. of Art.

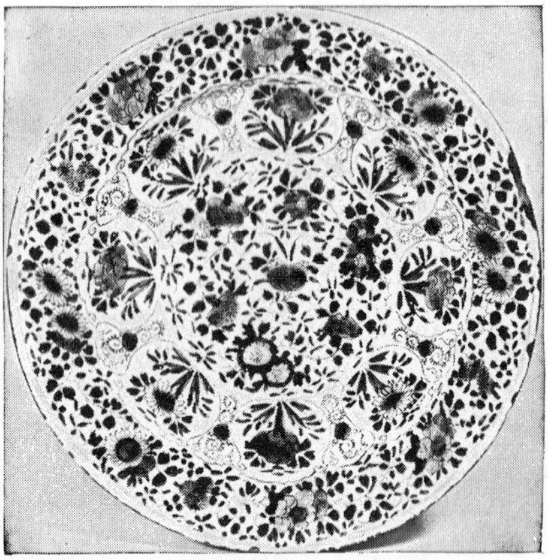

FIG. 573. Late 17th or early 18th cent. Dutch plate with Chinese design in blue on white ground. Dia. 10¼". Metropolitan Mus. of Art.

The Hollanders did not add much, if anything, to the art of ceramics but they did act as a means of distribution of ideas and particularly those of Far Eastern art. It is true that they became sidetracked in the painting of pictures on ceramics but this was probably due to the Italian influence and their quaint genre subjects were their own and have some appeal. Among their own quaint ideas are the musical plates which had on them scores with

FIG. 574. Three 17th cent. tin enameled tiles. 5" square. Metropolitan Mus. of Art.

verses written in open book medallions accompanied by various designs of musical instruments and other decorations. These were used after dinner in general singing. The Dutch were great singers and everyone carried a song book in his pocket so one can imagine the popularity of these plates.

It was in the 18th century which we shall come to later that the tasteless oddities were made.

CHAPTER XVII

EUROPEAN MODELED AND MOLDED WARES TO THE 18TH CENTURY

THERE has always been a tendency to imitate metal in the making of pottery and although this led in many instances to the worst faults in design and technique it also led to unforeseen benefits such as the discovery of lustre and the development of modeled wares. The spontaneous scratching of the surface and pinching up of the clay to decorate primitive potteries shows us that sculpture is so much a part of potting that it is difficult to separate the two. The work of the della Robbia family may be considered pottery by some and sculpture by others though, of course, it is both. The imitation of metal vessels developed this sculptural tendency and led to the wares of Kertch, Apulia, Campania and finally and worst of all Canosa but somewhere along the line this imitation had changed to sculpture. At the worst we can blame the metal copying for relief in imitation of repoussé and for a too slender structure such as fragile handles and spouts practical in metal but not in fired clay. At best it led to all the beautiful modeled work of the ages. While sculpture as such must be judged independently.

ARRETINE WARE OR TERRA SIGILLATA

During Roman times along with the wares of bad taste good sensible use was made of metal forms thoughtfully adapted to pottery as a medium, as we can see in the examples from Arezzo or Arretium in Etruria and which are variously called, "Arretine ware," "Samian ware," or "terra sigillata." The second name is a misnomer and is not used today. The last has become the name for the whole group of wares, usually of red body but sometimes of black in the earlier examples from Arezzo, and found in Italy, Spain (though not made there) and the Near East where they had been traded, as well as in France. A similar ware was made by the Gaulish provinces of Rome such as Graufesenque, Lezoux, etc. The molded reliefs or "sigilla" were separate stamps applied to a model vessel which was then cast in a mold used to make others complete. The forms are simple and usually without handles, consisting of bowls, cups and saucers of cylindrical or globular forms. Dr. Dragendorff's chart gives an excellent idea of the development. The first decoration was copied direct from embossed silver ware from Alexandria and Antioch and the bodies are covered with foliate and floral designs, masks and various decorative details, human and animal figures, shown in processions, sacrifices, hunts, battles, dances, feasts and various

391

rituals and episodes of the life of the times. The lustrous effect of these wares was produced by an alkaline glaze which also imparts a deep richness to the color. Potter's signatures were made in the mold and appear on the rims, bases or in the designs inside or outside of the vessels usually enclosed in a rectangle, foot-print or other fancifully formed tablet, either sunk or in relief. Some of the wares were plain and were signed inside the base. Full names or abbreviations were used as for instance the potter Marcus Perennius signed M.Pe, M.Per, M.Pere, M.Peren and also M.Perenni. Various slaves' names also appear on his vessels sometimes alone or at times with his signature. Some names represent factories. All the available material from these vessels has been tabulated and has been a great aid in establishing dates of other Roman objects, archaeological sites and other data. The ware dates from about 200 B.C. to A.D. 100 in Italy but continues in Gaul to about the middle of the 3d century.

GAULISH TERRA SIGILLATA

The French product is much like the Italian except that the ware is harder, the color darker and brighter and the decoration in lower relief and with smaller figures. In other words it is a technically better product but artistically deteriorated. The names are Gaulish and even Roman names are spelt in Gaulish fashion. The early bowls are cylindrical and then become hemispherical.

GERMAN TERRA SIGILLATA

In the Rhenish pottery which was first grey or black and later red an invention was made called "barbotine" which was simple slip applied by piping much as a caterer decorates a cake with frosting. It was first used to make small flowers on the rims of flat dishes but by the 3d century began to replace the molded design on standard Roman shaped vessels. This is a completely new technique for Europe and was much used not only in Germany but elsewhere such as at Lezoux. Another "invention" caused by the desire for complicated shapes which could not be cast with their designs in molds, was the application of plaques or medallions bearing designs pressed in them. Of course, this was only a revival of a very ancient stunt but now it became very popular and we see portraits of emperors, theatrical scenes, gladiatorial contests, etc. with explanatory inscriptions. It is interesting to see that the North Countries which had not been at all interested in painted wares now became enthusiastic enough in modeled wares to add technical processes. However, when the Roman power withdrew, the people of all Europe sank again to the making of crude primitive pottery unglazed but nevertheless showing strength of design.

MEDIEVAL POTTERIES OF EUROPE

FRANCE

It will be remembered that from 330 Constantinople was gaining power while Rome was losing. In 486 Gaul was lost and by the 7th century the

French 16th cent. Avignon
ewer much like some found in
Germany in general form. Ht.
14¼". Metropolitan Mus. of
Art.

Faïence pitcher attr. to 15th cent. of type known as
poteries de Savignies but probably from *Beauvais* or
Avignon. Simple and well worked out design of good
proportions. Ht. 6⅜". Metropolitan Mus. of Art.

French 16th cent. Normandy vase of
faïence labeled *"Pré d'Auge."* A bit top
heavy and weak at base. Ht. 10⅜". LeBreton Coll. Metropolitan Mus. of Art.

French 17th cent. pilgrim bottle after metal
repoussé one, possibly. Ht. 9½". LeBreton
Coll. Metropolitan Mus. of Art.

MEDIEVAL POTTERIES OF FRANCE

PLATE 123

Roman Empire was at a low ebb. In 406 the Barbarians crossed the Rhine and invaded even into Spain while in 718 to 732 the Muhammedan invasion was beyond the Pyrenees. Invasion, famine, plague and pestilence did not make a very fertile soil for the growth of the art of pottery and even under Pippin and Charlemagne in the 9th century there was more interest in conquest than in the arts. The wares were at first crude and unglazed but later were covered with a soft galena or lead sulfide glaze stained brown with iron or green with copper. The old methods of decoration were used combined with scratching, impressing, and application of strips of clay. Slip was used and where the glaze would often be yellowish or brown on the clay proper it was green over a white slip or greyish blue toward the end of the 15th century. Rarely painting was done with white, brown or red clay but more frequently various colors were combined in relief decoration, and some of the vessels were in human or animal forms taken from those of metal aquamaniles (vessels for pouring water on the hands before and after eating with one's fingers or for church ceremony). Many of the forms were typically French Gothic and those from Avignon, Beauvais and Savigny are alike in that they are good craftsmanship.

FIG. 575. French cistern with red body and brown slip and glaze of transparent lead type, under which is white appliqué of flowers. (c. 1770). Ht. 17″. Plummer, Ltd.

FIG. 576. Ewer with brownish lead glaze and touches of yellow and green, probably from Avignon. Late 16th or early 17th cent. Ht. 11⅛″. Metropolitan Mus. of Art.

There were many instances recorded of the bringing in of Italian and Spanish workmen by certain nobles. The Duke of Burgundy brought Jehan de Moustiers and Jehan-le-Voleur in 1391 to paint tiles for his palaces at Arras and Hesdin. At Poitiers, Duke Jean de Berry had John of Valencia, the "Saracen," do tiles in the Spanish manner in 1384. But these seemed to have no effect on the pottery of the country and even later when Francis I

(1494–1547) brought Girolamo della Robbia from Italy to decorate his "Petit Château de Madrid" in 1529 and when Masseot Abaquesne came to manufacture at Rouen about 1542, there seemed to be no effect on other potters.

It was in the 13th century that glaze was revived by the Savignies near Beauvais and in the 14th century La-Chapelle-des-Pots near Saintes became another important center. A little Italian influence was found in the use of the "sgraffito" method of decoration in slip, and either Spanish or Italian influence in the adoption of the alberello form about 1500. In Normandy there was also an industry for the making of gable finials of pottery with polychrome glazes.

GERMAN POTTERY

In Germany conditions were the same but in the 14th century the first stoneware was made. It was a high fired, semi-vitrified ware. Before this the pottery was brown and with ornate Gothic cut, stamped and applied decoration. The best known example of this ware is to be seen in the reddish-brown earthenware cup from Dreihausen, near Marburg in Hesse, which dates about 1400 and is now in the Kunsindustrimuseum, Copenhagen. This is not a cup one would drink from comfortably and we need not go into an aesthetic criticism of it.

Floor-tiles were unglazed in Germany with stamped or molded designs, while those in France and England were often two colored inlayed and glazed wares. Tiles were also used in Germany for stoves and were unglazed at first. Others were designed for architectural use.

ITALY

The obsession for painting which gripped Italian potters due to the wonderful new discovery of tin-enamel and the possibilities of colors of all sorts, blinded them to the possibilities of sculptured form but it is natural that in Italy sculpture should also occur and, if the potters in general were found lacking, it was the sculptors who took up the art.

LUCA DELLA ROBBIA (1399–1482)

There are no real prototypes for the works of the della Robbias. Technique had just come to a point where tin-enamel could be made to cover flaws in material and still be made so thin as not to clog up the details of fine sculpture. Luca was the son of a Florentine named Simone di Marco della Robbia who apprenticed him to Ghiberti. No sculpture of the 15th century surpasses his singing gallery in the cathedral at Florence, now in the Museo del Duomo, but his most important work is the tomb of Benozzo Federighi, bishop of Fiesole, which is now in the church of SS. Trinita in Florence. An effigy of the bishop lies on a sarcophagus sculptured with reliefs of angels holding a wreath which contains the inscription while above are the three-quarter figures of Christ and St. John and the Virgin. The whole is surrounded by a rectangular frame of tiles of exquisite beauty, painted in realistic colors with designs of flowers and fruit. From 1442 to 1446 he worked upon the

"Madonna and Child" by Luca della Robbia showing the superb sensitiveness of facial expression, sure knowledge of anatomy and fine modeling of the hands which mark this great genius. Ht. 31½". Metropolitan Mu:
of Art.

"MADONNA AND CHILD" BY LUCA DELLA ROBBIA

Plate 124

"Ascension and Resurrection" and reliefs of the "Madonna between two Angels" in the Via dell'Agnolo.

It is not necessary to list all of his great works. They are all known and mostly in museums. Many of those attributed to him are by younger members of his family or students, if not by actual forgers. We must, however, state that it is untrue that his earlier works were white or blue and white; actually among the earliest are medallions of the four Evangelists in the vault of the Brunelleschi's Pazzi chapel at St. Croce which are colored in various shades of blue, black, purple, yellow and green. His chief pupils were Andrea, his nephew, and Agostino di Duccio.

ANDREA DELLA ROBBIA
(1435–1525)

Andrea's works are not less beautiful than Luca's and he extended them to various architectural elements such as friezes, lavabos, fountains and large retables. There is only one sculpture in marble by him and that is an altar in S. Maria delle Grazie near Arezzo.

Fig. 577. Plaque representing "Prudence" by Luca della Robbia (1399–1482) made in Florence of tin enameled terracotta with some ordinary lead enamel also. Dia. 69". Metropolitan Mus. of Art.

_The characteristics of his work are a great sweetness and grace of pose. Although he did many reliefs of the Madonna and Child, they are all different and all beautiful. Sometimes he omitted the glaze from the bare parts such as the faces, hands and feet of his figures particularly when well modeled in the realistic manner. This was, of course, an old custom of the T'ang and Ming sculptors of China. The treatment is to be seen in his tympanum relief of St. Dominic and St. Francis in the loggia of the Florentine hospital of S. Paolo which is a design suggested but not slavishly following a fresco by Fra Angelico in the cloister of St. Marks. One of Andrea's most remarkable achievements is the series of infants in white on blue ground executed for, and set in front of, the foundling hospital in Florence. Around many of his medallions he used decorative but realistic fruits and flowers in colored enamels while the main relief is left white. Again it is not necessary to give a comprehensive list of his works, most of which are well known, but only to warn against forgeries mysteriously occurring in dealer's hands.

THE SONS OF ANDREA DELLA ROBBIA

Andrea lived to a ripe old age and had seven sons, five of whom worked with the father and carried on the studio. Of the work of Luca II we know

The "Adoration" by Andrea della Robbia (1435–1525) in glazed terracotta showing less stiffness than the work of Luca and a sensitive beauty of both features and hands, of composition and of movement which ranks it high amidst the great art of the world. Ht. 36″. 15th cent. Florence. Metropolitan Mus. of Art.

"ADORATION" BY ANDREA DELLA ROBBIA

PLATE 125

chiefly the very beautiful tile pavement in the upper story of Raphael's loggia at the Vatican made under the supervision and at the request of the painter in 1518.

Giovanni's (1469–1529) work is not distinguishable from that of his father in many cases in his early days but soon deteriorated. In the tympanum of the arch of a lavabo in the sacristy of S. Maria Novella at Florence, made in 1497, is a relief of the Madonna between two adoring angels which is of his enameled ware while the basin is of marble. Probably his most important work is the frieze on the outside of the Del Cappo hospital at Pistola. It is polychrome and represents the "Seven Works of Mercy." Six are by Giovanni and the seventh was made by Filippo Paladini of Pistola in 1585. Giovanni's chief pupil was Santi Buglioni (b.1494) who entered the shops in 1521.

Girolamo (1488–1566) was an architect and sculptor in bronze as well as in "della Robbia ware." He went to France and spent some forty years in

FIG. 578. Madonna and Child of the 15th cent. Tuscan school. Ht. 51". Metropolitan Mus. of Art.

FIG. 579. The "Boy St. John" by Giovanni della Robbia, Florentine 15th–16th cent. of terracotta enameled and painted. Ht. 15". Metropolitan Mus. of Art.

FIG. 580. This kneeling madonna by Giovanni della Robbia is of terracotta partly glazed, polychromed and gilded. 15th cent. Florentine School. Ht. 16⅝". Metropolitan Mus. of Art.

the service of the royal family. Francis I employed him to work on a palace in the Bois de Boulogne called the Château de Madrid, and which was decorated richly with enameled ware in tiles, friezes, medallions, etc. largely baked at Suresnes.

Examples of della Robbia pottery may be seen in most important museums though the finest examples are, of course, still in the buildings of Italy loved and respected by the people of all classes.

OTHER SCULPTURED WARES OF ITALY

Aside from this truly great dynasty of sculptor-potters which terminated toward the end of the 16th century there was little of note. Maestro Giorgio

Andreoli is supposed to have done a lustred relief of St. Sebastian now in the V. & A. Museum but this is highly questionable and nothing to be proud of. Orazio Fontana, Antonio Patanazzi and others made vases with more or less ornate handles and that is about all.

FIG. 581. Florentine 16th cent. altarpiece "The Assumption of the Virgin" in enameled terracotta of the della Robbia school. Ht. 118½". Metropolitan Mus. of Art.

FIG. 582. This is a fine large terracotta of Hercules and Antaeus done in the style of Giovanni Bologna, 16th cent. Florentine school. Ht. 35½". Metropolitan Mus. of Art.

FRENCH MODELED WARES

St. Porchaire—Orion—or Henry II Ware

The honorable William Burton has stated that Henry II ware is worth more than its weight in gold and, alas, it is, therefore, our duty to describe it. The body is of white clay with a cream colored glaze. The designs are impressed, while the clay is still soft, with metal stamps like those used by book-binders, and different colored slips are rubbed into the impressions. The ware is then turned down smooth. Ochre-yellow, brown, green, violet, black and blue with very rarely red are the colors used more or less in the order of their rarity. Finally, after the assembling of much architectural detail in miniature, such as applied reliefs, statuettes, inlays imitating pavements, scrolls, pillars, etc. all more or less inlayed as described above, the lead glaze is applied and it is fired in the "grand feu" (high fire).

The ware so made was designed to serve the humble uses of cups, ewers, salt cellars, candlesticks, bowls with covers and such. It usually bore the

St. Porchaire or "Henri II" ware of the earlier and less ornate type so far as modeling goes. (1524–1563 A.D.). Ht. 5″. Metropolitan Mus. of Art.

Salt cellar of the worst possible involved taste such as is seen in late St. Porchaire wares. Made about 1550. Ht. 6⅞″. Metropolitan Mus. of Art.

Tazza without cover of the St. Porchaire ware, with heads applied around the stem irregularly and with the wide border designs around the cup and the base irregularly brought together. Ht. 5″. Metropolitan Mus. of Art.

St. Porchaire, Henry II ware, known also as Orion ware. It was thought incorrectly to have come from there. Ht. 5¾″. Metropolitan Mus. of Art.

ST. PORCHAIRE "HENRY II" WARE, FRANCE, 16TH CENTURY

PLATE 126

devices of Francis I, Henry II or the crescents of Diane de Poitiers. For many years its source was unknown and much mystery enshrouded it. It was said to have been made by pupils of Benvenuto Cellini, God forbid!— or by Pagolo or Ascanio or even by poor, worthy Girolamo della Robbia (Would his father not have turned over in his grave?) or by the printer Geoffroy Tory. Later it was "proven" to have come from Orion, near Thouars, but now we know that it did originate at St. Porchaire in Poitou between c.1525 and c.1560 or 1565. Hannover divides it into three groups:

1.—Earliest—The least ornate, of Italo-French Renaissance style, only in black and brown.

2.—Middle—Ornate decoration and in varied coloring.

3.—Late—Oriental enlacements or arabesques, baroque and grotesque shapes, certain liquid jasper tones and the giving up of the inlay technique for painted slip.

There is nothing to recommend this ware either from an artistic or technical viewpoint yet in 1859 a salt cellar brought 12,500 francs and in 1884 a candlestick fetched 92,000 francs. I have not had the curiosity nor heart to search further but needless to say such prices have also set the forgers on the trail.

Let us pause in passing to note that this same technique and the very similar one of hand incising and inlaying was employed in the Korai period, Korea, with some of the most beautiful and tasteful of results. It is not the technique which makes for beauty but the feeling and intelligence with which it is used.

FIG. 583. French 16th cent. tankard attributed to Bernard Palissy (about 1510 to 1590) of simple form and better proportions than most things he did. Ht. 6¾". Metropolitan Mus. of Art.

BERNARD PALISSY (1510–1590)

Before we can come to the German beer drinkers and their wares we must pause to contemplate Bernard Palissy whom France includes among her "plus pures et plus belles gloires," though in Germany he is known as "eine gefallene Grösse." One may take his choice.

Our records from Palissy's own autobiography tell us that he was born about 1510 (though he does not remember the date himself), either in Saintes or in Agen in southwest France. He says he was a dreamer yet paid little attention to religion not guessing what an important part it was to play in his life. He seems to have gained that typical Renaissance spirit of inquiry into natural science which we see reflected in the notebook of Leonardo da Vinci who died about the time the boy was eight or nine years old in Cloux, France, not so very far from his birthplace. Bernard became a glass painter and land-surveyor.

He tells us that a "geometrician" became interested in his precocious intelligence and took him away for further training. Of course the naturalist is no more than a grown-up boy with an investigating mind and Bernard seemed to carry his interest in snakes, frogs, fish and the like beyond that of most boys.

He roamed through France working at his trade of glass painting for the windows of cathedrals, learned to blow glass, became something of a chemist and also a landscape-gardener and in about 1539 settled in the old town of Saintes and commenced to raise a family. This town had seen much history and interested him mightily. Also the cathedral of St. Peter was being erected so there was work to keep him busy. In 1544 the government gave him the task of investigating the salt swamps and he worked out a system of water supply for the town as well. He had become an honored citizen, a church goer and was respected by all.

These were troubled times, for the Reformation was under way and the thunder of the cannon of Boulogne-sur-mer which the English attacked a bit to the north, the tramping of troops and threats to peace might well have worried Bernard but they did not. It took a little white cup to wreck his life and make him famous! The Fates placed before him in the collection of a friend a small white porcelain undecorated cup without a handle, from China, and the dreadful whimsy was accomplished for in his own words, "like a man who gropes in the dark," *he set himself to make one like it.* Little did he know that the little cup was the result of generation on generation of clever work by thousands of careful Chinese. It looked so simple! "From that moment," he says, "without regard to the fact that I had not the least acquaintance with potter's clay, I gave myself up to searching after enamels."

He learned about the peasant ware about him and rushed home from work to plunge into experiments. He built himself a kiln, tore it down and built another. He hired men to bring him wood for firing and more and ever more wood. He spent money for expensive chemicals sent from afar. He lost his job for it was obvious that his mind was not on it. Poverty like a blank wall seemed to shut him from his simple conquest. He borrowed all he could and poured the proceeds into his furnace which now consumed the very food of his starving children. He was destitute and begged, yet some enamels would run while others would not melt at all, some changed color for no known reason and others chipped off. Never, never could he get it just right. Long since he had forgotten the subtle poison he had imbibed from the little cup which seemed to dance in a haze before his mad and staring eyes. He burnt the furniture in his house and ripped up the boards from the floor and finally developed—what? A porcelain like that of China? No. A soft porcelain? No. A stoneware? No. A ware which, we must admit before the chuckling fates, was less good than the simple contemporary ordinary wares of Spain and Italy; just a crude peasant pottery of another sort. But the mad man had something. That everyone had to admit.

We would like to be able to tell that he took this humble material and wrought great works of art that remained for ever after monuments to his tenacity and unconquerable spirit. We would like to show the moral of self-sacrifice and the sure reward of that inner fire which burns from the soul. But alas! Bernard was no more an artist than a potter. At least we can grant him that he did not go to copying the St. Porchaire ware. the works of Hirsvogel or of the Italian majolica makers. He had the first element of art; independence of spirit and he did turn to nature. But his mind was not imaginative, it was that of a scientist and an exact one. He saw reptiles and fishes as objects and took little notice of the *space* with which nature divides things and the conflict often brought about by their proximity. Thus

Fig. 584. Ornamental plaque-platter by Bernard Palissy. The back is covered with glazes of blue, chocolate, white and green. Length 21″. c. 1560. Plummer, Ltd.

upon a single platter he would make a stream about the bottom with the rim for shores and an island in the center and would fill the water with many fishes which might devour each other and the shores with lizards, snakes, insects, shells, foliage, etc. all in high relief. The wheel was unknown to him. His glazes were marbled and clouded in brown, blue and purple on the back. On the front things were carried out in their natural colors. French students have made careful zoological and botanical lists of his subjects which are all quite recognizable and we find for instance:—various snakes:—adder, necklace, etc. —fish such as mullet, eels, tench, roach, gudgeon, ray, etc.—lobsters, crabs, snails, crayfish, cockles, welks, water snails, limpets, turritellas, scallops, murex, etc.—among the plants are ferns, the strawberry, oak leaves, acorns, ivy, bramble, olive, mulberry, etc. —Palissy called these wares "figurines rustiques," and people admired them and put them on their sideboards, for no one could possibly eat off them.

Then came the Constable of France, Anne de Montmorency in 1548 from Saintonge, where he had been sent to suppress a revolution, and he gave Palissy a fine job, the making of a grotto in the park of the Château d'Ecouen. He built a shop for him and assigned the location of the grotto to an artificial crag to which water was brought from springs for a fountain. No part of this or his other grottos now remain, but the work brought him fame at the French Court and he was appointed *"Inventor of Rustic Pottery to the King and Queen-mother."* Meanwhile he had joined the Huguenots and was thrown into prison when the town of Saintes was taken by the Catholics, and later escaped to Paris under the patronage of Catherine de' Medici and her sons.

Catherine was just having the Tuileries built for her by Philbert de l'Orme and as a grotto was desired Palissy was set up in the garden of the Tuileries. Here he began to cast silver embossed dishes for his pottery forms and made strapwork and pierced borders, etc. He lived in Paris some 25 years in peace but in the palace Catherine was afraid of the influence of Admiral Coligny on Charles IX and the possibility of war with Spain. It was a good time for such an endeavor but Catherine thought it best to have the good admiral assassinated. This, however, failed and she bethought herself of another plan which was rather like burning down a house to kill a mouse; the simple idea of massacring all the Huguenots including the offending admiral who was of this faith. On St. Bartholomew's Day, August 24th, 1572 occurred one of the most bloody and terrible massacres known to history and it spread throughout Paris and thence throughout France. Poor Palissy was captured and thrown into the Bastille when he was nearly 80 and there he died in 1589 or 1590. Catherine licked her lips and went about the gentle pastime of encouraging her sons to partake of all manner of dissipation and licentiousness to keep their mental capacities such that they would not hamper her strange ambitions.

A few of Palissy's wares were copied probably by G. Dupré about 1600. There have also been casts from his worn-out molds, some imitations and forgeries as is understandable when we hear that a piece brought £1365 in 1911 in an English sale.

FIG. 586. 16th cent. dish. Style of Palissy but deeper in relief and more ornate. Dia. 10". Metropolitan Mus. of Art.

FIG. 585. Dish having figures symbolizing Temperance, the four elements the various arts, sciences, etc., which was cast by Palissy from the well known pewter dish by François Briot. French about 1570. Dia. 15¼". Metropolitan Mus. of Art.

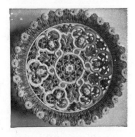

FIG. 587. Dish by Palissy probably modeled after or actually cast from a silver one after he went to Paris to work for Catherine de Medici about 1550. It lacks ceramic feeling but does show meticulous craftsmanship. Dia. about 10". Metropolitan Mus. of Art.

I do not believe his things were taken very seriously even in his time but his success was due to a colossal belief in himself and his omnipotent intelligence along with his earnestness. People believed him because he was very sure.

The real Palissy ware is of white body with reddish-yellow tint. It effervesces when touched with acids. Black was not successful and red gave him difficulties. He never did obtain a real white body. His glaze is finely crackled and bright and glossy.

GERMAN MODELED WARES

Hafner Ware

Hafner ware consists of stove tiles or heavy jugs made about the middle of the 16th century. The earliest are green and less often yellow or brown. About 1500 combined colors began to be used and not until 1533 were copies made of tiles in the Swiss technique and actually painted such as the first with a picture of David and Bathsheba on it. In the castle of Hohensalzburg is a Gothic stove dated 1501 which has much plastic or pressed mold decoration. Most examples have none of the hand technique of modeling. At first the tiles are small but later they made up a whole side including cornice, plinth and pilasters. By this time the various colors were employed and to the green, yellow, purple and blue of lead glaze colors a white tin-enamel was added. Tin was also added in various proportions to the blue color. Faults in firing and glaze are often seen.

Nuremburg seemed to be a center but the industry spread over Germany and Austria and such places as Cologne, Danzig, Lübeck, Rostock, Stralsund and Villingen in the Black Forest. About 1550 there was a revival of the plain green stoves which showed up the modeling better. Some were supplemented with a brownish black and black graphite. By the 17th century they were made of tiles in low relief which showed the transition to the tin-enameled tiles of the 18th century but even then the South Germans retained their relief decoration. Gilding was applied and the subject matter was usually religious, showing the fervor of the times.

Hafner Ware Vessels

Hafner ware was first known as "Hirsvogel" because Augustin Hirzvogel was supposed to have originated it but this was found to be untrue. It dates after 1550, most of it, and aside from stove tiles, consists of mugs of torso-shape, melon or ovoid shape with flaring feet and either small or wide mouths heavily rimmed. Frequently a twisted handle springs from the shoulder to the neck. The decoration is accomplished by means of small ridges or cloissons applied to the surface and outlining the design. These were squeezed from a cone and to these are added small leaves, flowers and figures made in pressed molds. The colored glazes are of lead type and comprise blue, green, brown, manganese and yellow plus white tin-enamel and are kept separate by

FIG. 588. Three Hafnerkrug pieces from the workshop of Paulus Preuning, Nüremberg, the first two in Vienna and the third in Munchen. About 1550. From *Alte Deutsche Kunsttöpfereien.*

FIG. 589. Green glazed earthenware tile with coat of arms and date 1580, made in Germany. Metropolitan Mus. of Art.

German green tile stove. 16th cent., exact kiln unknown. The reliefs are supposed to represent the "four parts of the World," and because America is prominent, it is known as The America Stove." International Studio Art Corp.

Nuremberg Stove of the 16th cent. Composed of two parts with a partly open-work gallery at the top. It is in many colors. International Studio Art Corp.

GERMAN TILE STOVES 16TH CENTURY

PLATE 127

the ridges which frequently stand out in white. Some are divided into horizontal bands with scroll and two color treatment. Others have arches in which are figures representing Charles I, Ferdinand I, Anne his wife, Elector John Frederick of Saxony, the Reformers, etc. as well as biblical and mythological subjects like those on the stoves. It is interesting to note that identification of the ware as having been made by Paul and Kunz Preuning was brought about by documents of their arrest and conviction in Nuremberg in 1541 for having made a jug with a Crucifixion and at the same time musicians and peasant dancers on it.

FIG. 590. Hafnerkrug, Sachsen, of 1570 made by Master Merten Koller in Annaberg. Now in the Kunstgewerbe Mus., Dresden.

FIG. 591. Hafnerkrug of 1569 by Master Merten Koller of Annaberg, now in Dresden. From *Alte Deutsche Kunsttöpfereien.*

SILESIA HAFNER WARE

"Silesia Hafner Ware" comprises a group of dishes in which the designs are scratched with a sharp instrument and which have glazes containing tin. One in Berlin has the arms of Balthasar von Promnitz, bishop of Breslau and is probably the earliest known. The technique is perhaps more closely associated with painting than modeled wares but we have included them in this section because they are incised and are close to the above ware.

Both these wares are rather crude and sometimes over crowded but they are honest and we see in them something not very far distant from the famous "Three Color Ming" wares of China. The colors are rich and attractive, and they are in good keeping with the rich velvets and brocades of the times or equally appropriate for sturdy oak or walnut tables.

Here we see a meeting of two different spirits of the German people who love their good food and drink but are also religious and even hard. Perhaps it is the old nomadic self-discipline, in fighting in the field and then relaxing with roisterous drinking and stuffing of food. The German may be lean and hungry like a wolf or fat like a pig. They are not two different men but one and the same; the animal before and after the hunt, and the world would do well to keep it in mind. So these wares express the duality of the German personality perfectly.

"STEINZEUG" OR GERMAN STONEWARE

Typical of the German people is the stoneware reminding us of the rich burgher who loves good beer in generous measure and cool as spring water. The early jugs are large round-bellied affairs with cylindrical necks and rimmed mouths. The "bartmann" or "greybeard" jugs have an old man's head modeled on the neck with beard spread out on the shoulder much as the owners probably spread their beards over their own paunches. Other decorations on them tell us what seemed sacred and what comical. As Hannover says, "what men thought of Christ, of the Pope, the Emperor, the lansquenet, the peasant, women, the chase, trade, county fairs and much else between heaven and earth, whilst coats of arms and merchants' marks are a proof that these jugs and tankards were not show pieces, but household gear to which men felt themselves thoroughly and closely attached."

FIG. 592. A "Bartmannkrug" of brown and some blue earthenware dated 1603 and made in Germany for the Coronation of James I of England.

FIG. 593. Cologne-Frechen late 16th cent. *Bartmann* with one floral medallion on front. The glaze is mottled brown. Ht. 8⅛". Metropolitan Mus. of Art.

FIG. 594. Frechen jug with the *bartmann* less important and a coat of arms added. Dark brown glazed earthenware of the late 16th or early 17th cent. Ht. 7¼". Metropolitan Mus. of Art.

The stoneware itself is something in a way like the first porcelain of the Han Dynasty in China, being composed of ordinary clay which is, however, fired at so high a temperature that it became "fritted" or fused into a hard substance proof against scratching with a steel knife and impervious to liquids. The special clay containing flint could not be found everywhere and so manufacture was confined to districts about the Rhine from Cologne to Coblenz and in Flanders at Raeren. The chief places were in Höhr, Grenzhausen, Siegburg, Cologne, Frechen and Raeren. It was also later tried in France and the Netherlands but it was not of sufficient merit to interest us.

The method of making is this: The clay was beaten in water and washed thoroughly. The flint is burnt or calcined, ground fine and suspended in water and then mixed with the clay, after which the whole is dried in a kiln until doughlike when it is well kneaded, beaten, and tempered to be ready for molding. The glaze is usually produced by common salt which is thrown into the kiln at a certain time in the firing when the highest temperature

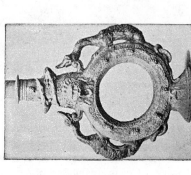

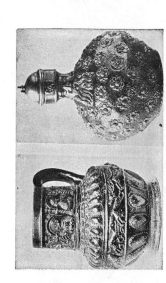

Left to Right: A "Gebuckelte Kanne" from the Maximinenstrasse work shop, Köln. Also a fine 16th cent. "Bartmannkrug" from Köln-Frechen. A *"Steinzeugkrug"* from the workshop of Jan Emens about 1590. Ht. 9½". From the Figdor Coll., Vienna. Siegburg jug of cream white stoneware c. 1600. This shape also made without handle. Ht. 5⅜". Metropolitan Mus. of Art. "Kanne" of grey and blue salt glazed stoneware from Westerwald (Grenzhausen) late 17th cent. Ht. 7½". Metropolitan Mus. of Art.

Left to Right: Jug from Raeren after Emens', dated 1598. Brown glaze, and with the arches which came into use in 1580. Ht. 10½". From W. R. Hearst Coll. A *"Ringkrug"* from the "Töpferfamilie Knütgen" during the middle of the 16th cent. From *Kunst und Kunsthandwerk.* Siegberg tankard with the usual white clay and transparent glaze and having low relief molded decoration rather unevenly applied. c. 1560. Ht. 9⅜". Metropolitan Mus. of Art. Ewer from Raeren of the early brown ware dating during the 16th cent. The body is white. Ht. 12⅞". Metropolitan Mus. of Art.

GERMAN STONEWARE 16TH AND 17TH CENTURIES

had been reached and no more smoke was given off. The heat volatilizes the salt so that the chlorin escapes, leaving the soda behind to combine with the silicic acid in the clay which forms a thin covering of soda glass on all exposed surfaces which is of great hardness and resists ordinary acids. The kiln used was the horizontal reverberatory type.

As the firing was done all at once and at high temperature few colors would not be destroyed. The Siegberg clay was white and a colorless glaze was used. Most of the other clays contained iron enough to turn them reddish which when covered with the salt glaze makes brown. A blue was obtained with cobalt and purple with manganese.

The Westerwald stoneware became grey in body and had floral patterns in the above colors. It was wheel-turned and yet shows traces of the inheritance from metal. However, we can also see quite clearly that leather jugs were also prototypes as in the triangular ones and some of the pilgrim bottles. This recalls that the wares from Susa were influenced by leather prototypes and also that one of the Chinese jars found in the Philippines appears at first glance to have been actually made of leather.

When the pieces were thrown on the wheel a "stege" or templet of metal was used to true them and though this lost some of the feeling of the hand of the potter, these German wares were so worked over with design that a certain human touch was regained. The handles were freely hand fashioned and were often so pressed to the body while still damp that slight distortion of the body took place. The molded plaquettes were so applied with incising that they appeared more a part of the body than is usual with the employment of this process.

Most of the designs were taken from contemporary engravings such as in Cologne, Heinrich Aldegraver, in Siegburg, Beham Solis, Virgil Solis, Jost Amman and Theodore de Bry, while in Raeren they were after Cornelis Bos, Balthrazar Sylvius, Adriaen Collaert, Abraham de Bruyn and Konrad Goltzius. Also at Raeren many Siegburg designs were copied.

A little after 1632 when the Swedes sacked Siegburg the potters from there and from Raeren moved to the Westerwald district near Coblentz, where at Grenzhausen and in Höhr the industry continued until the 18th century.

DESCRIPTIONS OF VARIOUS STONEWARES

Cologne was the site of the earliest stoneware. Shapes of a brownish-red pottery made at the start of the 15th century were similar and some time between 1520 and 1540 stoneware was in real production. Other early sites were Siegburg and Frechen nearby. Sherds found in the Maximinenstrasse and Komoedienstrasse, Cologne or "Köln" have been arranged by Otto von Falke as follows:

KÖLN (COLOGNE)

MAXIMINENSTRASSE

1.—Globular jugs with wide cylindrical necks and decorated with oak branches and rose stems combined with figures at times and also with the "Tree of Iesse" showing the genealogy of Christ, in relief.

2.—"Greybeard" jugs called "Bartmänner" invented here and soon copied at Frechen, Siegburg and Raeren.

3.—The use of oviform bosses in single or double rows and small round medallions with busts in antique style.

4.—Figure ware with subjects from history, religion and mythology on the tall "Pinten" and "Schnellen" or tall truncated conical mugs usually decorated with three matrices each having a complete design in itself.

These are all between 1520 and 1540.

FIG. 595. Frechen "Bartmannkrug" dated 1593 and inscribed, "Who knows if it is so true?" Ht. 14¾". The cover and handle, of course, are of pewter. From the W. R. Hearst Coll.

FIG. 596. Three pieces of Cologne-Frechen ware from the shop of Eigelstein of about 1560–1570. All have brown speckled glaze. The triangular one suggests a leather prototype. From the Oppenheim Coll.

FIG. 597. Rare Köln-Frechen brown glazed "Kanne" with vine and bird pattern and dating about 1540. From *Alte Deutsche Kunsttöpfereien.*

KOMOEDIENSTRASSE

The factory here seems to have been in the latter part of the century and not so active.

1.—"Bartmann" jugs globular but with nearly rectangular greybeard on the neck, a narrow frieze about the body and acanthus leaves pointing up and down from it.

2.—Other wares not distinguishable.

FRECHEN

At Frechen we find:

1.—"Bartmann" jugs exactly like those described above but with the ornamental frieze replaced by a saying such as "Drink und est, got nit vergest" (drink and eat, forget not God).

2.—Another type more ovoid and covered with prunts arranged like bunches of grapes.

3.—From a little earlier than 1600 stylized, grimacing "Bartmann" on a narrower neck and with three large medallions of round or oval shape with shields of arms such as those of Cologne, Amsterdam or England or rosettes and roughly molded heads.

EIGELSTEIN

At Eigelstein they made:

1.—"Schnellen" with only slightly rounded panels having a medallion in the center of each with a head or allegorical half figure, joined edge to edge to form triangular vessels.

2.—Similar types with a spout.

3.—Others with female allegorical subjects on almost cylindrical bodies and designed after Peter Flötner, or with lovers near a fountain.

These are difficult to distinguish particularly as the factory was moved to Frechen at the end of the 16th century.

The common characteristics of these wares are: 1.—a body of grey, 2.—a few are grey or yellow toned but these were probably kiln failures, 3.—usually a chestnut brown or somewhat lighter, 4.—an elliptical string mark on the bottom where they were cut off the wheel not unlike those of Japanese potteries.

The shapes can be seen in the illustrations but it should be noted that the Cologne mugs generally contract more than the Siegburg ones which are more slender and graceful. Hannover says, "On the banks of the Rhine makers of jugs were called 'Euler, Eulner or Ulner' and they are assumed, on the strength of this appellation, to have made owls as a kind of emblem of their handicraft." Perhaps this is a surface reason for their making them but the owl is a very pot-like bird and too an ancient emblem of night.

SIEGBURG

At Siegburg the potters found pure white clay and it retained its whiteness even after firing. The glaze was made colorless though at times blue was used and rarely a yellowish-brown or reddish color to touch up parts of the design. Some of the oldest shapes are even without salt glaze and have

Fig. 599. *"Kanne," "Schnelle"* and *"Schnabelkrüge"* or *"Schnabelkanne"* of salt glazed stoneware from Siegberg. Hts. 9", 15¼" and 9½". Metropolitan Mus. of Art.

Fig. 598. Siegburg pieces: 1.—*"Flasche"* of gourd shape from the workshop of Anno Knütgen. Late 16th cent. 2.—*"Trichterbecher"* of same period. 3.—*"Eulenkrug"* (owl jug) of the same period. 4.—*"Henkelkanne"* of about 1600. 5.—*"Ringelkrug,"* 15th cent. 6.—*"Kanne"* with Renaissance oramentation, c. 1570.

globular bodies, funnel neck and a wavy spreading foot shaped by pressing down with the fingers. 1.—The earliest were decorated with a holly-leaf incised in rude manner. Later ones had applied medallions in relief. Some were made with double walls, the outer one pierced with Gothic architectural tracery. The color of these was grey dappled with yellowish and brownish patches probably from contact with the flames of the kiln.

Other Siegburg wares were:

2.—Tall slender "Schnelle" with three panels. By the 16th century the potters had lost so much of the spirit of design that they often repeated one panel twice on the same pot.

3.—"Schnabelkrüge" (beak-pots) with globular bodies and long spouts rising from the side nearly to the height of the tall cylindrical neck and attached with a tubular link or "Dille." These usually date between 1560 and 1610 but are known as early as 1528 and as late as 1631.

4.—Pilgrim bottles are rare products of Anno Knütgen and his assistant the signer of F.T. about 1559 to 1568.

5.—"Leuchtervasen" (large jars with handles formed as sockets for candles).

6.—Goblets.

7.—"Birnkruge" (pear jugs).

8.—"Pullen" (footless globular bottles with short narrow necks).

All those from #4 on were supposed to have been made by artists in good old Gothic style.

A few of the artists' names are known; those of the Knütgen family, the Simons, Flach and Omian. Christian Knütgen was the chief representative of the Late Renaissance style at Siegburg. His oldest work is dated 1568, but it was 20 years later that he made his spouted jugs with a lion mask under the spout. Hans Hilgers pieces are found frequently but are not of top quality. They date between 1569 and 1595. Various other initials appear but cannot be traced such as LW, FT, etc.

In 1830 Peter Löwenich opened a kiln in Siegburg and made wares good enough to fool the museums and private collectors even in the Rhine valley. His clay is more bluish or yellowish grey than white and the style is lacking. At Höhr other 19th century copies were made but the rims are flat instead of rounded and they are more shiny. The old ware may shade off to a slightly brownish tone but it is quite different.

RAEREN

Raeren made a brown ware which later turned to grey in imitation of the Westerwald wares. On the grey, blue was occasionally used. A three handled jar is supposed to be original here. Out of a lot of copyists there rose unaccountably Jan Emens who signed between 1568 and 1594 with IE, IEM, IAN, YAN and EMENS. His first work was the copy of a large Schnelle of the shop of Anno Knütgen but made larger. It shows Judith, Esther and Lucretia. There is a fairly architectural quality in his work but I far from agree with the enthusiasts who say his proportions are perfect and that his works compare favorably with the best Greek vases, poor as many of them are. He often used a lion head with jaws curving together as though they

FIG. 600. Siegburg jug of the 17th cent. white stoneware. Ht. 9½". Metropolitan Mus. of Art.

FIG. 601. Siegburg "Bierbrug" dated 157? from the Museums für Kunst und Industri, Vienna.

FIG. 602. Two Raeren "Kanne" grey with blue glazes, the first dated 1605 and the other also of the first parts of the 17th cent. Hts. 20". From the W. R. Hearst Coll.

FIG. 604. A brown glazed krug with the coats of arms of Munzenburg and Amsterdam. Ht. 12¼". From the W. R. Hearst Coll. Dated 1599. Raeren.

FIG. 603. A John Emens "*Doppelfrieskrug*" or jug with double frieze in relief and covered with brown glaze. Ht. 18". It has also the initials IE.

had held a ring but there is no evidence of rings having been made. He made a broad band about the body of his pieces and filled it with any material that came to his hand from engravings, etc. Thus we have the "Peasant dance jugs," "Susanna jugs," "Paris jugs," etc. In 1580 he began the "Blauwerk" having light grey body with blue decoration but did not entirely give up the brown ware. At the same time came a changing of the frieze into arches and a more detailed treatment of both the architectural elements and the figures. It seems again that the artist starting out with inspirational fire has found it necessary to replace original thought with labored detail *hoping* to win applause by showing how much trouble he has gone to rather than *commanding* applause by some new vitality. I always feel that the artist who shows the sweat of detail dripping from his brow is like

an untrained athlete and that he gets just about the same raspberry from
the crowd. This may be heartless but after all does he not owe it to himself
and to his audience to keep on his toes? Jan Emens had something, but his
"Blauwerk" proves that he did not know he had.

Engel Kran was a pupil and imitator and his proportions were less good.
He often tried hard to get more figures in his friezes than the master could.

Baldem Mennicken who signed work between about 1575 and 1584 was
a better copyist and therefore more dangerous competitor. His work may
be called softer. Merten Mennicken, his son, copied the copyists. One
wonders why these men did not either learn more about their art of modeling
or give it up. Possibly they looked at their wares with eyes half closed as
some painters do at their pictures or just put on texture as an upholsterer
might tack tapestry on a chair. The Mennicken family went to Grenzhausen
and the wares there were then indistinguishable from those of Raeren. It is
true that Anno Knütgen, quickly followed by the Mennickens, made "Ringkrug" or "ring-jug" designs and later "double ring jugs." We know of
no triple ones but they will probably be tried someday, and will probably
be thought three times better than single ones. By 1630 the Westerwald had
taken the lead and Raeren declined. In 1880 a Hubert Schiffer made pretty
good imitations but having been cast in plaster molds, they can readily be
distinguished. He signed his wares HS but dealers found they could grind
this off and sell, to those who were not informed, these 19th century imitations for old ones.

WESTERWALD

Westerwald or "Nassau" stoneware was made for about twenty miles
around Grenzhausen including the towns of Grenzau and Höhr where there

FIG. 605. Westerwald jar
with screw top. Salt glazed
stoneware in grey and blue
and comes from either Hohr
or Grenzhausen. 18th cent.
Ht. 10". Metropolitan Mus.
of Art.

FIG. 606. Early 17th cent.
gray and blue jar probably
from Westerwald. Ht. 6¾".
Metropolitan Mus. of Art.

FIG. 607. Westerwald pos-
sibly Grenzhausen "Kanne"
of grey and blue salt glazed
stoneware. 17th cent. Ht.
about 10". Metropolitan
Mus. of Art.

was a guild of their own and where about 1590 refugee potters from Siegburg and Raeren settled. We cannot distinguish between the ware of nearby towns for the clay was all the same and the families of potters spread out. "Blauwerk" is typical of the section and can be told from that of Siegburg only by the signatures. Manganese was occasionally used and also brown glazes like those of Cologne. Plastic decoration soon gave way to stamped or incised design. During the 16th and early 17th centuries there was some life and interest but soon the short fat mugs of "Pinte" type and colossal jugs were devised with baroque style and more and more lifeless designs. These latter are attributed to Johann Kalb.

With the baroque, however, the unholy touch of architecture was removed and portraits were made of such people as the rulers of England, France and the Netherlands. William III of Orange, Queen Mary and Louis XIV

FIG. 608. Westerwald, German figure (one of pair) in salt g'azed stoneware of grayish wh:te. 18th cent. Ht. 7½". Metropolitan Mus. of Art.

FIG. 609. Grenzhausen, Westerwald, "Kanne" or tankard of gray and blue salt glazed stoneware. 17th cent. Ht. 6½". Metropolitan Mus. of Art.

FIG. 610. Westerwald 18th cent., German sand container of gray salt-glazed stoneware. Ht. 6¼". Metropclitan Mus. of Art.

were favorites. Arms, heraldry and figures disappeared and designs of lozenges, rosettes, palmettes, bosses, bunches of grapes, lions' masks, cherubs' heads and stars took their places. Many of these wares now took the simple shapes of the pewter jugs of the period and the designs of pomegranates and flowers were made from Indian palampores which carry right through to the Pennsylvania German potters of the New World. Rococo was the style of the day but for some reason was not noticed by these potters. Hannover aptly says, "A bourgeois craft became a rustic craft; stoneware became a peasant art." How strange this is! Here just as we were giving up in despair, for some unknown reason a backwash occurs in a place to which the potters and their children fled and their art is fed again with the rich strong blood of peasant art, stripped of all pose and ostentation, throwing off all architectural props and becoming alive again. Thus the saltcellar which looks almost Romanesque is to quote von Falke, "countrified baroque." Oh, there were queer twists to the thing and we find hand warmers in the shape of prayer books so that one could gather admiration and credit for being pious while merely warming the hands. There were vessels in the forms of barrels, cannon, etc., but even in these there is an honest humor and lack of pretense.

Stonewares were made elsewhere also, particularly as copies of the Rhine types, such as at Bouffioulx, Châtelet, Namur, Bouvignies, Verviers and Dinant. In Bavaria at Kreussen and in Saxony wares which were made were their own. The Kreussen ware seems to have sprung from Hafner ware. It is of greyish-white which fires red because of its iron content and was coated with a brown glaze which was at first clear but becomes toward the end of the 17th century and into the 18th century more and more opaque. It falls into two groups as follows:

1.—The designs are looted on and are covered with brown as well as the backgrounds of the pots.

2.—The designs are painted with various enamel colors such as blue, red yellow, white and green often with gold added.

These two styles overlap but the painted ones start in general about fifty years after the plain ones had started, although the oldest known is dated 1614 (in the Germanischesmuseum, Nuremberg) and the oldest painted one is dated 1618. The Kreussen mugs are low and broad and always have pewter covers. Polygonal bottles have pewter screw tops. Jugs are decorated with a horseman, a stag or a shield of arms.

In Saxony jugs of the above sort are distinguished by parti-colored palmettes scattered over the body and lozenge or cross hatched line texture back of the relief figures. "Trauerkruge," mistakenly believed to have been used for the funeral repast, are decorated with horizontal rows of circles or segments of circles (usually three rows) in black and white or red. It is probable that these and the Kreussen wares were decorated by glass painters.

There was a period here in America when stoneware decorated all the grand dining rooms in oak and with stained glass windows. A Siegburg "Mars tankard" brought £201 in Copenhagen in the Frohne sale in 1910, an owl jug in the Oppenheim sale at about the same time brought 9,100 marks, another by Jan Emens with the Flight of the Centaurs brought 23,500 marks. However, now it is difficult even to find examples for illustration here. The Randolph Hearst collection is the last in which there were a great number and these have been more or less dispersed at low prices comparatively speaking.

And so we have traced the course of the lustre wares and their end, the ever growing course of the enamel wares and the developments of stoneware with its tendency to become less and less interesting and more and more decorated with various colors. In the 18th century we see the end of hand-made potteries and the loss of human appeals.

FIG. 611. Kreussen tankard with brown glaze, 17th cent. Ht. 5½". Metropolitan Mus. of Art.
FIG. 612. Kreussen jar, 17th cent. Ht. 9". Metropolitan Mus. of Art.
FIG. 613. Tankard of grey, blue, and violet salt glaze stoneware from Grenzhausen c. 1640–1700. Ht. about 10". Metroplitan Mus. of Art.

FIG. 614. Kreussen krug dated 1665 showing saints. Ht. 6½". From the W. R. Hearst Coll.
FIG. 615. Stoneware jar with screw top for cover. Salt glaze of dark brown painted with enamel colors. Ht. 6½". Metropolitan Mus. of Art.
FIG. 616. Kreussen 17th cent. brown glazed tankard with polychrome enamel decoration. Ht. 5⅜". Metropolitan Mus. of Art.

FIG. 617. Hexagonal screw top flask from Kreussen with enamel painting of biblical figures. Early 17th cent. Ht. 13". From the W. R. Hearst Coll.
FIG. 618. Kreussen "Elector tankard" showing the Elector and his wife. The glaze is brown, 17th cent. Ht. 10". From the W. R. Hearst Coll.
FIG. 619. Salt glazed jug, German 17th cent. possibly Ober-Hessen 18th cent. Ht. 8¼". Metropolitan Mus. of Art.

419

CHAPTER XVIII

YÜAN PERIOD IN CHINA

(1280–1368)

THE last of the Sung emperors cast himself into the sea and China was conquered by the Mongols in 1280. The three grandsons of Jenghiz Khan were Mangu, the elder, Hulagu who was sent to take charge of Persia and Kublai who took charge of China. Mangu had died in 1260. The conquest had caused famine in the Western Asian areas but Kublai was an enlightened ruler and China prospered under the 35 years of his reign. He was the acknowledged sovereign of a greater territory and population than any ruler has ever known in this world. It ·is said that "The Chinese seals which Kublai conferred on his kinsmen reigning at Tabriz are stamped upon their letters to the kings of France, and survive in the archives of Paris," and further that "Adventurers from Turkestan, Persia, Armenia, Byzantium, even from Venice, served him as ministers, generals, governors, envoys, astronomers or physicians; soldiers from all Asia to the Caucasus fought his battles in the south of China." He encouraged culture, was tolerant as concerns religion, even trying to get European priests to aid in the education of his people and failing that obtained Tibetan Buddhistic priests, appointing a young lama, Mati Dhwaja, the head of the church and prince of Tibet, and above all he was a great builder. The accounts of Marco Polo tell us of the glories of his capital of Khanbaliq or Cambaluc situated about where Peking is now.

Kublai died in 1294 and the following Mongol rulers were of no special account. However, during this time some things took place which are of considerable interest to us. Trade routes with the Near East were made safe. Muslims in great numbers came to China and the Arabs conquered the western tip of Sumatra. The Franciscan Friar John of Montecorvino arrived the year of Kublai's death and within 30 years built a community of several thousand. Friar Odoric and the papal legate John of Marignolli helped. The merchants were not far behind the holy brethren.

As may be guessed the taste of the Mongol conquerors was not of the most sensitive. It was not unlike a bunch of cowboys, lumbermen or oil-drillers dictating the artistic works of today. Virility was not lacking but the ornate became desirable instead of the beautiful Sung economy. Drama was originated but the art of painting was chiefly carried on by copyists or by those who wished to make flamboyant show.

YÜAN CERAMICS

As rewards, the lieutenants of the Mongol army were apportioned territories and those whose land included pottery towns lost no time in taxing them to the limit so that they withered and died.

The old Sung kiln sites along the Yellow River had, as we have seen, in many cases been left by the workmen when the first part of the invasion took place. Probably most of them continued but under not very happy circumstances. It is certain that Ting, Tz'u Chou, Chün, Northern celadon, "Ying ching" and the various Tsung se or dark brown ware continued, many of them being probably hardly distinguishable from the Sung wares. A warning should certainly be sounded that every piece showing bad taste is not Yüan and every piece showing simple beauty is not necessarily Sung. It should also be pointed out that the Yüan period has become a sort of dumping ground into which all things neither distinctly Ming nor distinctly Sung have been shoved by those who were afraid to say simply that they did not know at what time certain things were made.

The drive south had acted as a temporary benefit to the southern kilns and of them all Ching-tê Chên grew the most. This place was located just east of the large Po Yang Lake in northern Kiangsi province not far south of the Yangtze River. It became the largest and most important pottery center in the whole world even up to the present time, due to having the necessary materials close at hand, being situated on the Ch'ang River which made export easy, and finally to having gained its strength at just the right time. The wares made there were known under different names such as: Chên yao, Ching-tê yao, Fou-liang yao, Jao Chou yao, Jao yao, Ch'ang-nan yao and Nan-ch'ang yao. The town is and probably has always been a market town or "chên" from which the name derives. Its first name was Ch'ang-nan Chên but this was changed by the Sung Emperor Chên Tsung who ordered the "nien hao" or name of the period to be used on the wares. This name was Ching-tê (1004–1007). The district town was Hsin-p'ing now Fou-liang in the prefecture of Jao chow and it is recorded that this was a center for the making of pottery from the Han period. We need not go into all the Chinese chronicles but it is interesting to note that during T'ang times in the 4th or 2nd year of Wu Tê (A.D. 621) or (A.D. 618) "porcelain jade" called also "false jade" was sent as tribute to the Emperor and from that time it had become the custom for the town to provide the court. We may also note that one potter, Ho Chung-ch'u became renowned but we do not know what his work was like. It was also written that some 300 kilns were at work in the town in the Sung dynasty.

Many of the kilns were in outlying small towns such as Nan Shan, south of the city, and Li-ts'un, Hu-tien, Hsiang-hu, Fu-tien-ts'un and Wang-ts'un, east of the city (see map by A. D. Brankston). Mr. Brankston in "Early Ming Wares of Ching-tê-chên," published by Henri Vetch, Peking, 1938, says, in speaking of the general wares found in the district of Fou-liang, in which the kilns worked, "Outside the town there are literally hundreds of kilns, large and small." And in touching upon Hu-tien says, "Blue decorated wares are found only at the western edge of the site and are mixed with scattered pieces of ying-ch'ing (shadow blue), and plain white porcelain. As one advances eastward the blue and white become scarcer, and finer pieces of ying-ch'ing more numerous, until, at the eastern edge there is a steep slope which contains nothing else except the finest ying-ch'ing with engraved designs. So it appears that the work progressed roughly westward." Later he says, "In addition to the above types there are stemcups and bowls of coarse grey ware with a chocolate coloured glaze. These are scarce, and appear to have been made of unrefined clay; they may have preceded the Sung ying-ch'ing wares or perhaps were a coarse variety of later date."

Again in speaking of the seggars found he says, "The first for firing ying-ching dishes of the Sung dynasty is of porcelain. The second, which comes from the western edge, is probably of the 14th century and is made of a coarse red earth. So it appears that during the Sung dynasty white clay was as plentiful as red earth and that by the 15th century it was necessary to look elsewhere for seggar material. This may mark the change over from natural fusible white clay to a mixture of kaolin and petuntse." He goes on to say that much the same conditions seemed to hold true of other sites in the vicinity and I think his deductions perfectly sound.

Nothing definite can be found out about Ching-tê-chên until we are able to sink shafts in various places.

We cannot definitely attribute Sung nor Yüan wares to this place yet but let us glance at the Chinese descriptions:

The *Memoirs of Chiang* (start of 14th century) state:

1.—They were pure white, 2.—without flaw, 3.—called "Jao Chou Jade," 4.—rivalled the red porcelain of Chêng-ting Fu and 5.—the green of Lung-ch'üan in beauty. (Of course this last does not tell us that they were anything like Lung-ch'üan wares, but simply that they were rated as highly.)

The *Ko Ku Yao Lun* (1387) says:

1.—They were thin in body, 2.—plain white with contracted waist, 3.—"hair mouthed things" which Bushell translates as meaning "with unglazed rims," and 4.—were lower in price than Ting yao.

The *Ching-tê Chêng T'ao lu* (1815) which brought together many otherwise unrecorded facts says:

1.—Chün yao was copied toward the end of the Sung dynasty and 2.—Chi chou ware was also copied with its crackle. This last tells us little because we have not yet identified Chi chou yao.

Some pieces have been reported found in the locality and Hobson describes them as follows: "The glaze is usually of a warm ivory tone, tending to cream color; it is hard and usually discontinued in the region of the base both underneath and on the side, and the exposed body is rather rough to the touch." (For further reference: *Chinese Pottery and Porcelain*, p. 157.) He further states that he sees no reason why they might not have copied Lung-ch'üan yao as did many other factory centers and we may add that our vase from "below the Suburban Altar site" and of Kuan yao confirms one more such site along with Chü-chou. In explanation of the reference to

Chün yao he cites a late 12th century passage quoted by the *T'ao lu* which says that in the Ta Kwan period (1107–1110) there were among the Ching-tê Chên wares "furnace transmutations" (yao lien) red as cinnabar and caused by the planet Mars approaching its greatest brightness when things happened magically and contrary to the usual order and that the disturbed potters broke these to pieces in their fear. This may be the same or a similar reference to that concerning the original Chün yao.

Hobson further quotes the *Po wu yao lan* (1621–1627): "Bk. ii., fol. 8 verso." "The body was thin and glossy (jun), the color white, the ornament blue or green (hua ch'ing), and compared with Ting ware it was little inferior." But he thinks that the reference may have been confused with the "ch'ing pai" or "blue-white" of early writers and says that the rest of the sentence seems based upon the *Ko ku yao lun* statement. One wonders whether perhaps he, in his fear of the meaning of the word ch'ing, may not be discrediting the author too severely, particularly now that we know of a number of blue and white examples which are certainly pre-Ming and very possibly Sung. (See the last of that section.) I am inclined again to believe that our Chinese writers spoke the truth quite clearly for those who wished to understand.

From the *Memoirs of Chiang* we learn that across the river another group of potters made a brownish yellow, or yellow-black ware "huang hei" at a place called Hu-t'ien and that the ware was called "huang liao" or "yellow stuff" and not much thought of. It could not be sold in the southern provinces, but only in Anhwei and Kiangsu. We are told that Chêkiang, Fukien, Kiangsi, Kwangtung and Kwangsi all preferred the "ch'ing pai" or greenish white ware. He also tells us that the finer wares were made from clay imported from Chinkêng while the local clay was used for the coarser wares and saggers. This imported stone was called "shih." The glaze was made of "glaze earth" from Ling-pei mixed with ashes of brushwood from the Yŭ-shan hills, which had been burnt with lime and persimmon wood. Mr. Hobson notes that this is essentially the same as the 18th century description.

The shapes of Yüan wares have been listed in the Bushell translations and although these are quoted with reserve by Hobson I know of no better ones. They are as follows:

1.—Bowls "wan" with high feet and with fish and water ornament.

2.—Platters "t'ieh" with "glazes shaded in different tones." The text reads literally "fa yün" meaning "emit mist" or perhaps "clouded," with "sea eyes" and "snow flowers."

3.—Dishes "p'an" of the horse hoof and betel-nut kinds, the latter suggesting a brownish red color.

4.—Large bowls "yü" with lotus ornament (or shaded like a lotus flower), or of a "square form with indented corners."

5.—Bowls and platters "wan t'ieh" with painted decoration "hsiu hua" literally "embroidered ornament" with silver designs "yin hsiu" literally "silver embroidery or painting" with fluted sides and with "encircling strings" (lung hsien)—which means literally "play lute"—and which I cannot make anything out of in any way.

6.—Incense burners of many forms and modeled after bronzes and those shaped like fabulous beasts which "eat tigers and can go five hundred li at a bound," as well as those shaped like "ting" with three or four feet, "i" like cups in the ancestral temple, "li" like large iron cauldrons, or with "elephant's legs" or like incense caskets or barrels.

7.—Vase forms such as the "ku" goblet, "tan" gall bladder, "hu" wine pot with spout and handle, "ching" or Buddhist washing vessel, "chih tzŭ" gardenia, "ho yeh" lotus leaf, "hu lu" gourd, "lü kuan" musical pipes, "shou huan" with ring and mask handles and the "liu li" forms.

Fig. 620. Shu-fu yao bowl of rough, pinkish buff ware with a bismuth-white glaze. The decoration is of fly'ng cranes, clouds, a scroll border and the two characters shu and fu in low relief. Dia. 8″. Warren E. Cox–John Platt Coll.

Shu fu yao we learn from the *Ko ku yao lun* had a small foot and molded design "yin hua" and those having the characters shu fu meaning pivot palace are highly valued. It says that the contemporary wares (it was published in 1387) have a large foot and plain white glaze lacking in "jun" brilliancy. It tells us that there are also some of "ch'ing" color and that those with "wu sê" or "five colored" ornament are very common. This we may say is strange for we find none of them that can surely be given the attribution. There are also "ch'ing hei" or "dark green" wares with gilt ornament, chiefly wine pots and cups which are said to be very lovely.

In Hsiang's Album (*op. cit.*, Fig. 21) is shown a gourd-shaped bottle with engraved dragon and cloud design which we are told was copied from a specimen of Northern Ting and bears the mark shu fu under the foot.

From the John Platt collection I have a bowl which was attributed to the Yüan period by the late Mr. Bosch Reitz of the Metropolitan Museum of Art and I had a discussion of it with Mr. Theodore Y. Hobby and he sent me the following reference: "At Nan Shan, ying-ch'ing wares were also made, but apparently were of a coarser quality than those of Hu-t'ien. Also there were wares with pure white glaze, either undecorated or with very slight moulded petals, dimples or nipples. These types also occur at Hsiang-hu, but, apparently unique to Nan Shan, are the wares with pale blue opaque glaze over moulded designs which are generally accepted, on the evidence of the *Ko ku yao lun*, as Yüan Shu-fu or palace ware."

"There may have been other kilns in the town of Ching-tê Chêng which made the imperial wares so marked. Of this type there are large lotus-form bowls, dishes on small foot-rims and stem cups. The bases are unglazed and usually oxidized to a salmon-pink color, the glaze is thick, fatty and opaque, of a pale blue-green color. The decoration, moulded inside, is generally of flowers or phoenixes. The best pieces have the characters Shu-fu moulded among the flowers, one on each side of the dish. Some of the bowls have a little incised decoration outside and some are marked inside with good wish characters such as fu (happiness), lu (emolument), or shou (longevity)." This throws more light on the ware that was said to have been made by private factories about Ching-tê Chên and to have been the most important of the period. The bowl we have is of a salmon pinkish tinted buff body, rough and heavy. The glaze is a cold white, hardly bluish but surely not warm in tone. The characters appear in it though it is difficult to photograph them as they are in low relief, set between flying geese and clouds.

Other large pottery centers were Nang-fêng Hsien in the Chien-yang Fu also in Kiangsi where the *T'ao lu* tells us another ware was made of white or yellowish white with designs of blue, and a third factory was at Chien-yang in Fukien province which we have discussed under the Sung section as the source of the "hare's fur" and "partridge" tea bowls.

Taking the same sequence of wares as we adopted in the Sung section let us examine the other wares in order:

FIG. 621. Wine ewer of Ying Ch'ing type of Late Sung or Yüan (1127–1368). Eumorfopoulos Coll. # B14.

FIG. 622. Ying Ch'ing wine ewer of white porcelain burnt brown where exposed and having a bubbly glaze with faint bluish tinge. Sung or Yüan (1127–1368). Ht. 5¼". Eumorfopoulos Coll. # B22.

FIG. 623. # B16 of Eumorfopoulos Coll. a wine ewer which also should be called Late Sung or Yüan (1127–1368) of Ying Ch'ing type and thin enough to be possibly Ju yao. Dia. of saucer 5¾"

"Ying ch'ing" wares certainly carried into Yüan and Ming and later times. I quite agree with Mr. Hobson's attribution in the Eumorfopoulos Collection of #B22 as "Sung or Yüan" but feel he should also certainly include #B16 which he calls "Sung" for they well may have been made by the same potter and are both more likely to be Yüan than Sung because of their strong western feeling and obvious derivation from thin handled metal forms. In the same category should fall #B13 and #B14. (See illustrations.)

Even later should be #B34 and #B35 which are exceedingly heavy and of a shape already tending toward Ming. I show a Chu chou celadon example of my own for general comparison. The ornate design, exceedingly heavy potting and form of them would in my opinion have to be outweighed by strong evidence to disprove them Yüan or Ming.

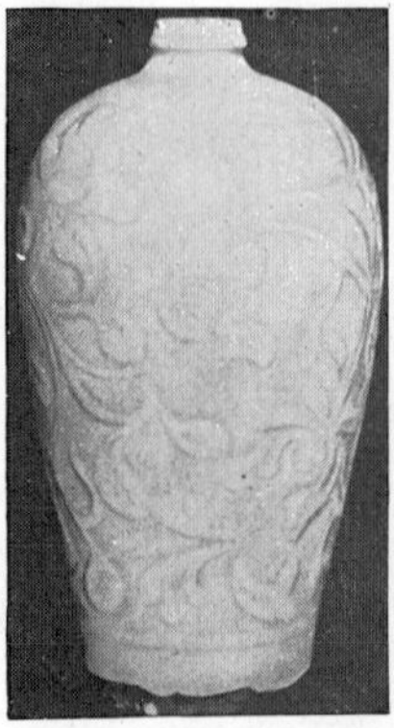

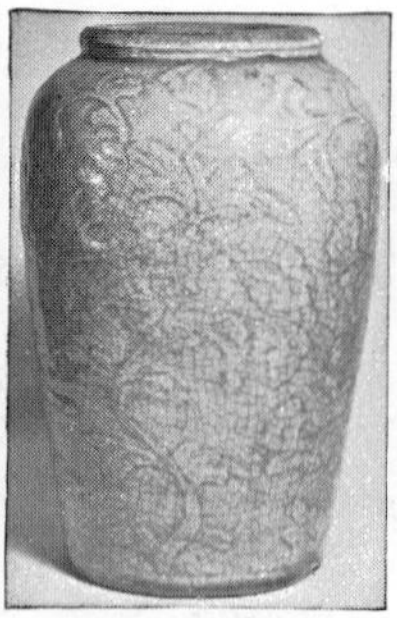
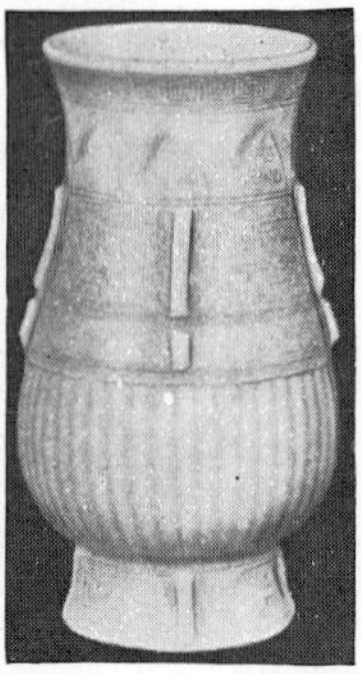

FIG. 624. Ying Ch'ing type vase which I do not believe could possibly be of "Ju type." The heavy potting, shape and ornate relief design would indicate Late Sung into Early Ming period. Ht. 9¼". # B34 Eumorfopoulos Coll.

FIG. 625. Heavily potted jar of white porcelain burnt red where exposed and with Ying Ch'ing bubbly palest blue glaze, not possibly Ju yao and of the Late Sung to Early Ming period. Compare with Chu Chou celadon in form and decoration. Ht. 16¼". # B35 Eumorfopoulos Coll.

FIG. 626. Typical Chu Chou celadon jar heavily potted and with relief decoration not unlike that of the two Ying Ch'ing examples shown. Ht. 12". Warren E. Cox Coll.

FIG. 627. Vase of bronze form (hu) of white porcelain slightly browned where exposed at the foot-rim, and a bubbly pale blue glaze. Ht. 5¾". # B1 Eumo. Coll.

FIG. 628. Lung-ch'üan vase (fêng wei p'ing) of grey porcelain burnt red-brown where exposed and with a sea-green glaze over applique design. Dated 1327 A.D. Ht. 28". Sir Percival David Coll.

Neither of the Kuan yao factories so far as we know survived the Mongolian conquest.

Ko yao undoubtedly persisted as a general type but the Chinese tell us nothing of the original source during this time.

Lung-ch'üan we have been given to believe stopped all work when the men moved to Ch'u-chou, the capital of Chekiang province, but this was not the case for in the Sir Percival David Collection there are several examples of typical Lung Ch'üan ware with Ming dates on them. Some workmen undoubtedly left while others remained and continued to work the kilns. It is difficult enough to distinguish the Ming from the Sung wares and in this we are uncertain but, lacking dated pieces, we certainly cannot as yet split them down to Yüan in period, although we know they were made.

The Yang Chiang factories in Kwangtung were not much harmed by the invasion and certainly continued without any definite break with the reddish brown body and glassy sort of glazes. It may also likely be that Yüeh factories continued. The bowls dug up at Showchow in Anhwei are called by Hobson, "probably Yüan" and they may be although other authorities place them in Sung times.

The Chün yao turned out at Yü chou we are told was coarser and the

Chün yao incense burner
cal'ed Sung ? at the museum
but more likely of the Yüan
or even Ming period. It is
of gray stoneware covered
with a rather opaque light
blue glaze. Ht. about 6".
Metropolitan Mus of Art.

Center: Late Sung, Yüan "incense jar" of grey porcelaneous stoneware burnt red where exposed and covered on the outside only and down nearly to the feet with a transparent olive green glaze finely crackled and full of bubbles. Made at Chün chou. Ht. 10". Warren E. Cox Coll.

Right: Chün type vase of the Yüan or Ming period. This type largely of the light blue color with olive brown edges. Similar examples have been sold for Sung pieces but the difference in body and glaze and the so involved form would certainly indicate a later period. Ht. about 8¾". Freer Gallery of Art, Washington.

Yüan Chün type vase on stand
of buff stoneware covered with an
even but somewhat opaque greenish pale blue mat glaze. Ht.
about 7½". Metropolitan Mus.
of Art.

Right: Four incense burners or flower-pots of buff ware or grey ware burnt red and with various glazes of blue, lavender, and greyish tones. Hts. 7", 5", 7½" and 13¾". Yüan period Chün yao made at Yu Chou in Northern Honan. Eumorfopoulos Coll. # C89, C90, C91 and C92. Note: Some of the less ornate and sturdier ones are undoubtedly Yüan but the two lower ones are, in my opinion, Ming and show close resemblance in form to many that we find glazed in green and yellow-brown.

YÜAN CHÜN WARES

PLATE 129

glaze ran in a thick welt ending some distance from the base which was entirely unglazed. This change may have taken place in the Yüan dynasty or possibly have started in late Sung times and no authority states anything to the contrary on the fact that it may have continued well into the Ming and perhaps even later times. The present day placing of all cruder pieces of Chün into the Yüan times is ridiculous. However, certain radical changes take place in the design of Chün wares as can be seen by the vessels illustrated and these certainly show no simple Sung taste. I think it quite correct to place all of these wares later and am glad to say that the Freer Gallery, Washington, has called theirs Yüan or Ming. Even so I incline toward the latter attribution for, if these wares were in ordinary green or mustard yellow glaze they would unhesitatingly be so placed because of their shapes. The example from my own collection has an olive green glaze exactly like a Sung example shown in that section. The blue glazes are little different except perhaps slightly more opaque.

I have already spoken in the Sung section of the Tsung Sê (dark brown colored) wares and the fact that many of these are later. In general the more ornate designs and more glossy or treacly glazes on the globular examples show them to be Yüan or Ming. In the Eumorfopoulos Collection #C418 there is an example with the design of a "happy boy" amongst foliage, with an incised leaf band above which is a plain band with incised inscription "ta te pa nien ch'i yüeh — jih" or "eighth year of Ta Tê, seventh month ? day" i.e., A.D. 1305. An abbreviated form of the character tê is used in the inscription. This vase Mr. Hobson also calls a Tz'u Chou type. His decription reads: "Vase of gallipot shape, with globular body and small neck with projecting ridge." (This is the usual Sung everted lip.) "Buff grey stoneware with thick black glaze, the ornament formed by cutting away the ground and exposing the body, namely a broad belt with boys holding lily scrolls: a band of angular fret on the shoulder. The base is glazed. Incised leaf patterns above the base and a plain black band with the inscription." This does not relegate all similar pieces to the same period but simply gives us a milestone to judge by.

To show us that we cannot go entirely by the style of design, I am illustrating #C413 of the Eumorfopoulos Collection, a most disconcerting jar to pedants. Here we see an example with "Ming style" design on one side and "Sung style" on the other just as though the potter said to himself, "If they want an ancient design, let them look at this side. If they want a contemporary design, they may turn it around." Hobson calls this jar "Sung or Yüan" but, of course, no Sung artist could have *foreseen* the decadence in taste that was going to take place and I should say that it is definitely Ming. The ornate side shows typical Ming taste and the very idea of making the combination in one jar is a Ming stunt. It is even more amusing to see that on the simple side the potter has made his glaze more mat in effect. He was a knowing fellow!

If the Chien yao bowls continued, perhaps not so much to fill the desires of the conquerors as the demand in Japan, so also did the wares of that general section. Hobson has designated that territory as the source of what

FIG. 629. Jar of buff-grey stoneware with thick black glaze. This is a Sung form carried over. Ht. 10″. Probably made at Tz'u Chou. Eumorfopoulos Coll. # C418.

FIG. 631. Top is jar # C413 Eumorfopoulos Coll. which shows what might be called Ming style on one side and Sung on the other. The pieces below are both more likely Yüan or Ming. Hts. 14″ and 15″.

FIG. 630. Rougher body and somewhat thicker glaze incline me to judge this piece as Yüan. It must be remembered that after about 1100 A.D. the northern sections of China were under Mongolian rule. Ht. 13″. Warren E. Cox Coll.

he labels "Kian temmoku" though we must remember the legend that when Wên, the Sung minister, passed by all of the wares turned to jade and the potters ran away to Ching-tê Chên. Despite my aforementioned theory that

FIG. 632. Yüan jar. The base is glazed and finished with a spiral. Collectors must not conclude that this is an indication of Japanese manufacture. Ht. 14½″. Eumorfopoulos Coll. # C411.

FIG. 633. The crude potting and ornate though poorly incised design lead us to place this jar as of the Yüan or Early Ming period. Ht. 14″.

FIG. 634. Jar with grey body and rather glossy though thinly applied dark brown glaze. The background is filled in with white. Yüan or Ming. Ht. 14″. Ex Edward Wells Coll. Judge Edgar Bromberger Coll. Brooklyn Mus.

this reference is to a *name* "jade ware" given or taken away by Wên and to the evidence of the jar and cover with the character for "jade" or the similar character numeral "five," incised on the bottom—I may have had one of these pottery bowls turned to jade in my hands once.

I met a very old Chinese gentleman who claimed that his brother had a cousin whose uncle lived at Yung-ho Chên, which is in Chi Chou district in the department of Kian or as we now know it, Chi-an Fu, in central Kiangsi near an old kiln-site, and that he, on a windy night but when the moonlight was strong, heard a high-pitched ringing like distant musical bells and, being impelled to follow the sound, came suddenly upon a bowl resting between the roots of a tree where a mole had no doubt turned it up from the earth. It had no color for it seemed part of the moonlight rather than simply to reflect it as would a common bowl, and, said my old friend, "He who says that moonlight is green will be contradicted by one who says that it is blue or one who claims that it is white." Perhaps we had better call the color ch'ing. "And white is a color," continued my friend, "for if white was absence of color, as Europeans describe it, it could not be seen when held up in the air while actually white can be most clearly seen of all." Well, to get back to the sound, it had been caused by the wind striking the so-very-thin bowl in just such a way and this seemed a remarkable and portentous thing to this man who picked up the bowl forthwith and sent it to his nephew who sent it to my friend with the express purpose of selling it to me.

We talked a little of what the price of such an object should be and drank rice wine while we talked. Soon I was so intrigued that I asked to see the bowl, thus showing my impatience and at the same time losing a certain amount of respect from my friend and doubling the price he had in mind. I was told that it would be too much of a shock for me to receive the impression of such an object upon more than one of my senses at once and after the lights were lowered the bowl was placed in my hands. It felt very beautiful, plain, thin as a breath and cold, cold as death. Then the lights were put on and it was no longer in my hands though the touch of it remained as does a kiss on a lover's lips. Perhaps I had not said the right words in praise. Perhaps my price had been too low. But in any event it was gone. Was it porcelain? Was it jade? Or was it the tissue of dreams?

"PHILIPPINE" POTTERIES

Brown Wares and Others

Though some are Sung and others are Ming, I decided that this would be a good place to discuss the potteries found in the Philippines, the East Indies and Malaysia. These were not made in such places but were probably produced in Fukien. Malcom Farley said he had found many sherds in that province which unmistakably corresponded. There are a number of different wares and Dr. Berthold Laufer properly allocated some of them with thick, opaque and oily glazes in a peculiar light blue, grass-green, dark green, olive green and lilac as "Kuang yao" made in Kuangtung province at either Yang-ch'un or Yang-kiang. This latter type is not found in graves and is probably all of Ming or later times. However, the "dragon jars," he says are of the Ming period, if in modern use, or of Sung period if found in burial caves. This, of course, is not a hard and fast rule but largely correct. He further shows the understanding of the natives (that is "the Dayak" to

FIG. 635. Ming period brown pottery jar with deep cobalt blue glaze and brown glaze at mouth. These were made in Fukien province. Ht. 22". Warren E. Cox Coll.

FIG. 636. One of a pair of slender brown pottery jars with amber-brown glaze over a relief applique, relief modeled and incised design. Ming period. Ht. 23". Warren E. Cox Coll.

FIG. 637. Typical brown pottery with yellow-brown glaze of the type found in Fukien Province. Ming period. Ht. 20½". Ann Arbor from Dr. Guthe.

quote him) of the age of these wares by the fact that tney would not buy any later imitations made in China which speculative dealers tried to palm off on them.

We find in Fay-Cooper Cole's Field Museum publication #162 that a man named Pigafetta made record of finding potteries in the Philippines in 1521, and that these were very highly valued by the natives and their source already lost in antiquity. Pigafetta was with Magellan when he made his wonderful expedition and he tells that a chief of a small island near Leyte "embraced the captain-general to whom he gave three porcelain jars covered with leaves and full of rice wine." When Pigafetta came to Cebu he saw the king, "seated on a palm mat on the ground, with only a cotton cloth before his privies. . . . From another mat on the ground he was eating turtle eggs which were in two porcelain dishes, and he had four jars of palm wine in front of him covered with sweet smelling herbs and arranged with four small reeds in each jar by which means he drank." A note states that such large jars are still used to drink from in all parts of this section. At Mindanao he wrote, "—in the house were hanging a number of porcelain jars and four metal gongs." And there the Spaniards saw two Chinese junks which made "warlike display" (I suppose it didn't have to be much of a show) and were captured and "The decks of the vessels were full of earthen jars and crockery, large porcelain vases, plates and bowls, and some fine porcelain jars which they called 'sinoratas'."

Mr. Cole further relates that by 1574 some of the ware had assumed great value in the eyes of the natives and the chiefs sent as tokens of allegiance to the King of Spain, "jewels, gold, silks, porcelains, rich and large earthen jars, and other very excellent things." The custom had also started in air, ancient forgotten time of placing jars in the graves. Japan had also decided that these jars were the best for keeping tea and Morga writes, "On this island, Luzon, very ancient clay vessels of a dark brown color are found by the natives, of a sorry appearance. (We suppose he means the jars.) The Japanese prize them highly, for they have found the root of a herb which they call 'Tscha' (tea), and which when drunk hot is considered as a great delicacy and of medicinal efficacy by the kings and lords of Japan, cannot be effectively preserved except in these vessels; which are so highly esteemed all over Japan that they form the most costly articles of their showrooms and cabinets. Indeed so highly do they value them that they overlay them externally with fine gold embossed with great skill, and enclose them in cases of brocade; and some of these vessels are valued at and fetch from 2,000 tael to 11 reals." This passage is most interesting for it also throws light on the fine Korean brown glazed bowl which I have described and which has a hardly perceptible tracery of gold on it.

Mr. Cole further quotes Carletti as having met a Franciscan in 1615 who was sent as ambassador from Japan to Rome, who assured him that he had seen 130,000 scudi paid by the king of Japan for such a vessel. Furthermore, "St. John relates that the Datu of Tamparuli (Borneo) gave rice to the value of almost £700 for a jar, and that he possessed a second jar of almost fabulous value which was about two feet high and of a dark olive green." This is not unlike the one we illustrate.

Due to the fact that the islanders could not possibly make such wares, more and more magic came to be told about them. One was said to speak and the Sultan of Brunei stated that it howled dolefully the night before the death of his second wife. Another is kept filled with water which is sprinkled over the fields and women to insure fecundity. This the sultan is said to have refused an offer of £20,000 for. His water sprinkling racket must have been a good one! Actually a man's wealth is judged by the number of jars he has. Among the Tinguian of Abra Mr. Cole tells of a jar named "Magsawi" which talked and went on long journeys by itself, was married to a female jar owned by the Tinguian of Ilocos Norte and had a child at San Quintin. The owner said it used to talk softly but that since it had been broken it could not be understood. This legend may have come from the actual sounds given off by some large jars. I have one myself which in our old studio, which had a forty-foot arched ceiling, would pick up the tones of my voice, if I raised it, and mimic me into shame. Now that we have moved it, it has ceased to remonstrate.

In partnership with Mr. E. L. Worcester who obtained them in the Philippines I own a number of these jars which I am illustrating along with those, pictures of which were kindly sent me from Ann Arbor by Dr. Guthe. They seem to fall into definite types as follows:

1.—The earliest which is probably of the Six Dynasties or late Han times about A.D. 220 to A.D. 618 is very thinly potted for its size and of a dense, heavy brown almost black body, decorated with three concentric ridge rings about the shoulder filled in between with wave combed incising and having four stamped small loops. The glaze is thin and hard and of a red-brown

Two renowned jars from the Sub-province of Abra, N. Luzon. The jar on the left is Magsawi, the famous talking jar. Photograph courtesy of Field Mus. of Natural History.

Jar made in Fukien province according to Malcomb Farley, but found in the Philippines and identical ware to the famous "talking jar." Loops repaired. Ht. about 9". Warren E. Cox Coll.

Chung Tze (brown pottery) vase found in the Philippines but made in Fukien province. The modeling and glaze are made to emulate leather sewn on as a covering. The upper part of the vase only is finished which would indicate that it probably stood in a rack of wood. Sung period. Ht. 24". Warren E. Cox Coll.

PHILIPPINE BROWN POTTERY (CHUNG TZE) JARS

PLATE 130

Sung period vase found in the Philippines and made of brown stoneware with a grey-brown glaze washed on helically about the body. Ht. 23″. Warren E. Cox Coll.

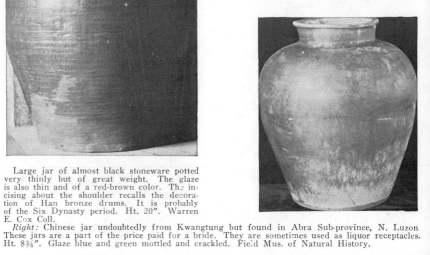

Large jar of almost black stoneware potted very thinly but of great weight. The glaze is also thin and of a red-brown color. The incising about the shoulder recalls the decoration of Han bronze drums. It is probably of the Six Dynasty period. Ht. 20″. Warren E. Cox Coll.

Right: Chinese jar undoubtedly from Kwangtung but found in Abra Sub-province, N. Luzon. These jars are a part of the price paid for a bride. They are sometimes used as liquor receptacles. Ht. 8¾″. Glaze blue and green mottled and crackled. Field Mus. of Natural History.

EARLY CHINESE JARS FOUND IN THE PHILIPPINES

PLATE 131

to olive color. It is wheel-made and has a flat bottom unmarked. This is a fine, powerful piece of potting not lacking in high technical skill so high fired that it rings with a clearer and higher note than does the first porcelain made in China of about the same period. The concentric ring decoration recalls that found on bronze drums made in China during the Han period.

2.—A heavier type of red-brown body and with thin olive brown glaze applied only half way up the neck and two thirds of the way down the body in thin wash streaked around the jar as though done on the wheel is early Sung or earlier. The glaze is similar to that applied to the late Han porcelain jars and the method of application on the upper part only is the same. These jars have flat bottoms and the larger ones have loops on the shoulders for tying down a covering. There is never any ornamentation and the shapes are simple and well proportioned.

3.—Perhaps a little later in the Sung period comes the very large jar of simple form and covered with an olive green glaze. The body of this is a buff stoneware also hard enough to give a note when struck.

FIG. 640. Brown pottery jar with transparent green glaze which produces greenish-brown effect. Ht. 14".

FIG. 639. Brownish black jar found with a bowl inverted over the mouth. The decoration and treatment of glaze would seem also to indicate that this piece was made in Fukien Province. Ht. 10½". Ann Arbor from Dr. Guthe.

FIG. 638. One of a pair of large jars of grey-brown pottery with a light brown glaze over relief dragons the details of which are incised. Ht. 24". Warren E. Cox Coll. This is the type that Laufer established as of Ming dynasty.

FIG. 641. Greenish brown jar of the 18th cent. made in Fukien province and sent to the Philippines. Ht. 20". Ann Arbor from Dr. Guthe.

4.—Of late Sung or Yüan period are probably three distinctive types of Tsung Sê t'zǔ (dark brown colored pottery).

a.—The first type is surely Sung in all characteristics. The ware is reddish-buff and it has applied ridges and dots representing stitched leather over the upper half and shoulder. There are four flat leather-like loops on the shoulder and the glaze is of a dark porous brown carrying out the illusion. The shapes are not unlike the ones described under section three. The lower parts are simply daubed with the remaining glaze on the brush and I believe these jars were intended to fit into racks of wood on a ship deck for the upper parts are beautifully finished, and the daubing is far from attractive.

b.—The famous talking jar described above and one in our collection is of high fired buff stoneware, wheel-turned as are all of these and decorated with appliqués (bosses in the case of the talking jar and dragons, tao-teh monster heads and flames on clouds on ours) and covered with a dark brown glaze which goes light brown and reddish in places where it is thin. The character of the design on our piece makes me believe it is possibly Indonesian and likely from Sukotai-Sawankalock though excavations there have so far turned up nothing just like it. The technique would point to 13th or 14th century without much doubt.

c.—Of the height of the Sung period again is the beautiful buff-grey bodied ware of nearly globular body with slightly angular shoulder and truncated conical neck having a rounded lip-rim. The foot is concave without foot-rim. On the shoulders are four well made loops either plain or like rope and the body may be plain or slightly incised. The glaze is a beautiful soft, waxy, porous deep brown showing light where thin. Few of the northern Tsung Sê wares can rival this in fineness of potting and beauty of form.

A later continuation of the same ware is shown in the half spherical heavier jar found with bowl over the top. This is probably Ming.

5.—Undoubtedly of early Ming period are the squatty and, a little later, the tall forms of "dragon jars" made of brown pottery nowhere nearly so hard as the former wares and covered with a transparent blown glaze of various shades but never deep in color. These are decorated with incised and appliqué designs of clouds, dragons and occasionally flowers.

6.—Of late Ming and later come the plain jars of similar shape and covered with deep blue, green or white splashed with blue glazes and also the squat brown pottery jars having a dull olive brown glaze and found in various places in Kwangtung province.

7.—The crude blue and white and other pottery and porcelain dishes are all of typical Kwangtung, Ching period make or even later.

8.—Just recently through the kind introduction by Miss Josephine Hadley of the Metropolitan Museum of Art, I met Mrs. Kamer Aga-Oglu who had brought a box of sherds from the University of Michigan, Ann Arbor, which had been found in the Philippines. They included a number of "celadon" types including Sung, Ming and possibly later Lung-ch'üan pieces typical in all respects, some Ch'u-chou examples which showed the effects of burial and may have been Sung in period, others of typical Ming aspects, one unmistakable Southern Kuan piece showing narrow and well made foot-rim and brownish olive transparent, crackled glaze, a few of the dull white glazed pieces with buff-gray, coarse body and indications of unglazed rims inside showing that they had been stacked one upon another in firing without much care, and finally a number of odd pieces which I could not identify. These astute young ladies had shown the pieces to a number of able authorities and Mrs. Aga-Oglu is going to make a special study of them, reports of which I shall look forward to with interest.

YÜAN TING YAO

When the Sung capital was moved from Kai-feng Fu in 1127 the potters from Ting Chou are said to have gone along and it is said that a test of a collector's skill in China is that of distinguishing between the north and south Ting wares. Certainly we cannot make this distinction.

Many other factories also tried to produce this ware and one of the best known is Hsüan Chou in Anhwei province. Others were Su Chou and Ssŭ Chou in the same province. In Shansi in Ho Chou a famous potter by the name of P'êng Chünpao made fine copies of Ting yao in the Yüan dynasty. Another place in this province was P'ing yang Fu where Dr. Rücker Embden dug up a ware with fairly coarse yellowish body, slip and yellowish crackle transparent glaze. This, having a slip, we should class among the Tz'u Chou type wares but it was an attempted copy of Ting. The same gentleman found a light grey bodied ware with thick, translucent yellowish glaze usually crackled near Yao Chou, Shensi province. These were Sung kilns which continued through the Yüan and into the Ming

Fig. 642. Dish of the Yüan period made at Ching-tê Chên to imitate Ting yao and probably actually after a Ting specimen judging by its design. The ware is white and the glaze whiter than the whitest Ting. The foot-rim is glazed and the edge is left unglazed although the ware is such that it would probably fire perfectly true. Dia. 6⅛". John Platt-Warren E. Cox Coll.

dynasties, though their output was not very important.

In the southern part in Kiangsi province at Nan-fêng Hsien and at Yung-ho Chên were made Tu Ting yao and the other wares including a purple or brown (T'zu) type, but nowhere could any kiln compete with the Ching-tê Chên makers of "nan Ting."

Data is lacking for the allocation of many of these Ting wares. The factories were not continuous and some of the provincial wares were very good. In all of them there was an increased tendency to crowd the design and in some a reversion took place toward the more ornate T'ang period shapes. Molded decoration almost entirely supplants incised and one may say in general that the glazes were more likely to be glossy or even glassy.

TZ'U CHOU TYPE YÜAN WARES

It will be remembered that the *Ko ku yao lun* (1387) stated flatly that Tz'u Chou wares of the contemporary times were not worth collecting. Its date brings us into Ming times but we would suppose the same applied to the slightly earlier wares. We do not quite agree with this statement but we must admit that the more ornate design on the globular Tz'u Chou jars with the addition of dark red, green and sometimes yellow, began to lose charm and become something like Ming paintings; dull and over ornate copies. Shapes too become more baroque. That tightness of line between bottom and top that lends to the Sung wares simplicity has relaxed into crooked S curves as may be seen in the dark glazed incised specimen illustrated.

One type found in northern China and quite possibly made at Tz'u Chou itself reverts to a more or less T'ang shape somewhat exaggerated. I illustrate the well known one from the Freer Gallery of Art, Washington, and submit with all due respect that I think the neck too slender and small for the heavy body and the incised floral decoration distinctly decadent. It was at first thought that these vases were of early Sung date, "near to T'ang," but we have already noted that the Mongolian invasion brought with it this flamboyant and somewhat Near Eastern feeling and I should allocate these specimens in the Yüan period on the grounds that the potting of the bases is rough and sloppy with wide and deep footrims, the taste decadent and the technique late rather than early. In the Samuel T. Peters Collection at the Metropolitan Museum of Art is a better proportioned and plain white glazed example which is a prototype.

FIG. 643. The dark brown body, angular shoulders often seen in Tz'u Chou vases of the Yüan period, and "mishima" inlay of this piece indicates to me that it is of late Sung or Yüan period. Ht. 16¼". The Cleveland Mus. of Art. Dikran G. Kelekian Coll.

In the past several great collectors paid high prices for these vases, thinking, I suppose, that they were the super super of carved wares and forgetting the real beauty of the fine and spontaneous line incising of the Sung period. The designs on every one are stiff, labored and wooden. If the old Chinese saying is true, that a leaf dies, if it is touched twice with the brush, how much more true it is when the leaf is whittled all around with the knife. In any event the prices were nearly top for Sung wares until recently in the Mrs. Christian R. Holmes sale immediately after a Chi-lü Hsien vase brought $1,350. An excellent specimen of this carved Tz'u Chou ware some 17 inches high brought only $500, and was, I believe, bought in at that. Formerly $5,000 would have been thought low.

The tendency shown in these vases toward sharper reversed curves can be seen in the simple black painted Tz'u Chou type wares in which the body is more gritty due to less care in refining it and lower fire temperature. The glazes are often not crackled (though this is not always a rule to be depended upon), the black is often blacker and the design more crowded. However, all style was not lost as can be seen in the incised jar with the somewhat wobbly but nevertheless expressive drawing of wilting long leaves and small flowers. This has a yellowish glaze with good imitation "tear stains" like those of Ting ware on it. Also a certain type of ware which I have not been able to allocate and two specimens of which are shown herewith, are well made of grey stoneware and covered with a brown or pinkish buff crackled glaze and painted with brown in sparse, well designed flowers. The cylindrical

FIG. 644. Tz'u Chou type vase like # C410 and # C416 of the Eumorfopoulos Coll. which are designated Yüan. Ht. 10½". Warren E. Cox Co.l.
FIG. 645. Vase. Late Sung or Yüan. Ht. 15½". Freer Gallery of Art, Wash.
FIG. 646. Tz'u Chou of the type called Yüan by many authorities but very likely of the Ming period. Ht. about 13". Gift of Mrs. Samuel T. Peters. Metropolitan Mus. of Art.

FIG. 647. Two jars with a flower pot, the one is Sung, the other jar and flower pot are Yüan. Hts. about 6". Warren E. Cox Coll.
FIG. 648. Wei Hsiang gallipot of the Yüan period. Ht. 9½". Warren E. Cox Coll.

FIG. 649. Tz'u Chou type jar of Yüan or Ming period. Ht. 13". Metropolitan Mus. of Art.
FIG. 650. Tz'u Chou of Yüan or Ming period. Metropolitan Mrs. of Art.
FIG. 651. White porcelain vase of the typical Yüan shape. Ht. 8½". Warren E. Cox Coll.

Tz'u Chou type jar of brown stoneware with slip and glaze giving a deep cafe-au-lait tone. The masterful painting of bird and flowers in black speaks of the great artistry sometimes found in paintings of the period. About the neck is a peculiar orange toned iron red overglaze band. Ht. 10". Warren E. Cox Coll.

Jar of buff-grey stoneware with white slip and warm white glaze closely crackled and clouded with pinkish grey and buff stains, painted with a spirited horse design in black and brown slips. Yüan period. Ht. 10". Eumorfopoulos Coll. # C359.

Left: Yüan incense burner (ting) of Tz'u Chou ware with brown glaze at bottom, a white slip and transparent glaze on upper part and swift, sure paintings of birds and plants. About the neck is a band of orange-red overglaze color. Many Yüan examples show as great a mastery of painting as the Sung ones. Ht. 6¼". Warren E. Cox Coll.

Center: Yüan Tz'u Chou of grey stone ware with pinkish glaze and decoration in brown. Ht. 8½". Ex Warren E. Cox Coll.

Right: Jar of grey stoneware which burns red where exposed in the cracks on the shoulder. In this case the incising was done before the slip was applied and the cream glaze runs with "tear drops" like the Ting yao glaze but more ivory in color. Yüan or Ming. Ht. 9". Warren E. Cox Coll.

YÜAN DYNASTY TZ'U CHOU TYPE POTTERIES

Plate 132

vase has also a band of dark reddish-brown around the neck. These are Yüan or Ming, probably the latter, and often have molded marks or the bottom probably indicating the maker.

BLUE AND WHITE YÜAN WARES

We have already made note that the *Po wu yao lan* refers to Ching-tê Chên wares which may be construed to mean blue decorated white wares, and which were said to have been made during the Yüan period. Much evidence seems even to point to a late Sung origin for blue and white ware as we have said, but the making of these things was in a highly experimental stage, the blue was dull and it is evident that the Chinese did not know how to handle it. Note as an instance the way the glaze cracked and broke open on the little bowl belonging to Mr. d'Ancona, particularly where it goes over the blue design. (See last part of Sung section.) Note also that the Chinese blue was uneven and lumpy to apply.

FIG. 652. Yüan or Early Ming period blue and white jar and cover. The decoration is in dark mottled blue and the glaze slightly bluish white. Ht. 15". Mus. of Fine Arts, Boston.

FIG. 653. Yüan or Early Ming period vase with grayed and reddish underglaze blue and a thick translucent glaze of cream tone. Ht. 7½". Metropolitan Mus. of Art.

FIG. 654. Blue and white jar called Yüan but which may possibly be a little earlier. The ground is slightly toward a buff tone and the blue somewhat grayed. Ht. 16½". Metropolitan Mus. of Art.

One group of heavy porcelains seem to contain iron for they burn red in some places where exposed. The shapes seem more Mongolian than Chinese and yet the blue is no better developed than on the thinner Sung types. These we place in the Yüan period.

Another and finer type are the large jars with covers of Near Eastern feeling in form and quite full in their decoration. On these the blue seems to have been better mastered, the potting is thinner and the glaze no longer gives trouble. They are probably Yüan or Early Ming.

CHAPTER XIX

THE GREAT MING PERIOD

(1368–1644)

THE odd conception that artists are born and not made is ridiculous for artists take a lot of making after having been born, but some people do seem to have an inherent longing for the beautiful. Just as the Negro cannot resist bursting into song though he be doing the mostly lowly and rough work so the Chinese must pause to contemplate the beautiful though his world may be falling about his ears. Mere conquests and the killing of thousands of his brethren cannot stop him any more than can the crowding of life which our various western "civilizations" have impressed upon him. Thus the Mongolian conquest was turned to use, digested and brought about not disaster but simply new ideas.

The pure and simple taste of the Sung period had reached the pinnacle of perfection in China and perhaps in the whole world. I believe, and others agree with me, that the finest vases and bowls ever made in the world were made then. But Ming taste is also most appealing. It may be said to divide itself into two fields each of which became more and more exaggerated. The one is that of reaching utter perfection in technique, an almost inhuman perfection, while the other is in developing the greatest of boldness and flamboyant color. Porcelain was the real medium for both though some of the Ming potteries and stonewares are superb.

The Chinese did not "invent" porcelain. We have seen that around A.D. 200 a ware was made which contained the necessary ingredient, "Kaolin" or "kao-lin" which is said to mean "high ridge" or possibly a certain mountain named "Kao-ling" where the substance was found near Ching-tê Chên. More or less consciously all through the Six Dynasties, T'ang and Sung periods for some thousand and more years the substance had been used and harder wares were made. These wares also became whiter in body and more translucent but not all porcelain is necessarily distinguished by these charac-teristics. Kaolin is a non-fusible silicate of alumina which has the property of uniting at high temperatures with "petuntse" or "pe-tun-tse," which is a fusible bisilicate feldspar, to form porcelain. Dr. Hirth found embalmed in *Sung Pharmacopia* two early references to "pai o" which he proves to have been kaolinic earth and says it was not only used for medicine but also in painting pictures, so it would seem that it was recognized at least at this time.

With the kaolin and petuntse there was mixed some chalk, some silicic acid in the form of quartz or sand and a little magnesia, and then the materials were washed, ground, filtered and then kneaded with water into a mass suitable for handling. The potter then proceeded with molding, throwing on the wheel, modeling or hand shaping. Much stress was laid upon proper cleaning, for one speck of foreign matter might cause a flaw. How differently the Sung potters regarded such things. Though they did strive for perfect wares, they also had such faith in their various abilities to move the beholder that they had no fear of any such minor distraction; they thought of imperfection as a part of nature just as they would paint a worm-eaten leaf to make it look *more natural and true* than a perfect one. ˙ .

When the potter had finished with the body he would dip it into a glaze composed of feldspar and lime and then the piece was fired at what the French call the "grand feu" or high fire of about 1350 to 1450 degrees Centigrade, or 2430 to 2610 degrees Fahrenheit. This brings about a chemical change making a hard, white, translucent and so vitrified material that it will ring like a bell when struck lightly. This substance we in the West have come to call "porcelain" though the original makers of it termed it "tz'u" (kiln) or "t'ao" (products of the kiln) or "yao" (ware), and drew no hard and fast differentiation. None of the early chronicles in China seem to speak definitely of translucency yet pieces found at Samarra were translucent. We have already explained in the section on Kuan yao, Sung period, that the phrase, "see right through" may well have meant see right into the glaze, and not necessarily through the body.

Due to various attempts to achieve this true porcelain or "hard porcelain" which is so hard that steel will not scratch it, impermeable to liquids and unaffected by all acids other than hydrofluoric, we find some confusion in terminology. Thus "Medici porcelain" made in Italy in the 16th century and the 17th century French wares of St. Cloud, etc. were nothing but white clay mixed with a "frit" or ground glass and covered with a lead glaze. It was fired at 1100° C. and again at 1000° C. for the glaze, and this was called "Soft Porcelain," though of course, it was not porcelain at all. Meanwhile the Chinese, hearing of it, made what is loosely called, "Soft Paste," in the late Ming and later periods. This is at times changed in body but usually in glaze only. The substance used was thought to be soapstone or steatite but has later been determined to be pegmatite. It may not be quite so high fired as hard porcelain but is still much higher than the so-called "soft porcelain" of Europe. Much of it is of the Yung Chêng or late K'ang Hsi period and decorated in blue on white but some is Ming of undetermined but probably late reign and a soft yellowish-white. Aside from this one type it is the practice in China to fire body, underglaze decoration and glaze all at one time. Only when surface decoration in enamel and gold is used did they fire a second and third time, each, of course, at a lower temperature.

The glaze of feldspar, limestone and plant ash was said to have been made in early times with the burnt leaves of bamboo, peach or later with ferns laid between layers of the limestone and burnt then mixed with water. It is said that the brilliance and clarity of the finest porcelain was obtained because of the exact quality of this ash. According to Hobson and quoting Bushell's translations, the porcelain clay came from Hsin-chêng-tu in the Ma-ts'ang hills in four places named "The Gully of a Thousand Families," and "the Dragon Gully," etc. The stone was obtained from the Hu-t'ien district. Good earth for the glaze came from Hsin-chêng-tu also but the best was brought from Ch'ang-ling and I-kêng. The "ch'ing" color came from Ch'ang-ling as did the yellow, but the white was from I-kêng. All of these places were near Ching-tê Chên.—Later in the Wan Li reign (1573–1619) the last important one of the dynasty the pits at the Ma-ts'ang hills were worked out and those at Wu-mên-t'o were not so good. Also the special mixtures of earth for the very heavy vessels came from Yü-kan and Wu-yüan and were mixed with stone from the Hu-t'ien district.

White Ware or "Blanc de Chine"

The pure white ware or "Blanc de Chine" as the French call it, is termed in China "pai tz'u" or "Chien yao" and the latter term must not be confused with the ware of which the little brown bowls are made in the same locality. This white ware comprised all manner of porcelain objects and was a dense creamy white almost pure white and as Hobson aptly calls it, "like milk jelly or blancmange," and the glaze is so united with the body that one can hardly tell where one stops and the other begins. The glazes of all the later periods appear glassy, or dead white in comparison with the Ming ware. At times it has the palest suggestion of a rosy tinge. A late Chinese book tells us, "When the glaze is white like jade, glossy and lustrous, rich and thick, with a reddish tinge, and the biscuit heavy, the ware is of first quality."

The ware was made at Tê-hua or Tehwa in the Ch'üan-chou district of Fukien province about 100 miles south of Chien-yang. By A.D. 1700 the wares were plentiful and no longer dear. Decorated pieces were also made as is proven by an example in the Eumorfopoulos Collection, a double bottomed hot water bowl with designs in green, yellow, red and typical Ming turquoise green. Those impressed with Ming marks are always of later date, but makers' marks do appear on some early ones. The finely modeled religious figures are undoubtedly the best of the output. Graceful Kuan-yin figures represent the idea of the "Mother of Mercy" of the Italians or of simple fecundity and hold inverted vases, "the source of water in which everything grows," or a child, as do our Madonnas. Others represent Darhuma and other Buddhistic or Taoist deities. One unique specimen seems actually to be a Christian Madonna perhaps inspired by one of the fathers of the Church in China.

Most of the early wares have fire cracks inside the bottom due to the weight of the body but this is not an invariable characteristic. The K'ang Hsi ones are usually purer white and more detailed in modeling while Yung Chêng and Ch'ien Lung ones are inclined to be ivory in tone and filled with little bubbles in the glaze, seemingly an attempt to get the Ming creaminess but an unsuccessful one. Modern wares are of white body, thinly potted and with glassy, white glaze, but even these are beautiful little works of art for the few dollars they cost. Ming examples can bring four or five thousand dollars and are well worth it. Besides the kilns at Tê-hua many smaller

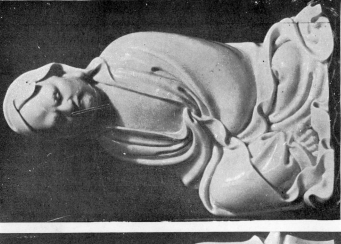

Left to Right: Late Ming or possibly K'ang Hsi figure of Kuan-yin, shown holding a ju-i sceptre and walking in water or standing on a cray-fish. Ht. 13″. Warren E. Cox Coll.
Te-hua figure of Kwan Yin which shows typically the rich creamy glaze attributed surely to the Ming period. Ht. 7½″. C. T. Loo & Co.
Fukien figure of a dignitary with a four clawed dragon in relief on his robe. Attributed to Ming dynasty. Note the slots left for the insertion of human hair. Attributed to Ming dynasty. Fuller Coll. Seattle Art Mus.
Fine Te-hua figure of Darhuma in thoughtful attitude. Ming dynasty. Ht. about 6½″. Ex Warren E. Cox Coll.

TÊ-HUA WHITE PORCELAIN FIGURES OF MING DYNASTY

PLATE 133

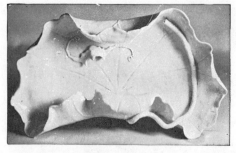

Left: Late Ming writer's water-dish of white porcelain with a glossy pinkish and ivory toned crackled glaze. It was fired on 28 small spurs with bottom glazed. Dia. 10″. Warren E. Cox Coll.
Right: Typical Tê-hua "birthday cup" with swallows on one side for happiness and stags and pine trees on the other for long life. Dia. 5¾″. Warren E. Cox Coll.

Left: Fukien Tê-hua porcelain of the Ming period with white body finely potted covered with a creamy glaze of pure white. Ht. about 8″. Metropolitan Mus. of Art.
Center: Ming period vase of white porcelain carved in relief with archaic dragons and having a transparent glaze slightly crackled. Ht. 4¼″. Ex D. Abbes Collection.
Right: Tê-hua, Fukien vase of fine quality and beautiful proportions. "Wheel marks" remain. Glaze is somewhat pitted but of pure, creamy white. Ht. 17¼″. Warren E. Cox Coll.

Left: Ming "soft paste" shallow dish in the form of a flower probably to be used for water on a scholar's table. Dia. 2½″. Fuller Coll. Seattle Art Mus.
Right: Ming period Fukien bowl probably from Tê-hua. Inscription reads, "If there are not three persons present to carry out the traditional drinking rule, drink three times yourself to match the rule. This is a cup to drink from." Dia. 5½″. Warren E. Cox Coll.

MING BLANC DE CHINE WARES
FROM TE-HUA AND OTHER KILNS

PLATE 134

factories copied the ware and some of the big ones such as Ting Chou, Ping-liang Fu in Shensi, and Ping-ting Chou and T'ai-yüan of the same province, Yü Chou and K'ai-fêng Fu in Honan, Wu-yüan Hsien and Ch'i-mên Hsien in Anhwei, etc., etc. But until more work is done in excavating we cannot allocate any given piece, and indeed it is difficult to place them in their proper periods. However, some of the greatest sculptors the world has known and worthy to be ranked with the della Robbias and others of great fame lived and died nameless leaving behind them a few of these beautiful and vigorous works of art. It is a field which should surely fascinate the collector.

Ming Colored Glazes

Colored glazes were made just as was the white with the addition of antimony for yellow, manganese for violet, aubergine (eggplant which the Chinese call "kai-pi-pe") or brown, copper for turquoise, green and several reds including the famous "sang de boeuf" or "Lang-yao" of sacrificial ox blood (not that the vases had anything to do with sacrifices except the giving up of considerable money for them) and iron for nasturtium or dead leaf brown and the highly prized green celadon colors. Varying temperatures account for the production of different colors with the same ingredients and transmutations produced Chün-like effects and also the "flambé" streaks of pale blue or lavender in red. These latter were only begun in the Ming period but later in the 18th century were well governed.

Crackle was perfected as an art in the Ming period and the potters not only could make any shape and size they wanted but graduate from large to small crackle, etc. The turquoise and yellow glazes as well as the copper reds or sang de boeuf are always crackled, the former rather finely and called "trout scales" or "fish scale" and the latter "crab's claw" as before. There are bottles on which the crackle takes a helical twist and a figure of blanc de chine in the Eumor-fopoulos Collection #D288 has the robe and hood crackled while the face is unblemished.

Underglaze colors are painted on the biscuit, will stand the high temperature of the "grand feu" and have the glaze over them. Only two were successful, blue and red. The blue was an oxide of cobalt and we do not know when or where it was first used, but it was surely used *as a glaze* on T'ang pieces and a colorless glaze may have been applied over the blue in some T'ang wares. We also know of early pieces from Persia and Syria but probably none go back much before the 6th or 7th century A.D. in China. The *Tao lu* (Julien, *op. cit.*, p. 76) speaks of the crackled wares made at Yung-ho Chên in the Sung period and says, "There were besides pieces with

Fig. 655. Tê-hua porcelain figure with crackle all over except on face and fingers. Ht. 30″. Eumorfopoulos Coll. # D288.

plain crackled ground, to which they add blue decoration." Again it is said that at Nan-fêng Hsien, in Kiangsi, in the Yüan dynasty, porcelain was made "of refined clay but somewhat thick, and decorated as a rule with blue designs, 'ch'ing hua'." In the Eumorfopoulos Collection Catalogue, Mr. Hobson some-

what hesitatingly designates #D1 as Sung, explaining that although some of these vases have designs which we are used to seeing on Ming porcelains, we are told by the Chinese that they are of Sung origin. This vase is not unlike the specimen I illustrate from the Metropolitan Museum of Art and which is called Ming or possibly Yüan. I show another under the Yüan section. The design is far less disturbing to me than the involved and poorly proportioned shape, with clumsy ring or loop handles, and the weight of the potting all of which would place them in the Ming times.

Far more Sung in shape and in decoration is a large jar from my own collection and a similar one #D14 in the Eumorfopoulos Collection which Hobson calls 15th century. The wonderful spirit and style of the "dragon horses" and the dashing wave borders, to say nothing of the beautifully done little rocks and flower passages make this seem surely an original work of art by some great master. The blue is dull and somewhat lumpy. The glaze is of soft ivory tone and crackled. The foot is slightly indented to give just a suggestion of a foot-rim. If it is of the Hsüan Tê reign (1426–1435) or the Chêng Hua (1465–1487) I know of nothing to equal it in those times. It is far more likely I believe that we will be able to push back many of these pieces as we learn more about kiln sites.

The underglaze red was made with the tiniest suggestion of copper oxide and fired in a reducing kiln. Again we do not know the source or time of beginning but tradition assigns it to the Hsüan Tê (1426–1435) reign in the Ming period when we do at least know that several kinds were developed. "Chi hung" was the color of the ritual cups used in the worship of the sun and it was divided into 1. "hsien hung" fresh or glossy red and 2. "pao shih hung" or precious stone red. The *Po wu yao lan* says, "For these they used a powder made of precious red stones from the West to paint the fish forms,

Fig. 657. An excellent example of the celadon made at Ch'u-chou but which has a design of Near Eastern feeling in underglaze red which appears reddish-brown and lustrous where it penetrates the green glaze. It is likely that the kilns in this district made the ware and the Ching-tê Chên took it up later using a lighter green glaze and white body. Dia. 11¾″. Warren E. Cox Coll. Ex Samuel T. Peters Coll.

and from the body of the porcelain there rose up in relief in the firing the precious brilliance of the fresh red ravishing the eye." This is, of course, a reference to the white cups with three fish or fruit on them. I show one from the Eumorfopoulos Collection which bears the Hsüan Tê mark.* It is further stated that later in such periods as the Chêng Tê the red is relatively dull and weak and in the Chia Ching the earth required ran out so that the potters had to use overglaze red enamel "fan hung" instead. At times the red was also used under a light celadon glaze but was, of course, rather dull. The beautiful dish illustrated is the best example I know.

The art of overglaze coloring was the chief achievement of the Ming potters. These overglaze colors are simply oxides of various metals ground up in glass which melts at a fairly low temperature in the kiln and makes them adhere to the glass-glaze. Iron red is the "driest" of these colors and appears almost mat but even it had a small amount of flux of glass for filling in areas, though it was used drier for outlines. Violet blue did not come into use until the K'ang Hsi period. Ming yellow is usually rather muddy though some odd bright yellow specimens exist. Gilding was rarely used and was either fired or leaf applied cold. Manganese produced a dry brown and black and this black was washed over with transparent green enamel to produce the lustrous blacks used in large areas. All colors except the red and black were transparent and usually applied thickly.

It is difficult to generalize about the Ming period yet collectors can say that a piece has a Ming look or is "Mingish" as old Voron used to say. First we must realize that the length of this period of 1368 to 1644 is some 276 years and that subtracting these years from our present we would find ourselves back when the British conquered New Netherlands and about the time that Marquette and Joliet discovered the Mississippi River. Quite a lot has taken place since then and, if potters had been making pots at that time in America, they would probably be making different ones now. Do not let anyone ever tell you that China is a country in which nothing much ever happened and no changes were made. Her present history shows a bit of what she has been through many times. There were huge migrations, many conflicts and one major change due to the new weapon of religion for in the Chia Ching (1522–1566) reign the Emperor adopted Taoism. We also see the even newer weapon of commercialism taking art in its deadly clutch toward the end of the dynasty. Therefore when we say Ming we mean a multitude of things.

Since 1923 our conception has become more clear so that the admonitions given by Mr. R. L. Hobson in his book "The Wares of the Ming Dynasty" are not so necessary. However, a few points are worth making: First, we must realize that most of the Ming porcelain and pottery which we see was expressly made for export and is not representative of Chinese taste or the best of Chinese craftsmanship. It had to be made heavy to travel well. It was naturally designed to please our Western taste. Actually some of the most delicate and thinly potted wares the world has ever seen are Ming. Secondly, Ming is not a dumping ground for stray pots, nor, to quote him, "is it a locus penetentiae into which anything wrongfully posing as Sung

*See Pl. 136, p. 465.

or Yüan should be degraded when found out." This we see often in Tz'u Chou, Tu Ting and "crackle" wares which dealers call Sung and when pressed retreat by allocating in the Ming dynasty when actually some of them are not as old as our grandmothers. Particularly so treated are the wares of grey, buff, green or yellow having a coarse crackle and made for export to the East Indies. These have been stock in trade for many years and are made even today, if any kilns are working in South China at all. Again an almost universal acceptance of roof tiles or finials as Ming is evident in America and ladies like to have them made into lamps, even though the modeling may be very bad, "because they are Ming." Chinese houses and temples are built up to the present with just these wares. Another group which Hobson says is dangerous is the "three color" enameled wares about which we shall have more to say later. These are expensive and as he says, "Worse still, they have been published as Ming in large and expensive books. This is particularly true of those fine porcelains which have grounds of the precious green-black, green or yellow enamels." He is probably referring to such publications as "Chinese Porcelain & Hard Stones" by Edgar Gorer and J. F. Blacker which was quoted as an authority to me by an eminent German professor, though many K'ang Hsi pieces in it are called Ming.

Mr. Hobson goes on to say that it has taken years to smother the "Lowestoft myth" and I may add that even now I run across some old lady now and then who still believes it. Another type is the Kwangtung ware which varies and has been made up to modern times. But the most often seen late pieces called Ming are the Taoist deities, lions, birds, etc., "with iron-red biscuit" (or brown we may add) "freely exposed in places and the rest of the surface coated with the thick Canton glaze of mottled blue-grey, flambé red or celadon green which are almost invariably labelled Ming, and they are almost invariably of 19th century make." Another amusing reference is to ginger jars; he says, "Extract the ginger and place the pots on the shelf. They become Ming in the twinkling of an eye."

I further quote, "And so for the benefit of the beginner a warning note is needed; but it must not be taken as a general tirade against the dealers in antiques. There are dealers and dealers. Those who take the trouble to study the things they handle—and most of them do that—are the best friends to the searcher after truth in this particular field. But there are still people who will pass off anything Chinese as Ming, partly out of ignorance, but mainly because the name Ming is something to conjure with. *A convenient philosophy tells them that there are many doubtful specimens, and that they are at liberty to give themselves the benefit of the doubt, and further, that the less they know of the subject the more doubt there is to benefit from.*" (The italics are my own.) "These sophists are a nuisance and should be exposed on·every occasion, if only for the good time that is wasted by the conscientious members of the trade in correcting the errors which they disseminate."

The above attitude has been very well developed by many small dealers who supply the decorative trade with lamp bases for they can gamble on

the fact that once a sale is made for this purpose the customer will never
raise the question of authenticity. Also the convenient covering of the bottom
in mounting makes it difficult to examine such pieces. But the sophists are
not all small firms. One of the largest in the country recently sold a man
who hired me for appraisal a dozen pieces which were misrepresented and
sold for many times their value. The amusing thing is that they willingly
and without demur refund the money when caught, but go merrily on in their
practices because the average pays. The only way to put a stop to this sort
of thing is to persuade all collectors and people who buy even solely for
decorative reasons to take the trouble to find out and then to press the matter.

The Ming body is fine and unctuous, white and smooth as is the fine Sung
stoneware, the difference being only in color. When the fingernail is scratched
on it there is no unpleasantness. The New York collector Mr. Robert West
calls it a "macaroni foot" and the feeling is not far different from that of
uncooked macaroni. Sometimes there are little pits and again there may be
small traces of iron which give a rusty red or brown look where exposed.

The Chinese described the glaze as being like "massed lard" and it is
valued for its thickness and flawlessness. Even if there was the slightest flaw
in the early times of Hung Wu the piece was ground smooth and reglazed.
But this glaze is always slightly undulating. It has been likened to an orange
peel but this is exaggeration unless a very smooth orange is considered. There
are also slight tubercles like grains of millet and depressions which have
been named "palm eyes"—"tsung yen." Mr. Nai-Chi Chang has recently
explained to me that this is not the correct translation for the word is actually
t'ze tsung making the meaning "bristle holes" or we might say, "pig's bristle
holes." The word t'ze is often omitted in writing though perfectly understood
by the Chinese although it was not by the English translators. The Chinese
also call it "chicken skin" which does imply the thousands of hardly perceptible
pores that take away any glassy look from it.

Many Ming vases are slightly distorted both because of careless turning
and through firing. Perhaps the potters felt this gave them a life which a
dead symmetrical form might not have, but I believe it was not calculated
in this dynasty. In any event it is never very great. When a vase had to
be made in a top and bottom section the Ming potters did not try very
hard to obliterate the joint but left it so that, even if it could not be seen
clearly, it could be easily felt by running one's hand over the surface.

None of these considerations are to be found in *all* Ming porcelain. For
instance, the *Shih ch'ing jih cha* tells us that the important way to judge
porcelain is by the foot, and continues by saying that the Yung Lo (1403–
1424) bowls have a glazed bottom and sandy foot. (You will note that at
once we depart from our general description.) He goes on to say that Hsüan
Tê (1426–1435) altar cups have a "cauldron bottom" probably meaning
convex, and thin, wire-like foot, and that Chia Ching (1522–1566) pieces
have a "loaf center," probably meaning convex inside, and rounded foot. It
should be added that one should not condemn a Ming piece because the
foot-rim is perfectly made because some are. It can only be said **generally**

that the K'ang Hsi rim is usually better potted and a little more likely to have a groove to fit a stand. We find the following foot types:

1.—Grooved and well potted foot-rims accompanied with glaze in the bottom which may differ from that on the outside or may be of different color due to the covering of it in firing.

2.—Rounded and finely potted with glaze applied underneath. This is the spaghetti or macaroni foot of Mr. West's.

3.—Sharp edged like the thin Ying Ching wares of the Sung period, but usually more even.

4.—Crudely rimmed and unglazed beneath.

5.—Flat bottomed and with no glaze or just a thin patch dabbed on.

Numbers four and five disappear by K'ang Hsi times.

I need not say more about Ming forms for the illustrations will show them well enough. However, they are seemingly all somewhat extreme as related to Sung ones and it is interesting to make comparisons.

It is the habit of writers to dwell upon the glorious Ming color and it is true that designs of brocades and cloisonné were employed as well as parts from paintings and some studies from nature itself. But at the same time we must realize that the factories had set up the division of labor system. Later in the K'ang Hsi period we are told that a vase passed through *seventy hands* before it was finished. It was not so bad in Ming times but bad enough for anyone would admit that such a system would lose all of the personal character and feeling of an artist. We are also told that there was stealing of the precious blue and that, therefore, an artist was selected to do a large piece and another to do a small one and the average of the amount of blue they used was carefully calculated and dealt out to the painters. Can one imagine a real artist working under such circumstances?

There are several classifications of the types of wares:

1.—"Three color type" or "san ts'ai."

2.—"Five color type" or "wu ts'ai."

3.—"Mixed color type" or "ts'a ts'ai."

But these do not hold true entirely for the first may be porcelain or pottery having three or four colors such as green, aubergine, yellow, turquoise, dark blue, etc., while "wu ts'ai" has come to mean porcelain with the enamel decoration on a glaze, usually white, and "ts'a ts'ai" may be applied to both.

THREE COLOR WARES

The enamels were inclined to run in firing and the "three colored wares" often show a method of confining them by reticulation, incising the surface or laying small ridges of clay or cloisons on it. But the old myth that these wares were "copied from cloisonné" has no basis in fact. Actually the fictile wares came first. These enamels were fired in the "demigrand feu" or lower heat and are alkali-lead silicates. The objects so decorated were "gallipots" or "mei p'ing" meaning vase for prunus bough, barrel shaped garden seats, large temple jars with covers, flower pots, incense burners and some beaker shaped vases of tall and graceful shape. The first of them may quite possibly have been developed from the Tz'u Chou type with the added red, green and

Late Ming *"san ts'ai"* or three color porcelain figure of Kuan Yin. Ht. 13″. Altman Coll. Metropolitan Mus. of Art.

Gallipot with pierced and modeled walls, cobalt ground, turquoise, straw and orange yellow. Ht. 10″. Early Ming. Bequest of Isaac D. Fletcher. Metropolitan Mus. of Art.

Left: Late Ming enamel on biscuit bowl with dark green ground, aubergine, yellow and a glossy white outlined in dull black. Dia. 7″. Bequest of Mary Clark Thompson. Metropolitan Mus. of Art.

Right: Ming incense burner (Ting) before Hsüan Tê 1426. Buff pottery with the neck and body pale aubergine, the legs and handles yellow green and the lip orange yellow. Glazes show iridescence from burial. Ht. 5½″. Ex Warren E. Cox Coll. Mrs. Ogden K. Shannon, Jr.

THREE COLOR (SAN TS'AI) MING POTTERIES

PLATE 135

Fig. 658. Two pairs of small Ming "three color" vases, the larger ones with scratched design and green ard yellow glaze, the smaller with ridges and gl es of yellow, grcen and aubergine. Hts. 8¼" and 6 ". Warren E. Cox Coll.

Fig. 659. One of pair of vases of light buff pottery glazed with pale green, aubergine, and greenish yellow and showing iridescence from burial. Ht. 7". Metropolitan Mus. of Art. Gift of Joseph Koshland.

yellow glazes to which turquoise and the other colors were again added. Some are of coarse pottery body while others are of white porcelain but all are thick and sturdy in potting. Many are glazed inside and on the bottom with green thinly applied. The turquoise varies from a hard glaze looking like

Fig. 660. Late Ming "three color" porcelain figure of Kuan Yin having the thinner and more transparent enamels not found in earlier times. Ht. 23". Altman Coll. Metropolitan Mus. of Art.

a high fired one to a soft crackled type which seems to be more popular in the later reigns and continues into the K'ang Hsi and Chien Lung periods. The violet or purple blue also varies from fairly clear to almost black. The vases with leaf green or aubergine ground are supposed to be more rare and therefore more valuable. The European and American collectors have always valued this ware highly and only a few years back the firm of Parish-Watson bought the piece illustrated in "The Wares of the Ming Dynasty" (Pl. 52, Fig. 1) in London for 945 pounds sterling. This piece was from the Benson Collection and was a good but fairly late piece. Others have brought up to $15,000 but the general price of $5,000 would take most and later during the depression things changed considerably. Since then prices have reversed themselves and during the inflationary years have escalated far beyond the expectations of collectors of four decades ago.

Naturally such prices attracted the copyists and some undiscriminating collectors have been taken in. A piece was sold in one of the important auction galleries in New York in 1938 which had been made in Japan and was put up by the anonymous "Famous Long Island Collector" and it brought over $800 though it was

PLATE 135 A

**RARE THREE-COLOR VASE WITH UNDERGLAZE BLUE, OF THE
HUNG WU PERIOD.**

The reasons for the Hung Wu attribution of this vase are as follows: 1.—It is made in five sections (the early potters had trouble "pulling" the clay). 2.—It has "moons" or translucent areas on shoulder and neck. 3.—The use of iron-red, reminiscent of Sung "three color ware," is unique. 4.—The gray-blue Chinese cobalt used as underglaze color on shoulder and base is of 14th cent. type.

(Cont'd)

PLATE 135 B

DETAILS OF VASE

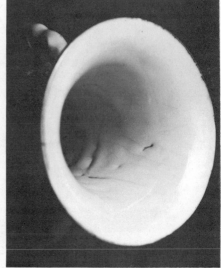

1. Elephant head handle made hollow and with iron-red details.

2. Inside of mouth showing "heaped and piled" glaze like "melted snow."

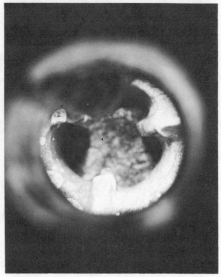

3. Bottom showing smooth but pitted texture.

4. Inside of vase showing three buttresses. Warren E. Cox Coll.

5.—The "worm holes" like those near elephant's trunk are characteristic of early wares. 6.—The "cuerda seca" (see p. 328) black outline technique was supplanted by the cloisonné technique in the early 15th cent.

exactly of the type that we handled for lamp bases at $35 to $50. Of course, a collector is foolish to believe he can buy properly from a dealer, an individual, or an unauthenticated auction. When a sizable investment is contemplated, be sure of your source.

FIVE COLOR WARES

The "five color wares" naturally show a great deal of painting and it may be useful here to give a list of the subjects used, though this cannot be entirely complete, of course.

CONFUCIAN SUBJECTS

CONFUCIUS himself

KUAN Yü, the warrior who was turned in the 16th century to

KUAN TI, the God of War seen in armor seated with uplifted hand or sometimes striding forward.

K'UEI HSING, the God of Literature who is usually seen as a demon with brush and writing equipment, and standing on a dragon-fish.

TAOIST SUBJECTS

SAN CHING, the spiritual trinity

SAN KUAN, the active trinity consisting of:

a.—Shang Ti who rules over the heavens

b.—Shou Lao who is the god of the southern star and long life and who is a transformation of Lao Tzŭ, the founder of the religion, and is an old man with a long beard and bald head with a large protuberance on it, said to have been caused by deep thought, and clothed in flowing robes on which the character "shou" or "longevity" is shown. At times he is seated and at times on the back of some animal such as an ox or water buffalo.

PA HSIEN, which are saints, demigods or genii which are about him and are known as:

a.—Chung-li Ch'üan, a bearded old man with a peach in one hand and fan in the other with which he wakes the spirits of the dead to life.

b.—Lü Tung-pin, who carries a sword and protects the world against monsters and plagues.

c.—Li T'ieh-kuai, the good spirit of magicians and astrologers and is shown as a beggar with pilgrim bottle and crutch.

d.—Ts'ao Kuo-chiu, the god of actors who carries castanets in his hands.

e.—Lan Ts'ai-ho, who may be a man or woman but always carries a basket of flowers and is the god of gardeners.

f.—Chang Kuo Lao, who is the god of writers and artists and always carries a twig and bamboo cane.

g.—Han Hsaing Tzŭ carries a flute and is the god of musicians.

h.—Ho Hsien Ku is the goddess of housewives but carries a lotus, why we do not know.

i.—Wên Ch'ang is another god of literature which is as a matter of fact watched over by five in all.

KUAN TI was borrowed by the Taoists from the Confucianists and is shown with a dragon on his robe and with a three-legged frog at his feet.

HSI WANG MU is the goddess of long life and is shown as a graceful, slender girl with a flowerbasket at times carried on a cane over her shoulder and is often shown under a flowering peach tree.

BUDDHIST SUBJECTS

BUDDHA, the founder who was supposed to have come into this world a rich and carefully protected boy but who was so shocked when he saw its unhappiness that he devoted his life to helping mankind, is shown standing on a lotus flower with one hand upraised or with a book.

KUAN-YIN is a perfect being who with only one more incarnation will attain Nirvana, and is also the goddess of mercy, the mother spirit and is frequently shown with a child in her arms or about her skirts, but is also seen with an inverted vase, the source of water in which things grow, representing the idea of fecundity.

SHAN-TS'AI is the name of the child who after several trials was permitted to help Kuan-yin in her deeds of mercy.

LOHAN, or in India, Arhat, or in Japan, Rakan are saints of which there are 16 in India and 18 in China, one of which is the popular:

PU-TAI HO-SHANG (or "Hotei" in Japan) the god of children and of earthly joys who is usually shown with his fat and naked belly and smiling face as he reclines against money bags.

ANIMAL SUBJECTS

Dog of Fo seen singly or in pairs as incense stick holders at Buddhistic altars and is like a lion showing his teeth and frequently has a collar of bells and is playing with a ball or cub. Pekinese dogs were bred to look like these.

Ch'i-lin (or kylin) is a strange animal which represents happiness and perfection and has a head half dragon's and half unicorn's, the hoofs of a horse, the tail of an ox and a scaly body but shaped like a deer. Two of these may be seen on the large blue and white jar.

Fêng-huang is the bird like a peacock or pheasant. It is supposed to live in the highest heavens and is a symbol of beauty and perfection. (Mr. Jean Delacour Bulletin of New York Zoological Society, Vol. XLIV, No. 6, Nov.–Dec. 1941 offers an interesting theory that it was Rheinart's Ocellated Argus pheasant.)

Lung is the dragon and appears in many forms as the symbol of Spring, the emblem of the Emperor and also a herald of storms and rains. It is said to have the head of a camel with horns like a deer, eyes like a rabbit, ears like a cow, a neck like a snake, the belly of a frog, scales like a carp, the claws of a hawk and the soles of the feet of a tiger. It also has long whiskers.

Five claws indicate the rank of the Emperor and also princes of the first and second rank.

Four claws show the ranks of princes of the third and fourth ranks.

Hsiang, the elephant is a symbol of power and strength as was also the leopard, tiger and lion.

Lu is the deer and represents long life.

T'u is the hare which is seen in the moon where it is preparing the elixir of life.

Fu is the bat which expresses happiness and good fortune.

Ho, the crane, the heron or the stork is supposed to live to a wonderful age and represents longevity.

BOTANICAL SUBJECTS

Sung, the fir tree, has many meanings including longevity and steadfastness.

Chu is the bamboo, strong because it bends before the wind.

The four season flowers are the
1.—Spring—peony
2.—Summer—lotus
3.—Autumn—chrysanthemum
4.—Winter—plum blossom
Note:—The latter is miscalled "hawthorn."

BUDDHISTIC EMBLEMS (Fig. 661)

Pa chi Hsiang are the 8 Buddhistic emblems
1.—The wheel in flames, "Lun."
2.—The conch shell expressing the wish for a lucky journey, "Lo."
3.—The umbrella of state presented to a mandarin on leaving his district to testify to his faithful services, "San."
4.—The tasseled throne canopy, "Kai."
5.—The lotus flower, "Hua."
6.—The urn with Buddhistic relics, "P'ing."
7.—The pair of fishes, symbolic of conjugal felicity and fertility, "Yü."
8.—The never ending knot or "entrails" another symbol of long life and the 8 Buddhistic commandments, "Chang."

Fig. 661.

Pa Pao are the eight precious things (not to be confused with the above).
1.—The pearl of purity with a ribbon, "Chu."

2.—The picture, "Hua."
3.—The sonorous jade stone, the character for which has the same pronunciation as the one for good luck, "Ch'ing."

4.—Crossed rhinoceros horns, "Chüeh."
5.—A coin, the symbol of wealth, "Ci'ien."
6.—An open lozenge shape, symbol for victory, "Fang-Shêng."

7.—Two books as a warning against evil, "Shu."
8.—A leaf, probably artemisia, a symbol of prophecy, "Ai-yeh."

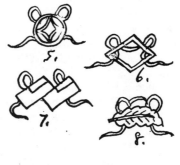

FIG. 662.

The 4 emblems of accomplishment are
1.—The chessboard
2.—The pair of books
3.—The lute
4.—Pair of scroll paintings.

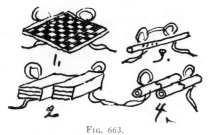

FIG. 663.

WAN-TZŬ is the swastika enclosed in a rhomboid sometimes with embellishments at the cor-

ners or ribbons and represents ten thousand things or the whole of creation. The swastika is also representative of the heart of Buddha and it turns opposite to the Nazi one.

YANG-YIN is a circle with an S line drawn through the center. It expresses the duality of the universe such as male and female, perpendicular and horizontal (in landscape painting), night and day, etc. It also relates in some way to moon worship. (See its use also in the pottery of the Black Earth Region in Europe.)

PA-KUA is the octagonal arrangement of the eight traigrams which mean the elements Heaven, Vapour, Fire, Thunder, Wind, Water, Mountain and Earth. They are formed of three broken and solid lines.

PA AN HSIEN are the emblems of the 8 Taoist saints which we have described above but which are also often shown alone.

SHOU is the character meaning long life and it is often composed into a sort of design. There are many variations.

Wan-tzŭ

Pa-kua

Yang-yin

Shou

FIG. 664.

There are many more such symbols and these can be found in the "Chinese Reader's Manual" by W. F. Mayers (Shanghai 1874) and Giles' "Chinese Biographical Dictionary," among other well known books.

Thus Ming decoration comes into the story telling field. It may be said that it is a rule that *the more story a work of art has to tell in a literal sense, the less its appeal to the emotions.* This is perhaps because the immediate meaning ties down too definitely the imagination to permit *the emotional expansion which gives us the experience of aesthetic thrill.* Here again we have come across one of our technical appeals. Many artists today believe that the less meaning their work contains the more beautiful it is. This is not what we mean. There is a superabundance of such material all about us in nature such as, for instance, the clouds forming everchanging and meaningless patterns save what we ourselves read into them. Is not the great work of art, among other things, surely one which challenges us at once and then holds our attention and offers such depth of meaning that upon returning to it again and again we find that we have never fully plumbed its depths nor encompassed its entire meaning? Has it not *many stories* worked into it rather than simply one? Is it not that a work of art with *a story* has too little meaning rather than too much? Perhaps again the Chinese show real wisdom in attaching to their symbols not one meaning but several with very intricate ramifications which may never be fully unravelled even by themselves to say nothing of its being done by an imperceptive and blunt western mind.

Hung Wu or Chu Yüan Chang (1368–1398)

The overthrow of Yissun Timur, the last of the Yüan period Mongols, was accomplished by an ex-Buddhistic monk who, seeing conditions, threw off his

vestments and joined the rebel army in Central China. His name was Yüan Chang but he adopted the title name of T'ai Tsu and is better known by the reign title of Hung Wu. His capitals were in Nanking and at K'ai feng Fu. Nanking had been captured from the Mongols in 1355. It was Peking which fell in 1368 and not until 1381 did Yunan province return to the Chinese.

Ching-tê Chên had been closed from time to time during the Yüan dynasty and it was not open when Hung Wu took Nanking. But soon it was opened and the white wares made there were popular. The *Ko ku yao lun* says, "Among modern 'Jao yao' the good examples, white in color and lustrous, are highly prized. There are besides, ch'ing and tzu wares with gilding, including wine pots and wine cups which are very lovely." The phrase "ch'uang chin chê" is also used which has a literal sense of "cut or wound with metal" which might be taken to mean incised, as Hobson says. On the other hand Julien (*op. cit.,* p. 89) translates the phrase "noir-bleus et rehausses d'or" or, "dark blue wares with gilt ornament," and Bushell renders the passage as "porcelain of greenish black color pencilled with

Fig. 665. White porcelain vase of almost Han form of *san ts'ai* (three-color) ware. Slightly mottled turquoise ground is hard and uncrackled, possibly felspathic, like bowl found at Chün Chou and is probably of Hung Wu period. Other colors yellow, green, aubergine. Ht. 22″. O. C. Raphael Coll.

design of gold." This is typical of our difficulties in Chinese translations. Was the ware wound with metal or was metal laid on it?

Hobson lists a small number including a small bottle with relief decoration and of white porcelain mounted with silver which bears the arms of Louis the Great, King of Hungary (1326–1382). The vase described on page 454 has every reason to be Hung Wu, and it is interesting that during this reign of some 30 years during which we know that the kilns were again busy some things must have been made which we are only beginning to identify. Finally there is a large vase of the "three color type," which we illustrate and which he shows in color in the "Wares of the Ming Dynasty" (Pl. 2) and which the Chinese who owned it has incised under the foot with "Hung Wu nein nei yung chih ch'i" or "vessel made for use in the interior (or in the palace) in the Hung Wu period."

CHIEN WÊN OR YUN WÊN (1399–1402)

Chien Wên whose dynastic title was Hui Ti was young, had bad advisors and was led into a long conflict with his powerful uncle, Prince of Yen. The results were the horrible massacres of Nanking and the taking of the throne in 1403.

YUNG LO OR TI (1403–1424)

The throne was taken through a sea of blood and the capital moved to Peking in 1421, but the Prince of Yen was a good builder as well as conqueror. Most of the palaces of Peking may be attributed to him. He it was who built the "Porcelain Pagoda" at Nanking, though we must add that it is largely stoneware. It was during this time that the famous eunuch Chêng Ho went on an expedition into the Indian Ocean and visited Ceylon and Sumatra. In 1408 in revenge for an insult offered an envoy from China, the Chinese army invaded Ceylon and carried off King Vijaya Bahu IV and for 30 years tribute was paid to China. Thus we see another connection with the Near East for the island had previously been visited by the Arabs.

The kilns at Ching-tê Chên were continuously operated and the *T'ao-lu* tells us that a thick and heavy ware was made as well as the very thin ware known as "t'o t'ai" or bodiless and with embossed "kung yang" decoration and also red decoration "hsien hung." The *Po wu yao lan* says that cups were made with broad mouth and contracted waist to fit the hand, with "sandy foot and smooth bottom." The best were supposed to have two lions rolling balls drawn inside and also a six character mark of the period. Some had a four character mark reading, "as fine as rice," while others had mandarin ducks or flowers. There were also cups decorated on the outside with deep blue. It also says that the wares were costly even in Ming times and that coarse copies were made toward the end of the dynasty.

Hobson speaks of a bowl in the Franks Collection, British Museum similar in shape to the one I illustrate from the Metropolitan Museum but with five clawed dragons and clouds in slip and an incised mark of Yung Lo in archaic

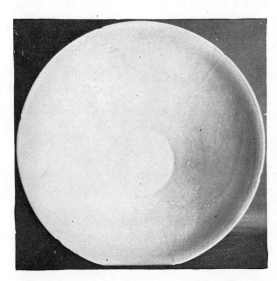

FIG. 666. One of rare Yung Lo period (1403–1424) Ming bowls of white porcelain in shape and size exactly like that of a Ting yao of Sung period, having the same six radial indented lines and notches at rim. Dia. 8¾". Altman Coll. Metropolitan Mus. of Art.

FIG. 667. Fine white porcelain vase having Yung Lo mark in underglaze blue under foot and possibly of that period. Ht. 6". Ex D. Abbes Coll.

FIG. 668. Pair of Yung Lo stem-cups with greenish white glaze of uneven surface "like melted snow." They have the marks in bottom in low relief and carved design of the *fêng huang* (heavenly birds) inside. Ht. 4" Dia. 3¾" Warren E. Cox Coll.

characters on the bottom inside. The example which I show from the Abbes Collection was sold for Yung Lo by Bluett & Sons, Ltd., London who are very careful dealers. I have not seen it but Mr. Abbes tells me it was very thin and fine. Note that the glaze is crackled.

We have recently acquired a remarkable pair of stem-cups (Fig. 668) which are of the narrow, sturdy shape typical of the period as given by A. D. Brankston in "Early Ming Wares of Chingte-chen" Table I, f and g. They are of very smooth paste with well-finished, rounded foot-rims and are glazed inside the foot as well as inside and outside with a very pale greenish glaze, almost white and resembling the *shu fu* glaze of Yüan period. In the bottom there is the Yung Lo mark in such low relief as to be hardly visible. The glaze is of uneven surface outside "like melted snow" as described by the Chinese. Inside they are carved with a lotus and *fêng huang* (heavenly bird) design as delicately as those of *shu fu* ware (See p. 424) or the *ying ch'ing* ware of the Yüan period (See p. 425). We have every reason to believe that these are of the period.

In the blue and white wares Mr. Hobson cites another bowl in the Ezekial Collection which is soft looking, has a sandy paste resembling "soft paste" and is painted outside with a landscape, much as are several fakes, and with a close diaper of spirals inside and the Yung Lo mark in greyish blue. The *Shih wu kan chu* mentions the color having been used in the period and calls it "Su-ma-ni" blue. It mentions also that Sumatra was a place from which the blue was transhipped in the next reign and it is possible that some might have come in the spoils which Chêng Ho brought back with him. Hannover speaks of a bowl at Dresden which is decorated in blue with a poem and landscape illustrating it. This is a thick and rather impure porcelain. It also has the mark.

Other bowls are painted in blue with a boy at play on the inside while the outside is coated with coral-red (iron red) glaze over which is pencilled delicate scroll and floral forms in gold. But the *Po wu yao lan* speaks of "hsien hung" wares which we take to mean underglaze red. In the British Museum is an underglaze red bowl in a 16th century leather case made in Venice showing that it is at least earlier than that. It has the mark "tan kuei" meaning literary success. Mr. Hobson makes this general observation, "The base of early" (He refers to the Ming period.) "bowls was often conical or convex underneath in contrast to those of the Chia Ching period which were convex inside; and this conical base is sometimes observable on red bowls, as in the case of one specimen in the British Museum which, in point of fact, bears the Yung Lo mark."

The "Porcelain Pagoda" had some tiles in the lower part and the ware is white and compact but granular when fractured. The glaze is pure and white while the body where exposed is pinkish. As a matter of fact these are also the characteristics of the bowls already mentioned and found in Korean tombs. Rücker-Embden reports in his notes to Ernst Zimmermann's "Chinesisches Porzellän," Munich 1915, p. 22, that he saw in Peking a fragment of tile reported to have come from this building and which had a translucent underglaze blue, and he says it was undoubtedly a porcelain and not stoneware.

We have no example in America and it makes us wish that some sort of exchange might be set up so that museums could swap duplicates.

HUNG HSI OR KAO CHIH (1425)

Nothing much that interests us happened in the reign of Kao Chih who took the dynastic title of Jen Tsung, except that Chêng Ho is reported to have gone on to Arabia and landed at Jiddah about 50 miles from Mecca.

HSÜAN TÊ OR CHAN CHI (1426–1435)

Chan Chi had the title of Hsüan Tsung and his was the most enlightened reign of the entire dynasty. He would have been an eminent scholar and statesman even had he not been Emperor. The bronzes and lacquer were of fine quality as well as the porcelains. If it had not been for the great Sung dynasty we might here point to the highest pinnacle of Chinese culture but, alas, the Sung period was never again to be equalled.

Ching-tê Chên was highly active and orders were also given to some 58 separate kilns, most of which were outside the jurisdiction of the "Ying-tsao-so-ch'êng" who was placed in charge of the Imperial factory itself. It is possible now to assign pieces to this reign with some assurance, and more material is available though it is costly and rare, and many fakes exist.

FIG. 669. Ming, Hsüan Tê (A.D. 1426–1435) bowl with greenish white glaze and underglaze blue and copper red. Inside is medallion at bottom with fish leaping from water, surrounded by border of fish, crayfish, crab and marine vegetation. Dia. 7". Metropolitan Mus. of Art.

FIG. 670. One of pair of Ming, Hsüan Tê dishes with deep and vivid underglaze blue flowers and foliage surrounded by iron red overglaze ground which allows small spots of greenish white glaze to be seen here and there. Dia. 7". Metropolitan Mus. of Art.

The *Po wu yao lan* states that the reign was famous for the underglaze red and also for Mohammedan blue. Also the greatest development of the "san ts'ai" or "three color" ware was made. The first place and highest rating was given to the porcelain stem cups of pure white and decorated with three fish in underglaze red, but there were also large bowls and small "cinnibar pots" which were "red as the sun." Added to these forms were pickle pots, small pots with basket covers and handles in the form of bamboo joints, and it is stated that all of these were unknown in more ancient times. In the "wu ts'ai" or five color ware there were flat sided jars with basket covers, round pots with flanged mouth for preserving honey, incense trays, vases and dishes. The white cups having the character "t'an" meaning "altar" engraved inside are known as "altar cups" though whether they were used for this purpose we do not know for sure. The material for these is refined and the ware thick and the form "beautiful enough to be used as elegant vases in the scholar's room." There were also, we learn, white cups for tea "with rounded body and convex base with thread-like foot, bright and lustrous like jade, and with finely engraved dragon and phoenix designs, which are scarcely inferior to the altar cups." At the bottom are the characters "ta Ming Hsüan Tê nien chih" meaning "made in the Hsüan Tê reign of the great Ming Dynasty." It also tells us that the glaze is uneven like orange peel "chü p'i." Further reference is made to the "chicken skin" and "palm eye" spots.

Three terms were applied to the red: "chi hung" seeming inclusive and "hsien hung" or "bright red" and "pao shih hung" or "precious stone red" the two divisions. None of these refers to overglaze red of the iron type and I do not agree with Hobson that the Chinese used "pao shih hung" to designate the red used in "painted design" or that "chi hung" designated the red "covering large areas." This is an entirely arbitrary meaning affixed entirely by himself. The *Po wu yao lan* states, "For these" (referring to pao shih hung) "they used a powder made of red precious stones 'pao shih' from the West to paint the fish forms, and from the body 'ku' there rose up in relief in the firing the precious brilliance of the fresh red ravishing the eye." In this connection Mr. Hobson states in "The Wares of the Ming Dynasty" (p. 29)— "The red precious stones from the west, rubies or cornelians, added in the form of powder, were traditionally supposed to have served this purpose, though of course *the color of the resultant red had nothing to do with the red of the*

FIG. 672. Hsüan Tê Ming dish with decoration in underglaze blue and copper-red on white ground. Dia. 10½". Metropolitan Mus. of Art.

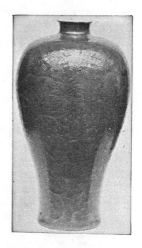

FIG. 671. Hsüan Tê bottle decorated in underglaze copper red. Ht. 5⅛". Metropolitan Mus. of Art.

FIG. 673. Vase with Hsüan Tê mark with incised design, white glaze which shows on inside, and yellow enamel all over. Probably Ming, though there are many imitations of this sort. Ht. 14". Metropolitan Mus. of Art.

stones." The underlining is mine. In the "Later Ceramic Wares of China" he says (p. 52) "The Chinese accounts of the Ming underglaze red all allude to the 'red precious stones' as an ingredient of the glaze. Probably it was cornaline (ma nao)" (The *Century Dictionary* says, "Cornaline is an obsolete form of the word carnelian or cornelian.") and he continues "and, *though it can have had no possible effect on the red colour which is solely due to reduced copper oxide, it may well have added brilliance to the glaze.*" But again in "The Wares of the Ming Dynasty" (p. 62) he says ". . . certain hard stones (cornelian among them) were pulverized and mixed with the glaze. *Though not in any sense a colouring agent, it is not impossible that such powder might in some way have helped the development of the copper red colour.*"

One naturally wonders exactly what he does mean. One thinks of garnets as also possibly the stones used. And one comes to the conclusion that he was guessing and not frank enough to say so.

Concerning the use of garnets we may say, that alamandine, the precious garnet, is an iron-aluminium stone which breaks up "incongruently" or into other compounds when melted, including iron oxides some of which we know tend to produce a red color. Early experiments in producing the synthetic ruby were interesting to us for it is recorded that Fremy and Hautefeuille fused oxides of lead, aluminum and chromium in a large crucible for about seven to eight days in "a furnace used for glass making" and masses of imper- fect and very thin rubies resulted. Certainly there might be a possibility that either ruby or garnet might influence the color of the red glaze.

Mr. A. L. Hetherington did the proper thing and consulted a chemist, Sir Herbert Jackson, who is also quoted by Hobson, and who says, "It is difficult to reconcile this well-established tradition with the actual scientific reactions which take place in the formation of a copper-red glaze. The colour is pro- duced by the aggregation of minute particles of copper under suitable condi- tions which it is not necessary to elaborate. Suffice it to say that the best colour will not be produced if the amount of copper present exceeds a certain quantity, viz. about 5% or less. An excess of copper will produce a red or brown sealingwax effect instead of a brilliant clear red. In actual practice the copper is introduced into the glaze in the form of its oxide, and under the reducing atmosphere of the kiln the oxide is robbed of its oxygen and reduced to the metal itself in a very finely divided state. This process of 'reduction' would no doubt be assisted by the presence of a reducing agent such as ferrous oxide, and conceivably a ferruginous earth might act in this way. But the tra- dition of introducing powdered rubies or cornelian could not be explained on these grounds. These stones consist largely of alumina and silica respectively. The presence of these substances in excess in a copper glaze will tend to retard or even to prevent the copper coming out, or 'striking' as it is technically called. Alumina, therefore, in some excess, and to some extent this is true of silica also, would counteract a superabundant quantity of copper which otherwise might have produced the undesirable opaque effect. Some such ex- planation as this is the only one which provides a scientific foundation for this oft-quoted tradition." Here we perhaps approach the truth and by all means we should accept the Chinese statement.

The speaking of "minute particles" of copper reminds me of a physical and not chemical effect which may have a bearing. Some years ago I studied with the famous still-life painter Emil Carlsen and he showed me that no mixing of color would produce a deep and luminous red. The method of obtaining it was to lay over a pure white ground layer upon layer thinly applied of trans- parent rose madder. The depth depends upon the number of glazes given and they strangely produce an effect almost like the sang de boeuf porcelain. He explained that the light penetrates such a glazed surface and is reflected back by the white ground. One may think of white light going through the glaze and reaching the white ground already changed to a red color and on reflecting back becoming even redder.

Ming, Hsüan Tê stem cup called by museum "sacrificial cup" though I do not know why. Slightly concave unglazed foot, greenish glaze and dark red fish. Edge of glaze at foot shows yellowish color. Potting slightly irregular. Ht. 4". Metropolitan Mus. of Art.

Stem-cup with three fish in deep red. Base unglazed and bears Hsüan Tê mark inside. Ht. 3". Eumorfopoulos Coll.

Stem cup with Wan Li mark, aubergine fruits and dragons lightly incised in the body inside. Mark is incised as well as painted in blue. Glaze shows yellowish brown where it meets body clay at foot. Gives every evidence of being actually Wan Li and is rare example for I know of no other of period. Ht. 4". Warren E. Cox Coll.

HSÜAN TÊ AND WAN LI STEM-CUPS

PLATE 136

Hsiang in his album shows 12 examples of the red. Some are covered all over, some incised with designs and some painted either with lumpy designs or finely lined ones. One odd example shows the red used with blue and white and etched design. Another shows it combined with brown and green enamels.

Most of the stem cups in modern collections are actually of the Yung Chêng period (1722–1736) when many Ming pieces were copied by Imperial order, but Mr. Hobson feels that the three in the Eumorfopoulos, the Vernon Wethered and the Percival David collections are correct. The glaze is as the Chinese say, "like congealed fat," or like, "new fallen snow," which is especially descriptive as it has also slight undulations. The shape is said to have been derived from a Han form in carved jade but it might just as well have come from a bronze form similar to the one I show. I also illustrate one from my own collection which has a Wan Li (1573–1619) mark and which well may be later, for a comparison of the shape. This piece of mine has two dragons lightly incised in the biscuit before glazing and the fruits are of an aubergine tone rather than red, showing difficulties with the tricky copper red glaze. The Ming ones of our present period also had three fruits instead of the three fish, at times. In each case the color is so heaped up that it stands in definite relief. The only difference between the Eumorfopoulos piece and that de-

FIG. 674. Ming bowl with Hsüan Tê mark and of the period, with greenish white pure ground and deep red fish. Dia.· 6″. Metropolitan Mus. of Art.

FIG. 675. Han bronze stem-cup. May have suggested porcelain ones. Ht. 5″. Warren E. Cox Coll.

FIG. 676. Lung ch'üan bowl of gray porcelain, burnt red at foot, with green glaze and copper red (appearing brown) decoration of two fishes. Dia. 6⅛″. Metropolitan Mus. of Art.

FIG. 677. Hsüan Tê, Ming stem-cup. Dragon horses, dashing waves, rocks in underglaze blue. Ht. 2¾″. Dia. 2¾″. Metropolitan Mus. of Art.

scribed by Hsiang is that in the former the mark is painted in blue on the inside and in the latter the mark is incised under the flat base of the foot. The other two mentioned agree with the Eumorfopoulos one except that the last one is only partly covered in on the bottom showing the hollow of the stem. The stem of mine is left entirely open at the bottom. It will also be noticed on comparison that Hsiang's is a little more chunky and less graceful in form, but whether this would constitute any definite difference I am not prepared to say. In point of fact there are two other examples in the Eumorfopoulos Collection #D4 and #D5 decorated in blue on white and in blue and white with red added, both of which carry the Hsüan Tê mark and both of which are much like Hsiang's form, the first not even having a flare to the lip. The later ones tend to become larger and heavier but are not so chunky as these.

The only example of single color red which satisfies Mr. Hobson is a small water pot for the writer's table and is in the Oppenheim Collection. It is a flattened oblate form with no base and no lip. The glaze is said to have a faintly bluish tint. It is also soft and rather dull and there are small spaces where the glaze has failed to fill in, and also "palm-eye" spots inside which are said to be signs of authenticity, but then my later bowl also has these. The mark in four characters in a square frame is faintly incised in the paste beneath the glaze of the bottom.

Enamel On Glaze Wares

Yellow and green enamel was used with iron red on the glaze in Sung wares of Tz'u Chou type. Hsiang shows a pagoda model with green roofs, yellow doors and red railings which he calls "wu ts'ai fu sê" or "applied colors." All of our authorities seem to compare the thick enamels of the Hsüan Tê period with the thin and more perfected ones capable of being used for very delicate painting in the Ch'êng Hua period (1465–1487). Mr. Hobson mentions a cut down vase in the B.M. which is square and decorated with a design of cranes and lotuses in "strong enamel colours and underglaze blue and has the Hsüan Tê mark in a fine Mohammedan blue." He also mentions the Winkworth one with well carried out design in red, green, brownish yellow and typical Ming turquoise blue, and says the enamels stand out thickly from the glaze while under the base is the Hsüan Tê mark together with the cyclical date corresponding with 1433 of our era.

I now submit an interesting piece from my own collection. The body is of fine, smooth texture and white. It has all the qualities of a true Ming body. The glaze is of copper red rather light in tone and more nearly a deep "peach bloom" color showing considerable of the mottling seen in that glaze. On one side the glaze was thinner and therefore lighter whether by accident or purpose we cannot tell but over this area is a beautiful painting of three immortals descending on clouds to a palace floating on a choppy sea. The technique of the painting of the waves is similar to that of the blue and white stem cups except that it is better and it has much the treatment that was copied from such paintings by

Fig. 678. Late Ming vase with Hsüan Tê mark and red glaze like that of fish on white bowls or "peach bloom" rather than of sang-de-boeuf type. Decoration in translucent enamels of green, yellow, white. Mark, though dull blue and generally Ming in character, does not correspond with handwriting of Hsüan Tê period. Ht. 20½". Warren E. Cox Coll.

Kōétsu, Sotatsu and Kōrin in later times in Japan. Under the foot is a strong Hsüan Tê mark in deep blue. The glaze inside and on the bottom is pitted with the "palm eye" spots and is of a greenish white. The potting is generally heavier than any K'ang Hsi vases of similar size.

It is likely that all the colored glazes we know as belonging to the Ming period were employed either as single colors or under enamel decoration during this reign. A dish in the Eumorfopoulos Collection #D214 is described as having dragons faintly traced in white slip on the inside and covered on the outside with a deep but brilliant blue glaze. It has the six character and double ring mark and was sent from China as an example of the listed "chi ch'ing" or "sky clearing blue." Another in the same collection is a celadon bowl with three feet #D215 and it has a four character mark in double ring. Also #D61 has pale underglaze blue and some green. I know of no examples in America.

MOHAMMEDAN BLUE

Used with enamel colors or for the marks when they were not incised, or for a general covering color rarely, was the deep blue. The *T'ao lu* tells us that "su-ni-p'o" blue was used for painting up to the reign of Ch'êng Hua (1465) when the supply ran out and only the common blues were available. It further tells us that the blue and white of the Hsüan Tê ranked first. Variously called "su-ni-p'o," "su-p'o-ni," and "su-ma-ni" probably with reference to the place it was thought to come from, or "hui hui ch'ing" meaning Mohammedan blue, or again as "wu-ming-i" in the Sung period, this color is supposed on good authority to have come from Western Asia in early times of the T'ang dynasty, and to have been increasingly imported since then. The Ming Annals tell us that in 1426, 1430, 1433 and 1434 "hui ch'ing" was brought as tribute from Sumatra. However, it must not be supposed that this blue was used on all wares of the period and, in truth, there is some little confusion concerning it, for some said it was pale as contrasted with the Chia Ching (1522–1566) blue while others say it was "deep and thickly piled and very lovely." The answer is probably that it was used both ways. We also learn that it was difficult to handle because it would run in firing and, therefore, it was mixed with the regular Chinese blue, which was dull and lifeless.

In *Hsiang's Album* are seven examples. Five show the blue confined to pencilled borders while the other two show dragons in clouds and "dragon pines." The stem cup in the Metropolitan Museum and others in England are all rather delicate and in contrast with them is the pilgrim bottle in the Franks Col., B.M., which is decorated with a heavy branch of peaches and foliage painted heavily in a blackish cobalt blue which shows inclination to run. This vase bears no mark but has a box bearing the seal of no less a person than Mr. Hsiang himself! This is not very conclusive evidence and, in fact pieces in such boxes are always suspect, but in this case the box is taken seriously in England at least. There are also the often shown "Swaythling" and "Trenchard" bowls mounted in silver rims and handles in the 16th century in England. These are painted in dark outlines and filled in with dark blue.

Wine ewers were made for the Mohammedan market, and on these the glaze is rather thick and bubbly, of greenish cast and inclined to run while the blue is mottled light and dark. Finally at Old Fostat in Egypt was found the bottom of a bowl now in the B.M. and it has the mark in four characters and a medallion of kylin playing painted in a greyish blue.

During the Chia Ching period a certain Mr. Ts'ui made wares, we are told, which some thought superior even to those of Hsüan Tê and Ch'eng Hua periods and could be distinguished only because they were larger than the originals. There is a deep bowl in the Salting Col. (Pl. 16, *Wares of the Ming Dynasty*) which may be by his hand. Mr. Ts'ui started a long line of imitators beginning just 100 years after the originals were made and extending down to the present. During the Yung Chêng and Ch'ien Lung times a type was made usually painted with lotus scrolls and these were given a flat wash first and then darker blue was heaped up over it. The same technique occurs on what appear to be originals and those of the Chêng Tê period (1506–1521). Of course Japan and other countries also took a bit of trouble in trying to make copies, but once a few of the real pieces are handled the immediate difference can always be seen.

FIG. 679. Hsüan Tê Ming dynasty jar with strong underglaze blue of Mohammedan type. Metropolitan Mus. of Art.

FIG. 680. Double walled "Three color" jar with outer wall pierced and modeled. Cobalt, turquoise, yellow, straw, green and aubergine. The inside yellow green. Early Ming, probably Hsüan Tê. Ht. 11½". Bequest of Edmund C. Converse. Metropolitan Mus. of Art.

The "san ts'ai" or three color porcelains of this reign are numerous but the rich westerner's demand for color makes them fairly expensive. The *Po wu yao lan* says, "Again there are the beautiful barrel shaped seats, some with openwork ground, the designs filled in with colors, gorgeous as cloud brocades: others with solid ground filled with colors and engraved floral designs so beautiful and brilliant as to dazzle the eye: both sorts have deep green background." Others have a blue ground, filled in with designs in colors, like ornaments carved in lapis lazuli "shih ch'ing," according to Bushell's translation. Generally our present authorities are contented in dividing these wares into Early Ming, Middle and Late. However, this reign undoubtedly produced many of them.

Other Hsüan Tê types are as follows:

1.—Gilt on white as seen on a dish in the B.M. with thick, lustrous greenish glaze and gilt decoration of lotus scrolls similar to those seen on the red bowls. This has the mark in blue.

2.—Wares with, "crackled grounds like ice," and supposed to rival Kuan and Ju yao. This may include celadon, Ko or even Ying Ching types.

3.—The *Chiang hsi t'ung chih* according to Bushell's translation tells of a porcelain with yellow ground which Mr. Hobson assumes to be blue and white with yellow painted in the background.

4.—Again the same source tells of pots made for fighting crickets, which were painted gold and these are spoken of in the collected works of Wu Mei-ts'un.

CH'ÊNG HUA OR CHIEN SHEN (1465–1487)

The intervening 30 years between the end of the Hsüan Tê and the beginning of the Ch'êng Hua reign was somewhat of a mix up, for Ying Tsung, if we call him by his title name, was a weak individual and succeeded in being defeated and shamefully captured by the Mongols. His brother Tai Tsung ruled for 6 years and then the less popular brother was returned to the throne. The periods are known as Chêng T'ung (1436–1449), Ching T'ai (1450–1456) (known chiefly for fine cloisonné) and T'ien Shun (1465–1487). Then the son took the title of Hsien Tsung and at once fell under the influence of his chief concubine, Wang Kuei-fei, and an ambitious eunuch, Wang Chih, but at least the Great Wall was repaired, the Grand Canal deepened and porcelain and literature were again encouraged.

The free use of the mark by imitators shows us that they had heard of the importance of this period, and the *Po wu yao lan* says, "In the highest class of Ch'êng ware it is impossible to surpass the stem cups with spreading mouth and flattened sides decorated in colors with grape vine pattern. They excel the Hsüan Tê cups in workmanship. Next to these come the wedding cups 'ch'uan pei' decorated with plants and grass insects, which are delightful; the tub-shaped cups with hen and chickens; the wine cups with figure subjects and lotuses (or the translation may mean wine cups shaped like lotuses with figure subjects for decoration); shallow cups with the five sacrificial vessels 'wu kung'; small cups with plant designs and insects; blue-painted cups thin as paper; small flat dishes for chopsticks, painted-in colors; incense boxes and all manner of small jars, all extremely fine and pleasing. In my judgment the Ch'êng yao blue and white does not equal that of the Hsüan yao; but the colored ware of the Hsüan court is inferior to that of the Hsien court." (It will be remembered that Hsien Tsung was the posthumous title of Ch'êng Hua.) It continues, "The reasons are that the blue of Hsüan ware is su-ni-p'o blue and this was exhausted after that reign, so that in the Ch'êng Hua period only the ordinary class blue was used, and that the colors of the Hsüan ware

are deep and thick and piled on and consequently not very beautiful, while those of the Ch'êng Hua are rather thin and subdued in color and produce a pictorial effect. This I consider a well grounded opinion." (Translation by Bushell.)

Although it is related that the last of the envoys came from Sumatra in 1486, nevertheless there is no evidence that they brought the blue on every call and there seems sufficient evidence to the point that Mohammedan blue was not being used. We know of no pieces with it of the period although certainly a number of things *seem* to be of this period and still have it, though the majority do not.

Among known examples of the period are: the cup in the B.M. decorated with imaginary animals on a dashing wave ground and similar to the one in the Metropolitan Museum, the first having a Ch'êng Hua and the second a Hsüan Tê mark. Another example in the same London museum was presented by Li Van Ch'ing of which Hobson wrote, "as its attribution is supported by one who is reputed the best judge in China, we feel safe in regarding it as an extremely likely specimen." It is of fine white paste with thick glaze of greenish tinge and is decorated in pure silvery blue with five figures, and bears the Ch'êng Hua mark. The "palm eye" spots are present and it seems that the glaze is full of microscopic bubbles. Mr. Hobson says the texture is like that of much handled marble as is that also of the Eumorfopoulos Col. #D8. The blue is said to be indigo in the latter. The base is convex beneath and marked with the six character mark.

Hsiang shows a number of colored wares which are yellow, green and aubergine applied apparently both over a glaze and direct on the biscuit. He also shows a cup much like the "chicken cups" but with geese in flight over water dotted with sprays of ling ching fungus. The "chicken cups" are described by the *Po wu yao lan* as "thin and diaphanous as a cicada's wing, so that the finger nail shows clearly through them," and also, "The design is of cock and hen instinct with life and motion, reminding one in every detail of a water color picture by one of the court artists of the Sung Dynasty. The flower is in the style of Huang Ch'üan." Hannover comments, though I do not know from what source, "Even towards the end of the Ming period a 'chicken cup' or 'chi kang' was regarded in China as a treasure, for which a price of $100,000 cash was not too high." Unfortunately we have no examples in Europe or America that I know of.

Examples of the heavier ware are to be found in the Hainhofer Cabinet at Upsala—and an egg-shaped box mentioned by Hobson as in the Oppenheim Collection which is still thin and is decorated with rocks and grapes in green, yellow and red.

Still heavier are the baluster shaped vases of the type of one in the B.M. with greyish crackle glaze and bold lotus scroll in leaf green, yellow, bluish green and manganese added to a little underglaze blue. The potting of this piece is obviously thick and the base is flat and unglazed except for a sunk panel in which is the mark of the period in blue. This cannot be anything but an Early Ming piece and therefore of this period, for it could not very well be earlier. Mr. Hannover does not agree; he says, "To

PLATE 137

Top left: Hung Wu vase with turquoise ground. (See p. 454 and plate 135, A and B. Warren E. Cox Coll.

Center: Pre-Hsüan-tê vase of similar structure in turquoise, white and black outlined. Metropolitan Mus. of Art.

Right: Vase similar to Eumo. coll. #D64 and also marked Ch'eng Hua. Greyish white crackled glaze with design in underglaze blue and enamels. H. B. Harris Coll.

Bottom left: Vase with turquoise ground and design in green and yellow with brown outlines. Probably Chêng-tê due to advanced technique and naturalistic design. Ht. 17½". Grandidier Coll. (Louvre).

Center: Late Ming vase with rough foot rim grooved to fit stand contrary to R. L. Hobson suggestion that this occurs only in K'ang Hsi specimens. Aubergine ground, straw color and turquoise. Ht. 19". Metropolitan Mus. of Art.

Right: Late Ming vase with turquoise ground, aubergine and straw colored flowers in relief. Ht. 19". Metropolitan Mus. of Art.

attach definitive weight to such loose identifications is, however, doubtless to overestimate our present-day knowledge as to the earliest true porcelain. As a rule, we should doubtless content ourselves with the definition 'Early Ming' for such articles as those here in question." He is referring to those cited by

FIG. 681. Ming, Ch'êng Hua (1465–1487) jar with white ground, two pale green enamels, yellow, pale uneven iron red and aubergine. Ht. 4½". Metropolitan Mus. of Art.

FIG. 682. Ch'êng Hua blue and white jar. Ht. 4¼". Metropolitan Mus. of Art.

both Zimmerman and Hobson with whom I am inclined to agree definitely because of the following course of reasoning:

1.—It is reasonable to assume that when one period copied the mark of another period it did not occur, as a rule, at least until that period had acquired

FIG. 683. Ming, Ch'êng Hua beaker or *ku*, after bronze form, with white ground, opaque yellow-green, clear yellow, palest aubergine and dull iron red decoration. Ht. 8½". Metropolitan Mus. of Art.

FIG. 684. Ch'êng Hua blue and white vase having charming quality of delicate drawing typical of this period. Metropolitan Mus. of Art.

sufficient antiquity to become interesting. Usually a few hundred years had to go past before a mark would become interesting. And even Mr. Ts'ui made his copies of Hsüan Tê and Ch'êng Hua ware in the Chia Ching period some 35 to 75 years later.

2.—Thus these vases *and marks particularly* would probably not have been copied much before 1525 which would make them no longer "Early Ming."

3.—The marks could not very well have been used earlier than the period designated unless the potters were clairvoyant.

Therefore, I see no reason for not stating that they are of the period and I think Hannover is being a little too cautious. We must remember that it is the truth we are after and from that viewpoint *it is quite as bad to make a late attribution as it is to make a too early one.* All too often an example is given

Fig. 685. Numbers D63, D64 and D65 of Eumor-fopoulos Coll. D64, crackled vase on left, bears a Ch'êng Hua mark in square frame in the underglaze blue. The other two are probably Chêng Tê (1506–1521) or later. Hts. 12¼", 14¼", 15½".

the general label of Ming when it obviously cannot belong at all in any of the reigns of the dynasty each of which had certain more or less definite characteristics and some of which are fairly exactly defined. If a piece does not fit into these characteristics it should be suspect at once; if it cannot be placed in a reign, it *may* be a later Ming copy but is 90% more likely to be a Yung Chêng copy, a Jap copy or a perfectly modern commercial copy. Oddities do occur but, if none of the standard books seem to describe them, the collector had better be very, very careful and quite prepared to gamble on a 100 to 1 shot.

The B.M. vase of the sort we are discussing is very similar to another which also bears the mark and belongs to H. B. Harris (See Pl. 17, *The Wares of the Ming Dynasty.*) while the Benson one has a Hsüan Tê mark probably indicating that it was a type that carried through Early Ming times. The Eumorfopoulos Collection has one #D63 without mark, another #D64 that has the Ch'êng Hua mark and finally #D65 without mark. A perfect one (Pl. 18, *The Wares of the Ming Dynasty*) from the Grandidier Collection has again no mark and is decorated with a lotus on turquoise ground. It seems obvious that these vases started in the Hsüan Tê period with a crackle ground and continued so into our present Ch'êng Hua period toward the end of which or shortly afterwards the style changed to include a completely enameled ground like the other "three color" wares. The shape, somewhat elongated as to neck and then with the addition of handles which tend to become more and more ornate, was continued in Late Ming days and quite possibly into K'ang Hsi times with a similar enamel treatment. With more study this may form a series valuable for comparisons. For the present I should not place the enameled ground ones any earlier than the Chêng Tê reign (1506–1521).

It is interesting to note in passing that few of these vases have escaped the break at the flaring and unstructural lip-rim.

Red ornamented wares are mentioned by the poet Kao Tan-jên who says in one passage, "ruby red bowls and cinnabar dishes were cleverly made and fine and more costly than Sung ware." The larger stem cup of the Eumorfopoulos Collection has been suggested as of this reign and it has a hollow foot, is unmarked and the bowl is more expanding. This is borne out by #55 in *Hsiang's Album* which also has a rim "more expanded." This would also agree with the vase forms the lips of which are of wider flare.

The *T'ao-shuo* speaks of "wine cups with high-flaming silver candle lighting up red beauty; brocade-design cups; cups decorated with swings, Dragon-boat Procession, famous scholars and playing children; cups with trellis-frame of grapes, with fragrant plants, fish and water weeds, gourds and aubergine fruit, the 8 Buddhist Emblems, 'yu-po-lo' flowers (a dark colored lotus) and Indian lotus scrolls." Some of these are explained by Kao Tan-jên's verses:

FIG. 686. Double gourd bottle of "three color" Ming ware with deep blue ground and decoration in yellow, aubergine and turquoise outlined in white. Ht. 19⅛". Ex Warren E. Cox Coll. Jacob Rupert Bequest. Metropolitan Mus. of Art.

1.—The "high flaming silver candle" is a picture of a girl looking at "hait'ang" (cydonia) blossoms by candle light.

2.—The swing design shows boys and girls in swings.

3.—The "Famous scholars" are usually Chou Mao-shu with his beloved lotus, and T'ao Yüan-ming with his chrysanthemum.

4.—The five children are usually under a pine tree in the "Playing children" design although not always and this is undoubtedly the basis of the "Prince of Hirado" design of Japan.

It is interesting that with the breaking away from the old traditional bronze forms and the inclination toward more flamboyancy, naturalism as seen in gourd and melon shapes became more marked. Of course these are not new forms, but so naturally are they done now that it seems that the potters went

back and took another look at nature. If we are to credit *Hsiang's Album* the
results are pretty terrible.

HUNG CHIH OR YU T'ANG (1488–1505)

Yu T'ang's unnotable career was under the title of Hsiao Tsung. The
appointment of the director at Ching-tê Chên was abolished in 1486 and discontinued until 1505, but some work was done and the reign is known for its
yellow wares. Also it continued the enamel decorated ones. Hsiang shows:
1.—an incense burner of archaic form in a yellow like that of a steamed
chestnut "cheng li," 2.—a wine cup shaped like a sunflower "k'uei hua" and

FIG. 687. Ming, Hung Chih (A.D. 1488–
1505) jar and cover of heavily potted porcelain with pale greenish, faintly crackled,
glassy ground decorated with dark muddy
red, dirty yellow and speckled green. Obviously not made under imperial supervision.
Ht. 6½". Metropolitan Mus. of Art.

FIG. 688. Pair of vases called Hung Chih
by museum but probably actually of Yüan
dynasty underglaze blue and white. Shape
more accentuated at waist and drawing more
crude. Ht. 9¾". Metropolitan Mus. of Art.

yellow outside with white inside, 3.—a spirit jar of the bronze "yu" form also
yellow, and 4.—a wine pot of gourd form with yellow body of pale tint "chiao
hung" with the stalk and leaves which form the handle and spout in brown
and green respectively.

We have had a yellow glaze since T'ang times of course and the Ming glaze
though somewhat harder was not much clearer as a rule. The yellow enamel
was also dirty and so transparent as to partake of whatever color was under
it. Only occasionally do we find a piece which seems correct in all respects
and is yet clear and bright. Mr. Hobson cites a dish with the mark which has
a ground of "soft yellow" the glaze looking as though particles of yellow were
suspended in it and as though it would otherwise be transparent. He says,
"These particles are naturally thinner on the higher edges of the piece and
more thickly accumulated where the glaze has been pooled in the hollow parts,
so that we get a graded rather than uniform coat of color."

The two plates shown are similar to another in the V. & A. Mus. which has
the mark of the period. They have fairly strong underglaze blue decoration
with the ground of yellow painted in afterwards and given a second firing.

The glaze has the same light "chicken skin" texture as seen on the Hsüan Tê cups.

This same sort of rich, pure glaze is found on beautifully potted pieces of clear white, slightly browned at the edge inside the foot-rim and of very slightly greenish tint. There is an example in the Franks Collection which is

FIG. 689. Plates called 16th cent. but probably actually of the Hung Chih period as right one is identical in design to one bearing that mark in V. & A. Mus. Underglaze design and overglaze lemon yellow enamel. Dia. 8½" and 9½". Metropolitan Mus. of Art. A plate of same design as one on right with Hsüan-tê mark sold for $40,000 at Parke-Bernet Galleries, sale #2869, May 23, 1969.

similar to the yellow ones mentioned above in technique. The fine glaze is used on the outside but the mark underneath is covered with an ordinary glaze.

This period also produced the beautiful "three color" figure of Kuan Yin in the Morgan Collection with yellow, green and aubergine glazes, which is dated to correspond with our year 1502. I tried to get a picture of this piece but Mr. Morgan would not allow its publication.

The writers of the times do not mention blue and white ware or red wares but they doubtless continued.

CHÊNG TÊ OR HOU CHAO (1506–1521)

Chêng Tê was only a child encouraged to a life of self-indulgence and vice by ambitious eunuchs so that he would give them no trouble in the management of affairs to suit themselves. He was finally persuaded to proclaim himself the Living Buddha.

In 1505 the Portuguese led by Francisco de Almeida landed in Ceylon and in 1509 a trading post was planted in Sumatra while in 1517 a fort was erected at Cólombo. It is also to be remembered that Magellan started in 1519 on that memorable voyage around the world. He was killed by natives in 1521 but the little *Vittoria* finally reached Seville with 31 men. The earth was getting smaller.

A fresh supply of the "Mohammedan blue" was obtained. The factories at Ching-tê Chên were reorganized and rebuilt. "Mohammedan scrolls" and the use of Arabic inscriptions came into style. These were not entirely for export purposes but for the large Mohammedan population in China. Some of the

Ming period, probably Chêng Tê reign, pottery Buddhistic figure with the head and neck left unglazed and yellow and green glaze covering the remainder. Ht. 52″. Fuller Coll. Seattle Art Mus.

LARGE MING "THREE COLOR" BUDDHISTIC FIGURE

Plate 138

objects such as brush rests and ink slabs are of typically Chinese taste. Many of the blue and white wares were mounted in silver in Europe and England. The "Mohammedan scrolls" or "hui hui wên," as the Chinese call them, are flowers of round silhouette connected by S formed stems with rather evenly distributed scroll shaped leaves. It was probably first a textile design. We have seen it before on the baluster shaped vases with crackle ground and enamel decoration and the large one with dragon handles and enameled ground shown is probably of this period.

The Arabic inscriptions are sometimes badly written so as to be hardly readable but make artistic decorations. They usually consist of quotations from the *Koran* or sayings such as those on the brush rest shown herewith.

The best color of the Mohammedan blue was supposed to have been mixed with one part only of the native cobalt while the poorer class was proportioned about six to four. The stealing of the blue, one would suppose, probably meant

FIG. 690. Chêng Tê brush rest for Moham-medan scholar's desk. White porcelain with bubbly greenish white thick glaze and under-glaze blue decoration including two square medallions containing hardly legible arabic script. Length 8¾". Metropolitan Mus. of Art.

FIG. 691. Chêng Tê bowl of greenish white porcelain with light and greyish un-derglaze blue decoration. Dia. 6". Metropolitan Mus. of Art.

that all pieces on which it was used were not made in the Imperial kilns. It was this type of blue and white ware which served as the prototype of the "Medici porcelain" and some of the Turkish wares. The color is indigo rather than the cobalt tone we would expect and often it is dirty and spotted looking in the large areas. It was so difficult to handle on a slender brush that the artists were more successful in laying washes than in making outlines. A technique was devised of incising the outline and filling it in with color and it is seen on dragon dishes and jars.

There are several pieces of this sort in the Eumorfopoulos Col. and also one in the Grandidier Col., in the Louvre. The French one is slightly more mottled than the British one but both have flat bases. Both are also rather ornate.

In the Winkworth Col. is a globular jar painted with mottled ju-i pendants about the shoulder, scrolls setting off four incised panels and conventionalized lotus petals around the bottom. Mr. Hobson states that this has a fine grained body and is burnt brown on the unglazed base. The openwork and ogee medallions are painted in underglaze blue and red. The incised work is rather poorly designed and to add to the technical stunts, the medallions are set off by appliquéd ridges of beading. A cup that belongs to Mr. Vernon Wethered has a similar incised and beaded treatment (see *The Wares of the Ming Dynasty*, Pl. 27).

FIG. 692. Ming, Chêng Tê dish with incised design of dragon in ye'low green,
showing some iridescence. Greenish white
ground. Dia. 8″. Metropolitan Mus. of
Art.

FIG. 693. Chêng Tê vase with
four ogival medallions reticulated
and colored with underglaze blue and
red while rest of decoration is in
blue only. Ht. 13½″. S. D. Winkworth Coll.

There is a square bowl in the B.M. with mark of the period and underglaze
Mohammedan blue decoration set off with clear yellow ground somewhat better
than the average of the preceding period, and Hsiang shows a complicated
lamp and also a helmet shaped cup with the same treatment and the yellow
described as like "steamed chestnuts."

The V. & A. Mus. has 2 saucer dishes with Chêng Tê marks and they have
incised dragon and cloud designs. The claws of the dragons are in emerald
green "ts'ui lü" over a white glaze of the same color as was used on the Chia
Ching bowls with green and gold decoration. Mr. Hobson says that this green
is "iridescent with age." All green enamels so thinly applied are naturally
iridescent when they are transparent due to the uneven breaking up of the
light rays which penetrate them and are reflected back from the white glaze
beneath. Such iridescence is characteristic of the so-called "apple greens" of
the K'ang Hsi period. The corroded surface iridescence due to age is quite
a different thing and does not appear on these wares so far as I have observed
them.

The "three colored wares" are represented by one in the Oppenheim Collection with the Chêng Tê mark on the neck, and several others. The technique
was simply carried on in traditional manner. In the M. Leon Fould Collection
is a brush washer of which Mr. Hobson says, "In this class of ware, which
would seem to have been a specialty of the Chêng Tê potters, we see the Ming,
'three-colour' scheme at its best." Here then we agree with him and point out
that another ware had reached its apex and was to decline thereafter.

Many wares of the period in the blue and white and celadon types are those
found in Egypt and the Near East, for this was an active time of trade.

CHIA CHING OR HOU TSUNG (1522–1566)

Hou Tsung took the title of Shih Tsung and contrary to all our former
emperors who were Buddhistic, he became a Taoist full of religious zeal. He

wielded his religious weapon with very unpleasant results for his Buddhistic rivals. Taoism had now degenerated into a mystic group of superstitions surrounding the ideas of immortality. Odd it is that this time was almost contemporary with the search for the fountain of youth by Ponce de León (1460–1521) in Florida.

Hou Tsung in 1536 had the Buddhistic temples burned down and destroyed while the gold and silver in them was melted up and then, on his death bed, when he was sure that the promises of immortality of the Taoist priests were not going to be kept, he reversed his orders and had their altars destroyed. But what particularly interests us is that *during this reign no Buddhistic art is likely to have been made, at the Imperial kilns in any event.* Also while the Emperor was busy worrying about his life-span the Mongols were raiding the north and the Japanese pirates visited the coast in many expeditions.

The Taoist designs of Eight Immortals, the "ling chih" fungus, the crane, deer and pine tree all of which represent long life, Hsi Wang Mu and the peaches of immortality came into favor. The authorities give much data about the new designs and we have not the room for all of it here, but a few follow:

Dragon—The dragon is shown with flames, clouds, fungus water chestnuts, lotus scrolls or holding the 8 triagrams. Two dragons have between them the "kan chu" or pearl of purity. Other dragons are with the characters

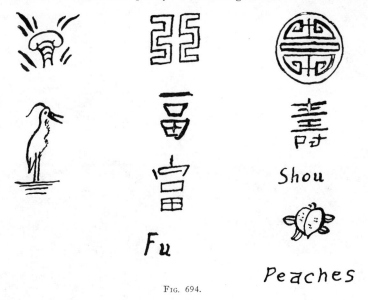

Fu

Shou

Peaches

Fig. 694.

"fu" happiness or "shou" longevity or with lions or "fêng huang" birds. These dragons are not like the early ones which look more like lizards and have divided tails.

Phoenix—The phoenix or "feng" or "Feng-Huang" (or "Ho-ho" bird of the Japanese) was an emblem of the Empress and we have described it in our earlier list. It is sometimes seen with other birds in pairs paying court to it. Actually it is incorrect to call it a "phoenix" for the meaning is quite different.

Lion Dog—The "shih tzŭ kou" appears in many ways.

Flying Lion—"Fei shih" or flying lion was popular.

Three Rams—These symbolized the return of Spring.

Peacocks were shown among the "Feng-Huang" but should not be confused with them.

Fish—The carp "li" or "p'o," the perch "kuei" and mackerel "ch'ing" were all used.

Also the seasonal flowers, mountains, landscapes and particularly water falls were popular, while the curling waves and rocks which Hobson calls the

Right: "Five color" jar. White porcelain with slightly greenish white glaze, dark underglaze blue ("Mohammedan blue"), dark red, green, yellow. Design of carp. Ht. 9½". Metropolitan Mus. of Art.

Left: Stem cup signed by maker, Lin Shaw T'ien. Glaze inside slight'y greenish-white with crackles hardly perceptible. Ground deep yellow. Design bright green, da.k aubergine. Dia. 6½". Warren E. Cox Coll.

Right: Box and cover in enamels of red and green with turquoise added. Under bottom is legend in blue, "seal box for use as required." Length 5½". Eumorfopoulos Coll. # D94.

Bowl with bold and spirited underglaze blue painting. Heavily potted. Dia. 7½". Metropolitan Mus. of Art.

Right: Blue and white dish having inscription behind seated figure. Dia. 6½". Metropolitan Mus. of Art.

CHIA CHING PORCELAINS

PLATE 139

"rock of ages pattern" referred to the heavenly land, a Taoist island off to the east. And added to these are all the Taoist emblems, children at play and the other immortals.

Our old friend Hsiang Yüan-p'ien whose album we have often quoted was probably still alive but he does not illustrate anything of this period. Other books such as the *Shih wu kan chu* published in 1591 and the *T'ao shuo,* as well as the *Annals of Fou-liang,* translated by Bushell give us information.

Officials at the factories were rotated bringing about healthy competition for the job. The Jao Chou earth and that from Ma-ts'ang are supposed to have been used up so that the bodies were not so good. The *Shih wu kan chu* tells us also that the "hsien hung" red was gone and the potters had to use iron-red overglaze color instead. However, to make up for these losses the Mohammedan blue was plentiful and it was used to make a fine dark blue, which is likened to violet ink but I think this reference is to the *density* or *consistency* of the color and does not mean that the blue itself was actually violet in shade, for it is not on existing specimens. It was also mastered so that it neither ran nor turned black. Yet the technique was not shaded but consisted still of outlines filled in with flat washes. What may be called the first "Hawthorn jar" is in the Kunsindustrimuseum, Copenhagen, though the pattern is a T'ang one as we know. The background of this jar does not show the "cracked ice" treatment but the blossoms of the prunus are well drawn. A fine Imperial Dragon jar is in the V. & A. Mus. and has borders of lotus scrolls. Some of the fish bowls are enormous and unbelievably well made. On the other hand it was said that the tiny boxes painted with blue designs were so good that even the Imperial factories in later times could not better them.

The *Po wu yao lan* tells us of small white cups already mentioned as "altar cups" and used in some way for rituals by the Emperor. It says these are not quite so fine as those of the Hsüan Tê period but beautiful in form and inscribed inside with characters "ch'a" tea, "chiu" wine, "ts'ao t'ang" decoction of dates or "chiang t'ang" decoction of ginger. The *T'ao shuo* says these cups are "white as jade," but some are said to be bluish or yellowish and these "are not worth collecting." In truth the Chinese collectors think less of the wares of this reign than any other of Ming times due to the poorer body clay. Hannover also says that forgeries of the mark are not so numerous, though the Japs made use of it at times.

The "five color" wares were about perfected and wares with polychrome decoration on monochrome grounds were outstanding, particularly those with gold decoration on red or green ground. Sometimes this latter was combined with blue and white as in the V. & A. Mus. example with slightly convex center, concave underneath, no foot-rim and inside a band of emerald green enamel with lotus designs in gold while in the center is a stork and cloud design in dark blue. Outside are two peach boughs and birds in blue. The mark reads, "ch'ang ming fu kuei" or "long life, riches and honors," which occurs on many pieces of this period. The green enamel is likely to be the "ts'ui lü" mentioned in the *T'ao shuo's* list. The overglaze reds vary from a dark opaque brick-red to a translucent tomato-red, which, having more flux, is more translucent, but all of them show brush marks. It may be interesting to note here for comparison that the red of the K'ang Hsi period (1662–1722) was thinner and dryer and more of a light coral color. A somewhat less rich color was also obtained by the Kioto potter Eiraku and others who copied it got a sometimes darker and more muddy color and sometimes a lighter color but never a redder red. The color was also applied to stem cups as in the Oppenheim one which is formed by a section of a sphere set stiffly on a slightly flaring stem.

Here we have the chief copyist reign but a reign that was itself not so honored. Some new colors were supposed to have been invented such as "dead-leaf brown." Some new shapes were invented; tobacco became known in 1530 and some of the forms made for bases of narghilis date shortly afterwards.

From the lists of the palace supply we find there were also octagonal jars, libation cups of helmet shape and ancient bronze forms including the "hsi" or rhinocerous carrying a vase on its back. One may wonder why it is that I say that due to the change of religion we are to look for recognizable changes in the art and then call it a "copyist reign," and tell of the imitating of these old forms, but it must be remembered that there were Taoists long years before the Chia Ching reign and that the very nature of the religion created interest in things long past. Also we are now witnessing the decline which led to a leaning on the past. There was nothing new in Taoism; the newness came only in the absolute adoption of it.

It was not easy to supply the Imperial Household. We read that in the year 1554 among other requirements there were demanded 26,350 bowls with dragons in blue, 30,500 plates, 6,900 wine cups, 680 large fish bowls, 9,000 tea cups, 10,200 bowls and 19,800 tea cups of another pattern, 600 libation cups and some 6,000 ewers or wine pots. Matched table sets came into use and in 1544 we hear of an order for 1,340 of these sets or "cho ch'i" comprising 27 pieces: 5 fruit dishes, 5 food dishes, 5 bowls, 5 vegetable dishes, 3 tea cups, 1 wine cup, 1 wine saucer, 1 slop bowl, 1 vinegar cruet.

Of the "three color," nothing is said but they no doubt persisted and in fact there is strong evidence that the technique changed about at this time. One sort had low fired enamel designs used over outlines in brown, probably manganese, and this would be a technique not unlike the cuerda seca of the Spanish. These are frequently bowls of yellow, green or aubergine grounds on which designs filled in with complementary colors are aided with greenish white. They are much like the enamel on biscuit K'ang Hsi ones except that in the Chia Ching ones there is often a white glaze which emerges under the base. A fine example is in the Grandidier Col. And others are in the Percival David Col., the B.M., etc.

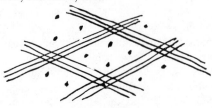

Fig. 695.

These wares were reproduced in the Yung Chêng and other periods.

Other "mixed colored wares" of the "red and green" family occur with white ground. These colors are also added to by use of an impure yellow and a turquoise green which we are told takes the place of the later blue enamel. Mr. Hobson shows an example from the R. F. W. Brandt Col. which has a "trellis" border of triple lines crossing each other to form diamonds in which are four dots, and he says that this is a typical design of the period.

The "five color" type with strong underglaze blue enhanced by numerous enamels was well done and prepared for its full use in the Wan Li reign to follow. Of course all of these colors were also used as monochromes.

There were not many individual potters known, as the factory methods did away with personal signing of pieces, but a few names emerge and they are of famous copyists. Chou T'an-ch'üan made fine copies of Ting yao and we have already spoken of Mr. Ts'ui who specialized in making Hsüan Tê and Chêng Hua copies. An amusing story is told about the former gentleman: Wên Wang vessels in the form of Shang bronzes were his specialty. These were said to have been made in a ware which after a bit of wear or artificial rubbing could not be distinguished from Ting yao. It seems he was permitted to examine a famous tripod censer or "li" belonging to the Great President of the Sacrifices, Mr. T'ang, and risking severe punishment, took measurements of the vessel with his hands and a record of the design on a piece of paper concealed in his sleeve. After some six months' time he procured another audience and astonished Mr. T'ang by producing the copy, perfect in every detail in replica of the older object. So delighted was Mr. T'ang by this seeming magic that he bought the reproduction for forty ounces of silver and placed it by his original. Some years later another collector became infatuated with the two beautiful Ting censers and after dickering a bit bought T'an-ch'üan's copy for 1,000 ounces of silver and went away happy.

But the real story comes to me from the same old gentleman who permitted me to hold the invisible jade bowl from the Kian factory and this is his version: It seems that another cousin of still another brother in going through some ancient family papers came to one which bore a seal dated as of the Chia Ching reign in the year of 1537, the year after the Buddhist temples were destroyed, and this paper was a confession of one of his ancient ancestors who was a good Buddhist and yet a servant of the famous Mr. T'ang who had changed his religion as it was necessary to do in order to hold an important office. The ancestor, whom we must for reasons of delicacy allow to remain nameless, confessed that, feeling that Mr. T'ang knew not the difference between the true and false religion or anything else, tested his theory by one day switching the positions of the Ting yao and the Chou Tan-ch'üan incense burners. There was no commotion in the house and the ancestor then began to feel that he should profit by his insight into human nature. He, therefore, went to the honorable Mr. Chou Tan-ch'üan and bet him that unaided he could not make still another perfect incense burner, saying that, if he did so, he, the servant of Mr. T'ang would pay another forty ounces of silver for it, while, if he failed Chou Tan-ch'üan must pay him ten ounces of silver. The challenge was taken up and the poor ancestor had to pay and take the incense burner for forty ounces, for the second copy was as good as the first. He then replaced the original with the second copy, remembering it to be the one now on the left, and added what he was sure was the original to his own private collection, which he kept very private indeed. His certainty, however, was

Left: Vases, aubergine (dark) ground with green blotches and orange-yellow heads, enamel on biscuit. Ht. 11″. Metropolitan Mus. of Art.

Right: Blue and white square beaker. Design shows scholars and immortals. Ht. 11″. Warren E. Cox Coll.

Right: Perfume sprinkler having clear greenish white glaze with slightly lavender tinted blue decoration. Has had foot cut and top rim cut down. Cup fitted with platform half way up, perforated with seven holes. Ht. 7″. Warren E. Cox Coll.

Bowl with enamel decoration. Outside predominantly iron red, blue inside. 16th cent. Dia. 4″. R. W. Brandt Coll.

Circular box and cover decorated in blue with children and flying cranes amid clouds which are Taoist motive. Dia. 15¼″. Metropolitan Mus. of Art.

Cup with eight immortals painted on octagonal form. Dia. 4″. Metropolitan Mus. of Art.

CHIA CHING PORCELAINS

PLATE 140

shaken when after all this, Mr. T'ang sold the collector the one piece and kept the supposed original for himself, gloating over the fine points of the one he kept. Being a poor man the ancestor could never sell his, whether it was the original, as he first thought, or the copy, as he was beginning to believe, so when he died he passed it to his heir and so it came down from hand to hand through all the years to the present day. My Chinese friend then produced what appeared to be a fine example of Ting yao but asked so high a price that I could not reach it, although I might have tried harder had I known it was by Mr. Chou Tan-ch'üan. Do you suppose the canny Mr. T'ang, noticing a slight rearrangement of the pieces and having a sharp eye, simply put them back in their former places? Could the second collector have known what he was doing after all and did he get the real Ting yao? Who will ever know?

Mr. Tz'ui's ware was known as "ts'ui kung yao tz'u" or "Mr. Tz'ui's porcelain," and was eagerly sought even during his lifetime. The colors of his monochrome and blue wares were perfect but, whether purposely as a matter of distinction, or simply carelessly, his cups were all of different size from the originals. Of course, if he had cast his pieces from the old pieces, a shrinkage would have taken place which in our present wares is about 1/10th to 1/12th but the *T'ao lu* and other authorities do not tell us whether they were larger or smaller, which is unfortunate.

Some works say that his wares brought higher prices than the originals while others say they were fit to be "used to put fruit stones in." Of course we of today would gladly pay a full Chêng Hua price for a piece, if we could be sure he made it.

WAN LI OR YI CHÜN (1573–1619)

The five year intermediate reign of Lung Ch'ing or Tsai Hou was interesting to us only because the Mongols were put back into their places and many years of peace followed.

The son of Tsai Hou took the title of Shên Tsung and became Emperor at 10 years of age. He was a fine young boy, but the eunuchs soon saw to it that he became known as bad tempered and licentious. The Japs invaded Korea under Taiko Hideyoshi and the Tartar chieftain Noorhachu was a threat which soon developed into conflict and loss for the Chinese, for it was he who was destined to be founder of the Manchu Dynasty.

Meanwhile the Dutch Admiral Spilberg landed on Ceylon and was asked to help oust the Portuguese which he did for his own good reasons, and in 1602 Sir John Lancaster was well received on the island and 11 years later a factory was opened for trade.

A few new designs were added during Lung Ch'ing times as follows: 1.—Clusters of chrysanthemums "to to," 2.—tuberose or iris "yü tsan hua," 3.—jasmine "ch'ang ch'un hua," 4.—all the flowers "k'uei hua," 5.—flowers of the four seasons supporting four characters heaven, earth, fair and fruitful "ch'ien k'un ch'ing t'ai," 6.—interlacing scrolls of mutan peony, 7.—the Tartar pheasant "chai chih," 8.—flying fishes, 9.—monsters in sea waves, 10.—faint wave patterns "tan shui," 11.—curled waves and plum blossoms, 12.—genre subjects "jên wu," 13.—historic figure subjects "ku shih," 14.—children hold-

Left to Right: Beaker shaped vase with neck truncated. Ware smooth and white. Glaze greenish. Underglaze blue deep, vivid and inclined to run. Ht. 9″. Warren E. Cox Coll.

Wan Li bottle of grace and strength. Ht. about 23″. Thompson Coll. Metropolitan Mus. of Art.

Blue and white vase, blue of vivid brilliant quality. Diameter of mouth and foot and height of neck all alike. Height of body 3½″ times this dimension. Ht. c. 24″. Altman Coll. Metropolitan Mus. of Art.

Superb gallipot with ju-i design about shoulder, eight precious objects and nien hao of Wan Li. The painting shows all the strong, dynamic power of best of the reign. Ht. 20¼″. Warren E. Cox Coll.

Jar with spirited painting of a horse dashing over waves amid clouds. Ht. 5½″. Warren E. Cox Coll.

Blue and white vase with delicate painting but somewhat spiritless. Metropolitan Mus. of Art.

Deep bowl and cover, Wan Li or slightly later, painted with simple charm though in poor, uneven quality of blue. This type is found in Annam. Ht. 9″. Metropolitan Mus. of Art.

VARIOUS STYLES OF DRAWING ON WAN LI
BLUE AND WHITE WARES

PLATE 141

ing branches and finally a design called a "joyous meeting" which Mr. Bushell describes as a pair of magpies and Mr. Hobson says was of two sages. We are also told that they incised dragons under the glazes and made jars with peonies and peacocks in gold and covers with lions on them.

There are two pieces in the B.M. while other collections include a few more but they might be of either the preceding or following reign so far as technique goes.

At the beginning of the Wan Li reign the factories at Ching-tê Chên were humming with activity, and the workmen were so pressed that they went daily to the temple of the God Chao, a potter of the Chin dynasty who had been deified. But a new God Chao took his place and this is how it happened: An order was given for the large fish bowls which for some reason would always come out warped or cracked. The Imperial Officer was wrathful and threatened dire punishment to all the potters. Again the fire was made and all prayed that the labor of many months would turn out all right, but the divine T'ung threw himself into it and was consumed whereupon the bowls came out beautifully. He was then deified.

The clay now came from Wu-mên-t'o but there were difficulties in transportation and so, quite often an inferior type was used. The Mohammedan blue had completely ceased probably due to Dutch intervention and coastal difficulties with Japan. The underglaze red was revived but was not so good as the fine color of the 15th century. Trade was extensive overland and many heavy pieces were made for export. The Chinese themselves have chiefly disparaging things to say about Late Ming wares and Wan Li in particular.

The *T'ao shuo* gives us these new shapes: trays for wine cups "pei p'an," flower vases "hua p'ing," flat backed wall vases in the form of a gourd, screens "p'ing," hanging oil lamps "ching t'ai," pricket candlesticks "chu t'ai," jars for candle snuff "chien chu kuan," chess boards "ch'i p'an," furniture for the writing table, brush handles "pi kuan," brush pots "pi ch'ung," brush rests "pia chia," pallette water droppers "yen shu ti" and various boxes for perfume, betel nuts, hats, handkerchiefs and fans. Here we can see the foreign influences at work and many things are made which are inappropriate for the material. The censor Wang Ching-min protested that many items were only extravagances, and particularly mentions candlesticks, chess boards and jars for holding the men, as well as handles for brushes, which would break easily. We are told that about half the obnoxious articles were cut off the lists at his protest, and that they numbered 96,000.

New decorations are said to be: full-faced dragons "chêng mein lung," squatting dragons "tun lung," ascending and descending dragons, winged and threadlike dragons, the "Hundred dragons," fabulous monsters paying court to the celestial dragon and to the archaic dragons, sea horses "hai ma," and many birds, animals, etc. The "ch'i-lin" appears often, and was said to portend the coming of a virtuous ruler and they certainly needed one but the two that followed were not so fine as might be.

Most of the above were rendered in blue and white but we read also of the following: 1.—blue and white bowls with five colored phoenixes flying through seasonal flowers; 2.—blue and white dishes with dragons or lotus

Ming bowl decorated in grey-blue under glaze. Dia. 5¾″. Metropolitan Mus. of Art.

Ming blue and white vase which probably dates in Wan Li period. Ht. 15¼″. Metropolitan Mus. of Art.

Box and cover with dragon and floral design in strong blue. Length c. 9″. Metropolitan Mus. of Art.

Blue and white Late Ming jar possibly from South China. Such little pieces found in Philippines and Malaysia. c. 1600. Ht. 3″. Metropolitan Mus. of Art.

Ting form incense burner. Feet in form of archaic dragons, tails winding about body in relief and forming handles. Underglaze blue and yellow enamel. Mark of Wan Li in double ring. Ht. 6¼″. Eumorfopoulos Coll.

Left: Plate with light blue decoration. Late Ming. Dia. 15″. Metropolitan Mus. of Art.
Right: Jar of heavy type with vigorous painting. Ht. 5″. Metropolitan Mus. of Art.

WAN LI WARES

PLATE 142

Stylization easily seen in pieces of Wan Li period, last great epoch of Ming dynasty (1573–1619). It may be designated as an elongated, tall stretching almost to the grotesque and at times a top heavy look due to mouth being so much wider than base. Blue and white of strong color. Metropolitan Mus. of Art.

Beakers of "wheat sheaf form" taken from bronze models, with flanges or suture marks maintained about middle and lower parts. Heavy white porcelain with strong underglaze decoration in blue and overglaze iron red and green enamel. Period mark on flaring mouths. Ht. 34″. Metropolitan Mus. of Art.

Left: Beaker with design outlined in black and washed with aubergine in ground of full yellow glaze. Base has white glaze and mark of Wan Li in blue in a double ring. Ht. 9½″. Eumorfopoulos Coll. # D115.

Right: Wan Li beaker in brilliant enamel "five color" decoration, having six character mark at lip, reading "Great Ming dynasty, reign of Wan Li made in." Ht. 12″. Boston Mus. of Fine Arts.

WAN LI BEAKERS OF "THREE COLOR" AND "FIVE COLOR" TYPE

PLATE 143

scrolls engraved; 3.—cups with nine dragons painted in red among blue and white sea waves; 4.—cups with nine blue monsters in red sea waves; 5.—cups with red sea waves with white crests; 6.—cups with yellow hibiscus flowers or enameled chrysanthemum flowers inside; 7.—incense burners with clouds and dragons worked in relief; and 8.—incense burners with designs carved in open work.

Special color arrangements were as follows: 1.—white inside and designs reserved in blue on the outside; 2.—blue ground with white designs all over; 3.—garden seats with aubergine lotus flowers on yellow ground; 4.—golden brown tea cups with engraved dragons and lotus scrolls; 5.—incense burners with enameled decoration on a yellow ground; 6.—vases of white porcelain with phoenixes and flowers engraved under the glaze; 7.—banquet dishes "shan p'an" white inside and with dragons in clouds outside painted in red, green, yellow and aubergine.

In this one reign we find more different qualities of material and technique than in a great many others put together. Tall, crude vases very heavily potted stand a yard in height and have the nien hao of Wan Li in six characters on the lip. Their glaze is heavy, greyish and bubbly. Then there are small, fine pieces with soft glaze easily scratched and crisp, thin porcelain with glossy glaze. The blue itself may be good Mohammedan quality, or dark like the Chia Ching, or pale and silvery, but usually it is simply dull and not very colorful. This was due to the first real improvements of the Chinese native blue which was to become so very bright and beautiful in the K'ang Hsi period. And the painting was direct and vigorous, weak and sloppy, careful and

FIG. 696. Small Wan Li bowl of blue and white mounted in silver gilt foot, rim and handles probably of late 16th cent. Dia. about 7". Metropolitan Mus. of Art.

FIG. 697. Wan Li blue and white cup with silver gilt mounts. Ht. 8½". Dia. 14". J. P. Morgan Coll. Metropolitan Mus. of Art.

painstaking or just plain poor. Variety was certainly the spice of Wan Li life.

A number of cups and ewers were mounted in Europe with silver or silver-gilt mounts that have assisted us in dating them. A number of these are cited by Hobson and I show a few from the Morgan Collection. A very fine example which belonged to Messrs. S. J. Philips has a nipple on the side which is an indication that it was probably originally designed as the base of a hubble pipe for Near Eastern use. I show an unmounted one of the same shape from the Metropolitan Museum of Art. In the Rosenborg Palace, Copenhagen, is a hexagonal box with handles and cover painted with figures crudely drawn in a dull blue and having the typical muslin-like texture of the glaze of this period. It was brought to Denmark in 1622 by Admiral Ove Gedde, who commanded the first Danish expedition to the East Indies, and given as a present to Princess Sophie Hedvig in 1723, some hundred years afterwards.

Thin porcelain types are frequently dishes with moulded borders. The ware is white, resonant and thinly potted while the glaze is clear and lustrous. There is often sand adhering to the foot-rim and pin holes in the glaze. Radiating wheel marks under the base, not to be confused with spiral marks, are signs of summary execution common on the ware. However, the work is fairly skillful and the brush was handled with speed and ease. The blue on these is usually pale and silvery.

Mr. Hannover says that these pieces are of rare occurrence and describes the white as being just slightly greenish. He goes on to say that the blue

FIG. 699. Ming blue and white *kendi* or water vessel. They drank from a stream from the spout at side. c. 1600. Metropolitan Mus. of Art.

FIG. 698. Fine ewer of blue and white Wan Li porcelain mounted with silver gilt base, cage, handle and top. Ht. 13⅝". J. P. Morgan Coll. Metropolitan Mus. of Art

has two tendencies, one to go toward black or indigo in tone and the other to go toward violet, but in almost all shades it has the tendency to run. He also says, "The bottom of a Ming piece often shows, under the glaze, faint radial lines in the paste, and where the foot-ring occurs it is often slightly brown." He further states that the paste has a "greasy" feel but I think that that is a bit exaggerated while Mr. Robert West's comparison to a piece of uncooked spaghetti is more like it.

"Porcelain House" is a good instance of the interest that the Near East took in these wares. It was called "Chini hane" and is in the Ardebil Mosque which was published by Dr. Sarre in "Denkmäler persischer Baukunst" in which is a picture showing some 500 bowls and jars. This mosque was built by Shah Abbas whose reign very nearly coincides with the Wan Li. It was 1586–1628 while Wan Li was 1573–1619. Most of the pieces collected were blue and white although there are some celadons and a few colored pieces. Hannover points out an interesting point and that is that none of the five piece sets called "garniture sets" are included and he deduces that these were first made in the 17th century to order for the Dutch market. Hobson says, "Another kind of vase, dimly seen in the back rows of Shah Abbas' Collection, is the large ovoid jar with loop handles on the shoulders. These, one imagines, were used as water jars on board ship and were traded widely in the East Indies and on the mainland. Sometimes they were protected by wickerwork or rope bands, as in the case of the Tradescant jar in the Ashmolean Museum, Oxford." This is the type we have described under the Philippine section.

"Kuei kung" or "devil's work" was made in some of the earlier reigns but now a further development of these incised and delicately modeled pieces took place. The modeling was often left unglazed, though some were covered with red with gold over that and some had blue and white decoration added as does the Metropolitan Museum one shown. Others had blue, yellow, green or aubergine washes to vignette the ornamentation. Another trick was to build up the ornament with slip and others had pierced work or "ling lung." It is doubtful if the K'ang Hsi workers ever reached the all round proficiency in this sort of lace work that the Late Ming potters accomplished.

Another type which seems to try to give the effect of "ling lung" work with a cheating on the labor is carved in the same way but in very low relief. These in turn were copied more and more crudely to the present day.

The "san ts'ai" or "three color" work went right on and into later times.

FIG. 700. Bowl and cover of *"kuei kung"* or "devil's work" with pierced fretwork and medallions in high relief showing traces of color and gilding. Ht. 6". Metropolitan Mus. of Art.

FIG. 701. Bowl and cover with blue and white design and high relief figures in medallions. Of the late Wan Li Period. Ht. 6½". Metropolitan Mus. of Art.

Hobson makes three divisions in it which may be helpful: He says that all of these glazes contained *soda, lime, lead* and *silica*. The early ones contained more silica and lime, were less fusible and less durable as well as being more opaque such as can be especially seen in the opaque violet. . . . The Chêng Tê type contained more lead making them more fusible, durable and transparent. . . . The Late Ming ones are fired in the muffle kiln and are softer yet, containing a higher proportion of lead and are fired at lower temperatures. These enamels were used in both the "san ts'ai" or three color type and the "wu ts'ai" or five color type and these were more easily controlled so that the designs could be outlined with dry pigment instead of resorting to incised or raised outlines. This seems a very sound analysis and much to be depended upon but I believe by careful comparisons most of these wares can be properly allocated within their proper reigns.

The molded wares came into vogue more extensively in the 18th century after the Wan Li period and continued through that century as is testified to by Père d'Entrecolles. This is also proven by the often published crayfish in the Hainhofer Cabinet at Upsala, which is yellow and has signs of gilt while the waves are thin and lustrous green with white crests.

The "sur biscuit" technique was certainly used a century before Wan Li but the Chinese writings are not very clear on the subject. However, the jars called "wave and plum blossom" jars are identified without any doubt and we have many examples of this type with rounded shoulders, wide cylindrical mouth and covers, which are certainly Wan Li or earlier, and are treated in this technique. Some have green and some aubergine grounds. Odd specimens of the sort are also treated over the glaze.

The "wu ts'ai" or five color ware had come to mean polychrome decoration including more than five colors and is so typical of the Wan Li period that it is often referred to as "Wan Li wu ts'ai yao." It now includes besides the underglaze blue: 1.— light green, 2.—dark green, 3.— aubergine, 4.—yellow, 5.—Ming iron red "fan hung" which is a rather glossy deep red of tomato color and iridescent at times, 6.— manganese brown, 7.—turquoise green. Deep blue was not being

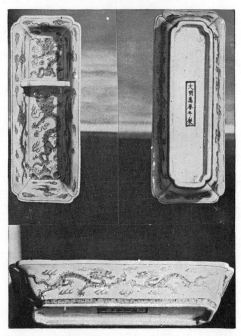

FIG. 702. Exceedingly rare but absolutely authentic Wan Li period brush tray with rest (which has been restored by Samson). The ground is of a soft but clear yellow and the dragons are of green and pale aubergine. All enamels are on a white glazed ground. The Wan Li mark is in deep underglaze blue. Ex Warren Cox Coll. Walter Blumenthal.

Left: Early Ming "Three color" gallipot with the more opaque type of enamels. The ground is cobalt blue and the design is in clear bright turquoise, yellow and creamy white. Under the foot and inside the neck is a thin wash of yellow green not used elsewhere. Ht. 12". Courtesy of Walter Blumenthal.

Right: "Three color" type jar and cover of dense almost white porcelaneous ware covered with various enamels held in place partially by low cloisonns. The ground is a soft but bright turquoise and the other colors are dark blue, aubergine, pale gray and white. Late Ming. Ht. about 15". Metropolitan Mus. of Art.

Left: Late Ming vase with enamel on biscuit, aubergine ground, green rocks and waves in three tones and yellow. Ht. 13". Bequest of Mary Clark Thompson. Metropolitan Mus. of Art.

Right: Fine Wan Li candlestick in colored enamels on a yellow ground, one of pair from the set in the British Mus. Ht. 28". C. T. Loo & Co.

SAN TS'AI (THREE COLOR) MING POTTERIES AND PORCELAINS
PLATE 144

used in enamel very often because the underglaze blue took its place.

The general styles that prevailed were:

1.—Underglaze blue, green, muddy yellow and red.

2.—Underglaze blue, green, yellow, aubergine, iron red and green-black (made by putting the transparent green over the manganese). This type usually has figure designs. This was copied in K'ang Hsi times but the red was lighter and less deep

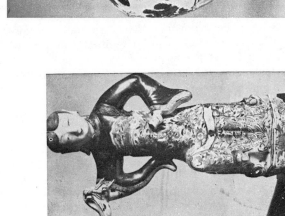

(a) (b) (c)

FIVE COLOR (WU TS'AI) MING PORCELAINS

WITH COMPARATIVE K'ANG HSI EXAMPLE

PLATE 145

(a) Wan Li ewer in the form of a dancing girl whose one arm acts as a handle and the other as a spout. The decoration is of rich "five color" type with strong underglaze blue and the jacket is of deep, fine iron red. Herbert Devine.
(b) Ming 17th cent. "five color" jar and cover with greenish white ground, deep underglaze blue, clear yellow, three greens, a pale and clear iron red, deep aubergine and strong black. Ht. 18″. Metropolitan Mus. of Art.
(c) Two similar "five color" vases, the one with the fan being Ming and the other with the crane K'ang Hsi, showing almost identical technique of drawing and similar shapes. Hts. 7½″ and 7¾″. Metropolitan Mus. of Art.

3.—All the enamels used but dominated with the red and green as a development of the Chia Ching style. Often the background is of diapered lightly painted lines. The blue is omitted.

Mr. Hobson gives us an amusing note to the effect that this type was copied "with disconcerting fidelity" probably by a factory in the 19th century which signed its wares with the mark "shên tê t'ang." In one interesting specimen he says the words "po ku" were added proclaiming the dish to be an "antique made at the Shên Tê Hall."

4.—Garden seats were supposed to have been made with brown dragons and lotus flowers on yellow ground, but we have none.

5.—Incense burners were supposed to have been made with the five colors on a yellow ground. They are probably like the K'ang Hsi famille jaune wares. One interesting piece is a bronze beaker form in the Eumorfopoulos Col. #D115 with brownish yellow glaze and a design outlined in brown and washed in with aubergine. This was bought by Frank Partridge at Southby & Co., May 30th, 1940, catalogue #264. One should not be surprised to find other odd combinations from time to time.

Hannover points out an odd specimen in the Salting Collection, V. & A. Mus. It bears the mark of Chêng Tê and may be of the period or might possibly be later Ming, but it is a bowl having large fishes in underglaze red while others are in the five color enamels and these are also employed in the polychrome border. He goes on to argue that, "Here we have evidently a specimen anterior to the time when the formula for five color painting was finally determined, and this seems, as far as can be judged, to have happened as early as the reign Wan Li. For when the Chinese speak of 'Wan Li wu ts'ai,' this undoubtedly implies that the five color painting, which otherwise in its final form belongs chiefly to the time of K'ang Hsi, has already in the latest period of the Ming dynasty to a certain extent assumed its later typical form." This logic does not hold any more than the argument that whenever we speak of a "Chippendale chair" or a "Renaissance scroll" we mean a chair actually made by Chippendale or a scroll actually made in the Renaissance. It is safe to say that in the Wan Li period the style was forming but not that it was formed or "finally determined."

Sometimes the enamels were applied very thinly and delicately and also very crudely and heavily. All sorts of craftsmanship were used and, as we have seen, many combinations. In fact the reign is noted for the very extremes to which it reached and not until later did things settle down into definite ruts of mechanical procedure and commercial practice.

Among the monochromes we find the following listed:

1.—White bowls of Yung Lo were imitated as were many of the other fine wares and the bodies and glazes are so nearly alike that we have to judge by style alone in making attributions which are always uncertain.

2.—Yellow of the "hung chih" type was also made along with golden brown and dead leaf brown.

3.—Aubergine was copied after the Chia Ching wares.

4.—Green of a fine leaf color was applied both direct on the body or over a grey or white crackled glaze.

5.—"Apple green" was also said to have been made.

6.—Celadon was made at Ch'u Chou and at Ching-tê Chêng among other places. In the V. & A. Mus. is a bowl with blue inside and pale celadon outside and French metal mounts that seem to indicate it is of about this period. In the Eumorfopoulos Col. is a low bowl with pale clair de lune celadon glaze and marked, "To be treasured in the Ju-ch'eng family in the 'hsin mao' year of Wan Li." (*i.e.* 1591) But we shall say more about celadon shortly.

7.—Hobson says there is a bottle of the flambé type in the B.M. but it must have been an accidental piece, I believe.

8.—Black, not unlike the "hare's fur" of the Sung Chien yao but blacker, was made.

FIG. 703. Ming dynasty gallipot of porcelain covered with a blue glaze. Ht. 13". Metropolitan Mus. of Art.

FIG. 704. Wan Li vase with brilliant black glaze turning to brown at edges. Ht. 15". M. Calmann Coll. (Paris).

FIG. 705. Ming, Wan Li pale "celadon" large dish probably made in South China for the Indian market. The design is of white slip applied through a tube. The glaze is poor and considerably pitted. Dia. 15". Metropolitan Mus. of Art.

9.—Black of the mirror quality is said to have been invented during the K'ang Hsi times by Père d'Entrecolles but Hobson says it was made in Wan Li times, backing his statement with a vase from the Calmann Col. (Pl. 42, *The Wares of the Ming Dynasty*), which has been frequently illustrated and which has every appearance of being Ming. He says of it, "The brown emerges prominently where the glaze has run thin on the raised parts, and conversely the black is more intense where the glaze has run thickly.

Marbled wares of the old T'ang type with mixed clays were again made and others had mixed slips or glazes as the case might be. One in the Eumorfopoulos Col. has the mixed slips and the mark "Modeled by Ch'ên Wên-ching in Ting yu year of Wan Li."

A steatitic slip of paint-like, opaque quality was used from K'ang Hsi onwards, but the Ming slip is liquid looking and translucent, probably of very thin porcelain clay. It was applied with a brush much as we see later in Minton and Sèvres wares but, of course, with more simple and tasteful designs. The ground used under this work was brown, deep blue or celadon. Flowers and rarely birds were painted. The shapes were bottle vases, flower pots, narghili bowls, ewers, jars and some large plates made evidently chiefly for trade in Indian and Persian markets for much of this ware is found in these countries. It is probably all the output of one factory which lasted well beyond Ming times but specimens have been found with Wan Li marks and some may be even earlier. Sometimes the slip is left dry and sometimes it is glazed over.

Another group of export wares is heavily built of a strong but coarse body which burns reddish brown and usually has sand or grit adhering to the foot-rim. The color varies being: slaty blue, celadon, light coffee brown or dark brown and the decoration is of crudely applied slip. An associated ware is also coarse and greyish blue and white and is decorated with Ming turquoise green or leaf green and red and white over incised designs. It has been suggested that some of this ware may have been made in Korea but there is no evidence to support the guess. However, we know of no place in Fukien province either for that matter. Wherever the factory was it continued long after Ming times.

As early as Wan Li the exceedingly tasteless association of porcelain and lacquer was made as is proven by a vase in the B.M. Lacquer is a more or less transparent varnish made from the sap of certain trees or from certain insects which suck this sap in China and Japan. It is applied cold having been dissolved in solvents. The vase mentioned is a beaker of typical Wan Li shape, square in plan and with the usual decorations of Imperial dragons and rock and wave borders rendered in green and red lacquer on a brown ground with details incised and lined with gold. There is a Wan Li mark in the usual place on the lip and it and the lion handles are in underglaze blue while the rest of the surface is left without glaze to receive the lacquer. To quote Hannover, "When this" (lacquer on porcelain) "is inlayed with mother of pearl, we have the *laque burgauté* of the French, which in its time seems to have enjoyed a somewhat undeserved popularity."

T'ai Ch'ang or Ch'ang Lo (1620–   )
T'ien Ch'i or Yu Chiao (1621–1627)
Ch'ung Cheng or Yu Chien (1628–1644)

The last three reigns of the Ming Dynasty amounted to very little. The first lasted only a few months. The next emperor Yu Chiao took the name of Hsi Tsung and proceeded to devote himself to carpentry while a nurse and eunuch ruled. One is reminded of the French king and his clocks. Finally Yu Chien took the name of Chuang Lieh Ti and, through the irony of fate, was a good man and earnest ruler but through treachery the gates of Peking were opened to a rebel force and he retreated to the "Mei Shan" or "Coal Hill" and there in sight of the city hanged himself with his girdle. After futile attempts to re-establish the survivors of the royal family against the Manchus a final stand was taken in Kwangtung by Kuei Wang but he had to retreat to Burma and also committed suicide in 1662.

Nothing is recorded of Ching-tê Chêng and the wares of the times are very much on the decline showing only poorer and poorer workmanship. Shortly after the end of Wan Li the Dutch in 1624 obtained a foothold in Formosa and there was evidently a great trade in blue and white wares with European modifications of shape.

Polychrome wares continued, of course, and they had the Wan Li color schemes. One variation was a blue and white ware with a wash of transparent green over it, as may be seen by a vase in the Grandidier Col., Louvre, Paris.

CONTINUOUS WARES

I have tried to give a brief suggestion as to the characteristics of the wares of the various reigns of the dynasty. I think it has been clear that technique replaced good taste to a considerable extent. Modeling became "devil's work," glazes became almost too refined, many colors led to less well

FIG. 706. Ming, T'ien Ch'i period (1621–1627 A.D.) dish of greenish white ground decorated with underglaze blue, light and dark iron red, yellow green, brown black and yellow enamels. Dia. 6". Metropolitan Mus. of Art.

FIG. 707. Ming, T'ien Ch'i (1621–1627 A.D.) dish with same colors as other specimen. The writing on it is a quotation. Dia. 6". Metropolitan Mus. of Art.

FIG. 708. "Ko yao" cup attributed to the Ming period. It has a sandy buff body and gray crackled glaze not so strong as the photo would suggest. Ht. 4". Metropolitan Mus. of Art.

considered painting, relying for its effect on the splash of the whole bouquet of colors. In other words there were many mediums of expression but not a great deal to express. . . . Or perhaps there was too much to express in the way of undigested emotions. It is really impossible ever to tell what is the matter with an art; it either springs from the earth in all perfection as does a beautiful flower to move one, or it does not. One cannot say, "I would have been moved by such a singer had her register been an octave lower, her overtones richer, her diction less pronounced." One might eventually improve a voice by such criticisms but then one would not be moved by it unless the voice suddenly blossomed out beyond all such rules of criticism. What could be more ridiculous than a lover making love to rules? Nothing unless it be an artist working to rules. . . . No, if art is successful, we can find a thousand reasons why we liked it and were moved while, if art does not move us, all we can say is that we were not moved. So with the pageant of Ming art and achievement we must admit that the show was well set but our hearts neither felt the weight of sadness, the lift of great joy nor any other emotion.

Some wares, however, carried through from the days of T'ang and Sung and did not die completely during Ming times. We have already spoken of the Tz'u Chou types of Yüan and Early Ming, of the Tsung Sê t'zǔ or dark brown types including those found in the Philippines, of the Chün yao and of blue and white wares, but others too were carried on.

Ko yao, as may be seen by the small cup shown from the Metropolitan Museum was imitated in a shape which shortly later was turned into an "apple green" by the addition of a transparent green enamel over the crackled glaze. We have also seen a crackle developed on the baluster shaped vases mentioned under the Chêng Hua reign and have noted how they gave way to enameled backgrounds. Again a crackled ware will be taken up shortly under what Mr. Hobson calls "Kiagnan Ting" wares. But often one sees a Ko yao example very much like the Sung ware except that it had a more porcelaneous body of the type of paste we expect from Ching-tê Chêng or a shape which could only be Ming.

FIG. 709. Lung Ch'üan yao dish of early Ming type with foliated edge, incised design of rather ornate character but covered with a creamy grey green glaze, which is un-crackled and pitted as may be seen inside the foot rim on the back. Dia. 12½". Warren E. Cox Coll.

FIG. 711. Celadon made at Wen Chou in late Ming times ac-cording to Sir Percival David. Exceedingly heavy, having walls about ¾" thick at the foot. The ware is white burnt red-brown at foot and the glaze is light yellowish green and more opaque than that of Ch'u-chou. Finely crackled. Ht. 12¾". Lem S. Tsang–Warren E. Cox Coll.

FIG. 710. A "Sêng-mao-hu" or monk's-cap jug of celadon glaze having the characteristics of Lung-ch'üan, and a blue underglaze mark of Hsüan-tê. Handle and cover new. Ht. 7¾". Note: These also occur in Hsüan-tê red and in Yung-lo white with incised design of eight Buddhistic emblems supported on lotus flowers, indicating a ceremonial use.

Celadons continued to be made right through the period in various places. Of course, one thinks of Ch'u Chou as the site for the largest output of Ming celadon and that is undoubtedly the case but it must be clearly borne in mind that Ch'u Chou had kilns and made pieces in Sung times and also that very similar wares were made well into K'ang Hsi times and probably even later. So similar are these that experts cannot distinguish them from Ming wares. It has, I believe, also been made clear that the kilns at Lung-Ch'üan did not cease work but proceeded to make excellent examples at least into Ming times. And again we know that Ching-tê Chêng was striving all along to copy these popular wares, while factories in Kwangtung and elsewhere were also working with the same thing in mind. Sir Percival David told me that the very heavy vase with frosty glaze shown herewith is from Wen Chou and is of late Ming period. From Yang Chiang in Kwangtung come some of the slip decorated pieces described above and other recognizable lower fired southern celadons, while another large source was from Show Chou in Anhwei.

The Lung Ch'üan wares did not change in quality or technique from those of the Sung period and would be indistinguishable save for the fact that some of them are dated such as those in the collection of Sir Percival David.

An example very likely to be from the Ching-tê Chêng factories is the ewer or jug "hu" of pure white ware showing only the slightest trace of brown near the edge of the glaze where the foot is exposed and covered with a light celadon glaze much like a lighter type of Lung Ch'üan. This piece has an underglaze Hsüan Tê four character mark and it is interesting to note that another of the same form was lent by the Chinese Government to the London, International Exhibition of Chinese Art 1935–6 and is described as having a "ruby-red glaze and mouth in the form of a priest's hat." This red one is of the same height and has the same mark—proving rather conclusively that they were both made at Ching-tê Chêng where the red glaze was developed. Brankston shows a white one (Pl. 2, *Early Ming Wares of Ching-te-Chên*) with incised design of probable Yung-Lo period.

The large oval vase with a Chia Ching mark which is so over fired as to

FIG. 712. Ming Chêng Tê vase and lamp for floating wick made at Ch'u-chou for Mohammedan trade. The vase has the character *shou* (longevity) on one side and *fu* (happiness) on the other. The ware has burnt red where exposed and the glaze is faintly crackled and frosty from burial. Hts. 7″ and 8″. Lem Sec Tsang Coll.–Warren E. Cox Coll.

FIG. 713. Show Chou, Anhwei, dish of grey porcelain burnt brown where exposed and having a glassy crackled glaze of olive-green. Dia. 12″. John Platt–Warren E. Cox Coll.

appear more like a crackled "Ting type" but which shows the clear pale green crackled glaze inside is more likely from Kiangsu or Anhwei, for the buff body is much like that of the so-called "Kiagnan Ting" wares.

Quite possible it is that the dish with unglazed bottom, rounded foot-rim glazed over and rich, crackled glaze is from Show Chou in Anhwei for it has many characteristics similar to the deep bowls which we described at the end of the Sung section.

The strong influence of Mohammedan design is to be seen on the two small vases with loop handles and the lamp in the form of a sanctuary and these seem to be Ch'u Chou ware of refined but typical sort, probably dating from the Chêng Tê period when that influence was strongest as is proven by the many blue and white wares with Arabic writing. Other refined examples from the same factory are the hat rest and the small toilet water holder in the "duck shape" in which urinals were often made but too small for such a purpose and having a lip for pouring. The large dish will serve to show how the design became more ornate and less well organized.

The striving for greater and greater weight to stand shipment resulted often in fire cracks which opened up during the firing in the kiln. This may be seen in the hot water bowl designed to keep rice hot while eating and also in the very large jar which has a globule of the glaze showing where it oozed through the crack. Often at Ch'u Chou the glaze was so thickly applied that it ran down in large drops at the bottom so that they had to be ground off or stands had to be made to fit their irregularities so that the vase would stand straight. Such large drips can be seen on the foot-rim of the jar and about the bottom of the amphora vase as well as on the side of the small mouthed "gallipot." These last two are of the deepest and richest green I have seen from this kiln site.

One of a pair of vases in the V. & A. Mus. is shown by Hobson in The Wares of the Ming Dynasty, Pl. 46, Fig. 2 and is of a pale watery green thin glaze rather greyish in color and is incised with flowers and an inscription dating it 1547 or the Chia Ching reign. This is interesting for wares of the type have been offered for sale as "Early Sung."

Glancing at a few of Sir Percival David's we find the following:

1.—LVIII Ch'u Chou vase, Hsüan Tê (A.D. 1432).

2.—LIX Vase from same kiln and similar, in shape, to the Ching T'ai period (1454).

3.—LX Flower pot of the Chêng Tê period (1517) and also from Ch'u Chou.

Finally I show another vase from the Lem Sec Tsang Collection which is inscribed according to the translation of Mr. Han of the Metropolitan

FIG. 715. Ch'u-chou vase of beautiful proportions and fine rich glaze running to heavy drops at the bottom. Ht. 23¾". Warren E. Cox Coll.

FIG. 716. Fine Ch'u-chou bottle of the Ming period which was some years ago exhibited at the Metropolitan Mus. of Art and catalogued at the Mrs. Samuel T. Peters sale as, "Lung Ch'üan Sung period." Ht. 18½". Warren E. Cox Coll.

FIG. 717. Ch'u-chou vase of the Ming period with exceedingly thick, rich green glaze. Ht. 12¼". Lem S. Tsang–Warren E. Cox Coll.

FIG. 718. Small Ming period vase made at Ch'u-chou. Vigorously incised and has soft pea-green crackled glaze. Ht. 6½". Mrs. Warren E. Cox.

FIG. 719. Early Ming Ch'u-chou vase of greyish porcelain burnt brown where exposed and covered with a rich, transparent grey-green glaze over an incised design. Ht. 9". Warren E. Cox Coll.

FIG. 720. Reticulated vase to hold flower petals or sandalwood to perfume room. Ex Warren E. Cox Coll.

FIG. 721. Lung Ch'uan yao "celadon" dish of white porcelain with incised lotus design covered with a greyish olive-green glaze rather thinly applied. Dia. 18". Warren E. Cox Coll.

Museum of Art, "The faithful person, Chou K'un-hsi a native of Hsi-yü, respectfully offers a pair of precious vases before Mme. Ma Ch'i seated to the rear of the hall. In donating this present he asks that she will protect the

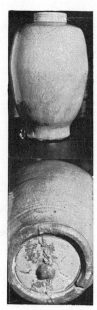

FIG. 722. Ch'u-chou toilet water bottle with incising to indicate the plumage of a duck. Length 7″. John Platt–Warren E. Cox Coll.

FIG. 724. Ch'u-chou large jar showing glassy crackled glaze and typical large drips around base, also a rather not unusual fire-crack through which a large drop of the glaze has come. Ht. 19″. Warren E. Cox Coll.

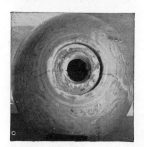

FIG. 723. Ch'u-chou yao hot water bowl made with shallow concavity at top and a hole in the bottom so that it can be filled with hot water to keep rice or other food warm. Dia. 6⅝″. Warren E. Cox Coll.

FIG. 726. Ming Ch'u-chou ware temple vase dated with the year equivalent to 1625. It has a rich green glaze of olive tone. Ht. 18″. Lem Sec Tsang Coll.–Warren E. Cox.

FIG. 725. Ch'u-chou vase (fêng wei p'ing) of greyish porcelain burnt red brown where exposed and with pale green glaze over an incised design. The inscription reads: "Made on a lucky day in the seventh month of the seventh year of the Hsüan Tê period (1432 A.D.) for use in the palace (fu) of the T'ien-shih (Taoist pope)." Ht. 17.3″. Sir Percival David Coll.

FIG. 727. Ch'u-chou vase (fêng wei p'ing) of greyish porcelain with light pea-green glaze over incised ornament and writing: "In the fifth year of the Ching T'ai period (A.D. 1454), the believer Yang Tsung-hsin of the hamlet of Chên-an in Fu li, etc." Hobson says that the Ching T'ai mark seldom appears on porcelain though it does most often on Ming cloisonné. Ht. 26.8″. Sir Percival David Coll.

peace and luck of his daughter," and it is dated, "on the day of the eighth month of the fifth year of T'ien Ch'i" or 1625.

Later in the K'ang Hsi section I shall show a specimen unique so far as I know and which many experts have called Ming but which is dated as of that later reign. Thus we have some stepping stones but they are rather far apart and seem to teach us only that we must not be too pedantic so far as dating celadons goes and that to try to judge by style, as Mr. Hobson would have us do, is, to say the least, difficult.

Fig. 728. Ch'u-chou flower-pot (p'ên) of greyish porcelain with grey-green glaze having some crackle near the bottom. On it is incised under the glaze, "The believer Ch'ên O of the eastern Suburb of Li-shui Hsien in the prefecture of Ch'u-chou has resolved to offer joyfully ten pieces to the Liu Ho Ssŭ (Buddhist Temple), that they may be placed before the Kuan-yin with the prayer that his mother may live a very long life, that he and his wife may grow old together, that every member of his family may be lucky, that he may have many prosperous sons and grandsons, that he may be able to perform meritorious deeds (in the service of Buddha) and that they may all enjoy happiness. Made in the middle ten days of the eighth month of the cyclical year Ting ch'ou of the Chêng Tê period." (A.D. 1517) Dia. 8.8″. Sir Percival David. Coll.

Fig. 729. Vase on left has mark of Ch'ên Chên-shan and a crackled watery celadon glaze. Ht. 10½″. S. D. Winkworth Col. Vase with handles has an inscription with date equal to 1547, and a pale celadon somewhat crackled glaze thinly applied. Ht. 12″. G. Hart Coll. Victoria & Albert Mus.

"KIANGNAN TING" AND OTHER CREAM GLAZED WARES

What we have said about the wide distribution of celadon wares is almost as true of the cream glazed wares. We have spoken of the Yung Lo and other rather close imitations of thin, white Ting yao. We have also indicated the continuance of slip covered and painted or incised decorated Tz'u Chou types. Now, during the Ming period, there developed wares which were perhaps influenced by both of these. They might better be called Tz'u Chou types since they are treated with white slip and transparent crackled glaze. The crackle is usually stained brown. They have loosely been put under the general name of Ting yao and as the provinces of Kiangsu and Anhwei were formerly united and called Kiangnan, and we are given to understand that most of the ware was made in these places, Mr. Hobson has given the general name of "Kiangnan Ting" to the wares. Obviously this is a rather ambiguous and not very well defined classification and it covers some very different looking wares but until we get further actual information we shall

Left: Yung-ho Chên vase showing the finer and darker crackle toward the mouth. Ht. 16″. Metropolitan Mus. of Art.
Center: Ming pottery vase of the type called "Kiangnan Ting." Buff body, white slip, crackled creamy glaze. Ht. 4½″. T. C. Lee–Warren E. Cox Coll.
Right: The finest example I know of the Yung-ho Chên type. Ming. Ht. 7″. Metropolitan Mus. of Art.

Yung-ho Chên vase of the type called "Kiangnan Ting" by Hobson but having a rich camellia-green crackled glaze. Ming Dynasty. Fukien province. Ht. 13¾″. Warren E. Cox Coll.

Ting type vase. Grey stoneware, cream glaze. Ht. 12¾″. Warren E. Cox Coll.

Yung-ho Chên Ming vase. Ht. 19¾″. Warren E. Cox Coll.

Kiangnan Ting vase of the usual light buff body heavily potted, covered with a thinly applied very finely crackled cream white glaze. Similar in form to some of the "three color" examples, but more beautiful in proportions and details of potting. Ht. 14″. Ex Samuel T. Peters Coll. Warren E. Cox Coll.

"KIANGNAN TING" AND RELATED WARES OF THE MING DYNASTY
PLATE 146

have to be contented with it. In the Sung section we have mentioned a few of the sites such as Hsiang-shan, Ssŭ Chou, Su Chou, Hsüan Chou and it is likely that these all continued more or less active, but particularly in what is now Kiangsu the *T'ao lu* tells of a place called Pai-t'u Chên where potteries were reported to have been made since Sung times constructed of the local clay and "very thin, white and lustrous, beautiful in form and workmanship." There were several hundred potters and the kilns were chiefly owned by a family of potters named Tsou. I know of no actual excavations at this site, but undoubtedly some of the wares we have originated there.

In Shansi there were four sites: 1.—P'ing-yang Fu, 2.—Ho Chou, 3.—

P'êng Chün-pao and 4.—Yu-tzŭ Hsien. The first ware, we are told by the *T'ao lu,* was white but had a discolored glaze and this is borne out by excavations there which disclosed a heavy painted and carved ware like a crude Tz'u Chou with rather close all-over design in the painted ones and high relief but crude work in the carved or molded ones, which are often after bronze forms. At Ho Chou the potteries existed from T'ang times and made at all times a refined and well potted ware though inclined to be yellowish in tone. At P'ang Chün-pao in the Yüan dynasty a goldsmith from Ho Chou made wares that the *Ko ku yao lan,* an almost contemporary work, said were exactly like Ting but "short" and "brittle" and not worth much, "But dealers in curiosities give them the name of 'Hsin ting' or 'New Ting,' and amateurs collect them at great cost, which is most ridiculous." At Yu-tzŭ Hsien in the north again a crude pottery was made.

Yao Chou in Shensi was a source of flat-bottomed bowls called "little seagulls." But going south we must not forget the kilns at Chi Chou and

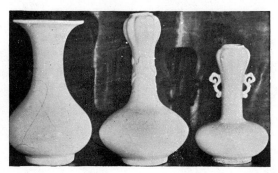

FIG. 730. Kiangnan Ting vases of the late Ming period. Hts. 13″ to 10″. Warren E. Cox Coll.

FIG. 731. Bowl and cover found at Swankalok and dating late Sung to early Ming. The decoration is in dull, blackish blue and the ware is reddish-buff. Ht. 4½″. N. M. Heeramaneck Coll.

those at Nan-fêng Hsien both in Kiangsi province. The latter made a heavy "t'u ting yao" in the Yüan dynasty and undoubtedly later. The Chi Chou kilns were situated at Yung-ho Chên where there were five factories according to the *Ko ku yao lan.* This will be remembered as the locality of the potteries that turned to jade. The *T'ao lu* tells us that crackle was a specialty and to quote, "These are the wares made in the Southern Sung period. Originally they were a special class of ware made at Yung-ho Chên. . . . The clay was coarse but strong, the body thick and the material heavy. Moreover, there were 'millet coloured' (mi sê) and pale green (fên ch'ing) kinds. The potters used *hua shih* (steatite) in the glaze, and the crackle was in running lines like a broken thing. They smeared and blackened the ware with coarse ink or ocherous earth; then they finished it. Afterwards they rubbed it clean, and it was found to have hidden lines and stains of red or black, like cracked ice, beautiful to look at. There were besides pieces with plain crackled ground, to which they added blue decoration." (Hobson's translation probably from Bushell.) This was of the Sung dynasty but leads us to believe that some of the heavy crackled wares and some of the

Fig. 732. Kiangnan Ting vase of another typical form sometimes having cloud scroll handles. These were usually made in a two piece mould and the handles applied afterwards. Ht. about 11″. Warren E. Cox Coll.

Fig. 734. Two fine vases of Kiangnan Ting ware the large one having loose suspended rings evidently fired in one piece and cut away from the post supports which were in the loops. Ralph M. Dudley Coll. The other is one of a perfectly matched pair in the L. G. Sheafer Coll.

dull blue on crackled ground wares found in Malaysia and Borneo may be the ones described, and these both continued to Ming and even later times.

In actual wares I think that it is obvious that they divide themselves into two main classes: First, the glossy and white or nearly white ones with hardly perceptible crackle or no crackle at all. These have bodies ranging from buff to white or nearly so and which are not hard but typical pottery very easily cut. They are largely molded and often have relief ornamentation or handles of cloud scrolls, lions, t'ao teh heads, etc. I do not contend for a minute that these are all alike or made in one place for, as one can readily see in the illustrations, the very weight of the potting varies consider-

Fig. 735. Yung-ho Chên bulb-bowl with pressed and incised design. Usually these pieces have no decoration. Ming Dynasty. Dia. 9¼″. Warren E. Cox Coll.

ably, but they are similar in technique and general appearance. . . . Second, the group which I think likely to be those described as from Yung-ho Chên which are generally wheel-turned to buff to brown ware and with a crackled glaze often stained deeper toward the lip-rim and only seldom decorated with relief appliqués, hand modeling or stamped and incised design as in the bowl illustrated. These too are pottery and neither porcelain nor stoneware. The foot-rim may be flat or often slightly bevelled on the inside and outside edge. My impression after long discussions of the subject with the late Malcolm Farley is that the first class of ware is found in the Kiangnan section while the second was found extensively by him in Kiangsi and Fukien provinces further south. It is unfortunate that he never was able to bring over his sherds from China to prove his points conclusively. A particularly heavy type, he said, was found at Dong Khe in Fukien province.

Both these wares and similar wares were continued into modern times. I show a most interesting specimen which I recently acquired. In shape it is less strong but much more refined than the Ming ones. The potting is thinner and the ware harder, being porcelaneous. It is incised under the bottom with a freely drawn K'ang Hsi nien hao mark and on it is incised two ch'i-lins or kylins on either side with their prancing feet on 4.—a *chüeh* or rhinocerous horn, 5.—a *ch'in* or stringed instrument partly covered with its

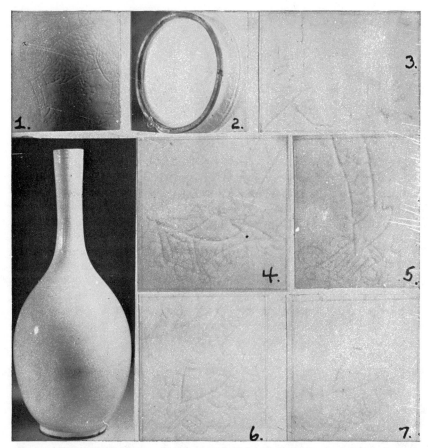

FIG. 736. K'ang Hsi "kiangnan ting" bottle refined form. 1.—Kylin decoration incised on either side. 2.—Note the thinner and deeper foot-rim which is slightly beveled and burnt brown where exposed. 3.—The mark is freely and swiftly incised and reads K'ang Hsi nein chih. 4.— The *chüeh* or rhinoceros horn under the right front foot of the kylin. 5.—The *ch'in* or stringed musical instrument with its bag cover half drawn over it which is under the left front foot. 6.—The *ai-yeh* or artemisia leaf which is under the right hind foot. 7.—The *p'ing* or vase which is under the left hind foot. Ht. 14¾". Warren E. Cox Coll.

covering bag, 6.—an *ai-yeh* or artemisia leaf and 7.—a *p'ing* or gourd shaped bottle, a strange mixture of Buddhist and other objects. This links the type with K'ang Hsi at least and the hard biscuit would seem to indicate a kiln site in or near Ching-tê Chêng, which is also in Kiangsi province, of course.

Finally I show what is, so far as I know, an entirely unique specimen of the second group, like in body clay, like in potting and identical in shape to the cream crackled ones but covered with a deep, rich leaf-green glaze having just about the same crackle as the cream ones. The glaze is entirely different from any of the more or less transparent ones used on the "three color" wares or on the porcelains and it has a typical "orange skin" undulating surface. Perhaps this piece is the prototype of the K'ang Hsi and Chien Lung crackled greens of well known fame and known as "camellia green," etc. In any event it is rare as a Ming specimen.

Tz'u Chou Type Wares

Though Ching-tê Chêng is the largest and most important group of kilns the world has ever known those at Tz'u Chou are undoubtedly the most continuous having lasted from the 6th century or earlier right up to the present. Moreover many of the other kilns that made this ware continued also and I am told that nowadays one can buy bowls, figures and various vessels very nearly like the early ones for household use.

In the Sung and Yüan sections I have mentioned the tendency just before Ming times to elaborate Tz'u Chou type wares by the addition of iron red and enamel colors. In fact it was very likely this type of ware that became the prototype of the "three colored" wares of Ming fame. However, tradition is strong in China and many monochrome paintings were done all during the Ming times distinguishable only by the style of the decoration and the form and consistency of the pot itself. One thing the artists could not get away from was the laxity of the side line of the vases into strongly curved S tendencies. They undoubtedly actually thought these new forms better and had no idea of giving them up. I show a vase of typical character decorated with a lotus loosely drawn, a happy boy and a bird along with characters. Another example is the blue ewer from the Metropolitan Museum less well potted than Six Dynasties examples and with crude decoration. All

Fig. 738. Fish-bowl of Early Ming times of stoneware with figures in relief representing the Eight Immortals. Probably of the Chia Ching reign. Dia. 23″. John Sparks, Ltd.

Fig. 737. Wine ewer of gourd shape with tiger spout and handle, of buff-gray stoneware covered with glossy slip and glaze and painted in brown. Note the scratching out of the veins of the leaves. Ht. 11¼″. John Platt–Warren E. Cox Coll.

Fig. 739. Tz'u Chou type jar from northern Honan and of the Ming period. The decoration is in black swiftly painted and scratched out for details. Nasli Heeramaneck Coll.

Ming T'zu Chou figure of Lao Tzŭ in buff pottery with cream slip and glaze, and brown details. Ht. 7″. Ex Warren E. Cox Coll. Mr. George Gillett.

Ming period Tz'u Chou showing a man of means, probably an official, together with his wife, holding the sceptre, his concubine and his horse. The artistry and gentle humor of this work shows to what heights some of the Ming artists could rise. Ex Warren E. Cox Coll. Mrs. Charles Porter Wilson.

Ming Tz'u Chou vase of good form but somewhat less dynamic design than is seen on the Sung examples. The other side shows a "happy boy" and there are several characters. Warren E. Cox Coll.

Tz'u Chou jar with yellow, green and iron-red design, of early Ming type. The red is darker than that on the southern Sung pieces. (See p. 206.) Ex Warren E. Cox Coll.

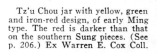

TZ'U CHOU TYPE WARES OF THE MING DYNASTY

PLATE 147

the painting was not of this character as we found in the two brownish examples which I show in the Yüan section as they may possibly be of that period. These are decorated simply and well, as is also the pillow from the Heeramaneck Collection.

That modeling became important we can see in the fine large fish bowl in the John Sparks Collection, London in which the Taoist figures are in fairly high relief. This is called "Early Ming" by them but I should be inclined to place it in the Chia Ching (1522–1566) or strongly Taoist times. I should also see no reason for not so placing the fine figure of Shou Lao, god of the southern star and of long life, and one form of Lao Tzŭ himself seated with an adoring child holding a plum beside him and loving animals: the stork, the tortoise and the deer, all representing long life, about him. This is decorated in two shades of brown or in brown and black. (Another Ming custom.)

FIG. 740. Buff stoneware vase, showing the more flamboyant line of the Yuan and Early Ming potteries. Ht. 13". Warren E. Cox Coll.

FIG. 741. Tz'u Chou type pillow of buff grey ware with white slip and transparent glaze. The fine painting is in black. On the bottom is a three character inscription stating it was made by the Chang family. Length about 12". N. M. Heeramaneck Coll.

FIG. 742. Ming pottery of Tz'u Chou type of reddish color with white slip, darkest aubergine or black slip decoration and blue glaze. The aubergine is used inside. Ht. 8". Gift of Robert E. Tod. Metropolitan Mus. of Art.

Another fine figure group shows a dignitary of importance with his wife on his right, a lovely concubine or second wife on his left and his horse behind him saddled and ready to carry the master. The human charm of this group speaks for itself. Thus we must not look with lack of interest upon Tz'u Chou works of later times.

FIG. 743. Tz'u Chou jar. Ht. 9¾". Eumo. Coll. # C295.

FIG. 744. Tz'u Chou type jar. Ht. 9½". Eumo. Coll. # C308.

Dating is difficult but we have a few milestones as follows:

1.—In the Eumorfopoulos Col. #C295 is a jar dated to correspond with 1446 which is in the brief and unimportant period of Chêng T'ung (1436-1449). I have not seen this piece and cannot describe the ware but the design might well be a Sung one and Hobson says it is of a grey stoneware with white slip and cream glaze, painted in brown and with a brown glaze inside. We assume the foot-rim to be about as expected as nothing is said of it.

2.—Another #C308 in the same collection is of "grey porcelaneous ware with white slip and painted in black under a creamy glaze." It has also a black glaze inside and at the lip. This piece has the Wan Li (1573–1619) six character mark on the shoulder. The large fish is characteristic and I should assign all of the bowls on which these appear, if not to Wan Li, at least to the Ming period judging not only by their style but also by the body and glaze. These are sometimes called timorously "Yüan."

3.—There are a number of specimens with enamels combined with slip painting which also bear Wan Li marks showing us that this type reached at least into late Ming times. They probably continued later.

One more note must be added. A whole group which we have classed as Ming to date must now be assigned to Southern Sung and very likely to our central Kiangsi kilns on the evidence of the small dated example of A.D. 1203 now in the Metropolitan Museum of Art. This ware is of a rather rough and sandy buff body with white slip and a yellowish cream glaze sometimes crackled and sometimes not. The painting is rather greyish black and though spirited is often of an all-over pattern less pictorial and less naturalistic than the Tz'u Chou ware itself. The incorrect idea that the glaze should always be crackled in old pieces is pure nonsense for at this time very few kilns could control crackle and the various factors both chemical and physical of this particular ware seemed fairly well balanced so that it fell on one side or the other as chance dictated.

TSUNG SÊ T'ZŬ (DARK BROWN COLORED POTTERY)

The little tea-bowls made at Chien-an or Chien-yang were certainly continued in Ming times, if not so much for the Chinese, at least as an item of trade with the Japanese who so appreciated them. It is my firm belief also that the "Kian Temmoku" bowls, despite the jade legend, continued and I may insert as helpful evidence that one can buy just such bowls of quite modern appearance in and about Chi-an, Kiangsi province up to modern times.

A small pot in the B.M. has a buff stoneware body and translucent brown glaze. This was found in a tomb in the Chien-ning district which has been dated as of 1560 or Chia Ching (1522–1566) period. Many of the so-called "Honan Temmokus" have all the characteristics of Ming potting. I think they were actually made in Honan and the rounded, bevelled or very heavy foot-rims, the glossy blue-black glaze, the generally poor potting and the angular or involved and exaggerated shapes all indicate a Ming and probably late Ming date for their manufacture. The ware is more like oatmeal than the rough and sandy buff ware of Chi-an. It usually has small black specks in it which are probably frit and had something to do with the wobbly shapes because it was hard to work with and inclined to wilt in firing. This body runs from buff to brown and reddish brown. Where the

Fig. 748. Vase of buff-white ware burnt reddish-brown where exposed. Glaze is blue-black and light brown. Probably from Honan and the exaggerated form suggests Mongolian influence, late Sung or Ming. Ht. 9½". Eumorfopoulos Coll. # B258.

Fig. 749. Probably worst specimen of four known is this vase with long, wobbly neck and splash of glaze running off bottom. Without doubt a kiln waster. Ht. 10½". Metropolitan Mus. of Art.

Figs. 746, 747. Tsung Se vase of light grey porcelaneous ware with even blue-black glaze shading to tan at lip and running down to an uneven edge near bottom. Note below the even edge of blue-black glaze and wide, bevelled foot-rim and glazed bottom, more like Ming than Sung. Ht. 10". Warren E. Cox Coll.

glaze is thin it takes a light tan color.

Potters at times made flecked effects or again large splashes and drips of so tricky a method as to be almost Japanese in character. This whole type of amphora is interesting. There are seven known; one in the Oppenheim Collection and three are shown. One has a gray-white body, two buff or buff gray and mine, the most perfect in form and in potting is of gray stoneware. The foot-rims are bevelled and I believe that this, together with the exaggerated S shapes, places them as late Sung to early Ming. The uncertain potting and glossiness are similar to Honan types.

ware. The foot-rims are all bevelled and I believe that this together with the exaggerated S shapes place them as very late Sung into Early Ming. The glaze is that expected from Honan as is also the wabbly potting which shows particularly in the neck of the one owned by the Metropolitan Museum of Art.

Finally there are the so-called "Tz'u Chou Temmokus" or globular large jars with incised glazes which we have seen from Sung times. Hobson placed all of these into the "Sung or Yüan" period but just as there are some that agree perfectly with Sung technique so there are also Yüan examples and also Ming ones, the latter distinguished by the glossy and treacly glaze, the thinner potting, though still rather heavy, and the ornate floral decoration. That some of this style are even later than Ming is fairly certain.

Fig. 750. Ming or even later example of what Hobson called, "Yuan temmoku" but which we term Tsung Se (brown pottery) and which dates from Early Sung to the 18th cent. Ht. 12¾". Warren E. Cox Coll.

Fig. 751. Brush holder with reserve design perhaps made with an actual leaf. The body is brown stoneware and the glaze brown with a suggestion of oil spots. Ht. 10¾". Warren E. Cox Coll.

Fig. 752. Tsung Sê jar of reddish-brown stoneware with light brown shaded to blue-black glaze. Note uneven and poorly made lip-rim. Ht. 7¼". Warren E. Cox Coll.

Fig. 753. Light buff stoneware jar, body burnt brown where exposed and covered with a blue-black glaze showing streaks of light brown. Honan of the Ming Dynasty. Note again uneven potting of lip-rim. Ht. 8¼". Warren E. Cox Coll.

CHÜN YAO

The contemporary Chinese books evidently feel that Chün yao of later than Sung times is not worth mention. The only reference given by Hobson is from the K'ang Hsi Encyclopaedia, the *Ch'in ting ku chin t'u shu chi ch'êng* which contains two references to large supplies of vases and wine jars "p'ing" and "t'an" being sent to Imperial order during the Hsüan Tê and Chia Ching periods from Tz'u Chou and "Chün Chou" now Yü Chou. Then there is also the reference that in 1563 both the subsidy and the tax on "Chün Chou" wares were abolished. Hobson says he does not know if the modern Yü Chou wares are just a revival or a continuation. I am inclined to the latter belief and to the opinion that many of the so-called "Yüan Chüns" are Ming and later. The modern wares as sold in Peking are of buff ware often washed over with a brown where exposed and the glaze is often thinner than the old and more greyish. However, other specimens that come on the market are of porcelaneous ware greyish in tone and with a dull red glaze. These probably were made at Ching-tê Chêng.

Later in the Eumorfopoulos Catalogue Mr. Hobson makes the interesting suggestion that the "Chün Chou" potters may have adopted the san ts'ai or three color enamels and to support this theory he shows a bowl #C96 which has a grey stoneware body quite like that of Chün yao but a bright peacock glaze with a splash of almost black aubergine on it very much like the three color glazes. He, however, does not go so far as to say that *all* the potteries were so made and wonders where the Ming and later examples are. . . . He then goes on in "Chinese Pottery & Porcelain" to say, "At any rate, the taste for the old Chün glazes was far from dead, for Hsiang Yüan p'ien included a number of them in his selected series formed in the 16th century and a celebrated potter, named Ou, at Yi-hsing in the late Ming period, made a reputation by his clever copies of them."

Now as to the actual wares let us say to begin with that many of the ornate incense burners now allocated in the Yüan period are undoubtedly Ming in taste. Secondly there is no reason to include all of the so-called "Yüan tz'ŭ" or "wares of the Yüan dynasty" with their thick and crackled glazes in that period. The Chinese books do not back this up and it is a purely arbitrary allocation. I think it happened this way. Many high prices were paid by rich men for Chün specimens. The collectors of these things did not always have the best of taste and they were readily appealed to by the large and involved specimens which seemed to them important and valuable. In time these were proven definitely not to be Sung taste and therefore our authorities pushed them gently into the Yüan catch box which was not so bad as calling them Ming to one of the old time collectors of Sung wares. Why not face the issue squarely? The shapes and the potting of these pieces, if they were covered with green or yellow transparent lead glazes would tell us that they were Ming at once. There is nothing contrary to this decision in Chinese books. Let us call them Ming, and at that they are a lot better potting than the large "Honan Temmokus" just described and which are confidently given the Sung attribution.

The "Yüan tz'ŭ" bowls of heavily crackled glazed ware are also earlier than the Yüan period as was proven by the finding of them at Turfan by Sir Aurel Stein. In other words these thick, transparent, crackled glazes continued over a long period of time and I believe up to the present. The various Chün wares indicate that they were made contemporaneously and that would surely show that several kilns were at work with them. During the Ming times still others made imitations.

We have examples of the Yi-hsing wares and shall describe them more fully in the later sections of the book. The bodies are brown or at times yellowish and the glazes streaky and of lavender color but opaque. The ones with light body are made to imitate "Ma Chün" or "soft Chün," but are not so good being harder, with a glaze of crystalline texture and having "rather thin and feeble patches of dull crimson," to quote Hobson.

The class of "sha t'ai" ware or "sandy body ware" has been given the name of "soft Chün" by Hobson and it seems a fitting one. Mr. Bahr has said it is known as "Ma Chün" by the Chinese and is widely known as of the Ming period, but again to quote Hobson, "No reason is assigned for either the name or the date and both seem to be based on trader's gossip to which no special importance need be attached." (*Chinese Pottery and Porcelain*, p. 127.) However, later in the Eumorfopoulos Collection, Mr. Hobson says, "Then there is the so-called 'Soft Chün'—the Chinese call it Ma-chün, deriving the name from a potter called Ma—a beautiful ware with buff (It sometimes burns red at the edges.), earthy looking body and a thick opaque glaze finely crazed and rather crystalline in texture but with a surface more waxen than that of typical Chün glaze. Its color is usually pale lavender blue, sometimes peacock blue, and it is usually broken by a splash or two of crimson red. The forms of the 'Soft Chün' wares are sometimes Sung or Yüan, but often typically Ming." Evidently Mr. Hobson became further convinced of the "trader's gossip" as time went on, but whether Mr. Ma made them or not and wherever they were made let us add that the potting is exceedingly heavy and crude and is far more likely to come from some other kiln than from that of the ancient Chün tradition.

Kwangtung yao or "Kwang yao"

In the southernmost province of China, Kwangtung, there are many kilns and some are reputed to be of ancient date reaching back as far as T'ang but less excavation has been done here and we skip from the Han potteries found by Prof. Jansie in the Southwest and Anam to those of Ming and later times for this general southern section. We must not forget that Dr. Laufer assigned a number of the wares found in the Philippines and East Indies to Fukien and Kwangtung provinces.

Perhaps the best known kilns are those of Shekwan West, close to Fatshan, and often the wares are called by either name. It was here that an imitation Chün yao was made and probably two other wares which are well known.

The first of these is a sort of flambé on a dark brown body of reddish tone. The glaze may be olive brown, blue black or green and on it are streaks and flecks of white, light buff, grey and grey-green with often bright

Fig. 756. Kwangtung pitcher with dark brown body and brown glaze flecked with pale blue except at rim. Called "Sung" by Metropolitan Mus. of Art but is actually Ming. Most of these wares are even later. Ht. c. 3". Metropolitan Mus. of Art.

Fig. 754. Kwangtung jar of dark buff stoneware with incised design under yellowish brown glaze. Ht. 5". Warren E. Cox Coll.

Fig. 755. Kwangtung early Ming pottery jar with buff body heavily potted, rounded, crude foot-rim, bottom daubed with glaze. Glaze opaque, pasty greenish white, thickly applied over lightly incised floral design. Ht. 10". Metropolitan Mus. of Art.

blue breaking through. Mr. Hetherington says quite truly that the Chinese insist that this ware originated in Sung times and that their opinions are to be respected. However, he and Hobson and all western authorities seem to agree that most of these wares are 18th century or later and that only a few, if any, are Ming. I see no reason for not including the gallipots with wide shallow foot-rims and rich glazes in the Ming category.

Gallipot of usual heavily potted
but light weight brown ware covered with light blue glaze shading
to lavender over relief appliqué
design. Ht. 12½″. Ming. Ex
Samuel T. Peters Coll. Warren
E. Cox Coll.

Left: Symbol of Earth in Shekwan "Fatshan" ware with
buff body and dull creamy glaze having crackle stained
blue-grey on corners. Alternating center panels contain
flowers and inscription in archaic characters reading:
"As long a life as Kwan Chen T'ze who lived at Kong
Tung for 1200 years." (Translation by Mr. Nai Chi
Chang.) Ht. 12″. Warren E. Cox Coll.
Right: Early Ming jar of grayish white ware with foot-
rim and bottom dressed with brown. Glaze greenish white
with brown crackle. Decoration carved in surface. Ht.
18″. Ex Samuel T. Peters Coll. Warren E. Cox Coll.

"Canton ware" Ming vase of
dense grey pottery which burns
reddish brown where exposed, covered with finely crackled deep
green glaze shading through aubergine and pale blue to lighter blue-
green. Ht. 11¼″. Warren E. Cox
Coll.

"KWANGTUNG" WARES MADE NEAR CANTON IN MING DYNASTY

PLATE 148

Figures of this ware with the hands and faces left unglazed and covered
with the flecked glaze, a dull red glaze, a green glaze and also a celadon type
glaze are seldom, if ever, Ming but are always so called by dealers of the
smaller shops.

These glazes contain lead and large amounts of phosphates. The mottled
effects are due to iron and not copper according to William Burton but some
little copper may be present.

Hobson reminds us that the names of the famous potters Ko Ming-hsiang

Indonesian architectural ornament said to have been found at Sukotai-Sawankalock, twin cities which were capital of Siam in 14th cent. during strong influence of Mongols. It appears to have been made by some wandering Chinese potter. The glaze is grey-white. Ht. 22". Fuller Coll. Seattle Art Mus.

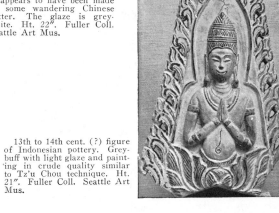

13th to 14th cent. (?) figure of Indonesian pottery. Grey-buff with light glaze and paint-ing in crude quality similar to Tz'u Chou technique. Ht. 21". Fuller Coll. Seattle Art Mus.

Indo-Chinese jar of crude manufacture similar to late Korean ones. Decoration in blue. Ht. 10¾". Freer Gallery of Art, Wash.

Jar claimed to be Sung but more likely Ming or later from Indo-China, but possibly made in China. Brooklyn Mus.

INDO-CHINESE WARES INFLUENCED OR MADE BY MING POTTERS

PLATE 149

and Ko Yüan-hsing have nothing to do with the Ming or Yüan dynasties. He also speaks of other potters but they do not particularly interest us for they were not great artists in any sense.

On the evidence of Captain Brinkley (see F. Brinkley, "Japan & China" vol. ix., p. 261) we attribute the other well known ware to Kwangtung potters though as to whether it was made at Shekwan near Fatshan we are not certain. This has a buff body which at times in later specimens has been washed over with a dark brown clay. The glaze is thick, opaque and paint-like but filled with crackle which is often stained grey or blue. The color of the glaze may vary from pinkish to buff or greyish white or light blue and where it runs thin a light tan of the body shows through. This occurs often on the high ridges of the often used relief decoration which may be molded by hand, applied or cast in the form. We often see a sort of broad gallipot with relief band of flowers about the body but other shapes such as the fine symbol of earth illustrated also occur. Hobson calls these "imitative wares" but I fail to see how they are any more imitative than many of the others and in truth they have a soft quality and charm all their own.

FIG. 757. Kwangtung yao jars, the larger showing a greenish brown glaze of "celadon" type and the smaller being of light gray blue with deep maroon patches. May be late Ming. Hts. 8" and 6½". Warren E. Cox Coll.

FIG. 758. Vase with the characteristics of Sung period and having an undulating soft glaze of bluish white with brown stained crackle, but is typical Ming porcelain. Probably a Chêng-Tê reproduction of Kuan yao. Ht. 10". Warren E. Cox Coll.

Still other types are also attributed to the province such as the greenish-white jar shown from the Metropolitan Museum and the two heavy jars from my own collection. These last seem to have been made in a variety of glazes and yet all to have been potted with the same technique and great weight. These are declared to be Sung but are more likely of the Ming period. Still other types which are probably of the 18th century or even later, though some may have originated during Ming times are the rough, brown bodied wares with similar pasty blue glazes having red blotches in imitation of Chün yao. These are certainly from Kwangtung but where we do not know.

I submit one more vase which may be from Kiangsi or Kwangtung. It has a white porcelain body with rough and gritty foot-rim but the glaze is of rich bluish white, unctuous and thick and has a buff crackle. The potting is purposely irregular though it is wheel-made. Possibly this piece was made in Ching-tê Chêng but the potting seems more primitive than we would expect there. The glaze is of "Kuan" (or Imperial Sung) type.

YI-HSING YAO

The city of Yi-hsing is on the west of the great lake in southern Kiangsu and south of the Yangtse River. It is about 200 miles west of Shanghai and the clays found there were found after firing to be cinnabar red, dark brown, "pear-skin green" and light red in color while other colors could be produced by mixing these. A priest was the first to make, "choice utensils for tea-drinking purposes," of these clays but his secret was stolen by Kung Ch'un in the Chêng Tê period (1506–1521) and his famous wares are described as, "hand made, with thumbmarks faintly visible in most of them," and "of the subdued lustre of oxidized gold," and of great accuracy and simplicity of shape. Hsiang published two said to have been sold for five hundred taels, and they are hexagonal grey-brown and ewer-shaped vermilion red. Our friend Mr. Hsiang writes of them that they turned to jade green when tea was made in them but adds that he had not seen the phenomenon personally. This is probably a misunderstanding of a reference similar to that made during Sung days to the effect that white cups were good for red tea and brown cups for green tea as they "brought out the color."

There are a number of potters of Ming times who were known for the ware: Shih Ta-pin, Li Chung-fang, Hsü Yu-ch'üan, Ch'ên Chung-mei and Ch'ên Chün-ch'ing were all famous along with Tung Han who in the Wan Li period made the first with "elaborate reliefs" on the surface. Hobson tells us moreover that Ch'ên Chung-mei made incense boxes, vases and weights for scrolls with fine carving and that he even made figures such as Kwan Yin. The Japanese are said particularly to like the work of Hui Meng-ch'ên who was also a Ming potter.

It must be explained that these wares vary not only in color but in hardness and finish. Some are as soft as lowest fired pottery while others are of real

Fig. 760. Yi-hsing teapot of red terracotta. Probably as late as the 18th cent. Length 6". Freer Gallery of Art, Washington.

Fig. 759. Yi-hsing pottery tea-pot of late Ming, probably Wan Li. Has seal of Ming Tsao and signature of Ming Yuan. Usual reddish ware with dull white blossoms. Ht. 5¼". Fuller Coll. Seattle Art Mus.

stoneware. Accuracy was considered a vital point and the spouts had to be straight while the covers fitted with a convex curve inside probably because such covers would drip the moisture collected on them back into the center of the liquid. Rarely glazes very like the "soft Chün" types were employed to imitate Chün yao, and others were similar to Kwangtung types of glaze. Ou, the famous imitator, also made Kuan and Ko types of glaze, and some of his work was considered good enough to be copied in the Yung Chêng period.

I was recently sent an example from China which is of red ware with a turquoise glaze etched to give an uneven surface much like that of corroded bronze.

Though the wares began as simple and well designed works of art the usual tendency for modeling to become ornate took hold and soon we have all sorts of involved and tricky stunts employed.

Mortuary and Architectural Pottery

While our interest has properly centered upon the great producers of ceramic wares we must not lose sight of the fact that nearly every town in China had a kiln to supply daily needs and mortuary wares. We find during Sung times less and less pottery used for the tombs but some exceedingly fine wares were so employed. In Ming days De Groot tells us in *The Religious System of China* (Vol. ii, p. 809) the tomb of an important man contained: "a furnace kettle and a furnace both of wood, saucer with stand, pot or vase, an earthen wine-pot, a spittoon, a water basin, an incense box, a tea cup,

Fig. 761. Ming pottery incense burner, probably part of a temple set of five pieces including two vases and two candlesticks. The teak cover has, of course, been added later. The glazes are of green and mustard ye'low. Ht. 23½". Metropolitan Mus. of Art. Altman Coll.

Fig. 762. Double tubular vase of the form called "Ying-hsuing," which words taken individually mean "eagle" and "bear" figures of which usually appear on one side holding the cylinders together, but taken together mean "champion." Such vases were given as rewards for military prowess and were originally a bronze form of T'ang or earlier period. Ht. 14½". Warren E. Cox Coll.

a tea saucer, two chop sticks, etc. . . . . two wooden bowls, twelve wooden platters, various articles of furniture including a bed, a screen, chest and a couch all of wood; 16 musicians, 24 armed lifeguards, 6 bearers, 10 female attendants; the spirits known as 'Azure Dragon,' the 'White Tiger,' the 'Red Bird,' and the 'Black Warrior'; the Spirits of the Door Way and ten warriors, . . . all made of wood and a foot high." Sometimes chiefly wood was used and again nearly everything might be made of pottery. Hobson says, "Even in the humblest tombs one might expect to find bowls and jars to contain the offerings of food with which the dead were always supplied."

The collection in the B.M. shows pieces from Szechwan province which are of reddish earthenware with opaque chocolate brown glaze sometimes having variegated milky grey splashes. Many of the jars have roughly modeled dragons on them. The Philippine finds which I have described are of better pottery. Another well known type is of hard, buff body unglazed on the bottom and covered with turquoise, brownish yellow and dark aubergine glazes inclined to chip off. The objects are generally molded and fairly thin. These should not be confused with the "three colored" wares described above. Many of these crude wares are not Ming at all but of much more recent date. Some large and ornate pieces such as incense burners have added to the colors mentioned above, green, violet, various blue and brown glazes all of the glassy type and all seeming to have a bad hold on the body much as did most T'ang glazes, and they are undoubtedly of a very similar consistency.

There is also the actual "Three color pottery" in contrast to the "Three color porcelain." This has a red or buff pottery body and much the same range of shapes and color treatments that are seen in the porcelain ones. They are not valued quite so highly on purely technical grounds.

The architectural pottery is much the same as the wares described above and occurs in the forms of tiles, vases for out-of-door use, finials, etc. The glazes of these are usually green, yellow, turquoise and aubergine or dark blue. A few dated specimens exist: In the Messel Collection one corresponds with 1529 and in the Louvre is one with a Wan Li mark. Mr. Hobson speaks of one in the Lindley Scott Collection, "It would almost certainly have been assigned to Ming date, were it not for the incised inscription, which gives the year of its manufacture as 1659." This is fifteen years after the end of the Ming period. The Ming designs were copied exactly right up to the end of the 18th century and later.

I recently discovered in the home of Harrison Cady, a fine figure about two feet high which has an inscription on the back of the seat which reads, "At Tien T'an mountain the Taoist temple 'Ho Shih T'ang' the Taoist believer Li Tao Ming spends his money freely in ordering one set of 'Three Officials' and one set of 'Kuan Chao.' " (The three officials are the Official of Heaven, the Official of Earth and the Official of Water, and are Taoist gods. The "Kuan Chao" are the three heroes of the Three Kingdom period, Liu Pei, Chang Fei and Chao Yün, under Kwan Yü who is also being called Kwan Ti, god of war.) "The followers of this temple are Ts'ui Tien and Ts'ui Yu. This dedication is on the 17th year of the Chêng Hua period (1465–1487) of the Great Ming Dynasty." (1482) "Offered by the usher stationed in

Chêng Hua figure dated the 17th year of the reign (1482) and made in Shan Si province to offer to the Taoist temple Ho Shih T'ang on Tien T'an mountain, Yang Chen hsien in Che Chow division. It is of the usual buff clay with green and amber glaze. Ht. 23½″. Harrison Cady owner.

CHÊNG HUA MING FIGURE FROM SHANSI PROVINCE
PLATE 150

the city, Ch'iao Ping and his son Ch'iao Pin in the district of Yang Chen, division of Che Chow Shansi province." Thus we have in this remarkable example a monument which tells us not only the date but the probable location of its manufacture. (See Pl. 150)

The sculpture of the Ming dynasty is filled with action and design, though sometimes the fullness of the latter somewhat overshadows the former. But the very exuberance, the diversification of interests, the added pressure of life which caused the Ming potters to overdo their vases and expend efforts in useless virtuosity in a dozen different ways, has imbued their modeling of figures with an appeal that anyone can understand. The aim was for natural, ism and proportions were as near those of life as possible. You may wonder at my enthusiasm for these modelers of figures when I have had to condemn most of the makers of vases but it should be understood that the art of modeling figures is really less difficult than that of making a fine vase. The

Pottery figure of Lohan glazed straw, green and amber colors. Ht. about 50″ with stand. Metropolitan Mus. of Art.

Ming pottery figures of Paranirvana (the "sleep" of Buddha) dated 1494. Remembering that these figures are only 10″ tall I think that their facial expression compare very favorably with those of the life sized Lohan ones. The ware is very light buff and the glazes are light mustard yellow, bright leaf-green, straw and black, and they adhere closely to the body. Ht. Lower group 15″. Ht. Standing figures 10″. Metropolitan Mus. of Art.

MING POTTERY FIGURES

PLATE 151

latter is a more sensitive expression just as might be a still life by Chardin which would be more difficult to copy than a caricature by Hogarth. These Ming works never have the *style* of T'ang examples, but they are alive and interesting.

Distinctions are difficult at times between Ming and modern figures of this sort simply because the modern artists working in some small Chinese town might still be following the Ming tradition and using the same materials. But strange as it may seem there is also great difficulty in distinguishing between Ming and T'ang figures in some instances when the simple green and brownish yellow transparent glazes were used. An excellent example of this difficulty is found in the six large seated Lohan statues which came on

Fig. 763. A roof tile finial of glazed pottery in yellow and green, of the Ming dynasty, one of a pair. Ht. 21½". Fuller Coll. Seattle Art Mus.
Fig. 764. Ming pottery figure showing traces of polychrome on a reddish clay. Ht. 21". Metropolitan Mus. of Art.
Fig. 765. Pottery figure of Lohan glazed in straw, green, and amber colors. Ht. about 50" on stand. Metropolitan Mus. of Art.

Fig. 766. Pair of Ming roof tile figures of buff pottery glazed in green, straw and orange yellow. Ht. 11". Metropolitan Mus. of Art.

Fig. 767. Ming roof tile of buff pottery with yellowish glassy white glaze, strongly crackled on the figure, yellow green, orange yellow, warm brown and black glazes. Ht. 17". Metropolitan Mus. of Art.

the market some years ago and were sold to the British Museum, Pennsylvania University Museum and Metropolitan Museum of Art. All were unhesitatingly called T'ang. The origin of these figures is unknown because they were reported to have been cached in a cave temple, "almost inaccessible on a mountain top near Ichou in Chih-li," as it is described by F. Perzynski who went there after the figures were brought out and found a "few fragments" of the figures, "which had evidently been broken off in the attempt to remove them through the narrow aperture of the caves." In Hobson's words, "On the

Fig. 768. Two Ming roof tiles, one in aubergine of dark color, bright green, yellow and straw, and the other in black brown and blue glazes. Ht. 13″. Metropolitan Mus. of Art.

Fig. 769. Ming pottery roof-tile with the usual green, yellow, etc., glazes. Ht. 15″. Metropolitan Mus. of Art.

altar of the shrine he found an incense burner of glazed ware, which he attributed to the Yüan dynasty, and there was a tablet recording the restoration of the altar in the Chêng Tê reign." Hobson adds that, "It is interesting to note that Mr. Perzynski assumed at once that these figures are of T'ang date." (See *Chinese Pottery and Porcelain,* p. 35, footnote.) Now let us weigh the evidence for there has been some controversy on the subject:

For T'ang Attribution

1.—The ware is near white and comparatively hard pottery.

2.—Hobson says, "The surface is covered with a brownish green glaze which is clearly a survival of the Han glaze." But he gives no chemical analysis or proof. We suppose he means that the glaze has the general aspect of a Han lead glaze.

3.—Referring to the design on the robe of the figure at the B.M. he says, "The same prunus design occurs on a typical T'ang bowl in the Eumorfopoulos Collection stencilled white in a green ground." Neither design was stencilled but the blossom design was used in T'ang times.

4.—He continues, "The colorless glaze on the fleshy parts has acquired a brown stain from the dripping of the cave moisture, and developed minute crackle, both of which features are observable on some of the glazed vases from the T'ang tombs; the pupils of the eyes are black." It is to be noted that he speaks of a stain which could occur in a short time but not of erosion or corrosion of the glaze. The crackle would have occurred in firing and it is only on the light "fleshy parts" as he says, though a very little here and there occurs elsewhere.

5.—He goes on to describe the glaze and concludes, "The technique, then, is that of the T'ang wares, but instead of being made in a mould like the grave statuettes, this monumental figure is modelled in the round by an artist worthy to rank with the masters of sculpture and painting who made the T'ang period famous."

Neutral Observations

1.—The body could be *either* T'ang or Ming. It is actually harder than that of most figures so glazed of the T'ang period but in all fairness this might be because of the large size and special care in potting.

2.—The glazes are undeniably of the Han type, T'ang type and also Ming type being ordinary lead glazes. They are certainly more heavily applied than those on most of the yellow and green glazed figures but this again may be because of the large size.

3.—The designs are, of course, after the fabrics which they represent and might be either T'ang or Ming. The prunus blossoms were so far as I know used at all times after they were originated and we certainly see them in Sung and Ming times as well as on K'ang Hsi "prunus jars."

Against the T'ang Attribution

1.—The glazes adhere to the body far better than do any of those on other T'ang figures I have seen. Most of these figures have strongly crackled glazes that tend to come off in small chips here and there. In applying the glazes heavier this tendency would be increased, that is they would crackle more and set up a greater tension between body and glaze so that one would expect to see small places where they had come off, particularly on such large surfaces.

2.—Mr. Theodore Y. Hobby has told me that the green is much like that on Ming vases, with which he has made comparisons.

3.—The frosty iridescent sheen seen on T'ang glazes and seldom absent at some place however small on pieces of this period is not in evidence on these figures. This iridescence also occurs on Ming pieces though not invariably. It appears on temple pieces as well as interred grave pieces much as does the green of bronze patination and one would especially expect to see it on figures which had been many centuries in caves where moisture had dripped on them. There is in fact no sign of erosion or decay of the glazes at all that is apparent and this is amazing for T'ang examples.

4.—On the grounds of style we expect exaggerations in T'ang figures which are seldom correct anatomically and usually gain style and design thereby. The Indian influence is often met with and can be seen in the narrow waists and broad shoulders, or again the heads may be too large in scale or the legs elongated. This was done as consciously as it is done by our modern advertising artists for women's clothes today. Yet these figures are perfectly exact and correct in their proportions as are, in fact, many Ming figures. I believe this to be the strongest argument for a Ming attribution. Certainly the artist who made them was aiming for naturalism rather than style.

5.—Not as conclusive evidence but worth note is the fact that during T'ang times most figures were made with the pupils of the eyes prominent and bold while it is characteristic of Ming figures that they often have narrow, slit eyes sometimes upturned at the corners in a more Mongolian expression. I think this change took place after the Mongolian invasion of Yüan times, in common wares at least.

6.—The conventionalized rock bases which without a doubt belong to the figures are often seen under Ming examples and *I have never seen any of this ornate style on T'ang examples.* These clumsy conventionalized rocks would certainly be picked as typically Ming, if seen alone.

7.—Much of the impressiveness of the figures is brought about by the concentrated squint of the eyes which command one as would a pointing finger in an advertisement. If one looks at the figures alone, exclusive of the heads, they become stodgy, sagging and totally lacking in the spirit of T'ang figures. The hands are posed and without vitality or life though they are very correct anatomically.

A comparison of these figures with the Ming "Paranirvana" group also of the Metropolitan Museum, remembering, of course, that the latter are only 10 to 15 inches high, shows a great similarity in the facial treatments and perhaps a balance in favor of the latter which are naturally less detailed but certainly far more moving in emotional expression. The colors of the glazes of these Ming figures and the large ones are similar as are also the textures of the glazes.

Finally, of course, there is the evidence that the other objects found in the caves were of Yüan and even Ming times, though this I do not give much weight to for frankly I do not believe the figures were very long in the caves. There was no sign that they had been *made* for these caves at all.

The question, of course, simmers down to whether the characteristics of these figures are due to their unusual size or are due to their having been made in the later period and I must say that I favor the latter analysis. This, however, does not in any sense condemn them as works of art. Often we are too quick to condemn a whole period such as the Ming or that of Rome because of some atrociously bad things which were perpetrated in it while a greater study and resulting insight will help us to appreciate the fine things which also were done. The very difficulty in distinguishing at what time these large figures were made shows us that some exceedingly great qualities prevailed for hundreds of years.

I am gratified to see that, after having written the above and having told Mr. Alan Priest, curator of Far Eastern Art of the Metropolitan Museum of Art, that it was my intention to publish the figures of seated lohans as Ming, he in his recent book on Chinese Sculpture has said, "These figures were called T'ang when they first appeared, and most of the owners up to this moment have stuck to that dating. A careful comparison with T'ang and Ming glazes shows the glazes on the Museum lohans to be far closer to Ming, and as the sculpture itself seems closer to Ming we suggest the later date." I had not told Mr. Priest *how* or *why* I thought both the glazes and the modeling were, not closer to but actually, Ming. Actually, I was wrong. The figures are now accepted as Liao (A.D. 907–1119).

CHAPTER XX

THE CH'ING DYNASTY

K'ANG HSI, YUNG CHÊNG, CH'IEN LUNG AND LATER REIGNS
1662–1722, 1723–1735, 1736–1796

Nurhachu the Manchurian (1559–1627) had a great army which had threatened China for some years. His country is in the basin of the great river Amur and its tributaries, the Sungari and Ussuri. This was an agricultural land but cold, and the people always looked to the South as a land of warmth and fertility. The people were of those great nomadic tribes that wandered about the Siberian plain, across the Bering land bridge that is believed to have existed, to America and back to settle finally and fish and raise crops. The Khitan Tartars ruled in the 10th century along with their conquered lands in Mongolia and Northern China. The Nüchens, founders of the Kin Dynasty overthrew them and ruled in late Sung days until they were in turn overcome by the Mongols.

The Ming Dynasty ended in 1644 when a rebel set himself up in Peking and the Emperor committed suicide. The General Wu San-kuei joined forces with the Manchurians to oust the usurper and this ended in the placing of a Manchurian prince upon the throne of China. It was a remarkable happening for the Chinese were ten times stronger in numbers and much richer. Nurhachu had in 1618 beaten three Chinese armies larger than his own but died in 1626 or 1627 an old and worn out man, but his son, T'ai Tsung carried on and finished the conquest taking China but wisely following the Chinese religion, literature and culture. His reign was under the dynastic title of Ta Ch'ing and he died in 1643 leaving his son Shun Chih at the age of nine to rule, and it was he who ascended the throne in 1644, the last year of the Ming Dynasty.

As a sign of subjugation the Chinese were forced to wear pigtails. Various attempts were tried to regain the throne and it was not until 1662 that the last of the patriots were driven to the Burmese border.

K'ANG HSI (1662–1722)

K'ang Hsi was the son of Shun Chih and when he died in 1661 this son was only eight years old, but when he was only 14 he took command and began to prove himself. He was described by a contemporary European priest who said, "This prince was one of the most extraordinary men who ever lived and who are only met with once in the course of several centuries.

He placed no limit to his desire for knowledge, and of all of the princes of Asia there was none with so great a taste for the arts and sciences."

His reign was not all sweetness and light for in 1673 the San Fan Rebellion had to be put down and it took eight years until 1681 during which time the Emperor led his own troops.

Europe was exerting more and more pressure. Catholic missionaries, Dominicans and Augustans from the Philippines, Franciscans from Italy and members of the Société des Missions Étrangères from Paris came in great numbers and were put in charge of the Bureau of Astronomy (the Jesuits), of mapping the country and given other scientific work until by 1700 there were probably about 300,000 Catholics in China. But by 1800, because of controversies, the French Revolution and its repercussions, etc., the number was reduced to about 200,000. The Portuguese retained Macao and the French, Dutch, British and Americans were increasing their trade.

Here we pause, for clearer understanding of some of the after effects, to relate a most unsavory chapter in English history which does not make John Bull seem quite the benevolent white father to the heathen that our school books lead us to believe. The East India Company had the monopoly of trade in England and at first the Chinese teas, silks and cottons were paid for by specie, but soon, to quote the *Encyclopaedia Britannica* 14th Edition (Vol. 5 p. 536), "The importation of opium, chiefly from India and on British ships, brought a reversal of the balance of trade." The Chinese were aware of the results of this insidious poison and took steps to regurgitate it. The Chinese government destroyed the stocks of drugs and forced the merchants to give bond that they would not engage in the further importation of dope. The Opium War was started for the British thought this action too high-handed. But thank heavens we have the pleasant task of telling about the things which China gave to Europe rather than the exceedingly unpleasant one of relating what Europe gave to China, except wherein such gifts effected the ceramic arts.

The first obvious results upon the industry of pottery making were that almost all production ceased while wars and rebellions raged throughout the 18 provinces between 1640 and 1680. Ching-tê Chêng itself was invaded during the San Fan Rebellion but that it was working earlier we know because of two orders in 1654 and 1659 that were sent down from the Palace by Shun Chih for large "dragon bowls" 2½ feet high, 3½ feet in diameter and with walls 3 inches thick and 5 inches at the bottom—and for plaques 3 feet by 2½ feet and 3 inches thick—which could not be made. We also hear that the industry was under Viceroy Lang T'ing-tso.

In 1680, after the rebellion, K'ang Hsi made plans for the establishment of the various crafts in the Palace precincts in Peking but the plans were abandoned. Shortly after Ching-tê Chêng was rebuilt with Imperial funds. The *T'ao shuo* tells that the officials were carefully selected, that funds were ample and that several thousands were put to work. It says that the producers became rich, sparing no labor and not grudging expense so that the wares turned out were novel in design and improved daily. It says, "Even when compared with that of former dynasties, which used to be lauded as being as precious as gold or jade, there is some that excels, none that fails to come up to the old, and, if it be not now described, after generations will be unable to discuss it." Thus the duties of recorder were taken seriously.

The good Père d'Entrecolles was on the spot and wrote a description of the place in 1712 at the height of the reign. He says it was on the right bank of the Ch'ang River, encircled by hills, with its double and triple lines of junks in the port, the whirling flames blazing away at the sky from the kilns which made it seem like a city on fire or an inferno, the huge population estimated as a million, all interested in one way or another in the "three thousand kilns." He said that there was work for all even the halt, the lame and the blind who could at least grind color.

No less a person than T'ang Ying, the director of the Imperial Factory in the later reign of Ch'ien Lung tells us more of the same in his book "Twenty Illustrations of the Manufacture of Porcelain."

S. W. Bushell, C.M.G. who was keeper of the Far Eastern Art department of the Victoria & Albert Museum at South Kensington, London made a translation of the *T'ao shuo* to which all modern scholars admit indebtedness and though his opinions may not all be ours they are well worth looking into.

He thought that this period, the K'ang Hsi, was the "Culminating epoch by common consent of both eastern and western connoisseurs," but we cannot agree for we now have added perspective not possible for him in his day.

He also wrote that Lang T'ing-tso, viceroy of Kiangsi and Kiangnan, was distinguished by the famous ware known as Lang yao but Hobson says, "The idea may be dismissed as in the highest degree improbable." Hannover says, "This advance was connected with the names of two remarkably able men. One of them was Lang T'ing-tso who had been entrusted with the supervision, during the previous reign, of the imperial factory and is said to have invented the so-called Lang yao." And later he says, "Others maintain that it (the name) is derived from a whole family of potters of the name of Lang." Well one man's guess is as good as another's.

All authorities agree that the brilliant renaissance in ceramics was due to the work of Ts'ang Ying-hüsan who was secretary of the Metropolitan Board of Works, appointed in 1683 superintendent of the Imperial Factories at Ching-tê Chêng.

The Shun Chih and early K'ang Hsi wares are simply transitional and of no great importance. Hobson says the only dated one he knows belongs to Dr. Lindley Scott and is a figure with glazes "in three color Ming style." He also speaks of a bowl in the B.M. marked "Ta Ch'ing nein chih" (made in the great Ch'ing dynasty) and says "Such a mark would be appropriate in the first reign of the dynasty and no other." Such may be the case but I cannot see his line of reason for such marks were used throughout the Ming dynasty (referring to the dynasty only and not the reign) and could also have followed as a habit.

He also mentions a group of pieces which were brought up from ships including the Haarlem which were sunk in Table Bay in 1648 and describes them as being thin, crisp, lightly moulded with leaf-shaped panels and painted with slight floral designs, deer, birds, etc., and human figures such as "long Elizas" which the Dutch called "Lang Lijsen," in various blues including a pale silvery, dark indigo and sapphire. The marks on these are the apocryphal date mark of Ch'eng Hua and of K'ang Hsi besides a number of complimentary marks such as "yü" or "jade," and a few "hall marks."

It is among these thin wares with bright enamel decorations that we should look for examples of the early "famille verte" porcelains and not, he says, among the black hawthorn vases which are not likely to have been made before the reconstruction of 1680. The *T'ao lu* says they made "eel yellow," turquoise and "spotted yellow" wares which were the most beautiful. It also says, brown, purple, green soufflé red, soufflé blue and pale yellow which were also good.

BLANC DE CHINE OR WHITE WARES

The pure white wares were not popular and are seldom seen because there is a growing itch to decorate if not with design at least with rich color. Then too white was the color of mourning and such wares were demanded by the court and probably also by lesser households for such ceremonies. White was the color used in worship of the "Year-Star" and also at times for special scholar's desk furniture. Such wares were made both at Ching-tê Chêng in Kiangsi and at Tê-hua in Fukien province. The finest clay was put aside for them for by now they had to be flawless to sustain appeal. The finest are called "t'o t'ai" or "bodiless" ware and Père d'Entrecolles says some had to be put on cotton wool for fear of damage and the glaze had to be blown on it as it was not safe to hold and dip. But there were also heavier wares and the decoration ran from "an hua" or "secret decoration" incised and engraved or molded or made with delicate traceries of liquid white clay (slip) or

FIG. 770. K'ang Hsi figure made at *Tê-hua*, Fukien province, of *Putai*. Glaze thinner and more glassy than that of Ming. Cream-white. Ht. 4¾". Mus. of Fine Arts, Boston.

FIG. 771. Brush pot, K'ang Hsi. Heavy foot rim about ¾" wide, unglazed. Tê-hua. Ht. 5½". Metropolitan Mus. of Art.

FIG. 772. "Blanc de Chine" figure of Kwan Yin walking on water. Tê-hua. Slightly greenish. ½" foot roughly glazed inside with fire crack. Ht. 15". Metropolitan Mus. of Art.

K'ang Hsi Tê-hua, Fukien, figure of Ma Ku with fawn of slightly greenish white and having about half-inch foot with fire cracks and glazed inside. Better than average example. Ht. 14½″. Metropolitan Mus. of Art.

K'ANG HSI "BLANC DE CHINE" FIGURE

PLATE 152

gypsum to boldly cut relief work and "a jour" piercing often of surprising delicacy descended from the "kuei kung" or "devil's work" of the Ming Dynasty. Occasionally a loose or free moving belt was made of free working rings, and chains, while low reliefs were built up on the ware with shavings of clay worked up with a wet brush, and reliefs were worked separately and luted onto the vessel with liquid clay.

Fig. 773. Bowl of *Kuei kung* (devil's work) reticulation on which are round medallions each containing two figures in high relief crudely modeled. Type originated in the Ming dynasty but this example is labeled K'ang Hsi. Dia. 3½". Ex Avery Coll. Metropolitan Mus. of Art.

Fig. 774. Reticulated K'ang Hsi "blanc de Chine" incense burner. Ht. 3½". Metropolitan Mus. of Art.

It is obvious from this description that more and more accent was being put upon lacy effects and delicate detail; upon perfection and not upon feeling. Meanwhile Tê-hua, which since 1550 or earlier had been turning out such beautiful figures continued making them but harder and whiter, more perfect and more detailed as may be seen by the examples illustrated. That old designs also were used is proven by the small octagonal box and cover from the Metropolitan Museum of Art which is very close to the form of a Sung period ying ching model.

BLUE AND WHITE WARES

The most numerous of the K'ang Hsi wares and probably the most important, if we judge by their effect on the rest of the world, are the blue and white wares. They were popular right up to the end of the period when the famille rose porcelains began to take their place. Hobson says of them, "When my lord of Bristol (*Diary of John Hervey, First Earl of Bristol*) in 1690 bought from 'Medina ye Jew' and 'Collemar ye Dutchman' tea-pots, large jars, china beakers, old china bottles, dishes, rice-pots, etc. 'for dear wife,' he had to pay substantial sums. But they are nothing to the price which the amateur will gladly give today." Bushell tells us that a first grade "Hawthorn" was bought from the Orrock Coll. for 230 pounds sterling but that one like it sold recently for 5,900 (Louis Huth Coll.). The excellent book *Blanc de Chine* by P. J. Donnelly has increased interest in these wares considerably. Thus it is an excellent time for a collector to acquire these always beautiful wares.

Neither Europeans nor the Japanese have ever been able to make anything

Left: Fine prunus jar or "Hawthorn jar" with original cover and deep, vibrant blue ground. Ht. 10⅜". Altman Coll. Metropolitan Mus. of Art.

Right: K'ang Hsi gallipot painted vigorously in Ming style but somewhat more stiff. Form exaggerated in width of shoulder and smallness of neck. Ht. 6½". Altman Coll. Metropolitan Mus. of Art.

K'ang Hsi blue and white temple vase with beautiful landscape painting in deep vibrant color. Ht. 29". Metropolitan Mus. of Art.

One of pair of blue and white bottles with squirrel and grape design. Ht. 7". K'ang Hsi. Ex D. Abbes Coll.

K'ANG HSI BLUE AND WHITE PORCELAINS

PLATE 153

comparable with good K'ang Hsi examples. The body is clean and dense, close grained, pure white and of an unctuous smoothness. The potting is perfectly true. The glaze is clear and limpid, lustrous and with only the very faintest tinge of green. The blue may be either light or dark but it should always be clear and without any reddish tinge or grey impurity. This is of the greatest importance in valuing a specimen.

K'ANG HSI COMPARED WITH MING TECHNIQUE

In K'ang Hsi painting the outlines are reduced to the slenderest possible guides and graded washes for shading are employed while Ming washes are flat. The foot-rim is well potted, neat and true with clean, straight sides or a groove to fit a stand. This is not to say that occasional Ming pieces may not also have a groove for the same purpose. There is a glaze underneath the bottom which comes up to a little way from the edge of the foot-rim and the body where exposed at this point is often slightly browned in firing.

There is seldom any bad drawing. One might almost wish that there was just to prove that the work had been done by human beings. Hobson tries to be kind in this passage, "But this mechanical skill could never have won for K'ang Hsi blue and white its world-wide recognition, had it not been for the beauty of the blue. One feels that manufacturers realizing this allowed the design to become more and more the mere vehicle for the blue." (*Later Ceramic Wares of China*, p. 12) Well now, I think we can hardly

FIG. 776. Blue "Hawthorn jars" of fair quality. Note different treatment of background, one said to represent branches against ice; the other, blossoms floating on water. Ht. 9½". Ex Warren E. Cox Coll.

FIG. 775. K'ang Hsi "Hawthorn vase." Ht. about 12". Courtesy of Graham & Son.

agree that this could have been conscious control on their part; one can hardly imagine a Manchurian overseer saying, "Draw without spirit, with perfection but without feeling, for it is the blue we wish to show off and not your drawing," as a gem merchant might plan the design of a piece of jewelry. No, I think it reduces itself to the simple fact that there *was* no feeling and I shall make this more clear as we go into the 18th century.

Everyone is familiar with the "prunus jar," the "hawthorn jar," or the flower bedecked "ginger jar." We all know that the design represents early spring blossoms against ice and it is interesting to know that these jars were given, filled with tea or sweetmeats as New Years' presents to friends with the perfect understanding that the jar was to be returned later much as were the pie tins between farmers' wives in early American days. There are many of these jars and even pairs or near pairs to be had for a few hundred dollars but a small group in Dresden are said to have been purchased at the price of a regiment of soldiers by Augustus the Strong who built the collection between 1694 and 1705. Let us hope this was a mere figure of speech. The one I show from the Altman Collection is thought by Mr. Theodore Hobby to be of finest quality and I am only sorry that we cannot possibly reproduce its color of deep, vibrant blue. There is supposed to be a difference in the quality of drawing and perhaps some of these jars are a bit more free than others within the set brackets of K'ang Hsi limitations. It is said that in some instances the prunus design was degraded to a mere pattern of blossoms without stems and that this pattern is not suitable for large surfaces though effective in borders and on small areas. And guess who said this—the man who spoke of the design as a proof that the large Lohan seated figures were T'ang and not Ming and the man who lauded the pattern on T'ang plates. Neither Bushell nor Hannover agreed on this point of "degradation." The latter shows a fine little specimen rare because most of these jars run from about 9 inches to 11 inches and he states that in China these jars were never valued so highly as in Europe. He mentions one which sold in the Huth sale at Christie's for 6,195 pounds sterling or some $30,000. He also gives a warning against modern fakes.

Of course such prices were the result of competition between rich men and were based on the fact that only a limited number of these jars were available. I know collectors who carry around small sample sherds in their pockets so as to compare them with vases seen in the auction and sales rooms. Technically this is a good stunt, if you are interested in getting a piece a fraction deeper in color than the next fellow's but if one has to judge one's *emotional response* to a work of art in this manner, one might as well carry around a sample to test the softness of his lady's skin and another to compare the color of her eye. This is not art but a picayune and fussbudget way of collecting which can appeal only to small minds.

The wares were all factory made and the people who made them knew what they were worth. We seem little different from the Philippine natives who went frantic over the glazed pots brought to them by the Chinese and which they themselves could not make. The Chinese often smile at our love for ordinary objects and lack of appreciation of the finer things of art and life.

This factory work was organized so that there were specialists for every step of the making and decorating of a pot; for drawing the lines around them, for outlines of flowers, for outlines of birds, for those of human figures and for animals, for painting landscapes of one sort or another, for filling in the designs with shadings, for making backgrounds, for inscriptions, marks and seals.

Père d'Entrecolles' comments on the painters are not very complimentary. He classes them with ordinary workmen and compares their ability with that of a "European apprentice of four months' standing." But Hobson says his remarks are colored with foreign prejudice and that he did not understand the conventions of Chinese drawing. This seems a bit out of place in that Hobson spent very little time living in China and the good priest lived and studied there for many years. However, this is one sort of convention which I might call the Convention of Commercial Short Cuts. It is quite different, as you may imagine, from that sort of convention which originated in the economy of space necessary among nomads. The one is a living force struggling to speak within limits. The other is a short cut forced by boredom and repetition. The one has the simplicity of the beginning of life while the other is simple death. I do not accuse Mr. Hobson of anything, but I say that he may have been unconsciously influenced in his admiration for prunus jars by his knowledge of the prices they fetched in the auction rooms.

So much for prunus jars and they do not deserve the diatribe which I have given but what goes for them goes for the other famous K'ang Hsi wares such as the "sang de boeuf," the "peach bloom" and the "famille verte." But let us say that they are not entirely to be condemned simply because they have been grossly overrated. They would have been just as good and just as bad had they not been adopted by high society. They are often as decorative as a nice piece of chintz or hand blocked linen or wall paper but few are great works of art.

Other Blue Ground Wares

One reason that the line and wash ground representing ice was done was simply that it was easier than trying the almost impossible feat of obtaining a perfectly even ground of blue. Another means had to be adopted, for applying such a ground with a brush was impossible. Therefore wave textures were tried, but they too were hardly satisfactory. Some vases simply were treated with brush patches like scales overlapping, but they gave as mussy an effect. Most of these wares had medallions of rectangular, square or fan shape in reserve and containing design of some sort such as peony flowers, figures, etc. There was also an odd variation of short necked club shaped vase with what Hobson calls "rose and ticket" design, the tickets being small oval medallions on the shoulder sometimes left blank like ticket labels. He says of these that they were painted with the best blue but must have been export wares because they occur in garniture sets.

Entirely foreign to Chinese taste are these "garnitures de cheminée," as the French call them or "chimney sets" or "mantelpiece sets" as the English call them, consisting of three beakers and two large jars with covers. These are not at all to be confused with the Chinese sets of two candle sticks, two vases for holding flowers or incense sticks and a center burner for use in front of a shrine. They are in fact typical of the bad taste of the Europeans of the time; made in huge sizes, each trying to outdo the last in scale, in ornateness of decoration and variety of color. These sets were designed to

K'ang Hsi soft paste blue and white vase with brown crackle which may or may not have been intentional. Ht. 10″. Metropolitan Mus. of Art.

K'ang Hsi vase with four character Ch'eng Hua, Ming mark in blue under foot. Cornflower blue with underglaze blue design. Foot shows very smooth clay. Delicately potted. Ht. 8″. Warren E. Cox Coll. Ex John Getts Coll.

Bottle with three brown-edged discs on neck. Suggests Near Eastern influence. Ht. about 10½″. Avery Coll. Metropolitan Mus. of Art.

Going one step further, this bottle not only has the rims of discs in brown but a brown (called by French "cafe au lait") ground on body, rest of design being underglaze blue. Ht. 8¼″. Metropolitan Mus. of Art.

SOFT PASTE, BLUE-GROUND AND CAFÉ-AU-LAIT UNDERGLAZE
BLUE DECORATED EXAMPLES

PLATE 154

place before the shrine of the great god I AM, the master whose portrait often hung above the mantelpiece commanding the European household.

Other wares of white on blue type are slender jars with contracted necks and decorated with archaic dragons and floral scrolls as well as the ewers and rose water sprinklers for the Western Asian market. Some of these have leaf shaped panels or mirror shaped ones filled with floral decoration. Ju-i borders

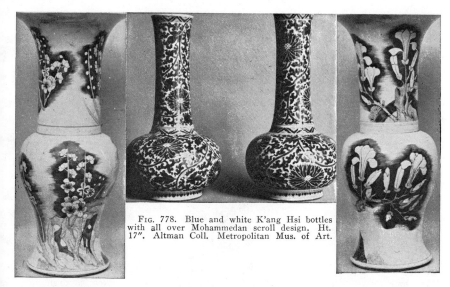

FIG. 778. Blue and white K'ang Hsi bottles with all over Mohammedan scroll design. Ht. 17". Altman Coll. Metropolitan Mus. of Art.

FIG. 777. Similar to common magnolia patterned vases is this with prunus blossoms which, however, are not in relief. Ht. 17". Havemeyer Coll. Metropolitan Mus. of Art.

FIG. 779. Magnolia blossoms on a "temple jar" shape set off by horizontal shading in blue on white ground thus eliminating heaviness of solid ground and using texture easier to obtain than a perfectly even ground. Design in low relief. Ht. about 17". Metropolitan Mus. of Art. H. O. Havemeyer bequest.

or "lambrequin" borders often finished the upper parts of the shoulders or about the neck just below the mouth. One of the rather pleasant ideas was to draw magnolias or blossoms and set them off by a series of horizontal brush strokes in blue but only filling part of the ground. Some of these have the flowers in low relief and are probably a bit later than the others.

BLUE ON WHITE WARES

In the blue on white wares we see all of the Ming devices with others added. Land and sea scapes are sometimes interestingly stylized and pheasant and

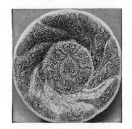

FIG. 780. K'ang Hsi plate with carved border and underglaze blue decoration. Dia. 14". Avery Coll. Metropolitan Mus. of Art.

FIG. 781. This plate shows a European trio, perhaps Austrian or Hungarian for lady seems to be playing a zimbol. K'ang Hsi. Dia. c. 12¼". Avery Coll. Metropolitan Mus. of Art.

FIG. 782. K'ang Hsi blue and white dish with wide rim in feeling of some Western Asian and Spanish wares of lustre type, but this may have originated in China. Dia. c. 18". Metropolitan Mus. of Art.

rock motives are often well done. Baskets of flowers are stiff but popular decorations for European taste. The old "Mohammedan flowers" of circular form joined by S shaped stems were made more ornate. The use of mirror shaped medallions was to suggest that they were actually mirrors in which you might see the landscape reflected from over your shoulder.

Not satisfied with making all possible varieties and combinations these artists naturally tried to make things more real by modeling them. This also made the work more costly and difficult to do. Père d'Entrecolles tells us how the Chinese were put to it to satisfy the European's taste for eccentric shapes and had to keep many moulds to make them. Some, like the winged

Fig. 783. Blue and white bowl with reticulated medallions. K'ang Hsi. Dia. 5⅛". Avery Coll. Metropolitan Mus. of Art.

Fig. 785. K'ang Hsi bowl with blue decoration about rim, also under reticulated sides. Note precision and delicacy. Dia. 6". Metropolitan Mus. of Art.

Fig. 784. Grotesque bottle with flamboyant handles in white porcelain with crudely drawn underglaze blue design. K'ang Hsi. Avery Coll. Metropolitan Mus. of Art.

handled bottles were copied from Venetian glass, others from various European wares and others came out of the heads of the merchants themselves. Most of these wares were painted in dull blue often with meaningless designs and the sharp and inappropriate rims of the plates and vases were inclined to chip and scale. Just a little later this was overcome by protecting the rims with a brown glaze that would stand the punishment of shipping and handling better.

In 1677 the district prefect ordered that no sacred writing and no reign-name of the Emperor could be put on porcelain as it might be broken and so the name would be desecrated. One suspects that he might have felt that the wares themselves were hardly complimentary, but, of course, he did not say that. The rule could not have been long obeyed but it may have started the custom of using various other names and symbols much to the resulting confusion of modern collectors. Even the reign-names of Hsüan Tê and Ch'êng Hua of the Ming Dynasty are more often seen than K'ang Hsi. Often simply the double ring is used. The character yü meaning jade is supposed to indicate authenticity and good quality but it was copied too. An odd mark like the letter G seems to occur on straight necked bottles which were probably made for some single firm in Holland. This mark occurs on both enameled wares and blue and white. Other symbols and marks can be seen in the tables of marks.

Excellent blue and white vases with bold and direct paintings. Hts. 17⅝″ and 13⅝″. Fuller Coll. Seattle Art Mus.

Beaker with landscapes set off by lambrequins of ju-i pattern and columns. Ht. c. 18″. Metropolitan Mus. of Art.

Temple jar of good proportions with vivid decoration in underglaze blue of court life. Ht. 18″. Metropolitan Mus. of Art.

Amphora of semi-eggshell porcelain with decoration in dark cobalt b e. Six character mark of reign under foot. Ht. 6¼″. C. T. Loo & Co.

Bottle of late K'ang Hsi. I give this attr. because of its elongated form, a mannerism which becomes quite popular in Yung Ch'eng period immediately following. Not very good porcelain and decorated with weak blue dragon design. Avery Coll. Metropolitan Mus. of Art.

K'ANG HSI BLUE AND WHITE WARES

PLATE 155

CHINESE "SOFT PASTE"

We have described the so-called "Chinese soft paste" called "hua shih'·" by the Chinese and also termed "steatitic porcelain." In 1923 in the "Wares of the Ming Dynasty" the term "soft paste" is used both with and without quotation marks. In 1925 in the "Later Ceramic Wares of China" Mr. Hobson calls it an "American name, which like so many stereotyped terms in ceramic phraseology will not bear examination." Hannover goes a step fur-

FIG. 786. Sprinkler bottle such as those used extensively in Near East. We again see disc with brown edge. Avery Coll. Metropolitan Mus. of Art.

FIG. 787. Bottle of white porcelain of K'ang Hsi period having blue decoration and projecting edge of center disc in brown glaze. Metropolitan Mus. of Art.

FIG. 788. Soft paste or "steatitic" ware with *"peau d'orange"* surface and design of vases painted in underglaze blue. Note coarse crackle and irregular highlight. K'ang Hsi. Ht. 9". Ex D. Abbes Coll.

FIG. 789. Deep cup of blue and white soft paste of creamy texture and light crackle. Base has apocryphal six-character Cheng Hua mark but piece is of K'ang Hsi period. Ht. 4¼". Guy Mayer Coll.

ther and says in his book published in translation by Rackham that same year, "It is an imitation of the old fên ting,"—(This I must say is doubtful.)—"which is erroneously regarded by the Americans as a soft paste porcelain, and for which they therefore pay enormous prices." To go back to Hobson and to continue the quotation above, he says, "Soft paste to the European ear suggests the artificial porcelains of Sévres and Chelsea, of which the body or paste was indeed relatively soft, whereas that of the Chinese ware is intensely hard. The glaze, on the other hand, is softer than the ordinary felspathic glaze; it contains a softening element of lead and is often crackled." Neither Mr. Hannover nor Mr. Hobson come right out and say that they think the body of this ware is as hard as the high-fired white porcelain and in truth it is not. They are both so intent upon distinguishing the meaning "to European ears" that they lose sight of the actual distinction and I doubt very much if any American actually thought that Chinese soft paste was like Sévres or Chelsea soft paste which incidentally is not "porcelain" at all.

Vogt made an analysis of the Chinese ware and declared that it does not contain steatite or soap-stone at all but actually pegmatite without any trace of magnesium. He obtained his samples from San-pao-p'eng, the source for many years. I cannot resist giving one more quotation which perfectly shows the Englishman's point of view. Hobson says, "We have, however, preserved the term 'steatitic' to distinguish the special ware made with the hua shih." Has he indeed! An American is wrong because he uses a term which is correct but somewhat confusing to a European while an Englishman, knowing definitely that he is wrong preserves the usage of misinformation for future generations. I hope this clears up the matter of soft paste, both Chinese and European, once and for all. The Chinese soft paste is just that and the European will be explained in its place, but certainly is not "soft paste *porcelain*" in any sense, for it is not porcelain.

Père d'Entrecolles tells us that the body was made of the hua shih, an unctuous, soapy material in the proportions of eight parts to two of petuntse, taking the place of the kaolin used in the regular porcelain, and goes on to say that it "is rare and far more expensive than the other porcelain. It has an extremely fine grain; and for purposes of painting when compared with ordinary porcelain, it is almost as vellum to paper. Moreover, this ware is surprisingly light to anyone accustomed to handle other kinds; it is far more fragile than the ordinary, and there is difficulty in finding the exact temperature for its firing. Some of the potters do not use hua shih for the body of the ware, but content themselves with making a diluted slip into which they dip their porcelain when dry, so as to give it a coating of hua shih before it is painted and glazed. By this means it gains a certain degree of beauty." The Chinese have always treasured it and asked high prices for it and the best artists painted on it often in the style of the Early Ming artists. It was also made in later reigns.

POWDER BLUE WARES

The difficulties of laying an even underglaze blue ground can only be appreciated if one has tried it. A general idea of the troubles involved can be obtained if one tries to get an even effect with ink on blotting paper. The biscuit of porcelain is immediately absorbent and each stroke of the brush sinks into it with graded values depending upon the amount of color in each part of the brush at the beginning and end of the stroke. One cannot smooth it out or smooth it over for the color does not remain wet long enough. This difficulty led to a very beautiful ground technique.

In the Ming Dynasty the potters had sometimes blown powdered glazes onto their wares but this was only in odd instances. Our old authority Père d'Entrecolles says, "as for the soufflé blue called tsouri tsim (ch'ui ch'ing),

Left: Powder blue vase having deep, rich color. Ht. 17½". Warren E. Cox Coll.
Center: Powder blue "club-shaped" vase over white porcelain and with gold decoration necessitating another firing. Ht. 17". Metropolitan Mus. of Art.
Right: Powder blue jar and cover with reserved medallions painted in famille verte enamels. Ht. 18". Metropolitan Mus. of Art.

Left: Small "club-shaped" vase of powder blue white porcelain with reserve medallions having well styled paintings. One shown seemingly of an immortal with scroll in hand, seated above a raging stream on grotesque dragon. No mark but ware is typical. Ht. 9". Metropolitan Mus. of Art.
Center: Excellent quality white porcelain vase with gold ornamented powder blue ground and reserved medallions with famille verte flower paintings already showing ornate qualities of following periods. White is tinged with green and pitted here and there. Ht. 17". Metropolitan Mus. of Art.
Right: Temple vase of rather rough powder blue with reserve medallions also painted in underglaze blue. Ht. 30". Metropolitan Mus. of Art.

POWDER BLUE K'ANG HSI PORCELAIN

PLATE 156

the finest blue prepared in the manner which I have described, is used. That is blown on the vase, and when it is dry the ordinary glaze is applied either alone or mixed with tsouri yeou, if crackle is required." Hannover says, "As the French term indicates, it was not painted, but blown through a bamboo tube with gauze at the end, on the biscuit, and glazed after dry-

FIG. 790. Powder blue bowl with reserved medallions inside and out, edged with iron red and painted in famille verte enamels on rumpled white ground. Dia. 6½". Metropolitan Mus. of Art.

FIG. 791. Pale powder blue plate with rumpled glaze and smartly drawn design in dark blue and underglaze red. Dia. 8". Metropolitan Mus. of Art.

ing." Hobson says, "Another type of blue glaze is manufactured by a different method, the cobalt being sponged or painted onto the body of the ware or sprayed on it in a dry powder and the glaze added as in the case of the blue and white." Whom are we to believe? Was the blue blown on wet in solution as a spray or was it blown on dry as a powder? Logic would seem to indicate the former for a man who was on the spot speaks of its being allowed to dry before glazing. Also if a dry powder was blown onto a surface it would have to have some wet or sticky surface to hold. Otherwise the powder would drop off. I may add that I have never seen a piece which shows any suggestion of having been "sponged."

In any event the glaze was most delicately applied, probably by spraying again, so that it did not disturb the blue, and the result was a fairly even surface of brilliant but soft blue with only slightly uneven cloudiness and which on close examination is seen to be filled with small particles sometimes blurred with slight running and sometimes quite sharp and clear, but never leaving any white showing except where a mask has been applied. Some are, as it were, close in texture and some are more broadly speckled as may be seen in my vase and the plate and bowl from the Metropolitan Museum. This has no relationship to quality or period. Masking was done

FIG. 792. Fine K'ang Hsi powder blue club shaped vases with reserved medallions in famille verte colors. Ht. 17". Metropolitan Mus. of Art.

by the simple application of pieces of paper cut out in the forms desired and pasted on temporarily whil^ the spraying was done. These were removed after the piece had dried and the decoration (either in blue or, after glazing and firing, in enamel) was painted in. This ground was also beautiful when gold or silver painting was done over the glaze in a low firing (see the club shaped vase illustrated, also the jar and cover), but often these metallic designs are rubbed off or have, in the case of silver, corroded to black. The making of garniture sets tells us that a number of these vases were made for export trade and on these the drawing is usually perfunctory but occasionally we see something with real character such as the small club shaped vase illustrated with its tall rectangular "mirror shaped" panel.

Odd examples exist on which there are powder blue medallions set among famille verte grounds and as time went on nearly every possible combination of all the techniques took place some being much like neapolitan ice cream in artistic effect. Bushell also mentions especially those with medallions decorated with fishes and other designs in red and gold.

"MAZARINE BLUE"

The term "mazarine blue" is foolish, for Cardinal Mazarine died in 1661 a year before K'ang Hsi came to the throne so it would have been difficult for him to admire this color invented in that reign. This is a very deep and

somewhat reddish blue of great brilliance even though dark. It is often a blue glaze applied over a white glaze but sometimes the white glaze was eliminated except for a light ring around the edge of the foot which causes the blue glaze to hang in a rich rounded rim at this point. (See description of this technique under sang de boeuf section.) The bottle from the Metropolitan Museum and my small gallipot are good in this respect while the gallipot from the museum is not, but this again is no definite proof of period, for it so happens that my piece bears a Ch'ien Lung mark.

FIG. 793. K'ang Hsi vase of dark blue called "Mazarin blue." White ware heavily potted and with pale green glaze inside more like Ch'ien Lung "celadon" than anything else. Ht. 13". Metropolitan Mus. of Art.

BLUE PUT IN PRESS WARE

Père d'Entrecolles tells us of another blue and white ware which he says was a lost art even in 1712. In this ware the design is only visible when the vessel contains liquid. It was made very thin and a blue design was painted inside and then covered with a thin slip, we assume by dipping and wiping off the outside. Then glaze was applied over the inside slip. It was then put on the lathe and pared down without cutting into the color. Then the exterior was glazed and the whole baked. However, so far as I can find out, no western collector has ever seen a piece of this ware.

Still one more technique which is rare is that of incising the design and rubbing blue into it, then wiping off the ground and glazing over the whole.

FIG. 794. K'ang Hsi bowl with medium to pale underglaze blue and fish in light olive green showing tiny specks of red and really intended to be red of *"rouge de cuivre"* or underglaze type. Dia. 7½". Metropolitan Mus. of Art.

FIG. 796. K'ang Hsi dish with underglaze blue (not as strong as it appears in picture) and blossoms in underglaze red to green tones. Dia 10". Metropolitan Mus. of Art.

FIG. 795. K'ang Hsi beaker with deep vivid blue, pale red (or peachbloom) and pale green decoration, first two being underglaze and latter a glaze applied over white ground. Ht. c. 17½". Mark is double circle enclosing lichen. Bequest of Mary Clark Thompson. Metropolitan Mus. of Art.

This inlay technique is like that of the Korean inlayed wares but usually is more delicate. (See example in Ch'ien Lung section.)

UNDERGLAZE RED

The underglaze red or "rouge de cuivre," as the French say, is the same copper color as was used in Hsüan Tê times and is employed alone or with the blue. During this reign there was not much improvement if any, but later it was mastered at least technically. The same two kinds of painting continued, one with slender lines like the blue decoration and one with heaped and lumpy design like the old fish cups of Ming. The color may vary from sang de boeuf to what we call "peach bloom." At times it is under a celadon glaze but these are not often K'ang Hsi and the red is not improved by a green wash over it.

SANG DE BOEUF

The Hsüan Tê reds of copper glazes were famous but the material ran out and the art was lost in the Chia Ch'ing reign of the 16th century. The revival of the art in the K'ang Hsi reign is entirely unexplained. Some have said it was done by the Lang family. Others maintain it had something to do with Lang T'ing-tso, the viceroy, or that he actually invented it. The *T'ao lu* mentions neither "Lang yao" nor Lang T'ing-tso which would seem strange. Therefore we must agree with Hobson that this is all nonsense and, for lack of a Chinese name of real meaning, turn to calling the ware by the French name of "Sang de Boeuf," meaning "ox blood." We already call many of the Ch'ing Dynasty wares by French names because they were so very much appreciated in that country.

Père d'Entrecolles, in a letter dated 1722, says this about the ware, "This red in the glaze, 'yu li hung,' is made with granulated red copper and the powder of a certain stone or pebble of reddish color. A Christian doctor told

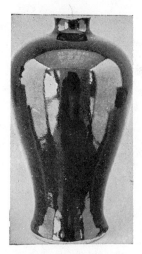

Left: Type known as "crushed strawberry" red with mottling through it. Ht. 7". Metropolitan Mus. of Art.

Center: Vase of K'ang Hsi period showing slipping down of glaze from lip allowing crackled buff glaze to show and narrow white rim at bottom of glaze intended to hold ox-blood red from dripping over and causing it to form a thick welt. Shape typical. Ht. c. 18". Metropolitan Mus. of Art.

Right: Vase of unusual shape derived from that of Han pottery or bronze. Lip has been cut and mounted with metal rim. Note pores similar to those in human skin in glaze. Ht. 7". Metropolitan Mus. of Art. Altman Coll.

Left: Jar and cover with deep red color against small areas of greenish cream at lip and on cover. Ht. 16½". Metropolitan Mus. of Art.

Center: Deep cherry-red bottle of typical shape for sang de boeuf glazes. Note glaze on this has run over bottom edge and been broken away despite fact it is obviously of period. Ht. 16⅞". Metropolitan Mus. of Art.

Right: Vase with deep red glaze running unevenly down over body and thinning to buff at lip. Inside and under foot has slightly greenish cream glaze with buff crackle and uneven indentations where bubbles have burst and glaze flowed together again. Note definite white rim of glaze around foot-rim placed there to keep red from overrunning it. Ht. 17½". Ex Eumorfopoulos Coll.

TYPICAL K'ANG HSI SANG DE BOEUF VASE FORMS

PLATE 157

Left: K'ang Hsi peach bloom *"ring necked bottle,"* the third of the classic forms and one which appears more rarely than the "chrysanthemum" and "amphora" bottles. Ht. 7¾". Metropolitan Mus. of Art.

Left: "Amphora" which is probably finest and most beautiful proportioned of the three vase forms and which also occurs in clair de lune glaze. Ht. 6". Metropolitan Mus. of Art.

Right: "Chrysanthemum vase," one of seven classic forms in which this ware usually appears. Note mottlings of pale green and lighter pink color. Ht. 8½". Metropolitan Mus. of Art.

Box for vermilion paste for use on seals and not for the ladies' rouge, though such pieces are called "rouge boxes." So true are these to size that covers and bottoms of different boxes are often put together when other members are broken. Dia. 2¾". Metropolitan Mus. of Art.

Jar with small mouth also for water for scholar's table of typical shape. Ht. 3½". Dia. 5". Metropol.tan Mus. of Art.

Plate said by museum to be "Late Ming" and perhaps of that time though same shape occurs in K'ang Hsi pieces of this ware, though plates are rare. Dia. 7". Metropolitan Mus. of Art.

Coupe for water for the scholar's table of typical shape. D.a. 4½". Metropo.itan Mus. of Art.

TYPICAL K'ANG HSI "PEACH BLOOM" FORMS

Plate 158

me that this stone was a kind of alum, used in medicine. The whole is
pounded in a mortar and mixed with a youth's urine and the ordinary porcelain glaze; but I have not been able to ascertain the quantities of the ingredients, for those in possession of the secret take good care not to divulge
it. This mixture is applied to the porcelain before it is fired and no other
glaze is used; but care has to be taken that the red does not run to the bottom of the vase during firing. They tell me that when they intend to apply

FIG. 797. Cherry red bowl
shading from light to deep
color. K'ang Hsi mark. Dia.
4¼". Perry Moore–Warren
E. Cox Coll.

FIG. 798. Rouge de fer or iron
red K'ang Hsi vases with some enamel decoration also added. Ht. 19".
Metropolitan Mus. of Art.

this red to a porcelain they do not use china stone 'petuntse,' but they use
instead of it, mixed with the china clay 'kaolin,' a yellow clay prepared in
the same manner as the petuntse. Probably it is a kind of clay specially
suited to receive the color." (Hobson's translation.) We have discussed the
matter of the red stones in the Hsüan Tê section. It should be added that
Hobson has declared that K'ang Hsi examples may be distinguished from
later ones and modern fakes because the glaze on those of this reign forms
a welt at the bottom and does not run over so that it has to be ground off.
This is largely so but not at all invariably for there are at least four fine
examples in the Altman Collection at the Metropolitan Museum of Art which
have the glaze running off. One of these, the cherry red bottle shown, is one
of the finest in this large group. It has also been neglected by both Père
d'Entrecolles and Hobson to point out *how* this glaze is so controlled. This
was done by applying a narrow band of white non-running glaze about the
bottom which would not melt quite so readily as the red glaze and acted as
an adhesive rim for the red glaze to hang on and build up on. Mr. Theodore
Y. Hobby, keeper of the Altman Collection, has gone over this matter with
me and agrees entirely. The reader will be able to see the white rim on the

jar with cover and the tall vases from this collection and the Eumorfopoulos
Collection although one cannot always see the rim for it is often entirely
covered by the red glaze.

The Sang de Boeuf glaze is glassy but full of bubbles not unlike that of a
rich Chü-chou celadon type and on the surface are many little pores which
vary in size and number but are always present. There is a faint but distinctive crackle hardly apparent but always present. The color seems to form
in small spots or blotches actually like clotted blood and sometimes these are
small and blended or again they may be large and, to my mind, rather
unpleasant as in the "strawberry red" type. The foot is usually, but not
always, well turned and perfect. It is, so far as can be seen, exactly like
other K'ang Hsi porcelains, white or greyish white and having some pores
and very smooth. There is glaze applied on the bottom. Hobson says,
"There is no red under the base, but here the glaze is sometimes a faint

K'ang Hsi vase with canary yellow glaze of glossy, transparent
type over incised design. Ht. 9⅝". Altman Coll. Metropolitan Mus.
of Art.

"Celadon" vase of pale green in form called "chrysanthemum."
Has little relationship with earlier celadon glazes and is valued about
as high as other single colored K'ang Hsi wares for its perfection.
Ht. 8¼". Altman Coll. Metropolitan Mus. of Art.

Canary yellow vase with transparent glossy glaze always associated
with this color. Ht. 9½". Metropolitan Mus. of Art.

K'ang Hsi gallipot heavily potted and covered with brown
crackled white glaze as in "apple-green" wares but in this case with
pale grey-blue transparent enamel. Ht. 7½". Metropolitan Mus.
of Art.

"Amphora" shaped vase of clear palest blue white called *"Clair de
lune"* or moonlight color. One of rarest and most costly K'ang Hsi
wares and shape which also occurs in peach bloom glaze is by some
considered most beautiful ever devised in ceramics. Ht. 6". Altman
Coll. Metropolitan Mus. of Art.

K'ang Hsi vase with cafe-au-lait crackled glaze. Ht. 8¼".
Metropolitan Mus. of Art.

"Celadon" of light pea-
green glaze over pure white
porcelain. Handles modeled
separately and attached, being left in biscuit and colored black. Double ring and
lichen mark under foot in
under-glaze blue. K'ang
Hsi. Ht. 13¼". Warren E.
Cox Coll.

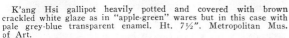

K'ANG HSI SINGLE COLORED PORCELAINS

greenish or buff crackle." Actually it is often olive green either plain or mottled and at times it breaks into pink or red in patches. Several of the Altman ones are like this. Of course, it would depend on how the piece was fired and how much heat was kept away from the protected glaze under the foot which is usually otherwise exactly like that applied on the body.

Again it is said that streaked ones are not of the period. This is so if one counts the prominent streaks such as we see in flambé wares, but many fine K'ang Hsi Sang de Boeufs have greyish streaks in the glaze. These may or may not be desirable depending upon the point of view.

The inside of most specimens is finished with a buff crackled glaze or greenish glaze having the same characteristic crackle and, in fact, specimens are found which are covered all over with this light glaze. Very often the red glaze slips down irregularly from the lip or over the shoulder leaving greenish white or buff areas. This, it would seem obvious to me, could only occur if a light colored glaze was first applied either all over the vessel or blending into the red glaze near the top, for certainly the color could not *slip in the glaze.* It may be answered that a broken sherd shows no light glaze under the red and I can only say that where the glaze is red I believe the red glaze and the light glaze have melted together to form one. In other words I believe that Père d'Entrecolles in this instance was describing the ware from hearsay, as he more or less admits, and that he missed entirely the method of manufacture. I think the vase was made, the light glaze applied, the red glaze either painted over it or blended into it, and that the white rim at the bottom was an entirely different glaze over which the red ran and collected. It is interesting to note that, if this is the case, the potters used much the same process that Emil Carlsen did in painting pictures of the ware in oils, that is, a translucent red over a white reflecting surface.

There are certain general shapes but also odd ones that crop up from time to time. They are all simple and without decoration even of the molded or modeled kind we see on celadon.

A further note should be added that Mr. Walter Howat has told me that the red color could only be brought out in the impurities existing in a muffle kiln. He states that he could turn the reddest piece blue or green by refiring in a kiln that would drive off the impurities united with the copper. I should very much like to go into a series of such experiments but we have not the sherds with which to work.

Occasionally Sang de Boeuf wares are considerably blended. One in the Altman Collection is grey, green, red and rose colored. Others may be "ashes of rose" color all over and are valued quite as highly as the red ones.

I have gone into this full description not only for technical reasons but because it should be understood that a sort of arbitrary, or what I call "stamp collectors," valuation has been placed on these wares of the K'ang Hsi period. A good Sang de Boeuf should bring from a few thousand dollars to ten times as much, if K'ang Hsi, while just as well made and colorful a piece of the later periods may bring two hundred and a modern example can be had for $15 or less. It behooves the collector to be wary!—and to know what he is doing when he buys a piece.

"Peach Bloom Wares"

We Americans seem to have invented the name "peach bloom" for the wares that the Chinese call "p'in kuo hung" or "apple red," "p'in kuo ch'ing" or "apple green" and "chiang tou hung" or "bean red," probably referring to the kidney beans which are mottled pink and green with brown spots. All of these terms have some of the qualities which the wares show for it varies from pink shading to liver color and red and contains splotches and irregular mottlings of light green, olive green and brown. This may sound like nothing very beautiful but in truth it is one of the softest and most harmonious color combinations imaginable. The glaze is usually thin and regular but at times occurs thick and fluid enough to run down the sides in ridges and drips. The color is said to be of copper as in the other red glazes but it can also be obtained by the use of chrome tin. The glaze is not crackled.

The small articles covered with this glaze are pearls of true perfection. The ware is white and perfectly pure. The potting is so perfect as to be entirely lifeless. The small and narrow foot-rims are perfectly made. The mark should be perfectly centered and beautifully written in blue under a palest greenish white glaze under the foot. This underglaze blue must be of clear color and not purplish or greyish in cast. No decoration was used save the lightest of incising, usually a dragon on the water pots, in round medallions.

The shapes can be seen in our illustrations and they comprise only a few though some doubtful odd shaped ones are claimed as of the period. The collector should be very careful indeed if offered anything other than the three vase forms, the "writer's coupe," the small round box, the small incurving bowl and the dish. Sizes also run fairly close together, although rarely the shape may have been made in a larger size for some very special gift from the court or for some special occasion.

Prices run very high depending on the quality of potting and the color. A few hundred dollars may be paid for a piece of the period but having ordinary color while $15,000 and even $20,000 have been paid for a single specimen. In the sale of Mrs. Christian R. Holmes' Collection, April 15th 1942 a pair of "ring necked vases" brought $9,200 though there was some roughness of the rings about the neck and the marks were far from the finest. Of course, these were depression days and it is rumored that Mrs. Holmes paid $60,000 for the pair. They were bought in by the dealer who sold them to her.

Many modern or later reproductions are exceedingly close to these wares. There is a typical example which was offered to me for a few thousand dollars recently. Of great importance is the quality of the mark and the close adherence to shape. But the collector must also know his glaze and the quality of the glaze under the foot which can only be learned by comparison with the best pieces. This latter must be not too glossy or regular, it has small pores and should not be too greenish, in fact nearly pure white. Beware of an irregularity in rim or lip. The reader may wonder why all this sudden stress upon perfection and I can answer simply that that is all these wares have to recommend them. Every last touch of the hand of man has been ironed out and obliterated. They are turned about as true as a piece of machinery.

In its way a peach bloom amphora is as difficult to make as a battle ship and with all our boasted ability we, here in America, or in the western hemisphere for that matter, have never been able to make one. But what of it? Is a line ruled by a perfect draughtsman as beautiful and alive as a line by Whistler, Li Lung-mien, by Rembrandt or by Chou Wên Chü? I think not. From the earliest days of childhood when with teeth set on tongue, eyes squinted and breath held the artist of perhaps six years tries to guide his crayon where he wants it to go, to the days of the mastery of brush or etching point, the artist is struggling for that control which will give him a free moving and undistracting medium with which to express himself. This is what tires artists as much as careful shooting tires the marksman. This is a sort of self-discipline that many artists simply cannot hold themselves to, and therefore, finally break down and go "modern" or resort to the ruler, the templet and other mechanical means. But the breakdown, even though expressed in so great a perfection as a peach bloom vase, is there, and is death undisguised to the eye of one who can see.

Sang de Pigeon Wares

Still another red was obtained with copper oxide and that is the ware commonly known as liver-colored but which the French call "Sang de Pigeon," with perhaps too much complimentary poesy for although this ware can be rich and beautiful it certainly does not rival the pigeon blood of a ruby.

Most of these are Yung Chêng but they undoubtedly originate in late K'ang Hsi times. Hobson speaks of them in "The Later Ceramic Wares of China" (p. 55) but does not show an example. I do not know of one which could be proven to be K'ang Hsi.

We shall describe the glaze in more detail in the Yung Chêng section. Suffice it to say that it is perfectly even in color, not crackled, thinner in application than the Sang de Boeuf and yet can be deep and rich in color. The surface is pitted in the "chicken skin" effect or sometimes glossy.

"Coral Red" or Iron Red

Iron red, actually made from iron oxide, is not an underglaze color or a glaze color as are the above copper reds, but must be fired at a comparatively low temperature over a glaze. The Chinese call it "fan hung" and collectors have come into the habit of calling it "coral red" which it does closely approach if one thinks of the deepest possible coral color although a good eye will see that it is slightly more toward the yellow side and not quite so bluish. We are told that the oxide was applied to the glaze with "ox glue" and that it borrows its gloss from the silica of the underlying glaze but is often mat in surface. It had been used in the "five colored" wares of Ming and naturally continued with the famille verte wares. As a monochrome it is usually later than K'ang Hsi. The color is always lighter from K'ang Hsi times on due to greater refinement; the Ming color being more dull and dark, if applied heavily at all as in Wan Li times. The color was first used in southern Sung times. (See p. 206.)

MING, HUNG WU (1368-1398) "THREE COLOR" VASE
Unique vase with both enamel and underglaze blue decoration made in five
sections and having a black outline separating the enamel colors. (See p. 455.)
Warren E. Cox Collection

RARE T'ANG (618-906) EQUESTRIAN FIGURE

T'ang pottery pieces with blue glaze are rare, and those showing Central Asian people are doubly so. This outstanding piece shows both features. Dr. Howard Balensweig Collection

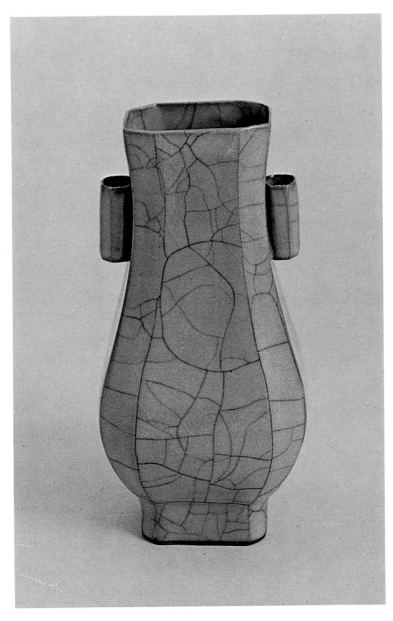

UNIQUE SOUTHERN KUAN (IMPERIAL) ALTAR SITE VASE
Typical Southern Kuan (Imperial) vase not excavated but handed down, showing superbly thin potting and in perfect condition. Warren E. Cox Collection

RARE LUNG-CH'UAN KU (BEAKER) VASE

This rare pottery vase is in the form of a bronze ku (beaker) and is one of only a few known. It surpasses the two in the David Collection. (See plates XLIII and XLIV in the David catalogue.) Warren E. Cox Collection

THE FINEST SOUTHERN SUNG "THREE COLOR" BOWL KNOWN
It was found in Southern Sung period (1127-1280) that iron-red could be added to
the yellow and green enamels known, giving the first polychrome ware known. All
the others published have a single lotus or bird design. Warren E. Cox Collection

TURQUOISE POTTERY FLOWER VASE FROM NISHAPUR
This piece was excavated in Nishapur but may have been made in Rhages or
Gurgan, twelfth to thirteenth century. The pierced design was employed in both
white and turquoise wares. It is, so far as we know, a unique shape. Warren E.
Cox Collection

K'ANG HSI, SANG DE BOEUF VASE
A typical sang de boeuf vase of the K'ang Hsi period (1662-1722). This piece is
interesting in that it shows exposed the rim of white glaze on which the thick roll
of red glaze adheres at the foot rim. The glaze shows the bloodlike texture.
Warren E. Cox Collection

IMPERIAL YELLOW GROUND FIGURE OF SHOU LAO
K'ang Hsi porcelain figure of Shou Lao holding the "peach of immortality" in his right hand. It is decorated with *famille verte* colors on Imperial yellow ground. Ht. 10½". Warren E. Cox Collection

The Book of

POTTERY AND PORCELAIN

VOLUME II

COLOR PLATE

The Book of

Pottery and Porcelain

BY

WARREN E. COX

*3000 illustrations. Pictures selected by the
author. Lay-outs by A. M. Lounsbery*

REVISED EDITION

VOLUME II

CROWN PUBLISHERS, INC.
NEW YORK

Original Edition: xx printings
Revised Edition: Fourth Printing, April, 1979

Library of Congress Catalogue Card Number: 75-127511
ISBN: 0-517-539314

Published simultaneously in Canada by General Publishing Company Limited

PRINTED IN THE UNITED STATES OF AMERICA

This book is dedicated

to

ELIZABETH AND ETHELYN

who kept things going while I had the fun of doing it

CONTENTS OF VOLUME TWO

CHAPTER XX

THE CH'ING DYNASTY (Continued)

BISCUIT OR UNGLAZED WARE

"Fan ts'u" in Chinese means "turned porcelain" and suggests that bisque ware was turned inside out, which is a lovely and amusing conception borne out frequently by just a touch of glaze on some inner part to carry out the illusion. Most pieces so made were signed by artists, which is a rare occurrence indeed in these so commercial times. The objects consist of lions, figures of Buddhist Arhats, or those who have achieved Nirvana, etc. All the pieces were very small and they are quite rare.

TING YAO OF THE CH'ING DYNASTY

The imitations of Sung Dynasty Ting yao continued and some quite good examples were made. The body used was opaque and earthy looking and the glaze was much like the early type being creamy and crackled. The ware was used to make objects for the writer's table and simple small vases, bowls and the like. One shape often seen is of a bottle with a hydra twisting about the neck in relief. Of course these pieces were fired at the high temperatures prevalent and cannot be confused with the Sung wares.

CLAIR DE LUNE

Even more expensive and rarer than the peach bloom wares is the clair de lune which is of equal quality and made in the same forms with a few added. This glaze, as the name indicates, is of the palest possible blue just off white and it is made of very refined cobalt perfectly handled. Less good specimens are deeper and later ones always are. All that has been said about the potting and marks of the peach bloom applies here.

OTHER BLUE WARES

From this palest blue we find shades all the way to "ta ch'ing" or dark blue and variations of lavender blue and slate blue. These are heavier wares and not so sought after but pleasant.

FIG. 799. Clair de Lune K'ang Hsi writer's coupe with the six character mark delicately pencilled under the bottom. Dia. 4". The Michael Friedsam Coll. Metropolitan Mus. of Art.

CELADON AND OTHER IRON GLAZES

Among the many continuations of celadon glazes we can distinguish three entirely different types:

1.—First, at Ching-tê Chêng a pale and very clear glaze was developed which rivaled the clair de lune and it was used on small vases and objects

of the same shapes as the peach bloom ones although vases of the "chrysanthemum shape" like that illustrated seem to dominate. These may be a trifle less well made and heavier than the other two classes but they are nevertheless very perfect and do command high prices.

2.—Second, also at Ching-tê Chêng larger vases were made of a fairly thinly potted ware very true and perfect and usually having all-over incised decoration under a rather yellowish green celadon glaze thinly applied and not crackled. The handles were often left in biscuit and sometimes colored brown or black. They are usually given the double ring and some mark in underglaze blue under the bottom where the glaze is typical K'ang Hsi pitted white.

3.—The factories at Lung-ch'üan continued and turned out a ware exactly like that which they had made all during the Ming period and on back into the Sung. It is interesting to note that Père d'Entrecolles wrote in 1722, "I was shown this year for the first time a kind of porcelain which is now in fashion; its color verges on olive and they call it long

FIG. 800. Pale "celadon" vase with incised decoration and bisque handles of the K'ang Hsi period (1662–1722 A.D.). Ht. 9". Metropolitan Mus. of Art.

tsiven." Bushell says (*op. cit.*, p. 214), "Long tsiven is a rendering of Lung-ch'üan, the district celebrated for celadons in the Sung and Ming periods. In another place d'Entrecolles describes the making of celadons in the Sung style with intent to deceive." Many other kilns were also engaged in the making of celadon wares and particularly Chüchou, the capital of Chekiang province and just northeast of Lung-ch'üan. Some new styles of decoration were used such as the application of slip as on the vase illustrated and the greater use of the mold as shown in the square example with sides and top secured by the glaze. The perfection of technique, shown in the small tea-pot which has a tapered chimney built in it to provide a better draft for the lamp below and to heat the tea more quickly, is something to note, but the exact old styles also continued without change.

To make this point entirely clear I illustrate a temple vase which belongs to Mr. Lem Sec Tsang and which innumerable collectors have passed upon as being Ming and not one single one has even suspected as being later although several have said it could be "Yüan or Ming," and yet which bears

FIG. 801. Ch'u chou candlestick of white porcelain covered with a pale transparent green glaze irregularly crackled. Probably late Ming to K'ang Hsi period c. 17th cent. Ht. 8". Lem Sec Tsang Coll. Warren E. Cox Coll.

FIG. 802. The transparent glaze looks like that of Ch'u Chou ware, but the construction and design reveal it to be a Koryo II, Korean piece. Avery Brundage Coll.

FIG. 803. K'ang Hsi Ch'u-chou vase as heavily potted as many Ming ones but having a slip relief decoration over which is a more transparent and less green glaze than is seen on the usual Ming specimen. Ht. 11¼". Warren E. Cox Coll.

the date of the year 1671 a good ten years into the K'ang Hsi period. The body, the potting and every detail of this piece corresponds perfectly with similar ones of the Ming period. The glaze is applied somewhat thinly and is, therefore, less green than some specimens but these potteries always varied in this respect and whether this would be a characteristic of later ones I am not prepared to say. The translation of the inscription on this piece by Mr. Han of the Metropolitan Museum of Art and corrected by Sir Percival David is as follows: "The faithful person, Hsü Ming-jui, who is a native of Chu-kou town, Ch'ing-yüan Hsien, Chekiang, offers a pair of vases in great cheer in the main hall in front of the Three Precious Ones in the White Cloud Temple, Nanking. In giving these vases he asks for the peace and luck of his family, for satisfaction of his business, and for the prosperity of his descendant." It is then dated, "On the lucky day of the middle month of Summer in the year hsin-hai, that is the 10th year of K'ang Hsi," which is 1671.

When, then, did the Chü-chou kilns cease to work? Judging by the fact that we have also excellent copies or continuations of the wares but which have all the characteristics of modern pieces I should say that they continued at least up to the Second World War.

GREY, BUFF AND BROWN IRON WARES

During the K'ang Hsi period a large number of crackled wares ranging from light grey to brown and almost black were made. Similar ones were also made uncrackled. The best known are called "tzu chin" (lustrous brown),

Fig. 804. K'ang Hsi Ch'u chou vase of greyish white porcelain. Glaze is typical transparent grey-green and strongly crack-led. Ht. 20". Lem Sec Tsang—Warren E. Cox Coll. See below enlarge-ment of neck with writing.

Fig. 805. Unique tea-pot of Ch'u-chou yao made in four pieces, a lamp with support for circular wick on saucer, a reticulated stand, the pot itself and a cover. A most ingeni-ous device in the pot causes the tea to heat quicker. By means of a bent hollow cone the heat is conducted up through the center of the pot. Late Ming or K'ang Hsi period. I have never seen anything else like it. Warren E. Cox Coll.

but these are also termed, "dead leaf" brown, "cafe-au-lait," "brown gold," "chocolate brown," "old gold brown" and "wu chin" or black gold, etc. The cafe-au-lait is used not only for single colored pieces but as a background for panel decoration much as was powder blue. Hobson tells us that this ware is called "Batavian" because it was largely imported by the Dutch who had an entrepôt in Batavia, Java. The panel decoration is most often in famille rose colors of the late K'ang Hsi or later periods. It occurs on the outside of bowls and also is combined with silver decoration.

Sometimes these glazes were shaded and mottled, coffee brown to olive or perhaps brown mottled with black and other effects. There are also examples of the lighter tones over engraved or relief decorations.

MIRROR BLACK

Mirror black was called "wu chin" or "black gold" and was made by mixing the cobaltiferous ore of manganese with the iron of coffee brown with the result that a glaze was made which was black with brownish or bluish reflections. It is spoken of as related to the Chien yao of Sung times but actually there is no connection whatsoever. An interesting point is that reports have it that the dark blue, the celadon, the lustrous brown and the mirror black glazes were applied with numerous coatings. It was said that some-

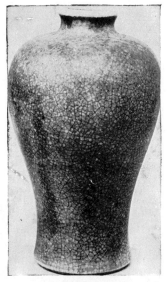

FIG. 806. White porcelain vase with white crackled glaze covered with a transparent brown enamel. K'ang Hsi. Ht. 4½". Metropolitan Mus. of Art.

times as many as nine were used, six by blowing and three more by painting with the brush.

FIG. 807. K'ang Hsi mirror black bottle of dull surface. Ht. 16½". Metropolitan Mus. of Art.

FIG. 808. K'ang Hsi. One of pair of unique triple gourd shaped vases with *wu chin* or "black gold" treatment of the bottom sections, greenish white center sections decorated with iron red, gold and yellow green, and the top treated in blue glaze with gold decoration. Ht. 18". Bequest of Mary Clark Thompson. Metropolitan Mus. of Art.

Another black of dull quality and usually crackled was said to go back to the K'ang Hsi period but I have never seen one which could be so attributed and I believe it was actually later. On the black, gilt designs were painted much as they were on the powder blue and these designs are usually almost worn out by handling. Frequently they are more or less crudely retouched. D'Entrecolles also mentions reserved panels in brown and painted in black designs but we have none of these, if they were made, though there do exist rare examples of enamel decorated medallions reserved in black.

FIG. 809. K'ang Hsi vase with deep turquoise blue glaze and very fine "fish roe" crackle. Ht. 4¾". Ex D. Abbes Coll.

FIG. 810. Imperial yellow K'ang Hsi writer's bottle made almost identically in the same form as peach bloom ones. Dia. 3¾". Metropolitan Mus. of Art.

FIG. 811. Orange yellow K'ang Hsi vase. Transparent and somewhat mottled glaze. Ht. 13½". Altman Coll. Metropolitan Mus. of Art.

YELLOW WARES

"Nanking yellow" was simply a thin coating of a glaze very similar to the brown ones and it is always brownish. "Imperial yellow" is quite different for it was made of a medium fired lead-silicate not so hard as the others. This appears darker over the biscuit and lighter when applied over a white glaze. Sometimes light engraving is traced under it and when the piece was for Imperial use the design was of dragons and pearls. This color is the clearest and strongest but there were many others such as primrose, canary, lemon and mustard, although they are all variations of the same thing. D'Entrecolles says these yellows were produced by the use of iron but we must agree with Mr. Hobson that it was probably antimony which gave the colors with perhaps a trace of iron. We found that uranium produces the same range of yellows but without characteristic iridescence.

TURQUOISE AND LEAF GREEN

Turquoise was obtained with copper and had been a favorite color since Ming days. It has also been continuously produced up to the present. The K'ang Hsi wares have a fine grained white body but we must add that some of the later examples also have the same characteristics. The glaze was called "fei ts'ui" or "kingfisher blue," "chi ts'ui" and "k'ung ch'iao lü" or "peacock green." It is almost always crackled, and this crackle is usually small and of the "fish roe" type that is almost round in appearance. It always stands out more on the greener—or that is the thicker glazed—examples. At times there were engraved examples but these are likely to be later. Some of the pieces have the K'ang Hsi mark and the wares seem to vary from the finest porcelain to almost pottery-like bodies though all are vitreous. The greens are called "leaf green," "cucumber green," "yellow leaf green," "snake skin green," etc. The latter called by the Chinese "shê p'i lü" is quite iridescent and transparent. The *T'ao lu* says this is one of the four famous glazes made under Ts'ang's regime.

APPLE GREEN

Apple green is not a glaze but an enamel applied over a greyish or brownish crackled white glaze. This green is transparent and, just as was explained in our section treating sang de boeuf, it was given greater brilliancy because of the white ground beneath it. It varies from a light to dark emerald color, is highly lustrous and iridescent and where the enamel has been broken internally by the crackle it has shining flakes called by the French "ailes de mouches" or "fly's wings" which is just exactly what they look like. These are not blemishes but were thought by collectors to indicate authenticity, but they are natural to the enamel and glaze and have been perfectly reproduced in modern fakes.

FIG. 812. "Emerald green" bottle of the "apple green" type. Late Ming or early K'ang Hsi. 17⅝". Metropolitan Mus. of Art.

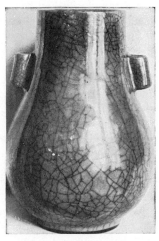

FIG. 813. K'ang Hsi "apple green" jar of a form similar to the Sung Kuan and Ko type but softer and more rounded. White porcelain covered with strongly crackled white glaze over which a transparent enamel has been fired at lower temperature. Ht. 9". Metropolitan Mus. of Art.

Apple green treatment was given chiefly to small vases and cups and as the prices were always high the ware has been made continuously to the present. To one who has handled the K'ang Hsi wares it is not difficult to distinguish between the originals and later examples, however, the ware was always heavy and it is difficult indeed to distinguish pieces which have been made during the period intended as grey crackled wares and enameled over with the green at a later time. Ch'ien Lung apple greens, Hobson says, "Will be recognized by the characteristic finish of the base (wedge shaped rather than straight sided), and it will be noticed that the enamel in these pieces commonly covers the raw edge of the base rim, giving it a brown appearance."

Other green enamels were also used and some are as dark as the color of a ripe cucumber while collectors have labeled others "Camellia-leaf, myrtle, spinach and sage green," but these again are most likely to occur at later times. In Kiangsu at "Kashan" they used the same sort of green over a pottery base. The treatments were also sometimes not over another glaze but applied direct and either crackled or not.

It should also be noted that crackle had been so mastered generally that the potters could make it occur just where wanted and some vases even had bands of different sized crackles about their bodies. However, never was it possible to reproduce one of the ancient crackles perfectly because too many elements were involved. D'Entrecolles says that the Chinese used "sui yu" or "crackle glaze" mixed with the other glaze and says it was made of pebbles. The T'ao lu says it was from the rock of San-pao-p'eng. Scherzer obtained samples of this rock in 1882 and Vogt proved that it was not, as was supposed, steatite but pegmatite, as it contains no magnesium. Scherzer also tells us that the two layers were given to produce the finer, or as the French say "truité" crackle and that four were applied to make the larger crackle. Hobson says that the "sui yu" was light grey but was not noticeable when mixed with the colored glazes. He also says that they colored the crazing purposely with red ochre, ink, tea, etc., while the ware was still warm and before the cracks had completely closed. This may be true but the reader should not gain the impression that the cracks at a given temperature were any more open just after the vase had been taken from the kiln than at any subsequent time and frequently the cracks were colored naturally due to substances in the body such as iron, or due to the use of liquids in the vessels, such as tea which during years might penetrate even a fairly dense body. Hobson also points out that in some cases the color went beyond the crackle and has "given the glaze a clouded appearance." He also says that the buff or oatmeal crackles are sometimes combined with underglaze blue and enameled colors and that when the enameled colors are used with this combination they are generally laid on pads of white slip locally applied. He adds, "The intentional crackle is quite distinct from the accidental crazing or faint crackling which develops on most of the medium fired glazes, such as aubergine and turquoise." But this is getting a bit too complex. Who is to know whether the old potter meant to have crackle or just obtained it and let it go at that?

In truth Hobson seems somewhat confused in his own mind concerning crackle; he says, "All pottery shrinks in the kiln and to ensure an even surface it is necessary that the body and the glaze should contract to the same extent. If the glaze contracts more than the body it will split up into a network of cracks." We must say that this is only half right for cracks will be produced also if the glaze contracts *less* than the body. This may cause the rumpled or "orange skin" effect and also a crackle.

Again Mr. Hobson says, "In the end they discovered several methods.

One was to heat the ware as much as possible in the sun whilst it was drying and then plunge it into pure water. A crackle was produced by this means after firing." In "Chinese Pottery and Porcelain," (p. 197, vol. 2) he says, "Another method is mentioned in the K'ang Hsi *Encyclopaedia*, viz. to heat the unglazed ware as much as possible in the sun, then plunge it into pure water. By this means a crackle was produced on the ware after firing." Of course this is ridiculous to anyone who understands the nature of crackle and either the source must have been all out of line or the translation was incorrect. Hannover comes a step nearer the truth in his "Pottery & Porce-

Left: Figure of Shou Lao of the usual porcelain painted in enamels and with bisque face and hands, the latter added after firing. At times these figures were made nearly a yard high. Ht. 19". Salting Bequest. Victoria and Albert Mus.

Taoist deity *Chen Wu* or *Hsüan T'ien* in the usual enamel on biscuit colors with the hands and face left in biscuit. Ht. 17". Michael Friedsam Coll. Metropolitan Mus. of Art.

Right: Figure of Kuan Yin of the K'ang Hsi period with enamel decoration. The faces and hands of such figures are frequently in bisque and, as in this case, the hands were made separately and added after firing. Ht. c. 19". Metropolitan Mus. of Art.

K'ANG HSI PORCELAIN FIGURES WITH ENAMEL DECORATION

PLATE 160

Middle K'ang Hsi "beaker shaped" vase with design perhaps showing Korean influence of flying cranes and lambrequin borders of "brocade design." Ht. 18". Bequest of Edward C. Converse. Metropolitan Mus. of Art.

Rare and beautiful K'ang Hsi famille noire with alternating yellow and black ground panels. Ht. ?1". Metropolitan Mus. of Art.

(a)

(b)

(c)

(a) K'ang Hsi "club shaped vase," with stylized elongated neck. About 1700 A.D. Ht. 28½". Metropolitan Mus. of Art.
(b) One of the finest "temple vases" of the K'ang Hsi period known. This vase has a bright green enamel ground against which the aubergine branches, white blossoms and black and white birds seem to breathe the very essence of Spring. Ht. 29½". Altman Coll. Metropolitan Mus. of Art.
(c) K'ang Hsi "temple vase" of the middle part dating about 1700 A.D. The colors are the usual famille verte enamels with iron red. Ht. 29½". Metropolitan Mus. of Art.

K'ANG HSI ENAMEL DECORATED PORCELAIN VASES

lain of the Far East," when he says, "Another Chinese source gives, for instance, as serving the same purpose, the method of heating in the sun and rapid cooling in cold water of the unfired, glazed vessels." However, what one did in the way of heating and quickly cooling "the unfired, glazed vessels," would have no effect at all. What can be easily demonstrated is that AFTER *a piece is fired with its glaze and is still in a state of tension between body and glaze, the crackle can be* ACCENTED *(not actually produced in the case where the glaze and body expand and contract to the same degree) by heating and sudden cooling.* This gives it a jolt which makes more crackle where some already existed but it will not make crackle on an uncracked piece. As for the myths concerning "pure water" and such operations "before" firing, they could only be passed on by those who had never fired a crackled pot in their lives.

The pegmatite might bring about crackle as would any other substances which would act simply to change the coefficient of expansion either of the glaze or the body so that they were made unequal. In fact the difficulty generally speaking is to match a body and glaze so that they will *not* cause crackle when it is not wanted. But the Chinese became very proficient in handling it, by Ming times.

POLYCHROME PORCELAINS

Besides the single colored wares there were many which combined several of the glazes. The "hu p'i" or "tiger-skin" ware was splashed and spotted with aubergine, yellow and green and as the glazes were thinner and the spots more sharply defined than such splashed effects in T'ang wares the effect was less pleasant. This ware is also called "spinach and egg" somewhat derisively but collectors often have a piece or two.

FIG. 814. K'ang Hsi rhyton after a T'ang model. "Egg and spinach" effect in green, yellow and white. The horns are brown. Length 5". Metropolitan Mus. of Art.
FIG. 815. K'ang Hsi bowl and plate of "egg and spinach" glazes of yellow, green and aubergine on white. Dias. 7" and 8". Warren E. Cox Coll.
FIG. 816. K'ang Hsi black enamel on biscuit cat with green glass eyes. Length 5¼". The Michael Friedsam Coll.

The "yao pien" or transmutation glaze of red (probably with blue streaks) was made by accident and destroyed as of no worth after an attempt to make red soufflé, d'Entrecolles tells us. He describes them simply as looking like a sort of agate.

High fired mixed colors were also made on small figures and ornaments in colors of celadon, red and blue. These were probably from Kwangtung in imitation of the real Ming ones. At any rate they do not come from Ching tê Chêng.

"San ts'ai" or enameled wares were made with medium fired glazes of yellow, green, turquoise, aubergine and purple blue. Bowls with engraved designs may have the designs washed over with one color and the background

FIG. 817. K'ang Hsi water jar with yellow body and top handle and spout in leaf green. Length 6". Bequest of Mary Clark Thompson. Metropolitan Mus. of Art.

FIG. 818. K'ang Hsi enamel on biscuit figure of *Li Po* or *Li Peh* the famous poet leaning on his wine jar. Length 6". Courtesy of Walter Blumenthal.

with another. "Brinjal bowls" are a variety of this with simply engraved sprays of flowers rather crudely filled in in green, white or yellow on an aubergine or "brinjal" ground. The same type was also made with green grounds. Raised outlines were no longer used but the same colors were employed on shapes that would keep them apart as we see on the peach shaped

FIG. 819. K'ang Hsi enamel on biscuit iridescent black horse made with transparent green over brownish back, pale aubergine, yellow and green, also with touches on the base rim, crop, etc., of muddy dark iron red. Ht. 7". Metropolitan Mus. of Art.

FIG. 820. K'ang Hsi enamel on biscuit porcelain lion in yellow green, pale aubergine, white and yellow with a rider on his back in European costume. Ht. 6". Metropolitan Mus. of Art.

wine pots. The bowls have meaningless seals called incorrectly, "shop marks" or "hall marks." A better class is the Imperial sort of dish or rice bowl with five clawed dragons engraved in them and colored yellow on green, green on aubergine, or aubergine on yellow but these again are hard to date and most that one sees are of Ch'ien Lung or later times.

A group of little animals, birds, deities and humans on rocks, in boats or in grottos are colored with green and aubergine but also with vermilion added, only traces of which can still be found. The good Père tells us that these were first fired in the biscuit and then daubed and refired in the less hot parts of the kiln. They are late K'ang Hsi, of course, or later as he wrote about them in the last year of the reign. Of them Hobson says, "They are apt to be confused with the enamels of the muffle kiln which were also used in washes on the biscuit body; but the latter, in spite of a superficial similarity, are in reality much more fusible and soft." There are also differences in color: The yellow is browner and darker, the aubergine is a little more red and the greens do not include the pale apple green color. A black was developed and made with a transparent glaze over a dull brown-black. A dirty white was also added in time.

"SUR BISCUITE" OR ENAMEL ON BISCUIT WARE

FIG. 821. Fine famille noire beaker with the usual white, green, yellow and aubergine enamels. Ht. 18¼". Metropolitan Mus. of Art.

The term "famille verte" means simply "green family" of wares and may be applied to all the enamel wares except those of the very end of the reign when rose enamels were introduced and we designate them as "famille rose." Under the "famille verte" name we have subdivisions depending on the color of the ground used; "famille noir" for black, "famille jaune" for yellow, etc. Also under the famille verte classification we have the "sur biscuite" and the more ordinary on glaze types, the first having been derived from the "san ts'ai" or "three color" type and the second from the "wu ts'ai" or "five color" type, of the Ming period, but the enamels used for all are very much alike. The K'ang Hsi enamels are different from the Ming in the following characteristics:

1.—The yellow is lighter and clearer.

2.—There are new shades of green including the "apple green."

3.—The iron red is lighter and more coral-color. (But not so light as the original Sung color, being applied more heavily.)

4.—The violet-blue was only very occasionally used in Ming times but it now replaces the turquoise-green.

Hobson says that the connoisseur looks to this blue especially in appraising a piece and, "If the blue is bright and clear, the piece will be highly valued." All very well it is to have a good blue color but there are after all the considerations of proportion, of line, the trueness of potting, the drawing of the design and its adaptation to the vase form among many other things to be considered. He says that around the blue there was at first a "curious oily stain which is lustrous like the track of oil on water," and that it was later overcome but that collectors are not disturbed by it and consider it a mark of genuineness. I do not know to what he refers unless it might be the slight touching of some transparent white glaze over the blue as it was applied over the black simply to produce greater gloss and depth of color. If this is so, we must sadly add that it is no mark of authenticity whatsoever for it was done on perfectly modern pieces as well.

The technique was a simple one. The usual famille verte sur biscuite vase was first fired in biscuit state. Upon the mat surface the design is drawn completely in brown-black manganese. Some colors are painted within outlines and others are washed right over the detail which shows through them. The full range of colors was not always used and green, yellow and aubergine form the usual combination. The white is a very slightly greenish tinged and lustrous glaze, the lustre being compared to a snail's track. The black is dull brown-black but becomes true black when the white is applied over it. Only rarely is the coral red used and still more rarely the violet-blue. Sometimes these are applied over a patch of porcelain glaze.

The amphora is like Ming ones but the neck has grown heavier and cer-

FIG. 822. Famille jaune square vase of the K'ang Hsi period with decoration in green, aubergine, etc. Ht. about 19½". Boston Mus. of Fine Arts.

FIG. 823. Typical *famille jaune* square vase decorated with the enamels of the day and iron red. Ht. 19". Altman Coll. Metropolitan Mus. of Art.

FIG. 824. K'ang Hsi *famille jaune* "temple vase" or "amphora" having a clearer than usual yellow ground fairly evenly applied and enamel colors painted direct on the biscuit. Ht. 27". Altman Coll. Metropolitan Mus. of Art.

FIG. 825. Rectangular *famille jaune* K'ang Hsi vase with handles imitating twigs and later called "crabstock" by the English. Ht. 21". Altman Coll. Metropolitan Mus. of Art.

tainly less beautiful than the Ch'ü Chou one shown in the celadon section. (See p. 505, Fig. 715.) The tapering square vase is a new style and varies considerably in the form of the shoulders, the neck, etc. Beakers and club shapes are also frequent but it is obvious that shape meant less to these potters than the decoration and here we have almost as static an idea of shape as we found when the Athenians became so intent upon their painting.

In point of rarity and therefore also of value the yellow ground ones stood first, the black second and the green third. White ground vessels were, of course, done over the glaze as in Ming times. Many of the figures and particularly the larger ones such as that from the Victoria and Albert Museum were predominantly yellow. Yellow, a favorite color of the court, was called, "Imperial yellow." Others had no particular distinction. It is merely one of those arbitrary whims of western collectors and certainly the finest specimen I know, the beautiful vase illustrated from the Altman Collection with birds and hawthorn blossoms, has a pale green ground that is as fresh as the earliest sprouts. No illustration can give the slightest impression of the glorious spring-like quality of this design filled with bursting blossoms and crazy birds filled with the ecstasy of the season.

It seems unnecessary in this day to mention that such wares are certainly not Ming, but recently a foremost German authority quoted that beautifully illustrated but totally unauthoritative work "Chinese Porcelain & Hard Stones" by Edgar Gorer and J. F. Blacker, published in 1911 by Bernard Quaritch of London in which Ming attributions are given wholesale.

Naturally such an expensive ware would be copied and it was by the Japanese and Chinese since K'ang Hsi days. Some such specimens are surprisingly correct in details and colors. The glazes are easily artifically worn Thus the collector has to be very careful indeed. Mr. Hobson has made some notes which I pass on for what they are worth. He says that in the finer pieces the black is not allowed to appear in too solid masses but is broken and graded to vary the surface. I believe this was merely due to the difficulty of getting an even black ground. During Ch'ien Lung's time, he says, the black was not allowed in such large areas and diapering came into style. However we have seen diapering in the Wan Li period and before so this is no new invention. In fact after the Yung Chêng period there was a reversion to the old Ming taste and this may have been a result of such a trend. He also says, which is quite true, that the black in later copies was sometimes mixed with the enamel which gives a dull and mat surface while in others the over transparent enamel is laid on too much and gives a sticky appearance.

More dangerous fakes are made by building vases up on old bases or by stripping some or grinding off the surface of some worthless but correct vase of the period and redecorating it.

The designers had difficulties with these wares simply because the whole ground had to be covered with enamel as we can see in the uneven grounds and the return to diapering. The painting in of such a ground is tedious and clumsy and, being conscious of this, the artists would naturally fill in as much detail as he could, particularly to avoid large and mussy areas of ground color.

Another difficulty was that of painting up to two sides of a line. The most spirited drawing with fine brush work and all the life a master might give it, would be ruined by such an after treatment. The filling in was simply a tedious and stupid method and naturally here and there the enamel would go over the line on one side of it or the other thus killing all its life and vigor. Is it not amazing that the Chinese people after making the joyful and alive paintings on pottery that they did in the Sung times could possibly sink so low as to return to kindergarten technique of outline filling?

So tedious and uninspiring was this whole medium of expression that weariness shows up in the fact that the backs of most of the round vases are not considered. Most of them contain no thoughtout design whatsoever and one sees only scraggly tips of branches approaching each other haphazardly. Certainly the greatest collection, if turned with the backs out, would show a sorry spectacle. Here we find the clearest sign of decadence; that of putting up a good front and not finishing off the job properly. It would be difficult to find an example in which a Sung artist had done this.

When one studies these wares with an open mind unbiased by their cost in the auction market and with an eye only for artistic merit one can see that they are bombastic attempts toward grandeur made by artists who were mere copyists at best and not very good ones at that.

FAMILLE VERTE DECORATION ON THE GLAZE

With the same enamels decorations were carried on much as in Ming days on the glazed wares. D'Entrecolles tells us that this glaze had less of the softening element of lime and fern ashes in it than that intended for the blue

FIG. 826. K'ang Hsi porcelain plate with a picture of the "Three Heroes," Chang Liang, Han Sin and Ch'ên P'ing, founders of the Han dynasty. D.a. 7¼". Metropolitan Mus. of Art.

FIG. 827. K'ang Hsi famille verte porcelain plate with the very best of swift and virile painting. Dia. 8⅛". Fuller Coll. Seattle Art Mus.

FIG. 828. Late K'ang Hsi porcelain plate with uneven white ground and decorated with palest iron red flowers, three greens, a gray-brown and purplish blue. Dia. 9½". Michael Friedsam Coll. Metropolitan Mus. of Art.

and white wares. This harder and higher fired glaze is stronger, more opaque and slightly cream. The second firing for the enamels is said to have harmed the softer blue and white type glaze and this is probably the reason that we see only seldom the underglaze color used with enamels. In fact the only ones I have seen were direct copies of Ming examples. The blue usually used in K'ang Hsi times with enamels was the newly developed

FIG. 829. Two rather better than average famille verte K'ang Hsi vases and one of the same period of the very rare type of relief bisque examples. It was thought by some collectors that these were intended for enamel coloring later but the careful touching in of the pupils of the eyes would not then have been necessary. Hts. 34″, 31″ and 28¾″. Fuller Coll. Seattle Art Mus.

FIG. 830. K'ang Hsi "temple" vase. Decorated with famille verte colors on a white ground. Ht. about 30″. Ross Coll. Boston Mus. of Fine Arts.

violet-blue enamel which is nowhere nearly so beautiful as the underglaze color.

It will be recognized at once that this painting of enamels on a glazed ground is a natural method of painting not beset by all the hampering tech-

FIG. 831. Middle K'ang Hsi cup or earlier. Ming shape, a simple design fairly well drawn, in famille verte enamels. 4″. Bequest of E. C. Converse.

FIG. 832. Late K'ang Hsi lantern of thin porcelain decorated with famille verte enamels and iron red. 13″. Metropolitan Mus. of Art.

FIG. 833. Late K'ang Hsi famille verte enamels on glaze jar with three greens, clear iron red, muddy yellow and underglazed blue on the horizontal lines. Ht. 12″. Bequest of Mary Clark Thompson. Metropolitan Mus. of Art.

nical difficulties which had to be overcome with the on-biscuit technique. The ground did not have to be filled in and it was also a pleasant and smooth surface on which to paint. The method used, however, was an outcome of the old system of manufacturing. The outlining was done in red or brown by several artists who specialized in various things. These outlines were then filled in either carefully or carelessly. Space-fear was not so pressing and we see some freedom, and once in a while a fine piece of composition.

FIG. 834. Late K'ang Hsi tea-pot of white porcelain decorated with famille verte enamels in the style of rather overcrowded flowers which is more often associated with the following periods of famille rose. Length 8". Bequest of Mary Clark Thompson. Metropolitan Mus. of Art.

FIG. 835. K'ang Hsi plate with low relief design and underglaze blue and brown rim edge, redecorated in Holland with colored enamels. Dia. 8". Bequest of Maria P. James. Metropolitan Mus. of Art.

Père d'Entrecolles however says, "Sometimes the painting is intentionally reserved for the second firing; at other times they only use the second firing to conceal defects in the porcelain, applying the colors to faulty places. This

FIG. 836. Possibly early K'ang Hsi gallipot with deep iron red ground over white glaze allowed to show in the clouds and yellow, blue and green enamels. Ht. 7". Bequest of Mary Clark Thompson. Metropolitan Mus. of Art.

FIG. 837. Early K'ang Hsi double wine or tea pot of heavily potted white ware with underglaze blue, iron red and green enamel decoration. Ht. 6". Ex Avery Coll. Metropolitan Mus. of Art.

FIG. 838. Early K'ang Hsi wine ewer heavily potted with white glaze and decoration in iron red and famille verte enamels. This shows a continuance of the Near Eastern shapes. Ht. 8". Metropolitan Mus. of Art.

porcelain, which is loaded with colors, is not to the taste of a good many people. As a rule one can feel the inequalities on the surface, whether due to the clumsiness of the workmen, to the exigencies of light and shade, or to the desire to conceal defects in the body of the ware." Of course he was reflecting Chinese taste.

Among the export famille verte wares there are many pieces which have decoration in places which were obviously the location of a flaw of some sort, and this again tended to make the style overornate and crowded. Again the enamels were pale in color and had to be "heaped and piled" as the old Ming potters had put it to get a sufficient depth.

GENERAL DATING

There is no point and little possibility in dividing these wares into actual years but we can generally allocate them as Early, Middle or Late K'ang Hsi.

Early K'ang Hsi (1672–1680)—Like Ming wares, enamels applied in broad washes, designs simple and direct, iron red still fairly dark and blue enamel and gilding are little used.

FIG. 839. Middle K'ang Hsi plate of rare type. "Brocade pattern" of famille verte colors. The rim is finished with a cafe au lait edge. Dia. 10½". Metropolitan Mus. of Art.—FIG. 840. K'ang Hsi early plate showing simple almost Minglike floral treatment. Dia. 8". Bequest of Maria P. James. Metropolitan Mus. of Art.

FIG. 841 below. Middle K'ang Hsi box for perfumed herbs. "Brocade pattern" in famille verte enamels including blue. Length 14". Gift of Robert E. Tod. Metropolitan Mus. of Art.

FIG. 842. Early K'ang Hsi vase showing bold and vigorous drawing. Ht. 22". Warren E. Cox Coll.—FIG. 843. A typical late K'ang Hsi vase with flowers drawn in a style only a little more vigorous than those which appear on many famille rose pieces. There is no rose on this piece, the blue is pinkish or lavender in tone and the glaze very thin and dry. Ht. 21". Warren E. Cox Coll.

Middle K'ang Hsi (1680 to 1700 or 1710)—Best quality, large vases with brocade patterns on grounds with reserve medallions, full designed plates with many figures, directly and well drawn birds and flowers, vases with coral red used partly or in the whole for ground, and vases with large figures of ladies.

Late K'ang Hsi (1700 or 1710 to 1722)—Delicate drawing, lightening and effeminacy throughout, like famille rose but in famille verte colors, egg shell "birthday plates," which were supposed to have been made for the birthday of the emperor in 1713 are typical, egg shell lanterns, etc.

Toward the very end of the reign two new colors were devised, a *muddy, mauve-pink* (1710–1720) followed by other opaque colors and *"arsenical white"* which was also opaque. These were the beginning of the famille rose colors.

Even over the glaze the grounds were sometimes filled in with enamel probably to cover up defects. Again enamels might be used over colored grounds such as in the "lang yao green glazed bowl in the British Museum" mentioned by Hobson as probably a faulty specimen and therefore decorated. I submit the suggestion that it was probably a good red to begin with but the second firing turned it unexpectedly green. (See discussion of Sang de Boeuf.) There are also powder blues with enamel decoration, grey crackled grounds and "Nanking yellow" but all are tricky stunts and not harmonious.

Fig. 844. K'ang Hsi bottle of white glaze decorated with gold only. Ht. 17″. Bequest of E. C. Converse. Metropolitan Mus. of Art.

Fig. 845. Late K'ang Hsi reticulated porcelain basket decorated in two greens and pu.ple, blue and pale yellow enamels and iron red. Length 4½″. Bequest of Mary Clark Thompson. Metropolitan Mus. of Art.

Fig. 846. One of a pair of baluster ornaments acquired in India. They are definitely of K'ang Hsi famille verte ware and were said to have been imported during the days of the Monguls and were probably made to order. Ht. 5¾″. Fuller Coll. Seattle Art Mus.

Fig. 847. Middle K'ang Hsi gallipot with covers. White glaze and pale, uneven red decoration. Ht. 9″. Bequest of Mary Strong Shattuck. Metropolitan Mus. of Art.

CHINESE IMARI WARE

We have described the Kakiemon ware and the more ornate "Old Imari" ware made in Arita in Hizen province, Japan, and probably influenced by the Dutch traders. This in a sense grew out of Chinese wares but it became so popular that the Chinese at Ching-tê Chêng copied it back as it were. The Chinese ware is better than the Japanese being thinner and clearer of color. The red is coral in the Chinese examples while it is more dull and like Indian red on the Japanese. The black is greenish on the Chinese examples and brownish on the Japanese ones.

RED AND BLUE WARE

Another ware had red and gold over glaze and blue underglaze design. It was an export ware and of poor quality.

During this enlightened reign we could have expected great things but the blight of commercialism, mass production and foreign influence was too great.

FIG. 848. K'ang Hsi Imari style vase of white porcelain decorated with dark underglaze blue, gold, green and iron red. Ht. 10". Metropolitan Mus. of Art.

FIG. 849. Late K'ang Hsi jar in the style of Japanese Imari ware decorated with pale underglaze blue, deep iron red and gold. Ht. 6". Metropolitan Mus. of Art.

FIG. 850. K'ang Hsi bowl decorated in Holland with iron red, green, purplish blue, a too bright yellow, dark brown and gold. Dia. 5½". Metropolitan Mus. of Art.—FIG. 851. Late K'ang Hsi bowl decorated in underglaze blue, iron red and green enamel. The blossoms on the outside are in slight relief. The inside lambrequins are distinctly European in design. Dia. 7½". Metropolitan Mus of Art.

FIG. 852. Large K'ang Hsi plate with the arms of the city of Louvain Dia. 17". Metropolitan Mus. of Art.

FIG. 853. Late K'ang Hsi plate in the Imari style. Dia. 10". Metropolitan Mus. of Art.

FIG. 854. K'ang Hsi plate showing strong Near Eastern influence. Dia. 8". Metropolitan Mus. of Art.

THE YUNG CHENG REIGN
(1723–1735)

Neither national history nor religion have much bearing upon art from this time forward. Commerce alone counts, and money became the prime incen-

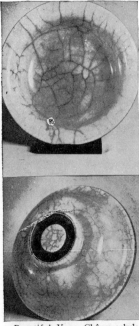

Yung Chêng bottle of white porcelain with creamy light green glaze and brown dressing on the body where exposed at the foot-rim. The six character mark is in underglaze blue. Ht. 6". T. C. Lee–Warren E. Cox Coll.

Beautiful Yung Chêng celadon bowl of white porcelain, the foot dressed with brown, and having a thick, rich, soft green glaze full of bubbles and crackled with brown. It also has the "brown mouth." Dia. about 7". Mrs. Warren E. Cox.

Right: Rare egg-shell apple green jar with finely crackled white glaze over which a transparent green enamel has been applied. The mark is K'ang Hsi in a blue slightly more purple in tint than it would be if of the period. Yung Chêng. Ht. 8¾". Perry Moore–Warren E. Cox Coll.

Yun Chêng reproduction of a Kuan type oblong dish with greyish body coated with a fat bluish-grey glaze with large crackles. Length 8½". C. T. Loo & Co.

Kuan type jardiniere with dragon handles of greyish porcelain covered with a fat greyish glaze. Yung Chêng period. Length 6". C. T. Loo & Co.

YUNG CHÊNG PORCELAINS
PLATE 162

tive, with a consequent decline in the integrity and quality of the art.

The fourth son of K'ang Hsi was a strong and hard ruler who put to death his own brothers but the good of the country burned in his heart. The *T'ao lu* says that he at once made a good appointment of Nien Hsi as the supervisor of the factories and in 1728 T'ang Ying was appointed assistant director of Ching-tê Chêng. Thus we hear of T'ang yao and Nien yao of the period though attributions are difficult to ascertain.

Above: Beautiful Yung Chêng soft paste bottle thinly and sensitively potted and having a "secret design" incised all over with a clear, transparent glaze having a helically twisted crackle. Ht. 12¾". Altman Coll. Metropolitan Mus. of Art. *Below:* Yung Chêng vase of a light starch blue incorrectly often called "clair de lune" which should be much lighter. Ht. 8½". T. C. Lee—Warren E. Cox Coll.

Yung Chêng tea-dust glazed vase of beautiful shape. The body is dark brown and the mark in relief under the bottom. Ht. 7". T. C. Lee—Warren E. Cox Coll.

Yung Chêng vase in the style of and with the mark of Ch'êng Hua but somewhat heavier and more glossy in glaze. Ht. 10½". Warren E. Cox Coll.

YUNG CHENG VASES
PLATE 163

A list of the wares made at Ching-tê Chêng was made by Hsieh Min, governor of the Kiangsi province from 1729 to 1734. It has been translated by Bushell in his "Oriental Ceramic Art" and repeated in about the same form in Hobson's "The Later Ceramic Wares of China." As this list is referred to by collectors the world over, it is important enough to give in detail following:

FIG. 855. Pair of plates with famille verte design. The mark is in underglaze blue of the six character Cheng Hua type although it is of late K'ang Hsi period. Dia. 8⅛". Guy Mayer Coll.

FIG. 856. Pair of plates with Ho ho birds in deep underglaze blue in center yellow medallions, bands of white glaze and pencilled underglaze blue cloud whorls at rim. The back has three blue birds in apple green ground and the six character K'ang Hsi mark in usual double ring. Dia. 7⅞". Guy Mayer Coll.

1.—Glazes of the Ta Kuan (Imperial) ware on an "iron body" including "yüeh pai" (moon white), "fên ch'ing" (pale blue or green) and "ta lü" (deep green).

2.—Ko yao glaze on an "iron body," including millet colour (mi sê) and fên ch'ing.

3.—Ju glaze without crackle on a "copper" body: the glaze colours copied from a cat's food basin of the Sung dynasty, and a dish for washing brushes moulded with a human face.

4.—Ju glaze with fish-roe crackle on a "copper" body.

5.—White Ting glaze. Only fên Ting was copied, and not the t'u Ting.

6.—Chün glazes. Nine varieties are given, of which five were copied from old palace pieces and four from newly acquired specimens.

7.—Reproductions of the chi hung red of the Hsüan Tê period: including the fresh red (hsien hung) and the ruby red (pao shih hung).

8.—Reproductions of the deep violet-blue (chi ch'ing) of the Hsüan Tê period. This glaze is deep and reddish, and has orange-peel marks and palm eyes.

9.—Reproductions of the glazes of the Imperial factory: including eel yellow, snake-skin green and spotted yellow.

10.—Lung-ch'üan glazes: including pale and dark shades.

11.—Tung-ch'ing glazes: including pale and dark shades.

12.—Reproductions of the Sung millet-coloured (mi sê) glaze: copied in form and colour from fragments dug up at Hsiang Hu.

13.—Sung pale green (fên ch'ing): copied from vares found at the same time as the last.

14.—Reproductions of "oil green" (yu lü) glaze: "copied from an old transmutation (yao pien) ware like green jade (pi yü) with brilliant colour broken by variegated passages and of antique elegance."

15.—The Chün glaze of the muffle kiln (lu chün): "the colour is between that of the Kuangtung wares and the Yi-hsing applied glaze (kua yu); and in the or amental markings (hua wên) and the transmutation tints of the flowing glaze it surpasses them."

16.—Ou's glazes, with red and blue markings.

17.—Blue mottled (ch'ing tien) glazes: copied from old Kuang yao.

18.—Moon white (üeh pai) glazes. "The colour somewhat resembles the Ta Kuan glaze, but the body of the ware is white. The glaze is without crackle, and there are two shades—pale and dark."

19.—Reproductions of the ruby red (pao shao) of the Hsüan Tê: the decoration consisting of (1) three fishes, (2) three fruits, (3) three fungi, or (4) the five Blessings. . . . Hobson adds this note:—"Symbolized by five bats. The Blessings are: longevity, riches, peace and serenity, love of virtue and an end crowning the life."

20.—Reproductions of the Lung-ch'üan glaze with ruby red decoration of the kind just described. "This is a new style of the reigning dynasty."

21.—Turquoise (fei ts'ui) glazes. Copying three sorts: (1) pure turquoise, (2) blue flecked, and (3) gold flecked (chin tien).

22.—Soufflé red (ch'ui hung) glaze.

23.—Soufflé blue (ch'ui ch'ing) glaze.

24.—Reproductions of *Yung Lo* porcelain: egg-shell *(t'o t'ai)* pure white with engraved *(chui)* or embossed *(kung)* designs.

25.—Copies of *Wan Li* and *Chêng Tê* enamelled *(wu ts'ai)* porcelain.

26.—Copies of *Ch'êng Hua* enamelled *(wu ts'ai)* porcelain.

27.—Porcelain with ornament in *Hsüan Tê* style in a yellow ground.

28.—*Cloisonné* blue *(fa ch'ing)* glaze. "This glaze is the result of recent attempts to match this colour (i.e. the deep blue of the *cloisonné* enamels). As compared with the deep and reddish *chi ch'ing*, it is darker and more vividly blue *(ts'ui)*, and it has no orange-peel or palm-eye markings."

29.—Reproductions of European wares with lifelike designs carved and engraved. "Sets of the five sacrificial utensils, dishes, plates, vases and boxes and the like are also decorated with coloured pictures in European style."

30.—Reproduction of wares with incised green decoration in a yellow glaze *chiao huang).*

31.—Reproductions of yellow glazed wares: including plain monochromes and those with incised ornament.

32.—Reproductions of purple brown *(tzŭ)* glazed wares: including plain monochromes and those with incised ornament.

33.—Porcelain with engraved ornament: including all kinds of glazes.

34.—Porcelain with embossed *(tui)* ornament: including all kinds of glazes.

35.—Painted red *(mo hung)*: copying old specimens.

36.—Red decoration *(ts'ai hung)*: copying old specimens. Note by Hobson:—"The *ts'ai hung* has the design painted in iron-red on a white ground."

37.—Porcelain in yellow after the European style.

38.—Porcelain in purple brown *(tzŭ)* after the European style.

39.—Silvered *(mo yin)* porcelain.

40.—Porcelain painted in ink *(shui mo)*.

41.—Reproductions of the pure white *(t'ien pai)* porcelain of the *Hsüan Tê* period: including a variety of wares thick and thin, large and small.

42.—Reproductions of *Chia Ching* wares with blue designs.

43.—Reproductions of *Ch'êng Hua* pale painted *(tan miao)* blue designs.

44.—Millet coloured *(mi se)* glazes. "Differing from the Sung millet coloured." In two shades, light and dark.

45.—Porcelain with red in the glaze *(yu li hung)*: including (1) painted designs exclusively in red, (2) the combination of blue foliage with red flowers

46.—Reproductions of lustrous brown *(tzŭ chin)* glaze: including two varieties, brown and yellow.

47.—Porcelain with yellow glaze *(chiao huang)* decorated in enamel colours *(wu ts'ai)*. "This is the result of recent experiments."

48.—Reproductions of green-glazed porcelain: including that with plain ground and engraved ornament.

49.—Wares with foreign colours *(yang ts'oi)*. "In the new copies of the Western style of painting in enamels *(fa-lang)* the landscapes and figure scenes, the flowering plants and birds are without exception of supernatural beauty and finish."

50.—Porcelain with embossed ornament *(kung hua)*: including all kinds of glazes.

51.—Porcelain with European *(hsi yang)* red colour.

52.—Reproductions of *(wu chin)* mirror black glazes: including those with black ground and white designs and those with black ground and gilding.

53.—Porcelain with European green colour.

54.—European *wu chin* (mirror black) wares.

55.—Gilt *(mo chin)* porcelain: copying the Japanese.

56.—Porcelain with gilt designs *(miao chin)*: copying the Japanese.

57.—Porcelain with silver designs *(miao yin)*: copying the Japanese.

58.—Large jars *(ta kang)* with Imperial factory glazes. "Dimensions: diameter at mouth, 3' 4" or 5" to 4'; height, 1' 7" or 8" to 2'. Glaze colours: (1) eel yellow, (2) cucumber green, and (3) mottled green and yellow *(huang lü tien)*."

Certain conclusions are obvious from a perusal of Hsieh Min's list:—First and most evident is a desire to retreat from the contemporary decadent designs and practices and return to the old traditions. Sick art often like the captive octopus sets out to devour itself. There is commendable revulsion of feeling against what is bad but, with the old spirit lacking, the reproduction is still revealing of the decadence in the heart of the people. The wares of Lung-ch'üan, Ch'ü-chou, Ting Chou and Chün Chou (now called Fu Chou) were attempted but they could not come alive again. The bodies of the reproductions are perfect and cold, hard and white. The potters sensed this and tried to dress the foot-rims with ferruginous clay but this would not look the same or *be* the same, of course. Second, the Ming wares were closer in imitation because the bodies were similar white porcelain. The K'ang Hsi wares were continued rather than copied but with differences and with even more perfection.

Third, we see another revolt against the overcrowded design which had

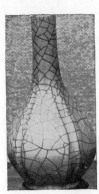

FIG. 857. Ko type pentagonal bottle with greenish grey glaze and the usual broad crackle of black. Ht. 8″. Guy Mayer Coll.

FIG. 858. Yung Chêng cherry red porcelain bottle of glossy but somewhat pitted glaze of even red more lightly mottled than streaked as in the sang-de-boeuf ones of the former reign. Ht. 12½″. Metropolitan Mus. of Art.

FIG. 859. Pale "celadon" glazed vase with paler glaze inside and brown lip rim. The glaze, not crackled is very glossy. Yung Chêng period. Ht. 12″. Metropolitan Mus. of Art.

FIG. 860. Yung Chêng, Ko type bottle with brownish grey glaze and large black and brown crackle. Ht. 17½″. Ex T. C. Lee–Warren E. Cox Coll.

FIG. 861. "Mazarine blue," vase of the Yung Chêng period. Ht. 15″. Metropolitan Mus. of Art.

FIG. 862. Large Yung-chêng vase of what is known as "orange peel" surface on a glaze of pale celadon green mottled with a dull strawberry color. Ht. 14½″. Altman Coll. Metropolitan Mus. of Art.

FIG. 863. Yung Chêng vase with clear green celadon glaze similar to the finest Lung chuan type but more even. Ht. 14¼″. T. C. Lee–Warren E. Cox Coll.

FIG. 864. Corinthian purple vase with greenish white glaze onto which was blown manganese in a technique like that of the powder blue wares. Yung Chêng. Ht. 6¾″. Perry Moore–Warren E. Cox Coll.

FIG. 865. Yung Chêng sage green plate with arabic inscription seemingly on an etched ground in low relief. Dia. 7″. Metropolitan Mus. of Art.

FIG. 866. Bottle with "Kuan yao" glaze of pale blue-green crackled irregularly with brown on a white porcelain body but with the foot-rim dressed with brown-black. Ht. 21″. Warren E. Cox Coll.

grown in greater and greater trade demands. The Chinese themselves seemed to prefer monochromes. Crackle was mastered in technique. Flambé of copper red streaked with blue or grey or purple was richly made although the actual fact was that tendencies had always been apparent in the sang de boeuf to streak in this way and what really happened was that rather than strive to

FIG. 867. Yung Chêng vase decorated with underglaze blue and peachbloom pink. A good sturdy shape and beautiful design. Ht. 14¼". Seattle Art Mus. Fuller Coll.

FIG. 868. Yung Chêng black glazed vase with gold decoration. Ht. 19". Formerly Garland Coll.

FIG. 869. Yung Chêng bottle in the wrongly called "Mazarine blue" which has a more porous and duller glaze than usually seen on K'ang Hsi pieces of the same color. Ht. 8½". Metropolitan Mus. of Art.

FIG. 870. Blue and white vase of the period showing a typical softened "Mingish" shape and over ornate dragon design. The dragon has iron red added over the blue. (1723–1735). Metropolitan Mus. of Art.

overcome the effect the potters decided it was easier to make use of it. Tea-dust of olive and brownish-green finely speckled and smooth, but a sort of super refined Sixth Dynasty glaze with less appeal for many, was developed.

There were also glazes made to imitate the poor European imitations of Chinese glazes. Blue and white was made frequently without shading to imitate the Ming ones but with a dull blue. The fashion for these was past and no care was taken in their manufacture. The imitations of Chia Ching dark violet Mohammedan blue and also of the Ch'êng Hua light tracery in blue were good enough to fool those who had not seen the real thing. The peculiar Ming foot was meticulously copied and every effort seemed to have been made to deceive. "Soft paste" blue and white was very well copied. And the wares with underglaze blue and enamels of yellow or red were not neglected.

The various underglaze reds were so well copied that collectors are still doubtful about many of the existing stem cups with red fishes on them and other red wares. Most that we see are, of course, of this period, if they have any age at all. The use of ruby red under a celadon glaze was supposed to have been invented at this time but, as we have seen, actually goes back much

Left: Yung Chêng very pale celadon vase with underglaze red mottled with green (like peachbloom glaze). Note that this shape has slightly more rounded shoulders than the K'ang Hsi peachbloom vases, the rings on the neck are higher. Ht. 8″. Metropolitan Mus. of Art.

Center: Yung Chêng large vase of a shape typical of the period. It is pale celadon decorated with gray, blue, brown, green, iron red and gold. Ht. 17″. Metropolitan Mus. of Art.

Right: Yung Chêng gallipot with low relief design of dragons in pale greenish white and ground of waves in underglaze red. Ht. 13″. Bequest of Mrs. H. O. Havemeyer. Metropolitan Mus. of Art.

Bowl decorated "in underglaze copper red and enamels." Dia. 6½″. Bequest of Edward G. Kennedy. Metropolitan Mus. of Art.

Yung Chêng porcelain cup of the type known as *Ku Yüeh Hsüan.* Dia. about 3″. Freer Gallery of Art, Washington.

Right: "Wine pot" (hu) or "sêng-mao-hu" (monk's cap jug) which originated in the Yung Lo reign and were often made in red and celadon in the Hsüan-tê reign *(see text).* Ht. 6″. Smaller than the Ming ones. Bequest of Mrs. H. O. Havemeyer. Metropolitan Mus. of Art.

One of pair of stem cups for wine. Ming type and decorated similariy but of the Yung Cheng period (1722–. 1735). Ht. 3″. Metropolitan Mus. of Art.

A large fish bowl of the Yungchêng period decorated with *famille rose* enamels and having a black ground. Inside is a broad and lively treatment of lotus and gold fish which must be very effective when waterplants and real fish are added. Ht. 15¼″. Altman Coll. Metropolitan Mus. of Art.

One of pair of eggshell porcelain lanterns with vivid famille verte enamel decoration. The stands are modern. Bequest of Edward C. Kennedy. Metropolitan Mus. of Art.

YUNG CHÊNG DECORATED WARES

PLATE 164

earlier. Variations grew out of this ware to include underglaze red and blue on white slip with a celadon ground or a lavender blue ground. These colors were all rather unpleasant together but the French liked them and even mounted specimens with ormolu mounts.

FIG. 871. Bowl of Ku-yüeh-hsüan type of semi-eggshell delicately painted with a poppy design on the outside and fruits inside, in polychrome. The mark is Yung Chêng as is the period. Dia. about 3". Guy Mayer Coll.

FIG. 872. Wine pot and jar of the Yung Chêng period and decorated with underglaze blue and red. The pieces are fitted nicely together to form what appears to be a gourd wine pot. It is thought that hot water was placed in the lower jar to keep the wine warm. Ht. 7½". Metropolitan Mus. of Art.

In enameled wares the new opaque colors almost at once became popular and we have the full flowering of the famille rose decorations, ornate to begin with and growing ever more so. On the other hand copies were made of the Ch'êng Hua underglaze blue and pale transparent enameled ware. T'ang Ying explains in his twenty illustrations of the processes of porcelain manufacture, that "yang ts'ai" or "foreign coloring" was used and adds that the

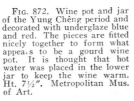

FIG. 873. Yung Chêng plate with greenish white ground, flowers in uneven iron red and gold, deep blue enamel, three greens and no rose. Dia. 14". Gift of W. B. Osgood Field. Metropolitan Mus. of Art.

FIG. 874. Yung Chêng "marriage plate." The border is in iron red and gold, the rest is in famille rose colors, the rose being pale in color and the blue also pale. Dia. 8". "Eggshell potting." Metropolitan Mus. of Art.

FIG. 875. Yung Chêng plate with famille rose enamel decoration including a pale rose. Dia. 13". Metropolitan Mus. of Art. Gift of W. B. Osgood Field.

colors were the same as those for enameling on metal, "fo lang yao," which was a term used to speak of cloisonné and painted enamels such as were applied near Canton. These were, according to Hobson, believed by the Chinese to have come from Ku li (Calicut) and might possibly have been French enamels imported through that port. Hippisley probably correctly

FIG. 876. Yung Chêng Ko type cup with gray glaze and dark gray crackle. It seems to be of gray ware and to have about a ¼" wide foot rim. Ht. 1¾". Metropolitan Mus. of Art.

FIG. 877. Yung Chêng plate c. 1725 of the so called "Jesuit ware" painted in iron red and gold with "the baptism of Christ." Dia. 8½". Metropolitan Mus. of Art.

FIG. 878. Yung Chêng Tê-hua, Fukien cup rather heavily potted and pure white. The glaze is more glassy than in Ming examples and less full of bubbles than in the Ch'ien Lung ones. Ht. 3". Metropolitan Mus. of Art.

suggests that pictures by Jesuit artists such as Gherardini and Belleville were also sources of design.

The arsenious white continued and also a rose-pink made from precipitate of gold or "purple of Cassius" and this latter was developed into many shades of ruby, carmine and light rose called by the Chinese "yen chih hung" or rouge red. Most enamels were more opaque than the K'ang Hsi ones and many new colors were brought about by mixing. This was not so easy as it sounds for the chemical reactions of one color upon another cannot always be foreseen: Iron red was mixed with a flux to make "tsao hung" or "jujube-red" as it is called and the brown-black mixed with a flux made "European black."

The wares painted at Ching-tê Chêng were delicate and effeminate but with some taste and allowed a fair amount of the pure white to show. This white is more glossy than the K'ang Hsi and very perfect. However, other wares were made and shipped as "blancs" to Canton where they could be decorated in closer touch with the foreign buyers. These were of course a step down, and it was here that the designs took on more of the characteristics of cloisonné and were made more and more ornate to give the customer more for his money in competition with other wares. "Seven border" plates on which you can count the borders were made with center medallions of flower baskets, Chinese interiors with ladies and children (a subject the Chinese love), dishes of fruit, bird and flower subjects such as pheasants and rocks, cocks and peonies, and quail in millet, etc. Sometimes these borders were broken with inserted medallions to add further richness. Some of these plates had decoration in overglaze blue, or black and gold, or at times in ruby pink or gold alone. Many of them have the solid ruby color on the backs and are known in Europe as "ruby backed porcelain." Another large group has the plain ruby ground broken by medallions of white containing varicolored decorations, and these are not only small objects and plates but great garniture sets.

These were painted in and about Canton and some are even so signed. One in the B.M. is signed Pai-shih and has the inscription "ling nan hui che" which means "Canton picture."

T'ang Ying is supposed also to have invented the use of silver for grounds and for painting, but Père d'Entrecolles referred to it as early as 1722.

One favorite trick that the Yung Chêng artists employed was to start the design on the back of a plate, bring it on over to the front, and sometimes around to the back again as though it were wrapped about the piece.

It can be said that these painters did render natural objects with simple mastery and that their flowers are beautiful if they were only not so crowded. Of course they were nowhere nearly so alive as were those of the Sung period even though all the colors were employed now and the Sung ones were in brown or black. Yung Chêng flowers are like those drawn for the scientists of a natural history museum with all the parts correct but no living, growing unity; they are painstaking rather than swift and alive.

THE CH'IEN LUNG PERIOD (1736–1796)

A fourth son again ascended the throne and there seemed luck in this for he was one of the most enlightened monarchs of history. Master not only of

FIG. 879. Ch'ien Lung vase called "clair de lune" by the museum but actually of a pale celadon color. Ht. 6″. Bequest of Mary Clark Thompson. Metropolitan Mus. of Art.
FIG. 880. Rare Ching Period "Celadon" and Blue Jar. Possibly a mortuary jar for the characters on the shoulder read, "Precious grasses in the mountain ҕhal have 1 o seeds, Peach blossoms in a cave have their own spring," and the four large characters read, "never," "mountain," "get old or die," "green." The seal reads, "Mr. Wu Chang, Fairy Kiln near Soo Chou."
FIG. 881. Ch'ien Lung camellia green bottle with fine crackle of the sort called "fish roe." It has a black lip rim. Ht. 15″. Metropolitan Mus. of Art.

the arts of peace but also of war, his empire included Chinese Turkestan and Tibet while he exerted some power over India. Burma, Siam and Annam also became tributaries.

The technician T'ang Ying succeeded Nein Hsi-yao at Huai-an Fu as director of the factories. In 1739 he was transferred to Kui-kiang but before he took his post he wrote notes covering his work. The *T'ao-lu* eulogizes him as the all time master of porcelain and claims that "The Imperial wares attained their greatest perfection at this time," but actually his inventions consisted chiefly of new additions to the already too broad palette of the "foreign colors" and further copies of the old glazes which were in some cases even more meticulous than those of Yung Chêng times. One popular stunt

Left: Cherry red flambé jar with only the faintest streaks of blue toward the top. Glazed under the foot with transparent yellow brown and at lip with greenish white. Ht. about 16″. Courtesy of Mrs. David Zipkin. Ex Warren E. Cox Coll.

Right: Ch'ien Lung vase with olive green tea dust glaze of a greener and more even and thinner texture than that seen on Sung examples. The inside has an irregularly crackled greenish white glaze. Ht. 14″. H. O. Havemeyer Bequest. Metropolitan Mus. of Art.

Left: Impressive turquoise blue vase with low relief decoration under a brilliant transparent glaze. Ch'ien Lung period. Ht. 24″. Altman Coll. Metropolitan Mus. of Art.

Ch'ien Lung porcelain *ku* or beaker cup made at Ching-tê Chên after an ancient Shang period bronze type. It is of white porcelain with a rich turquoise glaze, crackled. Ht. 11″. Gift of Mrs. Dora Delano Forbes. Mus. of Fine Arts, Boston.

Ch'ien Lung turquoise blue or "peacock blue" bottle with delicately incised design under the glaze. The potting is thin and true. Ht. 10½″. Metropolitan Mus. of Art.

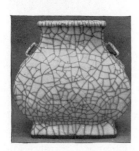

Right: Deep cobalt blue vase with rich glaze. Ch'ien Lung seal mark and of the period. Ht. 7½″. Perry Moore–Warren E. Cox Coll.

Ko type 18th cent. vase with greenish gray glaze and dark gray crackle. It is very much like the real Ko yao (See Sung section) but more glossy. Ht. 7½″. Metropolitan Mus. of Art.

Left: Peacock blue vase with the usual fine "fish roe" crackle. Ch'ien Lung period. Ht. 8½″. Perry Moore–Warren E. Cox Coll.

CH'IEN LUNG SINGLE COLOR PORCELAINS

Plate 165

of bad taste was the attempt to copy ancient bronzes and jades by casting direct from specimens and making glazes to more or less imitate the textures.

CH'IEN LUNG GLAZES

The sang de boeuf reds were, according to Hobson, conspicuously wanting in control of glaze and streaked with grey or blue and purple much as were the flambé types. This seems highly doubtful to me for in one breath we say that these craftsmen were over careful in detail and in the next we declare them careless. Why suddenly at the end of the K'ang Hsi reign at just the time when the great technician was put in charge of the factories should the potters suddenly become careless in the handling of this one ware? All of the K'ang Hsi sang de boeuf pieces were certainly not perfectly controlled as to glaze, as we have said, and now I am certain that some of the Ch'ien Lung ones were quite perfectly made. How to make a clear distinction between the wares of the two periods in a case like this where style of design cannot be considered is impossible to answer. Yet to the old collectors of K'ang Hsi sang de boeuf vases, who were millionaires and, by their very natures, precisionists at heart, it would have been almost a personal insult to say that one of their treasures might have been made after 1736 instead of just before 1722. Those 14 years might mean the difference between $200 and $20,000 literally, while the same generation thought nothing of slapping a whole classification such as the "three color" K'ang Hsi wares back a hundred years into Ming. Actually there was an increasing decadence but it was a general and gradual one and the trend was not toward loss of meticulous care in Ch'ien Lung times but quite the opposite; too much embroidered care exerted on subjects of too little taste. Carelessness did creep in but certainly not invariably.

FIG. 882. Ch'ien Lung olive green vase with gray crackle and dark brown foot. It is more glassy than the Ch'u-chou examples of the Ming and K'ang Hsi periods. Ht. 7". Bequest of Mary Clark Thompson. Metropolitan Mus. of Art.
FIG. 883. Ko type Ch'ien Lung vase of pale "celadon" green with a black crackle in a bubbly but glassy glaze. Ht. 6½". Metropolitan Mus. of Art.
FIG. 884. Ch'ien Lung "mirror black" bottle with rough glaze and pasty white inside. The body is grayish. Ht. 8". Isaac D. Fletcher Bequest. Metropolitan Mus. of Art.
FIG. 885. Ch'ien Lung iron rust glazed vase. Ht. 7". Metropolitan Mus. of Art.

While we are on this subject I should like to point out to the reader that ever since Ming days we have repeatedly described the paste as being smooth and dense and the glaze high-fired, perfect and white. Of course, it is true that both improved in this 100-year span just as they improved in the 275-year span of the Ming Dynasty, but to say that some of the finest and most delicate Ming wares are not just as pure and well potted as the finest of the 18th century ones is ridiculous. To say that all Ming paste has minute pits in it is false as it is to say that pits never occur in later pastes. Actually when we get down to facts there is little or no real *proof* that such a vase is K'ang Hsi and such an one Ch'ien Lung, or that such a piece is Yung Chêng and such an one Ming. It is not always the easiest thing in the world for a collector to be sure that some odd specimen was made before or after the 450-year stretch from Sung to Yung Chêng days, though this is, of course, easier. We can only go on the rather vague and often badly translated Chinese written descriptions, on the comparatively few drawings which were

FIG. 886. Ch'ien Lung vase with soft rose colored glaze which is glossy and unlike *sang de pigeon* ones of similar shape. Ht. 11″. Ex T. C. Lee–Warren E. Cox Coll. Now Mrs. Clark Getts Coll.

FIG. 887. Bottle vase with glaze of Kuan type of pale blue-green with hardly perceptible helically twisted crackle. White porcelain but with foot dressed in black. Ht. 22½″. Warren E. Cox Coll.

FIG. 888. Ch'ien Lung bottle of a shape never earlier than Yung Cheng covered with an iron rust glaze to emulate that of the Honan temmokus of the Sung period. Ht. 13″. Bequest of H. O. Havemeyer. Metropolitan Mus. of Art.

none too perfect either in color or scale and on the putting of two and two together. Therefore, we must be just as careful not to become too pedantic as we are not to become too loose in our judgments.

Liver red and sang de pigeon or "crimson" mat glazes filled with small pores and even in texture were more popular than in K'ang Hsi times for many thousands must have been made judging by the number still available. The series of almost identical vases illustrated show how difficult it is to judge between Yung Chêng and late 19th century pieces unless they are marked and comparisons can be made.

Iron rust glaze of dark brown with metallic flakes in it, "ch'a yeh mo" or tea-dust, an ocherous brown or bronze green dusted with tea-green and

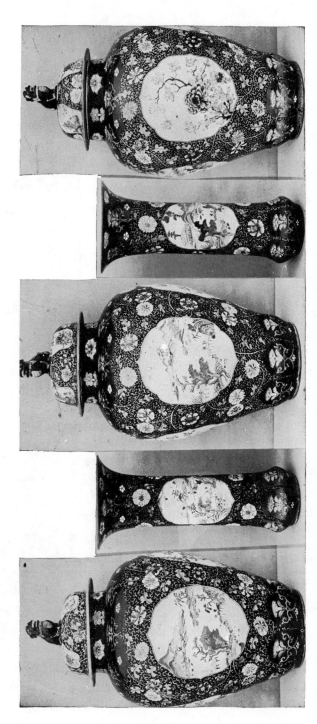

A large garniture set of famille rose vases with reserve medallions painted with landscapes set on a black ground ornamented with green leaves and rose enamel flowers. Type often called Yung Chêng but that was a short period and most of them are more likely Ch'ien Lung as these are marked in the museum. Hts. 24″ and 19″. Metropolitan Mus. of Art.

CH'IEN LUNG FAMILLE ROSE GARNITURE SET

PLATE 166

such glazes were frequent. All the range of green from the yellowish tones of the "camellia green" to those of turquoise blue and peacock were continued as were also the grey crackled wares after Ko yao. Sage tints and also "robin's egg blue" both plain and soufflé continued. It is said that the turquoise ones of the later period had a more reddish body which was sometimes rough because iron was mixed with it to help develop the color, but this is again a mere rule of thumb and highly doubtful.

Large bottle of pale "celadon" color with rose and yellow peaches, two greens, white and pink blossoms, etc. Ht. 18". Ch'ien Lung period. Bequest of Isaac D. Fletcher. Metropolitan Mus. of Art.

Yung Chêng large jar with greenish white ground and famille rose enamel decoration freely and well painted. The handles are coral or iron red. Ht. 19". Metropolitan Mus. of Art.

Ch'ien Lung bottle of a shape which originated in the Yung Chêng period with greenish white ground and decorated in famille rose colors and black. Ht. 10". Metropolitan Mus. of Art.

Ch'ien Lung bowl of the "Chinese Lowestoft" type rather heavily potted with famille rose colors, iron red and gold, the whole rather deep in color. The rim is unglazed at the top of the cover. Dia. 11". Metropolitan Mus. of Art.

Center: Ch'ing dynasty, Ch'ien Lung porcelain vase with famille rose colors. Ht. 9¾". Freer Gallery of Art, Washington.
Right: Cafe au lait vase and cover with reserved medallions. Ht. 18". Bequest of Mary Clark Thompson. Metropolitan Mus. of Art.

CH'IEN LUNG FAMILLE ROSE ENAMEL DECORATED VASES

PLATE 167

ENAMEL MONOCHROMES

The "mei kuei" or rose pink which T'ang Ying writes about was an enamel color such as that used for decorations and also for the backs of the "ruby backed plates." It now was applied with a rumpled surface like an orange peel and is sometimes clouded with deeper tones making a sort of famille rose flambé. The ware is usually thin and small cabinet vases are in the majority.

Other enamel monochromes are: lemon yellow which is opaque and rough, mustard yellow which is crackled, cloisonné blue, amaranth blue, "jujube-red" which is a thickly fluxed iron red, opaque turquoise green and finally an enamel black called "lac black." Of course all of the K'ang Hsi enamels and glazes too were continued.

FAMILLE ROSE WARES AND OTHERS

Among other enamel stunts we find the imitation bronzes made with imitations of inlay and also various copies of cloisonné, green jade, Peking lacquer, grained wood, millefiore glass, etc. The *T'ao shu* says, "Among all the works of art in carved gold, embossed silver, chiselled stone, lacquer, mother of pearl, bamboo and wood, gourd and shell, there is not one that is not now produced in porcelain, a perfect copy of the original piece." Of course this outrages one of the first principles of good art namely that one should express the medium in which the work is done.

At this time most of the "lac burgauté," which was also made in K'ang

FIG. 889. Ch'ien Lung blue and white jar of a shape often seen in Yung Chêng soft paste. Note the relief floral decoration. Ht. 11½". Metropolitan Mus. of Art.

FIG. 890. K'ang Hsi white porcelain vase with black lacquer (cold color) inlaid with mother of pearl. Ht. 8". Metropolitan Mus of Art.

FIG. 891. Ch'ien Lung porcelain vase decorated with carved cinnabar lacquer applied cold, of course. From *Chinese Lacquer* by Ed. F. Strange. Ht. 13½".

FIG. 892. Porcelain vase in lac burgautée of green and reddish-purple on black lacquer ground. Ch'ien Lung. Ht. 12¾". From *Chinese Lacquer*.

Hsi and even Ming times, was made. This is porcelain covered with black lacquer inlayed with mother of pearl. Even in Chou times this unhappy combination of lacquer on a pottery body was employed but there was more excuse for it before glaze was developed.

The Ch'ien Lung blue and white is supposed to be far inferior to that of the K'ang Hsi reign and this is true of the ever declining export wares but in some instances there is fine drawing and good color. The blue came from the mountains of Chekiang now. Much of it has a reddish tinge and

FIG. 893. One of a pair of beautiful tile panels measuring 33″ by 14″ and painted in famille rose enamels. Ch'ien Lung or later. Ex Warren E. Cox Coll.

FIG. 894. Pilgrim bottle of heavy porcelain with greenish glaze and deep blue underglaze decoration in the feeling of Chêng Tê examples. Ht. 9⅜″. Warren E. Cox Coll.

FIG. 895. "Celadon" with underglaze red and blue design of pomegranates and "hands of Buddha." The glaze is glossy but rich, the ware is white but the foot rim, which is rounded, is dressed with brown. Ht. 6¾″. Ch'ien Lung period. Ex Warren E. Cox Coll.

all of it is softer looking than the earlier sort. Large services were made with identical designs on many pieces. When the blue was not covered with the glaze it fired black and we see specimens from time to time of this mat ware with dry black, whether intended as finished or not we do not know.

The soft paste was made in large quantities and had a better general quality probably because of the cost of the material. One sort had very definite brush strokes and was called "onion sprout ware."

Underglaze red with the combinations of celadon, etc., were carried on from the Yung Chêng reign. The only way to distinguish the one from the other is by general feel and style.

The T'ao shuo says in reference to the designs on enameled wares that, "out of every ten designs you will get four of foreign colors, three taken from

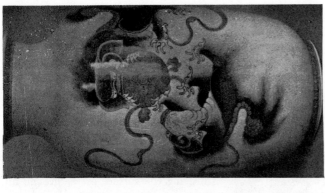

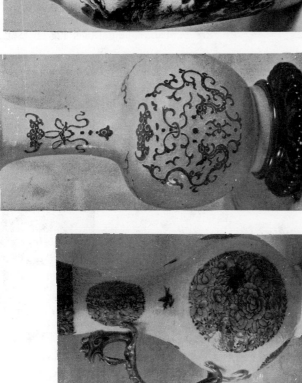

Left to Right: Ewer of fine white porcelain having a glossy glaze and "mille fleur" medallions in a slightly reddish blue. Ht. 10¼". Ch'ien Lung. Metropolitan Mus. of Art.

Ch'ien Lung porcelain vase with pale celadon glaze and decoration in dull blue with raised white edges similar to some of the Ming "Three color" jars in technique. Ht. 15". T. C. Lee—Warren E. Cox Coll.

Soft paste vase of the Ch'ien Lung period showing a soft "orange-peel" type glaze and slightly more reddish blue color. Ht. 15". Metropolitan Mus. of Art.

Ch'ien Lung blue and white porcelain vase with soft rich glaze and deep color. Ht. 16". Metropolitan Mus. of Art.

CH'IEN LUNG UNDERGLAZE BLUE DECORATION

PLATE 168

nature, two copies of antiques and one from silk brocade or embroidery." The nature subjects were landscapes, flowering plants, birds and trees, "mille fleurs" or thousand flowers, the "hundred deer," the "hundred birds" and combinations of pines and willows, etc. The brocade patterns use many borders as in earlier times.

FIG. 896. Memorial plate with tomb of Antoni van Leeuwenhock, the Dutch microscopist as design, in famille rose decoration. Dia. 8". Metropolitan Mus. of Art.

The European influence is seen on every hand and the use of careful shading to produce a round or three dimensional effect is frequent.

One rather pleasant texture is obtained in incising the surface of the ground all over with feathery scrolls, etc., and covering them with enamel colors such as turquoise, pink, yellow, green, lavender or grey. Some of these are monochromes and some have reserved medallions unincised and uncolored in which paintings are made of flowers, etc. "Peking bowls" were made at Ching-tê Chêng like the others and sent to Peking to the palace or for sale. These were continued in subsequent reigns and the best of them are of Tao Kuang times (1821–1850).

FIG. 897. "Mille-fleurs vase" of the Ch'ien Lung period with reserve medallions in famille rose enamels. Ht. 31". Metropolitan Mus. of Art.
FIG. 898. The character Fu means bat and also happiness. This Ch'ien Lung gourd vase has "a thousand bats" in iron red against a gold ground while the scarf tied about it is in yellow and blue enamel. The seal mark is in overglaze blue. Ht. 8½". Warren E. Cox Coll.
FIG. 899. Famille rose type Ch'ien Lung vase with rose enamel and gilding. Ht. about 16".
FIG. 900. Famille rose Ch'ien Lung vase with well styled design more dynamic than usual in this period. Ht. 17⅜". Fuller Coll. Seattle Art Mus.

Left: Octagonal porcelain dish with greenish white ground, deep rose flowers, deep blue enamel, brown, gold and white enamel, etc. Ht. 14". Metropolitan Mus. of Art.

Right: Armorial plate with the arms of Antoni van Leeuwenhock. Dia. 8". Metropolitan Mus. of Art.

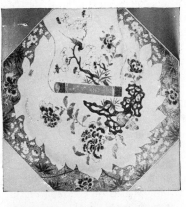

Plate with reticulated rim and decoration in pale famille rose colors. Ch'ien Lung period. Dia. 10½". Metropolitan Mus. of Art.

Left: Ch'ien Lung plate commemorating the signing of peace at Aix la Chapelle (1748) in iron red and gold,—a little pale pink, green, blue, etc. The patterns afforded by the book shelves, pictures and the hats hung on the walls have amusingly been taken account of. Dia. 8". Metropolitan Mus. of Art.

Right: Marriage plate with arms of two Dortrecht families, Beaumont and Backus and a design from the title page of an 18th cent. wedding song in black with flesh tones and a goll border. Dia. 8". Metropolitan Mus. of Art.

Portrait plate in famille rose colors of Antoni van Leeuwenhock, the Dutch microscopist. Dia. 8". Metropolitan Mus. of Art.

CH'IEN LUNG PLATES

PLATE 169

Another type is covered with a faintly greenish white which appears shrivelled and chilled and slightly lustrous.

Instead of incising under the iron red color similar designs of scrolls or foliage are painted in gold on top of it, and the same technique was used for a black ground, bronze-green and celadons. Gold also replaced brown on the edges of plates. "Foreign black" was applied like an enamel in famille rose design and also as a ground color with enameled scrolls in it looking like a sort of inlay. The old famille verte black was used in a special way in which a close floral scrollwork is reserved in white on the black ground and the whole covered with a transparent green.

"Ku-yüeh Porcelain"

At Peking were Imperial glass factories under the supervision of an artist whose name was Hu. As the component parts of the character Hu, if separated, read ku yüeh meaning ancient moon, naturally enough Hu adopted the studio name of Ku Yüeh Hsüan meaning Ancient Moon Pavilion. This glass was made in the Yung Chêng as well as the Ch'ien Lung reigns and the Emperor once expressed his admiration for the painting in enamels on it and wished that the same effect could be produced upon porcelain, whereupon T'ang Ying set out to make porcelain that looked like the glass and also did his best to copy the Ku-yüeh style of decoration consisting of floral designs and landscapes with figures, at times in foreign taste, very delicately painted and with an unusual amount of light and shade while being at the same time in the softest of colors. The glass was translucent and the porcelain gave a semblance of the material in its milky texture and glassy finish. The porcelain was known as "fang ku yüeh hsüan" or "imitation of Ku-yüeh-hsüan" and was greatly prized. Bushell (' Chinese Art" vol. ii, fig. 74.) shows a yellow glazed snuff bottle with the actual mark "Ku yueh hsuan chih." The glass itself is rare and Hobson refers to one example in the Hippisley Collection and another in the Ezekial Collection which is described as typical. The designs are, to quote him, 'Landscapes with dark brown rocks, flowering plants exquisitely drawn and coloured to Nature, and white robed figures," which he goes on to say should be characteristic of the porcelain. He shows what he is sure is a real example ("Later Ceramic Wares of China," Fig. 1 Pl. 26) and which has a stanza of verse on it with seals of the artist and under the foot the mark of Ch'ien Lung period in mauve enamel. This is a small bottle 3⅗" high with a flowering begonia, iris and hovering insect well painted on it. Actually the modeling which we are led to believe characteristic in strong light and shade is entirely missing. Perhaps this piece in the Sir Percival David Collection is actually the ware and perhaps not. Certainly the other pieces that are shown in the same book are very distant cousins.

At the Boston Museum of Fine Arts there is a vase about 9" tall which is thought to be at least of the style but probably not one of T'ang Ying's actual pieces. Yamanaka & Co. sold one reportedly to Mrs. Christian R. Holmes for some $60,000 and were offering it recently for $25,000. This example certainly has the modeling in light and shade and the greatest delicacy of painting and it is probably entirely correct so far as I can see. On the

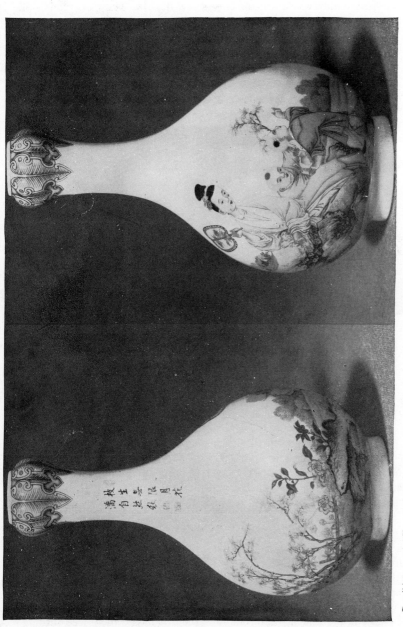

滿枝玉葉保昌花

KU-YÜEH PORCELAIN

PLATE 170

Possibly a real "Ku-yüeh Hsüan" porcelain reportedly sold to the late Mrs. C. R. Homes for $60,000 and now offered by Yamanaka & Co. for $25,000. Note the modeling of the faces and delicate flower painting. Also the poem supposedly a characteristic. Ht. 6″. Yamanaka & Co.

other hand the style carried on into the 19th century and perfectly modern copies are made today which sell for only a few dollars. The meticulous skill in detail of painting is not wanting either even on these modern examples though they are likely to show some carelessness in such details as the even spacing of the borders, if examined carefully. Certain of these modern pieces

Fig. 901. Bottle (tan p'ing) said to be in Ku Yüeh style. Poem reads, "With morning light the lovely moon has gone: But every year we know that spring comes on." Usual square Ch'ien Lung four character mark appears on bottom in pale blue enamel. Ht. 5½". Sir Percival David Coll.

Fig. 902. Vase of the "Ku-yüeh-hsüan type," but certainly not a real one. Note careful shading of flowers, the poem on shoulder and very white, soft looking ground. Ht. c. 9". Mus. of Fine Arts, Boston.

were sold quite unsuspectingly by reputable dealers when they first appeared on the market and others have been sold with intent to deceive.

This was not the only departure from the standard porcelain for there were others and we also find such combinations as the Ku-yüeh painting on ordinary porcelain or on a peculiarly ivory white ware of fine quality. The glassy porcelain also occurs with delicate underglaze blue decoration and that very delicate sort which is first incised and then rubbed with a little blue so that only a faint tracery is perceived under the glaze. Other wares are seen in the snuff bottles which came into use during the 18th century and some of these were probably not made at Ching-tê Chêng at all.

CARVED AND MODELED WARES

Modeled figures or partly modeled and partly molded figures decorated with famille rose enamels are fairly common. Carving and reticulation were carried to a technical extreme and there are vases hung on porcelain chains, with freely moving belts or necks made so that they can turn and yet cannot be removed from the body. One of the most amazing I have seen consisted of three vases in a stand made to embrace them and yet allow free turning. The bases which were hidden in the bottom of the stand had been made like cogwheels which engaged so that when one vase was turned the others also moved. How this was fired it would be difficult to conceive for there was no

Tea pot heavily potted, of glossy white with relief flowers in iron red, gold and famille rose. 6" long. Metropolitan Mus. of Art.

Lantern of white rcelain with famille se decoration. Ht. ". Metropolitan us. of Art.

Ch'ing-tê Chên porcelaneous vase with brown glaze molded meticulously after ancient shape of Shang bronze "ku." 18th cent. Ht. 9¾". Mus. of Fine Arts, Boston.

Ch'ien Lung bottle with tea-dust glaze and plums modeled in round and colored, pink, white, green and turquoise. Ht. 8¼". Fuller Coll. Seattle Art Mus.

Porcelain box and cover in famille rose decoration. Length 8".

Left to Right: Boy with lle-fleurs decoration on his e, in famille rose of light t. Ht. 14". Metropolitan us. of Art

Reticulated vase with solid container inside decorated in famille rose colors of white, blue, yellow, rose, greei :., enamels. Ht. 10½". Ex Avery Coll. Metropolitan Mus. of Art.

Pair of famille rose birds. Ht. c. 10". C. T. Loo & Co.

CH'IEN LUNG CARVED AND MODELED WARES

PLATE 171

way of getting inside to cut the parts free after firing. Very thin and often pierced lanterns on stands were a general output but bring high prices, if finely detailed.

One of the influences of metal work in the countries of Syria and Persia was the technique known in "Gombroon ware" of the Near East and the "devil's work" of the Far East. As early as the 12th century the Western Asian countries made reticulated ware the design of which was filled in with glaze. Such spaces had to be small or the glaze would melt out of them, and in China the ware was copied and called "rice grain" or "grain de riz"

FIG. 903. Yi-hsing yao vase, 18th cent. Famille rose enamel decoration. Ht. 4¾". T. C. Lee–Warren Cox Coll.

in French. The Japanese call it poetically "hotaradu" or "fire-fly" ware. This was also made with the soft paste of China, and at times supplemented with underglaze blue painting. It probably did not occur there until the 18th century and is typical of Ch'ien Lung work.

"Lace-work ware" was deeply incised, closely drawn floral scrolls covered with a glaze of faint celadon green tone. The result is a sort of overdoing of the incising of the Yung Lo bowls, etc.

"Mandarin porcelain" was so named because the figures on it were supposed to be in mandarin dress and the idea was to deceive the purchaser into believing that the ware was made for Imperial use. Actually no self-respecting Chinese would tolerate such a ware in his house. It was often covered with flowers and even figures stuck on in the round and overlayed with enamels in the worst possible taste with juxtaposition of pinks and reds plus gilding,

FIG. 904. Man with large head and small hands with enamels used to decorate robe. Holes for introduction of human hair for beard are found in figures back even in Ming days. Ht. 14¾". Metropolitan Mus. of Art.

FIG. 905. Figure of a woman in usual porcelain with enamel decorations. Ht. 15¼". Metropolitan Mus. of Art.

FIG. 906. Figure of Shou-lao after K'ang Hsi style but with famille rose enamel decoration which makes it Ch'ien Lung. Ht. 14". Metropolitan Mus. of Art.

etc. It is interesting to note similarities in expression between these decadent wares and those of Canosa. It took China a long time to arrive but when she did she not only added the extraneous junk but colored it to boot.

THE 19TH CENTURY

CHIA CH'ING (1796–1820), TAO KUANG (1821–1850), HSIEN FÊNG (1851–1861), T'UNG CHIH (1862–1873), KUANG HSÜ (1875–1908)

FIG. 907. "Mandarin style" vase with iron red, black and gold ground and relief flowers and figures in gold, blue, turquoise, pale green, rose and plum colored enamels. Worst taste of a well nigh tasteless period. Ht. 17″. Metropolitan Mus. of Art.

As I have said, history now had little effect upon the very sick art of ceramics. The Manchus were soft, and revolt and discontent were everywhere. A foreign war took place between 1840 and 1842 ending in the ceding of Hongkong to the British. In 1850 a band of semi-Christian fanatics brought about the T'ai P'ing Rebellion which lasted until 1865, with the result that legations were established in Peking. Many more ports were opened to foreign trade and the whole Far East was taught the real meaning of Western Civilization in detail.

CHIA CH'ING PORCELAIN (1796–1820)

In the Chia Ch'ing reign the potters tried to hold at least to Ch'ien Lung standards but were unable to do so. The wares were cruder and less well made.

TAO KUANG PORCELAIN (1821–1850)

By the Tao Kuang reign the wares show a marked degeneration. The body is chalky and coarse grained and the glaze though oily and bubbly has that muslin-like texture like the coarser Japanese wares. Peking medallion bowls are still of fairly good quality. A thin and very lustrous greenish wash was used to depict water in the landscapes. A ware with lightly incised Imperial dragons and covered with this same light greenish wash over which are enamel decorations is of this period though it has been contended that it might be earlier. It usually bears K'ang Hsi marks. Some other wares show a weak attempt to revive Yung Chêng styles and stunts.

HSIEN FÊNG (1851–1861) AND T'UNG CHIH (1862–1873)

In 1853 the T'ai P'ing Rebellion caused the burning down and wreckage of the kilns at Ching-tê Chêng and they were not rebuilt until 1864. Copies of sang de boeuf, apple green, peach bloom and famille noire wares are fairly good but not dangerous to any collector who had ever seen the real thing. Scherzer in 1882 was of the opinion that they might fool an unsuspecting collector but we have learned much since that time. He also speaks of one family named Ho which made sang de boeuf wares with coarse stoneware body and rather

Tao Kuang vase with turquoise ground and pale famille rose decoration. Ht. 12". Metropolitan Mus. of Art.

Tao Kuang vase with underglaze blue and red on white ground and with brown biscuit bands. Ht. 6". Metropolitan Mus. of Art.

Tao Kuang vase with underglaze blue decoration, underglaze red touches and white glaze. Dark bands are biscuit left unglazed and dressed with dark brown. Ht. 6½". Metropolitan Mus. of Art.

Hsien Fêng pale "celadon" plate with rounded foot dressed with brown slip and four character underglaze mark not centered and poorly written as usual with such late pieces. Dia. 5".

Left: Chia Ch'ing vase with yellow ground and iron red handles. Decoration in robin's-egg blue, and other famille rose colors of light tones. Inside is finished with blue. Ht. 12". Metropolitan Mus. of Art.
Right: Yellow ground vase with enamel decoration from Peking, of Kuang Hsü period and mark. Ht. 13". Ex Warren E. Cox Coll.

CHIA CH'ING, TAO KUANG, HSIEN FÊNG, AND KUANG HSÜ PORCELAIN

PLATE 172

too thick and uneven glaze and he calls this ware "kun houng" and says that no effort was made to control the glaze at the foot-rim. This may be the source of Hobson's statement but I have already gone into this and stated that even in K'ang Hsi times pieces were made with the glaze flowing over the foot-rim while later examples do also occur on which the glaze is stopped. Actually this is a generality and not an absolute rule at all. The

Jar of well modeled Chinese mandarin made in modern Shanghai factory. Courtesy of The Fan Co.

Pair of modern white porcelain figures with greyish body clay, probably made at Ching-tê Chêng. Ht. 15½". George Jensen, Inc.

Left: Mirror black vase of 19th cent., poorly made, glaze unrefined, having many raised specks in it and being roughly finished off at foot-rim. Glassy greenish white glaze faintly crackled inside. Ht. 11". Metropolitan Mus. of Art.

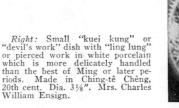

Right: Small "kuei kung" or "devil's work" dish with "ling lung" or pierced work in white porcelain which is more delicately handled than the best of Ming or later periods. Made in Ching-tê Chêng, 20th cent. Dia. 3⅛". Mrs. Charles William Ensign.

MODERN CHINESE PORCELAIN

PLATE 173

only way to judge between these later wares and the original ones is by that very hard to define element of quality. The later wares were made of less well refined clay, therefore the bodies are not so smooth to the touch nor the scratch of a fingernail. The potting was also less well done from start to finish. This is about all that can be said.

KUANG HSÜ AND MODERN (1875–1908)

Again the quality became steadily worse. Only recently, just before the war, some few pieces did come on the market which were of egg-shell thickness and made with incised dragon decorations and Yung Lo marks in the bottoms. At the same time certain all-over enameled decorations were applied on a similar very thin ware. They sold for fairly high prices ranging between $5 and $25 in this country, that is for modern wares, because they were well made. Also "devil's work" pieces were exceedingly well made, not in copy of the old but with original designs. Again the modeling shown in the pair of white figures illustrated and the jar in the form of a head is pleasing although the pair is so very much like two shown by a prominent dealer here, marked Ch'ien Lung and priced at $800, that they are probably direct copies.

OTHER CH'ING WARES
"INDIA CHINA," "LOWESTOFT," "JESUIT PORCELAIN," ETC.

Though lacking in any particular artistic merit some other wares have intrigued some collectors because of their historical interest. The various trading companies had made what are called "Company Porcelain" pieces. This ware in general is known as "East India Porcelain" not because it was ever made in India but because it came through the East India companies of the Dutch and English. Jacquemart thought that it came from Japan

FIG. 908. Imposing example of Canton decoration probably inspired by some Portuguese merchant for medallions show Spanish dancers. Scenes are almost monochrome being salmon buff with touches of color here and there. Ht. c. 15". The Fan Co.

FIG. 909. 19th-cent. Canton vases with carefully copied illustrations from a fairy tale book painted in western manner. Hts. c. 8". The Fan Co.

and the English characteristically, thinking it good and commendable as a product, adopted it, and their writers for some unknown reason attributed it to a little factory in Lowestoft which had never attained any distinction and never made any real "hard paste" porcelain. The ware was made in China and much of it right at Ch:ng-tê Chêng from where it was sent to places about Canton to be decorated in the merchant's taste. Hannover thinks the ware too poor to have been made at the chief center but I think he forgets how many factories were operating there and how poor were some of the wares made by some of them during this decline. That other factories also might have made blanks is undeniable for the quality varies greatly in its poor way.

Porcelain plate decorated with enamels in so-called "Sino-Lowestoft" manner and dated 1756. Metropolitan Mus. of Art.

"Chinese-Lowestoft" plate with Crucifixion in enamel colors and gold, made at Ching-tê Chêng and possibly decorated near Canton. Dia. 8¾". (c. 1750). Metropolitan Mus. of Art.

Plates having famille rose decoration of sort known for years as "Lowestoft" but made in China, probably for the French market as the borders show that taste. Dia. c. 10". John Gibbons Coll.

"CHINESE LOWESTOFT" OF THE 18TH CENTURY

PLATE 174

The decorations may be classed as follows:

1.—Ornamental borders only, outlined in brown and with gold, or with red and gold, or again with this combination and sprays of green added.

2.—Small scattered flowers in green and red.

3.—Large scattered flowers in underglaze blue of poor quality.

4.—Chinese landscapes in same medium.

5.—Same in iron red and gold.

6.—Same with little vases of flowers in black and gold.

7.—Customers' monograms in various colors.

8.—Large pieces with scenes from some historical painting or engraving and

Fig. 910. Chinese, so-called "Lowestoft" examples. Plate is of "Jesuit" type and platter "armorial." Plate dates c. 1750 and other pieces late 18th cent. Wm. H. Plummer & Co.

frequently with some added comical Chinese interpretation. These are usually punch bowls.

The Jesuit porcelain, the decoration of which was inspired by priests living in China, is a little better in quality and some is said to have been as early as Ming but I have never seen a convincing piece of this period. Père d'Entrecolles speaks of a piece as a rarity and we are therefore led to believe it was not made at Ching-tê Chêng during this time. The subjects comprise the crucifixion and other biblical subjects in black and gold. The same sort of porcelain was made with mythological subjects and some are frankly erotic.

Armorial wares were simply the same sort of porcelain with family shields, arms, etc., the designs of which were sent over and often misinterpreted by the Chinese artists. Monkhouse mentions one service in which the names of the colors were carefully copied but with the colors changed around so that the blue was labeled red, etc. The main interest lies in the fact that these wares can be dated closely. Thus the transition colors are placed about 1720 by examples in the B.M. Again we find that between 1711 and 1720 the "Chinese Imari" style was used. Those in the Yung Chêng reign show the pencilled underglaze blue. From Ch'ien Lung times the designs are more

FIG. 911. "Lowestoft" Chinese porcelain mon-tieth-handled jardinière of late 18th-cent. showing neo-classic influence. Philip Suval, Inc.

FIG. 912. "Sino-Lowestoft" porcelain bowl in soft enamel colors of sort possibly used to celebrate sailing of a certain ship and certainly not used on the ship itself. Dia. 10⅜″. (Late 18th cent.). Metropolitan Mus. of Art.

FIG. 914. Plate from well-known "Murhall Service," having coat of arms, crest and picture of castle. Ships to right are shown leaving for China and on left leaving China for home port, Plymouth, probably. Colors naturalistic. Made in South China near Canton, of type incorrectly known as "Lowestoft." John Gibbons Coll.

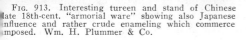

FIG. 913. Interesting tureen and stand of Chinese late 18th-cent. "armorial ware" showing also Japanese influence and rather crude enameling which commerce imposed. Wm. H. Plummer & Co.

and more Europeanized until about the middle of the 18th century we find Meissen floral sprays and later the little swags of flowers such as were used on Bow and Bristol, and again the French corn flower sprays. But all this gets out of our field. It got so complicated that the terrible "willow pattern" sentimentally concocted from Chinese originals was sent back to China to copy. Such is the effrontery of merchants!

There are many curiosities such as a pair of figures painted in enamels and made to represent Louis XIV and his queen. There were imitations of Delft ware, French faïence, and other things made for sale in Turkey, Siam, India and Persia.

Tê-hua, Fukien Porcelain

The Ming ware from Tê-hua has already been described and we have pointed out that during K'ang Hsi times the ware became whiter perhaps influenced by the white wares of Ching-tê Chêng. During the 17th and 18th centuries much of this ware was brought to Europe from Amoy and attempts were made to copy it in St. Cloud, Mennecy, Meissen and early Bow and Chelsea wares. None of these need bother the collector from the viewpoint of being mistaken for the original.

As for definitely dating Fukien porcelain our problem is somewhat more difficult. The Ming ones are heavily potted, with glaze melting into body, have a warm slightly rosy tinted glaze and the glaze is soft and melting; not glassy at all. I have never seen a fire crack in the bottom of one of these finest specimens.

The K'ang Hsi type, which may also extend back into late Ming times, seems somewhat higher fired, has fire cracks in the inside of the bottom, is made with thinner potting (probably in an effort to get away from the difficulties of fire cracks), has a pure white body and white glaze without warmth and the modeling is still very good but somewhat more detailed. D'Entrecolles wrote that in 1712 some of the Ching-tê Chêng potters went over to Tê-hua so that they could be nearer the Amoy port but that their ventures failed. Though the pure white ware had been made before, it is likely that from this date we get the much thinner glazed and harder looking ware.

We find in the *Li t'a k'an k'ao ku ou pien,* published in 1877 the following according to the Hobson translation, probably originally by Bushell, "When the glaze is white like jade, glossy and lustrous, rich and thick, with reddish tinge, and the biscuit heavy, the ware is of first quality . . . enameled specimens are second rate." Note that this does not specifically state that all such pieces are Ming. It also seems to indicate that the poorer type that is sometimes enameled is contemporary. However, I think we can assume that the enameled technique must have originated in Ching-tê Chêng, that, just as it was used in Meissen, the enamel was applied to cover up faults and that all such pieces are probably after 1712 or in late K'ang Hsi times.

In Yung Chêng times I think the general idea of reproducing antique pieces must have been responsible for a new technique which consisted of making the bodies somewhat heavier again but not so heavy as the Ming ones, allowing the body to stay white but covering it with a more glassy and warm colored glaze full of minute bubbles. Such a ware ran through Ch'ien Lung's reign and probably also later but sometime toward the end of the 18th century a reversion to the white ware in a cheaper and more pasty form was under way. The figures in the Yung Chêng and Ch'ien Lung glaze, which

Fine small white porcelain figures with cream glaze more glassy, filled with bubbles and less closely tied with body than in Ming ones. Ht. 5″. Warren E. Cox Coll.

Figure of Pu-tai a Buddhist priest of the Five Dynasties said to be an incarnation of Mi-lo-fu. Hands were made separately and stuck in by the glaze Glaze is glassy and full of minute bubbles. 7″. Metropolitan Mus. of Art.

Right: 18th-cent. figure of slightly greenish white. Foot c. 3/16″ thick and evenly glazed inside. Ht. 7½″. Metropolitan Mus. of Art.

CH'IEN LUNG, TÊ-HUA, FUKIEN PROVINCE FIGURES

PLATE 175

Left: Vase with delicately incised design of conventional petals above and below globular part. Into incising has been rubbed light blue under glaze. Has impressed Ch'ien Lung mark. Ht. 8". Warren E. Cox Coll.

Ornament consisting of pierced oval dish on which is modeled a fish. Biscuit pure white and glaze cream with warm colored crackle and high gloss, an exceedingly delicate and refined example, length 8". From T. C. Lee–Warren E. Cox Coll.

A fine example of *"blanc de chine"* obviously derived from bronze form but much added to by ornate low relief design which may have been carved direct and not simply cast in mold. Ht. 14½". Altman Coll. Metropolitan Mus. of Art.

18th-cent. vase with moulded design. Ht. 9". Metropolitan Mus. of Art.

Vase moulded with relief design, form being inspired by bronze model. Ht. 9". Bequest of Mrs. H. O. Havemeyer. Metropolitan Mus. of Art.

CH'IEN LUNG "BLANC DE CHINE" WARES MADE BY CHING-TÊ CHÊNG POTTERS

PLATE 176

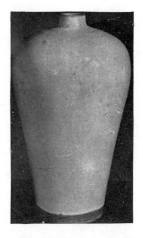

FIG. 915. Ch'ien Lung greenish white porcelain bell with incised design and the 8 trigrams around rim in pure white slip. Ht. 6". Metropolitan Mus. of Art.

FIG. 916. Fukien Tê Hua figure of Kwan Yin with child. Ch'ien Lung. Ht. 10". Warren E. Cox Coll.

FIG. 917. Kwangtung galli-pot of porous buff stoneware covered with opaque oyster-white crackled glaze showing pale green spots. Type still called "Ming" by trade though they date more often as late as Ch'ien Lung period (1736–1796). Ht. 11". Warren E. Cox Coll.

cannot be distinguished one from the other, are all sweeter and more effeminate in feeling.

Modern examples appear either cold, dead white or very glassy and sticky if of a warm color. The warm color is yellowish rather than rosy in tinge. The ware is coarse and gritty and there are almost always flaws due to careless workmanship.

The subjects of Tê-hua figures are the usual deities of both Buddhistic and Taoist faiths, lions for joss-sticks, imitations in form of rhinocerous horn cups, ewers and cups for tea and also for wine, furnishings of the writer's table, some rare European shapes (for these potters did not give in so readily to foreign trade suggestions), and finally, according to a Jesuit missionary who wrote in 1604, caricatures of Europeans particularly as the actors from Macao portrayed the Portuguese. The Chinese hated such things as, "the wearing of short garments which seemed ridiculous, praying on beads by men in the temples with swords girded on them and kneeling on one knee, their quarrels with one another and combats, women going with men in company, and the like." Hobson tells of the natives making shrines such as Buddha should have occupied and placing Europeans in them and also of placing Europeans on kylins as though they were Arhats. Some of these are real attempts at portraiture or caricature.

On some of the Kwan-yin figures and those of other deities traces can be found of gilding over a black ground or traces of an ungilded red and black lacquer. This would indicate that they were of the K'ang Hsi or later times of course.

Once in a while others turn up with sketchy floral ornaments in green and red, done in Europe to give the impression that they were so decorated in China. While still others fell entirely to the itching brushes of the "Hausmaler" who put European decoration all over them.

Any that may have well authenticated Ming enamels on them were probably taken in the same way to Ching-tê Chêng and touched up, but actually authenticated specimens of Ming enamel I have not seen.

Marks are not of the period but of the individual artist's seal. They are usually impressed in the biscuit before glazing on the backs of the figures and later ones are often slanting. They can seldom be read. The earliest figures have no marks. A few artists are known such as Ho Chao-tsung and Lai-kuan but their work has not been so classified as to be recognizable in unsigned pieces. Ming marks are always an indication that the piece is late.

Even the latest of these figures and vessels can rival the finest modeling ever done in Europe and the only factory that can rival them at all is the Royal Copenhagen one in Denmark. It is remarkable that since about 1550 or perhaps earlier a continuous industry has existed in Tê-hua and with so little change. Only in China would this be possible.

OTHER CH'ING POTTERIES AND PORCELAINS

Although pottery and some less well known porcelain formed a large amount of the trade from every port of China, little is known about it. The English, being a tea-drinking nation, paid some attention to the Yi-hsing stonewares as did also certain potters of the continent such as Ary de Milde of Holland, Böttger of Germany, as well as Dwight, Elers, Astbury and Wedgwood of England. In order to have a framework upon which to allocate what information we have, I have prepared the following chart giving first the *province,* then the *port or ports,* then the probable *sources* and finally the *descriptions* of the wares. This includes some of the late Ming as well as the 17th and 18th century wares.

I need not go into a general criticism of what happened in China for the last three centuries. We have seen the heart and soul go out of ceramics. We have witnessed the endeavors to supplant these real qualities first by absolute perfection, secondly by an attempt to return to the antique and thirdly by a wealth of detail in the K'ang Hsi, Yung Chêng and Ch'ien Lung reigns respectively. To the small mind of the perfectionist a work of art full of human appeal and close to the soul of the artist is less beautiful than a precise and machine-made or machine-aided thing. Few great men are perfect and no perfect man was ever great. Few great works of art are perfect and no perfect work of art can ever be great.

Antique objects can never be reproduced. We study the antique things because we want to learn how men thought and we wish to benefit by the good things of the past and avoid the errors the conclusions of which are already known to be unhappy. If we learn how to work in the best ways that the old artists worked, we can turn out things of our own in those ways avoiding their mistakes. It is beginning at the wrong end, however, to do as they tried to do in the Yung Chêng reign.

CHART OF CH'ING POTTERY AND PORCELAIN SOURCES

PROVINCE	PORTS	SOURCES	DESCRIPTIONS
Kwangtung	*Pakhoi*	*Yamchow*	Quoted from Maritime Customs Reports, 1892–1901, p. 422. "The ware comprises vases, incense-pots, bowls, teapots, plates, etc., or any domestic article in two shades of terra-cotta—light and dark—ornamented with appropriate figures and characters in Chinese style . . . The glazed surface is produced by rubbing with wax and polishing with wood and pumice stone after baking." (This would seem an exceedingly primitive method for th 19th century but the unevenness of creative developments must be considered.)
Kwangtung .	*Canton* Delta about a dozen ports	Many small factories	Buff pottery or stoneware with frequent brown and yellow and more seldom turquoise, blue and aubergine glazes with only partial covering of jars, incense burners, figures, etc., usually of grotesque feeling.
		Shekwan near *Fatshan*	(See Ming section for descriptions but note that most specimens are not of this early date.) Chün type, etc.
			General Canton wares characteristics are:—Hard fired stoneware. Bodies:—dark brown, buff and light greyish yellow. Glazes:—blue streaked with grey green or white over a substratum of olive brown, or green with grey and blue mottling, or brown. Seals:—*Ko Ming-hsiang* and *Ko Yüan-hsiang* placed their seals on some and probably lived in the 18th century.
			Other types are:— Bodies:—porcelaneous, white but burns dark brown where exposed. Glazes:—"Celadon" of a watery olive crackled type quite transparent and dark, thick flambé of dull surface. (This is often erroneously called Ming.)
Kwangtung	*Swatow* & *Chaochowfu*	*Funkai*—has beds of kaolin and other common clays.	Hobson says these wares are described as "pottery of every description, from common earthenware to finely finished articles with coloured glazes or enamels . . . including immense stoneware jars holding 100 to 150 liters." Also a coarse porcelain.—This may be one source of the jars found in the Philippines, Malay archipelago, etc.
Fukien	*Amoy* & *Chüanchowfu*	*Shih-ma* & *Tung-an Hsien*	Common porcelain dishes, bowls, etc., of much of the "archaic-looking blue and white and coloured ware. Often found in India and the Eastern archipelago.
		Tê-hua	White wares. (See "Fukien" porcelain of both *Ming* and *Ching* periods.) Also commonly known as *blanc de chine*.

CHART OF CH'ING POTTERY AND PORCELAIN SOURCES—*Continued*

PROVINCE	PORTS	SOURCES	DESCRIPTIONS
Chekiang	Ningpo	Not known	Simply reported in the Consular Reports as "china ware, fine."
Kiangsu	Nanking	Ching-tê Chêng	See main descriptions of *Ming* and *Ching* wares. This was the most important center of the Imperial Kilns.
	Shanghai	Southern Kiangsu (Kashan)	Buff pottery bowls, incense burners, etc., with opaque, finely crackled camellia-leaf green glaze.
		Yi-hsing	See description of wares of red and brown stoneware largely unglazed but sometimes imitating *Chün yao* and later sometimes enameled.
Anhwei	Wuhu	Ching-tê Chêng	See above.
Hunan	Changsha	Not known	Described as shipping "fine porcelain" down the *Yangtze* river.
Shantung	Kiaochow Weihaiwei Chefoo	Poshan decayed slate clay	Tz'u Chou type wares of various types, etc. (See Sung section.) Hobson says further, "A government factory for glazed pottery was started there at the end of the last century." It produced "vases of all shapes and dimensions, jars, flower-stands, flower-pots, etc., in two colours—a bluish grey and tea colour—perfect in form and glazing and looking like porcelain."
		Yenchowfu Tz'u Chou in Chihli	Similar to Poshan wares. See Sung section. Being so far south probably many were exported through these *Shantung* ports.
Chihli	Peking & Tiensin	Liulichu	Near Peking, exists today and makes copies of Tz'u Chou wares, etc. Also tiles with aubergine, green and brown glazes. Also vases with turquoise and aubergine iridescent glazes.
		Tz'u Chou	Stoneware of heavy but refined texture and very fine taste, of cream color incised or decorated with brown or black painting. (See Sung section.)—These same wares are being made today.
Shansi	Those of Chihli & of Shantung	Machuang near T'ai-yüan Fu	Buff stoneware ornaments, figures and vases with moulded designs with part glazes of green turquoise and aubergine.
			This type are also made in many of the interior provinces and many are shipped from *Kwangtung* and *Fukien* ports.
Shensi	Shantung ports	Yo Chou	Imitations of Tz'u Chou wares and also greyish white with sketchy designs in blue.

Multiplication of details in art is much like the man who talks too much in life, neither are convincing.

There is much historical interest shown in the 18th century but this must not be confused with art, or human appeals. There are those who know so much about a work of art that they cannot enjoy it. Such people look at a thing and immediately pigeonhole it saying, "It is so and so and so and so," and then turn quickly away as though to say, "Now that little task is done, let us see what else I can find to tell about." This is the kind of person that knows the names of all the flowers and birds but couldn't draw or paint one to save his neck. Such people never really look at anything.

Thus we reach a time of ever increasing byways and pitfalls for those who do not keep to the center of the road of honest enjoyment. Most pitfalls catch those who do not really enjoy art but want to give the impression that they do. No advice as to how to make love is necessary to the one who sincerely loves and no advice as to how to enjoy beauty is necessary to him who enjoys it.

In our aesthetic approach which admits all human appeals and does not attempt to distill them down to an unnatural essence called ART we avoid the latter in the belief that such metaphysical distillation is bound to produce artificial results as different from the real understanding of what man calls beauty as distilled perfume is different from the original fragrance of the flower. Each well known group of pottery or porcelain has its appeal to some people or it would not have become well known, but in China through the ages we find more appeals than elsewhere; appeals to the most sophisticated of cultured taste as well as to the newly rich merchants; appeals to the poet dreamers as well as to the show off swelled heads. We have not found every appeal in China, as for instance it was in Japan that the nature loving people loved asymmetry, but in China there is rich ground into which to delve and it is for that reason that artists the world over for centuries have gone there to study.

Chinese Marks

As early as the Shang Yin and Chou cultures (1766?–1122? B.C.) and (1122?–249 B.C.) the Chinese cast characters in their bronzes and it is natural to expect that in the Han potteries made partly to imitate bronzes we might expect to find the same thing but this is not so, probably because the pottery vessels were not considered precious enough to warrant such inscriptions. Occasionally we see examples of Han pottery bearing marks which were in the mold and appear on the bases but these are usually to be looked upon as fraudulent and, if the object happens to be an animal or figure, though it may be perfectly correct in every other way and actually of the period, it will usually be found that the base bearing the mark has been tampered with or attached so as to look as though it had been broken off and replaced, that is, it is really new and has been cleverly made to imitate the original base in every detail but with the mark added.

Other early inscriptions are sometimes carved into the already fired pottery. One can tell this only by close examination under a glass which will disclose small bubbles in the clay cut open here and there leaving a sharp edge quite unlike the bubbles which may have reached the surface while it was being fired. The actual carved edge even of soft pottery after firing is also sharper than would be carying in the soft clay before firing. But one has to be very careful and all such early pieces are suspect to say the least.

During the Six Dynasties and T'ang times no marks were used to indicate the reigns and very few occur that in any way help to date a piece. However some Yüeh yao had marks which Brankston used in his establishments of dates of the wares from the Chiu-yen sites. These are not reign marks but names of persons, such as that of the famous poet found on the frog, etc., and such marks as that meaning "five" on the bottom of the "Kian temmoku" vase in my collection which may be late T'ang or early Sung.

By the Sung Dynasty we rarely find actual reign marks such as that on the small Tz'u Chou type vase formerly in my collection and now in the Metropolitan Museum of Art and again on Lung ch'üan celadons and Yüeh wares. (See Sir Percival David pieces and sherd found by Plumer under those sections.) We also note the numerals 1 to 10 incised before firing on the bottoms of one type of Chün yao pieces. These are as given below:

1.—	一	i		6.—	六	liu
2.—	二	erh		7.—	七	ch'i
3.—	三	san		8.—	八	pa
4.—	四	ssŭ		9.—	九	chiu
5.—	五	wu		10.—	十	shih

These numerals refer only to the size of the vessels and in no way even prove authenticity for we learned that they were copied by imitations of the original Chün ware.

Yuan marks are also few and far between but in *The Early Ceramic Wares of China* by A. L. Hetherington there is shown on Plate 44 a heavily potted dish with hexagonal foliated sides which have warped and with three small and ill proportioned little legs. On the bottom is a felicity symbol of two fish and an inscription which is translated, "A product of the Ling Ho factory: made by Chiang Ch'i in the first year of Chih Chêng (*i.e.*, A.D. 1341), example copy number 109," in a poor underglaze red. Concerning it Mr. Hetherington gives the following arguments:

1.—Chemical analysis proves it to contain phosphate and this would indicate a pre-Manchu origin for, "this substance has not been found by Professor Collie in Manchu wares except those made at Kuangtung with which this specimen has no analogies."

2.—It is chemically similar to certain Korean and Northern Chinese wares.

3.—If it were of Ming origin why should they have used the name of a Mongol emperor and the least worthy at that? For it will be remembered that this last Yüan emperor was a pretty poor sort and not to be glorified by his own people let alone a conquering people.

4.—A Chinese emigrant to Korea would hardly have used the *nien hao* or honorific title of a bygone Mongol.

5.—It is not likely that it might be a fake by some Japanese for the piece is so roughly fired and potted and the red of so uneven and poor a color that this would not be likely. Also one would not expect a faker to use the name of so obscure a kiln and so out of the way a nien hao.

He gives various other reasons including the fact that red was highly developed by the time of the Hsüan Tê reign (1426–1435) but he neglects to point out that this was at Ching-tê Chêng and not in every obscure little factory in the country. Moreover each of his reasons has possible answers which the reader can think of himself and must weigh. Thus we are confronted with the three following possibilities:

1.—The piece is a Yüan specimen as marked.

2.—The piece is a Ming copy.

3.—The piece is an out and out modern fake.

I am inclined to agree entirely with Mr. Hetherington but I go through all this reasoning to show the reader how one should think about marks, and to make clear that they are at best one small contributing piece of evidence.

Ming Dynasty marks may be divided about as follows: 1.—Reign marks, 2.—Date marks, 3.—Hall marks (referring to the hall, study or pavilion), 4.—Potter's marks, 5.—Marks of praise or commendation and finally 6.—Marks of dedication, good wishes, etc.

Mr. A. L. Hetherington has made a very ingenious chart which is in universal use for determining the cyclical date marks. First it must be understood that the Chinese have a unit of sixty years and each year is named by two characters representing one of the *ten stems* with one of the *twelve branches*. The full explanation of the system with tables is given in W. F. Mayer's "Chinese Reader's Manual" (page 381). All we wish to be able to do is to quickly translate the cyclical dates which we may see, into our own system of dating. This can be done by means of the chart (see marks section).

"The first horizontal line of characters represent the ten stems. One of these stems will be found in combination with one of the branches in every cyclical date mark. If the eye is carried down vertically from the stem which has been detected in the inscription until it recognizes the branch character, the year can be read off at once." As an instance Mr. Hobson in "The Wares of the Ming Dynasty" shows the mark of a bowl (Pl. 15, fig. 2.) with the character 癸 (kuei) on it. This is found in the upper right hand corner, and the second character is 丑 (ch'ou) which is found in the sixth square below it indicating the 50th year.

Now the commencing of the cycles are: Beginning with the Han period 236, 176, 116, 56, A.D. 4, 64, 124, 184, 244, 304, 364, 424, 484, 544, 604, 664, 724, 784, 844, 904, 964, 1024, 1084, 1144, 1204, 1264, 1324, 1384, 1444, 1504, 1564 and 1624, etc. Therefore our cyclical years would not be of much use were it not for the fact that the title of the emperor is also given on this bowl namely Hsüan Tê (1426–1435). Taking 1324, the beginning of one cycle, and adding 50 years we find that the bowl was made in the year of 1373 which is too early. The next date would be 1384 plus 50 which equals 1433 which falls in the time of the reign and must be the right one. In some marks only the cyclical one is mentioned and we then have to guess the proper cycle by technical and stylistic means.

Only very rarely, as I have said, do the pre-Ming inscriptions include a nien hao or title name, therefore we do not need to give the individual names of the pre-Ming rulers here. Occasionally there are date marks incised in the paste or rarely in underglaze decoration.

The Ming period marks came generally into use because of the factory methods and the growing financial importance of the ceramic industry. They were stamped, incised before firing or painted, the latter being in underglaze blue as a rule though rarely in overglaze iron red or other colors. Usually they were in script and not in seal characters although the script is sometimes framed with a single or double box border. They are, of course, read from top to bottom beginning at the right and working to the left as in all Chinese writing. It is interesting to note in this connection that Sir Percival David in discussing the marks on certain Chü-chou celadons of the Yüan period told me that the Mongols read from top to bottom beginning at the left and working right and thus we may deduct that inscriptions that read around a vase to the right are Mongolian and those which read around to the left are Chinese.

The complete reign mark has six characters and these read for instance beginning with one on the upper right:

4.—	德	tê (Tê)	1.—	大	ta (great)
5.—	年	nien (title)	2.—	明	ming (Ming) (dynasty)
6.—	製	chih (made)	3.—	宣	hsüan (Hsüan)

or:—"Made in the Great Ming Hsüan Tê reign."

Sometimes the marks are reduced to four characters by eliminating the first two. At times again the last character chih is replaced by tsao but both have the same meaning. The marks also occur enclosed in a double ring and we find occasional examples having the rings alone. Much stress is laid upon the quality of the calligraphy by the Chinese and after one has seen the real examples of fine marks the difference is often perceptible even to the untrained eye between fake marks and real ones but we must hastily add that splitting hairs on this subject is bad, for excellent and undoubted pieces exist which are badly marked and some modern fakes of the worst sort have really beautiful marks.

Complete tables will be found in the *Chinese Reader's Manual* (by Mayers) but we will content ourselves with the nien hao of each of the Ming Emperors (see marks section).

Hall marks include the words "t'ang" 堂 (hall), or "chai" 齋 (study), or "t'ing" 亭 (pavilion) and they are open to a variety of meanings indicating a certain room in which there may be an inscription perhaps bearing upon some outstanding event in family history, a title, an ancestral hall, etc., and the mark may refer to the name of the studio or building of the potter or dealer who ordered the wares, etc. There are few hall marks in the Ming dynasty but one occurs fairly often in the late Ming wares of many kinds. It is "yu t'ang chia ch'i" meaning "beautiful vessel of (or for) the Jade Hall," and may be simply a complimentary statement or may have some definite reference to some certain hall. We do not know.

Sometimes the marks will definitely indicate that a piece is spurious. Such is the "Shên tê t'ang" meaning "Shên Tê Hall" which is found on pieces imitating Wan Li blue and white and enameled wares well made with radiating lines in the bases and defects in the glazes.

Potter's names rarely appear on porcelain but are found on potteries although not enough have been brought to light to determine any specific dates or locations. We have already mentioned a few and it may be noted that Ming-yüan signed with a seal while Hui Mêng-ch'ên used script at Yi-hsing.

Pleasant good wishes are sometimes expressed such as "wan fu yu t'ung," "may infinite happiness embrace all your affairs," or "ch'ang ming fu kuei," "long life, riches and honors," or some reference to well known quotations such as "tan kuei," "red cassia." The saying was "To pluck the cassia in the moon," meaning to obtain a high place in the State Examinations.

Some of the marks recurring on Chia Ching porcelain and Wan Li porcelain are given as follows, by R. L. Hobson:

1.—"Fu kuei chia ch'i"—"Fine vessel for rich and honorable."

2.—"T'ien hsia t'ai p'ing"—"Great peace throughout the Empire."

3.—"Lu wei ch'ing kao"—"Rank and emolument without corruption." This is typical of some which have a moralizing tone about them.

There are also symbols which are used for marks such as the peach and stork for longevity, the bat for happiness, the hare which helps the toad to pound the elixir of life in the moon in Taoist lore. Some of these are Ming though most of them are later.

All Ch'ing marks are placed on the bottoms underneath, except those occasional potter's, artist's or calligrapher's seals included in the decoration, none of which have as yet been identified. Unlike the Ming marks, they appear both in "k'ai shu" script and in "chuan shu" or angular seal characters and may be in enamel colors, iron red or even gilt as well as the underglaze blue. This was brought about because most of the time of making the piece was put into the decoration which was done after glazing. If the blue mark was put on first it was not sure but that the piece might turn out badly or the artist might do something not so successful or the glaze might have faults and it would be wished that the mark was not on it. Sometimes the Ch'ien Lung mark is in red on a turquoise background. They are usually all enclosed in a double ring or a square frame. Mr. Hobson points out that the enameled wares in the style of Ku Yüeh Hsüan have the marks in heavy relief enamel, usually blue, and that these wares are always of some importance. We must hastily add that such wares have the marks in lavender and the Yamanaka one is in grey enamel. Also the cheap reproductions on egg-shell porcelain carry the blue marks. All these are similar to the Ming marks and are read in the same way.

We find some more unexplained new marks during Ch'ing times such as the one which looks like a G and which seems to have a western origin as there is no Chinese character which is similar.

An exception to the above rule is the use of the names "Chieng Ming-kao" and "Ch'en Kuo-chih" which are found on biscuit porcelain of early 18th century and occasional seal signatures on Tê-hua, Yi-hsing and Fat-shan pieces.

Another curious mark found on export blue and white ware of the K'ang Hsi period represents "shou" or "longevity" written in a fanciful form which is appropriately called the spider mark.

As we have noted, there was an edict against using the Emperor's name on porcelain in the K'ang Hsi reign because of the danger that the object might be broken thus desecrating its use. Whether for this reason or not we do not know but it is likely that both the habit of marking the piece with a double ring alone, or of using a symbol such as those below was brought about. However, the Ming examples exist and the Emperor's edict was not of long standing so we cannot hold fast to this rule. The Eight Buddhist Emblems, Eight Precious Things, swastika in a lozenge, the cloud or fungus scroll, "fu," artemisia leaf, etc., are typical. Even the dragon and the lion are painted on the bottoms of snuff-bottles and small cabinet pieces. Thus many of the decorative or artistic elements were used for marks as well.

Finally this must be made clear: Do not trust marks save as *one* of many factors which must be considered in making an attribution. Learn to look first at the body clay, then the way the foot is made, then the way the glaze is applied, then what sort of glaze it is, then the crackle if there is any, then feel the weight of the piece and note its general potting, then note the decoration, its color, its way of application, etc., and then look at the mark in the way we have described above and, if *all* elements are correct, you may be fairly sure, while, if one or two are not correct, get an expert's opinion before buying. Two experts are better than one. Three are better than two. And your own eye and intelligent understanding plus experience are best of all.

CHAPTER XXI

EUROPEAN "SOFT PASTE" & PORCELAIN

WE HAVE shown how the art of *Lustre* originated in the Near East, was carried by the Arabs to Spain and thence spread to Italy where it died because it could not be used for the naturalistic painting there in vogue. We have traced *Enamel* decoration also from the ancient Near East as it spread east to China and west, as it also came back from China to the Near East in return and thence to Europe. We have seen how *Modeled* decoration after Rome increased in Europe and also in China, and how it spread north in Europe in preference to the painted or enameled wares. This was the situation at the beginning of the 18th century while at the same time the Europeans yearned to make porcelain, that great ware called "China" after the country of its origin.

Porcelain or *"China"* was a medium of great creation particularly during the Ming period in China but the technique came too late to Europe for the production of any really great works of art. The decadence of industrialism, commercialism and their attendant ills had already set in long before the technique was mastered. A quaintness here, a touch of humor there, a titillating bit of sex appeal or a pompous sort of strutting, though mere crumbs from the table of the gods have to help satisfy our everlasting hunger for beauty or appeals in any form and this is all the 18th century has to offer.

MEDICI "PORCELAIN"

One of the first, if not the very first, attempts to make porcelain in Europe was made in Venice, that great center of world trade, to which Chinese examples had been brought. This city was a glass making center as well and it was naturally thought that the translucence of porcelain was due to a content of glass. In 1470 Father Ulielmo da Bologna made a present of a small vase of "porcelain" made by the alchemist Maestro Antonio, and wrote a letter about it. The next record is of a payment in 1508 for seven bowls of "porcellana contrafacta" or imitation porcelain which shows that it was perfectly understood that they were not making real porcelain. Bernardo Buontalenti, sculptor, architect, painter and potter, under the patronage of the Grand Duke Cosimo I of the Medici, developed this imitation porcelain at the Medici factory and it was called "Medici porcelain."

625

Marks used on it are fairly well known and consist of a dome of the cathedral of Florence under which there is an F which may stand for either "Firenze" or "Franciscus." Another is the arms of the Medici with or without the letters "FMMDE II OR FMMED II" standing for "Franciscus Maria Medicis Magnus Dux Etruriae Secundus," on six palle or round spots. Only

three dated specimens are known: The earliest a square flask having on the front the arms of Philip II with the chain of the Golden Fleece, flanked by ribbons on each of which is "1581." This piece is at Sèvres. An undated similar piece is also there. Another dated piece is a medallion of white porcelaneous ware with the portrait of the Grand Duke Francesco in low relief surrounded by the inscription "Franc. Med. Mag. Dux Etruriae II 1586." The making of the ware continued through the reigns of Ferdinando I and Cosimo II although sometime during the latter's time the kiln was moved to Pisa.

The body of this ware is translucent but lighter in weight than porcelain and the glaze is imperfect. From a manuscript found in the Magliabechian Library in Florence we find that it is composed of 24 parts sand, 16 of glass, 10 parts of powdered rock crystal, 8 parts of soda and 12 parts of the white earth of Faenza, to which was added in the proportion of 12 parts to 3 of the kaolinic clay of Vincenza. The piece was covered with a lead glaze containing tin. Most of the pieces are coated and then decorated with blue or blue and manganese, though the jug in the Adolphe de Rothschild Col. is polychrome. Designs are of simple symmetrical sprays of flowers or at times asymmetrical arrangements. At times grotesques were used. Some show distinct influence of middle Ming wares. Some have relief decoration and the one in the Spitzer Col. is composed of two baroque masks above which are three spouts. The

Fig. 918. Dish of "Medici porcelain," actually soft paste, of course, decorated with grotesques and depicting Death of King Saul. Mark shown below, but letters on the palle do not show very well (See text). Metropolitan Mus. of Art.

shapes are what Hannover calls, "Venetian Oriental" and include double flasks, square bottles, pilgrim bottles, while dishes have flat rims parallel to the flat bottoms. Less than 40 pieces are known all told. Naturally forgeries are plentiful. Also they resemble some of the worst of the Chinese wares. One museum in Germany had a Chinese dish not only labeled Medici ware but also published it in color.

FRENCH SOFT-PASTE

At Rouen, famous for its pottery for some time, was discovered a material similar to Medici ware but made about 100 years later. A privilege was granted Edme and Louis Poterat in 1673. A few odd pieces of blue and

Ewer (Brocca) with blue on white ground of "Medici porcelain" with mark of a dome in blue, F in black, and mitre and sword in black. Ht. 8″. Gift of J. Pierpont Morgan. Metropolitan Mus. of Art.

"MEDICI PORCELAIN" EWER (BROCCA), VENICE

PLATE 177

white ware of very poor quality and opaque consistency are marked AP but how this stands for either Edme or Louis we do not know.

At St. Cloud, we are told by Dr. Martin Lister, a soft ware was made by Pierre Chicaneau in 1677 and by 1698 a factory was well under way. When Pierre died his widow married Henri Trou and he and his son bettered the factory. Marks are first *St.C.*, which is rare, then in 1696 the mark was a

FIG. 919. Saucer in style of and possibly from Poterat kiln, Rouen, which Hannover places it c. 1675. Museum simply calls it "St. Cloud (1712–1760,." Metropolitan Mus. of Art.

FIG. 920. Soft paste vase made at Rouen (1673–1687) resembling Medici ware but much later, of course. Ht. 17½". Metropolitan Mus. of Art.

sun alluding to *"Le Roi Soleil"* and in either 1712, 1722 or 1724 (depending upon which authority you believe) it was again changed to SC with a cross above and a T below. The first marks are in underglaze blue and the last in blue, red or incised. The factory failed in about 1766.

The objects made were small and often decorated with enamels Some large pieces are in turquoise pale celadon and warm white or yellowish white. All are highly translucent and always greenish by transmitted light rather than amber tinged as are the Fukien wares which they resemble in general appearance. In decoration there was some influence by Berain and Rouen faïence but chiefly it was Chinese. An underglaze blue at times harsh and again greyed was used plus turquoise, iron red, yellow and gold leaf afterwards fired.

Not much faking of this ware was done but Samson has made some copies and Hannover tells of 19th century Tournai plates decorated in blue and gold and marked falsely with the STC in muffle colors. Also some wares from the Rue de la Ville-l'Eveque (Faubourg St. Honoré, Paris) and some from Lille and Chantilly are similar.

The Lille factory was founded by Barthélemy Dorez and his nephew Pierre Pelissier for the making of both faïence and porcelaneous ware, about 1716 but they copied the St. Cloud things and only a few are definitely established by an L above a cross while there are some doubtful examples marked BF perhaps meaning Barthélemy-François.

Chantilly had a factory in 1725 founded by Louis-Henri de Bourbon, Duc de Condé, under the management of Sicaire Cirou. The first ware was pure white because of tin in the glaze but later a lead glaze was used and a warm

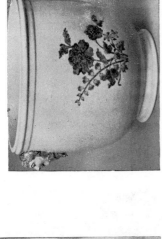

Left: St. Cloud cachepot of relief soft paste seeming more opaque than usual. Ht. 7¼″. Metropolitan Mus. of Art.
Center: Cup of St. Cloud with und rglaze blue decoration and relief ribbing. Ht. 3″. Metropolitan Mus. of Art.
Right: Cachepot from Chantilly factory decorated in natural colors. 18th cent. Ht. 7⅞″. Metropolitan Mus. of Art.

Left: Mennecy-Villeroy snuff-box with delicate polychrome decoration on yellowish body similar to that of St. Cloud but not so pure. Early 18th cent. Length 2½″
Center: Chantilly cup and saucer in polychrome decoration which is cross between Kakiemon and naturalistic styles. 18th cent. Dia. 4¾″.
Right: Chantilly cup and cover with enamel decorated relief floral sprays. 18th cent. Ht. 3½″. Metropolitan Mus. of Art.

FRENCH 18TH CENTURY "SOFT PASTE"

PLATE 178

18th cent. cane handle possibly from St. Cloud, decorated with enamel blue and yellow-orange vases with orange flowers. Length 5¼". Metropolitan Mus. of Art.

Right: Cane handle possibly St. Cloud. Decorated in enamel colors with red and green dominating. Early 18th cent. Length 3". Metropolitan Mus. of Art.

Bowl with cover and tray in dirty white, pitted glaze (1700–1750). Dia. of tray 7⅞". Metropolitan Mus. of Art.
St. Cloud (1712–62) cup and saucer moulded in design probably of Japanese origin. Dia. 4¾". Metropolitan Mus. of Art.

Cups called "French 18th cent." but typical of relief scale pattern of St. Cloud and probably made there. Ht. 2¾". Metropolitan Mus. of Art.

Small patch boxes made at St. Cloud in early 18th cent., one of Chinese god of plenty and other a lamb. About 3" long. Walter Blumenthal.

ST. CLOUD "SOFT PASTE"

PLATE 179

toned translucent body obtained. Some designs were from Kakiemon. There is a theory that the change in glaze took place because of the competition with Mennecy and Vincennes and, providing this is true, the white ware would date from 1725 to about 1735 or 1740, and the warm ware would date from this time to the close of the factory in 1789 due to the French Revolution. The designs also changed from the Kakiemon type to other oriental

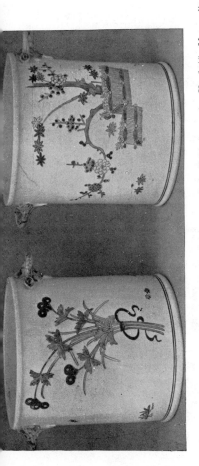

Left: Jars dating c. 1730–40 decorated with bright enamels in Kakiemon style. Ht. 5⅝". Metropolitan Mus. of Art.
Right: Basket work rimmed plate with flower decoration in natural colors. Type may have been inspiration of "Flora Danica service" of Copenhagen factory later.

Cup and saucer decorated in slightly blurred underglaze blue. (1725–1773). Dia. 4½".

Blue and white plate, with typical basket work rim. Metropolitan Mus. of Art.

CHANTILLY "SOFT PASTE"

PLATE 180

patterns and "Indian Flowers," which were really Chinese in character but thought to be Indian because the India Companies brought wares so decorated. This was a simple following of the trend of Meissen toward more and more naturalistic flowers, birds, insects, etc. Toward the end copies were made of the Sèvres wares with colored grounds and flowers were made for the ornamentation of clocks, wall sconces, etc. Very rarely figures of birds and humans were made.

The underglaze blue is softer than that of St. Cloud but was not very popular. Rare but not very valuable plates have flowers which look something like comets (see illustration). Green "camaïeu" painting was done also over the glaze.

By 1780 Sèvres had completely overshadowed Chantilly and the latter declined to poor potting and painting. After the revolution an Englishman named Potter tried to revive the work and there were half a dozen other attempts but they all failed. Samson has made some close copies but otherwise there was little imitation and less stealing of the marks, which were a hunting horn sometimes later obliterated and changed to the monograms of the Kings of France.

Mennecy-Villeroy had a factory started by François Barbin of the Rue de Charonne, Paris, where wares were made which are unknown today. In 1748 he moved to Mennecy under the patronage of Louis-François de Neufville, Sieur de Villeroy. Between 1753 and 1762 Barbin took his son into partnership. After the elder Barbin's retirement Joseph Jullieh and Symphorien Jacques managed, but later in 1773 they went to the factory at Bourg-la-Reine which was patronized by the Comte d'Eu.

Fig. 921. "Mennecy-Villeroy" jar and cover. Metropolitan Mus. of Art.
Fig. 922. Soft paste, Mennecy, 18th-cent. jars probably copied from Fukien, Tê-hua examples. Strangely enough such copies bring many times prices of far superior Chinese originals. Ht. 6¼". Metropolitan Mus. of Art.
Fig. 923. Mennecy pot-pourri of white glazed ware. Late 18th cent. Metropolitan Mus. of Art.

Most of the work of these places imitates that of Vincennes and Sèvres or that of St. Cloud despite the fact that the paste is yellowish and soapy looking and quite different from that of either. Here we see that even in the early days of the 18th century creative spirit had become so atrophied that factory copied factory and there was no slightest respect for the rights of personal design or desire to cultivate it. One small bright idea was dragged from place to place until it was worn to pieces.

Distinguishing characteristics of Mennecy-Villeroy wares are a purple-red frequently employed in shell borders and the thick enamel-like application of the colors, blue, green, red and yellow, particularly the red. The usual small articles were made including knife handles, walking stick knobs, boxes, cups, etc. Grotesque figures comprised most of the large articles.

In 1751 biscuit porcelain was made at Vincennes and promptly copied at Mennecy in the form of portrait medallions and busts, but the ware never approached the whiteness and softness of Sèvres.

Long after Böttger had made real hard porcelain and its secret had been stolen by other German-speaking centers the French continued to make soft paste although it is much less serviceable. It chips easily, is likely to crack in hot water and was difficult to handle in the kiln because it was inclined to wilt and become uneven. Perhaps the color did appeal, for it is less cold than hard paste, but there was certainly no reason to build an aura of false values about it. I suspect that the clever French shopkeepers had to do with this much as they have sold the Americans and English more recently on the great values of their post impressionist paintings. In any event many collectors pay high prices for these inferior wares from Europe while some, like Hobson, criticize the Americans for paying high prices for the actually superior soft paste wares of China.

German Soft Paste

In Berlin two brothers named Schackert applied to Frederick the Great for the right to set up a factory at Basdorff. They were only glass cutters and knew nothing about the work. We know of only two pieces although this was 1751. One is a jug in Hamburg and the other a piece in Berlin but they are nothing but milky glass.

Also in 1751 Wilhelm Kaspar Wegely was given permission to open in Berlin and encouraged by a free site and exemption from customs duties on materials. A certain unprincipled Herr Benckengraff aided him with men and materials from the Höchst factory. Then in 1756 the "Seven Years War" brought Frederick to Meissen and Wegely thought he would surely benefit but the monarch was so impressed by what he found there that he promptly sold out Wegely's place and put his army contractor Schimmelmann in charge. This gentleman soon entered the Danish service while Wegely, broken hearted and now deprived of his royal patronage, closed up in 1757.

The ware he made was neither a true soft paste nor like that of Meissen, being more chalky and less transparent, for it contained less felspar and quartz, but of course all of these wares both in France and Germany differed one from another. Many of Wegely's wares were undecorated and when they were, the colors were inclined to chip off. Even cold lacquer colors were used. One stunt was to apply flowers, birds and boys to a base with white ground, in the round, and then to color them. There were also uncolored figures, strongly colored ones, services with Watteau scenes and polychrome flower decorations in which purple dominated. These were copied from Höchst. The underglaze blue was poor but the gilding of good quality.

The mark was an underglaze blue, incised or impressed W made in four strokes to which were added numerals which were probably factory marks to indicate certain formulas, etc. By making the outside strokes of the W short, a nice similarity to the crossed swords of Meissen was obtained.

As the other German factories were true hard-porcelain manufacturers, we will come to them after the description of the discovery of porcelain by Böttger. In Thuringia, however, there were several other primitive attempts.

THURINGIAN WARES

Due to the natural resources, wood for fuel and other materials, the "Wald-fabriken" or "forest factories" of Thuringerwald came into being to supply the local people. There were a few "arcanists" who were alchemists claiming to know the secrets of porcelain manufacture. But also books such as "Die Kunst das ächte Porzellain zu verfertigen" by Franz Joseph Weber, 1798, told "The art of making true porcelain" for all to read.

The wares, at first very crude and uneven in color, became better as the designs became worse, due to growing commercial progress. The figures are often amusing and avoid the rococo preten-tiousness of the big factories.

Volkstedt, southwest of Leipzig and Dresden and near Rudolstadt, was founded by a theologian George Heinrich Macheleid. "Soft porcelain" was first made and in 1760 when experiments had suc-ceeded with hard porcelain, permission was given to establish a factory by the Prince of Schwartz-burg-Rudolstadt. In 1767 this privilege was trans-ferred to Christian Nonne who managed for 33 years. The factory still exists so far as we know.

The marks were first two pitchforks which luck-ily could be drawn quite similar to the crossed swords of Meissen and in 1787 the Elector of Saxony complained so that a single pitchfork was

FIG. 924. Hard paste Volk-stedt tea-caddy decorated in enamel colors and gilt (c. 1770). Metropolitan Mus. of Art.

used. In 1799 the factory was sold to W. Greiner and C. Holzapfel and the mark was changed to R standing for Rudolstadt. In the eighteen nineties the factory was split into three firms: Eckert & Cie., Karl Ens and Alteste Volkstedter Porzellan Fabrik, the last of which made a reputation for the making of fine fakes and forgeries.

The "soft porcelain" comprises chiefly small handleless cups decorated in the style of famille rose of China. The hard porcelain is slightly transparent, cold, grey and has a spotted glaze often covered for this reason with flowers, landscapes and figures. Much rococo twisting and writhing was also resorted to. The specialty of the factory was small painted or modeled portraits with fixed rococo frames and genre subjects and landscapes of the Dutch style along with maps of an ornamental character. This idea was at least more consistent than the painting of pictures on cases and pots although the results were hardly impressive art.

Kloster Veilsdorf, northeast of Frankfort, unlike the other places of the district, came into being at the desire of a prince, Friedrich Wilhelm Eugen of Hildburghausen, who hired the arcanist Johann Hermann Meyer in about 1765 or a little earlier and it turned out better wares at the then usual penalty of running always at a loss.

The most characteristic decoration was of large freely painted flowers on thread-like stems in a predominant reddish-violet, a purple and yellow, an iron red and two coppery greens.

Fig. 925. Kloster Veilsdorf, German cup and saucer of 1762–1770. Metropolitan Mus. of Art.

They also occur in purple only. Other designs are Boucher children painted in yellow, flowered trellises, green borders with a guarry-pattern in violet and edged with small rococo scrolls, chinoiseries after Herold of Meissen, figure subjects after Watteau and Teniers, etc. The shapes are fairly simple, going into neo-classic urns toward the end of the century with the French influence. The figures are not marked and are easily confused with those of Fulda but of no great excellence. One "Venus" in the Thüringer museum at Eisnach shows a fairly firm teat, an attractive umbilicus on a rounded paunch and nice legs not too much draped and seemingly inclined to spread. Of this our good Hannover says, "a seated Venus (?) with outstretched hand," (I hadn't even noticed that she had a hand!) "somewhat remarkable for its breadth and boldness of style." I go into detail because I want to bring out the fact that these factories all over Europe did not in this time lose the opportunity to include sex appeal for which there was an admitted desire so long as it was paraded under the name of "classic art." Other figures included a "Venus lying down with Cupid," a "Cupid having enchained two women," and a walking stick handle of a "charming female half figure." Of course the usual figures of the Italian comedies, many gods and goddesses and genre groups were made.

The mark was CV or C or V written separately and the V elongated could also luckily be made to look like the Meissen swords. Sometimes the latter were simply forged. Hannover says, "In 1782 for instance a whole case of porcelain from this factory was confiscated at the New Year fair at Leipzig, on the ground that its contents bore the mark of the electoral crossed swords."

At Gotha, northeast of Frankfort and north of Kloster Veilsdorf, was opened a small factory by Wilhelm Theodor von Rothberg in 1757 probably under court protection. Christian Schultz, Johann Georg Gabel and Johann Adam Brehm, three important artists were hired and the factory was taken over by them in 1782. In 1803 it was owned by Prince Augustus of Gotha and later sold to Gebrüder Simson. Schultz was a flower painter, Brehm was both a painter and modeler and Gabel was a pupil of the older Tischbein. At one time 38 artists were hired and even in 1803 there were 13 still at work.

As a result of this ownership the wares were as excellent as could be expected for this time and place. They were the best decorated in Thuringia. The first ware had a brownish or greyish glaze like earthenware but this was soon improved to a light, translucent paste with a creamy-yellowish glaze. The earliest wares are strongly rococo but changed to the prevailing Louis XVI style. Figures were sometimes painted in natural colors and sometimes were monochrome in blue, red or yellow. A specialty was the painting of flowers in gold or in gold and silver. In 1790 the pastoral scenes were changed to landscapes with very romantic nay almost heartbreaking ruins painted in iron red, or in brown over brown and in grisaille. There were also antique heads in the same treatments and with gold frames. At length Greek red figure vases were copied after the book by Hamilton. A marble-like biscuit was developed for figures and busts of which Hannover says, "It copied models from elsewhere with the ingenuousness of the period."

The first mark was R in underglaze blue or rarely impressed, standing for Rothberg, the founder, and of course not unlike that for Rudolstadt of Volkstedt. About 1790 it changed to R.g. or R-G. In 1805 it was changed to *GOTHA* or G and the Gotha was always in italics and in black and iron red, while the G is in underglaze blue, black, iron red or yellow. Wares with a hen on a mound with the word Gotha and the mark Porzellan Manufaktur Gotha are 19th century or later.

Wallendorf, the estate in Coburg-Sallfeld, southeast of Gotha, had a factory opened by Johann Wolfgang Hammann who with the help of some arcanists had made porcelain at Katshütte He was joined by his two cousins Johann Gottfried Greiner and Gotthelf Greiner sometimes called the father of Thuringer potters.

The ware was light and translucent but always greyish or yellowish and the blue was blackish while the other colors were dull. The specialty was in blue, brown or black glazes with reserved medallions in polychrome. The same stages of rococo, then chinoiseries (which were carried into the 19th century in blue and white), then polychrome flowers and birds and then in the 1780's painting in purple and in the 1790's in dark brown, grey and black of landscapes with ruins, were followed Pipe bowls were a specialty and "Turkish cups" without handles were copied from Meissen. The figures were clumsy and uninspired.

The W could, of course, again be made to resemble the crossed swords and the matter was protested from Saxony. Truly we are sinking lower and lower as the weight of the pennies grows greater and greater and the story takes on the aspects of a Greek tragedy. So low into the mire of indecency had porcelain sunk that it could never shake off the weight of deception and fraud to take wing and soar to the heights of stirring beauty. There can be beauty in hate and bloodshed. There can be beauty of a kind in oppression and even in cruelty. But there can never be beauty in snivelling and picayune stealing and the grovelling deceit with which money had inoculated the soul of man.

Gera was founded by Johann Gottlob Ehwaldt and Johann Gottleib Gottbrecht in 1779 and was at once bought by the two Greiner brothers and Wilhelm and Johann Andreas, an assistant director at Volkstedt and for a while it was a sort of branch of that place but in 1782 gained its independence. Hannover puts it very well when he says, "In one way it was capable of everything, in another of nothing, inasmuch as its material was very poor." Wood grained ware was a specialty with what appeared to be an engraving in red nailed on it. People marveled at this wonderful achievement. Other specialties were keepsakes, loving-cups, saucers, vases, pots and pitchers with landscapes having ruins all in natural colors. The modeling was weak and consisted of copies from Meissen but one group of "Indians" in the Grassi Museum is wonderful in concept and execution. This group would probably fetch a good price on 57th Street in one of the decorators' establishments which specialize in Victorian interiors.

The G resembled the Gotha mark and that of Gotskowsky. Later Gera was used and underlined. It is usually in red. Of course it was difficult to make the G look like crossed swords but this was overcome around 1780 by marking the blue and white wares with crossed swords with or without a dot. The only way to distinguish this ware from Meissen is its very poor quality.

Gotthelf Greiner was thought to be the father of Thuringerwald porcelain because what he did not accomplish in quality he did in quantity. He started a factory at Limbach and another in the neighboring town of Grossbreitenbach. He leased the Ilmenau factory. His five sons inherited all this and added Kloster Veilsdorf. Greiner was also associated with Hammann in 1764 at Wallendorf.

Limbach made only a "useful porcelain" chiefly blue and white. The early ware is similar to that of Gotha, is slightly yellowish and not so highly glazed. By Empire times it became fine and white. To the usual landscapes were added copies of Meissen chrysanthemum design taken from the Japanese and in the Biedermeier period portraits with natural colors and much gold. In the early times the factory made interesting figures with strange proportions, either too tall or too short and with exaggerated movement. Many were genre, others were gods and goddesses and a crucifixion copied from Meissen was often repeated. The colors are pleasant on the figures and the seemingly original naïveté is attractive.

The first mark was LB or two crossed L's with a star below slightly resembling the Meissen Marcolini mark. The LB is in purple, iron-red or black and the L's in underglaze blue and occur chiefly on the blue and white wares. After trouble about the marks a clover was adopted in 1797 for all the Greiner factories.

At Ilmenau. Christian Zacharias Gräbner in 1777 established a factory and after some financial difficulties absconded in 1782. The Prince of Weimar then directed it. Gräbner came back and ran away again and then in 1784 Franz Josef Weber was put in charge until 1786 when Gotthelf Greiner leased the place. He later turned it over to Nonne and Roesch who ran it until 1871 when it was taken over by a limited company.

The mark was a small "i" in underglaze blue and only a few pieces are known, and those are of poor quality. In the Empire and Biedermeier periods it was better but had a light tint of green or blue. The factory is chiefly known by imitations of the Wedgwood "jasper ware," of poor quality and uneven blue grounds. This same ware was also made with a suggestion of a glaze. The frames of pictures were always white and glossy. The usual subjects were treated and the "Venus Kallipygos" is also, as Hannover says, "rather broadly treated."

On the back of some of these picture panels is the name Sneff in italics incised. Greiner used two crossed Roman I's for the obvious reason until forced to use the cloverleaf. N & R stood for Nonne and Roesch.

Grossbreitenbach was established by Kammerjunker Major Anton Friedrich Wilhelm Ernst von Hopfgarten in 1777–1779 and sold in 1782 to Greiner, and its wares, though of the blue and white type, cannot be distinguished from those of Limbach which had the same mark. This place is just east of Ilmenau, south of Leipzig.

Rauenstein was started by no less than three Greiners and all not related to Gotthelf so far as we know. It began in 1783. Their names were Johann, Johann Friederich and Christian Daniel Sigmund. About all that is known for certain is that in 1787 it produced a common blue and white ware and about 1800 there were some 120 workmen including polychrome painters employed. The wares were even poorer copies of the other factories than theirs were of Meissen, and the figures without any interest.

The mark should be known to be avoided and is an R with or without a star below it in underglaze blue or overglaze red. It is like the Gotha R for Rotberg but smaller. It is difficult to tell it from the R for Rudolstadt used at Volkstedt in the first part of the 19th century. There were also a pair of crossed hoes with the letters R-n. If half the inventiveness had been used in the designs of these places that they employed in faking the Meissen mark, they might have turned out something worth while.

Ansbach was founded by Margrave Charles Alexander and directed by Johann Friederich Kändler, cousin to the famous Kändler at Meissen, in 1758. The specialty was gods and goddesses with big noses, comedians with half closed and seemingly swollen eyes, coffee pots with female masks under the spouts and purple landscapes painted in medallions in gold decked out with ribbons.

The mark was a Prussian eagle with A under it, the arms of the town and also a fake of the Meissen mark.

Passau was founded by Nikolaus Paul from Cassel and later went to Karl Hagen and is now called Dressel Kistler & Co. It did nothing of virtue in the early days and made dangerous forgeries with marks of Ludwigsburg and Höchst, though these places were hardly beyond reproach themselves.

A kiln at Würzburg started in 1775 by Johann Caspar Geyger is thought to have made gay little plain white figures or painted ones on uniform white pedestals. The mark was a bishop's mitre.

In Mannheim in 1767 Laurentius Russinger, a former modeler from Höchst

FIG. 926. Würzburg tea and coffee service which is exceedingly rare. Note interesting use of a lattice band not unlike in feeling the so-called "Mosaik" ones of Höchst but different in detail, and also the floral festoons. A. Beckhardt Coll. c. 1775–80.

made an ordinary blue and white and a polychrome decorated ware marked PZ. It had also a peculiar scroll pattern in green.

In Ottweiler in 1763, Prince William Henry of Nassau-Saarbrücken with the aid of the arcanist Dominique Pellevé made wares with the usual flowers and also mythological scenes or scenes of gallantry after Boucher and Wilson. One white figure of a boy has the mark NS with an added W and the date 1766.

In Kelsterbach, 1758, the output was chiefly of well modeled figures after Bustelli and these were probably done by Antonius Seefried in part at least, who it is fairly sure must have worked at Nymphenburg. They seem to have open mouths and raised eyebrows and a brilliant white glaze. A few were polychrome. The mark is HD standing for Hessen-Darmstadt surmounted with a crown, impressed or painted in underglaze blue. It also occurs in purple without the crown and in italics. Little useful porcelain was made.

FIG. 927. Interesting pipe bowl from Kelsterbach by Vogelmann, 1763–65. Mounted with silver and jewels. A. Beckhardt Coll.

At Fulda between Frankfort and Gotha we finally come to more interesting work. The quality of paste and the workmanship and painting are all excellent. The factory was started in 1765 by Prince-Bishop Heinrich von Bibra and called "Furstlich Füldaische feine Porzellan-Fabrik," and run by the same

Nikolaus Paul who worked for Wegely and also at Passau and Cassel under the directorship of Abraham Ripp. It ended in 1780.

Most of the ordinary wares were decorated with flowers in polychrome, red, or a strong purple. The usual landscapes and portraits were also made, and the later influence of Boucher, etc., carried through, but all were done in good taste and well painted. Landscapes in grey resting on gold scrolls and silhouette portraits set in tooled gold frames on cups seemed a favorite treatment. The wares are among the most expensive of these times in Germany though they are not rare.

The figures of the usual Italian comedy and amatory groups as well as religious figures are all full of natural grace. A 10-inch Madonna Immaculata standing on a globe on a baroque pedestal is well known. The figures resemble those of Karl Gottlieb Lück of Frankenthal though a little less alive.

The mark was an F until 1780 when a double F in italics sometimes with a crown and sometimes with a small cross on top was used or a simple cross like a plus sign, the arms of the city. It should be noted that this cross is never pulled together to resemble in any way the Meissen mark.

Cassel, like many of these places had had an old faïence factory for years but the porcelain factory was started in 1766 also by Nikolaus Paul just a year after he had started the Fulda factory. It was not until 1769 that real porcelain was made successfully, as it was advertised, "Complete colored and blue-and-white, reeded and smooth coffee and tea services at low prices." The useful wares are mostly blue and white and of poor quality, and the figures stodgy. Some are of a white chalky look and some greyish. The mark was the Hessian rampant lion or HC standing for Hessen-Cassel. Barber also gives a running animal that looks like a dog perhaps but this is not surely authenticated, and should not be accepted.

Thus we survey the preliminary wares and those country wares which were not true porcelains. Of course many of them were made long after the actual discovery of porcelain but I thought it best to place them all together. The reader has probably gathered that I think them of no artistic importance and of very little appeal in any sense. There used to be collectors who paid fair prices for some of them but time has proven them of little account.

CHAPTER XXII

THE EUROPEAN DISCOVERY
OF PORCELAIN

BRIEF HISTORICAL OUTLINE OF THE 18TH CENTURY

THE 18th century divides itself roughly into three sections; the Opening (1700–1715), the Middle (1715–1775) and the Close (1775–1800), with fifteen years, sixty, then twenty-five, respectively.

The *Opening* (1700–1715) was the time of Louis XIV (1643–1715), Queen Anne (1702-1714) and Joseph I (1705–1711) in France, England and Germany. The War of the Spanish Succession resulted in a succession of defeats of the French by the English, and the Peace of Utrecht (1713) gave large territorial additions to England. Prussia was made a kingdom under Frederick I in 1701.

In furniture it was the "Walnut Period" from about 1660 to 1720 and the Baroque style was breaking all precedents of proportion and classic tradition but the exaggeration was so great that people soon tired of it and began to tone it down to the more sentimental age of Rococo. Jean Antoine Watteau (1684–1721) was a favorite painter with his gay shepherds and shepherdesses, fêtes champêtres, rustic dances, etc.

Ever since the 16th century in Italy the Princes and Popes had been making collections of antique sculpture, and artists had been copying them. Also a strangely mixed conception of Chinese art had occurred, intriguing but entirely misunderstood.

The *Middle Period* (1715–1775) was the time of Louis XV (1727–1760) of George I (1714–1727) and George II (1727–1760) in England and of the North Countries there were Charles VI (1711–1740), Maria Theresa (1740–1780) and Frederick II (1740–1786). A troublous time in truth! The following dates give a very rough idea of what was taking place:

1720—Financial panic, bursting of the "South Sea Bubble" in England and the collapse of John Law's Mississippi scheme in France. (Penny gathering had become a craze in truth.)

1740—War of the Austrian Succession, England and Austria against France. Frederick II invades Silesia.

1748—Treaty of Aix-la-Chapelle.

1754—Continuous war between England and France in India, America and Europe.

1756—"The Seven Years War" France and Austria against England and
     Frederick the Great.
1770—Rise of Du Barry and fall of Choiseul.

The Marquise de Pompadour (1721–1764) had great influence on art and
politics at least between 1745 and 1764. François Boucher (1703–1770) was
a dispenser of sweetness and light with his pastoral, genre and historical subjects. His women, girls and nudes were famous.

In 1748, through the making of an underground aqueduct, it was found
that the ruins of Pompeii were accessible. In 1763 intensive excavations
were begun and much interest was stirred in both Pompeii and Herculaneum.
Thus the artistic ground was ready for the results of the Napoleonic conquests
which brought about an entirely new style during the Empire.

The *Close* of the century (1775–1800) was represented by Louis XVI
(1774–1792), the First Republic (1792–1795), Directory (1795–1799) and
finally the Consulate (1799–1804)—France was busy! In England George
III (1760–1820) was doing little or nothing but imitating the French in
culture. The spinning "mule" was invented in 1779, the weaving machine
in 1785 and Nelson annihilated the French fleet at the Battle of the Nile
in 1798. There was continuous social discontent partly due to the inventions
which threw men out of work, and to the costs of the wars. Frederick II
was the great personality of the northern countries. Napoleon invaded Italy
in 1796, Egypt in 1798 and then continued his campaigns of victory in Italy
and Germany about 1800. He loved show and was interested in antiques.
He changed the face of art as much as he changed the map of Europe and
neither were for the better.

Jacques Louis David (1748–1825) won the Grand Prix de Rome in 1775
and stayed there until 1780. He was made a court painter under Louis XVI,
was associated with Robespierre, voted for the death of his king and so was
made court painter by Napoleon. He was a pupil of Boucher and Vien but
changed and became the leader of the classic revival.

Meissen and the Discovery of Porcelain

France was satisfied with "soft-paste" and Holland with faïence or "Delft,"
but neither were very durable being given to chipping and easy cracking
through quick changes of temperature. However, Holland had a good im-
port business in hard porcelain wares from the East and did not want to
lose that through any home manufacture of similar wares. England never
did have a native pottery of any importance even in the last half of the 17th
century. True, John Dwight, the Elers brothers and others imitated Rhenish
stoneware and Chinese "buccaro" ware, but although Dwight tried to make
a porcelain he never succeeded in making anything but a white stoneware.
Perhaps all these men knew too much about ceramics to become inventors
of porcelain for often a man who knows it all does not see beyond what he
thinks is reason. It was not a potter who discovered porcelain for Europe
but an alchemist.

JOHANN FRIEDERICH BÖTTGER

Junckel, the inventor of ruby glass, had made a white milky glass, but nothing nearer, while Ehrenfried Walther Tschirnhausen can be credited with establishing the idea that porcelain could be made from different earths. He was a physicist who was searching for a means of creating an industry based upon his native soil.

To Böttger goes the real credit. He, Johann Friederich Böttger, was born at Schleiz in Thuringia in 1682 and was apprenticed to an apothecary when he was only 16. He was fascinated with the strange reactions of various chemicals and dreamed of finding the "philosopher's stone," and of the transmutation of metals. One who fooled with the "natural laws" was not particularly popular in those days but this did not deter the King of Prussia from attempting to capture the man when he heard rumors about his supposed ability to make gold. Böttger fled to Saxony where he was captured by the King of Poland and Elector of Saxony, August the Strong. Here he was kept prisoner, given working expenses and assistants including Tschirnhausen and told to make gold or else. . . . This caused considerable activity on Böttger's part as can be imagined and with some enormous burning glasses which Tschirnhausen had invented many substances were melted. The Elector grew impatient and Böttger tried several times to run away but was recaptured. Things were pretty black when his suggestion was finally accepted that he endeavor to start an industry of faïence making from which taxes could be squeezed first and then go back to the gold making later.

A factory was established at Dresden for this faïence making but Tschirnhausen and Böttger with enthusiasm set out to make porcelain. Luckily all of the melting experiments with the glasses had actually taught them a good deal, and in 1708 the first "red porcelain," very much like the ancient "buccaro" ware, and also like that made at Yi-hsing in China, and so appreciated by tea-drinkers, was made of "Nuremberg red earth," which contains iron oxide and a mixture of the local clay from the Plauenscher Grund near Dresden. This ware was very fusible and so hard that it was found that it could be cut with the wheel after firing. The Portuguese had been making a fine thing of the importing of Yi-hsing ware and, if the same thing could be made in Saxony the revenue would help to reinstate the impoverished country, start new wars and accomplish all manner of great things.

But at Dresden there were no throwers, moulders, modelers and in fact no one who knew anything at all about pottery. Therefore Peter Eggebrecht, a thrower, was brought from Berlin, Johann Jakob Irminger, a goldsmith, and other assistants were employed. We have found that as a rule pottery suffers when it is patterned after metal work. The handles are likely to be too thin, the forms too tenuous and applied decoration seems always necessary. But this conservative goldsmith did better things.

It would be expected that Böttger would now settle down to work with the new medium but he seems to have been a restless soul. Tschirnhausen and he had already noticed that white earth which remains white after firing is precisely that which is the most difficult to fuse. Thus they turned to the search for another substance which would act as a flux, which would be easily fusible and transparent after firing. Chalk, alabaster, marble and other siliceous minerals were tried from far and near. Yet right in Colditz a clay almost like kaolin was at hand.

There is no documentary evidence even as to the year of discovery for all was kept a dark and mysterious secret, but probably in late 1708 or early 1709 it was made. We hope that it was before October 1708 for it was then that old Tschirnhausen died and it would have been nice to have had him witness the results of all their struggles. However, it was not until March of 1709 that the king was informed. Böttger foolishly asked the king to appoint a committee to report upon the practical importance of his invention and of course the committee was unenthusiastic as might be expected, but the king on January 23d, 1710, nevertheless issued a royal patent for the erection of a factory in the castle of Albrechtsburg high on a hill overlooking Meissen. From 1710 to 1713 only the red ware was made and it cannot be said that the making of porcelain was fully solved until 1715.

Meissen Red Stoneware

Though stonewares are treated separately in this book it will aid the coherence of this section to keep all of the Meissen endeavors together. The color of this first ware produced was of red-brown to black and a dull, muddy yellow. It resembled the Bizen yaki of Japan and the terra sigillata of Rome and was not unlike the prehistoric wares save that it was harder. The 6 chief types are: 1.—even red, 2.—red with black surface, 3.—marbled ware, 4.—a different and lightly fired black glazed ware treated with gilding and lacquer colors, 5.—a polished surface ware having appliqués of mat branches in Chinese style and 6.—the yellow ware.

Methods of decoration and design included: 1.—casts particularly of Yi-hsing teapots, 2.—casts from Chinese soapstone and porcelain figures particularly such as were made at Tê-hua, Fukien, 3.—enamel decoration on teapots (all of these were before Johann Jakob Irminger's time but after he was employed the following processes came into being), 4.—molded and cut decoration after Turkish brass work, particularly ewers, 5.—wares labeled "classic" with appliqués, and 6.—"Laub and Bandelwerk" or cut with the wheel in foliate scrolls or "Muscheln" faceted decorations of the whole surface, which were Böttger's favorites.

Hannover says, "Grinding, polishing and cutting were for the most part executed in the 'Schleif und Poliermühle' at Dresden; the resources of this institution, however, did not suffice for dealing with the whole of his production. In the year 1712 there were at Dresden six, in Meissen three, in Bohemia ten glasscutters at work on the red stoneware, while goldsmiths and jewelers in Munich, Augsburg and presumably elsewhere were engaged in mounting it." Then he comes to an interesting sidelight on Böttger himself, "The fact was that Böttger had, as time went on, become so possessed with the idea that his beloved ware was a sort of precious stone, that he had the finest specimens mounted in precious metals overlaid with enamels, and set with turquoises and garnets after the manner of the Renaissance period."

There were also polished or partly polished pieces from Roman sculpture or from Bernini, or again from ivory carvings. Then reliefs from medals were made and rarely modeled pieces such as a dashing statuette of August the Strong, a crucifix in Gotha and figures from the Italian Comedies.

Böttger was kept prisoner and every means of keeping the secret was resorted to, yet it leaked and one of the traitors was Samuel Kempe who went to Berlin where he failed to make good but did encourage Friederich von Görne to set up a factory near the town of Plaue-an-der-Havel. When Böttger in 1715 sent an assistant to spy on the owner of this place, David Pennwitz, he received the report that they were making fairly good red stoneware, and it is supposed that they continued until 1730 when the place failed. Strangely the pieces traced to this factory, though they were less well made, brought just as high prices as did Böttger's own at the Lanna and Gasser sales, adding insult to injury.

Kempe, having failed at Berlin, went on to Bayreuth where a factory turned out very lightly fired and porous ware covered with a glaze of brown, black and rarely yellow, with delicate chinoiseries on it in gold and silver both unfired.

Böttger White Ware

Böttger himself didn't mind stealing ideas and credit as is proven by teapots copied from the Chinese by Arij de Milde and copied from him by Böttger including his mark of an animal in an oval with the name above. Arij de Milde was born at Delft in 1634 and never could have made these high-fired examples.

Criss-crossed lines and numerals, particularly 13 and 7 with letters also appear on these wares. Any which have the crossed swords are later. Graesse, the director of the Porcelain Collection at Dresden, was entirely mixed up and included many actual Chinese pieces as those of Böttger, even going so far in his book as to include several Chinese marks as those of Meissen. The fact that Edwin Atlee Barber passes them on in his books should be a warning.

The real wares are much harder than any of the contemporary attempts to copy them, and cannot be scratched with a steel blade or file. The dangerous copies are those from Kamenz, Saxony, of about 40 years ago. Still others were originally plain and have been cut or decorated later, particularly with coats of arms. There are also cheap Bohemian wares of black with lacquer designs. The Johanneum Sale showed prices of real Böttger examples ranging from 20,000 to 40,000 marks, while in the Grasser Sale similar examples brought only a few hundred and now they would bring less.

An eye witness tells us that in 1710 the porcelain made by Böttger was "indistinguishable from 'Indian' ware." Yet only in 1713 did white ware come on the market at the Easter Leipzig Fair. He had used "Schnorrsche Erde" named after the owner of the estate on which it was found near Erzegebirge, had discarded it for a clay found near Dresden until 1717 and then returned to it and continued ever after. For the fusible element he used alabaster only and never seems to have found out about feldspar or quartz.

The last ingredient has never been used at Meissen and this accounts for the strength of the ware for quartz makes a brittle and easily chipped porcelain.

By 1713 they had a stock of overglaze colors and an artist named Funke was working there. Underglaze blue was the king's favorite color as is proved by his large collection of Chinese blue and white pieces intended for the "Japanese Palace," but Böttger never mastered this and only later did his best workman, David Köhler make it. Never did Meissen equal the Chinese color.

The porcelain was not very translucent and had a creamy yellowish tinge. The glaze is thick, even and pure. Very rarely are pieces found which were made before Böttger discovered the glaze. Enamels are yellow, blue, green, pink and less pure iron-red, grey-green and violet. They were all used together but monochromes do occur, always to be regarded as later. A "mother-of-pearl" was very rarely used as a ground color instead of in the design. Gold and silver were strangely enough fired onto the porcelain even when he could not accomplish it on the stoneware and there are cups with metal all over either the inside or outside. There are also examples of burnished gold designs on mat ground and of relief gold.

This white ware was made in similar forms to the red ware. Even at an early date outer walls were reticulated as in Chinese "devil's work." Very early pieces were also impressed with bookbinder's stamps in the paste before firing. There were also the so-called "Callot figures" in the baroque taste and after the artist of that name.

The great genius and inventor of European porcelain had burned himself out by 1719 and in that year he finally worked and drank himself into his grave on March 13th.

HEROLD PERIOD

The factory was in financial straits. Two of the "arcanists" sold their secrets to du Paquier in Vienna. These were Stölzel and Hunger. However, through the strange irony of the powers that seem to control this universe, or just chance, Johann Gregor Herold was trained by du Paquier and in 1720 the Royal Commission at Dresden found him technically better equipped even than Böttger had been, and he obtained the directorship. His colors were higher fired and he added a brilliant iron-red, a purple, two kinds of

FIG. 928. Meissen bowl, Herold period, with gold Chinese figures. 1720–1725. Dia. 6". Metropolitan Mus. of Art.
FIG. 929. Meissen tea-pot, Herold period, c. 1725. Decorated with gold chinoiseries. Ht. 4¼". Metropolitan Mus. of Art.
FIG. 930. Meissen cup and saucer with gold chinoiseries of Herold type but marked with crossed swords in underglaze blue, which came into being in 1726. Dia. 5⅛". Metropolitan Mus. of Art.

Sugar-bowl c. 1720 to 1725. Gold decorations of chinoiseries. Length 6". Metropolitan Mus. of Art.

Right: Jar and cover of type known as "Augustus Rex vases" having Japanese decoration and dating c. 1725–1730. Ht. 16½". Metropolitan Mus. of Art.

Tea-pot c. 1724 with grotesque figures in style of Callot, marked M P M in underglaze blue. Ht. 4¼". Metropolitan Mus. of Art.

Left: Tea-caddy decorated with views of sea, figures and flowers in insets in rich enamels framed with gold lambrequins. Crossed swords mark in underglaze blue, 19 impressed and 52 in gold. Date between 1725–1750. Ht. 4⅛". Metropolitan Mus. of Art.

HEROLD PERIOD MEISSEN PORCELAIN

PLATE 181

green, a yellow and a light and dark blue. He also made a fine, thin porcelain which has never been surpassed in Europe.

Before Herold the factory continued the same wares described above probably under Funke and some pieces with silver lacquer, black and iron-red showing figures in medallions with the flesh in the last color, also pieces with designs from Watteau poorly painted and nowhere nearly so good as the later ones after the same painter. The Chinese gave over slowly to the baroque style and thus we place Herold's chinoiserie designs earlier than 1727 when his sketch book showed he was taking interest in the later style. It was just during this early period that August the Strong was also making further plans for his "Japanese Palace." It was about this time that the Kakiemon designs after the Japanese artist of that name became popular,

Turkish woman with hamper by Kändler. c. 1745. Ht. 6¼". Metropolitan Mus. of Art.

Sugar bowl with *"Mosaik"* or scale rococo reserves and landscape with figures. Marked with crossed swords in blue and 43 in violet. c. 1760–70. Ht. c. 3¾". Metropolitan Mus. of Art.

"Augustus Rex" vase and cover with raspberry colored ground and *chinoiserie* in enamels. Ht. 20". (c. 1730). Metropolitan Mus. of Art.

Figure described by museum simply as "Meissen 1730–80" but possibly by Friedrich Elias Meyer for it is like his things in rather affected pose and soft treatment. c. 1755. Ht. 11½". Metropolitan Mus. of Art.

MEISSEN WARES c. 1730–1770

PLATE 182

and the "red dragon service" and "yellow tiger service" date 1728 by Zimmerman and 1738 by Berling. Hannover has a good thought that the difficulty with the underglaze blue saved us the trite Imari style for years.

The perfect technique led to simple shapes and open designs for spots did not have to be covered with painting or modeling.

A group of vases made for the king only are marked AR for Augustus Rex in underglaze blue and are very rare. These show an attempt to do the

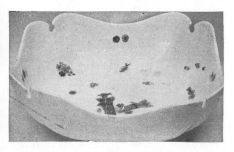

Dish, between 1725 and 1740, marked with crossed swords in blue. "Oriental design" with its *strohblumen* has evidently been used to cover worst pitting much of which could not be covered. Metropolitan Mus. of Art.

Tea-pot with design after Kakiemon but having baroque handle and spout. Between 1725 and 1750. Metropolitan Mus. of Art.

Above: Piece with baroque ornamentation and landscapes in polychrome enamels, c. 1730–1735. Ht. 8¼". Metropolitan Mus. of Art.
Below: These pieces, c. 1735 show typical "*Laub-und Bandelwerk*" baroque frames to landscapes. Cup and saucer have light blue ground color. Cup ht. 3⅛". Saucer 5⅛" dia. Metropolitan Mus. of Art.

MEISSEN WARES

PLATE 183

Chinese vases as translated by the Japanese and at once we see flamboyance of curve, exaggeration of color or other features which take them out of the class even of the Ch'ien Lung wares. The ways of the copyist are ever the same.

Likewise, the stunt of drawing without perspective came into use in the Meissen factory. Often the Chinese artist sacrificed the tricks of perspective for the making of a better design more suited to a flat or curved surface. This is not to say that the Chinese did not understand perspective for they often drew dragons or tree branches perfectly curving forwards or backwards from a plane and the aërial perspective of mountains behind mountains and of twisting streams was beautifully handled. Nevertheless the trite European critic likes to say that the Chinese did not understand perspective. Johann Gottlob Schlimpert and C. F. Herold, the brother of Johann Gregor Herold, seem to have been chiefly responsible for making pictures framed with baroque frames. The chinoiseries had had their run and European landscapes took their place. These were generally lifted from Watteau, Wouverman, Rugendas, etc. There were also water scenes difficult to explain from an inland country but due to pure copying. Many of these were in monochrome purple, iron-red or black, probably due to the influence of the engravings from which the artists worked.

Medallions were marked on colored grounds and then painted in as were the Chinese powder blue wares. Attempts were also made to color the porcelain all the way through, but these are exceedingly rare, as in truth also are the colored ground wares for many of them are also marked AR. These colors were laid on with the brush and none can be considered glazes. Only one minor glaze was finally developed and that was a brown similar to what the Chinese call "dead leaf brown," and it was used as in the East in conjunction with blue and white.

FIG. 931. Tea-caddy with canary yellow ground and "Kakiemon" type design. Ht. 4⅜". Metropolitan Mus. of Art.

FIG. 932. Tea-pot, cup and saucer with rose or mauve ground. Saucer has enamel painting directly on colored ground. Metropolitan Mus. of Art.

Fig. 933. Cup and saucer with metal mounts. Magenta ground with white medallions and Chinese floral designs in bright enamels, Meissen, c. 1735. Ht. 4⅞". Dia. 6¾". Metropolitan Mus. of Art.

This new underglaze blue was never good but some fairly close copies of Chinese wares were made. Some blue and white bears the AR mark but much was of common household variety and decorated with the "Zweibelmuster" or "Onion pattern" and the "Strohblumen" or "Strewn blossoms" or a thin Japanese plum blossom pattern. The latter was adopted by Royal Copenhagen and slightly modified. This porcelain has the crossed sword mark from 1726 and usually some letter probably indicating the artist. Blue was also combined rather unsuccessfully with iron-red.

Plastic wares resulted from the appointment of Gottlob Kirchner in 1727 who did some large vases of grotesque character in the style of J. Stella, and also some clock cases, wall fountains, etc., until 1729, when he was discharged. Later he was taken back after Ludwig Lück, an ivory carver, was also discharged for his lazy and disorderly ways, but did not last long and failed in the making of some large animal figures for the "Japanese Palace."

THE KÄNDLER PERIOD

Johann Joachim Kändler was appointed in 1731 and was a very different character for he started great activity at once. He continued with the factory until his death in 1775 and just about covers our middle 18th century period, adding considerably to it. The great animals were accomplished with Kirchner doing a rhinoceros after a Dürer woodcut, an elephant, a bear, a fox, a lioness and a leopard. After he left for Berlin, where he spent the rest of his life, Kändler completed a number more, making some of them life size, but the whole lot are very crude and full of flaws and fire cracks. Kirchner also completed a statuette of August the Strong and one of the Apostle Peter before his final departure.

Kändler wrote in one of his reports that, "There is not a single properly made handle in the whole factory," and he set out to make new shapes for

Left: Hard paste figures representing Autumn and Winter decorated with brilliant polychrome, moulded by Friedrich Elias Meyer c. 1755. Hts. 10⅛″ and 10¼″. Metropolitan Mus. of Art.
Right: Mark in underglaze blue. Decorated in yellow underdress with polychrome sprays of flowers, pale coat lined with gray and white fur and hat in buff. Ht. 7⅛″. Metropolitan Mus. of Art.

Left: Chinaman in white hard paste porcelain with enamel colors made during Kändler period, possibly George Fritzsche, c. 1735–40. Ht. 3½″. Metropolitan Mus. of Art.
Right: Lithophane from Guido Reni's "Magdalene," German 19th cent., probably Meissen. Metropolitan M of Art.

MEISSEN FIGURES

PLATE 184

all the knobs, feet, spouts, etc. He also made the "Sulkowsky service" (1735–1738) and the Brühl "Swan service" (1737–1741) executed for the Saxon Minister, Count Heinrich Brühl, who until his fall in 1763 had charge of the Meissen factory. These services were inspired by silver services and suffered all the involved and busy illnesses of these.

Johann Freirich Eberlein was at the factory between 1735 and 1749 and did some good modeling including figures of the "Three Graces" and "Four Seasons." Other pieces of his are the Atlanta and Meleager, Acis and Galatea, a sweetmeat stand for the Swan service, a drunken Silenus, etc.

There were still others who gave some character to the factory including Friederich Elias Meyer and Peter Reinicke.

Kändler made several figures two or three feet high and the age seemed on the whole to express lack of understanding of scale. He had said, "You can make anything you please in porcelain; if it is too big, it can be made in two pieces." No one has ever said just how large or small a piece of porcelain should be, aside from the technical difficulties of firing, etc., yet in each of us an invisible scale tells us what to expect. When this expectation is upset by surprise, there is always a loss of aesthetic appeal. Somehow we expect large sculpture to be of stone or bronze and it is a shock to find it in breakable porcelain. But Kändler evidently saw the error of his ways and turned to smaller figures.

In the 18th century "Schauessen" were used, that is, table decorations of sugar or wax figures arranged with scenes of rocks, trees, palaces, temples, pyramids, etc., either on the dining table or on a table to one side for the amusement and wonder of the guests. Now they carried into porcelain. Hundreds of these things were concocted and many of the figures we see today belonged to them but probably not the little ones with bocages, etc., for they are not made to be looked at from all sides. It is easy to see how people might get into the habit of keeping certain choice pieces on permanent display and particularly if they were of porcelain which could be easily washed off when necessary. In this way Kändler came to create a new art, that of representing the people of the day in the dress of the period. Thus from a caterer's art we derive all the little genre porcelains made at Meissen and elsewhere. These were not at once taken from real life but from the opera or such romantic scenes as lovers kissing, dancing couples and the famous "crinoline groups," Columbine and Scaramouche and more lovers. Before all this the figures were from classic sources.

Kändler used taste in keeping the colors pure and simple. The flesh parts are hardly tinted at all while the dresses are of plain color or sometimes with small all-over designs of "Indian flowers." The whole effect is not to make them too naturalistic and the sentimentality of the rococo from France does not come until later. Yet I cannot help but feel that the prices such toys have brought are out of all proportion to their intrinsic merit. Hannover tells us that some were sold for up to around $10,000 and that there are many fakes as a result.

It was natural to set candles near these "Schauessen" and so it was that some of the figures were made as candle holders themselves with ormolu mounts and leafy arbors to hold candle sockets.

A well known group of figures are the "Saxon Miners" (1735–1740) with a representation of August the Strong in a miner's costume among them. There were also foreign figures such as Turks, Poles, Negroes, etc. Kändler did not like the Royal Orchestra in Dresden so he made the well known "Monkey Band" as a dig. He also made small figures with boxes near them

Left: Cup and saucer attr. to Marcolini period (1774–1814) by museum. Kakiemon style but overcrowded. Plate dia. 5". Metropolitan Mus. of Art.

Right: Cup and saucer, cup having two medallions in white on red-violet ground, filled with "German flowers" in natural colors. Both have blue crossed swords, and cup an impressed 74, saucer 117. Ht. 2¾", dia. 5¾". Metropolitan Mus. of Art.

Left: Tureen and tray c. 1760–90 with landscape and marine views. Tray 12½" long, Metropolitan Mus. of Art.

Right: Tray and teacup with ribbon and flower design and marked with crossed swords and dot in blue. c. 1760–70. Tray 10" long. Metropolitan Mus. of Art.

MEISSEN WARES

PLATE 185

and finally copying the Chinese more or less, he made a number of birds and animals.

Here is the meeting and marriage of the two techniques of *sculpture* and *painting* and never are the two entirely separated again in the art of porcelain.

Many horrible vases with pierced walls and carefully modeled flowers and insects painted in pastoral colors on them and even worse "Schneeball" and "guelder-rose" jars were made, having small white flowers all over them in snowballs with cupids added, relief portraits, etc. Thus we find that Kändler's taste was both good and atrocious at the same time, and now added to his own bad taste comes the influence of the rococo with all the faults of the baroque and many added weaknesses.

So perfectly adapted was the medium to his new expression that it was thought by some that the rococo style actually originated at Meissen, but it came from France. After about 1750 the oriental influence is about gone as are also the "Indian flowers." The wares are now less massive and lighter in weight and design. European flowers were copied from such books as those by Preisler and Schmidhammer with stiff drawing and color incorrect. Shadows were introduced in what was known as "Saxe ombré." These date about 1742.

About 1750 both birds and flowers improve for they were painted from real ones and from Buffon's *Natural History,* a better book. These were known as "German flowers." Scattered small flowers were continued.

After Herold's time the frames were omitted from landscapes painted on vases and at most a rococo scroll was used at the bottom. Frames were also removed from the birds and flowers and the design became more free and open. Children after Boucher were also popular and after about 1760 the factory was obviously feeling the competition of Sèvres.

As the lighter colors were more easily fusible and not suitable for ground colors a "mosaic" pattern was devised which was really a sort of scale pattern, usually seen in green, purple or blue and sometimes was confined to the edges as on the sugar bowl illustrated. When so used it was bound by delicate scrolls. This was about the last spark of invention, as was even recognized at the factory, for men were sent out to steal ideas from Sèvres, Höchst, Frankenthal, Munich, Paris and Vienna. As these places were largely run by men who had stolen their ideas from Meissen, there was little to be gained. A new school of art was started but was ineffective. Kändler continued but was thought old fashioned. He made some busts of children and more horribly pompous and involved vases.

Acier followed Kändler and then the "bourgeois-sentimental" style of Greuze, Chardin and Moreau le Jeune with such groups as "The Happy Parents," "The Broken Foot Bridge," "The Broken Eggs," and "Children with Mottoes." The work was photographic in detail even to the imitation of the lace of a dress and entirely lacking in spirit of any sort. Others such as Zeizig, called Schenau, Carl Schonheit, etc., posed as artists for a short while. Friederich Elias Meyer at least tried to do nudes but they were chiefly known for their small heads and affected poses.

Marcolini or Neo-Classical Period

Competition was now strong from the Thuringian factories, the large European ones and such places as that of Wedgwood. Kändler died in 1775 leaving the management of the factory to Count Camillo Marcolini from 1774.

People were sick to death of the restlessness of the baroque and rococo. As early as 1766 we have record of a style referred to as "à la Grecque" and "Hetrurische Kante" or "Etruscan borders" and now by 1780 we see the surfaces gilded all over with reserved medallions simply framed enclosing stiff painting. All is now static and in "good taste."

In 1782 the much envied "bleu-de-roi" of Sèvres was accomplished and called "Gutbrennblau." An underglaze green was also found. Miniature painters worked "en grisaille" (in grey) or with flowery natural colors. Illustrations were copied from books and the works of Canaletto, Hogarth and Berchem were copied. Marcolini had the Magdalen of Correggio reproduced from the Dresden gallery on a large oval plaque. Thus naturalism went hand in hand with neo-classicism by 1800. They could do anything but they really did nothing.

Fig. 934. Meissen tea-pot having *"Mosaik"* decoration about shoulder and top. Ht. 3⅝". Mark, crossed swords in blue. c. 1765. Metropolitan Mus. of Art.

Fig. 935. Plates with *Alt Osier* pattern (wickerwork) on rims and *chinoiserie* flowers and birds. c. 1735. Dia. 13½". Metropolitan Mus. of Art.

Fig. 936. Dresden or Meissen Marcolini period "monteith" decorated with "German flowers" in natural colors. Mark is crossed swords and star (c. 1785). Used for cooling glasses. Length 11". John Gibbons Coll.

Fig. 937. Meissen coffee-pot decorated with rococo frame and marine view on either side in puce, yellow, green, black, red and blue enamels. Marks are crossed swords in blue and 20 in gold. c. 1740–45. Ht. 9½". Metropolitan Mus. of Art.

Then they turned to repeating their own old styles and the flowers were crude and poorly colored while oriental subjects were reproduced but in simplified and insipid form. There was, as Hannover so well puts it, "an unparalleled fumbling about in all directions and periods." They tried to copy Wedgwood but the figures are hard in feeling and the paste too white and unpleasant. Actually the situation was not unlike the one which we ourselves went through between the first and second world war and, therefore, needs no more description.

The factory closed in 1810. It was revived but when Marcolini died in 1814 it was in debt for 400,000 thalers. In 1828 it tried "lithophanes" or plaques molded on the reverse in intaglio so that when light passed through them the pictures appeared in relief. These were also made in Berlin and some were used for sconce shades or lamp shades. In 1831 casts were made from molded glass. Lithography was brought into use and transfer printing was done. H. G. Kühn was the director from 1833 and his modeler, Ernst August Leuteritz, made a psuedo-rococo mode out of all feeling of the times and with it the wares sank lower and lower.

We have often repeated that the Meissen marks mean nothing, for they were so extensively copied everywhere in Germany, elsewhere in Europe and even in England. However, they are included as one should know what they were. It is enough to have forgotten the Meissen marks, as it has been said, "It is enough to have forgotten one's Latin."

The factory gave the worst failures to the workmen and sold the "Mittle-gut" wares to "Pfuscher," "Hausmaler," "Wilde Maler," and "Chamberlans," at reduced prices and with the mark of the factory already on them. These gentlemen then decorated them as seemed best. In 1740 it was decided that such wares should not be sold except with a little decoration on them but this did not bother the outside painters for they built around this decoration. In 1760 a system of lines was cut into the mark and it may be taken as certain that any mark with a stroke through the swords where they meet was not decorated at the factory. This cancellation was not used on figures.

The mark when accompanied by a T is simply that stolen by Thieme, a factory which is still working under the name of Sächsische Porzellanfabrik Carl Thieme and making forgeries. The proprietor is or was C. Kitsch and the place is near Dresden at a town called Potschappel. The wares are also faked by Samson in the Rue Béranger, Paris, or were up to this last war. The only obvious distinguishing characteristic is a slightly weaker color than that of the originals. Samson, of course, attempted to fake everything and was usually fairly successful at it.

Vienna Porcelain

The factory in Vienna was established in 1718 by Claudius Innocentius du Paquier with the help of Christoph Conrad Hunger the same enameler and gilder who started at Meissen, and then turned up at Vienna, Venice, Stockholm and finally at St. Petersburg, one of the peddlers of secrets from place to place, and Samuel Stölzel another arcanist. Herold too was there, as we have said, and in 1720 Stölzel and Herold went to Meissen, and Hunger to Venice.

The oldest piece of Vienna known is a two handled cup of Meissen shape and material, for Stölzel even took the precaution to bring along some of the "Schnorrische Erde" when he came. It is marked "Gott allein die Ehr'und sonst keinem meh—3 May—1719," ("To God alone and to none other be the honor—3 May—1719"). A finger vase of Delft shape is marked "Vienna 12 July 1721" and decorated in underglaze blue which seems to have been mastered before it was at Meissen.

Vienna, like Meissen, Plaue and Bayreuth, made a red stoneware decorated in silver and gold as well as white porcelain so decorated. Hannover makes four divisions of the early wares:

1.—Polychrome chinoiseries like Herold's with flowers and birds similar to Japanese Imari, about 1725, but without Böttger's mother-of-pearl and with spaces filled with trellises.

Hard paste porcelain dish in style of Jacob Helchis (c. 1740) decorated in black and gold. Dia. 16⅛". Metropolitan Mus. of Art.

Left: Group of white porcelain enamelled in colors, c. 1765–70. Ht. 8¼". Metropolitan Mus. of Art.
Right: Chocolate pot c. 1780–1800, showing Empire influence. Ht. 9½". Metropolitan Mus. of Art.

Cup of du Paquier period (c. 1720–1730). Hard paste with decoration in enamel colors. Ht. 3⅛". Metropolitan Mus. of Art.

Cup and saucer of Sorgenthal type but given dating of 1823–26 by museum. Metropolitan Mus. of Art.

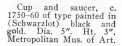

Cup and saucer, c. 1750–60 of type painted in (Schwarzlot) black and gold. Dia. 5". Ht. 3". Metropolitan Mus. of Art.

VIENNA PORCELAIN

PLATE 186

2.—Polychrome "Laub and Bandelwerk" or leafy scrolls with flowers, fruits, canopies, figures in landscapes in panels and cartouches, about 1730 to 1740.

3.—The black with gold decoration of the same sort of the same years.

4.—German naturalistic flower decorated pieces also of the same period.

Also the beginnings of the mythological, battle, genre scenes, and scenes with putti, etc., are rare but existent.

Much Vienna ware was decorated by outside painters like Bottengruber who was in the city between 1730 and 1736, Wolfsburg and Preussler. At the palace of the Count Dubsky there was a porcelain room such as was thought quite the thing in those days and walls, fireplace, furniture and all are made of porcelain. This seemed to be du Paquier's chief job.

Among the artists was Joseph Philipp Danhofer (1737) later of Bayreuth, Höchst and Ludwigsburg. Jakobus Helchis came from Trieste and did a few pieces decorated with fighting animals, etc., but chiefly in the black and gold style he did drawings of putti in all manner of scenes. He also did some "en camaieu" things in violet and also some "Schwarzlot" at first grey and later a rich black with red for the flesh parts of figures. About the only plastic work done at Vienna was the "panther handle." The most characteristic part of the style was the love of trellises, acanthus-palmettes, the scale pattern and lozenges as in the style of Baumgartner and Eissler, mixed with Japanese flowers or "German flowers," or "Indian flowers," and a strong tendency to overdecorate.

Du Paquier sold the factory in 1744 and it was placed under Mayerhofer who perhaps aided the factory by the discovery of a new kaolin deposit in Hungary in 1749. New artists worked in rococo taste. Christian Daniel Busch came from Meissen but went on to Nymphenburg. Johann Gottfried Klinger also came from Meissen but remained 30 years. Johann Sigmund Fischer was another famous painter and the modeler Johann Josef Niedermayer came from the Vienna Academy and remained between 1747 and 1784. Ludwig Lück drifted in for one year and then went to Fürstenberg and on to Copenhagen.

Early Part of "Second Period" at Vienna

During the first four or five years or between 1744 and about 1750 there were figures and landscapes painted in purple or grey with gilt rococo frames as well as naturalistic flowers, birds, animals, etc., after Meissen. Relief patterns also were used in the "Ozier" or "Brandenstein" manner. There remained also many of the du Paquier designs, of course, including "Schwarzlot" and Imari styles. European chinoiseries also continued until around 1780 when they had been replaced by lacquer designs in slight relief in gold on red or black ground. Baroque scrolls lost ground and the black was used for slight borders and landscapes.

Philip Ernst Schindler who did the finest figure painting about 1750 to 1760 made scenes of galanterie after Watteau, peasant scenes after Teniers and cavalry skirmishes in the style of Rugendas. The factory began to feel the weight of Meissen in competition which was going strong up to 1756 when the war started. Lück did a few figures and Niedermayer's can be recognized by their academic feeling, almost dancing movement and gentle smiles.

The earliest figures copied Meissen coloring as well as modeling but the later ones developed their own coloring dominated by brown, red and pale violet, light copper green, black, yellow and gold but always light in character and meticulous in execution. Characteristic is the lack of any base (1), a formal frieze of pendant tongue motives in gold on small bases (2), and a simple wave band of acanthus leaves about a small base (3).

In 1764 the manager was Josef Wolf and in 1770, von Kestler. In 1766 Meissen sent a scout to steal the new neo-classic designs which had begun about 1760. This sincerest form of flattery seemed to be most graciously extended in the whole European development of porcelain.

The tie between the Austrian and French courts through Marie Antoinette brought about strong influences from Sèvres as can be seen in the coquettish shapes, effeminate colors and such specialties as the bleu-de-roi over which was painted a gold network to lighten the depth of solid color, the "chiné" pattern and the "nach Taffet Art" (like taffeta effects).

In 1784 the factory was offered for sale and no purchaser found but a real manager was found in Konrad von Sorgenthal. The chief artist of this time was Anton Grassi who worked from 1778 and replaced Niedermayer in 1784. He was a pupil of Wilhelm Beyer who had been 8 years in Rome and was later a modeler at Ludwigsburg and later was made Court Sculptor, but his style by 1807 when he died was typically neo-classic, Empire.

Between about 1780 and 1785 he made figures with rococo feeling and polychrome glazes. Then Vienna like other factories tried to copy Wedgwood's jasper ware, largely in casts from French originals after Boucher, Bachelier and Pigalle, but the biscuit was somewhat yellowish. This was a transition type and soon Grassi, ever alert, made groups of his own such as "The Greeting" (1785) with a bit more life than his glazed pieces. Almost at once the neo-classic influence was seen in his "Judgment of Paris." Contemporary were his portrait busts and those of his pupil Elias Hütter.

EMPIRE PERIOD AT VIENNA (1791–1864)

Sorgenthal made a mistake which cost much in taste and prestige by appointing Josef Leithner in 1791. He made "Leithner blue" a copy of bleu-de-roi and various iridescent glazes running from mauve to copper red and finally an imitation bronze glaze. It was the custom to cover entirely the porcelain and also to try to make it look like other materials. Laurenz Herr imitated onyx cameos while Moritz Michael Daffinger did miniatures. Kothgasser could make very perfect borders in relief gold.

Sorgenthal died in 1805 and Grassi in 1807. Niedermayer, the son of the modeler, took charge but resigned in 1827 and in 1864 the Austrian Parliament shut the factory down. The blight of commerce had once again triumphed. A powerful royalty had cultivated porcelain, a luxury-loving aristocracy had sustained it, though with degraded taste, and now the masses had no interest. The murderous competition in appealing to the masses had raised the cry for cheaper and ever cheaper products. Nothing could stop the landslide to the present day depths of artistic degradation.

Under du Paquier in Vienna, as under Böttger in Meissen, there were no marks. Braun gives 15 odd examples, perhaps artists' marks, but they are unique. In 1744–1749, the "Bindenschild" mark, a shield with round fesse, the arms of the house of Austria, was used in iron-red, purple, black or impressed. In 1749 to about 1770 it was large, slanting and with thick strokes of underglaze blue. From 1770 to 1810 it was the same but symmetrically rounded and smaller. Then until the 1820's it was elongated and became triangular and about 1827 it was impressed and more regular. During the last few years the blue marks were imitated on wares of inferior sort to be sold to England. In 1783 impressed year marks were introduced, those before 1800 being only the last two numerals and those after, the last three. Impressed letters were only factory marks but painted numerals were artists' marks.

A Latin A meant "Ausschuss" on rejected wares. X was cut in undecorated wares.

Even before the last war the taste was such that du Paquier's period wares did not bring as much as the Sorgenthal stupid Empire things.

BERLIN PORCELAIN

We have described the abortive attempts of Wilhelm Kaspar Wegely to start a porcelain factory in Berlin and of the closing of his factory in 1757. It had never made anything but a sort of soft porcelain and now in 1763 the king bought up the place for 225,000 reichsthalers from an "industrial magnate," Johann Ernst Gotzkowsky who had started in without a cent. His published autobiography is not to be taken seriously.

The manager put in charge was Johann Georg Grieninger from 1761 to his death in 1798. The artistic director was Ernst Heinrich Reichardt who had been working under Wegely. He, however, died in 1764 and was followed by Theodor Gotthilf Manitius and under his management we find the figure painter Johann Balthasar Borrmann and the modeler Friedrich Elias Meyer, who was at Meissen (1748–1761), and Isaak Jakob Clauce who had been head painter under Wegely. Two other new artists from Meissen were Klipfel and Boehme and this background plus the beneficent help of King Frederick II assured success.

At first the paste was yellowish-grey but in 1765 a new body was presumably brought from the newly conquered province of Silesia, from Ströbel near Zobten and by 1770 this had added whiteness when mixed with the original clay. About 1771 kaolin was found in Brachwitz near Halle and later more at Sennewitz and Morl and these additions made the ware cold, bluish-white.

The Gotzkowsky "porcelain" is rare but grey and speckled and of little account. Some seemed to have been marked with an underglaze G. At Meissen a special pattern was made for this man before he took over the Berlin factory and it is called "Gotzkowsky erhabene Blumen." At Berlin the same pattern was called "Floramuster" while other designs were simply

Parts of set in natural colors. Probably after 1771 as they are hard paste. Pot and cover c. 3½" high. Metropolitan Mus. of Art.

Plate dated by museum c. 1765–70 and having well painted naturalistic flowers and pierced rim. Dia. 9⅝". Metropolitan Mus. of Art.

Hard paste milk-jug with flowers in natural colors and bands of green and pink with gilt trim. (1761–1786). Metropolitan Mus. of Art.

Part of tea and coffee service dated by museum between 1761 and 1830 but not likely to have been made before 1770 or later. Platter c. 10½" long. Metropolitan Mus. of Art.

BERLIN PORCELAIN

PLATE 187

pirated, such as the "Osier" and "Brandenstein." One new idea was the "Reliefzierat mit Spalier" (relief decoration with trellis) as used on the service for the Neues Palais at Potsdam. This is a really lovely pattern of interesting texture and color, being in gold on iron-red and with flowers in various colors. Some have thought it better than anything at Meissen. Another was the "Antikzierat" from about 1767 with blue "Mosaik" and gilt sprays with flowers in natural colors. Others were "new smooth" (1769), "vase shape with reeding" (1776), "smooth royal" (1780–81) and "smooth English" of the same year, and then the "smooth with beads" (1782). Most of these have some relief and much gold, with "German flowers" but no "Indian flowers" or chinoiseries. Purplish-red was also used for landscapes, figures, birds, etc.

It was noticeable that one single color would be predominant in the background such as green, iron-red, yellow, purple or gold. Painting en camaïeu was also done with two colors such as red and gold or pink and

Parts of a set of Berlin porcelain dating about 1763–1800 probably about 1780, with monogram in floral technique. Platter about 13″ long. Metropolitan Mus. of Art.

"Royal Berlin" tureen and stand of late 19th cent. with natural fruits and flowers like many earlier examples, and continuance of rococo feeling. Wm. H. Plummer & Co.

BERLIN PORCELAIN

PLATE 188

grey. The painting all tended toward drawing more and more and engravings were the source of much material. The underglaze blue was only used for common wares with "Muschel" (shell) patterns or "Zwiebelmuster" (the onion pattern) already used at Meissen and later to go with modification to Copenhagen.

As usual Watteau, Teniers and Boucher with the latter's children rendered in monochrome as well as natural colors, were the chief sources. Frederick the Great was not pleased with the imaginary battle scenes of Rugendas and so had some real scenes depicted. Exact naturalism was imposed by this particular monarch and the painters could not add or subtract figures from original paintings which they were set to copy. J. E. Nilson, Lessing, Chodowiecki and Piranesi were also followed in their engravings.

About 1765 the factory copied Sèvres wares and in the following year Frederick decided he would like to throw copies of Sèvres on the French market. Naturally this endeavor met with no success and a few large vases with poor underglaze, blue grounds and flower decoration in medallions only are left. The English influence with large jars having royal portraits in a wreath, etc., was felt slightly. And, of course, in the 1790's Wedgwood things were copied and then silhouettes by Ditmar, floral monograms and then relief portraits on gilt or monochrome grounds became popular.

The useful wares are not particularly worse than those of other factories of the period but the figures are certainly not good. Friedrich Elias Meyer's figures with too small heads continued, but his brother Wilhelm Christian Meyer joined the factory in 1766 having completed some monumental sculptures and the trend turned toward monumental forms not suited to porcelain. The young brother was the better of the two and he made many "allegorical children," "Muses," etc., and most of his things are more French than German in style. He had much to do with a large central table decoration given by Frederick to Catherine II to seal the alliance of Hubertsburg. This was completed in 1772 and shows Catherine enthroned under a canopy with attendants in biscuit and other figures paying homage rendered in polychrome. A grand affair!

Between 1785 and 1789 Johann George Müller made a whole series of tiresome allegorical figures without expression and in light colors. Some fairly good copies were made of Meissen birds and those of Pedrozzi.

Johann Carl Friederich Riese made naturalistic figures during the neoclassic times and collaborated with the architect Genelli in making table decorations.

During Gotzkowsky's time G was used in underglaze blue, brown and gold, those in blue are probably painted later for some 10,000 such pieces remained when he left the factory.

Berlin was never a very popular ware and never commanded high prices; therefore, it is less copied.

From 1763 to 1786 during the life of Frederick the Great a sceptre of various sizes was used in underglaze blue; 1763 to 1765 it is short like a clove; 1765 to 1770 it is long and slender with a distinct knob, grip, cross stroke and three-pointed finial with a letter sometimes below it; in the 1770's it is short again with cross stroke about middle; in 1780's it is thin with thickening of stem above and below cross stroke and fork at one end; from 1835 the K.P.M. is used; in 1844 to 1847 an eagle with same letters and in 1870 the sceptre with variations was used again with intent to deceive. The K.P.M. is also like the 1723 mark of Meissen but the ware is entirely different.

HÖCHST WARES

That I am not alone in my feeling about these 18th century wares is proven by the following from Emil Hannover, "Generally speaking, a breach of faith leads to no good. And yet it was through a breach of contract and disloyalty in many other forms that it was made possible in the 18th century for the art of porcelain to blossom for the service and delight of mankind, in practically every spot where it awakened the interest of some art-loving prince. For wherever it gained a footing it was due to the betrayal of the secret of porcelain production. Again and again this secret was revealed by workmen deserting from Meissen, and soon there were so many

FIG. 938. Hard paste Höchst jug c. 1770 to 1775, Louis Viktor Gerverot decorated after an engraving which represents "October" by Johann Esaias Nilson. Metropolitan Mus. of Art.

FIG. 939. Höchst "Woman with hen" and "Egg seller" made about 1750 before the French influence of rococo was felt. Ht. 6¼". A. Beckhardt Coll.

FIG. 940. Hard paste condiment jar with figure symbolizing "Summer." Ex Collection of Adolf Beckhardt. Metropolitan Mus. of Art.

initiated that—at any rate among the circle of the arcanists—it was no longer a secret at all." Perhaps the art did blossom but it was truly a malodorous flower which filled the air with stagnation of thought and the death of all inspired originality, alert observation and exploration of the beautiful and appealing, which is the business of the true artist.

This time it was Adam Friedrich von Löwenfinck who brought the Meissen secret to two merchants, Johann Christoph Göltz and Johann Felician Clarus, who applied in 1746 to the Elector of Mainz for the opening of a place in Höchst. Löwenfinck had left an unpleasant trail behind him also at Fulda but a 50-year grant was given and even permission to use the wheel from the electoral arms, but in 1749 he had to resign and Johann Benckgraff took his place only to depart hastily for Fürstenberg in 1753, while Löwenfinck trotted on to Strasburg.

Up to 1760 the factory made as much faïence as porcelain. In 1765 Göltz was forced to hold up payments to the workers and the factory came under the management of Johann Heinrich Masz. In 1765 it was reorganized as the "Churfürstlich-Maynzische privilegierte Porzellaine-Fabrique." The last elector, Friedrich Karl Joseph, took an interest and had to take the whole company in 1778 or shortly after, because the other stockholders had exploited it. The financial condition became worse and worse until 1796 when it was closed, with liabilities three times its assets. Some of its models were sent to Damm, near Aschaffenburg, for the making of "Steingut."

Practically all Höchst designs and models came direct from Meissen. One helmet cup with sturdy base and involved handle suggests a Delft form. The ware was at first grey but later became white. The only invention in color is an unpleasant red-purple approaching carmine and this was often used in monochrome landscapes.

FIG. 941. Höchst set of five vases with painting in purple. The gourd vases are interesting and new but involved. Made about 1755. A. Beckhardt Coll.

FIG. 942. Two figures from Höchst dating about 1750 or the second period showing the faience appearance which is typical. A. Beckhardt Coll.

Dr. Hans C. Krüger and E. W. Braun divide the figures into four periods: 1746–1749—To the resignation of Löwenfinck they are short and clumsy with large hands with crude movement. They are from the Italian Comedies, religious subjects, peasants, signed Zeschinger. All are on domed white bases with stumps supporting them. They look more like faïence than porcelain. 1749–1754—Similar to first but improvement in some figures of gods, groups of lovers, seasons, a fortune teller, etc., done by Simon Feilner and Job

Zeschinger. There are also some Italian comedy figures with square baroque bases which are so wooden that Krüger thinks they were from the carvings of Simon Troger.

1754–1767—Strong similarity to Frankenthal perhaps through Johann Friederich Lück who probably spent some time at Höchst before going to Frankenthal in 1758. Figures still stiff under direction of Laurentius Russinger as late as 1760 when the "Freemasons group" was made. A little later some "Kissing groups" and candlesticks were made after compositions by Pater and are fairly graceful and light in color, not too much of the ware being covered with enamel.

1767–1779—Johann Peter Melchior came after Russinger left to open a factory at Pfalz-Zweibrücken and brought fame though he was only 25 when he started at Höchst. In 1769 Grieninger tried to get hold of him at Berlin as did also Sèvres and Frankenthal. In Höchst he was Court Sculptor.

He did not go to Paris but was influenced by Flaconet and Claud Michel ("Clodion"); however, his child figures are entirely his own and are gay, lively and usually up to some prank. His "Venuses" have the rounded look and false modesty of the styles of the age. An excessively sweet pink seemed a favorite color. He was no great artist but a good craftsman and did about 300 pieces. Perhaps the nearest to great things he did were the portraits of Goethe and of the poet's family. From this association he turned his hand to writing and made a stupid and unreadable work on the theory of art.

In 1746–1770 the mark was the electoral wheel with or without the hat above it, impressed or painted in overglaze black, brown, purple, iron-red and gold. About 1770 it was only in underglaze blue. Legend has it that the gold was used only for the superior pieces but it was also on many poor examples. This is seldom a mark on the bisque figures. A letter G over the wheel may have stood for Göltz. Many letters are used including HM which dealers like to say stands for Melchior but does not as he signed only a few pieces and then with his full name. I.Z. stands for Zeschinger and A.L. for Löwenfinck.

Fürstenberg Wares

Fürstenberg is slightly southwest of Berlin and Plaue. The factory was in a castle above the Weser on the outskirts of the Sollinger Wald in the worst possible place for such a plant, but the whim of Duke Charles I of Brunswick placed it there and filled it with ne'er-do-well adventurers. In 1753 Benckgraff arrived with Johann Zeschinger, the painter, and Simon Feilner, the modeler, and soon the factory began to make porcelain.

Fig. 943. Höchst tea-caddy with scene of Mongolfier's Balloon in natural colors and gold. Made about 1785. Ht. 5". A. Beckhardt Coll.

Fig. 944. Cup and saucer which the museum attributes to "Furstenberg, 1750–95" but as the factory was not making porcelain until after 1753 is hardly correct. Actually the pieces are likely to date between 1770 and 1780. Plate dia. 5″. Metropolitan Mus. of Art.

Benckgraff died and Feilner helped manage while he turned out some fairly original figures of miners, Greek gods, comedy figures, etc., having expressive little faces quite different from the doll-like faces on most other figures of the time.

Zeschinger produced a better palette and the other painters divided themselves into specialties much as was reported done in the K'ang Hsi period in China but on a less extensive scale.

The oldest known piece is a plate dated 1758 which has a monochrome purple picture of two lovers in a garden with the borders decorated with alternating rococo panels and perforated trellises. Even as late as 1767 the factory lacked a yellow, a brown and an underglaze blue that would not run. Up to 1770 the paste was impure, yellowish and inclined to warp, while the glaze was greyish and full of specks.

The Seven Years War brought about the close of the factory in 1762 until peace was concluded. The Meissen and Berlin "Reliefzieraten" were copied but a more involved form was developed probably with the hope of hiding the glaze imperfections. The only ground painting was done with a sea-green and the underglaze blue. The designs were about like those of other factories of the period and much monochrome was used because they were taken from engravings so that the artists did not know what colors to use, and also some colors were missing. However landscapes were done in poly-chrome as well as iron-red, purple or sepia following Weinrotter, Waterloo, Watteau, Eisen, Leprince, Milson and Pillement though the chinoiseries of the latter are rare.

At length the ultimate has been achieved! We have witnessed the prostitution of ceramic art by painters ever since Greek days but here at length the painters made actual pictures of porcelain to hang on walls; not tiles, not plaques but pictures complete with ornate rococo gold frames also of porcelain. Art with a capital A was achieved by the great C. G. Albert with his chickens, turkeys and other birds and George Heinrich Holtzmann painted pastorals while others did portraits of gods and goddesses with great pomposity, bad colors and the worst of taste. They all date about 1767 or 1768 and Scherer thinks they were done as samples of skill in the days of adversity to help the artists to obtain work in the faïence kiln at Brunswick. This may or may not be true.

From about 1760 the plastic work seems to have been abandoned, except for a few figures by Feilner of about 1766, probably because of the difficulties in handling the paste. In 1770, however, Trabert, the director, died and was replaced by Kaulitz and Johann Ernst Kohl who improved the clay and revived the art. The new artists were Johann Christian Rombrich, Anton Carl Luplau (who later in 1776 left to become the master modeler at the Royal Porcelain Factory at Copenhagen), Carl Gottlieb Schubert (until 1804), P. Hendler and the Frenchman Desoches (until 1744). First there were putti in the Meissen manner but less lively and then birds and animals from Meissen models and ivories. Luplau did Greek figures, some things after Feilner and some original things such as "Flohsucherin" (woman looking for a flea). Desoches followed Chardin and Greuze as in the "Family at the Coffee-table." Schubert copied some "Seasons" from ivory ones by Permoser, "artisans" from Höchst, "street-vendors" and such from Berlin and a Leda from a bronze model. Hendler was just about as original.

As early as the 1760's biscuit portrait plaques and busts were made. The plaques had usually white, blue or gilt frames attached and bear the factory mark and often the name of the person represented, scratched in the paste. Both Desoches and Rombrich did these and seemingly from life. Another type represents Greek poets, statesmen, and philosophers in the Wedgwood manner, white on light blue, the frames of laurel leaves inscribed in gold with the name of the person represented. These are by Schubert and copied from the gems and cameos in the ducal Kunstkammer in Brunswick.

Busts of all sizes up to life were made again from life and this might have led to an original art but the ground was barren and the spark died out.

The "Transition Period of Painting" took place in 1770 and lasted until about 1785 and the biscuit and glaze was improved, the shapes simpler and the painting so much improved that it reached about the best for that day and age. However, this was not for long as the Neo-Classicism killed the larger spaces which had brought freedom to the painting by flutings like those on the "Apulian vases" of Italy

Fig. 945. Furstenberg porcelain of about 1785 to 1790 with an antique head in grey showing the neo-classic trend of the times. Metropolitan Mus. of Art.

and covering of the ground with colors. Painting sunk to silhouettes, antique portraits en grisaille and figures after Angelica Kauffmann or little elegaic landscapes enclosed in medallions. Wedgwood shapes were copied and about the only invention was the making of garniture sets of five or seven vases ranging from small àt the ends to highest in the center. Many of these vases bear inscriptions commemorating persons or certain days, for this was a period when memories were carefully kept alive and such things were regarded with sweet smiles of sadness.

Another type had "Arabian vases" resting on "Arabesque scrolls" painted on them with precision and centered in large areas of white with garland borders. Of course these were no more Arabian than the gypsies were Egyptian but this was a day of strange beliefs.

In 1795 the factory came under the management of Gerverot who remained until 1814. He had had a checkered career, born in Luneville, worked at Sèvres, then Niderviller, whence he stole a copy of all the recipes of the factory, and then to Ludwigsburg, Höchst, Frankenthal, Weesp (Holland), Schrezheim, Loosdrecht (Holland), Wedgwood, Cologne and several other places. He had a thorough system of pillage and naturally had learned a lot; almost everything, in fact, except the fundamentals of real art enjoyment or art practice, which cannot be stolen. His period parallels that of Sorgenthal at Vienna and rested upon the same misconceptions through leaning on Sèvres and Wedgwood. The best known painter was Heinrich Christian Brüning who worked diligently. Even the biscuit busts became tight, stiff and meaningless.

The factory mark F is used right up to today often on old models in order to deceive. The medallions had an F in gold on the backs and the busts had a running horse impressed and a blue F on the pedestals.

NYMPHENBURG WARES

The Elector Max III. Joseph of Bavaria provided a site at Neudeck-ob-der-Au in 1747 under the supervision of Franz Ignaz Niedermayer from Munich. Three workmen were hired away from Vienna and a fourth from the same place, Joseph Jakob Ringler, came as arcanist in 1753. The factory was state property under the management of Count Sigmund von Haimhausen and shortly Ringler decamped for Ludwigsburg. However, his own secrets were stolen by a "Chymikus," J. P. Rupert Härtl so all was well and in 1761 the factory was moved to Nymphenburg, northwest of Munich, where it became famous. In 1765 it had 200 workmen but during the famine of 1770 to 1771 there were only 30. When Max III. Joseph died in 1777 the Bavarian Electorate came to Karl Theodor of the Palatinate who already owned Frankenthal and it was not until his successor in 1799, Max IV. Joseph came into power that the factory was revived. It gained in 1800 when Frankenthal was closed and continued until 1862 as a state institution. It suffered the same Neo-Classic fate as the other factories and in 1822 an architect named Gärtner became head and proceeded to provide classical forms. In 1862 it was turned over to private hands and the usual revival of the old forms was tried with little effect.

Among the useful wares were "Rechauds" or food warmers which seemed to have been a specialty. These date about 1760 and preserve the rococo feeling. An early jar made between 1755 and 1760 in the National Museum, Stockholm, is treated like the Niderviller faïence that is painted to imitate grained wood on which is tacked a piece of paper bearing an engraving in red. It has the first mark of the factory, a hexagram. Another piece has cupids in gray on a purple ground and with etched gold borders. Still another type made about 1765 is a heavy and hard ware painted meticulously with naturalistic flowers and butterflies, but with crude colors.

A series of jugs or coffee-pots are decorated with park views, German flowers, country scenes, birds in landscapes, etc., in gold with brown details, gold and purple and other combinations. The influences were, of course, the same J. E. Nilson, Teniers, etc. All such medallions had rococo frames at first which gradually narrowed and disappeared because they involved too much labor.

BUSTELLI PERIOD

Another type was covered with imitation striped textile patterns, one of which was called chiné (chintz). But all the wares were overshadowed by the figure work due to an "unknown Italian," as Nagler calls him, who worked there between 1754 and 1763. This "unknown Italian" was Franz Anton Bustelli (or, as he was formerly known, Bastelli), and though he ranks with the famous Kändler and actually had better taste in proportions, etc., nothing whatsoever is known of his early life before he came to Nymphenburg in 1754.

At Neudeck between 1747 and 1749 the master modeler was Johann Theophil Schreiber who was an assembler rather than a modeler and after 1749 it was Johann Georg Härtl. They created little ladies and gentlemen in rococo costumes and stiff poses, with expressionless faces but stylized and elongated and with a certain toss of the head. These are on low irregular stands while those of Bustelli have regular oval or polygonal or rococo scroll bases showing his immediate tendency to design which would not leave an unmeaning detail, if it was possible to improve it. Bustelli's color was improved and sparingly used. He gradually developed his bases into rising rococo scrolls from flat ones and these were brought up so high as to act as supports and at the same time as counterpoise for the departure from the vertical of the figures, which was an invention of a kind. His figures become more and more vital and overflowing with life. Those from the Italian Comedies dance and turn their heads with the most capricious and Latin characteristics and truly they show by contrast how heavy is the Teuton conception of such things, but the genre subjects are as alive, and the street vendors, flower girls, fishmongers, cheese-sellers and Chinese figures are all personalities into which he has breathed life. His children are especially humorous and the putti very naughty and gay.

There is in his work an exaggerated turn or drop of the head to one side and an accompanying shrug of the shoulder which is over-coy. It is seen in most of the figures and the busts of laughing children which are so well

FIG. 946. Nymph-enburg porcelain stein with pewter cover and base and typical polychrome monogram in flowers. Late 18th cent. J. Gibbons Coll.

FIG. 947. Nymph-enberg horseman of about 1760 and prob-ably by Bustelli as can be told by the small head and exag-gerated pose. The colors are natural-istic. A. Beckhardt Coll.

known. There is also a sentimental languishing at times, as in the Mater Dolorosa, but at other times he seems to rise above his day and make fun of the sweet gentlemen and so charming ladies kissing the tips of their fingers, flirting behind fans and reading love letters with a bashful smile.

FIG. 948. Nymphen-burg hard paste figures of chinoiserie type. White paste with trans-parent glaze. Ht. 4″ and 4½″. Designed by Bustelli. Metro-politan Mus. of Art.

Certainly his humor comes beautifully to light in the groups of two lovers. These were done about 1760 and the bases have risen into backgrounds. "The Impetuous Suitor" is fairly crawling forward on his knees as he im-portunes his terribly shocked and outrageously insulted lady for the ancient favor (she nevertheless has raised her skirt well above her knee in the anxiety of the moment) and she pushes him away with one hand while she raises the other in a gesture of astonishment and opens her mouth noise-lessly, while cupid, hanging to the branch of a tree with one hand and caress-ing his chest with the other, looks on. In "The Love among the Ruins" we see a more casual approach as the figures recline against rococo scrolls as large as they are and the lady seems properly reluctantly willing, while on the coping adjacent to a broken stone tower sits a bored goat looking off into the distance, and the lady's dog barks through jealousy in the fore-ground. Bustelli did dogs well as we see in the "Lady Attacked by a Dog"

Fig. 949. A figure of the "Dottore" by the Furstenberg factory decorated in black and flesh with touches of red, blue and yellow.

Fig. 950. A small Bustelli bust of a coy young lady, Nymphenburg (c. 1760) after one by Kandler of the same year.

Fig. 951. Nymphenburg figure of the comedy character "Pantaloon" colored in red, black, gold and flesh.

and how well he rendered her startled turn as the dog snaps and tears her dress. He seemed to have difficulty in tying more than two figures together in movement and did only a few with a number of figures such as the "Hunting Group."

In 1763 Bustelli died and his place was taken by Dominikus Jakob Auliczek who had had a long academical training as a sculptor. He had studied architecture in Rome under Gaetano Chiaveri, who built the Catholic church at Dresden. His works show that he knew anatomy and the other academic essentials very well but had absolutely no feeling for the medium of porcelain. His "Shepherd and Shepherdess with Bird and Cage" is poor as compared with Bustelli's things. The shepherdess has plunked herself down in a most uncomfortable and unnatural

Fig. 952. Late Nymphenburg coffee-pot of the neo-classic influence long after Bustelli. Metropolitan Mus. of Art.

pose and seems to be looking beyond the bird in a dream state and this is rather typical of the lack of feeling in all his things. His large "Hercules and Omphale," "Mars and Vulcan," etc., are simply small editions of the works of

Bernini. His animal combats are after engravings by Ridinger, dry, unpleasant. Even so, many terra cotta casts were made of them in the 19th century.

Auliczek was pensioned off in 1797 and succeeded by J. P. Melchior who had exhausted his powers at Höchst before leaving. He made some portrait medallions and busts. Nymphenburg ended in the cold and uninteresting biscuit technique as did the other factories. Nothing about the colors was exceptional except the black. Many of Bustelli's things are left white but have a pleasant greyish or greenish tint accented in the hollows where the glaze runs thick.

Frankenthal, Kelsterbach and Ansbach copied Bustelli's works unsuccessfully and they are still being made so far as we know in the old factory. In 1792 much Nymphenburg porcelain was sold white and decorated outside the factory. Some of these outside painters were discovered by Hofmann who deciphered the marks.

FIG. 953. About 20 to 30 years ago the porcelain works at Nymphenburg started work again making an excellent porcelain. These well painted jars with white reserved medallions in yellow ground and natural colored flowers are typical. Ht. 17½". Warren E. Cox Coll.

Between 1753 and 1760 the mark was a *hexagram or six pointed star* with chemical or alchemical letters and numerals outside the points of the two intersecting triangles in underglaze blue, while the factory was at the old site of Neureck, also in paste impressed a *small shield* with oblique lozenges, the Bavarian "Rautenschild" at first sharp and after a few years blunted with design slanting from upper right hand corner to lower left.

In 1761 the same shield was used and occasionally a larger shield, while in 1763 the smaller one was resumed. Around 1800 the shield became carelessly drawn in a shape rather like a turtle shell. In 1810 to 1815 the old original shield was used but contrary to heraldic usage, slanting from the upper left corner to lower right. In about 1850 the five pointed star above a shield was impressed with a stamp.

There are many exceptions to these general rules: 1.—A St. Andrew's cross may replace the shield; 2.—An oval with lozenges may replace the shield; 3.—The hexagram may be used later by Auliczek; 4.—A series of "Turchenkopgen" (Turkish cups) to be sent to the Near East was marked with two crossed staves made to resemble the Meissen mark in various forms.

Many letters and signs are also used but have not been deciphered. The most usual is an intwined AC for Adam Clair, a pupil of Melchior's about 1799.

FRANKENTHAL WARES

Paul Hannong, the faïence maker of Strasburg, had with the help of Löwenfinck just begun to make porcelain in 1754 when Vincennes, later to be Sèvres, was given the monopoly for France. He was a resident of Alsace which was now in France and now out and found himself in a difficult position. He tried to sell his secret to the French government but was not successful and so finally went to the Elector Palatine, Carl Theodor, and was given the privilege to open a factory in 1755 at Frankenthal, though he had wanted to go to Mannheim.

The son, Charles Hannong, was superintendent and meanwhile the father returned to Strasburg to continue his faïence business, while supplying his son with materials, workmen and models. In 1757 the son died and was succeeded by another son, Joseph Adam Hannong, who finally bought the factory from his father in 1759 and, after the father's death in 1860, carried on both factories. The faïence factory was a success but the porcelain one could not be made to pay and finally he had to sell out to the Elector Carl Theodor who put it under a complicated management under Adam Bergdoll.

In 1770 Simon Feilner of Höchst and Fürstenberg was an assistant in charge of modeling. Bergdoll was ousted by Feilner who stayed on until about 1794 or 1795 when the French occupied Frankenthal and leased the factory to Peter van Recum. Then the French left and it reverted to the electoral administration until 1797 when it became French again and was leased to the heir of Peter van Recum, a relative named Johann Nepomuk van Recum, but it was not successful and in 1800 it was abolished and some of the workmen were transferred to Nymphenburg.

Thus the place lasted only half a century and under ever-changing management. The first master modeler was Johann Wilhelm Lanz who was under Joseph Adam Hannong in most of the first electoral period. He had no specialty but copied the usual subjects and technique from Meissen. His color was bold, not always in good taste and not well applied.

FIG. 954. Dancer from Frankenthal c. 1760, possibly by J. W. Lanz. White hard paste with overglaze enamel colors. Ht. 5½". Metropolitan Mus. of Art.

Johann Friedrich Lück was contemporary and took Lanz' place in 1761 when he departed, keeping it until 1764 and then going on to Meissen and Höchst. His work is stiff and over-ornate but well colored. His best known Frankenthal groups are "The Pair of Dancers," "The Five Senses," "The Princess and Her Retinue" and some arbor groups with pairs of lovers.

Joseph Adam Hannong was an arcanist but may have tried his hand at art with "The Woman Playing a Hurdy-gurdy" signed "J.A. Hannong 1761" which looks exactly like Lück's work in biscuit. Perhaps the style was so quickly contagious or perhaps it was just one more of those things.

The Carl Theodor Period (1762–1794–5) changed the figures to those with antique draperies or none at all. In 1762 Konrad Link was master modeler having studied at Vienna and Berlin and practiced at Mannheim. After he left Frankenthal in 1766 he returned to Mannheim but continued to furnish the factory with models and drawings. He did "The Nine Muses," "Twelve Months," "The Seasons," "The Elements," relief portraits of Carl Theodor and his consort, "The Graces" and the usual gods, allegorical figures, etc., one of the finest of which is "Meleager and Atlanta," simple and lovely in pose. His figures have expressive eyes and he seems to have liked to do them looking at each other. His use of drapery for support and to give movement is well handled.

Karl Gottlieb Lück took his place and is supposed to have been a relative of both Johann Freirich and also the ivory carver Johann Christoph Ludwig Lück who was employed at Meissen, Vienna and Copenhagen. His style was made up of that of Johann Freirich's and of Konrad Link's with a leaning toward the former, than whom he seemed to have more humor and a lighter touch with more vitality. He was a good colorist. He preferred to do things from actual life, though his "Europa and the Bull" and "Pluto and Diana at the Altar" are fairly good. Such groups as "The Birthday of the Child," "The Dismissed Servant Maid," "The Good Mother," and "The Naughty Children," are his forte and, in fact, this story telling sort of art was typical of the period. He also did conventional Chinese groups, pastoral groups and hunting groups as well as a cavalry engagement, all of which are lacking in form and life. He died in 1775.

FIG. 955. Frankenthal salt cellar with pastoral scenes and floral spray simply said to be 18th cent. by the museum but bearing the mark CT in blue, standing for Carl Theodor, which would make it between 1762 and 1770. Length 2½". Metropolitan Mus. of Art.

Adam Bauer, who took his place was not much of an artist though he had been the Court Sculptor at Württemberg. His figures were academic but often with heads too large which gives them a dwarf-like look.

Johann Peter Melchior took his place in 1779 with a dry technique and some of the old models from Höchst and Frankenthal. He also did some of the little children figures, portrait medallions, etc.

Adam Clair and his pupil, Landolin Ohmacht, carried on the medallions and biscuit busts in the same style.

The earliest pieces have P.H. for Paul Hannong and are according to Polaczek made in Strasburg between 1751 and 1754 before Hannong set up his factory in Frankenthal. They are rouge boxes in the form of a fragment of fluted column, a round tureen with German roses in polychrome and a set of vases with "Mosaik" and large panels showing theatrical scenes after Watteau, etc., including "Chinese style" and wicker patterns.

Just a little later the style became florid and "Indian flowers" were used in two shades of purple. A great centerpiece of rococo scrolls and lattice upon which are many detachable figures, dates 1760. An even more ornate chandelier after a Konrad Link model was made about 1765 for the Residential Palace at Karlsruhe and is mentioned by Hannover as being, "probably, as regards structure, the finest of all 18th century chandeliers." If this is so, we must conclude that his ideas of structure and ours are at variance. Nothing much was actually invented unless it be the rhomboidal platters with rounded corners which seem to be a specialty. There was much ordinary figure painting, the best known artists being Winterstein, Magnus and Osterspey. Another specialty was the painting of exotic birds.

Between 1770 and 1780 the factory of Carl Theodor tried to copy Sèvres and adopted a spotted pattern known as "oeil-de-perdrix" and a textile pattern with gold stripes and polychrome flowers along with other textile

FIG. 956. Frankenthal, German porcelain group with polychrome decoration and mark in underglaze blue. (1787). Ht. 7¼″. Metropolitan Mus. of Art.
FIG. 957. Pieces from a set dating about 1770 and made at Frankenthal during the John Hannong period. Ht. of coffee pot 9″. Metropolitan Mus. of Art.

patterns. They also did grained wood like Niederviller faïence and Nymphenburg porcelain and with the same sort of engraving in red. How worn out even so simple and cheap a trick does get in this century!

Feilner is said to have invented an underglaze black, a "bleu-de-roi" and a sky blue. We also hear that in 1769 Berthevin sold the secret of transferring prints in colors to the factory but no known pieces exist. The technique of the body of Frankenthal was brought from Passau and is as a rule soft white resembling French soft paste, and even at times yellowish. In 1774 a kaolin deposit was found but it was rather poor and from that date the ware is grey and often blistered on the surface. The factory was lucky in that work stopped before it came to the final period of the decline.

The first mark is a "Rautenschild" like that of Nymphenburg but painted in underglaze blue rather than impressed. Rarely is there an impressed P.H. for Paul Hannong. Later the same was used without the shield and the initials were sometimes impressed several times on a piece. An F (for Frankenthal) often is also used. The *lion rampant* in underglaze blue for the Palatinate was introduced while Paul Hannong was still in charge before 1760 and Joseph Adam Hannong added his initials JAH from 1759 to 1762. In 1762 CT for Carl Theodor was used, surmounted with the electoral cap and also in underglaze blue. Between 1762 and 1770 we find below this AB for Adam Bergdoll. After 1770 abbreviated dates such as 71 or 77 were impressed or painted. In 1795 the electoral initials ceased because of the French taking of the factory and there are very rare pieces with P V R in underglaze blue. In 1797 V R in underglaze blue stood for van Recum the heir. There are also the usual painter's and modeler's marks.

Before the first World War figures brought between 20 and 200 pounds in London but now they are nowhere nearly so much liked. The factory did not come to the point of copying its own old wares.

LUDWIGSBURG WARES

Ludwigsburg is just north of Stuttgart and with it we come to the last of the "important" factories of Germany which sprouted around Meissen like "suckers" about a willow stump, and this was much like the others. Charles Eugene, Duke of Württemberg, was a spendthrift and as luxury loving as most of the princes of the time. Of course he had to have a porcelain factory to add to his magnificence. His was a long reign from 1737 to 1793 and in 1758 he simply took over a small place that had been running a few years in Ludwigsburg near Stuttgart. He placed in charge of it Joseph Jacob Ringler who had previously worked at Vienna and Neudeck, and in this he was either wise or lucky for Ringler stuck for 40 years in spite of the troubles at the factory.

As was usual, the factory had been started without thought as to proper location and there was no fuel or kaolin in the surrounding country so the latter had to be brought from Hafnerzell, near Passau, far to the east. It was said that the richest of the merchants could not pay what the porcelain cost so the factory was attached to the faïence factory from about 1763 to help defray the expenses. In 1766 the ducal residence was transferred to the same City of Ludwigsburg and demands kept 154 workers busy; but in 1775 the residence was moved again to Stuttgart and a decline set in, the number of employees dropping to 81 in 1776. The Duke Charles took a journey to Sèvres and Wedgwood and was enthused, but when he died in 1793 the factory declined still more. Elector Frederick tried to revive it by bringing in some French workmen from Sèvres but in 1824 the undertaking was liquidated.

The porcelain is actually inferior to that of the other German factories, being grey and unevenly glazed, but it was cohesive and very delicate details could be modeled in it. Also large pieces could be made.

The art director Johann Gottfried Trothe (1758–1762) as well as Gottlieb Friedrich Riedel, who came to the factory in 1759 from Frankenthal, and Johann Göz, who was the first assembler "repairer" or "Oberpoussierer" as they were called, were all of the rococo school. Riedel left behind him engravings, sketches and models which were used by many factories. Göz was the leading figure modeler and is probably more or less responsible for the "Apollo Candlestick," in white porcelain at the Altertümersammlung in Stuttgart, as well as the companion piece, the "Diana Candlestick," and other figures (see Hans Christ on Ludwigsburg). Frankenthal is the undoubted influence due to Riedel who had been born in Dresden, worked at Meissen (1743–56), Höchst (1757–59) and then at Frankenthal before coming to Ludwigsburg. In 1779 he made engravings in Augsburg. He died in 1784. He and Göz both are probably responsible for the little dancing group of two men crowning a lady, and others of the same stiff and fussy sort. The ones with regularly shaped pedestals are possibly correctly attributed to Göz or Johann Jacob Louis who took his place.

Louis worked at the factory between 1762 and 1772 and, to the delight of collectors, marked his work, with an L. He did a parrot, and the birds as well as animals which are often fighting. He also did a fairly good "Turk with Horse" and possibly some Chinese figures which Hannover says remind him of Bustelli but he makes it clear, it should be noticed, that he is not contributing to the false legend which Balet built up concerning a mythical "Pustelli" supposed to have been a famous artist at Ludwigsburg. There was no such person.

Hans Christ in his book claims that these Chinese figures were actually done by Domenico Ferretti but Hannover says, "apparently without adequate reason." Ferretti had come to Stuttgart to work on the residency before he went to work in the porcelain factory in 1764. He brought a classical influence which soon became predominant as elsewhere. Most of his things were simply small scale adaptations of his work in stone and the heads are sometimes very small to give them a monumental look.

More than Ferretti, Christian Wilhelm Beyer brought classicism. He had been a painter and architect in Rome before deciding to become a sculptor. He went to Württemberg in 1759. There are two collections of his etchings in Vienna, one done in 1779 and the other in 1784 which give us a fine idea of his style. He was influenced by Wincklemann in Rome and by Natoire of the French Academy there. It is interesting to see how strongly contrasted are his alive and sexual Dionysiac Graeco-Roman divinities and his rather stupid Olympian ones. In such subjects as "The Satyr Kissing a Bacchante or others with his male and female figures embracing and crushing grapes he finds life and lust, while in his "Mourning Artemisia," "Venus," as well as his allegories such as "Veritas" and "Libertas" he becomes so banal that we can hardly believe the same artist did them.

In his "Musical Solos" (if in truth they are his), which is a series well known, he gets a pensive, coquettish feeling which is more tolerable in the female than in the male figures.

In 1767 he left for Vienna where he assisted in decorating with sculpture the court at Schönbrunn.

There were other sculptors of whom we know very little. Joseph Weinmüller was certainly there and did some work but has only been credited on doubtful grounds with a "Hercules Fighting the Nemean Lion." Pierre

François Lejeune has been credited by Balet with the above mentioned "Musical Solos," etc., instead of Beyer and this is not difficult to believe, for I cannot very well conceive of the same man doing such widely different things, technically speaking, as the bacchanalian figures and the almost silly "Player on the French Horn" in Stuttgart, who looks as though he were about to weep. But these arguments are of little interest to us and we need only note that another authority, Schnorr von Carolsfeld, denies him any part at all in modeling at Ludwigsburg.

FIG. 958. Ludwigsburg figure of a street sweeper by Beyer (1762–1767) decorated with enamel colors. Ht. 5⅛". Metropolitan Mus. of Art.
FIG. 959. Ludwigsburg late 18th cent. group representing Summer, one of a series of the seasons, decorated with pale lilac, blue, apple-green, yellow, red and black and flesh colors. Ht. 8¾". Metropolitan Mus. of Art.

All at least agree that Johann Heinrich Schmidt was the "repairer" at the factory from 1774 and did two white urns supported by three figures and a pair of memorial columns with a couple placing a wreath on them.

Later in the years 1790 to 1795 two more academic sculptors, Philip Jacob Scheffauer and Johann Heinrich Dannecker worked in biscuit. The latter did children groups representing, originally enough for that day at least, the "Seasons" and a boresome "Ariadne on the Panther."

It is very likely that part of the trend toward the biscuit was brought about by disgust on the part of the public for the garish and unpleasant color applied in the immediately preceding years. At Ludwigsburg the best period was between 1760 and 1770. Beyer's color was pleasant; his draperies were often a subdued violet or lilac or soft pink. During his time strong color was also used but it was dull and the nude parts were only delicately tinged. Later the color becomes cruder and darker, the nude's cheeks, knees, ears and other prominent parts are reddened and the figures at this time are below the average of the other factories in quality.

The enthusiasm shown in the figures was lacking for the "ordinary wares" which are dirty, grey and full of flaws while also being altogether too ordinary in design. One stunt was a relief scale surface over which strewn flowers were painted without regard to the surface. The "Osier" or wicker pattern was taken freely from other factories. The cohesive quality of the clay made possible some vases based on molded projecting supports.

Due to so many flaws, more decoration was dabbed on to hide them than good taste could stand. The flowers and birds are often also too large for the pieces and design sprawls all over the vessels in confusion and lack of organization. Again it bunches up tightly in a hard knot of flowers that look as strangled as a bouquet of wild flowers in the hand of a six-year-old child. The birds are probably from Riedel; certainly not from nature. The flowers are after Friedrich Kirschner. The usual Boucher, Watteau and Rugendas samples were made and landscapes with ruins were supported on rococo scrolls. With these noble themes we are often startled to find a bug or butterfly resting on the edge of the plate and so carefully painted as to make nearsighted ladies exclaim. In other words just everything was mastered including nature itself.

The mark is two C's placed back to back and intersecting, referring to Duke Charles, and surmounted, therefore, by a crown at times. Hannover says that some writers regard the crown as a mark of quality but that it is not. This mark was in underglaze blue but very rarely in red. An antler is sometimes with the C's or by a single L or three of them. Another L refers to Duke Ludwig. FR was used for King Fredrick (Fredrick Rex), surmounted by a royal crown and in red, gold or impressed. Also LOUISBOURG was painted in red. From 1816 to 1824 the monogram WR crowned for Wilhelm Rex was usually in gold.

Fig. 960. Cup and saucer said to be from Ludwigsberg between 1758 and 1824. These pieces are of course strongly Japanese in style. Dia. of plate 5". Metropolitan Mus. of Art.

CHAPTER XXIII

18TH CENTURY EUROPEAN PORCELAIN CONTINUED: FRANCE, ITALY, SPAIN, PORTUGAL, SWITZERLAND, RUSSIA, NETHERLANDS, BELGIUM, DENMARK, SWEDEN

FRANCE

VINCENNES & SÈVRES

RETURNING to France where no Böttger was captured and "soft paste" continued for years we find that just west of Frankenthal, Mannheim and Ludwigsburg the cities of Lille, St. Amand, Valenciennes and Strasburg were

FIG. 961. Soft paste vase made at Vincennes about 1750. Ht. 7½". Metropolitan Mus. of Art.

slow to steal the secret of hard porcelain. True, the potters were conscious of the fact that they must learn to compete with the northern and eastern factories, but it was slow to come. However, when the Dubois brothers, who had worked at St. Cloud and Chantilly, came to Orry de Fulvy, brother of the Comptroller General and financial advisor for France, it was not difficult to get the patronage in 1738 of Louis XV, and a riding-school at Vincennes was put at their disposal. Here they experimented and used up all the money granted plus 10,000 more livres and produced nothing. Later a workman named François Gravant in 1745 produced a semblance of porcelain, and a syndicate was formed with 90,000 livres and later 250,000 livres capital and was granted a 20-year privilege. Even so the king was again and again obliged to contribute to the organization's maintenance.

About 1750 the factory had about 100 hands or 10 throwers, 11 molders, 7 "makers of handles and spouts," 10 modelers, 10 painters and some 46 girls

682

under the heading of "fleurs" who possibly made the flowers copied from Meissen and made for decoration of vases, chandeliers, clocks, etc. and which were also popular when mounted on wire stems with metal leaves to serve as bouquets in vases. These flowers date from 1748 and in that year Madame de Pompadour bought 270 livres worth, while the king and queen paid 4,200 livres for flowers alone. In 1749 the crown princess, wishing to prove to her father, the King of Saxony, that the Vincennes factory compared with Meissen, sent him a blanc de chine vase with figures on either side mounted in ormolu and containing a large bouquet of flowers, some 480 in number. Of total sales that year of 44,600 the flowers brought 36,000 livres.

FIG. 962. Vincennes cachepot of about 1750 with scenes in pale enamel colors, handles decorated in purple, and gold bands. Ht. 4". Metropolitan Mus. of Art.

Probably at the instigation of the art loving Madame de Pompadour the king reorganized the factory and placed it under the technical leadership of Jean Hellot, Director of the Academy of Sciences. The artistic leaders were Duplessis, goldsmith to the court, and Bachelier and Hults who created the real "porcelaine de France."

With the usual unfortunate influence of the metal crafts, Duplessis made some ornate and involved forms one of which was called "vase vaisseau à mat" and somewhat resembles a boat, while another vase had elephant heads on either side with the trunks turned up into candle holders. These terrible things are very costly and considered rare and beautiful by some collectors.

Other examples of the period are white wares with relief blossom design made by workmen from St. Cloud and painted pieces after the Meissen wares after Kakiemon, with "Indian flowers," etc. made by workmen from Chantilly. Perhaps the earliest piece known dates about 1750 and has "Indian flowers" and insects about the edge with the center treated much like the "yellow tiger" design of Meissen. Even at this early period the gilding was laid thickly and burnished with a hob-nail "au clou," finely chased and engraved. A charming effect was obtained by even spacing of dots graduating from large to small and more closely spaced towards the center or the reverse. Such plates usually have a simple center medallion and border. There were dress fabrics similarly treated which one may recall having seen in pictures of the costumes towards the end of the century.

A strong blue was used for painting "children among clouds" and flowers. A purple was also used for these, for landscapes and for ornaments and birds. The polychrome effects were too brilliant to be pleasant. The birds look like imaginary pheasants and the figures, which were painted by artists recruited from the fan painters, remind one of the less good examples of this kindred art. Perhaps to get away from this unpleasant style, Viellard painted figures with the flesh parts natural and the drapes in monochrome shading.

Perforated wares and relief wares similar to the "Gotzkowsky erhabene Blumen" were tried. Then there were blue grounds with gold spots or reserved white stars, the use of large scattered corn-flowers and a "seme" or strewing of the same flowers.

Hellot with his assistants Gravant, Gerin, Caillat, Massue and Taunay obtained a large range of colors which united perfectly with the glaze of the soft porcelain. Hellot made the rule that all discoveries belonged to the factory and in 1753 he collected all the results and published them in a book still kept by the factory. A cup at the Sèvres Museum is signed by Taunay and dated 1748. It has sample strokes of many colors. Hellot invented the famous "bleu-de-roi" (royal blue) in 1749 superseding the "grosbleu." The turquoise blue was invented in 1752 and this is certainly one of the most beautiful of the Sèvres colors.

Fig. 964. Sèvres covered bowl which is decorated by Xrowet, 1767. Ht. 3⅞". Metropolitan Mus. of Art.

Fig. 963. Soft paste Sèvres ewer of 1756 with sprays of flowers in enamel colors on white ground, edges gilt, silver mountings. Ht. 6⅝". Metropolitan Mus. of Art.

The death of Orry de Fulvy led to a reorganization in 1751 and the king took a fourth of the capital in 1753 amounting to some 800,000 livres, allowed the factory to use the name *"Manufacture Royale de Porcelaine de France,"* and to mark the wares with two intertwined Ls which had, however, already been used for a few years unofficially. The factory was moved to Sèvres, half way between Paris and Versailles near the Palace of Bellevue which Madame de Pompadour had built three years before and where she received the king in her much talked of winter garden of porcelain flowers. The new building cost about a million livres and in 1756 the factory was solemnly inaugurated.

In 1757 the painter Xrowet or Xhrouet invented the pink ground, it is said, but Hellot must have had something to do with it for after his death in 1766 it disappears forever. This is the color which the English miscall "rose Dubarry" though the pieces decorated with it were made at a time when that little lady was still quite unknown. The French correctly call it "rose Pompadour." It is a color of great purity and opacity, neither bluish nor yellowish. A similar color had been invented in China in the K'ang Hsi reign (1662–1722) but of quite different consistency, and, to tell the truth, deeper, richer and more pleasant.

A yellow called "jaune jonquille" is rare. Then there was also a delicate violet, deep green, light apple green among others which are even more seldom seen than the early colors.

FIG. 965. Cup and saucer with *bleu-de-roi* ground with birds in gold in reserved medallions, Vincennes about 1753. Plate dia. 6". Metropolitan Mus. of Art.

The paste was made of sand from Fontainebleau, sea-salt, saltpetre, soda, alum and plaster-of-Paris or alabaster which were mixed together and fired at least 50 hours to yield a white frit which was pounded to a fine powder and mixed with marl from Argenteuil and then kneaded in a mill for weeks at a time, so it is said. It was then dried in troughs, crushed between rollers and sifted before being saturated with pure water and brought to the texture for use.

The glaze was no less complicated and from the same sand from Fontainebleau, litharge, soda, flint and potash also first mixed and smelted and then ground for use.

The soft paste was first fired as biscuit unglazed and then glazed by "arrosement" or spraying, rather than dipping, in order to make it adhere better to the biscuit, a little

FIG. 966. Oval dish of soft paste either Vincennes or Sèvres of 1756 or earlier. The flowers are in natural colors with the base and rim gilt. Length 10¼". Metropolitan Mus. of Art.

vinegar first having been added to the glaze. The ware was then fired again before it was ready for decoration. The decoration took another firing and, if gold was used, that had to be fired yet again. Each firing was at a lower temperature than the preceding, of course. The colors became so fused with the glaze that they are as smooth as the unpainted parts and seemingly no thicker.

The dotted pattern was developed further into the famous "oeil-de-perdrix" consisting of tiny circles or double circles dotted in green or blue and reserved in white on a monochrome or dotted ground. Another pattern in gold was called "caillouté" or pebble pattern and looks somewhat like grease spots floating on broth. Scales, marbling, network and such were used over the blue to soften its too intense effect.

The biscuit turned out to be such a beautiful material that it could not help but appeal yet the intent was to compete with Meissen so it was not used at first. A sculptor named Blondeau did the first groups which were hunting scenes after Oudry. Fournier in 1747, very likely the same who started the Copenhagen factory, is thought to have modeled a "Naiad" and a "River Goddess," a late copy of which is in the Louvre. Chavagnac and Grollier mention only 19 colored figures. A little girl with bird cage is said to be after Boucher but must be quite a bit after. In fact Boucher is said to have worked at the factory, not as a sculptor but in making sketches, supervising, etc. Such groups as "Le jaloux" by an otherwise unknown artist named Vandrevolle or van de Voorst are very perfectly in the Boucher feeling.

In 1754 Madame de Pompadour, though she had the same figures in enamel, bought eight Boucher biscuit figures of children modeled by Blondeau and this may have given the impetus, for biscuit immediately became popular. Bachelier requested many sketches from Boucher and the sculptor Fernex carried them out, as did also Suzanne. One cannot distinguish the work of these two one from the other. They are not marked with the names of the artists but simply "après Boucher" and the best known are "La laitière, La merchande de crême, Les mangeurs raisins, La leçon de musique, Le mouton chéri," etc. All of which are rustic but elegant, naïf yet blasé, child-like, yet full of a pretty sophistication typical of the painter at his best.

Even in Vincennes we find a neo-classic taste as can be seen in the group of four young Tritons and the companion group of young Bacchus with his retinue playing with a panther, in the Victoria and Albert Museum. These are by Louis Felix de la Rue. A far greater sculptor, Etienne Falconet, became regularly associated with the factory in 1757 after having supplied some models to Vincennes. One of these is the statuette of Madame de Pompadour as the "Goddess of Friendship" of which only three known examples exist, one in a private collection in France, one in Sèvres and one in the Pierpont Morgan Collection.

After the factory moved it was under the management of Boileau. In 1756 the expenses were 1,200,000 livres while sales were only 300,000. The whole staff got along on payments on account. In 1759 the king took the factory over and a host of artists were hired. The scope of our book is such that these cannot be listed and we refer the reader to "Pottery and Porcelain. European Porcelain" by Emil Hannover, pages 283 to 295. A few deductions from this list are offered by the above authority which we give briefly:

1. The list of flower painters is about twice that of the figure painters.
2. Bird painters are few, as are also landscape painters.
3. A large part of the output was in the form of services, either large dinner

FIG. 967. Bowl and tray (1777 ?) of Sèvres ware. Length 7¾". Metropolitan Mus. of Art.

FIG. 968. Sèvres covered bowl and tray by Aloncle (the bird painter) (1776). Length of tray 9". Metropolitan Mus. of Art.

FIG. 969. Sèvres tureen and tray with relief ornamentation gilded and the flowers and fruits in natural colors. (1777). Length of tray 24". Metropolitan Mus. of Art.

services, tête-a-tête or solitaire; and whole services were frequently given by the king as presents. Thus the Danish king was given in 1768–69 a service of some 377 pieces valued at some 32,918 livres. "Even the Emperor of China, who might be thought well able to provide himself with fine porcelain, repeatedly received large consignments of gifts from Sèvres," says Hannover. I wonder what he did with them and if they were not possibly a sort of hint for return favors.

In 1759 there were the critical moments of French finances and the king, followed by others, sent his silver and gold services to be melted at the mint, replacing them by porcelain. At exhibitions each year Madame de Pompadour frequently spent 80,000 to 100,000 livres on porcelain and this was a strong suggestion to the other ladies of the court. Catherine of Russia ordered a 744-piece service at some 328,000 livres which seems enough, but single pieces sold for as high as 40,000 reichsmarks in Frankfort while a pair of wine coolers brought 100,000.

All this made possible a technique between 1760 and 1780 which in some ways has never been equalled.

Etienne Falconet was at first influenced by Boucher and even in 1757 when he was appointed this persisted. "Les enfants Falconet" differ little from "les enfants Boucher,"—and "La lanterne magique" and "Le tourniquet" are actually after Boucher compositions along with other groups. Others such as the dairymaid at Sèvres are suggestive of Defernex. But in 1757 he made the famous "bather" in marble and in 1759 in biscuit. This was soon copied by other factories and is even made today. About this same time he made the marble "Amour" for the Hotel d'Evreux in Paris for Madame de Pompadour. That he was as appreciative of the qualities of the biscuit as of the other materials is shown by his adoption of it for his monumental works such as "Pygmalion" of the Salon of 1763, and the serious busts of Louis XV. Soon, however, his fame had outgrown this work and he was employed by Catherine II of Russia to make the monument to Peter the Great at St. Petersburg.

Bachelier then became manager of the sculpture and Pigalle was ordered to carry out some of his things among the most famous of which are the "L'amour et l'amitié" and the statue of Mercury from Frederick the Great's palace of Sansouci at Potsdam (1770). Antiques were now copied. When the Dauphin married Marie Antoinette in 1770 the factory wanted to make a present and decided to create a centerpiece of the *whole Palace Royal at Rheims with the statue of Louis XV* for a table decoration and on this foolish task Pigalle, Allegrain and Mouchy spent nearly 10 years. But Bachelier had even greater ideas of grandeur: The tapestry output of Gobelins and Beauvais had spread knowledge of the famous paintings of France. Why then should not Sèvres make all the worthy sculpture of France both antique and contemporary and, why, forsooth, should it not go a step further and make figures from the paintings and tapestries themselves? Nothing was impossible! Alors! And so the "History of Don Quixote" was made after Charles Antoine Coypel (1771) and the "Conversation Espagnole" of Carle Vanloo (1772), etc. It doesn't take much critical sense to realize what such transpositions would involve and we can only add that expectations were fulfilled.

La Du Barry, in pursuit of the Pompadour tradition, took interest in the factory and it in turn flattered her by rendering her as a "Spanish Singer" and making for her services with the initial D in gold and B in flowers. Pajou did a rather alive and charming bust of her in 1771.

THE FIRST TRUE PORCELAIN AT SÈVRES

Paul Hannong had tried to sell the secret of hard porcelain in 1753 but had failed perhaps because he could show the French no kaolin deposits on their soil. In 1760 a deposit was found at Alençon but the porcelain made from it was grey and coarse. Comte de Brances-Lauraguais made some experiments in 1764 with little result other than a few plates in psuedo-Chinese style which are signed LB and a couple of casts from medals and a portrait medallion of the Comte de Caylus signed "Nini." Then in 1768 the chemist Macquer found the wonderful deposits in Yrieix near Limoges and made a little figure of a child, now in the Sèvres Museum. Yet it was not until 1772 that production was actually under way at Sèvres and even then the hard paste was secondary to soft paste.

In this year the director Boileau died and was replaced by Parent who hired Louis-Simon Boizot, a pupil of Slotz and winner of the Prix de Rome. He was no genius but was able to carry out the work of such me.. as Clodion, Falconet, Bouchardon, Pigalle, Cafferi and Pajou and form a sort of representative style. At first he worked in soft paste but in 1775 he turned to "pate dure" and made such things as "L'Autel Royal" and the "Allegory of the Wedding of Louis XVI and Marie Antoinette" or "Le triomphe de Bacchus" as well as his pet theme of a woman and child, done as subjects mytho-

FIG. 970. Bisque hard paste figure, one of a series reduced from statues. This is the Baron De Montesquieu after Clodion. Sèvres 1783. Ht. 13¾". Metropolitan Mus. of Art.

FIG. 971. Sèvres (1779) porcelain pitcher with lilac ground covered with gilt dots in the center of white spots surrounded by blue dots, and medallions in pink, blue and lilac. The rims and some details are gilt. Ht. 4½". Metropolitan Mus. of Art.

logical, allegorical, from the theatre or from real life. His assistants followed him so well that their work can hardly be distinguished from his. Le Riche was one of these but he also did some original things such as "La nourrice," "Le déjeuner," "La toilette," etc., which are influenced by the scènes de moeurs of Moreau le jeune.

The hard paste things lose much of the charm that belonged to the soft paste. The new material was dead white, bluish and slightly glistening rather than warm and softly dull. It was on the other hand less liable to distortion in firing and could be more easily washed. Imitations of both the German wares and of Wedgwood were made and it was a boast that the latter particularly were perfect. Now that the factory had this medium it seemed that it had nothing to do with it for the blight had already taken hold.

Some oddities are interesting. There is a cup and saucer by Lamprecht with goats and sheep drawn in black. Fallot made a cup with pheasants and other birds in silver and gold evidently after Japanese lacquer effects. A plate of 1790 and marked G.I. has a black glaze with chinoiseries in gold. Brown tortoise-shell was made with iron and manganese which with the addition of cobalt blue became "green tortoise-shell" and which became a passion with some British collectors.

Then in 1780 Cotteau invented the "jewelled Sèvres" which was costly. This involved the fusing on of drops of enamel which to the not too observing eye might faintly resemble rubies, emeralds, sapphires, pearls and other gems. Later small glass jewels were stuck on so insecurely that they came off, if not handled with care.

Plaques of porcelain for insets for furniture and pictures of porcelain to hang on the wall were approved by Marie Antoinette. Some as large as two feet square have hunting scenes by Asselin after Oudry.

In 1778 Parent was succeeded by Regnier and in 1780 by d'Angivilliers, formerly Director des Batiments. He believed in the Classics and ordered to be made some copies of "Etruscan" vases supplied by Denon. An outstanding monument to his taste and discipline is the "Vase Medicis" standing 2 meters high, with blue ground, biscuit reliefs by Boizot and ormolu mountings by Thomire, finished in 1783. It is said that for two of these a bill of 108,000 livres was sent.

Another of his brilliant ideas resulted in the making of small figures after the statues of great men. He was also a loyal royalist and demonstrated it by having Pajou in 1781, at the birth of the Dauphin, make a "Venus rising from the sea," bringing a Dauphin to France. This is a really beautiful piece. But the jobs became more and more difficult and Boizot fell down badly in 1785 when, at the birth of the Duke of Normandy, he was given the task of representing "The French monarchy, on the stem of which the Genius of Fertility plants the third shoot."

Marie Antoinette is said to have had one service in which each plate took two months of solid work and cost nearly 500 livres. The "arabesque service" was designed by the architect Masson after motives from the Loggia of Raphael and there were others of great grandeur.

Boizot held a fairly good quality in the modeling as can be traced by the "Toilet of Venus" (1783), "The Birth of Bacchus" (1784), "The Rape of Prosperine" (1787), "The Childhood of Silenus" (1788) and "The Muses" of the same year. But wealthy people were already leaving Paris. In 1789 the hands revolted because they could not get their wages. Late in 1790 a

Fig. 973. Bisque figures mounted in ormolu which the museum calls Sèvres 1780–90 but which could not be much earlier than the later date and have a distinct Empire feeling. Ht. of central figure 13½". Metropolitan Mus. of Art.

syndicate made an offer for the factory but the king could not bring himself to let it go. In 1791 in May, the National Assembly declared that the factory of Gobelins and of Sèvres were both on the Civil List of the king, and were not to be treated like the other "biens nationaux."

After the Revolution there was, of course, a chaotic period but in May of 1800 Brongniart took the post of manager and held it for 47 years. During the Revolution the old artists had fled fearing that their work under d'Angivilliers might bring them under suspicion. Many had signed works designed for the glorification of the royal house and had seen such things smashed to pieces in 1793 by order of the men of the factories' own staff in the short space of four hours. Only a few such works were spared such as a bust of Frederick the Great by Boizot for the reason that he had been not only a king but also a philosopher and a friend of Voltaire, some busts of Diderot, Rousseau, Brutus and Socrates.

During the years 1790 to 1795 the wares are only of historical interest. Fasces, Phrygian caps and the tricolored ribbon were the chief motives and some of the old stock designs were used but poorly. The factory, you see, was of no use at all to the masses.

DIRECTOIRE PERIOD

The man of the Directorate was not averse to the old time luxury and the factory supplied grandiose things which were, however, not always paid for and so the financial difficulties became acute. Auction sales and lotteries were held and large amounts of undecorated pieces were sold off. Thus most of the pieces of the period which are seen now were decorated outside the factory and hundreds are of quite recent decoration even though they bear every resemblance to the real thing.

One of the first steps that Brongniart took was to stop the production of soft paste in 1804. That he was vitally interested is proven by his book, "Traite des arts ceramiques," (1844), but his was entirely a scientific mind and the taste continued lower and lower. He made the same mistake that

FIG. 974. Cup and saucer of Sèvres 1807. Metropolitan Mus. of Art.

FIG. 975. Sèvres biscuit bust of Louis XVI. Ht. 10¼". Made in 1820. Metropolitan Mus. of Art.

FIG. 976. Sèvres bust of Marie Antoinette, in biscuit. Ht. 12". 1821. Metropolitan Mus. of Art.

Sorgenthal had made at Vienna and turned loose a group of historical painters who had not the slightest idea of decorative beauty. Over the stiff, mechanical empire shapes they worked with dull colors and too bright gold. They were busy for the Revolution had emptied all the palaces of porcelain and at the same time the trend was toward grandeur and pomposity. It was an urge to hurry but a demand for much detail; a bad combination which led to shortcuts and trickery.

Many outside influences were not digested. The "Egyptian service" (1808) had a blue ground with hieroglyphics in gold and pictures by Sweebach drawn from Napoleon's expedition to the Nile. The "Olympian service" was another, and a "Medici vase" had 150 figures in the foreground and 2,000 in the background while a "Vase Etrusque" had a frieze of the solemn conqueror's procession into Paris with the stolen Italian works of art. The little plaquets for furniture were not grand enough so whole table tops were used to glorify some great personage.

MARKS

1753—L's entwined, up to Revolution.

Starting with 1753 the alphabet was used for year marks and in 1778 when it had been used up, double letters were used in the intervals between the L's. The following table is given for ready reference:

A—1753	J—1762	R—1770	AA—1778	II—1786
B—1754	K—1763	S—1771	BB—1779	JJ—1787
C—1755	L—1764	T—1772[1]	CC—1780[2]	KK—1788
D—1756	M—1765	U—1773	DD—1781	LL—1789
E—1757	N—1766	V—1774	EE—1782	MM—1790
F—1758	O—1767	X—1775	FF—1783	NN—1791
G—1759	P—1768	Y—1776	GG—1784	OO—1792
H—1760	Q—1769	Z—1777	HH—1785	PP—until 17th
I—1761				of July 1793.

Hard porcelain between 1769 and 1793 has as a rule a crown above the two L's.

1793—17th of July until 1800 RF meaning Republique Francaise either used separately or in a monogram and with the word Sèvres or seve beneath.

1801 to 1816—There were the following year marks:

T9 (Year IX	of the Republic) 1801		9	1809
X (" X	" "	") 1802	10	1810
II (" XI	" "	") 1803	oz (onze)	1811
(" XII	" "	") 1804	dz (douze)	1812
(" XIII	" "	") 1805	tz (treize)	1813
(" XIV	" "	") 1806	qz (quatorze)	1814
7 1807			qn (quinze)	1815
8 1808			sz (seize)	1816
			ds (dix-sept)	1817

To these were added:

1801–1802 "Sèvres" in gold or color

1803–1804 (8 May)—"M N^le Sèvres" in red, meaning (Manufacture Nationale de Sèvres)

1804–1809 "M. Imp^le de Sèvres" in red

1810–1814 A crowned eagle in red surrounded by the words "Manufacture Imperiale Sèvres"

(The three last were printed with a stamp)

1815—Two L's again printed in blue (under Louis XVIII)

The marks before 1800 were usually in blue and generally over the glaze (except in the early Vincennes ones which were *gros bleu* in decoration) or on hard paste. These are under the glaze, if in blue, but also in red and other colors over the glaze.

Sèvres biscuit has no factory mark until after 1860, but sometimes has marks denoting the moulder. Pieces with marks are modern.

Naturally there were as many fakes here at this important factory as at

Meissen. The chances of reward were so great that they have existed from the very beginning. It was against the law to use either color or gold in France for the long period of protection and any piece which shows either must, therefore, have been done with intent to deceive, if it did not come from the factory direct. Let us list a few statements:

1. Some hard porcelain bears the marks of the soft porcelain period, often marked A, going the whole hog.

2. The mark of a well known flower painter may appear on a piece bearing figures.

3. Any piece covered entirely with enamel and mounted with ormolu should be mistrusted. Many fake table tops were sold to tourists in the Rue de Rivoli.

4. At St. Amand-les-Eaux, Bettignies and his descendants made a material resembling the soft paste of Sèvres between 1815 and 1877.

5. Modern forgeries never have the color blended with the glaze as in the real Sèvres pate tendre.

6. The gold is etched "au clou" on the old pieces while modern ones are treated with thinner gold and agates are used giving a smoother, thinner effect.

7. At Minton, England, French artists were hired about 1860 to imitate the wares but they were clearly marked of that factory. However, such marks have been tampered with.

8. At Coalport in Shropshire imitations were made of the bleu-de-roi, turquoise and rose Pompadour and the Sèvres mark was nicely copied.

9. Thomas Martin Randall, at Madeley near Coalport, made an artificial porcelain between 1830 and 1840 which was covered with a turquoise ground like Sèvres. He also bought undecorated pieces, dressed them up and sold them through a dealer named Baldock in London.

10. Both Derby and Worcester made successful copies.

11. Most of the French factories made copies with bodies usually heavier and less white.

12. Fischer and Herend of Hungary made successful copies.

13. Genuine Sèvres pieces often have a small glazed hole (note the "glazed") in the foot-rim for hanging them up. When this is missing there is reason for doubt but its presence is no sure guarantee.

14. If the green is chrome of warm yellowish tone and lacking that slight iridescence generally on copper green, the piece was not decorated in the 18th century as this color came into being only in 1804.

15. If gilding has been fired too often in processes of faking and redecoration, it sinks into the glaze and loses brilliance.

16. Little black specks often occur on the white after repeated firings.

17. The turquoise on late pieces is usually greenish and the pink is too muddy, transparent or off color.

18. Naturally jewelled pieces with year marks prior to 1780 are fakes.

19. All biscuit with the Sèvres marks are fakes or made during the latter half of the 19th century.

20. Biscuit figures which have been glazed show black specks under the glaze according to Chavagnac and Grollier. There are "barely a score" of

known figures in glazed Sèvres porcelain, so one is not likely to find one on 2nd or 3rd Avenue, New York.

21.   The hard porcelain was not so much copied in France but inferior wares have often their marks removed so that they can be palmed off on the unsuspecting purchaser.

FIG. 977. Tournai plate with flowers in natural colors, soft paste said by the museum to be between 1750 and 1755. Dia. 8¾". Metropolitan Mus. of Art.

FIG. 978. Tournai, cup and saucer of soft paste with enamels of brown, green and rose with edges gilt. On the cup is the fox and the lion from the Fables of La Motte. On the saucer are two mules from the Fables of La Fontaine. Metropolitan Mus. of Art.

FIG. 979. Tournai milk jug with underglaze design in blue. This piece is of such faulty soft paste that it is likely to date between 1756 and 1762. (Note the greyish blotches near the bottom and pitting.) Ht. 5½". Metropolitan Mus. of Art.
FIG. 980. Valenciennes plate with polychrome decoration. Note the poor quality of the paste showing pitting, etc. Metropolitan Mus. of Art.
FIG. 981. Late example of La Seynie 1774–1799. Metropolitan Mus. of Art.

SMALLER FRENCH FACTORIES

It will be seen immediately upon reflection that no such free-for-all among the small factories as occurred in Germany could possibly take place in France, for in this country there was an all powerful central government and that government had given its protection to the *Vincennes Sèvres* factories. Two movements defied this condition: First, there was a revival in the second half of the 18th century of soft porcelain, which was naturally dominated by the artistic dictates of *Sèvres* and at the same time had a hard fight for existence, commercially speaking, in competition with the royal factory and its privileges. Second, after hard porcelain had been discovered, the secret, with help from Germany, spread like wild fire throughout the country and a tremendous number of little factories was started almost over night, only to run afoul of the same difficulties with the parent factory just as soon as they became of troublesome size. These conditions determined the fact that the small French factories all slavishly copied Sèvres but never in any way rivalled this center in technique, as those in Germany in some instances rivalled or surpassed, in certain details, Meissen.

TABLE OF SMALLER FACTORIES OF FRANCE

Name	Marks	Period of activity	Description of wares, artists, etc.
Sceaux in the Department of Seine.	SX	Founded by Jacques Chapelle under patronage of Duchesse de Maine later under Duc de Penthièvre managed by Julien Jacques Richard Glot.	Soft porcelain and faïence. Only in 1784 given full freedom to make porcelain. Had to edge its wares with pink and not gold, forced by Sèvres.
	anchor as also on the faïence.		Paste like Mennecy.
			Small articles, pomade-pots, mustard-pots, salt-cellars, covered bowls, etc.
			Polychrome birds, flowers, etc., like their own faïence and Vincennes. Also small comet-like flowers like Chantilly.
Tournai in the 18th century it was French.	1750–1781 Tower with gate, and windows and battlements from arms of town in color or gold.	Francois-Joseph Peternick. Factory declined in 1799 at his death.	See Netherlands section under faïence.
			Style resembles Meissen and Derby as well as Sèvres.
			Made a typical French soft porcelain so good that it could be used to counterfeit Sèvres.
Tournai	1756 to end also 2 crossed swords like those of Saxony the 4 angles having crosses in gold or underglaze blue on ordinary wares.	Head painter was Ghislain-Joseph Mayer.	1750–56 paste greyish and faulty polychrome flowers after Meissen and birds "sur terrasse" in pink or in four colors:—blue, yellow, green and brownish grey.
			1756–1762 paste yellowish and colors more numerous and paler, with flowers like Strasburg faïence, also in pink; also chinoiseries and birds.
			1762–1781 prime of factory— warm tone like Sèvres all colors and designs with also touches of gold, also gold alone, bright birds were favorites by Henri-Joseph Duvivier (1763–1771), also landscapes with ruins in pink, children after Boucher in pink and a bleu-de-roi was made. About 1735 painting in grisaille in medallions on yellow, green, blue or red ground.

TABLE OF SMALLER FACTORIES OF FRANCE—*Continued*

Name	Marks	Period of activity	Description of wares, artists, etc.
		A. J. Mayer.	Also *"décor bois"* like the other wood imitations with engravings. Also blue and white, which was late and distinguished by division of edge with radially placed curved lines in relief.
	Stork given at the Hague which were decorated there.		The *Hague* factory made hard porcelain but bought blanks of soft paste from *Tournai* to decorate.
Orleans	O with crown over it.	1753 M. Gerré	*Faïence* and soft paste—from 1768 hard porcelain.
	Also heraldic label with C under it on soft paste.		Soft paste decorated in blue like *Chantilly* rarely in polychrome like *Vincennes*.
	Fleur-de-lys on hard paste.	.	Pretty without distinction.

)Note:—*Chavagnac* and *Grollier* have furnished proof that the label was one of the marks used by the second *Vincennes* factory on its hard porcelain.

Name	Marks	Period of activity	Description
Crepy-en-Valois	D.C.P. ?	1762–	Children figures in glassy paste ? (*Sèvres* Museum).
Étiolles Seine-et-Oise	"Étiolles 1770 Pellevé"		Reeded jug with poorly painted flowers, also reeded cup, with greenish tone. (British Museum.) Also a coffee-pot and cup with pale polychrome flowers and landscape in purple (B.M.) This last is of hard porcelain.
	"Étiolles"		
	MP (Monier & Pellevé)		
Arras	AA in monogram.	1770– I. F. Boussemaert from Lille.	Soft porcelain like *Chantilly,* St. Cloud or *Tournai.* Chiefly blue and white, seldom polychrome—(see two plates with pale flowers at *Sèvres*).
	AR in monogram or separately.	Four maiden ladies took over factory in 1771. Their name was Delemer.	
Saint-Amand-les-Eaux (Nord)	J.F. in a double monogram flanked by SA, same as on faïence.	1771–1778, Jean-Baptiste-Joseph Fauquez. 1778 passed to the family of Bettignies and up to present.	One plate at *Sèvres* with greyish glaze painted in purple with castles by a river and a narrow border.
	Imitated *Sèvres* marks.		19th century imitations of *Sèvres pâte tendre.*
	S.A. to 1830.		In 1851 *Saivetat* wrote "The ground colors are in every way comparable to those which have won for *Sèvres* so great a reputation." But Hannover does not agree.
Strasburg	H in underglaze blue for Chas. period.	Chas. Hannong died in 1760, his son Joseph Adam Hannong returned to the faïence factory in Strasburg in 1762 but did not make porcelain until 1774.	Had secret as early as 1721 but tried to sell it and failed and opened in Frankenthal, discontinued making porcelain in 1754. Only a few trial-pieces.
	? Ph in monogram.		

TABLE OF SMALLER FACTORIES OF FRANCE—*Continued*

Name	Marks	Period of activity	Description of wares, artists, etc.
	H usually also with various letters and numbers incised in underglaze blue or with a dot above the first stroke of the letter. JH His *Frankenthal* porcelain was marked I.A.H.		For *Paul Hannong* see *Frankenthal*, some might have been made at *Strasburg*, we are not sure. Useful porcelain ordinary and strangely imperfect in technique, thick, coarse and faulty like faïence. The known pieces seem to be mere trials. Figures, a flute player *(Kunstgewerbemuseum, Strasburg)*, children *(Hamburg)*, a flute-playing faun. (Also *Hamburg* in glaze and the Victoria & Albert in biscuit), etc.—these are better and with well harmonized colors.
Niderviller	JLB monogram BLe or BN monogram CN or with or without coronet. CFL monogram all in underglaze blue, also Niderviller Nider Nid N	1754–1765—hard porcelain *Baron Jean-Louis Beyerle* 1774 to *Comte de Custine.* *(Claude) Francois Lanfrey Mgr.*	*Faïence* reorganized for hard porcelain figures in polychrome and biscuit by *Charles Sauvage Lemire—Virgin and Child* 1784 *(Sèvres),* Bacchante in biscuit (V. & A.), Polychrome Bacchante *(Musée de Cluny)* etc., also children in biscuit. See also section on *Luneville* and *Cyfflé.* Useful porcelain with flowers, the usual landscapes similar to those of *Sceaux faïence,* etc. The underglaze blue was inclined to run and resembled the soft paste of *St. Cloud. Porringer* with Louis XVI designs in iron red, blue and gold. Marbled grounds, reliefs in white in biscuit and landscapes in black only. (V. & A. Mus. and *Sèvres.*)
Lille	Crowned dauphin. The earlier pieces have (à Lille). On the back of a saucer in *Sèvres:* "*Cuit au charbon de terre. Fait à Lille en Flandre,* 1785" "Fired with coal. Made at Lille in Flanders, 1785"	c. 1784 hard porcelain *Leperre Durot* under patronage of the *Dauphin,* existed to 1917.	Scattered cornflowers "*(décor barbeau)*" in blue, polychrome flowers poorly painted, landscapes insipid in polychrome and purple landscapes like many others. Also still-life objects such as a hare hung up and pastoral subjects. All poor and spiritless.
Valenciennes	LV or FLV may stand for either Vanier or Valenciennes	c 1771– *Jean-Baptiste Fauquez* the owner also of the factory at *St. Amand-les-Eaux. Michel Vanier.*	No interest to collectors. Polychrome resembles Lille and inferior Paris wares. Mostly monochrome—black, violet or iron red, sometimes starred and dotted with gold, some have alternating blue and violet flowers ornamentally arranged.

TABLE OF SMALLER FACTORIES OF FRANCE—*Continued*

Name	Marks	Period of activity	Description of wares, artists, etc.
Caen	Caen, written, painted or printed in red overglaze.	c 1800–	White porcelain to be decorated in Paris after *Sèvres*. Coffee-pot with rare and difficult canary yellow with frieze of conventional ornament reserved in green, purple and gold *(Sèvres)*. Also cruder milk-jug, bowl and cup with small square landscapes in black suspended by thin green festoons and garlands in gold. (V. & A.)
Limoges	CD apart or interlaced. Used even after Louis XVI owned the factory. Earliest mark . G. R. et Cie.	1771 First of 40 factories at *Saint Yrieix* section by *Grellet, Massié* and *Fourniera.* 1777 Patronage of the *Comte d'Artois* 1784 Purchased by Louis XVI, in few years returned to private ownership	Porcelain of slightly yellowish hue with flowers in dull colors, also the strewn cornflowers. Cup and saucer with roughly painted pair of peasants dancing *(Sèvres)*. Porringer with Graces holding Cupid on their shoulders in delicate brown monochrome. *(Sèvres.)*
La Seynie	LS singly or as a monogram.	1774 Founded by some gentleman of high rank but unknown.	Chiefly white porcelain to Paris for decoration.
Tours	A. Tours 1772 on only two cases also 1782 Cupid figure.	1776–1783	Only two biscuit vases known *(Sèvres)*. And a biscuit figure which represents Cupid as a child.
Boissette near Melun south of Paris.	B shakily written with or without 2 dots.	1778 *Duke of Orleans* *Vermonet père et fils*	Chiefly decorated with polychrome flowers in the style of *Meissen* but poorly done. Also occasionally with ornamental flowers and an infrequent landscape.
Bordeaux	W Two V's joined so as to make a W similar to Berlin of Wegely and Wallendorf but the ware is quite French. AV monogram in circle the upper part of which was enclosed in a semicircle with the inscription "Bordeaux."	1781 *Pierre Verneuilh* and a relative 1787–1790 under *Vanier* and *Alluaud*	Not remarkable but table wares of fine quality in both paste and the decoration. *Semé* patterns not only of corn flowers but also of pansies and yellow daisies, also bouquets in polychrome. Particularized in festoons of foliage in Louis XVI style. A stone-cutter in biscuit *(Sèvres)*. Cup with rebus design *"elle à bon coeur"* (V. & A. Mus.)
Marseilles	R or JR monogram or rarely JRG (Joseph Gaspard Robert).	c 1776 Joseph Robert	Was *faïence* factory. No particular sense of material, the faïence and porcelain being decorated much alike. Greyish, uneven glaze, polychrome flowers like *faïence* ones, flowers in a strong dark blue. (Dish at *Sèvres*).

Around Paris at the close of the 18th century were innumerable private factories under the patronage of many princely or distinguished dabblers who were interested in aping the king and his interest in *Sèvres*. They are of no particular interest because the height of their ambitions seemed to be to ape also the wares of that place. We will list, however, a few taken in the order of their founding:

Vincennes in same château as the old home of soft paste.	HL or h et L. and LP crowned or uncrowned as decorative initials. ducal heraldic label	1767– *Pierre Antoine Hannong* and *Joseph Adam Hannong* were given permission to open a factory for *faïence* and porcelain. *de Laborde Mgr.* 1774 Sold to *Séguin* under patronage of *Louis-Philippe* Duc de *Chartres* then called "Manufacture royale."	Quite rough flowers and the initials LP in monogram in blue on a service made in 1779 (V. & A.). (*Sèvres* and others.) Custard-cup with finer garlands and decorative monogram in green and gold over a purple line. (*Kunstindustrimuseum, Copenhagen*)

FIG. 982. Paris, Rue de La Courtille chocolate pot of about 1773–1784 showing usual refinement but lack of invention in design. Ht. 8¼″. Metropolitan Mus. of Art.

Rue Faubourg Saint-Denis or sometimes called by the north section: *Rue Faubourg Saint-Lazare* or again *Fabrique du Comte d'Artois*	h and two crossed clay pipes with or without h in intersection. CP with or without coronet. Schoelscher in full or S	1779 *Pierre Antoine Hannong* Patron was Louis XVI's brother *Charles-Philippe Comte d'Arois* and later *Charles X* also patron of *Limoges* 1782 *Bourdon des Planches who constructed the first kiln for firing with coal.* After Revolution Schoelscher Mgr.	*Bleu-de-roi* and gold service now owned almost complete by Dr. Clarholm of *Karlstad, Sweden,* bears *Schoelscher's* name in full. Many copies without individuality. Nicely painted flowers and various ornaments in polychrome.

FIG. 983. Covered cup from *Cling-nancourt* or *Fabrique de Monsieur* 1775–1790, Paris. Ht. 3¾". Metropolitan Mus. of Art.

FIG. 984. Angoulême, Paris porcelain (Guerhard & Dihl) early 19th cent. Ht. 3½". Metropolitan Mus. of Art.

FIG. 985. Paris, *Rue de Bondy* (1780) decorated with floral designs in black. It is hard paste and the mark is Dihl & Guerhard stencilled at length in red. Length 9½". Metropolitan Mus. of Art.

FIG. 986. Paris chocolate-pot decorated with landscape and marine views in sepia on white, hard paste. c. 1750 to 1800. Ht. 10¾". Metropolitan Mus. of Art.

| *La Courtille* or *Rue Fontaine-au-Roy* or *Manufacture de Porcelaine* | Crossed torches. Crossed arrows points downward also DP Initials of artists | 1771– *Jean-Baptiste Locré* 1774– Russinger from Höchst ? 1830 end. | No surprises, shapes pseudo-antique, decorated with flowers, landscapes, animals and ornaments in *Louis XVI* style. Dainty and elegant in make, with white paste, clean glaze |

Allemande   and modelers.

and tooled or chased gilding.

A large vase with ornaments
in violet and green partly
on an orange-yellow ground.
(*Sèvres*)

Fig. 987. Cup and saucer marked *P. L.
Dagoty à Paris* in red. They are of hard
porcelain and date about 1802 when the
"Etruscan style" was popular. The de-
signs are in red and white on black ground.
Dia. of saucer 5″. Metropolitan Mus. of
Art.

Fig. 988. Paris, Rue Thiroux gilt hard paste porcelain cup and saucer of the delicate usual
effeminate style, 1778–1799. Saucer dia. 5¼″. Metropolitan Mus. of Art.
Fig. 989. Vieux Paris (DeGotte) coffee pot of about 1810–20. The ground is cobalt blue known
as "Roi-du Bleu" with rich gilding. Ht. 11″. John Gibbons Coll.

Fig. 990. Pair of early 19th cent. "Empire" vases of French porcelain such as have
been made ever since and are very popular even now in the decorative trade, particularly,
if the gold is rubbed down a bit to make it possible to sell them as antique. Metropolitan
Mus. of Art.

			Cup with purplish red roses suspended by ribbons in same color is dated 1772 and marked DP without torch or arrow mark. *(Sèvres)*
			Figures in biscuit by trees with sometimes applied leaves.
Clignancourt or *Fabrique de Monsieur*	Windmill stylized to 1775 then— LSX monogram with or without coronet plus sometimes a crowned B occasionally enclosed in 2 L's after Sèvres. Also **M**	1771– *Pierre Deruelle* Patron was *Louis-Stanislas-Xavier, Comte de Provence* brother of the king and later *Louis XVIII* 1790– *Deruelle* transferred it to his son *Moitte* 1798 last mentioned	Strewn cornflowers the serrated blue petals of which were here rendered in red and gold. Decoration in gold alone, see Kettle with spirit lamp (V. & A.). Ewers and wash basins with flowers, landscapes in monochrome. *Lamprech,* who later worked at *Sèvres,* painted in brownish-yellow monochrome.
			Biscuit statuette of the *Farnese Hercules.*
Rue de la Roquette	Crossed arrows with points upward only to be designated when accompanied by letters, often an S.	1774– *Vincent Dubois* 1790– last mention	Breakfast service with landscape vignettes in medallions suspended in delicate ornament (V. & A.). Biscuit less fine and rougher than that of *La Courtille* and that is rougher than that of *Sèvres.*
Rue de Charonne on same street as the above.		1795 *Darte Brothers*	Colored landscape with richly gilt borders (V. & A.) *bleu-de-roi* with gilt and cameo portraits of *Caligula* and of *Vespasian* plates.
Rue du Petit Carousel	PCG also "Manufacture (du) Petit Carousel à Paris" or "Petit Carousel à Paris"	1775 no patron	Respectable level. Polychrome butterflies between ornaments in gold (see ewer and basin *(Sèvres).* *Grisaille.* Much gold in slight Louis XVI style.
Rue Thiroux de Porcellaine de la Reine	MA or A crowned	1776– *Andre-Marie Leboeuf* patron: *Marie Antoinette*	Copied *Sèvres* too well and had difficulties when it started gilding and using color. There was practically no blue and white, the only kind supposed to have been allowed. Technique good but taste often questionable, very feminine with small semé cornflowers and daisies, also yellow roses on a pale pink ground, also "horrible" poppies, as Hannover says. *(Sèvres)* The paste has a soft tone resembling soft paste which it also copied. Strong also in exotic birds, ornamental friezes and white ware with simple lacework border in gold.

Rue de Bondy or *Manufacture d'Angoulême* later *Rue du Temple* and later *Boulevard St. Martin*	GA with **or** without a coronet and other symbols after the Revolution, the marks of the owners and finally just **Dihl**	1781 *Louis-Antoine de Bourbon, Duc d'Angoulême* and later Charles X founded by *Dihl* 1785 took as partner *Guerhard.*	Copies of *Sèvres* which brought trouble at once. 1806 a medal was awarded to the exhibition. *Bleu-de-roi* and gold on usual shapes, also monochrome or marbled grounds, cornflowers strewn as usual, flowers in gold, large naturalistic flowers. It had one invention which was scattered ears of corn in gold.
Rue Popincourt	Nast used his name in full for his mark.	1782– *Johann Nepomuc Hermann Nast* 1784 He re-established himself. 1817–1835 His sons	Nast's first little factory in which he was his own thrower, moulder, painter and fireman, burnt down twice. Influenced by *Sèvres* and *Wedgwood* — made plastic clocks in biscuit, richly gilt, daintily decorated glazed porcelain. Had a *Wedgwood* pale blue and lavender ground. Also made cups and saucers, etc., with cornflowers in blue, which are not rare. Three sorry plates spoken of by Hannover with the style of German transfer pictures (such as a lovely lady holding a dear little lamb [B.M.]) belong to son's period.
Petite Rue Saint-Gilles	Dagoty also Honoré also both together also "Manufacture de Madame Duchesse d'Angoulême or "Dagoty— Manufacture de S.M. l'Impératrice"	1785 ?*Dagoty* or ?—*Honoré* Whoever opened it, there was a partnership in 1810 dissolved in 1812.	Vases in relief in *Wedgwood* style. Colored grounds were much used, including terra cotta and olive-green. A few figures were done in biscuit. The decorations were landscapes, flowers and *grisaille* painting. Hannover says:—"All is lacking in any distinctive individuality, sober and neutral, but treated with neatness and accuracy."
Rue Amelot or *Rue Pont-aux-Choux*		1786 Patron *Duke of Orleans*	Its patron was its only distinction. Did invent the use of scattered roses stiffly drawn and the same in little medallions on dotted or *semé* ground.
Rue de Crussol or *Manufacture du Prince de Galles*	Potter or "potter à pari"	1789 *Charles Potter* an Englishman	Said to have had the great distinction of being the first man in Paris to practice the method of transfer printing on porcelain. Also an ordinary ware of the times with genre and portraits *en grisaille,* polychrome ornaments, cornflowers, butterflies, insects, etc.

ITALIAN PORCELAIN

VENETIAN WARES
1720–1740

The old Renaissance center of the world, Venice, which had been the first in the discovery of "soft porcelain" through the urge to imitate the real porcelain of the Far East was not long in acquiring the secret of Böttger and, in point of fact, it has been said to be the third factory in all Europe.

FIG. 991. Venetian cup and saucer from the Cozzi factory, of soft paste with pastel colors, c. 1765–1775. Dia. 4⅜". Metropolitan Mus. of Art.

FIG. 992. Venetian covered dish in soft paste with pastel colors. Ht. 3½". Metropolitan Mus. of Art.

There were two goldsmiths, Francesco Vezzi and Giuseppe Vezzi who bought patents of nobility in 1716 and they, together with two other gentlemen of nobility, having first provided the services of Christoph Conrad Hunger established the "Casa Eccelma Vezzi" near San Niccolò in Venice

FIG. 993. Venetian soft paste cup and saucer of about 1765 to 1812 with figures in the costumes of the period. Dia. 4⅞". Metropolitan Mus. of Art.

FIG. 994. Soft paste Venetian cups of about 1720–40 decorated in yellow, red, green and blue. Ht. 3¼". Metropolitan Mus. of Art.

in 1720. This Hunger is the same who wandered later to Meissen again, then to Stockholm and finally to Copenhagen—one of the untrustworthy disseminators of other people's secrets who was always ready to sell his information to the highest bidder, and when he came to Venice, he had not only the information but also the means of bringing "Schnorr'sche Erde" from Saxony and many of the stock designs of Herold and early Vienna porcelain. He had also the secret of Böttger's mother-of-pearl glaze, though his own was slightly warmer in hue and more glassy. The Venetian porcelain is much like that of Meissen, the pink lustre is not so even and the other colors are paler and lighter, but sometimes it takes a keen and practiced eye to tell the difference. Hannover says that Venetian baroque designs in gold in the style of Herold are, as a rule, outlined with iron-red. This is a distinction I have not seen commented upon by other authorities, but Hannover is a trustworthy and cautious observer.

MARKS HELP IN ATTRIBUTIONS

From about 1720 to 1725, they did not mark their wares. Therefore, unmarked porcelain which resembles early Vienna, or is decorated with leafy scroll work, the "Laub-un Bandelwerk" of Germany, with Chinese or European figures or harbor scenes in the style of Herold, or which are in the shapes of Böttger are likely to belong to this period and place.

In 1740 Francesco Vezzi died and it is supposed that the factory soon went out of existence. It is during this time, then from 1725 to 1740 that we should place all pieces marked with the name of Venice, or with abbreviations of it, or simply the initial V.

DEVELOPMENT IN SECOND PERIOD
1725-1740

After Hunger took his departure the factory was less influenced by Meissen. We see a new playful development of fantastic shapes far from reasonable or structural but at least relieving us from the monotony which

FIG. 995. Vase said by the museum to be "Venice, 1765–1812" but which is actually from the Cozzi factory in Venice and dates about 1770. Ht. 7½". Metropolitan Mus. of Art.
FIG. 996. Tea pot simply called "Italian 18th cent." by the museum but which may likely be from the Vezzi factory about 1725–1740. Ht. 5". Metropolitan Mus. of Art.
FIG. 997. Urn with flowers said by the museum to be from Venice, 18th cent. The neo-classic forms would indicate the latter part of the century. Ht. 13¼" over all. Metropolitan Mus. of Art.

prevailed among the copyists of other countries. The designs were not always conventional either as we can see in a cup of about 1725–30 or a little later, now in Dresden, with its design of a monster man's head and two hands filling a window and smoking a pipe amidst scrolls, and flanked by a parrot on one side and a monkey on the other plus two fantastic figures, a basket of flowers, etc. Composition too became loose, very thin and uncertainly drawn, reminiscent of late Near Eastern influences from metal, as may be seen in a cup and saucer at Dresden with decoration in iron-red only.

CAPO DI MONTE	VILLA REALE, PORTICI	NAPLES
1743–1759	1771–1773	1773–1821

King Charles III of Naples and his consort, a daughter of Augustus II of Saxony, were passionately fond of porcelain and in 1740, he, with the help of a Belgian chemist, Livio Ottavio Schepers, and a painter and cameo cutter, Giovanni Caselli, determined to start a factory in the palace of Capo di Monte on a hill just outside of Naples. The inscription over the doorway, which can still be read, states that the factory was opened in 1743 and remained in operation until 1759 when Charles III left Naples to become the King of Spain, taking with him some forty of the best workmen. In 1771 Ferdinand IV revived the works and transferred them to Villa Reale in Portici and again in 1773 they were transferred to Naples where they remained until 1821 when a great many of their old models were transferred to the Ginori factory at Doccia. In its first period the factory had made both soft paste and true porcelain but from 1773 it added also porcelain biscuit in large quantities. During the time from 1806 to 1815 when the factory was under Joseph and Murat this seems to have been its only output.

The palace in Naples has the only real collection of Capo di Monte. Hannover claims there are less than one hundred pieces of this ware north of the Alps in France, Germany or England. However, based upon his recollections of a visit about 50 years ago, a study of the pieces in the northern museums and a carefully edited catalogue of the Naples show in 1877 where there were 2000 pieces shown, he gives the following descriptions of the wares of the two period:

THE FIRST PERIOD OF CAPO DI MONTE

The soft paste was glassy, yellowish, greenish, bluish or livid in tone and was used for smaller pieces, as we would expect, being only different from that of the more northerly factories in the inclusion of such motives as dolphins, shells, periwinkles, coral and other designs taken from the sea. Among the earliest are a small number with no painted decoration, but the majority are "decorated in the Oriental style, viewed from the same angle as in the factories north of the Alps." This phase was displaced by the natural flowers, birds, landscapes and figures as elsewhere. Mythological figures and particularly those which are in some way associated with the sea, are the rule and *they are represented in relief and also colored.* We do not know who invented this style which was a natural result of the meeting of the old relief urge instigated by the copying of metal work and the color urge natural to the Italian soul. Hannover suggests Giuseppe Gricci but also mentions other distinguished modelers, Antonio Falcone, and Giuseppe Verdone and the painters Giovanni Fischer and Luigi Restile who executed the principle work of the period consisting of a "camera di porcelana" which was in the palace in Portici and later in 1865 taken to the palace of Capo di Monte, and which is entirely covered with porcelain panels having high relief colored rococo scroll work and primitive chinoiseries in the style of Boucher, some

FIG. 998. Typical Capo di Monte cup and with a mythological subject. Metropolitan Mus. of Art.

FIG. 999. Capo di Monte plate dating about 1750 to 1760 with relief decoration painted in enamel colors and gilt. It is soft paste, of course.

FIG. 1000. Capo di Monte coffee-pot of 1750 to 1760 showing the "Flaying of Marsya," on one side and Silenus with Bacchantes and Satyrs on the other. Metropolitan Mus. of Art.

FIG. 1002. Group of Venus and Cupid from Capo di Monte about 1759 to 1780. Metropolitan Mus. of Art.

FIG. 1001. Snuff-box possibly of *Capo di Monte*, porcelaneous ware with white ground, colored sea shells. Inside of box gilt. 1749–1759? Ht. 2″. Hispanic Society of America.

sconces, a chandelier and some furniture including a console which is now at Sèvres. Though the use of relief and colored figures was typical of the period there is strangely little figure modeling in the round and the few examples consist of the "to be expected" ones from the Italian comedy such as Colombines, Pulcinellas, etc., a few mythological groups such as Apollo and Daphne, Venus and Cupid, etc., some Biblical subjects and some genre subjects in costumes of the day. A rather typical figure is of an effeminate youth dressed in yellow and with a hen under his arm, in the Victoria and Albert Museum. The figures are all painted in polychrome, though sometimes sparingly. The painting on the porcelain of useful shapes was done in polychrome and in such monochromes as crimson, bluish-violet and black, "encre à la plume" or in pen and ink style.

THE SECOND OR SECOND AND THIRD PERIODS OF CAPO DI MONTE AT PORTICI AND NAPLES 1771–1821

Hannover deduces from the marks RF and FRF which were supposed to have been used at the factory only between 1771 and 1773, when it was at Portici, that it had already begun to use hard porcelain as well as soft, for they are found as often on the one as on the other. There was also more figure modeling in the second period, comprising allegorical ones, *putti,* and figures in the dress of the period as well as colossal groups.

The neo-classic influence put an end to the relief modeling. Upon plain surfaces were painted natural flowers, sea shells, fish and so forth taken

FIG. 1003. Capo di Monte late 18th cent. porcelain vase. Ht. 7½". Metropolitan Mus. of Art.

FIG. 1004. Naples tea pot of about 1780 in shape and style much like some English examples except for the handle and the leopard on the cover. Length 9¼'. Metropolitan Mus. of Art.

from books, exotic flowers, peasants in natural costumes and views of the town, views of Vesuvius, etc. The latter became more dominant after the move of the factory to Naples. At the Hamburg Museum is a dish with a fish after a work by an English naturalist, Catsby.

NEO-CLASSIC INFLUENCES

With Pompeii and Herculaneum close by, we are not surprised to hear that the neo-classic movement became strong in the development of shapes and of surface decorations. A good example is a jug closely following the form of an oenochoe in the British Museum. The surface decorations consisted not only of figures but also of designs. A whole service of this kind was sent to George III of England by the King of the Two Sicilies in 1787. These were painted in natural polychrome and carefully shaded to give rounded modeling. A typical ware is decorated only in black and gold on a grey ground "a chiaroscuro."

FIGURES OF CAPO DI MONTE AT NAPLES

The figures are chiefly colored. A few are in soft paste but most in hard. The best were from models by the Viennese, Tagliolini, who came to the factory in 1781 and became its chief support when later the style turned to biscuit. His principal works are Olympian figures in biscuit and in painted porcelain at the Museo Civico at Bologna. Hannover says that about the group can be arranged a whole Olympus in biscuit, the larger part of the figures from the Iliad and many Greek philosophers and Roman emperors plus numerous figures from the every day life of Naples and its environs (see Victoria & Albert Museum). The latter are often in a biscuit of a dirty yellowish tone.

Another skillful worker was Giuseppe Giordano who was called "Peppe" but he was even more dependent upon antique models than was Tagliolini and often merely copied them as exactly as he could.

Little real Capo di Monte ever comes onto the market though one can see many hundreds of fakes in shops along 59th Street and Lexington Avenue in New York and in London, Paris and most large cities of Europe. The tourist is almost sure to bring back spurious pieces from Italy marked with a crowned N which may have been made in France or Germany as well as in Italy. In early ceramic handbooks we were told that we could distinguish the real specimens because they were painted with a stippled technique similar to that of the miniature painters but the forgers also read the books.

DOCCIA WARES
1735 OR 1737

Second in age, if not importance among the Italian factories is that of Doccia near Florence, which was founded by the Marchese Carlo Ginori who was so thoroughgoing that he actually sent an expedition in a ship to the East to collect samples of the materials used in Chinese porcelain, and is thought, by some authorities, to have sent to Vienna for Carl Wandhelein to act as chemist. The early wares are painted with quasi-Chinese flowers with peculiar "trunk-like" stamens either in polychrome or iron-red.

When Carlo Ginori died in 1757, his son Lorenzo extended and improved the kilns so that they could at any rate make colossal figures and vases, if not better ones.

The factory has remained in the Ginori family right down to modern times and makes it a business to reproduce all kinds of wares from old moulds. As early as 1821 Doccia acquired the old models from the famous Neapolitan factory of the Capo di Monte porcelain when it ceased to be made in that factory, and for the past thirty or forty years it has copied them en masse, unscrupulously adding the original mark. Italian majolica of

FIG. 1005. Three plates from either Venice or Doccia and dating between 1760 and 1800. Lengths about 11". Metropolitan Mus. of Art.

FIG. 1006. Figure probably from Doccia of about 1740 to 1770. Ht. about 6½". Metropolitan Mus. of Art.

Faenza, Urbino, Castel Durante and Gubbio, Medici porcelain together with its mark, and other wares have been grist for this disreputable mill which, even in its more respectable days of the 18th century, never achieved any independence of style, though its modern wares are promising.

In some of the early wares considerable uncertainty naturally exists and they may be confused with those of Nove which used also a six pointed star for a mark as did Doccia at times.

FIG. 1007. Doccia, cup and saucer with design of oriental feeling in enamels and gold. Dia. 5". Metropolitan Mus. of Art.

FIG. 1008. Nove, (c. 1760–65) cup and saucer with yellow ground and medallions in violet, (outlined in violet) and red, orange and green. Dia. 4½". Metropolitan Mus. of Art.

NOVE WARES
1752 OR 1761

Giovanni Battista Antonibon and his son Pasquale founded a factory at Nove, near Bassano, for the making of faïence. In 1752 Pasquale persuaded

Sigismund Fischer to leave the factory at Meissen but nothing seems to have come from the attempt that we know. In 1761 Antonibon had two kilns in operation for the making of porcelain in the French style. The following year he took his son Giovanni Battista into the business and in 1781, Signor Parolini. In the period between 1802 and 1825 the firm was in the hands of some interests we do not know about but it reverted to the Antonibon family at the end of this time and they made porcelain until 1835. After this date it was discontinued and only faïence and earthenware were made.

The faïence was always good and during the 18th century ranks with the best in both appeal and technique. Only soft porcelain has been discovered bearing the Nove mark. Flowers seem to be the chief decoration and are in polychrome, green and gold, or purple. A few large pieces such as jardinières and teapots moulded with relief ornament are painted with figures, grotesque, mythological or historical. There are also birds and landscapes. A well known and finely executed piece is the teapot in the Hamburg Museum decorated with relief, moulded ornament of rococo type and painted figure panels. There are others of this typical sort, all dating from about 1765 to 1770. After 1770 the classical trend set in and a good example is the cylindrical cup with "bat wing" handle, *bleu-de-roi* ground and panels in reserve painted with the "Toilet of Venus, the Judgment of Paris, and the Death of Meleager" which is in the Franks Collection in the British Museum. The factory tried various experiments including the wood graining stunt. An interesting though perhaps doubtful example is a porringer in the Sèvres Museum decorated on the outside with a landscape with ruins in purple and on the inside with a Virgin and Child and three angels and with the following inscription around the rim: *"Scudella fabricata con la polvere delle S. Mura di Santa Casa di Loreto"*—"Porringer made of dust from the holy walls of the Holy House at Loreto." This is an exceptional piece in that it is the only one of hard porcelain from the Nove factory known. It bears the mark but there is naturally some doubt about it. Figures were also made but they are very rare and most of them found are doubtful specimens.

CONTRADA DI SAN GIOBBE
1765

At Contrada di San Giobbe in 1765, Geminiano Cozzi founded a factory, obtaining his clay from Tretto in the Venetian territory.

The earliest known specimen is a coffee-pot dated 1765 of greyish porcelain with pale bouquets of flowers, a handle and spout still bearing rococo influences and a cover which is without a knob. It is in the British Museum. Another dated 1766 and in the Musée des Arts Décoratifs, Paris, has flowers in relief on a gold ground. There is also a set of five potpourri vases with relief heads and garlands and painted flowers after Meissen and a porringer in the V. & A. Museum with stand in the same style having a character also like several cups in the Sèvres Museum treated with polychrome fruit and flowers, scale patterns *("Mosaik")* in red, green or purple, etc. Various cups in Hamburg, and Limoges show that the chinoiseries of Herold were also copied as were designs from Sèvres, Chelsea and Derby. There are no wares in underglaze blue. The gold was of fine quality and treated with great precision. Iron-red was used alone or with it at times.

The inclination of soft porcelain makers, due to the inconveniences of their wares and the danger of handling them for washing, was to make ornamental rather than useful things and figures, especially in plain white. An Oriental figure of this sort at Stockholm and a soldier talking to a woman which is of grey glassy porcelain in Sèvres are examples of the early types. In Hamburg there is a "Pieta" which is said to date about 1780. This is full of the sentimental and theatrical spirit of the day.

VINOVO (NEAR TURIN)
1776–1820

Near Turin at Vinovo, Giovanni Vittorio Brodel, beginning in 1765, made many vain attempts to manufacture porcelain but it was not until 1776 when he was joined in partnership by Pierre Antoine Hannong of Strasburg that a factory was started in the royal palace and called "La reale manifattura di Vinovo," but he found it quite as difficult as had others to get along with Hannong and retired from the business in 1778 and the business was sold in 1780.

The new proprietor was a famous chemist, Dr. Vittorio Amadeo Gioanetti and under him the factory made some technical advancement but he died in 1815 and in 1820 it had to be closed.

Only one specimen is known from the Brodel-Hannong period and that is an oblong tray with handles missing in the British Museum, painted with small and poorly done scattered flowers in polychrome and marred by large kiln flaws. It is dated 1776. In the same museum there are several later pieces, including a white cup and saucer decorated in gold with the arms of the King of Sardinia and a "Virgin" or Eve kneeling on the globe with a serpent in plain white. Other pieces at Turin and elsewhere include portraits, flowers, etc., in polychrome and gold, in purple alone, in gold alone and, in fact, all of the technique and much of the style of the smaller French factories, though it has a yellowish tone and thick and faulty glaze which makes it look like soft porcelain, though Brongniart claims it is hard.

ROME
1790–1831

Rome was the last founded of the 18th-century Italian factories and as its founder was Giovanni Volpato, the engraver, it is natural that it is known only for figures copied from the antique and from Canova. A little later Wedgwood was copied. Examples may be found at Gisselfeld in Denmark, at Hamburg, in the Traugott Collection at Stockholm and elsewhere. The Hamburg Museum has two figures of Centaurs with Cupids on their backs which are excellent and, in fact some of these figures are as good as were done in the age.

ESTE

There was also a small factory at Este between Padua and Ferrara which produced a greyish green glaze like thin "celadon" and some white figures probably by Jean-Pierre Varion who formed a partnership with Girolamo Franchini in 1780 to form the factory. Varion had formerly worked at Nove.

TREVISO

In the little town of Treviso in the Venetian territory, there was also some soft porcelain made in Venetian style and decorated with landscapes in large medallions. These date about 1799 to 1800 when the factory was owned by the brothers Giuseppe and Andrea Fontebasso. The mark is "Treviso G.A.F.F." (Giuseppe-Andrea Fratelli Fontebasso) or simply the two letters F.F.

Thus from the half promise of something new or at least different in Italy which seemed to be indicated by the background of all the potteries which had been made there in earlier days, we find that in actuality the blight of the 18th-century factory methods and copyist principles was too strong and there is not much to distinguish Italian wares from those of the other countries.

SPAIN

"LA CHINA" OR BUEN RETIRO

Charles III left Naples in 1759, taking with him the best workmen from Capo di Monte, as well as porcelain earth and other materials, and, having ascended the throne of Spain, set up a factory called "La China" but known better as Buen Retiro because it was situated in a palace of that name near Madrid.

We learn authentically that the construction of this factory cost 11,500,000 reales and that its annual expenses were something like 3,000,000. There was no source of revenue; it was merely a court plaything but the demands were not, as one might imagine, small. Not to be outdone by Portici, two rooms were ordered and probably carried out by Giuseppe Gricci, one being dated 1763 and so signed, in all the mussy grandeur of the rococo style, with chinoiseries, mirrors, masks, cupids, etc. Other jobs of whole ceilings and massive works are said to have been in palaces in Escorial, La Granja, Aranjuez and elsewhere. In the Royal Palace at Madrid was a clock crowned by biscuit figures and four vases 6 feet high holding bouquets of porcelain flowers. They date from 1802 when Sureda, director of the factory, went to Sèvres to get ideas. At about 1800 the cult of Wedgwood was also taken seriously. Then in 1808, during the French invasion, it was turned into a fortress.

"LA MONCLOA" OR "FLORIDA"

In 1817, Ferdinand VII started a new factory called "La Moncloa" or "Florida" and it continued until 1849 but did nothing of note. In fact, aside

Fig. 1009. Candelabrum made at *Buen Retiro* with pastel shades of natural polychrome on white. It has the typical blue *fleur-de-lis* mark. Late 18th cent. The ormolu mounts are contemporary. Ht. 18″. Hispanic Society of America.

Fig. 1010. Figure called simply "Spanish 18th cent." by the museum but undoubtedly from Buen Retiro about 1765. It is decorated with soft tones of pink, mauve and green. Ht. 7¼″. Metropolitan Mus. of Art.

Fig. 1011. Porcelain vase of *Buen Retiro.* The colors are purple and green grapes with gold handles. Second half of 18th cent. Ht. about 8″. Hispanic Society of America.

Fig. 1012. Buen Retiro porcelain of 1759 to 1808 decorated in soft colors. Metropolitan Mus. of Art.

from the rooms there seems to be little to be said about the earlier work of the factory, though the prices that pieces from it command are high. The Capo di Monte association helped in boosting its prestige, and, in fact, so close is the technique that it is often quite impossible to distinguish between them. This was made even more difficult in that the fleur-de-lys mark was also used.

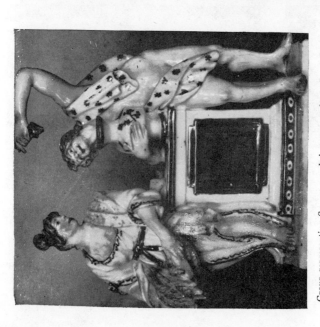

Group representing Summer and Autumn made at *Buen Retiro* during the 18th cent. with colors of blue, stippled flesh tones and gilt. Ht. 6¼″. Hispanic Society of America.

Right: Jar and cover made at the Royal Porcelain Factory of *Buen Retiro* with white ground, decorations in lilac and touches of gilt. The mark is a blue *fleur-de-lis*. Late 18th cent. Ht. 13¾″. Hispanic Society of America.

BUEN RETIRO SOFT PASTE OF THE 18th CENTURY

PLATE 189

The wares were hard paste, soft paste and biscuit. In general the Buen Retiro wares are thought to be whiter than those of Capo di Monte but yellowish exceptions do occur.

In the earlier days the factory was strongest in the modeling of figures, less successful in applied relief decoration and even weaker in purely painted technique, though there are some exceptions. A truly lovely and charming "Venus and Cupid" of yellowish white porcelain is in the Schlossmuseum in Berlin and the children such as the polychrome figures of a little boy drinking water and a little girl braiding her hair in the *Sèvres* collection, and the Bacchanalian children groups all show the happy influence of Gricci and are as good as anything the Capo di Monte factory ever turned out. The useful wares are, however, mediocre.

LA MONCLOA
1817

The second period of Buen Retiro came too late for us to expect anything of artistic merit from it. It was started at La Moncloa, as we have said above, in 1817 and the cylindrical cups, plain trays of uninteresting shapes and such, decorated in all-over enamels, marbled and agate grounds with reserves for undecorative painting of a poor character and much gilding, make them like all the rest of the period.

ALCORA
1764

The Count of Aranda had started a faïence factory at Alcora about 1750. The factory turned out almost every kind of ware; three kinds of "Spanish porcelain," "frita" (soft porcelain), "English pipeclay porcelain," "blue pipeclay porcelain," "marbled pipeclay porcelain," "buccaro" (Chinese stoneware type), "Strasburg ware" (faïence), etc., etc.

There was no style established because of constantly shifting managements. There are breakfast services now in the style of Sèvres and now following Wedgwood. The pipeclay was used for a ware similar to Leeds pottery. It was made in large quantities and much of it is erroneously called Leeds. Likewise much actual Alcora porcelain is probably erroneously identified.

Most Alcora porcelain is greenish-grey in tint, commonplace in shape and meagerly decorated. Bleu-de-roi grounds and gold, polychrome flowers, ornamental friezes sometimes broken by medallions with miniature painted heads, landscapes and such form the idiom which marked the time and not the place.

PORTUGAL

VISTA ALEGRE
1790

About 1790 Pinto Basto started a porcelain factory near Oporto at a place called Vista Alegre and there are a few specimens in museums.

LISBON

The only pieces known from the Lisbon factory are portrait "cameos" in Wedgwood style but on a brown or grey ground and are marked *"Lisboa Arsenal Real do exercito Joao de Figueiredo fecit."* There are a pair in Sèvres and another in the British Museum dated respectively 1783 and 1792.

SWITZERLAND

ZURICH OR SCHOREN (ITS ACTUAL LOCATION)
1763

The factory which was founded at Schoren near Bendlikon but spoken of as "Zurich" near which it also is, started as a faïence factory, made soft porcelain usually painted in blue or red or polychrome and later learned the secret of hard porcelain. It was founded by a group including Salomon Gessner, the painter-poet and had Adam Spengler of Schaffhausen as technical chief and Valentin Sonnenschein, the modeler and sculptor as part owner and practical assistant.

FIG. 1013. Jug of hard paste porcelain from Zurich, dated "1759–1799" by the museum but the factory started in 1763 and made soft paste at first. It should date 1770 to 1780. Ht. 3″. Metropolitan Mus. of Art.

FIG. 1014. Zurich cup and saucer with flowers in natural colors. They are hard paste of 1770–1780, not 1759–1799 as stated by the museum. Dia. of saucer 5⅛″. Metropolitan Mus. of Art.

Of the soft paste there is little except a teapot in the British Museum and some pieces in the Swiss Museums, a jug in the Victoria & Albert Museum and a few pieces at Sèvres.

The kaolin for the hard porcelain was obtained from *Lorraine* and even in its best period it is yellowish or greenish-grey and rather dirty in shade with many firing flaws. Gold was sparingly used if at all. The designs are of Swiss landscapes, birds and flowers and very infrequently figures. There were also imitations of Meissen *"Zwiebelmuster"* and other simple designs in underglaze blue. The subjects from nature were in polychrome or *en camaïeu*, at times also in two color combinations and these latter nearly always seem to have been executed by good painters.

The figures are bourgeois or rustic types done in an amateurish but fresh style with perhaps a bit of the spirit of Gessner. The painted ones are in a light and sometimes dingy color scheme which is not always happy. Much of the work, particularly the painting, is delicate in execution.

NYON

It is interesting to see that, though the porcelain of Zurich is quite German in character, that of Nyon is so French that it gave rise to the false legend that the factory was set up by workmen who were driven from Sèvres during the revolution.

Actually the factory was founded by two Germans, Ferdinand Müller of Frankenthal and his son-in-law, Jean-Jacques or Jacob Dortu from Berlin and after 1777 Marieberg in Sweden. Its porcelain was entirely imitative.

In 1786 the partnership was dissolved and until 1813 Dortu was the sole director and in 1813 it gave up porcelain and

FIG. 1015. Nyon cup and saucer with typical festoons and a silhouette, 1785–1790. Saucer 4¾" dia. Metropolitan Mus. of Art.

went into faïence copies of "Etruscan" vases and Wedgwood wares.

Most of the wares are of the useful type and the hard porcelain is cold and white. The decorations are in underglaze blue and polychrome and then later garlands, ribbons, trophies, love emblems and ornaments of the Louis XVI style together with strewn flowers, or rather geometrically arranged flowers, and such, in blue, red and gold and copying the other French schemes, which were in themselves nothing to boast of.

RUSSIA

St. Petersburg

In Russia the story is much the same; a ruler with ambitions, who was in this case Peter the Great. He had the desire to create national industries for the good of his land rather than to have a plaything for the purposes of showing how great he was.

In 1717 an emissary to Amsterdam entered into a contract with an Italian, Carlo Antonio Bonaveri to have him teach four Russians the secrets of porcelain in a year but nothing came of it. In the same year the Ambassador to Berlin persuaded Peter Eggebrecht to leave Dresden and set up a factory in St. Petersburg. He did go in 1718 but evidently stayed only a few years and returned without any recorded success. It was 25 years before porcelain was first produced at St. Petersburg. But bad fortune was not even yet overcome for with the first production we again run afoul of that major faker and charlatan Christoph Conrad Hunger who had been from Meissen to Venice, thence to Vienna, thence back to Meissen, and then to Stockholm where he was met by the Russian Baron N. A. Korff who was on a diplomatic mission for the Empress Elizabeth and arranged to send Hunger to St. Petersburg after payment of a 1,000 specie dollars and the guarantee of 1,000 rubles a year with the title of "Director of the Porcelain Factory of Her Imperial Majesty."

A factory was erected at Neva nearby and in 1745 Hunger was still making unsuccessful attempts to do something. In 1748 he had made six imperfect little cups in all and then was dismissed, having cost the Russian government the tidy sum of 15,000 rubles or thereabouts.

Vinogradov was put in charge and after a short while did succeed in making small pieces of porcelain of fairly good quality but was fired from the factory for drinking too much in 1751, and Johann Schlatter the Director of the Russian Mint took his place. Later the "arcanist" Johann Gottfried Müller was appointed for technical supervision.

The early production was naturally Meissen in style up to 1753 and consisted chiefly of little cups and saucers, small jugs and particularly snuff boxes which were used as presents from the court and frequently made in the shape of envelopes with red seals and the names of the recipients on them. Statuettes were tried, but the first are childlike models of a cow and a "dog Foo" of Chinese type. Then came Oriental racial types also crudely modeled.

The useful porcelain was usually decorated in monochrome purple, green, black or with gold alone or combined with the others. The "Gold Chinamen" decoration after Herold of Meissen was copied and became popular but gave way to scenes from daily life, landscapes and animals, and the palette was increased.

THE SECOND PERIOD—CATHERINE II
1762–1796

In 1762, when Catherine II ascended the throne, it marked a new period and in 1763 she visited the factory and there was an immediate and radical change of staff there. In her usual way, she took a lieutenant of the horse guards, Alexander Tchepotiev, and put him in charge with a Viennese, Joseph Regensburg as "arcanist" and Karlovsky from Meissen as master-modeler, adding a little later the French modeler J. S. Rachette. By 1780 most of the staff were Russians but by that time the factory style had been set as so nearly that of Sèvres that again it is difficult to tell them apart except for the marks. However, the Russian factory also made a commercial ware which was yellowish or greyish, crude and mediocre. *The only other way to distinguish the finer Russian ware from that of Sèvres is when it carries a picture from Russian towns, a picture of the Empress or an allegory concerning her or something of the sort.* The flowers were, strangely, on the other hand like those of early Copenhagen but can be distinguished because the Russian plates are edged with brown which was never done in the Danish factory. In general, the rest of the wares follow the neo-classical trend and toward the end of the century the same struggle was made to create huge services and colossal pieces. One of the services known as "Les Arabesques" consisted of about 1,000 pieces and cost 25,000 rubles, and had a table decoration to go with it consisting of six allegorical groups as well as a centerpiece which was a statue of the Empress on a pedestal flanked by "Justice" and "Charity." Figures copied the antique or Falconet or Clodion and the colored ones gave way to biscuit as elsewhere.

PAUL I PERIOD
1796–1801

Paul I was keenly interested in the factory but it was now the time of the Empire period which suited the Russian porcelain no more than it did any other and we see the naturalistic pictures, the covering of all surfaces with enamel and gold and the total loss of any national characteristics.

OTHER RUSSIAN FACTORIES

There developed many other Russian factories and on the accession of Catherine II there were 12 faïence and porcelain factories of which 7 were for porcelain only, by 1800 there were nearly 20, in 1813 there were 30, and in 1817 some 45 and most of these were around Gschely, which section was rich in kaolin.

THE GARDNER FACTORY

It was in this general location in the town of Verbilki that an Englishman, named Gardner founded one of the largest factories in 1758. About 1780 it was moved to Tver near Moscow.

POPOFF & GULIN

Two other factories marked their wares with full names or monograms in Russian characters, that of Popoff which was in the village of Gorbunovo (1806–1872) and that of the brothers Gulin or Gulina at Friasino. They are, of course, all Empire in style.

KORZEC

In Korzec, which was in the government of Volhynia, in 1780 or thereabouts, Prince Czartoryski founded a factory. From about 1803 it was placed under the management of Merault, a painter from Sèvres. The mark was either "Korzec" or a triangular drawn eye, and the style again typically Empire.

MEZER

Of about the same period and turning out much the same sort of thing was the factory of Mezer at Baranovka which mostly stamped its wares with the name of the place with or without the name of the maker.

In summing up the Russian factories we must conclude that they learned the secrets of porcelain too late and thus became decadent almost before they began. They added nothing new to the so-called art except the envelope shaped snuff boxes, which are not good taste at best, and the making of imitation Easter eggs painted with Biblical and other paintings in the worst possible taste.

THE NETHERLANDS

As we have already said, Holland was not particularly interested in Böttger's invention for in that country faïence had been developed to the most excellent possible technique and the porcelain demands could readily be filled by importation from the Orient. There is little of distinction about the Dutch 18th-century porcelain except a pleasant bourgeois character.

WEESP, 1764, OUDE LOOSDRECHT, 1771
OUDE AMSTEL, 1784, NIEUWER AMSTEL, 1799–1810

Count (or Baron) Gronsfeldt-Diepenbrock established the first hard porcelain factory in the plant of a bankrupt faïence factory at Amsterdam and

transferred it to Weesp in the same neighborhood. It was a propitious moment, for the Seven Years' War had thrown many of the German workers out of occupation and they were easily persuaded to come and work. It is reported that the output was so good technically that Gronsfeldt actually made advances to Sèvres for an amalgamation, but the answer given was that the French factory preferred to go on with the soft porcelain until the materials could be found on their own territory, and nothing came of the suggestion. But, if the factory had opened under the best of circumstances, these were not to continue; the German hands soon wished to return home and, added

FIG. 1016. Dish of Dutch hard paste (1775–1786) with trellis work in gilt, baskets of flowers in colors, etc., and circles in bright blue. Dia. 9½". Metropolitan Mus. of Art.

to the labor difficulties, there came sales troubles even greater, for just at this time the country was flooded with cheap Japanese porcelain. Financial sickness, the common complaint of the 18th-century porcelain factories in all countries, brought about the purchase of the factory by a Calvinist preacher named Mol.

OUDE LOOSDRECHT, 1771–1784

Mol moved the factory at once in 1771 to Oude Loosdrecht which lies between Utrecht and Amsterdam.

OUDE AMSTEL, 1784–1799

Mol died in 1782 and in. 1784 the factory belonged to a limited company which moved it again to Oude Amstel and appointed a German named F. Däuber as manager.

NIEUWER AMSTEL, 1799–1810

The company underwent changes in 1799 and was then known as G. Dommer & Co. which transferred the wandering factory still again to Nieuwer Amstel where it lasted only until 1810 and finally closed down for good.

In spite of all of this moving the productions are so alike and so continuous in their development that, were it not for changes in marks, they could not be surely distinguished one from another.

WEESP WARES

Between 1765 and 1770 roughly, a white porcelain was made ornamented with floral festoons, sprays or other motifs in relief. Perforated baskets were made and delicately picked out in blue. There were also rococo relief decorated wares very sparingly decorated with landscapes in cartouches or with birds or scattered flowers. Then there were also such pieces as the breakfast services with Watteau scenes and scenes from the Italian comedies, and other pieces such as tureens with large bouquets of flowers and a cut lemon or bird finial for the cover. In all of these the paste is white and the glaze even, while the colors are well fused, but perhaps a little lacking in brilliance for some tastes, though I find them very pleasant.

OUDE LOOSDRECHT

The quality seems to improve under Mol and there seems to me to creep in more of the Dutch characteristics as seen in certain elongation and, let us say, opening up of the tighter German forms. A good example of this may be seen in the perforated vase from a service which is in the Nederlandsch Museum and which is decorated with painted swans. In this the foot and the perforated neck are, as it were, stretched upward and the handles have become slender, though not losing in seeming strength, and are set further away from the sides. Such pieces could be neither German nor French and show that they were made after many of the Germans had returned home and before the French workers were brought in.

On the other hand a breakfast service in the Gemeente Museum painted with figures in landscapes in dark brown has nothing new to offer. Some pieces of the period have cupids in red camaïeu or monochrome decorations in purple. Others have gold borders and blue floral festoons around the edges. There were also polychrome landscapes, not by any means all Dutch in characteristics, birds, flowers and very rarely copies of the Japanese competitive wares but with a certain difference in the curves and scrolls used, making them wobbly and not improving even upon these lowly wares.

Some busts were made of biscuit and placed on fluted and often green-striped pedestals, and a vague beginning of the neo-classical feeling from France was taking form.

OUDE AMSTEL

With the change of location surprisingly the factory lost none of its technical excellence, which seems perfect except for the slight running of the blue at times, but it becomes somehow stiffer and dryer, and the originality of form has been lost. French models seem to have been copied and the work takes on the look of Sèvres.

The last days see the usual decline which we have learned to expect with the opening of the 19th century.

THE HAGUE
1775

The Viennese, Anton Leichner (Linker or Lyncker), founded at The Hague in 1775 a factory which, though it lasted only about ten years, turned out some fairly respectable works. He had a miniature painter who was well known at the time, Leonardus Temminck, who had been a pupil of Benjamin Bolomey, who in turn had studied in Paris under Boucher and this explains why we see the "Boucher children" painted in purple with such good understanding, and spirit.

FIG. 1017. Porcelain plate from The Hague about 1775-1786. Dia. 10¾". Metropolitan Mus. of Art.

FIG. 1018. Tureen with overglazed blue mark of stork with branch in beak, that of "The Hague" but the shape is a Tournai one and the body may even have been made there. The decoration is in natural colors except the flowers which are in underglaze blue with gilt scrolls. The ware is soft paste dating about 1785. Length 12". Leon van Biene.

The neo-classical blight is seen almost at once in the sober and stupid shapes, and figures were not attempted at all but the painting seemed to cover every possibility of the day. There were polychrome flowers, which were thinner and dryer than those of Meissen, landscapes with and without figures, birds on plates with bleu-de-roi shell edging around them, and much en camaïeu and grisaille painting, the latter used especially for antique profile heads in medallions with pale pink ground, a pleasant individual contrast and perhaps the best of the work turned out by the factory.

Occasionally this factory decorated white wares made elsewhere and particularly soft porcelain which it did not make at all itself. We have spoken of this connection with Tournai. The probable reason lies in the excellence of the Hague painting, as is pointed out, perhaps a bit too enthusiastically, but nevertheless with much truth, in the argument by H. E. van Gelder in his catalogue. However, we cannot conclude that the other factories sent their wares to be decorated and then returned to them for sale, because we find in the Gemeente Museum a pastille-burner and a sugar-bowl on which an attempt has obviously been made to cancel the original mark A (which van Gelder explains is the Ansbach mark and further claims that he believes he has found a confirmation in the archives of a relationship between the two places) by painting over it in overglaze blue The Hague stork. If there was a relationship, it would not seem to have been a friendly one. These pieces

FIG. 1019. Dutch tea-pot of the 18th cent. and probably from The Hague. Decorated with a green band of foliage with purple foliated design. Ht. 5″. Metropolitan Mus. of Art.

are the stranger because, though hard paste, they are decorated like the soft paste of Tournai. Perhaps we had better conclude simply that once in a while the factory might have bought a few undecorated examples and allowed the workers to amuse themselves dressing them up as experiments.

BELGIUM

MANUFACTURE DE MONTPLAISIR, 1784–1791

The country that is now Belgium was even later in starting porcelain making. The first hard porcelain factory was the Manufacture de Montplaisir which was started in 1784 by J. S. Vaume near Schaerbeek. It remained in existence only seven years and made simply decorated porcelain of the period style such as landscapes in the manner of India ink drawings, small evenly scattered or arranged flowers or monochrome landscapes particularly in green. It also tried the "décor bois" or wood grain stunt and specialized in scattered sprigs in combination with friezes or festoons of leaves and flowers.

ETERBEEK

Near Brussels, at Eterbeek a factory was started in 1775 by Chretien Kühne of Saxony. It made useful ware decorated with all the expected methods of the day and is said to have closed down in 1803.

DENMARK

Denmark can take justifiable pride in its ceramic history, for it is the home of the world famous Royal Copenhagen factory.

There is a little confusion concerning the first porcelain made in Denmark for it was the custom to refer to porcelain as "Delfs porcelain" inferring Delfsware which was faïence. However, we know that in 1737 Christoph Conrad Hunger approached the government and was luckily or wisely turned down. In 1752 and 1757 the ivory carver from Germany Christoph Ludwig Lück and his son Karl Gottlieb Lück were granted subsidies as were also Jürgen Gülding in 1753, and Johann Gottlieb Melhorn in 1754. The latter had attained distinction as a blue and white painter at Meissen. In 1755 Niels Birch found kaolin on the island of Bornholm. Melhorn had to quit his factory and go to Kastrup but there too he failed and we know of nothing from either place.

Fournier, a Frenchman, produced soft paste at Blaataarn about 1760 to 1765. He had worked at Vincennes and Chantilly as a modeler yet there is only one insignificant work attributed to him at Copenhagen, a medallion of Frederik V. of Denmark. Otherwise the wares are of common useful type with one service having a wicker patterned border with four reserves

Fig. 1020. Fournier Period (1760–1766) soft-paste service design presented to King Charles XV of Sweden by the Countess Dannemand. Marked F 5 in gold. 1760–1765. National Mus., Stockholm.

Fig. 1021. One of a pair of rococo vases with a medallion showing a shield supported by cupids and having a crown and F 5 in gold. The flowers are in natural colors. 1760–1765. Count Moltke Coll. in Bregentved.

in light rococo feeling of flowers. The edge is in rudimentary petal form which seemed to be a favorite treatment The painting was done by Jürgen Gülding, Joseph Brecheisen, George Christian Sciptius and others with a decidedly French style. The material is yellowish and with a soapy feel, having little brilliance not unlike Chantilly. There was a Meissen influence

GROUP. FLORA AND MINERVA
Height 11½ inches.

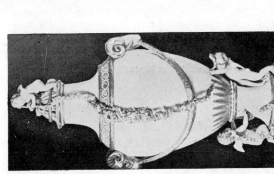

Left to Right: One of a pair of vases painted with portraits of Queen Juliane Marie and the Crown Prince Frederik. c. 1785. Ht. 15″. Rosenborg Castle. The Vase of gold and white with garland in natural colors. The playful treatment of cupids arranging the garlands shows at least a spark of invention. c. 1788. Rosenborg Castle. Typical of the gods made in European factories is this group of Flora and Minerva having the three line and personal mark of Jacob Schmidt, (1778–1807). Ht. 11 4/5″. Dansk Folke Mus., Copenhagen. Dansk Folke Mus., Copenhagen. Biscuit group with incised mark A HALD 1797. Dansk Folke Mus., Copenhagen.

COPENHAGEN PORCELAIN OF THE LATE 18TH CENTURY

PLATE 190

in the use of "mosaik." The thickness varies and it seems experimental. The colors have little depth and the only red tone is a characteristic pale pink. Otherwise there was a powerful copper green, and a very soft yellow sometimes hardly visible.

C7 stood for Christian VII on one piece. The usual mark is F5 for Frederik V. A month before his death Frederik V gave an order that the factory cease (1765).

J. G. Richter, a painter from Strasburg, and Frantz Heinrich Müller, were given Fournier's secrets and Müller started in 1771 to experiment and finally made a poor piece of real porcelain, with yellowish glaze and underglaze blue decoration. He was granted 1,000 rigsdalers in 1772 to start a factory and went in 1773 to Bornholm which helped him to get better results.

In 1774 he was trying to sell stock when Queen Dowager Juliane Marie took an interest and a company was formed with a capital of 19,000 rigsdalers with Holm, and the historian, Suhm, in charge. A privilege was granted on March 13, 1775 conferring a monopoly for 50 years and the post office in Købmagergade became the factory.

The mark was decided as "three wave-shaped lines representing the three streams of Denmark, namely, "The Sound and the Great and Little Belts." Hannover makes the point that the fact that it was adopted in 1775 does not exclude the possibility that Müller had been using it before.

The mark alone shows that Müller had an underglaze blue but this was, at first, greyish or even blackish. Probably the kaolin brought from GrødbyAa improved the paste. The sand came from Robertsdal and the felspar from near Nexø. Also the chalk from Faxe and fluorspar from Gislöf in Sweden helped the glaze. Later kaolin was brought from Limoges and felspar from Arendal in Norway while the chalk of the island of Møen was preferred to that of Faxe.

BORNHOLM PERIOD (1773–1776)

During the Bornholm period from 1773 to the beginning of 1776, the ware was bluish-grey with a tendency to "wreathing" which caused worry to Müller when C. F. G. Clar of Rendsburg applied for a privilege for himself, and he forthwith got help from workers from Saxony and Furstenberg. He even took a trip under a false name to Germany in the hope of getting some secrets. After this Johann Georg von Langen came bringing secrets from Furstenberg where he had been, and also from Höchst, through Benckgraff's notes. He urged the employment of Luplau.

This Anton Carl Luplau in 1795 applied to the governors to give him equal rank with Müller and in a report by Gronland we pick the few following statements as representative of the state of affairs: "It was not until Luplau brought with him a tried method that Müller learned that quartz is a principal ingredient." "Apart from alterations introduced by Justitsraad Müller, and to which I expressly attribute the ill-success of our factory, it is the paste of Luplau, his glaze and his kiln, that we are using at the moment." In the same year Luplau wrote a book, afterward edited by his son, giving "all the secrets of a true porcelain factory."

FIG. 1022. The upper group is said by Hayden to be of the "Bornholm period." The cup with three feet lower left is marked with the three lines and cross in blue under the handle. The tea-pot is the only one known with three blue lines under the handle. Mus. of the Royal Copenhagen Porcelain Factory.

In the meantime the factory was having the usual financial difficulties all kilns seemed subject to and in 1779, through the instigation of Juliane Marie, under the influence of her Cabinet Secretary, Holm, the king gave his consent to the acceptance of the factory, for the bright idea had occurred to the members of the board that it would be a good thing to make the gift. The factory was then called *Den Kongelige Danske Porcelains Fabrik.* This is the factory, popularly known as Royal Copenhagen, that became famous the world over for its fine wares.

In 1780 the first sales room was opened. Many new artists were brought in,

Fig. 1023. Dowager-Queen Juliane Marie bust signed "Luplau fec: 1781." At Rosenborg Castle.

Fig. 1024. Ewer and cover painted in aubergine (manganese) and certainly from a German model. Ht. 9½". c. 1779. Kunstindustri Mus., Bergen.

mainly German, but a sufficient number of Danes were there to give the work a flavor of its own.

In 1776 a rule was made not to paint the porcelain with colors other than underglaze blue and at about this time was made the ware with festoons of flowers in blue on a grey porcelain. In 1778 iron-red was resumed sometimes on flowers in slight relief. At the same time a purple was added and yet the underglaze blue was the chief medium, though not yet mastered. In 1779 the purple became dominant along with a good copper green. By 1780 the iron-red is predominant with purple a close second while polychrome flowers in rococo panels in slight relief and accented with pale copper green or gold are also made. This sort of shadow treatment seems probably original. The flowers were simple and broad but with a stiff, quaint style not without appeal. Soon, however, the rococo was replaced by the neo-classic trends of the day.

It was in 1780 that a new and whiter as well as more translucent porcelain was produced and most of the neo-classical shapes were done. By 1781 most of the old paste seems to have been used up and at the same time the painting of flowers is brighter and better, undoubtedly due to the German artists. One hand bell of the period is decorated in "mosaik" surrounding

FIG. 1025. Of the period between 1780 and 1796 a service painted with fruits in natural colors. Coll. of Her Majesty the Queen of Denmark.

harvest scenes in somewhat inky tones of polychrome almost exactly like those of the Berlin factory. But the Danish influence made the Germans do flowers that looked soft and fresh, like those of northern summers. The gilding was also moderate and in good taste. The usual purple and natural colored landscapes with, of course, romantic ruins, "altars of love," "altars of friendship," and "memorial columns," and the silhouettes, cupids in grey and in natural colors, etc., had their turn as elsewhere. A specialty was ini-

FIG. 1026. Front and top of casket which is mounted in gold and set with rubies, richly gilt and painted in natural colors. The royal crown appears on the front and the key is designed with the monogram of Christian VIII. c. 1781. Length 7¾". J. Pierpont Morgan Coll.

tials in flowers. And the northern people took the sweet-to-cloying sentimentality of the French seriously to their hearts and made it even more
sentimental.

Søren Preuss was responsible for many of the flowers and Luplau himself
for the cupids that are handles on the covers. In 1782 they introduced "flower
vases with cupids in black"
(painted of course) and in 1783
black pastoral scenes and "India
ink painting with cupids in
clouds." The iron-red was a
favorite with Ondrup.

FIG. 1027. Tray with landscape in deep green
and wreaths in manganese with the borders gilt by
Elias Meyer. It was given by Frederik VI to Pastor
Mandal of Sørum, Norway, 1790. Kunstindustri
Mus., Copenhagen.

Another decoration is called
"Quodlibets" meaning "what you
please" and consists of all manner of objects thrown together
and painted in various shades of
grey or natural colors. In 1788
there were cupid-surmounted
vases with portraits in brown of
Raphael, Durer, Leonardo, etc.

Breakfast sets were made for
two to twelve people and these latter were usually 51 pieces. The famous
"Müller service" made for the founder was of 46 pieces and 32 still exist. It
was made in 1784 by all of the artists in the factory supervised by Camradt,
and is a sampler with each piece differently treated. Some pieces are even
decorated differently on either side. For example one teapot is pink on one
side and white on the other. The
bleu-de-roi border holds the set together though even this border is
varied, so far as the gold design on
it is concerned. Three silhouette
portraits of Müller's sons with their
initials and ages are on one tea-
caddy and Charles A. Been also
pointed out portraits of Müller
himself and his second wife. There
was a rule in the factory that artists should not sign their work and
unfortunately this was adhered to
even in this service. Ondrup did
surreptitiously write his name in

FIG. 1028. Tray dated 1783 and painted with
"Quodlibet" or "attrap" decoration. Coll. of Hr.
Nörgaard, Sölyst, Denmark.

tiny letters in hidden places like the inside of a foot-rim, but we know his style
already from the constant use of iron-red in inharmonious combinations. Camradt did cupids en grisaille and portraits of the royal family. Lehmann did
polychrome flowers and "shadow pictures." Elias Meyer did landscapes, polychrome birds, "antique heads," and "quodlibet."

The decline began to take place and in 1785 mirror frames, toilet services, caskets, brush handles, etc., and cups with "kommik" paintings were so successful that they were often repeated. By 1786 flutes and dress buttons were added, plus pipe bowls with dates and inscriptions and breakfast services decorated by Meyer and Poggendahl. In 1787 came the first "Ovidian paintings" by Camradt and in 1788 large potpourri vases with figure handles, rams' heads, garlands and fluted or reeded pedestals.

The Flora Danica Service of world fame was commenced in 1789 or 1790 with botanical paintings by Johann Christoph Bayer, from Nuremberg, who had been at the factory since 1776. Tradition has it that the intention was to present this service to Catherine II of Russia but she died before it was completed. The first decorator of the factory was Holm, who had just laid out the gardens at Sorø and Copenhagen. He had just published his large and beautiful work dealing with Danish fungi and had the idea of using the plates to decorate a dinner service. Each piece had on the back a reference to the learned work and the Latin name of the plant. Yet, unlike the Palissy wares, these decorations, though accurate, were also beautiful. The colors were more brilliant than the printed plates of the book and the painting was graceful as the flowers themselves and without scientific stiffness. Here suddenly in the miasma of deceit and larceny of the penny grubbing 18th century, nay at its most odorous and marshy depths, two men, a manager and an artist have turned back to first sources; back to nature and regardless of the baroque or the rococo, the empire or directoire styles, have set out to take things from nature and arrange them so as to be beautiful and give delight. To arrange them on what principles?

Fig. 1029. Vase with cupids in natural colors and gilt decoration. Ht. 18″. Dansk Folke Mus., Copenhagen.

Well, here again we are confronted by the age old argument as to what constitutes art. Man has, through the ages tried to take the simple things around him and arrange them so as to suggest his feelings for them. He has tried to change nature just a little to please him the better. He has also taken a delight in placing things within certain bounds and making them fit those bounds properly. He carved a bear on the handle of a knife so that anyone would recognize it as a bear and yet, if the design was drawn on paper anyone could also see that it was the handle for a knife. He also unconsciously put something of himself into it, for he carved it differently than his brother would, or than any other man would. Whole tribes carved their bears differently from other tribes yet often nearly enough alike to be recognizable as from their tribe and no other. This was just as the language of one tribe might differ from all others and be understandable only to the members of that one tribe, and this marvelously enough despite the fact that each member of the tribe talked differently from every other member.

All this simple and sincere way of things had been lost to the 18th century for 1.—the artists were not close to nature, 2.—the artists were trying to

Plates, tureen and cruet stand of the Flora Danica service made for Catherine II of Russia. Rosenborg Copenhagen.

PIECES FROM THE FLORA DANICA SERVICE

PLATE 191

make things look more expensive and grand and did not keep within the bounds, 3.—artists were so pushed for time in the everlasting competition that they could not take the time to think out anything of their own and had to keep their brushes working without an idea behind them, 4.—as several generations had been taught simply to steal the ideas of each other, the whole thing dried up and there was nothing to steal.

But here in Copenhagen two men saw a gleam of light. On what principles could old Bayer arrange his flowers? He had no traditional tea-ceremony. He had no time to sit and watch each flower grow, blossom and die so as to try to catch the very spirit of the flower. He had never, like the Chinese, watched the bamboo day after day in summer rain, in hot sun, in a fall storm when birds could hold to it only a few seconds before being torn away by the wind. He had probably never thought of painting a flower in its surrounding atmosphere and under the conditions of its life, of painting it in his own way and as an expression of his own mood. He could only see it cold and alone, detached from all the world and laid out dead on a porcelain plate.

He, with the help of other artists who did the borders and general work, had turned out 1,000 pieces by 1792 in a little over 2 years, or about 40 a month or 10 a week. By 1794 he had totaled 1,335 including some big pieces valued at 10,400 rigsdaler. In 1797 there were 2,528 pieces and 180 still to be made. Then the court gave the order that it should be even greater so as to seat 100 guests. In 1802 it was still uncompleted and the court ordered work to stop. But work of real charm had been accomplished and

FIG. 1030. Two Sea Horses painted in brown and other colors and marked with three blue lines. c. 1800. National Mus., Stockholm.

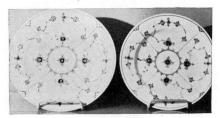

FIG. 1031. Antique and modern plates with fluted rims and "Muschel" pattern. Note deeper blue but heavier drawing on modern plate. George Jensen, Inc.

FIG. 1032. Empire feeling threw its blight upon this factory as upon others of Europe. Bowl at top was made in memory of brave Danes who fell at Battle of Copenhagen, dated April 2nd, 1801. Cups show "The King's Square, Copenhagen," and "Kronborg Castle" showing the Sound. Dansk Folke Mus., Copenhagen.

it may be that this return to first principles made by Holm and Bayer was responsible for the beautiful and natural charm of the present day Copenhagen work.

However, there is no doubt but that this undertaking, which was slow in being paid for, caused financial difficulties, which lasted until 1807 when the English bombarded Copenhagen and all production stopped. Between 1790 and 1800 there were "belt-plaques" and "ice-bells," plaques for furniture called "piano plaques," butter dishes in the form of apples, some square salvers, dishes with covers like a bunch of asparagus, scent bottles in the form of infants in swaddling-clothes (the appropriateness depending on the point of view I suppose), pipe-bowls in the shape of vases, tobacco-boxes in the shape of dogs' heads and such table decorations as sea-nymphs, mermen and sea-horses designed to stand on a mirror. The usual Wedgwood, "Egyptian" and "Etruscan" things were made.

The blue and white ware consisted chiefly of the "Muschel" pattern, the bouquet of flowers, the "onion" pattern or "Zwiebelmuster" of Meissen and a "Chinese" design from the same source. The blue and white of clear paste is later and that of good blue, later yet. The latest is too harsh and aggressive. The "Muschel" pattern became increasingly misunderstood and corrupted and in all late pieces the drawing gets more and more stiff with cautiousness yet somehow at the same time careless and heavy in composition.

After 1800 the purple continues but less pure and strong in color. Gold and white became increasingly popular because of the "good taste" of the day. Hannover states, and I think we should believe him, that collectors have placed a too high value on the plastic works of the old factory. Perhaps this is due to the modern fame, for at no time did the place have a modeler of note on its staff. We hear of J. J. Smidt and Andreas Hald whose marks appear on widely different things, and were possibly simply retouchers.

There have not been many forgeries except the baskets of flowers like those of the Flora Danica service which Samson copied, and carefully marked with the wave mark. Also a "restorer" in Dresden bought the bottoms of undecorated boxes with wave marks on them and made lids of Saxon porcelain, covering the whole with decoration so as to disguise the fact that the wares were different.

SWEDEN

MARIEBERG

In Sweden Ehrenreich applied for a privilege in 1758. In the same or following year the Marieberg property at Kungsholmen, Stockholm, was purchased from Baron C. F. Scheffer "for the establishment of a true porcelain factory," but after the place had burned down and been reerected Ehrenreich decided to give up porcelain and make faïence. There is only one insignificant piece to represent his experiments.

Possibly from France and copied at Marieberg are some pieces which Strole in the Rorstrand Museum has said were made by Ehrenreich's successor, Pierre Berthevin (1766–1769) which are soft-paste candlesticks and pastilleburners with decorations of freely modeled flowers applied. There are also animals such as a goat, a cat and a dog, but all of these are probably French and not Marieberg at all.

From Mennecy came the design for the custard cups with single handle and cover and decorated with flowers. Some of these cannot be distinguished except for the mark.

Strole classes the early wares as follows:

1. Earliest: Custard cups, miniature vases with dolphin handles and small modeled figures in highly translucent, greenish-yellow and faulty paste of soft type, marked MB incised which he says meant "Marieberg-Berthevin" while Hannover says it meant "Marie Berg."

2. Chalky white soft paste marked MB in color. (Possibly Sten's.)

3. True porcelain thinly glazed and probably of the last of the period of Henrik Sten (1769–1778).

The second period was a transitional period and probably started about 1770 when the modeler Fleurot was called in followed by Huret and Jacques or Jacob Dortie or Dortu, Frenchmen of no particular renown but workmen who may have helped the general technique.

It is definitely established that the F which sometimes occurs on figures

FIG. 1033. Woman with chickens painted in overglaze natural colors and, black and gold on belt and pendant ornaments. Mark M incised. Kunstindustri Mus., Copenhagen.
FIG. 1034. Statue of a Hero having the incised mark: I HOLM 1780 and three blue lines. Ht. 12¼". National Mus., Stockholm.
FIG. 1035. Not entered in books but probably dating c. 1786 to 1796 this dancing pair in contemporary costumes are in soft colors and gold.

and custard cups has nothing to do with Fleurot, and, as Huret is mentioned specifically in old documents of the factory as having "occasioned the flint porcelain" it is not likely that he especially concerned himself with hard porcelain. Sten did begin to experiment with hard porcelain on his own account. Hannover does not think it impossible that he might be responsible for the second or chalky type of ware. The third type may have been brought about by the man called Jacques Dortie by Strole and Jacob Dortu by Hannover, who identifies him as Müller's assistant at Nyon "for" as he says, "shortly after his engagement in 1777, the state of affairs at the factory is thus described: 'Old Franzen attends the faïence, Sten to the flint porcelain and Dortie the true porcelain.' If this line of thought is correct the third class must belong to the year 1777 and 1778 for Dortu only worked at the factory at that time. Dortu seems to have taken the secret with him when he left,

FIG. 1036. Large vases in white porcelain dating between 1780–1796. Ht. 48". Frederiksborg Castle.

for otherwise had the factory gone on making it until 1782 when it was transferred to Rorstrand or to 1788 when it was closed down, that porcelain could not have been such a rarity as it now is. It was probably superseded by the second type again. Some dated pieces would tend to confirm this.

These are cups decorated in gold and black with festoons and the arms of the family of Baron Liljencrants, dated 1781 and are of semi-porcelain; a tea-caddy and coffee-pot painted in purple, red and green, and in purple and gold respectively are dated the same year and are of the same material."

Thus according to Hannover's well thought out logic we conclude that:

1. Under Berthevin (1766–1769) we have the greenish-yellow soft paste after Mennecy models.

2. Under Henrik Sten (1769–1788) we have the chalky white semi-porcelain save for a brief period of 1777 and 1778 when the hard porcelain was made and then lost or discarded.

There are no hard porcelain custard cups probably because the material was not suitable for the thin walls. There are rare trays or platters with handles at each end and painted with landscapes in purple or with polychrome flowers and green edging. There are also perforated baskets with modeled and painted flowers, some ink stands and tête-à-tête sets with modeled flowers or a torch and quiver on a pedestal. These are seldom marked.

The semi-porcelain is of a limey character white as chalk and uneven like faïence. It is slightly and irregularly translucent, light in weight and without resonance. The glaze is often cracked. It is seldom decorated. The custard cups are usually molded in slight relief with helical lines and have handles with rococo feeling. The decorations are polychrome, purple, blue or green bunches of flowers on either side and smaller ones on the covers. The colors of the flowers are sometimes combined with gold, and black is rare but not unknown. When gold is used it is sparingly touched in and the knobs and edges are also gilded.

There are no landscapes in natural colors but only small ones in iron red, reddish purple and copper green. These are in quatrefoil medallions or round ones suspended from festoons in relief and framed with leaf garlands. All were in good taste but there is no real life or vigor.

The plastic work was small in quantity and surprisingly small in number of models. They are chiefly figures from life such as a poultry-maid, a vintner, a bag-piper, a dancing boy or girl, some figures from the Italian comedy and a few mythological ones. The children are graceful but lifeless. A shepherd trying to kiss a shepherdess is full of action but poorly modeled. Most of them are unpainted.

There is utmost confusion about the marks. The chief one is three small crowns sometimes decoratively drawn, sometimes just indicated with four little strokes and at times just three little dots in underglaze blue are used with or without the crowns. At times a little fleur-de-lis from the House of Vasa was used. The mark is most frequently in iron red or underglaze blue but it occurs also in black, gold, brown, and green, with the color at times corresponding to that used for the decoration of the piece. An F in gold, a cursive M in black or red and an incised MW along with other unexplained marks also occur and finally there are many pieces not marked at all. Only one full signature by an artist is known and that is a tray signed "Schirmer."

There is naturally little reason to imitate this ware although pieces which brought 20 to 40 kroner in 1888 jumped to ten times that value in more recent sales. Soon we may be able to buy good fakes for equal prices, if this keeps up.

IRELAND

BELLEEK

The story goes that Mr. John Caldwell Bloomfield of the Castle Caldwell estate on the River Erne of County Firmanagh below the Donegal Highlands and about six miles from the sea directly west of Belfast, noted the exceptional brilliancy of the whitewash used on a tenant's house and discovered a limepit which led to the discovery that the whole estate rested upon a felspathic clay stratum. A factory was built, it is reported, in 1857 though just what the output was seems in some doubt. According to W. P. Jervis (*The Encyclopaedia of Ceramics*, p. 41), the so-called "parian ware" was first made by a William Bromley, a modeler named Gallimore and some workmen hired temporarily away from W. H. Goss of Stoke-upon-Trent who was supposed to have produced the ware there. Who Mr. Goss was and how he got the secret from William Taylor Copeland who invented the ware in 1846 I do not know. Jervis also states that the firm of Messrs. McBirney & Armstrong of Belleek, the town from which the ware takes its name, first made it popular in 1863.

The "inventor" of the pearly luster was J. J. H. Brianchou, a Frenchman who took out a patent in England in July 8th, 1857. Actually some biscuit unglazed pieces were made which might resemble the other "parian wares" but were quite different, due to the difference of local materials, and the Belleek usually known is glazed. I suspect that just as it was a vogue to make soft, white or cream biscuit in America and call it "parian" because it was supposed to be similar to marble in texture, so the Belleek potters also tried their hand at it. Of course, the Frenchman's patent is somewhat foolish in view of the fact that luster, or a thin solution of metal washed over a glaze and fired on, is one of the very ancient ways of decorating ceramic wares. However, it is probably true that no luster was used at Belleek until 1863.

The ware is made with the plaster casting process; after the clay has been ground and refined down to the consistency of cream, it is poured into a mold, turned this way and that and allowed to dry about 20 minutes. The mold can then be removed and appliqués of flowers, etc., applied by hand after having been hand modeled. The firing is done in troughs or long saggers and the best pieces are placed in sealed saggers inside of these same troughs. It is said that firing lasts about 56 hours and uses about 17 tons of coal per kiln. To form the beautiful baskets, the clay is put through a machine and comes out like spaghetti in strings which are cut to length and then woven by hand over plaster forms. A damp cloth keeps them the right consistency.

The glaze is of two sorts. The finest is of white lead, red lead, flint and borax while the coarser omits the red lead. The firing is done for less time and at a lower temperature and takes about 10 tons per kiln.

The painting is then done and fired again while the luster takes a fourth firing at very low heat. This luster is colorless or very pale primrose yellow. The most usual colors are pastel pink and green.

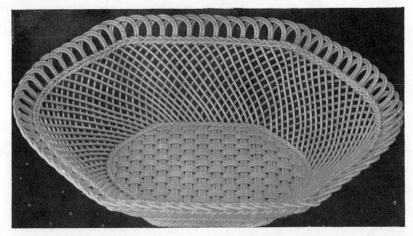

FIG. 1037. Belleek basket of typical type with beautifully even weave of strands. Length 10″. W. S. Pitcairne Corp.

FIG. 1038. Irish Belleek flower-pot of better and simpler type of organic design which is sometimes ruined by application of modeled flowers, etc. Ht. c. 4″. W. S. Pitcairne Corp.

FIG. 1039. Tea-pot "Limpet Cob" which shows a pleasant adaptation of sea forms. Ht. 8½″. W. S. Pitcairne Corp.

FIG. 1040. "Nile Vase," an art nouveau design of more modern feeling which has been very popular and was made in three sizes. Ht. 10″. W. S. Pitcairne Corp.

As the factory is so near the sea and the town lives through the kilns and fisheries, naturally the early pieces are of marine plants, sea shells, corals, mermaids, sea-dogs and such while later flat wares and flower vases were copied more or less from other kilns. However, a spirit of independence and the difference of the material makes these all quite distinct and easily recognized.

The early mark though not invariably used according to Mr. G. L. Pitcairn who represents the factory in America, is a round tower with an Irish harp to the left and an Irish Wolf Hound to the right. Beneath is a ribbon with the name Belleek and some shamrock ornamentation. On modern wares a circular Celtic symbol has been added. The basket pieces have a narrow, flat ribbon with the name impressed, stuck on the bottom.

As the factory is exactly on the border line between Eire and North Ireland it has had some troubles but fortunately appeals to both factions. It was also dependent on the River Erne for power until a board of fisheries recently made a grant of some machinery so that this power could be discontinued part of the year. It is, however, a beautiful place on this rushing stream amid rolling hills and I understand keeps some 100 to 150 men busily engaged in the making of this paper-thin, soft-toned and beautiful ware.

CHAPTER XXIV

ENGLISH "SOFT PASTE" AND "BONE CHINA"

Our ceramic world centers seem ever to move westward and England took its turn after Crete, Greece and Rome but England was never an inspired disseminator of design so much as a repository into which was gathered much that went on on the mainland of Europe. Yet the English never made any real hard porcelain during the 18th century, and was still trying to improve soft porcelain after hard porcelain had about replaced it on the continent. On the other hand, being a tea-drinking nation, close connections were maintained with China and designs from the Far East as well as from the continent found their way there. However, even in the Far East the influences were not so much from the fine wares of Ching-tê Chên of the K'ang Hsi or Ch'ien Lung periods as from the later Canton decorated wares and those from Japan from Arita or "Imari" porcelain. Kakiemon ware had an influence both direct and from the European copies of it. The Tê-hua wares of Fukien province also were indirectly an influence though, through France from such places as St. Cloud.

Besides these we have the influences of the chinoiseries of later Meissen origin which look like German ladies dressed up in Oriental clothes, and the also strong influences of Boucher as found in Chelsea porcelain, and Meissonier, Watteau and the rest. We have "Indianische Blumen" followed by "Deutsche Blumen," by "Fantasievogel" (exotic birds derived from China), Sèvres influences superseded by pseudo-classicism and then Angelica Kauffmann. Only one major development took place and that was in the stoneware of Wedgwood which too was not true porcelain but which so caught the popular taste at the end of the century as to become very popular over many years.

CHELSEA, 1745–1751

The earliest dated piece of English bone china is a "Goat and bee jug" owned by Lord Fisher similar to the one illustrated. The design was taken from a piece of silver bearing a hall mark of 1724. This jug has incised in the paste before firing, the word CHELSEA, a triangle and the date, 1745. It is thought that the factory opened about a year preceding this date and was about contemporary with the Bow factory.

A tea-pot in the form of a Chinaman with a parrot in his lap and another

742

with a Chinaman bestriding a snake, both showing close influence by Kandler, are also known. A rare group which is also marked is of two lovers full of ardent feeling, the lady seemingly trying to press her beautifully rounded breasts to the cheek of her lover.

Other figures of the period are a "Waterman with Dogget's coat and badge," a fortune-telling group and a small figure of a girl dancing and a boy with a hurdy-gurdy; all of which have the same soft paste and distinctive bases cut at the corners and beveled wider at the top than at the bottom. It is difficult to tell these figures from the French. There are also cups with raised flowers and a tea-pot with moulded overlapping strawberry leaves.

FIG. 1041. "Goat & Bee Jug," Chelsea marked, with triangle and delicately colored. One in the British Mus. has no coloring as is rule with these pieces between 1745 and 1751. They are practically speaking simply an opaque yellowish-white glass rather than porcelain. Pair of swans, one with cygnets, of the raised anchor period of Chelsea. Frank Stoner–Stoner & Evans, Ltd.

The bodies of these wares are creamy and translucent with a glaze of yellowish cast. If held against strong light they show bright spots like pinholes and these are the prototypes of the famous "moons" of the ensuing period attributable to unincorporated frit or glass in the paste. Not all of these are monochrome for some have details painted in natural colors but this may have been done later. It is known that William Duesbury who later purchased the factory had, at about 1750, a large business in decorating various porcelains. Little strewn flowers served as they did in Germany to hide blemishes. Mr. Herbert Eccles, F.C.S., made an analysis of the ware and it shows a large percentage of lead oxide from which he concludes that a flint glass may have been used in the composition. There is an absence of bone-ash.

An advertisement of 1750 mentions a Mr. Charles Gouyn who might have been the founder. The marks are a triangle incised and a crown and trident in underglaze blue which occurs on the lover group described, though this color was not used in decoration. Also a small embossed anchor on a round button seemed to have been used. The period ends in 1751.

Chelsea Second Period, 1751–1753
Raised Anchor and Occasionally Red Anchor Marks

Chaffers (3d edition p. 701) quotes Mason, a worker who wrote, "I think the Chelsea China Manufactory began about the year 1748 or 1749. I went to work about the year 1751. It was first carried on by the Duke of Cumberland and Sir Everard Fawkner, and the sole management was entrusted to a foreigner of the name of Nicholas Sprimont, report says, at a salary of a guinea per day with certain allowance for apprentices and other emoluments. I think Sir Everard died about 1755, much reduced in circumstances; when

Mr. Sprimont became sole proprietor; and having amassed a fortune, he traveled about England, and the manufactory was shut up about two years, for he neither would let it or carry it on himself. I then went to work at Bow for a short time, which was carried on by a firm, but I don't recollect their names. I went to work again at Chelsea for Mr. Sprimont, after being absent between two and three years, where I stopped till I engaged with Mr. (William) Duesbury to go to Derby, which was about the year 1763. I think there was very little business done after that time. What time Mr. Duesbury made a purchase of it I don't recollect, but some of the materials were taken to Derby." Another document says that the Duke of Cumberland was a great encourager of the Chelsea China and "bespoke a set for his own table."

Fig. 1042. Chelsea raised anchor period figure of Chinese boy, c. 1750. One of earliest and rarest figures from this factory and one of rarest types in English wares. Attempt to imitate white Fukien wares though paste is grey, heavy and glaze shiny, of slightly cream tone and has many pits as of burst bubbles in firing. There are a number of fire cracks. Also a resemblance to St. Cloud soft paste. Ht. 8". Frank Stoner–Stoner & Evans, Ltd.

Sprimont is thought to be a silver-smith. The eminent authority Frank Stoner says that Sprimont carried on until 1769, then sold to James Cox, who in 1770 sold to William Duesbury, who kept the factory between that date and 1784 during the "Chelsea Derby" period and then moved to Derby.

From 1751 the ware is thick, sandy and with a glaze like candle grease. It is sparingly painted in Oriental style. The added weight did not entirely prevent its warping in firing. Dr. Diamond has called attention to the "moons" or light discs in the body which were characteristic of the period. William Burton thinks that some of the frit was kept coarse to help prevent warping but actually I think it would act in the contrary way for it is the glass which melts and is soft in the kiln.

An analysis made by Eccles and published by King shows that the lead oxide is almost eliminated and a large content of lime introduced much as in the French soft paste, in a raised anchor marked piece.

With this mark there were busts in white glaze of the Duke of Cumberland, pieces of Imari (German influenced) style (and these occur also with the red anchor or in one odd case in the B.M. with an underglaze blue anchor). "Yellow tiger" and "red lion" as well as hexagonal jars were copies of the

Meissen designs after Kakiemon. The Meissen jars date between 1720 and 1725 while the Chelsea ones date between 1753 and 1758, the only change being the use of alternating panels of white strap work on coral red ground. The raised anchor also appears on copies of blanc de Chine in both Kwan Yin figures and cups with raised flower decoration, and these continued into the next period.

THE THIRD OR RED ANCHOR PERIOD, 1753–1758

The only differences now taking place are that the porcelain is a little better made, thinner, more translucent but blemishes still had to be covered by decoration. The Meissen influence was strengthened by the collection of Sir Charles Hanbury Williams, Plenipotentiary at Dresden, who allowed the factory to work with his German pieces. In 1748 Sir Charles was presented with a dessert service in the form of artichokes, laurel leaves, sunflowers and double leaves. The "Doctor" in the collection of Mrs. Radford is from the original by Peter Reinicke (1743–4) and is probably the "Italian Doctor" described

FIG. 1043. Hexagonal jar copied from Meissen which had in turn copied from Kakiemon in general style. Many have alternating light and dark ground panels. c. 1753–1758. Ht. 12". Metropolitan Mus of Art.

in the catalogue of 1755 though it has a raised anchor mark. The "Hurdy-gurdy Player" is also so marked. Besides the Meissen influence the engravings of J. J. Balechon after Boucher had an effect.

FIG. 1044. Two of the "Five Senses," "Seeing" and "Hearing" made c. 1755 at Chelsea. Ht. 11⅛". Metropolitan Mus. of Art.

As the wares of the triangle period are easily confused with those of Chantilly and St. Cloud so those of the second and third period are with wares of Bow particularly the uncolored vases, cups and other vessels. Both the early and late wares of Chelsea have sealing-wax red, lemon yellow and milky blu' but a pink used in the flower decoration of a small girl figure with the triangle mark is missing on later pieces and a pleasing dark red is peculiar. Parrots copied from Meissen were made in blue, purple and green and copied also by Bow but were discontinued by 1756.

The red-anchor figures were the best produced by this factory, and softer than their Meissen prototypes. Flat washed colors, large areas of white, touches of black and no gold made them tasteful. Plates were edged with brown, and underglaze blue is exceedingly rare. Applied flowers in full relief and reticulation were practiced. "A Pair of Peasants Dancing" are mentioned in the catalogue of 1756 and copied from Mandler, as were also the "Monkey Band" and tureens of sitting birds but perhaps the long-eared rabbit tureen was actually a Chelsea invention. Other figures are, "A Gardener and his Wife sitting with a Basket, River God, River Goddess, Ceres" (which gives the opportunity of a luscious nude in the flesh-like soft porcelain), "Map Seller, a Jew with his Box of Toys, Pierrot," and a typical subterfuge, "The Pedlar extoling his wares in a Box" which was copied from the Meissen "Man with a Tamed Rat" with omission of the rat. A "Maypole Group" belonging to Lord and Lady Fisher contains a figure exactly like a "Peasant Dancing" in the same collection. More elaborate groups are the "Madonna and Child on a Sphere" and two groups of three figures on rococo bases and equipped with candle sockets. The rococo bases are unusual for the period and one has a gold anchor mark which should warn us not to take the divisions of the period

FIG. 1045. Chelsea figure of duck painted with green back and pink wings dated by museum between 1750–1755. This may be one of "Stooping birds" mentioned in cat. of sale in 1755. Ht. 4⅜". Metropolitan Mus. of Art.

FIG. 1046. Nurse with child, Chelsea of the red anchor period about 1758. This group is from a continental prototype. Frank Stoner–Stoner & Evans, Ltd.

as too definite. King warns us as well that the "Persus Group" has distinctly the coloring of the gold-anchor period and is marked with a red anchor.

The useful china was taken from silver models and Meissen ones with often used relief borders and painting of German style. There was some spirit and even humor as may be seen by the "Nonsense panels" on the rim of a plate showing a lion scared to death with mane on end, a camel with stag horns and a twisted tail, etc. (See V. & A. Mus.)

Impractical "Crawfish Salts" were made and a "Sweetmeat Tray" is a pile of shells supporting a seven-shell group of cups painted with insects.

Blue and white specimens mentioned in the catalogue are difficult to identify. However, some with blue-anchor marks have pierced lattice rims with flowers in blue either in relief or flat at each intersection and crude center medallions of a "Willow Pattern," composed of Chinese rocks and trees. The sandy paste and spur marks are characteristic.

The useful wares were usually marked below the base while the figures were marked on the upper part of the bases. The anchor appears also in brown and purple. The two red-anchor marks are not established and their meaning is unknown. Occasionally the Meissen crossed swords were used perhaps when a set had to be filled out.

The catalogues of 1755 and 1756 mention an "exceeding rich blue enamel" and gilt edged plates which would seem to prove that the gold-anchor period began about this time.

The Fourth or Gold-Anchor Period, 1758–1770

Spur marks continue but "moons" disappear. The paste now contains bone ash and is whiter and more translucent but tends to crackle. This is the great period of ground colors and gilding. On April 15th, 1763 two large vases said to have been made in 1762 were given to the B.M. and they have "mazarine blue" ground and reserve panels of the death of Cleopatra on one side and exotic birds on the other set off by elaborately chased gilding.

Horace Walpole wrote to Sir Horace Mann on March 4th, 1763, "I saw

Fig. 1047. Vase with blue ground and rich gilding after Sèvres style. Between 1765–1770, Chelsea. Ht. 9¼". Metropolitan Mus. of Art.

Fig. 1048. Vase with tall, comparatively pleasing form and rococo handles, between 1762–1770, Chelsea. Ht. 11⅜". Metropolitan Mus. of Art.

Fig. 1049. Vase and cover of heart shape with reticulated neck and raised flowers. Not enough technical stunts could be heaped upon these pieces. Chelsea, 1765–1770. Ht. 9". Metropolitan Mus. of Art.

yesterday a magnificent service of Chelsea China which the King and Queen are sending to the Duke of Mecklenburg. There are dishes and plates without number, an epergne, candlesticks, salt cellars, sauce boats, tea and coffee equipages; in short it is complete; and cost twelve hundred pounds! I cannot boast of our taste; the forms are neither new, beautiful nor various. Yet Sprimont, the manufacturer, is a Frenchman. It seems their taste will not bear transplanting." It is amusing to add William King's comment some 160 years later, "Walpole's failure to appreciate this triumph of rococo art, the Mecklenburg service, is a melancholy reminder that after the pseudo-classicism of the next ten years there was yet to dawn the day of Strawberry Hill and the Gothic revival." He might have added that there was to follow Modern Art, streamlining, and revivals of the Mid-Victorian and Empire! However, it was in this year 1763 that a trend started away from the over-elaborate.

Fig. 1050. Vase of involved form influenced by most decadent of Sèvres designs. Ht. 9¼". Metropolitan Mus. of Art.

Fig. 1051. Vases between 1760–1770 with heaped up molded decoration in worst possible rococo taste. Chelsea. Ht. 13¼". Metropolitan Mus. of Art.

It is to be noted that during the transferring of ownership from Sprimont to Cox to Duesbury in 1769 and 1770 a workman, Francis Thomas, stole a quantity of the porcelain from the factory, some of which may have been decorated elsewhere.

The gold-anchor wares contain about 40% of the bone ash, the paste is still sandy but the glaze is richer and collects thickly in hollows. The elaborate design and gilding were copied from Sèvres. William Burton says that the gilding was done in the Chinese manner; leaf gold ground in honey was applied before low firing. Gold so applied has a dull lock not improved by burnishing. The later rich Chelsea gold was made in the modern manner; amalgam of gold and mercury ground fine with a small amount of glass or flux. In this way the gold can be laid as heavy as desired and then burnished and chased.

Figure modeling was improved. The "Pieta" was taken from a painting by Rubens in the Prado or from an engraving after the painting. Bernini did a similar subject at Doccia. The largest figure made by the factory is of Una or "Britannia" with a lion. This was listed in 1757 in the catalogue. Another group after Rubens was the "Roman Charity," and the series of Apollo and the Muses is well done. After Kandler were made little cupids and particularly one which is playing a bagpipe and controlling with a string a pair of lovers. "Bocages" or a "bosky grove" of flattened hawthorn leaves

"Roman Charity" group of 1765–70 based on engraving after Rubens with arrangement of feet changed. This group is a little different from one shown by William King in color (Pl. 4, *Chelsea Porcelain*) the robe of Cimon in this case being richly decorated and the bodice of Pera being spotted while they are plain brown and red in the other. Pera's skirt is also more richly decorated. The one in King's book is also shown on a blue and gold stand. Ht. 16¼". Irwin Untermeyer Coll.

CHELSEA GROUP, "ROMAN CHARITY"

Plate 192

and flowers came into use behind the figures and among these is "L'agréable Leçon" or the "Music Lesson" also rendered by Johann Friedrich Luck after Boucher in Frankenthal. These figures were done about 1765 and the colors were bright and growing brighter. A very ornate clock in rococo pink and gold; architectural, scroll and animal designs with a wing sprouting to one side to say nothing of cupids and flowers is in Buckingham Palace and is of the period. Other well-known pieces are a "Leda with Swan" after Boucher, "La bergère des Alpes" and "Le noeud de cravate" after Falconet from sketches by Boucher and dating from 1770 to 1784 depending upon the authority. There were also the "Seasons" and a series of portraits of popular Englishmen. These though childish in color and crude in modeling are better than the biscuit insipidity taking hold on the continent. The unknown modeler of the "Reaper" is somewhat better than average.

Vases and useful china with solid ground colors plain or patterned are chiefly of this fourth period. Polychrome flowers on bright gold grounds were used. In 1759 pea-green was added and in 1760 turquoise and the famous "claret" which is deeper than rose Pompadour and even than the Danish Rødgrød, and which was equalled only in rare Worcester imitations. The uneven bright blue and turquoise green were continued.

  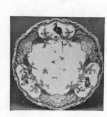 

Fig. 1052. Vase in deep blue with gold decoration after Sèvres style. Chelsea, c. 1765. Ht. 8¼". Metropolitan Mus. of Art.

Fig. 1053. Gold Anchor period covered cup with scale pattern from Meissen in pink and gold. Possibly what was meant in cat. of 1756 by "oxe's eye pattern." c. 1760–1765, Chelsea. Ht. 5¼". Metropolitan Mus. of Art.

Fig. 1054. Plate with red ground, gilt decoration and natural colors. Chelsea c. 1765. Dia. 8½". Metropolitan Mus. of Art.

Fig. 1055. Toilet bottle with white ground and claret color on neck and base and gilt on handles and borde ing medall.ons. Again shows French taste and neo-classic.sm though said to date c. 1760. Ht. 7". Metropolitan Mus. of Art.

"Chief among the masterpieces," says King, "of this period are the set of seven vases known as the 'Dudley Vases.' The ground is claret colored, richly gilded; on each are reserved two panels, one containing a mythological subject, the other panel of naturalistic birds in the style of Hondekoster. The painting is beautifully finished and the modelling a perfect expression of rococo feeling." If this is the Englishman's idea of perfect rococo feeling, it is quite different from that of the simple little tureens so classed on the continent. These vases are distorted monstrosities with weak, wobbly handles and I doubt that one put in a store on Broadway or at Atlantic City would bring $8 very readily though the actual price runs into four figures.

After the Boucher influence came a second-hand one first of Watteau and then of Greuze. The Chinoiserie painting and Chinese shapes in beakers top-heavy and clumsy are characteristic, and some of these latter were inappropriately decorated with naturalistic German flowers. In fact naturalistic painting was very much in style. By 1763 the Mecklenburg service has plates with centers containing exotic birds and festoons of flowers on the rims, interrupted with five blue panels containing different butterflies. An even more ornate service has the same centers with claret rims heavily gilded and still another has a peacock-feather rim copied from the Meissen original and poetically called the "oxes eye" pattern.

A bowl of the general aspect of what is called "Lowestoft" has a scene containing two boats and the Chelsea Old Church.

Fig. 1056. Chelsea cache-pot with gold anchor mark and decoration in turquoise and gold on handles and edge and naturalistic colors. c. 1760. Ht. 7". Symons Galleries.

Fig. 1057. Chelsea candelabra with gilt and bright colors, c. 1765. Ht. 13⅝". Metropolitan Mus. of Art

As early as 1754 wares incorrectly called "toys" consisting of snuff-boxes, smelling bottles, "etwees," trinkets for watches and handles for knives and forks were recorded in a sale by a Mr. Ford. Bonbonnières and patch-boxes were also copied from the French. On some of these little pieces even the bottoms were painted and they frequently have mottoes of a gallant or sentimental nature in incorrect French.

Chelsea-Derby or Derby

Chelsea-Derby is a vague term only correctly used in referring to pieces bearing the official mark of the factories in amalgamation, an anchor traversing a D. Rackham has shown that the gold anchor was still used in 1770 and mentions it on a cup in the Herbert Allen Collection marked also with an N. used at Derby. The true Derby mark, a crowned D in blue, puce, purple and green having crossed batons and six dots between the D and the crown has never been found with a gold anchor.

William Duesbury, the new owner, had been an enameller and had decorated 382 pieces in 1751. He obtained pieces from Chelsea, Bow, Derby and Staffordshire. Jewitt claims to have identified the first maker of porcelain at the Derby factory as Andrew Planche, a Frenchman who is said to have made small animals in a pipe-maker's kiln in 1745 and also to have entered into an agreement with Duesbury and Heath in 1756. Another theory assigns the beginning to the Cockpit Hill Works, a pottery which also made porcelain. John Heath was one of the owners of this place. In 1758 Duesbury

Derby "Ranelegh" figures c. 1765 showing grace of modeling and usual colors
except for orange brown on skirt. Ht.
11¼". Frank Stoner–Stoner & Evans,
Ltd.

"Una with the lion" figure, largest and
most important made at Chelsea factory.
Made and listed in cat. in 1757. c. 27".
Frank Stoner–Stoner & Evans, Ltd.

Part of group of four elements, represent-
ing Earth and Fire, c. 1765 at height of
Derby factory. Ht. 14". Frank Stoner–Stoner
& Evans, Ltd.

Rare and lovely group of four seasons made at Chelsea, 1765. Frank Stoner–Stoner &
Evans, Ltd.

CHELSEA AND DERBY FIGURES

PLATE 193

and Heath bought the Longton Hall Works and they seemed successful in 1763 but Heath went broke and Duesbury gained control.

When he died in 1786 his son, William Duesbury, and the grandson, continued until 1796, when the latter was joined by Michael Kean, until 1811 when it passed into the hands of Robert Bloor. It closed in 1848. Much later a revival was attempted of the high sounding "Royal Crown Derby Porcelain Works," but the wares were inferior. The molds including those from Chelsea were sold to Samuel Boyle who sold them to Copeland of the Spode works where they were not used but remained piled up until discovered in 1924 by Mr. Frank Stoner.

Fig. 1058. Two musicians, Chelsea, 1765, and two children, 1780. Frank Stoner–Stoner & Evans, Ltd.

Not a single figure has been identified from Derby before the uniting of the factories in 1770 though some were made. The earliest identified piece is a white cream jug which has an incised mark D 1750. The paste is sandy and the glaze very white. The handle is a twig and the foot has strawberries in relief. Duesbury made many experiments and technically some of the wares are so much like Gold Anchor Chelsea that they cannot be so distinguished. D'Hancarville's catalogue of Sir William Hamilton's collection (1766–7) changed the style overnight to classical adaptations of Wedgwood and to spiritless figures of sentimental character in pale, thin coloring. From 1771 the innovations are biscuit and lacework. The first had just been taken up at Meissen and the second, which originated at Sèvres in the 1750's, reached Meissen in the 70's and did not come to England certainly until about the same time.

Of course the portrait biscuit technique made possible the patronage of famous people and royalty and it is largely for this that the factory became famous. The paste was soft and pleasing and clever modellers were hired such as John James Spengler, from Zurich, in about 1790. He worked from designs of Bartolozzi and Angelica Kauffmann, Coffee and Stephen though the latter went to Coalport in 1800. Coffee probably did copies from Meissen and Sèvres as probably did also John Bacon. Stephen made a figure of

FIG. 1059 . Bacchus, designated by Mus. as "Late 18th cent., Chelsea." Ht. 14⅛". Metropolitan Mus. of Art.

FIG. 1060. Pair of Chelsea candlesticks with *"bocage"* or bowers of flowers and figures with cupids, doves and swan. Marked with gold anchor c. 1765. Irwin Untermeyer Coll.

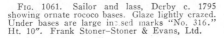

FIG. 1061. Sailor and lass, Derby c. 1795 showing ornate rococo bases. Glaze lightly crazed. Under bases are large in⸗sed marks "No. 316." Ht. 10". Frank Stoner–Stoner & Evans, Ltd.

FIG. 1062. So-called "Chelsea Derby" figures, c. 1780 and having soft coloring and pleasing modeling. Ht. 5¼". Frank Stoner–Stoner & Evans, Ltd.

Admiral Lord Howe and his well-known Four Elements. Spengler is well known for his Girl with Her Dead Bird, the Young Man Burying a Bird, Two Young Girls Waking Cupid, etc. During the Bloor period the biscuit became cold, hard and chalky.

Glazed figures from Derby are usually on simpler bases than those of Chelsea, the green used is washed out and pale, the color in general is soft and there is a lack of life and charm.

The decoration of the useful porcelain is symmetrical and weak in the best of taste for the finicky housewife who thought a great deal about taste

FIG. 1063. Biscuit group, by John James Spengler in "Crown Derby biscuit." Late 18th cent. Ht. 10¾". Metropolitan Mus. of Art.
FIG. 1064. Derby biscuit statuette of Lord Lyndhurst, c. 1810. Ht. 14¼". Metropolitan Mus. of Art.
FIG. 1065. "Gardener and Wife," Derby c. 1760. Ht. 8". John Gibbons Coll.

FIG. 1067. Derby 1780–90. "Crocus vase" beautifully painted with landscapes. In overglaze blue on bottom "Near Dalkeith, Scotland," beneath which is mark # 2 a crown with crossed swords below flanked by three dots and beneath which is a script D. Length 9½". Frank Stoner–Stoner & Evans, Ltd.

FIG. 1066. Baroque vase and stand of type called "Dudley vases," with turquoise ground and gilding. Chelsea c. 1760. Ht. 18". Symons Galleries.
FIG. 1068. "Chelsea-Derby" vase (c. 1775), soft paste decorated after Angelica Kaufman with stripes of blue, white and gold. Ht. 10⅜". Metropolitan Mus. of Art.

FIG. 1069. Chelsea 18th cent. boar in natural colors of general pinkish cast. Length 13½". Plummer, Ltd.

FIG. 1070. "Crown Derby" soft paste plate decorated in enamel colors of ocherous-red against rich green ground. 18th to 19th cent. Dia. 10". Metropolitan Mus. of Art.
FIG. 1071. Derby tureen c. 1770. Colors chiefly pink, purple and brown on white, with some added yellow and yellow green in the foliage. Length 9". Frank Stoner–Stoner & Evans, Ltd.

Crown Derby service of so-called "King pattern" (George III). Factory pattern # 1, c. 1780–90 and showing strong Imari influence. Philip Suval, Inc.

Part of Derby dessert service decorated in salmon pink and gold. c. 1800. Wm. H. Plummer & Co

DERBY SERVICES

PLATE 194

in those days. A new lapis-lazuli blue and an underglaze blue replaced the warm "Mazarine blue." The canary yellow bettered the Chelsea but the claret color is less rich. During Bloor's time poor imitation Imari was made.

One cannot become seriously critical of the work of these factories for they contributed nothing to the art of ceramics. Their works are at times amusing but it is even then a second-hand amusement.

Bow

Edward Heylyn who had a glass factory, and Thomas Frye, an Irish engraver, took out joint patents in 1744 and started a factory in Stratford-

Harlequin and Colombine figures. Smaller ones made at Bow in 1755 (Stratford-le-Bow, Essex) are extremely rare. Larger ones are Derby of 1780. Note that postures are identical and that small figures have simpler bases while Harlequin has a typical square hole at back of base. Bow figures have glossy black, double outlines of patches, pale olive green, bright yellow and deep blue of gentian shade. Derby ones have mat black, poor drawing of details in light pink line, dull turquoise, dull orangy yellow. Hts. 6¼″ and 5¼″. Frank Stoner–Stoner & Evans, Ltd.

DERBY AND BOW FIGURES COMPARED

PLATE 195

Left: "The Cooks," Bow figures dating c. 1755, maid with leg of lamb and the boy with fowls. Note low, unscro[l]
bases having only a few strewn flowers. Frank Stoner–Stoner & Evans, Ltd.
 Right: Bow figures c. 1765. Note high rococo bases hollowed beneath, typical of period. Irwin Untermeyer C

Left: Squirrels, Bow 1760, rare and particularly vigorous and alive in modeling. Note raised rococo bases. Fra
Stoner–Stoner & Evans, Ltd.
 Right: Pair of Bow birds dating 1760 and showing good modeling and coloring. Frank Stoner–Stoner & Eva
Ltd.

BOW FIGURES AND ANIMALS

PLATE 196

le-Bow, County of Essex, and Frye alone repeated the procedure in 1749. This is the factory popularly known as "Bow." He made some soft-paste ware which is the first we know to have contained bone-ash. The patent states that earth from America, "produce of the Cherokee nation," was used and called "unaker" by the natives.

From 1750 the owners were Weatherby and John Crowther with Frye as a foreman until 1759 when he retired. In 1762 Frye and Weatherby died and the year following Crowther went bankrupt though he kept the factory going until in 1776 Duesbury bought it and took the models and molds to Derby.

We have little real data: excavations in 1868 and 1921–2, some note books, lists of sales, etc. The "Craft Bowl" is dated 1700 and Thomas Craft wrote about his bowl that there were some 300 workmen employed in this year, that the factory was started in 1750 and called "New Canton." A few

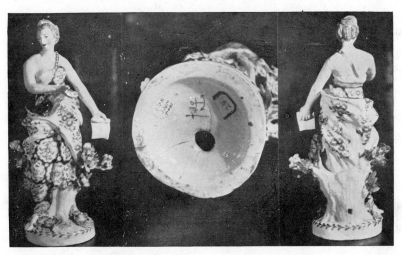

Fig. 1072. Unique Bow figure of Cleo, one of the Muses, c. 1765. There is a similar model in Chelsea but this is only one known in Bow. Note anchor and dagger mark under base in light red, also square hole at back of base for attachment of fixtures for candle sockets. Ht. 12½". Frank Stoner–Stoner & Evans, Ltd.

ink pots marked "Made at New Canton" and dated 1750 exist. I am happy to show one through the kindness of Lord Fisher. The ware was glassy, yellowish, thick, heavy and only slightly translucent having the general look of poor French soft paste which it imitated also in style. Small white statuettes were also made.

The Craft Bowl of ten years later shows that the ware had improved but was more chalky and white. However, a pair of octagonal plates in the B.M. one of which is dated 1770 shows the ware then to have become opaque, reddish-brown and covered with a bluish glaze full of black specks and such as to cease almost to resemble porcelain.

Vase shapes are a degenerate rococo with reserved medallions, applied flowers and twisted stem handles. There is a characteristic frilled collar

FIG. 1073. Plate with decoration in ochrous-red after Kakiemon in what is called the "Partridge pattern" made about 1760. Dia. 8⅜". Metropolitan Mus. of Art.

FIG. 1074. Rare type of early Bow dating about 1750 and probably representative of one of the Muses. There are other similar examples in the Victoria & Albert Mus. and all are thought to be the work of one man. Ht. 6". Frank Stoner–Stoner & Evans, Ltd.

FIG. 1075. Ink pot bearing the inscription, MADE AT NEW CANTON 1750 which is the earliest dated ware known from the factory at Stratford-le-Bow. It has been suggested by Lord Fisher that Mr. Crowther had seen a factory at Canton China and modeled the new one more or less after it, also that these ink pots may have been distributed to celebrate the opening of the "New Canton Factory." Similar examples are in both large British museums and this one came from the Mus of the Worcester Porcelain Company. The property of Lord and Lady Fisher.

around the foot. This great addition to the ceramic arts seems to be an entirely original invention! A vase in the B.M. has handles formed as jets of water spouted by dolphins. And of this period 1760 to 1770 there were knife handles of plain white with rococo relief scrolls on them.

Figures from Kandler are a Harlequin and Colombine (see the compared Bow and Derby ones illustrated), a Gallant Kissing His Hand, a Negro with

FIG. 1077. Sauceboat of Bow ware made about 1770. Length 8¼". Metropolitan Mus. of Art.

FIG. 1076. Platter of famille rose type made at Bow (c. 1760). Length 12". Plummer, Ltd.

a Horse and a Turk with a Horse. English subjects include a stately "Britannia" with a portrait medallion of George II in one hand and a Union Jack on a shield in the other, a figure of John Manners, some of Woodward and Kitty Clive (the actor and actress) playing The Fine Gentleman and The Fine Lady in "Lethe," the farce by Garrick. A sphinx has the head of the actress Peg Woffington. These figures and those of male and female cooks are thought to be by John Bacon. They are sometimes white and sometimes colored in bright hues. The dresses are partly in plain colors and partly patterned. Whether the foliage backgrounds originated in Chelsea or Bow is uncertain but Bow did make the first pedestals divided into four curled feet which later became characteristic of much English porcelain. Bow figures also frequently have a square hole made in the back to hold metal branches with painted leaves and porcelain flowers and a candle sconce.

Fig. 1078. A rare example of a Sweet-meat dish set, Bow, 1755, decorated in famille rose enamels, the drawing in a flat brown, the rose pitted and duller than the Chinese, the green and yellow green dull and thin, the aubergine and blue about like the Chinese. The potting is very uncertain as may be seen by the foot of one dish shown and the center dish has evidently sunk in the middle during firing. There are also a number of fire-cracks. Dia. laid out 15¼". Frank Stoner–Stoner & Evans, Ltd.

Animals and birds, particularly parrots, and pie-dishes in the form of partridges had strong colors often badly handled as were, in truth, also those on the figures copied from Watteau and on the pieces copied from the Kakiemon style. The usual Imari styles were followed as were those of famille rose and powder blue Chinese porcelain and it must be said that the

Fig. 1079. Group of parrots amidst foliage in bright colors made at Bow between 1755 and 1760. Ht. 9⅛". Metropolitan Mus. of Art.

Fig. 1080. Parrot with strong green color made at Bow about 1760. Ht. 6½". Metropolitan Mus. of Art.

underglaze blue was of good quality and a deep indigo tone. The transfer process was used but whether actually at the Bow factory or at nearby Battersea, where we know it was used as early as 1753, has not been determined. They were printed in black, red or purple and usually further painted.

The Bow wares were usually not marked but a red anchor with or without cable and usually accompanied by a dagger has been attributed to them and may have been from the arms of the City of London. Some blue and

FIG. 1082. Bow porcelain salt cellar of about 1750 colored in soft tones of pink and green. Ht. 4¾". Metropolitan Mus. of Art.

FIG. 1081. Male figure on rococo base made about 1760 at Bow. Ht. 8". Metropolitan Mus. of Art.

FIG. 1083. Group of two birds and a dog made at Bow about 1755 to 1760. Ht. 6½". Metropolitan Mus. of Art.

white pieces are marked TF in monogram standing for Thomas Frye, though Hobson has tried to call it a "maimed version of the Chinese character yu (jade)" and calls such pieces Worcester. Some figures bear the mark To possibly standing for Tebo, a French modeler who is supposed to have worked at Etruria, at Worcester and also Bristol, for the mark appears on these wares too. The figures marked B are supposed to be by Bacon.

The only other distinguishing characteristic is a maroon purple supposed to be unique.

<h2 style="text-align:center">WORCESTER</h2>

Bernhard Rackham, the editor of "Pottery and Porcelain" by Emil Hannover and author, for me, of the *Encyclopaedia Britannica* article on the sub-

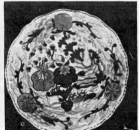

FIG. 1084. Three Chamberlain Worcester plates, 1st with apricot ground and reserved medallions, 2nd with iron red and gold in a derivation of the Imari manner, and 3d with gold and Sèvres blue and flowers in natural colors in the Sèvres manner. Thus all sources were drawn upon. c. 1811–1820. Philip Suval, Inc.

FIG. 1085. Large 1785? Chamberlain Worcester vase of good proportions and well gilded. The flower paintings are beautifully executed. Ht. 17½". Frank Stoner–Stoner & Evans, Ltd.

FIG. 1086. Worcester dish of about 1770 to 1780 of soft paste decorated with enamel colors of blue, violet, copper red, green, black and gold. Dia. 7½". Metropolitan Mus. of Art.

ject, is the acknowledged authority on Worcester, yet even he has found little real data to go on. Worcester is supposed to have started in "Lowdin's China House," a glass manufactory which made "steatitic porcelain" as early as 1750. An advertisement found by William Pountney would seem to prove that the work was transferred to Worcester in 1752 where the factory was managed by Davis until his death in 1766. In 1783 the business was sold to its London agent Thomas Flight for his sons, John and Joseph. In 1790 Martin Barr was taken into the partnership and the following year John Flight died. Thus in 1791 the company was called "Flight and Barr." In 1807 a younger Barr came into the business and the name was changed

FIG. 1087. Chamberlain Worcester covered urn with entwined handles. Cobalt blue ground with rich gold. This was modeled after the famous Warick Vase in Worcestershire. Has script mark of Chamberlain Worcester ε. 1810. John Gibbons.

to "Barr, Flight and Barr." In 1813 Martin Barr the elder died and his son George was taken into the firm which was then called "Flight, Barr and Barr" under which it continued until 1840.

In 1786 a second factory for the decoration of porcelain alone was started with wares from Caughley and called Robert Chamberlain and Son. It was fused into the other company in 1840 and in 1847 the older factory was given up and the new continued under the names of the Chamberlains. In 1848 Walter Chamberlain and John Lilly became the proprietors and in 1850 the

Bowl of Worcester ware which looks like a Near Eastern copy of a Chinese one. The colors are blue and red. c. 1770. Dia. 5⅞". Metropolitan Mus. of Art.

Plate in Kakiemon style painted in enamel colors at Worcester about 1770. Dia. 9". Metropolitan Mus. of Art.

Worcester milk-jug with design in pink, made about 1770 after continental style of Vienna of about 10 years earlier, Frankenthal, Gotha, etc. Ht. 4¾". Metropolitan Mus. of Art.

Worcester dessert basket painted in Chinese style with enamels, c. 1765-70. Length 9¼".

WORCESTER WARES SHOWING FOREIGN INFLUENCES

PLATE 197

son was taken in and W. H. Kerr, the name being in 1852 "Kerr and Binns" and from this time it so remained until in 1862 the "Royal Worcester Porcelain Co." was formed and existed up to a few years ago.

The earliest period is incorrectly known as the "Dr. Wall period" through the false idea that the apothecary William Davis and a Dr. Wall started the factory. During the time that steatite was used the ware was yellow or grey but of a fairly constant bluish-green tone by transmitted light. Not until 1800 did experiments lead to the adoption of modern Staffordshire body and chemical analysis at the V. & A. Mus. prove that Flight, Barr and Barr were still using a steatitic porcelain as late as 1823.

A considerable number of pieces attributed to the Lowden factory at Bristol or the earliest days of Worcester comprise pieces painted with Chinese

Worcester platter dating between 1770 and 1780. Length 11¼″. Metropolitan Mus. of Art.

One of pair of Worcester "Glacières" or fruit coolers with "royal blue" ground enriched with gilding and surrounding panels with birds and flowers in natural colors. c. 1775. Philip Suval, Inc.

Worcester hexagonal vase with cover decorated in the typical style. c. 1770–75. Ht. 16¼″. Metropolitan Mus. of Art.

Worcester platter painted with fruit and insects, made about 1780. Length 13½″. Metropolitan Mus. of Art.

WORCESTER PORCELAINS

PLATE 198

figures in underglaze blue or enamels, cylindrical mugs widening out toward the base, jugs with ordinary lip and scroll handle and sauceboats in the form of two conjoined leaves the stems of which form the loop handle.

Such wares date about 1750 to 1752 and are generally marked with one or two short strokes or with a saltire cross incised in the paste before firing. They have also various painted signs including an arrow passing through a circle in either underglaze blue or overglaze red. Another general feature is a short incision made with a sharp instrument on the inner side of the foot-rim.

Fig. 1088. Bowl with relief and underglaze blue decoration made about 1760–70. Dia. 4". Metropolitan Mus. of Art.

Fig. 1089. Worcester cream jug with underglaze blue decoration and rococo relief scrolls, made about 1760. Ht. 2¾". Metropolitan Mus. of Art.

The earliest porcelain definitely made at Worcester is from silver models with rococo relief designs painted in vignette style in reserved panels in underglaze blue or polychrome. They resemble St. Cloud. Much early Worcester blue and white ware was formerly ascribed to Bow including some marked with TF. The Kakiemon style was copied with later (in 1765) other Imari designs. Some of these were marked with quasi-Chinese symbols including the "fretted square" in underglaze blue. At about this time the famille rose designs from Canton were copied.

At the early date of 1756 the bad practice of transfer printing was in general use in black, red and various shades of purple with, slightly later, underglaze blue. Frequently supplemented with hand painting such wares show landscapes with ruins, portraits of Frederick the Great, George III, Queen Charlotte, the Marquis of Granby, the elder William Pitt, etc., and such subjects as a tea-party on a terrace, a gallant kissing a lady's hand, etc. Robert Hancock an engraver introduced the process and worked at the factory until 1774. The usual influence of Watteau, Boucher and Pillement were strong.

London dealers were able to dictate various subjects for treatment in their taste, but in 1768 some of the best artists from Chelsea were hired and the habit terminated. At this time the best period commenced with the famous colored grounds having reserved panels, gold bordered and painted with exotic birds, Chinese or natural flowers and scenes in the Watteau manner. The most famous color was the blue both in powder-blue form and laid in scales; but apple green, pea-green (sometimes over black scale outlines),

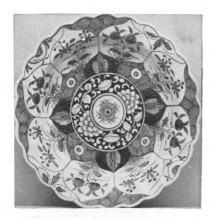

FIG. 1090. Plate in blue and white showing Japanese and Chinese characteristics, made at Worcester c. 1770. Dia. 7¼". Metropolitan Mus. of Art.

FIG. 1091. Plate decorated in enamel colors after Imari pattern, made at Worcester between 1770 and 1780. Dia. 8⅜". Metropolitan Mus. of Art.

turquoise, "maroon" and "claret color" and finally a pale canary yellow were also used. This last was used over a ground of basket work in relief to represent straw. An overglaze blue was rare but effective at times. A manganese violet is even more rare. Many modifications took place probably more or less accidentally just as the ware itself varied from greyish to yellowish. The underglaze blue is usually of indigo tone, the violet purple is "peculiarly misty" and a plum color is often predominant in the exotic bird panels.

Between 1768 and 1780 the "Blind Earl's pattern" of flowers and leaves in low relief was supposed to have been devised for the Earl of Coventry but he lost his sight in 1779 and both Bow and Chelsea used the design and technique much earlier. The green over black outline technique is known in Sung Chinese wares, of course. The use of diagonal gold stripes in the background was supposed to have been a real invention but the same were used in Meissen in the 1720's and were popular all over the continent, particularly in Sèvres. A design perhaps actually original was a "curtain of green leaves with little red berries among them, supported by a rococo trellis-work in gold." Artists were Donaldson about 1770 who did crude peasant scenes and clumsy exotic birds; O'Neale, Billingsley between 1808 and 1811; and Thomas Baxter between 1814 and 1821 with a gap between 1816 and 1819.

Between 1775 and 1780 the neo-classic influence stopped all originality and the Flights and Barrs coarsened the designs for mass production. Some odd pieces were decorated with trophies of feathers, the 19th century brought brassy gilding and the colors became strong and without meaning. Thus a factory that had been one of the distinguished ones of England became one of the most flagrant destroyers of good taste, and late Worcester is nothing for a collector to be proud of.

Before 1783 a crescent mark was used in gold, colors, printed in blue over the glaze but also painted in underglaze blue. The Chinese "fretted square,"

FIG. 1092. Worcester dessert basket in enamel colors, c. 1770–75. Length 10½″. Metropolitan Mus. of Art.

FIG. 1093. Worcester pitcher dating about 1770–75 having bright coloring and a scale blue ground. Ht. 11⅝″. Metropolitan Mus. of Art.

FIG. 1094. Flight, Barr & Barr 1807–13 tea cup and saucer with a dull rose Pompadour, gold and polychrome painting. The saucer has an impressed crown and F.B.B. The cup has "Flight, Barr & Barr, Worcester, London House, 1 Coventry St." in red script. Ht. 3½″. Frank Stoner–Stoner & Evans, Ltd.

W, imitation Chinese characters, Meissen crossed swords with the unaccounted for numerals 9 or 91, and the Sèvres double Ls were common.

After 1783 the crescent was used at the old factory usually with the name of Flight.

From 1792 to 1807 the usual mark is Flight and Barr surmounted by a crown. Later marks are of no interest to collectors.

Figures were made but few have been identified.

CAUGHLEY SHROPSHIRE 1772-1799

Thomas Turner, a pupil of the engraver Robert Hancock, settled in Shropshire near Broseley and influenced the ten year old pottery factory in 1772 to make china. It seems that Hancock went there too when he left Worcester in 1774.

In 1780 the well known "Willow Pattern" and "Broseley Blue Dragon Pattern" were made and probably originated with Turner. Both were printed in underglaze blue and touched with gold from the very first. The latter was printed in two blues, a cobalt and a more lavender color, and used for tea services. The willow pattern was used for whole dinner services. It was copied everywhere and an interesting chapter in "How to Identify Old China" by Mrs. Hadgson tells of its spread. Nothing could better exemplify the utter dearth of aesthetic consciousness than the stupid copying of this design which lacks every element of true Chinese painting and any real claim to beauty whatsoever, and the maudlin stories wrought about it to please the sentimental old ladies of the late 18th century.

The commercial chiseling in of Chamberlain in 1783 when he used Caughley to decorate was based upon a very inferior ware. The potting was bad and yellowish or brownish by transmitted light. The decoration at the factory

FIG. 1095. Dessert basket with underglaze blue decoration made at Caughley about 1775. Length 10⅝". Metropolitan Mus. of Art.

FIG. 1096. Caughley tea caddy with floral designs in gold alternating with vertical lines in dark blue. Ht. 4⅜". Metropolitan Mus. of Art.

FIG. 1097. Caughley dessert dish with cover and platter of soft porcelain decorated with polychrome and marked in underglaze blue. Length of tray 11¼". Metropolitan Mus. of Art.

chiefly was printed and often so badly that the background is not clean. The blue is strong and clean when it has not run. At times gold and gaudy colors were added in polychrome flowers. The "Salopian sprig" design about 1780 was done in blue with fine gold lines, "Salopian" being the name by which Caughley porcelain was known in the trade. The "Queen Charlotte's Pattern" used by both Caughley and Worcester was simply an elaborate "strohblumen muster" from about 1740 of Meissen, and later in Copenhagen, only that in this case the plate is divided into six panels instead of four. The flowers are large and scrolls and foliage fill the whole ground but each panel is exactly symmetrical and all life lost. Everything bigger and better but dead!

Caughley used the oil-spot ground of Sèvres rather than the scale pattern of Worcester.

The C for Caughley and S for Salopian were both painted and printed in underglaze blue. There are also crescents similar to the Worcester ones, numerals disguised as Chinese characters and the word Salopian which pertains to Salop or Shropshire.

COALPORT OR COALBROOKDALE

John Rose, a pupil of Turner's, set up a factory at Jackfield about 1780 but soon moved it to the Severn at Coalport opposite Caughley and in 1799 bought the older factory, managing both. In 1814 he gave up Caughley but subsequently absorbed both the Nantgarw and Swansea plants. Coalport exists today.

The wares were seldom marked and are hardly distinguishable from those they obviously copied. From 1810 to 1820 they copied the Swansea style. In

Fig. 1098. Coalport vase with turquoise blue ground, gold details and a medallion of flowers in natural colors. Ht. about 12″. Frank Stoner–Stoner & Evans, Ltd.

Fig. 1099. Coalport basket of about 1820 with the typically well modeled and delicately tinted flowers and touches of gold. Length 11¼″. Frank Stoner–Stoner & Evans, Ltd.

1819 William Billingsley, founder of Nantgarw introduced the body of this and the Swansea wares. In 1820 Rose "invented" a feldspathic glaze containing no lead which could be fired at low temperature. The usual styles were copied from Meissen, Sèvres and the Chinese as well as Chelsea.

The first wares sometimes bear C B D for Coalbrookdale and rarely the name of the factory. Imitations bore the marks of original factories forged. After 1819 CS stood for Coalport-Salopian and C S N for Coal-

Fig. 1100. A typically elaborate ink-well and candlestick made at Coalport about 1820. Length about 12″. Mrs. David Mahany.

port-Swansea-Nantgarw. From 1820 the new glazed pieces bore the imposing legend "Coalport Improved Felspar-Porcelain—J. Rose & Co.

NANTGARW, SWANSEA AND PINXTON

Nantgarw and Swansea were founded in 1811 and 1814 in South Wales and made the old glassy soft paste of France rather than the "bone china" invented by Spode about 1800.

In 1796 the wandering William Billingsley left Derby and with John Coke

FIG. 1101. Garniture of five Swansea vases dating 1820 and beautifully gilded and painted. A pierced gallery runs around the shoulder and lip and the covers are pierced as though they were intended to contain rose petals or other perfumed substance. This is the only set known. Frank Stoner-Stoner & Evans, Ltd.

started up in Pinxton in eastern Derbyshire. He had the old soft paste formula and between 1796 and 1801 made that. Coke didn't get the secret, for after Billingsley left the ware became clayey and opaque. Decoration of flowers, strewn roses, and landscapes in polychrome or in brown, pale yellowish-green and salmon pink were not unusual. Gold was costly and sparingly used, the edges of plates being finished in blue or red. Ground color of yellow and rarely salmon pink were the full range.

P and Pinxton occur as rare marks.

Following Billingsley's trail we find that in 1801 he left Pinxton for Staffordshire and after several unsuccessful attempts to set up for himself settled with Flight and the Barrs at Worcester. He had one stock in trade, his roses painted with the highlights taken out in the wet color. In 1811 he tried again to set up a factory in Nantgarw but gave it up in 1814.

FIG. 1102. Pair of delicate and thinly potted vases from Swansea (c. 1800) with decorations in natural colors. Ht. 8½". Plummer, Ltd.

Swansea had developed out of the "Cambrian Pottery" founded in 1764. In 1814 Lewis Weston Dillwyn, manager, sent for Billingsley and they worked together for three years. In 1817 the firm was taken by Bevington & Co. and Billingsley went to Nantgarw until 1819, then back to Coalport where he had set up a kiln in 1811. Nantgarw continued under Wm. W. Young and Thos. Pardoe, a flower painter from Bristol and Swansea until 1822. Bevington & Co. kept Swansea open until 1823 or 1824.

Billingsley's porcelain was cold white and translucent but hard to work and imperfect. At Swansea after 1817 steatitic ware was made with a mark of a trident and bone-ash ware was continued by Bevington & Co. During the delightful Mr. B's stay at Swansea the mark Nantgarw, NANTGARW or NANT GARW with or without the lettered C W for "china works" was also used at Swansea. The ware of Dillwyn is harder, less translucent and markedly greenish by transmitted light and is marked Swansea with or without crossed tridents or a single one. The Bevington & Co. wares bear the firm name in full. To add to the disorder, both firms also sold undecorated ware and various uninspired artists added to the general bad odor.

BRISTOL AND PLYMOUTH

Remembering "Lowdin's China House" we understand that it was difficult to tell Bristol and Worcester china of 1750 to 1752 apart.

About 1755 William Cookworthy, apothecary of Plymouth and possibly interested in the Lowdin plant, discovered the first kaolin known in England in Cornwall. A second factory ran from 1760 to 1765 in Bristol and in 1768 Cookworthy began to make a sort of hard porcelain in Plymouth. This plant

FIG. 1103. Pair of Plymouth (c. 1760–65) figures of "Antony and Cleopatra." Length 10¾". Plummer, Ltd. Note this model should not be mistaken for those of Ralph Wood, Jr., who made figures from the same moulds at a later date.

was transferred to Bristol in 1770 and in 1773 sold with all rights to Richard Champion who appointed John Brittan foreman. In 1781 it was sold to a syndicate of Staffordshire potters who continued the Plymouth-Bristol porcelain at New Hall, Shelton (Hanley).

A mug in the B.M. is dated March 14, 1768 and has the arms of Plymouth and name of the town. It is decorated in pale and blackish underglaze blue as might have been expected on a hard ware. The ware has many black specks and the enamels do not fuse perfectly with the glaze. Figures were made with greyish-yellow or greyish-blue tone, are mostly decorated and have bases touched up with red. Some are clumsy but some have finely modeled "bocages" and dresses with small patterns. The best are large figures representing the "Four Continents."

In 1770 some simple and well formed coffee pots and mugs seem to have been copied directly from Chinese examples. Garniture sets also seem to be fairly close in shape and design to Chinese originals.

The Plymouth mark is an alchemist's symbol which looks like a two or four and is in underglaze blue, red, blue enamel or gold.

Thus the later porcelain of Bristol is a continuation of Plymouth and not that of Lowdin. In fact the earliest hard paste of Bristol is not marked Bristol as at Lowdin's but sometimes bears the Plymouth mark

FIG. 1104. Plymouth teapot decorated in red, blue, green, yellow and puce with gold on a hard paste crude porcelain discolored and pitted typically. Ht. 6¾". Metropolitan Mus. of Art.

alone or with the cross Champion used in overglaze blue. He also used the crossed swords of Meissen but with an overglaze B superimposed. He evidently had some conscience as compared with other Englishmen of the day.

The Bristol hard ware has a shiny glaze of milk-white and the enamels stand out in relief on it as they do not fuse with it perfectly, due to the too large difference in fusing temperatures. Wheel marks left showing are common to both wares. A transparent copper green is most characteristic and it was at times combined with painting *en grisaille*. Rare ground colors are yellow and "scale blue." Gilding is rich and often tooled. "Cottage china" had some underglaze blue and some polychrome decoration. Transfer printing, if used at all, was well handled.

Fair technical achievement was ruined by the English genius for the combination of unpleasant colors found nowhere else in the world. This has been explained on the ground that the climate was so dense and foggy that raw color was the only kind that would carry, but this cannot be so, for nowhere else in the world do we find such strong color as about the equator. No, it cannot be the climate. It is just a penchant for unqualified colors in a sometimes fresh and child-like effect but at other times the most unpleasant results. Hannover says of Bristol and Plymouth, "—As one of the most serious offences in this respect we may point out a hexagonal vase in the B.M. with applied flowers in relief painted in natural colors, further decorated with two landscapes in blue monochrome and two others in crimson, and two (with exotic birds) in natural colors."

Artists who worked for Champion were Henry Bone (miniature painter), William Stephens, the modeler Thos. Briand and possibly Tebo as at Bow and Worcester. The theory that these artists signed themselves with numbers is not correct. Of course Meissen and Sèvres came in for their proper and improper attention.

LOWESTOFT

Lowestoft turned out an agreeably decorated soft paste useful china entirely different from the "India china" made in China which was attributed to it. It was founded in 1757 and lasted until 1802, had no marks of its own and occasionally made use of those of other factories preferring those of Worcester. In 1902 some wasters were excavated along with moulds and sherds.

FIG. 1105. Lowestoft inkstand decorated in colors but without gold made about 1780 and showing very crude potting for that late period. Ht. 1¾". Metropolitan Mus. of Art.

FIG. 1106. Lowestoft cup decorated in a very crude Chinese style with enamel colors of blue, red and green, made between 1770 and 1802. Dia. 3⅜". Metropolitan Mus. of Art.

FIG. 1108. Tea-pot in underglaze blue and white ware decorated in "Chinese style" and made at Lowestoft between 1760 and 1770. Ht. 3". Metropolitan Mus. of Art.

FIG. 1107. Blue and white tea-caddy in Chinese style and with low relief ornament. Only two cup handles prove that this factory ever did even very crude modeling. Ht. 3⅞". Lowestoft. Metropolitan Mus. of Art.

It varies greatly in tone but has a greenish-yellow tint by transmitted light resembling Bow, and contains bone-ash. Painted and printed underglaze blue designs resemble Worcester from which some were copied direct. From about 1770 the decoration was in enamel colors predominantly red and violet in flowers and scrolls. Rococo lasted here longer than elsewhere, in fact until about 1800. A feather-like motive is characteristic and natural flowers including French cornflowers were done. Numerous examples are labeled "A Trifle from Lowestoft" and seem to indicate a souvenir trade. These are usually small ink-pots or mugs of the common sort.

LIVERPOOL

It is thought that Richard Chaffers was making porcelain in Liverpool in 1756. The "Printed Ware Manufactory" decorated many pottery wares and perhaps some porcelain from different factories. But later Samuel Gilbody, Philip Christian, Seth and John Pennington and Zachariah Barnes made porcelain.

Fig. 1110. Liverpool tea-pot with fluted body and flower decoration in natural colors (c. 1765). Ht. 8". Plummer, Ltd.

Fig. 1109. Early 19th cent. Liverpool jug with black printed design on cream ware, showing the American eagle and a map of the U. S. with figures of Washington, Liberty, etc. A bowl at the museum has the same circular medallion. Ht. 10⅛". Metropolitan Mus. of Art.

Excavations prove that certain poor porcelains formerly called Longton Hall are actually Liverpool.

The Herculaneum Pottery started about 1796 at Toxeth Park on the right bank of the Mersey near Liverpool and made porcelain from about 1800 to 1841 the ware being similar to Staffordshire and some of it bearing landscapes in black.

STAFFORDSHIRE, LONGTON HALL

(The pottery wares commonly known as "Staffordshire" are discussed in the Pottery section.)

At Brownhills near Burslem, William Littler had a factory which was moved to Longton Hall about 1750. About 1758 Duesbury is supposed to have added it to his combination of Bow, Chelsea and Derby.

The first Longton Hall ware is glassy and transparent resembling early Chelsea. Its later ware is hard and much like Worcester. The mark is two L's above a row of vertical dots. Forms comprise strongly veined leaves and rococo

FIG. 1111. Two jugs the one in black and colors and the other in black only. The first was of the sort made to catch American trade favor by heaping on patriotic pictures and legends and the other is a rare naval type. Liverpool. Hts. 9¼" and 9½". Ex W. R. Hearst Coll. International Studio, Inc.

FIG. 1112. Set of three Longton Hall (c. 1770) baroque vases with flowers in natural colors and shading in deep crimson of purplish hue. Hts. 6½" and 5". Plummer, Ltd.
FIG. 1113. Longton Hall (c. 1760-1800) watch-holder by Wm. Littler, having a deep cobalt blue glaze of almost Chinese richness. Ht 9½". Plummer, Ltd.

pieces painted in purple after Littler. Freely molded and applied flowers and even birds were highly colored and ornate in effect. White enamel like that of Battersea or Staffordshire was applied over a strong blue ground as in Ming wares in China, and blue and white stripes were used.

NEW HALL

Champion's factory at Bristol ended at New Hall and under the name of the "New Hall China Manufactory" it existed from about 1782 to 1825.

The early ware is like "Cottage China," hard and decorated with patterns found at Bristol and also Minton. Rarely the mark was an N.

FIG. 1114. Tea-pot of New Hall style, 19th cent. Staffordshire. Length 8¾". Metropolitan Mus. of Art.

LONGPORT OR DAVENPORT, 1793–1887

John Davenport, at Longport, made an old pottery into a porcelain factory. The mark was "Davenport" and its wares resemble Derby in paste, glaze and decoration. Ornate gilding, a blue or apple green ground and reserved medallions are typical.

MINTON AT STOKE-UPON-TRENT

Thomas Minton, pupil of Turner at Caughley, made porcelain at Stoke-upon-Trent in 1796. Later he worked under the first Josiah Spode. At his

FIG. 1115. Pair of "Spode" vessels called "fruit coolers" but actually made for boiled and chilled marons. Ice was placed around the inner containers and also on the covers. The ground is apple green and the colors natural. Ht. about 9". John Gibbons Coll.

death in 1836 the factory passed to his son and remained under him until 1883 when it became a limited company.

In 1798 it made bone-china after the formula by Josiah Spode 2nd, marked with an overglaze blue M between 2 crossed S's.

SPODE AT STOKE-UPON-TRENT

Of the three Josiah Spodes, the first had a pottery works at Stoke and died in 1797, the second made the first bone-china there and died in 1827 and the third died a few years after but the factory continued under the name until 1833 when it was bought by William Taylor Copeland. It still operates

FIG. 1116. Pair of Spode c. 1815 vases marked in purple under the base "Spode 3802" with thin and translucent thrown bodies of fine texture and well painted with flowers on one side and landscapes on the other in natural colors. Ht. 6″. Frank Stoner–Stoner & Evans, Ltd.

FIG. 1117. Spode of the second member of the family or early 19th cent. with a pattern less Japanese than most of the earlier ones. It has a bluish body. Wm. H. Plummer & Co.

FIG. 1118. Tea-pot by Josiah Spode II, Stoke-on-Trent, 19th cent., showing the Imari style. Metropolitan Mus. of Art.

under his family name. The ware showed a leaning toward Japanese influence like Derby. The old mark was "Spode" with or without the addition of "Stone China" or "Feldspathic Porcelain."

About 1846 Copeland invented a ware called "Parian" after the marble but not resembling it and we will hear more of this in America. For further discussion of Spode wares see the Pottery section

WEDGWOOD OR ETRURIA

Wedgwood's factory called Etruria made porcelain between 1812 and 1816 It is generally marked "Wedgwood" in red print. We have treated the well

Fig. 1120. Rockingham figure called "THE POT BOY" on the post on the back and inscribed, "I vish as there was a hact O'Parlement to make people find their own Pots—." Figures are rare from this factory. A peculiar indented mark under the foot looks like o—o or a key hole. The colors are yellow, mustard brown, light grey and black. Ht. 9". Frank Stoner–Stoner & Evans, Ltd.

Fig. 1119. "Spode" tureen of the late 18th cent. with "Imari" pattern. John Gibbons Coll.

known "Jasper ware," etc., under another section in this book. The porcelain, of the class of transfer printed wares with hand coloring in enamels, was unimportant.

ROCKINGHAM

The Rockingham works at Swinton in Yorkshire made porcelain from about 1826 to 1842 at a time when taste was at the lowest level, and it followed the other factories both in technique and in design.

This has been a story of the effect of commercialism and industrialism upon one art. The effect upon all arts and on the people themselves can be clearly seen in it; not only did the arts suffer but the very souls of the people suffered. Man does not turn back to Greeks and Chinese if he has gods and dragons in his own soul. He may look at them with interest but he has no time to copy them. In the 18th century man learned a number of negative lessons: 1.—That the dynamic curves of the Baroque were tiring, 2.—That the softening of them into Rococo made them weak and even less pleasant, and 3.—That the straight lines of Neo-Classicism were dead. He proceeded

Fig. 1121. One of pair of Rockingham vases with the griffin mark of the Marquis of Rockingham in puce. The ground color of the vase is a light apricot with rich gilding and flowers in rather strong polychrome. Ht. 11⅜". Made about 1825. Ernest F. Follows. The mark reads: Rockingham Works, Brameld. Makers to the King.

from the fat ladies of Rubens to the delicate and challenging ladies of Watteau and finally to the very pure ladies of David and sentimental ones of Angelica Kauffman. He turned from wine and beer drinking to tea drinking. But he also learned that factory workers have no incentive to become artists and are in truth afraid of losing their jobs, if they do so incline. He learned that short cuts like transfer printing kill beauty and life. He learned that the clever nonproducer could collect more pennies and set himself over the producer. Some declared that machines were to blame but no real artist would use a machine unless it could actually improve his art, if it were not that he was in fear of starvation. Thomas Carlyle in his "Past and Present" published in 1843, and Mill and many others saw it and tried to stem the tide. The French Revolution really accomplished nothing, for the rich bankers simply took the place of the old royalty. Actually gold getting became the acknowledged aim even of men who counted themselves respectable. This was the disease of the century and artists cannot think deeply about their work when they have to put their minds on the tricks of money getting.

CHAPTER XXV

EUROPEAN 18TH CENTURY POTTERY

THE technical development from the first crude neolithic potteries to the mastery of porcelain has been traced. We have seen how porcelain became the plaything of rich monarchs and died as an art, but in its development we have seen what man did with this medium of baked clay; how he made his vessels for eating and drinking from it; how he made images of his ancient gods, of fearsome monsters, of Christ and the Madonna, of kings and philosophers; images of all that interested him in life, of love making, of humor and of death; images of a whole town or of the tiniest blue flower, and in this one medium we see reflected practically all that man is and all that man does. Vessels to hold things and images to remember things by are perhaps two of the most important necessities of man.

Most potters of the 18th century had frantically tried to imitate the beautiful porcelain of China but a few resisted this impulse and adhered more closely to the art of pottery. In doing so they were perhaps a little less imitative; a little more inclined to keep their art a sincere expression.

NETHERLANDS

We return of course to the Netherlands where "Delfsche porsleyn," that is the faïence of Delft, had never given way to porcelain. Around 1700 the commercial influences began to control. There was a natural pressure for mass production regardless of artistic merit but the tradition was strong and integrity and quality of the wares was maintained for some time.

The first few real artists included Johannes van der Haagen of the "Jonge Moriaanshoot" or "Young Moor's Head Pottery" and he refrained from the competition in ever more ornate polychrome, adhering to painting in blue alone in the style of Hendrik Goltzius and influenced by the old Italian masters.

Piet Vizeer and Gijsbert Verhaast were two others. The latter, however, might better have been a painter on canvas for his landscapes in full color are of that nature and simply executed on faïence panels for framing.

Others are included in the following list:

LIST OF 18TH CENTURY DUTCH PAINTERS ON FAÏENCE

Gillis and Hendrik de Koning (1721) Style of *Pijnacker* and *Keizer*. Proprietors after *Louwijs Fictoor* of the *"Double Tankard."*

Iohannes Pennis (1725–1788) Blue and white and polychrome. We see his signature on "music plates" in the Rouen Museum and elsewhere. Founded the *"Porceleijne Schotel"* (*Porcelain Dish*) which later came to *Johannes van Duijn.*

781

Delft plate with buff body, tin glaze and polychrome decoration. Early 18th cent. Dia. 13¾". International Studio Art Corp.

Delft dish of tin-enameled earthenware in Imari style. 18th cent. Dia. 9½". Metropolitan Mus. of Art.

Armorial plate not unlike in design those painted at Canton and in red, blue and gold on white ground. 18th cent. Dutch and possibly from the Pijnacker factory. Dia. 8¾". Metropolitan Mus. of Art.

Coupe shaped bowl with buff body, tin glaze and blue, green, yellow and aubergine painting from an Italian original with a Biblical subject. Dia. 14". International Studio Art Corp.

DELFT DISHES OF THE 18TH CENTURY

PLATE 199

Hendrik van Hoorn (1759–1803) Blue and white and polychrome on rococo models. Was last proprietor of the *"Three Ash-Barrels"* factory. "The Three Porcelain Barrels" says Barber.
Pieter van den Briel (1759–   ) Blue and white. Last owner of the *"Fortune"* factory.
Justus Brouwer (1759) Blue and white and polychrome, enormous output. Made the *"Herring Fishery"* plates, the *"Months,"* etc., represented in many collections and was proprietor of the *"Porceleijne Bijl"* or "De Porcilain Bgl" *(Porcelain Axe)* factory.
Gerrit Brouwer (1759) Blue and white and polychrome of poor quality, proprietor of the *"Lampetkan"* (Ewer).
Dirk van der Does (1759) Proprietor of the *"Rose"* started by *Arendt Cosiin.*

Rare type of 18th cent. Delft dish having the usual tin glaze and
turquoise, green, black, gold and iron red decoration. Dia. 8½". Dia. of
tub 4½". International Studio Art Corp.

Plaque of escutcheon shape with buff body, tin glaze and underglaze blue and aubergine decoration, the border being in blue
and white. The humor which may be intentional or unintentional
or half and half, as expressed by the gent leaning against the
sleigh drawn by a galloping horse and the skaters who seem to
be enjoying all sorts of hazards, is nevertheless ticklesome. Width
15". Early 18th cent. International Studio Art Corp.

DELFT PLAQUE AND DISH (18TH CENTURY)

PLATE 200

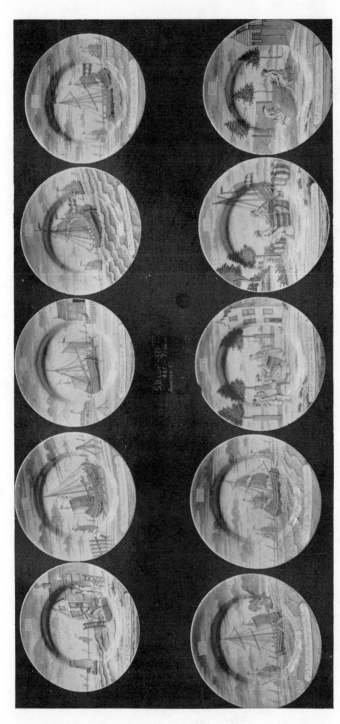

Set of ten plates by Justus Brouwer called "De Haringvangst" (The Herring Fishery). Two are missing. Dias. 9″. (171⁄ 1770). From the W. R. Hearst Coll.

DELFT PLATES "THE HERRING FISHERY"

PLATE 201

Anthoni Pennis (1759) Blue and white, polychrome and plastic works. Founded *"Twee Scheepjes"* *(Two Boats)* factory.

Anthonie Kruisweg (1759) A number of pieces have been wrongly credited to him in *Sèvres,* the Victoria and Albert Museum, etc. Was supposed to have followed the tradition of *Hoppesteyns.*

Hugo Brouwer (1716–1807) Blue and white and plastic work, rococo feeling usual, directed *Pijnackers* old factory the *"Three Porcelain Flasks."*

Albertus Kiell ('76') Blue and white sometimes with good Chinese drawing, owner of the *"Star"* (or "The White Star," Barber).

Johannes van Duijn (1764) Large number of blue and white and plastic pieces, signed name in full, blue and white tureens and *"pike-dishes."* Took over factory of *Johannes Pennis,* the *"Porcelain Dish."*

Lambertus Sanderus (1764) Poor quality of blue and white, proprietor of the *"Claw"* factory.

Zacharias Dextra, owner of *"Two Ash-urns"* factory from 1720. And *Jan Theunis Dextra* who from 1759 on controlled the *"Greek A."*—Copied Meissen designs on butter-dishes, sugar-bowls and tea-caddies, etc., marked with VA or V or other letters or figures in usual way but meaningless to us now.

At Delft the faïence was made thinner and lighter and copies of Meissen were made with the muffle, or decorating kiln. The old technique of underglaze decoration was therefore discarded and the technique began a decline. The competition with the cheap English cream colored earthen wares contributed. Of the 30 factories, 10 remained in 1794 when Gerrit Paape wrote his book. By 1808 there were only 8; the Ewer, the Flowerpot, the Claw, the Porcelain Bottle, the Greek A, the Three Bells, the Rose which made only tiles and finally Sanderson & Bellard who called themselves "Fabrikeurs in zoogenaamed engelsch aardewerk." By 1850 the Three Bells was the only

FIG. 1122. Early 18th cent. Delft money vase decorated in iron red, blue and gilding. Ht. 10¾". International Studio Art Corp.

FIG. 1123. Two Delft steins of the 18th cent., the left in yellow, and green with aubergine stipple, the right in yellow, blue and green which was a favorite combination toward the end of the century. J. Gibbons Coll.

one. In 1884 Joost Thooft and Labourchère started a place that made only slip-covered hard-fired earthenware with lead glaze which was not pleasing.

Holland was a country of painters but the shapes devised aside from the usual copies of Chinese and Italian ones were bizarre and sometimes amusing. "Finger vases" were probably inspired by Near Eastern ones but the ladies' shoes, sledges, monkey jugs, bird cages, violins, etc., were at least original. The modeled animals such as parrots after the Chinese, cocks, horses, cows, etc., were childlike and naïf, like wooden toys.

But the tiles show mastery and were sent even to Spain, a tile making country itself. They were sometimes framed but usually used about the stoves, in fireplaces, as dados or as a single row about the baseboard of a room.

FIG. 1124. Delft pot decorated in gold with the arms of England and Holland. Ht. 10″. From the W. R. Hearst Coll.

FIG. 1125. Delft vase dating between "1675 and 1750 from the factory of Adrian Piinacker" and of the usual enamels on thin body. Ht. 8⅞″. Metropo.itan Mus. of Art.

There were roughly three periods of tiles: First from late 16th to early 17th century they were of Italian type in yellow, dark blue, copper green and manganese purple and are about ⅜ inch thick. Second, from about 1650

FIG. 1126. Delft plate possibly by Anthoni Pennis depicting Christ's Entry into Jerusalem and made about 1759–60. Dia. 13″. Metropolitan Mus. of Art.

FIG. 1127. Plate showing strong influences of the South Chinese blue and white wares made around Canton, of the early 18th cent., Dutch, of white enameled blue underglaze ware. Dia. 6½″. Metropolitan Mus. of Art.

to 1750, is that of the best painting of ships, figures, landscapes or flowers usually in blue alone, and are about ¼ inch thick. The figures are often in the style of Palamedes or Peter Codde. The third period is from 1750 to around 1800 and the manganese purple of the rococo period becomes popular along with polychrome and the subjects are more pictorial such as landscapes with people in them, genre subjects, biblical subjects, etc. They are usually in a circle with the corners decorated. The rectangular ones have ornamental borders continuing from tile to tile. The thickness is still about ¼ inch.

Tile pictures of the 18th century covering four, six or more pieces are less well painted than the 17th century masters' works but still sure in drawing.

Fig. 1128. Pair of Delft 18th cent. plaques with embossed frames and paintings in blue of 1.—David & Abigail and 2.—Rebecca at the well. Ht. 20″. Metropolitan Mus. of Art.

"Useful Delft," "Boeren-delftsch" or peasant wares were often so cheap that the backs were left unfinished and covered with a yellowish half transparent lead glaze. The painting on these, either blue or polychrome, is usually too dull or too bright and sloppy. They have holes in the foot-rims for hanging.

Various Centers Outside Delft

Through the habit of calling all Dutch faïence Delft we may lose sight of the other potteries, a list of which follows:

Gouda—A few pieces with the name have been found and in about the middle of the 17th century there were supposed to be two potters there, one was *Cornelis Cornelisz van Dijck* and the other was *Michiel Wouters van Want*.

Dordrecht—At one time both of the above potters were working in this town.

Schiedam—A few pieces marked with the name are known.

The Hague—A 7 years' privilege was obtained by *Willem Jansz Lammerlaan* for the erection of a "*tegelbakkerij*" in 1644 and in 1680 or thereabouts two men from *Delft*, *Willem van der Lidt* and *Jeremias Godtlingh* went into partnership with a gold-smith, *Nicolas Keyser*.

Panel of tiles in manganese purple on white with floral corners and various landscapes. Each tile 5⅛″ sq. Metropolitan Mus. of Art.

DELFT 18TH CENTURY TILES

PLATE 202

Rotterdam—In 1627 a factory was in existence and running under two brothers, *Jacob* and *Henrick van der Heuvel,* and, as we know, in the middle of the century the city had so many *"plateelbakkers"* that they formed a corporation within the Guild of St. Luke. There were five or more factories here during the 17th and 18th century but only *Cornelis Boumeester* and *Jan Aalmis* have left behind recognizable signed work. *Boumeester* did marines with ships and landscapes of Italian type in the style of *Nicolaas Berchem. Aalmis* also did large tile pictures but was chiefly a figure painter and did allegories, pastoral subjects, military and tavern scenes, Dutch harbor scenes and even Chinese pavilions. His tiles decorating an old house at *Altona* are famous.

Utrecht—Seemed early to be a center for tile making and the museum there has many.

Arnheim—Was the place where fine *faïence* coffee-services, tureens and dishes in the style of *Pater* and *Lancret* were made and marked on the bottom with a cock. The factory was established in 1755 by *Johan van Kerckhoff* who did chinoiseries and polychrome painting in his first period, blue and white and pastoral genre in his second and then turned to imitating *Meissen* as did the *Dextras.*

Overtoom, near *Amsterdam*—Was called *"Blankenburg"* and later *" 't Fort de Eendragt"* and from there we hear from an old chemist who wrote in 1789. "I have seen many samples of the productions of this place. The material recalls *Delft* of the good period. . . . They made in this factory not only all sorts of table and kitchen wares, but also decorative articles, finely modeled and naturally painted birds, vases, candelabra, statuettes, groups. It is to be

FIG. 1129. Vase of late 18th cent. Delft pottery decorated in blue on white. Note crudity compared with 17th cent. one of similar shape with floral decoration. Ht. 9½". Metropolitan Mus. of Art.

FIG. 1130. Dutch 18th cent. bird cage decorated with floral design. Ht. 16½". Metropolitan Mus. of Art.

FIG. 1131. 18th cent. Delft cow with polychrome decoration. Ht. 3¼". Metropolitan Mus. of Art.

FIG. 1132. Horse marked with an AP monogram in blue and from Anthoni Pennis said to be between 1750 and 1775. The decoration is in polychrome. Ht. 9". Metropolitan Mus. of Art.

regretted that these things were excessively heavy. The enamel was white and brilliant, the colours as fine and vivid as on porcelain." The factory seems to have run only from 1754 to 1762 and used no mark and none of these pieces has been definitely identified.

msterdam—Unfortunately we have no examples we are sure of and there seemed to be no mark, though Barber says "Hartog v. Saten (1780–83)."

All of the marks found have not been deciphered and many are not to be depended upon for there were forgeries here as elsewhere and outside of Holland many attempts were made to copy the ware, in both the old days and recently. In Northern France factories have worked for years filling the market for "Old Delft." Hannover points out that a jug in South German style

FIG. 1133. A barber's basin of 18th cent. Delft in blue decoration. Length 11″. Metropolitan Mus. of Art.

FIG. 1134. Dutch late 18th cent. tea-pot and brazier with polychrome design adapted from Chinese porcelain. There is a lavish use of yellow. It is said to come from the Moor's Head and to be in the style of Gertrnij Verstelle. Ht. 14″. Metropolitan Mus. of Art.

Delft might bring $30 to $50 while a modern one might be had for $1 and he adds, "These ridiculously cheap Northern French imitations are by no means bad. The body is as light in color as it should be, the glaze satisfactory as regards pin holes, etc., the wearing of the glaze plausible—where found—the blue color excellent, the brush work bold and practised as in the old ware, the style of the figures often unimpeachable. The forgeries really betray themselves only in the ornamental designs, and sometimes by their

FIG. 1135. Panel of manganese purple decorated tiles of the late 18th cent. showing the influence of Indian palampores or cotton prints. About 20″ high. Metropolitan Mus. of Art.

'crazing' (genuine Delft is as a rule free from this), and by a slightly excessive weight, the genuine wares being, thanks to certain properties of their clay, of a lightness that is often astonishing." He then continues, "Even so the Northern French forgeries of blue-and-white Delft are nothing compared with those made by Samson in Paris. He makes imitations of everything as is well known; but blue-and-white Delft is his specialty, which he has carried to the highest degree of perfection." These, however, need not be feared for they bear his own mark and bring quite as much as the old ones.

The prices of Delft are varied from a few dollars to about $500 though never so much as Italian majolica or German Hafner ware. Its influence was a common one of pleasing the masses of people in many places.

BELGIUM

Belgium never did much but copy the Dutch faïence. There were two factories in Brussels known to have started as early as the 17th century and in 1705, Corneille Mombaers and Thierry Witsenburg founded a factory which only attained success when it was taken over by the son, Philippe Mombaers in 1724 who had been in France and Delft. This factory specialized in covered dishes in the form of pigeons, ducks, hens, etc., cabbages, melons and such. The marks B and K beneath a hay fork are not Brussels mark but refer to Abtsbessingen, near Sonderhausen and to some unknown painter. Authentic pieces have a tin glaze that runs with the colors and produces areas of agate-like veins, as has been pointed out by M. Marcel Laurent. The CB in monogram beneath a crown is the proper mark but is easily confused with that of Friedberg, Bavaria.

Another factory founded by Jacques Artoisenet in 1751 joined the older one in 1766. Laurent states that it is practically impossible to distinguish between these wares.

Stadtholder Charles-Alexandre of Lorraine erected a factory at Tervueren, near Brussels, in 1767 and it continued until 1781.

At Tournai, whence the clay for Delft came there had been potters from the 16th century and between 1698 and 1725 Joseph Fauquez had a factory there. He also had another at Saint-Amand from 1718 which was famous for its bianco sopra bianco ware with white on a slightly bluish ground. The wares of these two places are alike. In 1750 at this place another factory was started by Franço's Carpentier and taken by Joseph Péterinck in the following year. It was reported to have imitated the wares of Strasburg, Rouen and Delft, and to have made "brun de Rouen," a brown ware white inside though that from Rouen is all brown. "Grès d'Angleterre" is also mentioned and was probably similar to the cream ware from England. After Péterinck's death, his son-in-law, Bettignies made decorated quart pots marked "Fabrique de Bettignies à Tournay," with a date later than 1800.

At Liège, Baron de Bülow had a privilege for 30 years and it must have run out by 1767 for Lefébvre and Gavron then obtained one. The former is said to have turned out 150,000 pieces but not one has been identified. One interesting point is that at Tournai, Lille and Brussels the clay was supposed to have been stored for at least five years, and this probably permitted the full oxidation of all iron and rotting of all vegetable and animal matter. This habit was also found in many of the German and Dutch factories. Liège finally came into the hands of J. Boussemaert of Lille, the son of the well known potter of that city, and he made good wares marked L.G. or with L.G. on either side of the arms of Liège which is a stone pillar on two steps. These wares are often decorated with polychrome flowers in Strasburg style.

At Andenne, Joseph Wouters of Louvain started two factories in 1783 and 1787 and from the latter come the little figures by Guilain Richardot. After 1800 they made a large amount of lead glazed ware with or without printed decoration along neo-classic lines and marked AD W (Andenne-Wouters).

At Septfontaines, near Luxemburg, the Boch brothers began in 1767 and in 1795 the owner was Pierre-Joseph Boch. He made a white ware that looked like soft paste. The shapes were "elegant" and the decoration was in cobalt blue usually of flowers which have three petals and long branching stamens. In the 1780's Dalle made faïence landscape panels there. Biscuit groups copied from Sèvres were thought to have been made there but this is not likely. The factory still operates under the name of Velleroy & Boch.

FRANCE

Though the Far Eastern contacts were not great in France, and she misunderstood Chinese design, the desire for color brought about the discontinuance of painting the design on the unfused tin enamel of faïence and the adoption of painting on a fused tin enamel surface with muffle-kiln colors of

Rouen platter decorated in blue and red with a "lambrequin" design. It dates about 1705–1720. Metropolitan Mus. of Art.

Sinceny plate of about 1750 with polychrome decoration of lambrequin type. Metropolitan Mus. of Art.

Rouen platter of about 1750 decorated in polychrome and showing Italian influence but the weakness of the center landscape and the spiritless composition are lacking in all vitality. Metropolitan Mus. of Art.

Moustiers plate dating between 1738 and 1749 and attributed to the Olerys. Metropolitan Mus. of Art.

FRENCH FAÏENCE ROUEN, SINCENY, MOUSTIERS

PLATE 203

greater variety in a technique more like that of China. This change took place about 1750 but it did not entirely displace the older method of Nevers, Rouen and Moustiers. After all, the art of porcelain was an off-shoot from the main stem of pottery making; a rich man's plaything for many years before the common people could touch it, while the art of faïence continued to develop along its own lines until the end of the century.

ROUEN FAÏENCE

With Edme and his son, Louis Poterat, shortly after 1644 when they took over the privilege taken out originally by Nicols Poirel only a short while before, begins the real history of Rouen faïence which was destined to become important in several ways.

The oldest dated specimens are two dishes at the Musée Céramique, Rouen, marked "fait à Rouen 1647." One is painted in the center with what appears to be a female winged centaur holding an arrow, and about the rim four octagonal panels alternating with flowers and containing a design of probably Near Eastern influence. The other is in the style of Nevers with polychrome figures and flowers and the arms of the Bigot family of Rouen in blue and yellow.

There are also some unmarked pieces with quasi-Chinese figures in blue camaïeu which may be either Rouen or Nevers, of about this period.

An Italian style cistern of poor quality and having the arms of the Duke of Luxemburg may also be from Nevers. Thus there is no distinguishing characteristic between the two wares to begin with. Nevers was first in point of time and Rouen in importance and the workmen went from one to the other factory.

Rouen was the first factory after the Medici one to make soft paste and there seemed to be more interest in this than in the pottery which copied the Italian and Dutch styles. But soon competition with Nevers began and several potters who set up in Saint Sever in spite of Poterat's privilege showed that something had to be done. The war had exhausted finances so much that in 1709 everyone was obliged under a penalty of 6,000 livres fine to send their silver to be melted down. By 1722 people had to have pottery to take the place of the plate and some 2,000 men were at work in Saint Sever. Therefore the new design necessarily had to be simple and easily taught to workmen. Figures are difficult to draw so they were dispensed with. The elegance and formality of silver had to be carried over. The solution had been reached in China in Ming times of the Wan Li reign (1573–1619) or before in the "sceptre" or "Ju-i" design used about the shoulders of vases. Somehow it came to these French potters and "lambrequins," named after the pieces of cloth with various shaped bottom edges that were hung over windows and

FIG. 1136.

doors, were employed. The designs are of perfectly spaced alternating symmetrical units consisting of one larger and more important and one smaller used as a sort of filler in. They were adapted to borders of plates and to centers where they formed star-like medallions. The alternation was also used in technique, one unit being in blue on white while the other was in white on blue.

Fig. 1137. Lambrequin design on a plate of blue and white which shows a tendency to bring the border and center medallens together. Metropolitan Mus. of Art.

Fig. 1138. This plate decorated in the typical Rouen manner in blue and red, shows the enlarged medallion reaching all the way to the border lambrequins. Metropolian Mus. of Art.

Fig. 1139. In this example the center medallion is replaced by a flower but the radial lines have become heavy. (1705–20). Metropolitan Mus. of Art.

The Rouen white was bluish or greenish in tint. In the earliest example known, inscribed "Brument 1699," there is an odd and fanciful psuedo-Chinese design. It has lambrequins about the rim in blue and a red which Nevers could not obtain even in later copies, for the color is replaced by a dark ochre. The blue could easily be copied, and was at both Nevers and St. Cloud, but it was stiff to draw with and in both places the outlines were in black. Most Rouen pieces have an ornamental motive, rosette or basket of flowers but in the early 18th century they are all perfectly symmetrical.

Fig. 1140. Polychrome plate of Rouen of 1710 to 1712 showing an adaptation of Chinese design of the worst sort which was made up in and about Canton to appeal to western merchants. Metropolitan Mus. of Art.

Fig. 1141. Rouen plate decorated in blue and yellow (1705–1720) with a chinoiserie figure in the center and the typical hatching in the border. Metropolitan Mus. of Art.

This best period ware reaches its culmination between 1720 and 1740 in large dishes about 20 inches in diameter of the "style rayonnant" in which the center design has spread outward and the border inward until they meet and interlace.

Hannover quite rightly suggests that the designs all came from those of engravers of ornament, book-binders, decorators of Boulle furniture, textiles, wrought iron, etc., but never from nature. Thus life and new ever-changing interest were not present and the germ of death lay in the ready limitations of such research. When each field had been mastered to its limit there lay

Fig. 1142. Rouen polychrome plate of about 1750. Metropolitan Mus. of Art.
Fig. 1143. Plate said to date 1725 but of the general style termed, "a la corne" which was very popular by 1750. Metropolitan Mus. of Art.
Fig. 1144. Rouen jar of about 1750 with polychrome decoration on blue ground. Note: The stupid quality of this painting is typical of the decadent results of factory work. Metropolitan Mus. of Art.

ahead only further complication and elaboration. Yet within this ever thickening crust was born, probably from Delft, the powerful Chinese and Japanese germ of life which was destined to burst it apart.

CHINESE, JAPANESE AND ROCOCO DESIGN AT ROUEN

The first we know to make use of these Far Eastern motifs was Guillibaud who made a platter shortly after 1720 with a rococo scrolled rim, the arms of

Fig. 1145. Rouen plate of 1720 to 1750 which has a little style but shows the beginning of the decadence in its weak landscape and set quality of the border. Metropolitan Mus. of Art.

Fig. 1146. Rouen, Levavasseur of about 1780, platter decorated in colors and following the style of "German flowers" strewn on its surface. Metropolitan Mus. of Art.

the Duke of Luxemburg and a center filled with flowers, insects and birds, faintly Chinese in character but perfectly symmetrical which is opposed to Chinese tradition in painting such objects. Guillibaud also used cross-hatching in panels alternating with sections decorated with flowers which is another Chinese custom. The hatching is usually green with little crosses in red at the intersections or other little red motives and the rest is in polychrome colors often with flowers alternating in red, blue and green.

Another rococo type has what was known as "décor ferronnerie" with scenes of "pastoral gallantry" and all in the coloring of Guillibaud. Still another group has chinoiseries after Watteau, Boucher and Pillement freely adapted and set in solid borders broken by alternating panels. Again there were those decorated "au carquois" ("quiver"), etc., with trophies, horns, torches, bows, birds and flowers dully drawn without perspective, modeling, or composition. By 1750 the most popular were called "à la corne" and had a horn of plenty sprouting flowers and surrounded by birds and insects. By this time everything has become asymmetrical and the borders are wavy. It was not that the artists knew anything at all about the laws of Chinese arrangement but simply that they were tired of the dead symmetrical and broke it up.

Porcelain competition by 1770 forced the kilns at Marseilles and Strasburg to turn to overglaze painting in similar technique and soon Rouen followed. Of course earthenware could not compete with porcelain in finesse of detail but only sold as something similar at a lower price. M. T. Ph. Levavasseur started the change and it was not for the best. In 1786 there were 18 factories with some 1,200 employees. By 1802 there were only 6, by 1807 there were 4 and they were making the common "grès à l'anglaise."

A few odd styles are known such as the "Boulle style" and Rouen copied the Nevers "bleu persan" but with a more opaque blue of greyish tone and the designs outlined in red. Similar ones were made with yellow and green on a thick white ground. Delft "music plates" were also tried but with polychrome borders and, of course, such a good idea was not neglected at Nevers, Lille and Moustiers.

At Sèvres there is a large set of floor tiles in carpet design supposed to date about 1730 and to have been made at Saint Sever by Sieur de Villeray, one of the largest manufacturers, who made it for his own use. Another group was made at Lisieux by a Rouen worker, Joachim.

Everything was made; drug-pots, chamber-pots, church lamps, miniature commodes, "guéridons" (stands for the center of tables), watch-stands, mirror frames, weather-vanes, sconces, chess boards, maps of France and even bellows. Of these things Hannover says, "The Rouen potters showed their wonderful genius by decorating their ware in such a manner that even in senseless articles it became at least a delight to the eye." He also claimed that their appeal to the "artistic sense can disarm the intelligence." Well we are les disarmed!

Four polychromed busts of the seasons in the Louvre attributed to Fouquay (1725–1740) brought 2,646 pounds sterling at the Hamilton Palace sale in 1882. Fairly good plates can reach a few hundred dollars but the taste for such things has changed. However the prices were high enough to attract many forgers. Some of these have a red with orange cast, the blue and white pieces often have too much crackle and foot rings have been added to the round dishes while the originals were without them and slightly concave or flat. Any marked piece is not early Rouen. The fleur-de-lys was a later mark and never used in the early period. Imitations were made at Gien and Orleans about 1875 but marked with the town name.

The general characteristics of old Rouen are: 1.—They are thick and heavy, 2.—the glaze is greenish and less often bluish and always tends to crackle, 3.—the outlines are always in blue or red and never in black, 4.—the yellow color is always greenish and 5.—in the red there are always small pits where the color fails.

SINCENY (AISNE)

Other places made faïence similar to that of Rouen but quite honestly and one of these was Sinceny (Aisne) which was founded in 1733 by Fayard and placed under the management of Pierre Pellevé, who brought with him from Rouen workers and artists. The prices are about the same for these wares and the differences slight. A few of these may be noted: 1.—The Sinceny glaze is usually more bluish, 2.—the blue pigment stronger, 3.—the red is slightly glazed and not so inclined to bubble and pit. In the style of Guillibaud the quasi-Chinese figures have bright yellow garments and also similar figures were made as statuettes. The marks are an S with dots in color and the signature of Pellevé.

About 1775 artists from Lorraine did muffle-kiln decoration in the style of Strasburg, after the Rouen method, so well that the wares cannot be distinguished.

FIG. 1147. Sinceny plate of about 1750 with polychrome decoration. Metropolitan Mus. of Art.

ROUY AND SAINT-DENIS-SUR-SARTHON, QUIMPER (FINISTÈRE), ETC.

Pellevé went from Sinceny to Saint-Denis-sur-Sarthon (Orne) taking his followers and there in 1750 and later in 1790 at Rouy wares were made which can hardly be distinguished from each other or from Rouen. Again at the Loc-Maria factory in a suburb of Quimper (Finistère) founded in 1690 and taken over in 1743 by Pierre Caussy (son of a worker at Rouen who stole many quasi-Chinese designs from the older factory), a ware was made which can only be distinguished by its thick and dirty glaze and strongly accented drawing in manganese. By 1809 this place turned entirely to ordinary earthenware. Later a stoneware was tried and marked with an H in a triangle below a fleur-de-lys. In 1872 old models were tried from tracings of Caussy. He also used the mark in old style and Hannover points out that Graesse includes it as really old.

Saint Cloud

Even at Saint Cloud which we respect for its development of soft paste the lambrequins of Rouen were copied, using a different black instead of blue for the outlines. Later the faïence freed itself for there are blue and white pieces with pictures of workmen, craftsmen, etc., crudely painted which seem original. These are marked BV, CR and T with crowns for the château at Bellevue, Choisy-le-Roi and the Trianon, for which they were made.

The Paris Factories

Most of the Paris wares are distinguishable from Rouen only by their marks. The quality was not high. The red was replaced by ochre of a poor quality as at Nevers. More manganese and yellow were also used with the latter thinner and more transparent than that of Sinceny. The drawing was in black and none too good. Some of these factories are listed below:

The Factory of Oliver, rue de la Roquette, made stoves, drug vases and turned to the Strasburg colors and then to English ware.

The Pont-aux-Choux Factory started in 1772 and made wares cast from silver in Rouen-like material and then English ware.

The Factory of Digne, also rue de la Roquette, made apothecary jars for a monastic pharmacy at the order of the daughter of the Duke of Orleans after Rouen style of decoration.

Claud Michel (Clodion) (1738–1814)

Of course, not in glazed faïence and neither in biscuit porcelain, there were works done in low fired terracotta in France and particularly in Paris that were of great importance, in fact of such importance that they are thought of as sculpture and not ceramic art, which, however, they certainly are. Perhaps the greatest artist of this type was Claud Michel (called Clodion) who was born in Nancy in 1738 and came to Paris in 1755, a young man of only 17 years of age, to work in the shop of his uncle Lambert Sigisbert Adam, J. B. Pigalle. In 1759 he won the grand prize of the Académie Royale and in 1762 went to Rome. In 1792 the revolutionary agitation drove him back to his birthplace and he remained in Nancy until 1798. There is no positive record that he ever worked for any of the ceramic factories and the authority Mr. George Wildenstein is certain that he had his own kiln and did his own firing contrary to the way Falconet worked. Certainly his figures rank among the highest products of the century and of all time in his country just as did those of Luca and Andrea della Robbia in 15th and 16th century Italy.

Moustiers (Clerissy Factory)

The third large center with Nevers and Rouen was, of course, Moustiers-Sainte Marie (Basses Alps) where the sons Joseph and Pierre of the potter

FIG. 1148. A group in terracotta by the famous "Clodion" (Claud Michel) called "The Intoxication of Wine," which shows his full, rounded modeling and the sex appeal almost always present. Ht. 23¼". Metropolitan Mus. of Art.

FIG. 1149. A group by Clodion showing Bacchus and a nymph with Cupid, in terracotta. Ht. 18½". Metropolitan Mus. of Art.

Antoine Clerissy seem to have started in 1679. Joseph went to Marseilles to manage the Saint-Jean-du-Désert Factory and Pierre I, as he was called to distinguish him from the later Pierre, started at Moustiers. An Italian monk helped him and he hired the artists Gaspard and Jean-Baptiste Viry. The son, Antoine II, succeeded his father upon his death in 1728. Honoré Clerissy, whose relationship is not known, was also active there. The place did so well that in 1736 Antoine II retired and turned the plant over to his son, Pierre II. Under him it improved still more and when he was ennobled as a landed proprietor in 1783 he lost interest and sold out to Joseph Fouqué.

Another factory at Moustiers was started in 1738 by Joseph Olerys who had probably worked at the Clerissy place, had then gone to Marseilles and thence to Alcora in Valencia, Spain, in 1727 or 1732 (depending upon the authority) where the Count of Aranda had established a factory. His brother-in-law, Jean-Baptiste Laugier started with him, and when he died his son, Joseph II, took his place until 1771 when he sold out to Laugier, though the factory used the old name until 1790 as is proven by the mark, an O crossed with L on decadent wares. It occurs in yellow, orange, black or blue along with painter's marks.

There were still other factories but they were all small copyists. The Ferrat toward the end of the century copied Strasburg and then the English ware. Revivals were tried but by 1874 all work stopped.

Moustiers is light in weight as compared with Rouen. It is resonant and milk-white with slightly pinkish tone. There seem to be three generally accepted periods:

1.—Wares decorated in blue only from the beginning to 1738.
2.—Polychrome period from 1738, called the "Olery's period."
3.—Decadent period, in which both types were made, from about 1770.

FIRST PERIOD OF MOUSTIERS (1680–1738)

The Clerissy blue is lighter and brighter than Rouen blue. The only similar blue is that of Saint-Jean-du-Désert but there the outlines were in manganese while at Moustiers the blue was used for outline also. Gaspard Viry probably started the style of large dishes with hunting scenes after engravings by Antonio Tempesta and biblical subjects after Matthieu Mérian. Some have no borders while others have rims of lambrequins or motifs from Italian grotesques such as griffins, masks, etc.

Contemporary are those said to be of the style of Bérain though prototypes are found in the work of Sebastien le Clerc, Bernard Toro and others. In fact the style goes back to Roman wall paintings and had developed through the Renaissance and Baroque periods. It consists of airy and fantastic architectural members assembled without any thought of structure into patterns of delicate dreamlike arches with pedestals on leafy scrolls, awnings partly suspended by ribbons, balustrades guarding nothing, baldacchinos, terminal figures, consoles, brackets and such showing no slightest pull of gravity. However, gravity is taken account of in the draping of these things with garlands, hanging trophies, draperies, festoons, etc., of rich materials and flowers, not to mention lanterns. Then again it is not regarded, for there stand about in mid air or upon cushions of flowers with floating ribbons all manner of beings such as nymphs, genii and vaguely mythological personalities surrounded by flaming urns, fountains and vases of flowers among which are monkeys and parrots, cupids, satyrs, etc. It was great fun and led to many fantasies until the lambrequins surrounded it and slowly smothered it out of existence. The early ones with groups of goddesses, the Judgment of Paris or something of the sort are alive and sometimes even playful with contemporary dress included. They are generally rectangular with "broken" edges and come first to mind when Moustiers is mentioned.

SECOND PERIOD (1738–c.1770)

It is fairly certain that Olerys came back from Alcora and started the polychrome style. The "hunt dishes" stopped but the blue and white continued for a short while. The colors introduced were brown, yellow, green and purple. The style of Bérain was adopted but also cross influences seem to have continued between Alcora and Moustiers. Soon both used "décor à quirlandes" or small garlands alternating with medallions about the rim while in the center is another medallion with garland treated edges. In the medallions mythological subjects are used. The colors were usually blue, yellow, brown, black, green and purple in various shades. Those which are warmer and have no marks are usually attributed to Alcora, though this is a some-

FIG. 1150. Moustiers plate decorated in blue only and dating between 1738 and 1749. Metropolitan Mus. of Art.

FIG. 1151. Faience coffee-pot decorated in yellow and attributed to the Olerys and Laugiers. It is said to date between 1738 and 1749. Metropolitan Mus. of Art.

what arbitrary rule of thumb. Some have rococo designs instead of the flower garlands and these can be easily told apart because of the different treatments between Spanish and French scrolls. These commence about 1745 to 1750.

The "décor à la fleur de pomme de terre" (decoration of potato flowers) is used with both garlands and scrolls or alone and is of bouquets of flowers of symmetrical form separated by single flowers. This has a strong East Indian feeling explainable through Spain. Potato flowers could have had nothing whatsoever to do with the origin because they were unknown in France in 1750. The constant use of alternation is Near Eastern (see section on Ashur) and it is interesting to see it so strong in this Spanish influenced French place.

Finally the "genre Callot" design is of strewn grotesque figures faintly reminiscent of Callot, flowers, fragments of landscapes, etc., more or less, and chiefly less, in "Chinese style" in yellow, green, orange, blue, manganese and black combinations, usually the first three but sometimes all. This style lasted from about 1750 to 1770.

THIRD PERIOD OF MOUSTIERS (c.1770–)

When the decadence set in of course Meissen and Strasburg were copied but at Moustiers at least no more was taken than given for it had been considered a sort of school of potters for years. However, perhaps the real credit should go to Alcora for it was the source of much at Moustiers. There were also many small hangers-on such as Angoulême (Charente) founded c.1750 which with dull colors also copied Nevers and Rouen, Ardus (Tarn-et-Garonne) c. 1737 with red body and strongly crackled greyish glaze and stiff drawing, Aubagne (Bouches-du-Rhône) near Marseilles, c. 1782 where there were supposed to have been two factories, Auvillar (Tarn-et-Garonne) where several factories copied Varages, Rouen and Moustiers, Avignon (Vaucluse), Castilhon (Gard), Clermont Ferrand (Puy-de-Dôme) where the blue is more indigo than at Moustiers c.1730–1740, Goult (Vaucluse) c. 1740, La Foret (Savoy) 1730 by Noël Bouchard where Nevers was also imitated, Limoges (Haute Vienne) 1736 which changed in 1773 to porcelain making and then was an annex to Sèvres. (The faïence is poor. It is in manganese, light blue and green.) Lyons, 1733 by Joseph Combe and Jacques-Marie Ravier where the enamel was slightly bluish, Montauban (Tarn-et-Garonne) 1770 where Armand Lapierre did polychrome coats of arms with borders in blue and yellow and other imitations, Saint-Jean-du-Désert, Samadet (Landes) 1732 which copied the "Chinese style" and "genre Callot" along with imitations of Marseilles and Sinceny, and Varages (Var) where six factories between about 1740 and 1800 all made clumsy imitations.

About Alcora we have spoken of the attempt of the Count to have porcelain made and before that soft paste. We know that he encouraged only the best of craftsmanship and highest conceptions of the artists. It is told that he started a school and made each workman take several apprentices under him. He hired only Spanish artists after Olerys left up until 1750 when he gave up the factory entirely.

STRASBURG

Next in importance is probably Strasburg. It has often been mentioned in connection with the decline but, of course, in all fairness the decline was due to the general influences toward the end of the century and not to any one place, and it was the copyists of Strasburg rather than Strasburg itself which were responsible.

In 1720 a factory was established there by J. H. Wachenfeld of Ansbach. In 1721 a partnership was formed with Charles François Hannong who was a maker of clay pipes and stoves in Maestricht. In 1722 the partnership was broken and Hannong carried on. In 1724 he founded a new factory at Hagenau and in 1732 he turned both over to his sons, Paul Antoine and Balthazar. A price list of the time proves that they were active in making table services, coffee and tea services, knife handles, dishes, drug-vessels, doll's house sets, chimney sets, etc.

FIG. 1152. A typical Strasburg plate with the famous flowers casually laid askew. They are in natural colors with strong carmine and green. 18th cent. Metropolitan Mus. of Art.

The confusion about the early wares was dispelled by Brinckmann when they were found among those formerly called Rouen, Höchst, Ansbach and Hanau but chiefly among the first named. They are blue and white in much the Rouen manner, but with flowers more natural and fewer lambrequins. The next period shows "Indian flowers" in the Meissen manner.

In 1737 Balthazar Hannong took the business at Hagenau. In 1739 this factory came into Paul's hands and the next ten years saw its best and greatest production. Later Löwenfinck, having fled from Höchst, prevailed upon him to try "true porcelain" and this awakened the jealousy of the Vincennes factory which was making soft paste and they urged the ruling powers to call Alsace "foreign" and impose duties. Paul tried his best to sell the secret of hard porcelain in Paris but did not succeed and at last was forced to leave Strasburg. He then went, as we know, to Frankenthal where he made faïence and porcelain until he died in 1760.

His sons, Pierre Antoine and Joseph Adam stayed in Strasburg in the faïence business and later on Joseph was alone and tried again in 1774 to make porcelain, was hit by the drastic tariff and ruined, and thrown into debtor's prison. He died in Munich about 1800 in misery and want, a victim of jealousy in trade.

The history of Strasburg is that of the Hannongs solely and the style was entirely the one they adopted. Attempting to imitate porcelain they used muffle-kiln colors fired at low temperature on an already fused tin glaze. This glaze was not greenish like that of Rouen nor bluish like that of Nevers nor yet pinkish like that of Moustiers, but a fresh, soft, pure white without any brilliance. The colors were remarkable; especially a carmine-red which has never been matched and which was generally used. Flowers were gathered into loose bunches and laid coquettishly askew while similar smaller bunches were employed to obtain balance and individual blossoms covered imperfections. A beautiful copper-green, a violet, a light yellow and a blue were also used but the carmine and green predominate. Paul Hannong was the first in Europe to use gold on faïence and it is reported that in 1744 he showed Louis XV "gilded faïence" which is assumed to mean faïence with gold decoration only.

A few odd pieces have Chinese figures and these together with ones having flowers in crimson monochrome, also others imitative of Rouen blue and white, are signed by Joseph Hannong.

In the better ware the flowers are painted without outlines and with simple brush strokes modeling the petals with vitality. This must have been arrived at as a sort of invention because there is no evidence of Chinese or Japanese models having been seen or copied and the style is different also. On the shadow side the pigment may be laid so heavily that it stands out like enamel. The green was used pure and then shaded with black so that it has weight and acts as a foil for the delicacy of the flowers. Often the colors are not mixed but used with one over another to obtain blended effects. To the layman this may not seem a vitally different method but when a painter gets to thinking in masses rather than in outlines filled in, he has passed the first stage of his development. (See discussion of Sung, Chinese Tz'u Chou wares.)

In the cheaper and less good Strasburg wares the outline is thin and stiff as though done with a pen. This took longer but was safer for untrained artists.

Besides flat wares the usual odd pieces such as clock-cases, frames, etc. and some figures were made the latter being after Meissen ones but with more crudity and vigor.

These figures occur with the mark of Paul but not with the mark of Joseph Hannong. Paul's mark PH is never accompanied with other marks but Joseph's JH in monogram form usually has also numerals 1 to 1,000 in blue, below which is usually another number in blue or black. The first referred to the model list of the factory and the second had a meaning unknown. It did not refer to any sequence, date or quality as some dealers have tried to claim. A fiction grew up about the number 39 and imitators readily supplied the demand. Samson makes the body a little too light a grey and even he does not get the carmine. Strasburg glaze seldom crackles. But the collector must handle a number of pieces to make sure. No other faïence has been so much copied.

NIDERVILLER

One of the factories to be early influenced by the success of Strasburg was that of Niderviller in Alsace Lorraine also, near Sarrebourg. It was founded by Baron Jean-Louis de Beyerlé in 1754 with workmen from both Strasburg and Meissen. He and his wife loved the work and for some years their faïence wares were nearly as delicate as the porcelain of Meissen. The place came to Comte de Custine in 1774 and he placed it under François Lanfrey who allowed a slow decline to the final production of "English ware." In 1793 the comte was executed and Lanfrey became owner.

FIG. 1154. St. Clement jardinière with white tin glaze and decorated in natural colors. c. 1750. Metropolitan Mus. of Art.

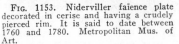

FIG. 1153. Niderviller faïence plate decorated in cerise and having a crudely pierced rim. It is said to date between 1760 and 1780. Metropolitan Mus. of Art.

Table wares very much like Strasburg are cleaner but slightly yellowish. The painting is delicate and good but the colors less fresh, particularly the carmine.

During the time of Beyerlé wood-grain effects were accomplished in grey, brown and yellow and the usual stunt of indicating an engraving pinned on it was faultlessly rendered. Some are signed "Kirian pinxit 1764," etc., and he may have been the originator of the idea in this particular factory. Framed panels with landscapes were also made and large drug vases, center pieces, etc., came in time. There are also biscuit and painted figures by Charles Sauvage Lemire and others.

Rarely the mark is "Niderviller" in full while again it may be BN (Beyerlé-Niderviller) or two C's set back to back for the Custine period.

LunÉville & Saint-ClÉment

Jacques Cambrette founded three concerns, two at Lunéville and one as an offshoot at Saint-Clément, all of which he left his son, Gabriel Cambrette, and son-in-law, Charles Loyal, at his death in 1758. Stanislaus Leozinski gave the two permission to use the "Manufacture Royale" but the business declined and Cambrette declared himself bankrupt, whereupon Loyal took over the business but had to sell the Lunéville holdings in 1778 to Sébastien Keller & Guerin, whose descendants were recently still owners. At Saint-Clément, Loyal formed a partnership with Mique and the sculptor Paul Louis Cyfflé but this was soon broken up and the place went to the stockholders until 1824 when Germain Thomas got hold of it. (See below for description of wares.)

Bellevue

In 1758, Bellevue near Toul (Meurthe) was founded by Lefrançois and in 1771 transfered to Charles Bayard and François Boyer and, like Lunéville, also obtained the title of "Manufacture Royale," and here too Cyfflé worked. He was born at Bruges and was a well known sculptor and his figures at both places became famous.

Lunéville made copies of Strasburg and also "English ware," but also large couchant lions with yellow jaws, and hounds of heraldic character which were used in the 18th century in halls in pairs to guard the vestibules. In biscuit there is a large statuette of King Stanislaus and at Sèvres there is also a cream colored bust of Louis XV, with a lion beside the pedestal.

Saint-Clément copied Strasburg and also the "English ware" as did Bellevue. At the latter place there are large figures such as "The Gardner," the "Little Savoyard" and the "Abbé Reading his Breviary," figures such as were used to "beautify" gardens in the 18th century.

The white and buff wares from Lunéville are often stamped "Terre de Lorraine" but the other wares from this place and all of those from Bellevue and Saint-Clément were not marked.

Thus the wares might not have been known had it not been for the fact that Cyfflé's style is recognizable. He did such things as "A shoe-maker whistling a tune to a starling in a cage above him," the "stocking-darner listening to a bird in a cage," and other small tradesmen or craftsmen in sweetly moving situations showing their kind hearts and causing all who observe them (providing of course that the observers could get themselves

FIG. 1155. Tall vase and cover made at Lille in 1767 and having polychrome decoration. Ht. 21". Metropolitan Mus. of Art.

FIG. 1156. St. Amand-les-Eaux tureen and cover dating about 1750–1775 and decorated with the usual polychrome flowers. Metropolitan Mus. of Art.

into the right state of mind) to feel a sad compassion. The supreme compliment of the 18th century, namely forgery, was granted them also.

Many other factories should be mentioned but we can content ourselves with those of the following chart:

CHART OF MINOR FAÏENCE FACTORIES OF FRANCE

Place	Mark	Dates & Founder	Description of wares
Aprey near Langres (Haute-Marne)	AP in monogram or APR	*Jacques Lallemand de Villehaut,* the Baron of Aprey, and his brother, *Joseph*	Early wares rococo and painted on a previously-fired tin glaze which is likely to chip off. Decoration is usually in blue and is of flowers, birds and Chinese figures or landscapes either free or in medallions.
	Also used on late imitations from old moulds	1769 Jacques died and his brother called in *François Ollivier* from Nevers	A tureen in colors with a good brown and of pinkish cast in Cluny. A Jardiniere with red shell edge picked out in green and flowers in colors is in the *Camando Coll., Louvre.*
	Samson also copied	Closed about 1860 Then owned by *Abel Girard* who copied old wares.	*Aprey* recalls the work of *Strasburg, Niderviller* and *Sceaux.* Colors are used in broad and strong work inclined to run.
	From 1772 no mark.		In 1772, according to *Paul Deveaux,* the painter *Jacques Jarry* influenced the work to be fine and delicate. These wares are not ever marked.

CHART OF MINOR FAÏENCE FACTORIES OF FRANCE—*Continued*

Place	Mark	Dates & Founder	Description of wares
Les Islettes (Meuse) Bois d'Epense (Marne)	No marks	1785 *François Bernard* took over factory from his father. *Jacques Henri Bernard,* his son, made great success.	It has fresh color and strong outlines of brown or black. The motives are large bouquets tied with red ribbons or in baskets, birds, poultry, Chinese landscapes and figures, and landscapes with military figures in them.
Lille	Lille between two palm-leaves under a crown and date Many fakes are on the market,— particularly on pieces with Dutch landscapes and on snuff-boxes looking like porcelain. FB in Monogram ? Fleur-de-lys?	Founded in 1696 by a modeler, *Jacques Feburier,* of Tournay, and a painter, *Jean Bossu.* After Feburier's death in 1729, his widow and son-in-law, *François Boussemaert* 1773 After the death of Boussemaert his widow married *Philippe-Auguste Petit,* who carried on until 1802.	Two altar pieces one in private possession and one in Sèvres, marked, *"Fecit Jacobus Feburier—Insulis in Flandria—Anno 1716—pinxit Maria Stephanus Borne—Anno 1716."* Painted in indigo tinted blue and touched with yellow. Rococo cartouche with cupids holding a ribbon inscribed *Maitre Daligne* with three scrolls and three insects alternating on rim all in colors on a plate in *Sèvres,* marked *Lille—1767.* Tea-pot marked *Lille—1768* in Cluny painted with rococo ornament in color with landscape on one side and two cupids in pale violet on other. Plates with playing cards on them.
Lille		1711 founded by *Barthélemy Dorez* and his nephew, *Pierre Pelissier* 1749 came to *Michel Joseph Herreng* and his widow carried on until 1780, when it went to *Hubert François Lefebure* Closed about 1820.	Founded for making soft porcelain but also made *faïence.*
Lille		1740 founded by *Jean Baptiste Wamps,* who worked for first factory. 1755 after his death it went to *Jacques Masquelier* who let it go in 1808.	Tiles only of rather Dutch characteristics. *Wamps* was Dutch.
Lille		1773 founded by *William Clarke* from Newcastle Only lasted a short time	Claimed he had a *faïence* "which is otherwise produced only in England and is very nearly as beautiful as porcelain."
Lille		1774 founded by *Charon* Only lasted a short time	Brown ware called *"terre de Saint-Esprit à la façon d'Angleterre et du Languedoc.'*

NOTE:—There are other wares attributed to Lille but upon what would seem to the author unsound grounds and the characteristics which *Jaennicke* points out are not worth consideration for they do not even wholly coincide with those of the very few known or fairly certain specimens.

CHART OF MINOR FAÏENCE FACTORIES OF FRANCE—*Continued*

Place	Mark	Dates & Founder	Description of wares
Saint-Amand-les-Eaux	PF in a double monogram	1718 founded by *Pierre Joseph Fauquez* from. Tournay. 1741 on his death his son, *Pierre François-Joseph Fauquez* who died and passed it on to his son, *Jean-Baptiste-Joseph Fauquez.* During Revolution he fled to Germany but returned to try to set the factory up again and died in Tournay 1804.	Imitated *Rouen* and *Strasburg.* Wares painted in an opaque white over a grey or grey blue glaze, at times alone or sometimes as a ground for a floral or lace pattern in several colors, such as the wall-fountain at *Sèvres*, in blue monochrome and "*blanc fixe.*" Also at *Sèvres* is a tureen with white branches and flowers over a grey ground and with added colored flowers over it, a plate with flowers in pale indigo blue in center and the rim in opaque white, a sauce-boat with grey-blue ground striped in white with flowers in colors over it, etc.
	Late mark same but flanked with an S and an A		Blue monochromes probably came first, then pieces with decoration in opaque white and finally the ones imitating Strasburg or borrowing from it. Last of all imitations of English ware which are generally yellow-glazed and painted in one or more colors with occasional gold edges.
Bailleul (Nord)	Marked Jacobus Hennekens		A tureen at *Sèvres* is oval and partly painted over a relief decoration in blue, grey and a good yellow.

Note:—Most of the factories in the west and south-west parts of France are much the same, perhaps having some one little specialty but otherwise following the current trend and their wares are difficult to distinguish one from another.

Rennes Brittany Pavé Saint-Laurent factory		c. 1745 by *Forasassi*, a Florentine.	Various clays from different places and also glazes of various tones. The tureens were moulded from silversmith's ones like those of many places and the decoration is similar to that of *Rouen, Moustiers* or *Marseilles.*
	Chiefly no marks. others are questionable	1759 came to *Dubois de la Vrillière.*	Manganese-purple is supposed to be more pronounced than elsewhere but this has been claimed elsewhere as we know. It also is all inclined to "blister" or "boil" so this is not a distinguishing feature.
	Jean-Baptiste-Alexis Bourgoin came from Rouen about 1755.		No red at all was used and the green is darker and duller so that the wares are somber.
	The inkstand is marked "*Fecitte. P. Bourgoiin A Rennes ce.12.8bre 1763*		A large inkstand at *Sèvres* has drawers and decoration in blue and manganese. (See mark.)

CHART OF MINOR FAÏENCE FACTORIES OF FRANCE—*Continued*

Place	Mark	Dates & Founder	Description of wares
Rennes *rue Hü*	*Francois-* *Alexandre* *Tutrel* Some painter's signatures Chiefly no marks	1749 founded by *Francois-Alexandre* *Tutrel*	Earliest known piece is 1769 and latest 1774. Perhaps here or at another factory was a painter named *Hirel de Choisy* who signed some of the best wares in- cluding a polychrome tureen in *Rennes Museum.* There was also *Michel De-* *rennes* and perhaps *(Jean)* *Baron.* See also wall cistern in colors dating about 1760 at *Rennes* *Museum.*
La Rochelle *(Charente-* *Inférieure)*	 Rochelle 1777	1743 founded by *Bricqueville* and an- other factory was working until 1789.	Imitations first of *Nevers,* then of *Rouen* blue and white, and then of *Moustiers* and finally of *Strasburg* wares in the usual sequence. Dishes with birds in center and rims with butterflies and other insects and flowers. Urn-shaped *"vase sur ter-* *rasse"* with freely modeled and painted flowers is typical and one at Sèvres is marked Rochelle 1777.
Maran	Maran and date No mark on fountain Another fountain is marked Maran 1754 of latter type.	1740 by *Pierre* *Rousencq*	Possibly, a wall fountain in the *Musée des Arts Decora-* *tifs in Paris,* with a garland of flowers freely modeled and painted around the upper part of the body and within the garland a few fishes in brown colors. Other pieces have heavy and violent color with an intense red.
Angoulême *(Charente)*		*(See Moustiers)*	
Cognac *(Charente)*		End of 18th cent.	Center of *"Faïence parlante"* during Revolution similar to that of *Nevers,* etc.
Bordeaux	 Clock dial marked Hustin 1750.	1711 *Jacques Gautier* who took in *Hustin* from Lille	Copies of *Moustiers, Nevers* and *Rouen.* Colors bad; blue is blackish, and there is no red. Some of the largest pieces of *faïence* ever made such as the clock dial from the city exchange.
Montauban *Auvillar* and *Ardus* in Tarn-et- Garonne			Strongest *Moustiers* influence.
Montpellier		1750—*Andre Philipp* from Marseilles	Fine *faïence* with flowers on yellow ground extending to back. These were models for *Moustiers.*

MARSEILLES
SAINT-JEAN-DU-DÉSERT

Perhaps ranking next to the greatest factories is Saint-Jean-du-Désert. In the 16th century some Italians were making faïence there but in 1677, 1678 or 1679 a factory was started in this suburb of Marseilles, by Joseph Clérissy, a son of Antoine Clérissy of Moustiers, or, if it was not started by him at least it came into his hands. When Joseph died in poverty in 1685 the direction of the place was under his eldest son named Antoine after the grandfather and he held it until 1733 when he went to Marseilles. From about 1750 there were about 10 factories selling to the Levant and French Colonies. By 1756 a school of painting unique in excellence had sprung up which produced a fresh and sincere sort of flower painting though landscapes were not improved much and figures not at all.

Among the places influenced were those of Louis Leroy (1741), Antoine Bonnefoy (1777), Fauchier, Veuve Perrin, Joseph Robert and Honoré Savy. Fauchier took over the factory of Etienne Héraud at Saint-Lazare in 1711, carried on with his nephew, Joseph Fauchier II, who finally inherited it in 1751 and his son carried on until 1794. The wares from the factory were just recently recognized among Moustiers types. A centerpiece in the Limoges Museum inscribed, "Joseph Fauchier à Marseille à la Bourgade," set us right.

In 1740 Claude Perrin founded a factory which did not gain distinction until after his death in 1748 when his widow ran it. Later she joined with Honoré Savy until about 1770 when she formed another company with François Abelard and her son. This latter made some experiments with porcelain up to about 1793 when she died.

Joseph Robert had started with a porcelain factory but in 1754 turned to faïence. Both were successful.

Honoré Savy after the partnership with Madam Perrin was dissolved, started in for himself around 1777 and became so successful that he even had a ship of his own for exporting.

Hannover says, "Like all the wares from Saint-Jean-du-Désert, everything from the factory of the elder Fauchier is painted in grand feu colours." This meant, of course, a limited palette. The oldest wares are in blue generally outlined in manganese. There is a dish signed by Antoine Clérissy in the style of the Moustiers "hunt dishes" and dated 1697. Another dated 1718 is in the style of Bérain of Moustiers but thinner and less vigorous. Large baluster jars of about the beginning of the century are in Nevers style following the Chinese but having taller and more flaring feet and angular curved covers with double knobs. The decorations on these are of a wide band containing figures from mythology and smaller borders of the dry arabesque style. The styles of Rouen and Savona were also employed. Under the young Fauchier the wares were muffle-kiln decorated and similar to those of other factories.

Around 1750 the Veuve Perrin factory took the lead in producing wares selected from all the best factories, copied in a highly developed technique.

It was particularly strong in colored grounds among which were the yellow of Montpellier (transposed into overglaze painting), a transparent water-green and a copper green which Honoré Savy brought to it. The gilding was fine. The sea motives predominate and marines and airy landscapes are characteristic decorations.

This could not have been due entirely to Madam Perrin for Joseph Robert achieved the same results and the wares of the two places cannot be told apart unless marked. The whiteness and refinement of his porcelain was also

FIG. 1157. Marseilles plate of about 1760 with a polychrome landscape. Metropolitan Mus. of Art.

FIG. 1158. Veuve Perrin late 18th cent. barber's basin from Marseilles with polychrome decoration. Metropolitan Mus. of Art.

obtained in his faïence and the richness of the glaze was even more pleasing, as is often the case. He was not quite so ambitious for variety but had a fairly wide range of shapes. His most appreciated work was decorated in monochrome, sepia, blue, or gold alone and the green and pink decoration he himself had a special affection for, but there were many styles. The flower modeling was done with style and beauty and not overdone. In general the plastic work of his factory was not quite so good as that of the Veuve Perrin one, though it is only fair to say that the confusion in attributions may have confused this issue.

Honoré Savy did plastic work but was a better painter and was a member of the Academy at Marseilles. Many of his plates are painted with polychrome in the center and green ornamentation on the rims. Another rich effect was obtained with dark green, light green and a purplish red. He was visited by Monsieur (the brother of the king) who obtained for him the use of the fleur-de-lys as his mark in 1777.

The Veuve Perrin mark was VP and Clérissy sometimes signed his name or the word Marseilles and the date, the earliest being 1681. An upright or horizontal F is supposed to be a mark of Fauchier, when on pieces of his style. The VP is easily confused with the IP of Store Kongensgade factory at Copenhagen and Madam Perrin's initials are sometimes detached from one another. Black and red were often used. At the time Robert worked, in his earliest period, with Etieu, the founder, they signed "Robert et Etieu"

sometimes. He also signed R or JR or RX ? in monogram. Other marks
attributed to him are not correct. Most of the finer pieces have no mark
and forgers are always ready to add a mark for good measure.

SCEAUX

Even the Marseilles wares were surpassed by a factory at Sceaux, near
Paris (Seine), founded in 1750 under the protection of the Duchess of Maine,
and then under that of Marie de Bourbon, the Duke of Penthièvre and High
Admiral of France (1725–1793). The first director was Jacques Chappelle,
who was both a chemist and member of the Academy, and its next was
Richard Glot who had the reputation of being the greatest modeler of his

Fig. 1160.   Sceaux (1753–1795)   jar which is one
of three designed as a garniture and decorated in
polychrome.   Metropolitan   Mus.   of   Art.

Fig. 1159. Sceaux vase possibly of the 18th cent. but more likely early 19th cent. Ht. 20″.
Metropolitan Mus. of Art.

time. Chappelle made porcelain and tried to make faïence just as refined.
He was also a man of business and in 1763 he retired with a fortune leaving
the work in charge of Jullien and a sculptor, Charles S. Jacques. It was they
who sold the factory to Glot for 40,000 livres in 1772 after having owned it
for nine years. Under him and the Duke's protection it achieved great fame.

The wares are mostly services of the period just preceding and of that of
Louis XVI. They are simple, formal in outline and decorated with pastorals,
cupids among clouds (often in crimson monochrome), flowers, birds, etc., set
in panels with molded borders of laurel leaves twisted about with ribbons

The carmine-red is less pure than that of Strasburg and softer. They had a fine ultramarine blue.

Glot was mayor of Sceaux and was arrested by the revolutionists. This broke his spirit and he finally sold the factory for an amount equal to one year's rent in 1794, to Antoine Cabaret who did nothing of note.

Chappelle did not seem to mark his wares. The SP (Sceaux-Penthièvre) was used after 1772 when the Duke became patron. It is in colors with or without an anchor referring to his being Admiral. Later the mark was Sceaux impressed and also with or without an anchor.

The body is maize-yellow and very light in weight. The glaze is white or slightly yellowish. It is one of the most costly of faïence wares and at the Bordes sale, 1911, a pastille-burner with decoration after Greuze of birds and festoons about a genre subject brought 10,100 francs.

"ENGLISH WARE," "FAÏENCE FINE," "STEINGUT" OR "FLINTPORSLIN"

We have had to end the histories of a number of factories with a disparaging reference to "English ware" which was often their last product. This is not due to the material itself which was in some ways an improvement over faïence, but to the use to which it was put, the way the market was flooded with it and the decadent period in which it was made. The French called it, "faïence fine," the Germans called it, "Steingut" (Steinzeug meaning the Rhenish stoneware), and the Swedish, "flintporslin." It originated in England but the continental imitations are of a blend of plastic clay with flint or quartz pebbles and often some kaolin. This produces a white body and thus the tin, necessary to make a white opaque glaze, was eliminated and an ordinary lead glaze took its place. As the result was too glaringly white, yellow-staining metallic oxides were mixed with the glaze. Sometimes the body was also colored and, naturally, this led to the mixing of two or more colored clays to produce the old marbled effect, wood graining, agate and tortoise-shell. This ware could be decorated on the biscuit and then glazed and given one firing, or a second or even third firing could be given it allowing the use of muffle-kiln colors. It was, unfortunately, peculiarly fitted to transfer printing. The temperature needed was not high and it could be fired with coal instead of wood, thus it was cheap. It was light and durable and, when chipped, the broken place remained white.

At first the effect of this ware was not bad for it brought along the designs of Wedgwood, though even these were cold and hard. Then France made a trade treaty with England in 1786 very much to the benefit of the latter country and entirely ruinous to the potters of France. Thus the ware was not taken up with enthusiasm as an artist might welcome a new material, but through the force of circumstances. It was one more insidious way in which the pressure of the penny might be applied. It is not interesting to us from any aesthetic viewpoint and I, therefore, simply append a list of a few of the most prominent factories which made a feature of it:

"ENGLISH WARE" OR "FAÏENCE FINE" FACTORIES

Douai (Nord)	*"Leigh & Cie— Douai" "Leigh 17 Douai" "Martin Dammann"*	1784—*Charles* and *Jacob Leigh* from England had managed two places in Staffordshire, formed the company *Houzé de l'Aulnoit & Cie.* Was hard hit by treaty of 1786 but lasted till 1820.	They obtained a privilege to make, *"fayence en grès pâte tendre blanche connue sous le nom de grès d'Angleterre."* Cream colored ware of English type mainly, and like that of Leeds particularly with pierced type of decoration, and with braided or twined handles and flower knobs. (See Sèvres)
		1799—*Martin Dammann* started a new factory but failed in 1804.	Red stoneware, black stoneware with garlands in relief after Wedgwood and jasper colored ware as well as polychrome wares with gilding.
		1800—*Boulé* brothers until 1806.	At time of Revolution they made the first orignial wares of the *"faïences parlantes"* type, snuff boxes, plates, etc., and busts of such people as Voltaire and Rousseau.
Choisy-le-Roi	*Choisy*	1804—Brothers *Paillart* started a factory which in 1824 came to *V. Paillart & H. Hautin*	Plate at Sèvres with printed medallion in black portrait of Marie Antoinette with an inscription on the rim reading: "Marie Antoinette d'Autriche Reine de France—*Impression sous couvert par Brevet d'Invention."*
Sèvres		There were seven factories by the end of the 18th century. 1806 *Clavareau Lambert & Cie.,* etc.	Painted decoration type. One with yellow ground with goat's head handles, festoons, medallions in relief and partly colored in blue and manganese. Another in same shape is pale green with black decoration. (Both at Sèvres)
Longwy (Lorraine)	Longwy incised and stamped	End of 18th cent.	Bust of Bonaparte and a tureen with imperial emblems, the handles being eagles with outspread wings.
Sarreguemines (Lorraine)	"Sarreguemines"	1770—*Paul Utzschneider* to present.	About 1800 great production of marbled wares. At *Sèvres* one brown jar of earthenware color in body.
Orleans (Loiret)	"Orleans" (stamped) "Grammont Laine' (Paine) Fabqt A Orleans"	1753—*Dessaux de Romilly* was authorized to set up a factory. 1757—Followed by *Gerault-Deranbert* who hired the sculptor *Jean Louis* End of 18th cent. *Grammont Laine* was there.	To make *"faïence en terre blanche purifée."* Statuettes of children, marbled and agate ware. In *Sèvres* there is a cream colored jug with flowers in relief.
Apt (Vaucluse)	No mark R is not correct	1780 and earlier factory amalgamated by *Bonnet.*	Earthenware of yellow body and also yellow and brown marbled ware.

Montereau (Seine-et-Marne) No mark Criel marked:—*"Manufacture de décors sur porcelaine et fayence* *—Rue du Cadran No. 9 à Paris"* also:—"Creil" or LCS (Legros-d'Anizy-Coquerel-Stone)		1775—*Clark, Shaw &* *Cie* amalgamated with Criel factory.	Transfer printed landscapes, etc. At *Creil* the first transfer-printing in France was done on earthenware under *Stone,* *Coquerel* and *Legros d'Anizy.* Scenes from French History, Fables of Lafontaine, etc., and portraits of great men, views of Italy, etc. At *Sèvres* there is a cup with red and green flowers among black-dotted clouds.
Chantilly	Hunting horn in gold *"Chantilly"* with P.......... below		V.A.M. there is a tea-pot with raised flowers and gilt lines. At *Sèvres* an oval dish painted in blue under a yellowish glaze, with a pair of lovers, and an octagonal dish with circular center and moulded rim. At *Rouen* a tureen in silver style of Louis XVI.
Loire (Nièvre)	*"La Charité"* may be the mark	1802—*Francis War-* *burton* from Staf- fordshire and later successor *Michael* *Willis*	English models in "faïence fine" and also *"biscuits noirs* *égyptiens"* after Wedgwood's so called "Basalt ware."

The makers of porcelain had worked under the retarding influences of "arcanists," rich dilettantes of the nobility and then commercial competition of a cut-throat variety. The makers of faïence did fully as important and perhaps more interesting things in their more honest appeal to the common people but were finally met by the competition of "English ware."

Delft had been inspired by the Far East and was also strongly influenced by the Near East in a roundabout way. The faïence of France was more strongly influenced by Italy and the Near East until later when naturalism and the Chinese motives came from the north and low countries. However, it was Delft and French faïence which had the strongest influence on the whole world of design until Wedgwood and the other classical influences became dominant.

German Faïence

Nowhere nearly so important nor original a source of design as Delft and French faïence, yet German faïence had some charm of its own. Its chief early influence readily traceable is that of Italian majolica as it affected Hirsvogel of Nuremberg who made the little owl jugs, the Pfau family and the peasant potteries of the Salzkammergut, the Alpine regions and south central Europe. These latter are not considered important by some general writers but I find in them a vitality and real joy of creation which is most stimulating. They are also most interesting in their relationship to the American wares incorrectly called "Pennsylvania Dutch."

The earliest dated examples of faïence in these regions are blue and white jugs from Franconia some of which bear the monograms LS for Lorenze Speckner of the Vest family factory at Kreussen. These all have metal screw tops. Another possible piece is a jug in the form of a dove with plumage in blue outline in the Victoria & Albert Museum. All of these pieces have designs that are similar to each other and unlike anything else in European faïence. These designs are of three large flowers arranged symmetrically with sometimes a fourth hanging straight down. The flowers and foliage are composed of curved lines terminating in spirals and the earliest ones are amplified with graduated dots in the background. It is difficult to explain this characteristic design for although the spiral was a heritage of Central Europe since Halstadt times, the symmetrical arrangement had been dropped since the Gothic period, and only in Spain in the 15th and 16th centuries was there any sign of it. Only one other place on earth showed this tendency strongly at the commencement of the 17th century and that was Central India, as may be seen by carpets, metal works, etc. This would seem an entirely impossible source of design for Bavaria until we read that, "During the 16th century Bruges, Antwerp and Amsterdam became the great emporia whence Indian produce, imported by the Portuguese, was distributed to Germany and even to England," in the article by Meston in the 14th edition *Encyclopaedia Britannica* (Vol. 12, p. 191 b). He continues with, "Private companies for trade with the East were formed in many parts of the United Provinces, but in 1602 they were all amalgamated by the states-general into the *'United East India Company of the Netherlands.'* Within a few years the Dutch had established factories on the continent of India, in Ceylon, in Sumatra, on the Persian Gulf and on the Red Sea, besides having obtained exclusive possession of the Moluccas."

Fig. 1161.

Mr. Quill Jones, the eminent authority on Oriental carpets, tells me that in Holland, England and Germany worn fragments of the Central Indian rugs, which are now almost priceless, were used by some people for common floor coverings. He further confirms the fact that the metal work from Central India and of this period is found in use in the same countries and states that the bringing of such objects down to the coastal cities of India for trade was comparatively easy and typical of the people. He even relates a story of finding a very heavily woven rug some 75 feet by 40 feet which had been brought hundreds of miles over mountainous country by a trader on camel back to show him. Thus these objects once landed in Holland would have been easily carried up the Rhine to Frankfort, into the foothills of the Vosges and east to Nuremberg.

Why did we not find more definite trace of these things in Holland design? Well, on looking back we do see some in the work of Pijnacker and earlier wares, and it may have been that the painter nation was appealed to more by the naturalism of Italian painting than by the primitive designs of India, while the contrary was the case among the Austrians, German peasants and Hungarians.

The use of these designs continued over a long period of time from about 1618 to well toward the end of the century; Speckner died about 1670 and

Three krugs with pewter covers and feet, the first from Kreussen dated 1701 painted with enamels. Ht. 9½". The second from Saxony and of the late 17th cent. It is brown glazed with enamel decoration of madonna and child in relief. Ht. 11". The third is either Frankfort or Hanau of the last quarter of the 17th cent. It is blue and white with Chinese influence. The cover has initials K. R. Ht. 12". From W. R. Hearst Coll. International Studio, Inc.

Two *kanne* and a *krug*, the first from Hanau of the middle 18th cent. painted in blue, the second from Nuremberg and said to be about 1730 and the third a *"walzenkrug"* also from Nuremberg of about 1725-50. Hts. 12½", 13" and 8¼". From W. R. Hearst Coll. International Studio, Inc.

GERMAN DECORATED WARES LATE 17TH AND 18TH CENTURY

PLATE 204

some may have been his work though no one man could have turned out all of them. Fragments have been found in excavations in Copenhagen. A large alberello type vase and an inkstand were found there and in Christiania. At Lübeck were discovered a pair of drug-pots dated 1660. Others from Nyköbing are dated 1668.

As time went on the glaze becomes coarse and glistening while at first it was mat and fine. The blue pigment also becomes heavier and the brushwork is more clumsy.

HAMBURG FAÏENCE

Temporarily we will now skip the South German wares and turn to Hamburg where specimens even when rarely marked are not identified, though some bear the arms of Hamburg or Hamburgers. Jugs found here seem to be prototypes of blue and white Hamburg stoves. These jugs have flat conical bases, inverted pear-shaped bodies and narrow cylindrical necks supported by a sturdy handle. Some have pewter lids but they were for containers and were too heavy and large, and too small of mouth to drink from. The body is heavy, the glaze opaque and cream and the design in bright blue

Hamburg Jug
FIG. 1162.

Hamburg or
South German
FIG. 1163.

with touches of strong yellow at times. The front side opposite the handle was the decorated surface and had a shield of arms, a merchant's mark, and an emblematic subject such as "Fortune" or the "Fall of Judith," etc. This panel is generally surrounded by a frame of leaves or wreath and outside of that small leaves springing from below the handle and spreading upward and outward toward the front.

The only similar example with flowers alone is a more softened form with neck curving into the body instead of cylindrical and set on it and the base missing and a metal one added, which is in the Copenhagen Museum. The body too is more sagging and perhaps this is a South German form, for again the flowers are symmetrical Indian ones, this time set on rock formation of Chinese character. Dishes are rare but there is one in the Hamburg Museum with a shield of arms within a wreath and a rim of Chinese flower forms, but set in un-Chinese symmetrical manner. The Hamburg factory seemed to reach its height about 1640 while the last dated piece is of 1656.

The stoves started about 1700 and have strong baroque forms enclosing subjects from Greek and Roman mythology, the Bible, views of the town and marines and landscapes. The best known makers were J. H. Volgrath, Cord Michael Möller, H. D. Hennings and Johann Otto Lessel.

At about 1775 the blue and white style was petering out and white stoves or white and gold stoves in the classic manner stopped the cheerful painting of the older artists. Wilhelm Tischbein at Eutin (c.1810 to 1820) made the best of these with friezes of figures from Greek vases in light colors inlayed in an ingenious manner on a dark brown clay.

HANAU WARES

For what may be considered our third oldest factory we return to the southwestern part of Germany to Hanau near Frankfort-on-the-Rhine. Here two Dutchmen, Daniel Behaghel and his son-in-law, Jacobus van der Walle, having tried to get a concession at Frankfort, started in 1661. They imported Dutch workmen. In 1679 one of these workmen Johannes Bally took away the privilege. In 1689 he died but his widow carried on until 1693 when the factory returned to Daniel Behaghel in company with the widow of Walle. After further changes it came to Heinrich von Alphen in 1726 and between 1740 and 1745 to his son. In 1787 the company, Martin, Dangers & Co., in 1794 Daniel Toussaint and in 1797 Jacob Achilles Leisler owned it until its end in 1806.

Ernst Zeh, authority on these wares, divides them into three general periods as follows:

T'ang Chinese

Hanau

FIG. 1164.

FIRST PERIOD OF HANAU WARE (1661–1700)

Between 1661 and 1700 the ware was entirely Dutch with blue outline and blue painting but without the use of "kwaart" which gave to the real Dutch faïence its brilliant color. The shapes are new and were later copied at Frankfort. They consist of "Enghalskrug" or long necked jugs with thick lip-rim which is pewter covered, and a globular body on a shallow but widely flaring foot, often bound with pewter for reinforcement, which might have been a help to some of the weak Greek prototypes; a similar form but with horizontally fluted neck and helically fluted body and a twisted handle extended on the body in two curls; radially fluted plates with small flat or slightly convex centers; and plates with nine lobes together with other common forms.

I have pointed out that the little T'ang bottle from my collection and now in the Metropolitan Museum has a horizontally fluted neck which originated as an Indian design. These ewers or jugs are closely similar to forms which we see carried out in metal in India and the Near East and even the fluted plates recall Near Eastern wares.

The decorations on the plain surfaced jugs are usually shields of arms but those of the fluted jugs are strewn flowers, possibly partly inspired by India cotton prints, or more formally arranged flowers in large symmetrical bunches, and having background filled with groups of dots. Sometimes these dots are replaced by a ring, a cross or a bird with outspread wings. This is the most typical feature of the factory and occurs on plates also. At times both plates and fluted jugs have interpretations of Chinese landscapes and figures.

Second Hanau Period (1700–1740)

The second period of Hanau carries on the designs of the first but the sprigs become smaller, the birds more numerous and the groups of dots closer.

Both Zeh and Hannover saw only the two influences: 1.—Chinese and, 2.—indigenous naturalistic, and neither of them properly account for the symmetrical Indian influence which evidently never dawned upon them. Goodness knows, there was enough talk in the period of "Indian flowers" to give them a clew even though most people entirely misapplied the term; there was so much smoke that one could not help but guess that there might be some fire, but, having seen Chinese design miscalled Indian, they looked no further for the real Indian influences.

During this period the Chinese influence in figures and landscapes continued but with much more European modification.

A new development is the lobed plate with radially arranged design and small center flowers, landscapes or fruits. This again speaks eloquently of Western Asia. One plate and a few odd jugs have muffle-kiln colors but these may have been made outside the factory for generally the color is blue alone or other of the high fire colors. The glaze is greyish, greenish or bluish and at times it was sprayed with manganese and had masked medallions in reserve.

FIG. 1165. A krug of pale blue glazed earthenware with blue design of the typical transition period 1700–1740, the flowers still showing Chinese influences but also the new symmetry of Indian flowers. Hanau. Ht. 14″. Metropolitan Mus. of Art.

The Third Period of Hanau Ware (1740–1786)

Zeh calls this the height but Hannover points out that the old designs are not even improved, and that the "German flowers" used are not so good as those of the French factories, while the same is true of the experiments with muffle-kiln colors. I quite agree that this period ushers in the decline.

The Fourth Period of Hanau Ware (1787–1806)

Zeh lists 109 marks and Graesse 101, many of which are not of the factory at all. The general mark found on hundreds of pieces from the beginning of the 18th century is an incised crescent. Another typical characteristic is the impression of a tool by which the base of the handle is pressed into the body on the shoulder. Most pieces have unglazed bases underneath.

This last period is really simply a final continuation of decline and nothing new was done that I know of.

No clear demarkation has been established between Hanau wares and those of Frankfort-on-the-Main which have no general mark at all and the chief authority on the latter, Stoehr, differs with Zeh on a number of points. As an instance, Stoehr attributes the jugs with plaited handles to Frankfort excepting only three. He also says the jugs with the depressions mentioned above on the handles are Frankfort ones, while Zeh also admits that this does occur infrequently on the Frankfort wares, and on those of Flors-heim as well. Where such specialists disagree it is well to tread lightly.

FRANKFORT-ON THE-MAIN

The factory at Frankfort-on-the-Main was established in 1666 with a privilege to Jean Simonet of Paris who had previously been a Hanau work-man. In 1693 the patron Johann Christoph Fehr died and the factory was held by the widow and two sons until 1723 when it went to Georg Haszlocher. Between 1732 and 1742 it changed hands many times until Johann Heckel bought it and he and his son kept it until 1772 or 1774 when it was finally closed down.

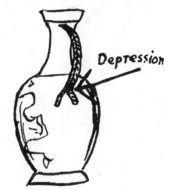

Frankfort or Florsheim Jug
FIG. 1166.

I hazard one guess about the new type symmetrical design and that is that it would be more likely to have started in the parent factory. Otherwise what we have said just above held true and the wares cannot be distinguished from those of Hanau.

The chart below lists the other more run-of-the-mill factories and we need mention only that we find more Western Asiatic

FIG. 1168. Small tureen of Höchst faïence decorated in natural colors by Danhofer and signed with red wheel over line with D under it, 18th cent. Mrs. Bruce.

FIG. 1167. Bavarian stein with pewter cover and base, having polychromed decoration. Ht. 8". J. Gibbons Coll.
FIG. 1169. Mug with coat of arms on manganese ground attr. to Bayreuth c. 1720. Ht. 10¼". W. R. Hearst Coll. International Studio, Inc.

traces at Nuremberg, almost perfect copies (except for the ware of course) of Chinese blue and white K'ang Hsi wares at Dresden and nothing much else of interest unless it be a new method of heaping vegetables to the side of a dish or flowers to the top of a vase at Proskau.

Fig. 1170. Pitcher with pewter cover and foot attr. to workshop of Cornelius Funke. Powdered manganese ground with blue painted monogram A.W.M. and windmills on side. Cover marked MEA 1745. Ht. 16″. Krug with pewter cover and foot from workshop of Cornelius Funke, decorated with monogram and crown supported on sides by two eagles. Cover marked CES 1725. Ht. 11″. W. R. Hearst Coll. International Studio, Inc.
Fig. 1171. Mug of blue and white tin glazed earthenware with Chinese figures, Potsdam, c. 1720. Ht. 10″. W. R. Hearst Coll. International Studio, Inc.

CHART OF GERMAN AND CENTRAL EUROPEAN FACTORIES

Nuremberg	N or NB in monogram only occasionally	1712—*Johann Caspar Ripp*, a potter from *Hanau*, manager for three merchants, *Christoph Marx*,	*Marx* got other good talent such as *Johann Wolff*, who later founded the *Copenhagen* and *Stockholm* factories,
	often with name or initials of artists.	*Heinrich Godfried*, *Anthon Hemmon* and the guardians of *Johann Conrad Romedi*, who died and his share came to *Johann Jacob Meyer*.	*Valentin Bontemps*, *Wenzel Ignaz Proschen*, *Adam Schuster*, *Andreas Tauber*, etc.
			Glaze is white, pale blue or greenish decorated with monochrome blue generally but also in other high temperature colors.
		1720 this had taken place and *Hemmon* had sold out to *Johann Andreas Marx* who was a good painter at the factory.	Manganese occurs in all shades from light to nearly black. Also bright yellow and yellowish-green. Red and pure black very rarely.
			Later muffle colors.
		Later owners were *Kess, Kordenbusch*, an artist, *Eckert* and finally *Struntz* until about 1840.	Motives are Chinese, a feather-like foliage, designs are arranged radially or symmetrically, small detached flowers occur on jugs of *Hanau* type, and a basket of fruit with birds is a favorite. The *Vögleinkrüge* or jugs of *Hanau* form with strewn tiny birds and flowers in blue on slate blue are typical.

CHART OF GERMAN AND CENTRAL EUROPEAN FACTORIES—*Continued*

These last jugs are even made to the present day as a tourist ware and were produced also in the 18th century at *Hanau, Frankfort* and *Ansbach.*

Landscapes of local character; biblical scenes and genre are typical of *Nuremberg.*

Rococo is seldom used and when it is it follows the engravings of *Nilson* and *Augsburg.*

Another specialty is the *Sternschüssel* a large or small round dish with a sunken star in the center and six depressions of heart shape around it. Here again we find a typical Near Eastern "sweetmeat dish" such as were made at *Rhages* and *Sultanabad.*

Still another type are the "rosette jugs" with *Hanau* shape but what Hannover calls "pierced Gothic rosettes" on either side of the globular body. We find their prototypes in the metal ones of Persia in which charcoal was placed to keep the contents warm.

	WR is one of their signatures but we do not know which.		Purple pictures and those in *"Schwarzlot"* were done mostly by the outside painters or *"Hausmaler."*
Bayreuth	*"Bayreuth. K."* or *Bayr.* |K. or *B.K.* for (Bayreuth-Knöller) or *B.F.S.* for (Fränkel and Schreck) *B.P.F.* for (Pfeiffer and Fränkel) or *B.P.* plus painter's marks	c1720—erected by *Johann Georg Knöller* 1745—purchased by the *burgomasters Fränkel* and *Schröckh.* Later came into the hands of *Johann Georg Pfeiffer* who held it until 1767 then to *Wetzel.* 1767 to 1783 it was managed by *Oswald.* 1735 to 1763 at its height but was still esteemed in 1795.	Shapes were usual jugs, lobed body and plaited handle jugs, pear-shaped jugs and cylindrical tankards, waiters or trays, inkstands, candlesticks, etc. Pale blue glaze like that of *Nuremberg.* The chief color being a light blue veiled by many small white specks. Decoration of *Laub-und Bandelwerk* forming a rim around the dishes similar to the *lambrequin* designs with a monogram or shield of arms in the center. (See *Hamburg Museum*) Muffle color was employed earlier here than elsewhere. Scattered flowers and birds occur. (See *Würzburg Mus.*) Some of the colored wares were painted by *Joseph Philipp Danhofer* and are very like *Vienna* porcelain in the period of *du Paquier* (1718–1743).

CHART OF GERMAN AND CENTRAL EUROPEAN FACTORIES—*Continued*

			Another type is in shiny brown stoneware decorated in silver or, infrequently, gold which it will be remembered was made in imitation of *Böttger's* early ware.
Amberg (Upper Palatinate)	Name of *Amberg* and *date,* 1774. *AB* in monogram	1759—*Simon Hetzendörfer* and now exists.	One coffee-pot known at *Sèvres* painted with polychrome, a butterfly and flowers. (See also *Luitpoldmuseum, Würzberg*)
Ansbach or *Onolzbach* (Middle Franconia) Ansp:popp— 1768		c1710—*Matthäus Bauer* also *Johann Caspar Ripp* 1747 worked but became the proprietor in 1769, *Georg Christoph Popp. Georg* took also *Johann Gottfried Popp* as partner. 1791—*Johann Julius* and *Georg Ludwig* Popp. Ended in 1807.	Not only *Ripp* but also *Johann Georg Taglieb* was an artist there. Copied *Rouen* but in 1730 probably under *Georg Christoph Popp* gained some difference in style, also *Bayreuth.* Chinese *famille verte* made as well as at *Delft* and many other classes of Far Eastern porcelain and in bright colors including a brilliant emerald green. Some rims of dishes were made in the *Laub-und Bandelwerk.* Coats of arms in *famille verte* colors. *Imari* ware with red and gold with deep strong blue glaze and frequent relief ornament in vases, tureens, bottles and bowls—also with *unfired* gold and cinnabar which is mostly worn off. Rarely they were made with lacquer alone and not on the blue glaze. Of course these are copies of the "Canton Mandarin wares." The blue is deep and heavy and often outlined with blackish manganese. Blue and white tureens and tankards of c.1730 have border ornaments of concentric semicircles. On the front of the tankards is generally a pink with petals striped lengthways in yellow and green in high temperature colors, there are also figure subjects of a crude type and a tree of the palm type is set on either side of the handle. The last known piece is a little jar painted with common polychrome flowers and inscribed: *"Abschiidt der Porzelainmahllerey in der Feijange-Faberick in Ansbach den der 13 Febr. 1804.—Der He(rr) ist gestorben, drum sindwir all verdorben."—*

CHART OF GERMAN AND CENTRAL EUROPEAN FACTORIES—*Continued*

			"Farewell of the porcelain painters in the *faïence*-factory at *Ansbach*, 13 Feb. 1804— The master is dead, therefore we are all ruined."
			But the factory struggled on for a few years more.
Höchst	Not always marked Wheel and painter's mark *JZ*—Johann Zeschinger *FH*—Friedrich Hess *I.H.*—Ignaz Hess *AL*—Adam Löwenfinck B.R., **G.C.,** M.S., LR and AMB are not yet known. (See porcelain section)	1746—*Adam Friedrich von Löwenfinck* with help of *Christoph Göltz* and *Johann Felician Clarus.* (See porcelain section) c1760 *faïence* seemed to have been discontinued. 1798 the factory was sold at auction but some moulds were evidently saved by the workmen and eventually went to *Damm.*	Ducks, geese, turkeys, partridges, pheasants and boar's heads in natural size and colors,—also lettuce, melons, artichokes, bunches of grapes, cabbages, etc.—better it is claimed than those of *Delft, Brussels, Proskau* and *Holitsch, Strasburg* and *Sleswick, Eckernförde* and *Kastrup* (near *Copenhagen*). Muffle-kiln colors like those of porcelain,—same artists did both. Baroque services (See tureen at *Troppau Museum*) *Hess* type rococo bordered dishes in yellow and black with crossed ears of corn in the center and a wreath around them (See *Strasburg Mus.*)
Damm near Aschaffenburg	*Wheel* of Höchst and a *D*	1827—the mother of *Forstmeister-Daniel Ernst Müller*	*"Fin Fayence"* or lead glaze earthenware. Many figures from the *Höchst* moulds (See *Frankfort* and *Würzburg Museums*).
Fulda	*Fuld* or FD with painter's marks or *black cross on white shield* and the signature F.v.L. for (Löwenfinck)	1736—*Adam Friedrich von Löwenfinck* having just escaped from *Meissen* and become Court enamel-painter.	Finest quality of muffle-kiln decoration with gold. It is said that 10 guilders worth was used on one set of vases by *Löwenfinck* in 1744. Great richness of coloring. (See gourd vase in *Hamburg Mus.*) Another fine vase by him is in the *Berlin Museum.*
Cassel	*HL* monogram for (Hesseland) *IHK*—1719 (Johann Heinrich Koch, who rented the factory from 1719 to 1724.)	1680—*Georg Kumpfe* founded. Changed owners several times. 1724—*Johann Christoph Gilze* 1735—Inherited by *Ludwig Gilze*—Later financial difficulties to *Landgrave of Hesse* to 1766 when porcelain took its place. (See that section)	Earliest wares unknown. Wares of blue and white like *Delft.* Copies of *Hanau* and according to *Brinckmann,* table services painted in colors. Toward the end also made stoves.
	"Steitzische Vasenfabrik in Cassel"	1771—another factory by *Simon Heinrich Steitz,* Court Confectioner Also there were other factories making the common English wares toward the end of the century.	Imitations of agate and jasper after *Wedgwood* (See *Hamburg Mus.*)

CHART OF GERMAN AND CENTRAL EUROPEAN FACTORIES—*Continued*

Offenbach	*O* followed by two *F's* written in one. (See porcelain section) *Offenbach 1807—Frantz G. Julb*	1739—*Philipp Friedrich Leyh* (or *Lay*) with workmen from *Hanau* 1.62—*Georg Heinrich Leyh,* his son. 1765—*Christoph Puschel* and then many others. 1807—still in existence	Decorated with flowers and among them tulips are prominent in four high temperature colors. Dish with bird in middle at *Landesmuseum, Cassell.* Also pieces at *Frankfort Museum.*
Kelsterbach and *Flörsheim* between Frankfort and Mayence		1758—*Kelsterbach* by *Johann Christian Frede* .1760—took in *Kaspar Maintz* Later made porcelain it is supposed	Wares of everyday use,—some like latest wares of *Hanau,* others like imitations of porcelains with blue flowers. In *Hamburg Mus.* there is a statuette of *Judith* with the head of *Holofernes* marked HD (*Hessen Darmstädtische.*)
Flörsheim	FH (Flörs Heim) monogram Same but with an impressed bunch of grapes, surmounted by his initials MJW	1765—*Georg Ludwig Müller* 1773—sold to the *Carthusian Monastery at Mayence,* who had it managed by *Kaspar Dreste* of *Hofheim.* 1781—leased to *Matthias Joseph Weingärtner.* 1797—*Kronenbold* and his nephew *Machenhauer* to 1846 and is still operating	At best resembles that of *Hanau* and simple peasant wares with more than usually smooth glaze. A center piece at *Hamburg* in high temperature colors is better than ordinary. *Weingärtner* produced "English" ware painted with roses and other flowers in blue on shapes of earlier wares.
Durlach	No identifying marks. Numerals from 1 to 8 painted in black which seem to indicate size. Also names of painters Löwer, Keim, Dumas and Karl Wettach Only in 19th century *"Durlach"* impressed on "English" ware.	1749—uncertain beginnings before this date (See *Stoehr-Der Cicerone* II. (1910), p. 310.) * *Johann Adam Benchiser* (or *Benckieser*) Did not end until about middle of 19th century	*Brinckmann* tells us the body is pale yellowish-grey sometimes of reddish cast. The tankards and jugs with the exception of the earliest are unglazed on the bottom and show rough string marks caused in separating them from the wheel. Blue is pale and washed out in earlier pieces and stronger later. Much manganese was used and often has white specks. The green is pale, bluish and dim. The yellow is lemon color shaded with ochre. In earlier pieces there is a brownish-grey and in later a dry brick-red. Black outlines and inscriptions are usual. Mostly the wares are jugs with pewter cover and foot-rim decorated with figures employed in industrial work framed in slight rococo frames on front. There is generally an inscription—name of person who ordered the piece, date, an aphorism in rhyme or something of the sort. On either side of the handle are flowers, roses,

CHART OF GERMAN AND CENTRAL EUROPEAN FACTORIES—*Continued*

tulips or forget-me-nots. This type lasted into 19th century even with asymmetrical framework to the pictures long after they had gone out of style.

"English ware" buff or rarely white, with yellow, yellowish-brown or white (rarely) glaze. White wares as a rule are unpainted or with landscapes in blue or flowers in colors. Yellow has frieze of vine leaves in brown or black.

Mosbach in Baden	T for (Tännich) ? *MB* below an electoral hat like a *crown.* Also *"Mossbach"* and *date.* CT for (Carl Theodor) in Monogram as on the Frankenthal but without crown of latter. In 1806 when Mosbach was made part of Baden, the mark was CF for (Carl Friedrich) *"Steingut"* is stamped *M* or *Mosbach*	1770—*Pierre Berthevin* (See *Marieberg*) and *Johann S. F. Tännich* from *Meissen* and *Strasburg* who later went to *Jever* and *Kiel*, before coming to *Mosbach.* 1774—*Tännich* was manager and 1781—*Carl Theodor* put *Johann Georg Friedrich List* in charge and *Tännich* went to *Mannheim*, and *Frankenthal.* 1787—*List* departed with most of the capital and *Roemer & Co.* had it until 1828. Still in existence with commercial wares.	None of the earliest wares are known. After *Tännich* arrival there is a rococo clock in the palace at *Karlsruhe* marked *"Mossbach . . . 1774"* At *Munich* is a portrait medallion of *Elector Carl Theodor* done in 1783 and at *Würzburg* are parts of a service with polychrome landscapes. The jugs are much like those of *Durlach* and tankards are done with a name or motto enclosed in a wreath of flowers, and plates with mottos. The latter more ordinary wares are frequently painted with forget-me-nots and cornflowers. The factory also tried to make the "English" *"Steingut"* but they have a grey or dirty white glaze and are not painted.
Ludwigsburg	Two *C's* crossed but without the crown which is on the porcelain. Similar to Niderviller mark of the Comte de Custine Or crossed C's above a W. Or crossed C's above a B.	1763—Also made *faïence* (See porcelain section for full story of factory.)	Rare and uncertain because of confusion of marks. Colossal white bust of Charles I *Duke of Württemberg* now at *Stuttgart.* At *Sèvres* a covered jar marked with crossed C's above a W and decorated with muffle-colors and partly worn off lacquer gilding. In *Hamburg* is an oval dish with large floral monogram in middle and four blue cartouches with groups of fruit on a black ground while there is a similar one in the *V.A.M.*—Also at *Hamburg* a tureen with branch of lemons on lid and painting in high fire manganese, yellow and green, marked with B under the crossed C's.

CHART OF GERMAN AND CENTRAL EUROPEAN FACTORIES— *Continued*

Göppingen in *Württemberg* Do not confuse with **Gög

gingen** in Bavaria | *Stag's horn* from the arms of *Württemberg* sometimes with IMPH which may mean (*Johann Matthias Plieder-Häuser*) ? | 1741—*Andreas Pliederhäuser* 1749—took partner, *Christian Rupprecht* from *Hamburg, Delft, Fulda,* etc.—Later, *Cyriacus Loubert* and *Adam Fichtmayer,* painters from *Hanover* were employed In 1753 *Andreas Pliederhäuser* died in poverty and his son, *Johann Matthias* inherited the privilege.

Nothing is heard for 35 years, in 1788 there is record of tariff troubles.

End unknown. | Reddish-buff body with thick greyish glaze.

The decoration is in blue and sometimes of two shades as a special feature.

Later pieces of the stag's horn mark are chiefly of peasant pottery and no really artistic wares seem ever to have been turned out. |
Schrezheim near Ellwangen	*B* under a small *arrow.*	1752—*Johann Baptist Bux* and carried on by his heirs after his death in 1800 to 1872 when it was destroyed by fire.	In the *Chapel of St. Anthony at Schrezheim* is an altar-tabernacle of great size and bold rococo design. In *Würzburg* is a large statuette of *St. Nepomuk.* Also made vegetable tureens in shape of cabbages, melons, etc. Most productions available to collectors are artless and homely. One group has a pale blue glaze but white is more usual. They are painted in blue or the high-temperature colors with a yellow. The designs are of "Indian" or "German" flowers and in the style of *Rouen.*
Crailsheim about 12 **miles** south of Ellwangen	*"Crailsheim"*	Not known	Tankard with man waving a moss-green flag and gripping a man who stands at his side. Others have bouquets of flowers in *Strasburg* style in moss-green and yellowish-brown.
Oettingen Bavaria later transferred to *Schrattenhofen*	*"Oettingen"* or an L over an Ö separated by a stroke Later wares are marked *Schrattenhofen*	1735—Not known 1740—*Johann Ulrich Sperl* 1748—taken over by *Köhler.*	In *Berlin* is a good tankard of about 1750 and with the L-Ö mark which is ascribed to Gottfried Leinfelder. It has a fine rococo feeling of scrolls and sprigs of foliage around a sort of shield holding a center medallion of flowers. The foot has a typical Chinese cross-hatched band with open panels. They made also a brown stoneware of Bayreuth style.

CHART OF GERMAN AND CENTRAL EUROPEAN FACTORIES—*Continued*

Göggingen not to be confused with *Göppingen* Was later transferred to *Friedberg*.	*CB* with or without a *crown* may be a correct mark? for (Chur-Bayern) also JH for (Joseph Hackl) ?	1748—*Prince-Bishop of Augsburg* 1749 *Joseph Hackl* was made modeller 1752—He owned it.	Pieces painted with flowers in soft, subdued, high-temperature colors. Chinese flowers of really good character were done here in blue and also in high-fired colors. (See oval platter in *Gewerbemuseum,* at *Reichenberg.*) In *Lund, Sweden,* there is a marked oblong dish with wavy edge and painted in blue with shield flanked by lions and a mottled band along the edge. *E. W. Braun* shows besides the Chinese decorated dish spoken of a wavy edged one with a basket of flowers in the center in typical' South German style from the *Hamburg Museum.*
Künersberg near *Memmingen*	Usually fully marked "*K nersberg*" or *KB*	1745—*Jacob Küner* and lasted until about 1770.	Imitations of ornamental designs of *Rouen* in a strong blue on a perfect white glaze on some dishes with deep curved edges and a conventionalized edge Other pieces have yellow and green. Others have several colors with a yellow-green predominating All simple and well made. Also vases with rococo relief ornament probably by *Johann Ulrich*|*Sperl.* Gold was also used. A wide variety of design including almost all styles.
Coburg		1739—	On'y a few isolated pieces known.
Dorotheenthal near *Arnstadt*	*AB* monogram for "*Augustenburg*" where *Elizabeth Albertine* of *Schwarzburg-Sondershausen,* had her seat as dowager. She was a patroness for some time. *J. G. Fliegel Arnstadt d. 9 May 1775*	1720—*Johann Theobald Frantz, Wilhelm Kanja* and *Johann Schnöter* are mentioned as manufacturers but the factory had already been known from around 1707 or a little later by workmen from *Brunswick.* (See *Max Sauerlandt*) There were some fifty known painters, which include *Alex, Wellendorf* and *J. G. Fliegel.*	*La'b-und Bandelwerk* dish at *Bremen* is typical as is also the blue and white winecooler at *Nuremberg.* Blue and white and polychrome, the blue chiefly for European designs and the polychrome for Chinese. All are high-temperature colors. No muffle-kiln painting was used in any of the Thuringian factories. Vivid iron-red verging on orange plays a large part but is never used on an extended surface. The green is grey-green or blue-green and the yellow approaches dark ochre. Jug with the figure of St. George in *British Museum,* is signed by *Fliegel*

CHART OF GERMAN AND CENTRAL EUROPEAN FACTORIES—*Continued*

Erfurt	Town mark a *wheel with six spokes* and painter's marks, one exactly like that of Joseph Hannong	There were three factories:— 1717—*Johann Gottfried Vorberg* and *Johann Ludwig Schumann.* 1719—a concession was granted for a new factory. 1734—Still a third was granted to *Johann Paul Stieglitz* and later his son, *Johann Christoph* between 1750 and 1754. 1791—His son in turn *Friederich Christoph Stieglitz* 1792—no mention and must have ended its work.	Colors same as those of *Dorotheenthal* but brighter, a fine brick-red, light olive-green and bright lemon-yellow with rich use of blue while the manganese is less prominent. No new shapes. A design much like that of Persian 17th century wares is seen around the edge of plates and on cylindrical tankards. It is a series of graduated strokes forming four "suns" with intermediate play of the same sort of strokes:— A typical plate in the *Museum Fredericianum in Cassel* shows also a triple fish motive much like that of the Persians and certainly not indigenous to this inland town. Others have ships or landscapes reserved on manganese grounds. One small group has grass-green designs outlined in manganese. Also fine flower painting was done in imitation of porcelain.
Abtsbessingen about 12 miles south-west of Sondershausen	*Hay-fork* from *Schwarzburg* arms	1766 or earlier— *Heinrich Christoph Muth* The last owner was supposed to be named *Wolff* and died in 1816.	Vases with reserved panels painted in blue on a yellow ground, a pyramid of modelled flowers painted in green, red, yellow and blue, a blue and white garden vase and also a stove in the same treatment, jugs, tankards, inkstands, etc. can be seen at the castle at Gehren and in the museum at Halle. They have a thick, low-fired, pale clay body with soft cream colored glaze and may be painted either with blue only or with several color combinations.
Dresden Saxony	No marks in first period	1707—It will be remembered that *Böttger* sent for *Peter Eggebrecht* (See Porcelain) and later he left the factory at *Dresden* to him and it passed down through the *Eggebrecht* family until in 1768—it became the property of *Christiane Sophie von Hörisch.* 1782—it was taken over by her son, *Carl Gottlieb Hörisch* 1783—it stopped.	*Brinckmann* at the *Hamburg Museum*, and *Zimmermann* conclusively respectively guessed at the wares and finally proved them definitely to include:— A 32 inch blue and white cylindrical vase with tall cylindrical neck very close to the Chinese shape and decorated with reserve rectangular medallions holding the "precious things" and flower decorations all in perfect Chinese style, with an uneven glaze with a tendency to "slide off" as Hannover says, and a blue with a tendency to form "eyes" or bubbles.

CHART OF GERMAN AND CENTRAL EUROPEAN FACTORIES—*Continued*

			Some covered vases more of Italian style, and a series of jugs with the arms of *Poland* and *Saxony* and the AR for *(Augustus Rex)* on them all in the same blue on the same glaze.
			Other small vases have lacquer colors of the type used before fired colors were produced here.
			And finally other faïence figures from *Böttger's* models.
	D.H. for (Dresden-Hörisch)		Later wares include similar drug-jugs or vases marked D.H. and dated 1781—long after *Augustus the Strong* had died. They must have been made to fill in sets by the later owners. Also pieces had high-fired colors; cornflower-blue, and yellowish green being characteristic. Became poorer and poorer in quality.
Hubertusburg	A *tree* surrounded with *three stars* with *"Hubertusburg"* below it, and below this *T* for (Tännich) Also *H* with *T* below it.	1770—*Johann Samuel Friedrich Tännich* backed by *Count von Lindenau* till 1774— then the count took over full management —But *Count Marcolini* and his *Meissen* factory made so much trouble that *Count Lindenau* finally placed his factory at the feet of the Elector asking only for a service as a "gracious memento"	A few pieces of *Tännich* period are known (See Dresden Museum) one is a vase painted with muffle-kiln flowers over a lemon-yellow leadglaze, while another is painted with a bouquet in tones of purple on a sea-green ground. On a white plate painted with flowers scattered in the porcelain manner, is an H and a T below it.
	19th century *"Wedgwood"* stamped.	1776–1835 it was under *Marcolini* and made "English" earthenware From 1814 to 1835 it was named:— *"Königliche sächsische Steingutfabrick Hubertusburg."* In 1835 it was sold to a man of business from *Leipzig* and declined until 1848.	Best wares were imitations of *Wedgwood* (See *Dresden Mus.*) but they are hard to classify being like many others made in German factories and stamped *"Wedgwood."* Of brittle material and with a glaze likely to crackle. Ordinary useful ware only.
Funke in Berlin		c1700—*Cornelius Funke* was not the first but was the first we know much about 1756—*Carl Friederich Lüdicke* obtained another privilege.	A large center piece in the palace of *Charlottenburg* has the eagle of *Brandenburg* on it. Jardinieres and plates with the monogram of *Frederick III at Berlin* in the *Hohenzollernmuseum.* Wares are not surely identified.

CHART OF GERMAN AND CENTRAL EUROPEAN FACTORIES—*Continued*

Potsdam	*"Potsdam" —1740* *P* with an *R* beneath it for (Potsdam-Rewendt)	c1740—*Christian Friedrich Rewendt* 1768—His sons, *Friedrich Wilhelm* and *Johann Christian Rewendt* inherited. 1770—*Johann* was full proprietor. 1775—bankrupt, and *Sartory* took over factory 1790—sold to wife of *General von Linckersdorff* 1790—*Sartory* founded a new factory 1800—sold to *Gottfried B. von Eckardstein.*	Most excellent imitations of *Delft* (were actually thought to be *Delft* for many years) but with a special character of their own. *O. Riesebieter* on the evidence of the one vase at Berlin in the *Schlossmuseum* marked "*Potsdam—1740*" set aside in 1912 a group that had been called *Delft*, with the following characteristics: Strongly reddish-toned body, shapes are ribbed or fluted inverted pear shapes with flaring feet and are more narrow than the corresponding *Delft* wares and finally a special decoration from *Delft* but differing and more constantly used is the peacock among Chinese flowers, with also a band of spirals such as we see on some *Ming* porcelain of the *Wan Li sur biscuit* type. The colors are intense blue alone and the high-temperature colors:—yellow, green, iron-red, along with a few in seagreen ground and some in cold lacquer colors.
Danzig	No marks	1658—There is mention of glazed wares made there. 18th century had several factories but wares are not differentiated.	Partly blue and white and partly polychrome and some are plastic but all are crude and, as Hannover says, "boorish." The stoves are better and the tiles for them have raised in relief like frames.
Königsberg	Stamped *HE* for "Hofrath Ehrenreich" The "*Hofrath*" is a title bestowed on him in *Sweden*. Also dated with day, month and year and has painter mark. "English" wares stamped with a K, sometimes several times. "factory of the *Brothers Collin*"	1776—*Johann Eberhard Ludwig Ehrenreich,* after having gone broke at *Straslund*. 1788—Sold to *Provinzial-Controller, Buvey* at auction. Changed owners several times and about 1808 *Ehrenreich* died at 80 and the factory ended in 1810. 1776—Another factory was started by *Paul Heinrich Collin* and his brother. c 1786	Blue is the leading color and only a sparing use of manganese. The decoration is all of "German" flowers; no Chinese. The glaze is greyish or grey-blue in cast. The blue is intense. Later "English" wares. All its efforts were directed to the imitating of *Wedgwood*. (See large brown vase in the *Prussian Museum at Königsberg*) Portrait medallions of black "basalt" ware and white in *Berlin Museum*.
Zerbst Duchy of Anhalt	*Z* in combination with other letters. *La* or *J.C.La* is for the painter	1721—*Johann Caspar Ripp* of *Nuremberg* fame, *Ansbach* and *Frankfort* as well as	Blue and white and high-fired polychrome colors and too various to bring out any characteristics.

CHART OF GERMAN AND CENTRAL EUROPEAN FACTORIES—*Continued*

	Johann Christian Langendorf	*Hanau* and *Bruns-wick.* Closed in 1861 (See *Stieda's* history)	A greyish-green color apparently painted over a bluish foundation, the use of yellow in combination with red, which is rare in north German wares, the use of applied and painted flowers with a flower acting as knob for tureen covers—are typical. Later did the usual lead-glazed wares.
Bernburg Anhalt	"*Bernburg*—1725 *Freytag*" *VF* monogram for *Victor Friedrich prince of Anhalt-Bernburg* from 1721	There must have been a factory in the early 18th century but we have, as yet, so little data that no history is possible.	Set of three vases of *Delft* shape and painted with Chinese designs in blue and manganese with the middle piece bearing the mark opposite. (See *Sauerlandt* report.) A plate in *Halle* and a foot warmer in the castle of *Dessau* marked VF. Also other wares such as the oval dish in *Hamburg* with blue and white foliated scrollwork or *Laub-und Bandelwerk.*
Magdeburg	"*J. P. Guichard*"	Not known	"English" earthenware with or without the name mark and a white glazed portrait medallion in the Berlin Museum.
Mecklenburg		There were places which are still not known. (See *F. Schlie*)	Renaissance period glazed stoves and unglazed architectural pieces 18th century wares unidentified.
Schwerin	*Z-like sign* and *A Sverin* with *K* below also *A.S.-K.*	c1760—*Appelstädt* founded and later it came to his son-in-law, *Malon,* and exists even today.	At the *Schwerin Museum* there is a collection including "tureens after pewter models," and that is about all we know. (See *Brinck-mann*)
Brunswick		1707—*Duke Anton Ulrich* with *Johann Philipp Franz* from *Saxony* as mgr. 1711—*Heinrich Christoph von Horn* and his partner *Werner Julius Günther von Hantelmann.* Then changed hands repeatedly. 1744–1749—two brothers, *Heinrich Werner* and *Christoph Friedrich Ludwig von Hantelmann.*	Began with blue and white but soon developed several colors.
	VH for von Hantelmann		Took up plastic work, modeled and colored fruit, asparagus, melon, grapes, etc., tureens and others in shape of birds on dishes amongst fruit.
	R & B *J.E.B.* *I.H.R.*	1749–1756 *Johann Erich Behling* and *Johann Heinrich Reichardt* 1756–1773—*Duke of Brunswick* 1773—let to *Johann*	At *Hamburg* a plate after *Nuremberg* with a basket of fruit and ornamental designs on rim in vivid blue, dark manganese and lemon-yellow, green and brick-red.

CHART OF GERMAN AND CENTRAL EUROPEAN FACTORIES—*Continued*

	J.B.R.	*Benjamin Rabe* who bought it in 1776. 1803 *Rabe* died and it came to an end.	
	Two *C's* crossed like those of *Ludwigsburg* and the *Comte de Custine*	1745—Another factory by—*Rudolf Anton Chely* till 1756.	Vegetable and animal tureens as above
Hanover at Wrisbergholzen	*WR* in monogram with painter's marks of *letters* or *numerals*	1737—*Vielstich* probably a relative of *Johann Christoph Vielstich* c1800—*L. V. Gerverot* who was for many years d rector of *Fürstenberg,* the porcelain factory. Lasted until about 1830.	*Kestner Museum at Hanover* —a large octagonal covered vase in Chinese-Dutch style with flowers in bluish-violet, —also a blue and white globular vase on high stand painted in similar manner. Combinations of blue, manganese, yellow and green were used. Also certain porphyry-colored tankards with panels reserved in blue. No muffle-kiln colors were used.
Münden	*M* or three *crescents* taken from the arms of *von Hanstein* and painter's marks	1746—Grew out of early pipe and pottery factory of *Carl Friedrich von Hanstein* 1775—Moved nearer to town and was inherited by his son *Johann Carl Friedrich von Hanstein,* and was soon extended for manufacture of the "English" ware.	*Faïence* with pierced decoration having double walls, the outer being perforated in the case of vases or other vessels and the rims of the plates being perforated. At the point of intersection of the mesh is usually a forget-me-not or other small flower in slight relief and colored. Manganese-purple and a dull green are more conspicuous than the blue, which, however, is sometimes used alone. There is also a yellow and all colors are high-fired; no muffle-kiln colors were ever used. Also wares in green and purple alone painted with landscapes or flowers in *Meissen* style. Plain white stones and also ones with gallant scenes in blue.
Aumund north-west of *Bremen*	*M.T.T.* D. & W.T. *A v E*	1751—Three merchants *Johann Christoph Mülhausen,* and *Diederich* and *Wilhelm Terhellen,* organized it with *Johann Christoph Vielstich* as mgr. 1757—bankrupt and sold to *Albrecht von Erberfeldt* who got a *Strasburger* mgr. and workmen from *Swabia*	A melon in natural colors marked M.T.T. *at Hamburg.* (Ill.) Blue and white tureen at *Kunstgewerbemuseum, Bremen* marked D. & W.T. (For *D. & W. Terhellen,* after the death of *Mülhausen* in 1775) Also a polychrome tankard in the same museum with Chinese figures, which has A v E (for *Albrecht von Erberfeld*)

CHART OF GERMAN AND CENTRAL EUROPEAN FACTORIES—*Continued*

Lesum	*V* or *Vi* The painters marked the wares "putting a stroke under the name of their employer and the first letter of their own name under the stroke," as Hannover says.	1752—*Johann Christoph Vielstich* after working one year at *Aumund* settled at *Lesum* until he died in 1792.	Tureen with flower sticking up on cover similar to the way they were made at *Zerbst* (mentioned above) and painted with a shield of arms in blue, at *Hamburg Mus.* Tops of tea-tables, ink-stands, *potpourri*, vases, melon-shaped boxes, fruit baskets, wall and stove. tiles, etc., according to *Brinckmann,* the last brown and black as well as marbled and blue-and-white. In the *Vestlandske Kunstindustrimuseum* at *Bergen* is a stag lying down, in manganese on green grass. At *Bremen* is a similar hound and also some tankards sprayed with manganese and with galloping horses and flowers in reserve,—ink-pots painted with flowers and a pierced basket with stand, but far better than these are the blue and white stove and some tiles in purple and green with *Hamburg* influence. (Ill. several and stove) The body is reddish, its glaze usually yellowish or bluish but infrequently pure white. The colors are blue, an insipid bluish green, several yellow shades, and—*no red.*
Jever	*Jev* or *Jever*	1760—Our old rambling acquaintance, *Tännich* turned up here and started a factory that had a difficult existence and lasted until 1776. *Sebastien Heinrich Kirch* who had worked at the *Chely* factory at *Brunswick* is, according to the authority *Riesebieter,* the sculptor.	A very few high class works such as the blue and white center piece of a boy with a basket on his head from the *Reisebieter Collection, Oldenberg.* Butter-dishes in the shape of swans and heavy tureens with freely modeled flowers and foliage show *Brunswick* and *Zerbst* influences.

There are perhaps a dozen other unimportant factories for which Graesse gives more or less well founded marks but their wares are very few and not distinguished.

It is strange upon reflection that we have found a strong Near Eastern influence and Indian influence in the faïence factories and that none of this was reflected in the porcelain of the day. Also the authorities became so absorbed in the correcting of the wrong habit of calling Chinese design "Indian" that they completely overlooked the fact that there really was Indian design in use. In fact the dilettante decorators of the 19th and 20th centuries have forgotten, or never heard of any Indian design in the 18th century in Europe at all.

Though it may be said that on the whole the workmanship in faïence wa} not so perfect as that in porcelain yet it must be said that the taste shown by the faïence potters or their common customers was superior to that shown in porcelain. There was a more reasonable approach and the medium was better expressed. The limited number of colors obtained brought about a natural harmony or at least safety of color scheme. Many of the factories never used muffle-kiln colors which broadened the palette but often brought unpleasant effects. Then again there were fewer forgeries because faïence did not as a rule command such high prices. The art of faïence did not wholly escape the attentions of the forgers, however, for Fleischmann of Nuremberg copied Hanau, Nuremberg, Frankfort and Bayreuth but his work is so cheap and badly made that it could not fool anyone who had seen the originals.

SWITZERLAND

The Swiss wares offer little but reflections from those of Italy and the other large surrounding countries. Most of the early work was in the form of stoves at such places as Winterthur where the Pfau, Ehrhart, Graf, Volger and Sulzer families worked into the early part of the 18th century. Other

centers were Stechborn, where Daniel Meier worked, Zurich and Berne, where Emmanuel Jean Früting (1745–1798) made blue landscape tiles and polychrome flowered ones. Probably other wares were made at these places but not many have been set aside. They were smoky in tone and had subdued colors though some had charm and delicacy. The factories at Beromünster and Lenzburg made household wares. At the former Andreas Dolder started at the end of the 18th century while at Lenzburg one factory was started in 1763 by A. H. and H. C. Klug and another later by Hans Jacob Frey. Most unmarked Swiss faïence is attributed not entirely correctly to one or the other of these factories unless it is the "Winterthur" type in which case it may not have come from that place either. This type consists of plates with broad rims decorated with arabesques in blue or with large flowers or fruits in colors or left plain, while the center has a shield of arms. The colors are high temperature ones only.

FIG. 1172. Swiss stove of 17th cent. decorated in blue, red and yellow, from mansion of Col. Von Sprecher Maienfeld. Ht. c. 8'. International Studio Art Corp.

Zurich wares are not easily identified unless marked Z. Both porcelain and faïence were made at the same factory and by the same workmen. The factory was not in the city but at Schorn near Bendikon. It was founded in 1763 and lasted until 1766. The poet and painter Salomon Gessner lost most of his fortune in the venture. The technical director was Adam Spengler, the same who discovered a way of printing pictures on porcelain after the English invention. After the initial failure the company dragged along into the usual decline and making of common "steingut," or lead-glazed white earthenware.

Swiss stove of 18th cent., decorated in blue on white. Made for a Basel Bishop in 1722. Ht. 4′ 5¼″.
International Studio Art Corp.

SWISS FAÏENCE STOVE (1722)

PLATE 205

AUSTRIAN TERRITORIES

The central location of the Austrian territories made them naturally absorb the various impulses. Wares from Italy, Nuremberg and other South German places, and even those of Delft had a stimulating effect on the peasant wares. There was nothing exclusive about them for most were turned out by the gross and peddled by the "Haussirer" and sold at country fairs but they were individual pieces instead of sets and made to commemorate some occasion such as a wedding, baptism or birthday and many had inscriptions and mottos. These were made at Graz, Gmunden and Salzburg among many other places in the Alpine districts. They were also extensively turned out in Moravia and Hungary. These peasant wares of Slovak or non-Slovak sorts with their simple flower ornament in enamel-like colors of yellow, green, blue and purple, even in the 19th century had more life and interest than those wares done for the Imperial and Royal Austro-Hungarian nobility at the "Majolika-Geschirrfabrik" at Holitsch.

This peasant ware is commonly known as "Habaner ware." I have been unable to obtain pictures of it for this book but the principle of alternation is well understood, the spacing is original and effective, the drawing is swift and direct as though the design had been well thought out in advance. These plates change their tempo much as does the Tzigane music and after the commercially choked stupidity of many of the better known wares they bring a joyous life that moves us and is lost like the music itself for they existed only from about 1635 into the early 19th century and had little after effect. They were started by Anabaptists who settled in the 16th century on the border between Moravia and Hungary and had with them potters who at first seemed influenced by the "Winterthur" wares of Switzerland.

The "Majolika-Geschirrfabrik" was at Holitsch near Göding straight north of Pressburg. The factory was founded in 1743 by Francis of Lorraine, consort of Maria Theresa. The wares were strongly influenced by those of France probably because Nicolas Germain, the foreman, had come from there. In 1750 Charles François Leduc was director and between 1756 and 1760 they even called the wares by such names as, "Strasburg salad-bowls," "Strasburg tankards," etc. But the factory also obtained models from Vienna and some plates are in the style of Castelli and show that the factory also kept its eyes open to the south. It imitated Meissen, Rouen, Nevers, Niderviller, Marseilles, Moustiers and Montpellier as well as Chinese and Japanese wares. Also many of its things were copied from Proskau as they were in turn copied there from workmen who had left the Hungarian factory.

In general the wares are decorated in both high-fired and muffle-kiln colors, the body is red and fine grained but otherwise there is no distinguishing characteristics unless it be the mark, which is generally HF standing for "Holitscher Fabrik." The H also occurs alone or accompanied by another H, a P, etc. Generally the mark is in clear blue but it was made also in manganese and rarely in light green.

The tureens in the form of birds are best known but these were copies as all else. From about 1786 the factory made "English ware" stamped

"Holitsch," and in 1827 it closed. Fakes of even these uninteresting wares were made and marked H.

POLAND

PROSKAU FIRST PERIOD (1763–1769)

With the help of workmen from Holitsch, Count Leopold von Proskau started a factory in 1763, in the village of Proskau near Oppeln, southeast of Breslau. The first wares are closely like those of Paul and Joseph Hannong of Strasburg and are painted in muffle-kiln colors in large flowers, especially carnations, in strong and heavy colors including sulphur-yellow, crimson and lifeless pale green. Another type seems to have copied porcelain with plastic flowers. The first period came to an end when the count fell dead in a duel in 1769 and the estate came to Johann Carl von Dietrichstein, who was an excellent patron. The mark of the first period was a P in baroque style.

PROSKAU SECOND PERIOD (1769–1783)

The second or "Dietrichstein Period" is strongly plastic in its flowers for decoration of vessels and its figures, of allegorical, mythological and such subjects. Many animal, bird and vegetable tureens were made as well as dishes in the form of leaves and candlesticks like trees. The colors are much as before except that the yellow is subdued and the yellow-green becomes dark green. The red becomes duller and duller until in 1780 it is a reddish-brown. The blue also became less and less conspicuous until it finally is lost entirely. The mark is D P in manganese brown or dark grey-blue.

PROSKAU THIRD PERIOD (1783–1788)

In 1783 the count sold the estate to Frederick the Great of Prussia having transferred his own undertaking to Weisskirchen, Moravia. Frederick appointed Johann Gottlieb Leopold, the district councillor who in 1786 took the factory on lease. The wares are now changed, being only useful things decorated in monochrome, chiefly pink. Some colored wares were made but they were dull in color and dry of design. They are all marked with P in manganese brown or blue.

PROSKAU FOURTH PERIOD (1788–1850)

English models in white, red or black clay, the latter without glaze were now made. The classic Empire was taken so seriously that real Greek vases were closely copied in 1793 under the direction of Prof. Bach of Breslau. In 1796 transfer printing was introduced and the plates were supplied chiefly by Degotschon and Endler whose names are sometimes seen on the wares. Brown-glazed ware decorated in silver, or plain in the style of Bayreuth was also made but not marked. Perhaps it was not a stock product. All the late "steingut" is impressed with "Proskau."

About the only partly original thing that the factory was noted for was the heaping of vegetables, fruits or flowers on pieces in the second period.

This went so far that on one egg-shaped tureen in Copenhagen, with fruit and flowers on it, a bunch of grapes is at one end and divided also so as to form a bowl and receptacle attached. Another idea was shown in a vase which was kept fairly plain but the cover is smothered under a large bouquet of flowers.

The Belvedere factory produced a service in 1776 which King Stanislaus Augustus Poniatowski sent in 1789 with a special mission to the Turkish Sultan. This is decorated in enamel colors and gold and inscribed in Turkish, "These gifts are sent to the Tsar of the race of Osman by the King of the Lekhs in proof of his most complete affection and utter devotion—in the capital of Warsaw." In Hamburg there is also a pair of covered "temple jar" vases with flowers and rocks in something like the Chinese manner. They also have bright colors. In Berlin is another vase with famille verte bird, rock and tree designs on a yellow ground in reserved medallions. Others are known with freely modeled flowers of Marieberg and Chinese "hawthorn" patterns.

One other factory of note was erected at Telechany by Michael Oginski toward the end of the 18th century. From there come vases with exotic rams' heads and human faces in relief. Also at Warsaw was another factory erected by a Saxon named Wolff in 1775 which copied Chinese vases in Delft style decorated with birds, flowers, etc., in blue. The Belvedere factory mark is B or "B-Varsovie" over the glaze. The "Fabryka Wolfa" used W alone. The Telechany wares are generally marked CO for Comte Oginski in dark brown.

A number of insignificant places made the "English ware" toward the end of the century.

RUSSIA

Peter the Great engaged potters while he was at Zaandam and installed them in Petersburg. The museums so far as I can find made no classifications of the early wares but Hannover says he visited there in 1913 and he describes stoves as follows, "Enormous and often magnificent flat faïence stoves, painted in some cases with flowers in colors, in others entirely in manganese with a figure enclosed by ornament on each tile, in others again with figures in manganese within ornamental framework in copper green; some of them are blue-and-white in the manner of Hamburg stoves, and some of the Empire period entirely white with a figure standing free between two columns." He continues, "Some of the blue-and-white examples are perhaps to be attributed to Hamburg potters, others to Dutchmen," but this is only a guess on his part, of course.

Also at Petersburg there was a factory which made cheap household wares.

At Reval was a factory at least as old as 1773 for it is mentioned in the "Connaissances politiques" of Beausobre, though Von Manteuffel dates it 1780. The marks are R with an F below it, or Re-Fi, or Reval-Fick (for Carl Christian Fick who had studied pharmacy at Keil and practiced in Stockholm). He settled about 1765 in Reval taking over a chemist's business and later started the pottery factory. Most of the output extant is in the possession of the Fick family with a few in the Esthonian Museum at Reval and some in Petersburg and Riga. The pieces are of richly developed rococo much like those of north Germany of this time and earlier. They are in green and yellow with natural flowers in colors similar to Marieberg and Stralsund. There are also "network" wares like those of Münden, and animal, human figure and fruit and vegetable boxes of a sort of Dutch type. The most remarkable and unforeseen development is that they also made "Toby-jugs" after the English ones.

DENMARK

In Store Kongensgade, Copenhagen, the Delfs Porselins eller Hollandich Steentøys Fabrique was established in 1722, with as manager Johann Wolff, a painter from Nuremberg, but he was dismissed in 1723 and went to Stockholm. In 1727 Johan Ernst Pfau became manager and stayed until 1749. The brewer, Christian Gierløf became owner in this time and there was a suit between him and Pfau in 1752 when the latter died. Other suits seem to have taken place between this place and Kastrup and also Østerbro established by Peter Hofnagel. In 1772 or 1773 the factory began to feel the competition from England but stuck to its blue and white wares to the end. These are high fired, buff and coarse of body. The glaze is white and only occasionally tinged with greyish-blue. It has pin holes like Delft which it most resembles and at times appears to have been "gekwaartet" like that ware. The blue is strong and clear but broken into minute specks. All drawing was done in blue. The general mark appears to be VP with at times a dot over the P, between the letters or over the down stroke of the V. Hannover suggests it should be read JP for Johan Pfau but it was also used after his time.

FIRST STORE KONGENSGADE PERIOD (1722–1727)

In Copenhagen is a beaker of vaguely Chinese feeling marked "Copenhagen J W" with the crown and cipher of Frederick IV of Denmark in the decoration. The reserved acanthus leaves, spirals, festoons of flowers and flower filled lambrequins are all typical Copenhagen in design. A similar piece shows the chequer pattern after Rouen and a Chinese emblem of four parts within a circle which also became a stock pattern of the factory. A plate marked "W-Kopenhagen-Anno 1726" has the so-called "parsley pattern." The W does not stand for Wolff but for Peter Wartberg who controlled the place after Wolff left.

SECOND STORE KONGENSGADE PERIOD (1727–c1750)

Wolff undoubtedly provided many of the designs of Nuremberg origin used by Pfau such as the basket full of flowers for plate centers. An amusing little piece of rather ingenious workmanship is a spice cabinet having four drawers and decorated in blue flowers. It is signed J. F. Pfau and dated 1737. Stars and dots were used after the Delft notion between flying birds, flowers and in the "parsley pattern." There are numbers running from 3 to 119 but their meaning is not known. Some pieces have freemasonry em-

blems for decoration and are dated 1747. Other "royal plates" or "Konge-
tallerkener" sometimes have the monogram of Christian VI and are decorated with well painted lambrequins while those with the cipher of Frederick
V are not so good perhaps indicating a decline. A rectangular tray and single
candle wall sconce are dated by Hannover as of 1730. Both have Chinese
influence. The baroque and rococo motives are to be seen on the "bishop
bowls," etc. Figures and general modeling were badly done and avoided.
The "bishop bowls" were in the shape of a bishop's mitre with a design of
a drinking party on them and served a derisive purpose as well as being
useful, as—"who should not put a cabbage in a bishop's hat or fill it up with
Koldskaal?" The Roman Catholic church had abused its power and misused
its riches and after Luther's time and the last defenses of Helgesen, it had
fallen into disrepute.

An often used motif was that of the arms of noble families.

THE THIRD OR GIERLØF PERIOD (c 1750)

At just about the time that Gierløf came in 1750 there was a change to
rococo style. Asbjorn was one of the chief artists as was also M. Momtoft.
The new style was used chiefly on trays and not at all on the rococo modeled
tureens. Some designs were also like those of the Japanese artist Korin
consisting of large flowers drawn in the flat and well spaced, with the use
of reeds and bamboo in the background to give slightly curved perpendicular
lines in contrast to the rounded masses. Where Gierløf got this design we
do not know but to say, as Ch. A. Been and Hannover do, that it is "merely
a modification of the peonies, lotus and bamboo of Chinese porcelain," is
not true for it is too well organized to have occurred in so immediate an
application and is so close to the Japanese solution of the problem, arrived at
over a period of years, that it would be a miracle if two so widely different
people attained so close a result.

Craftsmanship fell off but the design was more broad and direct. Hannover scorns it somewhat in his description of a plate in Copenhagen, saying,
"Even in the simplest among them, such as the plates painted with three
pears or apples lying down or in the air, the slapdash manner of the brushwork may often be combined with a lively sense of the decorative effect of
the great, broad strokes." Little did he know what we would become used
to after Picasso! But whatever the likes and dislikes are concerning this
technique, it was new to Europe and I believe it came somehow from Japan.
In Seto since the early 13th century had been kilns turning out "Ishizara"
or kitchen ware which is used all over Japan. An article in the *Eastern Art
Annual*, Vol. III, p. 45 by M. Yanagi describes this ware and illustrates some
pieces which strongly resemble the Store Kongensgade pieces. He says,
"The date when these plates were made is not yet known precisely, but it is
fairly certain that they were of late Tokugawa period, that is from the end
of the 18th century to the beginning of the 19th." Later he says, "A Seto
potter told me that 300 such plates can be made on a wheel within a day
by one person, and more than that number can be painted."—"The kilns
are built densely along the slope of the surrounding hills like labyrinths and

their chimneys in great number stand like a forest. The sky is always black with smoke and the river is always white with clay. Even now from this old pottery town an immense number of wares are distributed all over our country." This is a little like the Chinese description of Cheng-tê Ching but probably a fair report, and some of these plates must have found their way into Gierløf's hands, just as Imari found its way to other parts of Europe.

We learn that the glaze became dull and that experimental use of the sponge was made, to give the texture of foliage. This too is a Japanese stunt.

It was thought that all of the Store Kongensgade wares were decorated in blue until the Hamburg Museum found an ink-well of the Pfau period (1727–49) with high fired colors bearing the mark and of unmistakable style. The colors are two shades of yellow, greyish-green, manganese brown and blue. In Copenhagen is also a tankard with the mark and a Japanese painting in yellow, blue, green and iron-red reserved in a white ground on a manganese background.

HP is a usual mark perhaps referring to the son, Johan Heinrik Pfau. B, C or H also occur. Note our reference to marks under each period. Pieces have brought as much as $250 or $300 but these wares are not so high class as the wares of Rörstrand, Marieberg or the Norwegian faïence of Herrebøe.

Osterbro Factory

Peter Hofnagel established a factory in 1763 at Sortedamssø, now called the Østerbro factory. He was the Norwegian founder of the Herrebøe factory and some of his workmen came from Store Kongensgade and Kastrup, including his manager, Heinrich Wolff (not to be confused with Johann Wolff). A series of law suits with Gierløf wasted much of the substance of both places, though the final decision was in Hofnagel's favor, and he had to close down for lack of money. His advertisements show that he made all kinds of wares including blue-and-white until 1765 despite Gierløf's claim to have the sole rights to make them. At this time he turned to manganese purple and later he included blue decorations again, but it is almost impossible to identify his wares. Thor Kielland has brought together some pieces marked Ø:B:F interpreted as meaning Øster Bro Fabrik by J. Olrik, and one, a tureen with manganese flowers marked Hasrisz and IH in the cover and on the stand. This name also occurs on a rococo candlestick and blue-and-white dish among other pieces. The tureen is like wares from Sleswick and Hofnagel did advertise "tureens after the Sleswick fashion with embossed stand." The clay is grey or greyish-yellow and the glaze closely "smutted" without tendency to craze.

Kastrup Factory

Jacob Fortling erected a factory in Kastrup on the island of Amager between 1749 and 1754. He was the court architect and was given permission to make every sort of ware except the "so-called Delft porcelain or Dutch stoneware which Christian Gierløf and his associates alone are permitted to

make." As Fortling wanted to copy the wares of the Westerwald, three pot-
ters were brought from Coblenz and Joseph Adam Hannong was called from
Strasburg to supervise the building of the factory, but Fortling found him
"unyttig" or useless and appointed Heinrich Wolff, who later went to
Østerbro, as manager. Frederick V was sponsor and he appointed Johann
George Richter to keep Strasburg spirit alive.

In 1761 Fortling died and his widow carried on for a year and then sold
out to Jacob Stentzler and Jes Diedrichsen, who kept Richter on as art
director. As late as 1772 it had two kilns, one for faïence and one for stoneware, and set about building another for "English ware" but in 1776 Stentzler
died. In 1777 a creditor of Diedrichsen sold the factory to Christian Detlew
Westerholdt who took in as partner N. C. Høpffner. From this time the
place became entirely commercial. In 1781 Jacob Casper Leopold Mantzius
took a lease and tried to revive the faïence but he died in 1794.

The Fortling mark was F and the wares are naturally much like those of
Strasburg on a greyish-buff almost white body not so highly fired as the Store
Kongensgade. The glaze is thick and reddish or bluish-grey tinged and often
full of "pin pricks" and other flaws and is sometimes crazed. The red is dull;
the blue-green uneven and inclined to volatilize and settle on the white glaze;
an aquamarine seems to be of similar composition; and the yellow and other
colors are about as usual. Butter dishes in the form of an artichoke on a
saucer are in a deep blue as are also the leaves veined in black with the
floral painting. Large full blown roses and yellow parrot tulips are favorite
rococo designs, as are also pansies, honey-suckle and fanciful strewn flowers.
Tiles were also made with good figure painting. Large baroque vases surmounted by figures too big to be regarded simply as finials show good modeling. Many of the usual birds were made and there are two fine busts after
models by Saly, of Christian VI and Frederick V.

Hannover points out that the wares known as the "watchstand group" and
little dishes with high-fired colors also attributed by Frohne to this factory
do not belong here.

A price list of 1784 tells us that wares similar to "English ware" were
being made and stamped with an oval stamp with the letters CW and M
for Christian Westerholdt—and Mantzius. Many plates have fine perforated
rims with little flowers at the crossings of the strands. Slight relief was also
practiced.

The lesser Danish factories are given in the following chart:

LESSER DANISH FACTORIES

Hestkiøbgaard near *Birkerød*	1807—*Dybvad* founded as a contin-uation of the factory at the *Vesterbro,* in *Copenhagen,* which was destroyed by the English in that year. Closed about 1819	Stoves ?
Antvorskov near *Slagelse*	c 1810—*Haagen Christian von Astrup* Closed about 1820	We read that its sales were "endless" in 1812 *Faïence* ———— ?

LESSER DANISH FACTORIES—*Continued*

Søholm	*"Søholm"*	1826—A company started	Bowls with roulette-impressed borders in brown glazed, yellow glazed and in glazed red earthenware to be seen at the *Royal Porcelain Factory, Copenhagen.*
Farm of Hesbjerg west of *Odense*		1810—*A C. de Heinen,* who was *Chamberlain.*	None yet identified.
Mors	Plate is marked L and AM below	1774—*Thomas Lund* 1779—*Saxo Aschanius* and *Hans Meulengracht.*	*Frohne* illustrates a plate dated 1782 and inscribed with the name of the owner within a leaf wreath and a tea-pot with poor flower decoration. Both are in blue
Gudumlund nine miles south-east of *Aalborg*	A bee impressed usually with a number 1, 2 or 3. From 1808 three brown spots or a bee. Later no mark.	c1805—*Count Schimmelmann* established various industries which included a *faïence* factory which lasted until 1820.	Clay and its manager came from *Bornholm* and workers from Germany. It was very unskillful. Part simple *faïence* and part cream-colored earthenware like that of the English. Slight scattered flower, etc., and all in defective high temperature colors. The later unmarked wares are hardly distinguishable from those of the English.
Øland Island in the *Limfjord*	*Øland—E. Beck* 1818—B written and incised within a circle *Øland—B*	1814—*Eskild Beck,* from *Bornholm* and mgr. of *Gudumlund*	Ink-stand painted in blue and green with the name of the owner *"Ole Jensen Rønne—1819"* at the *Dansk Folkemuseum,* also two plates with crowned initials and the date 1820 within a wreath of flowers and another with a flower in the middle in purple, yellow, green and blue. Two are unglazed on the back. The clay is grey. Four pieces at the *Kunstindustrimuseum* are marked *"Øland—B"* and have slight blue patterns.
Bornholm Island, Rønne	*"Spietz"* impressed on body Not usually marked	*James Davenport* came in 1789 to dig coal there but failed and started a limeworks and brickworks and pipe and *faïence* factory. All failed. *Johan Spietz,* a German set up an earthenware factory on his own at *Rønne*	Pretty cream colored inkstands sometimes picked out in green or blue see *Dansk Folkemuseum, Copenhagen.*
Sleswick	SO with L below (for *Slesvig Otte* and *Lücke*) in monogram	1755—*Ludwig von Lücke* but had to give up because of "Thoughtlessness, folly and lack of good conduct." 1758—*Johan Rambusch* became sole proprietor 1773—His son *Friederich Vollrath Rambusch* inherited.	Predominant use of manganese purple and plastic usage. The clay is pale buff almost white and the glaze is discolored almost to a grey. One small group of wares with Chinese plant ornaments after the *Meissen* style is thin and light but most of the other wares are thick and heavy.

LESSER DANISH FACTORIES—*Continued*

SO with S below and R (for Rambusch) below that.

S alone and often left unmarked.

Lohmann was one of the figure painters who signed a "bishop bowl" in the *Dansk Folkemuseum.* *Meyer* is another who signed a rococo dish in the *Frohne Collection* with flower decoration.

One of the marked pieces is a relief decorated rococo tureen with the design picked out in manganese and a knob of strange twisted form, a helical round pyramid.

The factory also did "bishop bowls" as is proven by the one in *Hamburg* bearing the mark.

Another quaint conception is a punch-bowl in the form of a warship resting on rococo volutes, picked out in manganese and having scattered flowers in blue (at the same museum).

In the *Rambusch* period a grey green of either bluish or yellowish cast became a favorite color, also mufflecolors for *Meissen* type flowers came into use, but the grey green was high-fired and generally occurs with a manganese outline. There is also a slight resemblance to *Moustiers* wares, *Brinckmann* has observed. There was also a pure yellow-green of lower temperature but often used with manganese and this combination occurs on a "bishop bowl" in the *Folkemuseum* with figures and trees the trunks of which are in manganese and the foliage in the green.

There is one tray known in the Louis XVI style painted in yellow, green, blue, violet and black, and which must have been made between 1775–80.

Criseby later transferred to *Eckernförde* in 1764

C with L or AL in a monogram and also an E added.

1758—*Johann Nicolai Otte,* having sold his portion of the *Sleswick* factory to *Rambusch* when his two brothers did, set up on his own account.

1764—Transferred to *Eckernförde,* and came to a syndicate but in

1771—returned to *Otte*

Had modeller *Johann Buchwald* and painter *Abraham Leihamer,* who left c.1769.

O (for *Otte)* and E *(Eckernförde)* with B below (for *Buchwald)* and AL or L (for *Leihamer)* or other painter's marks below

A delicately painted plate in manganese is signed by both artists and *Otte* and dated 1761 (in *Hamburg)* as is a dish painted delicately in blue and two rococo candlesticks in the *Folkemuseum* and the *Kunstindustrimuseum.*

Many imitations of foreign models, for *Buchwald* had been to *Holitsch, Hungary, Rörstrand* and *Marieberg.* Later he went to *Kiel* and *Stockelsdorff.* Boar's head, cabbage, etc., tureens in the *Holitsch* manner, muffle-kiln colors and freely modelled blossoming sprays in the *Marieberg* manner and blue painting of all the others, were favorites, and a powerful blue is characteristic just as manganese is at *Sleswick.*

One small group has blue painted flowers with manga-

LESSER DANISH FACTORIES—*Continued*

again and numerals (66, 67 or 68) designating the year below again is the full mark but it also occurs in various parts.

All pieces signed AL or L may have been supervised by Leihamer but not necessarily painted by him. Sometimes his full name is signed and these are probably his own handiwork.

nese over them. These are thought to include certain watchstands that might otherwise be from *Kastrup* with the same color combination. (See *Nationalhistoriske Museum*, at *Frederiksborg*.)

Hannover says, "the motives of decoration on *Eckernförde* faïence are about as many as the wares themselves." Had both high and low temperature colors.

The clay is higher fired than Sleswick and is warm grey with very slight greenish or reddish tone and the glaze clean white with only a slight tendency to craze.

Leihamer painted flowers, figures and also landscapes.

Also *Jahn Zopff* probably from Meissen was a good flower painter.

A restless rococo movement was characteristic, a spray with full blown rose is often used and a snail or butterfly among the flowers on blue and white plates is favorite.

Also occasionally plain white faïence.

Flensborg	c1764—Developed from an earlier tile works	Large garden-vases of heavy body with coarsely painted garlands in the style of *Rouen* are thought by *Brinckmann* to come from here but *Dr. Sauermann* claims that there is no supporting evidence.
Holstein Kiel	The mark was a 3 storeys mark: K on top, T *(Tännich)* below and some painter such as P below. The others were A, R, M, and B for flowers. P did figures.	1758—*Peter Grafe* later became a ducal possession and was placed under *Tännich* 1766—Sold to two *Hamburg* business men *Reimers* and *Neumann* who let *Tännich* go and appointed *Buchwald* and *Leihamer*. 1769—Came to *C. J. Richardi* and both artists went to *Stockelsdorff* 1793 or earlier ceased. In the *Tännich* period there were also numerals such as # 1 and # 5	Low-fired, soft, pale buff, nearly white with faint reddish cast body, with glaze smooth and cold white but uneven and may vary from a bluish to reddish tone on same piece. It often has small holes which fill with dirt and show black but no crazing and many of the best pieces are quite perfect. Muffle-painting was favored and though not quite so good as some French factories, it is better than most German ones. Not so fine as Sceaux and *Marseilles* but bold and decorative. *Kiel* dishes always have the wavy edge of the rococo period and are edged with brown.

LESSER DANISH FACTORIES—*Continued*

In *Buchwald* period a B replaces the T.

One tea-tray has on it, *"Abr. Leihamer fecit, 1769—Buchwald Directeur—Kiel."* (See *Hamburg*) Only infrequently did *Leihamer* sign with full name. At *Hamburg* is also a fine *"Potpourri-vase"* by him.

Tännich developed a *"Potpourri-vase"* called "lavender-jar" which seems to be a new form consisting of an ovoid body on concave foot with flaring base, the body cut flat across the top to form a wide, squat concave neck and the cover is tall with concave sides and dome top surmounted by freely modeled plant forms or flowers often oak or cherry branches. The cover is perforated in six or eight holes to allow the fragrance of flowers placed inside to escape. The decoration is of flowers, landscapes or less often of small cupids (See *Kunstindustrimuseum*) (Also *Dansk Folkemuseum* also *Hamburg*)

During *Buchwald* times blue was freely used but *Tännich* seems to have scorned its use.

There is only one plate known with a Chinese figure on it, but many figures from everyday life were used in landscapes also from the immediate surroundings.

In *Hamburg* is one plate with Chinese flowers but that is the only one known; and copying was not so prevalent as elsewhere.

The gilding is handled with taste.

Beautiful wall cisterns with bowls below were made and are among the finest productions of the whole North. They are in natural colors of the fine flower painting and sometimes edged with blue. The modelling is the best of the rococo period. (See *Hamburg, Kunstindustri* and other museums.)

The *potpourri* vase by *Leihamer* has a landscape from an etching by *J. de Vischer* after *van Goyen*, as *Brinckmann* found out, and many were taken from copper plates but flowers seemed to have been done largely from nature.

Rendsburg

1765—*Christian Friedrich Gottlob Clar* and *Jesper Lorentzen,* an apothecary and a merchant 1772—When

A list of the wares of 1767 says they produced all types of wares from *"Pot-pourris"* and *"Bischofshüte"* or "bishop bowls" to cane handles, snuff-boxes, etc.

LESSER DANISH FACTORIES—*Continued*

Lorentzen
died *Clar* tried to make "English ware" and turned the business over to a company
1784—*Clar* went bankrupt and the company declared itself insolvent. The business was then turned over to the judge and shareholder, *Johann Heinrich Hallensen* in 1788 who kept *Clar* on.

The pierced baskets are marked in stories:
At top a **D** reversed or a rectangle combined with the R, below a painter's letter and below again usually 67, 68, **or** 69 for the date.

Stamped with cursive **RF** at times followed **by** a numeral, but this was often omitted to fool the customers into thinking that **they** were "English wares."

English black "basalt ware" and a slightly glazed red terra-cotta of *Clar's* own were produced.

First period (1765–72) whitish-buff body with soft white glaze. There are only a few pieces known: a small dish in *Hamburg* has a rose and an anemone in green, purple and yellow. A wash basin in the same museum is in natural flowers in blue only. Chinese flowers also in blue were used. (See *Folkemuseum* dish) Manganese was also used alone as on a tea-caddy in *Hamburg*.

Rendsburg pierced baskets touched up with blue and with a bouquet of flowers in blue are not rare.

The lead-glazed earthenware is after 1772. It has flowers in blue and landscapes but is often simply picked out with blue. It is too strongly straw colored or too white and generally muddy and densely crazed in glaze. Its forms are an urn with mask handles, a blue lined basket with grapes and other fruit in relief springing from the handles, a large pierced basket with inner container and plain cover with holes for flower stems and a tulip-bowl supported by three boys.

Brinckmann claims that a large center piece of yellowish ware with three nearly nude ladies on a pedestal, two supporting an open-work basket with a strange bird on the cover, is from here. Hannover says, if so, it is the largest piece yet known that this factory could handle.

Kellinghusen
in Holstein

Magretah Stemman

c1760—*Carsten Behrens* dreamed of a porcelain factory and got some men from *Saxony* to come there. Soon he was forced to convert the porcelain factory into a *faïence* factory and form a company. Technical manager was *Sebastian Heinrich Kirch.*
1765—the factory was granted a privilege
1768—*Kirch* departed

Kirch introduced the plastic trend of *Jever* and it became popular. *A large Venus* in the *Gewerbemuseum* at *Bremen* is proven by *Karl Schaefer* to have come from the factory of *Behrens.*

The hair is applied with a painting-horn in lines as thin as thread. It is similar in feeling to the *"Clutie"* wall-plaques with a head in high relief and a sunburst above, left open to hold a watch. (*Hamburg* and *Folkemus.*)

LESSER DANISH FACTORIES—*Continued*

KH—B (for *Kellinghusen-Behrens*)

KH—M (for *Kellinghusen-Møller*)

KH—Dr. G but as a rule it is not marked at all.

for places unknown and the company was dissolved so *Carsten Behrens* had to carry on alone. At his death it went to his heirs and lasted at least until 1825.

1783—Meanwhile two workmen, *Christian Heinrich Geppel* and *Georg Geppel*, who had been with *Clar* at *Rendsburg*, had established at *Kellinghausen* and were given a privilege for the making of white wares only.
1785—a royal resolution was given the old factory and *Dr. Joachim Møller* obtained a share in it and with it freedom to make every kind of earthenware at the new factory which he now owned also.
His widow married one of his workmen, *Jacob Stemmann*.
1800—it is still called, *"Doctor Grauers Fayence-Fabrique." Dr. Grauer* was a practicing physician and owned the factory only as a side issue.
1822—it went to *Nicolai Friedrich Mohns* who left it to his son, who sold it to *Martin Püssel* of *Lehmberg*.
1787—A third factory was set up by *Georg Geppel*.
Others tried as the clay from *Ovendorf*, nearby was excellent.

The pair in the *Folkemuseum* are inscribed *"Magretah Stemman"* and are of the *Dr. Grauer* period. These were among the commonest wares made at the place.

A bucket with flowers in colors at *Bergen* is marked KH-B.

Wall flower-holders and wall-plaques dated 1794 must be from the factory of *Joachim Møller*, as does also a cream jug in the shape of a satyr's head marked KH-M.

Local factories all used same clay and all used same rustic painting in high-temperature colors so that they cannot be told apart. Hannover says that the wares attributed to *Kastrup* and having large, coarsely-painted yellow and purple flowers with feathery greenish grey leaves and thread-like stalks in manganese are really from some factory here at *Kellinghusen*.

The ordinary peasant wares of *Kellinghusen* are more vigorously painted and have an iron-red added to the colors. The flowers are similar to those described above and also landscapes, ships, galloping horses or such subjects as a saint in her cell are used. Of course, the single colors were also used alone.

Stockelsdorff near Lübeck

* *Stockelsdorff* 1773—*Buchwald Direct.—Alr. Leihamer fecit.*
** A similar inscription.
*** *Buchwald Dir.—Creutzf 'dt fecit—Stockelsdorff* 1776.

Grew out of an earlier stove factory, owned by *Peter Graff* or *Grafe*, who founded the *Kiel* factory.
1771—obtained privilege for *State Councillor, Georg Nicolaus Lübbers*.
c1773—*Johann Buchwald* is director and *Abraham Leihamer* as decorator from *Eckernförde* and *Kiel*. But left in a few years and the painter *Creutzfeldt* took his place.

Under *Lübbers* and *Buchwald* stoves were the main output as they were in the time of *Graff*. They were in the rococo and "*Zopf*" styles and had grates of iron. All are painted in muffle-kiln colors in marbling and figures or landscapes with figures in them. They are real works of art and are signed with care as on the rococo *Hamburg* one with Chinese genre scenes,* and another in the early "*Zopf*" or classical style of the death of *Caesar* in the *Lübeck Museum*,** and still another in the *Folkemuseum*

LESSER DANISH FACTORIES—*Continued*

* Stockelsdorff— *1774—Leihamer* *fecit.* St or Stoff on blue and white wares	1788—*Lübbers* died and the son of *Johann Buchwald* carried on.	with subjects from the *Iliad.**** Next to stoves come tea-trays in importance. One with cows in a landscape within a ro- coco frame * and another with blue and white land- scape at *Hamburg* are typical. The factory used both high and low fired colors and serv- ices in manganese are known (See tureen at *Lübeck*) Very poor plates in blue are also found rather plentifully. The clay is lightly fired pale yellowish-white sometimes al- most pure white. The above plates are poor in- deed but some wares in well painted blue show that it was also used in the best period. (See wall cistern and vase at *Bergen*.) Among the colored wares are helmet jugs, jardinieres, etc. in splendid green, beautiful yellow, soft violet (for lining and shell borders) and a mat red.

Thus Danish wares contained little that was original but there was a tendency to simplify the too florid foreign wares to their simple components with a beneficial result. Surprising and rather refreshing it was to find here a Japanese influence. Of course the end was in sight when the "English ware" began to be made but here again the penny-pinchers had less to do with faïence than with porcelain so that there was less stealing of ideas and workmen and a consequently more original outlook in most of the factories. Of course we run across the trails of such secret-peddlers as Tännich and Hannong but the air smells generally sweeter than elsewhere. The appeal of the beautiful is an elusive thing and it sometimes settles upon the more lowly material in spite of every effort to capture it with the most costly of webs.

SWEDEN

RÖRSTRAND

We need not give in detail the unpleasant reports of Johann Wolff. Aereboe would have us believe that he was a thief and betrayer of trusts; that he brought to Stockholm materials and workmen from Copenhagen and it is true that he offered a considerable consignment of cobalt blue supposedly bought from Elsinore, but he was not unlike the other "arcanists." He came to Rörstrand in 1725 and was followed by Anders Nicolaus Ferdinand. In 1729 a privilege was granted and by that time Wolff had been dismissed. Ferdinand too was soon replaced by Christoffer Conrad Hunger who had been at Meissen, Vienna and Venice. In 1733 he was dismissed and replaced by Johann Georg Taglieb from Ansbach until 1739 or 1741.

The factory did a fair amount of work though it was financially unsound. The manager Anders Fahlström helped a bit but reorganization was necessary in 1753 after which he with Elias Magnus Ingman as director brought it to success. However Marieberg began to bring competition in 1758 to 1759 and the quality fell off. At the death of Fahlström in 1760 the management went to Jonas Tåman then to Erik Fahlström, Jacob Öhrn or Øhrn in 1763. Johann Buchwald introduced high temperature colors but by 1758 went to Marieberg. Anders Stenman invented a method of printing on faïence independently of the English but he and Henrik Sten about 1766 or later also went to Marieberg where the latter became manager and then director.

Ingman was enobled in 1758 and he became sole owner of Rörstrand by 1773 when he died. In 1782 his son, E. M. Nordenstolpe bought up the factory but a few years later closed it. Finally it was sold in 1797 to Bengt Reinhold Geijer and he made "English ware" or "flintporslin" as it is called in Swedish. The factory still continues.

WOLFF PERIOD (1725–?)

The only pieces of this period, and they are doubtful, are some walkingstick handles marked (Stock)?"*holm Anno 1725,*" a plate having a view with buildings in the center and a rim with alternating design of trellis and flowers in the Chinese manner, other similar plates and two blue and white vases in early Ming style. All but the first are marked "Stockholm."

FERDINAND PERIOD (1729–)

By 1729 Wolff had "long been under arrest" and Ferdinand was in charge. A jar and cover is the only example known. It has blue and white decoration like that of Rouen and Dorotheenthal, consisting of a monogram in a medallion surmounted by a crown and with lambrequin borders on the cover and top and bottom. It is dated 1729.

HUNGER-THELOT PERIOD (1733–)

Hunger and a man named Thelot seem to have turned out pieces together, and signed some stove tiles. They signed also an octagonal tray dated 1733 and painted in blue with a picture of "the feast of the Israelites at the foot of Sinai with Moses kneeling on the mountain—a subject conceived in the profane South German spirit," as Hannover describes it. This is a lively bit with musicians in the foreground, an old girl getting water and much other action set within a stupid floral border. Other pieces show a man with a trained bear, and some have lambrequin borders. Also there are some bowls with feet having landscapes with lovers, hunters, etc. The old Laub-und Bandelwerk was as popular as in Germany. Plates with biblical texts on a banner held by an angel and armorial pieces were made, one of which was signed "Anders Fahlström—Stockholm 1739." All are in blue on white.

From the early 1740's the Chinese influence becomes strong. One typical motive is of a bird with a long tail while others show a beflagged pavilion and a weeping willow. A very queer one shows a dead bird with its head hanging over a ledge while over it is a large flat umbrella. To one side is a tree while to the other is a dart. Perhaps Dali had ancestors! Actually Pillement, Oudry and Boucher were behind much of this, and the latter is said to have invented the "swan spouting water," though a very similar design occurs on two incised Sung period vases (A.D. 960–1280) (see Chinese section) in my collection. This design represented ducks eating greens.

The ground of all these wares up to c. 1750 was white of varying tone but at this time they began to add a bluish-grey tinge and decorate in white on it in the technique called in Italy, "bianco sopra bianco." But this was always much more crude and broad than the Italian examples. The earliest is a plate dated 1745. Later the technique was tried a little at Delft, Bristol and Saint Amand-les-Eaux, all in about five years. New stunts soon got around in the 18th century.

Hannover gives four supposedly original designs from Rörstrand:

1.—The scattered trefoil.

2.—The "blue leaf" which is also like a flower and appears in a center decoration and looks like "large twisted catkins (of hop?)."

3.—The "polestar motive," a sharp five pointed star with a space around it and five heavy rays with about eight or nine graduated lighter rays between them. (c 1748)

4.—The "Rehn design" supposed to have been devised by an architect named Jean Erik Rehn. It is a sort of bursting pomegranate centered and with a rococo border of three wave-like scrolls with three smaller ones between them (1745). This occurs in manganese and sometimes yellow too was added.

Marieberg had started with muffle-kiln colors in a style of painting like that of Strasburg and to meet the competition, Rörstrand made some trials on panels adding even gilding. These are dated 1758. Within a year plates were made with bird designs in colors similar to those known as "famille rose" of the Ch'ien Lung dynasty, China (1736–1796). A foliated butter dish copies Delft and has a decoration of small scattered roses after Meissen and marked as a real Delft one would be with an unintelligible rake and bird's head, and it might even be confused if it did not also have a mark "Stockholm 2/5 9/5 59. There are also some light, thin snuff boxes almost like porcelain.

The brushwork of the 1760's was broad and good and flowers and butterflies are well drawn in a sort of fluttery style. Toward the end of this decade flowers in the round were applied boldly to three sides of a temple jar shaped vase with a scalloped foot.

Marieberg forced the old factory to find a sort of half-hearted interest in plastic work. There were center pieces with half figures holding a shell supported on rococo scrolls and tureens had modeled flowers or fruits for the knob handles. On one there is a reclining lobster and on another a cauliflower. The jars with roses on three sides give somewhat the effect of a fat lady with a large corsage pinned on her great bosom. These were done both in muffle colors and in high-fired colors. But the factory concentrated chiefly on the latter. A red was never developed. The manganese purple was usually broken up into many small circles where bubbles had broken. The green is greyish or yellowish with a tendency to part in small fissures so that the white glaze can be seen through. The yellow is pale and has the same tendency. Therefore, the result is pallid but giving an antique and harmonious result. The blue alone is pure and strong and it was not overdone. The four designs listed continued, at least until 1773.

By this time there seemed to be a change of taste and polychrome was discontinued entirely in favor of black design. Many of the old forms were revived and so treated.

The stoves are copies of those made at Marieberg but of fine quality. This is not to say that sincere flattery was not returned in good measure by the younger factory. Punch bowls were made to imitate wooden tubs with vines and grapes applied about them and two vases in the Rörstrand Museum are five feet high. They are decorated with Chinese figures and landscapes. These seem to date about 1765.

The Rörstrand marks are complete and until 1773 the name of the factory, or the city, the day, month, year, the painter's mark and frequently the price of each piece or of a dozen was added. To 1758 "Stockholm" was used. Then "Rörstrand" and in 1758 and 1759 "Rörstrand-Stockholm" is found. Odd exceptions dating 1760–61 may also have just "Stockholm" on them. The date may be "–18/4. 52." The painters do not interest us as there were none of outstanding merit. Stråle and also Looström have made extensive studies but allowed their enthusiasm to run away with some of their conclusions.

MARIEBERG

Marieberg was founded on the island of Kungsholm off Stockholm by Johann Ehrenreich, court dentist, jack-of-all-trades and the same referred to in Königsberg and Stralsund. He had applied for a privilege to make porcelain in 1758 but his factory burned down in the following year. He then started on faïence and the first firing took place in April, 1760, bringing an immediate success for by 1762 he had 6 designers and 248 workmen. In 1766 the financial crisis forced him to give up his post to a Frenchman, Pierre Berthevin who came from Mennecy and went later to Mosbach. He tried to make soft porcelain for about 3 years and then Henrik Sten was director and soft porcelain was continued until the "English ware" was adopted. When Nordenstolpe the younger from Rörstrand bought the factory, he put Philipp Andrea Schirmer in charge until 1788 when it closed.

Probably the first wares were not marked and were decorated in rich colors in the manner of porcelain applied as enamels. Landscape and figure subjects were popular while modeled fruit, vegetables and flowers appear often. A little group of the "comedy figures" are in yellow or natural colors. The old stunt of marbling or making wood grain was done but in several colors used together such as red, yellow, blue, brown and violet. These pieces may have bird or flower finials on the vase covers or tureens.

Another group of wares are called the "violet group" though they are predominantly white with touches of violet. There has been some speculation about these pieces but it is fairly certain that the color was added intentionally and was no accident of the glaze. Hannover says, "Rörstrand faïence has not infrequently such an even faint violet tone, and it was perhaps this that the Marieberg factory sought to imitate." This same lavender tone does appear also on Sung Dynasty (960–1280) Tz'u Chou wares and seems to be due to small patches or specks of impurity in the body or slip. Perhaps there are tiny bits of manganese or iron in the clay. They are sought after by Chinese collectors and these or brown stains are often pleasant relief to the white. If, therefore, it occurs on Rörstrand, it may have originally been unintentional. Other examples of this staining appear on the "Tu Ting" wares also of the Sung Dynasty. Examples of plastic work of Marieberg are a pair of wild swine, rococo cachepots, women or a triton supporting a shell-shaped bowl, etc., and are often not decorated. On the other hand colored pieces are candelabrum, boxes and figures.

Blue and white was done with a bright blue tinged with ultramarine giving it a purplish tint and only seldom inclined to run. With it cornflowers, roses and convolvulus were painted on a service dating 1765. Again tureens were made with vegetable and lobster knobs or handles. All manner of natural shaped boxes were made in the forms of artichokes, melons, birds and fruits. One odd one is like a bunch of grapes. All were in natural colors.

About this same time the modeled and applied flowers were popular. One at least was done in black, brown and green. Many were in polychrome but all were in good taste due to Ehrenreich.

Ehrenreich also brought certain ideas to the factory including the tureens in rococo style with flowers in Strasburg manner, the use of a dolphin or bird for the cover handles, and the "terrace vase," "rabbit vase," etc. The "terrace vase" was a simple and pleasant inverted pear shaped jar with dome cover and decorated up each side and on the cover with flowers modeled in the round while the whole stands upon a large swirling baroque scroll perhaps five times larger than would be expected and having in its curves a bunch of grapes. This does sound terrible but somehow the effect is to give a preciousness to the jar. The "rabbit vase" we may at least commend as original in this age of worn out ideas and it was popular, for many examples exist. It consisted of the same shaped vase decorated with muffle-kiln colored flowers and the cover surmounted with a bunch of berries. This vase is set on a rock-like base around which and tapering upward to accent the perspective, goes a staircase with railing, while at the foot of this sits a rabbit about to ascend. Later the rabbit was replaced for some unknown reason by a boar.

Again we exclaim, by all the shades of poor unbalanced Dali, his brethren surely seemed to have existed back in those days, and we are led to believe that perhaps we should add another human appeal to the possible armament of the artist, namely that of *shock*, during the bored and despondent times of decadence; of unexplained and unexplainable and unrelated objects which, if not alluringly satisfactory as possessions for ourselves, are, at least *talk creators;* challenging conundrums and the sought-after symbolical representations of those who wish to appear mysterious and strange. Such extroverts, who always make great pretense of being introverts, cannot stand life, if they are not noticed and, no other means being easy for them, will play up their personal oddities. I remember when I was very young I had a great desire to have a black room, in which there was to be a black piano upon which would rest a bleached human skull. This room was a dream of mine for months until I suddenly awoke to the fact that I wanted it to impress a young lady with whom I was very much in love and who did not seem sufficiently impressed to return my love in like measure. My dreams always ended in picturing her astonishment when the door was thrown open and somehow I felt that *then* she would appreciate the dark depths of my soul. I spited her by not thinking of the room any more at all and by adopting a very flippant and shallow manner. She never knew what she missed! So it is with melting watches and rabbit vases. Can you imagine the astonishment of a proper young man left in a waiting room in a tasteful mansion to contemplate what at first glance appears to be a suavely perfect vase quite expensive looking and up to the taste of the moment when suddenly, penetrating his thoughts of the lady for whom he is waiting, he sees that the vase has at the bottom a rabbit or a boar about to ascend a staircase? He looks more closely for a hidden meaning. He wonders if there is some significance perhaps a symbol of the thwarted ambition for, of course, neither a rabbit nor a boar could go up a staircase and why should they anyway? He thinks all pottery is somewhat crazy and remembers the Wettergren's soup tureen with a lobster and cauliflower on the cover and how he tried hard to think of two foods that would go less well together and be more indigestible. Well artists are certainly crazy, but why should his Anna fall for a thing like that? It must be the influence of that fellow Erik who thinks he is artistic! And then she comes and says, "Why Johann, why are you sitting and frowning so at my new vase? What is the matter with you?" And he answers, "What is the idea of having such a crazy thing? Rabbits don't go upstairs. Why should you buy anything so silly?" And she, "Because I like it." And that is that.

Yes we have something here, something which Poe played at, something which is part of the old "groteschi" of Urbino and which Grünewald, Bosch and Brueghel seemed to know; the tales of strange things, the figures part animal part human, the danses macabres and such may not be able to move us to tenderness, to tears or to happiness, but at least they command attention and have been known to lead to fear, sexual desire and a sense of superiority, though usually those who practice such art are satisfied with obtaining attention alone, and if notice is taken of them that is sufficient.

MARIEBERG FROM 1766—BERTHEVIN

So much for our court dentist and his rabbits! When Ehrenreich departed in 1766 no great change took place. In 1768 a pompous and not too good service was done for Louis Auguste le Tonnelier de Breteuil, French Ambassador to Stockholm, each piece of which bears his arms printed with the transfer process while the rest is of flowers poorly painted. The handles are of bent vegetables. Many museums have parts of this service and the best that can be said of it is that it did have a clear porcelain-like white glaze.

Berthevin brought a spirit of imitation of porcelain not at all suitable to the material of faïence. Anders Stenman from Rörstrand started much printed design and Henrik Sten introduced classical shapes. Another service with pierced rims and scattered flowers was done in 1773 and in 1774 another was in much the style of Joseph Hannong. Just as Rörstrand was famous for its blue, so Marieberg was famous for a crimson about as good as that of Strasburg. Bianco-sopra-bianco was copied from Rörstrand. In 1764 an attempt had been made to handle the high temperature colors but it failed.

Hannover wisely says, "Nothing follows in history more surely after love of colour than colour-weariness and a tendency to renunciation of colour." Thus the chief characteristic of the Sten period was a demand for austere vases decorated after engravings after Boucher in black or brown and the same colors in renderings of trophies. Thus we approach the deadly Empire with its chinoiseries and neo-classical treatments in grey or red, its imitations of jasper or agate and its final descent into "English ware" or the "flint-porslin" and imitation of Staffordshire so good that without the marks one can hardly tell the difference.

The mark is of three crowns of Sweden above a line, below which is MB in monogram or not and an E (for Ehrenreich) or B (for Berthevin) followed by the date and a painter's mark. Johann Otto Franzén wrote his name in full on a terraced vase of 1766 (30/8) but this is not usual. The "flintporslin" is usually simply impressed with MB. Other marks are usually in blue underglaze, and rarely in black.

The body is buff with slight greenish tint. The glaze is very white and not inclined to craze. The flintporslin ware is astonishingly light, yellowish and with a close, fine crackle. Gilding is uncommon except as an edging but was combined at times with grisaille painting. Very infrequently it was combined with blue and white.

CHART OF SMALL FACTORIES

The following small factories are interesting only to a few readers. Of them Stralsund is the most important for it is there that Ehrenreich went when he left his post as director at Marieberg in 1766.

CHARTS OF SMALLER SWEDISH FACTORIES

| *Stralsund* | *Three nails* of the Crucifixion from the arms of the town, with an *E* (for *Ehrenreich*) followed by the date and often the painter's mark. Sometimes the E is replaced by a C (for Carl) or a B (for *Buchwald*) | 1757—*Councillor von Giese* with largest kiln to hold 6,480 plates. 1766—*Ehrenreich* took over management with help of *Johann Buchwald.* 1770—Was blown up by powder magazine explosion and Ehrenreich bankrupt, but stayed and *von Giese* put the factory on its feet again. 1780—*Giese* died and there were many disputes about the money with heirs. | Buff body with greenish tone with sometimes a grey and cold glaze. The colors are heavier, harder and more dead than those of *Rörstrand* and *Marieberg.* *Bianco-sopra-bianco* technique was copied. Also the *Rehn pattern,* the blue leaf and others among all the popular models of *Marieberg* including the boxes with recumbent figures, the "rabbit vases," etc. |
| | | | Early in the 1770's were made about the only original things: monumental *potpourri* vases with a nude woman and |

CHARTS OF SMALLER SWEDISH FACTORIES—*Continued*

		1785—When an agreement was made the resources were so depleted that it had to close. It was revived by *Carl* but had further troubles and closed for good in 1792.	other figures modelled in the round about the bases.
Pålsjö north of Helsingborg	*P F C* (for *Pålsjö Fabrik-Cöster*)	1765—*Michael Anders Cöster*, the district magistrate under direction of *Fröling* a *Swede* from *Stockholm*, until 1770. 1770 to 74—was under *Hindrich Wulph* our old acquaintance, *Heinrich Wolff*	See *Sigurd Wallin*—Undamaged pieces are among the greatest rarities. Sherds of flint porcelain moulded from English originals, have been found in large quantities at the site. The *faïence* body is pale buff and rather fine in texture. Another type is coarser and reddish-buff. The glaze is crazed and faulty. The decoration is in blue or manganese of very variable tone. There is one example of polychrome, a tankard in the *Kulturhistoriska Museum, Lund.* Motives were a spray of five petalled flowers and small scattered clover leaves and flowers with among them tulip-buds with stalks bearing similar clover-like, leaves. These occur sometimes alone or sometimes in wreaths around royal monograms,—that of *Adolf Frederik* of *Sweden.* Another motive is a small view of buildings similar to those of *Copenhagen*, and these are probably from the *Wolff* period.
Sölvesborg	S B for (Sölves-Borg) with numbers 1 or 2 added.	1773—*Major Gabriel Sparre* and managed by the painter from *Marieberg, Peter Akermark.* Later went to *S. Fr. von Zicpel*, a Prussian officer. 1793—closed	Buff lightly fired and fine clay. The glaze is inclined to craze. Decoration in blue or manganese and exceptionally in several colors, see large tureen with dolphin on cover in *Rörstrand Museum.* No independent style for shapes, taking all from *Rörstrand* or *Marieberg.* Motives of flowers not original and are different only in being more hastily and commercially painted. Most of the wares were without decoration or with the conventional "blue leaf" of *Rörstrand* in blue and also in manganese. Trees were also sometimes printed with a sponge. Also copied English earthenware.

Ulfsunda in parish of Bromma in the district of Sollentuna province of Stockholm.	C A L *Linning's* initials stamped and sometimes name of factory	End of 18th cent. *Christian Arvid Linning,* a sculptor of little ability. 1819—Was called "*Wedgwood-Fabriken paa Ulfsunda.*"	Appropriation of models by *Wedgwood* and *Flaxman* for useful wares of classical style. (See blue and white drug jar in *Lund*) Less hard fired than real *Wedgwood* but occur in black "basalt," buff terra-cotta with applied reliefs in brown or red, etc., cast from the prototypes direct. The largest piece is a clock in the *Nordiska Museum* signed by *Linning* but copied from a French model (See Hannover "Pottery and Porcelain," p. 497)
Gustafsberg		1827—May have had a predecessor at 1780-90	Typical of the times and of no interest

There were also several other late factories such as that at *Malmö,* another at *Höganäs* as well as *Norrköping* and *Norrtälje* the outputs of which are of very modest description.

NORWAY

C. Nyrop gives the following list of Norwegian factories though the wares are known from only one:

1741—Didrik von Cappelen at Dorholt near Skien

1753—Johan Heinrich Schwabs and Oluf Falch at Styrstuen

1758—Peter Hofnagel at Herrebøe (which we will speak of later)

1760—D. P. Fasmer at Bergen (stoneware and faïence)

1778—Iver Bredal and Gunner Eide also at Bergen

HERREBØE (1758-1770)

The wares from the factory at Herrebøe far from being unknown are among the most interesting of Scandinavia. Peter Hofnagel started the factory here near Frederikshald in 1758 and he obtained a privilege to open a factory at Drammen in 1762. He was a lawyer then a merchant after trying to become the postmaster of Arendal and he bought an estate where he took up agriculture. In 1757 he founded a tile factory and the next year a stoneware and stove factory from which the faïence factory developed. The director was Georg Kreibs, probably a Dane or at least his family was at Copenhagen. Two stepsons partly Scottish, named Joseph and Gunder Large, became artists at the ages of sixteen and eighteen in the year 1760 but the early painting was probably due to Heinrich Christian Friedrich Hosenfeller of Berlin.

The common mark is HB with at times an H below probably standing for Hosenfeller. Another was H K L with a slanting stroke below, standing for Herrebøe Kreibs Large. The often seen A and R and AR are identified. Finally we are sure at least of the full name of the factory and the name Large but they are rarely used. There are also numerals which do not refer to size (0 to 4).

The earliest piece is a large wall cistern inscribed Herrebøe 1760 and a similar one signed Large, probably of about the same date, now in Oslo. These are usual in shape and have a medallion in low relief with slight painting of flowers and a figure. Hosenfeller's style is supposed to have broad, free brush work with claw-like terminations to the rococo scrolls according to Thor Kielland but soon the young apprentices also did things in his style.

The body is fine-grained, buff and lightly fired. It is porous and the glaze tends to crackle and is of bluish or palest buff tint. It is only a little less opaque than oil paint white so the blue or manganese decoration were used above the unfired tin glaze. Outlines were not used but sometimes a detail is handled with a fine brush. Almost nowhere else and certainly not in Germany can be found such masterful handling of the best that the rococo style could give; there is a daring swing in the movement, a better accented rhythm and a more capricious viewpoint easily evident. Here once again we find appreciation of swift brushwork as in the Danish factory of Store Kongensgade in the 3rd or Gierløf period (c1750) though used not so much in a Japanese sort of technique as pure rococo. Undoubtedly this sort of technique occurred from time to time because the unfired glaze sucked up the paint almost as fast as would a blotter and *forced* a sure, swift stroke. Sometimes this is overdone in a work of art while again we all can recognize a too labored painting but once in a while an artist will gauge his tempo so perfectly that he will "hit it right on the nose" with all the sting and follow-through that is necessary and not a jot too much. It is then that the opponent in the prize ring unexpectedly collapses and the critics speak of timing. It is then that the golf ball sails further down the fairway. And in art something of this mastery was to be seen at Herrebøe though it was never anything like as fine as in the Sung Tz'u Chou wares, because of the inherent deficiencies of the whole rococo style.

The breaking up of the surface of the ware with indentations and convexities helically twisting about them, with melon-ribbed modeling or well spaced and sometimes alternating slight ribs and grooves, gives the design a less obvious rhythm as it plays a leitmotif over the undulating swells like ripples over waves. It is not a question of painting a flat design on an uninteresting surface or trying to make such a surface appear uneven; the pieces would be plastically beautiful in themselves, the designs would be beautiful in themselves, and the two are perfectly harmonized so that, as a rule, neither the one nor the other dominates and even when this does occur it seems intentional.

As an example of one piece which may be considered overmodeled, we can take the largest example known, a center-piece with cruets, mustard pots and salt cellars grouped around the figure of an almost naked baby boy holding a pierced basket for fruit. The modeling of this object is surely overdone and the anatomy of the boy is none too good but what gives it a peculiar charm is the vigorous painting and the bubbling overjoyed intoxication of the boy as he prances through the scrolls and scallop-shells, the foliage and pots, as though gaily bringing the pièce de résistance of the whole dinner. This work of art has been called "the jolliest figure in the whole art of faïence" which it certainly well may be. Who gives one small damn for anatomy and perfection of modeling if an artist can catch that illusive charm that makes men smile thereafter? Here is something that the merchants and copyists cannot catch any more than they could lay hold of a sunbeam. I wonder if this is not always true and that *those who lost the most through forgery had not actually the least to lose.* Meissen, Sèvres and Wedgwood are names that collectors conjure with but we might enjoy ourselves far more with the real things from odd places such as Store Kongensgade, Herrebøe, South Germany and Hungary as well as the Far East of pre-Ming days.

Large trays, wall cisterns, "bishop bowls" (which became more bowl and less mitre) and round tureens comprised most of the wares. A simple, well proportioned and undecorated turned candlestick of 1770 is signed Gunder Large and is in the church at Id.

Odd examples show that gold was tried and the bianco-sopra-bianco. Chinese designs occur on a few plates while swift and direct little landscapes and large flowers never lost the life of the place. Yet Herrebøe was not successful; it soon had to have sales at sacrifices and by 1772 it had about failed. Not until 1900 did the Kunsindustrimuseum of Oslo have an exhibition which led to modern appreciation with pieces bringing from 4,000 to 12,000 kroner. How much one such sale would have encouraged the factory! Hofnagel tried again in Drammen but again without success. He then went to Copenhagen in 1763 where we know he opened Østerbro sometime around 1764 or 1765. In 1770 he was obliged to return to Norway where he died in 1776 a sad and disconsolate failure.

Conclusion of Continental Faïence

The fate of Hofnagel was no different from that of most of the other "arcanists" of the day such as Tännich, Johann Wolff, Ehrenreich and all. They, after all, earned their way by the misappropriation and sale of the secrets of one factory to another and were naturally mistrusted. And so they moved from place to place establishing the manifold crossings of their art, losing manhood, individuality and personality, probably hating themselves in their innermost hearts, and giving up to a hang-dog existence until what was at first a clear desire to create faïence or porcelain was transformed into a mere struggle to get money by hook or by crook. Some hated themselves so much that they were discharged "for riotous living." Some were partly successful due to dual personalities because they were able to play the artist and creator on one side and the businessman and accumulator on the other. These men are none of them pleasant to contemplate and their mongrel art is no more pleasant. Of course there was greater skulduggery in the field of porcelain because there were more secrets to know and more rich patrons to work on, but all arts of the 18th century were similarly handled.

Despite all this and the misfortunes that visited the "arcanists," faïence had become a living art in some places and grown into the hearts of men. Some modernists think that plastics may supplant it but this is simply another material with completely different expression. Faïence will not be discarded any more than wood will be discarded for the manufacture of furniture and that will not be for many a year to come. The handful of clay which can be modeled or thrown on the wheel and painted with colors that never fade and given a glaze pleasant to the touch will always have its appeal to artists and to public alike and its possibilities for expression have only been half explored.

It was the penny piling business men who really harmed the ceramic arts and man had to live to the 20th century to find that gold is as worthless as words and words are as worthless as arms in the gaining and holding of power over fellow men. There is no such a thing as a burglar proof lock and no shield has ever been invented that cannot be pierced by some future weapon. The "arcanists" were not different from other men of the period.

Lincoln Steffens says in his autobiography, "The great corporations, called syndicates, are essential parts of the business political machinery in France, where the tendency to merge business and politics has gone further than anywhere else. We in America have what all those countries once had, a dual government, the political establishment and business, and the theory is that the government exists to regulate, control, and adjust the conflicting interests of these businesses as against one another and as against the people. Apparently this is a theory in conflict also with the facts of economic growth. The economic forces, therefore, cause in the United States that political corruption, which we regard as an exceptional evil, which in England has gone on to the point where it is quiet, decent and accepted, but which in France has succeeded in uniting the management of business and the direction of political policies into one government. The syndicates have divided France into spheres of influence, financial, industrial and political, which are not identical with but as governmental as departments; and in practice, a political leader can have a man appointed to a business job just as he can to a political office. The effect on business is the same as on political administration with us: inefficiency, dishonesty, the retardation of enterprise." This is the best description I know of just how it works. We remember all the granting of privileges and organization by royalty first; then the business men who ran the kilns for what they could get out of them; then we saw that the men who actually devoted their whole lives to doing the work in the factories, after the stockholders were paid, the landlords paid, the merchants taken care of, etc.—obtained nothing in the end.

But let us continue with Steffens, "The ownership of big business in France (in England, in Europe, too, but most clearly you see it in France) is in the hands of the third and fourth generation of the descendants of the great founders and builders. There are literally princes of business in France as there were princes and descendants in politics, and they are alike, these two kinds of privileged descendants. They want security, income, profits; not adventure enterprise, new machinery and methods. How the Europeans ever came to say that Americans worship money when they sell everything for money—the state, honors, business, the arts—is a mystery; and another is how they can see standardization 'in the States,' when they have it in their very bones. The general effect of European political business corruption has been to make everybody think of money, and not as with us as capital to build with and give away, but as cash to get, hold, or waste, to standardize dress, conduct, customs, and all thinking." Here though Steffens knew nothing about pots he has most clearly told us just what is the matter with them.

It is significant that only in odd places have we seen any originality at all as in South Germany, Hungary and Norway. Such spots simply were less touched by the blight. Other originality will be found in America but first we turn to England, the furthest western point of European culture, the latest to be affected but the final focal point of all this commercialism in the next century.

CHAPTER XXVI

THE POTTERIES AND STONEWARE OF ENGLAND AND WALES

IN THE excellent book "English Pottery" by Bernard Rackham and Herbert Read an introductory statement says that the English are likely to dismiss their earlier potteries as "mere peasant work" not to be compared with the stoneware or faïence of Europe. Of course Roman kilns are found there but during the wars of the Saxons and Normans the art seems to have been lost, and in the middle ages little was done of importance. Hannover points out that in the upper classes only pewter and silver were used to any extent while in the lower, bowls of wood seemed to take the place of pottery. He jumps directly to "Toft ware" of the 17th century as a beginning. Mr. Ferrand Hudig's handbook to the English wares in the Nederlandsch Museum at Amsterdam dismisses the 17th century slipware with, "It may on patriotic grounds have a certain attractiveness for the English collector; for the foreigner it is a backward production, destitute of aesthetic worth, and by no means so purely English as British writers would like to assume." Actually Rhenish stoneware, the Delft and other faïence products of both the north countries and of France, the wares of Spain and even Italy all had their influence in England. No art in this world can be called "pure" any more than any blood can be so termed for the peoples of the world did quite a bit of getting about from time to time. The degree of purity interests us, of course, as do all influences which go to make up any work of art, but this degree is nothing to boast about. England is, after all just one more European state separated by a creek which a number of people have swum across. It has dabbled with a number of European countries and been dabbled with in turn. Any isolation in an Englishman's mind is merely a defense mechanism as the last war has well proven.

ROMAN INFLUENCES

The Romans brought the use of the wheel in potting though for some unknown reason glaze was not also imported. Therefore, of course the crude pottery could not compete

FIG. 1173. Reddish buff cup of Roman pottery found in England and probably made there. Ht. 7⅜". Warren E. Cox Coll.

with wood, metal or leather for bowls and containers. At once the urge of the potters was expressed in scratching of designs and only a little later clay of a different color was applied to make a design or a slip covering was applied and scratched away to give a two colored effect. The trend toward painting, as we see it on the continent was retarded so that the plastic outlet was a natural one for the artist. Of course, pieces found in England do not materially differ from other Roman wares and they were strong in plastic expression and nondescript color. In fact we are not entirely certain as to just what pieces were made in England and what imported.

THE "DARK AGES"

Rackham and Read suggest that we term the period between the Roman occupation and the 16th century the "Dark Ages," although I wish to point out that the name should be granted, as on the continent, more because of our lack of knowledge than as a condemnation of the times. After the Romans withdrew there was no contact with the Near East as in Venice, no Islamic conquest as in Spain so that painting with enamels, lustre and all such did not influence England. Thus a natural development of the Roman trends; a coarse body, thin lead glaze and simple clay applications for ornament we find all the way through. R. L. Hobson says in his *Catalogue of English Pottery*, "Pavement tiles are the only form of pottery made in this country in mediaeval times which can claim any artistic qualities," but then we have also found Mr. Hobson unappreciative of the early Chinese wares and his code of beauty was perhaps so refined as to eliminate a number of wares we feel most worthy and strong. Sir Arthur Church in *English Earthenware*, p. 15, says of the Tudor costrels, that their forms are, "perhaps the least inartistic of any native ceramic vessels of the time which have come down to us," as though all were bad and these only less so. But let us examine these wares with an open mind:

12TH TO 14TH CENTURY WARES

On fairly certain circumstantial evidence we find the following:

1.—A jug of unglazed grey earthenware in the B.M. (No. B11) found with coins of Henry III and Edward I in it. This oviform body with spreading foot and lip-rim establishes a common form, reasonable and good. It has dignity and some vitality; stands well and is easy to pour into and out of; has a handle which grows out of the curves pleasantly and structurally. The form recalls certain ones from Hamburg and Kreussen of the 17th century. It has no relationship with South European forms or Western Asian ones but seems to have been evolved by an original craftsman.

2.—The ewer in the Salisbury Museum representing a knight on horseback so armed as to date it about 1200 is original though not commendable.

3.—Another aquamanile in the form of a bearded man on horseback, is of buff ware with dark brownish green glaze and is in the Sussex Archaeological Societies' Museum at Lewes.

4.—Other aquamaniles are in the form of rams and one is overlaid with chain-like spirals, a design found also on a spreading footed pitcher in the

Left: Buff earthenware jug decorated with green clay ridges and red clay roses under yellowish lead glaze. Found on site of Christ's Hospital (Greyfriars Monastery) London. 14th cent. Ht. 12⅞". London Mus.

Center: Buff earthenware jug covered with white slip and painted in brown, amber and dull green under transparent lead glaze, uncrackled. Found at Bishopsgate Street, London. 14th cent. Ht. 12". Guildhall Mus., London.

Right: Red ware jug with red slip under greenish-yellow glaze. 14th cent. Ht. 15¾". Found on site of Civet Cat, Oxford. Ashmolean Mus.

Left: Cistern with heraldic achievement of Henry VII and Elizabeth of York. Early 16th cent. Ht. 13". Sir Henry P. Harris K.B.E.

Right: Tyg and mug of Cistercian ware having red body and dark glaze but no slip decoration. Hts. 8¼" and 5⅝". London Mus.

Left: 16th cent. jug of buff earthenware partly covered with green, lead glaze. Ht. 5⅛". Victoria & Albert Mus.

Center: Jug of buff ware painted in brown under yellowish glaze in spirals. Found at kiln-site at Cheam, Surrey. 14th cent. Ht. 10¾". Cheam Parish Council.

Right: Red earthenware jug with white slip design under deep yellow lead glaze, found on site of Master's Lodge, University College, Oxford. 14th cent. Ht. 12½". Ashmolean Mus., Oxford.

EARLY ENGLISH POTTERY

Plate 206

Ashmolean Museum, Oxford. This is a design common to 13th century stained glass, illumination and murals. Of course we have spirals emanating from the "Black Earth Region" and central Europe thousands of years before and spreading in all directions but the application of this motive with slip did not come in the western hemisphere until it appeared on the Hafner ware around 1550. Therefore this 13th century appearance might be a direct Roman development saved over as it were.

5.—There is a stag with yellow glazed body and green glazed horns which is probably 14th century and shows one of the earliest developments of diversity of color. It is in the V. & A. Museum.

Though Hobson claims metal prototypes, Messrs. Rackham and Read speak of stone and wood carvings as also having given ideas to the potters. Some are ornate and mischievous while others are dignified and not unlike Han pieces with strong shapes, though these potters had certainly never seen the Chinese tomb wares. Yet here we find the horizontally ribbed body suggestive of metal types, the heavy rim and well formed handle. Strangely we even find the glaze covering the whole of the inside and not the whole outside as in Near Eastern and some Han examples.

The tall spindle shaped jugs, roughly potted and without decoration but of unusual grace of form are 13th century also and those with the slightly dented lip to aid pouring are perhaps a little later. The bases of these are generally thumbed down, giving a gadrooned effect and making them stand firmly. This technique appears only again so far as I know in Siegburg faïence of the 16th century, but there was no connection. In 1923 a kilnsite was opened in Cheam, Surrey where examples were found including some with freely painted foliage and one with spirals between border lines. The body is buff, the design in brown slip and the glaze yellowish and thin. Probably those with chevrons and trellis work are earlier. Still another found on the site of the Master's Lodge of University College, Oxford, has a red body with complicated spiral design and pendant points on the neck in white slip under a deep yellow glaze. Also at Oxford was found a trellis type with red body, red slip and greenish-yellow glaze. This one has been called 14th century after a study of its potting, though few of this type are later than 1300.

14TH AND 15TH CENTURY WARES

By the end of the 13th century the lip-spout had been made and turned grooves about the neck with also a further development of the different colors of clays for ornamentation. The height is a little less in proportion to the width. A fine example is the one in the London Museum with chevrons and perpendicular lines about the neck in green dented with a tool and dull red roses applied on a greenish brown body, while another in the British Museum is a jug with nearly globular body and of red earthenware while two diamond shaped panels contain a dragon and a lion in lighter clay on reddish brown ground while black is used in a crisscross pattern about the neck; and eagles, leaves and studs appear in brown. Naturally it was not long before such treatments led to purely painted techniques but it was a parallel development perhaps because so much of the Roman influence to model had

Fig. 1175. Red ware jug with applied studs partly covered with grey-green glaze, found on site of Crown and Cushion Inn, Week-day Cross, Nottingham. 15th cent. Ht. 7½". Castle Mus. and Art Gallery, Nottingham.

Fig. 1174. Red ware jug with relief decoration on reddish-brown ground in panels between which are eagles, leaves, etc , in black under transparent colorless glaze. 14th cent. Ht. 10¾". Brit sh Mus.

Fig. 1176. Jug of red ware with white slip decoration under yellow glaze. Found at Whittington Park, Buckinghamshire. 15th cent. Ht. 9¾". Victoria & Albert Mus.

been absorbed. A good example is one in the Guildhall Museum, London and found in that city. In this the lip-spout has become exaggerated and the neck loses definition. It is of buff earthenware with white slip painted in green, amber and brown. It begins to show the decadent result of a more facile medium and is not so beautiful as those with applied design.

Plain bodied wares with wheel marks and also simply carved patterns continued and had copper green glazes of a simple lead type. These are well established through having been shown in manuscripts of the period and not in the 15th century ones.

At Ipswich Museum are fragments with boss-like handles and projecting human faces which are called 14th and 15th century probably correctly. Another example, of the anthropomorphic type, is in the B.M. It has a human face molded on either side of the neck and a globular body with upside down pine-cone-scaled carved body. It is of buff clay with green glaze. The use of the faces seems to disappear later.

Rackham and Read also mention 14th century examples at Oxford which are buff with pale yellow or greenish-yellow glazes and decoration of strips or trellises in dark red clay, some of which have a short tubular spout springing from the front of the shoulder and attached by a strap to the neck. This we have seen in Italian majolica of the 14th and 15th centuries, at Siegburg of the latter half of the 16th century and in Near Eastern metal examples which are probably the source of the idea, though this may not be true for the development may be listed as follows: 1.—The rounded lip which does not pour well, 2.—The pinched up or V spout which pours well but makes covering more difficult, 3.—A tubular spout which overcomes both of these difficulties but breaks off easily, 4.—An added support and the troubles are over. However the abutting line like a check-rein on the spout is not pretty or simple and the whole thing is better in metal than in pottery.

16TH CENTURY WARES

A large number of pieces with bright green glaze are assigned to the 16th century:

1.—A small "bleeding-cup" of the B.M. with fleur-de-lys horizontal handle from the rim which might be Roman or Chinese in character but simple and sturdy in design.

2.—Small pitchers with glaze running down unevenly on the outside.

3.—A large variety of costrels and pilgrim-bottles with loops for straps for suspension.

4.—Others with lion head modeled handles.

5.—The natural evolution into marbled wares of red and white (or nearly white) clays as slips on buff body clay. And this again may have been a long suspended idea inherited from Rome, in turn from Crete and from there back to Egypt where it seemed to have originated.

FIG. 1177. Bleeding cup of buff ware with green lead glaze, of early 16th cent. Dia. 6¼". British Mus.

FIG. 1178. Jug and two tygs, 17th and 16th–17th cent. showing typical appliqués of white slip under brownish-yellow lead glaze. Hts. 6¼", 6¾" and 6⅜". C. J. Lomax and Yorkshire Mus.

6.—During the 16th century the mould came into use and we have stove-tiles, candle-sconces, etc., with the royal arms of the Tudor period (1485–1603) in relief.

7.—A fine and well-known example of this work is developed as a cistern (again the earliest we know), and it is about 20 inches by 13 inches at the front and filled with the heraldic achievement of Henry VII and his queen, Elizabeth of York. It is of red ware glazed in green.

There has been some doubt cast upon these wares and it has been suggested that they were not made in England. However a costrel in the B.M. shows the same quality of fine modeling and the style of lettering and the form of the rose would hardly have been learned by a foreign workman.

CISTERCIAN WARES

The "Cistercian wares," found chiefly on the sites of the abbeys, were made by monks and are technically excellent. The ware is red and harder than the other wares. It is covered with a dark iron-brown glaze and sometimes decorated with white slip or again incised. The cylindrical mugs are full of strength and vitality.

These early potteries of England are the ones which many Englishmen have been apologetic about and which Hannover does not even deign to mention, while Wedgwood and Ralph Wood pieces make them enthusiastic. To deny the potters have humor, strength and vitality is as foolish as it would be to say one does not like Shakespeare, and these wares prove that slip-ware was continuous from Roman times in England and perhaps a more characteristic craft than any other. Of course there were copies at odd times of continental things such as the jug in the Dr. J. W. L. Glaisher Collection which has an inscription about the neck: G. R. WROTHAM WAK, and which looks like a crude cast from a Raeren piece but these last Cistercian wares include pieces which form the prototypes of the tygs and posset-pots which are definitely English forms, just as is also the cup with two low handles which is like the Tickenhall tyg type. Tygs or tigs were cups with two or more handles so that they could be passed from hand to hand among several people. We must therefore conclude that slip-ware descended directly from the 16th century wares of the Cistercian monks, without halt, in a continuous line.

TICKENHALL WARES

Perhaps the crudest way of using slip is to apply a little cut shape like a cookie to a pottery surface and then cover the whole with a glaze and this is the way it was done at Tickenhall, Derbyshire where the wares resembled the Cistercian wares. A favorite shape was a cylindrical cup rounded at the bottom and fitted with a sturdy foot-rim. Opposing loop handles are placed low extending from near the bottom to about two thirds of the way up. A primitive flower or animal was usually applied. The ware is red and fairly hard, the slip white and the glaze brownish-yellow. They date from late 16th through the 17th century.

The later type it is said is a globular jug with cylindrical neck and handle. These seem to be of brown ware with chevron design hatched and fronds all in white slip under a yellow glaze. In these the technique is improved. That this ware extended into the 18th century in a less sincere and degraded form is proven by a dish marked E.W. 1796 owned by Mr. C. J. Lomax.

WROTHAM WARE (c1612–1721)

Dr. J. W. L. Glaisher has made a special study of the pottery made at Wrotham, Kent, and his collection includes one showing slip tracery and dots and dated 1656 on an applied pad while the initials probably of the owner are on another. An earlier one in the V. & A. Museum is dated 1621 and is simpler being decorated with pads only. Soon the pads included such designs as angels, masks, stars, etc., and some were "stitched" on with little dashes of slip, a technique hardly suitable to the medium. One technical stunt that was attractive and, so far as I know, not practiced elsewhere, was

Fig. 1181. Loving-cup with badly restored foot and picture of Charles II between the handles. Ht. 7⅝". Yorkshire Mus., York.

Fig. 1179. Wrotham (Kent) slipware candlestick with four handles, light taffy colored earthenware with white slip decorations. Note ingenious inlays in handles of white and taffy rope-twisted clay. Late 17th or early 18th cent. Ht. 6⅜". Ernest F. Follows.

Fig. 1180. Jug and Tyg of Wrotham ware covered with brown glaze having greenish tinge over red body. Jug has inscription reading "G R WROTHAM WAK" and relief casting about neck from Raeren piece. Tyg has initials $_M^S{}_M$ and inscription, "DECEMB: THE FIRST 1645." Hts. 12" and 6". Ex Dr. G. W. Glaisher Coll.

that the handles were made with a groove along the length and filled with a straight cord of slip, or a twisted one of white slip or even of white and red slip twisted together. The handles were usually double loops and there may be three or four with each mounted with a knob finial or knobs in the V of the loops, showing no practical purpose and a bad tendency to heap ornament. Some had incised slip and some simple incised decoration without slip. Many bear the name WROTHAM.

These date from about 1612 to 1721 and the earlier ones are better craftsmanship and also simpler. It has been suggested that the handle inlayed decoration and the use of the prunts or dots come from earlier leather techniques while Rackham and Read suggest that the shapes are not unlike the mortars of bell-metal; which are contemporary. The Spanish and Italian bronze mortars also of the period were made with appliqué pads so that the designs could be changed and probably this technique also was taken from them.

North Staffordshire and "Toft Ware" (1676–1707)

Thomas and Ralph Toft, who may or may not have been brothers, rate high in English ceramics. Other potters in Staffordshire imitated their wares such as Richard Meir, Ralph Simpson, Robert Shaw and Ralph Turner.

"Highwayman" dish with raised outlines, white slip and two-toned brown slip decoration, Staffordshire, c. 1640. Dia. 9". Mr. and Mrs. Frank P. Burnap.

Red earthenware dish decorated in white slip under yellowish glaze, made in Staffordshire (1670–1680). Mr. and Mrs. Frank P. Burnap.

Two Wrotham tygs showing pads of white clay stamped with relief design, upper 1656 and 1621. Hts. 7" and 6⅝". Dr. J. W. L. Glaisher and Victoria & Albert Mus.

Left: Buff earthenware dish with brown slip and combed decoration of white slip over it and under yellow glaze, Staffordshire, 18th cent. Dia. 13½". Mr. Frank Falkner.

Center: Beautiful bowl of hard chocolate-brown earthenware covered with white slip through which design is incised. Salt glaze. Made by Ralph Shaw, Burslem, Staffordshire, c. 1733. Ht. 3⅝". Mr. Wallace Elliot.

Right: Dish of dark brown ware covered on front with white slip having incised design and dabs of slate-blue under yellowish glaze. Staffordshire, 1753. Dia. 14½". Central Mus., Northampton.

Left: Dish of red ware covered with brown slip and decorated in white and olive-green slips under yellowish glaze. Inscribed *Thomas Toft,* c. 1670. Dia. 22". Dr. J. W. Glaisher.

Right: Brown ware dish decorated masterfully in white slip under yellow glaze. Staffordshire c. 1700. Dia. 13". Central Mus., Northampton.

ENGLISH SLIP WARES OF 17TH AND 18TH CENTURIES

PLATE 207

There is a large loving cup in the Yorkshire Museum, belonging to C. J. Lomax, of brown ware with decoration in dark brown and white slips and the legend, THOMAS TOFT ELIZABETH POOT, but most of his work was on large 18 inch plates, made for a marriage, christening or some other occasion. It is suggested that Toft was the manager of a factory that turned out ordinary pots and did these things himself only for such occasions. However, there must have been quite a trade in them too. His decoration was of very spirited animals or beautifully arranged plant forms such as those on the dish in the Central Museum, Northampton. The animals are as alive and vigorous as those on 12th to 13th century wares of Western Asia or the "Scythian" bronzes and one can say no more in praise.

The technique was difficult consisting of the pouring out of a pipette or long-spouted can the almost liquid clay. The longer one's hand hesitated, the wider became the line, as the liquid continued to flow. Thus the constant speed of drawing had to be maintained. Moreover the beginning or termination of a line would have a blob unless the attack and withdrawal were done surely and without hesitation. This is much like the technique of batik

Fig. 1184. Earthenware covered with white slip. Decorated in red slip under clear glaze, inscr., MARY PERKINS, 1704. Staffordshire. Dia. 19".

Fig. 1182. Two pieces of buff earthenware decorated in brown and white slips under yellow glaze. Upper 1704, lower 1697. Hts. 8¾" and 5½". Dr. J. W. Glaisher and Mr. C. J. Lomax.

Fig. 1183. Dish molded with raised outlines, covered with white slip and decorated with light and dark brown slips. Made by William Bird, Staffordshire c. 1751. Dia. 16¼". Manchester Art Gallery. Beneath is mold of hard brown earthenware incised to produce raised outlines. Incised on back: William Bird made this mould. In the year of Our Lord 1751. British Mus.

Fig. 1185. Brown earthenware decorated in white slip stamped with cross pattern, signed about neck SAMVEL HVGHESON 1678. Ht. 7⅜". Formerly Dr. J. W. Glaisher Coll.

(see article in 14th edition Ency. Britannica by the author) but the fabric in this case is stretched flat while a pottery vessel has a curved surface. With the pencil or etching-point, the brush or carving tool one can go slowly through a difficult passage, therefore, in one sense they are much more easily handled. However, the real artist does not, of course, want a line of constant width and Toft, just as Miss Ethelyn Stewart, makes the lines taper and grow and taper again to bring life and vitality like that of nature itself into the drawing.

The perpendicular brush of the Far East is surely a wonderful instrument and with it more sensitive expression can be achieved, but closely akin to it is this pipette technique and it imposes one more difficulty which drives the artist to great achievements in some ways. Thus the beautiful dish illustrated is decorated with only nine strokes and seventeen dots. It could not have engaged the artist more than ten minutes of actual work. The dish with a running hare which I believe now belongs to Mrs. Frank Burnap of Kansas City is as economically rendered and these things almost approach the wonderful work of the Sung period Tz'u Chou artists. Yet it is this ware which Hannover dismissed with, "There was no future for the ceramic art proper in peasant-pottery in England any more than in other countries. Here as elsewhere, it was from without, from the centers of ceramic culture, that the decisive fertilization came, after being awaited for a remarkably long period." How totally blind the porcelain-minded gentry are to art!

Of course, to be quite fair, it depends upon what Mr. Hannover was searching for; if he was looking for the beauties he does somewhat appreciate in Rhenish and Delft wares, he could find them in England only later and adulterated, but, if he had appreciated the wonderful brushwork of the Far East and the superb animal design of the Near East, he could hardly condemn Toft ware as mere "peasant-pottery" without a future.

These artists also invented other effects such as the outlining with dots on a dark slip giving a soft and yet brilliant result. This we have not seen elsewhere. Another stunt was to fill the design with a colored slip and grain it to look like matting or material. This was, of course, one of the first ideas in potting but it had long been lost and this occurrence without knowledge of the former wares is interesting. Another Staffordshire process was to make mound shaped molds of baked clay with the design incised, the lines often roughened by many tiny notches at right angles to them on the outside edge of a design. Over these the clay was patted and smoothed in exactly the same manner as was done with Ting yao, Sung period Chinese bowls. When the clay was removed ridges or cloissons were left standing outlining the design, and the areas between them were filled with different colored slips after which the whole was glazed and fired. These bowls with cloisonné technique were continued some years after the period of Toft ware. In the B.M. is one of the molds. Some had unnotched lines and some were notched on both sides. The notching was simply a method of softening the effect artistically. The former is well illustrated by a dish with St. George and the dragon and the latter by another with a spirited "Highwayman" brandishing sword and pistol, in the collection of Mrs. Frank P. Burnap. Most of these dishes are of buff body covered with white slip and decorated with light and dark brown slips and sometimes with red or reddish-brown. Some authorities attribute these wares to Derbyshire but most have been found in Staffordshire.

The "Hugheson Group"

Another type of wares was found marked "HUGHESON" or "SAMUEL HUGHESON" and the earliest of these is dated 1677. A typical example marked 1678 has an ovoid body of brown, a heavy foot-rim, short, sturdy wide cylindrical neck and heavy curved loop handle. The inscription is about the neck in white slip unimpressed, but the design on the body consists of diamond forms and scrolls with spots, stamped with a cross pattern throughout. Rackham and Read say, "On the earlier of these jugs man- ganese has been added over the impressions before glazing." This is the first use of man- ganese that we find, though some of the browns may have been partly and unconsciously due to it. A posset-pot of the Glaisher Collection was dabbed with bright green before the slip lines were applied. A similar one dated 1691 and with the name IOHN HUGHESON also on it, has green and cream slip dragged in alternating directions much as we see the designs of Egyp- tian glass, which, of course, these potters had never seen.

Fig. 1186. Posset-pot of red earthenware with combed white slip decoration and inscription reading, "IOHN HVGHESON 1691." Glaze yellowish streaked here and there with green of copper. Staffordshire. Ht. 9¼". Dr. J. W. Glaisher.

There are other names which occur such as on the example in the B.M. dated 1686 with "IOHN WENTER" and one in the Ashmolean Museum, Oxford, with "ANN BENOM F.K." and 1687, but whether these are names of the potters or of prospective owners we do not know. Some have doubted also that these are Staffordshire wares but we believe the evidence supporting that attribution is secure.

Fareham near Southampton

Posset-pots of red body with band decoration and inscriptions in crinkled strips of clay of white, dull red or stained green are attributed to Fareham, near Southampton.

"Metropolitan" or London Ware

A very simple sort of jug of red body with slight design and sometimes inscriptions trailed in white slip and covered with yellow glaze is found in and near London. These have all the appearance of the late Tickenhall group or even less well developed ware and one owned by B. T. Harland is inscribed "BE NOT HY MINDED BUT FEAR GOD, 1638" bearing out the earlier dating. A few examples are in the London Museum.

A still cruder and more summarily designed ware may come from London or from Staffordshire though the former seems more likely. These are thinly potted in buff clay, covered with a white slip, and dabbed with large spots placed in an irregular row and streaked with crude stripes. Rackham and

FIG. 1187. Buff earthenware jug partly covered with brown slip and decorated with combed white slip, Staffordshire, 17th cent. Ht. 9". Mr Frank Falkner.

FIG. 1188. Red earthenware jugs decorated with white slip under yellow glaze, London, middle 17th cent. Hts. 8¾" and 8¼". London Mus.

Read place them as late as the 17th century but, if this is their date, they show a definite decadence.

"FEATHERED" OR "COMBED" WARES

On the posset-pot above mentioned we spoke of dragged or "combed" design. This dated 1691 but the technique became popular about 1680 to

FIG. 1189. Mug and posset-pot of buff ware covered with brown slip incised down to body. Upper dated 1727 and lower 1732. Staffordshire and lower possibly Derbyshire. Hts. 3½" and 7½". Ex Dr. J. W. Glaisher Coll.

1700 or later in general, and "marbling," "feathering" and "graining" methods were devised. The technique was not used much at all in the North Countries of the continent where modeling made the surface textures, but here again it picks up the ancient stunt and carries it on probably not through any connection with Egyptian or Chinese or Near Eastern wares but just as a natural development arrived at through playing around with colored slips. Various rows of spots of slip were applied and while still fluid were dragged with a point or comb. This again appears easy enough but one should try it on the curved surface of a vessel to see how tricky it really is. The slip has to be just so moist and the body just slippery enough and the touch must be exceedingly light. Hannover's "peasant wares" forsooth! He should have tried it.

The method was used in various parts of the country. Some are known as "Welsh ware" and were made at Hounslow while others come from the northern potteries. In the V. & A. Museum is one marked "SCOTTS SUPERIOR FIRE-PROOF, SUNDERLAND."

Of course the more direct and primitive process of mixing clays together like marble cake produced the "agate ware" in the late 17th century but both seem to have not been copied from any known imported examples.

INCISED, GRAFFITO OR SGRAFFITO WARES

A potter named Ralph Shaw of Burslem took out a patent in 1733 to make chocolate brown and white striped curious pottery with a salt glaze but three years later Mr. Shaw's patent was taken away from him, so some of the large number of pieces known must have been made by others. A salt glazed bowl from the collection of Mr. Wallace Elliot is hard chocolate brown, covered inside with white slip, and outside with a band of the same through which a design has been scratched. Every other piece known has lead glaze with nowhere nearly such artistry. The uninitiated might even think this bowl to be Sung Chinese, so good is it. Very likely this is a real Ralph Shaw piece and it is a pity that he was not allowed to continue.

FIG. 1190. Devonshire jug of red ware with white slip and greenish-yellow glaze, much in style of certain South China, Ming wares. Inscribed, "Now i am come for to supply your workmen when in haruist dry when they do labour hard and sweat good drink is better far than meat. In winter time when it is cold i like wayes then good ale can hold all seasons do the same require and most men do strong drink desire. W H 1724, 1724, 1724." Ht. 13½". Ex Dr. J. W. Glaisher Coll.

The later type such as that shown with a bird design and dated 1753 shows strong resemblance to South German wares and the "Gabri" 10th to 11th century ones done with a light slip over a dark body with dabs of color on the slip in this case slate blue, to relieve the hardness. Of course it is not possible that these English potters had ever seen the Persian or Sung wares.

The incised method was used also in the West Country and Wales at such places as Donyat, Somersetshire and Crock Street where the thicker and more crude ware even more resembles "Gabri." The latest date found on any of them is 1779. But in many places in Devonshire and elsewhere about the country the method is used even to-day. A Devonshire one also from the Glaisher Collection looks very much like a certain type of Ming example from China, and by 1724, its date, there were quite possibly imported pieces to work from.

From about Salisbury are pieces of red body and with a very iridescent manganese glaze and these are variously dated between 1603 and 1800. The decoration is incised and several bear the initials W.Z. followed in one case by the word "MAKER." A fine covered goblet in the Salisbury, South Wilts and Blackmore Museum is inscribed "HERE IS THE GEST OF THE BARLY KORNE GLAD HAM I THE CILD IS BORN, 1692 I.G.R.K.S.K." and this is typical for most of these seem to have been made for christenings.

At many other places red bodied ware had brown or manganese glaze over simple incising. Some odd conceptions seem to have been

FIG. 1191. Buff earthenware jug with thick, glossy dark brown glaze. Head forms cover. Midlands 18th cent. Ht. 11". Mrs. J. W. Gaunt.

favorites such as the modeled bear-holding-a-cub jug with detachable head cover and a small monkey on the handle. This sort of jug was also made in the white Staffordshire ware and elsewhere. Little molded plaques were continued in use and undoubtedly gave Wedgwood his ideas later.

Finally Rackham and Read state that the wares of the 19th century were made in Blackburton in Lancashire, Pot-Howcans, near Halifax, at Midhope near Sheffield and at Polesworth in Warwickshire. They also state, "It is also interesting to note the spread of this technique to the United States, where pottery quite similar in technique was made in the early 19th century at Huntington, Long Island. This New England ware is quite distinct in character from the slipware made in Pennsylvania by German Immigrants." Of course we now know that the English were also partly responsible for the Pennsylvania wares and they need not have been so much on the defensive. In fact the plate with bird design is very much like both Long Island and Pennsylvania ones.

Here again we have found an unsullied art practiced by free men who were not forced to copy and could suit themselves.

Fig. 1194. Red-ware ink-well with rich chocolate-brown slip decorated in white slip under usual transparent glaze. Dia. 3". Plummer, Ltd.

Fig. 1192. Red earthenware jug with inlayed design and inscription reading, "Mrs. SHOO-SMITH? CATERBURY? 1809," in white slip, Sussex. This is a technique chiefly of Korea, of course, but arrived at here without outside influence. Ht. 12⅜". Coll. of Mrs. Hemming.

Fig. 1193. Cup with four handles and a whistle, of brown ware with incised decoration under lead glaze with flecks of iron. Inscribed, "HERE IS THE GEST OF THE BARLY KORNE. GLAD HAM I THE CILD IS BORN I G 1692," and on foot, "RK SK." Found at Mere, Wilshire but made near Salisbury. Ht. 8½". Salisbury, South Wilts and Blackmore Mus.

English Faïence or "Delft" and the Foreign Influence

The first direct foreign influence was indicated, of course, in the Tudor period (c1428–   ) with the green glazed heraldic wares but these did not continue much beyond the start of the 16th century. The general use of the word "Delft" is misleading, though it is customary in England, for the first wares of this sort came direct to England from Italy even before Delft was started in any great degree. Guido di Savino, from Castel Durante, went to Antwerp and was established by 1513. He has been linked with Guido Andries and Jacob Janson who left Antwerp to avoid persecution and settled in Norwich, later in 1570 moving to London. From this date, presumably in the "waterside" parishes Southwark and Lambeth, tin-enamelled wares were made. At Norwich we hear they made tiles and apothecaries' jars. (Cf. John Stow, "A Survey of the Cities of London and Westminster and the Borough of Southwark, 1598," 6th ed., London, 1755, Vol. II, p. 327.)

Some wares found in London, Oxford and elsewhere might almost be thought to be Italian majolica. They are decorated in polychrome, or are blue and white with the same bright colors but are somewhat different in form. For instance vases were made with a wide neck and bulbous bodies having two small loops, useless as handles or for tying on a cover, neither original nor sensible shapes. They often have the sacred monogram "yhs" in Gothic characters or at times a bird recalling those of Faenza ware. A polychrome tile showing a man in the dress of about 1530 is in the Guildhall Museum, London and is of the same class exactly as tiles with busts from the Herckenrode abbey, Belgium, Limburg, now in Brussels. Duplicates are also found in the bed of the Scheldt, Antwerp and in Brussels itself. Another from the house of Sir Nicholas Bacon built between 1563 and 1568 is in the exact colors of the Flemish tiles, blue, green and orange. It seems likely that this is of the early work of Jasper Andries and Janson.

A group of wares showing Italian influence are glossy enameled plates with foliage painted peculiarly with each leaf one half yellow, one half orange, with green and blue added. Another type has fruit including pomegranates bursting. A fine jug of the Early Stuart Period bears a picture of a youth in the dress of James I, fruits, flowers and foliage, in yellow, brown and blue. This has a medallion encircled with an English inscription and three initials in triangular arrangement, which is peculiarly English.

MOTTLED IMITATION STONEWARE

Similar in shape to the stoneware jugs of Cologne and Frechen are earthenware enamelled ones with globular bodies and cylindrical necks quite different in substance from any European ones. The glazes are brown, tawny yellow, dark green, purplish black and dark blue usually, though other odd colors do occur, and all seem to have been daubed or splashed on, combined

FIG. 1195. Earthenware jug covered with mottled purplish blue enamel, having chased silver-gilt mounts bearing London hall-mark for 1550. Ht. 7½". Lord Swaything.
FIG. 1196. Raeren (c. 1580–1600) stoneware flagon with brown mottled glaze and renaissance silver mounts. Ht. 9½". Plummer, Ltd.
FIG. 1197. Enamelled mug sprayed with purple in which there is a band about top reserved in white and painted in blue, "ELIZABETH BROCKLEHVRST 1628." London (Lambeth or Southwark). Ht. 5". Victoria & Albert Mus.

with a flux. They are usually mounted with English silver or silvergilt covers and bases, the hall-marks of which show them to date about the middle of the 16th century.

These were not made by foreign workmen as they are technically entirely different from anything on the continent. The English silversmiths did seek the continental "tiger ware" to mount and these were probably used for models for general shape.

ENGLISH FAÏENCE

"LAMBETH DELFT WARE"

OR

"METROPOLITAN TIN-GLAZED WARE"

Around 1630 we find that there were kilns at first in London and then a little later in Bristol and the nearby village of Brislington, Liverpool and a small place at Wincanton in Somersetshire. The products of the London potters came to be called "Lambeth Delft Ware" which is doubly wrong for Delft was not yet known as a pottery center and all the potters were not in the Lambeth parish of London, but in Southwark and Bermondsey where some sherds were found near a street called "Potter's Field." In 1690 there was also a potter at Aldgate. It is difficult to argue against even an incorrect tradition in England, however. Rackham and Read have suggested the term "Metropolitan tin-glazed ware" which, though grand sounding, is no more sensible. As the word faïence is generally accepted for this type of ware, and, as we cannot list all the places where it was made, I suggest that the ware be simply called "English Faïence."

FIG. 1198. Rare English faïence shoe decorated in blue with yellow heels, 1759. Length 8″. Courtesy—A Collector.

It is argued that as Joseph Medway, an Englishman, was employed as a thrower in Rotterdam in 1649 and Andrew Morton was a foreman in 1629 in another factory in the same city, the making of the ware must have preceded these dates in England. Of course, both may have been entirely foreign trained in their work. However, a piece recorded by B. J. Warrick and shown at the Burlington Club in 1914 has a silver collar on which in Latin there is a report of having bought it in 1618. This is decorated with mottled manganese and cobalt sprayed on the surface of the enamel, a process not found exactly the same on the continent. The same technique is found on a barrel-shaped mug in the V. & A. Museum clearly dated 1628 together with the English name ELIZABETH BROCKLEHURST. This technique is in the line of general development and was probably not copied from anywhere, though it has been used almost everywhere.

Also in 1628 is a globular jug so dated in the Collection of B. T. Harland which is near white with blue decoration of birds and flowers. Others of similar decoration date around 1631 or 1632. The designs are described as Chinese but are very much more crude and have some different characteristics from even the worst of the Canton wares of the time. By 1640 no more such

Group of "Lambeth delft" chargers partly blue and white and partly polychrome, all dating in late 17th cent. Upper left is Duke of Monmouth, center below is identical figure serving for Prince "Eugin." This was often done. Probably upper right is James II fleeing and lower right is William of Orange. Average dia. 13½". Guitel Montague.

Enamelled earthenware plate painted in blue, yellow, orange and green outlined in deep purple, inscribed, "THE ROSE IS RED THE LEAVES ARE GRENE GOD SAVE ELIZABETH OVR QVEENE." London, 1602. Dia. 10⅛". London Mus.

Enamelled earthenware jug painted in blue, yellow, orange and dull yellow-green. On front is youth in dress of early Stuart period in medallion about which is inscribed, "I AM NO BEGGER I CAN NOT CRAVE BVT YV KNOW THE THING THAT I WOVLD HAVE." On the neck are the initials R $\overset{C}{}$ E. Lambeth or Southwark, London c. 1630. Ht. 12½". Colonel John Parker.

Platter of relief and polychrome decoration called "Lambeth Delft." Mark on back is A–NLP. Length 20½". International Studio Art Corp.

ENGLISH FAÏENCE ("LAMBETH DELFT") OF THE 17TH CENTURY

PLATE 208

designs are used and only later was there a return of Chinese influence through the copying of the Dutch so-called "Nanking blue ware."

From about 1632 Italian designs came in at first through the Low Countries and these were most popular in Bristol. They are largely of fruit, flowers, etc. and have formalized borders usually edged with diagonal blue strokes for which they have been called "Blue Dash Chargers" by Ed. A. Downman. Some of these too were made in Brislington and London. The wares are buff, covered on the front only with tin enamel, while the backs have only a transparent lead glaze of yellowish or greenish tone. The enamel is white and the painting is in orange, yellow, purple, green and blue. The drawing was

Fig. 1199. Posset pot of "Lambeth Delft" made about 1700–1720. Ht. 5¾". "Liverpool Delft" mug wit handle in blue and white made in early 18th cent. Ht. 4¾". Owl after those made in Germany. Ht. 4" Guitel Montague.

crude and the anatomy particularly of the Bristol and Brislington pieces is bad. The foot-rim was flared outward and made fairly deep so that a cord could be tied around it to hang the piece on the wall. The earliest is one owned by Dr. Glaisher dated 1628 which has a design of all-over foliage with spiraled stems and conventionalized flowers reminiscent of Spanish lustre decoration. Some have portraits of sovereigns and important personages, others the Temptation of Adam and Eve while fruit heaped on a high footed dish seems to have been a later motive. They lasted at least until 1674 for there is one so dated also in the Glaisher Collection.

URBINO AND FAENZA TYPES

Another group in softer colors of purple, brownish-orange and blue have grotesques, caryatids, winged beasts, etc., in the styles of Urbino and Faenza but more crowded and loosely painted. These are not copied from Dutch "Urbino Delft" which is quite different. The Glaisher group includes ore dated 1649 with the initials $\frac{B}{E\ M}$ in the center of the front and the added colors of yellow and yellow-green.

A cistern dated 1638 and with the initials $\frac{I}{T\ I}$ had a modeled figure,

English faïence dish showing Urbino influence, painted in blue, yellowish-green, yellow, brownish-orange and purple. In center is ${}_{E}^{B}M$ and date 1649. Made in London at Lambeth or Southwark. Dia. 15¼". Ex Dr. J. W. Glaisher Coll.

London faïence dish painted blue, green, yellow and orange. Inscribed on back under lead glaze: ${}_{R}^{A}M$ 1640. Dia. 17". Mr. J. H. Taylor.

Dishes showing "The Fall." Upper one London, painted in blue, yellowish-green, yellow and brownish-orange. Lower, Bristol ware painted in blue, yellow, green, dark purple and dark red, trees being "sponged." Both are middle to late 17th cent. Hts. 14" and 13¾" W. M. Beaumont.

Left: So-called "Lambeth Delft" said to be rare in this size. Portrait, James II. Ground pale turquoise, drawing in plum and bright orangy yellow. Note three spur marks. Dia. 7¼". Frank Stoner—Stoner & Evans, Ltd.
Right: Faïence cistern described in text. Ht. 15¼". Hanley Mus.

English "delft" or faïence flagons with tin glaze and lettering in light blue on first reading WHIT 1651 and on other monogram of Queen Mary. Hts. 5½" and 6¾". Guitel Montague.

ENGLISH FAÏENCE (17TH CENTURY)

PLATE 209

flanked by two pilasters, paintings on the sides of the Spinario and Cupid and panels of allegorical figures in landscapes above panels of grotesques in the Urbino manner. The colors are partly blue and white and partly blue, purple and brownish yellow. But the interesting thing about this mixed up piece is that the back has a typical symmetrical "Indian flower" design like those of South Germany or the Kreussen c. 1618 to c. 1660 ones even to the spirals. This piece seems to have borrowed from everywhere. It is in the

Fig. 1200. English faïence pharmacy jars inscribed in blue, c. 1720. Ht. 1?". Probably Lambeth. Courtesy—A Collector.

Fig 1201. Small feeding-cup of English faïence, probably from Lambeth with relief Tudor Rose decoration and white glaze. c 1645. Mrs. Bruce.

Hanley Museum. Generally speaking these designs are found only on Bristol pieces and never on the London ones which is strange and can be accounted for only by some now unknown potter having gone there.

OTHER TYPES

A number of the Adam and Eve plates were made and it is conceded that the London ones are far better than those from Bristol and thereabouts. One in the collection of W. M. Beaumont, due to a notch in the tree excused by a notch on the other side, and some cleverly placed foliage, gives Adam quite a masculine look, which shows the playful and not too touchy humor of the period.

A few were of religious nature showing the Nativity, "Prodigal Son feasting with harlots," etc. One in the V. & A. Museum, painted in blue, green and yellow shows a figure of St. Mary Magdalene with crudely drawn house and castle in the background in the style of the period as can be seen in embroideries.

TECHNICAL CHARACTERISTICS

As we have said most of these wares are only lead glazed on the back, not like the good Delft but like what the Hollanders call "schotelgoed." They had no protection of saggers in the kiln and were simply fired like tiles. Of them Hannover says, "This English 'Delft' is in every respect inferior to the genuine article, and is obviously quite different from it from a technical point of view. Whereas the true Delft is so soft in body that it can be cut with a knife, it is difficult to scratch the English variety with a steel point." (I fail to see how this is an inferior characteristic.) "Genuine Delft is of a porous clay, which drank up the enamel far more readily than the English, and is therefore completely and evenly covered with glaze in quite another manner than the latter. Lastly, English Delft is often much crackled in its glaze, whilst the Dutch, as has been remarked on an earlier page, hardly ever has this defect." In other words the English material is put in the strange category of being a copy of Delft, which it is not, and then declared to be no good because it is not. Certainly hardness is not a bad point; crackle is considered pleasant in texture and all told the English seem to have pulled down such criticisms because of their unfortunate choice of the name "Lambeth Delft."

Some of the shapes not used on the continent are: barrel-shaped mugs, truncated egg-shaped mugs, wine bottles with wide body and narrow necks, posset-pots usually with spouts for sucking the liquid and slabs for pill-making decorated with the arms of the Apothecaries' Company.

FIG. 1202. English faience wall-pocket, c. 1730. Courtesy—A Collector.

Posset, according to the *Century Dictionary* is, "A drink composed of hot milk curdled by some infusion, as wine or other liquor, formerly much in favor both as a luxury and as a medicine." L. Jewitt in his "Ceramic Art of Great Britain" (first ed.) I., p. 108 says, "Posset is an excellent mixture of hot ale, milk, sugar, spices and sippets or dice of bread or oat cake, almost if not quite universal for supper on Christmas eve." It is evident that such a mixture could not be drunk from a spout unless the liquor was simply drained off from the bottom. Perhaps the earlier sort was not thickened with bread and such.

Of continental type wares there are those similar to the late ones of Bernard Palissy, square salt-cellars and various dishes molded with the subject called "La Fécondité" ranging from about 1659 to 1697 according to the dates on them.

The wine bottles were labeled SACK, WHIT, CLARET or RENISH WINE with sometimes a personal coat of arms and name added. They may have been used for samples as they seem to contain too little for table use in those days, at least this suggestion has been made by Mr. Frank Falkner. The apothecaries' jars had the names of drugs on them.

FIG. 1203. Mugs covered with dark and light blue enamel respectively, decorated with white slip. Upper London, lower either London or Bristol. Hts. 3½" and 5¼". City Art Gallery, Manchester. Mr. Edward Sheldon.

WHITE ON BLUE WARE

Infrequent Italian majolica and Delft but a usual technique of Nevers, France, was that of staining the enamel with cobalt and then applying the design in white arsenical slip on it. At Bristol this was done with a blue of dark inky tone, while at London it was lighter showing up the crackle even through the white. The designs were of crude Chinese character. There were also wares of a similar nature with blue combined with manganese.

ORIGINS OF BRISTOL WARES

In speaking of the cistern above we mentioned that the symmetrical flowers must have been brought by some individual potter or group of potters who came to Bristol not by way of London. The factories seem to have started from one of Edward Ward, "galley pot maker," in Brislington. Rackham

FIG. 1204. Enamelled earthenware plate of greenish tone, painted with deep yellow, dull red, blue and dull yellowish-green. Probably by Michael Edkins (c. 1760). Bristol. Dia. 9". Brig.-General Sir Gilbert Mellor K.B.E.

FIG. 1205. Plate by John Bowen of Bristol painted in blue on white. c. 1760. Ht. 8¾". Mr. R. Hall Warren.

FIG. 1206. Enamelled earthenware dish painted in blue, yellow, orange and clear turquoise-green, 1676. Probably Bristol. Dia. 12¾". Dr. J. W. Glaisher.

and Read say the word "gallipot" occurs in 1465 and was thought to have been used to designate pottery of all shapes that were brought from the Mediterranean in galleys. I think this theory unsound. They further say, "Dutch writers of the 17th century interpret 'glei' as meaning porcelain clay" (that is clay used for making tin-enamelled ware, then not distinguished from true porcelain). The general idea to-day seems to be a small mouthed

FIG. 1207. Dish, Bristol (?), painted in dark and light cobalt blue, yellow and turquoise blue outlined in purple, inscribed S and dated 1676. Dia. 8¼". Ex Dr. J. W. Glaisher Coll.

FIG. 1208. English faïence pilgrim bottle roughly decorated in purple or aubergine of manganese. Bristol (?) Early 18th cent. Ht. 7¾". Plummer, Ltd.

jar such as would be *used* on a ship. In any event Ward went to Bristol and built a pottery at Temple Back which remained in his family until 1741. It was the parent of the present Bristol factory at Fishponds. Ward's pupil, Thomas Frank, opened a factory at Brislington at Redcliff Back and his son worked at both places. Still another pottery was opened at Limekiln Lane by William Pottery, and John Bowen began his apprenticeship here in 1734. He worked later for Joseph Flower and others.

CHARACTERISTICS OF BRISTOL

We have said that the drawing of anatomy at Bristol was less good than that of the London wares and that the symmetrical flowers are characteristic. The colors include a slaty blue, "quaker green," dull yellow, brownish-orange and occasionally manganese and pale turquoise blue and are softer than the colors used at London. Plate edges are often scalloped, foliated or octagonal. Punch bowls had flattened flaring sides tangent to the curve of the bottoms. Posset-pot lids sometimes took the form of the royal crown with open-work bows, and the handles were in the form of snakes or rolls of clay twisted into the shape of coiled tendrils. Oblong flower holders with holes in the top for stems (see our illustration) were characteristic. Even tea-table wares were attempted toward the end of the 18th century but were clumsy and not popular.

FIG. 1209. "Bristol Delft" "crocus-pot" with polychrome decoration. c. 4″ high. Guitel Montague.
FIG. 1210. English "delft" crocus pots with grids and decorated with almost identical scenic subjects. Even when art was not wholly mechanical such was dearth of imagination that painters copied their own work over and over. c. 1730. Lengths c. 6″. Guitel Montague.

Perhaps the best painter was John Bowen who confined himself to blue on white wares and created an odd fairyland with stately ladies and gentlemen strolling among tall and misty trees and gaunt houses all in the most economical brush work, while on the other hand his ships show accuracy and attention to detail.

Michael Edkins is reported to have been a scene-painter, enameller of both faïence and Bristol glass and a good musician. Most of his known things are of chinoiserie character.

Joseph Flower started a factory at Redcliff in 1743. He painted in imitation of engravings and showed more skill than taste but at times also a naïve simplicity. He made starch-blue and lavender blue plates with broad white flowers on the rims in the bianco-sopra-bianco style and having centers of landscapes in blue or flowers in purple-blue, olive green and brownish orange. The same blue enamel with white flowers in borders is used inside

Bristol posset-pot painted purple, blue and yellow in pseudo-Chinese style. Late 17th cent. Ht. 9½". Brighton Mus.

Posset-pot and tray of pale blue faïence decorated in cobalt-blue with border of tray in purplish-blue. Both pot and tray have   and are dated

T
C A

1685. Ht. 13½". Ex Dr. J. W. Glaisher Coll.

Right: Punch bowl covered with pale lavender-blue and painted by John Bowen with white slip borders and Swedish ship inside with landscape with figures outside. 1728. Bristol, factory of Joseph Flower. Dia. 11⅜". City Art Gallery, Manchester.

Left: Bristol mid-18th cent. tin enamel plate painted in blue, brown, dull, dark red, yellow and olive green. Dia. 12½". Warren E. Cox Coll.

Center: Bristol plates, upper in blue, green, yellow, orange and dark purple (c. 1670). Lower in blue, orange and olive green (last of 17th cent.). Dias. 16½" and 14½". Mr. B. T. Harland. Mr. W. W. Beaumont.

Right: Bristol faïence plates, upper in blue, yellow, dark orange, green and dark purple with figure of William III, c. 1700. Lower in blue, green and brownish red with portrait of Dr. Sacheverell c. 1720. Dias. 14" and 11". Mr. B. T. Harland. Brighton Mus.

BRISTOL FAÏENCE (17TH AND 18TH CENTURIES)

PLATE 210

of bowls having ships in blue with touches of color for the flags, the sea, etc. He liked conical trees like the clipped boxwood ones one sees in England. Tiles were made at all the factories but were a feature here and were both individual and with grouped designs.

It has been claimed that Liverpool wares are thinner than the others and that Bristol is slightly more bluish or greenish in tone but neither rule is entirely true. In fact it is difficult to distinguish between Bristol and Liverpool wares for the flowers are identical except for perhaps a greater stiffness of stem and more direct brush work, less inclined to curlicues and scratchiness distinguishes Bristol work.

London plates were made in blue decoration of formal wreaths with legends, often beginning, "What is a merry man, etc.," including also ones which refer to the frailty of earthenware, expressions of sentiment, etc. At Bristol a special group includes a bowl of lavender grey with painting in white and inscription in blue celebrating the candidacy for Oxfordshire, 1755, of Viscount Wenman and Sir James Dashwood, Bart. The outside of this bowl has Chinese decorations in heavy manganese-purple and blue. This was a type often found.

Fig. 1211. Two plates from factory of Joseph Flower covered with pale lavender-blue, with borders of white and center painting in purple, blue, olive-green and dull, brownish orange. c. 1760. Dias. 8¾" and 16¼". Bristol Mus. and Art Gallery. Mr. W. R. Ackland.

SPATTERED GROUND WARES

Evidently suggested by the Chinese powder blue was a speckled ground used in the same way about reserve medallions. They date around 1754 and were in blue, manganese-purple, brown or yellow, not made by blowing powdered color onto a glaze but by spattering with a brush. Round, fan-shaped and shell-shaped reserved medallions were used both in Bristol and Liverpool.

Generally speaking Bristol took more interest in Chinese design than the other places. John Niglett who had a factory at Redcliff had an original color scheme of mahogany-red of

Fig. 1212. Bristol "delft" pomegranate tea-pot with yellow stippled ground. Ht. 4½". c. 1730–40. Guitel Montague.

sticky appearance, blue, sage-green and bright lemon yellow. His designs include the "long Lizas" of the Chinese, happy boys, rocks and palisades in a sort of clumsy imitation of K'ang Hsi style. Both John Flower and Edkins also made attempts after the same style. Of course, these all lacked the beautiful brush work and brilliant but harmonious colors of the Chinese but they should not be compared for they were not so much copies as individual works of art inspired by the Chinese and they have an appeal of their own in the soft qualified colors and almost childlike drawing.

Humanism in Art

There is also a homely humanism in this art. When we think of humanism we think of Will Rogers, Mark Twain, the present etcher S. Van Abbe in England, of Hogarth, Franz Hals and Will Shakespeare. What is this element which occurs in such different arts?

One may argue that all art is human as it is done by humans and for humans. Yet we think of some people as being more human than others even though they are of the same flesh and blood. If one is too alive he is not so human; if one is too dull, too careful, too good or too bad, he loses some of this human quality. Are we to come to the conclusion that to be human one should be just average or as Will Rogers said it, "know only what he reads in the papers"? Well hardly that. I think he said that just to make people more comfortable. I heard him in Cochran's Review in London kid the people about paying their war debt to the United States, kid about the Prince of Wales falling off his horse and say things that you would think quite impossible. Yet they liked it and paid him a high salary to come back and give them more. Perhaps this was because he said, "I never saw the man I did not like." Perhaps they felt his sympathy with all people underlying his kidding.

A human man is liked by dogs, children and cats. He has a sense of humor and not too much regard for himself. He will often play with an idea for some time before coming to any definite, hard and fast conclusion. He is seldom a religionist, though Christ was perhaps one of the most human of people. He is seldom a business man or scientist for their codes, ethics, rules and principles are too set and formalized to ever catch the fluid character of the really human world. He is interested in a *man* not in some one idea which represents that man, and he expects and allows for many contradictions in the thoughts and character of a man. And then fundamentally, of course, he has no fear for himself or his position or his reputation. He can smile at the world for he is not afraid and not very serious about it. He is willing to give up himself and even to give up any idea or any cause because of his breadth of vision. The army men used to express it by saying, "A hundred years from now nobody will know anything about it." And by this very attitude a number of men will be remembered for many centuries though they did not expect it or aim for it.

Perhaps we are trying to say something very similar to the ideas and beliefs of the Taoists and Zen Buddhists of the Far East; a human man is one who does not try to buck the current but stays in the flow of the universe.

It is fear that makes an artist copy another artist. It takes courage, that many men lack, to sing a song. The very courage of a man is in his approach to other men, to animals and to children, and it can be seen in the carriage, the look of the eye and, it is said, animals can even tell it by the smell of a person. This simple courage to do something of one's own was evident in the early potteries of England but it was lost by the 18th century porcelain makers to a great extent. They were frail but certainly not human in the large sense.

WINCANTON

Potters from Bristol established that less good factory at Wincanton, sherds of which were discovered by William Pountney. Blue and white, and manganese and white were of common style except for some which were sponged or splashed with reserve medallions in the usual manner. Some plates have a brown line at the edge. Again the design is scratched out of the colored ground and this was also done earlier at Liverpool and Bristol. An accidental strong pinkish tone occurs on many pieces.

Chinese plants with frond-like leaves set in trellis borders are typical. Dr. Glaisher has two plates dated 1738 and 1739 having St. George on one and a Chinese pavilion on the other. Both are marked WINCANTON. Other examples have the usual arms, etc.

FIG. 1213. Speckled purple ground plate with reserves painted in blue. Inscription reads: WINCANTON 1738. Somersetshire Dia. 8¾". Ex Dr. J. W. Glaisher Coll.

STAFFORDSHIRE

To quote Rackham and Read, "More satisfactory evidence than has yet been brought forward will be needed to prove that delft ware was ever made in Staffordshire."

LIVERPOOL

Liverpool did not become a pottery center until well into the 18th century and had not the early tradition that Bristol had. Its chief outlet was American

FIG. 1214. English faïence puzzle-jug decorated in blue and inscribed, "HERE GENTLEMEN COME TRY YOUR SKILL I'LE WAGER IF YOU WILL, THAT YOU DON'T DRINK THIS LIQUOR ALL WITHOUT YOU SPILL OR LET SOME FALL." Attr. to Richard Chaffers, c. 1750. Ht. 7¼". Plummer, Ltd.

FIG. 1215. One of pair of Liverpool "delft" sitting dogs on moulded bases made hollow and with slot in their backs as though intended for banks but so small a slot that few coins could be inserted. Underglaze blue, green and aubergine stipplings with overglaze yellow. c. 1730–40. Ht. 8⅜". Ernest F. Follows.

and other foreign markets. The best known potters were Alderman Thomas Shaw, who made ship punch-bowls, Seth Pennington, Richard Chaffers and Zachariah Barnes who made tiles.

The secret of transferring of copper plate etched or engraved designs onto paper and then onto the faïence was discovered by John Sadler and Guy Green in 1749. At first this was done only on the fired glaze but later they accomplished it on the unfired body. The paper was thin and soft so that when wet it would readily bend over the curved surface. Only a press, a little soap and the usual color to be fired on are necessary. One can begin to understand what happened to the art of faïence when it is understood that in 1756 they claimed they could print 1,200 tiles in six hours. The prints were in black, red or purple.

Rackham and Read say, "The mechanical process coming between the designer of the decoration and the finished product robs this type of ornamentation of any great aesthetic value," and this is putting it mildly and not quite right. Actually it was nothing more nor less than the temptation to make cheap things ever cheaper that ruined all chance of real art. Artistic things have been done in etching and artistic things could have been done in this medium, but they were not.

A chief product of Liverpool was the punch-bowl variously decorated with a ship in full sail and an inscribed ribbon. The outside was usually treated with the old designs of flowers, birds and insects. Such bowls may have been used to drink the luck of a voyage. They certainly were not used on board. John Robinson, apprentice of Seth Pennington, did one with the fleet and the legend, "Success to the Africa Trade." The Liverpool purple was almost black at times and the red was more russet than that used at Bristol. Other colors used were blue, yellow, olive green and occasionally brown. Trophies of weapons or naval gear in blue only around the borders or on the outside are also characteristic.

Fig. 1216. Six tiles about 5″ square all from Bristol except the one with children dancing and "Mr. Woodward in the character of Razor," which are Liverpool, the first having been printed by Sadler & Green in red c. 1755 and the second by the same people printed in black. Victoria & Albert Mus.

Some ship-bowls have Chinese landscapes on the outside and

some bowls were Chinese in character throughout. One in the Glaisher Collection and dated 1724 has lambrequins of the Rouen type. Another dated 1760 and wishing "Success to the Monmouth" has cranes on the outside similar to the "Fantasievogel" of German porcelain and to the exotic birds of Chelsea and Worcester, painted in yellow, dark purple and orange amidst purple and olive-green foliage.

Large flowers were painted on mugs in slate-blue, brown-orange, violet and olive-green on a bluish toned ground. Whole services carefully copied Ch'ien Lung contemporary blue and white ones of the South Chinese type with peonies, etc., but were so bad as to do no harm.

The tiles have an almost child-like simplicity of design and were often done in blue with the addition of just one other color. This was rather typical of many Liverpool wares. Sadler and Green made a series of actors in character. Others copied Chinese birds, French prints, etc. Bowen made some with his personal landscapes having tall feathery trees. Of course Sadler and Green printed designs for other factories and the process was not long kept a secret so that sure attribution of the printed wares is difficult and perhaps not worth the trouble anyhow.

By 1800 the lead glazed cream wares made all over England crowded out all worthy endeavor at Liverpool as elsewhere.

English Stoneware

There is some looseness in the application of the term "stoneware" as there is in porcelain, faïence and the other branches of ceramic arts. Hobson says stoneware is a partly vitrified earthenware attained by hard firing, that it is frequently translucent in its thinner parts, is impervious to liquids and able to resist acids. Burton simply says that stoneware consists of those varieties of earthenware which when sufficiently fired for use are practically impervious to liquids and so do not need a coating of glaze. Actually translucence, though it may be present, is not at all necessary as a characteristic. Furthermore there are some earthenwares, not stonewares, such as those made by the Cistercian monks, which hold liquids without having been glazed. Actually any or all wares are attacked by some acids such as hydrofluoric and this depends also upon the strength of the acid, the temperature, the length of time the application is made among other factors. Let us say then that all stoneware is vitrified sufficiently to ring when struck, to be impervious to liquids even when unglazed, to show translucence occasionally and finally to be harder than earthenware, though there are borderline wares which could go into either category.

Just as England was influenced in faïence by Italy and later by Delft so she was quite naturally influenced in her stoneware by the wares of Frechen, Raeren and Cologne during the 16th and 17th centuries. Licenses were petitioned for by William Simpson during the reign of Queen Elizabeth (1558–1603), by Thomas Rous in 1626 and by three associates, Ramsey, Arnold and Ayliffe in 1635 who wanted to make, "pantiles, stone jugs, earthen bottles, and other earthen commodityes nowe made by Straungers in Forraigne Partes." Yet we cannot find these wares and it is hardly likely that real stoneware was made until the latter half of the 17th century.

John Dwight at Fulham

In 1671 and again in 1684 John Dwight obtained a patent to open a factory in Fulham near London. He claimed he could make "opacous red and dark coloured porcellane or China and Persian wares." By the first it is supposed he meant something like Yi-hsing wares or similar to those the brothers Elers made, which were unglazed, but he never really accomplished the "transparent earthenware commonly knowne by the names of porcelaine or china," and we cannot guess what he had in mind as Persian wares, unless they were the contemporary 17th-century porcelaneous ones, which again he never approached.

In 1661 he was registrar to the Bishop of Chester. We hear of no former kiln training. Therefore it is believed that he opened his factory with the help of German potters, and his first wares are very much like those of Frechen and Cologne, wine jugs called "Bartmann" by the Germans with small necks and loop handles and a bearded face on the front of the neck with a rosette or crude shield of arms on the belly. Among some of these found in a walled up chamber at Fulham in 1866 was one with the crowned double C of Charles II, while another has the CR cipher and fleur-de-lys of the same king. A sherd of the ware made at Grenhausen, Nassau, with typical blue and manganese purple coloring was found also in Fulham. Similar wares were made by Symon Wooltus the younger and older in Southampton.

Dwight then developed a white or ivory body which he used for jugs of

FIG. 1219. Fulham stoneware plaque of tobaccobrown with relief bust of cavalier, early 18th cent. Dia. 8¼". Plummer, Ltd.

FIG. 1218. Jug of salt-glazed grey stoneware stained brown near top and decorated with appliqués after Hogarth, etc. Fulham c. 1740. Ht. 7". Brighton Mus.

FIG. 1217. Brown stoneware jug streaked with variegated colors (brown, white and mouse-grey) and decorated with appliqués in white including double bust of William & Mary, Fulham, c. 1690. Period of John Dwight. Ht. 6¾". Ex Coll. Dr. J. W. Glaisher.

German shape. Two of these mounted in silver are in the V. & A. Museum and are dated 1682. Another has dabs of brown and blue on it.

He also developed a marbled ware which was similar to that found in several other countries. Dr. Glaisher has one which is brown streaked with two bands of brown, white and grey, between which are appliqués of white figures, birds and a double bust of William and Mary over which is an angel's face with

Left: Mug of grey stoneware partly covered with brown glaze. Body has double walls with outer reticulated in flowers and foliage with stems incised. Fulham in period of John Dwight, late 17th cent. Ht. 4¾". Mr. Edward Sheldon.

Center: Neptune of grey stoneware covered with brown salt-glaze in imitation of bronze, Fulham, period of John Dwight, late 17th cent. Ht. 12¼". Victoria & Albert Mus.

Right: Fulham grey stoneware mug stained tobacco-brown on upper part as customary, and with interesting trees applied. Foliage made in simple and direct technique. Ht. 7½". (c. 1750). Plummer, Ltd.

Tea-pot of Astbury type and possibly by him. Glaze manganese and appliqués white under lead-glaze. Ht. 5". Guitel Montague.

Interesting oval plaque of chocolate brown ware with bust in white under greenish-yellow, crackled glaze. Attr. to Astbury c. 1740. Plummer, Ltd.

Coffee-pot with molded handle and spout and all-over incising of greatest technical skill. Potting thin and of reddish brown, hard ware. Bottom has psuedo-Chinese square mark. Probably made by Thomas Astbury c. 1740. Ht. 8½". Plummer, Ltd.

Staffordshire salt-glaze bowl of Elers style, c. 1730-40. Ht. 3½". Plummer, Ltd.

Left: Nottingham mug with incised stag-hunt decoration about the center and bands of applied clay grit over which is salt-glaze. Early 18th cent. Ht. 8¼". Brighton Mus.

EARLY ENGLISH WARES OF DWIGHT, ASTBURY AND ELERS
(c. 1700–1750)

PLATE 211

two wings. Others are simply marbled in black and white, brown and grey or brown and white.

Another technique was perfected, that of making double walled jugs with the outer wall perforated. This was done in China and Korea as well as on the continent in a crude way and also later at Nottingham. The appliqués were not always white as mentioned above; a mug in the collection of Edward Sheldon is light brown with stamped spots and pear shaped applied bosses in blue and chocolate colored clays. The process was described by Dwight in 1691 in one of his note books and these also prove that Dwight used flint in his mixture and also made an unglazed stoneware of reddish color.

Hannover and other authorities have said that the unglazed red ware had not been certainly identified but Rackham and Read show one "(period of John Dwight)" (Fig. 133) and say that they think among those now attributed to the Elers brothers we are likely to eventually find Dwight examples.

Some figures were done by Dwight and are of white or slightly buff stoneware, translucent in thinner parts and covered with a salt glaze of uneven thickness. Four other pieces are known which are dark brown and were copied from bronzes. One of Charles II and others of Mars and Jupiter show traces of unfired gilding. A light colored figure of Dwight's daughter inscribed, "Lydia Dwight, dyed March 3, 1673," dates these surely but none were possibly original works of art. Possibly young Grinling Gibbons did the modeling, or Italian sculptors may have been hired.

After John Dwight's death in 1703 the Fulham pottery was continued by his family but the figure work ended except for a possible few buff colored ones with cream colored tin enamel, reflecting the style of Queen Anne.

Beer jugs of the 18th century become more truly English. The grey or buff body is exposed on the lower half while the upper has a brown salt glaze. They are usually cylindrical with rolled and grooved mouldings near the top and bottom and have a grooved handle pinched where it joins the side near the bottom. Appliqués with arched or square shapes, oval or cut to fit the outline of the figures were used for decoration. From about 1720 there were busts of kings

FIG. 1220. Figures of "a sportsman with hound," and "Meleager," of white stoneware with salt-glaze, Fulham of period of John Dwight, late 17th cent. Hts. 9½" and 11". British Mus. Franks Coll.

FIG. 1221. Mug of grey stoneware with brown salt-glaze and applied reliefs. About top is inscribed, "GOD PRESERVE KING GEORGE AND ALL THE ROYAL FAMILY, EDWARD VAUGHAN, 1724." Ht. 8½". Fulham. Brighton Mus.

and queens such as Charles II, William III, Queen Anne, hunting scenes, beef-eaters, hares, stags, etc., all in settings with trees and church spires. On one dated 1729 is the "Midnight Modern Conversation" after Hogarth's well known print. Others had representations of the owners. The inscriptions are stamped on and the whole effect is commercial by the middle of the century.

The factory continues to-day and makes commercial wares and sanitary equipment.

Mortlake

At Mortlake a stoneware factory was started about 1800 by Joseph Kishere and in passing we may note also that a faïence kiln was started about 1750 by William Sanders. The former turned out many jugs with reliefs of Toby Filpot, groups of topers and hunting scenes but none are worth study.

York, The Manor House

At York in the Manor House, Francis Place had a small factory in the early part of the 18th century. A small cup in the V. & A. Museum proves that the ware was much like Dwight's marbled ware of light grey with markings in dark grey and brown. The potting seemed good and thin. After Place, Clifton made a white ware in imitation of Dwight's also.

Nottingham and the Midlands

In the 14th century Nottingham had earthenware kilns and in 1693 James Morley was named in legal proceedings by Dwight. Morley had worked for Thomas Harper of Southwark. The earliest dated piece attributed to him is

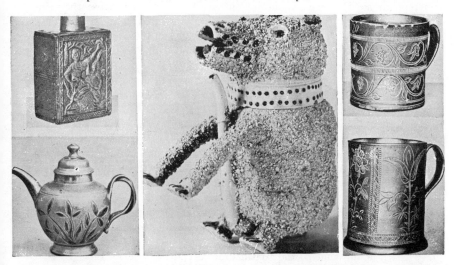

Fig. 1222. Molded Nottingham tea-caddy of brown stoneware inscribed, "Wm. & Ann Lockett, Jan the ye 6:1755. Also tea-pot with incised and brown slip design of same period. Castle Mus. and Art Gallery, Nottingham. Dr. E. J. Sidebotham Coll.
Fig. 1223. Nottingham bear-jug with removable head. Typical clay-grit and salt-glaze. Ht. 10". (c. 1760–1770). Plummer, Ltd.
Fig. 1224. Nottingham mugs of brown stoneware with incised and milled decoration covered with lustrous salt glaze. Upper, 1720. Hts. 4½" and 8". Castle Mus. and Art Gallery, Nottingham.

a posset-pot of 1700. The carved walled double potted wares seem to have been a pet stunt at Nottingham. The stoneware is light, neat, suave in form and is brown or russet-brown of deep tone on a salt glaze of almost metallic sheen. At times a dark brown slip was used to accent incised designs as on the puzzle-jug shown, but this is the only sort of painting attempted.

The puzzle-jugs were taken from an idea of the Chinese and will only pour in a certain way if the finger is held over certain holes and the vessel is turned in a certain series of motions. Any other attempt will spill the contents. The usual incising and stamping was employed but one characteristic was the close stabbing of the ground with a sharp point, the use of this same technique in borders, designs, etc., and the use of the roulette. Again tiny sherds of clay were sprinkled evenly on parts to give a rough texture. Only later did appliqués come into use.

The Nottingham designs are usually floral though stags, trees, etc., do occur and when not crowded, as they were later, have an honest and direct look. There is a definite resemblance to the pewter designs of Holland and Germany. Many of the forms also suggest metal in their thinness and elegance though all were heavy enough to be suitable for stoneware.

In the Midland, Swinton, later to become Rockingham Porcelain Works, Belper and also Brampton and Chesterfield all copied Nottingham more or less well but none were so good.

INDUSTRIALIZATION IN STAFFORDSHIRE

All the wares described to date were made in England for the use of the common man. The rich people did not use these wares because they drank from silver or glass and ate from silver or imported porcelain. It was tea and coffee which made the rich man become interested in the poor potter, because glass or metal was too hot to hold and there was also a tradition from the Far East that tea tasted better from pottery containers.

The East India Company of England imported a great many of the mis-called "buccaro" tea-pots made at Yi-hsing and elsewhere, even in Japan. (See those sections.) These fetched high prices and it is only natural that the potters of both Holland and England should try to imitate them. From Holland two men came shortly after the revolution in 1688 and settled in Bradwell Wood near Burslem, working as silversmiths in Fulham until they could start themselves as potters. They were the brothers, John Philip Elers and David Elers and whether they had anything to do with Dwight or brought their secrets from Lambertus van Eenhoorn or Ary de Milde in their homeland we do not know for they were masters at surrounding themselves with mystery. It is claimed that they hired only weak-minded workmen whom they locked up each day and searched before they left in the evening. They must have heard about some of the continental "arcanists!" They turned out tea-pots, cups, jugs, mugs and beakers with stamped appliqués in a pseudo Chinese style and with little figures in the contemporary style of England. Their wares were refined as might be expected from silversmiths.

The English potters seeing the competition tried to make their own wares neater and more refined. The adoption of salt-glaze, instead of the earlier lead glaze, in London, from Germany, led to the making of the famous "Staffordshire salt-glazed wares." Rackham and Read point out that the idea did not take hold in London because of the lack of brushwood and coal. Colonel J. C. Wedgwood said that the lack of large estates in Staffordshire helped and that the "Five towns" section near Burslem was made up of many small holdings on which workmen could have each his own little plot of ground.

For a time the wares of such men as Twyford, Astbury and the Wedgwoods kept their quality in being wheel-shaped and of natural colors, but soon the porcelain competition made for a desire to obtain white wares even though they lost much of their warmth and charm thereby. Early in the 18th century Thomas Astbury brought from Bideford in Devonshire the method of covering the body with a thin, white slip. Of course this lost much modeled detail and the natural plastic quality of the body. Probably either Astbury or Thomas Heath found that calcined flint added to the body would make it white and from then on the colored wares were second rate.

Earthenware, metal or stone molds had been used in making earthenware and not accomplishing any higher quality of aesthetic appeal. Now models were carved from alabaster and a series of clay impressions were made to form a master mold from which working molds could be made in any quantity. The pouring was done with liquid clay and washed around the inside, then left to dry. Any thickness could be obtained by repeating the process. When all is finally dry the mold is taken apart, the sutures trimmed but the original artist's work is thrice removed from the finished article and shrinkage and loss of detail and loss of all the subtle hand quality was the result.

This was bad enough but about 1750 Ralph Daniel brought "Plaster of Paris" which was the final step in the industrialization of the Staffordshire potteries, that industrialization which was the main cause of the death of ceramic art in so many places, as we have found out. It would certainly have been far better had tea never turned the eyes of rich men upon the humble pottery wares, for it was this which made the "improvements," the methods of quantity manufacture and the final squeezing of it for pennies that ruined it completely as an art in the short space of time between 1750 and 1800.

The Elers brothers are thought perhaps to have been at Cologne and they spent a short time at Fulham. About 1697 they came to Bradwell Wood, so it is supposed. Yet with all the talk of them there is not one piece which can surely be attributed to them. All that we judge them by are pieces which, as Rackham and Read say, "may with probability be attributed to them." Hannover says, "Connoisseurs of the subject, which will hardly be regarded outside of England as a profitable one for study or the activity of collectors, declare that they can distinguish genuine Elers ware from the slightly or much later imitations by the fact that in the former the handles, spouts, etc., show marks of having been made by hand, whilst in the latter they are made in moulds." Yet forgers would hardly overlook such a simple point. David became a merchant in London and a rich lady set up John Philip in the glass and earthenware business in Dublin, according to reports. They had used the lathe. They had or had not used molds, according to the authority whose word you wish to believe. But they certainly did not add one jot to the art of ceramics.

Tradition has it also that John Astbury and Joshua Twyford pretended to be half-wits and succeeded in getting into the Elers' place to obtain the secret of the red ware. In any event Twyford did make a red ware more human and less neat than the other type. He is supposed to have applied vines in relief and crabstock handles. Astbury made similar things in red stoneware we are told. At any rate he set up a factory for the purpose where either his son Thomas Astbury or Thomas Heath made the discovery of white wares with flint added.

Let us examine the dates: In 1710 it was, according to Hannover, that John Philip left for Dublin and his brother is supposed to have gone to London about the same time. It must have been before that date that the red ware was made. Yet the inventor of the red stoneware, Böttger, made his discovery in 1708 or 1709 at the earliest. Fast work! Just how much was due to Böttger, how much to the Elers and how much to Dwight who died in 1703 it is difficult to determine but it certainly seems likely that Böttger, and Irminger must have received some impetus from Fulham and one need only look back upon the floundering around of the Meissen factory with its use of lacquer colors, cut glass technique, casting of Chinese figures, etc., to see that the *art* was secondary to the discovery and very uncertain indeed. Surely Dwight must have learned something from Germany, though hardly from Böttger, surely the situation is much like that where most "inventions" are concerned; uncertain to say the least, but surely the art which consisted of appliqués, incising, etc., was simply and soundly developed in England while it was not in Germany, although the very techniques used in England had appeared on much earlier ordinary stoneware in Germany. It seems to have been one of those borrowings back and forth.

SALT GLAZE AND "CROUCH WARE"

Josiah Wedgwood states that the Elers were responsible for the introduction, of salt glaze and it may be true. The earliest examples are still in the first half of the 18th century, have a grey body and small white pads pressed on and stamped to form leaves, flowers, berries, etc., connected by thinly rolled stems, all in much the same technique as that of Dwight and the Elers. This is called "Crouch ware," a name which derives from the clay from Derbyshire which was used in the composition. Dr. Thomas Wedgwood seems to have been making this ware as early as 1710 in Burslem. Rackham and Read state positively that the mug dated 1701 in the Stoke-on-Trent Museum is German. But Wedgwood did not sign his wares and it is difficult to know whether many are from him or from the Astbury factory.

Thomas Astbury established a factory in Lane Delph, now Fenton, in 1725 and at this place the father and son made red, buff and brown wares with stamped relief ornaments applied and glazed over with a fine lead glaze. They also made marbled wares and scratch-ornamented wares. The "Portobello bowl" commemorating the capture of Portobello by Admiral Vernon in 1739

Interesting group of salt-glaze teapots from Staffordshire. First, second and sixth of bottom row by Whieldon
and have usual "tortoise shell" glazes of yellow, green and brown. Fifth in bottom row has portrait of Frederick
he Great and "black arrow" ground. Handle of this one is sort known as "crabstock." Hts. c. 4"–6". Guiter
Montague Coll.

Left: White salt-glazed jug with dressing of cobalt-blue. Inscr. "G. E.," Staffordshire c. 1750.
Ht. 8½". Col. John Parker.

Center: Early Georgian salt-glaze coffee pot after silver model. Color off white due to many
small pores in glaze which give effect of light brown dust over surface. C. 1730. Ht. 5¾". Frank
Stoner–Stoner & Evans, Ltd.

Right: Salt-glazed molded mug with bust of King George II and legend, "GOD SAVE THE
KING AND MY MASTER," also arms of Leveson–Gower, Staffordshire, c. 1750. Ht. 4⅞". City
of Manchester Art Gallery.

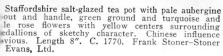

Staffordshire salt-glazed tea pot with pale aubergine
out and handle, green ground and turquoise and
le rose flowers with yellow centers surrounding
edallions of sketchy character. Chinese influence
vious. Length 8". C. 1770. Frank Stoner–Stoner
Evans, Ltd.

Staffordshire cream jug with salt glaze and enamel
floral decoration in bright blue, rose, green and yellow
and mat iron red inclined to chip off. c. 1770. Ht. 4".
Frank Stoner–Stoner & Evans, Ltd.

SALT-GLAZED PIECES (c. 1730–1750)

Plate 212

FIG. 1225. Teapots, cream-jug and cream-stoup or piggin of hard, red ware unglazed and decorated with fine appliqués perhaps made by brothers Elers at Bradwell Wood in late 17th cent. Bottom teapot early 18th cent. Hts. 2¾", 3⅛", 2½" and 6¾".

FIG. 1226. Teapot of white salt-glazed stoneware with decoration of blue relief appliqués, Staffordshire, early 18th cent. Ht. 5½". Three pieces of "Crouch ware," of drab color with white appliqués, Staffordshire, first half of 18th cent. Hts. 3", 4¾" and 3½". Mr. Edward Sheldon. Mr. C. F. C. Luxmoore.

was made there and is typical, being of red-brown clay with small ships, etc., in white clay applied.

The introduction of flint to the body which we mentioned above occurred about 1720 and this made the body nearly white so that it could more or less imitate porcelain. The reliefs were stained blue with cobalt. The results obtained were not good.

FIG. 1229. Staffordshire loving-cup with incised design filled with blue slip, salt-glazed. c. 1750. Ht. 4¾". Wedgwood Institute, Burslem.

FIG. 1227. Lead-glazed red earthenware tea-pot of Astbury type (c. 1750) painted with enamel colors and gold. Initials M.E. appear on it. Ht. 4¼". Harland Coll.

FIG. 1228. Astbury 2nd mug dating about 1750–55 of red ware with coat of arms applied in white slip and yellow glaze over all. Potting thin. Ht. 5½". Frank Stoner–Stoner & Evans, Ltd.

In the "Scratch blue ware" however the results were better. There are really two distinct types: the first being to scratch a design in the white ware, rub blue into the scratches and then fire it with a salt glaze; the second consisted (not quite so successfully) in applying blue to an area and then scratching through to the white. Both processes had existed in Germany in the Westerwald and had, of course been known for centuries in China. The second is much the rarer, perhaps because the potters were not quite satisfied with it. In fact Rackham and Read are not quite sure they have ever seen a piece

FIG. 1230. Late 18th cent. salt-glazed wall-pockets which are fairly rare. Wm. H. Plummer & Co.

and the one they illustrate may have been done this way or simply incised and then given a light wash of cobalt for instead of the lines being white, the blue has gone into them. This may, possibly, however, in due justice, have happened in the kiln. It is hard to say.

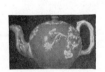

FIG. 1231. "Crabstock" lead glazed tea-pot of tan body with appliqué flowers touched with purple, green and bluish-grey. Ht. 4½". J. H. Taylor Coll.

FIG. 1232. Salt-glazed jug with enamel design after Tenier, c. 1770. Colors blue, rose, green and yellow but clearer and brighter than in many examples. Ht. 6¾". Frank Stoner—Stoner & Evans, Ltd.

FIG. 1233. Fox-head cup of late 18th or early 19th cent. in natural colors. Length 5¼". Plummer, Ltd.

Block-cutting for the molds for salt-glazed wares was done by Aaron Wood, apprentice to Dr. Thomas Wedgwood. Some of these were used also in lead glazed wares. In circles about medallions in much the sort of plan that was used in the Stuart period stumpwork embroidery, we find the various fanciful ideas carried out. A certain amusing association of ideas occurred in these but it was soon lost in the prevailing rococo art.

Enamel decoration was also applied to salt glaze. The earliest examples

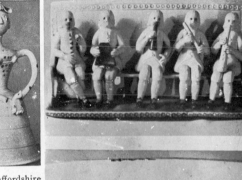

"The Fall" in white touched with
brown, first half of 18th cent. Ht.
6¾". Ex Col. Dr. J. W. Glaisher.

Unique Staffordshire
figure c. 1740. Wallace
Elliot Coll. Victoria
& Albert Mus.

Cat of red earth-
enware partly coated
with white slip
through which floral
pattern is incised,
then touched with
blue and purple un-
der lead glaze, Staf-
fordshire, c. 1750.
Ht. 5¼". Ex Coll.
Dr. J. W. Glaisher.

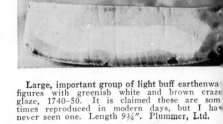

Large, important group of light buff earthenwa.
figures with greenish white and brown craze
glaze, 1740–50. It is claimed these are som
times reproduced in modern days, but I ha
never seen one. Length 9¾". Plummer, Ltd.

Whieldon dove cote
with typical "tortoise-
shell" decoration. Con-
tinental model popular
for its child-like "quaintness." c. 1760. Ht. 10".
Guitel Montague.

SALT-GLAZED FIGURES AND ALSO THOSE OF
ASTBURY AND WHIELDON TYPES

PLATE 213

were sent to Holland to be decorated and closely resemble Delft of the Meissen
influence in general appearance. The colors of this type are not so bright and
vivid as those made after 1750 by the two Dutchmen of Hot Lane and Daniel
of Cobridge, who were early "hausmaler" or artists working at their own
homes. Some of these wares were sent to London for decoration and also the
influences of Chelsea and Worcester porcelain were felt. They were cheaper
than porcelain and the colors were made garish to appeal to the lowest taste. Oil
gilding was employed. One type had thick white flowers touched with black or

gold on a blue ground. This is said to have been the noble invention of Aaron Wedgwood and his brother-in-law William Littler, the porcelain maker of Longton Hall. Then, of course came the transfer printing which we have described.

STAFFORDSHIRE FIGURES

In the first half of the century about 1740 or a little earlier salt-glazed figures were made of delightful charm. "Pew-groups" consisting of a lover and his sweetheart or two elderly people seated on a bench or pew about five or six inches long were made of white clay and decorated with dark brown. Again the figures would be set under a tree very crudely resembling the Chelsea ones. But these were real potters' wares and showed exuberant humor, invention and a childlike simplicity that is most appealing. Note the treatment of the hat on the one shown which was bequeathed by the late Wallace Elliot to the V. & A. Museum. As Mr. Frank Davis has suggested, she seems distantly related to the snake-goddess of Crete, and perhaps in thousands of years when the strange people who excavate the British Isles and try to piece together

FIG. 1234. Lovers under tree and "agate ware" rabbit in white and brown salt-glazed stoneware. First half and middle 18th cent. Hts. 7" and 2⅜". Ex Dr. J. W. Glaisher Coll. City Art Gallery, Manchester.

FIG. 1235. Hand made salt-glazed figures with impressed and also added brown clay touches. Owl-mugs recall those of Germany and China. Hts. 5⅜" and c. 8½". Ex Dr. J. W. Glaisher Coll.

the story of their 18th century inhabitants come across her, they will conclude that the natives bound their breasts very tightly, hid their limbs and worshipped birds but would not admit it, just as their men actually love flowers but would feel embarrassed if caught with one in hand.

Owl jugs were copied but improved upon from the more wooden models of 200 years before made in Germany about 1540. No shields were used but the plumage is ruffled and smart and the claws curl characteristically.

The eyes of all the figures are touched with simple dots of the dark brown which gives them a staring and often foolish expression. The tendency was to become more and more naturalistic which lost them much of the earlier life, and then came the use of the mold, copies of Tê-hua, Fukien, Chinese figures, added details, etc. By the middle of the century the "Astbury type" of lead glazed figures more or less supplanted them and then came Whieldon and Ralph Wood; the former preserving a little of the first charm but the latter losing it all.

LEAD-GLAZED POTTERY

Contemporary with these salt-glazed wares and, in fact forming a continuous series from the earliest days, were wares of red, various shades of brown from mahogany to light buff or faun, and almost white wares decorated with all manner of techniques and covered with lead glaze often inclined to crackle where it runs thick. They made no effort to imitate porcelain and therefore avoided the fate of the salt-glazed wares.

"Crabstock wares" of about the middle of the 18th century were made in the Astbury factory after Chinese models, but these are miscalled for the actual crabstock wares had the handles and spouts made to look like short lengths of wood with branches and twigs twined about them and the ornamentation was of the usual leaves and tendrils in relief. The thinly rolled stems, we have spoken of, were called "vineing" and this word was taken incorrectly to mean veining by Jewitt and others.

Fig. 1236. Whieldon horse with underglaze green and tortoise-shell colorings on cream ground, c. 1770. Cow jugs c. 1760. Voyez figures of sportsman and wife in mottled colors, Staffordshire c. 1780. Philip Suval, Inc.

Silver influences were quite natural and at first had simple charm but then the potters made "head and claw feet" and fragile finials so that stability was lost and inappropriate tours de force attempted.

In the Toft type occasional use of underglaze green occurred. Now manganese and iron were also used along with cobalt blue, grey, ochre yellow and orange, etc., on the applied reliefs on red-brown grounds and covered with the lead glaze. These date about 1750 and Twyford made some of them.

THOMAS WHIELDON—"AGATE WARE," "VEGETABLE WARES," ETC.

Considered a genius of the day, Thomas Whieldon made cream-colored ware not long after 1725. He was one of the most enterprising of English potters between 1740 and 1770 at his place Little Fenton or Fenton Low and it was here that many of the other potters received their training.

Yet his strange conception seemed based on the idea that pottery should be made to look like anything but pottery. He had never heard about "expression of material" or at any rate he discarded the idea. He made agate ware of

Fig. 1237. Whieldon type bull and dog of cream colored earthenware dappled with slate-grey and green under lead glaze, 1750. Ht. 4¼". Mr. C. J. Lomax.

Fig. 1238. Three cavalrymen in red, brown and white clays, stands splashed in slate-blue and purple under lead glaze, Staffordshire, Astbury type, c. 1750. Hts. 8". Mrs. Arthur James.

Fig. 1239. Tea-pot of earthenware with reticulated outer wall, glazed in green, mouse-grey, yellow, purple and blue, inner wall being light brown clay, Staffordshire, Whieldon, c. 1750. Ht. 6". Mrs. Arthur James.

mixed clays with a clear lead glaze over them a little like the T'ang Chinese ones, but by cleverly bluing the glaze a little he came really closer to the appearance of agate. Knife handles, tea-pots, snuff boxes, etc., were made of this product. "Clouded wares" included "tortoise shell" with oxides of manganese, cobalt, copper, antimony and ochre dabbed on his creamware.

But the "vegetable wares" in the forms and colors of various vegetables and fruits such as pineapples, etc., were most famous though they seem to burn our good old friend Hannover in aesthetic indignation as nothing of this sort on the continent ever did. I think that they are really better for they do not pretend to imitate natural forms but rather adapt them loosely to the forms of the vessels and conventionalize them somewhat. In fact Hannover seems to have an antagonistic attitude toward all of these English wares which

Fig. 1241. Late 18th cent. figures probably made in Whieldon factory. Wm. H. Plummer & Co.

Fig. 1240. Whieldon tea-pot c. 1765 of a so-called "pineapple" type. Glaze rich yellow and yellow green and finely crackled particularly where it runs deeper. These teapots extensively copied in America later. Length 7". Frank Stoner-Stoner & Evans, Ltd.

somewhat colors his critical sense and his translator, Bernard Rackham, takes quite justified exception to it. The walls of these wares are thin and the detail good. The colors are not objectionable though the glaze is somewhat shiny and sticky looking.

Reticulated and double walled wares were well made by this versatile potter also.

FIG. 1242. Woman with bucket and dog in brown and ivory glaze, Staffordshire, c. 1740. Ht. 4¼". Plummer, Ltd.
FIG. 1243. Musicians in various colors but having typical crackled lead glaze, Staffordshire, c. 1740. Hts. 4½" to 6¼". Plummer, Ltd.

When Josiah Wedgwood was 24 years old he became a managing partner of the Whieldon plant. Others to profit from the place were Daniel Bird who opened a factory at Cliff Bank near Stoke-upon-Trent, where he produced another agate ware, and John and Thomas Alders (or Aldersea) who made "tortoise shell ware."

Both at Little Fenton and Jackfield in Shropshire from about 1750 a black glaze was used over the red ware probably following Böttger's idea of black ware. The decorations were in relief with oil gold decoration. It is to be remembered that another imitation of the ware was made at Namur, Belgium. The county of Shropshire was a great stronghold of the Jacobite cult and the

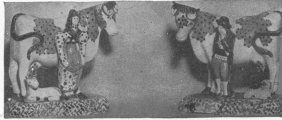

FIG. 1245. Prattware pottery cows in stippled decoration of blue, green and yellow, and two jugs of same ware with relief decoration and same colors. c. 1790. Philip Suval, Inc.

FIG. 1244. Grotesque pottery pitcher of seated figure on obverse side holding "Horn of plenty" from spout of which issues a dolphin. Handle is a panther. On reverse side is young faun. Blue, dark green, yellow and deep orange. Ht. 12". "Pratt ware" c. 1800. Plummer, Ltd.

decoration from there was made to appeal to the supporters of the young Pretender in a brownish and less brilliant sheen.

In Staffordshire and particularly in Little Fenton was also made "Pratt ware" a lead glazed ware named after the potter who worked there from about 1780 to 1800. This was colored with high temperature colors of blue, orange, black, purple, brown, green, etc., on a white ground.

"Astbury and Whieldon Figures"

It was probably Dwight at Fulham in the last of the 17th century who began to turn out little figures for more commercial purposes than simply as trick pieces for the potter's own amusement. Rackham and Read seem inclined to give some credit to the Elers but I think the playful spirit of the Staffordshire potters was actually responsible. In any event many red or light colored clay figures were covered with a lead glaze. Some had brown or yellow-buff clays added for ornamentation. On the slender and unsound reasoning that some details are something similar to those of the vine decorated tea-pots which may or may not have been made at the Astbury factory, these are called "Astbury Figures." The reasoning is doubly foolish and there was probably no connection whatsoever but the figures, though most of them are somewhat later and never so stylized and charming as the early salt-glazed ones, are nevertheless direct and living art portraying characters just as they were in the small towns; musicians, gamekeepers, soldiers, etc. The Mrs. Arthur James Collection is excellent and odd examples can be found now and then on the market. Once in a while the artists strayed to foreign subjects and a Buddhist sage or Italian comedy character might be tried but never were these actual copies. Plain white hussars made at Delft closely resemble certain models but it is likely that they were copied from the English in this instance.

Among them we are suddenly confronted with a totally different color scheme which was attributed to Whieldon. In Brighton Museum is a pillion group showing blending and spotting of purple, green, grey and blue. The cobalt was sometimes blended with the purple to form violet and dabbed on the figures before glazing. The first of these were hand made but soon they, like the salt-glazed ones were molded, but the potters seem to have sensed the pitfall and kept them simpler. Thus of the figures the salt-glazed early ones are by far the finest, the lead-glazed, not so good to begin with, but hold out and are better toward the end.

It has recently been claimed by an English dealer that some of the very few on the market are "fakes." Of course, there are none of these figures which are actually proven to have been made by Astbury. Rackham and Read along with other authorities call them simply "Astbury type," quite likely incorrectly as we have explained, but I venture to say that there are no fakes of this type of ware. My reasons are simple: 1.—Naïve art is the most difficult to fake convincingly and the ones doubted are full of the more or less careless but at the same time effective simplicity that cannot be assumed by a sophisticated artist trying to be childlike. 2.—I have compared the quality of the glaze with particular attention paid to the size and form of the crackle of the doubtful ones with undoubted ones and I find it identical in thickness, color, glossiness, crackle and number of bubbles. (It is impossible to duplicate a given type of crackle unless all the various elements which enter into the making of it are perfectly duplicated both chemically and physically. The glaze fractures in certain forms due to its structure plus the way the fractures are caused by the body; and even the same glaze fractures differently under slightly varying firing conditions.) Thus a forger would have had to perfect every detail beyond human possibilities. 3.—These figures do not bring very large amounts on the market, seldom going over a few hundred dollars. Therefore the reward to a forger would not be great unless he did a great many, and there are, and have always been very few indeed available. I, therefore, come to the conclusion that the doubted pieces are quite all right and are of the period, also that nothing resembling them is being made to-day.

Animals too were made with excellent life and spirit. Later on Crucifixions in various forms and other more pretentious things were made. The animals are not sufficiently appreciated because they came along when the people of England were talking of *Art* quite seriously. I can only say that they often rank very close to the beauty of the Egyptian and T'ang Chinese ones.

RALPH WOOD

Rackham and Read only touch lightly upon them and many authorities skip them entirely. The former gentlemen then say, "Staffordshire figures reach their zenith in technical skill and artistic quality in the pottery of Ralph Wood and his son of the same name, of Burslem, brother and nephew of the block-cutter Aaron Wood." The senior was also a block-cutter. Thus it may be said that the family was born and bred to the mold and I shall probably call down the wrath of the dealers, and the chilling breath of British contempt, by declaring that the works of the two and of the nephew of the younger, Enoch Wood, are worthy of no more attention than is given to them by old Hannover in his statement, "About this class a long chapter could be written, extending from the still sound old-English joviality of the 'Vicar and Moses'

Fig. 1246. "Farmer & Wife" and "Old Age" (smaller ones) by Ralph Wood, having usual transparent underglaze colors. Said to have been made c. 1750. Philip Suval, Inc.

Ralph Wood and Whieldon toby jugs decorated with colored glazes c. 1765. Almost identical in form though not from same mold. Flesh parts of Wood one of pale aubergine tint and britches grey-blue while or is better controlled. Mug of Whieldon one is cinnamon-rufous brown and dark parts are very dark bergine rather than brown black as on Wood example. Hts. 9½". Frank Stoner–Stoner & Evans, Ltd.

left, Wilson toby-jug, 1810, with typical stippled base and modeled handle while flesh parts are white. r is Davenport, 1820, marked with name and anchor flanked by 3 and 6. Flesh tone appears on face and s. Both have enamel colors of blue, yellow-green, yellow-tan, black and rose-red. Hts. 9¾". Frank Stoner-er & Evans, Ltd.

TOBY JUGS (c. 1765–1820)

PLATE 214

of Ralph Wood to the 'Toby jugs' already somewhat less funny and thence to the great mass of thoroughly talentless and finally even tasteless Staffordshire figures—" and, "The same chapter relating to the peasant strain in English pottery of the period, about 1800 and afterwards, would also include another class of ware made to be sold at fairs—earthenwares with copper, silver and gold lustre, for the most part tea and coffee-pots, which from about 1790 onwards, were produced not only in Staffordshire, but also at Swansea, New Castle, Liverpool and Sunderland." Thus he makes his one statement about the Woods and concludes, "But in pursuance of the programme set before this book we may release ourselves from describing all these ugly things,

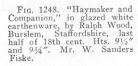

FIG. 1248. "Haymaker and Companion," in glazed white earthenware, by Ralph Wood, Burslem, Staffordshire, last half of 18th cent. Hts. 9½" and 9¼". Mr. W. Sanders Fiske.

FIG. 1247. Boxer by Ralph Wood, Sr. Cream colored clay glazed with translucent vinaceous-fawn on britches, chrysolite yellow green coat and fluorite green base. Fire crack and incised X are shown under base. Ht. 8". c. 1760. Frank Stoner–Stoner & Evans, Ltd.

and make our final halt." I dislike only his term "peasant pottery" for these wares had outgrown in their rank commercialism their original peasant stock. The facts are these: The colored glazes had been fully developed in general

FIG. 1249. "Madonna and Child" by Ralph Wood the younger. Almost identical figure illustrated in last work of Wedgwood except that hand of child is below madonna's chin. c. 1785. Ht. c. 12". John Gibbons Coll.

FIG. 1250. Figure of Newton with telescope, globe and books. Remarkable modeling full of vigor and yet sensitive. Signed R. WOOD, Burslem, at back of base. Ht. 12". c. 1785. Frank Stoner–Stoner & Evans, Ltd.

in Staffordshire, as we listed them above. Rackham and Read liken them to those of poor Palissy of 200 years before and this is not saving much though even this is not true for they are different in colors and more glassy; really not so pleasant even as these. In other words there was no technical accomplishment other than the simple art of block-cutting of greater detail. Of the "Toby jugs" there had been a long tradition based upon Toby Philpot, as Rackham and Read point out, he of the song "The Brown Jug" and not Uncle Toby of Laurence Sterne, and certainly the Woods lowered the standard rather than added to it. Of the "Vicar and Moses" and other kindred subjects there is proof that they were taken from contemporary engravings with nothing more than a common exercise of the block-cutter's art. But the majority of the figures are not even English in origin and were stolen from continental models of Paul Louis Cyfflé, Palissy, etc. Among the classical figures, the Diana is the Diane Chasseresse of the Louvre, etc. Other figures were taken from Dwight.

Mr. Frank Falkner discovered that the younger Ralph Wood shared a tenement at Burslem with the French modeller John Voyez, and the jug with figures in relief signed Voyez and dated 1788 together with his medallion of the Judgment of Paris have led to this statement by Rackham and Read. "The treatment of the figures upon these works is so similar to that of the statuettes bearing the impressed mark of Ralph Wood or his son (or the stamped mould-numbers of a series to which such statuettes belong) THAT THERE IS LITTLE ROOM FOR DOUBT THAT THE WOODS OWE THEIR FAME, AS FAR AS MODELLING WAS CONCERNED TO THIS FRENCH IMMIGRANT." (The capitals are mine.)

Thus there is not much interest or beauty in the products of these block-cutters who stole their technique and even their modeling, giving no credit to Voyez in the purely industrial manner of their class.

Of the portrait busts of Enoch Wood after this or that real source, often with enamel colors to imitate porcelain and of such figures as that of Benjamin Franklin which was miscalled and inscribed "Washington," perhaps the least said the better.

JOSIAH WEDGWOOD

Josiah Wedgwood was born at Burslem in 1730 and died in 1795. He was the youngest son of Dr. Thomas Wedgwood and soon after his father died, which was in 1739, the boy was apprenticed to the brother Thomas, the oldest of the family and it was he who taught him the technique of ceramics. In fact the family had been more or less noted since the 17th century.

In 1752 he became the manager of a small factory at Stoke-on-Trent, known as "Alders" or the Cliff Bank Pottery and was a partner of Harrison and Aldersea, but moved on in 1754 to join Whieldon at Little Fenton, where he made his experiments with salt glazes to no very good purpose. In 1759, disappointed as he said in the "conservatism of Whieldon" whom, God knows, we never would have thought of criticising for conservatism, he started his own place at "Ivy House" in Burslem where he chiefly made salt-glazed wares and green and yellow glazed wares. In 1762 he leased in addition the "Brick House," called the "Bell Works" also in Burslem, just about at the time the English cream colored earthenware was reaching perfection and he became one of its chief makers with the result that he received the patronage of Queen Charlotte and the ware was called "Queen's ware," becoming Wedgwood's financial support. It is not true that he "invented" this ware as we are led to believe by some "authorities."

FIG. 1251. Marbled ware candlestick said to be, "typical of very early period, c. 1769." Josiah Wedgwood & Sons, Ltd.

Now at 32 years of age he became a social leader of his community, improving roads, taking interest in the construction of the Trent and Mersey Canal, founding schools, and in time becoming "potter to the King." He traveled extensively visiting London, Liverpool, Manchester and Birmingham. When he left Whieldon in 1759 he opened a shop in Newport Street, London, and the merchant Thomas Bently became his friend in Liverpool in 1762, later to aid him in many ways particularly in supplying a classical training which Wedgwood lacked. He also acted as his only agent for some years, in which he sold the wares extensively to Sadler and Green who decorated them with transfer prints. His was undoubtedly the influence that started Wedgwood to making "artistic classic stoneware."

FIG. 1252. "Black basalt" candlestick marked "Wedgwood & Bentley," c. 1770. Josiah Wedgwood & Sons, Ltd.

In 1767 he was introduced to the Comte de Caylus' work called the "Recueil d'Antiquities Egyptiennes Etrusques, Greques, Romaines et Gauloises" and became enthusiastic about using the designs reproduced therein. Miss Meteyard also states that he became acquainted with the works of La Chausse, Laurent, Berger, Montfaucon, Dempster, Gori and Winkelmann. In a sense he was really a pioneer of the adaptation of classic designs to potting though, of course, some such influence had begun to be felt in design in general on the continent of Europe. Of course, the influence was not felt in England until about 1770 or the Chelsea-Derby times. Actually at Sèvres, although the Louis

XVI style made some use of classic design, there were no real imitations of antique models until Napoleon's time. In Germany the style came later than in France.

In 1773 he transferred all of his plant to "Etruria" and his products included both earthenware and stoneware for useful wares and stoneware of an ornamental nature. Rackham and Read say, "Before Wedgwood we may almost say that there was no such thing as 'ornamental pottery' in England." Later a branch of the factory was established at Chelsea for enamel painting on the earthenware and "encaustic" painting on the black stoneware. Bently had become a partner but he died in 1780. In 1790 Wedgwood took his sons John, Josiah and Thomas, and the cousin Thomas Byerley into partnership forming the company which is still moderately successful.

Hannover wrote an oft quoted passage which seems just, "On his monument in the parish church at Stoke-on-Trent are chiselled the words, 'Who converted a rude and inconsiderable Manufactory into an elegant Art and an important part of National Commerce.' Some have thought that he did the opposite, converting an art, perhaps rude and inconsiderable, but nevertheless always an art, into a manufacture. The truth is that he did both, creating a great manufacture with an incontestably artistic stamp." Hannover tried his best to give Wedgwood the benefit of the doubt but when one is acquainted with Hannover's feelings about the whole classical movement, one realizes just how charitable he was being.

Rackham and Read, being English, are of course more laudatory but they say of Greek ceramics which Wedgwood copied (*English Pottery*, p. 122), "From the point of view of the potter it was a misfortune for Wedgwood that the pottery from which he chiefly drew his inspiration for his innovations—whatever virtues it may possess in exquisite beauty of draughtsmanship and gracefulness of shape—was not good pottery." It is a little difficult to understand how all this "gracefulness" and "beauty" could exist without its being good pottery unless one takes account of the classic attitude which dreams its dreams unhampered by any structural or functional criticisms But these two were on the track for they continue, "In ceramic qualities, Greek vases of the 'best' period stand far behind the ancient wares of Egypt, Persia and the Far East, and are inferior even to the unpretentious pottery made far and wide by aborigines in the provinces of the Roman Empire. Their shapes are copied from, or intended to emulate metalwork; nor do they depend for decoration on the plastic possibilities of clay." So, having laid the blame on the Greeks, firmly but somewhat dressed for those classic minded people whom they did not wish to offend, they say of Wedgwood, "It is to these circumstances that we owe the fact that in his ornamental stoneware Wedgwood drifted altogether away from the conception of pottery as a branch of plastic art. In actual appearance his jasper and other stoneware speaks far more of the art of the sculptor and the gem cutter than that of the potter." My readers know my feelings in the matter but I am willing to let the indictment stand just as it comes from the mouths of his countrymen. He can be forgiven the art-for-art's-sake creation of "ornamental" meaning *useless* wares for that was the trend of the day, but other students of the antique have gained immeasurably from their studies while he grasped the shell only and understood none of the inner life or meaning. He was a good business man and perhaps should be mistrusted even in any sincere attempt to do better than make saleable merchandise.

Prodigious were the technical processes practiced at this factory. Wedgwood was a genius at getting other people to work for him. In 1771 he got an order to do a huge table service of some 1,000 pieces for the Empress of Russia and each piece was to have on it a view of an English castle, monument or landscape and, on the strength of this he was able to get a large staff of the Chelsea porcelain painters. From Sheffield and Birmingham metal workers he learned methods for making his wares thinner and piercing them more successfully. Unglazed red and black stonewares called "rosso antico" and "basaltes" or

Fig. 1253. Three plates from "Catherine II of Russia" dinner service said to have been "executed by Josiah Wedgwood in 1774." Josiah Wedgwood & Sons, Ltd.

"Egyptian black" were simple adaptations of wares which had long been made in Staffordshire and which he simply improved and named. The "basaltes" ware was used for panels in relief, portrait medallions, life-sized busts, gems copied from antique ones, lamps, ink-stands, salt-cellars and vases among other things. He is quoted as having said that he could copy any of the "Etruscan" vases (which, of course, were not Etruscan at all) and improve them by giving, "higher artistic value by the addition of light and shade, which are entirely lacking in the old vases."

Besides the red and black wares he made a number resembling stone by the admixture of various oxides. "Jasper ware" is perhaps the best known and was obtained by the adding of carbonate and sulphate of barium to a semi-porcelain clay. The result is translucent when thin, hard enough to grind and polish and yet soft enough to be stained throughout with the metal oxides. In 1775 when it was first made, the body was so stained but almost at once in 1777 the process was cheapened by dipping the body (before firing, of course) so that only the surface was stained. There are seven colors all of which are mixed with sulphate of barium: lavender-blue of three shades, lilac, pale pink, greyish-green, olive-green, yellow and black. The rarest is yellow and the most difficult to get and most variable is the lilac. Usually the relief decoration contrasts in color with the ground and often the decoration is white. Sometimes rare examples combine three colors such as the pair formerly in my own collection which are lilac, with small green medallions and white ornaments over all.

Nothing seemed too small or too ambiguous for Wedgwood's attention and he made buttons, ear-rings, finger-rings, beads, knife handles, shoe-buckles, panels for furniture, etc.

Many Italian modelers were hired along with such English ones as James Tassie and William Hackwood, who did many portraits, etc., but far better known is John Flaxman who was a great sculptor in his own right. He was born in 1755. His father was a molder and kept a shop in Covent Gardens for the sale of plaster figures. It is said that by his own efforts he learned enough Greek and Latin to read the poets. At 15 he entered the Royal Academy and in 1797 was elected associate and in 1800 a full member. In 1810 he was appointed Professor of Sculpture there. In 1787 ne went to Italy for a few years where he made illustrations of the Odyssey, and Aeschylus and Dante. Wedgwood captured him and some of the portraits are by him as well as some of the best vases, one of which is the "Apotheosis of Homer" known as the "Pegasus vase" from the finial on its cover. This vase was given to the British Museum in 1786 before the Italian sojourn. .

The original "Portland vase" was of glass and was discovered in the course of excavations in Rome toward the end of the 16th century. After having been in the possession of the Palazzo Barberini in Rome, from which it is also called the "Barbarini vase," it was sold in 1786 for 1,000 guineas to the Duke of Portland. It is now in the British Museum in a restored condition as it was smashed to many pieces by a madman. The original is, of course, glass with an almost black ground and is one of the masterpieces of the glass cutter's art. Wedgwood copied it sometimes in blue-black and sometimes in blue jasper and looked on these copies as the crown of his life's work. There are about 20 examples, but some of these were not turned out until after Wedgwood's death. He sold them for 50 pounds sterling while one fetched £215.5s in 1892. Actually the copies are pretty bad and even the simple

Fig. 1255. "Warwick vase," 1880, a reproduction of a silver piece in Warwick Castle. Josiah Wedgwood & Sons.

Fig. 1254.   One of reproductions, somewhat distorted, of the "Portland Vase." Josiah Wedgwood & Sons, Ltd.

FIG. 1256. Set of flower vases of white earthenware with brown slip through which pattern is cut while festoons are in relief appliqués. Over-all lead glaze. Josiah Wedgwood, Etruria, Staffordshire, late 18th cent. Middle vase 11⅛". Wedgwood Institute, Burslem.

FIG. 1257. Example of well-known "Queen's Ware" which flooded market. Said to be, "hand embossed" but most of design on this ware is simply cast in mold. Josiah Wedgwood & Sons, Ltd.

shape of the original was not followed perfectly. In the Wedgwood copy the handles do not follow the curve of the body but sag inwards and the upper parts of these handles do not meet the neck horizontally as the original ones do. The shoulder is also more rounded and not so strong and the neck is slightly shortened. The result is dumpy and not of the aristocratic stance of the original. Is this criticism picayune? I assure you that it is just such subtile lines which make or break a work of art, and it is in just such things that the copyist fails.

Thus in general we find that Wedgwood lost all of the warmth and interest of the touch of the human hand in potting. In the freest things he ever did there is a tightness which shows that, had he really known the Greeks, he would have been shocked at them. Wedgwood erected the final cold slab over the tomb of all the appeals of ancient pottery. As Hannover says, "Even

FIG. 1258. Wedgwood game-pie dish with glazed inside oven dish. Outer dish and cover of terracotta which looks like pie crust. Made in four sizes for Trinity College, Cambridge. c. 1850. John Gibbons Coll.

FIG. 1259. "Queen's Ware" plate, part of service called "Hampton Court" with rather stiff flower said to, "bespeak, through the intricate detail and beautiful underglaze enamelling," (whatever that may mean) "the craftsmanship for which our artisans have been renowned for six generations." Josiah Wedgwood & Sons, Ltd.

to the method by which he stamped his wares, instead of marking them with a name written by hand in the manner of the old faïence, we trace the factory spirit in his activities." This mark was WEDGWOOD. Later between 1768 and 1780 it was WEDGWOOD & BENTLEY-ETRURIA or at times the ETRURIA was left off. Pieces marked simply WEDGWOOD-ETRURIA are later and from about 1840. Small pieces sometimes have W & B. There are many workmen's marks such as letters, figures, flowers, etc., some impressed and some painted, which have no importance. Hannover says, "We should note, however, that three large letters such as OTN or ALX in combination with the factory mark indicate that the piece in question is not older than the period after 1860, the factory indicating the year with an O, the following with a P and so on." The first letter refers to the workman, the second to the month and the last to the year.

Fake marks are WEDGWOODE and WEDGWOOD & CO. which he did not use. Pieces so marked were made by William Smith about 1840 at Stock-on-Tees. Of course we have said that many continental factories copied the wares before they were snowed under by them and there was hardly a factory in the whole of Staffordshire which did not follow suit, while others in England were not far behind. The factory still turns out all the same wares more crudely made save that the "jasper" was discontinued for the war period. In the modern ones the blue color is often paler and dryer and sometimes darker and less grey, the green is too fresh, the white reliefs are rougher and not so soft to the touch. In the latter part of the 19th century pieces brought over $2,000 and now a tenth of that would be fairly high.

Leeds' Swinton and "Don" Pottery

About 1774, according to Messrs. Kidson, a firm by the name of Humble, Green & Co. was established at Leeds. Hannover says two brothers by the name of Green founded it around 1760. Sometime in the 70's Hartley joined and the firm was then known as Humble, Hartley, Green & Co. and then later as simply Hartley, Green & Co.

Hartley set out to copy Wedgwood and did succeed in spreading his wares all over the Continent. The firm changed hands several times, having its prime between 1781 and 1805 and went out of existence in 1878, though several revivals have been attempted up to this day.

Some catalogues and drawings show little of what might have been original. Nearly everything was copied including "agate-ware," "Tortoise-shell ware," "basalt," etc., but the specialty seemed to be a cream colored ware which was now made everywhere. Some of the forms were simple but they grew progressively worse and worse in greater complications. The ware is a little yellower than

Fig. 1260. Reticulated Leeds earthenware piece with impressed mark, "LEEDS POTTERY." A most delicate and accurate piece of work. Ht. 11". c. 1780. Plummer, Ltd.

that of Staffordshire and may look slightly greenish where the glaze runs thick. It is harder and never quite so thin as the Wedgwood glaze. As duty was charged by weight, the Leeds kiln tried to make theirs lighter and succeeded better than any other place but not satisfied with this they commenced to pierce every possible surface such as the rims of plates, covers, etc. This work was done hole by hole with individual punches. Wedgwood caught the idea and improved it by making block punches which killed even the slight unevenness which still expressed the hand made article. Much of the cream ware was left undecorated and it is preferable that way. Some, however, was painted in black, red, brown or blue and some was painted in subdued colors of enamel, green, red lilac and yellow.

Fig. 1261. Leeds, late 18th cent. pair of rabbit candlesticks of cream colored earthenware touched with copper-green, with bases in yellow "tortoise-shell." Ht. 5½". Mr. Victor Gollancz.

Fig. 1262. Chestnut-bowl of Leeds pierced earthenware of cream color. c. 1800. Ht. 9". City Art Gallery, Leeds.

Figures were also made which Rackham and Read are enthusiastic about but which have little to recommend them except their subdued colors. They seem to represent most of the bad points of their Staffordshire predecessors and no good ones. In fact these authorities seem unaccountably enthusiastic about all the Leeds work; they say, "The pierced ornament is executed with a care and delicacy never equalled by any other pottery." I think that as long as they are quibbling about so unimportant a technique they might be referred to the "ling lung" or "devil's work" done in the latter part of the Ming Dynasty in China, or some of the K'ang Hsi and even modern examples. Englishmen seem to enjoy making such flat statements concerning their own excellence.

John Green started another factory in 1790 near Mexborough in South Yorkshire known as the "Don Pottery," and some of the partners had an interest in Swinton from about 1787 to 1806. We suppose the wares made in both places were closely like those of Leeds, which were closely like others. Several places such as Castleford in 1790 and Ferrybridge in 1792, followed suit. The only recorded mark of distinction that Castleford could claim was that a blue outline was used and the tea-pots were rather oblong or squarish.

Still other factories were:

Shelton (1774–1816) by Samuel Hollins which made red and brown unglazed stoneware.

Lane End (1739–1786) John Turner, friend and rival of Wedgwood with "jasper," "Black basalt," and a "cane colored ware." The blue "jasper" was better modeled than Wedgwood's.

FIG. 1263. Late 18th cent. Leeds figure of musician with greyish-white crazed glaze. Ht. 11¼". Plummer, Ltd.

FIG. 1264. Ambitious cruet-stand of typical cream colored Leeds ware with names of condiments in German in red-dish-brown. c. 1800. City Art Gallery, Leeds.

Neale & Palmer (1760–1776) Henry Palmer took workmen and models from Wedgwood including John Voyez.

Josiah Spode (three individuals) The eldest served with Whieldon, did painting in blue underglaze and printing in underglaze colors, though this was done first at Caughley and brought to Spode by an engraver named Lucas and a printer named Richards.

Elijah Mayer (1770–1813) at Hanley copied black Wedgwood ware.

William Adams of Greengates, Staffordshire (1745–1805) was a pupil of Wedgwood and made "jasper." His blue is more violet and shiny. He himself modeled and Enoch Wood worked for him for a while.

Herculaneum (1796) An old factory was taken over and given this name and the business of copying the wares of Etruria.

Swinton (mentioned above), near Rotherham, made a "brown china" that is called "Rocking-

FIG. 1265. Castleford tea-pot of ware almost like so-called "parian body" of some American wares, decorated in dark blue enamel. Ingenious slotted arrangement holds slide cover in place even when pouring. Bottom has impressed 22 as only mark. c. 1820. Length 9". Frank Stoner–Stoner & Evans, Ltd.

ham glaze" from the estate of the Marquis of Rockingham upon which it is located. This type was later very popular in America, as at Bennington.

Jackfield, in Shropshire, made black glazed tea-pots, etc., painted in oil colors which are usually worn off to no great loss.

Joseph Ring at Bristol made a cream-colored ware the color being due to the glaze and not the body which was dark.

Cambrian Pottery, at Swansea, made all kinds of Staffordshire wares and particularly an "opaque china" which is whiter than most of the cream wares and owes its reputation to:

Fig. 1266. Staffordshire figure of "Flora," possibly Wedgwood, c. 1800. Ht. 11″. John Gibbons Coll.

Fig. 1267. One of pair of Staffordshire groups "Peace and Plenty" set upon hollow bases with vent hole in bottom. Bright green, iron red, blue, yellow and tan. c. 1800–10. Length 9½″. Ernest F. Follows.

Fig. 1268. Staffordshire girl with doll (unidentified) with enamel decoration and costume which dates it c. 1830–40. Vermiform motif dress is typical. Ht. c. 11″. John Gibbons Coll.

William Weston Young, a painter of flowers and landscapes.

Derby made the cream wares and a "brown ware" it is thought though this has not been definitely proven and some found about the site may have been sent in for decoration.

Shore & Goulding at Isleworth made a copy of the "Portland vase" of a red earthenware also used for tea-pots in Chinese style.

We have given too much space to the sad tale of the 18th century, but it was necessary first in order to set right many misled collectors who are still impressed, as the English were, by the continental vogue; secondly to gain a proper perspective on the porcelain achievements of Europe; and finally to help us understand our modern age. The trend was ever westward and finally, of course, it jumped the wide stretches of the Atlantic to America. One wonders, if after this last war or within another few hundred years, the complete circuit of the globe will have been accomplished and China will again take the lead.

Conquest of arms had to do with the 18th century in the introduction of the neo-classic through Napoleon, if nowhere else. Actually it had much to do with the North Countries also. Conquest by religion had little or nothing to do with the 18th century art of ceramics. The old kings and popes had little power, but conquest by pennies was all important and it brought disaster to most of the factories by 1850 because it brought about the very antithesis of all art appeals.

FIG. 1269. Staffordshire Obediah Sherratt group c. 1830 showing bull baiting. 3-color stippling of base is typical. Length c. 11″. John Gibbons Coll.

FIG. 1270. English stoneware jug of cream white with neck, lip and upper part of handle in cobalt blue, late 18th to early 19th cent. Brought to Newburyport, Mass. c. 1763, it is reported. Ht. 9½″. Metropolitan Mus. of Art.

As the art of ceramics moved west to America it had little chance to accomplish great works of art. The machine had done all it could; mass production had worked its greatest harm and soon there developed the era of sanitation; of the making of whole facades of buildings sheathed in tiles such as the Near Easterners or Chinese never dreamed of, the era of fuller knowledge of all art of the past, and then the inevitable turn of fate; depression, war and the attendant troubles. In art the greater knowledge of ancient arts did not become strong enough to bring the enthusiasm and love for art in general that one might have expected; instead the use of machines, the habit of mass production and the urge to sell ever cheaper to satisfy the penny gatherers, overcame our possible rennaisance almost at once and withered it as soon as it sprouted here in America. Every means of cheap short cuts were employed to develop a psuedo art called "modernistic." This had no strength during the boom days but gained powerfully when the final depression of 1929 came along. Thus the story of American ceramics is also sad in conclusion.

However, before the European came to this country some really great things were done and in the beginnings we shall find much to interest us.

CHAPTER XXVII

AMERICAN INDIAN POTTERIES

ETHNOGRAPHY

Along the great Siberian plain eastward following the Arctic Circle and crossing such great rivers as the Lena and the Kolima, in highlands, river valleys and frozen salt marshes, and at times north of Sakhalin, and north of the Sea of Okhotsk along Kamchatka and down the river Anadir out onto Cape Deshnef (East Cape), came various waves of migratory people, not travelling but drifting as would flotsam on the tide, sometimes advancing, sometimes retreating, following their hunting. Life was very hard in these far northern latitudes, for they lie at about the same latitude frozen most of the year and open only during July, August, September and sometimes part of October with temperatures usually not more than ten to fifteen degrees above freezing even then. Hunting and fishing were the only livelihood and the providing of shelter and food took all of man's time. Accidents were swift and terrible and courage was not a seldom used and talked about embellishment of character but the simple necessity for survival.

The Bering Strait is only 56 miles across and ice extends the shorelines in the cold season. Moreover, there are two bleak granite domes of islands, between which the boundary line between Russia and the United States now passes, which have no harbors but upon which live about 80 Eskimos. These islands, with their ice flanges must have been stepping stones so that at times, when conditions were right a small trickle of the peoples of Asia came to America. At times some must have returned while at times also some penetrated up the Yukon valley or even further east and south to the mouth of the Mackenzie. The ice cap moved north and south imperceptibly to them and with this movement all flora and, therefore, all fauna either gained further north or was pushed south. We must not think of the ice cap as a hard and frozen line of solid ice; there were simply harder and harder winters or more and more, what we might call, heat spells. During the harder winters the rivers froze deeper and the glaciers pushed further and, as the cap moved south, they did not retreat so far and the herds which grazed right up to the foot of them and all around them found better pasturage a little toward the south.

So it was over a short period in the life of man, a mere few 100,000 years or so, or perhaps a bit more, no time at all in our history for the "Java Man" is said to have lived some 450,000 years ago.

Down the coast to the Columbia River they came, up the Mackenzie to Great Slave Lake, on to what is now California on one side, and into the head waters of the Missouri and Mississippi on the other side. Into these warmer, easier lands moved the strong men who had survived the hardships of the north, very slowly and perhaps even holding still a subconscious mistrust of the too good lands which greeted them. They didn't bring much of culture along. The journey had been far too arduous or it may be that the culture of the old world had developed elsewhere or later than the waves of migration. It is true also that they did not seem so very capable in developing certain cultures of their own as fast as some other groups of men. Even when they did settle down in one place for a while, they were very slow to learn the benefits of agriculture and animals were only to be hunted so far as they could see, excepting the dog, of course, which was a fellow huntsman. They had no cattle, sheep, goats, pigs, horses, camels or reindeer, no wheat, barley or rice and they knew nothing about the plow, the wheel in any form, or iron, and stringed instruments seemed never to have occurred to them at all.

But certain things they did develop in common with all mankind of the Old World. They knew about fire and how to make it, the spear and spear thrower and probably the harpoon and bow, the making and use of cordage and nets as well as baskets, the implements of stone for cutting, scraping, piercing and hammering, and finally they brought with them the shamanistic practices and beliefs, and rites for adolescent boys and girls. But beyond all this they brought one more thing with them and that was a well developed sense of conventionalization of design. In an earlier chapter I have explained how this was developed by nomads through the urge to record important things on the very confined space areas available to the men who have to carry all their worldly goods through many hardships on their own backs. Here we have a race of men which has crossed the ice fields and the strait, has ascended great rivers and seen many hardships. A square inch of leather or small piece of bone would have a value to them, and they had learned well to be brief i.1 their expressions, they could conventionalize a world of meaning in a small space. Nothing was drawn naturalistically for ages until the building of civilization had changed things in many aspects.

We were taught in school to think of the American Indian as of the "red race" as though they were a race apart but actually they are chiefly of the Mongoloid division of the human species, having brown skin, straight, stiff, black head hair and little beard or body hair. Their faces are broad and they have shovel-shaped incisor teeth as well as bluish pigment spots in the sacral region during infancy. All of these are common also to their Mongolian cousins and not to other humans. At first the French school of ethnology explained much of the settlement of the country as from Polynesia, but this was discarded and then it was believed that *all* of the American Indians came by way of the north, if not across the strait at least by way of the Aleutian Islands. Now certain head formations and other characteristics have introduced an element of doubt best expressed by Dr. A. L. Kroeber in the 14th edition *Encyclopaedia Britannica*, Vol. 15, p. 505, "There are some interesting but as yet insufficient indications of Australian or Melanesian Negroid influence on the physique of the American Indians of certain localities. The very long and low skulls of the south end of Baja California may represent a colony or infusion of such immigrants. Similar conjectures have been advanced about the long headed peoples of the Atlantic sides of both North and South America." Of course, these "infusions," as the Doctor calls them, must have been very slight and certain it is that they brought few traceable art motives or trends with them, though a perusal of "Elephants and Ethnologists" by G. Elliot Smith, most convincingly demonstrates that some motifs came even from India to our west coasts.

And so our migrations wandered further and further south, some settling along the Pacific coast, some in the great central plains and a few drifting off to the east. Living conditions became comparatively easy and the migrants multiplied, finding their way down through Central America and finally into South America. In the area from Mexico to Peru agriculture did begin with the partial cultivation of certain indigenous plants such as the squash, pumpkin and beans. Maize, probably native to the highlands of Mexico and Guatemala was slowly altered and domesticated to man's use, spreading over all the Americas from the St. Lawrence to the La Plata. In the tropical regions other plants were cultivated such as the potato, sweet potato, manioc, tomato, pineapple, tobacco, chocolate and chili pepper, but all of this agriculture was hand done with no help but that of a rude hoe or sharpened stick. Eventually the turkey was partly domesticated in Mexico and the llama and alpaca in Peru. Cotton, of another species than that of the Old World, came to be used and true fabrics were made. The bronze age probably developed before this and we soon find that in "Middle America" copper, gold, silver, platinum, tin and lead were smelted, cast and plated. Whether these arts were in any part brought from the Old World and, if so how much, are most interesting speculations which we cannot enter into here. And, just as we would expect, pottery was made in just about the same places as agriculture was practiced and at just about the same time. Finally masonry began and spread as far as the southwestern United States and south to northwestern Argentina, and a civilization was launched and under way.

When we stop to think of the hazards of the way, we can easily see how little, how very very little of culture could possibly have been brought by the various migratory peoples and, bearing this in mind, it is amazing to see how alike the mind of man is in its natural development. Each phase of the Old World culture is, in a way, duplicated by that of the New World.

Naturally those who had come first had had longer to enjoy the benefits of this virgin continent of North America and naturally it was they who, in their drifting, had moved furthest south until met by delaying obstructions. Thus we find the greatest advancement in Central America where the Isthmus of Panama pinching down had helped to stop them and where the approach to the Equator slowed the progress. Some overcame the difficulties and reached South America to be lost in the valley of the Amazon and others luckily drifted along the Pacific coast to Peru and there we find a closely following culture just a little later but quite as great.

Thus our culture in the Americas traces its course geographically and chronologically from the most primitive of the far north, the most recent arrivals, through the next in culture, the eastern wandering tribes of North America, through the more advanced Central Plains Indians and Southwestern Indians, to the Mexican and South American peaks of culture represented by the Mayan and Inca civilizations. And peaks they were, as great as those of Egypt and Iran in a not very different way, and after them came the natural and inevitable decadence; the story of the history of man's progress and stumbling, much as it occurred in the Old World, written for him again that he might see it and have a second chance to learn his lessons from it. Then the Spaniards and the English and the French burst upon the New World and swept all this away caring nothing for it and wanting only gold and the fountain of youth and to impose their well earned and magnificently developed culture of the 16th, 17th and 18th centuries upon these "poor benighted heathens" and we come to our modern era.

Eskimo Pottery

The Eskimos are racially no different from other American Indians, though we now find them mixed with the whites in certain areas, but by and large, from Greenland to Siberia they are the same and even in Siberia are many who have actually come back from the North American continent. We need not go into a description of them and their life habits except to say that they live largely upon fish and meat and have little use for pottery particularly in that they do not as a rule cook their meat. What pottery they did make has long been obsolete except for the making of rude clay oil lamps where stone for the purpose could not be found. Along the coast as far east as Franklin Bay heavy pottery has been found of good sturdy form and some

Fig. 1271. Pottery lamp for whale oil, probably most primitive in our book being simply a hand patted shallow bowl fired in an open fire. Ht. c. 4″. Crude pottery cylindrical cup of hand patted clay impressed possibly with dim recollection of mat-made wares brought from Asia or possibly given the treatment simply through a desire for texture. Ht. c. 7″. Both are made by Eskimos, first from Cape Prince of Wales, second from Point Barrow, Alaska. Mus. of Am. Indian.

surprisingly large in size and ornamented with incised and impressed designs. This pottery is altogether further advanced than we would expect to find as a natural development of the people themselves particularly with the consideration of their hunting habits and lack of interest in such things, and must have been made by men who had learned their art in Siberia. This theory is borne out by the total lack of pottery of any kind made by the central Canadian country Indians of the Athabascan and Algonkin tribes and also by the fact that there is no pottery made from southern British Columbia to Alaska on the Pacific coast, where vessels of bone, wood and horn serve instead. We do find along this coast traces of advanced Asiatic art occasionally, though these have not been planted by any planned invasion and we do have the strange similarity of design, called "Pacific Art" by Ernest Fenellosa. But this all came later than the time when these potteries seem to have been made, and they stand interestingly alone in themselves as an isolated development.

North Atlantic Indian Pottery

From Newfoundland to South Georgia on the Atlantic coast is an area which may be considered as a whole though there are many subdivisions unnecessary to our survey. These Indians were of the Algonkin, Iroquois and, further south, Sioux stocks of historic times. They lived a little on agriculture during certain times but more largely upon fishing and hunting. One shell mound known on the Potomac consists of oyster shells which covered about 30 acres to a depth of some 15 feet. In the lower Penobscot Valley in Maine dwelt a people who strangely placed large quantities of red hematite paint in their graves and so were called the "Red-paint people" by archaeologists. These people have long slender celts and slate points resembling those of the Eskimos and even those of Northern Europe and Asia. They are not related to the Indians of Colonial times who had similar burial customs, but seem to form a link with a more distant past. The pottery is of the simplest of the Algonkin type.

Algonkin Pottery

The Algonkin pottery chiefly of the marginal regions such as New York bay, Long Island, Connecticut and Rhode Island is primitive in form and decorated with incising, cord-marking or mat impressions very much as we find it thousands of years before in China.

Iroquois Pottery

The Iroquois pottery is more interesting and shows a primitive virility and originality. The vessels, found chiefly in New York and Pennsylvania have a rounded conical base, constricted neck and high straight collar *square in plan* or sometimes slightly inward slanting, the sides of which are usually incised with a rectilinear or triangular pattern or both, or sometimes with modelled figures or heads in relief, giving a strong and not unpleasing effect. Why and how this peculiar form came into being I cannot seem to find out but I venture the guess, and that is all it is and all it should be taken for, that in propping such a vessel up on its point leaning against a mat wall, the round mouthed type was found to roll and fall over unless a corner could be found for it. Certainly this type with its square mouth to steady it would

FIG. 1272. Primitive jar from Suffolk County, N. Y., which lacks rim of any sort and has simple incised design about shoulder. Of dark gray clay. Ht. 8¼″. Mus. of Am. Indian.

FIG. 1273. Large jar seemingly comb impressed and similar in shape and treatment to those found in Western Asia. Ht. 15⅞″. Found in Clinton County, N. Y. Mus. of Am. Indian.

FIG. 1274. Pottery jar from Fichers Island, Suffolk County, N. Y. showing Iroquois squared mouth which seems a more or less local idea. Dark brownish gray clay. Ht. 12½″. Mus. of Am. Indian.

lean well against any wall. In other words we have here a mat-leaning-surface decorated with a sort of incised mat design. Also *two* of these vessels would lean together over a fire. This seems to be one that the Chinese did not think of!

Trumpet-like smoking pipes were beautifully shaped and often also well ornamented with modelled life forms. Dr. Kroeber says, "The typical Virginia pipe with long stem and upturned bowl, taken to England by early colonists along with the first tobacco, gave form to the common clay pipe of the present time." These would have been made by the antecedents of the Sioux Indians we suppose.

GEORGIA AND FLORIDA INDIAN POTTERIES

This section is naturally somewhat complicated by various influences such as the Muskogin family in southern Georgia and northern Florida, the traces of Calusa and Timucua further down, and on the west coast early Arawakan

FIG. 1275. Pottery jar from Bronx County, N. Y. which shows further development with actual figures modeled and stuck on corners. Slow transition from beginnings of incising to first appliqués. Mus. of Am. Indian.

FIG. 1276. Pottery burial urn from Bryan County, Georgia, with interesting stamped design probably made by wooden stamp. Proportions good and graceful form has been evolved. Ht. 16½″. Mus. of Am. Indian.

FIG. 1277. Jar from Calhoun County, Florida, with interestingly developed incised design which had evidently been conceived before the vase form because neck and mouth curve to harmonize with it. Amazing how few vases are so conceived. Even finest Greek ones seem to have designs which are after-thoughts. Ht. 7¼″. Mus. of Am. Indian.

from the West Indies. Here again naturally fish made up the chief diet as is proven by hundreds of shell mounds but agriculture was also practiced where the country was suitable.

On the Florida peninsula it was the custom to bury the dead, either extended or flexed depending upon the region, or sometimes exposed until the flesh had gone and then the bones only were buried—together with many crude figures of animals or things, vessels of fanciful shapes, etc., made of fired clay, as mortuary offerings. On the west coast especially large deposits of earthenware utensils are found with the dead and the forms suggest a distinct type of vessel. In other words we find here the beginning of the customs which gave us so much pottery in Egypt and China and it would not have been

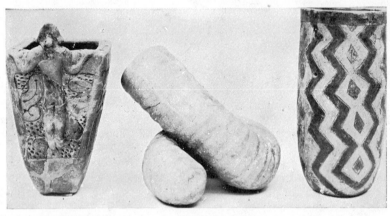

Fig. 1278. Left, a square jar from Calhoun County with figure moulded on one side. Ht. 7″. In center an odd idea of a vase in form of grub or perhaps a sea-worm. Ht. 6¾″. Right, cylindrical jar with incised design and several colors employed as with "three color" wares of China. This jar had been "killed." Ht. 8½″. Mus. of Am. Indian.

so very long, comparatively speaking, before this art would have developed perhaps along similar lines. It is impossible to date any of these Indian potteries closely for there are no historical records kept by the tribes, but they cannot be over 2,000 years old and the customs probably did not change materially from 1,000 years back up to historical times. We must remember the slowness of the development of the same primitive cultures in other countries such as Egypt in which a mere thousand years did not greatly change the look of things.

Georgia and Gulf Coast Potteries

It is interesting to note that these mortuary vessels were "killed" by putting holes in the bottom. In Georgia urn burial of either cremated or non-cremated remains is rather common. Along the Gulf coast, where pile dwellings were used as protection against marauders human or animal, an unpainted pottery was made of good and pleasing form and in the western part of this area we find well modelled life forms and pottery with engraved or indented designs.

An interesting group of potteries is decorated with figured stamps or paddles with designs so like those of certain West Indies wooden objects that they

Fig. 1279. Pottery vessel of animistic form from Hardman Mound, Nacoochee, White County, Georgia. Dark clay with white decorations. Very like those found in Western Asia dating c. 3000 B.C. though made thousands of years later and thousands of miles from there showing how much man's development takes similar trends. Mus. of Am. Indian.

seem to prove a connection of some sort though these pieces are found not only on the coast near Mobile but also all the way inland to near Knoxville, Tennessee.

Pipes were usually of trumpet shapes with the bowls expanding into animal and human heads or bird shapes, those in most of the territory being beautifully designed and well made though those on the West Coast are less so.

On the Florida keys the pottery was similar to that of the peninsula but showing stronger West Indies influences as we would expect. Cutting tools of shell and shark's teeth were mainly used.

Thus we see that the South Atlantic Coast is advanced over the North Atlantic Coast and this is probably due to the more nomadic tendencies of the hunters in the northern region, as well as their somewhat later arrival.

GREAT LAKES AND UPPER MISSISSIPPI POTTERIES

The Great Lakes and Upper Mississippi area also belonged to the Algonkin and Sioux stocks and its culture is similar to that found to the eastward and not so well developed as that further south. Wild rice, hunting and fishing supplied the food wants and agriculture was practiced in favorable parts. Evidently two important industries were undertaken, for in Minnesota, in Pipestone County, there are evidences of the mining of catlinite or "red claystone" which was made into pipes, ornaments and ceremonial objects which were spread far and wide, and the copper of the Lake Superior region was battered out of pits by rude stone hammers. This copper was used for the

Fig. 1280. Three pieces found at Big Bend Bank Cemetery, Posey County, Indiana, near junction of Wabash and Ohio Rivers. Human effigy bowl, complicated and far from easy to pot, bottle and animal effigy bowl show considerable development. Dias. a. 8″. Mus. of Am. Indian.

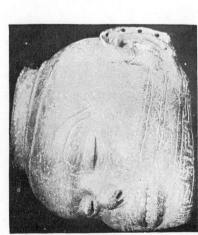

Fine strong pottery bowl from Nacoochee Mound, White County, Georgia. Dark clay with well drawn spirals spaced about rim and typical space-filling device. Ht. 7¼″. Mus. of Am. Indian.

Left: Jar from Cayuga County, N.Y., with not only Iroquois squared mouth but suggestions of faces at corner designs suggesting further development. Ht. c. 12″.
Right: From Cross County, Arkansas, comes this animal vessel which, though primitive, is amusingly decorated.

Left: Pottery jar representing human head, from Mississippi County, Arkansas, which gives feeling there might have been a prototype of stone.
Center: Pottery jar from Natchez, Mississippi, truly potted, of hard nearly black ware with beautifully worked out spiral design masterfully applied to form. From Apache Co., Arizona. Ht. 13″. Mus. of Am. Indian.
Right: Fully developed basket technique as applied to coiled pottery.

NORTH AMERICAN INDIAN POTTERIES, MODELED AND INCISED

making of ornaments, tools, etc., and the sheet copper with repoussé designs on it found in Illinois and even in Florida came from these mines. This is outside our field of pottery but is mentioned to show the degree of culture and also of intercommunication which prevailed.

FIG. 1281. Water bottles from Lafayette and Miller Counties, Arkansas, of hard black ware which appear to have been carved after firing, then polished. This would account for scratchy look of design. Hts. c. 8″ to 9″. Mus. of Am. Indian.

The pottery was frequently incised and indented with figures and painted pottery is rare. The shapes are more primitive than those to the south, but distinctive.

MISSISSIPPI POTTERIES

The "Mound-builders," as the Indians of the Mississippi basin are called, show evidences of higher culture than any other group north of Mexico as we would expect, for have we not found that all the great cultures of the world were likely to center about the fertile basins of great rivers? Here life was

FIG. 1282. Three-lobed water bottle from Ozan, Hemstead County, Arkansas, which suggests use over fire and recalls some of two-lobed ones of South America. Ht. 9½″. Mus. of Am. Indian.
FIG. 1283. Pottery jar from Arkansas with pinched-up applied bosses and incised design. Mus. of Am. Indian.
FIG. 1284. Animal effigy bowl with incised decoration after firing. Length 9½″. Mus. of Am. Indian.

comparatively easy and became sedentary. At first these mound-builders were thought to have been a race apart but it was found that the tumuli were entirely the work of the Indians, that many in the Ohio Valley were in use and even in process of building after the arrival of the Europeans. Some of the mounds are complicated in form and show considerable engineering knowledge. They were used for living quarters, burial, defense and also religious and civic purposes. There are evidences of cultural relations with Mexico and the influence of these people extended into the coastal region of Georgia and north into the Great Lakes region. We don't know what the houses and temples were like but there is evidence that they were of wattlework faced with clay and perhaps with bark thatched roofs. Remains of stockades have been found.

These people worked stone masterfully as is proven by the fine tobacco pipes with animal figures on them. In the Hopewell mounds in Ohio was found a head-dress "consisting of a high frontal piece made of sheets of copper cov-

FIG. 1285. Female effigy jar from Crittenden County, Arkansas, which again shows parallel development to those of South America. Possibly such jars started as ritualistic vessels having to do with fertility. Ht. 7″. Mus. of Am. Indian.

FIG. 1286. Water bottle from Ouachita Parish, Louisiana. Hard dark gray ware in form and design which, though well related, are beginning to show an over-sophistication and perhaps tendency toward unstructural. One could imagine points being easily knocked off. Ht. 5¾″. Mus. of Am. Indian.

FIG. 1287. Bowl from Ouachita Parish, Louisiana. Well formed, shows beginning of definite foot treatment, body and rim, and which has well worked out snake-like incised design. Ht. 2¾″. Mus. of Am. Indian.

ered with indented figures out of which rise a pair of wooden antlers neatly plated with sheet copper, etc.," as is said by Frederick W. Hodge in the article on North America in the 14th edition *Encyclopaedia Britannica*. He continues further by quoting Holmes, "The sword-like blades of Tennessee approach the highest place among American chipped products and the agricultural implements of the Illinois region constitute a unique and remarkable class without parallel in any country." So much for their general culture. Their pottery is not quite up to that of the ancient Pueblos of the Southwest. Yet it is certainly far advanced. We find elaborately engraved and painted vases. Effigy vessels are full of character and even humor, though we should be careful not to confuse our own sense of humor with that of distant peoples as we well know that the dealings with humor, even between such closely allied people as the English and Americans, are precarious; that which seems funny to one man may seem deadly serious to another. The basic roundness of a pot is carried out in the effigy ones by making the body very fat and the appendages closely pressed to it. Of course, the roundness of heads as related to the roundness of pots did not escape them and we have some which are indicative of a portrait approach. These occur in the middle Mississippi region. In the lower reaches of the river and on the Gulf Coast a most beautifully proportioned and decorated scroll-decorated pottery was made with particular use of the spiral, that ever recurring design like that of the swastika and vine border or wave border, which we find sooner or later on all primitive wares. These are largely incised and with a considerable degree of accuracy. There are globular and bottle shapes along with others. In the Southern Appalachian region between this culture and that of the Southern Atlantic there was made a good stamp-decorated ware.

GREAT PLAINS AND ROCKY MOUNTAIN POTTERIES

The nomadic Indians of the Great Plains did little farming except in the valleys of the eastern part and that was very minor; their livings were made through the abundant herds of bison and antelope and other game. We should not think of the Apache or Comanche stock as having been there for these tribes are comparatively recent comers but the Pawnee of Nebraska, the Wichita of Kansas and the Caddoan of Arkansas, Oklahoma and Texas were earlier, although we do not know just how early. Pottery is rare throughout the whole area except at the eastern fringe where it is probably partly that of the Mound-Builders. In the Ozark rock shelters a late pottery is infrequently found associated with the bow instead of the earlier *atlatl*.

BASKET-MAKER I (1500–2000 B.C.)

In the arid region further west it is said that maize agriculture was derived from Mexico as much as 1500 to 2000 years B.C. The people made beautiful coiled basketry and the *atlatl* or throwing stick was used instead of the bow. There was no pottery made in this time.

BASKET-MAKER II AND III PERIODS

Pottery of the so-called "Basket-maker II and III periods" may have been invented or have been introduced. It was of a most primitive and rude type. "Slab-houses" with pole and brush roofs over a pit were made in villages and the bow was used in Utah, Colorado, Arizona and New Mexico areas.

PROTO-PUEBLO OR PUEBLO I

Rooms of the Proto-Pueblo period became rectangular and emerged from the ground. Heads were deformed by pressure. It is believed by some that a new race of broad-headed people supplanted the former long-headed people coming from the South but this is debatable to date. Pottery was made by the coil method much as the baskets were made and left, the structural coils unobliterated, in what we term "corrugated pottery." Here we see almost as though unfolding before our eyes the slow development from basket to pottery taking place. At once black-on-white and neck-coiled pottery was made because the people were accustomed to see the natural designs developed in their basketry and felt a need for them on their pottery. This culture took place in the San Juan drainage, parts of the Rio Grande, Little Colorado and upper Gila valleys. It became rapid spreading geographically. The *kiva* or

Left: Animal jar like those of Western Asia in general conception and decoration, from Arizona. Ht. 8". Mus. of Am. Indian.

Right: Only a painter of the bowls found at Nishapur, Persia, or a Sung, Chinese artist could render a parrot with such simplicity and spirit as is shown in this fine bowl from Hawikuh, New Mexico. Dia. 10". Mus. of Am. Indian.

Left: San Domingo Pueblo pottery jar, New Mexico, which may even have had Spanish or Mexican prototype. Stag drawn in X-ray style with intestines and arrow of spirit within. Stag's head inside seems to be giving up spirit and god on mountains may be representative of thunder, lightning and rain with mountains of clouds above. Mus. of Am. Indian.

Right: Bowl with design of ceremonial dancer. Dia. 8". Hawikuh, New Mexico. Mus. of Am. Indian.

Left: Typical late Zuni jar of sort made even today. Ht. c. 10". New Mexico. Mus. of Am. Ind an.

Right: Pottery jar from Hopi tribe, Arizona, with design of ceremonial mask and head gear. Late piece and even modern ones are similar. Mus. of Am. Indian.

NEW MEXICO AND ARIZONA PAINTED POTTERIES

PLATE 216

Fig. 1288. Right, from Hawikuh, New Mexico, typical primitive coiled pottery jar with outside untouched, inside smooth. Left, jar from Chaco Canyon, N. M. grooved to satisfy coiled texture which had become habit. Center, partly coiled, partly smooth surfaced jar. Note that device very like twisting reed in basketry was used to make design. Hts. c. 3½″ to 5¾″. Mus. of Am. Indian.

ceremonial chamber was started which implies certain solid developments of priest-craft which is to have as much influence upon this hemisphere as it did upon the other.

THE GREAT PERIOD OR PUEBLO III

Some geographical contraction took place but the great architectural and ceramic achievements were accomplished about which I shall have more to say later.

Fig. 1289. Bowl with interesting head and shoulder picture of man in ceremonial trappings, much conventionalized. New Mexico. Mus. of Am. Indian.
Fig. 1290. Zuni, New Mexico, jar with stags. Late type not well potted and sloppy in design. Ht. c. 9″. Mus. of Am. Indian.
Fig. 1291. Mimbres Valley, New Mexico, bowl with designs of what appear to be dead stags with large targets on them, perhaps for easy shooting? Mus. of Am. Indian.

PROTO-HISTORIC OR PUEBLO IV AND HISTORIC OR PUEBLO V

A definite cultural degeneration set in and large areas were abandoned in the Pueblo IV and V periods. Corrugated pottery disappeared and the arts all became less certain and in the first of the 17th century the colonization of the Spaniards began. Up to this time, over long periods, were gradually developed small masonry houses on the sites of which we find black-on-white pottery which evidently originated in the San Juan drainage country of Colorado and spread as far as Salt Lake, almost to the Texas border, and south through New Mexico and Arizona, or—did it come up through the South and reach as far as Colorado and Utah? We cannot be too sure of such origins. Then began the period of contraction and defense. Large pueblos or group houses were built on mesa tops or in valleys and protected at places with walls. The entrances were gained by ladders and hatchways and only in the latter decades were ground floor openings introduced.

FIG. 1292. Bowl from Mimbres Valley, New Mexico, with grasshoppers for decoration. Note that they have very full stomachs. Mus. of Am. Indian.

FIG. 1293. Jars with spiral treatments, one square and other round. One on left with knob handle like those seen on Chinese eating bowls of Han period, but decorated to represent bird's head. Ht. c. 5½". Rio Puerco District, Arizona. Mus. of Am. Indian.

FIRST PRIMITIVE START TOWARD BRICK MAKING

Where there was stone it was used but where it was lacking a form of concrete was employed and even in prehistoric times mud mixed with sage was rolled into loaf forms and used for wall building. Here we see our natural steps in brick making which leads to tile making, etc. First man makes two rows of posts and wattles or osiers between which he pounds mud. Then it occurs to him that mud can be made into loaves and so more easily transported to where he wants to build his walls. And finally it occurs to him to fire the loaves and we come to a stage of brick building. This must always take place in a section which is lacking in stones, for bricks are simply man made stones. The bricks were not used in prehistoric times by the Pueblo Indians, but some of the primitive pueblos would house several hundred persons, and were wonderful pieces of construction with the means in hand.

The pottery was made, as we have explained, without the wheel but was true and fine in workmanship. It was graceful and well proportioned and beautiful in color in the later periods. During two periods the decoration was in glaze. In the Mississippi valley and again here we find the natural inclinations of the people for conventionalized design of ancient derivation meeting the desire to expand the arts into more and more naturalistic forms. The animal and human and bird figures are beautifully developed, side by side or actually knitted in with the conventional. Given a few thousand years more the conventional would have disappeared entirely or been reduced at least to odd symbols such as the crescent, the cross, etc., for these people had space to develop naturalism. As life becomes more and more sedentary there is less danger of breakage and even the basketry gives way to earthenware.

So much for our North American Indian pottery which does no more than approximate the earliest known painted pottery of China dating some

3000 years B.C. (and the string decorated or impressed wares of such times). It is less like that of ancient Egypt or Crete and, in fact, is interesting to us only because it helps to show us better how such stages were arrived at.

CENTRAL AMERICAN CERAMICS

ARCHAIC

An archaic people in Central America left traces from the Valley of Mexico to Salvador under volcanic ash and lava flows. We know little about them except that their culture was not of a low grade, for they understood the arts of weaving and of pottery making and may be compared to the Pueblo Indians of later date and further north. Some time before the Christian era there came an influx of people from South America, a sort of backwash of earlier migrations, which settled practically all of Panama, and Costa Rica, parts of Nicaragua and also Honduras and these sections show closer analogies to South American culture than do the others. Some believe that the first of these may have been the Mayas while others are inclined to believe that the Mayas developed from strains which had stayed in place during the earlier drifts southward, remaining in the Huasteca country around Tampico and then moving southward and eastward.

MAYAS AND CHOROTEGAS

By the beginning of the Christian era two more or less definite linguistic groups had assumed a historic pattern owing to their use of writing and of a calendar. Dr. Herbert Spinden has shown that the Maya calendar was put into working order between 613 and 580 B.C. Our earliest Chorotega records are considerably later, but it seems that this linguistic group preceded the Mayas and was forced by them to move from Western Honduras north and south so that they finally came to settle in parts of Southern Mexico and along the south coast of Costa Rica. They are of comparatively little importance.

THE MAYAS—OLD EMPIRE (A.D. 50–700)

Centering in northern Guatamala and within an inverted triangle the points of which are in Palenque, in the Mexican state of Chiapas, a point somewhere about in the northern part of British Honduras and southward to Copan in the western part of the Republic of Honduras was the earliest phase of Mayan development. Dr. Sylvanus Griswold Morley believes that the Mayas originated on the Atlantic Coast about Vera Cruz and points out that the earliest dated object is the Tuxtla Statuette of 98 B.C. found at San Andrés de Tuxtla which is roughly half way between this place and the site of the Mayan Old Empire described above. Two objects bearing the earliest dates found within the area of the Old Empire are the Leyden plate dated A.D. 60 and Stela #9 at Uaxactun dated A.D. 68. We may think then of the rise and fall of the Old Empire of the Mayas as being roughly between A.D. 50 and 700, the original area being occupied continuously up to about A.D. 450 at which time a period of the greatest vigor occurred and movement north into Yucatan took place

Sculptured (before firing) pottery jar which, contrary to method of modeling, is actually carved with much same technique as stone carving. From San Agustin Acasaquastlan, western part of El Progreso Province, Guatemala. Ht. 7¼". Mus. of Am. Indian.

Pottery figure of baby owl probably used as ritual vessel, recalling again prominence of owl in ancient Chinese bronze forms. Probably c. 10th cent., Colima, Mexico. Ht. c. 8½". N. M. Heeramaneck Coll.

Small jar found at Costa Rica. Red ware. Bears close resemblance, save for wide mouth and flaring lip, to Yüeh vessels in form of frogs of 6 Dynasties and T'ang times found just west of Hang Chou at Chiu Yen site. Dia. 3". N. M. Heeramaneck Coll.

Pottery or terra-cotta dog of Toltec Civilization from Colima, Mexico c. A.D. 800–1300. Length 15¾". Brooklyn Mus.

MEXICAN PRE-COLUMBIAN POTTERY

PLATE 217

where the New Empire was founded. At the same time a body of the populace must have traveled west and the culture in an attenuated form even reached to the Valley of Mexico where it was developed by the Toltec, later immigrants from the North, the first of many waves all speaking the language known as Nahuatl.

NEW EMPIRE

From about 450 to 700 oversophistication and internal crumbling of the morale brought about the decline. But the art of pottery, that of stone and also wood came to equal "any work of Europe up to the Industrial Revolution and is worthy of comparison with any of Asia or Africa," as has been said. In the New Empire all became extravagant and flamboyant.

From about 690 to 990 is a period analogous in many ways to the Dark Ages of Europe. What brought this about we do not know but Dr. Morley and Ellsworth Huntington have suggested that climatic changes took place which caused far greater humidity and also that a system had been started for the burning off of the luxuriant growth. This was found at first to benefit the crops but they did not realize that the fire also consumed the humus in the soil itself and after each burning it took a longer and longer time before regrowth took place, therefore, living became more and more difficult. A strong centrifugal movement took place perhaps something like that of the colonial enterprises of the Ancient Greeks and finally the great cities, some 25 of which existed, were encroached upon by the jungle and fell into decay so that now the immense pyramids and temples are overgrown. I need not describe these as it is out of our field but these people had made the pyramid of the Sun in Teotihuacan with a larger base and nearly the same height as that of the Great Pyramid of Egypt, and many other surprisingly great works.

FIG. 1294. Pre-Toltec figure c. 8th to 10th cent. found at Colima. Ht. 12″. N. M. Heeramaneck Coll.

FIG. 1295. Terra-cotta female figure in Tepic style with painted and modeled ornamentation, from Ixtlan territory, Mexico. Ht. 16¼″. Brooklyn Mus.

RENAISSANCE PERIOD (990–1200)

From 990 to 1200 a great recrudescence of the old spirit took place; new cities were built, art was more virile and forged forward and a period of excellence occurred.

TOLTEC INVASION (1201–1458)

This period was closed by internecine strife and the setting up of the Toltec hegemony which was in itself a period of brilliant achievement and showed that these invaders from Mexico were in themselves a strong and cultural force but new intrigue took place and new revolutions occurred until after

1458 the Maya-Toltec culture burst into many hostile parts and so it was when the Spaniards found them.

THE POTTERY OF THE MAYAS

Whole lifetimes of study will be necessary to work out all the phases of the material we even now have in hand from this section and in our brief survey we can only pause to glance quickly at it. Here too the wheel was unknown though, strangely enough, certain altar stones and the so-called "Calendar stone" are made and designed on the circular principle, but the potteries were true and well formed without its use. Modelling, coiling and even molding were practiced from early times. Stamping, incising or engraving and painting with slip were methods well understood for decoration. The paste is fine and hard. Tripod bowls and vertical-sided beakers are characteristic. Vases in animal form are also common. Only rough chronological classifications can yet be attempted. There seem to have been definite pottery centers from which the wares were distributed and these should in time be investigated and their wares traced. Among the amusing pottery wares are the ocarinas made in human form. Large idols were also made.

TOLTEC AND AZTEC POTTERIES

It is not necessary to go into the formations and developments of the Toltec people in Mexico for there is much the same stock underlying all and the Aztecs may be looked upon simply as a final wave of many of the Nahuatl-speaking tribes who came from the North and broke up the Toltec clans which were pushed further south and east resulting in the introduction of Toltec art into Yucatan and Salvador and in time even into Nicaragua and Panama. It seems that these Nahuatl-speaking tribes were the ones that introduced the bow into the Mayan culture and that this aided the conquests. How like our history of the other hemisphere where the northern bowmen–hunters overcame the southern agriculturists!

To the Aztecs, the Toltecs were known as master stone cutters, while they themselves were warriors and political organizers. But the art of the potter also flourished in Mexico through the means of the coiling process and moulds, though the pottery of the Aztec is inferior in every way. Toltec pottery naturally shows close affinity with the Mayan but certain techniques were developed of their own. Primary is the method of adding a dark slip to the body and carving it out to form outlines between which slips of other colors were laid, the favorite being a turquoise blue. Ware of this sort, a kind of champlevé, is found about Vera Cruz in the Totonac area and shows a close connection between these people and the Toltecs. But in form and finish all of these wares are fine though in polish they are not equal to those of the Maya or Zapotec type, nor those further inland in Puebla where there were also Toltec people. Later under the Aztec reign the Toltec potters of Cholula were considered the great masters and were supposed to have received their traditions of color from the Mayans. It is said that the table ware of Montezuma and the Aztec nobles was made there. (See pl. 224A)

NICARAGUA, COSTA RICA AND PANAMA

The southern limit of Mayan culture is unknown. Nahuatl-speaking colonies are to be found in the Rivas Department of Nicaragua and on the Nicoya Peninsula of western Costa Rica. The potteries from these places also show strong Nahuatl influences even when found in what appear to be early sites, and these potteries are far finer than any of that of the Aztecs. They are decorated with polychrome designs in slip and so is that on the mainland found in the graves of the Guetar people.

In Southern Costa Rica and Western Panama where there are Talamancan tribes the pottery was developed to a degree which is equalled only by that of Peru. It has been said that in the "biscuit-ware" they have never been surpassed in the history of hand made pottery. I suppose this means pottery made without help of the wheel. The forms are beautiful in the extreme and the colors are also fine but less brilliant than those of Cholula or Oaxaca, and, especially of Southern Peru. The Talamancans were also masters of what is called the "lost color" process. This consists of painting designs in wax on a slip of a certain color after which a slip of another color is applied by dipping. When the piece is fired the portions covered with the wax release the last applied or upper slip which comes off leaving the first showing through. This process was practiced also by the natives of Ecuador and Colombia and at times in Peru and ties up our present territory closely with these sections.

And thus we see what took place on the North American Continent. One might almost say that culturally as the land tapers down we come to higher and higher achievements and there are all indications of a sort of clogging up of the processes of migration in the tip of the Central American cone with only one major back-wash in Yucatan, but such hindrances as the equatorial heat, the dangers of the sea, of the jungle and of marshes among many others could not stop such a movement in the conquest of this globe by the ever restless races of man.

SOUTH AMERICAN CERAMICS

Onward they came down the West Coast of South America in their canoes to avoid the jungle and marshes, though they had no seafaring technique to speak of, or over to the East coming up the Magdalena and Cauca rivers into the highlands of Colombia and southward into the inter-Andean plateau, or along the Atlantic sea coast.

THE COAST

In Ecuador on the coast were steaming hot jungles full of yellow fever, malaria, tangled forests and carnivorous animals. This was no place for man to stay. Certainly no civilization could be built here at least for millenniums to come.

At Tumbez the hills divide the hot and humid coast from the more southerly hot and arid coast which stretches for some 1500 miles on to the south into Peru and Chile, cut only by the swift and turbulent small rivers rushing down from the mountains and the verdure which clings to their banks. From June to November the country is repellent and forlorn, cloaked in fog and desolate, without movement or life though the sea teems with gulls, ganets, pelicans and cormorants, and fish of many kinds as well as dolphins and seals. This did not look like a promised land, and one wonders what urge there was behind these people to drive them on, but they came and they settled and they lived on fish and what small game there was, and finally came to grow cotton, maguey and tequilla, from which they wove baskets and of which our "Panama" hats are largely made. In the southern part the desert plain lies 2000 or 3000 feet above the sea down to which the rivers make their ways in narrow canyons which 20 miles back from the coast are 1000 feet high and closely shut in. Here they could go no further inland and survive.

THE CORDILLERA

Down this coast run the three great Cordillera or mountain ridges, the East, the West and the Central with *hoya* or valleys between them. In Ecuador are about 25,000 square miles between 7,000 and 14,000 feet high which are suitable for pastoral or agricultural societies. Roughly this equals Massachusetts, New Hampshire, Connecticut and Rhode Island. In Peru there is three to four times as much livable area, the Marañón on the northwest being too hot and enervating for any great development, the Huallaga and the Maritime Cordillera south of the Knot of Pasco being better, though even the passes through the Maritime Cordillera are higher than Pike's Peak or Mont Blanc.

THE CEJA DE LA MONTAÑA

The *Ceja de la Montaña* or "eyebrow of the woodlands" links the mountains with deep valleys to the eastward which descend among high ridges of barren stone to plunge into the dense wilderness of roaring streams and thundering water-falls, impenetrable and terrifying jungle and savage animal life, insect life, reptilian life and all that goes to make up one of the most unconquerable parts of the world's surface, the great Upper Amazon. The Incas even tried to dominate this country at one time but never succeeded.

CUZCO THE CENTER OF THE INCA EMPIRE

In south central Peru is Cuzco, the home of the Inca Empire, the capital of *Ttahua-utin-suyu* or the "land of the four sections" among the head waters of the Amazon. The small streams drain into the Urubamba, which drains into the Ucayali, which in turn drains into the Marañón turning east from a long journey north, which finally drains into the great Amazon. The Urubamba, on an average of about 11,000 feet above sea level, has a valley of temperate climate rich in the necessary raw materials for making pottery, textiles, metalwork, stone architecture and all that goes to produce a civilization.

LAKE TITICACA BASIN

South of Cuzco is the knot of Vilcañote and then the basin of Lake Titicaca stretching south to Lake Poopó at about 12.100 feet above sea level and on south to the salt beds of Coipasa and Uyuni. This is the cradle of the great *Tiahuanaco Empire*. Still further south is a tangle of mountains known as the Desert and Puna of Atacama in South Bolivia, Northwest Argentine and North Chile which is a continuation of the Peruvian coastal region ethnologically speaking where there are only traces of a few backward people.

This is the background of one of the greatest cultures that man has ever known. There are alluvial plains for agriculture and steppe conditions for herds. There are *viscacha*, large edible rodents, deer, edible guinea-pigs or *cui*, partridges and good lake fish. There is gold, silver, lead, tin and—a queer distinction but a good one, *checorumi*, or large working stones for building and *vini*, or small heavy stones. Here sometime and probably some considerable time before Christ came an almost primitive race of men, probably drifting down from the earliest beginnings of the Central American culture which was always a little ahead in both development and decline, of the South American culture. Through the legends of the natives and the writings of early European scholars we are led to the same conclusion. Father Cabello de Balboa writes between 1576 and 1586 the report as given him telling how the strong ruler Naymlap arrived from the North with his wife and many concubines, retainers, officials and soldiers. These followers worshipped an idol made in his likeness from a green stone (jade?). When he died he was interred in the room in which he died, and his followers gave out the story that he had taken wing, because of his goodness, and flown away so that the people went in every direction searching for him to bring him back. Father Antonio de la Calancha tells of a chief named Chimo who ruled the section around what is now Trujillo, on the northern coast of Peru, and founded a strong and rich empire which lasted so well that it took the Inca, Topa Yupanqui, a long time with many troops to conquer it.

Chimu Culture

This refers to the early culture which existed in this section, it is thought between 200 B.C. and A.D. 200 and up to Inca times with a dark age period of decline between 800 and 1100 after which there was a "renaissance," the Early Chimu period. It will be interesting and instructive to pause to note indications as to what this culture was, so far as we can piece it out from present beliefs, legends and archaeological evidence.

The Moon

The Indians of Pacasmayu or Pacasmyo just north of Trujillo worship the moon and built her a temple called Sian or "House of the Moon" for they saw that she controlled the movements of certain fish, the periods of their women, and caused crops to grow. She is greater than the sun for she can be seen both day and night and sometimes eclipsed the sun while the opposite never occurred. Dances and sacrifices of children five years old were held to her.

Early Chimu water bottle of man on llama with stirrup-shaped spout handle. Am. Mus. of Natural Hist.

Left: Early Chimu water jar with single spout stirrup-shaped and paintings of men carrying others in litters, etc., in red on buff ground. Am. Mus. of Natural Hist.

Owl, in red and white Chimu pottery of fairly early period. This bird had significance to worshipers of moon, and is probably one of symbols brought from China. Ht. 7½". N. M. Heeramaneck Coll.

Fine Chimbote, Chimu red and white ware portrait. Ht. 9". Alice Heeramaneck Coll.

PERUVIAN CHIMU POTTERIES

PLATE 218

THE SEA

The sea they naturally worshipped and called it *Ni* making sacrifices of maize-meal and ochre to it, for it was the source of much of their food, but fish were looked upon only as food. The whale, because of his size, was respected and adored and we see numbers of pictures of him in their art, and even pottery vessels made in his shape.

STONES

A certain sort of stones called *Alecpong* was holy and to quote one of our most excellent authorities, Mr. Philip Ainsworth Means (p. 61, *Ancient Civilizations of the Andes*), "They were regarded as the progenitors of the people among whom they stood, for it was thought that the stones were sons of the Sun who, in a rage because of the death of the woman by whom he had had them, had turned them into stone, commanding later on when his anger was past, that the descendants of each stone adore it."

THE STARS

Three stars were deified and called *Patá*. The Spaniards call them *"las tres Marías"* and there is a story about one having been a thief and the other two commanded to lead him away to be devoured by vultures. They also believed that the human race descended from four stars, two of which conceived the Kings and Chiefs, while the other two conceived the poor and lowly. Also both the Indians of Pascasmayu and those of Yungas around northern Bolivia east of Lake Titicaca calculated the year by certain stars called *Fur* and which the Spaniards called *"las Cabrillas"* which were so honored because of the good they had done for the people.

MARRIAGE AND RELATIONS WITH WOMEN

The marriage custom was to fill a newly made pot with maize-flour and tallow from young llamas and place it before the man and woman. It was then set on fire and they poked and stirred until it was entirely consumed. Then they were told, to quote Means again, "Now you are married, but bear it in mind that you must always be equally industrious and equally ardent in love, for you must always be equals in the state into which you are entering." It is not clear whether this means personal equals or equally balanced in the two endeavors or perhaps both, the woman representing the industry and the man the ardor.

Adulterers were thrown over the cliffs.

During times of drought or famine fasts were held and the animals were forced also to fast. Intercourse with their wives was also denied the celebrants of the fast.

DOCTORS

Doctors had become skillful in the use of herbs and simples and were highly respected but they might be beaten to death if a patient died or tied to the body which was buried while they were left above ground to be devoured by the vultures. Many of the potteries show easily recognized symptoms of various diseases.

DEMONS

Demons were thought to be present at the dances and feasts of Pacasmayu and other parts of the coast and would make replies to questions asked idols and "guacas," or idol houses—temples.

FIG. 1296. Red and White Chimu pottery vessel showing remarkable drawing of running demon. Ht. 7". N. M. Heeramaneck Coll.

All this Means tells us from the account given by Father Calancha.

We learn also that these people used javelins in their wars, probably nothing more than well developed fish spears which had been necessary to them in their migrations for thousands of years back along the coast. The people of the highlands used slings.

They were not bound by strict rules of primogeniture. The chiefs chose their heirs to the throne from among their sons or brothers beforehand and the chosen one was especially trained for the position. In the very most northerly section between Piura and Tumbez the Tallanas Indians had chieftainesses or *"capullanas"* as the Spaniards called them.

All accounts agree that these coastal tribes were more advanced in the early times than those of the highlands.

CHAN-CHAN

The capital of this empire, Chan-Chan, was between the sea and the present Trujillo on the right side of the Moche River. All the lords of the shore country built their palaces on the summits of hills or, if no suitable hill was available, artificial ones were made by piling up earth to the required height into mounds or *"huacas"* like flat topped pyramids. At Chan-Chan the capital of the empire there were reservoirs and aqueducts. Beautiful gardens flowered about the palaces. The interiors were of cool white plaster painted with frescoes. Some of the *huacas* were 200 feet high so that advantage was taken of the sea breezes when the rooms were opened. From the sea the aspect must have been one of charming beauty and the life could not have been very different from that of the Egyptians or the Greeks.

CHIMU POTTERY

Dr. Alés Hrdlička found in the Chicama Valley in Peru a very old *huaca* in which were two vessels, one a pedestal-foot dish and the other a tripod dish,

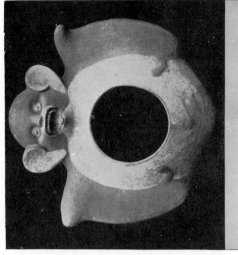

Right: Interesting little bowl from Chimbote, Peru, in form of bat, with head for handle. Am. Mus. of Natural Hist.

Left: Bowl of the red and white ware of Chimbote of the Chimu period, called a "jaguar bowl." Length 11". N. M. Heeramaneck Coll.

Left: Peruvian pottery sandalled foot modeled hollow for bottle. Am. Mus. of Natural Hist.

CHIMU POTTERY FROM CHIMBOTE

PLATE 219

FIG. 1297. Early Chimu water bottles one showing demon head above ears of corn and flanked by lesser deities, other showing a full hamper. Mus. of Natural Hist.

both of definite Central American type both as to form and decoration, just such as are found in Panama, Costa Rica and Nicaragua. With these pieces were brachycephalic skulls of the Central American type, proving beyond a doubt the tieup already outlined.

Thus we find out at once that pottery is one of our chief sources of infor-

FIG. 1298. Water bottles from Chimbote, first being portrait of diseased head, second looking like man without teeth and with puffed cheeks and third holding stump of one leg and cup or perhaps tip of wooden leg. Am. Mus. of Natural Hist.

mation as to the origins of these people but pottery tells us much more that is interesting for this pottery particularly with its highly realistic paintings and well modelled figures possesses a great documentary value besides its aesthetic aspect. Mr. Means has grouped it into four definite classifications as follows:

1.—Scenes and landscapes showing ceremonial and daily life (painted and modelled).

2.—Portraits single or in groups (chiefly modelled).

Fig. 1299. Early Chimu pottery bottles, one painted with warrior in full regalia, another modeled as fine portrait and third painted and in relief showing fight between mythical beings. All have stirrup spouts but portrait one is inclined toward back. Am. Mus. of Natural Hist.

3.—Decorative designs, naturalistic, formalized and also conventionalized (predominantly painted).

4.—Miscellaneous (painted and modelled or plain).

SUBJECTS OF CHIMU POTTERY

He then illustrates various examples similar to those in our own illustrations showing battle scenes, the effigy of a man on a raft with swimmers, a warrior showing his arms and body and face painting, men killing a deer in a netted enclosure, fishing scenes showing boats with carved bow and stern in the form of animal heads, ceremonial dances and a fanged warrior against an aureole-like "sun" design. Others show that the mighty were carried in chairs or litters elaborately decorated, there are also houses, meeting houses, open pavilions and other buildings. The portraiture is life-like and shows excellent characterization.

WOMEN IN CHIMU POTTERY AND DISCUSSION OF OBSCENITY

Women are seldom shown and this is peculiar for all recently nomadic groups value their women highly as is only natural, for women could not

FIG. 1300. Portrait bottles from Chimbote, Peru of type after handle-spout had moved down to back. First and third might well be of same person. Am. Mus. of Natural Hist.

stand the hardships of nomadic life as well as men and slowly become scarce as they are now in Tibet and Mongolia. When the sedentary life is taken up they are preserved carefully and, one might say, collected by the more powerful members into harems much as we found them with the Crusaders in Western Asia. Father Cabello's account proves that this was also the case

FIG. 1301. Chimu bottle in the form of a bird, in red and white. Ht. 10″. N. M. Heeramaneck Coll.

in Peru. When shown at all in the pottery they are hard at work, in the practice of witchcraft or else in acts of a physiological sort peculiar to their sex such as child bearing. Perhaps they were so precious that religious taboos had been built up about them, though in all of this art we do not find much evidence of servitude to priestcraft, or decadent introspection. Rather, there is a healthy and straightforward viewpoint which may be difficult even for us of today to grasp. While I am on this subject I want to point out that it is frequently impossible for members of our own society to gather clearly the pure simplicity of such societies. To them it is no more interesting to depict the processes of body elimination than those of body replenishment and one is no more obscene than the other. The processes of life, birth, sustenance, procreation and death are all simply part of living and, if anything is set aside as different, it is invariably death for the simple reason that death is sometimes difficult to understand as to cause, etc. The pleasures of the chase and of war are also those of the feast and of copulation; cause and effect, they are all one. We saw how in the Philippines the water sold from a vase was used indiscriminately to aid fecundity of the soil and of the women, and this is ever the sound and healthy attitude of man until he is persuaded by the religionists, or those who make power out of his weakness for being taught introspective questionings, to taboo this or that and anything may be tabooed for their purpose, anything which is more or less necessary for natural existence; the chase, war, food, sexual relations or anything else in part or even in the whole at times. Obscenity cannot be ill-omened until the priests have pointed out the omens, it cannot mean moral impurity until the priests have drawn up the lines of what they call morality and, as there is nothing impure in nature, obscenity does not exist for those who live closely and understandingly with nature. These Peruvians could not have come thus far without living closely and very understandingly with nature in both her hardest and softest moods.

Conventionalized Designs in Chimu Pottery

The conventionalized designs are not so vital as those further to the North in Middle America and here we have a transition period in which they are being lost. It is evident that they are continued simply as ornament and that the significance has been lost, but so bred into the past are they that the people felt a certain subconscious satisfaction in them.

Chimu Technique

The Early Chimu emphasis is on form rather than color. The wares are of a reddish clay, much like those of Central America though somewhat lighter and cleaner looking, are covered in part with a white or cream colored slip and maybe painted in black, brown or red-brown slips. On the effigy pieces the hands and faces are sometimes left uncovered by the slip and well burnished with an advanced technique. We have seen how those of T'ang China were left exposed but they were never burnished. Very rarely other colors were used such as crimson, yellow, orange and blue.

Early Nazca Culture

So far as we know the Early Nazca people, who were in the Pisco and Ica valleys on the coast of Peru about two thirds of the way toward the south, were of an even earlier culture or the finds represent a later date (probably the latter) for they had progressed to the point of coming under the influence of a priestcraft-religion the mainspring of which was terror and from which the Early Chimu people seemed still to be free.

General Characteristics of Early Nazca Pottery

Means gives three main differences between the Early Nazca and the Early Chimu potteries as follows:

1.—Realism survives but is rare and to be seen only in occasional examples.

2.—Color is far more varied and important including—crimson, scarlet, pink, yellow, orange, green, various blues, brown, grey, black and white.

3.—Stylistic dogmas of design are all powerful "with an increase of beauty." The last remark being a simple statement of Mr. Means' own taste without the support of argument, but perhaps it would be better to say—with a *different* beauty appeal.

FIG. 1302. Two beakers the one on the left being strangely close in general feeling to a Chou period (1122–249 B.C.) Chinese Tsun. Am. Mus. of Natural Hist.

FIG. 1303. Water bottle from Pachacamac which shows Nazca type highly conventionalized figures and an angular feeling not seen in Chimu pieces. The double spout with bridge handle is a later development. Am. Mus. of Natural Hist.

Dr. Eduard Seler in his excellent treatise on Early Nazca art describes the following fabulous personages which are depicted:

The Spotted Cat—called "the Bringer of the Means of Life" which may

FIG. 1304. Two cups from Nazca, Peru, the one having a conventionalized face painted on it, the nose and ears of which form three perpendicular flanges set at even intervals about the center. The other has a strangely camel-like animal and what appear to be figures with their heads bent over. Am. Mus. of Natural Hist.

FIG. 1305. Nazca jar with bridge handle and oddly arranged figures. Am. Mus. of Natural Hist.

Large cup found at Nazca, Peru similar to other shown from the museum. Ht. 7½". Nasli Heeramaneck Coll.

A rare pottery dish from the Valley of Nazca, Peru with a realistic human figure much less often seen than in Chimu wares. This is really Tiahuanaco in style. Ht. c. 16". Am. Mus. of Natural Hist.

Rare Nazca pottery jar with two posts which probably fitted into ring supports. This is very similar in style to the dish with figure and is also Tiahuanaco in style. Ht. about 8". Nasli Heeramaneck Coll.

NAZCA POTTERIES

PLATE 220

or may not be so, but he brings in his paws frequently what appear to be seeds, leaves and pods, although sometimes they are lacking.

The Cat Demon—a demon which brandishes a club and clutches one or more decapitated heads by the hair or at times whole figures by the waist which in turn seem to hold a mummified head by the hair. Many of the heads seem to be mummified for they are drawn or modeled with thorns passed through the lips. He seems to be a sort of war god and similar to, or perhaps the same as the god with a bird head or that of a masked man.

The Bird Demon—seems similar to that above though sometimes more conventionalized. The feet are never those of a man and it does not, therefore, seem to represent a man with a mask.

The Multiple-Headed God—has attached relaxed (perhaps dead) spindly legs and puny weazened arms. The faces are all highly conventionalized but give, nevertheless, unpleasant leers from their lozenge shaped eyes.

The Centipede God—seems to derive from the centipede figures on Early Chimu pots which perhaps indicate that the Early Chimu culture was before that of the Early Nazca for the Nazca ones are far more detailed and complicated.

Fig. 1306. Two Nazca bottles the one with a painting of the Centipede God and the other a crudely modeled staring figure. It is to be noted that this head is very small in scale and the handle approaches that of the double spout. In other words first came the stirrup spout-handle, then the heads pushed it back as it were, and then the modeling of heads became less important and the double spout came into being. Hts. about 10″. Am. Mus. of Natural Hist.

Mr. Means says concerning the Multiple-Headed God: "It seems to me quite possible that this personage is a late development in Early Nazca art, perhaps of the late 5th or early 6th century."

Mouth-masks like cats' whiskers seen on these faces have actually been found made of copper and gold and Means points out that they seem to be the peculiar property of the dead and of the gods or demons. A tongue-like long flat band hangs down over the chin and seems to be supported by two pin-like points into the septum of the nose.

Headdresses are ornamented with secondary faces, "human, feline or non-descript."

Hands and feet with too few digits are found in large proportion and others have too many digits. The significance of this is not known. It could hardly be a simple disregard of detail for these people seemed to love detail.

The figures hold what seem to be ceremonial staffs, clubs and similar weapons, spears and spear-throwers and also slings such as Dr. Hrdlička found on the southerly borders of the Early Nazca region.

There are other similarities of design to be noted: Where there is realism it is much like that of the Early Chimu culture and we find a spout situated back of the heads set at an angle away from them on the effigy pots and attached to them by a bridge which forms a sort of carrying handle. The Early Chimu pots have a stirrup spout. Later the Nazca spout develops into a double one with bridge between. These narrow openings were used because of rapid evaporation from larger mouths even though they must have been exceedingly difficult to pour into without spilling. A most interesting development is the whistle spout which comes along later.

Fig. 1307.

HIGHLAND CULTURE TO A.D. 600
TIAHUANACO I

In Peru Means mentions only one structure which seems to be pre-Incaic and that is at Vilcashuaman. Of it he says, "Save that it is built of stone and not of adobe it closely resembles the pyramids so common on the coast." Near the southern end of Lake Titicaca in Western Bolivia were two easily distinguishable cultural periods which we may term Tiahuanaco I and Tiahuanaco II. The structures of the first are of the local reddish-brown sandstone and of the other of hard stone which must have been brought from some distance.

TIAHUANACO I POTTERIES

The potteries are very crude and are coarsely incised or painted.

TIAHUANACO II

The Tiahuanaco II section is the most important excavation site in the mountains though this section may have been ruled at times from Cuzco in Peru. In the earliest times the people could hew stone and make buildings huge but very rough. Then trade of coastal cotton with highland wool must have acted to bring the Early Nazca culture to these people and, to a lesser extent, even that of Early Chimu some thousand miles or so to the north. Father Cieza de Leon, writing between 1540 and 1550, tells us that even in his day the great structures of this people were known to be more ancient than the Incas who imitated their masonry in building the city of Cuzco. He describes in some detail the tremendous size of these works including doorways carved out of a single stone "30 feet broad, 15 feet or more long and 6 inches in thickness." Father Diego de Alcobasa wrote, "There are also many other stones carved into the shape of men and women so naturally that they appear to be alive, some drinking from cups in their hands, others sitting, others standing and others walking in the stream which flows by the walls. There are also statues of women with their infants in their laps, others with them on their backs and in a thousand other postures—" Mr. Means says that the statues of women do not now exist and discredits some of the other things said, but the full allowance for enthusiastic exaggeration deducted, we still have a very interesting account which probably had some foundation, and we know from the accounts of Father Cobo and in these days of Dr. González that far more remains underground than above. (See also reports from Pennsylvania University Museum work, etc.)

"The Weeping God of Tiahuanaco"

Means says a general conspectus of Tiahuanaco II art may be seen in the monolithic gateway at the northwest corner of Calasasaya, which has on it what is well known as "the Weeping God of Tiahuanaco." It is not necessary to trace a full description of the piece here but briefly it has a central figure with large square face and elaborate headdress from which project many snake-like parts terminating in conventionalized puma profiles and circular patterns of unknown significance. From his large round eyesockets tears course down his cheeks. There is no doubt but that he is Viracocha, the chief god of these mountain people. His hands have only four digits and hold a highly conventionalized spear-thrower in one and in the other a quiver containing two spears. His rich dress and girdle are decorated with puma heads. Every part of the frieze is laden with ornamental detail representing men, animals, birds and fish as well as many symbolical motifs the significance of which we do not yet know. There are 24 attendants on either side arranged in 3 rows of 8 each, the upper and lower rows having winged men with spears while the center row is of birds or men wearing bird masks. Below is a maeander border seemingly of heads like the god's. The arrangement is symmetrical in general scheme but there is considerable vigor and some variation. Everything seems to be thought of in squares broken by jagged angles. This is probably because of the fact that in their stone building they were necessarily very conscious of the square and the jagged angles may represent fractures or thrusts of which they were also conscious. No one can say for sure but the association seems likely.

Tiahuanaco II Pottery c. a.d. 300 to 600

The bowls, jars, bottles and vases of this people are strictly consistent. They are decorated in rich sombre colors with pumas and other creatures much like those on the gateway. Many shapes are simple and well proportioned but some found at Cuzco are involved and poor. Typical are the ornamentation of the nose and forehead of the faces and ornamentation of the rim of the pot. Fanged mouths recall those of the Early Chimu art. Hands with too few digits and grasping decapitated heads are reminiscent of Early Nazca art. These pieces date back from about a.d. 600. Means thinks, namely to a.d. 300 or thereabouts.

Later Tiahuanaco II Art

At Chavín de Huánter in the valley of the Puccha River, a tributary of the Marañon, was found a monument called the "Raimondi Monolith" after the discoverer. This stone has the same god represented on it but the face is absolutely square and strangely made to appear like a face from either above or below. From above it looks like a highly conventionalized feline face or two snarling feline faces nose to nose and in profile. Means points out that we have something rare here in Andean art but a trick which can be duplicated in Mayan art, in Alaskan art and he says doubtless elsewhere in ancient American art. He might have also added in Chinese art of the Shang Yin and Chou periods and gone on around the Pacific and added in the tattooing of the islands of the South Pacific.

This piece has the same characteristics of Early Nazca art as found in the gateway but it is interesting to note that the art has now become in every detail perfectly symmetrical. Early Nazca art was strongly so, Tiahuanaco at first was more symmetrical and now it has frozen into the rigid convention so that a line drawn down the center will have exactly the same on one side as on the other. The fangs and the feather-like ornaments are from Early Chimu art and not indigenous. The multiple headed headdress is typical of Early Nazca art, as we know. Mr. Means says about it, "Its style is decidedly more mature—one might almost say more nearly senile—than that of the Monolithic Gateway." He places it about A.D. 800.

In describing another find made by Dr. Tello called the "Chavín Obelisk" in the Museum of the University of San Marcos, he says that Dr. Tello says it is a dragon eating fish, serpents and condors all highly conventionalized. From the photographs I must admit that the good doctor can see in it more than I can. However, an interesting comment concerning the genital organ of the creature is made by Means. It is in the form of a fanged puma-head from which issues a plant-like object which Tello says is perhaps emblematic of fertility. Means says, "In this element we have a faint suggestion of that wistful phallicism which so often accompanies the degeneration of art among people desirous of fertility who dimly realize that their vitality is at a low ebb."

Some finds have been made from the mountains of the Department of Piura in the north and Means shows a piece of polished black pottery from the Elías Collection which he claims is the earliest artifact known to us from that region dating between A.D. 800 and 1000 and showing Chavín Tiahuanaco art in its last stages. The decorative band he says represents birds with only the beaks showing and we hope he knows that they are birds but at any rate they show, he says, "the ultimate stage of aesthetic disintegration."

Symbolic Conventionalization

Previously we outlined a theory which so far as I know has not before been suggested, namely that conventionalism in art came from the necessity to make records on small areas. Here we come to another type of conventionalization, that of symbols which at first are abbreviated without the slightest loss of meaning, then are carried on to a degree more simplified because all know what they mean, and finally end up as meaningless designs used solely for ornamentation until they pass out of existence, the public slowly having forgotten what was at first a perfectly clear shorthand.

It is not always easy to distinguish between the two kinds of conventionalization when seen on an individual example, but there is no trouble at all when we have a group of the one to compare with a group of the other. The living conventionalized art of the nomads is always strong and dynamic and would suggest to the uninitiated that it held a meaning and a vital one. The dying conventionalization of decadent-art-symbolism is really a sort of laziness or lack of interest on the part of the artist and it is always marked with the signs of short cuts to effects and poorer craftsmanship. As an instance we have here the perfect symmetry which no living art would tolerate but which the lazy and uninterested craftsman finds saves worry and the effort of thinking on his part. There is as much difference between the two as there is between infancy and senility. There are likenesses but also great differences which can best be sensed when we ask if the artist was doing his best. Sometimes today artists like to assume a primitive pose. Between their assumed simplicity and that of the simple man expressing himself earnestly to the best of his ability is all the difference between charlatanism and sincerity. So it is with conventionalization and purposeless conventions in art; conventions which have lost their purpose are useless and dead.

ECUADOR

In Ecuador, the Kingdom of Quitu, at first a seafaring people, moved up into the highlands to escape the heat. They were warlike and reached from

FIG. 1308. Pre-Conquest red pottery vase from Ecuador ingeniously designed with the body of a seated figure as neck and the head as stopper. This piece undoubtedly shows a closer relationship with the Peruvian potteries than is usual. Ht. about 14″ Brooklyn Mus.

FIG. 1309. Native pottery bottle decorated with "negative painting" from El Angel, Ecuador, pre-Conquest. Note the similarity to some neolithic European and also some Egyptian forms. Ht. 25½″. Brooklyn Mus.

an archaic culture more closely associated with that of Colombia and Central America than with the Peruvian culture, up to about a par with Tiahuanaco II. In general they showed some traces also of influence from the latter in some of their potteries.

The highland culture was not very unlike that of Peru but always less advanced. The coastal culture is more like that of Colombia. A few odd outstanding pieces show that their art as potters was not of much consequence except where influenced by outside sources. A bowl with a rather well conventionalized bird in white on a black ground is crudely made and probably fairly early as is also a vase with face and arms on the neck, perhaps of Early Chimu times. Later wares are represented by the typical Inca "aryballus" and the refined small jar of good shape with two loops and no decoration. The tall vase shows a grace of form which would also indicate a period of about Inca times. It is an excellent piece of work.

The Period of Decline (A.D. 900–1400)

The Tiahuanaco II culture has shown us that a decline had set in. The central government now showed the same weakness, and conflicting groups set up innumerable small tribal communities throughout the highland zone while the coastal people returned to their original condition. Dr. Max Uhle has invented a term "Epigone Style" from the Greek meaning "one born afterwards" for this time, and describes it as follows: He says it resembles the Tiahuanaco II but "is inferior to its famous prototype in almost every respect." Means thinks that the specimens Dr. Uhle offers are actually "integral parts of Tiahuanaco II art" and that others are "unskillful attempts by coastal artists to copy the characteristics."

The states which were now separated from the central government and cultural life soon fell into degeneracy themselves. The Chimu one extended from the Gulf of Guayaquil to Parmunca and conquered up into the hills but the rulers whiled away the time with buffoons, concubines, dancers and all such court parasites and gave themselves out of boredom to unnatural vices, the worship of animals and human sacrifices, much as we have seen about the Mediterranean in ancient days.

Potteries of the Decline

The argument about general characteristics suggests to us how difficult it is to tell about individual examples. Dr. Kroeber says of all we have, 3% are Early Chimu and 97% late in the black style pottery. In other words, there is practically no Early Chimu black pottery. In the red type 25% are early while 75% are late. The stirrup handle with spout is common to both periods as is also the double bodied jar.

Late Chimu features which are not found at all in the Early Chimu period are:

This ceremonial urn of the Tiahuanaco Epigonal Period is from the Nazca Valley and shows the symmetrical style with some Early Chimu characteristics. The figure is Viracocha, the creator god worshipped in pre-Inca times. Am. Mus. of Natural Hist.

Three bottles from Tiahuanaco sites dating about 6th to 7th cent. and typical in style. Hts. 5″ to 6″. N. M. Heeramaneck Coll.

TIAHUANACO POTTERIES

PLATE 221

1.—Double spout linked by bridge (which came from Early Nazca via Tiahuanaco to coast again).

2.—Flattened oval rather than globular bodies.

3.—Absence of spirited and beautiful realistic paintings of genre-scenes or persons, etc.

4.—There are cases of Early Chimu whistling jars but they are exceedingly rare while in Late Chimu times they are common.

5.—Stolid modeling which attempts to be lifelike and is not.

6.—Formalized wares showing Tiahuanaco influences.

Fig. 1310. A group of Peruvian late period black clay potteries showing the decline in the art. Am. Mus. of Natural Hist.

Fig. 1311. Black pottery bottles, the one on the left of two parrots about 8¾" high, the center a whistling bottle (Chimbote) showing a man in a shelter, and the right one also a whistling bottle with a man on the shoulder seated in a contemplative attitude. Am. Mus. of Natural Hist.

WHISTLING BOTTLES

The whistling bottles are most amusing and typical of this period of nonsense and funmaking. I show an example which was in my possession

which has two spouts connected with a bridge in typical Late Chimu style. One of the spouts is closed by a top on which is perched a monkey with his tail arched high and when one either pours liquor into or out of the other the air is forced through a small hole so cleverly designed that a mournful whistle results. The obscene nature of this piece is such that it would never have occurred to the Early Chimu people and what early examples there are represent birds or other things.

FIG. 1312. Late Chimu whistling bottle of black clay. Ht. about 6".

THE RIMAC VALLEY ABOVE LIMA
CHANCAY AND NIEVERÍA

Found at Chancay by Dr. Uhle and classified by Dr. Kroeber are the following types of pottery:

1.—"Interlocking ware" of the various surrounding types.
2.—White on red ware
3.—"Epigonal" 3 and 4 color wares.
4.—Three color geometric ware (red, black and white).
5.—Black on white ware.

Means says that #1. is pre-Tiahuanaco of a mixed Early Chimu and Early Nazca type, that 2, 3 and 4 are Tiahuanaco II provincial wares influenced by 1, and that 5 is post Tiahuanaco yet pre-Inca. The latter is a very crude ware realistic in modelling though geometric in painting and

FIG. 1313. Figures from Recuay, Peru, of a man with a llama, a jar, and a woman with a water jar. Am. Mus. of Natural Hist.

Means cannot explain this strange crudeness unless it is perhaps "an artistic mannerism." It seems hard to believe that these people had descended to our modern plane wherein crudity could be assumed, as simplicity is assumed, simply because the artists can think of no more shocking type of self-advertising, but this may be the case.

Of the black-on-white ware Means has to say that it has also been found at Ancón and as people came from all about to visit the oracle-god at Rimac-Tampu, it would not be surprising if pottery from every region of the Andean area were found there.

Nievería Pottery

Higher up the Rimac Valley at Nievería and Cajamarquilla is found a post-Tiahuanaco ware with elements from earlier coastal wares again taking the modelling from Early Chimu and the painting from Early Nazca.

Chincha, Pisco, Ica and Nazca Later Wares

After the Early Nazca period there were Tiahuanaco influences strongly throughout all of this war loving section. When the realm of Chuquimancu divided up war was constant but brief periods of peace were procured by the expedient of exchanging of women. The wares of the later periods continued rich and somber in color with the same methods of depicting human and animal life. The most distinctive of these wares of what may be called the Late Nazca period were decorated with designs inspired by textile art. Such designs constitute a new type of decorative art and are peculiar to this region during this time.

Tiahuanaco-Epignol Period a.d. 600–900
Atacameno Period a.d. 900–1100
Chincha-Atacameno Period a.d. 1100–1350

Dr. Max Uhle makes a somewhat different classification which consists of the Tiahuanaco-Epignol period (a.d. 600–900), the Atacameno period (a.d. 900–1100) and finally the Chincha-Atacameno period (a.d. 1100–1350). He says that the first pottery in north Chile in the Tacna and Arica region was much like that in Peru. The second period is marked by influences from the South and Southeast and he calls it by the name of a more southerly section in Chile. The pottery is coarse and heavy with ill arranged designs of vigor. Means says about these that they have some relationship with Inca pot shapes as we shall see later. The last period has the same shapes but the designs have become more refined doubtless because of the influence of Chincha or late Nazca art.

In the highlands after the Tiahuanaco II period from say 600 the arts declined to an uninteresting level. Thus we conclude that after this period there was a distinct decline throughout the whole of Peru and Bolivia but a decline far greater and more telling in the highlands.

THE INCAS

Mr. Means points out an unhappy truth in his "Ancient Civilizations of the Andes" (p. 205) and that is that the historians of Peru fall into two biased schools: the one he terms "Garcilasan" and the other "Toledan." The Inca, Garcilaso de la Vega, tells of the creation of man and woman by the sun and the placing of them on an island in Lake Titicaca whence they travelled with a staff of gold seeking a place where with one blow it would sink out of sight in the ground. This was a story he had from his maternal uncle. There are others concerning shining youths in golden mantles that so blinded the people that they gave homage. Of the "Toledan" school he says, "The underlying objective of this school was to justify the establishment of Castilian power in the Andean area and elsewhere in America, this end to be served by showing the Incas to have been bastards and usurpers whom Charles I and Philip II of Castile, descendants of those questionable sovereigns, Sancho IV and Henry II of Castile, had every right to supersede, not only because they were so much superior in their hereditary right to rule, but also because America was only a fitting reward for the services rendered to God during the eight centuries of the Reconquest in Spain—and also because Alexander VI—that holy pontiff—had given them the right." This school was represented most loyally by Viceroy Don Francisco de Toledo, Capitan Don Pedro Sarmiento de Gamboa, in his history of the Incas, 1572, and by Cieza de Leon who tried to be honest and unbiased but bases his work upon that of Sarmiento.

The Incas themselves have a story which is related from their royal *quipus* or knot-records something as follows: In A.D. 945 a barbarous family of four sons and four daughters lived in the highlands. The sisters made beautiful raiment heavily spangled with gold and they all stole by night to some deserted buildings about five leagues from the present city of Cuzco. When dawn came they entered the market place telling the villagers that they had come from Heaven and were children of the Sun and such was the awe caused by their shining beauty that they were hailed as rulers.

Another story is that Mama Ocllo became pregnant by her brother Manco Capac, that another of the brothers disapproved and was killed by Capac who then gave out word that Mama Ocllo had become pregnant by the Sun and so Sinchi Roca was born. Here we have a Zeus-like myth taken in much the same spirit as that of the early Greeks.

Then there is the legend of Mama Huaco, who was mannish and warlike as well as wise and prudent. She threw two golden rods in such a way that one fell two cross-bow shots from Matahua while the other landed at Huaca Pata (Holy Terrace or Square) in the city of Cuzco. The first entered the earth only a little, while the other buried itself so deeply that it was argued that at this place the group was destined to go.

We find then, 1.—simple migration myths and 2.—memories of astuteness and chicancery of the shining mantle type.

Dr. Uhle, supplementing his study of the languages has made a thorough study of the pottery found in the Yucay, Urubamba and Arequipa sections among other places in southern Peru which have yielded up not only the beginnings of the ceramic forms later perfected by the Incas but also the incipient decorative motives which were later to become the developed indicators of the highest art of the Incas, and he has found out and satisfactorily proven that it is likely that the Incas were originally simply a small tribe of "llama-tending, potato-growing mountaineers" no different from hundreds of others at the time of the collapse of the Tiahuanaço II culture. They probably lived south of Cuzco or Tampu (now Ollantaytambo) on the Urubamba River, though this is not definitely established. Other small tribes were forming alliances and engaging in conflicts, building dynasties, etc., and as Means says, this was much the same as the conditions which produced Genghis Khan, "for the rivalries resulting therefrom engendered recurrent struggles for mastery, and the struggles bred strength and ever more strength in the victors."

Characteristics of Incas

These Incas were not luxury loving rulers but soldiers and wise administrators and their glory was not expressed in bodily comfort so much as in a "superlative aesthetic glory." They were not far advanced in certain things; the arch was unknown, glass was unknown, the wheel had not been invented and they could not, therefore, harness natural water power. Iron called "*quillay*" was, alas for their hopes of opposing the Spaniards, not known but as workmen in gold, bronze, silver, pottery, textiles, and stone sculpture or architecture they were as fine as any known up to the time of the Renaissance, at least.

Inca Pottery

We cannot be so definite about the Inca potteries as we can about those of Greece but excavation and study is going on and this is one of the richest fields of present day investigation. It is a field in which that master archaeologist and critic of aesthetics, Mr. Horace H. F. Jayne, has shown considerable interest and leadership as well as those others of whom I have spoken and who are mentioned in the bibliography. A number of our museums are rich in treasure such as The Museum of The American Indian, The American Museum of Natural History and the Pennsylvania University Museum, but so far all too much interest has been expended upon the ethnological and archaeological aspect to the exclusion of the aesthetic, except only in the last mentioned museum which was in charge of Mr. Jayne. Our great but somewhat unbalanced Metropolitan Museum does not even deign to show this art, though most of the larger museums of Europe have specimens of which they are justly proud.

Inca Forms—The "Aryballus"

Probably the best known and appreciated shape of pottery is the "aryballus" because of its general similarity to some Greek forms though it has ever been more structural than they. The base is a shallow cone, point downward.

INCA POTTERIES

PLATE 222

Inca potteries from Peru, a flat dish with bird head handle, an "aryballas," a graceful flaring cup which is a form also made of wood, and a small jar with typical loop handle characteristic of these wares. Am. Mus. of Natural Hist.

The body arches up from this in almost a deep parabolic curve and from this comes a cylindrical neck flaring to a fairly wide mouth-rim. There are two loops low down on the sides and they are small and strongly made. Most are yet intact in place on those found. A small nubbin either plain or with roughly indicated animal head (usually feline) is frequently seen on the

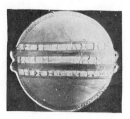

FIG. 1315. Small flat pottery dish which seems a typical Inca form. The double loops on opposing sides suggest a possibly arched handle. Dia. Am. Mus. of Natural Hist.

FIG. 1314. Two pieces found on the island of Titicaca in Bolivia just over the border of south east Peru. The "aryballas" is said to be of Cuzco type and the one handled vessel is similar. Am. Mus. of Natural Hist.

shoulder at the base of the neck. Concerning this Means says, "This nubbin and the two handles at the widest part of the pot served to hold the carrying-rope in place when the aryballus was carried upon someone's back, the rope being passed through the handles and over the nubbin, after which the ends of the rope fell over the carrier's shoulder and were held by his hands on

FIG. 1316. A very large "aryballas" with the neck broken and sitting upon the sort of stand which was probably used. It is my contention that the loops were used also to sling these vessels from above and to aid in tipping them for pouring. This vase would have been well over 4 feet high. Am. Mus. of Natural Hist.

FIG. 1317. Stem coupe with cover and an "aryballas" of good proportions and conventional decoration. These latter range in size from about 6" high to huge examples about 4 feet high, and far too heavy for any man to carry even partly filled. Am. Mus. of Natural Hist.

his chest. This arrangement brought it about that the side of the aryballus which would rest upon the carrier's back was left undecorated, all the ornamentation being concentrated on the other side, that which bore the nubbin, though some have decoration on both sides." I frankly admit that I am not satisfied with the description for most of these vessels are only from about 9 to 12 inches high, though there are larger ones, of course, some of which are about 40 inches high and which, if filled with water could not be carried by any man of ordinary strength. It seems in fact that they were made in about three sizes: 1.—small ones 8 or 9 inches high which could be carried easily by simply grasping the neck, 2.—fewer middle sized ones about 12 inches high that are at least a good size for carrying with cord slings, 3.—even fewer very large ones that few men could lift when filled. There are practically speaking none in between these sizes. Therefore, at once we see that most of them are not even appropriate sizes for carrying vessels. A man would certainly look like a fool with one of the little ones on his back and I doubt he could even hoist one of the big ones. I have carefully computed the capacity of one of the larger jars and find that it would hold about 21 gallons of water which would weigh approximately 186 pounds avoirdupois plus the weight of the jar itself which is about 40 pounds making a total of 226 pounds. Quite a load to carry any distance in mountainous country!

Another thing is clear and that is that the two loops are generally below the center of gravity. If then the vessel were to be held on the back by means of cord at all, the cord would have to pass around the back at the widest part (where it would rub well into the carrier's back), come through the loops and cross at the base of the neck to keep it from tipping outward before going around it and over the shoulders. This would mean that the nubbin had no reason for being at all, and it would also mean that a man was carrying a most unpleasant and awkward burden. Of course the cords could cross *under* the knob instead of simply at the neck, but there would be no particular reason for this and any such arrangement would press the lip-rim into the carrier's back in a way that would be hardly comfortable to say the least.

I think, therefore, that considering sizes, the possibilities of cord arrangements and the shape we must reach the definite conclusion that these are not carrying vessels at all. Perhaps the consensus has been reached by our authorities because there is some evidence such as the picture or model of a man carrying one of these vessels which I have been unable to run down, but it can have been reached only because our authorities are not pot carrying people and did not think of the difficulties involved. Furthermore I have searched in vain for the natural wear of chafing of cords on the decorations of these vessels and have found none. We might as well conclude that an amphora or a hydria was a carrying vessel because we have pictures of Greeks carrying them in various ways, or that a modern ice-water pitcher is a carrying vessel because we see people carry them from the kitchen to the dining room.

What then is the nubbin for? Let us pause to consider how often we see in these wares a man's head, a god's head, a puma head or some other animal head projecting in relief from one side of a vessel. In fact this was one of the chief characteristics not only of South American wares but also of Central American wares. Could the nubbin not, therefore, simply be an atrophied form of the same thing? I feel that it is and that a series could be arranged showing the prototypes of the "aryballus" in rounded bodied jars with loops and more prominent and detailed heads upon them.

The pointed bottom, which is never decorated, by the way, would raise another question were it not for the fact that in the American Museum of Natural History there is an actual clay rest which was found on the Island of Titicaca and with an "aryballus" fitted nicely into it. The pointed bottom would make another inconvenience for any possible carrier as he would have to stand and balance the jar, if he put it down, as the width of the body makes it a shape that will not lean nicely against a wall or other object. Naturally the carrier, if he could hoist one of the big jars, would not mind carrying also a clay base of a few pounds more, but he might forget it and that would be a pretty fix.

Everything helps to make us believe that these jars were used on stands in the homes of well-to-do Inca people. They were occasionally against a wall and therefore in such cases decorated only on one side. I believe that for the larger ones, which probably stood on the floor, there may have been rope hoists attached in some way to the loops which are nicely placed just about at or sometimes slightly under the center of gravity, to aid in pouring from them. The pointed base would also make it easier to tip them in their circular stands sufficiently to pour from them. The small ones can be nicely handled by the two loops, which were perhaps actual handles. By this means pouring from them, as a servant might pour wine into a cup, is not an ungraceful movement.

Some of these vessels have two more much smaller loops, one at either side of the lip and just under it immediately above the large loops. They can be used only for tying a cover on although there is no evidence of a rim for a cover inside the lip. They are too small and the location too dangerous at the fragile edge of the lip to have supported the weight of the vessel in any way.

Generally cylindrical but slightly flaring wooden cups were made and decorated with fine painting. These were also copied in pottery and, in fact the size was sometimes increased to make a fairly large and deep vessel.

Dishes and Bowls

Small and very shallow dishes were made frequently with little double loops at the rim arranged horizontally and opposing each other. Larger dishes have often a more bowl-like form and an animal or bird head as handle or ornament on one side only.

Really much more like an aryballus (I think the larger vessel might better be called an amphora, if we have to go Greek in our naming of these unrelated wares. I continue the custom simply because it has become so definitely grounded that otherwise misunderstandings might arise.)—is a small globular vessel with horizontally placed loop handle and excellent all-over decoration. Another is similar but has a narrower mouth and beveled bottom, the decoration consisting simply of a band about the body at the height of the handle. A third shape which seems fairly common from Cuzco is a pear shaped bottle with small straight, unflaring neck and the same sort of loop handle.

General Characteristics

Dr. Bingham in his recent work shows pedestal cooking-pots, bowls, jars, kettles, ladles, plates, jugs and cups and says that they are found from North Ecuador down to Northwest Argentine and Central Chile and that they are always at the top of the archaeological sites.

These potteries are all thin walled and extremely good. Some are of brown or buff color, though most are grey. The coloring is good though chiefly geometrical, limited in range and low in tone nowhere nearly approaching the Early Nazca wares or those of Mexico with their brilliant and dynamic painting, or even those of the complicated Tiahuanaco II patterns. Means says, "In the later reigns from the death of Pachacutec to that of Huayna Capac, Incaic art fell away from the austere but beautiful geometric ornamentation and became increasingly flamboyant, and increasingly naturalistic due probably to traditions of peoples brought into the empire."

An interesting case in the American Museum of Natural History shows examples of all these periods and a classified listing on the card something as follows:

Early Nazca—polychrome designs of mythical figures on globular vessels with double spouts connected by a bridge and also vases with curved sides.

Early Chimu—realistic figures modelled in reddish-brown ware with light buff or white slip, portraits and models of houses typical, the stirrup spout typical, and also delicate painting in red on white.

Middle Chimu—curvilinear style design in red, white and black.

Epigonal or Tiahuanaco—Tiahuanaco bird and animal design combined with coastal styles.

Late Nazca or Ica—designs in black, white and red from textile patterns.

Late Chimu—typically black ware modeled and incised.

Early Tiahuanaco—incense bowls with modeled puma heads and zoomorphic figures in burnished colors.

Classic Tiahuanaco—the puma, condor, and warrior figures in black, white and yellow on red ground are seen, and flaring sided goblet is typical.

Decadent Tiahuanaco—general breakdown of classic designs.

Chavín—designs copied from their famous sculpture.

Recuay—(central highlands of Peru)—Tiahuanaco influence with the jaguar predominant as an art motive and the use of a "negative" painting technique.

Inca—geometrical designs and animal handled dishes and loop handled bowls along with some poor head-cups.

COLOMBIA

The Colombian culture is naturally strongly influenced by Costa Rica and we find strong modelling such as is shown by the face with protuberant eyes on the fragment of grey pottery shown. Small figures were made, seemingly of a female deity. A finely incised and rather ornate jar has an owl-like face on it and another of good angular shape fitted with four loops for suspension is painted in black, orange and white with a well conventionalized but probably meaningless design. The plinth loaned to the American Museum of Natural History by A. F. Tower is an excellent example of powerful work and may be compared with some of those from Costa Rica.

FIG. 1319. Two jars of red ware decorated in black from Colombia. Hts. 9¾″ and 9¼″. Am. Mus. of Natural Hist.

FIG. 1318. Pre-Columbian pottery burial urn from between Ocana and Puerto Mosquito on the Magdalena River near Los Angeles, Colombia. Ht. 27⅛″. Am. Mus. of Natural Hist.

FIG. 1320. Large pottery jar from the Island of Marajo in the Amazon, Brazil. Note the crudely modeled but highly conventionalized faces on the neck. Ht. 19¼″. Brooklyn Mus.

FIG. 1321. Red pottery jar from Colombia which shows a close association of ideas with some of the North American incised and partly modeled wares carried to further development. Am. Mus. of Natural Hist.

BRAZIL

In Brazil the Carib and Arawak stocks in the North and the Tupi-Guarani and Ges in the South did work much as they do now with painted, moulded, applied and engraved techniques. Their potteries do not as a rule interest us although two or three beautiful examples of an incised slip ware are interesting in both decoration and form. But as I have said before, the conditions climatic and otherwise were not particularly conducive to the making of good pottery.

AFTER THE SPANISH INVASION

The "Great Inca" Huayna Capac died in 1526 and in the following year Pizarro appeared at Tumbez, to return again in 1531 and finally treacherously seized the Inca, Atahualpa in 1532. In 1533 Almago brought reinforcements

A large lavatory made of polychrome tiles of majolica type. About 7' long. Made in Mexico about 1830. Metropolitan Mus. of Art.

Jars of about 1700 made in Mexico and showing Spanish (Talavera) Influence. Metropolitan Mus. of Art.

MEXICAN POTTERY AFTER THE SPANISH INVASION

PLATE 223

and Pizarro entered Cuzco. Troubled times were brought by the "men of God" from Spain. Pizarro executed Almago in 1538 and was himself assassinated in 1541 by "Almago the Lad," half caste son of Almago. In 1542 Vaca de Castro beheaded "Almago the Lad."

FIG. 1322. Mexican faïence or majolica laver showing the influence of 17th cent. Persian design through Spanish influence. (c. 1660–1680). Metropolitan Mus. of Art.

FIG. 1323. Mexican majolica plates made about 1840 the one on the right showing a design of symmetrically arranged "Indian flowers." Metropolitan Mus. of Art.

Naturally some trickle of Spanish potteries were brought in but it was no time for the development of the unwarlike arts and it fell upon unfertile soil.

In Mexico things were a little different; the Spaniards came in 1519 and in 1521 Cortes hired some 400,000 natives to rebuild the city. I show a large blue and white Spanish type majolica bowl from the Metropolitan Museum,

FIG. 1324. Early 18th cent. majolica flower-pot made in the form of a Chinese garden seat of drum form. Ht. 18". Metropolitan Mus. of Art.

FIG. 1325. Flower-pot made about 1830 with polychrome decoration and faintly reminiscent of Chinese form and decoration. Metropolitan Mus. of Art.

FIG. 1326. A set of blue and white tiles of late 17th to early 18th cent., Mexico. 53" by 43½". Metropolitan Mus. of Art.

of about 1660–1680. Other European influences came in later although still through Spain. The barrel shaped flowerpot of Dutch-Chinese influence appears of this varied type about 1700 to 1750, while the three jars of somewhat Near Eastern flavor after the Talavera influence show that the Moorish style

Coiled snake vase, two headed, ceremonial, glazed, deep intaglia surface design 8″ dia. (Acambra).

Jointed ceremonial doll with eagle claw and jade bracelet, 11″ tall.

"God of Fire" funeral urn, full standing figure front, vase concealed, all-over glyph intaglia over painted. Terra cotta 2′ 2″.

Tepic Clay Figurines, male and female, phallic.

"Goddess of Agriculture—Xipe" and deity funeral urn, vase concealed, terra cotta.

MEXICAN POTTERIES

(See text p. 940 *et seq.*)

PLATE 224

had not been lost and the tiles show a rather crude style which might be Spanish. This same Talavera influence appears as late as 1800 and even a little afterwards as can be seen in the dishes shown. These are of no real importance but some large endeavors were attempted as can be seen by the lavatory in polychromed majolica dating about 1830 at the Metropolitan Museum. The colors are crude and bright and not very pleasant and the style had become florid and softened without the dynamic qualities of the Spanish.

Then troubles increased: the American army at Ayotla, a treaty in 1848, then the French under General Forey took possession in 1863 and Maximilian, Archduke of Austria, was crowned Emperor of Mexico in 1864, and finally Diaz captured Mexico City in 1867. The wares are a poor quality of peasant pottery with vague Indian or Spanish designs, flowers, some Christian symbols, etc., badly potted and unpleasant in tone, then things to sell to the tourist trade.

Sculptured head, high glazed clay, 6″ high.

Left: Portrait of Deity, full figure, terra cotta.
Center: Left—Seated Deity figure, 4½″. Right—Portrait of Deity, full figure, terra cotta.

(Left) Laughing mask, terra cotta, 2½″ high. (Right) Death mask, painted surface, 5″ high. Note the wonderful studies of expression in this plate.

Right: Head, sculptured clay.

ALL FROM PERMANENT COLLECTION OF INTERNATIONAL BUSINESS MACHINES CORP.
TOTONACAN CULTURE POTTERIES STATE OF VERA CRUZ, MEXICO

(See text p. 942 *et seq.*)
PLATE 224A

Ceramic bottle from the Santarem region (Amazon River). Exuberant detail. Procession of animal figurines. Mouth of bottle well turned and ornately decorated with incised designs. From Permanent Coll. of International Business Machines Corp.

Vase executed by Marajo Indians who lived at mouth of Amazon, showing the use of geometric design and fine bold potting. National Mus. of Rio (Quinta Boavista).

Idol of red polychromed clay, anthropomorphous figure, representing a chieftain or person of very high dynasty among the Chibcha personages. Found in the neighborhood of Tunjaque, a city which belonged to the reign of the Chibchas. From Permanent Coll. of International Business Machines Corp.

SOUTH AMERICAN POTTERIES

PLATE 225

CHAPTER XXVIII

AMERICAN COLONIAL TO 19TH CENTURY WARES

No one knows when the first attempts at pottery were made in America by the European colonists. We suppose about the first Monday after father had shot a rabbit and mother had declared that she would not cook in those poisonous looking Indian pots, the idea began to take hold. Anyhow not later than 1650 there were several potteries in Virginia making crude household wares. Records are scanty and though we hear about the distilleries and grain mills nothing much is said of pottery. Probably it was not even thought worth decorating.

We would have expected an earlier start in New Amsterdam but the first record is of a list of burghers of the city of "Amsterdam, New Netherland," including Dirck Claesen, "Pot Baker," 1657. We do not even know whether or not he followed his trade and we hear nothing again until 1697-8 when three more names are so listed. Edwin Atlee Barber, in his "Pottery and Porcelain of the United States," credits Prof. Isaac Broome with the discovery of an old kiln a few miles south of South Amboy, N. J. and suggests that perhaps the first Dutch pottery was located there. John Spargo, in his "Early American Pottery and China," (p. 54), says, "So far as the present writer knows, there are no records bearing on this point, nor are there any specimens of pottery bearing the mark of Dirck Claesen or any of his contemporaries or credibly attributed to any potter of this period."

He does say, however, that there was a pottery "at least as early as 1684 at or near Burlington, N. J." No piece has been attributed to this place either but there is a record in the Bodleian Library, Oxford, concerning a Daniell Coxe which proves some such place existed, and that it made "Pottery of white and China ware," though this seems highly doubtful to say the least. The manager is thought to be James Budd who is mentioned in a suit against the potter Edward Randall in 1685. Some believe that Coxe was merely an owner and that he never came to America at all. In any event we can only surmise that the report was exaggerated and not to be taken seriously. Spargo argues that it was not translucent and could not, therefore, have been "china ware" but this is a waste of time, and a futile argument.

Let us try to clear up some of the odd habits of collectors of Americana.

It is not necessary to go far back, for Spargo is typical. In his "Early American Pottery and China" (1938) (p. 7) he says, "All wares produced by the potter's art which are not pottery are china. That is only another way of saying that wares which are not absolutely opaque, but possess the quality of being translucent in any degree, are to be classified as china and not as pottery." Thus he would call stoneware "pottery." And all the translucent wares such as Medici, French soft paste, Belleek, English "bone-china" would be called "china." Again he states that "china" and porcelain are synonomous and continues, "They both equally designate any product of the potter's art which is translucent." Actually translucence is not present to any appreciable degree in many of the original, real China wares as we find in many of the Wan Li late Ming period. Any ware in a thin enough piece will be translucent as we find in some of the non-kaolinic early Sung wares. Many translucent wares are more glass than "china" or porcelain, and contain no kaolin at all. Also even thin sheets of so dense and opaque a material as gold are translucent, and he would have to get down to microm-eter measurements to make his definition stick. Also all dictionaries give the term pottery as meaning a non-kaolinic ware made of clay and hardened by burning, but also as *any ware* so hardened, covering the whole of ceramic products. Thus we may call porcelain, soft-paste, stoneware, terracotta, faïence, etc., all pottery in general. Thus confusion reigns! I have tried hard to give concise definitions at the back of this book and the composition of each ware has been given, when it could be found, under its description. Generalities are misleading and should be avoided as much as possible.

Having decided arbitrarily in his own mind that only porcelain can be translucent, and knowing that porcelain was not invented in Europe until much later, Spargo concludes in backward reasoning that the Burlington ware could not be translucent even though, as he himself admits, it might resemble Dwight's white ware which *was* translucent in thin parts. If he has ever seen any of the Dwight type ware, he blinded himself to its translucence because it did not fit his definitions. But Spargo is not the only one to blame for this confusion; four or five of the leading authorities in this field wander about just as vaguely. And, if on the shelves of any collector today there is a piece which seems to answer the description of the Coxe pottery and which has been condemned because of being translucent, that collector may take hope again and continue his comparisons and research along the lines of Dwight type wares of about the same period in Staffordshire.

Virginia Kaolin or "Unaker" (c. 1744)

Edward Heylyn and Thomas Frye of the Bow factory took out a patent in 1744 for making "China ware" in which they state that the material to be used was, "an earth, the produce of the Cherokee nation in America, called by the natives 'unaker,' " and we believe that the Bow factory actually used this material at least for some time, at least until the discovery of china clay in Cornwall in 1768, perhaps. William Cookworthy in 1745 wrote a letter which mentions a person who had discovered china-earth in the back of Virginia and who had gone for a cargo of it. He says that both petuntse and kaolin were discovered and says, " 'Tis the latter earth is the essential thing towards the success of manufacture."

SOUTH CAROLINA CLAY (c. 1765)

About 1765 clay was sent from South Carolina and it is supposed that pottery making started about when it was discovered. Even true porcelain might have been made for we know that Wedgwood was alarmed that the industry might rival his world monopoly. He said, "They had an agent amongst us hiring a number of our hands for establishing new Pottworks in South Carolina; having got one of our insolvent Master Potters there to conduct them." Also, "They have every material there, equal if not superior to our own," and again, "As the necessities of life and consequently the price of labor amongst us are daily advancing, it is highly probable that more will follow them, and join their brother artists and manufacturers of every class, who are from all quarters taking rapid flight indeed the same way! Whether this can be remedied is out of our sphere to know, but we cannot help apprehending such consequences from these emigrations as make us very uneasy for our trade and Posterity." Wedgwood himself used some of the clay for some years, and later some from Pensacola, Florida. However, the existence of the Carolina potteries was precarious and left no trace.

NEW YORK CITY (1735)

In New York, John Remmey (1735) had a pottery on Potter's Hill near Fresh Water Pond not far from the site of the old City Hall. Barber wrote that Clarkson Crolius was a partner but Spargo, who has done some excellent researches in the historical field, states this to have been impossible, though he does say there was a William and Peter Crolius (or Croylas), potters who became freemen in the city in March, 1729. He also says the wives of William and of John Remmey were sisters and that the two properties were contiguous. He is sure there was never any partnership though both Dr. Stillwell and Barber thought there was. Spargo goes on to say that John Remmey had a son John Remmey II and William Crolius had a son John who had a son Clarkson.

A stoneware batter jug now in the New York Historical Society is inscribed "New York, Feb'y 17th, 1798—Flowered by Mr. Clarkson Crolius." This is a brownish grey stoneware with the design incised and a deep blue color applied here and there. It has a typical salt glaze. Barber claims, "John Remmey, one of the partners, having died in 1762, the second partner appears to have carried on alone, as indicated by a salt glazed stoneware jug or batter pot." Spargo points out that Clarkson Crolius was only born in Oct. 5, 1773 or about ten years after the death of his supposed business partner. I also point out that one of the owners of a kiln would hardly be inscribing himself as having "flowered" a pot.

After the death of John Crolius, the son, Clarkson Crolius took over the management of their kiln and in 1812, when Potter's Hill was leveled and Collect Pond filled in, he moved to 65 Bayard Street where he continued until 1848. Meanwhile his son, Clarkson Crolius II joined his father and

Stoneware butter
churn made by Clark-
son Crolius, Sr. c.
1800. N. Y. Histori-
cal Soc.

Salt glazed grey jug with blue
decoration made by John Crolius.
Dated July 18, 1775. Metropolitan
Mus. of Art.

Salt-glazed stoneware batter jug
dated Feb. 17, 1798 and made by
Clarkson Crolius, Sr. N. Y. Historical Soc.

Teapot made by Clarkson Crolius, Jr. Flower and
acorn design, with squirrel on lid. 19th cent. N. Y.
Historical Soc.

Late 18th cent. Crolius stoneware
jar. N. Y. Historical Soc.

CROLIUS (NEW YORK) POTTERIES

PLATE 226

signed "C. Crolius, Manufacturer, New York" impressed into the clay just
as his father also did.

John Remmey II had a son, John Remmey III, and it is possible that
Barber may have been right about some financial connection between one of
the Crolius and one of the Remmey boys, though it could not have been the

FIG. 1328. Left, stoneware jar covered with light brown slip, an unusual treatment; inscribed: "Paul Cushman's Stoneware Factory 1809." Cushman, so far as is known, was the first Albany, New York Potter. Right, Gray salt glaze stoneware jug with incised and cobalt blue decoration; inscribed: Commeraw's Stoneware N. York." 1802–1820. McKearin Coll.

FIG. 1327. Salt-glazed stoneware jug, stamped J. Remmey, Manhattan-Wells New-York and with U. S. coat of arms which establishes this was not the work of the first John Remmey but either the second or third, probably the latter. 19th cent. N. Y. Historical Soc.

first two in the business. John Remmey III was a good potter and also wrote articles and a book, "Egypt as It Is," (1799).

PENNSYLVANIA WARES (1683–)

Pennsylvania was first settled along the Delaware River by English, Dutch and Swedes, the latter making the first settlement. In 1655 there was Dutch control, while in 1664 it was English. The William Penn petition to Charles II was made in 1680 and his treaty with the Indians was in 1683. To this land came many of the oppressed and among them were the Quakers of Welsh stock and formed the "Welsh Barony" in Delaware and Montgomery counties. Also about this time came the Mennonites (1682–3) and settled in "Germantown." They were Germans from both sides of the Rhine and were followed by Lutherans and Reformed Church people from the Palatinate, Bavaria, Austria, etc. Swiss came in great numbers around 1727 and later. Scotch-Irish Presbyterians arrived and took up the back country along the frontier and finally in 1770 Connecticut "Yankees" came to the beautiful Wyoming and Muncy valleys. Thus we have a melting pot and the people are not "Pennsylvania Dutch" at all.

The earliest established piece was found by Dr. Edwin A. Barber in 1891 and is a shaving dish dated 1733, but of course these various peoples must have made much pottery before that, and the first must have been made about 1683 or fifty years earlier. It must have been some of the simple wares with plain surfaces or incising as slip would not have been attempted at the beginning, though it may have occurred within a very few years. The settlers from England may well have included some potters who knew the techniques, both of trailed and incised slip, from Staffordshire, the West Country or

Plate of slip-ware with incised decoration. Parts of the design are colored in green. Penn. late 18th cent. This is not unlike the Staffordshire ones though a bit more ornate than most and the American potters seemed to use green rather than blue. Similar German examples more often have several colors employed. Metropolitan Mus. of Art.

Irregular octagonal plate with yellow slip on a dark chocolate ground, from Penn. and made about 1800. Ginsburg & Levy. Dr. Smith Coll.

Incised slip-ware plate with "Indian flowers" and dated 1805. Dia. 12". Metropolitan Mus. of Art.

Crude trailed slip decoration of cream and green on red ware of the early 19th cent. Penn. Dia. 7⅝". Metropolitan Mus. of Art.

PENNSYLVANIA POTTERIES

PLATE 227

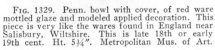

Fig. 1330. Red earthenware jar with yellow and green slip as well as incised decoration, made by Christian Klinker c. 1792. Ht. 10″. Metropolitan Mus. of Art.

Fig. 1329. Penn. bowl with cover, of red ware mottled glaze and modeled applied decoration. This piece is very like the wares found in England near Salisbury, Wiltshire. This is late 18th or early 19th cent. Ht. 5¾″. Metropolitan Mus. of Art.

Wales. Some Toft wares are similar (1676–1700) and on these tulips seem also to be a favorite design. A dish supposedly from Somersetshire dated 1725 and in the Glaisher Collection has an attached cup in the center and an incised slip design including a bird in just the style and colors of the Pennsylvania wares. Actually the retarded English development just about occurred at the right time to bring about prototypes of the American wares, while in Germany the development was far advanced. In Hesse at Frankfort and elsewhere there are odd instances of similar wares but even in the first half of the 17th century the designs are more ornate, involved, executed in various colors and often including incising, spotting and trailing of the slip all on the one piece. To be sure, the symmetrical "Indian flowers" are there but by the end of the 17th century they had become quite detailed and showed signs of decadent overloading.

Spargo goes to great trouble to prove the source as Germany. He says, "Neither in the color of the body or the glaze nor in any other

Fig. 1331. Rare Pennsylvania earthenware covered jar, colored slip and incised decoration. Probably late 18th cent. McKearin Coll.

feature does the sgraffito ware of the German potters of the middle nineteenth century differ from that of the earlier German potters who settled in Pennsylvania." He then says the roulette used in making a band of regular indentations around the edge of a piece is common to German and Pennsylvania potters but neglects to say that it was also used commonly in Staffordshire. He also

F<small>IG</small>. 1332. Pennsylvania, Montgomery Co., jug inscribed "Whitpain Township" and "Henry Dull" as well as with the county name. It is dated under the handle with what appears to be 1805. Geo. S. McKearin.

states that the late Albert Pitkin told him that he had examined *two*, no less, "sgraffito plates, both brought from Germany within twenty-five years, which were identical with one in his collection made by Troxel, in Montgomery County, Pennsylvania, bearing his name and date." Neither Pitkin's notes nor his widow who published them in "Early American Folk Pottery," (1918) mention this astounding coincidence or even touch upon the exact duplication of both materials and works of art being made thousands of miles

F<small>IG</small>. 1333. "Tulip ware" incised slip Penn. plate of red earthenware dating about 1800 and showing the typical "Indian flowers," symmetrically arranged. Dia. 12". Metropolitan Mus. of Art.

F<small>IG</small>. 1334. Slip-ware plate in cream and black on red ground. Penn. 18th cent. Dia. 12". Metropolitan Mus. of Art.

apart. Spargo, who has been often quoted as an authority, throws all reason to the breezes when he raves on, "The writer of these pages believes that

Pitkin's conclusion in the case of this single experiment would have been the same if the experiment had embraced three thousand pieces instead of three." But the whole is just plain nonsense and I note that Spargo does not even show ONE of these duplications in illustrations. Barber also says the wares were quite similar and that he could tell them apart because the backs of the German ones were, "a lighter and brighter red color than any of the Pennsylvania ware."

FIG. 1335. Nearly every country has made marbled ware since it was first devised to imitate stone in Egypt. This example is decorated in cream and green glazes on red ware. It has a coggled rope border. Dia. 15¾". Penn. c. 1800. Metropolitan Mus. of Art.

FIG. 1336. Slip-ware plate with brown ground and yellow and green decoration. The inscription reads, "In this plate stands a star; brandy I drink gladly." Dia. 13⅛". Metropolitan Mus. of Art.

FIG. 1337. Jug by Jacob Schall of Montgomery Co., Penn. It is of red earthenware with incised design of three doves with cream and green glazes lightly brushed on. Ht. 6¾". (Probably about 1830.) Metropolitan Mus. of Art.

Actually no two of these freely hand done things could be alike. There may be a very close similarity to a half blind man of little background or experience between some Ming wares, the "Gabri type" Persian incised slip wares, those of Germany, those of England and those of America. Such similarities do not go very far and the different characteristics of the artists cannot escape the eye of the careful observer.

One element of design they did owe to the people of the Rhine or possibly the Dutch, and that is the symmetrical "Indian flowers" which were actually originated in India and brought direct to these northern countries, not into Morocco and Spain. These designs may be seen in the "Lorenz Speckner Group" (c1618–1670), which are, by the way, excellent blue and white. They are seen also in some of the "Habaner ware" of Austria of the late 17th century and early 18th century, which were richly colored; and in Hesse about Frankfort in incised examples painted in with slip (seldom incised through the slip to the body) and in slip trailed designs. They are known also in England though there the symmetry was less popular and is seen only in such odd pieces as a cistern of faïence and a Staffordshire dish figure. After the Revolution these designs gave way to poorer yet more ambitious ones such as the one Spargo illustrates with a fiddler and two dancing couples, the men wearing "Washington hats," and which is dated 1786.

The mariner's compass design in the form of a star with added points is, so far as I know, entirely English and does not occur on German wares at all. Spargo says, "Toward the middle of the 17th century it was made in England, and it is a remarkable fact that the designs used by the English potters at that time, and the ware itself, were practically identical with those made familiar by the work of our Pennsylvania potters during the 18th and 19th centuries." The gentleman seems to have what might be called an "identity complex," such as some people who see in every one on the street a close resemblance to some friend or acquaintance!

Fig. 1338. Typical cream slip over red ware dish signed "Gemacht oon Samuel Paul, 1798." Penn. Dia. 12½". Metropolitan Mus. of Art.

Fig. 1339. Plate somewhat in the style of Hessen ones but different in color. It is of red ware with cream slip and a strong green glaze over it. Made by Geo. Hübener (1785–1798). Dia. 10½". Metropolitan Mus. of Art.

Fig. 1340. White slip and red ware plate from Montgomery County, Upper Hanover Township and made by Samuel Troxel (c. 1823). Dia. 11¼". Metropolitan Mus. of Art.

Most of these wares were not made so much for use as for gifts much as in Italy and later in England. It is also to be noted that most of them were simply two color in effect, though green splashes were added in the glaze as in the Near East and T'ang China (A.D. 618–906).

Fig. 1341. Cistern of stoneware molded and pressed with appliqué bosses and leaf forms in blue on a grey ground. Penn. Franklin Co., Waynesboro, by Salomon Bell, early 19th cent. Ht. 14½". Metropolitan Mus. of Art.

Fig. 1342. Early in the 19th cent. some had grown tired of the dead symmetry of the "Indian flowers," and turned to such arrangements. This piece is from Montgomery Co. near Tylersport and was made by Johannes Neesz (1775–1867). It is inscribed, "There is meat and sauerkraut. Our daughter is a bride in the year 1810." Dia. 10". Metropolitan Mus. of Art.

Among the known names because of signatures of makers are John Leidy, one of the best who died in 1838 (this name has a possible English sound to it), David Spinner, a Swiss (1758–1811), George Huebener, John Neesz (or Nase) (1775–1867), Jacob Schell (or Scholl) (c1830), David Haring (c1840), Samuel Troxel and Jacob Taney, but often the piece would have not the name of the maker but of the intended owner on it, as in England.

Most all of the so-called "scratch wares" were made in Pennsylvania but there is a local tradition around Bennington, Vermont, that a few were made by German potters employed there. Perhaps this was only because the Bennington people wanted to say that every type of American ware had been made there. Others were said to have been made in the Pruden pottery in Elizabeth, N. J., but none have been so identified.

OTHER PRE-REVOLUTIONARY POTTERIES

In Quincy, Mass., which used to be Braintree, Joseph Palmer, a Devonshire man, started a pottery in 1753. He brought his brother-in-law, Richard Cranch, who was only 20, in with him and they started salt factories, chocolate mills, spaghetti factories and finally a glass and pottery works, and, as they hired largely German labor, the settlement was called "Germantown" again as in Pennsylvania. Cranch sold out in 1760 and Palmer became fairly important although we have no specimen of his pottery recognized. It was supposed to have been a heavy stoneware and a salt-glazed cream-ware.

PHILADELPHIA

A pottery was opened in 1769–70 in Philadelphia with a Frenchman named Gousse Bonnin from Bow and a George Anthony Morris, who seemed to have put up the capital. It was on Prime St. near the present navy yard. They announced in 1769 that they were ready to sell porcelain as good as Bow, and advertised for workmen and for bones as well as "Zaffer" or "Zaffera" for making blue ware. In 1772 they wanted more workmen and "fifty wagon loads of white flint stone." In the Pennsylvania Museum is a piece which is probably authentic. It is an openwork or latticed sided fruit bowl with flowers at the corners and intersections in relief. The decoration is of a large rose and foliage in the bottom and this and the flowers in relief are in underglaze blue. In 1774 the factory failed and Bonnin went back to England.

MASSACHUSETTS POTTERIES

In Boston a factory was established in 1769 and made "tortoise-shell" and "cream-and-green" wares for table use, so it was claimed.

Other early Massachusetts places were at Salem, 1641, by John Pride; in Danvers by William Osborne shortly after; and finally in Peabody where in 1730 earthenware was commenced by Jonathan Kettle, Joseph Osborne, Joseph Whittemore and Miles Kendall. Later in Peabody (1759–1828) William Southwick made pottery with red body and almost black glaze. The ware was what might well be termed "Kitchen American" with nothing to recommend it. At Weston, Abraham Hews (1765) made domestic wares and moved to Cambridge later.

CONNECTICUT POTTERIES

At Litchfield (c1753) John Pierce had a place as did also Jesse Wadhams and Hervey Brooks. Jonathan Durell started here about the same time and moved to New York in 1774 where he opened a kiln near "Kitechemet's

Mead House." He may also have drifted to Philadelphia and worked in the Southwark Pottery of Bonnin and Morris but this is not surely proven. He seemed to be a bit along the "arcanist" type.

CHART OF PRE-REVOLUTIONARY KILNS

Burlington, N. J.	1684	Daniell Coxe absent prop. Edward Randall William Winn	Salt-glazed white stoneware
Peabody, Mass.	1730	Jonathan Kettle	Black glazed red ware
New York City	1735	John Remmey I	Stoneware—salt-glazed grey type
Huntington, L. I.	1751	Adam States	Red ware and stoneware
Braintree, Mass.	1753	Joseph Palmer Richard Cranch	Stoneware—grey type
Litchfield, Conn.	1753	John Pierce Jesse Wadhams Hervey Brooks	Red ware and Stoneware
Peabody, Mass.	1759	William Southwick	Redware with black glaze following Kettle's
New York City	c1762	John Remmey II John Crolius Also son of Clarkson, etc. Either together or separate but at any rate upon friendly terms we would suppose.	Stoneware—grey type
Weston, Mass.	1769	Abraham Hews	Red ware
Philadelphia, Pa.	1769	Gousse Bonnin George Anthony Morris	"Bone-china" white and decorated
New York City	1774	Jonathan Durell	Probably copies of Bonnin's wares
East Greenwich R. I.	1775	—Upton	White ware of some sort
Pennsylvania	1733 or earlier		The scratchware or slipware of engraved type described

All of these wares seem to fall into four simple groups, only one of which has any real artistic merit:

1.—Common lead glazed red or reddish brown ware of purely utilitarian type with slight decoration or none, of which one can only say that they are sturdy, honest and direct. A few show good proportions and some have wheel grooves. Impressing had just begun a little. Slip trailing was done infrequently. There was little inclination to exchange the colors so that wares from one section are much like those from another.

2.—Grey stoneware which was much the same in use and spirit but more durable and cost more. They are a little stronger in form and show the first traces of incised technique. Soon afterward they used rather hastily and scantily applied blue color.

3.—Imitative wares from the English such as the Philadelphia type and of salt glaze which are near white and with polychrome decoration. They are poor imitations at best.

4.—The Pennsylvania slip wares which are real achievements of the potter's arts.

LATE 18TH AND 19TH CENTURY AMERICAN POTTERIES
AFTER THE REVOLUTION (1775–1783)

Wedgwood is thought to have sent his best wares to the colonies and was worried about the possible competition there, but he need not have worried for soon after 1783 the flood of "English cream ware" from his factory and others swamped the market. The case of Bonnin and Morris in Philadelphia was typical for no sooner had they made American "bone-china" than large cargoes were dumped, and brought about their bankruptcy.

When the war spirit swept the country there was no liking for the English wares and small potters again sprang up and the larger places were able to pay expenses, but the result of this boom was a cheapening of the qualities because of the financial conditions and because some of the good English potters living here withdrew and went home. In 1783 when the war of arms ceased, England again commenced the economic war. Huge amounts of transfer printed wares were sent over with portraits of Washington, Franklin, Jefferson and other national figures. This was not, of course, very patriotic of the English merchants but they have always been broad-minded and have had the "progress of mankind" in mind. They even went further and wrote mottoes on pieces expressing British humiliation and American exultation over victory.

So clever were they that soon the Americans actually became ashamed of home products and thought that "imported" things were the only ones worth while. Even the excellent wares made at Bennington were demanded by dealers unmarked so that they could be sold as English. By the end of the 19th century there was hardly a factory worth mention left in America.

BENNINGTON, VERMONT (1793–1839)

Captain John Norton came from the "Litchfield Group" of potters having worked at Goshen, then later at Williamstown, Mass. before he settled in 1785 in Old Bennington, where there had been a settlement less than twenty years. In 1793 he built a kiln opposite the Hinman house. To this date he only made common red pottery and at his last stop probably salt-glazed stoneware. He died in 1828. In 1831 his son, Judge Lyman Norton, moved to the present Bennington village and built on the present site. He and his son, Julius, continued stoneware and made a new "yellow-ware" in imitation of the English "cream ware" or "Queen's ware," adding also imitation "Rockingham ware" which is about the same as the "cream ware" spattered before firing with a brown glaze similar to that used at Swinton on the estate of the Marquis of Rockingham and not unlike the "tortoise shell ware" of Whieldon, all of which simply made use of manganese with lead spar and flint.

Up to this time all was entirely utilitarian, but because of the growing middle class market, salesmanship became exuberant. Notable for this exuberance were the large wagons painted dark green and lettered in yellow,

Left: Fine example of a so called, "handwarmer," but undoubtedly a flask mottled in green, yellow, brown and white made by the U. S. Pottery of Bennington, Vt. (c. 1853–1858). Ht. 7⅝". Metropolitan Mus. of Art.

Center: A Bennington "hound handled pitcher," with the usual mottled glaze. Geo. S. McKearin.

Right: So-called, "celery dish," of Bennington ware mottled a beautiful black, brown and yellow on brown pottery. c. 1850. Ht. 9¾". Metropolitan Mus. of Art.

Left: Two good old New England bean-pots made by Lyman & Fenton about 1850 at Bennington, Vt. Ht. 7⅝". Metropolitan Mus. of Art.

Right: Curtain knobs made at Bennington about 1850 and mottled in black, brown and yellow. Length about 4½". Metropolitan Mus. of Art.

Left: Bennington candlesticks in various mottlings of green, black, brown and white. c. 1850. Ht. about 8". Metropolitan Mus. of Art.

Right: Bennington pottery stag with the mottled "Rockingham" glaze made by Lyman Fenton & Co., 1849. Ginsburg and Levy, Inc.

BENNINGTON (VERMONT) POTTERIES

PLATE 228

FIG. 1344. A grey stoneware jug signed J. F. Fenton and made at Bennington, Vt. Ht. 18". Metropolitan Mus. of Art.

FIG. 1343. A "Toby jug," and bottle in the form of a man, made at Bennington with what was called "flint enamel." Geo. S. McKearin.

"BENNINGTON STONEWARE," "NORTON POTTERY." These wagons were drawn by four perfectly matched horses, and with a smart young man handling the horses, talking up the wares, collecting the money and creating a demand.

Norton & Fenton, East Bennington (1839)

In 1839 Judge Norton took his son-in-law, Christopher Webber Fenton, in with him. Fenton had made red pottery at Dorset, Vermont, where Jonathan Fenton had established a pottery in 1801. The firm was now, "Norton & Fenton, Bennington, Vermont" (the first mark), and this was impressed on some of the octagonal pitchers of "single glaze," "Rockingham ware." It also appears in an elliptical form on similar pitchers supposed to be a little later, while mark 3, a few years later still, "Norton & Fenton, East Bennington, Vermont," showing that at this time they moved to what is now Bennington and what was then derisively called "Algiers." In 1828 Fenton married Judge Norton's daughter and the first "down town" pottery was erected, the mark being simply "Norton and Fenton." This year Captain Norton died. The association was between Fenton and Judge Lyman Norton, the captain's oldest son. Still later the firm was Julius and Edward Norton and about 1865, Edward and Lyman P. Norton, and again later Edward Norton & Co., when Thatcher (C. W.) became partner.

Meanwhile the younger men wanted to go into the making of "Parian ware" and though the judge did not care about it, Mr. Fenton, Julius Norton and Henry Hall started the work in the north wing of the pottery, bringing

FIG. 1346. A "Cow Creamer" with the imitation Rockingham glaze made at Bennington, Vermont about 1850. Length 7". Brooklyn Mus.

FIG. 1345. Sugar bowl with "flint enamel glaze" marked *Lyman Fenton & Co., Bennington, Vermont* and made about 1840. Ht. 4¾". Brooklyn Mus.

FIG. 1347. Bennington mottled "flint ware" or "Rockingham" glazed book flasks. The titles are such as, "Bennington Companion," or, "Departed Spirits." Hts. 5" to 11". Ginsburg & Levy, Inc. Dr. Smith Coll.

FIG. 1348. A well made jar with cover of about 1850 by the Lyman, Fenton & Co. kilns. It is black, brown and yellow on brown ware. Ht. 10¼". Metropolitan Mus. of Art.

John Harrison from England to do the modeling. The partnership lasted only a few years and then Fenton leased the wing from the Nortons and went into business alone, his mark being "Fenton's Works, Bennington, Vermont." During this period we find the mark on a great variety of wares such as Rockingham, Cream ware, Parian ware, glazed and unglazed and with elaborate ornamentation.

Shortly afterward Fenton obtained another partner, Alason Potter Lyman, who despite his middle name was a lawyer and the firm was now known as "Lyman and Fenton." Then Mr. Calvin Park came in and it was, "Lyman, Fenton and Park."

Meanwhile the Nortons made a new partnership but relinquished their interest in 1881 when they sold to C. W. Thatcher who used the name, "The Edward Norton Co." This later company seemed to make only stoneware.

Fenton, though a real artist, wore out the patience of his several partners by his expensive experiments. A patent was issued #6,907 on Nov. 27th, 1849 which tells of a process of immersing the article in transparent glaze and sprinkling colors on it with a small box with holes in it to obtain variegated effects. This would seem to be simply another method similar to the Chinese "powder blue" process but Fenton and the Patent Office probably did not know that.

THE UNITED STATES POTTERY

The United States Pottery was formed by Fenton and his partners in 1852 and was directly across the street from the Norton Stone Ware Works. It had six kilns. Finer wares were made including soft-paste, elaborately decorated "Parian ware" and "white granite." Fenton's ware was supposed to have been an improvement over Rockingham and was harder with also a greater variety of color. It was plain, mottled and "scrodled," the latter meaning a sort of mottling or marbling. The wares were known as "Fenton's enamel," or "Flint enamel," and the colors were black, yellow, olive green and other greens, browns and dark red and blue which were sparingly used. He found a fine kaolin deposit in Vermont which brought the kiln prosperity.

Workmen came from Germany and England and the payroll jumped to $6,000 a week. Theophile Fry and Daniel Greatbach were the chief artists. The latter had worked for the Jersey City Pottery and he made the first "hound handled pitchers," there. The idea was far from original, however, for fox handled ones had been made in Hungary and dog handled ones in Brampton, Derbyshire, and Doulton. But when he joined the U. S. Pottery he altered the design slightly and again when he went to Trenton he altered it again. The U. S. Pottery ones have a spirited deer hunt on one side and a boar hunt on the other. A grape vine covers the neck and shoulder and it was made in three sizes and usually brown. The head of the dog is free of the forepaws, while the Jersey ones do not have the vines and are heavier.

When the U. S. Pottery closed Greatbach went to South Carolina and then to Peoria, Ill., where he sold the mold for his jug. It then came to the Vance Faïence Co. which made a few copies but honestly signed them with their name. Greatbach came from England where he had been a mold maker as were also Charles and William Leake, John Leigh, Enoch Barber, Joseph and Henry Lawton, John Harrison, Alsop, Molds, Cartwright, Turncliff, etc.

"PARIAN WARE"

The "Parian ware" was an imitation of that made in England. It is an unglazed more or less soft porcelain or bone china of fine near-white body

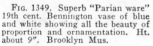

FIG. 1349. Superb "Parian ware"
19th cent. Bennington vase of blue
and white showing all the beauty of
proportion and ornamentation. Ht.
about 9″. Brooklyn Mus.

FIG. 1350. "Parian ware" pitcher of about 1850 with
molded relief decoration of corn. Ht. 9″. Brooklyn Mus.

out of which small figures, vases and pitchers were made. Cows, Toby jugs,
etc., were also made. The ware was supposed by Copeland to be so fine
grained that it looked like Parian marble (which by the way is neither
white nor close grained). Many imitations of the Bennington output were
made and few real originals are to be found. Fenton may have invented the
idea of making it with blue ground which was perhaps suggested by Wedgwood
"jasper ware." The ground which was usually blue was pitted. The model
was made and pitted by hand. Then the mold made from it had small projections corresponding with these pits. These points were covered with blue
or grey slip with a brush so that when the white clay was poured in, it took up
the color from the points and left the relief design in white. Sometimes a
velvety surface was obtained by coating the interiors of the saggers with
glaze which vaporized with the heat and gave the piece a glossy sort of half
glazed look. As a rule, only the pieces intended to hold liquid were glazed
on the inside, not on the outside. The original ware of Copeland's was invented in 1846. Silly quibbles have come up and some purists claim that the
blue and white ware should not be called "Parian," but once he stole the
name, 1 see no reason for Fenton not having used it on both colored and
uncolored wares which were otherwise identical. Spargo is very confusing
about it. calling the ware a "true hard-paste porcelain," and then adding, "It

was mellowed somewhat by the use of bone-ash." Of course the latter would immediately make it fall into the "bone-china" classification.

Some of the pieces bore a raised ribbon mark but most were unmarked. Even the originals did not continue a constant level of quality. After the factory was closed the workmen went hither and yon and the molds were stored and used time and again.

A few added notes from Pitkin may be of interest: The "white granite" ware was chiefly for toilet sets but occasionally for mantel ornaments. The "scrodle" or "lava" wares were not popular and are the rarest. In making it the "wedging process" was used. Clays came from Long Island, New Jersey and South Carolina, chiefly as ballast for ships from abroad, and "blue" or "ball clay" came from Woodbridge, N. J., while the stoneware clay was from South Amboy. The "Parian ware" was both pressed and cast.

FIG. 1351. Bennington American Eagle with Parian body and white transparent glaze with gilding. (c. 1840–1850). Length 4". Ginsburg & Levy.

A marvelously horrible statue was made by Fenton, Greatbach and others and shown in the Crystal Palace in the New York World's Fair of 1853. The base is "lava ware," the second section "flint enamel," on which is a bust of Fenton caged in by eight "Rockingham" columns, and the whole is surmounted by a madonna and child in "Parian ware." It is now on the porch of Fenton's former residence for all to admire.

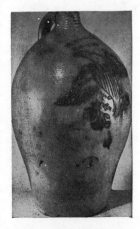

FIG. 1352. Grey stoneware salt glazed jug with blue decoration over incising, made by Daniel Goodale of Hartford, Conn., between 1818 and 1830 and inscribed *D. Goodale, Hartford.* Ht. 15". Brooklyn, Mus.

FIG. 1353. Pitcher of grey stoneware decorated with dark blue while the inside is brown and yellow, made at Hartford, Conn. early 19th cent. Metropolitan Mus. of Art.

FIG. 1354. Pottery jar of brown with lighter brown glaze, incised "GOODWIN & WEBSTER," Hartford, Conn. 1830–1850. Ht. 9½". Metropolitan Mus. of Art.

I refer those who would seek further to the excellent book by Pitkin and his widow and to their collection in Hartford.

OTHER VERMONT FACTORIES

Jonathan Fenton started a small kiln in 1801 in Dorset and Spargo describes an inkwell from it as being extremely hard in body, almost black and covered with a green glaze.

In 1806–1809, Norman L. Judd started a place in Burlington, and later again in Rome, N. Y., c1810. In the place of Samuel Woodman who made a crude ware at Poultney around 1800 to about 1820 there was nothing of interest. Neither was there in the Middlebury kiln of Caleb Farrer (1812–1850). Many other towns had kilns where useful wares were made.

I think little came of this art because America had bitterly cut off all traditions between 1776 and 1783. Also conditions were bad and there was the English competition. In any event no real works of art were made.

CHART OF OTHER AMERICAN KILNS

Hartford S.E. Corner of Park St. & Quaker Lane	Marks none	c1790—Nathaniel Seymour—Employed 4 men at wheel—kiln 10′ diameter and fired about 50 times a year. Retired in 1825—but the kiln was carried on by grandson Major Seymour until 1842. 1840 Moved "Up the lane." 1849 Major Seymour joined Stedman at Ravenna, Ohio in making stoneware.	Used clays from outside the state (Spargo p. 107)—But this was after 1825. Before entirely Conn. clay. Glaze of red lead and sand half and half. Ordinary red ware. Dishes of 1 gal. were $1 per doz. Milk pans 2 gal. $1.50 per doz. After 1830 they made chiefly unglazed flower-pots
Hartford N.E. Corner of Potter & Front Sts.		(c1790—heresay—) John Souter, who was English. 1805—sold out to Peter Cross who moved in a few years to 38 Front St.	Earthenware. Boston got most of her earthenware from Hartford, such as pots for beans, cake, butter, tea, and beer bottles, mugs, fountains, butter-pails, water coolers and milk pans.
Norwich, Conn.	"Norwich" and dated from '794 to 1812	1792—Charles Lathrop	Salt-glazed stoneware and also red ware.
Norwich	None	1796—C. Pott & Son	A few found about Norwich Ring-shaped bottles wrongly called "haymaker's" bottles. Were neither carried by haymakers nor, as Spargo says, carried over the arm when riding. It was originally a Western Asian design and idea. Spargo claims they were made in Conn., Vermont, West Virginia, Maryland, Ohio and South Carolina though he gives no evidence.

CHART OF OTHER AMERICAN KILNS—*Continued*

Huntington, L. I.		1751—Adam States Idle for some time after war then came to Jonathan Titus	Lead glazed red ware c1758–60 added salt glazed stoneware
	Report quoted by Spargo from investigations by Mrs. Irving S. Sammis:	1805—sold to:— Timothy Williams Scudder Sammis Samuel Fleet Samuel Wetmore Later Williams sold his quarter share for $65.25. Scudder bought out the lot and ran until 1825 then sold to Benjamin Keeler 1827 sold to Henry	"Crocus jar" before 1813 and inscribed in yellow slip with name of Iantha Sammis who was married in 1813 to Abner Chichester.
	"Lewis and Gardiner"	Lewis and Nathan Gardiner	
Morgantown West Virginia		c 1784—Foulke who was probably foreign trained. c1800—James W. Thompson took over, had been working for Foulke	Slip-decorated ware ranking with the best from Pennsylvania, not scratched but trailed. Also lead glazed red ware. Grey stoneware.
Philadelphia Sugar Alley	None	c 1790—Andrew Miller 1810—retired and left to 2 sons Abraham and Andrew who moved to 7th & Zane Sts. c 1817—Abraham sole proprietor. He was leading member of Franklin Institute. 1858—Died and business passed to ?	Wares not known but supposed to be red ware and "slip covered ware"—without decoration or with simple decoration ? Pure speculation. Abraham Miller, an enthusiastic potter, is supposed to be first American potter to make silver lustred ware. First piece exhibited in 1824 in Franklin Inst. Also red and black glazed tea-pots, coffee-pots, etc. Also a specimen of porcelain and of cream-ware. The porcelain was never sold on market. In 1835 he had an exhibit showing all steps of pottery making. In 1842 he showed earthenware plates, vases and ornamental flower-pots.
	Never marked		He originated the "Tam O'Shanter mugs" in Rockingham ware popular from c1840 to 1850. Modelled figures in creamware for friends. Dipped lace into slip and applied so that lace burned away in kiln leaving slip pattern, an old and not good "art."

CHART OF OTHER AMERICAN KILNS—*Continued*

Philadelphia	None	c 1790—John Curtis 1811 was still in city directory	Supposed to make "pottery of good quality?"
		Perhaps his was the place where a murder occurred in 1800 ?	Supposed to be cream-ware?
Elizabeth, N. J.	"Samuel Dunham"	1816—John Pruden old red ware pottery made till 1876 slipware Samuel Dunham was potter	"Quaint" slipware trailed technique. Some inscribed "Shoo fly"
Philadelphia	None	c 1808 or perhaps a few years before— Alexander Trotter Head of the Columbian Pottery c 1813 retired.	Cream-ware or "Queen's ware" No pieces authenticated
Philadelphia S. Fifth St.	None	c1810—Daniel Freytag	Cream-ware elaborately decorated also with silver and gold—overglaze colors, of course. No wares identified certainly
Philadelphia		1816 or 1817, or 1822 or 1823—David G. Seixas	Such good copies of "Liverpool wares" i.e. cream-ware as not to be distinguishable. So we hear.
Philadelphia	Called the ——	1809 or 1810—Capt. John Mullowny 1816 "Washington Pottery"	Common yellow and black glazed red earthenware. Teapots, coffee-pots, pitchers, etc. Advertised, "any device, cypher, or pattern put on china or other ware at the shortest notice by leaving orders at the warehouse." (This is important for collectors to bear in mind.)
Philadelphia South St.		1809—Messrs. Binney & Ronaldson	Same as above with slip decorations, trailed.
Philadelphia		1812—Thomas Haig 1833—succeeded by his two sons James and Thomas who carried on till about 1883.	Earthenware with red color and also black, tea-pots, coffee-pots, cake moulds, pitchers, strainers bowls, mugs, plates, etc. Perhaps also cream ware because the judges at the Franklin Inst. said his ware was better than that brought from England. "Believed" Haig made a Rockingham pitcher with Washington full length and shown as a mason, wearing his regalia in the act of presiding over his lodge ? ? ?
South Amboy, N. J. *Old Bridge* now *Herbertsville*		1800—Van Wickle's	Stoneware
Roundabout now *Sayreville*		Another in 1802—	Same

CHART OF OTHER AMERICAN KILNS—*Continued*

South Amboy	"Warne & Letts, 1807" and on other side,—"Liberty For Ev S.	Another in 1807—Warne & Letts Amboy. Ne Jer'sy."	One marked crock owned by William Goedecke, Esq. of N.Y.C. Is crudely potted Ordinary Jersey stoneware.
South Amboy		1828—John Hancock, English, from Cobridge, Swansea, South Wales, etc.	Stoneware similar to Van Wickle's it is thought, and yellow ware similar to Locker's.
South Amboy		1849—Thomas Locker	Yellow ware
East Liberties, Pa. now part of *Pittsburgh*		1827—Jabez Voudry, English, with a partner named Frost	Earthenware and stoneware Yellow ware and possibly some white ware Perhaps Rockingham (Spargo says he saw a pitcher marked Voudry & —— and the rest of the mark was not legible.)—But he thinks it may have been made in East Liverpool, Ohio "and that the mark was really that of Voudry & Brothers, sons of Jabez Voudry.
Whately, Mass.		1802—Thomas Crafts	Coarse red earthenware
		1821—He took in partners	Black tea-pots added
		1833—New partner and plant enlarged 1847 or 1848 closed.	Stoneware They made jugs, crocks, churns etc. Cider pitcher with face odd example

Note:—Spargo says, "*Assuming some or all of them to have been made at the Whately pottery, it has not been possible to tell whether they were made as early as 1805 or as late as 1840, for example.*" He continues, "*Nor could the most careful examiner point to a single feature of the ware, whether a quality of the material used or a marked individuality of workmanship, demonstrating that they could not have been made anywhere else.*" And again, "*The same thing might be said of the stoneware that was made at Whately from 1833 to 1847.*" So far as can be learned, it was as undistinguished, and as undistinguishable from the product of scores of contemporary potteries, as the red ware.*"

James Clews, an Englishman, worked at Cobridge where he succeeded Andrew Stevenson in 1818 and continued until 1829. He made a deep blue transfer-printed ware showing American historical events, scenery, etc. Two series called the "Syntax" and "Quixote" were in much demand. He came to Louisville, Ky., in 1836 and joined Jabez Voudry and Jacob Lewis, Voudry having left Pittsburgh and the Lewis Pottery Co., which had been established in 1829 and made "cream ware." They went to Troy, Ind., and were incorporated in 1837 absorbing the Lewis Pottery Co., but Voudry immediately withdrew and remained in Louisville.

The Troy pottery found that the wares were not white as Clews had promised they would be, so a yellow ware and "Rockingham" were made, both of inferior grade. In about two years Clews went home and Voudry had to close his successful place to try to pull the Troy kilns into shape. In 1846 the business was abandoned.

The Jersey Porcelain and Earthenware Co.
The First Real Porcelain

There had been many claims to real porcelain but none had been made until the Jersey Porcelain and Earthenware Co. was incorporated in 1825. None of the firm had any records as potters. They were George Dummer,

Henry Pots, Jr., Timothy Dewey, Robert Abbatt and William W. Shirley. In 1826 the Franklin Institute awarded the firm a silver medal for "the best china from American materials." The ware was a true white porcelain decorated chiefly with gold. A yellow ware and cream ware were also made and in 1828 the real porcelain was given up because of competition with the imported cream ware.

The works were finally bought by Henderson and were known as the D. & J. Henderson Co. They made cream ware, yellow ware and a good grade of "Rockingham" marked with the firm name and Jersey City impressed in circular form.

FIG. 1355. Jersey City c. 1850, "Hound handled pitcher," on the front of which is a mask and the body is decorated with a hunting scene on one side and an American Eagle pulling the tail of the British Lion on the other. Note the handle form as compared with the Bennington one. Ht. 7 3/16". Metropolitan Mus. of Art.

The American Pottery Mfg. Co. was formed in 1833 with David Henderson at the head, and the new mark was a flag with "Am. Pottery Manufg. Co., Jersey City," also an elliptical design elaborately drawn with the same legend, both printed and never impressed. Still later the mark of the American Pottery Co., 1840, was impressed. About 1839 it is said there was a print of a "Casanova pattern" stolen outright from John Ridgway of Staffordshire. Pitchers have been found with the portrait of Harrison who ran for president in 1840, but these may or may not have been made at Jersey City. Daniel Greatbach was there in 1839 before going to Bennington.

In 1845 the business came into the hands of Messrs. Rhodes, Strong and McGerron who made only cream ware until 1854 when it closed. Later a new firm made only commercial wares marked with a British coat of arms, a lion and unicorn and the initials R.T.

Philadelphia, Wm. Ellias Tucker

Benjamin Tucker, c.1815, opened a china shop at 324 High St., Philadelphia (later Market St.) and carried it on until c.1823. His son, William Ellias Tucker played with a decorating kiln in the back room, painting floral and other designs rather badly on English china. In turn he learned to make cream ware, a fairly hard bone-china, at any rate harder than the English product, and in 1825 or 1826 he started to erect a kiln. His brother Thomas Tucker said that he had many failures because of the sabotage of Englishmen sent over as workmen. However, he overcame the difficulties and made a gilt decorated "bone-china," with poor decoration.

Fig. 1356. Porcelain pitcher by Tucker & Hemphill, Philadelphia, and decorated in gold and blue, dated 1828 in red. Ginsburg & Levy, Inc.

Fig. 1357. Pitcher dating about 1828–1838 made by Tucker and Hemphill works. It bears the incised mark of Andres Craig Walker, W, who was reported to be one of the best workers in the factory. Ht. 9¼". Lent by Arthur W. Clement. Brooklyn Mus.

In 1828, when the Jersey firm was failing, Tucker and Thomas Hulme showed at the Franklin Institute and took a prize. The mark was "Tucker and Hulme, Philadelphia, 1828," pencilled in red under the glaze with at times the addition of "China Manufacturers." In 1829 Hulme withdrew his support, and Tucker wrote to President Andrew Jackson who complimented him but gave no support for his work. In 1832 he found a new partner, Judge Joseph Hemphill. Meanwhile a strong competitor had sprung up.

Judge Hemphill kept Thomas Tucker, the son, and sent to France, England and Germany for men. An imitation of some Sèvres wares was made with borders of roses and other flowers. Elaborate monograms, coats of arms, portraits of noted men, etc., were all made and later copies of well-known works such as the Vaughan portrait of Washington by Gilbert Stuart and the Charles Wilson Peale one of Wayne ("Mad Anthony"). One ambitious piece shows Napoleon watching the burning of Moscow.

Some were unmarked and some had Hemphill's name in red. At least one

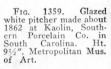

Fig. 1358. Tucker & Hemphill pitcher of the 19th cent. with usual white ground and flower decoration in bright colors. The banding is in gold. Ht. 9⅜". Metropolitan Mus. of Art.

Fig. 1359. Glazed white pitcher made about 1862 at Kaolin, Southern Porcelain Co. in South Carolina. Ht. 9½". Metropolitan Mus. of Art.

writer states that the wares were as fine as those of Sèvres but they were not, neither technically nor artistically. Hemphill could have brought over every brick of the old factory, all the workmen, their wives, children and sweethearts as well as all the personal enemies and casual acquaintances of the workmen. He could have enclosed the whole in a dome of soft French atmosphere and made settings of the surrounding country and yet he could not have captured the real Sèvres, for such is art.

In 1837 the judge sold his interest to Thomas Tucker who kept up only about six months and then Abraham Miller bought the machinery and molds while Tucker opened a shop and began to sell imported wares. The kaolin had come from Chester County, Pa., the feldspar from Newcastle County, Delaware, near Wilmington and the blue clay from Perth Amboy.

SMITH, FIFE & Co.

In European style a couple of workmen left Tucker and started a place known as Smith, Fife & Co. The money was put up by Jason Fennemore and he had a lady friend to whom he sent representative pieces and she preserved them so that we know they made pitchers, smelling bottles, leaf shaped dishes, etc. The ware (though less white) and decorations were almost identical to Tucker's of the same period. They were marked with underglaze red. The little piracy expedition did not last long. This was about 1830.

WILLIAM H. FARRER AND KAOLIN, S. C. (1856)

From Bennington a seed was planted in South Carolina when William H. Farrer withdrew his interest and went to Kaolin. This place was the source of some of the Bennington clay and it was thought that money could be saved in not having to ship this product. Alexander H. Stephens, later vice-president of the Confederacy, was a member of the company. Though Farrer had taken some workmen with him when he left Bennington, he was no potter and soon found himself in trouble. The start was in 1856. In 1857 Decius W. Clark and Christopher Webber Fenton went down to advise him. The designer and modeler Josiah Jones advised him to use mixtures of other clays but Farrer stuck to the native product.

They made common earthenware, poor "Rockingham," fairly good cream ware and yellow ware, along with a fairly good porcelain. Attempts were made to imitate the pitted ground "Parian ware" but nothing of real quality was ever turned out.

The place operated through the Civil War but gave up in 1865 when a new firm was formed by R. B. Bullock, later governor of Georgia. After about 12 years it was turned over to McNamee & Co. of New York. The original company marked with "S. P. Company, Kaolin, S. C." or "S. P. C."

GREENPOINT, L. I.
CHARLES CARTLIDGE & CO. AND HERBERT Q. FERGUSON (1848)

Charles Cartlidge came here from England in 1832, worked at Jersey City under David Henderson, became a manager for wholesale distribution of Ridgeway's china and finally formed the Charles Cartlidge Co. in partnership with Herbert Q. Ferguson, at Greenpoint, L. I. in 1848. They began to make buttons. Cartlidge sent to Staffordshire for his brother-in-law, Josiah Jones and Elijah Tatler, china painter. In 1853 at the fair they showed table ware, drawer pulls, door knobs and plates, escutcheons, etc., in bone-china and earthenware. They also made busts and small figures, all from the work of other sculptors, and these were in "Parian" or bisque. Several of these of about 6 inches to 11 inches in size are in the museums. The firm closed in 1856.

WILLIAM BOCH (1850)

Also at Greenpoint, William Boch, a German, and his brother started a kiln in 1850, and made bone-china. In 1857 Thomas C. Smith became manager and part owner, then sole owner and in 1864 or 1865 he started to make real porcelain. In 1866 he began to decorate his ware. In 1874 Karl Müller joined him as modeler and designer. The period was bad and this Müller was typical of its worst aspects. "The Century Vase" is typical with bison-head handles, portraits on two sides, modeled animals' heads on a rib of gold, pictures of Indians, a "Revolutionary Soldier," the Boston Tea Party and God knows what on it. We understand that Müller did some worse things but let us pass them swiftly. He also did Forrest acting William Tell and some figures illustrating Hood's "The Song of the Shirt."

The factory also made some poor copies of Sèvres from 1876 down to our days. The mark has been an eagle's head with S in the beak. See also Union Porcelain Company of Boston.

TRENTON, NEW JERSEY
OTT & BREWER AND THE "ETRURIA POTTERY"

In Trenton the Etruria Pottery which came into charge of John Hart Brewer hired Professor Isaac Broome to work in "Parian ware." John Spargo says, "His bust of Cleopatra and his various baseball designs rank in the

best ceramic sculptures of the 19th Century." The statement covers very
well the artist, the critic and the century.

East Liverpool, Ohio

James Bennet with the help of Anthony Kearns and Benjamin Harker
started in East Liverpool, Ohio, in 1840. There may have been some small
potters of kitchen ware before this time. He had worked under David Henderson in Jersey City and in 1837 for James Clews in Troy, Indiana. The
first firing netted $250 and he promptly sent to England for his brothers
David, Edwin and William who arrived in 1841 and brought along John
Tunnicliffe. They all made yellow pottery until 1845.

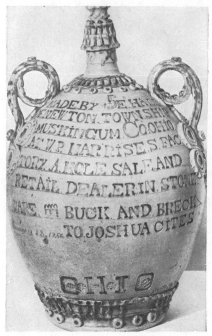

Fig. 1360. An Ohio stoneware jug made to demonstrate the technical proficiency of one E. Hall
of W. P. Harrises Factory and dated 1856. Ht. 18". Chas. W. Lyon, Inc.

Benjamin Harker was paid off and started a kiln of his own. Also in 1842
James Salt, Joseph Ogden, John Hancock and Frederic Mear started the
"Salt and Mear Works." In 1844 John Goodwin, another of the original
workers, started still another kiln. All of these places made yellow ware and
"Rockingham." Of course they were far from the first to make it even in
this country but "Rockingham" was largely made popular from East Liverpool
and Bennington.

In 1844 the Bennet brothers sold out to Samuel, Jesse, Thomas and John
Croxall. In 1847 William Brunt started a kiln and again in 1848 Jabez
Voudry started "Wood & Voudry." This place burnt down in the first year

and then "Woodward, Blakely & Co." rebuilt it in 1849. In 1847 George S. Harker, Benjamin Harker's son joined James Taylor and this firm stole the already stolen Greatbach hound handle pitcher model, which they changed slightly. This firm was "Harker, Taylor & Co." and they ceased in 1851.

Isaac W. Knowles, who sold down the river for James Bennet the first year set up in 1845 with Isaac A. Harvey, then bought him out and reorganized with John Taylor and Homer S. Knowles. The firm in 1870 was "Knowles, Taylor & Knowles." They made the usual wares and started with cream ware in 1872. In 1873 they started to make "ironstone china," or "stone china," or "white granite," as it was variously known.

TRENTON, N. J.

Returning to Trenton, the first pottery was established in 1852 by James Taylor and Henry Speeler, both of whom had been in business in East Liverpool. The usual common yellow and "Rockingham" wares were made and another design of the hound handled pitcher and a cow creamer in both wares. There are no pieces bearing the mark of this place.

In 1853 Richard Millington and John Astbury opened a small kiln which made the same wares and also white ware. No trade-mark was used until 1859 when the firm took in Mr. Poulson and became, "Millington, Astbury & Poulson," marking their wares with an impressed M.A.P. in an ellipse. Among other things they made in 1861 a pitcher with relief design showing the shooting of Colonel Ellsworth at Alexandria, Va. It was of white with garish polychrome painting. This wondrous work of art may have been made by Jones at Greenpoint but that is uncertain.

Charles Hattersly in 1852 started and at once leased to William Young & Sons. Some pitchers seem to prove that they made the first cream ware and porcelain in Trenton.

In 1855 Taylor & Speeler made "white granite" and in 1859 Rhodes & Yates followed.

Thomas Maddock and William Leigh started decorating china in New York in 1847 and later Maddock was in the crockery business in Jersey City. In 1873 he started selling and making sanitary wares and Trenton and East Liverpool made a great industry of this.

BALTIMORE, MD.

Edwin Bennet, one of the East Liverpool brothers, set up in Baltimore in 1846. In 1848 he was joined by his brother William and they marked their wares, "E. & W. Bennet, Canton Ave., Baltimore Md." In 1856 William withdrew and the initials E.B. were used. This firm made all the wares. Charles Coxon joined them in 1850 and made the "Rebekah at the Well Tea-pot," copying the design from a jug made by S. Alcock & Co. It has white figures on blue ground. Also the "Wild Boar Pitcher," and the "Stag Hunt Pitcher" were made there. Another had a standing stork. A hound handled pitcher had game hanging around the sides while another with dolphin handle had fish. The "Daniel Boon Pitcher," was another. All of these wares are difficult to tell from Bennington.

So much for the highlights of an inbred and decadent art which really never had a chance to develop. It was never anything but a sprout from the already failing English ceramic art and everything from the beginning was done for commercial reasons— enough to kill an art. Aesthetics are not of so much interest to the collector of Americana as history and popular interest in little facts. Quaintness is its chief appeal to such collectors. Humor was heavy as may be seen by the beer mugs made with a frog in the bottom, the "monkey-jugs," etc.

Fig. 1361. "Stag pitcher" designed by Charles Coxon in copy of the Rockingham ware of England. Made possibly at South Amboy, possibly at Baltimore. Ht. 10". Brooklyn Mus.

Then came the days of the scroll-saw-gothic, the mansard roofs of elegance from France and the iron stags on the front lawn. America came of age and a very rough and selfish age it was, characterized chiefly by money grabbing, ruination of natural resources and boisterous debauchery set off against stiff-necked narrow mindedness. Some of the people had come here because of religious principles, yet we find no great religious thinkers as in China and Italy. There was no incentive to do religious art. The country had political leaders but none who offered the artists patronage. This was a great country of bourgeois and the 19th century art was the worst of bourgeois art.

CHAPTER XXIX

CONTEMPORARY CERAMICS

IN ALL ages the term "MODERN" has been used to designate every *revolt* against accepted tradition. The underlying psychology is easy to understand: tradition is difficult to learn and understand; it takes long to ground oneself and many will not put in the effort to do so, therefore, they take the short-cut of modernism thinking it an easier path. An architect has to adhere to some traditions of building or his structure would fall down. A lawyer must at least know the procedures of the courts and a doctor must have some knowledge of medicine or he would be a menace to the race. An artist, however, is looked upon as harmless and is, therefore, free to do as he likes. Only very rarely do we find, as in the case of Picasso, an artist who is well grounded in the various elements of his art turning to a revolt against some of its phases. In this sense most "modern art" exponents are really charlatans or at the very least people who wish to reap rewards for the least possible endeavors.

Our commercial attitude and industrial attitude are chiefly responsible for the large number of such artists in the past fifty years. If the business man tries to get all he can for the least possible effort, so, it is reasoned, should the artist. The eye has been focused upon the results and the results have been largely measured in pennies.

Any revolt will do and we have had many in the past years: 1.—The revolt against the machine and its corollary, the revolt against those who revolted against the machine, as represented by the "handicraft" movement in England and America of William Morris, Elbert Hubbard, etc., and those who preached that the machine, properly mastered, would lead to new arts such as Edgar Brandt in France. 2.—The return to simplicity in America after the renaissance between World War I and 1929. 3.—The discovery after the Paris Exposition of Japanese art, a revolt against European tradition. 4.—The new ways of seeing light expounded by the impressionists. 5.—The new ways of drawing by the post-impressionists, the vorticists, the cubists, the futurists, the da-daists, etc., which revolted against drawing anything as it is seen. 6.—The revolt against the classic movement of the end of the 18th century and the beginning of the 19th century by reverting to naturalism. 7.—The revolt against natural forms imposed by the architects of skyscrapers who had found their soap-box forms imposed by the zoning laws of New York City. 8.—The revolt against this soap-box design imposed by the

1009

streamline experts who streamlined not only moving objects but all manner of static objects for no reason at all. 9.—A revolt against all of this cold design by a return to Victorian horrors which were at least human. These and many other revolts have been tried in the last twenty-five years to such an extent that "modern art" is impossible to define. This impossibility is well demonstrated by the New York Modern Art Museum which has had to fall back upon Italian masters, various primitive arts and all manner of twisted versions and roundabout reasons to prove its reason for being.

The history of modern art as outlined by Rudolph Rosenthal in the December, 1935 *Parnassus* is, to quote, "Briefly, the first period of modern decorative art lasted from 1860 to 1893, beginning with Morris and reaching the continent through Van de Velde of Brussels. The second period came in 1894, lasting until 1925 when the Decorative Arts Exposition was held in Paris. The third is the one that began with 1925 and is still continuing." We might split hairs about the last statement but it is on the whole quite right.

The Paris exhibitions of 1867 and 1878 featured Japanese art. Whistler was doing his nocturnes and Degas his dancers. Carlyle had written his warnings. The adjustment had to be made and industrialism could not win out. But the germ of our present revolt against the factories and the whole system of heckling, money grubbing, stupid and yet powerful parasites was born.

THE FRENCH "GRÈS POTTERS"

One potter was Ernest Chaplet (1835–1902) a champion who made all his wares by hand and sometimes without even the aid of the wheel. His "flammés" and "grès" stonewares and porcelains of blues, violets, greys and copper reds were beautiful. He worked at Sèvres where he revived the old barbotine technique, at Laurin's at Bourg la Reine, and was later manager of the Haviland factory. Finally he went to Choisy le Roi where he worked until he died. His mark was the chaplet or rosary.

Chaplet won the heart of the sculptor Jean Carriès (1855–1894) who gave up his art to carry on ceramics. He set up his kiln at St. Amand en Puisaye and Montriveau, near Nevers and in the exhibition of 1889 his results brought universal admiration. The Japanese had inspired him but his work is very much his own and he did not only vases but also masks, figures, heads, animals, etc. His architect friend, G. Höentschel, who was a similar potter, gave a collection of his work to the Musée du Petit Palais, Paris. Another disciple was Paul Jeanneny (1861–1920) who adhered more closely to the Japanese wares, which by the way, were the early type and not the Arita or "Satsuma," things.

L'Art du Feu was a school started by Chaplet and among the pupils was the great artist Auguste Delaherche, who worked with running glazes at times over relief designs and obtained effects of velvety richness. Others of the group were Adrien Dalpayrat, who worked with Voisin Delacroix and later with Mlle. Lesbros, and who did glazes of opaque blood-red, deep blue and soft yellow which were not very beautiful but technically interesting. Edmond Lachenal used relief foliage under dull green glazes which he etched with hydrofluoric acid to produce a velvety surface known as "émail velouté."

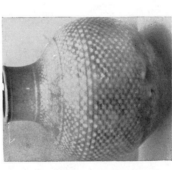

Left: Pair of Limoges vases by Ernest Chaplet of about 1870 to 1886 with relief decoration and copper-red glaze. *Center:* Stoneware vase by Emile Lenoble. *Right:* Earthenware plate of the early 20th cent. by Andre Methey (1871-1920). Metropolitan Mus. of Art.

Left: Beauvais stoneware bowl by Auguste Delaherche in the 20th cent. *Center:* A typical stoneware vase by Emile Decoeur of the 20th cent., Fontenay-aux-Roses, Siene. *Right:* Plate made by Haviland & Co. of Limoges and designed by Felix Braquemond (1833-1914) and probably made between 1872 and 1880. Metropolitan Mus. of Art.

THE FRENCH "GRÈS POTTERS" AND OTHER EARLY MODERNISTS

PLATE 229

FIG. 1363. Bottle of 1899 by Alexandre Bigot of stoneware glazed in light grey streaked with blue, brown and tan in the flambé manner. Metropolitan Mus. of Art.

FIG. 1364. Stoneware vase by Adrien Dalpayrat made at the end of the 19th cent. This, of course, shows the uneven potting and glaze mannerisms of some Japanese potteries. Ht. 8". Metropolitan Mus. of Art.

FIG. 1362. Stoneware jug made at Limoges under the technical direction of Ernest Chaplet around 1882 to 1886. It is a teutonic thing somewhat sweetened up with French Art Nouveau style. Ht. 9". Metropolitan Mus. of Art.

Albert Dammouse at Sèvres did more naturalistic and accidental things of similar feeling. His "pâte décor" made use of glaze and paste used side by side or over each other. The only reason that the business men at the factory could not grasp his art and ruin it was that no two pieces came out alike so that the merchants could not reorder and, too, the colors were dull while merchants like bright colors that arrest the eye—though they may tire of it later. Taxile Doat, an Englishman, at Sèvres made among other things some small insets of animal heads, etc., in porcelain and stoneware.

FIG. 1365. The two upper pieces are by Raoul Lachenal and the lower ones by Claude Lévy of France. In the 1939 Exhibition in New York the latter's style had become greatly exaggerated.

FIG. 1366. Stoneware vase with the well known "engobe" glaze treatment undoubtedly inspired by the Sung, Yüan and Ming or later wares of Tz'u Chou. This is certainly no improvement even upon the latest and worst of the type. Emile Lenoble. Metropolitan Mus. of Art.

Among the younger men was Emile Lenoble, Chaplet's son-in-law, who inherited his kiln and practiced with "engobes" which he cut away to the biscuit in straight line decoration. These engobes were glazes of dark brown, grey, deep blue, green, orange-red and white, all of which contrasted well against stoneware of grey. Many of the things remind us of Sung incised "Tz'u chou yao" and here a truly great art might have been born but times were not right and not many of the finest of these wares were then available.

Emile Decoeur produced the soft, thick and rich glazes of modified color which he used over the simplest of relief decoration in the best of taste. The colors were brownish-yellow, delicate grey-blue or green and his glazes all run slightly in firing. There is a suave, sure strength in his work which is not immediately obvious.

Young Raoul Lachenal, the son of Edmond, followed Decoeur and sometimes his work is as fine as is also at times that of Henri Simmen.

Another group led by Jean Mayodon followed the figure decoration of Syrian and Persian wares, such as slender leaping deer and gracefully drawn birds. René Buthaud worked in large, flat figures in strong relief with deep incising.

None of these "grès potters" were really great artists but they obtained beautiful textures and very simple and pleasant forms and France has a right to be proud of them for they faced the flood and stood out as a hopeful light in the darkness until they were extinguished.

Fig. 1368. Vase of typical Art Nouveau type designed by Georges de Feure about 1898–1904 and potted by E. Gerard. Metropolitan Mus. of Art.

Fig. 1367. Sèvres pieces exhibited in the Paris 1925 Exhibition. The art-nouveau stunts are well represented and in the first piece, upper left, we see superimposed rosettes of Edgar Brandt iron-work fame.

FRENCH EARTHENWARE

There had been various half hearted attempts to revive lustre but André Methey really did some pleasant things with simple repeat patterns of natural forms. Etienne Avenard followed him and Félix Massoul used deeper colors and more geometric patterns. Jean Besnard also made lustre. But all of these were inclined to cover the whole vessel with lustre rather than using it sparingly as in early works. The result is a bit like a metallic vessel or Christmas tree ornament rather than a pot decorated with simple brush strokes.

No earthenware of merit was turned out at Sèvres. Gordon M. Forsyth wrote in 1925 that Sèvres had "become artistically mute." Raoul Kachenal and Claude Lévy made decadent things in which the shapes boast without being strong and the colors do not suit either the designs or the shapes. Sentimental sculpture was made by E. de Canto and Marcel Renard.

MODERN GERMAN WARES

The revival in Germany is associated with Max Läuger and Schmuz-Baudisz both of whom are strongly influenced, and to good purpose too, by the peasant wares of Bavaria and the Black Forest region.

Läuger's jugs and vases are of deep, even color with natural slip decorations in contrasting color, as he made them at Karlsruhe. More recently he worked at Kandern for C. Mayer making tiles, and still later he made strong colored majolica for the Maiolica Manufaktur at Karlsruhe. Ludwig Koenig and Georg Schrimpf followed him but fell into the modern pose of trying to appear naïve.

This is an interesting characteristic of much modern art. There is an appeal of a sort in it. Some men love innocent, doll-like little girls with starry eyes and not a thought in their heads. Some women like naughty, boyish men whom they can mother. The instinct is a perverted one similar to that of a capon which likes to take care of chicks. It recalls the story of De Maupassant of the fat inn keeper who came to enjoy hatching out chicks in his own bed. The objects of such affection in art are those who just never came of age and are still in adolescent stages and they prefer to be thought cute.

There is no doubt but that this instinct to play motherly protector and to play child is strong in all decadent societies. Note for example the Roman phases and the "puttis" of the days of Louis XV. It is also strong in our days, up to World War II.

The artist who consciously makes this appeal is begging to be protected. He says, "Here, this is my little effort. I know, of course, that it is nothing," and he puts his head on one side and smiles coyly, hoping that you will answer, "But my dear fellow, it is charming and so, so clever!" Others less obvious but of the same ilk are those who never get beyond the sketch stage. Everything they do is, "just a sketch," said in a deprecatory yet hopeful manner. Modern ceramics are full of such works done by little old ladies who turn out the cutest donkeys in bright blue glaze purchased in a package from Drakenfelds, or perhaps they are foreign gentlemen with souls which they can only express in the most charming and child-like manner by scratching clay as though they didn't really half mean it, or again they may be the daughters that mothers are proud of (for their age) and who do children's lamps and ash receivers for nit-wits.

"But," one may argue, "you have said that you find an appeal in naïveté as found in the simple savage or primitive people such as that shown by the Chimu or Han cultures. Why not then appreciate it in artists of today?" My answer is that it represents sincerity *today* in this sophisticated age only among the members of the grammar schools or asylums and that people who find their mental enjoyments in associations with children up to 10 years of age or the inmates of special homes for feeble minded can and should enjoy the arts of such undeveloped or distorted minds of today. I personally take a rather objective viewpoint of such intelligences and find them somewhat depressing. Each man to his own tastes. Just as a fine savage differs from a retarded or perverted civilized man so does his art differ from that of the feeble minded. The one is at least healthy while the other implies disease of one sort or another.

Th. Schmuz-Baudisz painted in Munich and only after 1896 became interested in ceramics. He covered his vessels with engobe and incised animal and floral designs in highly stylized manner. In 1902 he became director of the Staatliche Porzellan Manufaktur, Berlin, after being at Swaine & Co., Hüttensteinach. In Berlin he tried large tiles with landscapes in color which are poor.

Dr. Seger in 1884 used copper oxide glazes and made some plastic things of fair quality, as did also Franz Metzner, Anton Pachegger and Herman Hubatsch. In 1918 Max Adolf Pfeiffer directed at Berlin and some fair things were made by E. P. Borner, Max Esser and Paul Schuerich.

All the factories tried to give some little flavor to their commercial endeavors by attaching a few artists as appendages. At Nymphenburg, Albert Bäuml was director in 1888, and Jozef Wackerle made fine peasant type potteries and humorous figures deriding 18th century life. He mastered both porcelain and faïence techniques and did not allow his things to become crude but took from the peasant wares their directness. Theodor Kärner and W. Neuhäuser made animals well. Much of the work was influenced by Copenhagen or by the peasant wares. Most of these moderns fall into schools or copy each other outright more slavishly than did even the Chinese who had traditions but also a basic originality.

Ernst Barlach set a new style with his Russian peasants full of life and plastic good sense. He worked at the Schwarzburger Werkstätten für Porzellan at Unterweissbach. Others there were Hugo Meisch, Arthur Storch and Hans Poelzig. At Nymphenburg Fraus J. Biehler and M. Goossen did reliefs.

At Munich George Kemper made rather effeminate putti, etc., and Königsbauer did double walled medieval looking jugs with outer walls pierced. Otto Müller made similar faïence things after Chinese ideas. Kurt Feuerriegel also shows 16th century characteristics. Perhaps the best in this part of the country is Frau Auguste Papendieck, whose kiln was near Bremen, who did monochrome and slightly glazed vessels of simple form and good honest potting.

In the Villeroy & Boch firm J. Kühne and Jean Beck along with Ernst Riegel worked, the latter doing fair modeling.

It has been said that Germany showed the greatest hope during this time but we find a dull and uninteresting art there. The pots were made for no common use and were looked upon as art, separated from the life of the people and from their tastes. This divergence of artist from the course of the times was brought about by his revolt against what the people were being educated to like and to use by the industrialists. No art can grow on mere revolt. No artist can thrive if he does things which the people about him do not want. And yet what was the artist to do in the dilemma in which he was placed? He had either to go along with the industrialists or oppose them, and they had sold the public a bill of goods through their ballyhoo on cheapness and the pressure of their everlasting noise in advertising. Of course the public would regret its purchases, for a thing which is not honestly made is an outrage and offense forever, but who could outshout the money makers?

AUSTRIA

Only in the 20th century did any movement start in Austria. After the Viennese Secession, 1902, Bertold Löffler worked in terra cotta, and Michael Powolny joined him to form the Wiener Keramik. The latter's things are in common clay with bright, opaque, low fired glazes. In 1907 they collaborated with the Wiener Werkstätte which the architect Josef Hoffmann was fathering and Kola Moser, who died in 1918, joined. The Werkbund Exhibition of 1912 showed the crude putti set among flowers and the black and white underglaze wares which became well known. Also in 1912 the Wiener Keramik collaborated with the Gmünder Keramische Werkstätte and made peasant pottery under the direction of Franz and Emile Schleisz. Powolny made tiles for Hoffmann's use as did others also. Otto Prutscher was a designer and also pottery maker. But this work as art is all affected, sloppy and undisciplined. In 1925 at the International Exhibition the faïence stove by Gmünder and the large figure by Dina Kuhn were typically loose. Why Hoffmann, whose own work is the essence of simplicity, could not hold down the exuberance and childishness of these young potters has always been a mystery to me. He wrote for me in the *Encyclopaedia Britannica,* 14th edition, "Sound development does not lie in a mere production of novelties; the whole circumstances of the age must lead in a natural line to new form."

HOLLAND

About 1884 the German potter, W. Von Gudenberg and artist, Th. Colenbrander commenced original work at the Rozenburg factory, The Hague. The latter shows Japanese influence but also did things with leaf decoration which may be said to be his own, if there is any glory in that for the glazes are unpleasantly crude and bright and strive to be "futuristic." He left the place in 1889 and all such work stopped.

In 1916 pseudo-porcelain in pale colors was shaped and painted in the "Jugend style." Japanese influence was great. The material was thin as paper, and not porcelain in any sense. E. L. F. Bodart and L. Senf made earthenware with brown glazes scratched with designs after the Sung and later Chinese techniques. They also made faïence with non-stanniferous glazes of transparent colors allowing Near Eastern sorts of designs to show through, and gold and silver lustre ware.

William Morris and Walter Crane of England started a movement first at Amstelhook then at Distel, which consisted in the use of simple materials and old techniques. W. C. Brouwer made original shapes covered with home made glazes giving accidental effects. The sculptor, J. Mendes De Costa, made small groups of Jewish women and also animals in lead glazed grès. C. J. Lanooy made imitation French grès and used flambé glazes. B. Nienhuys, a teacher, turned out some vases of simple and fairly strong shapes with soft harmonious glazes.

In 1912 Colenbrander, using chiefly blue and brown in dull tones, painted designs on faïence while by 1925, in his old age, he designed unglazed wares for the Arnhem factory at Ram. There was a great leaning toward dull and sombre colors which were considered "good taste" as a revolt against the splashers in bright colors, just as these splashers were in revolt against "antique colors."

H. Krop, at Eskaf, made really pleasant domestic wares with rich white glazes sometimes over relief decoration and sometimes painted in black.

BELGIUM

From Belgium about the only good work shown at the Paris Exhibition, 1925, was that of Ch. Catteau with fine white glaze and designs of flowers, birds and animals. From the Boch Frères the work of Domergue and Sandoz was better than anything else shown but the whole of Belgium endeavors were copyist and poor.

SCANDINAVIA
THE ROYAL COPENHAGEN FACTORY, DENMARK
(See Earlier and Later Sections)

At the Royal Copenhagen Factory, Denmark, Arnold Krog toward the end of the 19th century introduced white porcelain with underglaze design

FIG. 1369. Jars # 1, 3 and 4 are from Boch Freres while # 2 is from the Faiencerie de Keramis, Belgium. All show the peculiar angularized convention then thought "artistic."

which had to be in blue and other soft, cool colors. This led to painting of birds and flowers, etc., because the effect was so thin that the use of mere design would have been uninteresting. There being no accidental texture in the surface, texture had to be introduced into the painting itself. The modeling of animals and other forms was entirely naturalistic but of fine quality from

FIG. 1370. Two plates by Arnold Krog who was at the factory from 1885–1890 and, as these show, was strongly influenced by late period Japanese art.

FIG. 1371. Group of vases, the flowers and fish showing Japanese characteristics and the two with boats showing the naturalistic trend. These were designed by Arnold Krog 1885–1890 in underglaze colors.

the start. Henning used overglaze painting on his "oriental figures" and obtained a not at all unpleasant delicate sex appeal. The Danish peasant figures by Carl Martin Hansen are sensitive and charming and the ethereal figures by A. Malinowski again are very beautiful. He worked in a cream biscuit which gave warmth to his figures and the decoration was confined to slight touches of sepia and gold as a rule. Also a grey crackle was developed in various patterns, large and small, squared and rounded, and used by such artists as Thorkild Olsen and the excellent draughtsman N. Tidemand.

A "celadon" was practically a factory material and too glossy and vivid a green to be pleasant. Few artists worked with it but some figures were made recently.

The stoneware, however, attracted some of the finest artists and Jais Niel-

Fig. 1373. Candelabra by Krog with the mussel blue pattern made between 1891 and 1895.

Fig. 1372. Jar by Jais Nielsen, a dish from Herman A. Kähler designed by Jens Thirslund and another by Chr. Joachim from Kobenhavns Fajancefabric, all Danish.

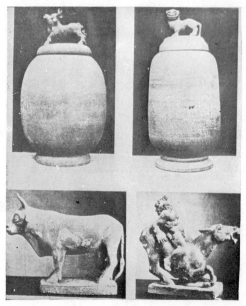

Fig. 1375. A Silenus group by Kai Nielsen of Bing & Gröndhal, Denmark. Metropolitan Mus. of Art.

Fig. 1374. Fine, strong works by Jean Gauguin wrought in perfectly suitable rough surfaced pottery. The animal forms are dynamic and alive, a quality which they strangely lost in the 1939 Exhibition in New York.

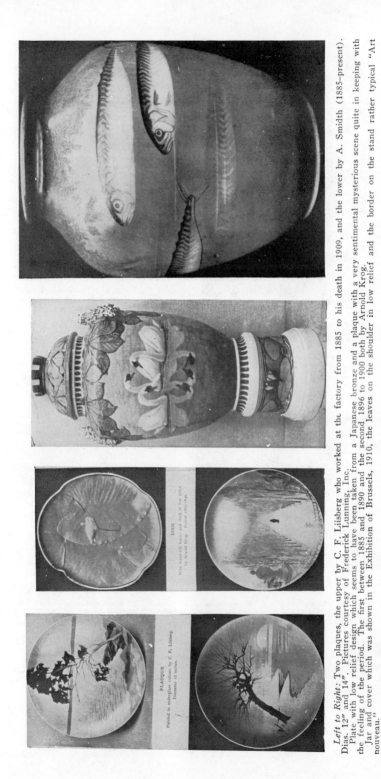

Left to Right: Two plaques, the upper by C. F. Liisberg who worked at the factory from 1885 to his death in 1909, and the lower by A. Smidth (1885–present). Dias. 12″ and 14″. Pictures courtesy of Frederick Lunning, Inc.

Plate with low relief design which seems to have been taken from a Japanese bronze and a plaque with a very sentimental mysterious scene quite in keeping with the feeling of the period. The first between 1885 and 1890 and the second 1896 to 1900 both by Arnold Krog. Jar and cover which was shown in the Exhibition of Brussels, 1910, the leaves on the shoulder in low relief and the border on the stand rather typical "Art nouveau."

Also shown at Brussels this jar has a fine adaptation of swimming mackerel and sea-weed.

ROYAL COPENHAGEN PIECES MADE BEFORE 1910
BY KROG, LIISBERG, SMIDTH

PLATE 230

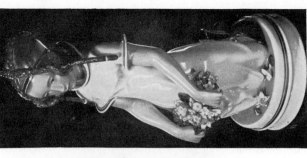

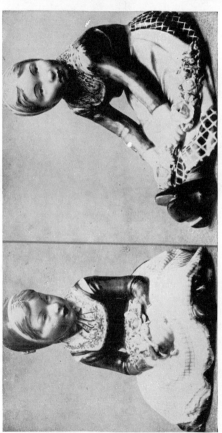

Two small figures by Carl Martin Hansen. Ht. about 4". George Jensen, Inc. Note: These have the black crown and three lines of blue, for marks.

Left: This figure called "Ave Mari" is said to be the first by Henning and was shown in the Paris Exposition of 1925. The head is nicely balanced so that it sways from side to side. Ht. 12½". George Jensen, Inc.
Right: Typical of Malinowski is this dainty figure which is touched with sepia and gold only. The mark is the black crown with three wavy lines in blue. Ht. 8½". George Jensen, Inc.

ROYAL COPENHAGEN FIGURES BY HENNING, MALINOWSKI AND HANSEN

PLATE 231

sen particularly did some beautiful things with strong turquoise-blue glazes.
The "faïence" was frequently covered with lead or hydric borate transparent glaze and painted with underglaze colors. Of course, this is not
faïence technique strictly speaking, but is exceedingly effective. Joachim
is the best master of this ware and his work is gay and lively with rich
assemblings of colors.

Bing & Gröndahl and other Danish Factories

About as large as the Royal Copenhagen factory is that of Bing & Gröndahl also in Denmark and established in 1853. The first good artist hired
by Harald Bing was Peitro Krohn who did the "heron set" combining underglaze colors with gold. In 1900 this firm showed at Paris the work of two

Fig. 1376. A charming figure by Knud Kyhn of the Royal Copenhagen Porcelain Factory and
figures of the usual great beauty by the late Kai Nielsen of the Bing & Gröndahls Porcellainfabrik,
Denmark.

really great artists, Kai Nielsen and Jean Gauguin, the son of the painter.
Kai Nielsen's Venus is truly (as Dalgas, the then director of the Copenhagen
works told me) "a symbol of complete harmony between the art and material."
In the 1925 exhibition he showed "The Grape Gatherers, The Birth of Venus,
The Christians v. Saracens," and his latest at the time, "The Sea." Everything he ever touched was alive and full of charm. His accenting of certain
proportions was masterful. This was a great artist now unfortunately no
longer alive.

To Jean Gauguin I give the palm as the greatest of artists at that time.
Of him Gordon M. Forsyth said, "He is undoubtedly one of the greatest
artists that have ever worked in pottery." At the exhibition was a bull rampant with the power that one would expect to find in the work of a Western
Asiatic bronze artist. Another piece is of a satyr reeling on the back of an
ass which is shrieking and stumbling to its feet. Two large jars with covers
and finials, one of another bull and the other of some strange animal would
add dignity to any collection of pottery of any age. Here is no pose but a
real dynamic working out of all that the material affords in expression.

At Copenhagen, Jais Nielsen (not to be confused with Kai) really belongs
to this small group of the really great. His work gives one a sense of tremendous scale, though it be small. Some trick of proportions is responsible.
Perhaps he is a little mannered but certainly his things carry the manner.

At Nastved, Herman A. Kähler used the local clay and applied lustres. Jens Thirslund also made some interesting dishes, one of which was triangular and with a stag design.

At the Kobenhavns Fajancefabric, Chr. Joachim made decorative things with strong overglaze colors and on the island of Bornholm, at the Hjort's pottery they made some beautiful small vases and figures with thick glazes. Hansen-Jacobsen also made some beautiful but not great things.

SWEDEN & NORWAY

Sweden shows much less of the creative spirit and copies of peasant pottery are about all that was shown. The same is true of Norway and of the "Arabia" factory in Finland.

ENGLAND '

Some private decorators in England worked at the Wedgwood factory on cream ware but to no good purpose. Alfred and Louise Powell are typical.

FIG. 1377. William de Morgan of Fulham, Sand's End Pottery (1839–1917) made these ruby, and other toned, lustre pieces of glowing, rich color but rather mussy design. Metropolitan Mus. of Art.

FIG. 1378. Two plates by Alfred Powell and Louis Powell respectively showing St. Paul's and the "Badge of Aldeburgh, Suffolk." The two jars are from Stabler and Adams.

Whether the "Flambé movement" started in France or England is of no moment. But transmutation glazes of Chinese type became a vogue and they were made by Doulton of Burslem, W. Moorcroft of Stoke-on-Trent, W. Howson Taylor of the Ruskin Pottery, Smethwick in Pilkington's of Manchester, Bernard Moore and many others. The only thing that kept this sort of thing from becoming a real bonanza in the commercial field was that every piece turned out different.

Among the best known early modern potters were Gwladys Rodgers at Pilkington's who used lustre and in 1928 turned to a grey glaze with slight designs in black, Gilbert Bayes and Mr. and Mrs. Harold Stabler at Doulton's who made figures of fair interest, Charles Vyse and Gwendolen Parnell, who did traditional 18th century things and finally John Skeaping who used glazed pottery as a medium for sculpture.

OLD NOTES ON 1925 EXHIBITION AT PARIS

As I go over the old catalogue of the 1925 exhibition at Paris I 'find these marginal notes: The whole English section was heavily commercial. The wares were well enough made but lacking in the textures of the French wares and the skill and beauty of the Scandinavian, and particularly the Danes. Gordon Forsyth wrote, "The British section as a whole was inclined to be rather staid and dull. There was in the pottery section a real lack of spirit of adventure on the artistic side." He also said, "If British potters are to lead in the various markets of the world, they must be creative artists and not complaisant tools of the retailers." Amusingly, his British mind in his very statements gives away the attitude, for he speaks of the "artistic side," (as though there were any other for an artist to follow!) and he sets the ambition of achievements as "the markets of the world."

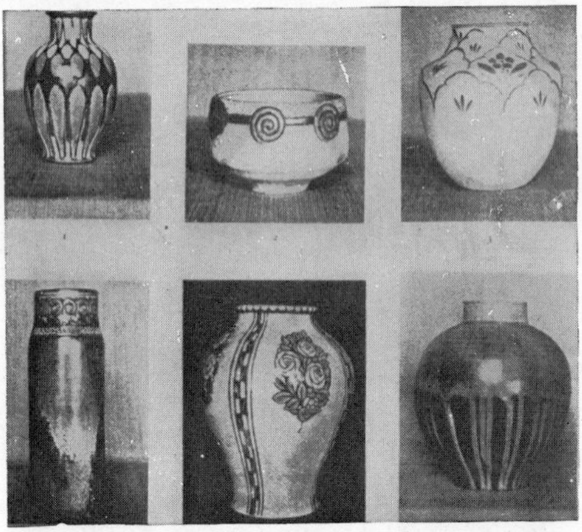

Opposite the Wedgwood exhibition I noted, "Not a spark." Powell had some sloppy silver lustre service designs. The "jasper ware" had become poorer in craftsmanship and positively sentimental. J. E. Goodwin made unobservant and badly shaped copies of Sung and later Chinese wares. It was interesting to note that some of these were made for lamp fittings. England had awakened to the American lamp business!

W. T. Copeland & Sons, the descendants of the Spode factory simply showed more underglaze transfer prints, some exotic flower decorations and some

FIG. 1379. Doulton & Co., Ltd., wares by Hy. Simeon, Vera Huggins and Wm. Rowe. Including salt glazed stoneware and a crystalline glaze so popular at the time.

stupidly modeled birds and animals.

Doulton & Co. had a fountain by Gilbert Bayes in stoneware with colored glazes that blended well with the foliage about it. If more of our great sculptors would let themselves go and make use of a bit of color here and there (not flesh color to imitate life but patterns) the art would become more interesting to the average man. I once heard a critic say of a man's paintings that they were as dull and lifeless as an exhibition of sculpture. This Doulton firm made use of the term "Sung glazes" which they were not and which I resented. Actually these were flambé, crystalline, etc. Hy. Simeon used some peacock tail patterns in soft colors and with salt glazes on safe and uninteresting shapes. Vera Huggins tried to be primitive in a nice way. William Rowe was "just too too sweet!" I also made note that the pinwheel roses with stiff foliage seemed to be the rage in Liberty's batiks. The general impression was, "Arts and crafty."

At Pilkington's, founded in 1900, a small department was formed for artists including Walter Crane and Lewis F. Day. All pottery was wheel made. Lustre was favorite. The shapes in the 1925 show came nearly up to the Danish ones. In Richard Joyce's work there was a too close adherence to Renais-

FIG. 1380. Pilkington & Co. vase of about 1906 decorated by G. M. Forsyth in purple and gold lustre somewhat following the style of de Morgan's things.

FIG. 1381. Examples from the Pilkington Tile & Pottery Co., Ltd. 1.—Silver and blue by Richard Joyce. 2.—Underglaze and lustre decoration, W. S. Mycock. 3.—Bowl in silver lustre on ruby ground by Gwladys M. Rodgers. 4.—Mottled glazed effects. 5.—Similar to # 3 also by Gwladys M. Rodgers.

sance design. W. S. Mycock got away from this effect by allowing his glazes to run. Gwladys M. Rodgers got patterns which seemed to drip with the fire of lustre, and there was nothing effeminate about her shapes.

Of Worcester I found nothing to look at.

Of Minton one could only say that since M. Arneaux there was a weak following of the French.

The Cauldon Potteries, Ltd., were entirely commercial.

Also exhibiting was Wm. Moorcroft & Co., run by Moorcroft himself who is an accomplished potter with real feeling and perhaps a too great worship of the Chinese without a clear understanding of them.

One of the best known and appreciated of the English potters in his own country is Bernard Moore who makes a piece now and then and obtains beautiful effects in lustre, flambé glazes and various slip treatments. A case full of these pieces shows like the smouldering of lambent fire.

John and Truda Adams' firm is Carter, Stabler & Adams, including the Stabler couple as well. It was originally a tile making firm under the super-

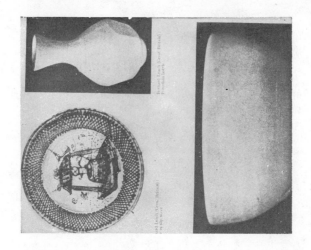

Bernard Leach (Rossef Britain)
Porcelain bottle

Ford Leach (Gross Britain)
 try slip glaze

Fig. 1383. A group from the Ravenscourt Pottery and two pieces from the Ruskin Pottery made by W. Howson Taylor and glazed with flambé effects.

Fig. 1384. Slipware plate by Bernard Leach and a rather insecure small bottle by the same artist. The large bowl is of "Kuan type", made by W. Staite Murray who often came fairly close to Sung wares or at least Yung Chêng copies of them.

Fig. 1382. Figures by Gwendolen Parnell, the "Atalanta" far from sound but the two lower ones showing some good qualities of observation and humor.

1026

vision of Mr. Adams. The Stablers make stoneware figures of some charm and decorated by Mrs. Adams. The firm also makes a "Della Robia" ware for architectural purposes which is gay in spirit. Messrs. Carter of Poole, Dorset aid. They do much underglaze decoration with a mat surfaced glaze and also have a brilliant fine blue with a greenish cast which is used over a red earthenware body. The shapes are not so good as those of Pilkington and the decorations are less sure but at times Mrs. Adams turns out a rather sweetish Persian sort of thing that is not too bad.

M. W. Howson Taylor, Birmingham, makes the well-known Ruskin Pottery which is not happy in shapes but well potted and sometimes surprisingly thin in the egg-shell bowls. Again flambés, lustres, etc., were favorites.

Among the individual potters the best known are probably W. Staite Murray and Gwendolen Parnell. Miss Parnell used porcelain body and a full palette of colors. She did figures of British characters successfully but at times overreaches herself as much as does her running figure of "Atlanta." Someone has said that her British types are, "dainty rogues in porcelain," and this well describes them.

W. Staite Murray studied the Ming Tz'u chou potteries and thought them Sung. His ware has a stoneware body and the glazes are thick and rich and of soft ivory, buff or grey. The decorations are in black, brown and white in the Chinese manner though painted without benefit of the perpendicular brush. Mr. Bernard Rackham, however, has one so close to the Chinese that it might well fool some incautious collector.

Bernard Leach does similar things again but his shapes are less good. He also worked in slip after the technique of the old Staffordshire potters but captures none of their real qualities. There are a host of others who are more or less amateurs and none of whom are of any interest to us.

CZECHOSLOVAKIA

At this Paris exhibition of 1925 the Czechoslovakian part showed a fine fireplace in cream white by L. & C. Hardmuth of Prague and some commercial wares challenging the English.

BELGIUM

Though a good part of the modern movement started in Belgium it never got more than a start there. At the exhibition Ch. Catteau had some ware with an opaque crackled glaze. Boch Frères had some things by Domergue and Sandoz with soft and bad forms suggesting glass by Galle or Lalique and designs that would go well with "Mission furniture" the Roycroft movement, etc. It is hard to say why these designs are so sickening. Perhaps they are most expressive of schoolteacher-conventionalization or the stencil patterns sold by women's magazines.

ITALY

In the Italian section Richard Ginori of Colonnata, Firenze, had services decorated with simple lambrequin patterns in one color or in gold on white.

One design is of a reclining classical lady with draped cords above and below her.

SPAIN

There were several pieces in the Spanish exhibition from Daniel Zuloaga's Sons of fair merit.

LATVIA

Strangely in Latvia there were some of the best ultra modern things such as cubist designs not at all unpleasant and not so demanding as they would be on canvas. These were made by A. Sutta, and Vidbergs did some charming and rather sexy plates with plain broad rims and center decorations of simply drawn nudes reclining amongst huge blossoms and foliage. There were also the peasant types of wares.

A Few Notes on Designs in Other Mediums

In order to understand that ceramics are often influenced by other mediums as they in turn affect other mediums, a note or two here may be of help. This had become a time of artificial fabrics, which needed to be sumptuous and rich looking. Perhaps this explains the vogue for transmutation and lustred effect in part. Again the modern process of autogenous soldering made possible Edgar Brandt's metal screens of various combinations of brass, copper, silver, etc. Cheney Bros. have a pair of doors here in New York done by him and they adopted some of his rosettes in fabric design. I have never seen it exactly copied in ceramics but have no doubt that it was and perhaps our stiff pin-wheel rosettes are owed partially to him.

Of course the newly discovered Han tomb potteries and those from Mesopotamia along with greater interest in archaeology brought about a semblance of the sort of enthusiasm that was shown in Renaissance times and again in those of Napoleon just preceding this modern era.

Finally trade had become so international in character that, had not the wares been labeled, it would have been difficult to tell what country they were made in. American influences were not shown because Mr. Hoover had made up his mind that America had nothing worth showing.

AMERICA, THE ART CENTER OF THE WORLD

The Ruskin, Burne-Jones, Rosetti and William Morris influences had reached America from England, more as a revolt against classicism than anything else. There were three revolts: that against the machine, that against commerce and that against classicism and naturally America did not feel so strongly against the first two because they had benefited this nation while they had harmed England in many ways. Even classicism had not bothered us as much as others. The Art Nouveau hardly touched us. But what did suit our taste was the Arts and Crafts movement. The ideas were good: 1.—The use of the hand instead of the machine. 2.—The idea of building furniture to function. 3.—The idea of not disguising materials, all suited the practical American way of thinking and people like Elbert Hubbard boosted them. "Mission furniture" and "Colonial mahogany" became popular and were set upon "Turkish carpets." Rich people even had Turkish dens dimly illuminated with pierced brass lamps lined with red. Sanitation, air and light had not yet become words to conjure with.

In the finer homes the great decorators were doing "period rooms" with a leaning toward the heavier styles. Wm. Baumgarten & Co., White, Allom & Co., etc., were making the American millionaire conscious that he could spend money for antique furniture and ornaments. Some of the great collections such as those of Morgan, Altman and Mellon were well under way and fine tapestries, bronzes, porcelains and all manner of great works of art were being brought to this country. These had such a strong influence that the craftsmen were busy translating harmonious characteristics into their own works and very little was heard about art movements in modern Europe. There was a market and it created no revolts. Such firms as Tiffany Studios and Edward F. Caldwell & Co. were making the finest craftsmanship almost regardless of cost.

The masses knew and cared nothing about art and men of commerce only turned to it after their fortunes had been made. Art in business had not been thought about.

Two architects, iconoclasts in our midst, were condemning all this and trying to get down to first principles. They have been much overrated by some but they did exert some influence. One was Louis Sullivan who died in 1924 and the other Frank Lloyd Wright. It is argued that Wright brought about much of the modern movement in Germany but it was too complicated for any one such influence to be solely credited. Wright is not a profound man though there is little doubt that he considers himself a prophet. Broadly speaking, his houses fit into a landscape about as well as would a large tombstone in a living room. They are angular and textureless with queer jutting shelves and planes. Color means little to him. Yet, having worked in Japan, he places in these houses, without understanding of the highest elements of Japanese economy in art, fussy spots such as few Japanese would tolerate, of wood carvings, screens, ornamented vases, etc., in "artistic groups." On a cement shelf that is as uncompromising and unpleasant in texture as only a block of cement can be he will have a vase with dried grasses and a paper fan. His masses are as assertive as his speech and his taste as erratic as his reasoning. But this man did start something, of that there is no doubt, for many of his ideas were taken up in Europe far more than here and have much to do with the "modern movement."

The "skyscraper" design came about through the drawings of Hugh Ferris for Harvey Wiley Corbett which showed the "envelope" allowed by the zoning laws. These drawings had hardly been shown at the Architectural League of New York before many other architects developed the style in their work. Such men as Raymond Hood, Ralph Walker and J. Ely Kahn developed the "setback" style which had its advantages in buildings but no reason at all to be copied in furniture and potteries. Everything became angular and squared except, of course, the human body which did not feel comfortable in the chairs, while at the same time the eyes became tired of such hard angularity.

A few potteries were making fair wares and people paid high prices for Rookwood, Roseville and even Fulper jars of which we shall speak later.

At the same time the "Boom" was in the making and American millionaires had started to clean the art out of Europe in earnest. The auction galleries were selling "Ming vases" for $25 to $50 and "Corot paintings" for a few hundred, although the real things were bringing hundreds and thousands of dollars. Every salesroom hummed and fakes supplied the market. Living artists and popular craftsmen were only just surviving for the larger American homes had Tudor living rooms, Spanish patios, Grinling Gibbons mantels in pine incidental rooms, Chippendale upstairs sitting rooms, Louis XV and Louis XVI bedrooms and Modern bars. Thus the poor craftsman had to work in every sort of period. It was educational but not soundly so. More money was spent for faked antiques and for liquor (for this was the prohibition era) than for honest craftsmanship.

Due to the fact that Americans did not think modern craftsmanship sufficiently expensive, there was no interest in the potteries of contemporaries. About the only modern wares which were sold in large quantities were those imitating old Chinese wares and made in China and Japan. At least 75% of the pottery lamps were made from these. In making lamps we tried to widen the taste and attempted to sell Persian wares, East Indian brasses, Italian potteries, etc., but with no very great success.

The genius of one man, Mr. Edward I. Farmer, led to the selling of fine antique Chinese wares as lamps and it was also he who taught the American public that they could spend thousands of dollars for lamps made with bases of fine jades and other hard stones. His shades were rounded and soft in tone, often made from embroideries or tapestries of Chinese origin and hung with thick fringes. I do not know what Farmer's highest priced lamp was but he sold many for $10,000 or more. Vase lamps became a sure and definite style trend.

A reaction against the overcrowding of rooms with many decorative objects led to the revolt against Victorianism and no objects of art were permitted. Thus lamps became about the only art objects in many modern rooms, retained simply because they are of use. An amusing sidelight was that the most modern of modernists did not give up vase lamps despite all their theories of functionalism, etc.; they simply used modern looking vases and shades.

In our own studio which started immediately after World War I in East Orange, N. J. and moved to New York in the following year, we made lamps of every period (Farmer had never stepped out of the Chinese field.) and we tried to do all decorating of shades by hand instead of using the fancy fabrics which Farmer had used. All of the graphic arts have been employed and our chief artist, Miss Ethelyn C. Stewart, is a master of etching, lithography, the oriental perpendicular brush, the tjanting used for batik, etc. She is also quite able to demonstrate the differences between Meissen flowers of various periods, Vienna flowers, Sèvres, Chinese of various periods, Japanese,

Rakka jar of 12th to 13th cent. mounted as a lamp with shade designed by Warren E. Cox and made of hand blended velvet by Ethelyn C. Stewart.

Sung Dynasty Tz'u Chou lamp with shade designed by Warren E. Cox and hand painted by Ethelyn C. Stewart.

Late Sung to Early Ming Tz'u Chou vase of unique character but with neck cut slightly and therefore made into a lamp by Warren E. Cox. The shade has alternating panels of hand painting on silk and batiked design (to reproduce the incised parts) on velvet by Ethelyn C. Stewart.

17th cent. Hispano Moresque lustre jar with shade designed by Warren E. Cox and batiked by Ethelyn C. Stewart.

Late Ming "Three colored" vase with shade designed by Warren E. Cox and batiked on velvet by Ethelyn C. Stewart.

K'ang Hsi (1662–1722 A.D.) porcelain vase with famille verte enamel decoration mounted as a lamp. The shade is designed by Warren E. Cox and decorated with hand colored etchings printed on the silk by Ethelyn C. Stewart.

ANTIQUE POTTERIES AND PORCELAINS INCORPORATED IN LAMP DESIGNS BY WARREN E. COX

PLATE 232

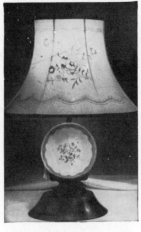

Takatori 18th cent. Japanese saki-bottle with shade designed by Warren E. Cox and batiked and hand painted by Ethelyn C. Stewart.

A porcelain dish mounted as a lamp by Warren E. Cox and the shade hand painted by Ethelyn C. Stewart.

Modern Sèvres porcelain lamp with shade designed by Warren E. Cox and decorated with a hand colored etching printed on silk by Ethelyn C. Stewart.

Sèvres lamp with shade designed by Warren E. Cox and etched and hand painted by Ethelyn C. Stewart.

Modern Wedgwood vase with shade designed by Warren E. Cox and decorated with an etched and hand painted border by Ethelyn C. Stewart.

Modern reproduction of a Sung Tz'u Chou incised slip vase somewhat modified and designed by Warren E. Cox, fired by Walter Howat and with shade hand painted by Ethelyn C. Stewart.

LAMPS DESIGNED BY WARREN E. COX USING ANTIQUE AND
MODERN CERAMIC PIECES

PLATE 233

English, etc., etc. A hundred or so of her etchings made for lamp shades have become truly famous.

Meanwhile a large collection of fine potteries and porcelains was made. The less good pieces were sold as lamp bases and the finest have been put to one side for sale to collectors. We became interested in a kiln and made many reproductions for less expensive lamps.

Many other lamp firms followed. Roland and Mrs. Moore copied Farmer's shades and lately the crushed velvet ones which we designed for Persian wares mottled to pick up the texture and iridescent tones. Mrs. Moore died some years ago and since that time less attention has been paid to the shade art in his establishment although many fine antique Chinese ceramic wares have been sold. The more commercial and larger firms, such as Yamanaka & Co., Long Sang Ti Co. and others, built large lamp departments until more vases were sold for this purpose than for any other. Edward F. Caldwell & Co. mounted many ordinary 17th century Persian oil jars with their superb champleve enamel work.

Such was the many sided and diverse "modern art" of the period after World War I up to the depression. No two people could even agree as to what was modern and it was really a free-for-all with plenty of money behind it.

REPORT ON THE 1939 POTTERIES SHOWN IN THE NEW YORK EXPOSITION

FRANCE

Robert Bloch, Paris, showed some wares strongly reminiscent of the Victorian era, with heavy body and thin, frosty, mat glazes of pastel colors with often decorations in chocolate brown and gold. Dishes in the form of ostrich feathers, stupid chess-men and pairs of negro figures led me to note that a great effort had been made to obtain a soigné effect of chic, and had failed.

There was nothing of note in the table wares of Charles Ahrenfeldt, Au Vase Etrusque, L. Bernardaud, The Porcelain Manufactury of Limoges and Robert Haviland & Le Tanneur. The block-like and gaudy colored figures of Breton peasants made by Hanroit of Breton had little charm.

Germany and Austria were, of course, not exhibited.

HUNGARY

In Hungary the Herend pieces were the most ordinary but even these were alive in spirit. The bird and flower decorations were gayly painted with clear, fresh but harmonious colors. A nude figure some twelve to fourteen inches high was beautifully modeled by Lux Eleby and the broad touches of color, a yellowish buff for the hair and a light, dull red irregularly brushed on the drape showed a perfect understanding of just how much and just how little color to use. No attempt had been made to touch up the high places with natural pink but the warmth of the off-white glaze itself adds feeling of life.

Madam Olga Braun told me about Géza Gorka who has spent many years in recovering the lost arts of the Hungarian peasant potteries. In the Christmas Exhibition of 1938 he and his brother received honors for this ware which is direct and strong like that of long ago. The colors are rich blues, greens, dull yellows and the ground frequently buff. This kiln which is at Nógrádverőcze, near Budapest, will bear watching, if it survives the war.

Lili Márkus had a large, cylindrical dark jar with circular concavities in

Fig. 1385. Dish by Mrs. Truda Adams of the Carter, Stabler & Adams company, which is pleasant in its pseudo Persian design but overly weak and delicate.

Fig. 1386. W. Staite Murray not only made Tz'u Chou type things but also attempted the Chün glazes with some success. Metropolitan Mus. of Art.

Fig. 1387. Tz'u Chou type jar by W. Staite Murray owned by Bernard Rackham. Comparison with Sung examples is hardly fair, but the form is too fat and rounded and the brush-work too much organized in the swirl of the fish and repetition of the V marks. However, it is better than most modern pottery.

which were tiny crude models of things in bright enamels sunk quite deeply as though in little inch wide caves. The overmantle of a mountain with figures on it in relief and enameled with soft colors is not a new idea but was well done. Another large jar reminds us a little of those by Gauguin but is less dynamic.

Fig. 1388. Large jar by Lili Markus in glazed earthenware of dark brownish black and greyish blue. Ht. about 16″. Note: The feeling of this piece is not unlike that of some of Gauguin's but it is weaker.

Fig. 1389. Faïence Madonna and Child by G. Y. Eleöd which is typically sweet, and even somewhat flippant. Ht. 16″. Modern Hungarian.

Fig. 1390. Technically the lustre effects of Zsolnay Gyár are very excellent but the results are somewhat thin and glassy, like Christmas tree ornaments and the forms are uninteresting. Ht. 15½″. Modern Hungarian.

Jenö Eschnebach had only been out of art school for a short while but had made a small crucifixion which was outstandingly beautiful and sensitive, though done in what at first appears a sketchy style. It looks to have been done by a great artist in haste and totally without pose.

Margit Kovács works in heavy pottery which has a mediaeval feeling in its slip decorations and dark glazes of gold, red and blue. The sculptors B. Markup and Béla Ohmann had good figures in faïence, one of a mountaineer on a donkey and another of a rather sweet and willowy Madonna and Child.

Of poorer effect there are the sloppy modeling and potting of István Gádor and the overornate lustres of Zsolnay Gyár much like the English 19th century ones.

Fig. 1391. Margit Kovacs medieval sort of things in dark glazes, gold, red and blue. Ht. 12½″. Modern Hungarian.

Fig. 1392. By F. Borszéky—A bonnière in various soft colors of glazes on what appears to be a hard porcelain ware. Dia. 7″. Modern Hungarian.

HOLLAND

The Royal Delft Factory in Holland has gone in for some Persian shaped pottery having rather indefinite patterns in well blended and deep colored lustres. They are also making some very thin white wares after the Chinese. There were also a dull continuation of the blue and white and polychrome "Delft wares."

The factory Zaalberg "de rinj," Leiderdorp, had some heavy and medium red pottery prominently scored with wheel marks and covered with a thin and often partly wiped off glaze of pale green, blue, lavender, yellow, grey or a thick, deep blue of unpleasant reddish tone. The shapes are tall beakers, one well formed pitcher and platters. This all appears to be a great effort to be primitive.

BELGIUM

The S. A. Faiencerie de Nimy had some ordinary cream ware and some with blue glaze. There were also some very poorly modeled animals in lumpy sugary white glaze, a Belgian artist's conception of a negro jazz-band and some figures in sets of five or six all of poor quality and no redeeming features.

P. Paulus had some poor copies of 17th century "Kashan" potteries in brown and green and cream and rust.

Marcel Wolfers found a new texture, something always dear to the mind of a modernist, and it consists of a thick brown glaze in which are sprinkled many pieces of mother-of-pearl giving somewhat the effect of some Ming Chinese lacquer only that in the latter case the pieces are not scattered but laid carefully like mosaic. Again Wolfers uses what appears to be flecks of egg shell set in a dark brown glaze though I should imagine that real egg shell would calcine and crumble with the heat. Another trick is on a large jar which seems to have been stippled or sponged on a thick glaze which after firing was covered with gold and rubbed so that the gold does not adhere to the high ridges. There was also a large plate treated this way and with coral red on the inside.

Van Nerom has a jar and dishes with cute little figures in child-like drawing and colored with pale blue, pink, etc., rather carelessly so that it runs over the edges. It is strange that we don't mind a bold splash of color that breaks carelessly over a strong outline but we resent the transgression of a weak and uncertain hand.

Pierre Caille probably thinks of himself as a great humorist when he does his badly modeled animals in unpleasant yellow, green and rose glazes; and his lumpy birds are well frosted. He has also copied some of the Austrian, Wiener Werkstadt techniques and some pie-faced lions of Italian heritage.

The Belgian artists were on the wrong track in 1925 and they certainly lived down to expectations.

DENMARK

The Hegnetslund Lervarefabrik showed some vases, jugs and figures in red iron rust glazes, some majolica pigs and jugs by Anker Nørregaard and some pottery in dull green glazes. Nothing new in any way approaching the fine wares from this country was shown.

Saxbo work was marked by refined and beautiful shapes and among them one, so far as I know, new treatment for a jug so simple and so fundamentally good potting that it is a wonder it has not been used for centuries. The pear shaped body has a fairly wide neck which is cut down the middle, one half curving forward to form the lip or spout while the other is extended and curves backward to join the body and form the handle. This seems to be a real invention.

Nathalie Krebs and Eva Wilhjelm together with Erik Rahr all had beautiful shapes in their wares with the finest of glazes of buff, brown, cream and white as well as pale blue running to deep blue. Nathalie Krebs was manager of the factory and is an especially able potter.

There was a strong Japanese influence in the "temmoku" flat straight-sided tea bowls actually invented in China but given a more popular flare and weaker character in Japan. Some of the tea-pots could have been shown by Japan and not thought misplaced. They had glazes of brown, pinkish white and buff.

The sculptors, Hugo Liisberg and Olaf Staehr Nielsen, work well but were not particularly thrilling, though I did note with pleasure a charming faun in brown glaze which was gentle, alert and living.

If this factory would turn a little more toward the strength of Chinese

Vigorous animals full of life are modeled by Knud Kyhn in solid stoneware of great weight and glazed in dull brown, bluish or green tones. The power and life in his work are well shown in this old bear. Length 13″. Frederick Lunning, Inc.

Left: The most beautifully potted and decorated Royal Copenhagen porcelain bowl I have seen. There is a pale grey-blue shading about the stand and the design inside which was painted by Bertha Nathanielsen and signed by her. Dia. 5½″. Mrs. Warren E. Cox.
Right: Large modern Copenhagen underglazed decorated jar of the type made by The Royal Copenhagen Manufactory and copied somewhat weakly by Bing & Grondahl. Ht. 31″. Frederick Lunning, Inc.

MODERN ROYAL COPENHAGEN WARES

PLATE 234

sources rather than the already second-hand ones of Japan, it would benefit. Yet there was nothing that one would not be happy to own and I believe that over a period of years one would not grow tired of any of the pieces. I do not know of any stoneware of finer quality though than that of Axal Salto, the painter, and Bode Willumsen perhaps rates as high.

The Herman A. Kahler factory has two fine artists in Svend Hammershøj and Jens Thiirslund who do what are almost classic shapes but with strange and pleasant distortions that are so sure that they are entirely convincing. The ware is lightweight and high ringing stoneware of grey or black and thinly made. The glaze is greyish white of dull surface and crackled and wiped off in places so that the body shows through. There is real textural charm very hard to put in words.

Fig. 1393. This cup shows one style of Thiirslund of the Kähler pottery, Näestved. It is of light grey with black decoration swiftly and none too surely applied. Metropolitan Mus. of Art.

Fig. 1394. Two pieces of the new red glazed ware which is more mat than a sang de boeuf glaze and more closely approximates the Yung Chèng sang de pigeon. Hts. 8″ and 3″. Frederick Lunning, Inc.

Fig. 1395. So well known are the animal figures from Copenhagen that it is unnecessary to show more than a few. This was taken from the figure in the fountain in the Peace Palace, Hague. Ht. 11″. George Jensen, Inc.

The L. Hjorth's Terracottafabrik, Rønne, Bornholm, had some cylindrical jars with covers in dark brown, dull glaze on thin but heavy stoneware and a few heavy vases in pleasing transmutation glazes but uncertain in shape. There was also a small figure of a woman with a jar but poor in modeling. This ware is called "iron glaze ware," which does not seem particularly original. Much of the glaze is actually olive green which might include some iron along with copper or other green producing elements.

A. S. Michael Andersen & Søn of the same place, also showed some simple vases of good quality stoneware with transmutation glazes of brown to blue. A terra-cotta bust of a girl is piquant and illusively charming with suggestive shrug, secretive smile, and off the face hair treatment. This last is worth note for the artist has simply pressed the clay up into small rounded waves with the thumb and then incised them with lines producing a convincing texture.

The Royal Copenhagen Porcelain Manufactory had a few of the older type underglazed painted porcelains of beautiful craftsmanship and some perhaps overchaste table ware, but other things were more interesting. The heavy stoneware thickly potted of roughly modeled animals glazed in buff, mottled

Fig. 1396. A group of the grey crackled wares decorated in a peculiar and none too pleasant orange color, black and gold. Royal Copenhagen. Hts. about 2″ to 13″. George Jensen, Inc.

grey, cream and iron rust were vigorous and strong. Some rich brown glazed pieces like the "Tsung Sê," "Chien yao," or "Temmoku" Chinese type are good but have less lustre and variation than the Far Eastern ones.

Fig. 1398. Christian Thomsen did a series illustrating the Hans Christian Andersen fairy tales, of which this, "The King's Nightdress," is one. Ht. 8″. George Jensen, Inc.

Fig. 1397. A group of modern plates decorated with natural flowers somewhat in the old style of about 1780 to 1800. George Jensen, Inc.

A new ware to me was of superb beauty and was shown in only two pieces. It is of pure white porcelain body which shows an "iron foot" and "brown mouth" as in some of the Kuan and Ko wares. The glaze is cloudy, pale greyish, greenish blue like that of the finest "kinuta" celadon and is as soft and unctuous and pleasant to the touch. This is perhaps the most beautiful ware the factory ever turned out.

One of the best artists is Hans Hansen who does vessels which O. Mathiesen glazes though the two work so closely in mutual understanding that the glaze

FIG. 1401. This lovely little dog has a silky and soft col‑ ored glaze. It is interesting to compare it with the dog by Edward McCartan (see mod‑ ern American section.) Length 13". George Jensen, Inc.

FIG. 1399. Ducks by G. Herold of the Royal Copen‑ hagen Factory, 20th cent. Metropolitan Mus. of Art.

FIG. 1400. Typical underglaze painting of ship on Royal Copenhagen jar. The colors have to be blue, gray, lavender, etc., to stand the high temperature in firing. They are both decorative and beautifully detailed. Courtesy of George Jensen, Inc.

FIG. 1402. Bing and Grøndahl porcelain vase by Mrs. Jo Hahn Locher in low relief with mat glaze. Metro‑ politan Mus. of Art.

is always perfectly suited to the shape. One particularly fine one was a tall slightly bulging cylindrical vase with perpendicular grooves covered with an olive green glaze. A smaller jar and cover had a most ingenious hexagonal design in relief on it and a finial in the form of an animal which looks to have been inspired from a Ming period jade carving.

Niels Thorsson is another strong modeler and his pieces are glazed by H. Madslund in a new and very rich glaze of copper red which varies from bright and strong color to dark blackish red and slips from the edge as do the sang de boeuf glazes of China, though it is thinner and less glossy than these, which is after all more pleasant and less assertive.

The other things were of little note such as the set of plates with silhouettes from Hans Christian Andersen's fairy tales, etc.

This factory has always maintained such a high stand‑ ard of technique that there could be little improvement but the trend away from the more pictorial things and toward the stoneware and beautiful glazes is a good one, if the public will support it. After all it does take a more sophisticated and better trained taste to appreciate a small white or green bowl with wonderful glaze than it does to like a big vase with boats or flowers painted on it, and the public appeal for fine things will probably always be a narrow one.

Bing and Grøndahl also at Copenhagen, which calls itself "The National Factory of Porcelain," has become perhaps as important as the older factory, due to a few great artists who have been on its staff.

Kai Nielsen, who died, I understand, in 1934 or 1935, had developed his talent even further. A life-sized statue of Venus was full of sexual charm and very lovely. This had been pushed over by a drunken woman who reeled against it at the fair and had been broken but I inspected it in a closet and found the modeling wonderfully sure and knowing. Another charming piece was the "Venus with the Apple." Nielsen's proportions are purposely changed but add to the vitality of his work somewhat as do "El Greco's."

FIG. 1403. Stoneware vase from Bing and Grøndahl by C. Olsen. Metropolitan Mus. of Art.

I was disappointed in Jean Gauguin. His jars were similar but less strong and a life-sized tiger's head was naturalistic and without power as though modeled from the head of a fur rug. A small model of a tiger showed poor and uncertain knowledge of anatomy. A rhinoceros head looked so good that it might have been sliced off a real animal but one wonders what the purpose might be. A couple of faun heads were stupid and dull. As I wrote this I wondered, if I might have been wrong in my first impression at the Paris show but going back over old photographs I find it was not so; it is he who simply seems to have dried up. Perhaps all his strength was borrowed from Han potteries and now that he has drifted away from them he has lost his source.

Professor Hans Tegner did a group of hard porcelain small figures with bright and deep overglaze colors representing various characters from the Andersen fairy tales. There was the "Nightingale," "Swineherd," "Chimney Sweep and His Princess," the "Emperor's New Clothes" (showing his majesty in crown and shirt tails), and "Big Claus and Little Claus," among them. They are all full of humor and delicacy and are also fine craftsmanship, but similar subjects had been treated by Christian Thomsen at the Royal Copenhagen works.

Axel Locher has a few rather 18th century-like little figures such as, "The Girl with Sheep," etc.

The vases and other vessels of this factory are of the finest of modern wares and rate very close to the Royal Copenhagen ones. Both of these places have withstood the withering effects of industrialism probably because of the royal patronage and the intense national pride which all Danes take in them.

ENGLAND

In England it is a different matter. We walked past the throne on which the Magna Charta was displayed and watched the faces of the people who were disappointed to find they could not read it. We crossed an immense room which contained racing automobiles and engines of other sorts, then after climbing some stairs to a balcony where there were many ship models, statistical charts, etc., and following directions to turn to the right, we found tucked away in the furtherest corner a half dozen little cases chock full of "china," for the most part as ornately bedecked as an officer of the Palace Guard on dress parade. People were passing these cases in double line, each fellow pushing his girl along before him and not giving her any too much time to look at anything. The exclamations were typically preceded by exhaled or aspirated exclamation so common to the British, "Ooh! Aren't they wonderful? Ho! That's a fine one!" all very much as though fireworks were being displayed. And the wares themselves really called for something like that.

Royal Worcester China was in the first case and along the top was a row of plates in red with one in blue so heavily encrusted with gold filigree that you could hardly make out the color under it. Below this was a large porcelain sign with the words Royal Worcester China and a row of life-sized birds contorting themselves as much as possible beside a nice large flower on each piece. The birds looked overstuffed and the colors dull. On the bottom shelf was a well modeled but cheaply colored group of three circus horses and some smartly, flatly conventionalized hunters showing the style common to advertisements for men's clothing. (See any copy of Esquire.)

The Wedgwood case showed not one new spark and a muddy copy of the same old "Portland vase."

The usual floating ladies in flowing drapes in pâte sur pâte on shiny olive green and dull blue grounds were proudly shown still again by Minton. A cup was delicately decorated with light gilt tracery about two photographic portraits of George VI and Elizabeth with many legends so that no one could mistake who they were. These commemorated their trip to the United States. There were also services in heavy colors and with too much gold surrounding too small medallions in which were painted birds and flowers.

Royal Doulton has tried pitifully to copy dogs in Copenhagen style and this factory too showed encrusted gilt plates. Some dainty and sweet little girl figures were shown but no artist's name was given, and a "balloon woman" may have been by Gwendolen Parnell, though the humor was missing and it may have been just a stylized copy of her work.

Royal Crown Derby rehashed the same old Imari designs in Derby red, gold and blue, tightly painted flowers in pasty colors and having much of the too red blue which would go well only in petunias, and a small cup in celebration of George VI's visit.

Spode had some plates with the stiffest flowers yet seen and the most opaque colors. They had left off the gold but the very broad rims were finished in heavy rose de Mantenon.

That was all. I asked the manager why they had not sent over some of their artists' work and was told that the exhibit represented the best work in England. They had never heard of Staite Murray. Where were the Adams, Hy. Simeon of the Doulton Co., Gwladys Rodgers and the rest? In the true British disdain which covers uncertainty I was looked upon as though I had mentioned the names of foreigners.

ITALY

The Societa Ceramica Italiana, Laveno, had some heavy potteries particularly some 16-inch pilgrim bottles with a large clumsy child with a goose on them in horrible, bright orange and other colored glazes that hurt.

The Melandri Pietro, Faienza, had some ordinary lustre and some grotesque shaped and bizarre pots of large scale. It seemed that Italy was trying to gain notice by scale alone.

Ivos Pacetti had some crude modern sculpture with sticky brown and blue glaze.

But when we come to Richard Ginori, Milano, there is a new and charming note. The shapes are restrained and yet they are all quite different. Some are of neo-classic feeling as in a large cream mat glazed vase with two acanthus scroll handles in gold, and two smaller vases of the same ware with female figures riding dolphins done in burnished and mat gold. Another was in a soft grey blue of beautiful tone. But though classic these pieces are all original in proportions and details of treatment.

Pietro

A number of bottles are tall and simple being modeled in helical convex ridges some of equal width and some alternating wide and narrow. These are very thinly potted and covered with a pearly grey glaze, a greyish white and a pinkish white not at all iridescent but seemingly glowing like the surfaces of real pearls. A small cylindrical jar with narrow neck was alternately convex ribbed with soft, dull red and pearly grey. Some similar wares were in mat black and one such jar had a wide rolled up lip curving back over the shoulder and colored in light terra cotta.

A large jar was in underglaze blue and gold on white porcelain body and the blue looked almost exactly like real lapis. The form was simple and quite satisfying.

There were also some photographic gold portrait plaques, service pieces with purple landscapes, etc., but they did not harm the real joy found in the work of other artists at this factory, though these artists remained nameless.

POLAND

Poland showed a couple of saints in badly modeled, low-fired cream pottery of pinkish hue, some heavy stoneware plates, vases of amateurish shapes, metallic lustres with blended effects, mannered "modern" vases and various copies of Persian wares. Nothing approached their embroidered arts or the other crafts.

Ginori

FIG. 1404.

CZECHOSLOVAKIA

Czechoslovakia had some faïence of the usual sort including a puzzle pitcher with three spouts and pierced neck, but nothing of interest.

RUSSIA

Russia has had a strange turn for the literal and naturalistic. The artists seem to have so much of a story to tell that art is forgotten. This artistic hysteria is like that of a public speaker so unsure that he heaps statistics, fact upon fact, until he bores his audience. And again there seems to be little of the true bourgeois appeal for only the British can surpass their wares for royal ostentation and bad taste.

Nadezhda Zamyatina had some small female "Tartar Dancers," very sexy but I had to examine them with care to determine in the case whether they were porcelain or actually carved out of ivory. There was also a "vase for desk" in the form of a book case with a girl sitting in front of it with an open book in her lap. Can anyone imagine a more appropriate subject!

The Dulevsky Porcelain Factory had a well modeled figure of "Chapayev on Horseback" by Alexander Sotnikov and some "Cossack Dancers" by the same artist. The first figure was also done by Orlov with overglaze colors.

Dulevsky had some dinner services much in the late 18th century French style with the "Order of Lenin" and the "Red Banner" motives.

FIG. 1405. Typical "Ku-Yüeh Hsüan type" eggshell vase with carefully shaded painting in delicate famille rose enamels and a square Ch'ien Lung seal mark in blue enamel. Ht. 7½". Ex Warren E. Cox Coll.

FIG. 1406. Reproduction of incorrect shape and too sweet colors of famille verte porcelain. It has a double ring underglaze blue mark. Ht. 11¼". T. C. Lee–Warren E. Cox Coll.

FIG. 1407. Modern Tz'u Chou pottery vase with sandy buff body, a sort of st.cky cream slip and glaze, and too sharp, crowded black design. The form also is not Sung. Ht. 11". Warren E. Cox Coll.

FIG. 1408. Reproductions of "peach bloom" vases of crude potting, the smaller having a dull, spotty glaze while the larger has a too glassy pale yellowish green glaze with traces of pink and an odd crackle. Both have six character K'ang Hsi marks in the underglaze blue. Hts. 6¼" and 7¼". Perry Moore–Warren E. Cox Coll.

There were several large vases a yard or more in height. One had views of Moscow, parades, etc., on it and was by Tamara Bezpalova. Another with hunting scenes by Ivan Riznich looked much like the chromos of the early 19th century calendar art. Others were called, "Twenty Years of the Red Army," "The Mosco-Volga Canal," etc., and were by Ludmila Protopopova.

Left: 19th cent. beautiful figure of Kwan Yin in brown-crackled glaze and face and hands in ivory white. It is very large. Ht. 53″. C. T. Loo & Co.

Right: Modern eggshell porcelain vase of the so called, Ku Yüeh Hsüan (See Ch'ien Lung section) type with a seal mark of that period in blue enamel. It has a coral red ground over which is delicate tracery of gold and in which are reserved medallions beautifully painted. Ht. about 8″. T. C. Lee–Warren E. Cox Coll. Now in Nai Chi Chang Coll.

CHINESE 19TH AND 20TH CENTURY PORCELAINS

PLATE 235

So much for the various sections of the New York 1939 Fair. It is obvious that our times will not go down as a great era of art achievement but there were some fairly nice things here and there.

The Far Eastern exhibitions had little to show but the Japanese continue to make copies of both the Chinese wares and their own which are altogether too good and sometimes really dangerous to the unwary collector, while China turns out some perfectly beautiful modern wares among which are very fine egg-shell bowls marked with Yung lo characters delicately incised in the inside of the bottom and dragons about the sides in good style. Among the

FIG. 1409. A modern Japanese reproduction of a Korai "mishima" bowl too glassy in appearance, fired on a foot-rim instead of spurs and having three spots of red in the center flowers, all of which are not characteristic. Dia. 7". Fritz Low–Beer Coll.

FIG. 1410. Paper-thin egg-shell bowl of slightly greenish white beautifully incised with clouds and dragons and on the bottom inside a four character Yung Lo, Ming mark, before glazing. This type does not, so far as I know, copy any existing Yung Lo type of bowl but some unwary collectors have been taken in by such pieces. The difference in price is about $15 against a minimum of several thousands. Dia. 5". T. C. Lee–Warren E. Cox Coll.

FIG. 1412. Modern porcelain bowl made at Ching-tê Chêng and decorated with too brilliant famille rose enamels. The marks are six character Ch'ien Lung ones in script in faint iron red. Dia. 6¾". Perry Moore–Warren E. Cox Coll.

FIG. 1411. Vase of the K'ang Hsi famille verte style of pure white porcelain (too white and glossy) and well painted in too brilliant enamels. Has a green enamel leaf mark. Ht. 6½". Modern Ching-tê Chêng. T. C. Lee–Warren E. Cox Coll.

FIG. 1413. Modern vase made at Ching-tê Chêng of the heavy "Ku-Yüeh Hsüan" type and with the usual square seal mark of Ch'ien Lung in blue enamel. The ground is dull iron-red with gold tracery and the reserved medallions are beautifully painted in the shaded style influenced by western painting. Ht. 9¾". T. C. Lee–Warren E. Cox Coll.

excellent wares are also "Ku Yueh Hsüan" wares of fine porcelain beautifully painted and all properly marked in blue enamel or lavender enamel marks. Potteries and stonewares are no less generally good and modern celadons, Tz'u chou wares and Tsung Sê wares are deceiving. I show a few for comparison. In Korean celadon and "mishima" again excellent copies are made by a factory there but the tendency with these wares is to introduce too much red and make the designs too overdone. Only once in a while does one come along which is an exact copy of some fine old piece.

Japan also has copied "Lowestoft" and other commercial European wares very crudely for the decorative market.

Again there is a thriving business in the Near East copying the "Kashan" oil jars and one can find the results in almost any rug shop window, but these lack all the true character of the 17th and 18th century specimens.

CHAPTER XXX

CONTEMPORARY AMERICAN CERAMICS

MUCH has been said as to the sources of modern design in the preceding chapter but the development here in America is somewhat different from that of Europe or Asia. There are three pretty well defined classifications:

1.—Commercial suppliers of building materials and table ware.
2.—Individual potters both amateur and professional.
3.—Sculptors who work more or less in ceramics.

There is practically no artistic merit left in the first classification for obvious reasons. So far as the architectural suppliers are concerned there is a noticeable attempt to try to make pottery tiles look like wooden ones or asbestos ones or any other medium other than what they really are. Stone, gold and other substances are copied probably at the direction of the architects. Thus the Ludowici Celadon Co. got out a booklet showing "Georgian" and "Provincial Shingle Tiles," etc. Again the Gladding McBean & Co. advertising speaks of "Granitex-finish ceramic veneer," for steel sheathing.

Another characteristic is shown by this same company which gets out a booklet telling us that the company was founded by Peter McGill McBean in 1875 and showing "improved Hermosa tile" and "Franciscan table ware" with pride, but not mentioning one word about any artist that may have worked for them. The architects are given ample mention even when the lowly urns are spoken of in connection with the Beverly Hills Post Office. The designer of the "Franciscan ware" is said to be "one of America's foremost merchandise stylists." In the Northwestern Terra Cotta Corp. material we find two artists mentioned, J. H. Lambert and B. Leo Steif neither of whom are Americans and both of whom are architects. These gentlemen and Mr. Andre Alizier did doorways very much reminiscent of Edgar Brandt's metal work with flattened rosettes and wavy lines. Even this sort of imitative trash was slapped around two reliefs of Will Rogers for the high school of his name in Tulsa.

The Northwestern claims that, "Chicago's Michigan Avenue is virtually a 'Terra-Cotta Boulevard'" implying that it is largely theirs. Why they do not pay more attention to the quality of their quantity I do not know. Other such companies are the older Atlantic Terra Cotta Co., the Federal Seaboard Terra Cotta Corp., the Galloway Terra Cotta Co. of Philadelphia, The Mosaic Tile Co., Ohio, Conkling Armstrong, etc. The materials that these companies turn out or turned out could produce really beautiful effects. Once in a great

1048

while a really fine work of art is made such as the pediment for the Pennsylvania Museum which I shall describe under the work of C. Paul Jennewein and which was executed at the Atlantic Terra Cotta Co., but it is seldom the case.

It is not necessary to go into detail about the "Kitchen and Garden" pottery such as that made by the Galloway Terra Cotta Co. and Homer Laughlin China Co. The latter is making simple and heavy ware colored with plain light and dark blue, yellow, green and orange glazes, the idea being that one should mix the colors in setting a table.

Fig. 1414. A simple and well designed set called the "Rancho pattern" made by Gladding, Mc-Bean & Co.

Also in the commercial field is the Fulper Pottery started in 1805 in Flemington, N. J. In 1928 a larger plant was built in Trenton, N. J., and a claim is made that many pieces are hand made though this is not obvious from looking at the wares. J. M. Stangl has been president for about 30 years and the wares are marked "STANGL." They claim to have made the first solid color ware; a modest boast! And also claim the very practical feature that the ware is "oven proof," that is, it will not crack from fairly quick transitions between heat and cold. They also make wares of a "peasant type" which, however, are of no particular note. "Art ware, lamps, vases, flower pots, ash trays and countless other items in all shapes," cater to the small gift shop and store trade. The wares are called pottery but are said to be fired at 2200° to 2300° Fahrenheit which would be a fair heat for stoneware or even porcelain.

FIG. 1416. Fulper pottery sent as examples of their best work, "very simple but effective patterns."

FIG. 1415. Terra cotta panels made for the Will Rogers High School, Tulsa, Okla. which do not bear the artist's name and which show somewhat inappropriate use of designs obviously taken from Edgar Brandt's iron work which have nothing to do with either Mr. Rogers or Oklahoma. Northwestern Terra Cotta Co.

FIG. 1417. It will be noted that both of these very simple designs are on the same shapes.

LENOX BELLEEK

Walter Scott Lenox worked as an apprentice in the Ott & Brewer factory and Willetts Pottery, Trenton, and became manager of the former. In 1889 he formed a partnership with Jonathan Coxon, Sr., in the Ceramic Art Co. until 1894 when he acquired his partner's share and continued until 1906 when he organized the Lenox Co.

His intention from the first was to make a similar ware to the Irish Belleek and he employed two potters who had worked at Castle Caldwell and were in this country. Actually what he did is more pleasing than the original Belleek in some ways. The Irish ware is very thin, cold white and covered with a lustre which has a high sheen. Dainty things were done with it and it seemed to escape much of the blight of the period but it was at times over-ornate. The Lenox ware is warmer in tone, perhaps even more translucent and not so lustrous, being more like highly polished ivory.

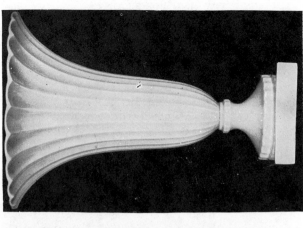

LENOX BELLEEK

PLATE 236

Left: The two color effects are well carried out and one wishes only for a somewhat more characterful design than such things as these little flowers. Lenox Co. *Center:* Swan bowl made by the Ceramic Art Co. of Trenton, N. J., about 1889–1896, the immediate predecessor of Lenox, and marked *C. A. C. Belleek.* Ht. 4¾". Brooklyn Mus. *Right:* This simple shape is beautifully proportioned and lends itself to charming flower arrangements. Lenox Co.

Harry A. Brown managed the factory for some years before the death of Lenox in 1920 and carried on after that time. Frank G. Holmes has been the chief designer for many years and he is responsible for the simplicity, grace and restraint which have marked the products. William H. Clayton who was an apprentice of Lenox has also been a powerful factor.

This ware is made of clay, feldspar and flint mixed with filtered water. The feldspar comes from New England and after being reduced to a fine, white powder by grinding under an ancient millstone is mixed with the clay and

FIG. 1418. Mr. Holmes often uses even thinner and more sparse decoration for the Lenox services. Of course this does show off the beautiful material to advantage.
FIG. 1419. Frank G. Holmes employs fluting in a great many of his designs for Lenox and it has a sort of neo-classic charm. One must admit that the factory always carries it out accurately.
FIG. 1420. A simple neo-classic feeling makes this service very chaste and in good taste in a formal way. Lenox Co.

placed in a large revolving cylinder, lined with porcelain blocks and containing some water and flint pebbles, where they are, "pebble ground." Even the number of revolutions is counted so that all results will be entirely uniform. It takes fifty hours to complete the, "pebble grinding," and then the mixture is forced by compressed air through a fine wire screen containing 200 meshes to the square inch and the slip is produced. But it is not finished for it then passes over electro-magnets which remove all iron particles and enters into an aging process. We do not know what this aging really accomplishes, though many opinions have been advanced but it is an old process and the results are certainly better when it is followed. At Lenox it is "aged" for only a few days (not years as in ancient China) when it is ready for casting or for the "jiggering" machine. This is simply a wheel, power driven, and upon which cups and plates are made over a plaster mould or into a plaster mould. A "profile" is necessary in many cases. The elaborate shapes are, of course, moulded, as has been done for years, in a plaster mould.

Firing is done in saggers and the men have become expert in balancing them upon their heads as they climb the ladders to stack the kiln. The heat is brought to 2200° Fahrenheit and it is interesting to note that the kilns would burst, if not bound with steel bands. Cones which wilt under certain heats are no longer used, their place having been taken by pyrometers. The firing is done for 30 hours and cooling for two days.

This produces the biscuit ware which is then sand blasted to remove any irregularities. Finally they are cleaned of any particles by compressed air. and dipped into the glaze. The second firing is done at 2100° F. and in ; kiln called the "glost kiln."

Decoration is all surface and consists of the old processes of etching with hydrofluoric acid, and applying of gold and overglaze colors. Some powdered colors are applied and both etched outlines and transfer prints are used though these are often touched up by hand. All imperfect ware is destroyed and not offered for sale.

Obviously this factory aims toward a super perfection which is undoubtedly achieved and for the small flaw-finding mind of the commercial buyers it has great appeal. That the material is beautiful no one can deny but just as obviously the "jiggering machines," use of molds, etc., eliminates all expression of the hand and though these things are simple and pleasant they are far from inspired works of art. The table ware is tasteful and has charm.

ROOKWOOD

One factory which did overlap the commercial and artistic field was the Rookwood Pottery of Cincinnati. It was started in 1880 by Maria Longworth Storer after experiments in the Dallas Granite Ware Factory where she noted that the high fire destroyed all colors except blue and black. The factory was financed by Mrs. Storer's father to, "give employment to the idle rich." In 1883 William Watts Taylor became a partner and in 1890 Mrs. Storer retired. Later John D. Wareham became president and treasurer.

From its earliest days the decoration consisted in "the application to wet clay pieces of metallic oxides mixed with clay and water or what is technically known as slip, so that the colors become of the very substance and fibre of the piece." Low relief simple modeling is often used. About 1883 "tiger-eye" and "goldstone" glazes were used. Less kindly critics called this "the molasses period," but these glazes did have a depth seldom equaled. Crystalline effects

FIG. 1421. Rookwood vase decorated with various colored porcelain glazes. It will be noted that in this and other pieces from this kiln an artistic effect is sought by a softening of the line somewhat as early photographers obtained it by throwing a picture out of focus.

FIG. 1422. "Sung Plum (reduction)" glazed vase so named but, if it is meant that it has any relation to Chün yao, we must disagree for neither in shape nor in glaze is there any slightest perceptible similarity. Rookwood c. 1935.

FIG. 1423. Weak and wandering pseudo Chinese design motifs, applied in a way that shows lack of understanding, have been used for years by Rookwood on very safe vase forms. This vase shown on a cheapest possible teakwood stand is typical and one dislikes seeing such technical skill so misused.

An early Rookwood jar showing the Japanese influence which was popular at the time, dating between 1880 and 1884.

"Tiger eye" Rookwood ware made from 1884 to the present and rather typical of the factory.

"Mat glazed" type of Rookwood which shows considerable influence of the French pottery of the time, 1896, made by Emile Decoeur and his followers. The soft texture and color has some appeal.

"Iris type glaze" of the type made between 1900 and 1920. It has a certain depth but is glassy and unpleasant in some ways. However, the vase is nevertheless well designed and well decorated to suit the shape.

Contemporary jar with red clay and porcelain glaze by John D. Wareham. The sturdy shape is well related to the very impressionistic bull and flower design.

"Vellum glazed" or transparent mat glazed vase over design of colored clay. This type was done from about 1900, the particular one shown dates 1904. It is evident that more attention was paid to the texture than to the design.

ROOKWOOD POTTERY
PLATE 237

were obtained in the glaze and not on the surface as in the Copenhagen wares of this nature.

In 1896 mat glazes were produced and "Iris" of pale tone and "Sea Green" were first shown in Paris in 1900. In 1904 the first "Vellum" glazes were made by Stanley Burt, while later came "Ombroso" 1910, "Soft Porcelain" 1915 and a revival of "Tiger-eye" 1920 along with "Oxblood," "Flambé," and a "special red" following the European and English enthusiasm for these effects

In fact there was probably too much following of the "early modern" French potters.

The firing was done around 2000° F. for a period of 24 to 36 hours and allowed to cool for three or four days. Later the piece was glazed and refired.

Artistically speaking the product was probably about as high as any turned out in America though all the ills of the times are also reflected in it. Artists were largely from the local Cincinnati school and among them were Valentine, Daly, McDonald and Shiryama. Mr. Wareham also has made some fine pieces. A celadon was unpleasantly overglossy and the shapes are often anty though some good strong ones do occur. An idea can be obtained by noting the fine jar with a bull on it and the celadon both by Mr. Wareham which are illustrated.

Fig. 1424. An early Rookwood piece by Mrs. Storer and called "Limoges painting" though why it is so called escapes me.

Fig. 1426. Mat glazed Rookwood vase showing influence of Emil Decoeur and his French followers but fairly strong in shape and having a design with concavities well designed to catch and hold the glaze interestingly.

Fig. 1425. "Celadon and turquoise glazes" are used on this vase by Mr. Wareham which in its glassy slickness has all the unpleasantness of modern Japanese commercial celadons with only the advantage of a turquoise note introduced, perhaps not so very much to its benefit.

Unfortunately this factory has been closed recently and I doubt that it will ever again be reopened. A Mr. Walter Schott, dealer in second-hand automobiles in Cincinnati, has purchased the stock and is trying to give the impression that the kilns are still working in order to help sell it off, but nothing new comes out of the place. If our government had been as far sighted as that of Denmark, this establishment might have rivaled that of the Royal Copenhagen one in foreign propaganda and building of a pride in home products.

KENTON HILLS

Meanwhile some of the men from Rookwood have started the Kenton Hills Porcelains factory in Erlanger, Ky. Harold F. Bopp was listed as production manager and chemist, David W. Seyler, art director and sculptor, William E. Hentschel, designer, and Rosemary Dickman and Alza Stratton are down as decorators. These are all Art Academy of Cincinnati people except Bopp, who, I believe, is no longer an associate.

Their work is very much along the lines of what they were doing at Rook-

Fig. 1429. Small Kenton Hills jar called "Ox blood" but really of a crushed straw-berry color. Ht. 4¼".

Fig. 1427. Kenton Hills small yellow vase with white and brown decoration signed Hentschel. Ht. 5¼".

Fig. 1428. Kenton Hills porcelain vase with starch-blue glaze and well designed form and decoration. Ht. 12¾".

wood and Mr. Seyler has told me that they still regret conditions at the older pottery. Due to the war and draft, this organization has closed temporarily but plans to continue when hostilities cease. They also are trying to straddle the commercial fence and on which side they finally alight will be interesting to note.

INDIVIDUAL AND AMATEUR POTTERS

Certainly one of the most fundamental of our modern potters is Leon Volkmar of Bedford, N. Y., whom I show here at work in a few stills from his wonderful moving picture detailing every step of the making of a vase. He was born in France, 1879, studied in the National Academy from 1898 to 1901 and the year following took up the career of potter. His father, Charles, was a well known painter. He joined the Durant Kilns in 1911 and continued after the death of his associate Durant Rice in 1919, discontinuing the trade name in about 1928. His glazes include the copper blues and reds, aubergine, yellows, etc., and some browns and blacks. Applied designs, crystalline glazes, etc., never interested him as he was always trying for simple forms with fine color and texture. The Near Eastern influence was strong but never that of Japan. He says, "I have since held quite steadily that an artist's work that stems out of the historic past need not for that reason be lacking as an expression of that artist's personality; that originality does not consist in seeking out ways, types and processes that have never been thought of before for this way lies the 'novel,' the 'bizarre' and not least the 'commercial' in the commoner sense." He has done work for some of the finest patrons and is represented in several museums and has taught in Pratt Institute, Penn. Museum School of Industrial Art, Teachers College, Columbia University and was Professor of Ceramics in the University of Ceramics, Cincinnati.

It is impossible to give an idea of the depth and beauty of the glazes he has devised but the pieces shown will speak for themselves as to the integrity of his work and the fine sturdiness which most everything he touches seems to develop.

In the building of a vase we see him at work first "wedging" and "kneading" the clay to get it entirely a smooth and homogeneous mass. We will remember that this was all done with machines at the Lenox plant and the mass was kept thin for molding. The turning process demands infinitely more manual labor.

Fig. 1432. Copper reduction glaze of the texture of some Chün or flambé types. The form is also somewhat reminiscent of the Chün hexagonal flowerpots. Leon Volkmar. Cranbrook Foundation Mus.

Fig. 1430. Pottery with enamel decoration in turquoise, cobalt, yellow, aubergine and cream. Leon Volkmar.

Fig. 1431. Jar in turquoise, cobalt and cream which won the bronze medal in the Paris Exposition 1937. Leon Volkmar.

Next we see him carefully centering the lump of clay on the wheel and then, by foot power alone because it can better govern the speed, the turning begins and the lump is brought upward, while, at the same time, the inside is hollowed out. As the pressure from within might break through, the outer wall must be supported with one hand while the other works its way downward. Then a scraper is used to even the surface. (You will note that this is not a template with the form of the side already determined.)

The finishing touches are those in which the final refinements are accomplished and they take great care. I show Mr. Volkmar shaping a lip-rim. Later the surface has to be more or less smooth, the foot-rim must be shaped, etc., before the start of decoration and glazing and final firing during which, of course, the whole may be lost.

When one knows how thorough and painstaking the craftsman must be, what a skillful and tricky business it is to turn well on the wheel and how little the appreciation for honest craftsmanship is felt in this country; when one considers the knowledge and training necessary to make one good pot and the hard work involved in making every single good pot even after one knows all about it—then one can appreciate the courage that it takes to give a lifetime to this art, but, one way and another, many work at it.

In nearly every small town and in all the cities there are individual kilns

The clay has to be left out in the sun to dry partially after it has been put through a sieve and carefully strained. Here it is being picked up out of the container. Leon Volkmar.

A few steps in the making of a vase from a handful of clay. The pounding and wedging. Leon Volkmar.

Centering the lump on the wheel is a careful business the lack of which may end in catastrophe due to centrifugal force. I have seen a piece fly across the room. Leon Volkmar.

Here the actual turning has progressed somewhat and the clay has been pressed upward. Leon Volkmar.

LEON VOLKMAR SHOWS STAGES IN VASE-MAKING I

Plate 238

Pressing from within and also from the outside, the hollowed cylinder is taking form. Leon Volkmar.

Here the scraper is brought into use to even up the grooves made by the fingers. Some Chinese potters feature these very grooves. (See Sung T'zu Chin wares.) Leon Volkmar.

As the neck takes shape the lip-rim is treated. When one notes the delicate handling in mid air and without arm rest, one begins to appreciate some of the paper thin lips of Ying Ching and other Chinese wares. Leon Volkmar.

The master-potter, after the tense effort, is putting the final surface touches upon his work. Through his mind is going a series of questions: Should the neck be pulled up and elongated a trifle? Does the lip flare sufficiently? Has the body enough lift in it? etc. Now everything is in a fluid moment of conception. Tomorrow it will have become a hard and well nigh permanent achievement. Leon Volkmar.

LEON VOLKMAR SHOWS STAGES IN VASE-MAKING II

PLATE 239

in operation. In the times of our grandmothers when ladies painted pansies on everything from the coal scuttles to the bottoms of frying pans the artiness led to much china painting, and when the Japanese influence was felt from the Paris Exposition many went in for potteries. In time the Syracuse Museum of Fine Arts, whose director is Anna Wetherill Olmsted, became a sort of center.

In 1932 a small exhibition was organized in "Memory of Adelaide Alsop Robineau," and in 1936 an exhibition was organized to send to Kunstindustrimuseum in Copenhagen, which later went to Stockholm, Gothenburg, Helsingfors, Stoke-on-Trent and the Whitney Museum, New York. It was financed by the Rockefeller Foundation.

The aims of this society are "To improve ceramic art in America, to educate the American public and to make sales for ceramic artists." A greater concentration on the first might further the latter projects. As sales made

FIG. 1434. "Student Singers" by Russell Barnett Aitken which has some element of cartoonist humor of a broad nature.

FIG. 1433. "Europa" by Russell Barnett Aitken.

FIG. 1435. Russell Barnett Aitken's cartoonist qualities again appear in "The Hunter."

Miss Olmsted mentions: 1.—The securing of a job with the late Dwight James Baum, architect, for "Edward Winter's enamels on sheet metal." 2.—The sale of a chess set by Peter Ganine for the purpose of manufacture in bakelite. What these did to further ceramic arts is doubtful. Miss Olmsted says, "Visitors have been frankly amazed after coming in a trifle high-hattedly with the expectation of seeing rows upon rows of dinnerware when they discover instead Archipenko's glazed terra cotta life-sized figures," and I should think they might be for I have heard of those who were amazed at almost anything done by this artist. By "glazed terra cotta," we suppose Miss Olmsted means pottery. The statement preceding this quotes, " 'More beautiful things for everyday life' runs the Swedish motto—and if Sweden, why not America?" What on earth would one do with a life-sized Archipenko figure in everyday life?

The paper ends with the flat statement that "American ceramic art has come of age and can hold its own with the contemporary output of any country in the world." This is, of course, ridiculous for we cannot match either technically or artistically the modern wares of China, Japan, or Denmark. But let us see the wares on which Miss Olmsted's boast is made.

Russell Barnett Aitken was given the frontispiece in the catalogue of the last show before the war for a childlike bit of humorous cartooning called

Fig. 1437. Salt glazed stoneware jar and cover by Charles M. Harder. A good, sturdy job. Charles M. Harder, Alfred, N. Y.

Fig. 1436. Jar and plate by Edgar Littlefield which won a prize in 1935. The forms and decoration are sound and the glazes appear interesting particularly in the mottled quality of the jar.

"Student singers." Besides this he also had two other of the sixteen illustrations. I leave the reader to judge the "Europa" and "Hunter" for themselves.

Edgar Littlefield received the first prize given by the Onondaga Pottery for the fourth annual exhibition with some heavy but well formed pieces with

Fig. 1438. "Fish scale" crackle glaze with slip decoration in gray and black. This has nothing to do with the Chinese "fish roe" crackle, of course. The design gives good texture to the piece. Charles M. Harder, Alfred, N. Y.

Fig. 1439. This group of pieces by Gertrude and Otto Natzler are well potted and show a sensitive appreciation of form but the glaze in its weak interpretation of the rough Japanese feeling is neither practical nor attractive. Syracuse Mus. of Fine Arts.

geometrical designs and soft glazes very reminiscent of the wares of Decoeur and other French followers.

Charles M. Harder's work is similar in its simplicity and attention to textures. He is the head of the department of industrial design at The New York State College of Ceramics at Alfred, N. Y., was born in Alabama but lived in Texas and graduated from The Art Institute of Chicago, the same school in which he is now teaching. He writes me, "When I do break down and decorate, I try to 'ram it into the wet clay' while the pot is fresh, and tie it up with the glaze treatment in such a way that it can't get away from the form." He likes, "plastic quality" and "function," as who does not. Glen Lukens is of simi-

Fig. 1440. Deep cup by Mary Yancey Hodgdon which has some good qualities though strongly influenced by the Japanese mannerisms of the 19th cent. The dish is by Glen Lukens. Syracuse Mus. of Fine Arts.

Fig. 1441. Two fairly well formed but thick and clumsy pieces by Glen Lukens finished in what he calls, "Death Valley raw yellow alkaline glaze." Syracuse Mus. of Fine Arts.

lar persuasion but covers his wares with what he calls, "Death Valley raw yellow alkaline glaze." Gertrude and Otto Natzler won another prize with some thin and well potted bowls with dry and what appear to be only partly fluxed glazes roughly applied to bowls and dishes which would certainly be hard to wash clean. Mary Yancay Hodgdon showed a wheel marked cup of Japanese style with a rich glaze inside and running irregularly over the lip. She also showed a dish with thick scratched out glaze design. Carl Walters in the eighth show had a plate reminiscent of 9th century Rakka ware and a weak imitation of the Egyptian hippopotamus with foliage patterns on the sides and top. Karl Drerup had a tall grey porcelain vase fired by Von Tury. Josef von Tury has made an ingenious arrangement with the Ford Works of New Jersey to use the space between toilet seats, and other large pieces which they fire, for his vases in the kiln. Tury is a well trained European ceramist and like Walter Howat has really been responsible for much that appears under the names of others.

None of the above work is any more than less-good imitations of styles already established by others, but Harold Riegger received a prize for a stoneware bottle unglazed, which is sure and has fine points. It recalls no ancient ware. The form is pleasing, the wheel marks well related to it and the whole

Three thinly potted and very beautiful small cups made by Frank Reuss Kelley, having underglaze decoration, slip and blended glaze decoration fired at about 2470° F. The slip-ware piece on the right has some characteristics of the Sung though it is in no way a copy. The center piece of softly blended ivory and dull brown tones is an example of the finest potting in all respects. Hts. about 2½" to 4".

Two charming cups by Paul Freigang showing fine porcelain forms and simple well related and original design.

Left: Deep cup by Frank Reuss Kelley decorated with some of his own crystalline glaze which is deep blue with rose crystals evenly distributed and graduated from large to small at the top. Ht. about 5".

Right: This fine, sure piece of potting by Harold Riegger is one of the best examples of use of wheel marks for ornamentation that I have ever seen. Its proportions give it a towering upward lift, it has a good sturdy neck to grasp, a practical mouth for pouring and a well proportioned practical base. Syracuse Mus. of Fine Arts.

Left: Vase of beautiful form and fine proportions covered down to near the bottom with a transmutation glaze. Leon Volkmar, Mrs. Beagle Coll.

MODERN AMERICAN PIECES

PLATE 240

thing very satisfying. I shall be interested to see more of this man's work.

Henry Varnum Poor also won a prize for an oval bowl which is typical of his style. Mr. Poor is a painter of fair success in a modern manner and his wares are more interesting to him as presenting a surface on which he can draw or paint than objects conceived as beautiful entities in themselves. The quality is that of faïence or majolica, the clay he uses is local from Rockland County, N. Y. Though the craftsmanship is rather sloppy, it is sincere work and he may do something really fine yet.

Fig. 1442. The Hippopotamus is a frank copy of the Egyptian ones and shows a flowery character which is no improvement. The plate is strongly reminiscent of 9th cent. Rakka ware but lacking in the original vitality and strength. Both are by Carl Walters. Syracuse Mus. of Fine Arts.

Fig. 1443. Platter by Henry Varnum Poor which shows more promise than any of his earlier work. Syracuse Mus. of Fine Arts.

Sculptural work seems to take up fully half of the work of the Syracuse group despite their ambition for usefulness and perhaps the best is by Waylande Gregory an erratic and changeable sort of man in both personality and work. It is hard to describe his endeavors for his restless virtuosity is now sensitive and delicate as in the "Head of Child," in this exhibition, now humorous as in the figures representing octaves in a "Musical Fountain," or the very baroque figure he has in the pool at his own home or again fearful as in his "Fountain of the Atom," at the New York World's Fair. He has told me that "Sex is the motive power," of much that he does and yet his work is so purposely distorted in most instances as not to make this element at all moving to the ordinary man. He has a kiln of his own and boasts that he does his own firing. I do not rate him as a first class sculptor but his things are amusing and he understands the medium, though it is his temperament to exaggerate.

Of the others, Paul Bogatay shows little. Sorcha Boru's naïve short-legged animals with stupid expressions are uninteresting, Carl Walters' similar ones are better designed and more interesting and a host of modelers of small figures such as Thelma Frazier, Alexander Blazys, Walter J. Anderson and Viktor Schreckengost have done things which are full of the tiresome cuteness called

"exquisite humor," by Miss Olmsted. It is to be noted that the general trick of the babies as seen in Frazier's, "Pegasi on Tracks," is very close to that

FIG. 1447. I do not know whether Thelma Frazier did this "Pegasi on Tracks" before Schreckengost's "Smoked Ham" or after but it is cute in an almost identical manner except that it is not carried out in true pottery, the structure being so conceived as to necessitate the use of a metal rod. Cup by Josef Von Tury who is a well-known technician and gets some pleasant, interesting glazes. Excellent form. Syracuse Mus. of Fine Arts.

FIG. 1446. Thelma Frazier seems to have paralleled another potter's perhaps too original idea for certainly there is here a similarity in what might be called baloney sausage forms to those shown by Brastoff. This is found "an outstanding piece of whimsical sculpture," by Miss Olmsted. Syracuse Mus. of Art

on Schreckengost's "Smoked Ham." Another similarity is noticeable between the figures of Frazier's, "Marguerita and the Jewels," and Sascha Brastoff's, "Emergence." I sincerely hope that this is not going to be the commencement of a whole school or style of what Miss Olmsted says is "always delightful and with no trace of vulgarity."

This society represents a fair cross section of what is being done among independent and amateur potters of the country but there are a few more about whom we should have a word. Paul Freigang is an European trained

FIG. 1448. Cookie-jar by Arthur E. Baggs of salt-glazed stoneware. No new invention in loop handles but they are adequate to get fingers into which was not always the case even in Greek wares, and knob on cover is beautifully harmonized with them. An honest, intelligent piece of craftsmanship which rises to a degree of really fine art. Syracuse Mus. of Fine Arts.

FIG. 1449. Three pieces by Maija Grotell. Large cylinder 21″ of dark grey body with semi-opaque white mat glaze. Two firings at 2400° F. Shape recalls Chinese "symbol of earth" save that it has not proper eight divisions and is round. Small cylinder 14½″ is in blue-grey, tan and brown slip decorated and having "an ash glaze." One firing at 2450° F. Globular jar 12″ has an "inlayed crackle glaze in pastel colors." It is a borax glaze and had two firings at 2400° F. Recalls spotted Yüeh and Lung-ch'üan wares.

FIG. 1450. Charming bit of reticulated ware surely and expertly handled, not quite the "devil's work" of the Chinese masters but having considerable charm of its own, by Paul Freigang.

FIG. 1451. Large and well modeled vase of sturdy proportions and interesting design by Paul Freigang. Stoneware.

potter who has been practicing in this country for many years and is not only a top notch technician but a very real artist The three vases, one with incised slip, one with low relief modeled design and one reticulated, show sturdy and sound form and well adapted design of original character. The bowls are charming in form and color. The two cups are exquisite in every feature. He is not active just now but has plans for starting a new kiln before long.

Maija Grotell is another excellent potter. She graduated from the Academy of Art and Industrie, Helsingfors, Finland, has taught in a number of good centers including the Henry Street Settlement and Rutgers University, and is now instructing in the Cranbrook Academy of Art, Michigan. The Metropolitan Museum and Detroit Institute of Art own examples of her work. She works largely in stoneware and seems to like the rough textured surfaces of a "modern art" vogue but understands good potting and some of her things have considerable charm.

Fig. 1452. Well made flower bowl of pottery showing Japanese influence but distinctly original in its carrying out. Mrs. Mary Door.

Fig. 1453. Well conceived and beautifully made bowl for flowers. Glaze is mat type well suited to form. Mrs. Mary Door.

A man who grew up in potting is Arthur E. Baggs born in Alfred, inoculated and partly educated by Charles F. Binns, Founding Director of the N. Y. State School of Clay Working and Ceramics, now the N. Y. State College of Ceramics at Alfred. He developed and finally became owner of the Marblehead Potteries, Mass., assisted in the development of the Cowan Pottery Studios, Rocky River, Ohio and taught at Ethical Cultural School, N. Y., Cleveland School of Art and finally at Ohio State University, where he now is. Mr. Baggs says his chief interests are: 1.—Creative experimenting in design and technology of ceramics, and 2.—trying to interest recruits in the same absorbing job. His cookie-jar of salt-glazed stoneware shows fine structural form and a useful and beautiful development of the old-time loop handles, and the cover-knob.

One of our best American potters, a great technician and true artist is Frank Reuss Kelley

Fig. 1454. Porcelain jar by Frank Reuss Kelley fired at about 2470° F. and decorated with his own glazes. This piece shows his fine feeling for good structural form. Ht. c. 9".

of Norwalk, Connecticut. He studied in Alsace and has made many hundreds of experiments with various body clays and glazes with the result that he can actually produce some of the most surprising and beautiful of effects. He tells me that he has an open method of firing without a sagger. But his forms would be outstanding alone for their vigor and sure potting sense. Unfortunately Mr. Kelley is somewhat disgusted with the uphill job of earning a living at making pottery and has now ceased to work. I sincerely hope that someone will come along and make it possible for this truly fine artist to continue.

A few pieces which I have designed are also shown. These were fired by Walter Howat as were most of the following sculptured examples. Mr. Howat is a chemist who worked at the Atlantic Terra Cotta Co. and then set up a kiln in his own back yard at Tottenville, S. I. He is aided by his wife and daughter and employs a number of other assistants. Technically I believe he knows more about the obtaining of various glazes in textures and colors to suit the piece than any other potter in America. These pieces of ours are designed for lamp bases and the glazes are an excellent celadon of both the Lung Ch'üan and "northern Sung" types, "imperial yellow," coral red, starch blue, a Ming type lead glaze, and the transparent type used on Tz'u Chou forms over slip. Some of my forms are traditional, some are adapted and slightly changed and some are entirely without precedent. These are, of course, all molded pieces though we have attempted to get some hand work into the incising of the slips, making of handles, etc.

Fig. 1455. Modified T'ang amphora designed by the author and fired by Walter Howat. Color is dull chartreuse.

SCULPTORS

Lu Duble is a sculptress who spent several years in Haiti and has caught the feeling of the natives very well in her "Head of a Young Woman" and

Fig. 1457. "Agriculture" by Henry Kreis. Only 15" long but has an almost monumental feeling. Masses simply handled and slight flattening of surfaces and economy of detailed decoration give it power.

Fig. 1456. Life-sized study of young woman in Haiti by Lu Duble. A good portrait, full of the movement of these people. An outstanding terra cotta.

Original design Tz'u Chou type bottle by the author, carried out by Agnes and Walter Howat. Body buff-grey, the slip hand carved by Mrs. Howat.

A helical twist bottle designed for use with a celadon or thick yellow glaze which accents form and surface texture.

Small Tz'u Chou type vase having incised slip executed by Agnes Howat. Bold crackle stained after firing.

Original "fig formed" vase designed particularly to be used with celadon glaze which runs thin on high ridges and deep in grooves.

Yung Chêng vase form slightly modified. Colors yellow, iron red, pale blue and celadon.

Ming form modified and carried out in celadon, cream, coral red and imperial yellow glazes.

PORCELAINS DESIGNED BY WARREN E. COX AND MADE BY WALTER HOWAT

PLATE 241

Right: Kneeling figure by Carl L. Schmitz, full of beautifully rounded masses showing fluid softness appropriate to terra cotta. It is interesting to compare this figure with the very similar one, in pose, of Mr. Snowden's which is more fleshlike and perhaps less expressive of the medium being not so heavy and potterylike in its development.

I have seen nothing which so well swung the animal rhythm of Negro dancers as this figure in terracotta by LuDuble.

Left: Interesting small terra cotta by George Snowden makes use of a modern sweater, and its removal, to build a figure composed of all fairly large masses, eliminating the smaller details of face and fingers. A lovely composition.

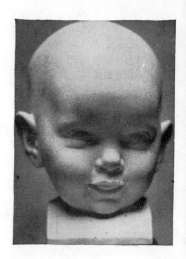

Right: "Mimi" by C. Paul Jennewein is a charming small glazed head of a baby with a delicate and elfish smile full of character and charm.

AMERICAN SCULPTORS' CERAMIC WORK

PLATE 242

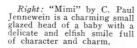

"Dancer." She does not do her own firing as in fact do none of the following sculptors who look upon terra cotta simply as one medium in which to have their work carried out. However, these are well trained artists who perfectly understand the characteristics of the medium.

W. T. Benda has done some charming little heads which were fired by Walter Howat.

Henry Kreis, from Essen, worked at stone carving and other sculpture crafts in Europe and then for Joseph Urban, Carl Paul Jennewein and Paul Manship here. From about 1933 he has made terra-cotta figures which have a simple strength and a somewhat carved feeling. He prefers the medium because it is less expensive than bronze or marble—perhaps $10 cost for a portrait (for material and firing) against $200 for bronze and $500 for marble.

FIG. 1458. "Accordion Player," by Helen Clark Phillips in waxed terra cotta. Ht. c. 15″.
FIG. 1459. Girl with a lute is graceful and noble in bearing. It has a monumental quality and is yet alive, expressing terra cotta and also flesh. To my mind the best of the figures Schmitz has done.
FIG. 1460. George H. Snowden certainly gets a fleshlike softness with all its appeal in many of his figures.

He writes me, "Besides, bronze and marble look very pretentious in the average home, while a terra-cotta portrait fits everywhere from the furnished room up. Furthermore a terra-cotta keeps the touch of the sculptor and is therefore a real original and this is not the case with the other materials. I would rather have a terra cotta of, let us say, Rodin, than a bronze cast, which on top of it all might exist 100 times."

He also writes, "I model a portrait by building it up hollow, usually a day previous. This way I do not lose any time in making the model wait, while the clay turns slightly harder." His firing was done by Paul Freigang.

Carl L. Schmitz is a friend of Kreis and was born in Metz. He studied in Munich under J. Wackerle and H. Hahn, came to this country in 1923 and became a citizen. He attended the Beaux Arts Institute and worked for Jennewein, Carl Milles and Paul Manship, opening his own studio in 1930. Here we have a most interesting contrast between the carver in Kreis and the modeler in Schmitz. Both are strong and sound men. Both have cast off all mannerisms, if they ever did have any. Both express themselves beautifully in the medium yet a little study shows that Kreis likes planes while Schmitz prefers rounded forms. Schmitz too has Freigang do his firing.

George H. Snowden was born in Yonkers and went to Yale, the Academy at Rome and the National Academy. His figures, particularly the female ones,

Perhaps the greatest ceramic achievement of our day is the tympanum done for one of the pediments of the Pennsylvania Mus. of Art by Mr. Jennewein and executed in colored glazes by Mr. Leon Solon of the Atlantic Terra Cotta Co.

Right: Wheeler Williams is a most alive and promising sculptor but uneven in his work. This baby's head with its damp, curly hair and eyes slightly out of focus is as fine as anything Houdon ever did.

Beautiful "Madonna and Child" by Helen Brett Babbington which shows fine composition and a full understanding of terra cotta in the surface modeling.

Left: The architect, Harry Lindeberg, was a fine subject for this terra cotta head by Wheeler Williams.

have a soft natural feeling almost alive and yet not entirely naturalistic, for they all seem to have fallen by chance into designs of real charm. A startling yet perfectly sound one is of a girl pulling off a sweater over her head. The conception is daring, for it might appear overmannered and smart but the direct and sincere treatment saves it from all of this, and the elimination of the features and hair brings the whole thing into a system of large curves. The body divides itself into three sized groups of masses: 1.—the smallest are the fingers, toes and features. 2.—The medium sized masses are the arms, lower legs and neck. 3.—The largest are the torso and thighs. Snowden by this natural and clever subject eliminates the details and keeps the larger proportionate masses. This figure is wonderfully modeled for one at once feels the softness of the breasts, the firmness of the thighs and the hardness of the ribs.

A true potter-sculptor who does his own firing is Albert Drexler Jacobson who studied at the Beaux Arts Institute, New York, the British Academy, Rome, etc. He was greatly influenced by the Post Impressionist movement in France and has done a number of things influenced by such artists as Brancusi, but also does very direct and excellent portrait work in terra cotta such as the head illustrated. He also makes some well potted vessels, strong in form and well decorated in both single and double firings at 2000° F.

Fig. 1461. Madonna from "The Shrine of the Americas," by Frederick Allen Williams and executed in glazed white porcelain by Walter Howat.

Fig. 1462. Two flower boxes made in 1914 by Paul Manship, showing some influence of Western Asia and one might also say of Japan in spacing and arrangement of figures. Very pleasant moving designs and suit their purpose well.

Marion Lawrence Fosdick graduated from the Museum School of Fine Arts, Boston, put in a year at the Kunstgewerbe Museum Schule, Berlin, was a pupil of George Demetrios, Hans Hofmann, etc., and then went to Alfred University where she has taught drawing, design and ceramics. She has exhibited widely and several of the museums own her work including the Metropolitan Museum of Art, New York.

Paul Manship is one of America's best known sculptors and I need not go into his history, for it is well known. I was disappointed to find that he had only done a little in ceramics. However, the flower boxes shown, which are in his "antique style," are sufficient to show that he could do great things in the medium.

There are many less well known individuals, too numerous to attempt to represent in full but about whom a whole book could be done. Just by chance I discovered the very lovely "Madonna and Child" by Helen Brett Babbington of Detroit, Michigan and although the problem of the hands has not been happily solved in this piece, the general modeling and composition is very fine and I think it a beautiful work of art. Again by chance alone, I found the work of Helen Clark Phillips who, having studied at the Paul Revere Pottery, Boston, and at Henry St. under Maija Grotell and T. S. Haile has done a very expressive Basque accordion player, and a number of well designed incised slipware pieces showing various animals, and some well designed stoneware. It is a good sign that these who do not profess to be great are, nevertheless, sound craftsmen.

Fig. 1463. Portrait by Albert Drexler Jacobson showing direct and proper plastic handling of terra cotta. Life size.

Fig. 1464. Jar by Albert Drexler Jacobson decorated with brown and black glazes and some green and white drips about lip-rim. Sturdy in form, design well related to form. Ht. c. 10″.

Fig. 1465. "Memory" is classic in feeling but one is sure that it is because the subject actually had classic features. The glaze forms a soft haze about the lines that is appropriate and moving. By C. P. Jennewein.

C. Paul Jennewein was born in Stuttgart but came to this country when he was seventeen, studied painting and did some good mural work, served in the army in World War I, received the Prix de Rome and studied there also serving in the American Red Cross in Rome. The three heads of "Mimi," "Marietta," and the one called "Memory," show the wonderful genius of the man and would rank with anything of the sort that had ever been done. The first is mat and the other two in a sort of soft glaze that does not harm the modeling, which, it should be noted, has been kept simple and undetailed so that little crevices would not catch and hold too much of the glaze. These are emotional and lovely.

However, special attention should be drawn to the tympanum panel by Mr. Jennewein placed in one of the pediments of the Pennsylvania Museum of Art in Fairmount Park, Philadelphia, the figures for which range from 2 feet 1½ inches to the center one of Zeus or Jupiter which is 12 feet tall. Much has been published about this greatest achievement of architectural sculpture in pottery in America and it is not necessary here to go into detail, but when one realizes that the figures had to be made in several sections, that the shrinkage is about 1 inch to the foot in the material used in firing, that the glazes had to be sprayed on evenly and could not be touched by fingers before firing, and that all had to be so planned that perfect drainage could be obtained, as ice would chip and finally destroy the work, otherwise, you can begin to realize some of the difficulties encountered. Mr. Leon V. Solon handled the coloring with the aid of Walter Howat, and the Atlantic Terra Cotta Co. of Perth Amboy did the firing at 2300° F. The red and gold similar to that used on Lenox china had to be fired again at lower temperature, of course.

Frederic Allen Williams was a Beaux Arts and National Academy student and though born 1898 in West Newton, Mass., has been associated in the public mind largely with the West, for he has been in various localities there and lived in Taos. He also has a great interest in American Indians as can be seen in his "Madonna," "Maid of Taos," etc. His animal figures are also excellent and some have been designed and rendered in glazed porcelain. Walter Howat again does his firing.

Wheeler Williams was born in Chicago, attended the Art Institute and Yale, served in World War I, received his master's degree in architecture at Harvard and in 1922 started as a sculptor. The large terra-cotta figure with the dog is somewhat overstylized and not convincingly so. His glazed porcelain table decorations of police dogs and the four standing figures are fairly good decorative art but we see his real strength in the head of Harry Lindeberg, which is, as the saying goes, a speaking likeness. The head of Helen Wills Moody is again well done but lacks all the brilliance of McCartan's. Williams has seen the face as more fleshy, there are suggestions of rings under the eyes and a

FIG. 1466. Good design but never as good as that of McCartan, monumental quality yet not to be compared with "Girl With Lute" by Schmitz, parts of this figure are almost naturalistic while other parts, such as the breasts are rather poorly conventionalized, yet—it has a charm which lies perhaps in the lift of the head and the movement and this may be more of the model than of Wheeler Williams himself. It is life size.

relaxed almost dreamy expression not exactly as we worshippers of our great tennis champion would expect to see her. In his baby's head "Diana," he has struck the truest note so far in his ceramic work. In the slight pout of the lips, the sleepy, dreamy expression of the eyes which do not quite focus, the moist curls on the toweled head and the suggested faintest shadow of a smile he has caught everything in the mood of the just awakened baby. I feel that this head ranks with that best one by Houdon and who could say more? It is a superb example of terra-cotta art. The firing of this piece was by Paul Freigang and the other things were by Walter Howat and Von Tury.

At the same time Mrs. Moody posed for both McCartan and Williams and I am delighted to be able to show here the work of both men. Edward Mc-Cartan was born in Albany and studied under Herbert Adams, George Grey

FIG. 1467 "Jonas," by Edward Mc-Cartan, a fine terra cotta and all dog. an utterly simple piece of modeling but as vigorous as are the little dachshunds themselves.

Barnard and Herman MacNeil. He also worked at the Beaux Arts, Paris. Probably everyone has admired his "Diana with Grey Hound," bronze but his terra cottas are no less beautiful. The dachshund, "Jonas," is one more which shows his love for and understanding of dogs. The portrait head of Miss Ruth Fletcher is one of the most brilliantly alive and vital little heads, for it is just under life size, that I have ever seen, and the head of Helen Wills Moody shows the keen alertness and moral stamina of this great champion whom we used to call "Little Poker Face." Again Howat does McCartan's firing.

These then are our great ones and Modern America need feel no lack of pride in them, for they are doing really living art which will last down through the ages and always give enjoyment. There are many others no doubt and it is a strange thing that one only hears by chance of this or that one having done an odd bit in fired clay. Perhaps this is the fault of the public.

America then has very bad industrial ceramics, rather poor individual and amateur ceramics but some great sculptors who have done wonderful things. Of course, the less strong artists of the second and first category took the pleasant short cut to various sorts of "modernistic art," but it is gratifying to see that the great and truly successful men have avoided these stylizations as they have in fact avoided any and all superficial stylization. A man's style should grow from the heart of his work outward and not be put on like a coat of many colors.

With the ironing out of our cities by air travel which certainly will flatten the present huge piles of skyscrapers and with the great wealth which this country is sure to enjoy after World War II it is hoped that a new renaissance will take place in the arts and that the ceramic arts will benefit with the others. There is no doubt but that Americans will have to learn how to use

Left: I do not know Ruth Fletcher but Mr. McCartan has certainly made me want to with this wonderful portrait. Terracotta, fired by Walter Howat after careful finishing of the cast by Mr. McCartan.

Center: Compare this head with that of Wheeler Williams of Mrs. Helen Wills Moody and you will see part of the reason that I hold Mr. McCartan as our present greatest sculptor. "Mac," saw not only the girl posing for him but the vital, piercing intelligence, superb muscle control and brilliant outguessing of an opponent which made this true and superb specimen of American womanhood the so-many-times champion.

Right: The Williams head of Mrs. Helen Wills Moody accents her classic beauty but gives her a dreamy look and shows a tired sagging of the muscles under her eyes and on her cheeks which perhaps might have been present as she posed. Her sensitive yet resolute mouth is beautifully rendered. Perhaps the hair is a little too wavy and too much conventionalized.

AMERICAN SCULPTORS' CERAMIC WORKS

PLATE 244

their leisure better, for they are going to have plenty of it along with plenty of everything else. Perhaps some of the now inarticulate masses will find means of becoming articulate. Meanwhile the plate for steaming food, the cup or mug for brimming drink and the image of clay may continue to charm a few simple souls like myself.

THE MARKS OF POTTERIES AND PORCELAINS

INTRODUCTION

My FIRST inclination was to exclude marks from this book entirely, for, as the reader will have gathered from my often repeated statements to that effect, *marks cannot be trusted*. The true collector is impressed first by the style, second by the paste of the ware where it is exposed at the foot-rim or elsewhere, third by the type of glaze, its condition, etc., fourth by the colors used, the slips if any; the details of decoration, etc. and finally, if he finds everything else characteristic and correct, the mark adds perhaps 1% more conviction in the attribution. Most marks are easier to copy than a single good, vigorous brush-stroke and perhaps that is the reason that many artists, as on the Caffaggiolo wares, painted the marks with a swift spontaneity. It will be remembered that in our section on Hispano-Moresque lustre potteries we have pointed out that the backs of the plates often show the quality of the artist who painted them better than the fronts for, "No imitator can get the same swift feeling in his strokes as can a man who has done hundreds in his own way." Thus in looking at a mark its style of drawing and character must also be taken into consideration and a swiftly drawn mark is more difficult to counterfeit than a careful and meticulous one, paradoxical as that may seem at first. Practically all marks have at one time or another been copied and particularly those of costly wares receive the attentions of cheats and fakers for obvious reasons.

Marks may refer to any one of a dozen different things: the name of a factory, the name of a manager of a factory, the name of an artist, the name of a town (and there are often more than one potteries in a town), the name of a certain potter, a series date, a formula of one sort or another, the trade mark of a merchant, an intended owner's name, etc. Many places in the 18th century purposely made their marks look as much as possible like those famous ones of Dresden and Sèvres to add to the confusion. Thus the meanings of marks in the study of ceramics have varied from authority to authority and from year to year, in many instances. I have mentioned in my text here and there the scorn with which Emil Hannover treats the inclusion of certain marks by Chaffers. Barber mentions a number of contradictions between Jacquemart and Fortnum. And all writers include a large number of marks the meanings of which are entirely unknown.

Such are the difficulties but so long as these pitfalls are borne constantly in mind, the study of marks is no doubt fascinating and to some people affords as much enjoyment as might the working out of a cross word puzzle. It, of course, has little to do with the appreciation of a true collector for those illusive appeals, a few of which I have attempted to point out in this book, may exist in large number and great strength on a piece with a certain mark, while they are entirely nonexistent in another piece which perfectly authentically carries the same mark. Again, of course, many of the very finest things have no marks at all. One thing, however, may be said with certainty and that is that no piece that carries a faked mark can possibly be a great work of art for sincerity is one characteristic that is absolutely necessary. Thus in a negative way the study of marks may benefit a collector, if he learns something about the imitative and downright counterfeit ones, for it stands to reason that the pieces which bear them are also imitative or counterfeit and to be avoided.

Just as there are some people who know the names of all the flowers but never actually perceived the beauty of one, so there are those who know where most pots are made but never really appreciated the beauty of one. Yet we cannot deny that taste

1079

and appreciation are fed by knowledge. Contrary to the self-flattering popular belief, no one was ever born with good taste. It is just that we must not confuse the food of knowledge with taste itself. Facts as to where a work of art was made, by whom and under what conditions all add to our understanding of it, to our final appreciation and in turn to the enlargement of our general taste just as food aids the athlete to build a strong body, *but the food is not the body* and a wealth of training, of spirit, of both inherited and environmental influences in addition to the food go to make the athlete. If this is true with the body of an athlete, certainly it is a thousand times more true with the mind of a man of taste.

At least a mark will show what a piece is supposed to be and that is a beginning In the various comments which I have added to our section on marks aid will be found and, if the student reads that such and such a mark was "of Duesbury's time," he can look up Duesbury and find out who he was and when he lived, and will probably go on from there to find out more and more about Derby wares. Nearly every mark has a whole history behind it and only by finding out about that history can one be truly said to know a mark. Most students prefer to get a picture in their minds of the development-in-general of a certain sort of ware and leave the details of the marks to be looked up when they are confronted by a certain piece. That is just why such a list of marks as we have brought together is useful. How, then, does the collector go about this?

It will be noticed that we divide the wares described in our book into several large groups as follows:—POTTERIES, GLAZED POTTERIES, SLIP COATED POTTERIES, TIN GLAZED POTTERIES, LUSTRED POTTERIES, PAINTED FAÏENCE, MODELED POTTERIES AND STONEWARES, PORCELAIN and BONE CHINA. The first thing to do is to determine whether a piece is *pottery, soft paste, porcelain* or *stoneware*. The latter need not trouble us much for it is seldom marked anyway. Pottery is readily distinguished by its softness and usually heavy potting. But between real porcelain or "hard paste" and the various approximations of it called "soft paste," it is not always so easy for the inexperienced to judge. There need be little difficulty in this, however, if one once takes a small file and tries to cut the foot, where the paste is exposed, for it will be found out at once that real porcelain is very hard and the file makes no impression, while soft paste can readily be cut. The only exception to this rule is that the Chinese soft paste is so nearly like porcelain, it being, in fact, porcelain with a little steatite added, that it also resists the file. One having determined which type of ware one is looking up, the field is cut down to a far more narrow search.

Next considerations should have to do with style and here we run into some difficulties, but usually one can at least determine whether a piece is actually Chinese or Japanese on one hand or European on the other. This is not invariably so easy as it would appear, but usually it can be done. If it is Far Eastern and has a mark, there is nothing for it but to search through those marks of the different reigns until one finds it, remembering such points as that famille rose enamel did not occur until the very end of K'ang Hsi so that, if a piece appears earlier but has rose enamel on it, it must be actually later or have been redecorated. In general the wares available to western collectors and made in the Ming dynasty are heavy, far heavier than Ch'ing wares of later period, but this is not always so as we find bowls of the Yung Lo reign very early in Ming times to be exceedingly thin. In general K'ang Hsi and later wares have the foot-rims turned in grooves to fit stands but this does not say that all Ming pieces lacked this characteristic or that all later pieces have it. In general the painting of Ming pieces is more bold and direct than that of later pieces, but once again there are many exceptions to the rule. Only study can give the student a sort of sixth sense about such things. The same thing is true about European wares and only by comparing can one tell the differences between English wares made to copy Sèvres or Dresden, and the real thing. Many of the soft paste wares such as St. Cloud and Mennecy in France copied Chinese wares of Tê Hua, Fukien, white porcelain and others. Light transmitted through the Chinese specimens is warm while light through the French ones is greenish. Of course the first cannot be cut with a file while the latter can. The amazing thing is that the poorly modeled French ones bring prices often into four figures, the originals can be bought for a few hundred or sometimes even below $100. However, in general again, the difference is not hard to tell

If a piece is European or English the next step is to run through the marks of this field until something is found that seems to compare. Then read the comments on it to determine whether or not there were variations. Beware of pieces which bear the well known marks of the best and largest factories for these are the ones most often imitated. Also look carefully at the drawing. For crowns, as an instance, occur on potteries of Italy, porcelains of Italy, Sèvres, certain Paris wares and some German porcelains, as well as on English wares. Anchors occur not only on Chelsea but also on wares of Venice, Sceaux, etc. quite naturally, and shields, fleur-de-lis and suns or stars are often encountered on wares that were not intended to be imitative in any way. Sometimes even the size is tell-tale.

When this is all accomplished and you have coldly weighed the evidence, it is often wise to get the opinion of your curator at the museum, of some reputable dealer who handles the type of wares you are interested in or of private collectors who have handled many similar specimens. Opinions may differ here and there but it is surprising how very much alike are the opinions of those who really know. Such opinions are well worth paying for, for it is evident that the pitfalls are many and varied. However, the sport is worth the chance and the hazards only add to the enjoyment of victories attained.

We have listed here all the important marks, the basic ones and only those marks that are generally accepted as authentic. A few doubtful marks are included, but they are so designated.

Numbers at the top of the page in the following index of marks refer to the pages where the corresponding marks are illustrated. Similarly, numbers accompanying the illustrated marks refer to the pages on which the marks are discussed.

INDEX OF MARKS SECTION

* Barber's Marks With Notes, and With the Notes Also of Chaffers, Hannover, Etc.

* Barber's Marks by courtesy of A. M. Maddock.

MARKS ON POTTERY OF ITALY

1–25.—*Caffaggiolo,* Caffagiuolo, Cafaggiolo or Cafagguolo. The most frequent form of the mark is seen in Nos. 1, 4, 5, 6, 7, in which a P has a dash across the upright, while the curved line at top is continued upward to make an S, thus forming a monogram which includes S.P.F. Senatus Populus Florentinus ?) or S.P.R. (Senatus Populus Romanus ?). Both these inscriptions are of frequent occurrence in Caffaggiolo decorations. Molinier suggests the meaning as an abbreviation of "Semper" one of the mottoes of the Medici and Hannover says, "The interpretation is the more probable as another of these mottoes, the word 'Glovis' (*si volg* read backwards) occurs on Caffaggiolo wares." The form of the mark varies widely often being little more than a P with the lower part crossed by a wavy line. It is found in one instance on Damascus ware.

3.—Doubtful. Fortnum says it is from Faenza.

5.—On a plate also marked *In Caffaggiuolo.* Hannover says the monogram is sometimes accompanied by a trident, but of the trident, which also occurs among Faenza marks, absolutely nothing is known.

6.—On a plate also marked *Cafagioli* and on a dish marked *In Caffagiuollo.*

9.—The usual mark with C or G and under it *In galiano nell ano 1547;* under this the artist's initials A F *f (ecit)*, possibly, suggested by Hannover, *Antonio Fattorini.* Galiano is a village near Caffaggiolo, where the artist may have worked.

11.—An undeciphered mark on an early plate with the Virgin and Child. This is not certainly of Caffaggiolo, but possibly of Faenza.

12.—Three marks uncertain. One on a plate in the collection of Baron Gustav de Rothschild is dated 1507.

21–30.—Caffaggiolo. Marks 24, 28, 29, 30 are doubtful. 26 occurs in a very large size on a dish attributed by Delange to Faenza, by Fortnum to Caffaggiolo.

31, 32, 33.—SIENA 31 is on a plate painted in blue *"a porcelan"* and is a mark of *Maestro Benedetto,* chief potter and artist there. Douglas states he was the son of a certain Maestro Giorgio of Faenza. A plate in the Victoria and Albert Museum is signed in full: *fata ī Siena da mº Benedetto.* 32 has been mistaken for a mark of Pesaro. #32 and 33 are also assigned to Benedetto, but Fortnum thinks them initials of owners of the objects. (See 200)

34.—PISA.

35.—Unknown. On a box with emblems of Cosmo de' Medici.

36, 37, 38.—MONTE LUPO. 38 is on a dish dated 1663, and has been assigned by some to Monte Feltro.

39–47.—GUBBIO. These are various forms of the signature of *Maestro Giorgio Andreoli;* 43 is perhaps the most frequent. The marks are frequently very large. The upper initials in 39 are, perhaps, those of the owner.

47.—Mark of *Maestro Giorgio* in very large size on a dish with bathing scene, called "Diana and her Nymphs surprised, etc." Hannover says, "Maestro Giorgio signed his name in full only on his most important works; thus we have *Mº Giorgio 1520 a di 2 de O'tobre in Ugubio.* As a rule he signed himself merely M.G. or M.G. *da Ugubio* in a large careless hand. His latest dated works belong to 1541; he seems to have died in 1552." Pieces also bear the initials M,R,D and more often N but, as these never occur with the master's signatures, they may be the initials of assistants.

48.—A similar form of mark was used in the 16th and 17th centuries on goods, etc., by merchants; also found on merchant's seals. More commonly the top forms a figure 4. Perhaps it is a trade mark of a merchant. A similar form occurring in mark 52 is thought by Jacquemart to indicate ecclesiastical dignitaries, or pharmacies attached to Monasteries. The mark 48 occurs on several pieces.

49, 50.—Maestro Giorgio

51.—G.A. for Giorgio Andreoli

52.—Maestro Giorgio, with mercantile or religious sign. (See 48)

53, 54.—Maestro Giorgio: some read *Maestro Gillio*.

55.—Gubbio, supposed later than Giorgio.

56.—On a dish by Giorgio dated 1518.

59–61.—Marks assigned to *Maestro Vincenzio, or Cencio*. Hannover says, "His son, *Vincentius Andreoli*, is commonly regarded as identical with the *Maestro Cencio* mentioned by Piccolpasso as the only possessor in his time of the secret of red lustre."

62.—Gubbio

63.—Gubbio. Mark of the master *Prestino,* whose signature also occurs in full. A relief of the Madonna in the Louvre is signed *1536 Perestinus* and Hannover gives another example signed: *1557 in Gubbio per mano di Mastro Prestino* (that is "the Rapid Painter") and adds about his works that, "We may suppose that they were typical of the period of decadence."

64.—Gubbio. Probably *Maestro Vincenzio*.

65.—Gubbio

66.—Gubbio or Diruta. Uncertain.

67.—Gubbio

68.—Gubbio. Jacquemart thinks the letters mean *Mater Gloriosa,* not *Maestro Giorgio*.

69.—Gubbio. Probably *Prestino*.

70, 71, 72, 73.—Marks found on Gubbio wares.

74–85.—CASTEL-DURANTE

74, 76, 77, 78, 79.—Trade marks perhaps of dealers, found on Castel-Durante wares. (See #48)

81.—Signature of *Giovanni Maria, vasaro,* and date 12 Sept., 1508. Note:—Hannover says, "It is signed: *1508 a di 12 de Seteb. facta fu i Castel Durāt. Zona Maria Vro;* that is to say, it was made at Castel-Durante, on September 12, 1508, by 'Zona Maria Vasaro (The Potter'.)" (See text.)

83.—Doubtful. Castel-Durante or Fabriano. Mark of painter or owner.

85.—On cups, etc., made of dust of the Santa Casa at Loretto.

86.—URBINO Mark on inferior work. Mr. Fortnum thinks of a young artist.

87–111.—Urbino.

87.—Attributed to Flaminio Fontana. Note:—Hannover says, "This style," (That of the Gonzaga service c.1519), "passed from Nicolo Pellipario (this was really his name)," (Not the usually used *Nicola da Urbino* who was really a native of Castel-Durante.), "to his followers, who assumed the name of Fontana." The first was Guido who signed *Guido da Castello Durante, Maestro Guido Fontana Vasaro,* and *Guido Durantino in Urbino.* "However this may be, Guido Fontana, son of Nicola da Urbino, had himself three sons, Orazio, Camillo and Nicolo. Of the last two nothing is known." Who Flaminio Fontana was I do not know.

88.—Unknown artist on a plate with St. Luke.

89, 97.—*Nicola da Urbino.*

90.—*Orazio Fontana.*

91.—Attributed by Passeri to Orazio Fontana, but #93 is on work much later.

92.—Unknown artist.

94.—On work of *Orazio Fontana.*

95.—Orazio Fontana.

96.—Orazio Fontana. The Greek *Phi* may be a monogram of O *f* and the *Delta* mean Durantino.

98, 99, 100, 106.—Signatures of *Francesco Xanto.*

101.—On one of the pieces of the Gonzaga-Este service, by Nicola da Urbino.

102.—On a dish painted with St. Jerome.

103.—*Francesco Durantino.*

104, 105, 109, 112.—Found on Urbino work.

107.—Initials of Gian. *Maria Mariani,* dated 1542.

108.—Attributed to *Luca Cambiasi.*

110.—*Alfonso Patanazzi.*

111.—CITTA DI CASTELLO. On a plateau sgraffiato.
113.—VITERBO. Date 1544.
114, 115, 116, 117.—DIRUTA.
118, 119, 120.—Diruta.
121.—FABRIANO.
122, 123, 124.—ROME.
125–141.—FAENZA. 125 and 126 are typical marks of the Casa Pirota. 127 is a frequent mark. 131 is the date 1491 between the letters M and G, which may imply *Mater Gloriosa*. 134, 135, 136, 144 are all of the same workshop.
142–156.—Faenza.
142.—On a plate with allegorical subject. B.M. for *Daldasaro Manara*.
143.—Casa Pirota. A frequent mark in similar form. (c.1525). Note:—Hannover mentions two plates of fine workmanship signed *Fata in Fae*(nza)—*Josef I* (n) *Ca*(sa) *Pirota 1525*, and *Fato in Faenza in Caxa Pirota*, respectively.
144.—On a plate representing Solomon. Lazari reads the mark G.I.O., but Fortnum thinks it is T.M. in antique letters.
145.—Doubtful. Faenza or Caffaggiolo.
155.—Said to be on a piece with the name of Giovano of Palermo, and the words *in Faenza*. Doubted by Jacquemart.
157.—FORLI. On a plaque date 1523.
158, 159.—Forli. Signatures on Forli wares are known also of *Moiero da Forli*, and *Leuchadius Solobrinus* 1564.
160. RAVENNA.
161.—*In arimin. Rimini.*
162.—RIMINI.
163–168.—VENICE.
165.—On a plate from the botega of *Mo Ludovico*. Other Venice pieces are marked *In Botega di Mo. Jacomo da Pesaro;* and *Jo Stefano Barcello Veneziano pinx.*
Note:—CANDIANA 1620, is a mark on a plate. There is no such place as Candiana. The word may be Venetian.
169.—Venice.
170.—On a plate seemingly Venetian.
171.—CORNARO.
172.—TREVISO.
173, 174, 175.—BASSANO. The *Terchi* family. The mark 173, which is the iron crown, is also on other fabrics.
176.—VERONA. Illegible mark, the enamel being broken. It occurs on a plate under the words 1563 *adi* 15 *zenaro. Gio Giovanni Batista da faenza in Verona.*
177, 178.—PADUA.
179.—GENOA. A lighthouse hanging out a signal.
180.—Attributed to Genoa by M. Demmin.
181.—SAVONA. The shield mark is drawn in various shapes, often with a few dashes of the brush, and is accompanied by a variety of letters.
182.—Savona.
183.—Savona. *Gio. Anton. Guidobono.*
184.—Savona.
185.—Savona. Solomon's knot.
186.—TURIN. Escutcheon of Charles Emanuel, 1638.
187.—Turin. Escutcheon of Victor Amadeus, 1713.
188.—Turin. Cross of Savoy and trumpet.
189.—MAURIENNE.
190.—MILAN.
191, 192.—Milan. *Felice Clerice?*
193.—Milan. *Pasquale Rubati.*
194.—Milan.
195, 196.—LODI.
197.—TREVISO.
198, 199.—NOVE.

200.—SIENA. Initials of Campani?

201.—PESARO. *Casali and Caligari,* 1763.

202.—SAN QUIRICO. Arms of Chigi. Date 1723.

203.—NAPLES. Vases; one inscribed *Paulus Francus Brandi Pinx.*

204, 205, 206, 207.—On same class of Naples vases.

208, 209.—Naples. *Del Vecchio* fabric, impressed marks.

210.—Naples. Attributed to Capo-di-Monte.

211.—Naples. *Giustiniani,* impressed. Other marks of this fabric are the name in full; the letter G, the name with I.N. and a vase.

212.—Attributed to Naples and to Castelli. We have it on wares found in Germany. Mr. Fortnum thinks German.

213, 214, 215.—CASTELLI; 213, *Saverio Grue;* 215, *Liborius Grue.*

216–230.—Unknown marks on Italian pottery.

MARKS ON WARES OF ITALY, PERSIA, RHODES, ETC.

231.—Persia. Painted in blue on a hard paste porcelain bowl.

232.—Unknown. On a hard paste porcelain bowl. Engraved through the glaze.

233.—Unknown. The square mark painted in blue, the characters engraved through the glaze, on a hard paste porcelain bowl.

234.—Persia. In blue on hard paste porcelain bowl.

235.—Persia. In blue on hard paste porcelain vase.

236.—Persia. In red on vase, apparently soft paste porcelain.

237.—MANISES, in Spain. On copper lustred ware. (Chaffers.)

238.—On a Hispano-Moresque plate, 15th century. (Chaffers.)

239.—On a Hispano-Moresque dish, gold lustred. (Chaffers.)

240.—On a Persian or Damascus ware jug.

241.—RHODES. Given by Marryat as found on Rhodian wares, supposed to represent the cross of the Knights.

242.—On a flask of "artificial porcelain paste, perhaps engobe," with design eminently Persian, but showing Chinese influence, brought from Persia. (Fortnum.)

243.—Persia. Name of maker, *Hatim,* on Persian pottery.

MARKS ON POTTERY OF FRANCE

1.—On a green enameled plate are escutcheons of arms of Frence provinces, and the one given here, which contains part of the arms of Beauvais and the name of *Masse,* perhaps of the artist. An inscription ends with *Fait en Decembre* 1502, or as Jacquemart reads, 1511.

2.—POITOU. The Goose of Thouars, found on a vase; supposed reference to Orion.

3.—AVON. Mark on the Nurse and other figures which were formerly attributed to Palissy.

ROUEN. All other marks which are not numbered, are found on pottery of Rouen. Many of these are similar to marks on Delft. The only artists' signatures known are the two, easily read, of *Dieul,* who decorated *faience a la corne.*

Still other marks painted, sometimes rudely, on Rouen were as follows (These are not in facsimile.): Ro, Go, G₃, DV, Gm., M, RD, GL, PP, Mo, HC, Mv, P.D, GMd, R, DL, HM, WGt, G., GW, S., Gi, HT and Mrs. Guillibeaux.

1, 2, 3.—LILLE. François Boussemart.

LILLE. Note:—Hannover mentions the five factories and the earliest pieces which date 1716 (See text.) and over 50 years later.

4.—Lille. Féburier and Boussemaert (or Fevrier and Boussemart).

5, 6.—Lille. Barthelemi Dorez, 1709–'15. His grandson signed N. A. Dorez, in 1748.

7, 8, 9.—Lille; 7, about 1788; (?) 8, Petit?

10.—VALENCIENNES. *Louis Dorez.*

11, 12, 13, 14, 15.—ST. AMAND LES EAUX. *P. J. Fauquez.* (Pierre Joseph.)

16.—PARIS. *Claude Reverend's* mark.

17, 18.—Paris. On ware resembling Reverend's.

19.—SCEAUX. Mark of Glot (Richard), who also marked with the word *Sceaux.* Prior to 1772 the mark had been S X.

20.—Sceaux? or Bourg la Reine? Doubtful.

21.—Sceaux. Glot's period. (Hannover says this SP was after the Duke of Penthièvre had assumed patronage. It stood for Sceaux-Penthièvre.) It occurs with or without anchor, referring to the Duke as Grand Admiral.

22.—BOURG LA REINE.

23.—ST. CLOUD. *Trou's mark.*

24, 25, 26.—SINCENY. 25 is signature of Pellevé (Pierre) who came from Rouen with workmen and artists, and later founded Saint-Denis-sur-Sarthon.

27, 28, 29, 30, 31, 32.—APREY. The factory monogram Ap, with initials of Jarry and other artists.

33.—MATHAUT.

34, 35—NIDERVILLER. Beyerle period. The mark is B N in monogram.

36, 37, 38, 39.—Niderviller. Custine period. These are very similar to the marks of Kronenburg and Ludwigsburg.

40.—SARREGUEMINES. *Utzchneider & Co.*

41.—STRASBOURG. *Charles Hannong.*

42, 43, 44.—Strasbourg. *Paul Antoine Hannong.*

45, 46, 47.—Strasbourg. *Joseph Adam Hannong.*

48.—Strasbourg or Hagenau. Possibly *Balthasar Hannong.*

49.—PREMIERES, in Burgundy. *J. Lavalle.* Other marks are J L P in a script monogram.

50.—MEILLONAS. *Madame de Marron.*

51, 52.—VARAGES.

53, 54, 55.—TAVERNE. *Gaze,* director.

56–86.—MOUSTIERS. The marks including a monogram of O L are attributed to Joseph Olery. Some are his but Jacquemart doubts many. 86 is supposed signature of *Foque,* successor to *Clarissy.* Names, perhaps of Spanish artists— *Soliva, Miguel Vilax, Fo Gianzel, Cros*—occur. A potter, *Ferrat* about 1760 signs his name. *Pierre Fournier* signs work dated 1775; *Antoine Guichard,* in 1763; *Thion,* in the last century. *Moustiers* appears as a mark written and also applied through pricked points. Viry, painter, signs a plate.

87–95.—Moustiers. 87 and 88 are marks of *Feraud,* potter. 95 is probably Olery. The others are uncertain.

96–98.—MARSEILLES. The fleur-de-lis is attributed to *Savy* after 1777.

99–102.—Marseilles. *J. G. Robert.*

103, 104.—Marseilles. *Veuve Perrin.*

105.—Marseilles. *A Bonnefoy.*

106.—Marseilles. *J. Fauchier.*

107.—MARANS. *J. P. Roussencq.*

108, 109.—Marans.

110.—RÉNAC. (Jacquemart.)

111.—ORLEANS.

112–123.—NEVERS. 112 is the earliest known signature; 113 Denis Lefebvre; 114, Jacques Bourdu; 115, 116, Henri Borne on statuettes; 117, Jacques Seigne; 119, Dominique Conrade, third of the name, 1650–'72; 120, Etienne Born; 121, François Rodriguez; 122, Nicholas Viodé; (?) 123, from the Conrade arms.

124.—LIMOGES. Massié.
125.—LA TOUR D'AIGUES.
126.—*Avisseau,* modern potter at Tours (Died 1861.)
127–146.—Unknown marks on French pottery.
147–183.—Unknown marks found on French pottery. On a basin is the mark ALEX 1724. On a bas-relief is the name *J. Alliot.*

MARKS ON POTTERY OF BELGIUM AND HOLLAND

1–3.—TOURNAY. Marks probably of *Peterynck.*
4.—TERVUEREN. ?
5.—MALINES. Attributed by Jacquemart.
6.—BRUGES. *Henri Pulinx.* (or Pulinckx) (1753– ?) Graesse gives 8 unsubstantiated marks for this place.
7.—LUXEMBOURG. Mark of the brothers *Boch* before the French Revolution.
8.—Luxembourg. Subsequent mark impressed.
9, 10.—Luxembourg.
11–19. Unknown marks on Flemish pottery.
20.—AMSTERDAM, 1780–'83. *Hartog v. Laun.*
21–40.—DELFT.
21.—*Samuel Piet Roerder.*
22, 23, 24.—*Suter van der Even,* 1580.
28.—Factory with the sign of *De Metaale Pot,* 1639.
29, 30.—*De Paauw* (The Peacock), 1651.
31.—*Jacobus de Milde,* 1764.
32.—*Martinus Gouda.*
33.—*Q. Kleynoven,* 1680.
34.—*Cornelius Keyser, Jacobus Pynaker and Adrian Pynaker* 1680. (or Pijnacker according to Hannover).
37.—*Jan Jansz Kuylick,* 1680.
38.—*Johannes Mesch,* 1680.
39.—*T'Fortuyn* (The Fortune), 1691.
40.—Widow of Pieter van der Briel.
41–81.—Marks deposited in the Hotel de Ville, Delft, in 1764, by potters designating their shop names. These are not always given in facsimile.
41–45.—DE WITTE STER (The White Star). *A. Kielle.*
46.—IN DER VERGULDE BOOT (The Gilded Boat). *Johannes der Appel.*
47–49.—DE ROOS (The Rose). *Dirk van der Does.*
50.—DE KLAAUW (The Claw). *Lambertus Sanderus.*
51, 52.—DE DRIE KLOKKEN (The Three Bells). *W. van der Does.*
53–56.—DE GRIEKSE A (The Greek A). *J. T. Dextra.* 1765, the works passed to *Jacobus Halder Adriaensz* (M.56).
57.—DE DRIE PORCELEYNE ASTONNEN (The Three Porcelain Barrels). *Hendrick von Hoorn.*
58, 59.—DE ROMEYN (The Roman). *Petrus van Marum.* The same year the manufactory passed into the hands of *Jan van der Kloot Jansz* (M.59).
60.—T'JONGUE MORIAANS HOFFT (The Young Moor's Head). Widow of *Peter Jan van der Hagen.*
61–63.—IN T'OUDE MORIAANS HOFFT (The Old Moor's Head). *Geertruy Verstelle.*
64, 65.—DE PORCELEIN BYL (The Porcelain Axe). *Justus Brouwer.* Occurs frequently.
66, 67.—DE DREI PORCELEYNE FLESCHJES (The Three Porcelain Flasks) *Hugo Brouwer.*
68–70.—T'HART (The Stag). *Hendrik van Middeldyk.*

71.—DE TWEE SCHEEPJES (The Two Ships). *Anth. Pennis.*
72–74.—DE PORCELEYNE SCHOOTEL (The Porcelain Dish). *Johannes van Duyn.*
75.—DE VERGULDE BLOMPOT (The Gilded Flower Pot). *P. Verburg.* The mark is not facsimile.
76.—DE PORCELYN FLES (The Porcelain Bottle). *Pieter van Doorne.*
77.—DE DUBBELDE SCHENKKAN (The Double Pitcher). *Thomas Spaandonck.*
78–80.—DE LAMPETKAN (The Ewer). Widow of *Gerardus Brouwer.*
81.—DE TWE WILDEMANS (The Two Savages). Widow of *Willem van Beek.*
Note:—All the unnumbered marks are found on pottery apparently of Delft; but their signification is unknown. It is important to note that similar marks are found on wares of Rouen, and other factories. The collector will exercise judgment as to paste and style of decoration before assigning specimens, and will frequently find it impossible to decide where a piece was made.

MARKS ON POTTERY OF SWITZERLAND, GERMANY, SWEDEN, SPAIN AND PORTUGAL

1, 2.—ZURICH.
3.—WINTERTHUR. On an escritoire. (Jacquemart.)
4.—Anspach (Bavaria).
5, 6, 7, 8, 9.—BAIREUTH. Sometimes the name in full.
10, 11, 12.—FRANKENTHAL. 10 and 11 are marks of *Paul A. Hannong;* 12, of *Joseph A. Hannong.* It is not possible to distinguish the first mark from Hannong's when at Strasbourg.
13.—GOGGINGEN, near Augsburg, established about 1750.
14.—Harburg. Initials of *Johann Schaper.*
15, 16, 17.—HÖCHST. 15 has the G for (Göltz) *Geltz;* 16 the Z for Johann Zeschinger; 17 is the wheel alone, the arms of Mayence. (Also note Hannover states the FH is for Friederich Hess, the I.H. for Ignaz Hess, the AL for Adam Löwenfinck and there are others such as B.B., G.C., M.S., L.R. and AMB which "await interpretation.")
18.—POPPELSDORF. Wessel's manufactory; impressed. Also found impressed with the name *Mettlach* on pottery of that place.
19, 20, 21, 22, 23.—NUREMBERG. M. Demmin gives a monogram of H C D, and date 1550, as on a stove. *Glüer,* probably an artist, signs a dish with *Nurnberg 1723.* Plates are signed *G. F. Greber Anno 1729 Nuremberg. Stroebel* signs a bell, with date 1724, and a dish painted, with date 1730. A stove of green tiles, with religious subjects, has the signature of *Hans Kraut,* and date 1578. *Hans Kraut* was the great potter of Willingen.
24.—SCHREITZHEIM.
25, 26, 27.—STRALSUND.
28–43.—Unknown marks on German pottery.
44–56.—Unknown marks on German pottery.
57–62.—RORSTRAND. According to Mrs. Palisser 61 and 62 are probably signatures of *Arfinger.* Chaffers gives a mark, *Storkhulm* 22, 8. 1751 D H B, as of the factory after Rorstrand was united to Stockholm. The marks include the date, price and signatures of artists. *Stockholm* is found, and also *Rorstrand,* impressed.
63.—Rorstrand, or Marieberg, or Kiel ?
64–69.—MARIEBERG.
70.—Swedish ?
71.—KÜNERSBERG.

72.—Künersbarg.
GUSTAFSBERG, 1820 to 1860. The mark is the name with an anchor.
HELSINBURG. Given by Chaffers as on stonewares, made from 1770.
73–79.—KIEL.
80, 81.—ALCORA.
82, 83.—Attributed to *Seville*.
84, 85.—LISBON.
For marks on pottery of Russia and Poland see porcelain section.

MARKS ON PORCELAIN OF ITALY, SPAIN AND PORTUGAL

1.—FLORENCE. On Medicean porcelain. The arms of the Medici and initials of Franciscus Medici Magnus Etruriae Dux Secundus. (Hannover gives it Franciscus Maria Medicis Magnus Dux Etruriae Secundus, but also illustrates the six palle with the two upper ones only bearing Ms.)

2.—Florence. On Medici porcelain. Dome of the cathedral of Florence.

3.—Tablet held by a lion in the decoration of a bowl. (This I do not think a Medici mark.)

4, 5, 6, 7.—DOCCIA. Near Florence. (Hannover says, "Among the earliest of its productions are certain cups signed by *Anreiter*.") (He also adds, "As early as 1821, when the famous Neapolitan factory closed down, Doccia acquired the models for the relief porcelain of Capo di Monte, and for the past thirty or forty years has copied them en masse, unscrupulously adding the mark of the originals.")

8, 9, 10, 11.—LE NOVE. 10 and 11 are signatures of *Gio. B. Antonibon*.

12, 13.—VENICE. *Vezzi*; impressed or in red.

14, 15, 16.—Venice. *Cozzi*; in red, blue or gold. This mark must be distinguished from that of Chelsea in England.

17.—Venice.

18–26.—NAPLES. CAPO-DI-MONTE factory. 18 is supposed to be the earliest mark, in blue. (Hannover says, "The mark of the factory during the first period (that of Charles III) was the Bourbon fleur-de-lis, either uncolored (Impressed) or painted in blue, more rarely in red or gold.") The fleur-de-lis was also used at Buen Retiro factory in Madrid, as given below. 21, 22, 23, 24 are marks of Ferdinand IV. in and after 1759. The crowned N is often reversed in the mark. The marks are sometimes in color, sometimes impressed.

GIUSTINIANI, of Naples made hard paste porcelain, using the same marks as on pottery. (See 211 in section on wares of Italy, Persia, Rhodes, etc.—pottery.)

27–31.—MADRID. Marks of the *Buen Retiro* factory. This factory was an outgrowth of Capo-di-Monte in Naples, and used the fleur-de-lis mark also. 27 and 28 are the cipher of Charles III. 29 is M, for Madrid.

32.—VISTA ALLEGRE, near Oporto, Portugal.

33, 34, 35.—TURIN, Italy; *Vineuf* factory of Dr. Gionetti, impressed or scratched. The cross is also sometimes accompanied by scratched lines, forming VN in monogram.

MARKS ON PORCELAIN OF SEVRES

1.—VINCENNES. The interlaced double L, the initial of the king's name, was adopted by the Vincennes factory shortly after its foundation, and used until 1753. The mark, unaccompanied by other letters, is rarely, if ever, found on porcelain made at Sèvres. After the removal of the factory to Sèvres, this mark, accompanied with date letters, as hereafter explained, continued the typical mark of the factory down to the Revolution.

2.—Vincennes. The mark was usually in this form, with a dot in the monogram. Marks 1 and 2 should be found only on pieces made prior to 1753.

3.—Vincennes and Sèvres. In 1753, at Vincennes, the system of dating by letters of the alphabet was adopted, A being 1753, B 1754, etc. (See table in text.) (Note:—Barber here gives QQ-1794 and RR-1795 which Hannover omits.) This mode of marking the date fell into disuse, and, from this period until 1800, it is found only on rare examples. In 1801, the custom of dating was resumed. (See our text.) Here again Barber differs from Hannover whose system we have shown in the text:—as follows –//– he gives as 1804, an arrow for 1805 and slanting parallel lines with dots at the center at the outer edges for 1806. From there on the two systems are the same.—Barber adds, "From 1818 the year is expressed by the two last figures only. Thus: 18–1818, 19–1819, etc. and is so continued to the present time." A further note adds:—The *Guide* published for the Sèvres factory still adheres to the old system of dates, which rejected the letter J, and regards K as 1762, and the letters which follow representing, L,1763, and so on. This system is abandoned by all authorities, French and English, and we do not know why it is retained in the guide. In addition to the above tables, it is necessary to add that 1811, 1812, 1813 are sometimes indicated by 11, 12, 13, and possibly other years were occasionally so indicated to 1817: 1769, the year of a comet, was sometimes indicated by a comet rudely painted, instead of Q. The factory was removed to Sèvres in 1756. A, B, C, D, therefore date Vincennes wares. D also dates work at Sèvres. The date letter is placed either within or outside of the monogram, and is sometimes a capital and sometimes a small letter.

4.—The crown was adopted over the monogram as the mark of hard paste porcelain after its introduction. Forms of this mark are 5, 6 and 10, showing accompanying signatures of artists. Thus, mark 10 includes the factory mark, the device of the artist *Vieillard,* and the date DD, 1781. This mark on a service in the T.-P. collection has also the mark of another artist, *Baudoin,* on each piece.

7.—The letter Z having been reached in 1777, double letters were used thereafter, AA being 1778, etc. A difference of opinion existed as to whether the letter J was used for 1762, but the best authorities now agree that it was used.

8, 9.—In the Republican period the royal initial was abandoned and the mark R. F., for *Republique Francaise,* was adopted (1792–1800), always accompanied by the word *Sèvres.* The R.F. was in monogram, as in mark 8, or in one of the forms in mark 9. Dates were not used from 1792 to 1801.

11.—About 1800 the word Sèvres was used alone, without the R.F. It was usually in a form similar to mark 11, but varied as made by different hands. This mark was in use from 1800 till the end of 1802.

12.—In the Consular period, 1803, the mark 12, for *Manufacture Nationale,* was used, stenciled in red.

13.—In the Imperial period, beginning May 8, 1804, mark 13, for *Manufacture Imperiale,* was adopted, and used until 1809, stenciled in red.

14.—The imperial eagle was adopted as the mark in this form in 1810, printed in red, and continued in use till the abdication, in 1814. Date marks were used from 1801, for which see our text chart.

15.—Mark of the period of Louis XVIII, used from May, 1814, to September, 1824, the date indicated by the last two figures of the year. This mark was printed in blue.

16, 17, 18, 19.—Marks used in the reign of Charles X., from 1824 to 1828, printed in blue; the figures under the mark indicating the year of the century.

20, 21.—Marks used in the reign of Charles X., in 1829 and 1830. Mark 30 was used on decorated wares; 21 was used on pieces which were gilded only.

22.—This mark was used only in 1830; under *Louis Philippe.*

23.—Used from 1831 to November, 1834, under *Louis Philippe.*

24.—Used from November, 1834, to July, 1835.

25.—The cipher of *Louis Philippe,* used from July, 1835, to 1848.

26.—Used under the Republic from 1848 to 1852.

27.—Used under the Empire of *Louis Napoleon,* from 1852 to 1854.

28.—Cipher of *Louis Napoleon,* used from 1854 to 1872.

29, 30.—These marks have been used in addition to the factory mark since July, 1872, usually printed in red.

31, 32.—The letter S with the date of the year of the century, in an oval, was adopted 1848 as the factory mark on all pieces, and continues in use. On white wares, sold without decoration, it is cut across by a scratch through the glaze. It is printed pale green. Mr. Chaffers says it has been used on white wares since 1833. This may be taken for what it is worth. Many modern pieces with this mark cut across are decorated by amateurs and others. None have any particular value.

33.—Marks of this kind, containing names of chateaux or palaces, were placed on pieces, table services, etc., made for use in the royal residences thus indicated.

34.—Monogram of Catherine II of Russia, in flowers, laurels, etc., on a service made for her.

35, 36.—*Visa* of Alexander Brongniart, the director, occurring on several fine pieces in the T.-P. collection. It does not appear as an intentional mark, but as if the artist's work had been submitted to the director, and he had written on the back wih a lead pencil *Vu Alex B* or *Vu B.* In the firing this has become a yellowish mark with some metallic iridescence.

37.—Marks stenciled in red on a plate dated 1811, decorated with a view of the Palace of St. Cloud, signed *Label.* The visa of Brongniart in form of mark 36 is also on the plate. (T.-P. Col.)

Many hard paste specimens of Sèvres which originally bore the marks of the Imperial period prior to 1814 are found with the letters M. Imple, or the eagle, ground off on a wheel, leaving only the words De SÈVRES OF SÈVRES. The wheel has removed the glaze.

MARKS ON PORCELAIN OF FRANCE

1, 2.—Unknown marks on early French porcelains, given by Jacquemart as possibly Louis Poterat, of Rouen, 1673–1711.

3.—Unknown, on similar porcelain.

4.—ST. CLOUD.—Two forms. Pierre Chicanneau, 1702–'15.

5.—St. Cloud. Trou, 1706.

6, 7, 8.—Uncertain. On porcelains resembling.

9.—PARIS. *Marie Moreau,* widow of Chicanneau's son.

10–13.—LILLE. 10 is the earliest mark. In 13 L is on a saucer, and B on the cup.

14, 15.—CHANTILLY. 15 is Pigorry's mark since 1803.

16, 17.—MENNECY—VILLEROY. In gold, color and later impressed.

18, 19, 20.—VINCENNES and SÈVRES.—See marks of Sèvres above.

21, 22, 23.—SCEAUX. 21 usually scratched. 22, later, painted in blue. 23 scratched.

24.—ORLEANS.

25.—ETIOLLES.
26.—LA TOUR D'AIGUES.
27.—BOURG-LA-REINE.
28, 29.—ARRAS.
30–39.—Unknown marks on early French porcelains, resembling St. Cloud, given by Jacquemart. 33, 35 are doubtless the same as 6, 8 above.
40–46.—Unknown marks on hard paste porcelains. 44 attributed by Riocreux to Fontainbleau. 45 resembles the mark of a Sèvres painter.
47.—Paris. Pierre A. Hannong's mark, 1773.
48, 49.—Paris. Same factory. Charles Philippe.
50.—Paris. Gros Caillou. Established by Lamarre, 1773.
51.—Paris. Morelle à Paris. Established 1773.
52, 53.—Paris. Souroux, potter. Established 1773. His successor was Ollivier.
54.—Paris. De la Courtille factory.
55.—Paris. De la Courtille. This mark, torches or headless arrows, is made in various forms, and somewhat resembles the Dresden crossed swords, which probably did not bother the users of it.
56.—Paris. *Dubois.* This mark—two branches, alluding to the maker's name—often resembles the previous one. Also assigned to De la Courtille factory.
57, 58.—LIMOGES. Factory of Massie. The earliest mark was G.R., et Cie.
59, 60.—LA SEINIE. Established 1774.
61.—Paris. J. J. Lassia, 1774.
62–70.—CLIGNANCOURT. The windmill is the earliest mark, rare, used only in 1775. 64 is stenciled on a specimen. 65, initial of *Monsieur,* the king's brother; 66, 67, 68, initials of Prince Louis Stanislas Xavier; 69, initial of Moitte, director, used with the name *Clignancourt;* 70, initial of Deruelle, director.
71.—Paris. *Manufacture du petit Carousel.* Mark used with the name of the factory variously abbreviated.
72, 73.—BOISETTE.
74, 75, 76.—Paris. Lebeuf. *Porcelaine de la Reine.* Initial of Marie Antoinette.
77.—Paris. *Porcelaine de la Reine.* Initials of Guy & Housel, successors to Lebeuf. These occur with *Rue Thirou à Paris.* LEVEILLE, 12 *Rue Thiroux,* is the latest mark.
78, 79, 80.—Paris. *Porcelaine d'Angoulême.* Early marks of Guerhard & Dihl. Later marks are their names in full, and MANUFACTURE DE MONS. LE DUC D'ANGOULÊME A PARIS, without name.
81.—Paris. *Nast,* manufacturer. Stenciled.
82.—LILLE. The early pieces have *à Lille.*
83, 84, 85, 86.—Paris. Factory established by Lamarre, 1784. 84, 85, 86 are initials of Louis Philippe Joseph, Duc d'Orleans, patron.
87, 88.—Paris. H. F. Chanou. Established 1784. The marks are penciled in red.
89, 90.—VALENCIENNES. Initials of Fauquez, Lamoninary and V. Early mark, *Valencien.*
91.—CHOISY LE ROY. Impressed.
92, 93, 94.—Vincennes. Factory of P. A. Hannong. Established 1786.
95.—Vincennes. Attributed to Hannong's, or another factory under the patronage of Louis Philippe.
96, 97.—Paris. Charles Potter. *Porcelaine du Prince de Galles.*
98.—Paris. Belleville. Jacob Pettit. The J has sometimes a dot above it.
99.—CAEN. Desmare et Cie. Established 1798.
100.—Paris. *Manufacture de S. M. l'Impératrice.* Also marked with full name of factory, and *P. L. Dagoty,* proprietor.
101–106.—STRASBOURG. 101, C. Hannong; 102, 103, Paul A. Hannong; 104, the same, with H in the paste; 105, J. A. Hannong, with numbers; 106, J. A. Hannong.
107.—BRANCAS LAURAGAIS.
108, 109.—ORLEANS. 108, of Gerault; 109, of LeBrun.
110.—Given by Jacquemart as the mark of Jacques Louis Broilliet on experimental porcelain, at *Gros Caillou* (Paris) 1765.

111, 112, 113.—MARSEILLES. Robert. 113 is doubtful.
114–121.--Niderviller. 114, Beyerle's period; 115, 116, 117, 120, Custine's period. These marks must not be confused with those of Ludwigsburg. 119 is Lanfray's cipher. NIDERVILLER in an open outlined letter is impressed on statues of Franklin and other biscuit pieces.
122, 123.—BORDEAUX. Marks of Verneuille.
124.—Unknown French. Resembles Limbach, in Germany.
125–131.—Unknown marks on French porcelain.
132.—Attributed by Baron Davillier to Marseilles.

MARKS ON PORCELAIN OF GERMANY AND OTHER EUROPEAN COUNTRIES

Note:—The MEISSEN Marks are listed as DRESDEN where the factory was located.
1–8.—DRESDEN. Marks stamped on Böttger red ware. Böttger's porcelain was never marked.
9, 10, 11.—Dresden. Initials of August Rex, in blue and in gold 1709–'26.
14, 15.—Dresden. King's period, from 1770; the mark with O about 1778.
16.—Dresden. Crossed swords, with star. Marcolini period, from 1796.
17, 18.—Dresden. Early marks for (17) *Königlicher* or (18) *Meissener Porzellan Manufactur.* Hannover says, "Not until about 1723 did a sparing use of a mark begin—in underglaze blue, with the cursive letters K.P.M. or K.P.F. (*Königliche Porzellan Fabrik.*)" He continues, stating that the mark or marks appeared usually on the sugar-basin and tea-pot of breakfast-sets and that it continued long after the crossed swords were adopted.
19, 20.—Dresden. First forms of the crossed swords, used from 1719. Here again there seems to be some difference of opinion for Hannover clearly states, "The crossed-swords mark occurs from about 1726 onwards; but even in 1730 the letters just mentioned are sometimes used—now and then in combination with the crossed swords." He also continues, "Until 1731, it was rather the exception than the rule for the Meissen factory to mark its porcelain."
21.—Dresden. Bruhl's time, 1750. Hannover says, "The sword mark, in its oldest form, consists of two swords with pommels, with the guard set at a right angle, and the blades crossing each other also at an approximate right angle. Towards the close of the 1730s the guards were set obliquely and the blades crossed at at an acute angle. From about 1750, the pommels disappear and the swords now become small and delicate. A few years later a comparatively long period begins, during which a dot was set in the rhombus formed by the swords and the cross-pieces; hence the name 'dot period' and *Saxe au point*. This is estimated by Berling as ranging from about 1756 till 1780. From about 1780 the well known star was placed under the swords. This is often taken to be the mark of Marcolini, though it was introduced a few years before his time, and remained in use a year or so after his death (in 1814), when it was succeeded by a Roman or Arabic numeral. All these marks were in blue under the glaze. Only on biscuit of the Marcolini period is the mark not painted, but incised, and at the same time enclosed in a triangle." We should add that he states earlier, "But when, in 1731, the mark began to appear on all new porcelain in underglaze blue, a quantity of old ware, originally unmarked, was at the same time furnished with the same mark" (the crossed swords) "in blue *over* the glaze."
22.—Dresden. Crossed swords; modern mark. The earliest form in Herold's period, sometimes closely resembles the modern form.
23.—Dresden. A modern mark.
24.—Dresden. On a service made for the Countess Cosel. (Kosel.) Hannover notes she

fell into disgrace in 1718 and doubts it.

25.—Dresden. Used about 1730.

26.—Dresden. Dated 1739.

27.—Dresden. Early form of mark.

28, 29.—Dresden. Marks used 1718.

30, 31.—Dresden. Early marks.

32.—Dresden. Mark used 1718.

33.—Dresden. Date of use unknown; on statuettes, with or without crossed swords. (Chaffers) (doubtful?)

34, 35.—VIENNA, Austria.

36.—ELBOGEN.

37, 38.—SCHLAKENWALD, Austria. (See also #61.)

39-44.—HEREND, Hungary. 39 is impressed in the paste; 40, 41, usually printed in blue; 42, painted in black, with *Herend* impressed; 43, painted in red; 44, initials of M. Fischer.

45, 46.—ALTEN ROTHAU. *Nowotny*, maker.

47, 48.—PIRKENHAMMER. *Fischer & Reichembach*, and *Charles Fischer*.

49.—PRAGUE. *Kriegel & Co.*

50-53.—HÖCHST, Mayence. (See 15, 16, 17 in Marks on Pottery of Germany) 51 is the mark of Geltz; 52, of Zeschinger.

54.—Höchst. Mark of Dahl.

1.—FÜRSTENBERG. The F is made in various forms.

2.—HESSE CASSEL?

3.—HESSE DARMSTADT. (Jacquemart.)

4, 5.—FULDA.

6.—GERA? or GOTHA? See #25.

7, 8.—Gotha.

9.—WALLENDORF. (Also used at Berlin.)

10.—ARNSTADT.

11, 12, 13, 14.—LIMBACH.

15.—VOLKSTADT. Marryat says KLOSTER VEILSDORF. (See 24 below.)

16.—ANSPACH. So says Marryat. See 26, 46, 47, 48 below.

17.—RAUENSTEIN.

18, 19.—GROSBREITENBACH.

20.—Grosbreitenbach ?

21, 22, 23.—RUDOLSTADT. R was used in various forms.

24.—Volkstadt. See 15 above.

25.—GERA. Two forms of G.

26.—Attributed to both Gera and Anspach, Barber says probably the latter. Chaffers gives it with a D under a crown. The mark varies from a rude eagle (46) to this form. See 16.

27, 28.—BADEN-BADEN. The blade of an ax or of two axes, in gold or impressed.

29-35.—LUDWIGSBURG (KRONENBURG). The double C is the cipher of Charles Eugene, who died in 1793, but the mark was used till 1806. It must not be confounded with that of Niderviller, in Custine's time, which was sometimes accompanied by a coronet. The mark frequently appears without the crown, as in 31 and 32. The form 30 (L, with a crown) is also a mark of the time of Charles Eugene. The letters CC in mark 29 were changed in 1806 to T.R., the T.R. being sometimes in monogram; and in 1818 the letters W.R. were substituted. The stag's horns, singly, 35, or on a shield, as in 34, were also used.

36.—HILDSHEIM, Hannover. Sometimes the letter A only; from about 1760.

37, 38, 39.—NYMPHENBURG and NEUDECK. The first is the oldest mark. These are impressed, without color, and sometimes difficult to recognize. Found on pieces with marks of other factories, which bought and decorated them

40-45.—FRANKENTHAL. 41, P. A. Hannong's mark; 42, Joseph A. Hannong; 43, initials of Carl Theodore, Elector; 44, supposed of Ringler; 45, supposed, of Bartolo.

46, 47, 48.—Anspach, Bavaria.

49.—BAIREUTH.
50.—REGENSBURG (RATISBON).
51.—WÜRTZBURG, Bavaria.
52–57.—BERLIN. The scepter is the general mark, made in several forms. 52, 53, 54 are the earliest marks of Wegely, 1750–1761; 56, globe and cross and K.P.M., for Königlicher Parzellan Manufactur, adopted about 1830; 57, modern mark, alone, and with K.P.M. The Wegely marks resemble Wallendorff and others, quite carelessly including Meissen, of course.
58.—CHARLOTTENBERG.
59.—PROSKAU.
60.—VIENNA. See also 34 and 35 preceding.
61.—SCHLAKENWALD, Austria. See 37 and 38 preceding.
62, 63, 64.—Unknown marks on German hard paste porcelain.
65–76.—Unknown marks on German hard paste porcelain.
77, 78.—Uncertain; possibly Frankenthal, *Hannong fecit.*
79.—WEESP, Holland.
80.—Weesp? Arnstadt? Saxe Gotha? Quite uncertain.
81.—LOOSDRECHT. Manufactur oude Loosdrecht.
82, 83.—AMSTEL (Amsterdam).
84.—AMSTERDAM. The lion frequently alone.
85.—THE HAGUE.
86, 87, 88.—BRUSSELS. 87 is the mark of L. Cretté.
89–92.—LUXEMBOURG. 92 is the modern mark.
93.—ZURICH, Switzerland.
94.—NYON, Switzerland.
95–98.—TOURNAY. 95 is Peterynck's mark from 1751; the tower is also assigned to Vincennes, and pieces thus marked are called "Porcelaine de la tour."
99, 100, 101.—MARIEBERG, Sweden.
102, 103.—COPENHAGEN. Three waving lines for the Sound and the Belts.
104–112.—ST. PETERSBURG. Royal factory; 104, time of Empress Elizabeth, 1741; 105, 106, Empress Catherine (Ekaterina), 1762; 107, Emperor Paul, 1796; 108, Emperor Alexander, 1801; 109, Emperor Nicholas, 1825; 110, 111, Emperor Alexander II, 1855; 112, shows system of dates by dots adopted 1871—one dot for 1871, two for 1872, etc.
113, 114.—St. Petersburg. Brothers Korniloff.
115–119.—MOSCOW. Gardners.
120–123.—Moscow. Popoff. Factory established 1830.
124.—KIEV, Russia, or near there at Mejxigorie. Pottery.
125.—BARANOWKA, Poland. Pottery.
126.—CHMELOFF, Poland. Pottery.
127.—Kiev, Russia. Pottery.
128.—KORZEC, Poland. Pottery.

MARKS ON POTTERY AND PORCELAIN OF ENGLAND

1–18.—Bow. Scratched marks, resembling 4, 11, and other unintelligible scratches occur. Other marks are in color; sometimes as in 14, 15, 16, 18 in two colors.
19.—Bow? Bristol? Impressed mark. Uncertain.
20, 21.—CHELSEA. The triangle impressed was formerly assigned to Bow till discovery of piece with mark 21. It is on an English pottery teapot in the T.-P. collection.
22.—CHELSEA. Anchor embossed. Early mark.

23, 24.—Chelsea. Forms of the anchor mark in colors or gold. The anchor was used by many other factories.

25, 26.—Uncertain. Bow?

27, 28.—DERBY. Chelsea-Derby period.

29, 30.—Derby. Crown-Derby period. 30 supposed to be mark on pieces made at Chelsea, after the purchase by.Duesbury, and before closing the works.

31.—Derby. A mark of Duesbury's time, date unknown.

32, 33, 34, 35.—Marks used from about 1788. The earliest in puce or blue, later in red. 34 is of Duesbury & Kean.

36.—Derby. Bloor's mark.

37–41.—Derby. Bloor's marks.

42.—Derby. Modern mark of S. Hancock, present owner.

43, 44.—Derby? Uncertain marks on pieces resembling Derby.

45, 46.—Derby. Copies of Sèvres and Dresden marks on Derby porcelain.

47.—Derby. On a statuette.

48–52.—Derby. 48, 49, 50 are imitations of a Chinese symbol. 51 is uncertain, perhaps of Bloor's time. 52, a star, often impressed on figures.

53–57.—Bow? These marks occur in blue on figures.

58.—Bow? Supposed Monogram of Fry in blue.

59.—Bow? Impressed.

60.—DERBY. On service made for the Persian ambassador.

61.—Derby. On a plate.

62.—Derby. Used in 1842. Imitation of Sèvres.

63–76.—Derby. On various pieces. 71–75 are marks of Cocker, on figures, etc., made by him at Derby till 1840, and after that in London; 76 is an imitation of a Sèvres mark.

77–82.—WORCESTER. Workmen's marks on Worcester porcelain.

83.—CAUGHLEY. Forms of the crescent mark, and C in blue.

84.—Caughley. Forms of S, for Salopian, in blue or impressed.

85.—Caughley.

86, 87.—Caughley.

88–96.—Caughley. Numerals 1, 2, 3, etc., in fanciful style on printed wares.

97.—Caughley Mark of Rose?

98.—COALPORT.

99–104 —COLEBROOKDALE. The first three are the older marks. 102, adopted 1851. 103 is a modern mark, being a monogram of S.C., for Salopian, Colebrook-Dale, and including C, for Caughley or Coalport; S, for Swansea; and N, for Nantgarrow, the combined factories.

105.—SHELTON. The *New Hall* factory. Modern marks of this factory are HACKWOOD, or HACKWOOD & CO., from 1842 to 1856; then C & H, *late Hackwood*, for Cockson & Harding; and since 1862 HARDING.

106–110.—PINXTON.

111–132.—WORCESTER. The early mark is the letter W, in various forms, as in 112. This stands for Worcester or Wall.

The crescent, also in different forms, as in 113, in blue, gold or impressed, was used prior to 1793. It must not be mistaken for the crescent of Caughley, which it so closely resembles that certain specimens can sometimes be identified only by the paste or decorations.

The marks numbered 111 are workmen's marks. These do not identify specimens with certainty, as of Worcester, for similar marks are found on other porcelains.

The square marks, 114, 115 116, are early marks imitating Oriental.

Marks 117, 118, 119 are found on prints, and are the signatures of Robert Hancock, engraver. The anchor in 118 and 119 may be of Richard Holdship.

The 120–126 are early marks, fanciful imitations of Chinese. Other marks occur, resembling these in character.

127, 128, 129, 130 are imitations, of course, of the crossed sword mark of the Dresden factory.

131.—Is an imitation of the mark of Sèvres.

132.—Is an imitation of the mark of Chantilly.

133–146.—WORCESTER Flight purchased the works (1783), and used his name, impressed (mark 133), or painted (134), sometimes with the crescent mark in blue. 133 and 134 were used till 1792. After the king's visit, in 1788, mark 135 was sometimes used.

136.—Scratched mark of Barr after 1793.

137.—Flight & Barr, 1793–1807.

138–140.—Flight, Barr & Barr, 1807–1813. The F.B.B. impressed.

139.—Impressed mark, used 1813–1840.

141.—Printed mark, used 1813–1840.

142.—Chamberlain, 1788 to about 1804.

143.—Chamberlain, 1847–1850. Impressed or printed.

A Printed mark, *Chamberlain's Regent China, Worcester,* etc. under a crown, was used from 1811 to about 1820.

A written mark, *Chamberlains, Worcester, & 63 Piccadilly, London,* was used about 1814.

A printed mark, CHAMBERLAINS, WORCESTER, & 155 NEW BOND ST. LONDON under a crown, was used from 1820 to 1840. After the union of the two factories in 1840, the printed mark was CHAMBERLAIN & CO., 155 NEW BOND ST., & NO 1 COVENTRY ST. LONDON, under a crown.

In 1847 the mark was simply *Chamberlain. & Co., Worcester.*

From 1847 to 1850 mark 143 was used.

144.—Was used 1850–1851.

145.—Mark adopted by Kerr & Binns, 1851, and since used.

146.—Kerr & Binns on special work.

147.—PLYMOUTH. In blue, red or gold.

148–164.—BRISTOL. The general mark is a cross (149), in slate color, blue, or in the paste, with or without numbers and other marks. Numbers from 1 to 24 are thought to be of decorators. B, with a number (marks 151–154), was frequently used. 155 shows Bristol and Plymouth combined; 157, John Britain, foreman in the factory. 159 shows an embossed T over the cross in blue. The Dresden mark was frequently used, as in 160, 161, 162, 163, in combination with numbers, etc. 164 is probably a workman's mark.

165–169.—STOKE. *Minton.* 165 is the earliest mark. 166, 167 are also early marks. 168 was used about 1850, and 169 later.

170–174.—Stoke. Marks of Josiah Spode, father and son. 170 is an old mark, neatly penciled in various colors.

175–183.—Stoke. Marks of the several successors of Spode since 1833.

175.—Copeland & Garret, 1833–1847.

176.—Used by Copeland & Garret.

177.—Copeland & Garret.

178, 179.—Copeland & Garret, 1833–1847.

180.—Copeland, 1847–1851.

181.—Copeland, after 1851.

182.—Copeland used, 1847–1867.

183.—W. T. Copeland & Sons, after 1867.

184.—ROCKINGHAM. Adopted about 1823. The mark of *Brameld* from 1807 was his name impressed, sometimes with a cross and four dots. Tea-pots have impressed marks; MORTLOCK, CADOGANS, MORTLOCK'S CADOGAN, ROCKINGHAM. Coffee-pots had sometimes the pattern name NORFOLK impressed.

185–187.—SWANSEA. The name SWANSEA, stenciled or impressed, was used about 1815; also SWANSEA, DILLWYN & CO., and DILLWYN'S ETRUSCAN WARE. Marks 185, 186 are impressed, date unknown. 187 is on an old pottery vase. *Cambrian Pottery* also appears.

188.—NANTGAR W. 1813–1820, painted, impressed or stenciled. *Mortlock,* in gilt, occurs on ware decorated in London, and also on Swansea ware.

189.—LONGPORT. *Davenport's* mark. The earliest mark was LONGPORT or DAVENPORT LONGPORT. The marks are impressed or printed and forms vary. After 1805, on ironstone wares the anchor was in a portico.

190.—LIVERPOOL. *Richard Chaffers.*
191.—Liverpool. *Pennington.* In gold or colors.
192.—Longport. *Rogers.* Pottery and ironstone.
193.—LANE DELPH. *C. J. Mason.* Various other marks, including the name. The oldest marks include the name, MILES MASON; a mark is MASON'S CAMBRIAN ARGIL; and a late mark, FENTON STONE WORKS, C. J. M. & CO.
194.—TUNSTALL and BURSLEM. *Bridgwood & Clark,* 1857.
195.—LONGTON. *Hilditch & Son.*
196.—Tunstall. Bowers?
197.—Longton. *Mayer & Newbold.*
198, 199.—On Elers ware tea-pots.
200.—YARMOUTH. *Absolon.*
201, 202, 203.—LEEDS. 201 is *Charles Green.*
204.—LANE-END. *Turner.*
205.—EDINBURGH (Portobello) pottery.
206, 207, 208.—Liverpool. 206, 208 are Herculaneum pottery. Marks of this pottery are found impressed, painted and printed on bottoms and sides of pieces. 207 is of *Case & Mort,* proprietors from 1833.
209–214.—BURSLEM and ETRURIA. Marks of *Wedgwood* and his factory. The most common mark is the word WEDGWOOD, impressed.

MARKS OF AMERICAN POTTERS

MARKS OF PENNSYLVANIA POTTERIES

	Established
1.—Bonnin & Morris, Philadelphia, Pa.	1770
2.—Joseph Smith Pottery, Bucks County, Pa.	1767
3, 4.—Henry Roudebush, Montgomery County, Pa.	1811–1816
5.—Samuel Troxel, Montgomery County, Pa.	1823–1833
6.—George Hubener, Montgomery County, Pa.	1785–1798
7.—Jacob or Isaac Tany, Bucks County, Pa.	1794
8.—John Drey, Easton, Pa.	1809
9.—Andrew Headman, Rock Hill, Bucks County, Pa.	1808
10, 11.—Unidentified marks on German American pottery.	
12.—Jacob Schell, Tylers Port, Montgomery County, Pa.	1830
13.—Womelsdorf, Pa.	
John Menner	1784
Willoughby Smith	1864
14.—American China Manufactory, Philadelphia, Pa.	1825
15, 16.—Tucker & Hulme	1828
17.—Judge Joseph Hemphill	1832–1836
18–24.—Private marks of workmen.	
25.—Smith, Fife & Co., Philadelphia, Pa.	1830
26.—Ralph Bagnall Beach, Philadelphia, Pa.	1845
27.—Kurlbaum & Schwartz	1851
28.—Workman's mark.	
29.—The Phoenix Pottery, Kaolin and Fire Brick Co., Phoenixville, Pa.	1867
30.—Beerbower & Griffen, Phoenixville, Pa.	1877
31–34A.—Griffen, Smith & Hill, Phoenixville, Pa.	1879
35–37.—Chester Pottery Co. of Pennsylvania, Phoenixville, Pa.	1894
38.—The Philadelphia City Pottery, J. E. Jeffords & Co.	1868
39.—Galloway & Graff, Philadelphia, Pa.	1810
40–59.—The Mayer Pottery Co., Beaver Falls, Pa.	1881

Established

60.—Star Encaustic Tile Co., Pittsburg, Pa. 1882
61.—The Robertson Art Tile Co., Morrisville, Pa.
62.—The Shenango China Co., New Castle, Pa.
63, 64.—Moravian Pottery and Tile Works, Doylestown, Pa.
65.—The Wick China Co., Kittanning, Pa.
66–70.—The Ford China Co., Ford City, Pa.
71.—The New Castle Pottery Co., New Castle, Pa.
72.—The Derry China Co., Derry Station, Pa.
73.—Pennsylvania Museum and School of Industrial Art, Phila., Pa. 1903

MARKS OF NEW JERSEY POTTERIES

74–81.—The Jersey City Pottery, Jersey City, N. J. 1829
    D. & J. Henderson.
    American Pottery Manufacturing Co. 1833
82.—William Young & Sons, Trenton, N. J. 1853
83–90.—The Willits Manufacturing Co., Trenton, N. J. 1879
91.—The City Pottery Co., Trenton, N. J. 1859
92–98.—Greenwood Pottery Co., Trenton, N. J. 1861
99–101.—The East Trenton Pottery Co., Trenton, N. J. 1888
102, 103.—Millington, Astbury & Poulson, Trenton, N. J. 1853
104, 105.—Thomas Maddock & Sons, Trenton, N. J. 1859
105A.—Thomas Maddock's Sons Co., Trenton, N. J. 1902
106–108.—The Maddock Pottery Co., Trenton, N. J. 1893
109, 110.—John Maddock & Sons, Trenton, N. J. .... · 1894
111–140.—The Glasgow Pottery, Trenton, N. J. 1863
141–155.—Ott & Brewer, Trenton, N. J. 1863
156–163.—The Cook Pottery Co., Trenton, N. J. 1894
164–166.—Isaac Broome, Trenton, N. J. 1880
167.—Coxon & Co., Trenton, N. J. 1863
168.—Trenton Pottery Co., Trenton, N. J. 1865
169–184.—Mercer Pottery Co., Trenton, N. J. 1868
185.—The New Jersey Pottery Co., Trenton, N. J. 1869
186–203.—International Pottery Co., Trenton, N. J. 1860
204–206.—American Crockery Co., Trenton, N. J. 1876
207–212.—Burroughs & Mountford Co., Trenton, N. J. 1879
213–217.—The Prospect Hill Pottery Co., Trenton, N. J. 1880
218–225.—Anchor Pottery Co., Trenton, N. J. 1894
226, 227.—Delaware Pottery, Trenton, N. J. 1884
228–240.—Crescent Pottery, Trenton, N. J. 1881
241–243.—Empire Pottery, Trenton, N. J. 1863
244.—Enterprise Pottery, Trenton, N. J. 1880
245–254.—Trenton Potteries Co., Trenton, N. J. Organized 1892
255.—The Bellmark Pottery Co., Trenton, N. J. 1893
256–258.—The Fell & Thropp Co., Trenton, N. J.
259, 260.—The Trenton Pottery Works, Trenton, N. J.
261.—Keystone Pottery Co., Trenton, N. J.
262.—Star Porcelain Co., Trenton, N. J.
263–267.—The Ceramic Art Co., Trenton, N. J. 1889
268.—The Trenton China Co., Trenton, N. J. 1859
269.—The American Art China Works, Trenton, N. J. 1891
270, 271.—Columbian Art Pottery, Trenton, N. J.
272.—American Porcelain Manufacturing Co., Gloucester, N. J. 1854
273, 274.—L. B. Beerbower & Co., Elizabeth, N. J. 1816
275.—Charles Wingender & Brother, Haddonfield, N. J.
276.—C. L. & H. A. Poillon, Woodbridge, N. J.

MARKS OF NEW YORK POTTERIES

	Established
277.—Salamander Works, New York, N. Y.	1848
278–286.—New York City Pottery, N. Y., N. Y.	1853
287–291.—Union Porcelain Works, Greenpoint, N. Y.	1876
292–298.—Onondaga Pottery Co., Syracuse, N. Y.	1871
299–302.—Volkmar Pottery, Greenpoint, N. Y.	1879
303.—East Morrison China Works, N. Y., N. Y.	
304–306.—The Faïence Manufacturing Co., Greenpoint, N. Y.	1880
307.—Charles Graham Chemical Pottery Works, Brooklyn, N. Y.	
308, 309.—Middle Lane Pottery, East Hampton, L. I. T. A. Brouwer, Jr.	
310, 310A, 310B.—The Chittenango Pottery Co., Chittenango, N. Y.	1897
311.—American Art Ceramic Co., Corona, N. Y.	1901

MARKS OF NEW ENGLAND POTTERIES

312–314.—Norton Pottery Co., Bennington, Vt.	1793
315–317.—United States Pottery Co., Bennington, Vt.	1849
318.—Nichols & Alford, Burlington, Vt.	1854
319–327.—New England Pottery Co., East Boston, Mass.	1854
328, 329.—Chelsea Keramic, Chelsea, Mass.	1866
330–332.—Dedham Pottery Co., Dedham, Mass.	
333–335.—Hampshire Pottery Co., Keene, N. H.	1871
336–342.—New Milford Pottery Co., New Milford, Conn.	1886
343–347.—The Grueby Faïence Co., Boston, Mass.	1897
348–360.—Artist's marks.	
361, 362.—Merrimac Ceramic Co., Newburyport, Mass.	1897
363.—The Low Art Tile Co., Chelsea, Mass.	1893

MARKS OF OHIO POTTERIES

364–367.—The Harker Pottery Co., East Liverpool, O.	1840
368–372.—The Goodwin Pottery Co., East Liverpool, O.	1844
373–377.—The Smith-Phillips China Co., East Liverpool, O.	
378–391.—The Vodrey Pottery Co., East Liverpool, O.	1848
392–401.—The William Brunt Pottery Co., East Liverpool, O.	1850
402–435.—The Knowles, Taylor & Knowles Co., East Liverpool, O.	1854
436.—D. E. McNicol Pottery Co., East Liverpool, O.	1863
437–443.—C. C. Thompson Pottery Co., East Liverpool, O.	1868
444–452.—The Homer Laughlin China Co., East Liverpool, O.	1874
453–463.—The Potter's Cooperative Co., East Liverpool, O.	1876
464–468.—Cartwright Brothers, East Liverpool, O.	
469–474.—The Globe Pottery Co., East Liverpool, O.	1881
475.—The Wallace and Chetwynd Pottery Co., East Liverpool, O.	
476–478.—The United States Pottery, East Liverpool, O.	
479–483.—The East Liverpool Pottery Co., East Liverpool, O.	1896
484–487.—The George C. Murphy Pottery Co., East Liverpool, O.	
488–493.—The East End Pottery Co., East Liverpool, O.	
494.—The East Liverpool Potteries Co., East Liverpool, O.	
495–498.—The Union Potteries Co., East Liverpool, O.	
499–510A.—The Burford Brothers Pottery Co., East Liverpool, O.	
511–514.—The Taylor, Smith & Taylor Co., East Liverpool, O.	1899
515, 516.—The West End Pottery Co., East Liverpool, O.	1893
517–521.—The Sèvres China Co., East Liverpool, O.	1900
522, 523.—The Ed. M. Knowles China Co., East Liverpool, O.	1901
524–526.—The Brockman Pottery Co., Cincinnati, O.	1862
527–540.—The Rookwood Pottery Co., Cincinnati, O.	1879

Marks of Southern Potteries

Marks of Western Potteries

MARKS ON WARES OF ITALY, PERSIA, RHODES, ETC.

MARKS ON POTTERY OF FRANCE·

B   B   B   B   D2 $\frac{D}{14}$ lille   P   ⚜

D   XX   Lille   FB B   XX   C   S.C.A

XA   R R   LZ   Axe   ⚓   OP   SP

B. R.   S$\frac{t}{T}$C   ·S·   S·pellevé   ·S.C.y.   j·A   ⚓

ARj   R   R·v.   LR   RG M.   N.   M.   ♔

C   C   +   [M & Cie]   CH   M   R   H

M $\frac{H}{T9}$ H   HB   J S L   R   V   V

#G   ·G·   G   φ.   A·φ.   φG

φP   φSc   Sφ   φA   Rφ   φSφ   Bφ

Bφ   Bφ   φP   Fφ   Bφ   φ·h   φic.

φφ   φ.O·φ   T·L·   φs   Mφ   RNf

RT   RB·f   A B   Pf   f.   fi   Ef   Fe

f.   f^{d} F^{d} G   M.C.   M·C·A 1750 J·A   P.F.

F·P   ·oy·   ⚜   ⚜   ⚜   R   R   R

·R·X·   V·   V·   B·   F.   R   M   M

R   ♔   J. Boulard a Neuer 1622 $\frac{ILF}{1636}$ B

K·B 1689   H·B 1689   B.   P·C   E.Borne 1689   d conrad A neuers

·F·R·1734   N   A·+ Limoges · le 18me may J74J   de Conrade antuers

avisseau
atouc
1855

A.C

AN
A.
P.

CD
CABRI
1762

CB
.C.
.S.

F.C- 1661

GDG
1780
2

FG=SG
FE.
fl.
GAA
H

"Fait par GDE, A⁰ 1761."

HE
H G i

JⁿTamact
1696

H
G
H

.II.
J
B

+Leger+

Lejeune+
+1730+

A.R. f

R

M

NICOLas H.V
1738

OIP, OP

OS

I.R+PAIVADEAVf
1643

PB
P
P

P

GP
P

PO
P.R.

PV
3|2

R
R
R.B
F
RL

R.M.
f

S. G.h

NE

T.C.E
1793 an 41

VM
W
2
W
W
H
P.

MARKS ON POTTERY OF BELGIUM AND HOLLAND

6☀
☀R
☀ G
CCC
c. r,
.IM
FP

B
B. L
GA
i

F
1677
F
1.6.8.0
R G
MD
Sloot
1720

Sr G

UNKNOWN MARKS ON POTTERY OF HOLLAND

MARKS ON POTTERY OF GERMANY, SWEDEN,
DENMARK, SPAIN AND PORTUGAL

MARKS ON PORCELAIN OF ITALY, SPAIN AND
PORTUGAL

MARKS ON PORCELAIN OF SEVRES

MARKS USED BY PAINTERS, DECORATORS AND GILDERS AT SEVRES

FIRST PERIOD. 1753–1799

Aloncle—birds, animals, emblems, etc.

Anteaume—landscape, animals.

Armand—birds, flowers, etc.

Asselin—portraits, miniatures, etc.

Aubert (senior)—flowers.

Bailly (son)—flowers.

Bardet—flowers.

Barre—detached bouquets.

Barrat—garlands, bouquets.

Baudoin — ornaments, friezes, etc.

Becquet—flowers, etc.

Bertrand — detached bouquets.

Bienfait—gilding.

Binet—detached bouquets.

Binet, Madame (née *Sophie Chanou*)—flowers.

Boucher—flowers, garlands, etc.

Bouchet—landscape, figures, ornaments.

Bouillat—flowers, landscapes.

Boulanger—detached bouquets.

Boulanger (son) — pastoral subjects, children.

Bulidon—detached bouquets.

Bunel, Madame (née *Manon Buteux*)—flowers.

Couturier—gilding.

Dieu — Chinese, Chinese flowers, gilding, etc.

Dodin—figure, various subjects, portraits.

Drand—Chinese, gilding.

Dubois — flowers, garlands, etc.

Dusolle—detached bouquets, etc.

Dutanda—detached bouquets, garlands.

Evans—birds, butterflies, landscapes.

Falot—arabesques, birds, butterflies.

Fontaine — emblems, miniatures, etc.

Fontelliau—gilding, etc.

Fouré — flowers, bouquets, etc.

Fritsch—figures, children.

Fumez—detached bouquets.

Fumez—another form.

Gauthier—landscape and animals.

Genest—figure and genre.

Genin — flowers, garlands, friezes, etc.

Bunel, Madame — another form.

Buteux (senior) — flowers, emblems, etc.

Buteux (elder son, — detached bouquets, etc.

Buteux (younger son)—pastoral subjects, children.

Capel—friezes.

Cardin — detached bouquets.

Carrier—flowers.

Castel — landscapes, hunts, birds.

Caton — pastoral subjects, children, birds.

Catrice — flowers, detached bouquets.

Chabry — miniatures, pastoral subjects.

Chanou, Madame (née *Julie Durosey*)—flowers.

Chapuis (elder) – flowers, birds, etc.

Chapuis (younger) — detached bouquets.

Chauvaux (father) — gilding.

Chauvaux (son)—detached bouquets, gilding.

Chevalier — flowers, bouquets, etc.

Choisy, De — flowers, arabesques.

Chulot—emblems, flowers, arabesques.

Commelin — detached bouquets, garlands.

Cornaille — flowers, detached bouquets.

Henrion—garlands, detached bouquets.

Héricourt — detached bouquets, garlands.

Hilken—figures, pastoral subjects, etc.

Houry—flowers, etc.

Huny — detached bouquets, flowers.

Joyau — detached bouquets, etc.

Jubin—gilding.

La Roche—flowers, garlands, emblems.

La Roche—another form.

Le Bel (elder)—figures and flowers.

Le Bel (younger)—garlands, bouquets, etc.

Léandre — pastoral subjects, miniatures.

Lecot—Chinese, etc.

Lecot—another form.

Ledoux—landscape and birds.

Le Guay—gilding.

Le Guay—another form.

Leguay—miniatures, children, Chinese.

Gerard — pastoral subjects, miniatures.

Gerard, Madame (née Vautrin)—flowers.

Girard—arabesques,Chinese, etc.

Gomery—flowers and birds.

Gremont—garlands,bouquets.

Grison—gilding.

Michel—detached bouquets.

Moiron—detached bouquets; also another form used by Michel.

Mongenot—flowers, detached bouquets.

Morin—marine. military subjects.

Mutel—landscape.

Niquet — detached bouquets, etc.

Noel—flowers, ornaments.

Nouaithier, Madame (née Sophie Durosy)—flowers.

Parpette — flowers, detached bouquets.

Parpette, Dlle. Louison—flowers.

Pajou—figure.

Petit—flowers.

Pfeiffer—detached bouquets.

Pierre (elder)—flowers, bouquets.

Pierre (younger)—bouquets, garlands.

Philippine (elder) — pastoral subjects, children, etc.

Pithou (elder)—portraits, historical subjects.

Pithou (younger) — figures, flowers, ornaments.

Pouillot—detached bouquets.

Prevost—gilding.

Raux—detached bouquets.

Levé (father)—flowers, birds, arabesques.

Levé, Felix—flowers, Chinese.

Maqueret, Madame (née Bouillat)—flowers.

Massy—groups of flowers, garlands.

Merault (elder)—friezes.

Merault (younger)—garlands, bouquets.

Micaud — flowers, bouquets, medallions.

Rochet — figure, miniatures, etc.

Rosset—landscapes, etc.

Roussel—detached bouquets.

Schradre — birds, landscape, etc.

Sinsson—flowers, groups, garlands, etc.

Sioux (elder)—detached bouquets, garlands.

Sioux (younger) — flowers, garlands.

Tabary—birds, etc.

Taillandier—detached bouquets, garlands.

Tandart—groups of flowers, garlands.

Tardi — detached bouquets, etc.

Theodore—gilding.

Thevenet (father) — flowers, medallions, groups, etc.

Thevenet (son) — ornaments, friezes, etc.

Vandé—gilding, flowers.

Vavasseur —arabesques.

Vieillard — emblems, ornaments, etc.

Vincent—gilding.

Xrowet—arabesques, flowers, etc.

Yvernel—landscape, birds.

SECOND PERIOD. 1800–1874

André, Jules—landscape.

Apoil—figures, subjects, etc.

Apoil, Madame—figure.

Barré—flowers.

Barriat—figure.

Beranger—figure.

Blanchard—decorator.

Blanchard, Alex.—ornament worker.

Boitel—gilding.

Bonnuit—decorator.

Boullemier, Antoine—gilding.

Boullèmier (elder)—gilding.

Boullèmier (son)—gilding.

Archelais—ornament worker (pâtes sur pâtes).

Avisse—ornament worker.

Barbin—ornaments.

Drouet—flowers.

Ducluzeau, Madame—figure, subjects, portraits, etc.

Durosey—gilding.

Farraguet, Madame —figure, subjects, etc.

Ficquenet—flowers and ornaments (pâtes sur pâtes).

Fontaine—flowers.

Fragonard—figure, genre,etc.

Ganeau (son)—gilding.

Gély — ornament worker (pâtes sur pâtes).

Bx. Buteux—flowers.

Œ Cabau—flowers.

CP Capronnier—gilding.

IC Célos — ornament worker (pâtes sur pâtes).

LC Charpentier—decorator.

F.C. Charrin, Dlle. Fanny—subjects, figures, portraits.

C.C. Constant—gilding.

C.Z. Constantin—figure.

AD Dammouse—figure, ornament (pâtes sur pâtes).

D David—decorator.

D.F. Delafosse—figure.

D.F. Davignon—landscape.

D.P. Desperais—ornaments.

DE Derichsweiller—decorator.

CD Develly — landscape and genre.

Dh Deutsch—ornaments.

D.I. Didier—ornaments, etc.

D: Didier—another form.

A Martinet—flowers.

E.deM. Maussion, Mdlle. de—figure

M Merigot—ornaments, etc.

MAR Meyer, Alfred—figure, etc.

McC Micaud—gilding.

M Milet, Optat—decorator on faience and pastes.

M.R Moreau—gilding.

AM Moriot—figure, etc.

PP Parpette, Dlle.—flowers.

P.L. Philippine — flowers and ornaments.

P Pline—decorative gilding.

R Poupart—landscape.

R Regnier, Ferd.—figure, various subjects.

JR Regnier, Hyacinthe—figure.

R Rejoux—decorator.

E 1000 Renard, Émile—decorator.

EMR Richard, Émile—flowers.

ER Richard, Eugène—flowers.

J.J. Georget—figure, portraits, etc.

Gob.R Gobert—figure on enamel and on pastes.

D.G. Godin—gilding.

F.G. Goupil—figure.

H Guillemain—decorator.

H Hallion, Eugène—landscape.

H Hallion, François—decorator in gilding.

h.D. Huard — ornaments, divers styles.

.C.h. Humbert—figure.

E Julienne — ornaments, style Renaissance, etc.

L Lambert—flowers.

Lg Langlacé—landscape.

L Latache—gilding.

L.B. Le Bel—landscape.

L Legay — ornament worker (pâtes sur pâtes).

L.G. Le Gay—figures, various subjects, portraits.

LG Legrand—gilding.

EL Leroy, Eugène—gilding.

R Richard, François—decorator.

JhR Richard, Joseph—decorator.

+ Richard, Paul — decorative gilding.

Rx. Riocreux, Isidore—landscape.

Rx Riocreux, Désiré-Denis — flowers.

PR Robert, Pierre—landscape.

CR Robert Madame—flowers and landscape.

R Robert, Jean-François—landscape.

PMR Roussel—figure, etc.

P.S Schilt, Louis-Pierre—flowers.

S.S.p Sinsson (father)—flowers.

M Solon—figures and ornaments (pâtes sur pâtes).

S.W. Swebach — landscape and genre.

J.T. Trager—flowers, birds.

T. Troyon—ornaments.

W Walter—flowers.

UNDETERMINED SIGNATURES. ETC.

W
Tg
CP   Three marks on plate dated 1821, view of Moka, signed L. M., richly gilded. The first mark also on several plates dated 1812, lapis-lazuli borders, heavy gilding, antique cameo paintings.

M On richly decorated and gilded plates, 1821.

Фhiиε On plate, time of Louis XVIII., richly gilded ; monochrome portrait of Racine : (probable mark of Philippine.)

Ɗᵐᵗ Яog ᵈ On plate not dated, rich gilding, monochrome portrait of Bourdaloue.

BT On fine plates and vases, 1812.

Ɗᵘᵉ Τᵣᵉ On plate *temp* Louis XVIII., rich gilding, monochrome portrait of Bourdon (? Dlle. de Treverret).

Я Twice this size on plate, 1822, view of Sèvres factory ; possibly a *visa* of Riocreux.

Lₚ In black on foot of ice vase, with river deities in superb gilding, dated 1831.

ARTISTS' SIGNATURES FOUND AT FULL LENGTH

Baldisseroni—figure.
Brunel—figure.
Bulot—flowers.
Cool, Madame de—figure.
Courcy, De—figure.
Froment—figure.
Gallois, Madame (née *Durand*)—figure.
Garneray—landscape.
De Gault—figure.
Goddé—decorator, enamels and relief.
Hamon—figure.
Jaccober—flowers and fruits.
Jacquotot, Madame Victoire—figure, subjects, portraits.
Jadelot, Madame—figure.

Lamarre—landscape.
Langlois, Polycles—landscape.
Laurent, Madame Pauline—figure, subjects, etc.
Lessore—figure, etc.
Meyer-Heine—figure and ornaments on enamel.
Parant—figure, etc.
Philip—decorator on enamel.
Schilt, Abel—figure, subjects, portraits.
Solon, Dlle.—figure, subjects.
Treverret, Dlle. de—figure.
Van Os—flowers and fruits.
Van Marck—landscape.

MARKS USED AT SÈVRES TO INDICATE DATES OF MANUFACTURE

A (Vincennes)	 1753	N	 1766
B "	 1754	O	 1767
C "	 1755	P	 1768
D	 1756	Q	 1769
E	 1757	R	 1770
F	 1758	S	 1771
G	 1759	T	 1772
H	 1760	U	 1773
I	 1761	V	 1774
J (see foot note)	 1762	X	 1775
K	 1763	Y	 1776
L	 1764	Z	 1777
M	 1765		

AA	 1778	JJ	 1787
BB	 1779	KK	 1788
CC	 1780	LL	 1789
DD	 1781	MM	 1790
EE	 1782	NN	 1791
FF	. . . . : 1783	OO	 1792
GG	 1784	PP	 1793
HH	 1785	QQ	 1794
II	 1786	RR	 1795

This mode of marking the date fell into disuse, and, from this period until 1800, it is found only on rare examples. In 1801, the custom of dating was resumed, and the letters replaced by the following signs:

T. 9 . . . . An IX. (1801)	9 1809
X . . . . " X. (1802)	10 1810
11 . . . . " XI. (1803)	*oz.* (onze) 1811
−∥− . . . . " XII. (1804)	*d. z.* (douze) 1812
⬆ . . . . " XIII. (1805)	*t. z.* (treize) 1813
⬊ . . . . " XIV. (1806)	*q. z.* (quatorze) 1814
	q. n. (quinze) 1815
7 1807	*s. z.* (seize) 1816
8 1808	*d. s.* (dix-sept) 1817

MARKS ON PORCELAIN OF FRANCE

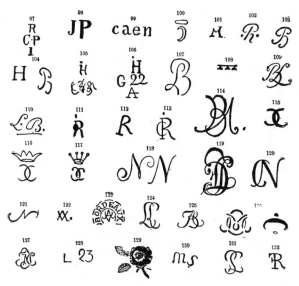

MARKS ON PORCELAIN OF GERMANY, ETC.

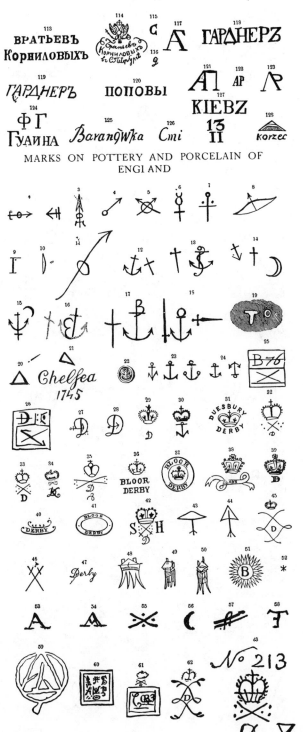

MARKS ON POTTERY AND PORCELAIN OF
ENGLAND

MARKS OF PENNSYLVANIA POTTERIES

MARKS OF NEW JERSEY POTTERIES

MARKS OF NEW YORK POTTERIES

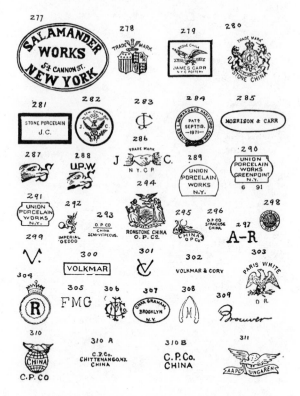

MARKS OF NEW ENGLAND POTTERIES

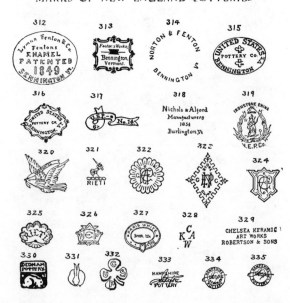

MARKS OF OHIO POTTERIES

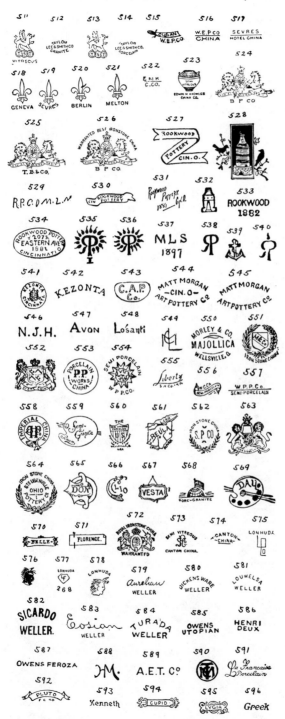

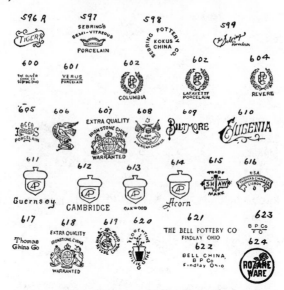

MARKS OF SOUTHERN POTTERIES

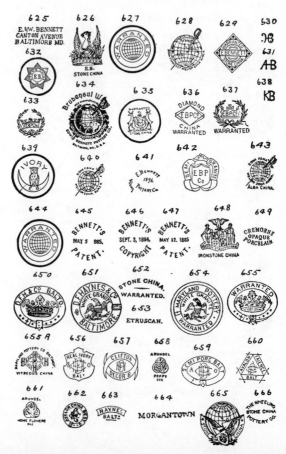

MARKS OF WESTERN POTTERIES

PRIVATE MARKS OF ROOKWOOD DECORATORS

MARKS ON CHINESE WARES

The inscriptions sometimes occurring in the field of decoration on Chinese porcelains are poems or references to the subject of the painting rather than dates or place marks, though exceptions do occur as in the Wan Li blue and white vase and the small Sung period Tz'u Chou formerly in my own collection ir which the six character reign mark is about the shoulder, and in the three beakers in the Metropolitan Museum on which the marks occur in small rectangular cartouches near the lip-rim. Generally speaking the stamped, incised or painted marks which throw light on the period of a piece are found on the bottom. Marks on Sung or Yuan pieces are exceedingly rare and Ming pieces which have marks usually have the characters in ordinary script (k'ai shu) rather than in seal characters (chuan shu) though the script characters are often enclosed by a square, rectangular or round frame of double lines, as though to suggest a seal. Chinese inscriptions are read right to left in perpendicular columns top to bottom. Sir Percival David has pointed out that Mongolian inscriptions read top to bottom, left to right and this has been a contributing factor in placing some pieces. (See Plate XXXVII, The Catalogue of Chinese Pottery and Porcelain in The Collection of Sir Percival David.)

Marks fall into five classifications:

1.—Reign or date marks.
2.—Hall marks.
3.—Factory marks and potter's names.
4.—Marks of praise, dedication, etc.
5.—Pictorial or symbol marks.

1.—DATE MARKS.—Usually the period is indicated by giving the honorific name assumed by the emperor on ascending the throne. This title (nien hao) is the name by which collectors are accustomed to know the reign; thus Chan Chi's reign is known as Hsüan Tê and Chien Shen's as Ch'êng Hua (See text). To quote Mr. Ralph M. Chait (Chinese Chronology), "He loses his personal name and does not assume any name or proper title as do European kings, but gives to the epoch of his reign a distinguished appellation, which designates at once his period. This, however, is not the name by which he is canonized after death. That is called the "Mia Hao". Therefore, in history the emperor is known by his Mia Hao, and in ceramic history he is called by his Nien Hao, because it is perfectly obvious that it would be impossible to do otherwise, as no one could tell what his canonized name would be." Most earlier wares are marked with six characters. The first two beginning at the upper right and reading downward refer to the dynasty, thus ta ming means Great Ming (dynasty). The next two, that is the bottom one on the right hand column and the top one on the left hand column are the nien hao, thus we might read Hsüan Tê and the last two are nien chih or "period made,"—the whole reading ta ming hsüan tê nien hao or literally Great Ming Hsüan Tê period made. Sometimes the last character is tsao but this also means "made."

Abbreviated marks sometimes leave off the first two characters, giving simply the nien hao and "period made." Abbreviated marks which read simply ta ming nien chih also occur on proper specimens but are to be mistrusted for the Japanese made use of such marks. Sometimes only the double ring is used without any characters in it and this occurs in Ming as well as Ch'ing times. It is explained by R. L. Hobson that one workman did the rings and another the characters so perhaps these pieces which slipped through without the attention of the second workman. In any event such a mark seems to have no bearing on the quality whatsoever. A complete list of the Imperial nien hao will be found in the Chinese Reader's Manual, by Mayer, in Giles' Dictionary, and in Handbook of Marks on Pottery and Porcelain by Burton and Hobson.

Once again we must warn that Chinese marks were copied in later reigns, were freely placed on modern wares made for trade and were also counterfeited by the Japanese. In his very interesting book Early Ming Wares of Chingtechen, the late A. D. Brankston shows some most convincing comparisons in the calligraphy. Hobson states "The connoisseur will take little heed of the ordinary date marks unless they are supported by good collateral evidence."

Seal marks are usually arranged in three columns of two characters each instead of in two columns of three characters each. They are read the same way from upper right to lower left and the nien hao occurs in the two center characters.

Brankston adds a few notes on marks of the Hsüan Tê period, "Apart from calligraphy, there are several forms of writing the mark. On dishes and bowls with glazed bases the mark is usually underneath in six characters enclosed in a double, rarely a single circle. On dishes with unglazed bases the mark is sometimes written in a line under the rim on the outside. On stem-cups the mark is usually written inside the bowl in the center, on yellow glazed stem-cups the mark is incised inside." This last is not invariably the case in later examples as we know. He continues, "There is a scarce type of bowl in which the six character mark is written inside in a single column, enclosed in a double rectangle: Plate 12g. The example seen was decorated outside with the Eight Buddhistic Emblems supported on lotus scrolls. The Hsüan Tê mark in four characters is rarely seen on Imperial porcelain. Those jars and bowls marked Hsüan Tê nien tsao were apparently made for export, fragments have been found in many places on the trade route along the South China coast, and in the Philippines." Again he stresses the style of writing, "If, in the writing of the mark, any stroke which forms part of a character has been formed by two sweeps of the brush, the piece in question is with little doubt a later copy. This being so, the same fault should be found in the drawing, if in underglaze blue."

Rare specimens have a cyclical date as well as the nien hao. Thus in The Wares of the Ming Dynasty, R. L. Hobson shows a well known bowl from the S. D. Winkworth collection which is marked ta ming hsüan tê kuei ch'ou nien tsao or made in the kuei ch'ou year of the Hsüan Tê period, viz. 1433. This Chinese cycle consists of sixty years each of which has an individual name in two characters formed by combining one of the Ten Stems with one of Twelve Branches. The Chinese Reader's Manual gives

CHRONOLOGICAL TABLE

Mark	Tran-scription	Year of the Cycle	Mark	Tran-scription	Year of the Cycle	Mark	Tran-scription	Year of the Cycle
子甲	Chia-tzŭ	1	申甲	Chia-shên	21	辰甲	Chia-ch'ên	41
丑乙	I-ch'oŭ	2	酉乙	I-yu	22	巳乙	I-ssŭ	42
寅丙	Ping-yin	3	戌丙	Ping-hsŭ	23	午丙	Ping-wu	43
卯丁	Ting-mao	4	亥丁	Ting-hai	24	未丁	Ting-wei	44
辰戊	Mou-ch'ên	5	子戊	Mou-tzŭ	25	申戊	Mou-shên	45
巳己	Chi-ssŭ	6	丑己	Chi-ch'ou	26	酉己	Chi-yu	46
午庚	Kêng-wu	7	寅庚	Kêng-yin	27	戌庚	Kêng-hsŭ	47
未辛	Hsin-wei	8	卯辛	Hsin-mao	28	亥辛	Hsin-hai	48
申壬	Jên-shên	9	辰壬	Jên-ch'ên	29	子壬	Jên-tzŭ	49
酉癸	Kuei-yu	10	巳癸	Kuei-ssŭ	30	丑癸	Kuei-ch'ou	50
戌甲	Chia-hsŭ	11	午甲	Chia-wu	31	寅甲	Chia-yin	51
亥乙	I-hai	12	未乙	I-wei	32	卯乙	I-mao	52
子丙	Ping-tzŭ	13	申丙	Ping-shên	33	辰丙	Ping-ch'ên	53
丑丁	Ting-ch'ou	14	酉丁	Ting-yu	34	巳丁	Ting-ssŭ	54
寅戊	Mou-yin	15	戌戊	Mou-hsŭ	35	午戊	Mou-wu	55
卯己	Chi-mao	16	亥己	Chi-hai	36	未己	Chi-wei	56
辰庚	Kêng-ch'ên	17	子庚	Kêng-tzŭ	37	申庚	Kêng-shên	57
巳辛	Hsin-ssŭ	18	丑辛	Hsin-ch'ou	38	酉辛	Hsin-yu	58
午壬	Jên-wu	19	寅壬	Jên-yin	39	戌壬	Jên-hsŭ	59
未癸	Kuei-wei	20	卯癸	Kuei-mao	40	亥癸	Kuei-hai	60

chronological tables with a full description of the system but the certainly ingenious table worked out by Hetherington is used by all collectors. It appears in his book, *The Early Ceramic Wares of China* (A. L. Hetherington) and also in *The Wares of the Ming Dynasty* (R. L. Hobson) from which our page was reproduced.

MARKS, INSCRIPTIONS AND CHINESE CHARACTERS

甲 chia	乙 i	丙 ping	丁 ting	戊 mou	己 chi	庚 kêng	辛 hsin	壬 jên	癸 kuei
子 [1] tzŭ	丑 [2] ch'ou	寅 [3] yin	卯 [4] mao	辰 [5] ch'ên	巳 [6] ssŭ	午 [7] wu	未 [8] wei	申 [9] shên	酉 [10] yu
戌 [11] hsŭ	亥 [12] hai	子 [13]	丑 [14]	寅 [15]	卯 [16]	辰 [17]	巳 [18]	午 [19]	未 [20]
申 [21]	酉 [22]	戌 [23]	亥 [24]	子 [25]	丑 [26]	寅 [27]	卯 [28]	辰 [29]	巳 [30]
午 [31]	未 [32]	申 [33]	酉 [34]	戌 [35]	亥 [36]	子 [37]	丑 [38]	寅 [39]	卯 [40]
辰 [41]	巳 [42]	午 [43]	未 [44]	申 [45]	酉 [46]	戌 [47]	亥 [48]	子 [49]	丑 [50]
寅 [51]	卯 [52]	辰 [53]	巳 [54]	午 [55]	未 [56]	申 [57]	酉 [58]	戌 [59]	亥 [60]

" The first horizontal line of characters represents the ten stems. One of these stems will be found in combination with one of the branches in every cyclical date mark. If the eye is carried vertically downwards from the stem which has been detected in the inscription until it recognises the branch character, the year can be read off at once." Take the inscription on Fig. 2 of Plate 15. The character 癸 (*kuei*) is detected and is found to be the tenth stem, reading the table from left to right. With it is the character 丑 (*ch'ou*), the second branch. By carrying the eye vertically down the column headed with 癸 the combination is found in the sixth horizontal line of the diagrams indicating the fiftieth year. In some inscriptions the cyclical date is all that is mentioned, and we are left to determine the particular cycle concerned as best we may from indications of style or other internal evidence. But here we have only to do with the cycle in which the Hsüan Tê period fell, and we have no difficulty in arriving at the date 1433.

The cyclical system is supposed to have been instituted in the year 2637 B.C.; but in the Ming period we are only concerned with the cycles which began in 1324, 1384, 1444, 1504, 1564 and 1624 A.D.

Simpler still, but very uncommon, are those convenient date marks in which the number of the year in the reign is specified. To read those one must know the Chinese numerals :—

1 = 一 i.	5 = 五 wu.	9 = 九 chiu.
2 = 二 êrh.	6 = 六 liu.	10 = 十 shih.
3 = 三 san.	7 = 七 ch'i.	
4 = 四 ssŭ.	8 = 八 pa.	

DYNASTIC PERIODS MENTIONED IN THIS BOOK

Han dynasty	206 B.C.– 220 A.D.
T'ang „	618 A.D.– 906 A.D.
Sung „	960 A.D.–1279 A.D.
Yüan „	1280 A.D.–1367 A.D.
Ming „	1368 A.D.–1644 A.D.
Ch'ing „	1644 A.D.–1912 A.D.

REIGNS OF THE MING DYNASTY

Hung Wu	洪	武	1368–1398.
Chien Wên	建	文	1399–1402.
Yung Lo	永	樂	1403–1424.
Hung Hsi	洪	熙	1425.
Hsüan Tê	宣	德	1426–1435.
Chêng T'ung	正	統	1436–1449.
Ching T'ai	景	泰	1450–1456.
T'ien Shun	天	順	1457–1464.
Ch'êng Hua	成	化	1465–1487.
Hung Chih	弘	治	1488–1505.
Chêng Tê	正	德	1506–1521.
Chia Ching	嘉	靖	1522–1566.
Lung Ch'ing	隆	慶	1567–1572.
Wan Li	萬	歷	1573–1619.
T'ai Ch'ang	泰	昌	1620.
T'ien Ch'i	天	啓	1621–1627.
Ch'ung Chêng	崇	禎	1628–1644.

CH'ING REIGNS MENTIONED IN THIS BOOK

K'ang Hsi	1662–1722.
Yung Chêng	1723–1735.
Ch'ien Lung	1736–1795.

Rarely there also occur marks in which the year in the reign is specified as on our Tz'u Chou example now in the Metropolitan Museum referred to above. Page 220 from *The Wares of the Ming Dynasty* gives the numerals 1 to 10 but I also find page 215 from *Chinesisches Kunstgewerbe* (Martin Feddersen) valuable as it shows how the higher numerals are arrived at and gives the seasons.

I also reproduce Feddersen's arrangement of the marks of the more important reigns of Ming and Ch'ing dynasties, as I think them most excellently arranged.

POTTERY AND PORCELAIN
CHRONOLOGICAL GUIDE

一年 ⎱ 1. Year

元年

九年六月十日 ⎱ 9. Year / 6. Month / 10. Day

五十六 ⎱ 56

百千萬 100 / 1000 / 10000

年歲月日 — Year / Year / Month / Day

一二三四五六七八九十 — 1 2 3 4 5 6 7 8 9 10

春夏秋冬 — Spring / Summer / Autumn / Winter

十二二十 — 12 / 20

NIEN-HAOS OF THE MING DYNASTY

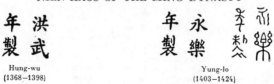

年製 洪武
Hung-wu
(1368–1398)

年製 永樂
Yung-lo
(1403–1424)

德年製 大明宣
Hsüan-tê (1426–1435)

化年製 大明成 年製 成化
Ch'êng-hua (1465–1487)

治年製 大明弘
Hung-chih
(1488–1505)

大明正
德年製

Chêng-tê
(1506–1521)

大明嘉
靖年製

Chia-ching
(1522–1566)

大明隆
慶年製

Lung-ch'ing
(1567–1572)

大明萬
曆年製

Wan-li
(1573–1619)

大明天
啟年製

T'ien-ch'i
(1621–1627)

崇禎
年製

Ch'ung-chêng
(1628–1643)

NIEN-HAOS OF THE CH'ING DYNASTY

大清順
治年製

Shun-chih (1644–1661)

大清康
熙年製

K'ang-hsi (1662–1722)

大清雍
正年製

Yung-chêng (1723–1735)

大清乾
隆年製

Ch'ien-lung (1736–1795)

大清嘉
慶年製

Chia-ch'ing (1796–1820)

大清道
光年製

Tao-kuang (1821–1850)

大清咸
豐年製

Hsien-fêng (1851–1861)

大清同
治年製

T'ung-chih (1862–1874)

大清光
緒年製

Kuang-hsü (1875–1908)

2.—HALL MARKS refer to certain halls or pavilions in the Imperial palace, to a studio in which the piece was made, to the family hall name of the person for whom the vessel was made, some building such as a hall of justice and possibly to the name of a shop for which the ware was ordered, and we can seldom determine which. They are very rare on Ming wares. We classify them as "Hall Marks" because they usually contain the word t'ang (hall) or an equivalent such as t'ing (pavilion), chai (study), etc. Hobson says, "The *t'ang ming* is the 'family hall name,' making reference to some outstanding event in family history, e.g. *wu tê t'ang chin*—Chin of the Military valour (wu tê) hall. It is inscribed in one of the chief rooms of the house, on graves, in deeds, etc."

Mr. Hobson says that one hall mark does occur more or less frequently on late Ming wares and that is *yü t'ang chia ch'i* or "Beautiful vessel of (or for) the Jade Hall." This may mean simply "Hall of pure worth," and may refer to a factory but the wares which bear it are considerably varied, so it may be simply a sort of mark of commendation.

He also gives another mark which occurs only on faked Ming wares. This is *shên tê t'ang* meaning simply Shên Tê Hall, a name the meaning of which we do not know.

Among Barber's marks which follow there are a number of hall marks with his translations which are entirely correct except that he renders the character yu or yuh, as he spells it, as *jewel* instead of as *jade* as we are accustomed to think of it. No doubt the wider meaning is also quite correct. It will also be noted that phonetic spellings are different from those in common use now. I do not agree with his calling the lichens "sesamum flowers" and I take with several grains of salt the statement that the "two fish mark" has appeared on a blue and white piece dating 969–1106 in the Sung period. Also the "standard table" is obviously a representation of a bronze ting or four-legged incense burner or sacrificial vessel (see discussion of the ting form in our first section). However, the marks are otherwise all right and I include them as many people have referred to them in years past.

3.—POTTER'S NAMES occur on potteries and wares from the smaller kilns but never on Imperial wares or those from the Imperial factories. No example has yet been found of the ware signed *Hu yin tao jên* by Hao Shih-chiu and of the Ming Yi-hsing potters we only know of examples which bear the seal-mark of Ming-yüan (see text) and a script mark of Hui Mêng-ch'ên one of which Hobson shows in *The Wares of the Ming Dynasty* a small simple tea-pot which is said to bear the inscription, "*ching ch'i hui mêng ch'ên chih*" translated as, "made by Hui Mêng-ch'ên of King-ki (another name of Yi-hsing).

Hetherington speaks of a curious mark resembling G to be seen on some K'ang Hsi blue and white wares and enameled wares of fine quality and says it may have been suggested by some European trader.

He also says the names Chiang Ming-kao and Ch'ên Kuo-chih are found on biscuit porcelain of the early 13th century, and that potter's names are also found on the white porcelain of Tê hua, Fukien province, on Yi-hsing wares and those called Fatshan from down near Canton. Little work has been done to trace these potters and, in fact, there is little data to go on.

4.—MARKS OF COMMENDATION, of praise or suggesting the use to which the vessel should be put sometimes accompany the date marks or those of the potters. Thus the altar cups of Hsüan Tê were inscribed *t'an* (altar); those of Chia Ching period *ch'a* (tea) or *chiu* (wine), etc. inside the cups while under the base, we are told by the *Po wu yao lan*, might appear *chin lu* (golden seal), *ta chiao* (great sacrifice) or as on one in the British Museum mentioned by Hobson, *han hsing* (to contain fragrance). Other legends such as the frequently found one *fu kuei chia ch'i* (fine vessel for the rich and honorable) and *ch'ang ming fu kuei* (long life, riches and honors) or *wan fu yu t'ung* (may infinite happiness embrace all your affairs) express good wishes or at times a moral precept as in *lu wei ch'ing kao* (rank and emolument without corruption).

5.—PICTORIAL OR SYMBOL MARKS also express longevity (the stork, peach or pine tree) or happiness (the bat). Most of these occur on later wares but Hobson speaks of the hare and stork used as marks under the base of some late Ming wares of Chia Ching or Wan Li reigns, of both blue and white and enamel type. In Chait's *Chinese Chronology* as well as in the Barber marks reproduced will be found the

MARKS AND SYMBOLS ON POTTERY OF CHINA

Marks, Symbols, etc		Marks, Symbols, etc.	
	Three forms of the two fish mark, found on old blue ware: one of the earliest known, from 969–1106		times repeated a hundred or more times. Such pieces are called "hundred show."
	The sesamum flower. Various flower marks are found, in ancient and modern periods		Circular show mark
			Oval show mark
	Hoa: a small flower inside a cup. Marks the Yung-lo period, 1403–1424		Thin form of show
	Butterfly		Fuh-che: happiness
	Show: long life; a wish for longevity, common in one or another of these and other forms on porcelain: some-		
	Fuh-che: happiness		Yuh-ehin: precious gem.
	Luh: wealth		Wan-yuh: beautiful gem.
	Keih: good luck.		Chin-wan: valuable rarity
	Yuh: a gem; precious thing		Ta-keih: prosperity; good luck.
	Wan: literature.		Choo-foo: a polite expression in China. Mark used 1260–1367
	Hing: flourishing.		Keang-tang: preserved ginger Used 1522–1566
	Ke: a vessel; vase; ability.		Tsaou-tang: preserves; chow-chow Used 1522–1566
	Paou: precious.		Tung-gan, a name.

Ting : perfect

Tsuen perfect ; a name.

King   good wishes

A name

Woo-fuh: the five blessings —long life, health, riches, love of virtue, a natural death

Woo-chin: the five blessings.

} Chin-yuh : precious gem.

} Yung-ching, a name

Tsae Jun / tang che } Made for the brilliant hall of the middle.

Wei / foo / ching } Made to add to the jasper.

Jin / ho / kwan } Hall of brotherhood.

Fung / seen / tang } Hall of ancestors

Tang Khe / che yuh } Made for hall of wonderful beauty.

Tang Ching / che ti } Made for hall of virtuous study.

Tang Pi / che yuh } Made for hall of jeweled girdle.

Tang Tze / che tze } Made for hall of violet embroidery

Tang King / che wei } Made for hall of worship

Kea Yuh / ke tang } Beautiful vase for hall of gems

Chang Fuh / chun kwei } Wealth, honor. long youth

Chang Fuh / ming kwei } Wealth, honor, long life

Tze Teen / fuh kwan } Heaven grant happiness.

Jou Khe / woo chin } Wonderful as the five precious things

Jou Khe / yuh chin } Wonderful gem, resembling a jewel.

Jou Khe / yuh wan } Same signification.

Ya Ching / tsei yu } Remarkable meeting of philosophers and friends.

Chin Poo / wan ku } Valuable curiosity for antiquaries.

Paou Wan / ting yah } Elegant, perfect, precious ting; metal incense pot.

Shan Wan / tow shang } Compliment; comparing to a mountain and the North star

Ya Mei / che yuh } Made for one who knows gems.

Wan show woo keang   an unlimited long life

Wan / show / woo / keang } Same. This is in the seal character.

Keang ming kaou (name); tsaou (maker)

} Wan ming cheang (name) che (made)

} Yung ching yu che; made for Yung ching

Badge of authority ; on pieces for mandarins.

Tablet of honor, including the swastika.

Another form of the same.

連成 奇后	Leen ching khe how (not translated).
珍若深 藏	Jo shin chin tsang : precious property ; Jo shin (name).
式載流歪	Same mark
珍乱莊殊	Same mark
鼎奇石寶 之珍	Ting Khe / che she / chin paou — Ting of very precious and costly stone
鼎奇玉寶 之宝	Ting Khe / che yuh / chin paou — Same meaning.
玉思有美 雅製	Yuh Chung / ya yuh / che mei — For the true hearted, elegant gem made.
福壽比南山 如東海	Long life as the south mountain. Happiness like the east sea

	Another form.
	A mandarin mark of honor.
	The sounding stone.
	Another sounding instrument.
	Sacred ax.
	Shell or helmet ?
	Shell ?
	Shell ?
	Standard table.
	Leaves. Frequent marks.
	Treasures of writing, stone for ink, brushes for writing, a roll of paper, etc. Found as a mark, and common, as are many of the previous designs, in the surface decorations of porcelains.

	Beautiful vase for the wealthy and noble. Otherwise translated : wealth, honors and intellect.
	Probably a name.
	Valuable vase for divining
	These three combinations or arrangements of lines, known as the eight diagrams of Fuh-hi, frequently occur on Chinese porcelain. They have reference to certain mystic ideas, utterly unintelligible to us, relating to the genders, the principles of creation, the origin of all things, etc., etc. Chinese philosophers profess to understand their meaning and suggestions, and the Chinese regard them as talismanic.

Bamboo leaves, used as a mark at King-te-chin, 1573–1619. We have also found the leaves used as an exterior decoration of porcelain dishes which we believe to be Persian.

Square marks, common on old specimens, in these and many other forms.

Paou : precious

"artemis leaf" or palm leaf with and without fillets, and called *chiao yeh,* the *ling chih* or fungus mistakenly called sesamum flower by Barber, the *lein hua* or lotus blossom, the *ting* or four legged incense burner called a "tripod" by Hetherington, the *pi ting ju i* or brush, ink-cake and jade sceptre reading according to Chait "May it be fixed as you wish," (a rebus), the head of a *ju-i* sceptre, the endless knot, the *fu shou shang ch'üan* another rebus meaning Happiness and longevity represented by the bat and peach combined, the "spider mark" actually a form of *"show"* or *shou* the longevity character similar to those shown at the bottom of the first column of Barber's marks, the *mei hua* or sprig of prunus (in a double ring) and, of course, the various forms of the swastika enclosed in squares or lozenges with and without fillets or with simple loops at the corners. None, not a single one, of these can be in any way depended upon to help date a given specimen as all are used freely on modern examples many of which do not even purport to be of any of the periods interesting to collectors. Added to these there are also the Buddhist emblems, Taoist emblems, etc. (See Ming section.) One very fancy mark is a circle or square with various writings in it and embraced on either side with dragons. This occurs only on modern pieces.

Chu shih chü (red rocks retreat).

Chiang ming kao tsao (made by Chiang Ming-kao).

Yu chai (quiet pavilion).

Ku yüeh hsuan chih (made by Ku Yueh Hsuan).

Ch'en kuo chih tsao (made by Ch'en Kuo-chih).

Lu i t'ang (hall of green ripples).

Yü fêng yang lin (Yang-lin of Yu-fêng).

Shên tê t'ang chih (made for the hall of cultivation of virtue).

Pai-shih (white rock) and Ling nan hui chê (Canton picture).

Ts'ai jun t'ang chih (made in the hall of brilliant colours).

Wang tso t'ing tso (made by Wang Tso-t'ing).

Ching wei t'ang chih (made for the hall of respectful awe).

Wang ping jung tso (made by Wang Ping-jung).

Ta ya chai (pavilion of grand culture).

Chao-chin.

Chih (made to command).

Chung t'un shih (Chung-t'un family).

Shop marks.

Li-chih.

Lai-kuan.

Ch'i yü pao ting chih chên (a gem among precious vessels of rare jade).

Chao tsung ho yin (seal of Ho Chao-tsung).

Ko Ming hsiang chih (made by Ko Ming-hsiang).

Ko yüan hsiang chih (made by Ko Yuan-hsiang).

Yi hsing tzŭ sha (brown earth of Yi-hsing).

G mark.

Fu (happiness).

Lu (rank)

Shou (longevity)

Spider mark (a form of *shou*)

A tripod.

Chên wan (precious trinket).

Yü (jade).

Ya wan (elegant trinket).

Ch'üan (complete).

Chi (good luck).

Endless knot.

Ling chih furgus.

Head of a ju-i sceptre.

Fu (an embroidery ornament).

MARKS ON JAPANESE WARES

In the text I have explained the confusion which is met in the study of Japanese wares; many of the marks are of a character to add even to that confusion for, if an artist was known by many names so also did he use varied signatures of each or any of these names as, for instance the three writings of Kenzan's signature. I reproduce a few pages of the best known marks as listed by Barber and Hannover and for those who are further interested there are many books on the subject such as that of J. Bowes *Japanese Marks and Seals,* London, 1882, the catalogue by A. W. Franks and the Japanese Chronological Tables by W. Bramsen. Of course, these marks may be potter's names, the names of tea-ceremony masters, names of towns or sections along with poetic names of places and then all the various kinds similar to Chinese marks as listed above, and once again the student must be advised that all the important ones were freely copied as with Chinese marks.

MARKS ON JAPANESE POTTERY AND PORCELAIN

Marks of Periods		Marks of Periods		Marks of Periods	
德建 中文	Ken-tok, 1370.	正永 永大	Yei-show, 1504	德正 保享	Show-tok, 1711.
中文	Bun-tin, 1372.	永大	Dai-jei, 1521	保享	Kiyo-ho, 1717
授天	Ten-du, 1375	祿亨	Kiyo-rok, 1528	文元	Gen-bun, 1736.
和弘	Ko-wa. 1380	永大	Di-yei, 1532	保寬	Kwan-po, 1741.

中元 Gen-tin, 1380.	治弘 Ko-dsi, 1555.	享延 Yen-kiyo, 1744.
四德 Mei-tok, 1393.	祿永 Yei-rok, 1558	延寬 Kwan-jen, 1748.
永廉 O-yei, 1394.	龜元 Gen-ki, 1570	曆寶 Ho-reki, 1751.
長正 Show-tiyo, 1428.	正天 Ten-show, 1573	和明 Mei-wa, 1764.
享永 Yei-kiyo, 1429	祿文 Bun-rok, 1592	永安 An-jei, 1772.
吉嘉 Ka-kitsu, 1441	長慶 Kei-chiyo, 1596	明天 Ten-mei, 1781.
安文 Bun-an, 1444	和元 Gen-wa, 1615	政寬 Kwan-sei, 1789.
德宝 Ho-tok, 1449	永寬 Kwan-jei, 1624	和享 Kiyo-wa, 1801.
德亨 Kiyo-tok, 1452	保正 Show-ho, 1644.	化文 Bun-kwa, 1804.
正康 Ko-show, 1455	安慶 Kei-an, 1648	政文 Bun-sei, 1818.
祿長 Chiyo-rok, 1457	應承 Show-o, 1652.	保天 Ten-po, 1834.
正寬 Kwan-show, 1460.	曆明 Mei-reki, 1655.	化弘 Ko-kua, 1844.
正文 Bun-show, 1466.	治萬 Man-dsi, 1658	永嘉 Ka-yei, 1848.
仁應 O-nin, 1467	文寬 Kwan-bun, 1661	久文 Bun-se, 1854.
明文 Bun-mei, 1469	寶延 Yen-po, 1673	治元 Man-yen, 1860.
亨長 Chiyo-kiyo, 1487	和天 Ten-wa, 1681	應慶 Bun-kin, 1861.
德延 En-tok, 1489	享貞 Tei-kiyo, 1684.	治明 Gen-di, 1861.
應明 Mei-o, 1492	祿元 Gen-rok, 1688.	政安 Kei-o, 1865.
龜文 Bun-ki, 1501	永寶 Ho-yei, 1704	延萬 Mei-di, 1868.

Enamel Marks.

} Enamel mark. Forgery? of Chinese date 1645

} Di-Nipon: Great Japan / Han-suki, maker. (Enamel.)

} Nipon. Japan. Next signs illegible. / Eurok, maker. (Enamel.)

Awata Potteries.

} Great Japan / Dioto, maker

Tokio, name of factory; and maker's names.

Ae-rako, a name.

Ki-yo, a name.

Yu-ah-su-zan, a name.

} Awata

Banko Potteries.

} Banko.

Banko.

Banko Potteries.

Nipon, Japan.

Ari-nori, name.

Banko.

Shing-en, a name.

Banko.

Banko.

Banko: eminent of flowers.

Banko: an old mark.

Guso, name.

Maker's mark.

Bishu Porcelain.

} Bishu.

Hiradoson Porcelain.

} Hiradoson. / Shi-ae, maker.

} Hiradoson and maker's name.

Hezen Porcelain.	
肥前	} Hezen, or Fisen.
肥州	} He-shu.
肥前 田力三	} Hezen: Haritikami, maker.
信南造 肥修山	} Hezen: Shinpo, maker.
肥瑛山 汪川造	} Hezen: Reksen, maker
西肥 南里製 有田山	} West Hezen: Nan-di, maker.
百太造 水川有田	} He-shu (Hezen): Tentai, maker
	Haridan, factory.
	The following are Hezen factory villages:
山内向大	Great mountain between rivers.
山内向三	Three mountains between rivers.
山泉和	Mountain of springs.
平高攵	Beautiful upper plain.
平野本	Beautiful chief plain.
平野中	Middle plain.
平長	Long plain.

Hezen Porcelain.	
郎大	Great vase.
郎中	Medium vase.
川白	White stream.
町赤	Street of painters in red.
屋岩	The cave.
剥南	South bank.
尾囲	Outside tail.
田毛黒	Black field.
瀬廣	Firo-se.
瀬一	Itche-na-se.
左井	Imali.

Kaga Pottery and Porcelain.	
九谷	} Kutani: the nine valleys.
九武	} Kutani.
	Kutani.
	Made at Kutani.
	} Made at Kutani.
九力 谷陽	} Kagayo Kutani.
九加 谷陽	} The same.
加攵	} The same.

Kaga Pottery and Porcelain.	
九九朱	} Kagayo Kutani.
九谷製 大日本	} Great Japan, made at Kutani.
九谷不山	} Kutani Bok-zan.
	Kutani: Touzan.
	Porcelain Mountain (Touzan).
	Rising-sun Mountain.
本山	Ponzan.
柳造	Dio, maker.

Kaga Pottery and Porcelain.	
壽	Long life.
福	Happiness.
禄	Riches.
Kioto Pottery.	
京都	} Kioto.
錦造 昇京都	} Kioto, Japan; Kinkou san, maker.
錦造	Kinkousan, maker.
Satsuma Pottery.	
墨世宏	Itsigaya, a place.
	Tai-zan, maker.

Great Japan; Garden Mountain; strong pottery.

To-o.

Made at Kutani, long house.

Kutani.

Shiba (Tokei) Pottery.

Hikomakoro, maker at Sie-untei, in Shiba.

Unknown.

Awari Porcelain.

Awari

Saeng-ets. beautiful moon; name of celebrated painter.

Ai-we, name.

Spring Mountain

Painter's name (Yamamoto Sho-tan)

Symbols, Inscriptions, Names, etc.

Long life.

Long life.

Wealth, honors and long life.

Made at beautiful garden.

The same; maker's name (Gos-ki) added

Tai-zan.

Tai-zan.

Tai-zan.

Den-ko, name.

Symbols, Inscriptions, Names, etc.

Happiness.

Wealth.

So-o.

Kami, maker.

Rakou-masa, maker.

Huzi-nori, name.

Imitation of Chinese marks: "Precious property of Joshin."

Shin-fo-se-seki, name.

Seven honorable societies.

Hall of increase of peace, harmony.

Wealth, honors and long youth

Wealth, honors and long life.

Same factory name.

Sanfo, maker. These are on Nagasaki wares.

Sito in Japan, with maker's name; Nagasaki.

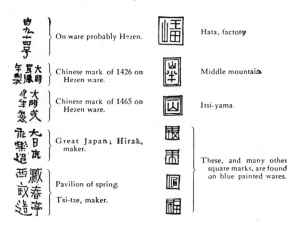

Factory-marks and signatures of artists on Japanese
porcelain.

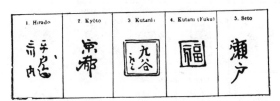

Place-marks on Japanese porcelain.

1. Gempin	7. Ninsei	13. Hōzan	19. Kitei	25. Eiraku (Hōzen)
2. Mimpei	8. Kenzan	14. Hōzan	20. Kitei	26. Kahin Shiryō (Eiraku)
3. Raku	9. Kenzan	15. Rokubei	21. Yosobei	27. Seifu
4. Kuchu	10. Kenzan	16. Dōhachi II	22. Zōroku	28. Makuzu
5. Ninsei	11. Kinkōzan	17. Dōhachi IV	23. Zōroku (Ōtani)	29. Ritsuō (Haritsu)
6. Ninsei	12. Taizan	18. Mokubei	24. Hōzen (Eiraku)	30. Koren

Signatures of artists on Japanese stoneware, etc.

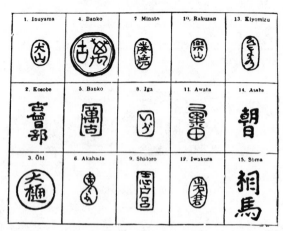

Place-marks on Japanese stoneware.

INDEX

1151

1152   INDEX

Billingsley, William, 767, 770, 771
Bindenschild mark, 661
Bing & Gröndahl factory, 1022, 1041
Binney and Ronaldson, 1000
Birch, Niels, 726
Bird, Daniel, 908
Bird motifs, 853, 893
Birnkruge, 414
Birthday Plates, 578
Biscuit ware, 559, 633, 669, 680, 686, 943, 1052
Bishop bowls, 842, 861
Bisque figures, 689, 691
Bizen ware, 235, 239
Blaataarn, 726
Black Earth potteries, 12, 21, 24, 28, 29, 75
Black-figure ware, 46, 49, 51, 53, 58
Black gold ware, Chinese, 562, 563
Black Pottery People, 27
Blackburton potteries, 878
Blanc de Chine, 444, 535ff., 614
Blankenburg, 788
Blauwerk, 415, 416, 417
Bleu Persan ware, 376, 796
Bleu-de-roi, 656, 684
Blondeau, 686
Bloomfield, John Caldwell, 739
Bloor, Robert, 753
Blue dragon pattern, 768
Blue jasper ware, 920
Blue leaf design, 853
Blue, Mazarine, 550
Blue, Mohammedan, 468
Blue, robin's egg, 594
Blue ware, Chinese, 579
Blue ware, Copenhagen, 1018, 1022
Blue ware, English, 885, 886
Boch brothers, The, 792
Boch, Pierre-Joseph, 792
Boch, William, 1005
Boeren-Delftsch ware, 787
Boileau, 686, 689
Boizot, Louis Simon, 689ff.
Bolomey, Benjamin, 724
Bonaveri, Carlo Antonio, 719
Bone, Henry, 773
Bone ash, 748
Bone China, 742, 991, 1003
Bonnefoy, Antoine, 810
Bonnet, 814
Bonnin, Gousse, 989, 990
Bonnin and Morris, 990
Bontemps, Valentin, 822
Boode, Peter, 141
Bordeaux, 699, 809
Borneo, 432, 510
Bornholm, 726, 1038
Borrmann, Johann Balthasar, 661
Bos, Cornelis, 411
Bosch, 856
Bossue, Jean, 807
Bottengruber, 659
Böttger, Johann Friedrich, 616, 633, 643ff., 682, 705, 824, 830, 900, 908
Bouchard, Noël, 802
Bouchardson, 689
Boucher, François, 642, 853, 857
Bouffioulx, 418
Boulé brothers, 814
Boulevard St. Garbin, 704
Boulle style, 796
Boumeester, Cornelis, 788
Bourdon des Planches, 700
Bourg-la-Reine factory, 632
Bourgoin, Jean-Baptiste-Alexis, 808
Boussemaert, François, 791, 807
Bouvignies, 418
Bow, 612, 742, 744, 757, 980, 989
Bowen, John, 887
Boxer vase, 38
Boyer, François, 805
Boyle, Samuel, 753
Braintree, Mass., 989, 990
Brampton, 898, 995
Brandenstein, 659, 662
Brankston, A. D., 101, 124, 421, 461, 467, 620
Braun, E. W., 666, 829
Brazil, 973
Brecheisen, Joseph, 726
Brehm, Johann Adam, 636
Breslau, 839

Briand, Thos., 773
Bricqueville, 809
Briot, François, 405
Brislington potteries, 806, 880, 882, 887
Bristol, 765, 772, 882ff.
Bromley, William, 739
Brongniart, 591ff.
Brooks, Hervey, 989, 990
Broome, Isaac, 979, 1005
Brouwer, Gerrit, 782
Brouwer, Hugo, 785
Brouwer, Huibrecht, 382
Brouwer, Justus, 387, 782, 784
Brühl, Count Heinrich, 652
Brüning, Heinrich Christian, 670
Brussels ware, 825
Bruyn, Abraham de, 411
Bry, Theodore de, 411
Buccaro wares, 49, 65ff., 239, 642, 643
Bucchero. See Buccaro
Budd, James, 979
Buddha, 231, 234, 455, 456
Buen Retiro, 714
Buglioni, Santi, 399
Bülow, Baron de, 791
Buontalenti, Bernardo, 625
Burlington, N. J., 979, 990, 998
Burslem, 876, 900, 913
Burton, William, 132, 170, 368, 400, 744
Busch, Christian Daniel, 659
Bushell, S. W., 534, 560, 581, 600, 612
Bustelli, Franz Anton, 639, 671, 679
Butler, A. J., 9, 282, 305ff., 332, 342
Bux, Johann Baptist, 828
Byzantium, 323

C

Cabaret, Antoine, 813
Caen, 699
Caffaggiolo, 354, 357, 360, 362, 367
Cafferi, 689
Caillat, 684
Calicut, 587
Callot figures, 646
Cambrette, Gabriel, 805
Cambrette, Jacques, 805
Cambrian pottery, 772, 921
Camellia green, 566, 594
Campania, 58, 69, 71, 391
Campaniform, 325
Camradi, 733
Canosa, 71, 391
Cantharus, 43
Canton, 520, 588, 608, 824
Capo di Monte, 372, 707, 714
Cappelen, Didrik von, 859
Capua, 50
Carl Theodor, Elector, 827
Carlsen, Emil, 464, 555
Carolsfeld, Schnorr von, 679
Carpentier François, 791
Carthusian Monastery Mayence, 826
Cartlidge, Charles, & Co., 1005
Cartwright, 995
Casa Eccelma Vezzi, 705
Caselli, Giovanni, 707
Cassel factory, 640, 825
Castel Durante ware, 360ff.
Castelli, 366, 372, 838
Castilhon, 802
Castle Durante. See Castel Durante
Castleford pottery, 920
Catherine of Russia, 688, 720, 916
Caughley, 764, 768ff., 921
Cauldon potteries, 1025
Caussy, Pierre, 797
Caylus, Comte de, 914
Ceja de la Montaña, 944
Celadon, 147 et seq., 213, 436, 468, 502, 507, 56... 594, 1018, 1040, 1047, 1055
Cencio, Maestro, 357
Ceramic lamps, American, 1030ff.
Cerquate, 359
Chaffers, Richard, 775, 892
Chait, Ralph M., 142
Chamberlain, Robert and Son, 764
Chamberlain, Walter, 764
Chamberlans, 657
Champion, Richard, 772
Champlevé, Toltec, 942